Tragedies
to
Triumph

A Collection of Faith Based
Short Stories

Dr. Teresa

ISBN 978-1-959895-49-7 (paperback)
ISBN 978-1-959895-48-0 (ebook)

Printed in the United States of America

WESTPOINT
PRINT AND MEDIA

Story One: The Camouflage of Delilah "Woman of Color"

A southern fictional biography about the life of a girl named Delilah. The setting is around 1940's when being biracial in the community was not acceptable. Delilah's mom was a lady of the night. At an early age, Delilah's mom told her she was a "woman of color" and that she could manipulate both sides of the racial barriers. Delilah's mom abandoned her at an early age pulling her into a life of agony and despair, but faith helps her to persevere.

Story Two: Delilah Too! "The Camouflage Continues…"

This story is the sequel of The Camouflage of Delilah. It was all about survival with Delilah after she meets a mysterious older woman who taught her how to survive in two worlds battling with racial barriers. Even though pieces of Delilah's life were finally pulling together, other fragments were unresolved.

Story Three: TAME (Taking All My Energy)

Diamond Oslo a talented African American female rhythm and blues artist with a strong faith background. She is young and destined for success without knowledge of deceit. She coveted pride and arrogance which lead her into a world of double-dealing. Even though Diamond was faced with a lot of mishaps, her inner faith gradually gives her a bolt of power to realize that roses can bloom even during thorns and thistles.

Story Four: Silent Predator

Have you heard the saying, "Sleep tight; don't let the bed bug's bite?" could this really be true? Just because you cannot see it does not mean its not there! Some things are better off staying in the dead zone. That is what Pamela Jones thought. She is a remarkable young lady destine for success. She is a popular girl in a secluded community. She encounters strange happenings in her life that only occurred during sleep. Paranormal experiences begin to overshadow her life. Is it a gift or a curse? Can she stand the pressures of her surroundings? Only her destiny will reveal the truth. Will Pamela have to seek outside of man's comprehension to gain her sanity? Some things are better off ignored, especially in Silent Predator, the story that can bite you forever.

CONTENTS

The Camouflage of Delilah

"Woman of Color"

Dedicated to My Beloved Parents

Essie Mae Moore Rolle
(1927-1970)

Nelson Ernest Rolle
(1923-2000)

Thelma Alexander, an inspiring mother
(1910)

ACKNOWLEDGEMENT

To the Holy Spirit, who led and guided me through the entire process. Thank you. To my beloved husband Grady who stood by me through the process… I am grateful you are in my life.

CHAPTER 1

My life took a turn in 1945 during the summer months. Jobs were scarce for blacks, unless you had a little bit of education. My mama always had a job because I've never seen her miss a night of work. We always had food and clothing. Even a small house we were renting. Mama always dreamed of owning her own house. I enjoyed looking at Mama getting ready for work. She usually left around 9 P.M. until day break.

As I looked out of the hot beaming window. I could see the stars in the sky twinkling. Maybe they guided the people who worked at night. Mama said, they are angels watching over us, showing us which way to go in life. I kinda like the ideal of someone looking out for me daily. I could see Mama's reflection through the glass window. She always pranced around the room looking for her attire, making sure she looked the best for work. Watching Mama fussing to herself was fun. Sometimes she would ask me if she looked okay. Of course, I would say yes.

Mama was the best dressed and looking woman in town to me. I noticed Mama rambling through her dresser drawer looking for her stockings. Mama wore the most beautiful stockings. They had a rose on each leg. She loved roses especially yellow ones. Mama was looking for her stockings. When she would put them on, most of the time I would rub her smooth legs. Mama always wore this shiny locket around her neck. She told me the locket held the secret to her life, and one day I would get to wear it. But for now, all I can do is look at it.

She kept on rambling through the house. Oh, by the way, my name is Delilah and I am six years old. I live with my mama whose name is

Candy. That is short for Candace. My daddy left a long time ago. Mama told me when daddy took one look at me, he left. I don't know why. I guess because I look different from my friend Lettie. My hair is very curly and my skin is so bright. Sometimes I don't know whether I am white or colored. Mama told me I am just a girl of color.

In order for Mama to work at night, I had to go to Lettie's house in the evening. I didn't care because she had lots of toys and stuff. Lettie often told me we were sisters, and everything she had was mine. I felt we had a lifelong friendship by the way we took care of each other all the time.

Suddenly I heard a horn blowing in the front of the house. I looked out the window and saw a very light-skinned man in the car. He kept yelling for Mama to come out of the house.

She said, "I'm coming."

She rushed me out of the house and told me to walk directly to Lettie's house. which was about three houses down. As Mama was getting in the car, I could feel deep inside that she wanted a better life for me. Mama looked directly in my eyes as I walked toward Mrs. Lois' house (Lettie's mama). As the car drove off, I could still feel the presence of my mama's eyes watching me, as if to say, "I am watching you always."

Mrs. Lois always stood at the door watching me walk safely to her house. As my mama got into the car, she blew a kiss at me with her ruby red lips. My mama was a pretty lady to me. Her skin was like a peach. I guess that is why so many men liked her. Every time my mama left with a man, I hoped it would be my daddy. No such luck yet! I did notice each car was different every time she went to work. I guess she had to catch a ride every night, since we didn't have transportation.

As I walked toward Mrs. Lois' house, I could still smell the fragrance of my mama as she continued to look at me. There was a difference in Mama's eyes this time. It was as though she was terrified. Maybe she didn't want to leave me this time. I saw a sparkling stare in her eyes as though she was telling me goodbye, forever. But I knew she would come back because she often told me she would never leave me like my daddy did.

While walking toward Lettie's house, I thought, one day I'm going to be a good Mama!

The door opened wide and Mrs. Lois and Lettie greeted me at the door. This happened every night, seven days a week. Mama only rested in the mornings. I would play with my dolls or dress up like a movie star, because Mama always told me that I could do anything if I would put my mind to it. I enjoyed being at Lettie's house. Her room had plenty of toys. Sometimes we would fall asleep with the toys in our hands.

It was getting late. Mrs. Lois put Lettie and me to bed. But before she could say good night, she heard a racket going on outside. I looked out bedroom window. I saw this light-skinned man, almost the color of me shoved my mama out of the car. All I could see was her ruby lips all smeared with blood. Her dress was ripped and had streaks of fresh blood covering it. I looked at Mama's roses on her stockings, they didn't even look like roses anymore. I was wondering what was going on. Mrs. Lois ran to the door. All she could do was hug Mama. Mama was crying, but she looked around to see if I was present in the room. She couldn't see us peeping through the crack of the door. Mrs. Lois went into the bathroom to get a wet towel and antiseptic to clean Mama's face.

Lettie and I continued to peep through the crack of the door. I started crying because I didn't want Mama to cry. Lettie took me by the hand and held me tight. She told me don't cry, but I couldn't help it. Somebody done hurt my mama. I thought. Mrs. Lois heard us and told us to close the door of the room. I wouldn't close the door because I wanted to see my mama. I grasped on to the edge of the door trying to hold it so it wouldn't close completely, but Mrs. Lois came over and grabbed the door and closed it in my face. She yelled at Lettie and me and told us to get to bed.

We still could hear their conversation from the walls of the room because they were so thin. Lettie told me she could sometimes hear her mama and dad in the bedroom making funny noises late at night from the bedroom walls.

Mrs. Lois looked at Mama. She told her she needed to change her lifestyle and focus on raising me to becoming a young lady. Mama told Mrs. Lois she had to disappear for a while. I don't know why she said that. Mama told Mrs. Lois she was going home to get cleaned up. I figured she'd pick me up in the morning. Mrs. Lois wouldn't let her walk home by herself, so she told us to keep the door close and she would be right back. I heard the door close and Mama was gone. I told Lettie; things will be better tomorrow because Mama always feels better in the mornings after she has slept for about eight hours. It was a while before Mrs. Lois came back, but I couldn't go to sleep.

Suddenly I heard Mrs. Lois come back in the house. She was talking to someone on the phone. She was saying that my Mama was no good and that she deserved what happened to her. I couldn't believe she would say these rude things about my mama. She even discussed my biological daddy with this anonymous person on the phone. I heard her say my real daddy was a white man. That's why my daddy left. I was so involved with the conversation on the phone I didn't realize I was falling out of the bed. I made a loud sound as I fell on the floor. Mrs. Lois came to the bedroom door and yelled at us to go to bed. But I was the only one up.

I was going to find out the truth about my daddy. I kept thinking it would be nice to have my real daddy around. I didn't care what color he was, just as long as he was my daddy. Well, I better go to sleep, I thought because tomorrow I will have to take care of Mama.

But you know what? That was the last time I saw Candy, my mama. I will never forget that night as long as I have breath in my body.

Six years have passed. Mama still hasn't showed up. Sometimes I look down the street, especially at night, to see if Mama is coming out the house to go to work. I miss her so much. Mrs. Lois used to tell me to stop looking. She always told me is my mama loved me so much, how come she wasn't here taking care of me? I never knew what happened between the time Mama left Mrs. Lois' house and the next morning. No one talks about it, and if they do, the conversation changes when I'm present.

There was something very strange about this. Mrs. Lois and her husband decided to raise me, but they wanted to do it the legal way. At the age twelve, the state awarded them custody of me. I didn't want to be adopted because I knew one day either my mama or real dad would finally show up. But for now, this is my family.

Sometimes I felt Mrs. Lois was happy they didn't adopt me because she would get excited looking in the mailbox during the first of the month. She wouldn't let anyone go to the mailbox, especially check time. Sometimes she would fuss with the mailman if it didn't come on time. Even though the check was for me, I never got to see it. All I saw was new clothes for Lettie, a new refrigerator, and always looking for new hats for her Sunday church showoff in which Mrs. Lois enjoyed being in competition with the women at church. It didn't bother me because Lettie was now my best friend and my sister. If you want to call it that. Now I got to be with her all the time. It was great having an older sibling (two weeks older). We could chat all the time even in our sleep. I guess you think that is kind of funny.

Getting older can sometimes be confusing. I don't know whether to be a child or a young lady. Mama used to say getting older means you become wiser. I can't tell by Mrs. Lois. She spends money as fast as it comes in and then complains when it runs out. One day she had the nerve to look me in the eye and tell me I'm the reason she can't make ends meet. This woman blames me for everything that goes wrong in the house or at school. She doesn't know that Lettie is already active with boys. When I say active, I mean *real active*. She sometimes tells lies about why we are late coming home from school. It isn't me. It's Lettie, but guess who gets the blame? Me! INactive, INNocent, ME! I just roll my eyes up in the air and say to myself, "Here we go again!" Lettie just looks at me with her slick self and smirks. But covering for her is okay because I know she will do the same for me.

CHAPTER 2

I am now sixteen years old. My body has matured a lot. Mrs. Lois said I look sort of like my mama. Mr. John (Mrs. Lois' husband) always stares at me, especially when I am asleep. He doesn't know it, but I see him looking at me through the corners of his eyes all the time. One night I got up to go to the bathroom. Since the bathroom is across from the living room, I would have to pass in front of the television. Mr. John would be looking at me. Sometimes I could feel his creepy eyes looking through my nightgown. It was though he was X-raying me. For my age, my chest was well-developed. I would rush to the bathroom and rush back to my bedroom to keep him from staring at me.

Lettie asked, "Why are you always rushing to the bathroom?"

I would just tell her I didn't want the boogie man to get me. Lettie would just laugh and go back to sleep. She knows I am too old to believe in the boogie man. Some nights I can't sleep because I am worried about Mama.

I can hear through the walls Mr. John and Mrs. Lois discussing a lot of issues. Seems like that is the only time they really communicate. During the day time they hardly ever say two words to each other. One night as I was going to the bathroom, I didn't see Mr. John in the living room, I felt safe. But low and behold, this man was waiting in the bathroom for me because I saw his shadow against the door. So, I ran in the room and woke Lettie up. I told her I saw someone in the house. I knew it was Mr. John, but I wanted her to go to the bathroom with me and catch her dad. Lettie proceeded toward the bathroom with me. But by that time, Mr. John had disappeared. Phew! That was a close one.

It is six o'clock in the morning and I hear the alarm go off. The alarm is Mrs. Lois' big mouth telling us to get up and get ready for school. While I was in the bathroom preparing myself for school, I heard the phone ring. I'm always listening when the phone rings because I am hoping it will be my mama calling.

Mrs. Lois answered the phone. It was a social worker. I guess they were checking up on me. All I could hear was what Mrs. Lois was saying.

She said loudly, "Just don't cut my check off! I will come in today and update the papers!"

Mrs. Lois yelled toward us, "Hurry up! Get to this table and eat breakfast!"

When you look at the breakfast food, it doesn't look like we're getting extra money at all. She gives us a spoonful of eggs, and it doesn't seem as though she knows how to cook because the eggs seem brown. Sometimes I feel she cooks them at night and thaws them out in the morning. I often wondered why Mr. John said he would get his breakfast on the way to work.

Mr. John would drop Lettie and me to school almost every day. He told us we are the greediest children he ever seen. I know why because we would have breakfast at home and breakfast with him at the truck stop. we didn't have time to sit down and eat, so we would eat it in the car.

Mr. John said, "Delilah, feed me while I drive."

I fed him because I didn't think anything was wrong with doing it. Lettie would look at me kind of funny. Sometimes she would get jealous and not speak to me all day.

As we parked in front of Central High School, Mr. John would give us a five-minute lecture on keeping boys' hands off of us. To me, he needs to practice what he preaches because every time I get out of the car, he pats me like an ironing board in the back.

I feel very uncomfortable when Mr. John touches me. Mrs. Lois told me he does it because he loves me. If that's love, I probably better tell Mrs. Lois she missing out on love. I don't see him patting her butt.

Lettie and I walked towards the school building door. Every time we enter the classroom the boys start whistling at me. Some even try to touch me. I get my books and hit them across their heads. Of course, Lettie backs me up by calling them gross names.

Lettie and I are in the same class. Lettie is very smart, but sneaky. She always brings home all A's on her report card. As for me, if it wasn't for Lettie I would probable still be in the first grade. My teachers are always telling me how smart my mama was in school. But she dropped out of school to take care of me. That's when she ran away from home. I never seen my grandparents. Mama married my so-called daddy when she was fifteen years old. I heard Mrs. Lois say my so-called daddy was probably my grandfather. Thank God he wasn't my real daddy. I probably would have been retarded or something.

Let's talk about school. I play dumb so I will get all the attention. One day I am going to be just like my Mama. Sleep in the day and work at night. The only thing I would change is that my children would have a *real daddy*. OOPs, the bell rang. I'm so glad it is time to get out of here.

Lettie and I start walking home from school. It is about two miles from the school yard. We laugh and talk all the way home. Sometimes the older guys would pass by in their cars and insult me by calling me half-breed. But I remember what Mama told me. *I'm just a little woman of color*. Mama also told me I had an advantage over Lettie. She constantly stressed when white people have job openings sometimes, they won't hire a colored person. So, I don't get angry when those guys call me half-breed because I can play both sides of the fence. I must decide which side I want to stay on.

I enjoy walking home because I don't have to worry about Mr. John touching me. I'm afraid to tell anyone because I thought about how they took me in when my mama disappeared. It's not easy to go up to a woman who has fed, clothed, and sheltered you, and then tell her that her husband is hitting on you. I know someday I am going to have to reveal it to her before it goes too far.

As we reach the house Mrs. Lois is on the porch mending one of my dresses. She is always mending my clothes. When Lettie needs a new dress, she just goes out and buy it. Sometimes I wonder where my monthly check goes. Most of the time I have to borrow Lettie's clothes. I am so glad that I have permanent press hair. You know what I mean.

Mrs. Lois asked, "How was your day?"

As always it was okay, I said.

She sat on the porch and talked with us for about an hour. Mrs. Lois has a meeting at church tonight. This meant we had to stay home with Mr. John because he comes home late sometimes. I think he does this purposely so he wouldn't have to go to church with her. He's a bank teller at the local tank. I know he got the job because of his skin color. He is not a dark-skinned man and he is very educated. I guess that is why Lettie is so smart. Mr. John told me to keep thinking smart, I'll get there.

Later we went inside and helped prepare dinner. While we were preparing dinner, the phone rang. When I heard the phone ring, I knew the latest gossip was coming through. Mrs. Lois answered the phone. She noticed Lettie and me looking at her so she walked over to the bathroom and closed the door. Lettie and I waited until she closed the door, then we put our ears as close as we could to the bathroom door.

We heard Mrs. Lois saying, "You don't say. I told you the state was going to try to find her. They just don't want to give me that check. Just don't tell anyone you told me."

Then we heard her hang up the phone. Lettie and I rushed back to the kitchen to set up the table. As she came out of the bathroom, we kept looking at her.

Mrs. Lois had this inquiring look on her face.

Then she said, "What are you'll looking at?"

We looked at each other and replied, "Nothing!"

Mrs. Lois said, "Well…finish up. You don't have time to look at me"

Lettie and I looked at each other with a grin on our faces.

While putting the plates on the table, I whispered to Lettie, "Maybe they're looking for my mama."

"Sh-sh, "said Lettie, "let's talk about this later."

I agreed.

We placed the food on the table then we sat in the living room, which during this time was called a front room. We were quietly waiting for Mr. John to come home from work. Mrs. Lois always timed Mr. John, especially when he was coming home from work. She knew what time he left, and the time he should be arriving home. I think she just thinks somebody wants her husband. If you ask me, she should be glad he comes home at all especially the way she cooks. My mama always told me, "The way to a man's heart is his stomach." That means you got to know how to cook if you want to keep your man from running to another woman's kitchen.

Mrs. Lois kept looking at the clock hoping Mr. John would get home in time to go to church with her. But we knew better. He is going to come through that door when we are finished eating. That was his normal routine. Mrs. Lois, Lettie, and I sat down at the table to eat.

I asked, "Have you heard from my mama?"

Lettie looked at me as if to say, "Please don't asked that."

Mrs. Lois replied, "Quit asking me that every day! When I find some more information out on your mama's whereabouts, I will make sure you will the first person to know!"

"Yeah, right," I said talking through my teeth.

This woman just wanted to keep leaching off of me through the welfare.

Then Lettie said, "Delilah, I thought you were happy here?"

"I am happy," I replied in a low-keyed voice. "But I want to see my mama. I haven't seen her in nine years."

"What makes you think she wants to see you?" asked Mrs. Lois. "Nine years is a long time for a woman not to contact her daughter."

Lettie turned to me with concern in her eyes. Then she said, "Don't worry. Maybe your mama is trying to get a grip on her life before she enters into your life again."

Mrs. Lois made a gesture at Lettie with her eyes, as if to say, "I think you are talking a little too much."

Suddenly, Mr. John came through the door, as normal, making excuses for being late. Lettie and I knew better.

Mrs. Lois felt deserted. Mr. John walked toward the bathroom.

Mrs. Lois said softly, "I guess you won't be going to the meeting tonight."

Mr. John ignored her. He went into the bathroom to wash up for dinner.

Then he sat down at the dinner table. Lettie and I looked at each other smirking and touching each other's feet under the table. We knew better. Mrs. Lois got up from the table because she was running late for her meeting. She went into the bedroom to get her purse.

While walking out of the bedroom, Mrs. Lois went over to Mr. John and whispered in his ear, "Honey, I got to go. I'll see you at church."

We knew better. This was the opportunity for him to have some peace from her. Before Mrs. Lois left, she told us to make sure we cleaned the kitchen up before we went to bed.

I hated being home with Mr. John because he would always think of an errand for Lettie to do in order to get her out of the house. As usual, he sent Lettie outside to look for his wallet in the truck. I knew his wallet wasn't in the truck, but I just played along with his game.

Something strange happened that night. Mrs. Lois left her sweater on the chair in the bedroom. Meanwhile, Mr. John was looking at me up and down like I was a popsicle stick ready to be eaten. I felt frozen just like a popsicle stick. I hated when he stared at me.

He told me to sit down by him on the sofa. I hesitated because his hands were patting the seat of the sofa as if saying, "Come, let me touch and caress your butt."

Suddenly Mrs. Lois opened the door quietly. She was ranting and talking to herself as she closed the front door. I tried to get away from Mr. John, but he had his hand inside my blouse caressing my breast. Mrs. Lois turned around and dropped her Bible and purse.

She looked at me as if I was dirt. She could not even open her mouth to speak. Her lips dropped and her eyes became firey red as though the devil got inside of her. She stood there in astonishment. Mr. John just took his hand away from my chest. He was caught red-handed abusing my body. Mrs. Lois was so furious she took the lamp and threw it at me.

"1...I... I can...can," Mr. John tried to explain.
Mrs. Lois shouted, "Shut Up! Just Shut Up!"

He was trying to get out of being caught. I thought, finally she had him. Would you believe she blamed me for the incident. I ran to the bedroom to escape from this horrible situation, but she just continued to follow me to the room. She knocked me down on the floor. She called me white trash and all sorts of ungodly names. She yelled at me continuously through the house.

Then she shouted, "LEAVE MY HOUSE!"

She kept repeating with anger in her eyes, "LEAVE! MY! HOUSE! LEAVE! MY! HOUSE!"

I started thinking maybe she was treating me this way because her check was about to come to an end. I cried on the inside, It's not my fault! It's not my fault!

Before I could finish my thoughts, Mrs. Lois took the same lamp and struck me across the head. I fell and reached for my head. My hand was full of blood. I began to think about what happened to my mama. In the mist of all this turmoil, I was trying to tell her this is not my fault.

With a scared squeaky voice I said, "Mr. John was coming on to me. I just didn't know how to tell you."

But I don't think she wanted to know the truth. Mrs. Lois kept screaming and yelling at me to get out of her so-so-so-house. You know what I mean. She was a cursing woman when she got mad. The church folks should see her now. She told me I was the cause of this. She told me I was just like the women in proverbs, waiting to seduce her husband. I refused to listen to those horrible lies. She didn't know about the night he seduced me into holdings private spot (you know what I mean) and help him to get a sexual thrill. I thought to myself maybe if she would make more noises in the bedroom at night, she wouldn't need me to substitute.

While all this action was going on, Lettie was so frightened she just balled up in a corner on the floor shaking. She couldn't back me up this time.

Mrs. Lois pulled me by my hair and dragged me to the front room. I continued to cry in agony. The blood from my head was dripping in my face like a waterfall

I kept yelling with a trembling voice, "It's not my fault! It's not my fault!"

Mr. John just stood there watching her beating me half to death. He knew it was all his fault, so he felt guilty and came over and pulled Mrs. Lois away from me.

Mrs. Lois then threw me out the door and shouted, "You are just like your mother! A harlot! An undercover whore!"

I ran as fast as I could. In the midst of my hurt and pain my heart started panting. I stopped in the middle of the road.

I heard Lettie calling out to me, "Please don't leave!"

Both of us cried and hugged each other.

Mrs. Lois yelled at Lettie, "Leave that whore alone!"

Lettie couldn't turn me a loose. She held me tight. As we held on to each other, we took our pinkie fingers and hooked them together, symbolizing sisters forever.

I told Lettie, "You will always be my sister in my heart."

Lettie kept telling me, "Please don't leave." Our fingers began to let go.

I walked toward the railroad tracks refusing to look back. I couldn't bear the pain in Lettie's eyes as we departed. I began to think about how my mama had left me with this family, and now I had no one to turn to.

A voice spoke to my heart and said, "You are a woman of color. Stand tall and let your color be your guide."

Continuing to walk on, I didn't know where I was going. Memories of my life flashed before me as though it was a repetitious thing for people to leave me.

It was a dreary night for me. I thought, there is so much drama in my life. I wonder what's next? I lost my mama, now I lost my best friend. Maybe it's all because of my color. At my age I didn't know where I was going, and how to accomplish the desires of my heart with no guidance. I continued to hold my head as the blood kept streaming in my face. I reached under my dress and pulled off my half-slip to wrap it around my head.

Suddenly I passed a church that was standing far off from the railroad tracks. This must be the church Mrs. Lois attended for prayer meetings. I heard the congregation singing songs of Zion. The sweet melody drew me nearer to the building. As I came closer to the harmony of the voices, I saw a man in a white suit standing outside the building.

He gazed at me and said, "Go on in."

It was amazing. I was like in a trance. It was like I was hypnotized by this man.

He glowed as white as a snowball, only he was different and unexplainable. Being in this state of mind, I walked in the church. There were eyes staring at me like I was God himself. They saw the blood on my dress and dripping from my head. I heard a woman with a great big hat on, like a fruit basket ready for the market, telling me with her hands to come over and sit by her. She went to get some water out of the bathroom. She dabbed some cold water on the bruises that tattooed my flesh. The congregation continued to sing, then all of a sudden everyone sat down and the minister got up to say some encouraging words to the people. I guess I got there at the end of the service. The minister started talking and while he was exhorting the congregation, he was glancing at me as though it was God himself talking to me.

He shouted to the congregation, "God has a purpose for everyone's life no matter what you are going through. Just remember, God is not finished with you until you have fulfilled his purpose!"

As he was talking, I could feel the confirment of those words. He continued.

"Life can be rough, and it can be tough. Character is more important than the color of your skin!"

I kept squirming in my seat. Those words were really hitting me hard. During this time, I didn't feel pain coming from the bruises on my head. Maybe God was trying to tell me something. One thing I did learn from Mrs. Lois is hold on to your faith, no matter what your trials maybe. I really didn't know what real trials were like until I had to do everything on my own, starting now.

I was about to get up and leave because I felt uneasy with this man looking at me so hard. It reminded me of Mr. John. I didn't want any more trouble in my life. The lady sitting next to me with the fruit hat took my hand. She held on to me as if to say everything is okay. So, I remained calm and began to adhere to what the minister was saying.

I will never forget the words he said.

"Color is only a barrier if that is all you can see."

I got to thinking about what Mama said. "You are a woman of color and can use both sides of the fence, it is up to you to decide which side of the fence you want to live on."

Now those words were finally making some sense to me. The service over and the minister greeted everyone at the door. While waiting to shake the minister's hand, the woman with the fruit basket hat looked at me and asked my name.

I told her Delilah. At first, she was astounded. I know why because everybody thinks about Samson and Delilah in the Bible when I introduce myself.

But I told her "No, I am not that Delilah I am just a woman of color."

She looked at me and smiled. She appeared to be in her mid-sixties. She asked, "Can I drop you home?"

I answered, "I don't have a home."

The lady sort of ignored my answer. She probably was one of those saints who don't ask questions, but tend to the situation.

"By the way," she said, "my name is Mrs. Lucy. I live not too far from here."

I looked at her and wondered if she had any idea what had happened to me. Mrs. Lucy grabbed me by the hand insinuating that I could spend the night at her house. It was difficult for me to trust anyone at this time. It seemed like I had been a nomad all my life.

To make me feel comfortable with her, Mrs. Lucy said, "I live alone. My husband died about a year ago."

I asked, "Do you have any children?"

She replied, "I have one daughter. She left a while ago. I haven't heard from her since."

As we continued to move forward to shake hands with the minister, I noticed the man in the white suit still standing at the door. He looked at me and nodded his head as if to signal me that it was okay. I turned around to tell Mrs. Lucy about this man in white, but before I could say anything he had disappeared. Finally, we were able to shake the minister's hand.

The minister turned to Mrs. Lucy and inquired, "Who is this young lady?" Mrs. Lucy answered, "This beautiful young lady is visiting me for a while." In my spirit I felt someone was watching over me. Mrs. Lucy looked at me and smiled. As we walked from the church, I saw Mrs. Lucy head for her car. I thought, this lady must have some money because most colored people either walk to work or catch a ride with their bosses.

Mrs. Lucy shouted, "Come on! Hurry up!"

I ran toward the car and got in. While we were in the car, we became acquainted with each other. I didn't tell her about the incident with Mrs. Lois. I wouldn't dare let anyone know about that. Mrs. Lucy asked me a lot of questions about my mother. I told her I ran away. I don't think she believed me because I noticed how she twisted her lip a little. Even though I told her I ran away, she continued to converse with me.

She told me about how her husband had died from a heart attack and she hadn't seen her daughter since she was twenty years old, which was about fifteen years ago. I kind of felt sorry for her. Seemed like she was in worst shape than me.

Mrs. Lucy insisted that I stay the night with her. I decided to stay. Where else could I go? I didn't know where my daddy or Mama was and my best friend's mother kicked me out. So, I told her okay. We walked inside the house. She had a very modest but beautiful home. I followed her as she walked toward the bathroom. She opened a bedroom door. This room was her daughter's room. Her daughter's room reminded me of Lettie's room with all those stuffed animals on the bed. Mrs. Lucy went into her medicine cabinet to get some antiseptic and placed some of it on a wet cloth. It bought back memories of the last day I saw my mama. As we sat on the bed in her daughter's room, she pressed the medicated cloth against the opened wounds on my head and attended to the bruises on my body. She never once asked me what happened. I guess she was waiting for me to come forward. But I didn't feel like discussing it at the moment.

Mrs. Lucy prepared her daughter's bedroom for me. It seemed as though she left the room just the way it was the day her daughter disappeared. Maybe I'll be that daughter for her, just this one night, I thought, because I don't know what kind of lady this is. She could be some psycho or mass murder. I'm just kidding. This could turn out to be a great relationship between us. We'll see.

Mrs. Lucy told me she didn't stay up late unless the Lord talked to her. I hope he isn't talking to her tonight because I am tired, miserable, and lost my best friend. But I am going to figure out a way to see Lettie. You just wait and see.

My eyes became very tired and heavy as I lay in the bed thinking about how my life was such a puzzle. I began to feel troublesome with tears rolling down my eyes dripping on the pillows. I kept thinking how Mr. John put his hands on me and forced me to touch his private area.

Fortunately, he never had sex with me, I think, or did he? Mama told me sex is when two people get on top of each other. Well, he never was on top of me, but the thought of him touching my breast gave me the creeps. I tried to tell Mrs. Lois, but she believed that no good husband of hers. I hope he never tries this on Lettie because if he does, I probably will kill him or something.

I wish people like him got their things chopped off then they would know how it feels to be sexually violated. I hope tomorrow is better. It can't get any worse. I got on my knees beside the bed and prayed.

I said, "Good night, Mama. Good night, Daddy, wherever you are and good night, Lettie and God."

Then I hurried into bed because it was jet dark in that room and I hoped Mrs. Lucy's daughter ran away and didn't die in this room. I put the sheets over my head.

CHAPTER 3

Finally, it was morning, I heard the rooster crowing outside. The aroma of bacon, sausage, and eggs filled the atmosphere of my room. I hurried to get out of bed. I walked toward the kitchen following the smell of the delicious breakfast.

Mrs. Lucy said, "Good morning, child, did you sleep well?"

Yawning, and holding my mouth, I replied, "I slept like a lamb."

I really didn't know how a lamb slept. It was just a figure of speech. Really, I couldn't sleep, because the house was not familiar to me like Lettie's home. But I could get used to it.

I started to help Mrs. Lucy prepare the table. In the midst of preparing the table, she talked with me about school.

"Do you go to school around here?" she asked.

I said, "Yes, but my grades were not too good."

Then she exclaimed, "You know education is very important to colored people."

While Mrs. Lucy was talking, I noticed her just eyeing me up and down.

She asked, "By the way, what color is your mama?"

I was astounded. Why would a stranger ask that kind of a question?

I replied with lots of confidence in my voice, "Colored, my mother was black!"

Then, she was really getting too personal. She asked, "What color is your father?"

That's when I almost let her have it, but I took a deep breath.

I answered, "I don't know. My mama never told me. She just said I was a woman of color and that I could camouflage with any environment."

Mrs. Lucy just laughed and said, "Oh, child, you just all mixed up."

But I wasn't kidding.

As we ate breakfast, Mrs. Lucy asked me all sorts of questions. I wouldn't tell her about the night my Mama left. I felt it was none of her business. Mrs. Lucy didn't even try to pry into my business.

That's what I liked about her. She just was concerned and wanted to help a poor girl out.

Mrs. Lucy asked, "Would you like to stay with me for a while? I would love to have the company."

I hesitated for a while. Is this lady nuts or just a saint, I thought. She must be a saint, I whispered silently.

Since I couldn't go back to Lettie's house, I finally replied with excitement, "Sure. I would love to keep you company!"

Mrs. Lucy said amazed, "You have to continue to go to school." Also help with the chores around the house and maybe get a part-time job, she thought.

I said, "I don't mind going to school and doing chores around the house but...."

"No buts!" she yelled. "The reason I want you to get a job is because it will help you invest in your future."

I thought again, maybe she is trying to help me to get a day job instead of a night job like Mama. I do want to be a good mama someday.

I answered with assurance, "Sure, I'll look for a job."

While we were eating breakfast, Mrs. Lucy picked up the newspaper and put it in my face.

She said, "Here! Look for a job!" She didn't waste any time. Looks like she is making sure I don't leach off of her. She looked like she had money, but was stingy with it. I picked up the paper pretending I was looking for a job.

She kept asking, "Did you find something yet?"

I said bravely, "Nobody is going to hire me because I am colored."

Mrs. Lucy took my hand, looked at the shade of her skin against my skin.

"Oh…Oh! Yes! somebody will hire you!" shouted Mrs. Lucy.

She kept on talking about how a light-skinned Negro could get a job quicker than a very dark-skinned Negro. The pieces were finally coming together (remembering what Mama told me). It's worth a try. Mama did it. Why can't I?

A knock was at the door.

Mrs. Lucy said, "I wonder who that could be this morning?"

She got up stretching her arms. Then she moved slowly toward the door. I saw a shadow of a man.

"Oh, Travis," Mrs. Lucy said like she was surprised.

I got up to go over to the door. Mrs. Lucy introduced me to Travis. He was around my age. He did a lot of odd jobs for Mrs. Lucy. Travis looked at me with his eyes staring at my bosom. I always had a problem with guys looking at them. I guess because my chest was a little too large for my body. That is one reason I wore loose clothing all the time. Mrs. Lucy looked at me and then looked at him, as if to say, "He'll make a great match for you." Then she looked at the jar on the kitchen counter.

"Here is the money I owe you," she said, looking at Travis out of the corner of her eye.

I remained shy and secluded because Mama told me women should not be forward with men.

Mrs. Lucy asked Travis, "When will you have time to rake the back yard?"

She knew Travis was looking at me. It was as though she was implying for him to come back soon. Travis replied, "I will come by tomorrow after school."

I thought I knew his face from somewhere. Yes! It was at school. He was one of those guys all the girls went after. As Travis headed for the door, Mrs. Lucy looked at me and boldly spoke saying, "What a nice young man. He lives right down the street." I didn't care if he lived next door. He wasn't putting his hands on me.

I didn't think I ever wanted a man putting his hands on me any more until I got married, and even then, I am going to have to think about it. Mrs. Lucy then went up to her daughter's bedroom. I just knew she was checking to see if I stole anything. She called for me to come up to the room. She was going through some clothes in the closet, pulling out everything that she could find. I moved closer to Mrs. Lucy as she put some of the items up to me.

"I know you can fit in some of these clothes. My daughter was about your size."

I said, "Mrs. Lucy, you are so nice to me. Why are you so kind?"

Mrs. Lucy winked her eye at me and said, "Just thank God for the blessings."

She suggested I look through the items and take whatever I could wear. I started rambling in the closet. I found shoes, socks, dresses and all sorts of stuff. The funny thing about it, she never told me her daughter's name. I wonder why! Maybe she is upset with her daughter.

Continuing to sort out the things in the closet, I noticed a letter in the pocket of a vinyl jacket. I didn't want to impose, so I put it back into the jacket. I sat on the bed looking at the different items I pulled out of the closet, then I thought, I won't be imposing, she abandoned these clothes. Her mama told me to take what I want. So, I took the jacket, but only so I could read the letter.

I slowly pulled out the letter. It was handwritten by her daughter named "Cee." The letter was written to a guy named Jerry. I read it out loud.

"My dearest Jerry, I cannot deal with this problem anymore. I can't tell Mama because she will kick me out. Please forgive me. Love Always. Cee."

It was sealed with a ruby red lipstick print sort of like the color my mama used to wear. Before I could fold the letter up and put it away, Mrs. Lucy came in the room. She noticed me trying to hide something behind my back. But before she could catch me, I dropped it slowly on the floor and kicked it with my foot under the bed while she was coming toward me. I just knew she saw what I did, but she didn't.

Mrs. Lucy hurriedly asked, "Did you like the things?"

"Oh, I loved them. Thanks!" I answered, thinking, I would rather have my own.

I thought about all the clothes Lettie had and how sometimes she would share them with me. I missed her so much. I'm not saying I missed her more than my mama. It's just she was always there for me. While I was thinking this Mrs. Lucy was calling my name. It seemed as though she was far away, but she was right in my ear. I was daydreaming.

"Delilah!" Mrs. Lucy shouted, putting her hands in front of my eyes to see if I was on earth. I snapped out of it.

"Oh...Oh! I'm sorry! I was just thinking of how nice it was for you to let me live with you and have some of your daughter's things. I hope I'm not depriving you of her things." I said.

"Now look," said Mrs. Lucy, "you are not depriving me of anything of my daughter's. If she wanted these things, she would have never left me."

"Do you miss your daughter?" I asked.

She hesitated for a moment and looked around the room quickly as if to say I miss her, but I don't want anyone to know.

Mrs. Lucy replied slowly, "No! No! I don't miss her at all. She left me am alone and didn't even say why she was leaving."

Because I had seen the letter in her daughter's coat pocket, I knew she didn't leave purposely. I didn't know whether to tell Mrs. Lucy, or leave it alone. I did mention there must be a reason her daughter left. She acted she didn't care and refused to talk about it.

She took me by the hand and said, "The good Lord sent you to keep me company. He told me last night as I was praying. Do you believe God hears us?"

"I don't know." I replied.

I figured out something. Mrs. Lucy only heard what she wanted to hear because if she could hear God, I am sure He would have told her about her daughter. As I was thinking this Mrs. Lucy took me by the hand and put her arms around me.

Then she said, "My daughter would be here today if she hadn't started seeing that guy in town. I told her he was not our kind, but she just wouldn't listen. I gave my daughter everything I never had, even a nice gold locket."

Mrs. Lucy began to weep. I moved closer and stared at her. She seemed empty inside. I just hugged her tightly. She enjoyed this moment and smiled as if she had her daughter back. We continued to hug as we walked out of the room.

Later during the day, I helped clean the house. While I was sweeping the floor, which was a large walnut wood floor, I dropped the broom as if I saw a ghost. I forgot I shoved that letter under the bed. I didn't want Mrs. Lucy to find it. It was not the right time. So, I hurried into the bedroom while Mrs. Lucy was in the kitchen, pretending I was cleaning under the bed just in case she caught me. Then I put the letter in my plaid dress pocket, this was the only safe place to put it, since I was afraid, she would find it.

Suddenly I heard a knock on the door.

Mrs. Lucy yelled, "Delilah would you answer that for me?"

Of course, I answered the door. Guess who was there? Travis. He stared at me through the front screen door and said, "Ain't you going to open the door?"

Before I could, Mrs. Lucy yelled across the room, "Who is it?"

I yelled back, "It's Travis!"

She told me to let him in. I was hesitant because of the way he stared at me.

It was as though he saw a delicious dripping popsicle. I was thinking this because he stared with his mouth opened, and his tongue showing. Mrs. Lettie said he is a nice guy. I can't tell by the way he was looking at me. I let Travis in. He grabbed hold of the screened door handle as I was opening it. I snatched my hand away quickly so he couldn't touch me.

Travis asked, "Is Mrs. Lucy in?"

I didn't say anything as I waved my hand toward the kitchen, giving him directions where she was.

As he was walking toward the kitchen he said, "What's the matter, the cat got your tongue?"

Refusing to say anything, I closed the front door and continued to sweep the front room floor. While Travis was in the kitchen with Mrs. Lucy, I thought I would find a safe place to put the letter.

I searched all over the front room, but I couldn't find one single place to put it. Mrs. Lucy was a very clean woman and she knew every crack in her house. So, I just kept the letter in my pocket hoping I wouldn't forget it when I took my bath tonight.

After Travis finished talking to Mrs. Lucy, he came in the front room. I perceived he wanted to talk to me but I wouldn't hold my head up as I gradually swept the floor. There wasn't much dirt or dust on the floor. I was really passing time so I didn't have to go into the kitchen.

Travis came up to me and said, "How would you like to go to the picture show with me tonight?"

It didn't amaze me that he asked me out, because Lettie already schooled me on how to detect when a guy is interested in you. I looked up at him (he was much taller than me) and saw him looking directly in my hazel eyes.

As he stared into my eyes, he said, "You must be mixed or something. I never seen a colored person with those colored eyes."

I didn't reply to that question. I hurriedly told him yes, so he wouldn't asked me that question again. Forgetting to get permission from Mrs. Lucy, I ran into the kitchen and asked her if she had anything for me to do tonight because Travis wanted me to accompany him to the picture show. Mrs. Lucy was excited and took me by the hand.

She said, "I told you he was a nice guy."

I wondered to myself if he really was a nice guy.

CHAPTER 4

Later that night Travis came by to pick me up. He didn't have a car, so we walked to the picture show, which was about two miles from Mrs. Lucy's house. I told you she lived in a well-to-do neighborhood. Maybe it's because she was my color, blend in with any color. As we were headed toward the street, Travis began to ask me a lot of questions. I really wasn't in the mood to talk about my past, especially with him, someone I hardly knew. He noticed I wasn't talking that much and started talking about himself, like I was interested.

Finally, we came to the entrance of the picture show. I noticed a sign saying, "Colored people go upstairs." Travis paid for the tickets. They were twenty cents each. The white man in the ticket booth looked at me strangely. I guess he was trying to figure out what color I was. He knew, but he studied me for a minute pointing at the sign. It was as if he thought I was going to try to sneak in the white section. We walked up the steps slowly. Travis held my hand so I wouldn't fall down the steps. But I knew the real reason he was olding my hand.. To my surprise, I noticed Lettie standing by the stairs waiting to go in. She was chatting with some other girls. Then she looked up and saw me.

She slowly walked over to me and then whispered in my ear, "Friends forever, but not now."

Lettie would tell me that every time she saw me. I wondered why not now? Then Lettie sneaked slowly back over to the girls as if she didn't want to talk with me at all.

"Tickets!" cried the white man at the door.

Travis walked over and gave the man our tickets.

"You want some popcorn or something to drink?" he said softly.

I said, "Not now."

I had just had supper with Mrs. Lucy earlier. We continued to proceed to the seats upstairs. There were seats available near Lettie, but I didn't know whether she wanted me to sit there. With astonishment, I saw Lettie pat the seat next to her signaling Travis and me to sit in the seats next to her.

Travis asked me, "Do you know her?"

I replied, "Yeah! We attend the same school and we are in the homeroom."

I couldn't discuss the tragic things that had happened to me. We sat down. Travis was a nice gentleman who pulled out the seat so I could sit down first. That means I got to sit next to Lettie.

Great! I hope this means what I think it means. Lettie looked at me and smiled the way she used to. I knew then everything was okay.

As we watched the previews before the movie, Lettie leaned over and asked, "Do you want to go to the bathroom with me?"

I was so excited about talking to her I shouted, "Sure!"

Maybe this was my chance to find out how she feels about me. I told Travis I was going to the bathroom to freshen up. He moved his legs over so we could pass by him. I started to say something to Lettie, but she cautioned me not to talk until we reached the restroom.

As we reached the restroom, she held her finger up to her mouth and said, "Sh-sh-sh."

She walked over and looked in the bathroom stalls to see if anyone was using them. Then she walked over to me and quietly said, "The coast is clear."

I started to talk loud as usual, and Lettie warned me not to talk loud with the gesture of her finger to her mouth.

I asked Lettie with a low-keyed voice, "Why were you avoiding me?"

Lettie said, "I am not allowed to hang around you anymore."

There had been talk around town that Mrs. Lois put me out of their house because I was going with her husband. Lettie knew this was a lie, but because of her religious background she had to obey her parents. You know what's so funny. When Lettie gets around her parents she acts like a saint. Wonder why she doesn't obey them about sex. You know she is real active with boys like I said before. I was thinking all these things while she was making excuses for not being my close friend or even my sister forever. When Lettie finished talking, I told her in a bold tone of voice that I knew she didn't believe them because her dad tried the same thing with her. She didn't know I knew this dirty little secret. We continued to primp in front of the mirror.

Lettie said, "Delilah, we better get back to the movie. We'll get a chance to talk some more later."

As we hurried toward our seats, there was a white boy standing by the stairs. He looked kind of friendly. He hollered at me in a seducing way. Lettie kept telling me to come on. I told her I was going to buy some popcorn and a drink. So, Lettie went back to her seat to watch the movie with the girls. Meanwhile, I walked over to the white guy.

He said, "Hey, pretty girl, what's your name?"

I acted like I was shy with my arms folded near the wall. I didn't answer, then he moved in an "I am in control" way. He asked me my name again.

This time I said loudly, "Ain't you in the wrong place. The sign says, 'colored people upstairs."

He turned to me and replied, "Aren't you in the wrong place."

I said, "You don't know what colored looks like?"

He yelled back at me, "You aren't colored!?"

In order to get away from him I tried to move swiftly, but he caught my hand.

"What you running for, colored woman?" he said in a rude way.

Trying to pull my hand away I yelled, "I'm not running from you."

I pretended like I was brave because I didn't want any trouble.

He stared at me and said, "I'm Henry...Henry Smith."

I don't know why, but I politely answered, "Delilah is my name."

He asked, "You live around here?

I never had a white guy stop and talk to me. Most of the time they were rude to me because of my color.

Then I came over closer to him and said, "Yeah, I live about two miles from here."

To my surprise, he asked, "If you don't mind... could I come around sometime?"

Somehow, I figured out he knew two miles from the movie was not a colored people area. Then I thought, He thinks I am white sitting in the movie with colored people. I didn't tell him differently.

I answered quickly, "I would rather we get acquainted first before you come around."

He was a gentleman. He respected my wishes. I couldn't believe this white boy was coming on to me. Maybe he thinks I am white. He wrote my phone number down. I warned him not to call until after school hours because I didn't know what Mrs. Lucy would think even though she looked half-white herself. Henry took my number and folded it up in his right pocket and smiled at me. I turned toward the entrance door. Without him seeing me I smiled, too, (playing both sides seem to be fun). That's when I returned to my seat.

Lettie asked me, "Where is the popcorn?"

You know, I completely forgot about that.

I said to Lettie, "Oh...the line was too long, so I decided to return to my seat."

Finally the movie ended. As we exited down the stairs, I saw Mrs. Lo is waiting outside the door. I knew she came to pick Lettie up. She thinks her daughter is the perfect child. She just don't know.

Lettie and the girls passed by me with no words. I knew what was up. Mrs. Lois stared with anger in her heart at me as I trotted down the stairs. Travis held my hand again. Mrs. Lois kept staring at me as she put the girls in the car. I ignored her and continued to walk with Travis. This was some night. You know what! Travis turned out to be a nice guy!

CHAPTER 5

I waited a week before I started back to school. Mrs. Lucy would drop me off.

Sometimes I would see Lettie in the mornings on campus. I would walk over to greet her, but something changed about her. She wasn't as happy to see me as I was to see her. Maybe Mrs. Lois brainwashed her or something. Lettie spoke to me in a low-keyed voiced. This wasn't like her. She was okay at the movie. I wondered what that old lady told her again. Or perhaps Mr. John had been using her as a substitute for me. If he was, I didn't know what I would do.

When we were in class, Lettie passed a note to me that said, "Friends forever, but not now." I thought, Not again! I felt alienated. "What's going on!" When the bell ranged Lettie looked at me as if to say, I still love you, but not now. I needed her to talk to me but she wouldn't. I walked outside of the building and stood in front of the flag waiting for Mrs. Lucy to pick me up. While waiting for my ride, I noticed Mr. John's truck along the side of the sidewalk. He kept looking at me as though he had gotten the best of me. Not so because one day he will get what he deserves. Lettie looked at me as she got into the car.

I heard Mr. John say, "Don't look at that slut!"

As long as it wasn't Lettie calling me that I am okay. It took Mrs. Lucy a long time to pick me up, so I started walking home. On my way I saw this restaurant that had a sign in the door, "Waitress Needed, White Only Apply." I thought maybe I would apply for this job in the evening.

Well, I don't know. It's worth a try.

I started walking toward the door. The bell on the door rang. Everybody in the restaurant turned around and stared at me. I looked around and noticed myself in the mirror above one of tables. My hair looked too much like a black woman.

I got to do something about this, I thought. So I look like a nigger. That's what they are looking at. I can beat that. I have hazel eyes, a very bright complexion, but kinky hair. I'll fix that.

Before I could walk out the door, the owner yelled across the counter, "What you want!"

I felt so fretful I could hardly speak. I said, "Oh…Oh I just want a glass of water."

The man with the apron on shouted, "Get out of here! We don't served niggers!"

As I was headed toward the door, I yelled, "I'm not a nigger!" Then I looked him straight in the eye and said, "I am just a woman of color."

He looked at me laughing. "Ha! ha! ha! What color!"

He thought he was joking on me. But tomorrow the joke is going to be on him. I walked out of the restaurant with one thought in my head. The waitress job is going to be mine tomorrow. You'll see.

As I continued to walk down town, there was a dress shop not too far from the restaurant. In the showcase window was a white female mannequin with a beautiful bright-colored dress on. It was so beautiful my eyes lit up. I knew I couldn't afford it, but I kept staring at it anyway.

Suddenly a lady came out of the store and yelled, "Hey girl! Are you looking to buy something?" With my head hanging down, I replied, "No, Ma'am."

She continued to shout at me. "Then… get the… hell away from my window!"

I was furious as I rushed away from the front of the window. I could feel her still looking at me as though I was going to steal something.

Being colored is not easy. You have to put up with a lot and shut your mouth or else be punished for something you didn't do. I see why Mama told me I have an advantage because being full-blooded colored can be very rough sometimes. But you know what! I am going to figure out a way to beat this all-white world system even if it means going on the other side of the fence and straightening out a few things. I will be glad when this civil rights thing is over so I can at least be myself, somebody.

I see why my Mama was always with men of lighter skin. She probably felt this was the only way she was going to advance in this world. I wish I could talk to Mama now. I would ask her why she had me? Then I would ask why she didn't have a darker man for my father? Even though I didn't know what color he was.

That night before supper Mrs. Lucy asked, "Did you find a job yet?"

I replied, "Nobody going to hired a kinky head nigger."

She proclaimed, "Don't you ever call yourself that name again."

She knew I felt disappointed. I told her about the incident at the restaurant.

Mrs. Lucy said, "Honey, now it is time to play both sides of the fence. White people think we all look a like, dark-skinned, wide nose, brown/black eyes and nappy hair."

Mrs. Lucy chuckled, "Now, what is the problem?

Pulling my hair out so Mrs. Lucy could see the naps, I said, "My hair!"

Mrs. Lucy laughed again. "Child, have you ever heard of a straightening comb?"

I replied, "Yes, but I was told my hair was too good to put fire on it."

"Well, we're going to fix that tonight," Mrs. Lucy said.

She went into the cabinet drawer and pulled out a straightening comb. Then she moved her pots to the back burner on the stove, and turned on the fire. She told me to pull up the dining room chair. She gave me a mirror and told me to watch what she is doing. While she was straightening my hair I noticed the texture and the brownish-black hair lighten up. She also put curls in my hair to give it that bouncy look. I looked in the mirror and I didn't see a black girl anymore. I saw a white girl ready to get a job. Even though I didn't fill comfortable doing this, a girl got to do what she got to do. Mrs. Lucy stared in the mirror at me. I smiled at her. She then hugged me tightly like my mama would have done.

Then Mrs. Lucy said loudly, "Now go get that job!"

Later that night a man came by selling some fish. I answered the door. He stared at me and me and said "How do you do, Ma'am? I'm sorry to disturb you, but is your cook in?"

I laughed because I finally fooled someone.

I said, "I'm not the Ma'am."

I yelled for Mrs. Lucy to come to the door.

He asked Mrs. Lucy, "Are you the cook?"

Mrs. Lucy looked at him rolling her eyes and shouted, "Do I look like a cook to you? I am the owner of this house!"

The man was surprised to see that a colored person lived in this neighborhood.

Then he said, "Sorry miss, I… I thought…"

Mrs. Lucy cut his words off and said, "I know what you thought… ah…ah…never mind."

She didn't want to embarrass him since he was our kind.

"Would you like to buy some fish?" asked the man.

Mrs. Lucy bought the fish from the man. She said we should always help each other out.

As the man was leaving, Mrs. Lucy looked at me and grabbed my hand with excitement and said, "You just passed your first test!"

I was so excited because I knew if I could fool a colored man. I could fool a white man. They think we all look alike anyway. I knew that tomorrow I would have that job. I slept very well that night thinking about how my color was going to be an asset to me. Now I could see the dividends starting to rake in.

Morning finally came. I couldn't wait to go and apply for the job. I asked Mrs. Lucy not to drop me off at school. I wanted to walk so I could go by the restaurant and apply for the job. As I got closer to the door, I became kind of scared.

But before I could open the door a white man passed by, tilted his hat and said, "How you do, Ma'am?"

I felt relieved knowing I was still passing the test. When I opened the door the bell rang again. The owner looked up, but this time he didn't stare. I looked around at the tables. The people didn't stare. I thought, Mama you were right!

The owner asked politely, "What can I do for you?"

I replied, "I saw the sign in the window and… is the job still open? But I can only work in the evenings?"

He kept looking at me. I felt he was seeing right through me.

He asked, "When can you start?"

I answered excitedly, "You mean…mean…I got the job?!"

Waving his hands at me, he yelled, "Yeah…Yeah… You can start tomorrow."

As I walked out of the door, I lifted my arms up in the air and said, "Yes!"

I was filled with so much excitement I skipped and pranced all the way to school.

On the way to school Lettie and her father passed me. They didn't even stop to see if I needed a ride. But it didn't matter It was probably for the best.

I thought about it. She probably didn't know who I was. I can't do this to my friends. So I saw a puddle of water on the ground and reached down and poured tons of water on my head. It looked awful, but at least I looked myself again.

I'm glad I don't have to go to work today because how would I straighten this hair in thirty minutes? I better hurry up before the bell rings.

As I ran toward the school building, water was dripping from my hair. I didn't care as long as I got the job.

Walking up the stairs at the school gave me the jitters. Mama told me I could play both sides and it really worked! I felt like I was on top of the world.

As I walked in the classroom all eyes were looking at me. They noticed the water running from my hair into my face.

A boy from the class shouted, "What happened to you? You look like it rained on your head!"

The entire class starting laughing even my teacher, but it didn't matter to me. Accomplishing my goal was all that mattered, and I did.

CHAPTER 6

The bell rang and school was over. Everybody was pushing and shoving trying to get home. As I exited the building, I noticed Mrs. Lucy's car parked near the school. Then her hand was waving out of the car trying to get my attention. While running over to the car, I noticed Travis walking toward the street.

I hollered, "Hey, Travis, come on and ride with us!" This was just fine with Mrs. Lucy because I think she was trying to hook us up anyway. Travis got into the back seat of the car. Mrs. Lucy told me the reason she came by to get me from school. She knew I would get the job so she wanted to surprise me by picking me up. This woman is a God sent jewel. She reminds me of the mother-daughter relationship I wish I had with my real mama. For now, I'll take the substitute. Meanwhile, I better figure out a way to play this dual role. Being colored at school and white at work might be a little bit too much, but it's worth it.

As we were passing the streets on our way home, I noticed a woman walking on the sidewalk with her head hanging down. When we were adjacent to the woman, Travis asked me, "What are you staring at?"

Continuing to watch the lady, I hesitated to tell him. She looked a lot like my mother, but my mother wouldn't look like that. On her head was a colorful scarf and her clothing looked like she was a bum. I kept repeating silently, this can't be my Mama…this can't be."

Travis asked me again the same question. Telling him nothing wasn't going to get him off my back, so I yelled, "Oh, look at the beautiful scarf she has on!"

Travis smirked at me, as if to say, "you are nuts." I didn't care. It got me off the subject.

Mrs. Lucy dropped Travis at the door of his house. Travis looked at me with a slick eye.

He started walking toward the door, turned around and hollered, "Delilah, I'll call you later!"

"You mean...you not coming over later?" I shouted.

Mrs. Lucy took a glance at me and smiled. By the looks of it, she thinks I like him. He's okay, but just for a friend. I don't need another situation in my life right. I thought.

Travis hollered, "I don't know. I have to do some work around the house for my dad, but I'll call you!"

About five minutes later we drove up to the house.

Mrs. Lucy asked, "What were you looking at back there? And don't tell me you were looking at the lady's scarf. I'm smarter than that."

Well I knew I couldn't pull the wool over her eyes so as we walked toward the door I acted like I didn't hear her. Mrs. Lucy looked at me waiting for an answer. I tilted my head to the side with my eyes rolling up and told her nothing. Mrs. Lucy didn't take it any further.

Later that night, Mrs. Lucy and I sat down at the kitchen table to eat dinner. Mrs. Lucy is a great cook. She has taught me a lot of tricks in cooking. Maybe I can spruce up some of the food at the restaurant, I thought. It was a strange moment at the table. Mrs. Lucy didn't say one word to me as we passed the food to each other at dinner. I just had to break the ice.

"Travis is a nice guy," I said trying to initiate a conversation.

Mrs. Lucy looked at me like "now you want to talk to me?"

I just didn't want her to think my mama was in town. At least not until I inquired some more about it. I bet Mrs. Lois knows. She probably will tell me now that she doesn't get compensated anymore. Wrong thought! It was worth a try.

We continued to eat dinner silently. Suddenly the phone rang. I jumped up to answer it because this silent treatment was killing me.

"Hello," I said loudly so Mrs. Lucy could hear me. "Oh, Hi Travis. Okay thanks. See you tomorrow."

I briskly walked over to the dinner table again. This time I started a conversation.

I said, "That was Travis. He told me he couldn't come over today because he was still helping his daddy."

Finally, she spoke to me. I thought maybe she was giving me the silent treatment.

Mrs. Lucy looked me directly in the eye and said, "Travis is a nice guy. I don't want any trouble with you and him."

Somebody at church must have told her what happened to me at Mrs. Lois house. Well, I guess I better tell her the real story before she believed the rumor.

So, I gazed right into her eyes and replied, "I know those church people told you what happened, but they are only telling you Mrs. Lois' side."

Mrs. Lucy kept staring at me implying I should continue to talk, so I did. I gave her the true story on how Mr. John was always looking at me and touching my body. I even told her about the situation that happened the night I met her. By her gestures, it seemed as though she believed me. Thank God somebody did. I felt like I lived more holy than Lettie, Mrs. Lois and her husband.

Mrs. Lucy moved closer to me as I was telling her the story. I began to sniff a lot but inside I was crying with grief. My mama was gone, my papa I didn't know, my best friend didn't communicate with me anymore, and my body had been abused. I cried with agony. Mrs. Lucy took me in her arms. She tried to comfort me by telling me everything was going to be okay, and God really cared for me. Mrs. Lucy also told me she believed me because there had been rumors around town about Mr. John messing around with the young girls in town. This explained why he was late coming home in the evenings.

Mrs. Lucy took her apron off the stove rack to wipe my tears. I felt so secure being in her arms. All I could think about was my mama. I missed her so much. It had been years since I saw her ruby lips and felt her silky rose stockings. Inside my heart all I wanted to do is find my mama and everything would be all right. Mrs. Lucy said she was going to help me out by asking around about my mama.

With the help of God and Mrs. Lucy it will happen. Trust me. Mrs. Lois always taught me with God all things are possible.

I finally felt relieved. Mrs. Lucy got up from the table and patted me on the back softly. I just knew things were going to get better for me. I pulled away from the table to help Mrs. Lucy in the kitchen.

She whispered in my ear, "Don't worry."

I went to my room to prepare for bed. While putting on my nightgown, I remembered I didn't take that letter out of my dress pocket. Rushing over to the closet to find it I noticed the dress on the floor. I picked it up to see if it had been washed. It still didn't smell fresh, so I knew Mrs. Lucy didn't wash it yet. Sighing with relief I took the note out of the dress pocket and placed it in my purse on the dresser. To me, this is the safest place right now. I laid across the bed sideways, thinking about what my daddy might look like. Before I knew it, I had closed my eyes.

CHAPTER 7

The school bell rang. I rushed out of class quickly so I could get home to straighten my hair for work. Travis was watching me as I rushed down the street. I was trying to get home in time to do my little switch-a-roo.

Mrs. Lucy helped me get dressed for the first day. She showed me how to do my hair just in case she wasn't home on time to help. She even taught me the proper English to use when I was around white folks, so they couldn't decode a fraud.

As I was headed toward the door, Mrs. Lucy had me stand still while she circled around me checking to see if everything was intact for the job.

"Okay Delilah, go and hit that job hard! White girl!" she said, smiling as she talked.

I hurriedly walked to the restaurant. When I got to the entrance of the restaurant butterflies started crawling in my stomach. I opened the door. Then walked over to the counter where the owner was.

The owner extended his hand and said, "Are you Delilah?"

I cleared my throat and answered with a screechy voice, "Yes, I am, but you can call me, Dee."

He shook my hand. For a moment, I thought he was going to throw me out. I passed another test. He told me his name was Irvin Miller, but I could call him Mr. Irvin. He was very friendly. Maybe because I am white (Ha! Ha!). Anyway, it was around 5. Mr. Irvin told me around this time it was slow but it would pick up around 6:30. The restaurant stayed open until 10. Mr. Irvin started asking me questions. Where did I live? Who were my relatives and so on. I didn't answer any of his questions.

Mr. Irvin asked, "Why are you so quiet?"

Because my mama told me not to be too friendly with people I don't know," I replied.

"Well, I don't blame you. A pretty olive-skinned young lady like you has to be careful," said Mr. Irvin.

Since the conversation wasn't going anywhere, he started talking about himself.

"Delilah is a pretty name. You know I wish I had children. My wife died a few years ago and we never had any. She was barren, you know. Now I am all alone…but I manage. We were going to adopt but I told my wife you don't know what you're getting these days with all these niggers having mixed babies. You know what I mean, Dee?"

"No. You tell me," I replied. (I knew all the time what he was talking about. He didn't know he was looking at one.)

Mr. Irvin cautiously looked around the room and then softly said. "Times are changing… These civil rights stuff! Changing everything! I see more whites and blacks together than I ever seen in my life time, and I am 62 years old. So, you be careful young lady. These niggers are trying to be equal with us."

He kept ranting on and on.

I just gazed at Mr. Irvin. I didn't know what to say. Changing the subject, I hurriedly said, "Do you want me to fill the sugar, salt and pepper bottles?"

Looking at his watch, he said, "Go ahead and make yourself useful. Time is money."

He went to the kitchen in the back. A few customers came in. I trotted over to their table.

"What can I get you, sir?" I asked.

"Well, I'll have the special, and my friend will have the same," the customer said.

I took the order up to the kitchen window. You won't believe who worked in the kitchen: Henry Smith! Mr. Irvin was watching me as I looked at Henry. Then he introduced him to me. We played that off really good.

Around 6:45 it started to get very busy just like Mr. Irvin predicted. No one noticed I was a colored girl. I was rejoicing on the inside. If Mama could see me now.

As I was waiting on the tables, I suddenly saw Lettie and her friends walking on the sidewalk in front of the restaurant. As much as I wanted to talk to her, I couldn't let her see me. Moving closer to the corner of the restaurant was a better place not to be seen, so I did. Lettie glanced inside the restaurant but she didn't look my way. She was headed toward the door. She opened it but she changed her mind and closed the door.

"Whew! That was close!" I said softy to myself.

It was almost closing time. As usual there were always last-minute customers. The gentleman who came in was well-dressed and very polite.

Placing his hat on the hat rack, he said, "How you do, Ma'am

To me this was an honor. Then I went over to his table. He kept staring at me up and down. His face looked sort of familiar.

I know! He is the man that was with Mama the night she was hurt. I hope he doesn't recognize me.

"Can I help you?" I said quickly. I even put the menu in front of him so he wouldn't recognize me.

"I "Il leave you to think about what you want," I said.

"Know what I want. Give me some coffee, black, and a piece of that apple pie on the counter, "he replied.

Moving swiftly over behind the counter to get the coffee and pie, I could feel his eyes watching every movement I was making. I saw from the corner of my eyes when he got up to come over to me. Then Mr. Irvin came out of the kitchen.

"Irvin!" the man shouted across the room.

"How's the night?" asked Mr. Irvin.

"All is well, "exclaimed the gentleman.

Mr. Irvin saved me this time. I must have an angel looking over me. This was another close one. The man went back to his table and Mr. Irvin went over to talk to him. They must be good friends because he laughed and joked with Mr. Irvin. I took his coffee and pie over to him.

The man looked up and down my dress again, then he said, "You look familiar. Do I know you from somewhere?"

I replied, "I don't think so. I live not too far from here." This will give him the idea I am white.

He hesitated, "May...maybe not, but you look like someone I know."

Mr. Irvin interrupted, "This is my new waitress, De. Isn't she a pretty young thing?"

The man looked at me and smiled. I dashed over to clean the tables since the other customers were leaving.

Finally, the gentleman finished his food. He went over to the hat rack and put his hat on his head in a fashionable way.

He turned and said, "Good night."

I was so happy he left because he had me on edge. We began closing the restaurant,

Exiting toward the door. Henry turned around and asked, "You need a ride?

I turned around quickly and answered, "No."

I hope he didn't think I was being funny. I didn't need anyone finding out my secret so soon. Mr. Irvin hurried us up. He was ready to turn the lights off. He lived next to the place. I don't know what he was rushing for

This was an interesting first day. I started walking home. All of a sudden, I saw Mrs. Lucy parked about a mile down from the restaurant. It was very nice of her to pick me up.

When I got to the car Mrs. Lucy said, "Hurry up!"

She reached open to the passenger side of the car to pull the lock up.

"How was your first day?" she inquired as she drove off.

"It was very interesting," I said. "I passed the test all night long."

She gradually grabbed my hand while she was driving. Mrs. Lucy always grabbed my hand when she wanted to give me assurance about something Then she smiled at me.

CHAPTER 8

The weeks went by really fast. I was doing really good at the switch-a-roo thing. I passed every test the entire week. I'm wasn't nervous anymore. I really felt accepted at the restaurant. Henry continues to ask me out. But I know about that yet. Travis is still burning his heart over me. But like I said, I am not ready yet.

Today is Sunday. This will be my first time going to church with Mrs. Lucy. I don't know how to face Mrs. Lois. Faith is going to have to move on her heart for me. Faith hasn't let me down yet, that is why I trust her.

We reached the church late because the car wouldn't start. As we entered the church doors, all eyes were on me because of that rumor going around.

The service was great. The minister gave an inspiring sermon, and the choir was magnificent. I got excited when I heard the gospel music. I got a chance to see Lettie. She smiled at me and winked. I knew everything was going to be okay with us. Now Mrs. Lois, she didn't smile nor smirk. She just looked at me with her nose in the air with her fancy hat on her head taking up air space. Mr. John wasn't with her. I gathered he probably made up some excuse to stay home. Like I said, I really enjoyed the service. The spirit was high. Ushers fanned congregation members slain in the holy spirit. I really don't know what that means, but if I attend here long enough, I'll probably be slain.

Everything was going great until testimony time. Many people stood up telling how God had blessed them abundantly. Faith was talked about in the testimonies. I could relate to faith because so far that is the fuel I am running on. That's why I am here today. I need a refill.

Suddenly, I decided to stand up. Something was tugging me on the inside, telling me I should be thankful. Of course, the entire congregation turned around and looked at me. I felt shy at first, but Mrs. Lucy encouraged me by hugging me. I stood up and started thanking God for his goodness, noticing Mrs. Lois twitching her mouth and nose as if to say, "Liar! Liar!"

I started to sit down. Before I could sit down Mrs. Lucy boost my behind to stay up. She has a way of giving me a boost. Looking nervously at the congregation, I began telling my testimony.

"I am happy to be here today. God has truly been with me all of my life. I don't know where my mama is, but God has given me a substitute for now." I put my hand on Mrs. Lucy. She smiled. "I never knew my father but…"

Mrs. Lois interrupted, "Why don't you sit down, harlot!"

The pastor told her to calm down. That's when the entire testimony turned into a confession.

I said in a scared but confident voice, "I know there is a rumor going around about me, but I am here to tell you that's just what it is. A rumor. I didn't engage in any sexual acts with Mr. John. He came on to me. This wasn't the first time. He was always looking at my body."

I started crying. Mrs. Lucy held me. Mrs. Lois became very silent.

Looking at Mrs. Lois, I said, "I always enjoyed being with Lettie. Lettie can tell you how your husband tried the same thing on her."

I didn't want to tell Lettie's part. Lettie looked at her mama with a guilty face and started crying. Mrs. Lois felt so ashamed. She ran over to me. An elderly lady tried to stop her, but she pushed her out the way. The pastor even came out of the pulpit. They thought Mrs. Lois was going to hit me or something. To my surprise, she took me out of Mrs. Lucy arms, and hugged me tight. I felt like gasping for air.

I softly whispered to myself while looking up to heaven, "Thank you God."

All I could think of is Lettie and I being able to communicate openly for a change. The pastor waited for our emotions to calm down, then he said in a strong authoritative voice, "The Lord is at hand. Forgiveness is in this place. Praise the Lord! Praise the Lord!"

Everyone in the church started praising God. Some had tears in their eyes as they watched Mrs. Lois and me mend our relationship. It was a wonderful feeling.

The pastor looked over at me as he continued to talk. He said, "Young lady, I know sometimes you feel like you or out of place because of your color. I want you to always remember this: *Character is stronger than color!*"

Then he went on to explain. "When you have good morals, good reputation, and self-discipline, color is not a barrier. Color is just what it says, color. We have to look beyond our color and trust God for our future. Color is not our barrier… We are our barrier when we allow our self-esteem and behavior to be belittled and stereotyped because of color."

Coming down from the pulpit, the preacher shouted, "The enemy (Satan) is trying to deteriorate our character! But I know! Thank God! I have seen the future! One day our character will overshadow our color! And we will no longer be known by our color, but by our character!"

The congregation yelled, "Amen! Amen!"

The pastor came up closer to me and looked me in the eye and repeated, *"Remember, Character is stronger than color!"*

He gave me a great big hug, and said, "Praise the Lord!"

The choir sang songs of praise while the sweet spirit of forgiveness was in the atmosphere. The service was so anointed I wept through the entire thing.

Church service was over. I finally got a chance to talk to Lettie in public without looking for Mrs. Lois. Mrs. Lucy and Mrs. Lois were getting acquainted by the car. You would think that they already knew each other. I was hoping Mrs. Lois would blurt out some information about the whereabouts of my mama.

Maybe I will find out later. This was a beautiful day for an reunion.

CHAPTER 9

The years went by first. It is now a very cool November. Lettie and I graduated from high school. Both of us are twenty years old and attending the local university. We are so proud to be studying in our second year. Lettie is studying to become a teacher and I am studying to be a nurse. It was very difficult for me to get into the nursing program. Not like Lettie. Teaching was easy for a colored woman because they needed someone to teach our kids. But being a nurse was tough because some white folks didn't want a colored person touching them. So, in order to get accepted into the program, I did my camouflage thing. Mrs. Lucy helped me again, and when I was accepted into the nursing program, we celebrated.

If Mama could only see me now, she probably would say, *"You really know how to cross those fences!"*

I am still playing both sides of the fence at work. Sometimes I feel guilty, but most of the time I just ignore my feelings and say, "What the heck. If I can play this game without being caught, more power to me."

Travis got a scholarship at the state college out of town. He writes me just about every week. Sometimes he writes the same thing over and over, but I always reply to his letters. I could use a true friend like that. I haven't given him my heart yet, but he keeps trying.

Now Henry, guess what! I finally said yes to him! We are dating on a regular basis. He still hasn't figured out I am colored. To me, that's his problem. I am still residing with Mrs. Lucy. We have become the best of friends, but she doesn't have a clue about Henry. Sometimes I call he Mama Lucy. I haven't given up on searching for my mama.

Mrs. Lois is now living alone most of the time since Lettie attends college full-time. I heard Mr. John was killed. The rumor is he tried the same thing with someone else's daughter, and father shot him. I told you someday I was going to get my revenge. Thank God, I didn't have to. Somebody else did. I am sort of satisfied. At least he won't be touching anybody for a long time. Maybe eternity, if he went where I think he went. When I think about it, I wish he was punished another way instead of being killed by someone.

I guess you wonder what I am doing this minute. Well, I'm laying across my bed doing some homework for my nursing class. Mrs. Lucy always told me she wanted me to get an education and make something out of myself. It's enough having your color as a barrier.

I continued to work at the restaurant as long as my grade point average remains 3.0 or higher. Can you believe I started thinking smarter. My mama would be proud of me if she could see me now.

There was a knock on my bedroom door.

It was Mama Lucy. She asked, "Would you run to the store for me?"

I always had to walk to the store. Mama Lucy didn't trust anyone with her car even though it wasn't a brand-new car.

Mama Lucy said, "Please don't take all day because I need to finish dinner before you go to work."

Ah, work. A refreshing word. I can't wait to see Henry, I thought.

As I walked along the street to go to the store, I passed the restaurant and saw Mr. Irvin looking out the window. I waved at him. He smiled at me. I was so relieved that there was no one colored walking with me. Later on, he probably is going to inquire about this moment. The grocery store was adjacent to the restaurant. I picked up the things Mama Lucy wanted to finish dinner. While I was paying for the items at the register, I noticed a woman looking at me in the window. As I looked closer at her, she fled. She looked sort of like the same woman I saw a few years ago, but older. I thought, maybe she is my mama, but then I thought again, my mama was a pretty woman. This lady looked like she hadn't had a day of sleep, and a hot meal in a long time. So, I ignored the situation.

I decided to stop by the restaurant for a while. At least I would get a chance to see Henry. This is the only time we get to see each other.

Entering the restaurant for a while. I noticed a white blonde at the counter talking to Henry. I pretended to be talking to Mr. Irvin so I could scout out what was going on. Henry saw me and tried to play it off as though he wasn't interested, but I could see in his eyes that he was nervous. Then the woman saw Henry staring at me and pulled his face close to hers for a kiss. Not just a smack on the lips, but a French tongue kiss. I was furious. She continued to flirt with Henry. He knew I was upset. He tried to push her off. Mr. Irvin saw the situation. He even tried to sugarcoat it by telling the young lady to stop playing around with Henry while he was on the clock. I could tell Mr. Irvin didn't want me to be hurt. He knew Henry and I had a thing for each other.

While I walked toward the corner. The blonde got up and looked at me with a sly smile, and left. Henry turned toward me and said, "Delilah, what's up?"

I replied in a snobby voice, "It's definitely not you!"

Henry tried to explain what was going on but I refused to listen and stormed out of the restaurant.

Later that day the phone rang. Luckily Mama Lucy wasn't home. It was Henry.

I said, "Don't you ever call this number unless I tell you to. You want to get me in trouble?"

He asks me to meet him at the park across from the restaurant.

Since I was already upset, I shouted into the receiver, "Go somewhere and hide!"

He refused to give up until I agreed to meet him. So, I agreed, but only for a little while because I needed to be back before Mama Lucy returned. I didn't like lying to her. She is such a good person. I made sure everything was caught up in the house, the cleaning, wash and whatever else needed to be done. I didn't want Mama Lucy to fuss about anything. I just covered myself just in case I didn't return on time. Before I could leave, the phone rang.

"Hello!" I said in a rush tone. The voice on the other end sounded very familiar.

"No, Mrs. Lucy isn't here, May I..." Before I could finish my sentence, the phone went click.

I kept murmuring, "That voice sounded familiar It couldn't...but it could....it sounded like my mama. No, it couldn't be... Well... maybe that woman will call back."

I went up to my bedroom to get my purse and sweater. While I was in the room, I decided to look at the letter I hid in my purse. I sat on the bed with Inquiries wondering through my mind. I was really inquisitive now. Who is Mama Lucy's daughter? Why doesn't she talk much about her? These questions started clouding my mind. I felt it was time to investigate. But first, I had to see what Henry wanted.

If thinks I am going to believe that blonde was just a friend, he has the wrong girlfriend.

As I began to exit out the door the phone rang again. I backtracked my steps, looked at the time, and continued outside.

CHAPTER 10

Sitting on the bench in the bench in the park, I could feel the wind blowing through my hair, and it was very chilly. I looked in my purse for the letter, so I could figure out this puzzle. Guess what? I left the letter on the bed. Oh! No! Mama Lucy might find it! I couldn't just leave, I thought. Henry was on his way. I crossed fingers, my toes, my legs and anything else that could be crossed hoping Mama Lucy didn't get home before me. She had a tendency to pick up any stray paper hanging around.

I don't think Mama Lucy is ready for this letter because I haven't figured out what it means yet. Continuing to have all my physical faculties crossed. I looked up to heaven telling God to please, please, let her not see the letter.

Meanwhile, from the corner of my eye, I could see Henry approaching. Henry came over to hug me but I just snatched my shoulders from his hands to let him know everything was not okay.

"What's wrong?" Henry asked.

He knew what was wrong. He just wanted to play with my emotions. I wouldn't say anything and responded with a don't care attitude. Then he grabbed me and caressed me with a kiss. I was in another world as my lips touched his. His kiss was like being on a mountain top. I couldn't help myself, so I gave in.

As we sat on the bench in the park, I was mediating on whether I should tell Henry who I really was. While we snuggled up, I kept thinking should I or shouldn't I? Then Henry took his hand and pulled my chin up to look in his eyes.

What are you thinking about?" he said in a soothing voice.

I said, "I have something to tell you."

Henry just stared at me curiously. But did he really know about my puzzled life. Before I could open my mouth to begin, Henry closed my lips with a soft touch of his fingers.

Henry said, "I know what you are going to say and don't try to interrupt me, Delilah, just listen."

As I listened to Henry, I noticed a shadow standing in the far corner. It was the white suit man again. I took another quick look, then he vanished right before my eyes. Maybe I was seeing things. I realized he was the same man I saw at the church years ago.

Henry looked at me and said, "What's wrong?"

He was always concerned about me daydreaming.

I whispered, "Nothing." Henry looked me as he explained, "I know you are wondering why I look in your eyes all the time. It's because I wonder how you can play your game with a straight face." I was stunned, he really read me good.

Continuing with hesitation, Henry said, "You know...I know you are not white. I knew that the night I saw you at the movie."

I couldn't do anything or say anything. My lips were frozen.

Henry continued, "I just knew you were the type of woman I wanted, even though it took some time to convince you. I want you to know I have loved you from the first moment I laid eyes on you. Your color doesn't matter to me. I guess love doesn't have a color."

I tried to say something, but Henry put his finger up to my lips.

Then he continued, "You know I am glad there is a civil rights movement. My parents wouldn't agree with me, but I don't care. I hate seeing human beings treated like animals. That's why, Delilah, I never looked at your color. I watched the way you acted. You weren't easy to lure. I also noticed you didn't let any one touch you and... it doesn't matter to me if we never have sex. I can wait till you are ready."

That's when I interrupted Henry successfully and said, "I was told that character is stronger than color and I am starting to find this out, but the reason I haven't had sex with you…because I am saving myself for my husband."

Henry didn't know I knew my mama had a lot of men and not one of them can say they are my daddy. I just didn't want that part of my mama to rub off on me. So far it hasn't. Henry looked at me and smiled. I didn't want to ask him how he knew I wasn't totally white. I felt I needed to leave that alone.

Henry promised me he wouldn't tell anyone, especially Mr. Irvin or I wouldn't have a job.

It was very cool, but I couldn't feel it because Henry had his arms all wrapped around me to keep me warm. I wanted to continue the conversation and be honest about my past. Somehow it wasn't the right time.

Finally, Henry woke up out of the daze, and pulled us apart.

I was furious and asked, "Which one do you want? Me or this thing?"

Henry was tied tongued. He didn't know what to say, but I figured out by his gestures and facial expressions it wasn't me he wanted. Being upset I just walked away. I heard Henry calling my name, but I turned my back to him and walked off. I was in despair on the inside. He hurt me.

While I was walking my mind kept pondering on the words Henry said. I love you. He loved me all right. I felt used and abused. Could Lettie be right? Maybe, I will never fit in.

Since my break wasn't over, I walked off some stress. My eyes were cloudy with water. I tried to dry my face with my apron but tears continued to fall. I passed the dress shop close by the restaurant. Then I backed up thinking. Let me get my mind off of this before I return to work. This was the same dress shop I saw that beautiful dress in a while back. This time there was a different lady inside. She looked like me, but only lighter.

As I acted like I was looking for something, she asked, "May I help you?"

Quietly I said, "No thanks."

She kept watching me as I borrowed through the clothing. It wasn't a look of "are you trying to steal something?" It was more of a look, "May I ask you something?" I could see from the corner of my eyes she wanted to converse with me. So I initiated it.

"You have some beautiful things in here, "I said.

Then she replied with a friendly voice, "Oh, most of my clothes are imported from Paris."

I didn't want to look her in the eyes because they were watery and swollen from tears. Then the lady looked around the store to see if anyone was looking, then she came closer to me. With a friendly hand, she pulled me over to talk to her.

"You know, I have been noticing you around here lately," she said. "I've always wanted to ask you how you got your skin so beautiful, and olive looking?"

Being smart aleck, I turn to her and said in a frisky way, "It depends on who your parents are."

I just knew I shouldn't have opened up that can of worms, but before I knew it, my mouth opened up with that smart remark. Then the lady reached out her hand to introduced herself.

She said, "My name is Mattie…Mattie Jones."

I didn't know whether to shake her hand or flip her over. So, I reached to shake her hand. She had a friendly smile upon her face. Then I felt safe to talk. Before I could tell her my name, she told me she was a woman of color, too. So, I gathered she got this job the same way I did. But before I could finish my thoughts, Mattie replied, "I am the owner of this dress shop."

I couldn't believe it! I just couldn't believe it! A colored woman owning a dress shop in a white town!

So, I inquired, "What do you mean by colored woman?"

I wanted to make sure she wasn't up to any tricks. You see, I don't share my camouflage with anybody. Then Mattie told me she had inherited this dress shop from her mother. She was colored, but her father was white, and before he passed away, he left this inheritance in his will. As she was telling me this story she kept looking around very nervously. I know why. She probably felt like me, and didn't want anyone to know her secret.

Mattie continued with her conversation. "My mother was a maid in my father's house, but his parents wouldn't allow them to date, so they sneaked around, until they sneaked around and got me. That is when my mama stopped working for them. He knew she was pregnant, but he couldn't do anything because his parents had all the money. So after his parents' deaths, he left my mother this shop, sort of a way of paying her back for the years he was forced to mistreat me."

Moving closer to Mattie, I began to feel her agony. Then I asked, "How come you work in here since you say you own it?"

She answered, "No one knows I own this shop, except for the attorney over my father's estate. It was stipulated in my father's will, that he keep it a secret so the attorney pretended he was the owner and hired Susan the white lady that works in here. She is the manager but she doesn't know I am the owner. My father told me to do it this way. This is the only way my business could continue to prosper."

The story was so interesting I asked her to tell me more.

Mattie said, "Well, then the attorney asked Susan to hire me as a sales lady. She didn't know she was hiring the owner. That's the way I keep an eye on things and report to the attorney if I see any fishy things to going on."

I smirked.

Mattie asked, "What are you smiling about?"

I laughed very loudly on the inside. The woman that was rude to me doesn't know she is working for a colored woman. Now I felt better about this situation. That old, mean, lady is being camouflaged by a colored woman.

Before Mattie could finish her sentences, she saw me glowing with excitement and said, "Don't ever give up your dignity because you are mixed. What happened to you and me has happened to many men and women. Just remember that you are somebody, even though sometimes you have to jump over to other side of the fence to get some justice. But don't forget who you are and where you come from. We will always be considered colored in the white man's world until things change.

Mattie also said, "Sometimes we have to use our color to pave the way for other colored people, knowing things will change. People are going to look back and say, 'He or she was colored, and accomplished many goals during racial times.' It will give others an honor to be black and say. 'I can do the same thing, too.'"

That's when I told Mattie, "I know things are going to change with the civil rights movement."

With confidence, Mattie hugged me. I was flamed with joy on the inside.

Finally, someone is like me. I began to think what Mama said was right. My color is an advantage right now. I should be proud that I can see, feel, taste, hear and live some of the finer things in life, but I won't forget where I come from.

Before I knew it, time had flown by. My break was over. This was the best break I have ever had. As I headed toward the door, Mattie looked at me and smiled.

Then she said, "Things will change. By the way, what is your name?"

"Delilah!" said I.

Then I walked out the door with confidence. I could remember thinking, Mattie is a real down to earth person, especially being a woman of color owning a business in these times.

CHAPTER 11

The next day continued with my daily routines. Going to school, studying for exams, doing chores for Mama Lucy. But I hadn't forgotten what Mattie told me. Right now, though, all I could think about was getting even with Henry. If I did, my entire secret would be uncovered. So I got to be smart and play like I don't care what happened yesterday.

While I was helping Mama Lucy in the kitchen, the phone rang. I ran to answer it, hoping that it might be that same lady's voice on the phone.

"Hello!" I answered with excitement.

Guess who was on the phone? Henry! I told him over and over never to call this number. Even though I pretended not to care, it was still burning me up on the inside. I hung up the phone. Before I could return to the kitchen it rang again.

Mama Lucy yelled, "Who is it? Why does the phone keep ringing?"

I shouted, "It's…it's…the wrong number!"

I hurried over to answered the phone so it wouldn't ring again. In a lowkeyed voice I whispered, "Henry… I… talk to you at work. Please don't call here."

When I went back into the kitchen, I pretended it was the wrong number again. I told Mama Lucy the person hung up. Whew! That was another close one, I kept looking at the clock as we prepared dinner. I was anxious to go to work, because I was going to give Henry the silent treatment. One thing about men, they do not like the silent treatment medicine. They would rather you yell, fuss or fight, but not the silent treatment! Mama Lucy taught me that.

It was time for me to get ready for work. Mama Lucy sometimes helps me to prepare the camouflage thing. As I exited out the door the phone rang again. I didn't know whether to answer it, or continue going out the door. Looking at my watch, I was already pushing for time. I rushed and gave Mama Lucy a hug "as she hurried me out the door. Mama Lucy went to answer the phone. I listened from outside the door. Yes! It wasn't Henry! Saved Again!

I arrived to work about five minutes late, but that was usual for me. People always say it is a tradition for colored people not to be on time.

Wait a minute! I'm not supposed to be portraying colored! I better start getting to work on time! I thought

Everyone in the restaurant can tell when you are late. The doorbell always rings when you enter. Mr. Irvin must be in the back. I didn't see him. The morning waitress looked at her watch as she put some dishes on the counter.

She came up to me and said, "You late again?

Ignoring her, I walked over to put up my purse. That is when I saw Henry looking at me from the corner of his eyes. I kept saying to myself treatment! Silent treatment!

I could tell it was eating him up. When I was taking orders from the customers, I could feel him watching every step I took. Even when I took the orders over to the counter to be processed, he would try to hold my hand, but I wouldn't let him. I would snatch my hand quickly away. I was really enjoying this treatment.

While waiting on the customers I noticed Mr. Irvin at the counter. He was in a daze. He didn't say too much to any of us. I was very concerned. While I was preparing to take my break, Henry decided to grab me from behind in the kitchen. The cook kept looking at us strange. He didn't know we were involved. Henry pulled me into a corner. He started kissing me. I kept telling him to stop. He wouldn't so I stepped on his toes very hard. He jerked away quickly then.

I said, "Henry, if I am not good enough for you in public then don't try to touch me in private."

I am so glad I didn't give myself totally to him, especially sexually. Henry looked at me with a caressing look and said, "Dee, you know I love you. I just couldn't give you an answer at that time.

I replied, "Then I can't let you touch me at this time.""

Ah quit trying to play hard to get. You know you are easy, said Henry.

"EASY!" I yelled. "So…so this is…what this is all about. Having an easy piece!"

Henry calmly interrupted, "I am not saying you are THAT easy.

"Then what are you implying?!" I yelled.

Henry just looked at me. He didn't know what to say, Henry kept trying to explain himself to me. But I wouldn't lighten up on him. Finally, I told Henry to get out of my life. When I said those words, there was an awaken came over me. Maybe this relationship is not meant for me, especially since I can't see a future with him.

While trying to pull me closer Henry asked, "Can we start all over?"

I said, "Starting All over means I would have to tell you I am not totally colored and furthermore you probably wouldn't have looked at me if I was upstairs at the picture show. So…so…forget… forget I exist!" I yelled.

From the front of the restaurant, I could hear Mr. Irvin yelling at one of the customers. It was Lettie. He was telling her he didn't have a colored girl working here. I had forgotten to tell Lettie I was playing white at this restaurant. I hoped she didn't say my name. Going closer to the front I could hear Mr. Irvin insisting that Lettie get out of his place.

Whew! Another close one! I figured; Lettie wouldn't blow my cover. We think alike, sometimes. This was the one time I was glad we were thinking alike. Looking at the clock, I noticed I used up my break time fooling around with Henry.

When Henry saw I wasn't going for his lies, he lightened up and left me along. I was almost time for me to go home. I started filling the empty containers on the customer tables. Then I cleaned the tables. Now this was the time I decided to have a conversation with Mr. Irvin. He was at the cash register closing out for the night. I sat on the stool next to the counter pretending to be filling the salt and pepper shakers.

I inquired, "Mr. Irvin, how you feeling?"

He looked at me with a very solemn face. He looked very weak. Then he gave in to my question.

"Dee, I don't know if I am going to see next year," he said with a very sad voice.

I asked, "Why do you say that?"

Mr. Irvin came over to the side I was sitting on. He grabbed me and gave me an hug like a father would hug his daughter. Continuing to talk, Mr. Irvin said, "I went to the doctor and he told me I have bone cancer."

I was so astonished at the news.

I said, "Sometimes those doctors don't know what they are talking about."

Mr. Irvin just looked at me and said, "They know what they are talking about because I have had two doctors' opinions."

Anything I can do?" I asked. Then Mr. Irvin in finally said, "There is nothing you can do, Dee, unless you have the same blood type as I. I don't think you do. You see, I don't have any living relatives and I am going to need a bone marrow transplant."

I felt sorry for Mr. Irvin in some ways, but in other ways I felt he deserved

The park wasn't that crowded, but I could see homeless people trying to find food in the garbage cans. I also saw that same woman again. She looked at me with a quick glance and ran off. I wanted to run behind her, but I was afraid Henry would question me about it. We continued to sit on the bench all lovey-dovey.

Guess what? I saw Lettie walking in the park. She didn't see me. Maybe I should call her, or maybe I shouldn't? Then she will know my secret. You see. Lettie didn't know I was playing the fence game. Lettie was with some friends, so I figured she wouldn't pay attention to a white girl sitting in the park. Low and behold, she started walking towards the bench. I tried to escape from her view by turning my head into Henry's chest. That was the wrong thing to do because it gave Henry a thought, he could go further with me.

So, I quickly roused up out of his chest. That's when Lettie started staring at me very hard as if she knew me. Of course, she knew me, but not as a white girl. Lettie came closer, and looked at her friends.

One of the young ladies whispered softly to Lettie, "Is that your friend Delilah?"

As her friends were murmuring about me, Lettie shouted, "Delilah, is that you?"

I pretended I didn't hear her, hoping she would get the idea that I wasn't Delilah. But Lettie was the type of person is she couldn't get your attention; she would get right in your face. Lettie stood about two feet away from me, then she moved closer. I couldn't help myself. I had to look her straight in the face.

Lettie said in a surprised voice, "Delilah, I thought that was you. What you did to yourself...your hair...your look...Girl, I could have sworn you were a white lady!"

Henry looked strangely at Lettie.
Lettie shouted, "And what you looking at? Haven't you seen a colored lady before?!"
That's when I interrupted their conversation.
I explained, "Lettie, Henry is my friend."
Lettie shouted, "What kind of a friend! A boyfriend?"
I couldn't keep my secret longer.
Getting up from the bench I shouted back at Lettie, "Henry is my boyfriend...you...you...got a problem with that?!"

Lettie looked at her friends who silently whispered to each other. I knew what they were thinking.

Then lettie pulled me by the hand and screamed, "Delilah, what's wrong with you! Don't you know you would never fit in with this people... no matter what you do! He will never be able to take you home!"

Lettie was right, Henry would never be able to take me home, but who said I wanted to meet his family? This is what I kept pondering as Lettie and her friends continued to ridicule Henry and me. As the conversation got heavier, Henry grabbed me by the elbow and pulled me closer to him.

Then he replied, looking at Lettie, "I care a lot about Delilah. Maybe she was wrong to for trying to be something she is not. Whether she is colored or white, I don't think like my family. I believe people should care from the inside, not from the outside."

Lettie replied, "I believe that, too, but Delilah shouldn't have to change her appearance in order to be accepted."

I looked at Lettie and felt very guilty about what I was doing, but she didn't understand. In this day and time, a young woman colored had it hard.

I believe I wouldn't have gotten my job or entered nursing school unless I camouflaged as a white woman. Maybe it was wrong, but to get what I wanted now...well... A girl has to do what's best for her!

When I explained the situation to Lettie and friends, they didn't understand. I guess they would have to be in my shoes. So, Lettie and her friends decided to lighten up on me.

Lettie said, "You know, I'm not going to let this stand in between our friendship...even...even... if you don't understand."

While I was hugging Lettie I whispered in her ear, "Thanks...one day you will."

Then Lettie and her friends continued to walk away in the park. I felt empty inside. Henry noticed it and pulled my chin up and kissed me on the cheek.

CHAPTER 12

Today is Friday and I am so glad Mama Lucy didn't find the letter. Thank God! He answered my prayer! I am now at the restaurant. It is very busy here Everybody's frantic, impatient, and wants things their way, from Mr. Irvin the owner down to the customers. I can't wait to become a licensed nurse. But you know what? I am going to keep my cool. The money is good for now, especially the tips. Sometimes I make twenty dollars a day on weekends. I give Mama Lucy her cut on Sundays. She is very good to me. One thing I noticed when I was younger, Mama always paid her bills. She even paid Mrs. Lois for keeping me. She didn't want any handouts. That's where I inherited it from.

Even though the money was good today, Mr. Irvin didn't look too happy. He wasn't very talkative like he used to be. Also, he sat down a lot at the counter. This was not like Mr. Irvin. I wondered what was going on. I hoped it wasn't because of me.

As I was picking up the food for the customers at the counter, I noticed Mr. Irvin daydreaming. I went over to him.

I said, "A penny for your thoughts."

Mr. Irvin slumped down with his hands on his jaw. He replied, "It's going to take more than a penny for these thoughts."

He smiled in a solemn way. I just knew something was going on. I thought, I will pray for him because Mrs. Lucy instilled in me to pray for people when you feel their spirit. Now I know what she is talking about. I can feel something is wrong with Mr. Irvin.

I shoved my body over to Mr. Irvin near the counter and gave him a hug. He told me thanks. He needed that. If only he knew that the person who hugged him is colored. He probably would throw his clothes in the garbage and bathe for days. Mr. Irvin didn't like colored folks. He thought they was always looking for a hand out. In the back of my head, I wanted to tell him so many times. Colored people are only asking for what is due to them. But who am I to say? I am already reaping the benefits, but all this switching to play white-colored is taking a toll on me. Sometimes I forget to talk properly. That's when I act like I am clearing my throat. When I think about it, it becomes hilarious to me.

I was taking an order from one of the booths when the phone rang. Mr. Irvin was in a daze. He didn't even hear the phone. It rang several times, until I quickly ran over to answer it. Mr. Irvin was still out of it.

When I answered the phone it was Henry, he said, "Tell Mr. Irvin I can't come in today because I am sick."

Mr. Irvin was out of it when I told him. He didn't get upset. That's not natural for him.

He just replied, "Ask the morning person if they could work over time."

The time was going fast. It was so busy in the restaurant until I couldn't think straight. I would put the orders on the paper without looking up. I was hoping these people didn't think I was rude, but I just didn't have time.

Finally, I got a break. I figured I would walk over to the park for some fresh air. As I was walking, I noticed a blonde-headed young lady sitting on the bench. When I came closer, I noticed she wasn't alone. It looked like Henry, could you believe that? They were on the bench that Henry and I shared all the time. But she wasn't by herself. I got closer, and low and behold, it was. So sick. Henry all wrapped up with blondie.

He couldn't see me because I was behind the bench watching every move, he made on her. She was having a good time with my man. That's when I didn't even stop to think. I ran over in front of the bench and looked Henry straight in the eye. At first, he couldn't say nothing.

He stammered, "I...I..."

I said in a not so caring attitude, "You got well quick."

Then he replied, "I feel better..."

I interrupted with, "Feel better when you are with this blondie!"

The blonde white girl looked at me and said, "Don't you shout at me! You pretending white girl!"

I was stunned. Henry had told this blondie I was colored. That's when I grabbed her by the hair, rolling my eyes with anger.

As I was having a good time pulling her hair. She was screaming for help. She even had the nerve to holler for Henry. He was in a state of shock because he had never seen this side of me. Henry was in a daze. It seemed as though he had become a statue. He couldn't move.

I called her all kinds of names. Some of them I don't think exist in the dictionary. I didn't care. I didn't want her with my Henry.

Finally, Henry woke up out of the daze, and pulled us apart.

I was furious and asked, "Which one do you want? Me or thins thing?"

Henry was tied tongued. He didn't know what to say, but I figured out by his gestures and facial expressions it wasn't me he wanted. Being upset I just walked away. I heard Henry calling my name, but I turned my back to him and walked off. I was in despair on the inside. He hurt me.

While I was walking my mind kept pondering on the words Henry said. I love you. He loved me all right. I felt used and abused. Could Lettie be right? Maybe, I will never fit in.

Since my break wasn't over, I walked off some stress. My eyes were cloudy with water. I tried to dry my face with my apron but tears continued to fall. I passed the dress shop close by the restaurant. Then I backed up thinking. Let me get my mind off of this before I return to work.

This was the same dress shop I saw that beautiful dress in a while back. This time there was a different lady inside. She looked like me, but only lighter.

As I acted like I was looking for something, she asked, "May I help you?"

Quietly said, "No thanks."

She kept watching me as I browsed through the clothing. It wasn't a look of "are you trying to steal something? "It was more of a look, "May I ask you something?" I could see from the corner of my eyes she wanted to converse with me. So I initiated it.

"You have some beautiful things in here," I said.

Then she replied with a friendly voice, "Oh, most of my clothes are imported from Paris."

I didn't want to look her in the eyes because they were watery and swollen from tears. Then the lady looked around the store to see if anyone was looking, then she came closer to me. With a friendly hand, she pulled me over to talk to her.

"You know, I have been noticing you around here lately, "she said. "I've always wanted to ask you how you got your skin so beautiful, and olive looking?"

Being a smart aleck, I turn to her and said in a frisky way, "It depends on who your parents are."

I just knew I shouldn't have opened up that can of worms, but before I knew it my mouth opened up with that smart remark. Then the lady reached out her hand to introduce herself.

She said, "My name is Mattie...Mattie Jones."

I didn't know whether to shake her hand or flip her over. So I reached to shake her hand. She had a friendly smile upon her face. Then I felt safe to talk. Before I could tell her my name, she told me she was a woman of color, too. So I gathered she got this job the same way I did. But before I could finish my thoughts, Mattie replied, "I am the owner of this dress shop."

I couldn't believe it! I just couldn't believe it! A colored woman owning a dress shop in a white town!

So I inquired, "What do you mean by colored woman?"

I wanted to make sure she wasn't up to any tricks. You see, I don't share my camouflage with anybody. Then Mattie told me she had inherited this dress shop from her mother. She was colored, but her father was white, and before he passed away he left this inheritance in his will. As she was telling me this story she kept looking around very nervously. I know why. She probably felt like me, and didn't want anyone to know her secret.

Mattie continued with her conversation. "Mother was a maid in my father's house, but his parents wouldn't allow them to date, so they sneaked around, until they sneaked around and got me. That is when my mama stopped working for them. He knew she was pregnant, but he couldn't do anything because his parents had all the money. So after his parents' deaths, he left my mother this shop, sort of a way of paying her back for the years he was forced to mistreat me.

Moving closer to Mattie, I began to feel her agony. Then I asked, "How come you work in here since you say you own it?"

She answered, "No one knows I own this shop, except for the attorney over my father's estate. It was stipulated in my father's will, that he keep it a secret so the attorney pretended he was the owner and hired Susan the white lady that works in here. She is the manager but she doesn't know I am the owner. My father told me to do it this way. This is the only way my business could continue to prosper."

The story was so interesting I asked her to tell me more.

Mattie said, "Well, then the attorney asked Susan to hire me as a sales lady. She didn't know she was hiring the owner. That's the way I keep an eye on things and report to the attorney if I see any fishy things going on."

I smirked.

Mattie asked, "What are you smiling about?"

I laughed very loudly on the inside. The woman that was rude to me doesn't know she is working for a colored woman. Now I felt better about this situation. That old, mean, lady is being camouflaged by a colored woman.

Before Mattie could finish her sentences, she saw me glowing with excitement and said, "Don't ever give up your dignity because you are mixed. What happened to you and me has happened to many men and women. Just remember that you are somebody, even though sometimes you have to jump over to the other side of the fence to get some justice. But don't forget who you are and where you come from. We will always be considered colored in the white man's world until things change."

Mattie also said, "Sometimes we have to use our color to pave the way for other colored people, knowing things will change. People are going to look back and say, 'He or she was colored, and accomplished many goals during racial times.' It will give others an honor to be black and say, 'I can do the same thing, too.'"

That's when I told Mattie, "I know things are going to change with the ciivl rights movement."

With confidence, Mattie hugged me. I was flamed with joy on the inside.

Finally, someone is like me. I began to think what Mama said was right. My color is an advantage right now. I should be proud that I can see, feel, taste, hear and live some of the finer things in life, but I won't forget where I come from.

Before I knew it, time had flown by. My break was over. This was the best break I have ever had. As I headed toward the door, Mattie looked at me and smiled.

Then she said, "Things will change. By the way, what is your name?"

"Delilah!" I said.

Then I walked out the door with confidence. I could remember thinking, Mattie is a real down to earth person, especially being a woman of color owning a business in these times.

CHAPTER 13

The next day continues with my daily routines. Going to school, studying for exams, doing chores for Mama Lucy. But I hadn't forgotten what Mattie told me. Right now, though, all I could think about was getting even with Henry. If I did, my entire secret would be uncovered. So I got to be smart and play like I don't care what happened yesterday.

While I was helping Mama Lucy in the kitchen, the phoe rang. I ran to answer it, hoping that it might be that same lady's voice on the phone.

"Hello!" I answered with excitement.

Guess who was on the phone? Henry! I told him over and over never to call this number. Even though I pretended not to care, it was still burning me up on the inside. I hung up the phone. Before I could return to the kitchen it rang again.

Mama Lucy yelled, "Who is it? Why does the phone keep ringing?"

I shouted, "It's…it's….the wrong number!"

I hurried over to answer the phone so it wouldn't ring again. In a low keyed voice I whispered, "Henry…I…talk to you at work. Please don't call here."

When I went back into the kitchen, I pretended it was the wrong number again. I told Mama Lucy the person hung up. Whew! That was another one close to me. I kept looking at the clock as we prepared dinner. I was anxious to go to work, because I was going to give Henry the silent treatment. One thing about men, they do not like the silent treatment! Mama Lucy taught me that.

It was time for me to get ready for work. Mama Lucy sometimes helps me to prepare the camouflage thing. As I exited out the door the phone rang again. I didn't know whether to answer it, or continue going out the door. Looking at my watch, I was already pushing for time. I rushed and gave Mama Lucy a hug as she hurried me out the door. Mama Lucy went to answer the phone. I listened from outside the door. Yes! It wasn't Henry! Saved! Again!

I arrived at work about five minutes late, but that was usual for me. People always say it is a tradition for colored people not to be on time.

Wait a minute! I'm not supposed to be portraying colored! I better start getting to work on time! I thought.

Everyone in the restaurant can tell when you are late. The door bell always rings when you enter. Mr. Irvin must be in the back. I didn't see him. The morning waitress looked at her watch as she put some dishes on the counter.

She came up to me and said, "You late again?"

Ignoring her, I walked over to put up my purse. That is when I saw Henry looking at me from the corner of his eyes. I kept saying to myself, Silent treatment! Silent treatment!

I could tell it was eating him up. When I was taking orders from the customers, I could feel him watching every step I took. Even when I took the orders over to the counter to be processed he would try to hold my hand, but I wouldn't let him. I would snatch my hand quickly away. I was really enjoying this treatment.

While waiting on the customers I noticed Mr. Irvin at the counter. He was in a daze. He didn't say too much to any of us. I was very concerned. While I was preparing to take my break, Henry decided to grab me from behind in the kitchen. The cook kept looking at us strange. He didn't know we are involved. Henry pulled me into a corner. He started kissing me. I kept telling him to stop. He wouldn't so I stepped on his toes very hard. He jerked away quickly then.

I said, "Henry, If I am not good enough for you in public then don't try to touch me in private."

I am so glad I didn't give myself totally to him, especially sexually. Henry looked at me with a caressing look and said, "Dee, you know I love you. I just couldn't give you an answer at that time.

I replied, "Then I can't let you touch me at this time."

"Ah quit trying to play hard to get. You know you are easy." said Henry.

"EASY!" I yelled." So...so this is...what this is all about. Having an easy piece!"

Henry calmly interrupted, "I am not saying you are THAT easy."

"Then what are you implying?!" I yelled.

Henry just looked at me. He didn't know what to say. Henry kept trying to explain himself to me. But I wouldn't lighten up on him. Finally, I told Henry to get out of my life. When I said those words, there was an awakening that came over me. Maybe this relationship is not meant for me, especially since I can't see a future with him.

While trying to pull me closer Henry asked, "Can we start all over?"

I said, "Starting all over means I would have to tell you I am not totally colored and furthermore you probably wouldn't have looked at me if I was upstairs at the picture show. So...so...forget I exist!" I yelled.

From the front of the restaurant I could hear Mr. Irvin yelling at once of the customers. It was Lettie. He was telling her he didn't have a colored girl working here. I had forgotten to tell Lettie I was playing white at this restaurant. I hoped she didn't say my name. Going closer to the front I could hear Mr. Irvin insisting that Lettie get out of his place.

Whew! Another close one! I figured, Lettie wouldn't blow my cover. We think alike, sometimes. This was the one time I was glad we were thinking alike. Looking at the clock, I noticed I used up my break time fooling around with Henry.

When Henry saw I wasn't going for his lies, he lightened up and left me alone. It was almost time for me to go home. I started filling the empty containers on the customer tables. Then I cleaned the tables. Now this was the time I decided to have a conversation with Mr. Irvin. He was at the cash register closing out for the night. I sat on the stool next to the counter pretending to be filling the salt and pepper shakers.

I inquired, "Mr. Irvin, how are you feeling?"

He looked at me with a very solemn face. He looked very weak. Then he gave into my question.

"Dee, I don't know if I am going to see you next year," he said with a very sad voice.

I asked, "Why do you say that?"

Mr. Irvin came over to the side I was sitting on. He grabbed me and gave me a hug like a father would hug his daughter. Continuing to talk, Mr. Irvin said, "I went to the doctor and he told me I have bone cancer."

I was so astonished at the news.

I said, "Sometimes those doctors don't know what they are talking about."

Mr. Irvin just looked at me and said, "They know what they are talking about because I have had two doctors' opinions."

"Anything I can do?" I asked.

Then Mr. Irvin finally said, "There is nothing you can do, Dee, unless you have the same blood type as I. I don't think you do. You see, I don't have any living relatives, and I am going to need a bone marrow transplant."

I felt sorry for Mr. Irvin in some ways, but in other ways I felt he deserved to be sick because of the way he treated colored folks. He was the most prejudiced white man I had ever met. But then, no one really deserves to be sick, no matter what color they are.

I comforted Mr. Irvin with another hug. You know, he looked at me strangely, as though he was looking at a lost love. Then I kissed him on the cheeks.

"Thanks, I needed that," He said, continuing to look at me strangely. If only he knew he kissed a colored woman.

Mr. Irvin turned to me and said, "Your parents must be proud of you. You are so kind-hearted...an...an... a very concerned young lady."

I thought if only my mama and dad could see me now. If only my mama and daddy were here. Before I could finish those thoughts, I saw a reflection through the glass picture window of the restaurant. It was the same man with a white suit on. I tried to go closer to see better, but he vanished before my eyes. I looked at Mr. Irvin to see if he saw the same thing. He was looking, but he saw a transient woman looking in the window, not a man. When I took a closer look, it was the same woman I had seen in the past.

Mr. Irvin shouted toward me with anger, "Would you please tell that nigger to get away from my window!"

My heart couldn't tell that woman that because I knew where I came from, and it wasn't from a palace. I wouldn't move, so Mr. Irvin headed toward the door.

I hastily stopped him in his tracks and said, "Maybe if we give her something to eat she will leave."

By the look of Mr. Irvin eyes, he didn't care whether she ate or not. Since Mr. Irvin was weak, I told him I would take care of this. So I went into the kitchen and took out some soup from the refrigerator and warmed it up. Meanwhile, I went to the door to talk to the woman, but she started running away.

I said, "Wait! She stopped for a moment.

"Wait right there. I have something for you to eat," I shouted. The woman waited while I dashed back in the kitchen to get the soup

I extended the bowl of soup toward her. Then I hurriedly asked, Aren't you hungry?"

She turned around. She wouldn't look at me. She was cold and trembling, probably with fear.

She continued to hold her head down and said, "Yes… yes… I would love to have something to eat."

She took the bowl of soup and started gulping it down quickly. I made sure everything was disposable, because Mr. Irvin would have had a fit if I fed a colored person with his silverware. Of course, he was watching every move I made. You would think his heart would change since he was sick. But he didn't. His heart was as hard as stone.

When the woman finished the soup, she grabbed a hold of my hand very tight, but she refused to look up. While she was leaning over I saw a shiny locket glaring in my face. It looked a lot like the locket my mama wore.

I thought, This woman can't be my mama. My mama had to be somewhere looking beautiful as always.

The woman then said in a soft voice, "God bless you." She moved on down the street.

I stood there for a moment thinking. Maybe that is why the white suit man was standing at the window. Maybe.

CHAPTER 14

The weeks went by very fast. Today is my first day of interning. This is the time when all of the missing pieces in my life started coming together. Mama Lucy dropped me off down the street from the hospital. She always dropped me off far from my destiny because she didn't want anyone to figure out my camouflage, especially when I am playing my white role, I thought, smiling to myself.

Walking toward the hospital door I felt kind of scared because now I would be around a whole lot of people. I hoped no one notice the difference. I can't let anything or anybody stop me from graduating.

I glanced up to heaven and said, "Please Lord, don't let anyone notice me as being…"

Before I could finish, I heard someone calling my name. I was frightened by my situation.

"Are you Delilah?" a voice said.

I snapped out of it quickly and said, "Oh, Oh…yes!"

Then I looked at the tag on the nurse. It said, HEAD NURSE. I knew then this was the beginning of the real thing.

"Follow me," she said.

I went over to the nurses' station and signed in. I was very nervous. It was very busy in the hallways and many of the patients were sick. I was in the intensive care area. I didn't know they were going to train me in this area the first week. They must think I am an experienced nurse.

The head nurse said, "Delilah, let's get started. I am going to take you to Mr. Irvin's room."

I said, "Mr. Irvin?" The head nurse repeated, "Yes, Mr. Irvin."

It can't be the Mr. Irvin I know, I thought.

Before I entered the room, I could hear Mr. Irvin's voice. It was him all right. Then the head nurse started telling me his diagnoses. His condition was worse than I thought. Mr. Irvin saw my face and smiled. The head nurse saw me smiling at him and said, "Do you know Mr. Irvin?"

I told her he was my boss at my part-time job. Then the head nurse asked me to take Mr. Irvin's vital signs.

Mr. Irvin said, "I know I am in good hands now."

The head nurse said, "Oh yes. Delilah is one of our best interns »

After I finished with his blood pressure, I took Mr. Irvin's right hand checked his IV. Then I took his hand and held it tightly. This was my way of telling him to hang in there.

As we walked out of the room, the head nurse told me he was looking for a bone marrow donor, but they could not find a match for him. She also said he had a rare blood type which was very difficult to match unless the person was his next of kin.

I asked, "Have you had anyone come in to donate?"

She said, "We have had a few but there was always something wrong. At this time he needs a donor… soon." |

I kept saying in my mind over and over, Maybe I should try.

Later during my lunch break, I decided to go by Mr. Irvin's room and cheer him up. When I entered the room., he was asleep. So I sat next to his bed watching his heart monitor. Every time it made a funny beep I thought Mr. Irvin was dying. It was scary, but what bothered me the most was he didn't have anyone to comfort him.

I heard someone talking in the wing of the hallway. It was Henry with blondie coming to visit Mr. Irvin. As he entered the room, he was surprised to see me. My guess is, he got caught again. It didn't matter to me because I decided in my heart to let him go and go on with my life.

I said, "Hi, Henry and blondie."

I was being funny with him and furthermore blondie didn't like me anyway because of the incident in the park.

Henry asked quietly, "How is Mr. Irvin during?

I replied in a soft voice, "Not too good. The doctors say he needs a donor."

"I know," Henry said. "Dee, why don't you try since you have a white father?"

I answered in a harsh tone of voice, "You don't know what my father is."

Henry said, "I know one thing, he ain't colored."

I sort of ignored him because I didn't know whether he was implying or being funny,

Turning to comfort Mr. Irvin, it appeared he had awakened and was listening to us. He asked me to come closer to him.

With a shaky voice he said, "Dee, I never asked you to do anything for me."

Before he could complete the words, I told him, "Yes, I will see if I can be your donor."

I only permitted myself to do this because of the break he had given me in the past

Mr. Irvin asked, "Henry... Do you mind leaving for a moment?

As they left the room, he asked me to come closer. I sat on the side of his bed. Then tears started coming out of his eyes. I felt so sorry for Mr. Irvin, not only because he was sick, but because he didn't have any next of kin. Now he was crying on a colored girl's shoulder.

Mr. Irvin said, "I must confess something, and you are the only person I feel comfortable talking to."

I looked at him with a strange look.

He continued, "About twenty years ago, I met a beautiful young lady like you, but she was colored. I liked her a lot, but I just couldn't have her."

I started thinking, Why is this man confessing to me?

He held my hand even tighter. Then he said, "She was dating this white boy. I was sort of jealous because he had her and not me."

I kept listening very hard.

Then Mr. Irvin said with remorse, "Since I couldn't have this girl I told her boyfriend I was going to tell his parents unless he let me have her. So one night he brought her to me. I was so overwhelmed with her beauty…couldn't help myself….she tried to stop me but I wouldn't let her go."

I said, "Mr. Irvin, that is your past. You don't have to tell me this."

But Mr. Irvin felt so guilty he had to have someone to confess to.

He said, "She was so beautiful…so beautiful I just had to have her…I… had to have her."

I looked at Mr. Irvin and asked him, "How do you feel about her now?"

He replied, "I wish I could see her now… to tell her how I really feel about her. I even would like to apologize for my behavior toward her."

That's when I asked, "What is her name? I might know it."

Suddenly he hesitated for a moment. I don't think he wanted to tell me her name. I looked at the clock. It was almost time to return to my duties. I continued to hold Mr. Irvin's hand.

I repeated, "Your past is your past. SInce you feel so guilty of your past, I know only one person that can forgive you."

I thought about Mrs. Lois, and now I forgave her. It wasn't us. It was God dealing with our hearts. I remembered one of the ways to please himwas to forgive one another. I continued to talk about God to Mr. Irvin. He was in tears. He told me he was afraid to die.

I told Mr. Irvin, "God is the only one who can give you peace in the midst of trying times."

I thought about myself and how God had given me the comfort to go on with my life without a mother and a father. I knew the angels were watching over me and Mr. Irvin.

I felt so uneasy. Mr. Irvin really felt sorry for what he had done. I said to myself, I got to find that colored woman he was in love with.

Before I left, I asked, "If you tell me the woman's name…I probably can find her."

He still was hesitant to tell me.

Then slowly he said, "Can...can...Candace is her name. I don't know her last name."

My eyes nearly popped out of my head when he said that name.

"Is she called Candy for short?" I asked.

He replied in a hesitant voice again, "Yes...yes...that's what her boyfriend called her sometimes... but he also called her Cee Cee."

Feeling strange about this conversation, I stood back from his bed and just looked at him. Candace is my mama's name, and they call her Candy for short.

"Oh, NO!" I said out loud.

Mr. Irvin said, "What's wrong, Dee?!"

I couldn't tell him because I didn't know for sure it was my mama. There are a lot of Candace's around. I thought maybe if I took the blood test to see if I matched, it would give me some answers. I quickly ran out of the room. All this time Mr. Irvin knew who my mama was. I couldn't stand being in the same room with him, even if he was my father.

CHAPTER 15

The next morning, I woke up with a headache. I tossed and turned all night wondering if Mr. Irvin was my father. Then I thought about Mama and how she would feel so I looked up to heaven.

I said, "Dear God, If Mr. Irvin is my father, please reveal it to me."

I heard Mrs. Lucy call me from the kitchen. I went into the kitchen but I wasn't my happy-go-lucky self.

Mrs. Lucy said, "Child, you don't look too good today."

"I just had a bad night," I answered.

"Well, maybe this cup of tea will help you," she said, pouring the tea in a cup in front of me.

My mind could not stay off of what Mr. Irvin told me yesterday.

"Delilah! Delilah!" said Mama Lucy.

She was trying to get my attention while I was staring at the steam coming from the cup of tea.

"Oh Oh I'm all right," I said in a squeaky voice.

Then I said, "Mama Lucy... if... if you knew where your daughter was...would you forgive her for leaving?"

I was trying to figure out what to do in my situation.

Mama Lucy replied, "You know what. I used to think I would never forgive my daughter. God dealt with me on that. He told me if I didn't forgive my daughter, he wasn't going to forgive me for my faults. That's when I came to terms with myself and realized my daughter is all that I have."

I kept listening. She was giving me some good advice.

Mama Lucy said, "I would greet her with open arms because I still love my daughter."

Her answer gave me the will power to go and be a donor for Mr. Irvin whether he was or was not my biological father.

I could see the water in Mama Lucy's eyes. She really missed her daughter. I changed the subject by asking her if she had heard from Travis.

She said, "Oh, yes. He's home for winter break."

I said. "Maybe he will come to see me."

"Of course he will." Mama Lucy said, a jolly tone in her voice.

See it worked. I did get back into a good mood. There was a knock on the door. A shadow was all I could see.

"Who is it!" I yelled.

Guess who? It was Travis.

"How is everybody doing?" he asked.

I kept my head down looking at the grinds of my tea bag.

Mama Lucy looked at me and said, "We're fine… We're just fine… How are you doing in college?"

Travis replied, "Just great! I thought I would come by and see Delilah."

Mama Lucy loved this. She had been wanting to hook us up from day one.

"Well, I got to go!" I shouted.

"Where are you going? You don't have school today!" Mama Lucy said.

She was trying to imply you can stay home. I told her I was going to see Mr. Irvin.

Travis asked, "Maybe I can come along?"

I invited Travis just in case Henry and blondie showed up. I enjoyed making Henry work for my heart even though I didn't want him back

As we entered the hospital, the staff was staring at me because I was with this colored guy. One of the nurses at the nurses' station was whispering to another nurse. I know they were wondering where I was going with Travis. Travis was very dark but handsome. Me, playing white, this was a no-no. I insisted that Travis sit in the waiting room while I visited Mr. Irvin, knowing that Mr. Irvin was prejudiced.

When I entered the room, Mr. Irvin was sitting up eating his breakfast. He was still in a very bad mood.

He said, "Hi, Dee. I see you're off today." He noticed I wasn't wearing my uniform

I said, "Mr. Irvin, I can't stay long because I have to go somewhere." I didn't want him to know if I was going to be a donor just in case my blood didn't match. I visited with him for a short time until it was time to do the test.

Travis waited the entire time while I was in the room being tested.

My mind kept wondering if I would be a match. This moment could be one of the worst or best moments of my life.

I heard the nurse say, "That's all. Delilah. You can wait in the waiting room. We will call you when we have the results.

Sweat was popping from my head. I hoped my hair didn't curl up because my hair didn't resist moisture.

While I was waiting, I heard a woman screaming and yelling in the halls… She had a voice that sounded familiar. I heard her yell again. Travis looked at me and I looked at him. We were wondering what was going on. So both of us stood up and went to the door of the waiting room. Looking down the hallsI noticed a woman in a wheelchair yelling at the nurses.

Since I was familiar with the staff, they didn't prevent me from helping the woman.

I rushed over to the wheelchair. Before I could assist her, I noticed she really looked familiar. I asked the nurse who she was. When the nurse started pronouncing her first name Candice, my mouth dropped in shock. I grabbed the shair and noticed her full name. It was my mama. I ran over to her. She didn't recognized me. I told her I was Delilah, her daughter. She just stared at me as though I was a stranger. She was delirious! She was fighting the nurses. Then the doctor came over to me.

He said, "Do you know this woman?"

I hastily shouted, "Yes… Yes…She is my mama!"

Then the doctor explained her condition to me. Mama was on heroine. The doctor said she had been addicted for sometime.

I cried loudly, "Mama! Mama! This is me! Delilah!"

She was out of it. Travis came over and took me in his arms while they were taking her away.

The nurse said, "Delilah? How…"

Before she could even think about what to say I said, "Yes…yes… she is my mama. Yes… I am colored."

I paused for a while and looked her straight in the eyes and said, "What does color have to do with treatment of a patient?"

The nurse just looked at me with astonished eyes and walked off as if to say, Who do you think you are?

While they were taking Mama away, tears were dropping from my eyes like raindrops. I tried to hold on to the wheelchair, but Travis took my hands away from the chair and held on to me.

The doctor said, "Delilah, I can't give you any answers now. We will let you know her condition later. Just continue to wait in the waiting room. Someone will let you know about any treatments that will be done."

As we walked toward the waiting room, I continued to weep heavily. I thought I finally found my mama, but she didn't know me. Then I started remembering all of the episodes of the woman on the street. That woman was my mama all the time. I didn't know. She didn't look like my mama. My mama always looked pretty. Now I know why she looked that way. She was on drugs.

"But why… Why?" I continued to cry.

Travis held me in his arms as we waited for my test results. Ever since I saw my mama in that wheelchair I wasn't excited about the test results. I just wanted more information on my mama's condition.

The test results can wait, I thought.

CHAPTER 16

While waiting for the results, I decided to call Mama Lucy and tell her about the good, and not so good news. Mama Lucy didn't hesitate when I talked to her. She immediately came to the hospital. She was excited for me. but disappointed about the way I saw my mama.

As she entered the waiting room, she grabbed a hold of me tightly. I started crying again.

Mama Lucy said, "Baby, it's going to be okay. Remember, God sees everything and he knows how much we can bear."

Mama Lucy always knew the right words to say. We continued to Converse in the room. Then a nurse's aide came in the waiting room and brought my mama's clothing. In her clothing was the locket she always wore.

Mama Lucy noticed the locket and said, "May I see that?"

I said, "Yes. This is my mama's. She always wore it, but she never let me look inside because she told me I had to wait until I was older."

I handed the locket to Mama Lucy. Her eyes became big then she put her hand over her face and she started weeping.

"What's wrong, Mama Lucy?" I asked. Mama Lucy couldn't say anything. She just kept staring at the locket. Then she began to open up the locket. She passed the locket over to me. Inside was a picture of Mama Lucy and another man.

Mama Lucy asked me, "What is your mother's name?"

I replied, "Candace, but everybody called her Candy." Mama Lucy began to squeeze her arms around me tightly.

Trembling, she shouted, "I am your grandmother!... You...you are my grandbaby!"

I was short for words. All this time I had been living with my real grandmother. I reached into my purse and pulled out the letter I had been holding. I handed it over to Mama lucy.. I didn't realize I was holding the missing parts of my life in my purse. Mama Lucy slowly took the letter out of my hand. As she read it tears started streaming down her face.

Mama Lucy cried. "All these years. I just knew my baby didn't just run away. I finally got my baby back!"

While Mama Lucy was dripping with tears, I was streaming with tears too. There were even tears coming out of Travis' eyes.

Waiting impatiently for the test results, I stood in the hallway for a while by myself. Down the hallway was the man with the white suit again. He looked at me, tilted his white hat and smiled at me.

"Delilah! Delilah!" The nurse shouted.

I turned toward her. She was coming with my results. I turned around to see if the white suit man was still there. He had disappeared again.

The nurse said, "Come with me, Delilah. The doctor wants to tell you your results."

We entered the doctor's office. She asked me to sit down. As I was sitting, the doctor had a questioning look on his face.

"What... What?!" I said.

With gestures of his hands, he told me to relax and take a deep breath.

"'The test results came out positive. You...you are a match," he exclaimed.

I shouted, "How can that be? It must be... it must be...a mistake!"

In a way I wanted it to be true, but I was reacting to all of the excitement.

The doctor continued to explain, "Mr. Irvin's blood type is so rare that only a blood relative can match it."

This time my mouth was open and I couldn't say a word. I fainted!

When I regained consciousness, Mama Lucy and Travis were standing over me. They had already heard the news.

I don't know if I can take anymore news.

As Mama Lucy held me in her arms, she said, "Honey, the lord done answered your prayers and my prayers. Praise the lord.

I grabbed her tightly and started weeping again, but it was a joyful cry.

Now I have to figure out a way to tell Mr. Irvin. I have already asked God to help me. I got to believe he will answer. So far he has. I want Mr. Irvin to accept he is my father, no matter what it may cost him.

While we were continuing to wait on the condition of my mother, Mama Lucy pulled out her wallet and started updating me on pictures of Mama when she was younger. I had never seen Mama Lucy so happy. There were sparkles in her eyes like diamonds. She always wanted to know the whereabouts of Mama.

Another doctor came in the waiting room to give me information. He asked me to step outside the door into the hallway. I asked Mama Lucy to come, too. I explained to the doctor she was Mama's mother. He told us they finally got her sedated and that we should come back tomorrow. The doctor told us, if she would have come an hour later, we probably would have lost her.

Mama Lucy turned to me and said, "God's time is not our time."

CHAPTER 17

I woke up early. I was excited about seeing Mama again. Mama Lucy and I ate breakfast. This time it was different. It was grandmother with granddaughter. We had a lot to catch up on. Travis didn't go with us this time, but he did comfort me all night. Mama Lucy was right! Travis is a great guy!

We left early for the hospital. As we entered Mama's room, she was lying on her side facing the wall. When she heard our footsteps in the room, she turned over. She looked at me, then she looked at Mama Lucy. Her eyes looked like she had been crying for a while.

The only words Mama would say were, "Please forgive me… please…please..!"

She reached her hands out for us. I touched Mama's warm hands and held them to my face. She always had warm soft hands. Mama Lucy went over to her and hugged her.

Mama Lucy whispered, "Sh…sh… You are in good hands now."

Mama whispered back, "I know…I know."

It was a great reunion. Then Mama sat up in the bed. It seemed like she had regained her strength. She put her soft hands up to my face and started pulling at my hair.

I said smiling, "Don't even ask me."

Mama smiled. She knew I had been playing the game she taught me. She spoke out loud, "Delilah, I've missed you."

She looked at Mama Lucy with sorrowful eyes. She started explaining what happened. Mama Lucy kept trying to tell Mama she didn't have to explain anything, but she insisted we needed to know.

Mama said while looking at Mama Lucy, "The day I left home started a nightmare. I left home because I had made a big mistake... Don't want you or Delilah to say anything, just listen. The white guy I was dating is not Delilah's father....took me to a restaurant to meet another white man who was older...He told me I had to sleep with him in order for him to keep it a secret...I didn't want to lose my relationship with Jerry...Jerry kept insisting I do it. I fought hard. That is when he hit me... later I became pregnant.... I....I couldn't tell you, Mama, because I was afraid you were going to kick me out... so...so I ran away and had Delilah." She looked at me and smiled. "She is the best thing that ever happened to me." I smiled back at Mama.

Mama Lucy said, "Don't tell me anymore. I'm sure..."

Mama said, "Mama don't say anymore. It is not your fault... To make a long story short... It was hard for me raising a daughter by myself. One day I met this white guy. He told me I could work for him. I didn't know it was being a whore and before I knew it, I was with men and using drugs. It became a permanent job for me." Mama gave me a remorseful look. "The night I left you with Mrs. Lois, I had gotten into some trouble with one of the guys. I happened to see a man murdered. They tried to kill me, but instead they told me to keep my mouth closed or they would kill Delilah. I couldn't let Delilah be in danger so I left.

"I tried to contact Mrs. Lois several times. She would never return calls or contact me. I even tried to contact you, Mama, several times. But I didn't know what to say." She started to sob. "And with me being on drugs..I....I....was no good for you."

Mama Lucy said with tears in her eyes, "That's okay. You are home now and that is where you are going to stay"

We hugged each other with joyful tears. I wanted to tell Mama about Mr. Irvin being in the hospital, but Mama Lucy signaled me with her eyes to be quiet.

CHAPTER 18

A few days later, Mama was still in the hospital. She was recovering quickly. I couldn't wait for her to come home.

It was around 6 a.m. The phone rang. I jumped out of my bed. Mama Lucy beat me to the phone. It was for me. The hospital had called to let me know Mr. Irvin's condition had worsened.

Mama Lucy went out to the car to warm it up. The car wouldn't start. She kept trying to start the car. Finally, she flooded the engine. Time was moving fast. Since the car was stalled, Mama Lucy told me to take a cab. It took the cab about 45 minutes. Meanwhile, the hospital called again. They told me that the transplant has to be done immediately. I began to fret.

When I reached Mr. Irvin's room, I noticed he was not there. I looked around to see if anyone knew anything. All of a sudden the doctor saw me.

He said, "Delilah, I need to see you."

I said, "I'm ready to do the transplant."

The doctor looked at me with a solemn look. I knew something wasn't right. He came closer. I was standing outside Mr. Irvin's room. He asked me to step into the room. That is when he told me: Mr. Irvin had passed away about fifteen minutes ago.

He held out an envelope and said, "He wanted me to give you this."

I slowly took the envelope from his hand. He gave me a brief hug then left in order for me to be alone.

I stood still for a while because I couldn't believe he was gone. I had just found out he was my father, now… he was gone!

I started walking out of the hospital. I had tears coming from my eyes for Mr. Irvin. I guess because he trusted me so much. I was so upset I sat on the bench in front of the hospital. I kept looking at the envelope. Finally I opened it slowly. Chills ran all through my spine as I read the letter. I could not stop the tears from streaming down my cheeks. The letter read:

Dear Dee,

By the time you receive this letter, I will be gone. I told you, I wasn't going to be here next year. I want you to know that I always knew you wasn't a white girl. You resemble your Mama so much, I had to have you close to me. That's right! I knew you were Candy's daughter. But I didn't know until yesterday that you were my daughter. I am sorry for not being there for you. I really cared for your mother, but she didn't have any intentions on furthering our relationship, especially after the incident, you know. I didn't get a chow to ask her forgiveness. Please tell her, I am sorry, and that I have always loved her from the first moment I saw her. Many times I said prejudiced remarks around you about colored people, but it was only because I couldn't have your mother. I was angry. Not because she was colored, but because I couldn't be colored with her. You understand the times.

Dee, just remember you are a beautiful person, not just on the outside, but also on the inside. Your color has nothing to do with who you are inside. I want you to know I was listening to you when you said God gives peace and he forgives. I believe that. Don't worry about me. I am going to a place that knows none of my past. Like you said, The past is the past.

Please forgive me and don't forget to tell your mama. You are going to make a great nurse!

P.S. please see the attorney listed on the business card enclosed
With past and present love,
Your real Dad, Mr. Irvin

After reading this letter, I couldn't feel anything but forgiveness for Mr. Irvin. I only wish he could have enjoyed me as his daughter. But when I thin about it, we did have some good times together and I believe it was all because he had the feeling that I was his child.

I followed Mr. Irvin's instructions. I went to see the attorney that was the business card. The attorney told me. Mr. Irvin left Mama and me the restaurant and enough money to live on for the rest of our lives. We bought a house in a mixed neighbor where color doesn't matter.

Mama is now the owner of the restaurant. I told her the story about Mattie and her dress shop, so she decided to do the same thing. The business prospered more then when Mr. Irvin operated it.

Henry still works in the restaurant. Mama made him the manager. We are just friends and I like it that way. Travis finished college and we see other regular now. We might even get married.

By the way, the Civil Rights Act Of 1968 was passed by Congress. You see it didn't just move, it passed.

And guess what? I did become a great nurse like my *real father* said. I am now the supervisor at the same hospital that didn't hire **black** nurses. That's right! We are no longer called ***colored people.***

YOU SEE, CHARACTER IS STRONGER THAN COLOR!

THE END

Delilah Too!

"The Camouflage continues..."

Dedicated To:
Richard Lee Jr.
Kincie Elaine
Jamie Lee
and my beautiful grandchildren

ACKNOWLEDGEMENT

To The Most Highest Being, "God"
Thank you.

CHAPTER 1

It seemed almost like a dream, finding out my true identity. I couldn't believe how all the pieces came together. My father Mr. Irvin! Who would believe it! My grandmother, Momma Lucy! That was impossible! Most of all, my Momma is alive! Now that's what I am talking about. Momma was the best piece of the puzzle I found. It was like putting together a jigsaw puzzle with one of the corners missing. When I found that piece (my Momma), the entire picture came together, well almost came together.

Mr. Irvin left us with all of his worldly possessions. I couldn't imagine me being rich and all that. During the late 60's, black people being rich didn't come over night. You were either accused of stealing or playing the number, "you know what I mean", illegal gambling. Well Momma played it smart, even though we had lots of money; she went through Mr. Irvin's attorney for everything so there wouldn't be any suspicion of illegal gambling. During these times, if you were doing something out of the ordinary, you had better make sure you have the white man backing you. We had nothing to worry about because Mr. Irvin's attorney had already taken care of any inquiries. For example: Even though we legally owned the restaurant, by word-of-mouth customers think Henry (the ex-busboy) is the owner. Technically he is just the manager. Our lawyer pays Henry extra each month to keep his mouth shut and believe me; he keeps it shut for those extra bucks. So, when anyone comes in inquiring about who owns the place, Henry would step out and say he is the owner. He only did this as a favor for Mom and me. Looking at the extra dough each month enhanced the favor very well. It was worth it because it kept us in safe territory. You see he still has this thing for me. I do not do reruns if you know what I mean. If a guy doesn't play straight the first time, I just get rid of him. Henry was my first boyfriend and the last to ever make my heart fragile. This is my motto now "No reruns!!

We bought a beautiful house in a mixed neighborhood. Well, we thought it was mixed but the blacks here act just like they don't know you: the upper-class type blacks. Most of them had to work decades to accomplish what we gained after one death. So, our house is another camouflage; we tell the neighbors we are housekeeping for an elderly couple up north. In a way it is the truth; we bought the house from our attorney 's parents. The house is huge with three bedrooms upstairs and two downstairs. It also has a porch with a swing in the front. It sort of looked like one of those plantation houses. Grandma Lucy comes to visit often; I was hoping she would move in with us, due to her failing health. I remember the last time I took her to see the doctor; he confirmed she had an enlarged heart. I wanted her to stay with us, so that I could take care of her like she took care of me all those years. But not Momma Lucy she loved her house. She has always been a cleaning fanatic.

Now, I hate it when she comes over because all she can think of is clean this and that. This is when I began to forget the illness and wish she would remain in her own territory. Even though I love grandma, she can be a real witch when it comes to cleaning, but a real doll when it comes to love and understanding.

Since Momma doesn't work, I am supporting both of us, even though we have enough finances to carry into the next generation. It is still difficult for blacks to justify being rich in the South unless you are a doctor or lawyer and I ain't any of that, but close. So, we continue to camouflage some areas in our lives just to keep peace. Not just with the whites only, but with our own people sometimes.

Sometimes I wonder if Mr. Irvin was in the mafia, because there are so many digits on our bank statement monthly. Our lawyer meets with us monthly to show us our debits and credits; this is just so we don't seem suspicious with our spending, especially with me being the only source of income from the outside. I think he gets a big cut in this matter, because he is not concerned about the cover-ups he is doing. I wouldn't either, knowing that he has a salary for life. But he never shows us his salary, and he rushes through the statements, so we won't ask any questions. I used to ask him for a copy of the statement, but he wouldn't reply, "If these papers were caught in your hands you would have to answer some big questions". I didn't bother anymore, so as long as Momma was taken care of I was satisfied.

You see there was a lot of camouflaging still going on in my life. I will be glad when a black person's character will be esteemed high, especially in the south. Talk about cover up. Now that I am a head nurse at Memorial Hospital it is even worse.

Some of the patients still have that plantation mentality. They just cannot stand for me to touch them. Not only do the patients have that stigma, but some of my co-workers do also. But I remember what Mr. Irvin told me in his last words, "I will be a great nurse". Through God's help, I am trying. Believe me it takes God to control that beast inside of me that wants to get back at the world for all the wrongdoing that was done to me in the past. I haven't forgotten that it was God's grace that kept me through all these years. Also, I sort of figured out that man in the White Suit. I believed he was and angel, because whenever there was a piece of my life was being sewn together, he would show up. As a matter of fact, I don't recall seeing his presence anymore since the time he visually smiled at me and disappeared. I know I am not crazy, Momma always told me angels are watching us daily. She told me the angels are the ones who record all your good and bad. That is one reason I am glad Momma didn't die. Now she attends church regularly and she sings in the choir. By the way she carries herself, I believe she gave her life to God.

There are no drugs or alcohol in her life anymore and of course, no men.

She doesn't even go out on the town anymore. Grandma Lucy said, "God done resurrected her daughter" but I say, "God done resurrected a soul". It feels good to have a positive role model in my life. With the both of them, I can't run off the road, because they are behind me one hundred percent to keep me steady.

Speaking about life, my life is beginning to move like a roller coaster. I am constantly battling my feelings for my future companion, Travis. Travis has been my close friend since the time I moved in with Momma Lucy. He was always by my side. When the pieces of my life were put together, he was standing beside me. Sometimes I want to marry him and sometimes I would say let's just be friends. I enjoyed us being friends with no strings attached. This is really bothering me. I can't return to my old self--dating white guys. I really care for Travis, but something is missing. Maybe it is because we have been like brother and sister to long or maybe I still have feelings for Henry since he dropped Blondie. Guess What? She was sneaking around with some black guy and got knocked up. Her parents made her give up the baby for adoption, so they say. Henry won't talk about it because, the same table he turned on me turned on him. Lettie warned me about going across the line for a man. I tell her all the time to just pray for me. Some people have chocolate fever; I guess I have vanilla fever, if you know what I mean. But it's considered normal because of my bloodline.

Lettie lucked up and got herself a real gentleman, black, handsome and smart. His name is Sam, but we call him SJ for short because he is Sam Jr. He is a postman for the United States. He makes a descent living. I told Lettie she better not let him swim away. Of course, she didn't, and they are engaged to be married soon. I am lucky to be her maid of honor. This is really going to be fun. Lettie and I have been friends since we were toddlers now, I get to see her become a wife. It sounds neat to me. Mrs. Lois and I still are friends. Even though she was put on probation for the hell she put me through, she continued to cash those checks even when I was still living with Momma Lucy. The social workers caught up with her, because every time they made home visits to see me, Mrs. Lois would make up all sorts of lies, they caught up with her finally.

One day I received a subpoena for court about the situation. Mrs. Lois asked me to speak on her behalf at the hearing. I could have thought of all the ungodly mischief she and her husband did to me. But I though about Lettie and her feelings and what will happen to her if she loses the confidence she has in her mother. Being reluctant to my feelings I realized Mrs. Lois had paid enough with the death of Mr. John. So, when the judge asked me about my living ability at their house, I thought about all the good times Lettie and I shared and how those hard times brought me where I am today. I remembered what Momma Lucy told me, "What seems hard today is just the answer for tomorrow." Mrs. Lois looked at me with a curious eye. I know she thought I was going to hatchet her in the courtroom.

Forgiveness means forgiveness, I thought to myself Mrs. Lois was good to me in her own way. After the announcement of her sentence, which was five years of probation, paying back the money, and she could no longer harbor children in her home, Mrs. Lois just gave a great big hug with tears streaming down her eyes. It reminded me of the time we reunited in forgiveness a few years ago in church. Her words sounded like a foreign language. But I did hear her say, "My home will always be your home". I appreciated that. But I have a home and I wouldn't want to be reminded of the immoral incidents that went on in that house. I love my home with Momma and me. It is like old times again, but now I get to watch Momma get pretty in her Sunday best. The aroma of her perfume still smells like Momma. I can smell her scent a mile away.

Sometimes I feel like something is going to happen. Everything in my life seemed perfect. I was always told when the sun is shining you better look out because a hurricane is coming soon. You better believe it; a storm was right around the corner.

CHAPTER 2

It was a bright Saturday morning. Lettie and I were supposed to go shopping for her wedding dress today. I picked up Lettie in the car I inherited in the estate. Mr. Irvin left his 1956 beige Chevy to me. It was sort of like new since he hardly ever drove the thing. He was a very conservative man. He believed in preserving everything. When we received our inheritance, it included a lot of ancient heirlooms, I guess from his ancestors. Those items looked practically new. I believe some of them never were used and worth a pretty penny.

As I approached Lettie's house, I began to get the jitters. You see, it has been a long time since I had sat foot into Mrs. Lois's house. I felt if I stayed away from it, then I could get over the bad memories from the past. I stopped the car and sat in it for a moment. I could feel my heart panicking as I turned the key to release it from the steering wheel. As I opened the car door, my knees began to tremble like someone having a nervous breakdown. I thought, "Calm down Delilah, Mr. John is dead… he is dead." Then I braced myself and began walking in slow motion toward the door. I could hear Mrs. Lois and Lettie's voices seeping through the door cracks. No matter what, I still think Mrs. Lois doesn't trust me, I can feel it when I am around Lettie's fiancée, SJ. Mrs. Lois always stays around when he and I are in the same room. Whether she knows it or not, I am not interested in SJ. Best friend's rules: Never talk to each other's past or present boyfriends. Lettie and I always kept this rule. I guess that's one of the reasons we are still best friends.

I knocked on the door. Mrs. Lois opened the door and gave me one of those baby hugs.

"Hello, Delilah" she said, "I see you and Lettie are going to pick out the dress for her big day."

Someway and somehow Mrs. Lois gets under my skin. She is one of those so-called Christians who laugh in your face and smiles behind your back. I know she forgave me but the way she carries herself in front of me you would think she is putting on a fake love attack.

As Letttie disappeared toward her room she yelled, "Delilah, hold on a minute, I left my checkbook in the room."

I didn't want to be in the same room with Mrs. Lois and being in the same house still wasn't satisfying. I browsed my eyes across the room as I noticed the same set up as when I was a teenager. Flashbacks of the horrible attack flooded my mind as I studied the room carefully. Mrs. Lois noticed the blurred look upon my face, but there was no time for a conversation, thank God. Lettie rushed out of the room and kissed her mom on the cheek.

I gathered she knew I didn't fit in with her home anymore. We kind of read each other's thoughts occasionally. Sometimes I am super thankful for a friend like that. Well, you can say, we are sisters forever. While dashing toward the car doors and hurrying to drive out of the driveway, Lettie noticed I had perspiration running down my face.

She said, "Delilah, you don't have to come into the house next time, I know it is not comfortable being in my house, just honk the horn next time."

I replied, "If I honk the horn that will be impolite.... and., (hesitating what to say)...girl just pray for me...just pray for me.

Lettie said, "Delilah, do you trust me?"

"Of Course, I do... I will always trust you" I replied, wandering why she would say such a thing.

With concern for me, Lettie gratefully said, "Then get you some help...you cannot go through life with that fear hanging over your shoulder."

As I was stopping at the light, I thought, "She was right", I have to get over the past in order to get better.

Lettie thought I was ignoring her.

"Are you listening to me? Asked Lettie, "You know the pastor can help you, he does counsel all the time."

Noticing how serious Lettie was, I said. "Maybe one day, I don't like everybody knowing my business."

"But everybody knew about what happened to you with my dad… so get over that and get some help." Lettie replied with a concerned tone of voice.

To indicate I was going to do so, I shook my head to insinuate that I would get some help. But when, I really didn't know.

Lettie continued to rant on about me getting some help and that if I would let go maybe I could relate better with others. I admit, I do have a problem with getting close to people especially men, but there are a lot of women out there who do. I didn't think that indicated something was wrong with me. Well in my eyes I felt I was one hundred percent okay.

Finally, we came to our destination, "The Wedding Dress Shop", that's the name; it has all kinds of formal dresses, from imported to made in the USA. It was one of the finest shops in downtown and only the rich could afford to buy a dress there. I had never been inside of it, but they tell me that you have to look rich even to get service. That is why Lettie and I put on our Sunday best to impress.

When you walk inside the door, there is a lady standing at the door to greets you. I entered in first just in case I had to camouflage to get top rate service. Low and behold I did. I thought all of this stopped in the 60's.

The beauty of laces, pearls, sequins and you name it on the apparels astounded Lettie. She ran over to one wedding dress with nothing but lace and pearls. I watched, as the sales lady was not too fond of Lettie touching the dresses. I went over to Lettie and tried to pull her off before the lady came over. I didn't make it in time.

"May I help you?" the sales lady asked.

"No ma'am…I am just looking" Lettie replied. Lettie began to feel insecure in this high-priced bridal shop.

Then the sales lady looked over to me and saw me browsing through the dresses but didn't say anything.

She lashed back at Lettie and said, "We have some consignment dresses over there."

She pointed toward the gowns in the further back room. Lettie knew she could afford any dress, because my wedding present to her was to buy her dress for her. Since I can afford it why not help a sister out. I was beginning to get furious with this sales lady, but I didn't want to act ignorant, so I went over to Lettie and said out loud, "I heard you are having a big wedding and your wedding dress is going to cost in the thousands.... must be nice to have a rich uncle up north to buy your gown"

The sales lady turned around and said to me, "Do you know this woman?"

"Of course, why her uncle is one of the richest black men up north." I said.

Now I knew this woman thought I was white, and a white woman's word is her bond in this society. The sales lady went over to Lettie and apologized. Even told her about the ten percent discount sale, which she would have never known. Lettie was sort of upset with me, because she didn't want me to bail her out of every prejudice situation. But I kept telling Lettie that some things never change. I didn't mind being a back up for my sister. We should all feel that way.

At that moment Lettie was getting first class service from all the salespeople, even the manager. You see, money talks.

They were bringing out all sorts of gowns, even the ones they had been saving for special customers. I could see that Lettie enjoyed this first-class treatment, as she turned around with a beautiful gown. It was as though she was an enchanted princess in a dreamland. I felt excited for Lettie, because she deserved more than this. I had established firmly in my mind a long time ago (when we grasped fingers) that whatever is mine will also be hers. One thing about our sister relationship, Lettie would rather do without before she would use me. Now I call that a real sisterhood.

Lettie found herself a gorgeous pearl and lace gown; she looked like a queen for a day. Her headpiece was a tiara with pearls and sequins.

When I glanced at Lettie in the mirror, I did a double take. She was so beautiful and looked like a princess in snowy white colors looking for her prince. I am very proud of my sister and going to do the best that I can to make her special day great.

As we approached the sales counter, the sales lady, asked us to come again and smiled. I believe she was smiling because of the over thousand dollars check Lettie gave her. She was even more delighted when she found out the check wasn't rubber. Oh, yes, she called the bank to make sure it was good. It just made her look bad for prejudging people. She could hardly look at us in the face, when she asked us to come back, I replied through my gnashing teeth, "Maybe in another time or life". Lettie heard me and smirked with her hands over her mouth. This was another episode of the new era and time. I guess we have to get used to it.

We were already late for the meeting that was going to be held at our restaurant at 3:00. This is where I would get to meet the bridesmaids, ushers etc. As we entered the restaurant door the bell on the door rang. When it rang, I picked up a remorseful feeling. It was a front door memory of Mr. Irvin and me. I grasped a hold of the bell tightly thinking about all of the great times Mr. Irvin and I had in the place. It was sort of funny; I hadn't felt this way in a long time.

Lettie saw me startled at the door. It was as though I couldn't take that bell out of my hand. Lettie gently removed the bell out of my hand. I know she was thinking I was retracting my memories. So, she redirected my mind to another direction as we entered the dining area.

"Delilah, I am so glad you are helping me with this," said Lettie.

I stepped out of a dazed and stated, "Oh…Oh…thanks."

"Oh thanks…you mean…you're welcome," Lettie replied strangely.

The entire wedding party was waiting on us. Lettie's fiancée, Sam pulled her by surprise and gave her a large hug and romantic kiss in front of us. I felt sort of jealous because he was always treating her like she was his world. I know I shouldn't feel jealous because she deserves a good man in her life. Maybe God would bless me with one. Before I could get the words out of my mouth, I noticed this gentleman looking at me from across the room. He was very handsome, and his eyes could put you in a trance. His countenance was very fair and self-assured. I believe he was the sort of man that thought he could get any woman he approached. Lettie saw me checking him out. Just before she called the meeting to order, Lettie moved over close to me and whispered.

"All right now, we don't need any camouflaging."

"What do you mean, no camouflaging?" I softly said.

"You know what I mean," (pointing to Henry at the counter) Lettie said.

"All I am doing is looking", I replied.

Lettie looked at him did a doubled take at me as she noticed there was some chemistry going on between us. I almost moved over close to him, but Lettie jerked me back in a sneaky way.

Lettie began the meeting, telling everyone what his or her duties were in preparing for the big day. Even though Lettie was doing all the arrangements, I was her coordinator and maid of honor. She didn't trust anyone but me. Maybe it's because I am her banker for this occasion. After announcing everybody's positions, I noticed this guy was not a part of the wedding party.

Now this put a lot of inquiring in my mind. I wanted to know who this nice-looking hunk was. Oh, I forgot to tell you, he is a white guy. That is why Lettie told me "No Camouflaging!" She knew what kind of drama I went through with Henry.

But you know what, I can't base one bad relationship on another, which would be prejudiced, I mean, downright prejudiced!

Before I could finish my thoughts, Sam announced, "Dinner is on me today…everybody!"

Now that the meeting was over I got my chance to move in on this hunk. Lettie knew I was up to something. Low and behold she quickly grabbed me by the hand and finagled me into sitting with Sam and her at their table. That was Lettie for you, she was always trying to protect. While we were eating, I could see from the corner of my eyes, the guy continuing to look at me.

I asked Sam, "Who is he?'

"Oh, that's Jeremy. He is one of the guys who works with me," Sam replied.

"He is probably already taken," Lettie informed me.

"No! He isn't", Sam said smiling at me.

Lettie glared at Sam with that look. She continued to interfere with her protection rights.

Sam continued to give me information about Jeremy. He informed me that Jeremy knew about me from him. That is one of the reasons he came to the meeting. Lettie disapproved of that, because she felt I needed to be counseled before I entered into another drastic relationship. But who says it was going to be drastic? She was always overstepping my decisions.

Sam and Lettie persistently bickered back in forth about this guy and me. Meanwhile, he continued to stare at me from the counter. He was sitting alone, and I wanted to intervene and entertain him with a conversation. As he got up, moving toward our table, I didn't say a word.

Sam and Lettie were still bickering at each other. As he got closer, I began to feel as though goose bumps were appearing on my face. I was hoping not, I must appear to be beautiful even if it is just for this moment. While I was thinking to myself, he appeared at our table.

"Well Sam, seems like you are ready for the big day" Jeremy said.

"As ready as I am going to be", "Why don't you have a seat?" Sam continued.

Of course, he didn't have to say that, Jeremy quickly sat next to me. I was smiling all behind my ears. Lettie couldn't stand this. SJ introduced us to Jeremy even though Lettie was not interested. But I was highly volcanic by this. Lettie was highly upset with SJ so she excused herself and SJ quickly followed. I guess they had things to talk about. It didn't bother me because now I get a chance to really get acquainted with Jeremy. I wasn't forward at all; I waited for him to initiate the conversation.

"Are you and Lettie good friends?" Jeremy asked.

Pretending to be timid, I replied, "oh yes…not just good friends… we are like sisters."

My hands became wet with sweat as I was holding them under the table trying to think about what he was going to say and how I was going to respond. Jeremy kept looking at my chest. I felt like he was trying to undress me in front of all these people. Finally, there were a sigh of relief when the locket around my neck emotionally aroused him.

"That's a beautiful locket around your neck…it looks very old" he said.

Trying not to let him notice my blouse being so low cut, I pulled the locket up with my front lapel.

"Yes…it is old, it belonged to my mother."

Jeremy asked, "If you don't mind me asking, how come Lettie and you are so close?"

My mind began to ponder, "Why is he asking me this question?" Ah…huh…he thinks I am a white girl!

Then I spoke very sarcastic, "Let me tell you up front, I am mixed …I don't believe we have to choose our friends by color."

I could tell by the look on Jeremy's face, he was sorry he asked that question. Then he started to apologize for the misunderstanding. He asked me if we could start all over with our conversation. I agreed. Everyone deserves a second chance. As we began to talk, Jeremy was telling me about his job as a supervisor at the post office. He also got personal with me and told me he was adopted and that he never knew his real mom.

I wasn't about to tell him my past life. So I just told him about my mom working at this restaurant (she was off today) and I related to him that we had similar jobs because I am a supervisory nurse at the local hospital. I really enjoyed the conversation we had at the table. He seemed to be a very nice gentleman. The only thing I didn't care for so far is, he drank a lot of beers at the table. Momma Lucy always told me to stay away from guys who use a habit for enjoyment. But then I thought, maybe he was nervous and just drinking to calm his nerves. At least I hope so.

Finally, SJ and Lettie resolved their differences. They returned to the table and saw us getting along fine. We were at the restaurant for about an hour more, joking around and laughing. I noticed Jeremy didn't stop drinking. He continued to gulp down more beers. He was in no shape to drive home. Since SJ invited him, he volunteered to drop him home. I decided to take Lettie home, so SJ didn't have to deal with two problems on the way home. Lettie kept asking me questions about Jeremy. She was always nosey about my business.

When we reached Lettie's house, Lettie asked, "Are you going to see Jeremy again?"

"I don't know …but …I sure hope so," I replied with great assurance in my tone of voice.

I knew Lettie didn't want me to remain friendly with Jeremy, but this is my life and all men are not the same.

CHAPTER 3

The sun was beaming on my face as I dreaded getting up for work. I had a terrible night. Lately I have been having nightmares about my past, especially the incident with Mr. John. I never really got over that. Sometimes I would wake up with cold sweats, because I could still feel his cold hands touching my body. It seemed so real at times. Maybe I needed to talk to someone about this. But I didn't know who to go to. It felt so strange talking about it. Well, it was first Sunday, and I didn't want to intrude on my Mom with this because she never really knew the true story and this was her favorite Sunday to attend church. I just couldn't spoil it for her, maybe another time. Ever since I was a little girl, first Sunday was a big day. It wasn't that big to me, but to Momma Lucy it was a very important day, and she always wore white. Momma Lucy told me she wore white because it stood for purity during the Holy Communion ceremony, which she participated in every first Sunday. If those saints didn't feel holy that day, I guess they wouldn't. Momma always told me whiteness should come from the purity of the heart and shine everyday with the deeds we do to one another. I sometimes think people are hypocrites that wear white on Sunday and their hearts are dirty throughout the week.

Meanwhile, I could smell the bacon and eggs aroma coming all the way up the stairs seeping under the door. This was my wake-up call. Momma knew how to get me up. My bedroom was adjacent to mom's; therefore, I was very close to her. Sometimes when I would see her getting dressed in her room, I would recall the moment she left me when I was six. Now I embrace every moment that I have with my mom, because now that I am older, I refuse to take our relationship for granted.

It was 8:30 a.m. the time we would meet at the table for breakfast on Sunday morning. This was quality time for Momma and me. Sometimes this was the only time we were able to chat. I didn't keep much from my mom and even if I did, Lettie with her bell clapper mouth would spill it. I wouldn't be surprised if she already knew about Jeremy. While I was preparing the table for breakfast, I heard the door open up. It was Momma Lucy. She owned a key to the house, so really, we had no privacy from her. She would just come in whenever. Momma Lucy always came around this same time every Sunday. She wanted to keep the family in unity, and this was one of her ways. As she entered into the dining area, Momma was strutting down the stairs. To me, my Momma still is the most beautiful woman in the world. Sometimes I would tease her about getting me a daddy. She always replied, "When God is ready." Now that I am older, she counsels me to wait on God, for a man in my life. But you know me I can't wait. The thought of me turning into a spinster draws me impatiently.

While we were settling down at the breakfast table the phone rang. It was Travis. He informed us that his father passed away that morning from a heart attack. Travis had a close relationship with his father; therefore, he was hurting deeply inside. I wanted to run over and comfort him the way he supported me during my trying times. As I hung up the phone, they saw the deep sympathetic expression on my face. I felt so bad for Travis. I gave Momma Lucy and Momma the news. I was swallowing with remorse as I told them the sad news.

I quickly ran down the street to Travis's house. He was sitting on the front porch with his head down. When he saw me, he ran over to me, and we hugged each other very tightly. I had no words to utter to him because I didn't know how it feels to loose a real father.

Travis said, "Thanks Delilah for coming over."

"Don't say a word…just…" I said.

I couldn't finish my words for watching the tears rolling down his face. Seeing a man cry is like watching a baby die. I began to roll with tears down my throat as we began to walk away from the house for some fresh air.

"Travis, I want you to know that I am here for you...no matter what."

Travis replied, "It just feels... It just feels...so bad." "Why it was just yesterday we were talking on the porch about my future plans...my dad was going to help me with my own business.

"You can still own your own business, Travis." I said.

"I don't think so Delilah...not right now" Travis continued.

"Why not?" I asked.

That is when Travis went on and told me that because his father died, he would have to help his mother take care of some things before he can go into his career. Now this meant we had to put off our plans of an engagement. Which in a way was okay by me because I hadn't really made up my mind what I wanted to do. I agreed with Travis to give him some space to clear up his mind.

As we departed from each other, I kissed him on the jaw, as if to say goodbye. I had possessed in my mind that this was going to be final. I walked slowly back to my corner as I watched Travis enter into the porch door. Momma Lucy and Momma were about to get into the car, when I showed up. Momma Lucy figured out something was wrong other than Travis's dad. She always was a fortuneteller for other peoples' business. She glanced at me with a sly look.

"Is everything okay Delilah?" Momma Lucy asked.

"Yeah...I just had to comfort Travis you know...I think he will be alright."

Both of them appeared to be skeptical about what was really going on. Instead of leading them on, I continued to walk in the house. I could feel their eyes breathing down my neck to give them more information. They continued to get into the car. I was relieved now.

Even though everything was in an uproar with Travis and me, the day turned out to be prosperous. I was on my lunch break in the cafeteria. Like normal, I would always get a salad, some orange juice and my favorite novel of the week; these were my favorite energy foods. Well, while I was in the lunch line picking up my favorite foods, I notice a familiar face staring at me. I couldn't believe my eyes. It was Jeremy. He was also in the cafeteria with another woman. He didn't notice me. I definitely wasn't going to approach him, especially with that woman. So, I tried to hide behind my book. It worked for about fifteen minutes. Then I heard a voice say softly near me. "Delilah...Delilah..."

I continued to hide behind my favorite novel hoping I was at a juicy part to keep me detained. It didn't succeed. Jeremy began to come closer. I peeped around the book and noticed the woman telling him to go ahead. This is when I felt some relief, because a girl friend wouldn't tell her man to go talk to another woman, not with the tone of voice she had. I anticipated they were just friends.

Looking up at Jeremy as he gazed around the book, I was agitated. His breathing down my neck from behind me continued to give me the jitters.

Then I spoke, "You got a problem?"

He answered, "No."

I was trying to frustrate him, but he was determined not to give up.

"Delilah...have I done something to offend you?"

I replied, "Jeremy...you seem...like a nice guy but..."

"But what?" Jeremy replied.

"Well...right now...I don't have room for a significant other in my life."

It seemed like my comment didn't mean a thing to him, because he began to sit his body in the chair next to me. More ever, he put his arm around my chair with ease. I begin to squirm around in my chair. This guy was getting on my nerves. He was to forward. Momma Lucy always told me, if a guy pushes to hard in the beginning he is bound to slow up at the end.

Jeremy continued to give me this flattery conversation about he loved looking at my beautiful eyes. I wanted to tell him to look at something else if he couldn't stand it. But I was enjoying every moment of it. Who is to say you can't enjoy flattery some time. Just as long as you don't let it suck you in. I kept glancing at my watch as he continued to talk. I was hoping someone would page me over the intercom. No such luck this time. Then his conversation begins to strike me with amazement. Jeremy began to tell me about how he was adopted when… "Nurse Baker will you please report to Room 204," the intercom announced.

That's me, I thought…. and at the wrong time…just when Jeremy was beginning to become interesting.

I arose from the chair and packed my lunch left over. Jeremy asked me if he could call me later. I said yeah, but I didn't think he would.

While walking down the hall to room 204, I could hear screaming and distraught yelling coming out of the room. I really didn't want to go in there. I could hear one of the desk nurses calling my name. It was room 204. This patient did not like black people. She was a very wealthy woman who thought all blacks looked alike and were looking for a handout. It was really strange how she got along with me. Could it be because she doesn't know I am partly black? Or could she just be blind? I really don't know the answer to those questions, but I will use these moments to my advantage. Prejudice still exists with all races of color. So, take could care of your Kodak moment.

Suddenly I saw Nurse Smith, one of my black nurses, crying as she ran out of the room.

"Nurse Baker!" "I don't have to take this crap from anyone…I am sick and tired of being called a nigger," Nurse Smith shouted.

I replied, "Calm down Nurse Smith."

"I'll calm down the day you are called a nigger to your face!" Nurse Smith answered in rage. Then she headed toward the staff break room. I proceeded into the room. There was Mrs. Schmidt pretending to be hysterical when all she wanted was some attention. Mrs. Schmidt was a rich old bitty. She and her husband owned practically the whole town. Mr. Schmidt was a circuit judge. He retired a few years ago but he pretends to still control the entire judicial system in this town. Well as for Mrs. Schmidt, she thinks blacks owe her something because she was always donating to the cause of the poor. But we know this was all political. She tries to put that face in the public, but behind closed doors she hates blacks. Today was a perfect example.

Mrs. Schmidt doesn't know I am a half-breed. This is my camouflaging kicking in especially with the job that I have.

As I headed toward Mrs. Schmidt, she began to place her hand on her heart pretending she was having an attack. I was so used to her game. But I played along with it, just to make her comfortable. She was grasping for air and reaching for me. I was her favorite nurse. I was thinking if she only knew.

"Oh…thank God you are here!" She said panicking.

"I thought the nurse was going to give me black needles …or something"

Mrs. Schmidt always thought someone was after her. I believe her deeds were catching up with her.

"Calm down…. it will be all right," I replied.

She was like a baby when I held her in my arms. I am so glad; I have not a prejudice bone in my body. My Momma always told me, "Who gives us the right to judge a person because they were born a different color. It wasn't their choice. It was the way God planned it."

Mrs. Schmidt began to mellow out as I took her vital signs and gave her the shot.

The she said, "Nurse Baker I am so glad you are here with me… you are the only nurse in here I can trust…you see. I don't trust those niggers in here…they might try to do something to me since my husband convicted so many of them."

I always listened to her, but it didn't mean I had to agree with her. Sometimes it is not the right time to say some things. I learned in church that there is a time for everything. Keeping silent can save you from a lot of pain.

As the medication starting penetrating through her body, she began to go into a daze. She grasped the palm of my hand tightly then fell asleep.

Before I could exit out of her room, I could hear my name called again through the halls. One of the doctors told me there was a gentleman looking for me. Low and behold, it was Jeremy. He is a really aggressive guy. As I moved toward him in the halls he began to smile. I just hope he doesn't think that smile meant anything personal to him.

"I just had to see you again." he said, with a delightful look upon his face.

"I didn't get a chance to talk to you Delilah like I wanted to."

I continued to listen to him with a little concern.

"Just give me a chance to get to know you."

He just didn't know. I don't want anyone to really get to know me, because my past had just too much drama.

Then I spoke, "Jeremy... I just am not ready for another relationship in my life...it is just too confusing..."

"I know about Travis, but I can be different." he said.

Being different wasn't the problem. My problem was being able to handle a relationship with a man. Ever since Mr. John touched me I can't stand for anyone to take my personal space. I know I should get some help. Lettie informed me that it was going to get worse unless I do something about it.

Then I said, "You... Jeremy...can we...we be just friends for now?"

"Well, if that is what it will take for you to spend time with me, I accept the friendship."

"I have things to do now, can we talk later?" I asked.

"Sure! When?"

"Not tomorrow, because I have a funeral to attend, I will get back to you"

"Promise me that you won't stay away too long," Jeremy said.

I sort of swallowed hard inside my throat and replied, "You have my scout's honor."

As he was walking away, I know he thought about what I said. I am not a scout so how come my word can be honored. Jeremy just smiled.

CHAPTER 4

It was a gloomy day for me as well as for Travis. It was the day of the final goodbye to Travis's daddy. I really didn't know how to comfort Travis. The pain I felt for him was recapturing the sorrow I felt for Mr. Irvin. I really miss Mr. Irvin. Momma Lucy and Momma attended the funeral services. I decided to meet them at the gravesite. While awaiting their arrival I traveled through the grave tombs passing the time away. I never knew where Mr. Irvin's body was buried, so I traveled over to the north side where the whites were. My eyes were scanning the tombstones. Finally, I came across a family plot that said, "Irvin." There was my father's plot. I stalled for a moment. Then the memories that we had together were swimming around in my head until I began to see drops of water falling on my dress. You know, I really miss him. When I think about it, I spent about four years with Mr. Irvin before he was identified as my real father. That's a long time. In a way, he looked out for me. He was a wonderful person deep inside. He just couldn't be the person he really wanted to be. As the tears were streaming from my face, I recognized next to him was his wife. He must have really loved her because on her stone engraved, "MY BELOVED WIFE WHOM I WILL ALWAYS LOVE, NO MATTER WHAT!" Thoughts began to rumble in my head.

Before I could think anymore, I began to notice the funeral procession rolling in around the cemetery on the south side.

I saw Travis with his arms around his mother. You could see that she was filled with sorrow. Travis could barely hold his head up. I was really feeling his pain. Tears were drooling down my eyes. Momma Lucy came over to comfort me. She knew it was more than Travis's dad that was paining me on the inside. She could always discern my spirit.

"Baby…just let go…it's alright to cry," she said softly in my ears.

I clung to Momma Lucy tightly.

"Remember God sees your hurt…and knows all about it."

I looked around the audience and saw many of our classmates standing with support. That was one of the great things about attending an all-black school. Whenever something happens to someone in my high school class, you could count on your brother and sister for support. Mrs. Lois and Lettie also were standing nearby.

All of a sudden, I heard this outburst. It was Travis. He let go.

"Daddy why!" "…Did you have to leave us?"

Travis was screaming. I had never seen a man howler like that. Then Momma Lucy explained to me that sometimes it is best to express our anger on the outside instead of letting it eat you up on the inside. She even explained how she didn't speak for weeks when her husband died, but when she did it was a scream indicating a relief from her heart. Everyone expresses his or her pain differently so we must honor the effect.

We began tossing flowers on top of the coffin giving our last good-bye. This is when I couldn't take it anymore, I just had to go over to Travis and comfort him with my own arms. Momma looked at me. She knew the desire that was burning on the inside of me. By her facial jesters I knew it was okay.

Before I could get within arms length of him, Travis turned loose his mother and grabbed me tightly. With his head on my shoulder, I could feel nothing but remorse for him. We were capturing the pain of death inside. By the time we came back to reality, the funeral procession was leaving. Travis and I sat in the chairs in front of the coffin as they lowered his father's body into the ground. Travis continued to stare at the coffin as it was disappearing from his sight. I continued to embrace him with the arms of care. Then Travis began to open up to me.

"Delilah, I love my daddy so much."

"I wish I could have done something for him."

"But you did Travis…you were the son he wanted…you also had a close relationship with him…death can't take that away from you."

Looking at me with amazement, Travis kissed me on the lips. He didn't expect me to understand his pain.

"No matter what happens next Delilah, you will always be my best friend…and…I love you."

I didn't know what to say. All I knew is that it wasn't the time for him to say those words.

Now he is really confusing me. "I love you too" couldn't come out of my mouth. If it did, then I wouldn't be truthful to my heart. My heart is now dwelling in another place.

Travis explained, "You don't have to tell me you love me…I just want you to know how I feel about you in case something happens to me. One of the things my daddy always told me is to always speak your feelings openly because you may not get a chance next time."

"Oh, come on Travis…you know you're not going anywhere."

"I didn't say I was going anywhere; I just want you to know my true feelings about you."

"I will never forget the first day I met you at Mrs. Lucy's house.… and the day we were at the movies…you are so special to me."

"Stop trying to flatter me Travis, it's not working."

"I'm not trying to flatter you…I just want you to know that no matter what happens, I will always be there for you:

"Me too." I spoke.

"Now come on, let's go to the house. I know they are waiting on us Travis."

When we reached the house, there were people everywhere, from the front porch to the backyard of the house. Lettie was inside the kitchen helping to serve the guests. Lettie looked at me with an inquisitive eye. I knew she wanted to get details of my business. As always, she did.

Lettie was the type of person who didn't lighten up if she was involved in your business. Of course, we were like sisters, but I didn't want her all up in my drama.

Lettie pulled me into a quiet corner and whispered, "I need to talk to you"

"Oh yeah, what about?"

"You know."

Then she yanked on my dress collar and pulled me outside to an isolated spot in the corner of the yard where there would be no interruptions.

"I don't know what you are doing Dee, but you are treading on dangerous ground." she said.

"Dangerous ground...I don't know what you are talking about."

"You're right! You don't know what I am talking about...how you could do Travis..."

"Wait a minute Ms. Lettie! You tend to your own business."

"Tend to my own business...you are my business!"

"Well Lettie, if you are implying about Jeremy...why I hardly know the guy."

"You better keep it that way...from what I was told he was adopted... and those types of people, you don't know what kind of background... and especially behavior that is in the closet."

"Lettie you are right...but we are just mutual friends now."

"And it better stay mutual friends, because I am sick and tired of people hurting you."

"Don't worry Lettie, I will be cautious."

"You better."

We began to hug each other and chat about our childhood fantasy, which is when I began to feel fatigued. Lettie insisted that I sit down in a chair outside and get some fresh air. She knows that I am still battling with my past. She constantly tries to sort spiritual help for me. But I refuse to take my problems to a minister. He is just a man. I pray about it all the time. The reason I have a phobia with men is because of the uncomfortable touching I had when I was younger. Maybe I will take up Lettie's offer and go see the minister, but I better pray about it first.

Dr. Teresa

Momma Lucy always told me not to be so hasty to talk about things to others until I have sorted it out with God. Sometimes it could be someone else he wants you to confide in. Just trust God.

CHAPTER 5

It was a very windy day. I decided to spend today with my Momma. We were going to go by the restaurant to see how everything is going. While riding along in the car I noticed coming from our lawyer's office building was Jeremy. I looked again to make sure there was no mistaken identity. It was Jeremy, I whispered loud to myself. Maybe he is checking up on me. But then I thought, since he was adopted, he could be using the same attorney to investigate his adoption records. I thought no more of it. Momma stopped by one of the dress shops looking for a semi-formal outfit to wear to Lettie's wedding, which is coming up in about two weeks. Of course, she just had to stop at the shop where Lettie and I bought her wedding dress. This time, when the saleslady saw me, she was very polite. You would think I was a queen the way she waited on us hand and foot.

She even went in the back of the room to pull out the reserved dresses for her most extravagant clients. Momma kept looking at the lady strange; because you could tell that Momma was black, but me, that were an all-different story. I just loved fooling them. The game that I played, Momma just laughed to herself. She knew it was all about me when it came to the saleslady giving her good quality service. As for me, I enjoyed every moment of it. Being with Momma gave me a sense of security. I realized that I could have lost her years ago. I will never forget the look upon her face when she saw me in the hospital for the first time after years of wondering. I told God, if I get my Momma back, I would do all I can to keep her safe, with His help of course.

I watched Momma as she was being fitted for a dress for Lettie's wedding. I noticed how her body structure was similar to mine. She was always a pretty woman, but now she looks even prettier to me. I looked around the showcases in the store. My eyes were attracted to the case with the lady's hosiery. I gazed closer at the case and there were a pair of stockings with roses resembling the ones Momma used to wear. I thought I would surprise her by buying a pair. I had the saleslady wrap them up in a nice gift box. I just knew Momma was going to be surprised.

As we got into the car, I turned to Momma and handed her the nice beautiful wrapped box. She smiled at me and opened the box slowly.

"You like it Momma?"

She was stunned, "Oh…Dee I love them."

"I didn't know you remembered"

"I remember rubbing your legs with these same roses on them…I always thought you had smooth legs."

Momma laughed, "Dee, you are amazing…I needed something to cheer me up today…and you are the one who knows how to do it."

"Momma, can I ask you something?"

"Sure."

"Do you ever think about when you were out there all alone?"

"Yeah… sometimes I do…and I regret every moment of it."

I took Momma by the hand and leaned on her shoulder as she started driving.

"The thought of me leaving you with Mrs. Lois and Mr. John sometimes deteriorates me inside."

"Why Momma, you did what you thought was best for me at the moment."

"Delilah, I didn't know Mr. John was that type of a man…and to take my daughter through all of that distress labels me an unfit mother."

"But that is in the past…I still love you Momma no matter what…I knew you weren't in your right mind…you couldn't have."

"You're right baby."

"I want you to know that at night I can hear you mumbling in your sleep…do you have nightmares at night?"

"Well…"

"You can be honest with me Dee."

"Sometimes I have these night terrors and. …But they don't last long"

"Is it nightmares about Mr. John?"

"To tell you the truth Momma, I have been having these night terrors pretty regular, I was afraid to come to you because you already have a lot to deal with."

"I have already dealt with my past. Since I have turned my life over to God, my past is erased, and I only have a future …that includes you, Momma Lucy, and God."

"I wish it was that easy for me…I am in my late twenties and have never let a man touch me. I don't know if it is because of what Mr. John did or what Henry did. I just know I don't want any man getting close to me. I am probably the only virgin alive in her twenties."

"There is nothing wrong with being a virgin. If I could do my life over, that would be a great thought for me."

"The problem is not just being a virgin Momma; it's being alone and not having a companion."

"Delilah, there are some things we can't handle by ourselves," Momma said.

"You must realize that God didn't intend for us to handle our problems alone."

I replied, "But it is so hard for me to let God handle this situation, I know without a doubt God guided my life this far, even back into the arms of you."

Then Momma spoke in a convincing tone of voice, "Trust God…. just trust God."

I wanted to trust God, but it seemed like He was far away from me, maybe because I haven't totally given Him the problem. Lettie is always telling me I need some spiritual counseling. Somehow, I don't trust too many people. I guess Mrs. Lois spoiled that for me because of her behavior as being a Christian. I would love to talk to someone for spiritual help, but lately all I have seen are spiritual hypocrites. They tell me one thing and think another. Meanwhile, I just have to trust God; He has never failed me so far.

Momma began to tell me about some of the things she encountered while she was out there in the world. She said there where times she didn't have anything to eat. Many times, she would look into the garbage cans to find left over food. She didn't care if it was spoiled. Momma said it was all about survival. Thinking about seeing me again kept her alive. Faith drew us back together. Some of the things Momma wouldn't talk about because it hurt her to remember the state she was in. When I noticed the tears filling her eyes, I began to ponder up another subject. It worked every time. The joy of us being reunited is more important than her past. Momma Lucy often told me that when you have given your life to God, your past no longer exists, because God has forgiven you for the things you've done as the old person. Now, you are a new creature in Christ. I thank God daily for my grandmother. She is really a woman of wisdom. Looking at Momma, I am sure it is rubbing off on her. I am hoping it will hurry up and paint me. I need all the help that I can get.

As our car turned into the restaurant, I began to think about Henry and how I trusted him with my feelings. Second thoughts came across my head, if I can rely on man with my feelings, why couldn't I rely on God.

Momma and I entered. The doorbell rang as normal. That doorbell has a history behind it. I can remember all the times it would tell on me, especially when I was late. Also, it reminded me of Mr. Irvin. He would always give me a smile when I entered. It didn't matter to him whether I was late or not. What a wonderful person he was.

While approaching the counter to get something to drink, Henry was up to his old tricks again. There was a brunette woman all over him at the counter. When he noticed I was looking, he tried to play innocent. By now he should know I am not up for games. Henry was always trying to wiggle his way back into my life. I am not into instant playbacks. I am into fast-forward, "Skip the junk and let the real stuff take its course".

The waitresses always knew what to serve me, especially during lunchtime. My favorite energy foods, except I don't have a juicy novel to read at the moment. Momma would always get herself a cup of coffee. I enjoy watching her play the camouflage game at the restaurant. She always pretends she is the manager. I watched her go over to a customer and greet them with concern, and then she would offer them complimentary dessert on the house to show how she appreciates their business. Laughter just jumps up inside of me, because they don't know we are actually the owners. Henry is just the camouflage owner. Momma would always come by and check up on her place. She would always tell me, "Don't trust someone to treat your business like you would." The reason she would repeat this is because, when a person doesn't have an investment in your business, they don't care about it as much as you. That was good advice from Momma, because by me being a supervisor, no one is going to care for my patients as well as me. Believe it or not, my job would be on the line if I didn't handle the patients or staff in a mannerly way.

CHAPTER 6

It was another day of trauma at work. But this time it wasn't the patients. My lawyer called me to inform me about a probate hearing that will be going on with Mr. Irvin's estate. It seems that someone is claiming to be a close relative of his and wanting to claim part of my inheritance. It never fails; when you try to do good evil is always present. Mr. John T. Sable is a great lawyer, but sometimes he can get pretty greedy. I scheduled a brief meeting with him on my lunch. While I was in my favorite spot in the cafeteria, he walks over to the table so formal.

"Delilah, I am glad you could meet with me on such a short notice." he said.

"Well, I figured it had to be important for you to ask to see me on my lunch break."

Mr. Sable takes a seat next to me. Then looking suspicious he whispers.

"Do these people in here know about you?"

"No Mr. Sable, and you can stop whispering."

"I came to tell you that there is someone claiming to be a relative of Mr. Irvin and wants to get a profit from your inheritance."

"Who is it?" I replied.

"I can't expose that information, because the person wants to remain anonymous until we get definite proof."

"Well…do you have proof?"

"Not yet…but it doesn't look too good for you and your mom."

"What do you mean it doesn't look good…you mean…?"

"I mean you could lose more than half of your estate."

"And...."

"And what...you mean to tell me after all these years...someone.... somebody wants to take what is rightfully mine."

Mr. Sable explained, "They are not taking it in a sense.... just sharing it."

"Just Sharing It!" I shouted across the room.

Mr. Sable already felt uncomfortable meeting with me in public and me bursting out loud with anger didn't make the situation any better.

"I tell you what, Mr. John. T. Sable.... If you don't settle this matter in a hurry...I might just change lawyers!"

Mr. Sable didn't care too much for that statement. He realized that he was getting big bucks from us. He probably thinks he would lose profit from the other claim, because of the agreement he had with Mr. Irvin. He will only get a monthly salary if he handles our business.

"Calm down Delilah...I will handle this and let you know the findings.... You are jumping to conclusions...we haven't received any positive proof of this person's identity."

"Mr. Sable, I appreciate you coming to tell me all of this. Have you contacted my mom about this?"

"NO...I haven't but..."

"Do me a favor. Don't contact her until you have definitely received proof of this other person. I wouldn't want any more fractures in her life. ...and she is happy now especially with the restaurant."

"I will keep that promise Delilah; only if you promise me that you won't do your own personal investigation."

Mr. Sable knew that I would pry into something quick and hurry. He also knew I didn't trust him.

I replied, "I will try to do my best at keeping my nose clean of the situation."

As he stood up from the table, I could see in his facial expressions that he didn't believe me. Mr. Sable was the type of man that loved his money and power. So whatever one wins has to be the one that he would benefit from the most.

Since the meeting wasn't very long, I continued to finish my lunch break with a salad, orange juice and my favorite novel. But this time the energy food wasn't complete, because I didn't have the wits to read a book at this time. My head kept thinking about the person who would probably gain profit from the pain and agony that mom and I had suffered in the past years. Suddenly I was called from lunch to take a call. As I walked toward the nurse's station, I could feel that the call was not good news. I was so nervous I didn't even answer the phone properly.

"Hello."

"Dee, this is mom, Come home as soon as you can."

"Why…what's wrong…"

"Momma Lucy took ill, and I can't get her to go and see the doctor."

"Mom…I will be there as soon as I can…but call her doctor anyway."

"Delilah, you know how Momma hates doctors."

"This is not a matter of what she hates or loves at the moment…I will be there as soon as I can get someone to cover for me…If she gets any worse, please call the emergency ambulance."

I hung up the phone abruptly as the nurses at the station recognized something was wrong.

"Is everything alright?" the nurse asked.

"Page to see if you can get Nurse Lighthouse to cover for me…I have an emergency at home…. It's my grandmother."

"Okay, you go ahead I got you covered." the nurse replied.

I gathered my belongings and rushed out to my car. Meanwhile at the house, Momma was calling probably everyone at church to pray for Momma Lucy.

While driving to the house, pondering through my mind, were the special times Momma Lucy and I had. I will never forget how she took me in even when she didn't know me from Adam's ant. She protected me for years until I found my true identity. I don't think if I were in her situation, I could take in a stranger. I guess, because she is an example of a real Christian. She took care of my needs. She also took care of some of the voids in my life during my mishaps.

Suddenly I began to have flash backs of the time Momma Lucy taught me how to play the camouflage game. She was really good at it. The reason she was good at it, is because her mother taught her the same thing. I could imagine in her time and era how difficult it was for a black woman to advance in this world. She is a strong woman and a great person in my sight. The thought of me losing her began to make me panic. Then I thought about what Momma Lucy always did when trouble came her way. She would go into her secret closet (her room) and talk to God. She often told me that prayer changes things. Out of all the people in the world, I should be the most faithful person to prayer.

As I was getting closer to the house, I could hear this voice on the inside telling me to pull over and pray. I pulled my car over and began to make my request unto God:

> *"Heavenly Father, you are the only person that knows me, you have been so good to me in spite of my difficult behavior. Lord, please take care of Momma Lucy, please don't take her away from me...I love her so much...please...please God make it better...If you make her better Lord, I promise I will get some help from the minister... I know that through him you can heal my pain... but God because of pride ...I stood in the way of being delivered...I realize that camouflaging is only pretending who you really are on the outside and not knowing who you are on the inside...I also realize that I was born this way for a reason, and you have a path for my life. Please Lord, hear my cry... thanks for listening."*

After I talked with God, there was an assurance in my spirit that Momma Lucy was going to be all right.

CHAPTER 7

As I approached the front of the house, I noticed the ambulance leaving. I rushed inside the house. Momma was sitting in the chair in the living room. She was with tears in her eyes and wiping her face with a tissue. All that would come out of my mouth was, "Momma Lucy…"

I ran to Momma to see what the matter was. She embraced me very tightly.

Then said, "That was a close one…Momma Lucy is in the room resting."

My heart felt a relief. When I saw the ambulance leaving, I just knew Momma Lucy was being transported to the hospital. Thank God, she will be all right. I thought again with amazement, "Thank God!"

I couldn't wait to see Momma Lucy. As I entered the room, I could hear Momma Lucy looking up to the ceiling and murmuring words up to heaven. I sat on the bed and held her hand until she was finished. Momma Lucy turned to me and looked at me with contentment.

"I know everything is going to be okay." she spoke.

I gave her a kiss on the forehead with confidence. I knew God answered my prayer. Now that He has, I must live up to my promise to Him. You see, it is better not to make a vow to God, than to make one and break it. I was told it is just like lying to God and He hates a liar.

Momma Lucy said, "Dee, I am worried about you."

"Why…Momma? I am okay."

"It's not the okay I am worried about. It's the not okay you are not talking about."

"You worry too much Momma...look out for yourself...I will be all right."

"Dee, you need to confide in someone...I can tell...you act like everything is okay, but I can feel you."

One thing about Momma Lucy, you can't fool her. She knew too much about camouflaging. I know she is the one I should talk to, but I don't want to trouble her with my problems. She has enough trials with her health.

Suddenly Momma Lucy said, "Have you heard from Travis?"

"No...we thought we would give each other some space, since he has so many things to take care after his father's death."

"You know...Travis is a good guy...he would make you a good husband."

I replied, "Momma Lucy, you are always trying to hook me up with someone...especially

Travis."

"You're not getting any younger...and..."

"That's it Momma! I am not looking for a husband."

"Well, you don't have to look Delilah, he has already found you...I know you kind of like him...don't you?"

"I don't have to answer that... (Smiling at Momma Lucy) do I?"

Momma Lucy knew how to manipulate a conversation. It doesn't matter whether she wins or loses as long as she has gotten her point across. One day I will marry, but for now I must attack the past in order to go forward. Too many memories have shattered me into standing still.

"Get some rest Momma Lucy...I will see you later...I have to return to work."

As I exited the room, I could see Momma Lucy watching me. She is always concerned about me. I know that she loves me. She is such a beautiful person, not just on the outside, but on the inside as well. I highly respect her opinions. Especially by her being my grandmother.

Momma was still sitting on the sofa when I entered the room. It seemed as though she had a lot on her mind. I hope that old lawyer hasn't told her anything.

I asked, "By the way, have you heard from Mr. Sable lately?"

"No, I haven't…but maybe I need to call him."

"Momma don't bother yourself…I'll look into it."

At least I know he didn't contact her. That was really close. I could have spilled the beans. It is best not to assume anything until you have evidence.

"Dee, come here for a second…I know you have to get back to work, but I need to talk to you."

I replied, "Can we talk tonight when I get home?"

"Only if you promise me you will talk to me and not ignore me."

"Mom, I will see you tonight…I promise."

Momma knew I had some issues that I needed to have resolved. She didn't want me to end up like she was. She prejudges me a lot with situations. I gather it's because she feels that I would go down the same path she did. I know it is her love that keeps her so concerned about my future. I can comprehend now why I need to pursue some spiritual help. Then maybe it will give Lettie, Momma Lucy and Momma some peace of mind. Don't get me wrong; it is a blessing to have such a dedicated trio behind you.

I wasn't too enthused about returning to work. Being a supervisor wasn't an easy task. Being black didn't help any. Because of my color, sometimes I had to imitate being white to get the patients to cooperate. Many times, I get flak from the staff because I am black. The confusion doesn't always come from the white staff. The majority of my battles come from my own kind. Some say, I am trying to be white, and some say, I think that I am better than them. Either way, I end up crossing the fence frequently, never knowing which side I will end up on. There has got to be a place for people like me.

CHAPTER 8

A lot of commotion is happening today. The episode with Momma Lucy has finally diminished into the air; also, there is not too much talk about me for the moment. Today is my best friend's wedding and everyone is excited about the occasion. Everything was so beautiful today, even the sky. Outside of the church, there seemed to be a confirmation in the atmosphere signaling that God is pleased with this special occasion. I know I shouldn't think this, but Lettie was sexually active, and she needed a husband.

I recall from one of the sermons at church, the minister would somehow put an emphasis on fornication with the youth. Now that I am older, I realize how important it is to remain abstinent. Your body is the temple of God, saved or not. Through my entire life, God has blessed me. Maybe it's because I was keeping my body for that special guy. Don't get me wrong, I am not a saint, but some good morals were instilled in me while I was young. I am not judging Lettie, but happy for her to be able to not let the devil use her body anymore.

I am inspired to keep my body for that special man because sometimes I catch my mom daydreaming and I know it is not all about happy things. By her being a prostitute, it didn't make things easy for her when it came to a relationship with a man. I can remember one day she told me she was proud of the way I carried myself in front of men. Momma always told me to save myself for my wedding day. She also said when a man finds himself a virgin it gives a sense of security and trustworthy. But being a virgin goes both ways. Momma even told me about an incident of one of her fellow girlfriends of the world. She said that on her wedding day, she could hear from the back of her seat some guys talking about what they did with her and how the groom was in for a surprise. Now think about it. Would you like to be in that girl's situation?

As I walked into the church to see if everything was the way Lettie demanded it to be, there was Jeremy watching me as he converses with SJ. Of course, he was drooling. This was the day that the beauty in me was magnified. I am the type of person who didn't wear much makeup on my skin. But today I did it for the wedding. Now makeup on top of beauty can make a girl feel really arrogant. I noticed him walking toward me as I checked out the decorations on the isles. I had to make sure this was a perfect day for Lettie. As I continued to pretend to do my little thing, guess what?

"Well…look at you" Jeremy said.

I pretended to listen.

"Don't you look astonishing?" he said.

I was thinking he used the wrong word, in order to gain my attention.

Then Jeremy said, "You would think you are stepping into royalty with this lovely lady submerged in beauty …"

That was it. That was all it took. I turned around. You see I needed the correct key to open my conversation.

Trying to not focus on me I asked, "Are you ready for today?"

Jeremy replied, "Why, this is no big deal."

"What do you mean by no big deal?"

"I didn't mean it the way it sounded…I was just saying that weddings are common."

It seemed to me that Jeremy was not the marrying type, especially if he thinks weddings are common. Dealing with this type of guy can make your hormones go wacky. But if I dealt with Henry, I could definitely put up with Jeremy. While I was chatting with Jeremy, I recognized SJ sitting on the front bench of the church. He seemed to be in a daze. I was very concerned and put the conversation with Jeremy on hold. Jeremy was full of awe because I brushed him off swiftly.

I sat next to SJ on the bench and said, "A penny for your thoughts."
He was stunned.

"Oh, hi Dee, what's up?" SJ said solemnly.

"That is what I was about to ask you…you must be getting those wedding bell jitters."

"Not really," he replied.

SJ was very short with his explanation. He was usually open with me about things. We had this brother-sister relationship since the time he started dating Lettie. I like to think he was closer to me than Lettie. SJ told me that I was more levelheaded than Lettie.

I asked, "SJ…there must be something wrong…this is not like you…especially with me, you can talk to me about anything."

"That's the problem Dee…I can talk to you …but Lettie…it's impossible to get a word through to her."

"She just doesn't listen." he continued.

"SJ…I am not trying to pry into your business… but this is something you two should have discussed a long time ago."

"I know."

"You just can't wait until your "I do day" to solve problems"

"What should I do Dee?"

"I don't know SJ"

"This is something you are going to have to figure out…. and fast."

"Do you think we are ready for today?"

"I don't know…this is something you need to discuss with Lettie."

"Can I ask you something SJ?"

"Sure…you know how I feel about talking to you."

"Do you love Lettie?"

"Of course, I love Lettie."

"I mean r-e-a-l-l-y love her."

"What do you mean by that?"

"Well, there are different levels of love…one type is love for your parents…for your siblings…for your friends…. your enemies…for the spouse…and don't forget love for
God."

"So, what are you trying to insinuate?"

"I'm not trying to insinuate anything...you're doing that yourself."

SJ was getting aggressive with me. It seemed as though he was hiding something. Now if he is afraid to talk to me it must relate to Lettie, because he knows how glued together we are.

I stated boldly, "You better get yourself together...if you hurt Lettie...I don't think I will ever be able to forgive you...so whatever it is...spell it out now."

Then Sam shouted, "I love Lettie...but I am in love with someone else!"

I was in shock. I couldn't open my mouth to say anything. All the time Lettie was giving me advice about relationships, she was blind. My mouth was closed for about five minutes. I think that was the only time I have ever been furious with SJ. I looked around to see if anyone was in the church before I could go off in rage. Apparently, Jeremy had already exited the church when I brushed him off.

"You mean to tell me...that all this time...you have been lying to my sister?"

"Not totally lying."

"Well, what do you call that...getting my sister all excited.... then dropping the bomb on her."

"You see Dee, the person I am in love with doesn't know it."

"Doesn't know it...why didn't you tell her!"

"Because it is...you...yeah...it's you!"

I was as frozen as an ice sickle on the roof of a house. My lips didn't only drop, but my heart began to panic with fear. I should have noticed all the signs. SJ would always take up for me when Lettie and I would argue. He always had this funny look toward me, especially when I was with Lettie. Then I thought about it. No wonder he was so comfortable with discussing issues with me. You must be friends before you become lovers. That is how true love starts. Why didn't I notice the clues?

I turned away from SJ and walked off. How could he do this to Lettie? Then I had to change the thought to, how can I do this to Lettie? It was my entire fault. I should have seen the signs earlier, but I was too wrapped up in my world. I just could not hurt Lettie. Mr. John broke us apart before and I will not let SJ's feeling do it again. We will just have to stay our distances and let his feelings become desolate. The idea of him continuing to go on with this lie began to ponder in my heart. I don't know if I could allow this wedding to go on.

Meanwhile, Lettie was in the dressing room of the church. She was so beautiful. The expression and glow on her face was as though she had seen God. I could tell Lettie was filled with joy on the inside. I couldn't be selfish and shatter this moment for her, but on the other hand, can't I stand to see this moment shattered forever with a lie. I looked around the room. Even the bridal party was excited. Lettie's dress gave her the image of a princess. Just watching her looking at herself in the mirror made me uneasy, especially marrying SJ. Happiness is not just the moment of the wedding, but what remains after the wedding. According to SJ, he is just going through the motions, but is heart is elsewhere. I couldn't take it anymore. I didn't care if the wedding had to be cancelled. My conscious was eating me alive. There is no way I could let this ceremony continue under the circumstances. I ran out of the room to the next room where the groom, best man and ushers were preparing. Before I knocked on the door, I almost retreated until I noticed SJ was behind me. Apparently, he was coming from the men's room. He bumped into me as I was going to return to the room with Lettie.

I asked, "I hope you are not planning on marrying Lettie?"

"Why not…you won't have me."

"I don't want you…and you are not going to marry Lettie either."

"Who is going to stop me?"

"I am…because you don't love…."

Before I could finish my statement, there was Lettie standing outside the lady's room with one of the bridesmaids.

"Don't love…who?" Lettie asked.

Both of us looked at each other with amazement. The cat was out of the bag. I thought to myself, "How are we going to get out of this?" Somehow, I am always in the middle of someone's mishaps.

Lettie asked again, "Who don't love…whom?"

SJ replied, "Let me explain…this…"

I said, "No let me explain…before you tell her anymore lies."

"What lies?" Lettie asked.

"Tell her SJ…go ahead and tell her!"

"Dee… can I talk to Lettie alone?"

I replied, "Alone…No, I won't allow it …I want to hear everything you tell her!"

Lettie said, "Yes…I have nothing to hide from Dee."

"Lettie, I can't marry you." SJ said.

Lettie wasn't a bit surprised. She took off her engagement ring and placed it into SJ's hand palm and folded it closed. As if to say this Chapter in my life is closed. She turned to me and gave me a hug with tears streaming down her eyes. My words were all choked up in my throat until I couldn't open my mouth. Lettie walked toward the double doors of the church. As Lettie was proceeding out, the guests were entering the church. There was no turning back now. I hope that Lettie never finds out that the person Sam is in love with is I. But then again, maybe I should tell her and save a lot of future hurt. I'll think about it.

Meanwhile, an announcement was made to the guests that the wedding was cancelled due too an emergency. That was all that I could think of to keep Lettie's reputation. Of course, Ms. Lois was really crazed, but Momma Lucy was able to keep her stable. As for the wedding party, they partied with the catering food. Even the family members and some of the guests enjoyed the reception. Only one bridesmaid knew the truth and she was sworn to secrecy. SJ of course, left before the cancellation of the wedding was announced and Jeremy followed him. As for Lettie, I don't know where she ended up, but I do know her secret place for sanity. The graveyard. She always told me if you are feeling down, visit the dead and you will realize how blessed you are to be alive, and problems are solvable as long as you are alive. In other words, "there is hope for the living".

I couldn't remain at the reception with the thought of Lettie out there alone and unstable. I left and went searching for her. She was right where I said she would be, the graveyard. She was sitting on her father's vault. I watched from far off as she was picking the weeds from around Mr. John's grave. She was talking to him. I didn't know whether to disturb her or leave. I saw physically that she was all right. Sometimes people need a moment of silence without everybody giving them advice. This is the time you can really listen to God, because you don't want to hear a physical voice. The spiritual voice from God comes from within. Every word of God that you have read or heard comes into play at this time. Noticing she was safe, I returned to the reception. I knew she would talk with me when she was ready. That's what sisters are for.

CHAPTER 9

It was weeks before Lettie was able to face the world. She didn't even attend church regularly. It was eating me alive not being able to see Lettie. Every time I would call her, Ms. Lois would make up some excuse. Ms. Lois was handling the situation as though embarrassment was coming directly from me. Because of the past experience with Ms. Lois, I wouldn't put it past her.

Momma and Momma Lucy told me to give it some time. They really didn't know the entire picture. Maybe I needed to confide in them. Momma Lucy was great at giving me advice. I waited until Sunday morning. It was the one Sunday out of the month I was able to attend church. Momma Lucy would do her Sunday routine by coming over and eating breakfast with us. Sometimes she would even prepare it for us. We were sitting at the table enjoying each other's company when suddenly, Momma Lucy asked, "When is the last time you talked to Lettie?"

I replied, "It's been a while."

"It's a shame how that Sam left her standing at the altar." Momma Lucy said.

"Momma Lucy, he didn't leave her at the altar…she left before it started."

"You're right…but…."

"Let's just eat." Momma replied.

It remained quiet at the table, but I noticed that Momma Lucy was itching inside to talk about it some more. She enjoyed controlling the conversation. Out of respect we let her do it.

Everyone remained quiet at the table for a while. I kept looking at the clock on the wall over the stove. It was not normal for everyone to be so silent. Suddenly I heard a sound as though someone was choking. I looked across the room. It was Momma Lucy trying to catch her breath. I couldn't remove my bottom from the chair. It was as if I was stuck to it. All I could hear was Momma yelling and screaming for me to help. I don't know what came over me. Momma practically yelled into my eardrum for me to become unglued to the chair. Before I knew it, I was giving Momma Lucy mouth-to-mouth resuscitation. Momma was calling the ambulance while I was taking Momma Lucy's vital signs. The ambulance took its time getting here. Momma was in shock. She stood in a corner just looking at me assisting Momma Lucy. As I was trying to help Momma Lucy, I could see Momma's heart panicking. The more I tried to bring Momma Lucy through, the more I began to recall the day she was sick and didn't want to go to the hospital. I should have insisted that she visited her doctor.

Finally, the ambulance arrived, and the paramedics met me at the door. Most of them knew me from the local hospital. I stood back as they tried to revive Momma Lucy. I could tell by her vital signs that her blood pressure was low, and it didn't look very good. As they were putting her on the stretcher, I held on to Momma. She was in tears. The only thing that I could think of was prayer. Prayer changes things. I took Momma by the hand and said a silent prayer. Then I ran over to Momma Lucy before they put her into the ambulance and said, "Momma it's going to be alright...hold on...."

Then I turned to one of the paramedics and asked him if I could come along. Momma trailed us in the car. I held on to Momma Lucy's hand as we transported her to the hospital. I kept pondering around in my mind what would I do without Momma Lucy. She was one of the greatest people that influenced my life. She also taught me a lot about survival. What would I do without her?

As we entered the emergency room, I continued to hold on to Momma Lucy's hand. Momma was next to her telling her to hold on and don't give up. It was like a dream that you wish would never come true.

While we were in the waiting room, flashbacks of the times I had with Momma Lucy began to rekindle my mind. I will never forget the time she straightened my hair so that I could pretend to be white to get a job. Also, she often taught me how to survive with the camouflage game we had going on. She knew how to make a biracial young lady survive during those times. Tears began to fall from my eyes as I thought about the days of laughter and sorrow we had together even before I knew she was my grandmother. Thinking about these things gave me a sense of appreciation for the elderly people in our lives. Sometimes we take them for granted. We think that they will be with us forever. I am so glad that I got a chance to know my grandmother and to capture some of her wisdom. I believe this is one of the reasons I am prosperous today. I am not talking about money either. I am talking about being able to make good decisions that will affect me for life. True wisdom does not come from man. God instills this in anyone who will listen to His instructions. Momma Lucy used to say, "If you listen, you can save yourself a whole lot of trouble." I believe that with all my heart.

The time seemed to be moving like a snail on the ground. Momma and I continued to look at the clock. Because of Momma Lucy's enlarged heart, we knew there was going to be some difficulties by the expression on the doctor's face as he took her into surgery.

Momma cried herself to sleep on my shoulder. The worst thing that could happen is losing Momma Lucy, especially for Momma's sake. She never had a real relationship with her mom until a few years ago. I watched how they bonded together over the years. It brought so much joy to me to see a mother-daughter relationship blossom so much. While I was thinking about all of the great moments with Momma Lucy, I noticed the front tail of a white jacket before me. It was the doctor. I could tell by his demeanor that Momma Lucy was gone. He didn't have to say a word. I awakened Momma from off my shoulder. You could tell by my eyes it was over. The doctor explained to us that there was nothing he could really do. It was a matter of time. Momma and I were full of pain and hurt. Momma continued to have tears streaming down her eyes. I could tell she was trying to be strong for me. Believe it or not, I was strong.

Suddenly, as I was holding on to Momma, I recognized a man in a white suit across from us just staring at me. Before I could blink my eyes, he was gone. I remember years ago, a man in a white suit used to appear frequently, but when I found my Momma, he never returned again. I always thought it was my guardian angel watching over me. I was wondering why he appeared again. Is it because I need guidance? Only the future can tell.

Because I am a supervisor at this hospital, many of the staff came over to comfort and offer us their condolences. With the help of prayer and God, we will make it through this.

Momma Lucy has left a legacy with me that I will never forget.

The following day we prepared her funeral arrangements. This was a time I needed my best friend, Lettie. She was always there for me especially in the time of trouble, even though she caused a lot of my trouble. But what are friends for, especially sisters. While sitting at the kitchen table with Momma, there was a knock on the door. I couldn't believe it. It was Travis. Before he could say anything, I ran and wrapped myself in his arms. We were always good friends even after our relationship as lovers fell apart.

Travis said, "Are you okay?"

"As okay...as I am going to be." I replied.

Travis looked over at Momma at the table as she scavenged through Momma Lucy's important papers.

"Ms. --------how are you today?"

"Just fine," Momma answered with a low-keyed voice. She wasn't up to conversations today.

Travis noticed the solitude in the room so he changed the subject. Looking at both of us and wondering what to say, he said, "Momma told me to tell you if you need anything just call...and that goes for me too."

We knew that Travis meant well, but at this time our minds were far from seeking help. Suddenly the doorbell rang again. By surprise it was Lettie. I was so happy to see her, I forgot Travis was standing there.

Lettie ran over to me, and we hugged each other tightly. It was only for a moment, but it felt like many moments. I had been waiting to hear from her. Behind Lettie was Mrs. Lois with an armful of food. Mrs. Lois went over to Momma and gave her encouraging words. It was like a reunion in the room. My entire life was in the room, well almost my entire life. Momma Lucy was missing, but her spirit was in the atmosphere. While Momma and Mrs. Lois prepared dinner for us, Lettie, Travis and I continued our conversation in the living room. I was surprised to see Lettie wasn't treating me cold. Maybe she doesn't know about Sam's feelings for me. I began to wonder how much of the conversation she overheard at the church.

Somehow Travis notices that there were some frictions in the room by the way the communication waves were in the room. Travis knew about Lettie's mishap, so he didn't talk about it, but he sensed that Lettie and I needed to be alone.

Travis said, "Dee I better be going now...but if you need me, please call me and I will check on you later...see you later Lettie."

When Travis left the room, I began to ask Lettie how it was going. I just knew I shouldn't have started that conversation. Lettie began to have watery eyes as she said,

"Dee, I didn't mean to leave you hanging at the wedding...but after..."

I interrupted her and said, "Lettie, you know you don't have to explain anything to me."

"But I look at all the money you spent for the wedding...and all the ..."

"What I just told you girl...you don't have to explain...and the money I spent... it was well spent."

We gazed at each other and low and behold we began to chuckle about the matter. Lettie began to talk about the signals she was getting all along by SJ, but she was willing to ignore them. She even told me how he always would compare me to her. This is when I was rolling around in my mind whether I should tell her the truth or forget about it. Knowing what SJ might be doing at this moment, I better be honest with her before the truth hit the ceiling later. Even though this was my moment of bereavement, I felt if the truth was told then Momma Lucy would be proud of me.

As we were sitting in the living room, I changed the subject and said, "You know...I have something to tell you."

Lettie looked at me strangely.

"Did you really love SJ?" I asked.

"Well, I did."

"How can you just turn your emotions off so quickly?"

"Dee, I have to tell you something...it was all a front..."

"All a front!"

"Yeah, all a front...I was just trying to prove to you that I can get a fish and catch it quicker than you."

I was laughing to myself, because the joke was on Lettie. She really didn't catch him; she just had him in the net.

While we were yet laughing, I said, "You want to hear something funny..."

Lettie replied, "Let's hear it."

"Sam had his eyes on me."

Lettie was stunned for a moment. She panicked for a second.

Abruptly I said, "Don't get the wrong idea...I didn't want him for a second."

"How do you know he wanted you, Dee?"

"Because he told me so...and...it was right before the wedding started."

"You mean to tell me you waited all this time to tell me!"

"All this time...lady you waited all this time to make space for me... you were all wrapped up in your little world...and that's...what happens when sisters don't communicate for a while!"

Lettie shouted, "Now you want to put it on me!"

"I'm not putting it on you...I ...well..."

Mrs. Lois and mom came out of the kitchen wondering what was going on. Lettie and I were very secret about matters between us. In order to keep them out of our situation we turned around to each other and said, "We're okay…."

While I was Looking at Lettie I said, "Ain't that right?"

As Mrs. Lois and Momma exited the room, we smirked at each other. Lettie and I were saints at covering our tracks. Because of the long separation we had in the past we were not going to let anybody separate us with foolishness anymore.

Lettie said, "Dee…I am not mad at you…kind of jealous, but not mad…it seems like you get all the men…but I have also come to terms with myself about you."

"…In what way?"

"Dee, you have always been attractive to guys, even when we were teenagers…you always got the whistles…the winks…even the smiles."

I thought Lettie was trying to insinuate something, so I said, "…and go on."

"Don't get me wrong…I am not saying I can't get a man…I know there is at least one out there looking for Lettie."

I inquired, "So are you saying all the men out there are looking at me but not for me?"

"That's not what I am saying…it's not all about you…I am trying to tell you…if a man is for you no one can take him away from you."

I came to terms with Lettie because she was correct. Whatever is right for you, is for you and the only one I know that can take it away from you is God Almighty. I realized from this conversation, if you really love someone you have to be honest with him or her whether it hurts you. Also remember honesty is the key for any relationship. The honesty caused Lettie and me to mend our sister-sister relationship instantly. We are friends forever.

CHAPTER 10

Today is another day I will have to deal with the death of my grandmother. I took some time off from the hospital to deal with Momma Lucy's personal matters and also her funeral arrangements. I couldn't let Momma go through all this pain. It was enough dealing with the sorrow within. It grieved me daily to see my Momma in tears every time she thought about Momma Lucy. I kept myself busy at all times, because she was the center of my survival. Now it will be just Momma and me, but we will have the spirit of Momma Lucy around forever. She will always be in our hearts.

I finally decided to take Momma Lucy and Momma's advice about seeing a minister. While I was in Minister Hines' office handling the funeral services, I began to talk to Minister Hines about God. He could tell that I was troubled on the inside by our conversation. It was time for me to confide in someone and what better person than my minister. I am not saying all ministers are good to talk to, because there are some that bring up your situation in their Sunday message. Minister Hines was a godly man; he didn't believe in having cliques. He treated everybody the same. The only person I would see around him all the time was his wife. I can remember in one of his sermons he would say, "If you have cliques, they become ticks." I guess you know what that means. Momma Lucy even told me, he has a lot of people's secrets wrapped up inside of him. I believe it. There is such an anointing when you talk to him. You feel like you are talking to Jesus Himself. One thing I noticed about Minister Hines, he always kept his office door open so that the secretary could see what he was doing, especially when he was counseling one on one. He was the type of person you could really trust and open up to. Minister Hines was very attentive as I spoke to him.

"Pastor, before my grandmother passed away, she insisted I get some help...she was very concerned...I guess you know about the situation with Mr. John. He was a very aggressive man and spent most of his time trying to seduce me."

Minister Hines said, "Go on."

"I really don't want to talk about the entire thing...it's just, I can't sleep at night and the thought of his hands touching my body seems to overshadow my conscious a lot...what can I do?"

He said. "First you must realize that you can't change anything... have you forgiven Mr. John?"

"He was killed before I could really talk to him."

"What about his wife...have you talked to her."

"Yes...but I have a problem visiting her home...does this mean I haven't forgiven."

"No...it means you haven't given it up...forgiving and giving it up are two different things...you see sometimes we forgive and think that's it."

"What do you mean by giving it up?"

"It means... setting your mind and soul free from guilt...the only way you can do this is to challenge the enemy by going back into that house and saying to you "this is the past, I am now in the future."

"But Pastor, suppose I remember the incidents again as I go into the house?"

"Dee it is the devil's job to bring it back to your remembrance...but through faith you must know with a shadow of doubt that you are free... this only comes through faith...only through trusting God."

I began to feel sorrow in my spirit. My desire is to have a real relationship with a man. Not to have sex, but as a companion toward marriage. I was afraid to discuss this with Minister Hines. Where I came from, sex was not discussed in the church. I don't know why, because it takes sex to multiply the saints of God. While thinking, Minister Hines waited for me to start talking again. Before I could open up about this situation, tears began to stroll down my face. I had so much fear inside of me for men, especially when it came to them trying to become intimate. Minister Hines passed me some tissue to dry my tears.

I said, "Thanks for listening...I needed this."

"Are you okay?" He asked.

Before I could give him an answer, I began to cry very loud.

"It's okay to cry Dee...but it's how you respond to the problem after the tears."

One thing about Minister Hines he didn't sugar coat anything, in other words he was telling me its okay to cry, but what are you going to do about the situation after the tears.

Minister Hines said, "I can see you are going through some difficult times...but the answer is always in front of us...because of the pain and the situation we can't see it...remember God cares for you, and He knows all about it...even if you don't care to talk about it...trust Him... the same way you are trusting me...He will listen."

"Thank you for the encouraging words, Pastor." I replied.

As I exit the room, Minister Hines said, "Dee I will be praying for you."

When I left the church, I decided to go by the restaurant and check on things for mom. When I entered the building, Jeremy and Sam were sitting at one of the booths. Apparently, they were having a lunch break. I spoke to them as I walked toward Henry at the counter.

"How's your mom doing?" Henry said.

"She's okay...by the way she won't be in for awhile...can you handle things?"

"Sure... anything for you." He replied.

Now Henry has always tried to get a shoe in with me. But he doesn't stand a chance. Like I said before, "I don't do reruns" because reruns are just recapturing the same events but looking at them at a different time with different views.

Henry said, "How about your favorite energy food?"

Brushing Henry off I answered, "Not today...I have... much to do...but I will take a rain check."

I walked around the back of the counter and went into the office. No one suspected us as owners, because most managers have an office. While pondering around on Momma's desk I noticed a note attached to her phone. It stated, "Please call Mr. Sable, signed Henry". I was relieved Momma didn't see the note. She definitely didn't need to hear any sadder info. I took the note and threw it in the garbage pail next to her desk and walked out.

I bumped into Jeremy standing in my way.

"What do you want?" I said.

"I just wanted to know how you were doing, I heard your grandmother passed," he replied.

"We are doing fine."

"Anything I can do for you Dee...I am not trying to get a date... but really anything

I can do...?" he continued to ask.

"But really, we are fine!" I exclaimed.

"Dee... stop giving me a hard time?"

"Why don't you get out of my way?"

Jeremy moved out of my way. I waved good-bye to Henry. SJ didn't say much to me. He is probably so full of guilt from what he had done to Lettie.

By the time I got to the door, Jeremy opened it for me and followed me out to my car.

I turned around and said, "What now?"

He grabbed me by the hand. Before I could jerk away, he pulled me closer to him and kissed me. I couldn't believe how forceful he was. But believe it or not, I enjoyed every moment of that kiss.

Then he looked me in the eyes and said, "How bout I take you out tonight...just to give you a little company."

Then I turned around a said, "Okay...come to my house... tonight... and have dinner with us."

I was surprised; Jeremy actually took up the offer to visit my home. I couldn't leave Momma alone at the moment, so I figured he would get a chance to meet Momma and know that I wasn't looking for a handyman.

CHAPTER 11

It was late in the evening. The house was full of people coming in and out paying their respects. Every time the doorbell rung, I was looking for Jeremy to walk in. I couldn't believe I was anxious about seeing him. That little kiss did something to me. That is one reason Momma used to tell me not to play with a little fire, because it starts a big one that is hard to put out. For now, the fire was kindling. While I was talking to some of the members of the church, Jeremy walked in. My heart began to flutter. Something happened to me, I was beginning to have feelings for this guy. I couldn't wait for him to come closer. Lettie was also in the corner watching. She smiled at me and continued to assist the guests. I introduced Jeremy to Momma. She wasn't offended by his color, because she had relationships with white men in the past. She warned me about my feelings. She said be careful, because being biracial doesn't mean you are white. She also informed me to keep my feelings on guard at all times. Be friends first, then you will know whether you are compatible. Infatuation is the feeling that arouses you when you are friends. Sometimes you think this is love, you are only fooling yourself. After friendship infatuation kicks out and love steps in, time will tell.

Jeremy blended in with the family very well. Although he was white, he had an olive color of skin with blue eyes that you could drown in. We were almost the same color. Well sort of. After everyone had left, Jeremy, Lettie and I played scrabble for a while. Mrs. Lois remained at our house also to help Momma out. It was though she felt she needed to be there. It was very warm in the house, but no one could take the place of the warmth that came from Momma Lucy. From that moment on Jeremy spent a lot of time at our house during the week of bereavement. He really meant it when he said he would be there for me. I was astonished Lettie didn't try to break the relationship up. Maybe she would be thinking this was payback time for me.

It is the day of Momma Lucy's funeral. It was a short ceremony. We honored her last wish by having a short service. She will be greatly missed. There were many people at the funeral. She touched many lives especially young ladies. I thought I was the only one she taught how to camouflage. Several biracial ladies stood up in service and recaptured the effect of Momma Lucy in their lives before the civil rights movement. Many revisited the survival techniques she taught them while their lives were shattered with disgrace. Momma Lucy was a wonderful person and a saint sent by God.

The repast was at Momma Lucy's house. I don't know what we are going to do with her house, because our house is enough for us. Momma is going to let it remain empty until she can figure out what to do with it.

While attending to the guests, Jeremy implied he had to leave for a while but would be back. Of course he gave me a little kiss on the cheek that kept me smiling while he was gone.

I could hear Momma screaming across the room "We are out of ice!"

Travis offered to go and get the ice, but because it took Jeremy so long to return, I decided to go alone. Also, this would give me a chance to breathe some fresh air. Momma Lucy touched so many people's hearts until the house was packed like sardines. When Momma announced we needed ice that was all it took for me to make a breakthrough. Travis even insisted to come along with me.

At the store Travis and I played around with the ice, we began throwing ice at each other. It was as if it was yesterday when we were teenagers. It was refreshing being able to laugh again. Especially with the tragedies we had encountered in our lives. As we exited out the door still fooling around with the ice, I noticed Jeremy's car across the street. It wasn't just across the street, it was across from Mr. Sable's law office.

This is the second time I had seen him there. My mind began to inquire, "Why is he seeing Mr. Sable?" Travis noticed me looking across the street.

"Everything okay?" he said.

"Yeah…oh…yeah."

I don't think Travis recognized Jeremy's car across the street. As we entered into the car, I kept looking through the rear view mirror to see if Jeremy was coming out of the building. No such luck. But there was no doubt in my mind that it was Jeremy's car. Maybe I should go back I thought. Then I would have to explain everything to Travis. I didn't want to get into a brunt with him, not at the moment.

When we returned to Momma Lucy's house I couldn't wait for the ice to run out again. I even asked Momma over and over did she need me to go to the store or something. She would tell me to calm down. She didn't know I was itching for an excuse to see what was up at Mr. Sable's office. Finally, which I hoped was not too late; Momma needed me to drop a plate off at one of Momma Lucy's friend Mrs. Johnny Mae. They were old time friends. She couldn't make it to the funeral, so Momma promised to bring her an obituary and a plate of food. Now this was a great idea! Mrs. Johnny Mae was a talker and if I stayed a little too long, she would be my excuse. Travis offered to come again, but before he could get into the car I was gone. I decided not to go to Mrs. Johnny Mae's house right away. Instead, I traveled along the road of Mr. Sable's office and Jeremy's car was still parked there. Now in order for me to be able to see who was in Mr. Sable's office, I would have to do one of my camouflage things again. It comes in handy sometimes. I was wondering how I was going to disguise myself. I parked across the street in front of the convenience store. Then I opened the car glove compartment and saw Momma Lucy's old reading glasses. I put them on and looked into the mirror. There was still something missing. I pulled my hair up into a bun like the older lady's wear. Now I really looked old. I walked across the street hoping Jeremy wouldn't come out and catch me. He didn't. I walked up to the receptionist desk.

"Is Mr. Sable in?" I said.

"Yes he is, but he is with a client at the moment." The receptionist replied.

"I'll wait…but"

"May I ask…do you have an appointment?"

"No…I don't but…"

"Can I get your name?"

Before I could say my name, Jeremy was coming out of the office. I rushed over to the magazine table and placed one of the books in front of my face so he couldn't notice me.

I heard Mr. Sable tell Jeremy, "It will all be over soon…don't you worry."

"Mr. Sable there is a lady here…" the receptionist implied.

But before she could finish her sentence I had dashed out of the office. Now that Jeremy is on his way back to the repast, I thought I'd better retreat to Mrs. Johnny Mae's house.

Believe it or not, Jeremy didn't suspect I was following him. It was best at that time because I really couldn't make heads or tails of the situation. Sometimes it is best not to jump to the gun, especially when you don't have all of your ducks in a row.

After Momma Lucy's repast, I decided to put my inquiring mind to rest and spend a lot of time with Jeremy. We engaged in a lot of time with each other. If I wasn't with him, he was at my house. Momma was very fond of him. Lettie didn't care too much for him; she thought I should stick to my own kind. But who is my own kind? I can be white or black; it was up to my mood. I didn't know what was happening to me. I was beginning to think Jeremy, see Jeremy, and dream Jeremy. I guess being in his company twenty-four –seven began to bring about something inside of me that I never thought would happen. Was it love or infatuation? We had only been dating for about a month. I enjoyed being around him, but why? Could it be because I needed to fill a void in my life? Time would tell. Right then, I was going to indulge the moment.

CHAPTER 12

It was a Saturday morning, my long weekend from the hospital. I usually sleep in during that day to catch up on some rest. I was stricken by the voice of our attorney Mr. Sable. I thought I was dreaming so I continued to embrace my pillow with sleep. But when I heard Momma yell with a hysterical voice, I leaped out of bed and ran to see what was going on. It wasn't a dream. Momma and Mr. Sable were sitting at the kitchen table. All I could think of was that Mr. Sable had spilled the beans about the mysterious new relative of mine.

As I walked into the room Momma could hardly focus her eyes on me. I was hideous with Mr. Sable.

Pretending like I didn't know what was going on I inquired, "What's going on?"

"We have some awful news, Dee." Momma replied.

Mr. Sable could hardly look at me. He knew that I had asked him not to tell Momma.

Mr. Sable said, "Mr. Irvin's estate will have to go into probate."

I remained silent. I did not want Momma to know that I received this information a while back.

Momma asked, "Why do we have to go into probate...he didn't have any relatives?"

"At the time...he didn't ...but we have new information...and... this person wants what belongs to him."

After Mr. Sable made that statement, I began to think. He identified the relative as a he. Could it be Jeremy? I have to find out before Momma. Mr. Sable continued to explain the situation to us. Momma was very upset. I didn't blame her; we have been through a lot and now this. I just wish I knew who was behind this. There will be no rest for me today. I will find out what is going on. I noticed Mr. Sable was always nervous when he talked about the issue. He was never that way before. Maybe it is time for my camouflage thing. A girl's got to do what is best for her. It's all about survival. It is all about survival, survival.

When Mr. Sable left, Momma kept busy during the day. This is the way she handled her problems. I don't handle problems the same way. I will get to the bottom of this.

Today I was going to have lunch with Jeremy it was also his weekend off. We had been spending a lot of time with each other. I think he is crazy about me. With the thought of him being Mr. Irvin's heir I don't know if I can deal with my emotions right now. We agreed to meet at the restaurant.

When I entered the restaurant Mr. Sable was also there eating lunch. Henry was at the counter chatting with him. He was always talking. Sometimes I felt he talked more than worked. But because he did us a favor by keeping his mouth closed, we put up with him.

I walked over to the counter and said, "Hi Henry, what's up?"

Henry replied, "You know it is all about you baby."

"I'm not your baby."

"Dee, you know how I feel about you."

"Yeah…and others too."

"Dee…why are you always giving me a hard time?"

I looked at Henry sarcastically and said, "Don't go there."

Then I turned around and looked at Mr. Sable in the face.

"I see you like having lunch here?"

"I come in here occasionally…when I get the chance." He replied.

"I'm not angry at you Mr. Sable…just a little upset…I wish you would have called me before you came over."

"There was not much time…and with your grandmother passing..,"

"That's not the point…anyway…when can we settle this dispute?"

"I am in the process of getting a probate date, it should be soon."

Henry interrupted, "What is this about probate?"

"Someone else wants our inheritance…I guess they decided to come forth after they saw what we possessed."

"Don't take it like that…they only want what's theirs." Henry stated.

I wanted to just go up to Henry and close his mouth permanently, but before I could act on it, Jeremy walked in. He was as handsome as ever. He had something behind his back. He came toward me and gave me a kiss on the lips. Before I knew it, I was kissing him in the mouth. I couldn't control my emotions for him. From behind his back came my favorite flower a yellow rose.

"For the most beautiful woman in the world." He said.

I glanced at Henry and turned with excitement toward Jeremy. This was the time I could really intimidate him.

"Oh…that was so thoughtful of you…Jeremy"

While walking toward the booth, I could see the bitterness in Henry's eyes. I don't think he had ever gotten over us. I could see from the corner of my eyes that he was having a real juicy conversation with Mr. Sable.

The waitress came over and said, "The usual Dee?"

"Oh…no not today…we will have steak and potatoes."

"Is that okay with you Jeremy?"

"What ever tastes good to you …tastes good to me." Jeremy replied.

Jeremy asked, "By the way…how is your mom?"

"She…she is okay."

"You didn't say that with confidence…what's the matter?"

"We are having some legal battles."

"Do you want to talk about them?"

"No…no not at the moment."

"Hey Sable!"

"What are you calling him for?"

"Maybe he can help you."

"You mean…you know him?"

"Why yes he is my uncle."

My lips dropped almost into my food. Mr. Sable is Jeremy's uncle. I couldn't believe it. Maybe that is why he was always at his office. Mr.

Sable came over to the table. I explained to Jeremy that I was acquainted legally with Mr. Sable. Mr. Sable didn't say much, but he did tell Jeremy he would do all that he could to settle the matter for mom and me. I was beginning to become confused. Jeremy is Mr. Sable's nephew. Then how does he fit in as Mr. Irvin's son? I remember Jeremy telling me he was adopted. Maybe he is Mr. Irvin's son.

After Mr. Sable left, I asked Jeremy, "I thought you were adopted?"

"Well, I am…you see Mr. Sable is my uncle by my adopted parents. He is presently seeking my biological parents."

The conversation with Jeremy didn't make the situation better. Now I don't know what to think. This is a time to pray for guidance. As I left the restaurant with a puzzled face, I saw the man in the white suit standing adjacent to my car. I looked back to see if anyone else saw him. Within seconds he vanished. Maybe God is trying to tell me something. I decided to drop by Lettie's for a while. Mrs. Lois wasn't home, and I was glad. She often listened to Lettie and me when we were in conversations. She didn't allow Lettie to have private talks with me. It was as though she thought I was hiding something from her. Maybe Mrs. Lois still has a guilty conscience.

Lettie was the type of person who didn't mind speaking her mind. She was a real friend and never sugarcoated her feelings. Even the way she looked on a Saturday evening was hideous. She would tell me this was her let hair down day. Everyday was a let down day for her. As I approached her door, I began to get those vibes again. I know I am going to have to let go of the past soon. Lettie opened the door. She had these large curlers in her head and a scarf covering them. She always looks like she had just had a fight or something. But this was Lettie, very intriguing and didn't care who was standing there.

"Well, what you want girl," she asked as she opened the door.

"I need to talk to you about something." I replied.

"What are you standing at the door for? Come on in."

I tried to stop from entering the house, but Lettie literally threw me inside. Butterflies began to fly around my insides. My heart was panting as I glanced around the house. My mouth was as though someone had glued my lips together. As I looked at the sofa. Memories of my last night in this house began to rekindle my mind. Lettie recognized how hysterical I was. She went into the kitchen to get me a glass of water. She knew what was going on in my mind. Lettie took me by the shoulder and led me toward the chair. I continued to stare at the sofa. Then Lettie interrupted.

"What you came over for?" she said.

"I.... I...don't ...know." I replied. I had completely forgot about what I was going to discuss with Lettie.

Lettie said, "Dee...you really need to get some help...this is the first time you have stepped foot in this house since that night."

"I know...but..."

"No buts...I pushed you in here because you need to stand up to your fears...daddy can't hurt you anymore...he is dead."

"I...know..."

"Listen Dee, this is one time I am going to have to be frank with you...a lot of your personal problems come from your past."

"Would you let me talk Lettie?"

"Go ahead!"

"You're not the one that had your daddy's hands all over you daily...now was you...no...Let me talk...I have had to live with this all my life...afraid for anyone to get close to me."

"Dee, I have been meaning to talk to you about that... my daddy did it to me also...even more when you left." Lettie said with tears streaming down her eyes.

"What did you do ...why you are not afraid to live in this house?"

"I got some help...not a psychiatrist...but spiritual help."

"You mean...you...talked to a minister?"

"Yes, I did...I couldn't take it any longer coming in and out of this house and watching

Momma covered up for him...I hate to say this...but I was glad when he was killed."

I said, "You shouldn't feel that way…when I heard he was killed, I didn't want my revenge that way, I wanted him to confess what he had done to me and to God."

Lettie said, "He confessed to Momma what he had done to you but she never told anyone
…I heard them through the walls one night."

"Why didn't you tell me Lettie?"

"What good was it… he was already dead."

"But the thought of him realizing he was wrong meant a lot to me." I stated.

"I am sorry Dee…I didn't know this could give you a breakthrough…I am very sorry."

"I forgive you Lettie; I knew you meant well."

As we embraced each other with open arms, another piece of my life was being healed. Now it is up to me to get spiritual counseling so I can move on with my life. Finally, my mind rekindled what I wanted to talk to Lettie about. Lettie listened to me attentively. As always, she gave me advice. She told me to not judge Jeremy until all of the evidence is in. In other words, don't judge a book before you finish reading it. Being with Lettie at this moment gave me the comfort of true friendship. While we were watching TV, Mrs. Lois entered the house. She could barely speak; because she was surprised to see me sitting in her living room. I was astonished when she came over to Lettie and me and gave us a big hug. I could see that she was full of tears with joy on the inside. She always wanted me to come back into her home.

CHAPTER 13

Mr. Sable finally obtained a date for the hearing of the probate. I was anxious to find out who this relative was. Today was the day the mystery relative would reveal himself. I sort of thought it is Jeremy, that is one reason I was not uptight. Momma had been pacing the floor of the Judge's office for about thirty minutes. Mr. Sable kept thumping his finger on his briefcase. I continued to watch the clock waiting for the judge to walk in and this supposed to be relative, which I knew was going to be Jeremy. Jeremy called me on last night to wish me good luck in the case. I began to think he was trying to pull something over my head. He even told me over the phone he loved me and didn't want me to be hurt, of all the nerve, to stab me in the back… Anticipation was prancing all over the office. Momma was walking a hole in the floor while Mr. Sable continued to make drum sounds out of his briefcase.

Suddenly the door opened. It was the judge; we all stood as he sat down. Then I noticed he put his nameplate in front of him. It was Judge Schmidt. My mind was pondering, could this be the prejudiced lady Mrs. Schmidt's husband? Before I could think any further, he announced he was late because he had to visit his wife in the hospital. I knew then the odds were slim for Momma and me.

Then he said to Mr. Sable, "Councilman… are you ready?"

"No…your Honor if you don't mind…the other party is not present." Mr. Sable replied.

"Councilman I do mind…but since this case involves your other party I will allow a few seconds and that means by the time I go over this case review….that person had better be walking through that door."

I was beginning to panic because this judge did not sound friendly and by me being black didn't help any. I could see Momma with her hands up to her chin, praying through them silently. Under the table I took Momma's hand to be in agreement with her. Mr. Sable continued to thump his briefcase until the judge gave him the evil eye.

Finally, the door opened, a gray suit stood out from head to toe. My eyes were beholden as Henry stood there with a smile on his face. Momma and I were in shock. I was furious with Mr. Sable. He was the person Mr. Irvin trusted with his estate. Momma Lucy always told me to watch out for the ones who seem to be your friend, especially in business. She always thought he was in it for the money. As Henry was sitting down, I could feel that he was laughing at me from within. All this time I thought it was Jeremy and it was the two-timing Henry. The judge stated that Mr. Sable could begin the hearing.

"Your honor Henry Smith claims to be the legal son of Mr. Irvin.... He was the son of Mrs. Irvin before she married Mr. Irvin."

"Do you have proof this is Mr. Irvin's legal son...or did he adopt him?" the Judge asked.

Mr. Sable handed the judge the legal documents of Henry's adoption and biological parent.

"I have proof that he is the son of Mrs. Irvin...he was given away at birth." Mr. Sable stated.

"In other words, Henry Smith is Mrs. Irvin's son before marrying Mr. Irvin."

"That's correct Sir."

"Tell me Councilman...what claim does Henry have on Mr. Irvin's estate...being that he is not his biological or adopted son?"

"Well, being that Mrs. Irvin was married to Mr. Irvin, therefore any inheritance she had would go to him."

The Judge shuffled through the papers on the table.

"I have here in my hands the will that Mr. Irvin left to Delilah and Candice Jones," The Judge replied.

"Tell me Henry Smith...why are you claiming the inheritance of a dead man you never knew?" The Judge asked.

"I knew him alright…he was a self-centered, prejudiced…miser… who didn't care about anyone but himself." Henry replied.

"So, this is a revenge plot?" inquired the Judge.

I wanted to defend Mr. Irvin in this case, but because of my color, the best thing for me to do now was to remain silent. Momma wouldn't open her eyes during the probate. She continued with her silent prayers. Mr. Sable looked across the table at me with a smile and assurance that things were in our favor. After the constant battle going back and forth with the issues, the judge finally said, "Mr. Henry Smith I find no claims for you on Mr. Irvin's estate, due to, Mr. Irvin having no knowledge of your existence as a son…and most of all, his biological children legally have the right to all claims."

"Case Closed!" He exclaimed.

It was like the dead coming alive. Momma raised her arms in the air and shouted, "Praise the Lord!"

Henry Smith stormed out of the building. Mr. Sable explained to the judge why he brought the case to him. He felt this was the only way Momma and I would get real justice, being that it was a white versus black case. Mr. Sable wanted to honor Mr. Irvin's wishes, but Henry kept pushing him until he had to file a probate. By doing this, Henry could not hassle us anymore about the estate. Mr. Sable knew all along we were going to win, but he had to remain neutral. The thought of me crying over Henry made my stomach turn. All this time he was after my money. Since times are changing now, we won't need Henry after all. Momma can manage her restaurant herself. Henry was so greedy until he was out of a job and his inheritance. It doesn't pay to have greed.

This was a time for a celebration. Momma called over Mrs. Lois and Lettie and I called Jeremy over. Seemed like Lettie's advice worked this time. Her advice worked most of the time. I just couldn't stand for her to be right all the time. But for now, she can be as right as she wants to be.

All of us were sitting in the living room celebrating with coffee and cake. This moment seemed like a repeat of the time Momma and I received our big inheritance. The person was missing was Momma Lucy.

She would have been proud of this moment. Especially Momma, she prayed through the entire case. Suddenly I heard someone knocking on the back door. I went to see who was there. When I opened the door there was no one there. Then I stepped outside the doorway and across the street I saw a man in a white suit. He just stared at me. He must be my guardian angel. I smiled at him and walked back into the house.

Before I could sit down, Jeremy asked me to stand up. I looked at Lettie strangely and Lettie just smiled.

"What is it Jeremy?" I asked.

He reached in his pants pocket and pulled out a ring. My feet were frozen to the floor until I couldn't faint. Jeremy kneeled down on his knees. I couldn't believe it. This was a Kodak moment.

"Dee from the very first moment I saw you …I knew you could be mine…will you marry me?" Jeremy asked.

I couldn't open my mouth. I was so astonished. Then Lettie answered for me.

"Yes…she will…yes!" Lettie yelled.

Mrs. Lois told Lettie to be quiet. Momma was excited also.

I think when I turned around and said "NO" the entire room became dormant.

Jeremy said, "Dee…you are kidding me."

"No, I am not kidding…I would love to marry you…but I have some things to work out."

"What things…is it me…you have some one else?"

"No there is no one else…just give me a little more time…you are moving too fast."

Everybody left the room to give us some privacy. Jeremy didn't understand my past. He didn't know that I needed a healing. I knew if I said yes, we would end up just like Travis and me. I don't even know if I still loved Travis. I couldn't pull him into this mess. I realized it was my entire fault. Momma always told me don't play around with fire unless you are willing to put it out. At this time, I didn't know what to put out. Now is the real test of infatuation or love.

Finally, I said, "Jeremy can we just slow down?"

"Slow down...I give you my heart and you tell me to slow down!"

"Just listen to what I have to say...you don't even know me...you don't know my past...all you see is a black and white girl destined for love...I am not saying I don't love you...I am saying I don't really know what love is when it comes to a man...just give me some time...give me some time."

"Because I love you, I will grant you that request...can we still see each other?"

"Yes, Jeremy...that is what I am talking about ...we need to spend more time getting to know one another."

On those last words Jeremy gave me one of the most romantic kisses. Everyone came back into the room. I believe they were listening from the kitchen. The celebration continued as though the ring never existed.

Jeremy and I began to spend time together like friends. It was similar to the way Travis and I related, but it couldn't replace Travis and our special relationship. I believe Travis is the only guy who puts up with me. No matter what I do or say to him, he continues to spend time with our family. Jeremy on the other hand, spends time with mom and I but there is something missing in this friendship. One day while we were sitting on my favorite bench in the park, I began to wonder why I was attracted to Jeremy. He definitely wasn't black, and he had no characteristics of being black. Is it because I really don't know who I am? Could it be I need to find my own identity? Before the questions could be answered in my head....

"What are you thinking about Dee?" Jeremy said.

"Oh...oh...I was wondering what it would be like if you were black." I replied.

"Why would you think such a thing...do you want me to be black?"

"No...but there is nothing wrong with thinking."

"Dee, why do you have this hang up with color...don't you know on the inside is what counts?"

"I know that...but for years...I didn't know what I was."

Then Jeremy turned my cheek up to his face and said, "I love you... and that's all that matters."

I was beginning to get the jitters. Love is one thing, but saying I love you is a big step for most men, especially black men.

I asked, "Jeremy are you sure it is love and not infatuation?"

"I think it is love…this feeling inside of me just wants to be with you."

Now being with me can mean sex and all sorts of things. I really think guys say they love me just to get into my underwear. I made an agreement a long time ago to save myself for my husband. My mom's life taught me the pain of giving up your virginity too soon. I constantly believe my mom struggles with the thoughts of those men she used to sleep with for money. She told me Jesus is the man in her life now. I guess Jesus is my man now also, because He is the only one that will see my body naked in the bathroom.

Jeremy and I continued to talk at the park. Suddenly, I heard someone call my name. It was Momma yelling my name.

Momma cried out, "Dee…Dee!"

I turned around and saw she was hysterical.

"Something happened to Travis!" She shouted.

Just the thought of something happening to Travis began to kindle my mind with fear. I couldn't stand to lose another person in my life again. I was probably getting ahead of myself.

"Momma what happened to Travis?" I shouted with anger.

"Travis was working on the roof of his mother's house when he fell off the top of it." Momma replied.

Jeremy hurried to take me to the hospital, while Momma followed alone in her car. On the way to the hospital, I was very quiet. I know that Jeremy thinks I am still in love with Travis. It is very difficult to give up your feelings on a guy who was with you from the beginning of adolescent stage. Travis has always been a great friend.

As we entered the hospital emergency room, Travis' mother was there with Lettie and Mrs. Lois. We were sort of like family when it came to any happenings around us. Momma ran over to console Travis's mom. This moment reminded me of the time the missing pieces of my life was rekindled. I walked over to the nurse and asked her what was going on; because I was a supervisor, she was able to inform me of his condition. Travis had some fractured bones from the fall. There was no definite answer for us until further test were ran. Meanwhile, all of us impatiently waited in the emergency waiting room. Then I noticed a lot of commotion going on in the room. The doctor came out to tell Travis's mom the diagnosis of his condition. Apparently, Travis fractured his spinal cord and probably would not be able to walk unless a miracle happens.

The thought of Travis not walking was pending in my mind over and over. I couldn't believe Travis couldn't walk. All of us gathered in the waiting room and prayed for Travis. Jeremy even prayed the prayer for us. This was a miracle waiting to happen.

CHAPTER 14

The weeks seemed very long as I waited for a miracle with Travis. Therefore, I visited him regularly even when I was on duty. Sometimes I would go in to feed him his lunch. One thing about Travis, he didn't have any bitterness toward his condition. His facial expressions always were pleasant. I felt sorry for Travis in many ways. Here I am worrying about a man in my life and Travis who always was in my life is now alone in a paraplegic body. Sometimes I would stand outside his room door and cry. I always try to hold back the tears when I am visiting him. Maybe if I had married him things maybe would change.

The relationship between Jeremy and I began to diminish because I spent a lot of my time comforting Travis. Jeremy and I still keep in touch. He even stops by the hospital to see Travis. One day while Jeremy was visiting Travis, I overheard a conversation between them. The entire conversation was centered on me.

"Travis, you must be a strong guy." Jeremy said.

"Why did you say that?" Travis replied.

"Dee is such a beautiful young lady…inside …and out."

"Yeah, she is special."

"Tell me Travis…why you never married Dee?"

"We weren't ready for marriage …and I had things to do since my dad died."

"Just between me and you…. is Dee really a virgin or is she playing on me."

"One thing I can say about Dee…she is a real woman…that's all I can say."

"You mean…you never tried her?"

"For what…I respect Dee…and anyway if I was going to marry any woman it would have been her."

"Travis…I got to hand it to you…you must be really love her."

"It goes beyond love with her; she is a special person…even though I am laying up here with no movement in my body…she …still cares for me."

"She is special…very special…I guess you know I have feelings for her too."

"I know."

"What do you say about that?"

"Jeremy, I wouldn't stop you from having the feelings you have for her…because I couldn't …and if you want to marry her go ahead…but it will not stop me loving her…I am no good for her now."

With that thought coming from Travis's mouth, tears of sorrow began to ponder in my head. All this time I really didn't think Travis was that much in love with me. He has always put others in front of his feelings and life. I didn't know what to do. I couldn't walk into the room because my eyes were filled with water. Even if Jeremy was to come back into my life, I couldn't marry him because of the guilt I have inside for the way I treated Travis. I actually played with his emotions.

Since Travis was going home today, it would help me to figure out some things. Momma Lucy always told me the best way to figure out things is to go to church. I couldn't wait for the clock to tick at two o'clock. I hurried home so that I could be prepared for Sunday evening service. I just knew Minister Hines had the answer for me tonight.

When six o'clock came around, Momma didn't have to scream for me to hurry up. I was already in the car waiting on her. Momma kept looking at me strangely on the way to church. She was wondering why I was so excited about church. Normally I would lag around, and she would have to hurry me up.

As we entered the church grounds, I could feel the relief coming from the building. Momma always sat up front in church. She said the noise from the back keeps her from concentrating on the service. The choir sang beautiful melodies during the worship service. The worship service was much anointed. I couldn't wait to hear Minister Hines give the sermon. When I looked up in the pulpit, I saw the man in the white suit looking directly at me.

I looked at Momma and said, "Do you see the man in the white suit?"

"Sh...sh..." Momma replied.

"Momma...I...am not kidding."

"And I am not kidding when I say ...sh!"

All my life the man in the white suit has been appearing in my life. Maybe he is a visiting minister. Suddenly Minister Hines got up to start with his sermon.

"This evening my text will come from Psalm's forty, verses one through four," he said.

Then he began to read the verses out loud. They began to cling to my heart. He began to explain them. It was as though God was talking to me Himself.

Minister Hines said, "I waited patiently for God to help me; then he listened and heard my cry. He lifted me out of the pit of despair, out from the bog and the mire, and set my feet on a hard, firm path and steadied me as I walked along. He has given me a new song to sing, of praises to our God. Now many will hear of the glorious things He did for me, and stand in awe before the Lord, and put their trust in Him."

As he amplified the scripture, tears were falling from my eyes like drops of blood. I began to recapture memories of the past. God delivered me from being homeless by giving me Momma Lucy. He delivered me from being motherless by giving me Mrs. Lois in the beginning and my real mom in the latter years. He delivered me from being fatherless by giving me Mr. Irvin even though I had no idea he existed. He gave me true friends Lettie and Travis. Then I began to think about the physical blessings. I was violated when I was young, and God gave me comfort and peace in the midst of my trouble. God set me into a high position on my job. Most of all He gave me wisdom and understanding through my grandma and mom. There is no need for me to complain. I am blessed.

I looked over at mom and she was emotionally disturbed by the sermon. My mom had been through a lot, but I look at how God had established her goings and placed her on a solid rock. My mom has no past in my eyesight, because she had accepted Christ in her life, therefore she is a new creature, old things are passed away, everything is new.

It was a touchy service. The entire church was on a spiritual high. When the minister called for altar call, I stood up and went forward. Minister Hines smiled at me. The man in the white suit had left the pulpit. I looked around to see if he was in the building. He had vanished. As I stood at the altar, I began to ask God to forgive me for my ungratefulness. Then I began to ask God to open up my eyes of understanding of His will for my life. As the prayer went forth, I began to feel a sense of relief from anxiety. The emptiness that was in my heart about men began to become a cloud of peace. The love I had for Travis began to become stronger in my heart even though he was paraplegic. The understanding of true love was flourishing inside me. The spirit of confusion left my soul immediately. I began to praise and worship God for his wonderful gift He had allowed me to behold.

Momma came over to me and said; "Now you can go on."

I knew immediately what she was saying. I needed to let the past stay in the past and go on with my life. The hurt and pain I experienced was nailed to the cross. As I turned around to leave the altar, I glanced to the back of the church and there was Travis in a wheelchair capturing my great moment of joy. I could tell he was happy for me by the look in his eyes. If I wasn't mistaken, I believe he had some raindrops on his face. Travis's mom was sitting next to him. I could see her lips silently saying to me, "thank you for being there for Travis and me."

Finally, the service was over, I hurriedly ran over to where Travis was. He was excited to see me.

"Did you like the service?" I said.

"Yes, I did." Travis replied.

"I will be over tomorrow, Travis."

"Okay, I will see you then…by the way, thanks for being you."

As I headed toward the doorway of the church, my heart wouldn't let me leave without final words with Travis. His mother was pushing him out the door, when I pulled on the wheelchair and whispered in his ear, "I love you."

I held Travis's hand and gave him a kiss on the cheek.

The End, Maybe!!

Tame

"Killing My Intimacy"

TAME SERIES: Taking All My Energy

"When we take all **_our energy_** to gain the things that God has already prepared for us; it becomes vanity in the sight of God"

Dedicated to women all over the world who sacrifice
their lives for lust, fame and fortune.

ACKNOWLEDGEMENT

Special Thanks to My Beloved Daughter:
Kincie Elaine -Editor

CHAPTER 1

I had been told relentlessly that I am a beautiful black woman. My skin is as radiant as a peach on a perfect blooming day. I have always thought that God gave me this beauty for a purpose. To me, beauty is attractive on the outside and that you can camouflage the inside to get the attention you need. Arrogance and no contentment could only put a dent into the character I have built within myself. I was the Goddess of real living and no one could bid me to believe anything different. But when I began to focus on the disturbances around me, the inner femininity of me began to realize the value of sunshine. My life had been wastefully trusted in prosperity and lust, but there was no one to blame but me. Beauty, fame and lust were nothing but vanity. I have come to the consensus that there are more eminent things in this world. I have recently acquired a taste for true living and become obsessed with it. The value of life is priceless, and I am willing to do anything to gain consciousness of it.

As the sunshine was beaming through the windowpane, a burst of energy was penetrating upon my face, something that I didn't take the time to really appreciate. God's light was absorbing the success fragments that were left within me. He felt like a sponge soaking up drops of water in a dry parched place. I enjoyed having him in my presence. He was finally a reality that I began to admire. I was grateful for just being able to feel the warmth of his attributes.

I have also become sensitive to the air I was breathing. It didn't matter to me whether it was a polluted atmosphere or a moment of fresh air. It was priceless for me to awake and see another day. Being alive and knowing it, was the utmost important thing in my life and I wasn't going to let anything or anybody keep me from possessing it. My heart longs to be a part of the world again. I have finally found my purpose in life.

While the revelation of life flourished my conscience, memories of past events flood my heart releasing an eccentric ecstasy. I was in another time zone that took me back to the day I entered this infallible world. I began to have flashbacks of the most precious moments in my life I had seemed to forgotten. The person that I was and became was no longer in conflict with each other.

I began to realize that having everything at your fingertip can become a liability when you have no knowledge of the value of it. Sometimes I would blame my parents for giving me the desire of my heart, frequently. They cultivated my life style by their standards of living. They are successful (My dad a stockbroker and my mom the owner of a prominent florist shop). They are financially situated and wanted to bring an offspring into this world to share it. My mom was in her late forties when finally was able to conceive a child. My birth caused serious complications. Doctors informed my parents that it was a fifty-fifty chance of me being a normal child. My parents had faith in God, and believed that my life had a purpose. I believe it was signifying my path of life. Many times during the pregnancy she thought that she was going to lose me, but my parents stood their grounds on faith. The Christian life they lived was being tested through me. They had a divine touch that instilled confidence in them. They knew I was a gift from God. Now that I look back, I realize a gift involves not just the giver, but also the receiver.

On the day I took my first breath of fresh air, my existence brought about a radiant and reviving presence between them, because of the spark and the radiant beauty that were imparted upon me, my parents agreed to name me "Diamond". I became their most valuable and prized possession and there was nothing too good for me.

When it came to me, the term spoil was given a new definition. My parents gave me everything I needed and my wants were not even a bonus, because everything was included in the need package of my life. It was a blessing for me to get the things that I need and a sin to get the things I desire; therefore my life was overwhelmed with pride, greed and success. I went from ballet lessons to piano lessons and I was talented in both. These tattoos remain on my entire adolescent stage and carried over into my adulthood. I was a very happy and satisfied little girl; the thought of having everything soothed the outer person of me greatly, so I didn't have time to think about my feelings or other people's feelings.

At the age of six a hidden talent was bestowed upon me. I never fail to remember that Sunday. While we were in church singing the hymns "Amazing Grace", something remarkable happened. I have always enjoyed singing, especially in church. I would close my eyes tightly and let the music and the lyrics of the words be submerged into my soul. The vibrant lyrics of the song overshadowed me deeply. I was in depth with the soul of singing. When the congregation stopped singing, my strong voice was still in concert. My parents were astounded at the virtue that protruded out of my body. With my eyes closed tightly, I sung my heart out. Suddenly, I couldn't hear anyone's voice but me. The people in the church began to applaud.

"Sing one more verse!" The pastor shouted as he clapped his hands with joy.

I was stunned and look around and said, "...Who me?"

"Yes, baby...you," replied Mom as she was boosting me to sing.

I felt like I was on top of the world. I open my eyes and noticed the congregation standing and applauding my efforts. I wanted to sing until the ceiling fell in.

At the age of six, the feeling of success was being able to accomplish something that only an adult could do. To me, that was singing with boldness.

"Go ahead and sing baby...that's my girl," yelled Dad from the Deacon's corner.

I began to open my mouth to sing some more of "Amazing Grace," I heard a special quality coming from my voice that I never felt before. Even the walls seemed to be listening to the echoing tone, as the sound bounced around the church. I was surprised at what was projecting from the inside of, "little Diamond Oslo".

After that Sunday, voice lessons began to be a part of my weekly curriculum. I took voice lessons from grade school through high school. My voice teacher was highly impressed with the quality of my voice. She told my parents that I had a mature and promising voice for my age. My parents were very supportive with the talent I had been given. Even though I was gifted with many talents, singing began to overshadow them all. There was no limit to what I needed or wanted to pursue with a career in singing.

In high school I entered every singing contest that was posted on campus with the results of winning first, second, or third. I wasn't satisfied with being in second or third place, so I worked very hard at being number one. My parents were determined for me to be successful and that determination drove me into different levels of pride. They spent lots of money nurturing my talent. They knew one day I was going to be famous and there would be no limit for payback. I had the confidence of a millionaire and money was no object.

Finally, the opportunity to demonstrate my talent among aristocrats aroused. At the age of fifteen I entered the annual high school talent contest. The Aseret Talent Agency was visiting and scouting for new talent, especially young talent for Rhythm & Blues. I didn't know much about R&B song, because my parents didn't allow me to listen to that type of music. I was only allowed to listen to classic or gospel music. I knew that if I won this contest it would bring bigger and better things for me, so I borrowed a Rhythm & Blues CD from one of the girls at school. I carried my headset everyday in my book bag and listened to it on the bus going and coming, until I was ready to finalize the piece with confidence.

I will never forget that day. I was nervous because I didn't have the congregation egging me on and my voice teacher was not around to signal any deficiencies. Furthermore this time it wasn't all about me. I had competition to be concerned about. It took faith and courage to believe this was my breakthrough. I began to start singing the R & B song but my mouth couldn't seem to let it come out. Then all of a sudden a melody began to give a breakthrough from my mind and then protrude through my lips. I can remember the song distinctively. I sung, "God Bless the Child". At first I was startled for a moment, but I took a grip of myself and remembered that I had to sing from my soul. My heart was pounding with lasting confidence when I was announced the winner of the Aseret Talent contest. I won first place in the talent contest and also won a three-year contract with Aseret Talent Agency. The agency was prominent and very difficult to acquire a contract with. I felt highly fortunate being the one to obtain their attention. I was overwhelmed with excitement, because the first Chapter of my singing career was originated.

On the day of officially signing the contract, I was very anxious. My parents and I were sitting in the main lobby waiting to see the owner, Mr. Singleton. This moment bought about a celebrative atmosphere among us. I had anticipated this instant since the gift of singing protruded through my soul. My parents were probably more excited than me, because their investment in my talent is finally going to have some payoff.

Dad looked at me and asked, "Are you nervous?"

I replied with great self-assurance. "Not really,"

"I really have to think about this R&B thing," Dad said solemnly.

"But dad…it's a record deal…a chance of a lifetime," I implied.

Mom didn't say much. I could tell by her facial expressions that she was waiting for dad to give the words. She was always a hundred percent behind my father in decision making.

"We will see what they have to say…but I am still not keen on you singing the devil's music," Dad replied.

Dad knew that my confidence was beyond reality. I stayed on a natural high twenty-four seven.

"Well baby this is the payoff for all those voice lessons," Mom said.

"I know…don't think I don't appreciate all you have done for me," I said with appreciation written all over my face.

The agency was a very busy place. I could tell because the executive assistant's phone rang constantly and also it seemed like no one had the time to stop and say hello. I was getting dizzy looking back and forth at the people passing the lobby. I was watching and expecting to be the next person called to enter Mr. Singleton's office. I kept looking at his executive assistant at the desk hoping she would get up and tell me it was my turn to go into his office. I could tell this agency was top in clients. Even the pictures on the wall looked like they came from an art gallery. I walked around the lobby for a little while looking at the photos of the many famous artists that Aseret represented.

Suddenly a breath of fresh air quenched my soul. There standing at the desk was the most handsome man I had ever seen. He had a deep chocolate complexion and skin as smooth as a baby. His hair was not that nappy stuff. He had a good grade of hair. He looked like he was mix with another race. My hormones were really wacky, especially at the age of fifteen.

Constantly, I was observing every movement as he talked to the assistant; I kept looking at him up and down. His presence made goose bumps jump all over me. It was love at first sight; at least I thought it was. There was only one problem; he appeared to be much older than me. He looked to be in his late twenties or early thirties. I didn't really care because men really don't grow up until about thirty.

The continuing glance at him began to get him to notice me. Glancing at someone a long time does get their attention. There must be a burst of energy that comes from the eyes that manipulates a person to look. Every time he would stare at me, I would put a magazine up to my face to block out the glimmer that came upon me. I was actually blushing. But blushing wasn't the word; I believed I had found my first love, even if it took me five years to wait on it. In my mind I knew one day I was going to have this man. I even started daydreaming about how it would feel to be in his arms. Being selfish has never failed me yet.

While I was pretending to indulge into the magazine, I heard a soft voice say, "hello,"

I slowly removed the magazine from my face. I couldn't believe what was before my eyes. There near my body was the dessert I was drooling over. I was a chocolate fudge ice cream bar melting with heat. I looked over at my mom and saw her smiling at the way I was acting. She knew that I was flirting with him by the way I was smiling. Somehow mothers know the thoughts of their daughters, it's because they were once a daughter.

"Hello, Sir," Dad said, as he stood up to greet him. I believe my dad was turning the action to another direction. He was very protective of me, especially when it came to boys or shall I say men.

"My name is Marcus Singleton," He said.

I didn't give my dad a chance to say anything else when I stumbled out, "You mean the...Singleton..."

"Yes, I am the son of Mr. Singleton, owner and operator of Aseret," Marcus smiled as he replied.

I was stunned for words and my father knew it, so he finally carried on with the greetings.

"I am Dick Oslo and this is my wife Janice, and my daughter Diamond," He explained.

Marcus greeted my parents with a handshake, but when it was my turn, he took my hand from being folded and pulled it up to his lips and kissed it. I was reluctant to let him and turn it a loose. I kept starring at the spot on my hand he kissed. I almost fainted, but it wouldn't be lady like if I did. My dad began to clear his throat, in other words, hands off is what he was simply implying to Marcus.

"Are you all waiting to see my Dad?" Marcus asked.

"Why yes...this young lady will be signing her first contract today," Dad replied.

Marcus faced me with a look I had never seen in a man's eyes before.

He moved closer to me and said, "You must be that dynamic new voice I have been hearing ...you have a beautiful face also,"

I was arrogant and didn't mind saying, "I am...and thank you for the compliment,"

"That's great you have so much confidence in yourself," Marcus said.

"She was born with it," Mom said.

"Well some people are born with it," Marcus said, insinuating through his body movement, he was born with it also.

My dad scanned the room swiftly while saying to Marcus, "Are there any gospel singers in this company?"

Marcus responded reluctantly, "Yeah…we have…"

Before Marcus could complete his thought the door of Mr. Singleton opened; He was escorting one of the well-known female singers out to the lobby. Not knowing I was sitting in the lobby he walked back into his office. Marcus personally escorted us into his father's office. I could smell success creeping into the atmosphere.

"Come in and sit down," Mr. Singleton said as he closed his cigar box on the desk.

"Would you like to have one?" He said as he greeted my dad.

"No thanks, I quit long time ago," Dad said.

"You don't mind if I do," Mr. Singleton asked.

"No, go right ahead" Dad said.

"Have a seat!" Mr. Singleton said with excitement, as he pulled out the chair for my mom and me. He was quite the gentlemen.

"Marcus, why don't you get some drinks for the people?" Mr. Singleton asked as he sat in his chair behind the desk.

"We are just fine," Mom interrupted, as she looked over at my father. She knew he had a thing for drinking in the past.

"But…we will take water or tea if you have it," Mom said calmly.

Marcus was headed toward the bar in the office, but stopped after my mother's remark. He stood in the corner watching everything. Just watching him was the most sensational Kodak moment that didn't include me.

"I see you already met my son Marcus," Mr. Singleton said.

"I am Marcus Senior, but everyone calls me Big Daddy," He continued.

Then he looked over in the chair at me and said, "So you are the talent everyone is talking about,"

I gathered why they called him Big Daddy. He was a very tall man. He looked to be about six feet plus. When he stood over me I felt like Jack and the Giant. But, not only was he tall, but his body was really buffed for a man his age. I could see where his son gets his good looks.

"I guess…yes," I said nervously.

"I like the name, Diamond…it stands out," Mr. Singleton said.

"I like it too," I said trying to act like I was shy.

Mr. Singleton turned towards my parents and said, "We have a remarkable deal here for your daughter…we are about to make a star,"

"What kind of a deal are you talking about?" Dad asked as he looked over at my mother. By him being a stockbroker, he was used to seeing con-artists and crooks all the time. He wasn't taking any chances with his little girl.

"A deal you can't turn down …we are willing to give her a three year contract with royalties…which will include musical videos, concerts, and the works," He said.

"You mean I will get to have my own music video and concerts?" I said excitedly forgetting that my parents have the last say so.

"Yes the works," He replied.

"Oh… Mr. Singleton…I can't believe it!" I shouted.

"Not Mr. Singleton, but Big Daddy…Call me, Big Daddy," He said as he puffed the cigar continuously.

"Wait a minute…we are moving too fast…will she be singing any gospel?" Dad asked, still skeptical of the moment.

Big Daddy looked over at Marcus as though this was a surprise to him.

"Gospel…well…you know you have to start somewhere…and besides she will be given a chance of a lifetime," Big Daddy implied while puffing on his cigar.

"I need to have my lawyer look over the contract," Dad explained as he took the contract out of Marcus's hand.

"I will give you a week to have your lawyer look over the contract… meanwhile we will work with Diamond as an artist in development on our label," Big Daddy said.

"Well…you got a deal," Dad said as he shook hands with Big Daddy.

"But what about your schoolwork?" Mom asked as she looked over at me.

"She can attend public school for right now, until she starts going on tours, then we will provide her a tutor," Big Daddy explained.

"You think you ready for this?" Mom asked me as she held my hand with assurance.

"Yes mom…this is always what I wanted," I said.

My parents noticed the burst of sunshine upon my face and agreed to Big Daddy's terms. Meanwhile I was on top of the world. My life was beginning to feel like a chess game. It seemed as though everything I desired was coming into play. If only I knew which direction it was headed. I couldn't believe this was really happening to me. My parents shook hands with Big Daddy and Marcus. Marcus came over and gave me a hug around the neck. The kind of hug you would give your kid sister.

"Dad, we are going to have to give her a party," Marcus said.

"You're right, as soon as we receive the contract signed we will celebrate her success with a pre-release party," Big Daddy said.

"You mean a party with other known singers?" I asked with excitement.

"Yes, that's right…just for you…and you will be the star of the night," Marcus replied.

I couldn't believe that I was about to walk into stardom. When Big Daddy announced I was going to be in the company of other known singers, I had to pinch myself to see if I was dreaming. I have always dreamed about meeting the top R&B artists. I was overwhelmed with joy because it has become a reality and not just a fantasy.

I thought, "This only happened on television with other people", but now it has become a reality for me.

CHAPTER 2

The contract was legit with Aseret Talent Agency. I couldn't believe my parents signed the contract. I found out before signing the contract that Big Daddy agreed to include in the agreement the production of at least two gospel recordings CD's, which will include the same package as the R&B. My parents and I signed a five-year contract with all the works. Big Daddy kept his promise about celebrating the contract signing event. The bash was held at Big Daddy's mansion. There were many known R&B artists in attendance. I was nervous and didn't really know how to present myself. I couldn't believe this was all done for me. I walked around the mansion with a face of awe. I thought I had everything, but this was another phrase for me.

My parents' were enjoying themselves chatting with the guest. For a while I felt out of place because I thought I was the only underage guest, until I met Marcus's baby sister Sherrie. Sherrie didn't resemble Marcus at all. She was pretty, but she was on the stocky side when it came to her weight. She was also very bubbly young lady. I noticed from the corner of my eye, she was constantly staring at me. Finally she decided to walk over.

"Hi, my name is Sherrie," She said.

"I am Diamond," I said.

"I already know that…you signed on with my Dad's agency," Sherrie said very frisky.

"Oh…you are Marcus's…fa… sister?" I asked as I almost blurted she was fat.

"I am his half-sister; we don't have the same mother," Sherrie replied.

I was trying not to be obnoxious, but I took pleasure in crushing a person's self-esteem, even if they didn't have one.

"I really like your house," I said changing the subject, because I didn't want to ruin tonight with my hideous comments.

"It's okay...I think he could have built it bigger," Sherrie said.

When Sherrie said those words, I couldn't think of anything but a spoiled brat. I wanted to hit a homerun with repulsive words, but I remained calm.

"So I see you met my brother Marcus," Sherrie said as she glanced over at him flirting with some of the ladies.

"Yes I met him," I said.

"He is a lady's man...he thinks he can get any woman in the world, you better be glad that you are not old enough," Sherrie said.

"What do you mean by that?" I asked.

"Every time my daddy signs on a new talent...especially..." Sherrie was interrupted by Marcus as he walked over into her conversation.

"So what are you two up too?" Marcus asked, as he hugged Sherrie around the neck with his arms.

"Why you ask, don't you have enough entertainment" Sherrie replied.

Sherrie got a kick out of kidding around with her brother.

"So...I see you met my little sister," Marcus implied.

"Not little sister...but only sister," Sherrie answered getting smart with Marcus.

Marcus ignored his sister's remark, because he knew that she was always trying to make sure she was the only permanent female in his life.

"Are you enjoying yourself Diamond?" Marcus asked.

"Yes I am...I think it was so nice of your dad to do this for me," I replied.

"How else were you going to meet the entire Aseret family?" Marcus implied.

"Come over here with me Diamond...I want you to meet someone," Marcus said as he pulled my arm walking toward the crowd.

We started walking toward a young man whose physical attraction could not compete with Marcus. He had dreads in his hair and fair skin. This was the kind of guy you would really call pretty boy.

"Jesse, I want you to meet Diamond," Marcus said.

"So this is the Diamond everyone is talking about," Jesse said as he took my hand and kissed it.

Jesse's kiss didn't feel the same as Marcus's hug.

"Hi. "I said shyly snatching my hand quickly from him.

"Jesse is one of our producers; you will be working closely with him, so get to know him," Marcus said.

I watched Jesse as Marcus was talking. Jesse continued to stare at Marcus constantly.

"I will be the first person you will see on Monday, before you enter the studio," Jesse said.

"What will I do in the studio…I don't have songs and…" I said.

"Don't be concerned about the songs; we already have some lyrics written especially for you," Jessie replied.

Suddenly I heard Big Daddy getting everybody's attention. Marcus takes a champagne glass from the hostess's tray as he was passing by. He handed me the glass.

"I would like to make a toast to Diamond, our next superstar… May she bring in many platinum records," Big Daddy Shouted with joy.

All eyes were on me as they toasted and applauded to my future success. I was going to be the next "Superstar".

I know I wasn't allowed to drink champagne, but for this moment I felt reluctant to say no. Marcus took my glass and clanged it on to my glass to make a toast. Then Marcus turned around and kissed me on the forehead. His kiss left an imprint on my feminine hormones forever.

After that moment, excitement in the party began to escalate. Everyone was juiced up and seemed to be having a great time. Marcus decided to manipulate me by walking toward the balcony as we were talking. I was wondering what he was up to. As we headed toward the balcony, I could feel the eyes of others scanning our every move.

"How do you like all of this?" Marcus asked looking around at the audience before me.

"All of what?" I asked with a puzzle upon my face. Marcus probably thought I wasn't used to the finer things of life.

"Well...for starters...the parties and celebrities!" Marcus shouted while raising his glass into the air.

"Oh...this" I replied looking inside the room.

Before I could turn, Marcus accidentally wasted his champagne on the lapel of my dress. He took out his handkerchief from his jacket and tried to dry up the residue that was sinking into my chiffon dress.

I jumped back and shouted, "Oh looked what you done!"

The rude and obnoxious person inside of me was beginning to surface. I couldn't believe I let that side of me show up.

"I am so sorry," Marcus said as he took the handkerchief to pat the spot dry.

"That's okay," I said as I took his hand away from my dress.

I was hoping he didn't notice my sudden change of personally. He didn't because I noticed he continued to flirt with me. I didn't know whether to entertain it or ignore it.

"I tell you what...Diamond I will make sure your dress is taken care of first thing in the morning," Marcus said.

"I told you... its okay," I said.

"No it is not okay...we can't have our star running around with a soiled dress," He said. Whether he noticed or not, I was going to have a soiled dress the rest of the night anyway.

"Okay...you can come by tomorrow to pick up the dress," I said, keeping Marcus from talking about my dress.

"Better yet, why don't we have lunch tomorrow?" Marcus said.

"I don't think so...and don't you think you are a little too old for me?" I forwardly asked.

"Diamond, I wasn't talking about a date.... I am talking about a business lunch, where we can talk about some of your ideas," Marcus replied stumbling for words.

"I will have to ask my parents... but remember... only business,"

"What do you think I am…a child molester?"

"I don't know what you are… I've only known you for a little while,"

I kept looking around wondering what others could be thinking about me, especially out on the balcony with a man about five years older than me.

"We better go back inside," I said.

"Of course Diamond, whatever you say," Marcus replied with a sly tone of voice.

As the balcony door opened I could see my Dad watching from the far end of the room. His protective eyes were like a surveillance camera. I could tell he had a sense of relief when he saw us enter back into the party where I was visible. Also I notice Marcus's friend Jesse watching every movement we were making. I felt from the corner of my eyes he was waiting for the moment to interrupt our conversation. Jesse's footsteps were anticipating on when to come over. As he walked over he stumbled into a chair. I began to snicker on the inside.

"I need to watch where I am going," Jesse said as he approached Marcus and me.

With snickering written all over my face, I said, "Well that is one way of getting attention,"

Jesse had a witty look upon his face.

"Diamond didn't mean it that way…" Marcus said trying to get Jesse from thinking I was being rude.

"Really" Jesse boldly said.

"I was only kidding Jesse, loosen up," I said.

Before we could continue, Marcus's cell phone rang. He walked away from us to answer the call.

While Marcus was over in another area talking on his cell, Jesse and I became acquainted.

"Well how does it feel to be a star?" Jesse asked.

Trying to keep my answers short and sweet, I said, "I ain't a star yet,"

"You might as well be, Big Daddy has great plans for you,"

"How come everyone knows my plans except me?"

"You'll find out soon enough,"

"Since you are the producer, do you know when I will be going on tour?"

"You would probably go on tours during the summer months, due to your schooling and working on the CD; it's the best timing,"

"I can't wait, I am so excited,"

"I know that…on Monday we will go over some lyrics that I think you will be interested in,"

"It seems like, you have all the answers?"

"By the way, don't let Marcus get to you,"

"He's not getting to me, I sort of like him…he is a real gentleman,"

I could see the jealousy mark upon Jesse. I really didn't know where he was coming from.

"Diamond…watch it with him, he can be a real charmer," Jesse said.

"Why are you telling me to watch myself…it's not like I want to go out with him…anyway I'm just a baby to him," I firmly stated.

Before we continued our little rivalry, Marcus started walking toward us.

"Is everything okay?" Jesse asked as he noticed Marcus's demeanor.

"Yeah" Marcus' puzzled face replied softly.

"So what do you think about this young lady here?" Marcus asked Jesse as he put his arms around my shoulders.

"She is a real gem…I mean a real gem," Jesse replied.

I couldn't do anything but indulge into the moment. I thought, here I am fifteen and have older guys gloating over me. It felt good to know that I was attractive and beautiful even though I had a large wet spot on my dress flashing. I didn't care, this was my night. Most of the people probably didn't notice the spot, especially when I see the hostesses keep going back to fill their champagne trays. I believe there was more than champagne on those trays.

Without warning, the champagne was finally taking a toll of me. I began dancing with any and everyone. My Dad was showing off his two-step dance from the seventies. He took the floor with my mom. Marcus and Jesse also danced several times with me. We had a fantastic time at the celebration. Sherrie and I danced next to each other, laughing and joking at others who were making fools out of themselves. I was immense in pride and looking forward to being a fantastic legacy as a female R& B artist.

CHAPTER 3

I anticipated the next day, because I knew Marcus was coming by to pick up my dress and to have lunch if my dad allows it. But meeting Marcus for lunch might have been a move I shouldn't have done, because lighting a match can start a fire that sometimes spread into a disaster. Marcus had one point toward him when he kept his promise to come by and pick me up.

When the doorbell rang I was already waiting for him in the living room, but my dad wouldn't let me answer the door. He believes a man should come in the house and meet the head of the house, before he takes his daughter out.

My dad opened the door and said, "Hi Marcus, how are you today?"

My dad stood at the door with the doorknob in his hand. It was an indication of him waiting for Marcus to be invited into the house.

"I am fine…and how are you?" Marcus asked nervously.

"I am doing great," Dad replied.

Dad finally released the doorknob and allowed Marcus to enter the house.

"I would like to ask you something Mr. Oslo?" Marcus asked.

"Go ahead," Dad frantically said standing boldly in front of Marcus, like he was my bodyguard.

"Well…dad, are you going to tell him to have a seat? I asked.

"I really don't have time to sit…I just wanted to ask your dad if I could take you to lunch?" Marcus replied reluctantly.

"Well I don't know…her mother is at church…uh…Diamond is too young to be hanging around with you by herself," Dad said as he sat in his favorite chair.

"I know sir…but I am only taking her to drop her dress off to the dry cleaners and then I would like to take her for some lunch…that way we can talk about her career path in depth," Marcus replied.

"You can do that right here…I won't get in the way," Dad said.

I could tell by my dad's behavior that he was reluctant to give me the go ahead, but he saw the way I was looking. Somehow I could always manipulate my parents to get what I wanted by the facial gestures I made.

"And how long will that take?" Dad asked looking at his watch.

"I will have her back by three o'clock," Marcus replied.

"Marcus, we normally don't let our daughter go any places on Sunday, because this is the Lord's Day…I don't know if I should make an exception being that we didn't go to church today," Dad said.

My eyes continued to manipulate my dad until he decided to say yes.

"Okay…okay, Diamond you have my permission… it is around twelve o'clock now…make sure you are back on time," Father said looking at his watch.

"I will dad…thanks," I excitedly said as I kissed him on the jaw.

"I don't know how your mom is going to take this since you didn't go to church," Dad implied.

"She'll be alright, especially since you said it was alright…you know how to handle mom," I said smiling at my dad.

My dad was watching Marcus carefully as he opened the door. I hurried out the door before he could change his mind. Suddenly I realized I ran outside without the dress. I walked back into the house and noticed my dad watching me from the window. He closed the curtains quickly as I opened the door.

"I thought you forgot something," He said as he handed me the dress.

"Thanks dad…I love you," I said.

As I opened the door to exit, dad said, "Be careful with older guys and you uphold your standards and be a lady,"

I looked at my father and smiled with an assurance that I would take heed to his advice. As we walked out the door I was impressed with Marcus's politeness toward my father.

Marcus was very polite as he opened the door of his beige Porsche. I felt there was a mystery with him, but I couldn't pinpoint it. Of course, he had the top down of the car. He probably was trying to impress me.

"Your father was pretty hard on me," Marcus said as he was driving down the street.

"He was just looking out for my wellbeing," I replied.

"It wasn't like I was going to steal you or sleep with you,"

"Of course not, that was not what my father was thinking, you have to put yourself in his place…an older guy comes by and takes your fifteen year old daughter to lunch without a chaperone,"

"A chaperone" Marcus chuckled.

"Yes, a chaperone!" I replied sincerely.

"We just signed a million-dollar contract…now you need a chaperone!"

"It's not about the contract; it is about not letting me be manipulated by the music industry,"

"How am I manipulating you?"

"I didn't say you were…for starters, why are you taking me to lunch?"

"…To get to know you better,"

"Are you sure?"

"I am sure," Marcus said as he smiled at the way I was coming on to him.

No matter what Marcus said, I will always keep my guard up on him. Especially because he is very attractive young man and have a past record of being a charmer.

As we drove down the downtown area of the Main Street, I could smell the newly fresh air of success. I knew the day was coming when I would be one of the world's fineness R & B artists. I was astounded at how quickly stardom was knocking on my door.

When we approached the dry cleaners building, I looked at my watch, making sure that we pace the day with the amount of time I had to spend with him. It was special being able to spend the day with a handsome and top executive. I even felt special.

Marcus stopped the car on the edge of the sidewalk in front of the dry cleaners. I began to become timid when it came to being with him alone.

"Diamond, I will be right back," Marcus said as he took the dress from out of the backseat of the car.

I waited patiently while he walked into the dry cleaners. I began to primp into the rear-view mirror. There in the view of the mirror was another car pulling up to the rear bumper of the car. Before I could turn from the mirror, I noticed Marcus walking toward the car. Then the car behind swerved and tried to hit Marcus.

"Did you see that?" I asked.

"Yeah...I couldn't miss it...it almost hit me," Marcus replied reluctantly.

"Maybe you should report it to the police?"

"Oh...I'll be alright; you know how some of these crazy city folks are,"

"But the way the car was coming it didn't look like it was some crazy folk,"

"Okay, I am alright...we are wasting time, remember I have to have you back by three o'clock," Marcus said as he drove the car off in a raging pace.

I didn't know whether I was getting on his nerves or if he was angry because I was trying to tell him what to do. I ceased the conversation and rode quietly to the restaurant.

When we reached the restaurant, I could tell he was taking me to the most exclusive place I have ever dined in, as we walked in, there was a Maitre'd standing at the door in a tuxedo greeting us.

"Your name...sir?" The maitre d asked.

"Marcus Singleton," Marcus replied.

"Oh, yes…we have reservations for three… will your other party be coming soon?" The maitre d asked.

I thought to myself, "other party".

"Yes, sir, will you please let him know we are here," Marcus said.

"Who is the other party? I asked as I reluctantly allowed him to take me by the hand to follow the maitre d to the table.

It was a very cozy and elegant French restaurant. I could tell that it wasn't Marcus's first time dining here. When we were passing the dining tables I notice the disposition of the people. Most of them knew him my name and had a friendly countenance with him. Marcus waited for me to position myself so he could be courteous and pull my chair out. As I sat down, I felt as though I was being serenaded into a trap. I had to keep reminding myself that this was only a business luncheon.

"Thank you," I said admiring the glow upon Marcus's face.

"My pleasure," Marcus said as he smiled and sat across from me.

The waiter came over and said, "Mr. Singleton will you be ordering now?"

"In a few minutes, I am waiting on a friend," Marcus replied.

Marcus and I started looking at the menu. I didn't have any idea of what to order. Most of the food items were in French. I was only fluent in Spanish so Marcus had to help me to decipher what to eat.

"Well how do you like this place?" Marcus asked.

"I like it," I said glancing around and admiring the scenery.

"This is my favorite restaurant…I enjoy the French music and candlelight it gives me a touch of France,"

"I can see that…I was told they dim the lights so you can't really see the quality of the food,"

Marcus laughed and said, "That's not the reason the lights are dimmed…they are dim to give that cozy and romance feeling,"

I swallowed hard and said, "It's…its…cozy"

"Diamond have you ever been to France?"

"No…but I hope to visit one day,"

"You keep singing like you do, you will probably be touring over there,"

The ringing of Marcus's cellular phone interrupted our conversation. "Hello," He answered.

Then Marcus put his hand over the receiver end of the phone and said, "Diamond excuse me for a moment,"

He stood up from the table and walked over to a counter. I could see he was literally upset about something. The gestures of his hand and head were agreeing to my assumption. Every time I noticed him gazing at me I would pretend I was viewing the menu. From the corner of my eye, I could see him putting his cellular phone back into his pocket and walking toward the table. I relinquished the idea of trying to inquire about Marcus's social life. Who was I to give a matured man advice, but I just knew that he had some type of drama in his life, but it wasn't up to me to resolve it.

"Well or you ready to order?" Marcus asked in a low-keyed voice.

"What about the other person?" I inquired.

"Oh…he won't be coming," Marcus replied.

I did not want to intrude on Marcus's personal life, but it seemed quite obvious that something was wrong. Instead of trying to cipher out what was going on, I deviated from the subject.

"So what are we going to have?" Marcus asked with his focus in another world.

"Of course, I'll have what you have," I replied knowing I didn't recognize most of the items on the menu.

Marcus signals the waiter that we were ready to order.

"We are ready to order," He said politely to the waiter.

"Yes sir, would you like to have our special, Cestino all'Aragosta," The waiter said.

"Sure that will be fine," Marcus replied.

"What about the young misses?" The waiter asked.

"I'll have the same thing he is having," I replied.

"What about drinks… we have a bottle 19--- one of the finest years?" The waiter continued.

Looking at the expression on my face Marcus replied, "Just give us something that looks like we are drinking wine,"

"Perhaps…sparkling… concord juice, sir?" The waiter asked as he noticed the fresh youthfulness upon my face.

"That would be excellent," Marcus replied with a smirk on his face.

"What was that I ordered… the Cestino---all…?" I asked.

"You mean the Cestino all'Aragosta…it's an elegant lobster-based pasta dish.

We laughed as the waiter left the table. It was amazing on how much I could learn from Marcus. He seemed like a cultured and well-rounded guy. The lunch date with Marcus turned out to be absolutely marvelous. We barely touched the subject of my career. However, I was able to share some of my adolescent moments with him, which help him to recall some of the fun times he had forgotten, due to the strenuous relationship between him and his dad.

After our luncheon Marcus drove me home on time. He walked me to the door of the house. I gather my dad was expecting my arrival because he was watching and waiting. He opened the door before I could put the key into the lock. I could tell by the expression on my dad's face coming home on time pleased him. Since Marcus kept his promise, I could foresee my dad allowing him to take me out again. Then again, I wasn't about to try to extend the tight rope too soon. I knew how to manage my manipulation. It had to be the right words and right time.

From this moment, the special relationship between Marcus and I had a stamp of approval.

Studio time was stressful but valuable. It was my first day at the Aseret Studio. I could tell that it was a lot of tension in the room. When I first walked in, Marcus introduced me to the staff. I briefly met some of them at the celebration night. I was curious about the beautiful black woman standing adjacent to me watching Marcus introduce me to everyone. I didn't remember seeing her at the celebration. She stood silently for a moment until Marcus decided to personally introduce her.

"Diamond this is…," Marcus said as he was interrupted.

"Toni...Toni Johnson, and I am your personal assistant, if you need anything I'm at your service," She said as we shook hands.

"You mean she will be at your beg and call," Marcus said flirting with Toni.

"Oh Marcus...can you be serious," She implied enjoying the attention.

"Diamond whatever you need just let me know," Toni said, "Here's my card, call me anytime...we are going to be working a lot together.

"So, if I need some coffee you would get it?" I asked trying to have a sense of humor.

"Young lady, I am not your secretary...I am here to assist you in every detail of your career...beyond secretary work," Toni replied intensely.

"Diamond...Toni means..." Marcus implied.

"I meant just what I said...if you would excuse me," Toni said as she answered her cell phone.

Radically speaking, I could feel that we were going to get along just find. Frankly this was only the beginning of a tensed relationship. To keep myself from giving her my rights, I quickly separated from her. I walked over to Jesse to see what he was up too. He was dealing with the guys on the sounds for my lyrics. Toni came over and handed me the lyrics for the song we were going to rehearse from the staff songwriter, who was a well-known songwriter.

"I bet you are excited?" Toni asked, as she helps to prepare me for rehearsal.

"Yes, I am," I replied.

I was keeping my answers short, because Toni had revealed her true personality. We were like the pot and the kettle, having the same purpose but in conflict.

"So what do you think about Marcus?" Toni asked trying to pry information out of me.

"I think he's cool," I replied, shuffling the music sheets around.

"Yeah...I think he is cool too," Toni said looking through the glass of the studio room at Marcus.

Apparently Toni had a thing for Marcus, because she kept looking at him as he was admiring my behavior in the studio. Females tend to know when another female has a thing for a guy. There is a release of ecstasy between the chemistry. I call it women's instinct.

"Now relax and just pretend you are singing in the bathroom," Toni said putting into play her assistant duties.

"By the way how old are you?" I asked putting on the headphones.

"Twenty-eight…may I ask you why you asked?" Toni replied.

"Oh, just wandering," I said.

"Now, if you are wandering if Marcus and I are dating, the answer is no," Toni said.

"Well why not?" I asked.

"We tried that dating thing and it didn't work…young lady let's focus on you," Toni replied.

Marcus continued to watch us through the studio glance. It was though he was trying to figure out what we were talking about. Then Toni went into the sound room where Marcus and Jesse were. I could see through Toni's little act. Toni's eyes revealed that she still cared a lot for Marcus.

Rehearsal in the studio took hours, before I could really get a break. Being a star took hard work, dedication and I was willing to go beyond the extra mile. Marcus didn't stay in the studio the entire time, (because he was one of the Chief Executive Officers; second in command of the agency). He would come in once and a while and check on the status of our recording and make sure we were using time wisely. Jesse on the other hand, was amazed at the way my voice was projecting in the sound room. My voice portrayed perfection in quality, sound and pitch. I new the perfection came from God, but like I was willing to own the credit. He stated, "A voice that could make heaven shake," He was wondering why I didn't sing gospel music. I couldn't answer that question, but I knew it was a God given talent.

CHAPTER 4

Success was becoming a normal word for me and I was on the trail beyond success. My first single was number one on the charts and the album was about to become gold. I wasn't settling for a gold record, I wanted platinum. I had become driven my pride, arrogance and success. I thought I was invincible. I was now into my third year of my career and about to hit eighteen years old in a few months. I was not only a female artist, but also one of the youngest composers of music. My world was submerged into success and brought about royalties that were kicking in like the coins flowing from a winning slot machine.

Finally, the magic number eighteen was about to burst into reality. Eighteen meant independency, freedom, and above all officially a woman. I no longer had to conceal my heart from the intimate feelings for Marcus. The pain of seeing him with another woman no longer quenches my soul. I knew with no doubt that I didn't have to contemplate about having him anymore. If only I knew how Marcus felt about me as a woman. Even though we spent a lot of quality time together I didn't know whether it was forced upon him for business sake or if he really desired to have more?

While waiting for daybreak to crack through my bedroom window. I rested my head upon my pillow wondering whether Marcus saw me as a friend, sister or perhaps a future lover. I could remember on one occasion during a late-night studio session Marcus was beginning to see me as more than a mutual friendship. My assistant Toni and I were polishing up some ideas for my next tour. Toni was one of Marcus's old flames. Even though there was not much charisma between Toni and

Marcus, I remained solid in order to not stir up a mutiny between our working relationships. Marcus walked into Toni's office to check on the tour plans, it was different this time. His casual friendly appearance was conversing to profound inner sensations. I could feel his eyes undressing me as I was leaning over the desk talking to Toni. I could see the sparkle in his eyes as he asked, "Working late tonight?"

"Yeah, I need to in order to have them finalize by tomorrow," Toni replied, as she was pointing to some ideas.

"What about you…why are you working late? I asked interrupting their conversation.

"I had to finish up a contract for Big Daddy," Marcus replied.

"Well we are about finish…so would you like to go for a night cap?" Toni asked.

"Not tonight…by the way Diamond do you have a ride home?" Marcus asked.

Toni was devastated when Marcus ignored her suggestion. She was observing every word that was coming out of Marcus's mouth. It was though she was dissecting his feelings in each word. I gather she was becoming very jealous. To entertain her thoughts I decided to play hard to get.

"Yeah…I was going to call my dad to pick me up as soon as we were done," I replied glancing boldly at Toni.

"Don't bother…call your dad and tell him I will bring you home," Marcus said.

"Are you sure?" I asked knowing that I was manipulating the situation.

"No sweat," Marcus replied.

While I was picking up the phone to call my dad, I could hear the conversation between Marcus and Toni. I didn't know whether my dad had left or not. This felt like a chance I could be alone with Marcus. I decided to pretend I was talking to my dad on the phone, so I could listen to their conversation. In the past, Toni had apprised me about the time Marcus and she were seeing each other. She stated, "Marcus never wanted to make a commitment," In the mind of Toni, Marcus was a lady's man. I didn't know if she was warning me or trying to keep me from thinking that I could have more than what she had with him. It seemed to me, she had never fully gotten over him.

As I hung up the phone, I could tell she didn't want Marcus to take me home.

"Father said it will be okay, but to make sure you don't take any alternate routes," I said knowing that lying was a part of manipulation, one of the characteristics I have perfected.

Toni was furious. She swiftly walked over to the coat rack and snatched her jacket from it. Marcus's character of being a gentleman continued to be in play, he walked over to help Toni put on her jacket.

"Forget it…it won't work!" Toni angrily said, putting on her jacket.

"Toni can we discuss this later?" Marcus asked.

"You had your chance…grow up…and you know…someday you…ah…never mind," Toni said as she stormed out of the office.

It was an embarrassing scene for Marcus. He tried to offset the mood in the room by hurrying me out of the office. I went alone with the performance.

"Are you ready?" Marcus spoke solemnly.

"Yes, I am," I replied gathering my things to leave.

"You sure it will be okay with your dad?"

"I'm sure,"

Marcus was covering himself from more confrontations, especially with my dad. Marcus was quiet during the time, from the elevator to the parking area. As he was opening the car door for me, he turned around and said, "Toni has never gotten over our relationship,"

I really didn't want to talk about their ancient relationship, but because Marcus was opening up to me I indulged in the moment to my advantage.

"Well maybe it didn't end right," I said, not knowing whether it was the correct words to say at the time. I wanted to remain neutral, so that I could watch his game closely.

Marcus continued to get into the car and put the key into the ignition. A strange sensation came over me. I was willing to go forward, so I put my hand over his hand to emotionally arouse his thoughts. Suddenly a captivating moment was about to happen. He stared into my eyes giving me a beaming flow of immense sexual ecstasy. My mind was carried beyond rational thoughts or self-control. Marcus took my hand and held it tightly pressing it to his jaw. Then he slowly pressed my hand up to his lips giving me an exotic soft kiss on the tip of my fingers. My heart was racing like an animal panting for water. He could tell that I wanted it by the way my bodily movements were surrendering to his every move. I was indulging into the mystical world of lust and it felt wonderful. However, I couldn't believe after that moment, Marcus apologized for his behavior. I knew at that moment that there was an eccentric chemistry between us. Could it have been lust or love? I didn't care, it felt right. It was the last time our chemistry sparked together, because it wasn't time.

A few months had passed. I was spending a lot of time alone with Marcus. Most of the time, I would stay after hours at the agency to work on new material. This gave me an excuse to see him regularly without the presence of Toni. We encountered many moments of intimacy, but we went no further than a kiss on the hand or jaw. I wasn't ready to give my body to him yet.

Finally, the day approached for me to become a true woman. My birthday was the most exciting day awaiting. Marcus and my parents were taking me out for lunch for this grand day. That morning I was reminiscing in my dreams all the intimate moments Marcus and I shared. It wasn't just the kisses, but the foreplay with the kisses that aroused my femininity greatly. Before I could finish my dreaming, I had a quick snap of the mind when my mom shouted, "Diamond...are you up!"

Mom knocked on my bedroom door and said, "Remember Marcus is taking us to lunch today,"

"Okay, mom, I will be up soon," I replied.

Time didn't fly fast enough for me to prepare myself for lunch with Marcus. I wasn't impressed with birthday presents and all the trimmings, because I could afford anything I wanted. Spending time with Marcus as a woman was the most valuable gift a girl could receive.

If I could freeze time, that's what I would have done on my eighteenth birthday. Marcus took my parents and me to the French restaurant where we had our first lunch date. As we were sitting at the table, I sensed something secretly was going on with Marcus.

"Marcus this is very nice…is the food good here?" Dad said.

"It's great!" I shouted interrupting dad's conversation.

"This place is exquisite, and has great food," Marcus replied.

The waiter came over to take our orders. Of course I ordered the Cestino all'Aragosta because it was the only item I was familiar with. Marcus ordered the finest wine. This time I was able to drink French wine without a chaperone.

"Mr. Oslo aren't you proud of Diamond?" Marcus asked, as he sipped the wine from the glass.

"Yes we are…she has made us proud," Dad replied, as he tried to sip some wine from the glass, but when he noticed my mother watching him closely, he placed it on the table. She always monitored his drinking. The waitress finally brought our entrees to the table while we continued to enjoy each other's company.

"What do you think Mrs. Oslo?" Marcus asked.

"About… what…?" Mother asked, trying to keep her eyes on father and the wine glass.

"About your daughter's success…?" Marcus implied.

"She knows I am proud of her…and her newest album is a hit, there is no limit to her earning a Grammy," Mother said.

"We are hoping for the same thing and it looks good," Marcus said as he smiled at me.

"I know I am going to be nominated for a Grammy, I always get what I want…because I plan on winning it also," I said with arrogance.

"Diamond that last song on your album, "Time Over Ribbons" is running up the chart rapidly," Marcus said.

Before I could initiate any more words out of my mouth, a flash came across my face. It was the paparazzi, looking for a story. I didn't care because I enjoyed the media and especially the tabloids. I was told the more headlines they have on you, whether they or true or not, the more you become attractive to the media.

This was the right time for paparazzi to intervene. The atmosphere was suitable for the occasion. We had a fantastic time reminiscing over the flashbacks of my career, especially laughing over the blubbers we encountered during the tours.

"Tell me something Marcus…how come a handsome and successful young man like you hasn't been taken?" Dad said.

"I guess I haven't found that special one yet," He replied, looking over at me.

"But you see women all the time Marcus… Don't try to play one over on my dad," I said.

"I'm not…I know I see women all the time, but they are not what I am looking for," Marcus said.

"Well, what are you looking for in a woman?" Mother boldly asked.

"She has to be smart, independent and willing to meet me half-way," Marcus replied.

"But what if she is missing some of these qualities?" I asked being sarcastic.

"Well, I guess she is not the right one," Marcus replied, with a signal to the waiter.

Suddenly the waiter walked over and cleared our table. Then another waiter walked over with a birthday cake. Then a violinist came over and serenaded me with the song, "I Will Always Love You, Happy Birthday Diamond". I was astounded it was a song Marcus had specially written for this day. That is when I began to figure out something fishy was going on. It was a beautiful cake with yellow roses surrounded around the edges. Eighteen candles were placed around a small treasure chest displayed in the center. The cake symbolized that I was the treasure of my parents life.

"Happy Birthday!" They shouted.

"Thank you," I said while my eyes were overtaken with tears.

"Make a wish?" Marcus asked.

I looked around at my parents and said, "I really appreciate this,"

"Don't thank us, thank Marcus it was all his idea," Father said.

I made a wish and blew out the candles. The time was joyful and pleasing to the spoilage inside of me. Teardrops wear streaming down my face. While the waiter was preparing to cut the cake, Marcus's laughter had turned into sincerity.

"Before we cut the cake, I have something to say," Marcus said.

I paused and my parents were inquisitive about what he was about to say. The violinist and waiter stopped, the waiter stopped and my dad took a sip from the wine glass which was nonstop. Mother and I looked at each other strangely.

"Mr. Oslo can I ask you a question?" Marcus asked.

"Go ahead," Dad replied taking a large gulp from the glass.

"Have I ever disrespected your daughter in anyway?" Marcus asked.

"No you haven't…To be quit frank with you…I have grown to be quit fond of you," Dad said.

"I am pleased to hear you say that…because I want to ask you and your wife…" Marcus hesitated to finish.

"Go on," Father said, waiting to hear Marcus complete his thoughts.

Marcus hesitated for a moment and took the treasure box off the top of the cake and opened it. I was speechless. Then Marcus got up out of his chair and kneeled down before me to propose.

"What I want to say is…May I have your daughter's hand in marriage…or should I say Diamond will you marry me?" Marcus said with complete assurance. His eyes signified he was ready to make a commitment. Something he couldn't allow himself to do with Toni. I didn't know whether to be flattered or honored.

When Marcus opened his mouth I could hear each word drumming in my head and making and etching stone upon my heart. I became skeptical when I didn't hear him say the word "love". I was beginning to panic until; he mumbles the words out of his mouth.

"I want you to know that from the very first day I met you I saw someone special and I felt a feeling that I thought was wrong especially with you being young and all that…but I waited to see if the feeling was just a infatuation, but I know that it is not, because I care deeply about you…I know that you are the one I want to spend the rest of my life with," Marcus said saturating his feelings directly into my eyes.

I was waiting for the magic word before I could reply with my answer. The words he stated were fine, but I needed the final approval stamped by my father's thoughts. It's the word that God created from the beginning of time for man. Marcus lips began to open up with the three words I had been waiting on.

"I Love you and want you to be my wife," Marcus softly said drifting into my eyes, as though we were alone.

Now it was time for me to say my magic words. They imparted from my lips so quickly making me seem desperate.

"Yes…Yes…. I…" I said as Marcus put a huge diamond upon my finger.

I looked upon the face on my dad. The nodding of his head with a smile gave me a confirmation of his approval. My mom pulled me over and hugged me with gladness.

"How soon are you planning to marry my daughter?" Mom said with excitement.

"Well…it depends on whether Diamond wants to wait," Marcus replied looking to see how I will respond.

"Mom…Don't worry… it won't be too soon…I have my music to think about and now that I am composing my own music…. who knows," I said assuring my mother, so that she won't have to hurry and make an invitation list.

"I am glad you said that…I was getting kind of worried that you were moving a little too fast…you see… I don't mind giving you my daughter's hand as long as you give her time to think about her future," Dad said.

Marcus took me by the hand and said, "I plan on giving her all the time she needs, as long as she doesn't leave me out of her time,"

"Oh Marcus…you know I won't do that," I replied gripping his hand tightly on top of the table.

"I just know you are going to have a church wedding?" Mom asked.

"Of Course, mom we can't leave God out," I replied

"I know the perfect wedding planner," Mom said excitedly.

"Mom calm down…Marcus and I will let you know when… then you can call the wedding planner…I want to make sure my concerts and tours don't interfere" I explained holding Marcus's hand tightly.

"Just remember baby, I will always be the first man in your life," Dad proclaimed.

As I was smiling, I reached over and grabbed my dad's hand and said, "I will always be your little girl,"

Marcus embraced my arms against his and put his arms around my waist, and then we gazed into each other's eyes as though we knew we were meant for each other. Our pupils were adjourning as our lips touched each other. I closed my eyes to indulge into the world of first love. His tongue released the tension between my lips as we French kissed. It was the first time I had ever French kissed someone. I was blessed it was the man I was about to marry. I was obsessed with Marcus and finally the intimate Chapter of my life has been initiated.

CHAPTER 5

Being Marcus's fiancée' instead of a prospect candidate gave me more ammunition than I needed to put Toni's aggressiveness on breaks. This afternoon was special but the excitement was yet to come. My parents invited most of my friends and business acquaintances over to celebrate my special day. It was a special day and most of all perfect timing. I was not only having my eighteenth birthday party, but also I would be able to announce my engagement to Marcus. Being on a natural high was one of my distinctive qualities and tonight was a superb time to foster it. During the evening I was anxious to give out such great news, especially in the presents of Toni.

"Having a great time?" Mother asked as she walked passes me with the hors d'oeuvres in her hand.

"Yes mother…it is wonderful," I replied, as I observed Marcus talking with Jesse.

Everybody seemed to be having a great time. I continued to be mindful of everyone's actions, especially when it came toward Marcus. Toni's behavior was a little distant. This was really a chance for me to announce my engagement. I was desperate about dismounting Toni. Being the person I am it was the perfect time to burst the bubble inside of her. Anxiety was all over me as I was convincing myself on how to break the news. I continued to scan the room. I was just that type of a person. I wanted to make sure I was the center of attraction especially with Marcus. After all, it is my birthday.

Big Daddy and my dad were having a grand time with the bottles of wine. I didn't want to think about how my mom was feeling about it. Big

Daddy and dad were gulping them down never-ending. I was inquisitive about whether Marcus had informed his dad of our engagement. In order not to stir up a wasp nest I remained silent about the situation.

I saw Sherrie sitting in a chair staring around. She was mostly looking at every available man in the room. I could tell by how she would look at their hand to see if they had on a wedding ring. Sherrie had a head start on womanhood because she turned eighteen before I did. We had grown to become great friends over the years. I could entrust her with my deepest darkest secrets. This is another reason Toni and I did not have a fantastic relationship. Toni knew that the way to getting a man to indulge interest in her was through his mom or sister. Since Marcus's mother was deceased and he didn't have a good relationship with his dad, Sherrie was the path. She was the only one other than my parents that I felt comfortable about announcing my engagement too. Somehow Sherrie and Toni didn't care much for each other. I didn't know why, but I didn't care. Toni was now the past Chapter in Marcus's life and I plan on keeping it that way.

"What's up girl...don't it feel good to be eighteen?" Sherrie asked, as she passed a high-five toward me.

"Yeah, it feels great, now I can drink wine without a chaperone," I replied, as I flashed the wine glass in front of her.

"That's all you can think of...what about the men...fine, sexy, single men?" Sherrie asked.

"Well...I leave that for you...I already have my sexy man," I replied looking over at Marcus.

"Just look at these fine men...I just know you going to hit on one of them tonight...especially on your birthday," Sherrie said as she was eyeballing the guys across the room.

"I see one I want to hit on right now," I said as I tilted my check over at Marcus.

"You mean Marcus...girl are you that serious about Marcus!" Sherrie shouted.

"I believe I am," I said as I walked toward him.

Sherrie smiled as I moved closer to Marcus to get his attention. She really didn't care that her brother flattered me; she was too high on getting a man for herself.

"Hi," I said to Marcus with a cute smile on my face.

"Hi," Marcus replied, trying to be timid at the moment.

I had forgotten Jesse was standing there. All of my attention was going toward my man.

"Well…what am I invisible?" Jesse asked.

"Oh Jesse, stop trying to get all the attention," Sherrie replied.

"Just want a little love for the brother," Jesse said.

I didn't want Jesse to think that I was trying to come on to him, so I brushed him off.

The capturing whirlwind from Marcus's attractive eyes began to sweep me off of my feet. Jesse was jealous of the relationship between Marcus and me. I didn't want him to think I was flirting. I could feel the tension between them and didn't know what to say or do to release it.

"Happy birthday, Diamond," Jesse said as he kissed me on the forehead.

I could tell by the expression on Marcus's face that he didn't care too much for Jesse putting his lips on me. I didn't want Marcus to think I was flirting, so I moved away from Jesse quickly.

The party was really energetic and the booze was working up a swift sensation in the room. I pulled Marcus aside to discuss our engagement.

"Marcus don't you think we should make our announcement?" I asked.

"Not now," Marcus replied.

"…Why not?" I asked, as I noticed Marcus fidgeting about the situation.

"Don't you think we should wait until everyone is ready?" Marcus asked.

I glanced around the room and notice everyone being joyful and full of merry. I thought, what better time to make an announcement.

"Marcus, are you telling me you are not ready to let everybody know?"

"It's not that…. it's just…it's the wrong timing,"

"Well if you think so,"

"Yes, just trust me on this one Diamond,"

"It's not that I don't trust you…are you thinking about what they will think? Remember, I am a woman now…it doesn't matter if I am marrying someone ten years older than me,"

"No, it is not the age bracket…I just want it to be private…between you and me for now,"

"But my parents know,"

"I know…please trust me…we will do it another time in another setting,"

"Honey I do trust you…it's just…you wanting to wait keeps haunting me,"

"If you have to know…I need to talk to my dad before I let everyone in on the big surprise…you see, it's not right for me to announce our engagement and my dad is the last to know…I should have told him before I told your parents,"

"I guess I am being selfish honey…that's what I like about you; you always want to do what is best for everybody,"

The rest of the night Marcus seemed distance from me. He spent most of his time talking with the guests. Meanwhile I was socializing with Sherrie and noticed Marcus having a serious talk with Toni. It seemed to be very comforting and soothing to her by the way she was carrying on. Toni was even smiling with Marcus. I was inquisitive about that moment. I decided to let reality kick in. I thought as I looked at my hand "I have the ring on my finger". Which was the strangest thing; no one really noticed the ring on my finger, until it was time to blow the candles out on the cake.

A song of happy birthday began to swim around the room as my mother bought out the cake with eighteen candles on it. Even though I was grateful for my mother thinking of me, a cake was at the bottom of the list for excitement at the moment. There was nothing more intriguing than the moment Marcus kneeled down his knees and proposed to me.

"Make a wish Diamond?" A voice from behind me said.

"Yeah... wish for that tall dark and handsome man!" Sherrie yelled across the table.

The words that Sherrie spoke were not of any interest to me. I had already captured my night and shiny armor. I smiled at Marcus standing next to me. I knew he read my thoughts, but another man was not in my thoughts at the time, because my thoughts were clogged up with the images of Marcus, the man of my heart. I watched the candles as the light reflected from the flames. Slowly I blew them out thinking about what to wish. I had everything I needed and wanted and the finalization would be marrying Marcus. As I held the knife with two hands to cut the cake, the ring on my finger was flashing like a neon sign. I could see the faces of many inquiring about it but none wanted to be heard except Sherrie.

"Diamond, that's a nice rock on your hand!" Sherrie yelled boldly.

I wanted to take a piece of the cake and shove it into her mouth, but I wasn't about to break my promise to Marcus. I remained calm and changed the subject.

"The cake tastes delicious mother," I said licking the frosting off my fingers.

"Thank you Diamond, I knew you would love it," Mother said.

Sherrie was not the type to be ignored and changing the subject just made her interrogate more.

Sherrie pulled me by the shoulder away from the guest and asked. "What's with the ring?"

"What ring?" I said trying to play dumb.

"You can't fool me something is going on,"

"Sherrie, there is always something going on with you...now let's finish cutting the cake,"

"Someone else can cut the cake...I'm not talking about me...I am talking about that ring on your finger,"

"Okay...Sherrie you caught me,"

"Now what's up?"

"You promise me you won't tell anyone?"

"That depends,"

"Come on Sherrie!"

"Okay...Okay, I won't tell,"

Sherrie and I walked toward the kitchen and waited for everyone to leave out of the room. As we sat at the table I told Sherrie the story of how her brother proposed to me. She was excited because she always wanted a sister, but was also concerned because of the many relationships Marcus had damaged in the past including the one with his dad.

Sherrie shared with me the conflict between Marcus and Big Daddy. Marcus is Big Daddy's child from his first wife. Marcus's mom died in an automobile accident in which he blamed Big Daddy because he was driving. Marcus felt his dad should have died in the accident instead of his mom, because Big Daddy was unfaithful to his mom. When Big Daddy remarried, he promised his son he would not be unfaithful to another woman and so far he hasn't. Marcus believed his dad was being unfair because he finally made up his mind to be faithful, but it wasn't to his mom. The problem wasn't his father being faithful, but being faithful to Sherrie's mother made Marcus feel that his mother was betrayed. Even though Sherrie's mom died about a year ago from cancer, this still didn't give Marcus any satisfaction about the unfaithfulness that was done toward his mom.

I realized from the conversation with Sherrie, that Marcus needed to mend the relationship with his dad before he could step into another. I was not about to let Big Daddy come between Marcus and me. I wanted all of Marcus's love even if it meant being on his side about the situation.

Meanwhile, Sherrie promised me she wouldn't tell anybody about our engagement until we formally announced it.

Later on, my father gathered all the guests together to make an announcement. I was hoping he didn't spoil the evening for Marcus and me. He had the guests follow him outside. There in front of the house was a red convertible Mercedes, then my mother handed the keys to me. As I opened the door and felt the leather seats, I sat in the driver's seat with a face full of glee. This was the second best gift I had received on my birthday. I hugged my parents with appreciation. Even more, I wanted to kiss Marcus, but if I did, the cat would start to come out of the bag. It was difficult but I managed to compose my emotions.

CHAPTER 6

Even though Marcus continued to be distant about our engagement, we still managed to spend a lot of quality time together. It was strenuous sometimes trying to manipulate the situation, especially when we wanted to be alone. It has been two weeks and Marcus still hasn't given the okay to broadcast the advancement in our relationship. I had noticed that some of the personnel at Aseret have become skeptical of us. Now that I was preparing for my winter tour, I had become accustomed to being watched by the staff. My personal life was beginning to be the most attractive topic in the Agency. The ring on my finger had become a fashionable conversation piece among the employees, especially Toni. She questioned me several times about the ring, but I would just smile and give her the brush off. Her demeanor had changed and seemed to be in a more positive mode when it came to Marcus. I didn't know whether this was a blessing or a signal of a curse in my relationship.

Another day at the studio was like a busy day at the mall during the holidays. Everybody wants something but no one wants to give. I spent long hours at the studio and much of it was with Jesse and Toni. Sometime Marcus would come in check on the status of things. I enjoyed sitting at the piano composing music. I focused on songs that captured your inner feelings and take you to your own private mesmerized world. I indulged into my music most of the time. Today I was putting my entire heart into my work until I didn't pay any attention to my surroundings.

"How's your day Diamond?" Marcus said as he sat next to me on the piano bench.

"Great," I said as he smacked me on the lips.

"Do you feel like taking a break...you have been working really long hours lately?"

"I know...but I got to have these songs ready for the tour...and the lyrics..."

"Don't say anymore," Marcus said, as he pulled a yellow rose from behind his back.

My face lighted up like sunshine in a gloomy day. I always felt yellow roses symbolized the true beauty of nature. Marcus knew that it was my favorite intimate keepsake. I was fortunate to have him in my life because he knew the right thing to say and do to keep me happy.

As Marcus and I kissed on the piano bench I could feel someone was watching everything we were doing. Of course, it was Jesse looking through the sound room. Toni and he seemed to enjoy keeping track of the drama in Marcus and my life. I didn't care whether he saw us being intimate or deeply in love. I wanted the whole world to know that I was in love with Marcus and sooner or later they would have to except it.

Suddenly Toni storms into the sound room and hands a tabloid paper to Jesse. I could tell by the expression on their faces that it wasn't pleasant. By that time Marcus and I were sitting on the piano bench collaborating romantically. I could sense a coldness coming from the sound room. As we were preparing ourselves to leave the studio room, Toni walks in and slams the paper on the piano.

"You mind telling me what this is," Toni said in a furious tone, as she looked at Marcus.

"What!" Marcus shouted.

"This...this is disgusting!" Toni yelled holding the headlines of the paper to my face.

I snatched the paper out of Toni's hand. On the front page of the paper said, "Aseret's Top CEO Robs Diamond's Cradle". I was speechless. I had completely forgotten about the moment at the restaurant. It all was coming back to me, the flashing of the cameras, paparazzi and the entire restaurant scene. I should have known that it was going to be announced in the tabloid. My mind was wondering where they could have received their information. Then I thought, "The waiter.... the waiter," Paparazzi pays good money for juicy stories. I was short for words when I read the headlines.

"When were you going to tell me?" Toni asked.

"Soon…I didn't know…" Marcus replied.

"Didn't know what…that it wasn't going to get out…you can't tell me you didn't notice…word has been spreading all over this place about you and her," Toni said.

"But Toni…" Marcus said.

I remained quiet. I wasn't about to make the fuel hotter, especially now that the cat was out of the bag.

"And you … are flashing around here thinking that no one would notice this ring on your finger!" Toni shouted as she snatched my hand and shoved it into Marcus's face.

I was really sustaining from hitting her, especially when I snatched my hand back. She kept going on and on until finally I couldn't contain myself any longer.

"Wait a minute…Toni…you and Marcus no longer have a relationship, so what's it to you!" I shouted.

"Calm down Toni…I can explain everything," Marcus said calmly.

"Calm!" "Explain!" "You told me that I was the most understanding woman in the world…and you also told me at Diamond's party that we were going to spend a weekend together…Isn't that right!" Toni yelled.

"Yes…you are an understanding woman…and…I…didn't mean a weekend as lovers," Marcus said calmly.

"So now you change your story…you are nothing but a player…!" Toni shouted.

"Hey…watch the language around the lady," Marcus continued to talk in a low-keyed voice.

"I should have hit you when I had the chance! Toni confessed.

"So you are the one who tried to hit Marcus in front of the dry cleaners!" I exclaimed.

Marcus was short for words and asked, "If you cared so much about me…why did you try to kill me?"

"You...you...!" Toni shouted as she furiously stampeded out of the room.

I didn't know what to say. There were no words that could come out of my mouth to soothe the event that just took place. Marcus tried to make things better by telling me he was sorry. Sorry was not the word I wanted to hear at the moment. He walked into the sound room where Jesse was. Marcus's face was in a state of shock. He didn't realize how obsessed Toni was with him. Jesse had captured every moment of the arguing between Marcus and Toni. By the look on his face he was not deeply concerned. I watched as Marcus walked into the sound room. Marcus and Jesse were smiling and chatting about the situation. It was as though Toni was a joke to them. I thought Jesse would be one of the first people to be angry with Marcus because I felt he was jealous of our relationship. It turned out he was happy for our announcement. Now that our secret had hit the fan there was no turning back for Marcus.

I decided to let the drama surpass my mind, because there were more important things I needed to be concerned about. Composing music was my way out of the drama temporarily. Music was a therapy for me especially when I am upset or depressed. I didn't know whether to trust Marcus or not, but the inner part of me loved him immensely. Reminiscing about Marcus and my intimate moments began to kick in. My mind pondered the wonderful times Marcus and I spent together. The day I first met him closed the fog that was covering the state of confusion in my mind. I needed someone to talk to and I needed it now. When all else fails I knew that I could count on the advice of my mother. I began to walk out of the studio and head toward Toni's office to call my mom. Marcus walked out of the sound room to get my attention, but I ignored him. I didn't need him telling me any more lies to escalate the confusion. I could tell by the look on his face, he really was concerned, but I couldn't give in to his charm. I needed to sort some things out.

I was reluctant about using Toni's phone since I knew she would probably be in there. When I entered into Toni's office, I could tell she was not interested in talking to anyone. Her mind was profoundly into her work. She intentionally ignored me as I stood in front of her desk.

I cleared my throat and politely asked, "You mind if I use your phone?"

"Sure," Toni said trying not to make eye to eye contact with me.

I reached over to call mom. Toni interrupted me and said, "Better yet why don't you use your cell phone?"

"I would if I had it with me," I said.

Toni reached over and pulled a cell phone out of her desk and said, "Now you have one...anything else?"

"Look Toni...I am sorry about what happened," I said.

"You don't have to be sorry...look we have to work together...you could have at least told me,"

"I wanted to... but Marcus didn't want anyone to know at the time,"

"I hope you know what you are getting into...Marcus is not what you think he is,"

"Everybody has some areas they need to grow in,"

"But do you want to marry someone you don't really know very well?"

"I feel I know him enough...we spent a lot of time together,"

"But do you really know him?"

"You know Toni...you are just jealous because I have Marcus...I am going to be his wife...something you have been trying to do for some time,"

"Diamond, I have been with Marcus I know what it is like to be in his bed and feel the emptiness,"

"What do you mean by emptiness?"

"Have you slept with Marcus...have you ever had true intimacy or should I say sex...not kissing...but physical romantic sex?"

"Look Toni, I know what it means to have true intimacy with a man...and Marcus is romantic,"

"Oh really...well tell me how it feels when he takes his fingers and moved them softly down your back?"

"I don't have to tell you that,"

"Of course you can't tell me that, because you never slept with him…cause if you did you would have known… he hardly moves when we are having sex,"

"Maybe he had a bad day…you know how it is around the office,"

"Diamond you need to get real with life…ask yourself, why haven't Marcus tried to sleep with you all this time,"

"I don't have to ask that question…I can answer it…I was too young,"

"Too young…get real, young lady…Marcus is not to be trusted," Toni said as she took the papers off the desk and packed them into her briefcase.

"On the contrary… I will continue to work with you on this tour, but when this is over I am requesting to be assigned to another artist…I wish you well with Marcus," Toni exclaimed as she walked out of the office.

The conversation with Toni began to quench my soul. She was right, I had never really seen the sexual side of Marcus, but I wasn't worried about the sex. I was more concern with whether Marcus really loved me. I picked up the cell phone to call my mom, but before I could call her Marcus walked into the office. I hurriedly placed the cell phone into the pocket of my blouse.

"Diamond, can we talk?" Marcus asked.

"Sure…we might as well," I said as I stood in front of the desk waiting for him to initiate it.

"Will you please sit next to me?" He asked.

I moved closer and sat in the chair next to him.

"I am so sorry about what happened today…Toni took everything I said to her the other night out of context," Marcus said.

"I know," I said as I became vulnerable to the contents of Marcus's face.

"Can we just start over?"

"Marcus I never said it was over…I just believe when a man and a woman make promises to each other they must keep them,"

"I know that Diamond, that is why I am asking you again to marry me...I love you,"

"But how do I know you love me...we have never had sex?"

"Sex doesn't prove to a woman that you love her...remember all the qualities I told your mother that I wanted in a woman...they are in you,"

"But still... a man should want to be physically intimate with his woman,"

"I do feel intimacy for you...but I want to wait until we are married,"

"So you telling me...you can sustain from having sex with other woman until we get married?"

"Of course...any woman worth having is worth waiting for,"

"You know Marcus, that is what I love about you...you are so understanding,"

"You didn't know this, but I always wanted to remain abstinent until I found the right man...thank you for being that person,"

"Diamond... just hold me close," Marcus said as he embraced me into his arms. The never-ending love between us was revived as we held each other closely. Marcus romanced me with the most impeccable kiss I had ever known.

Toni was walking toward us. I had forgotten I had her cell phone. I refused to take my eyes off of Marcus. I reached into my pocket and handed her the cell phone with no intermission from our romantic moment. I knew this was eating her up on the inside as she walked off.

Even though our engagement was announced in the tabloids, Marcus felt that it was not right for the public to officially announce it to his daddy. So we happily waltzed into Big Daddy's office. He was having a conference with some of the office staff. According to his expression, he was not surprised to see Marcus and me walking in with a bliss of radiance over our faces.

"Just saw the news...," Big Daddy said as he picks up the paper to show us the headlines.

"...What do you have to say for yourself?" Big Daddy asked.

"I say...," Marcus said being speechless.

"I say congratulations!" Big Daddy shouted.

We were astounded at the way Big Daddy handled it.

"I just knew there was something special about this woman," He said as he hugged me.

I was still in awe, because I didn't think Big Daddy would approve of it. Knowing that Marcus and his father didn't get along; his actions were beginning to frighten me. Because of the audience we had, I was wondering whether it was just a front. Even Marcus thought his father's behavior was strange. It really didn't matter to me, because at the present time being accepted as Big Daddy's daughter-in-law was more important.

Big Daddy began to celebrate in his office with wine. Everyone that was present in his office was congratulating us. It was a warm feeling of acceptance. Of course, Big Daddy had to be the one to say the words before the toast.

"May happiness, success and a lot of future CEO's babies come out of this.' Big Daddy said as he gulped down the wine.

When he said the last words, laughter was bubbling up inside of me. I was planning on having happiness and success, but children, not right now. After the toast Marcus and I embraced with another impeccable moment of love.

"So when is the big date?" Big Daddy asked.

Marcus and I looked at each other, and I said, "Well we haven't decided yet,"

"Well, I was thinking right after Diamond's winter tour," Marcus said.

"I can see already you are not going to let this marriage meddle with our big star's career," Big Daddy said.

"We have already discussed not allowing our marriage to interfere," Marcus said.

"Big Daddy when I first came to Aseret I was happy to be a part of this family...now I am more than happy to be your daughter-in-law," I said.

"That's daughter to you...and don't you forget it," Big Daddy said.

"I feel I have made the right choice...especially when it comes to choosing a wife," Marcus said.

"Well …I'll drink to that," Big Daddy said as he gulped more wine down his throat.

Marcus's outside appearance was transparent to the person that was living inside of him. I could tell that the relationship between him and his father was not that great. His father was a heavy drinker. There were some emotional disturbances going on within Marcus. I didn't know whether it was Marcus or his father that was keeping the distance in their relationship. One day the Pandora box will be opened and the pressure will withhold when it escapes.

CHAPTER 7

Even though I didn't get a chance to discuss my situation with my mom, there were other issues at hand. I need to find out how to handle pressure especially the pressure of becoming a wife. I didn't want my domestic responsibilities to take a toll over my music career. Then I thought, "What a more meaningful person to ask than mom," I decided to put some space into my schedule to have a heart-to-heart talk with my mom. If she didn't have the answers, I didn't know who would.

Spending time with my mom was very valuable to her. On this particular day, mom was cooking her specialty, spaghetti. Talking with my mom seemed to make the task of cooking move along quickly.

"I am so glad you found time for yourself," Mom said, as she was stirring the hot spaghetti sauce on the stove.

"I need to get some rest before the tour," I said while sitting at the brunch table reading a magazine.

"Did you read the article about Marcus and me in the tabloids?" I asked.

"Yes I did…but those papers always have lies…they feed off of lies," Mom replied.

"I felt they intruded upon our privacy,"

"Most of them do…that's how they meet their sales quota…I don't know why you thought your life was going to be secluded…don't you know that stardom breeds gossip," Mom said.

I began to walk over to the stove and watch my mother create her famous Italian spaghetti sauce. I took the spoon from her to taste it.

"Um…tastes good," I said.

"You always loved my sauce," Mom said taking the spoon from me and tasting it also.

"I think it needs a little more something," She said trying to figure out what ingredient was needed.

"Tell me something mom, when you met dad… did you know he was the one for you?" I asked.

"Not in the beginning, you see I was always attractive to your dad in high school, but because of his character of being a flirter, I didn't care too much for guys like that," Mom replied.

"So how did you hook up with him?" I asked.

"Well…that's a long and mystic story,"

"I would like to know…come on mom…your little girl is asking you to tell your secrets," I said as I smiled.

Suddenly, my cell phone rang. I pulled it out of my pocket. It was Marcus checking to see how my day was and wanted to take me out for dinner. I did not want to take away the special time I was having with my mom, because once a girl gets married, quality time becomes quantity time.

"I'll talk to you later…I love you," I said as I closed the cell phone.

"My…my, he really keeps tabs on you…sort of like what your dad used to do," Mom said.

"Since you talking about dad… finish telling me about how you became interested in him…since you say you weren't at first," I said.

"At first I wasn't …but as time passed by I began to see him regularly passing by…I was working at a hamburger joint trying to help pay my way through college…Often we would pass each other and he would blow his horn at me," Mother said as she sat down near me at the table.

"I guess you would call those love signals," I said giggling.

"You can call it what you want to…it was the strangest thing, I began to become attracted to him… I would tell my friends if they saw him to ask for his number,"

"I thought you told me not to be forward with guys,"

"I know but I wasn't being forward, my friends were,"

"So that's the way you do it,"

"Diamond do you want to hear the story are not…. any way I met him face to face for the first time at my best friends birthday party… During my days we had house parties and everybody was welcome to come,"

"Times have really changed,"

"Yes they have…. and Dick your father came by in his 1970 Cadillac, Cadillac's were the style then…It was blue with white wall tires and heavily accessorized,"

"Okay mother, enough with the car and …"

"Well that night a lot of parties were going on and people would travel from party to party…I didn't know your father that much but my best friend did so she asked him to ride with us to scout out the scenery…Of course I was excited…I kept telling my friend he is in the back seat, he is in the back seat…my heart was pounding with joy,"

"Would you say it was love at first sight?"

"I don't know what it was, but I do know that I never felt the same about him after that night,"

"What else happened?"

"How do you know something else happened?"

"I can just feel it,"

"You're right…after my friend dropped us off, we began to talk and he asked me to ride with him around the area since it was a Saturday night…I rode with him for a while and then that is when he told me these special words,"

"What words mother?"

"Oh…I can't tell you,"

"You told me everything else so far," Diamond said, waiting with anticipation.

"You might think I was green or something,"

"I don't think you were green, just vulnerable,"

"Now that's why I am not going to tell you,"

"Okay…. she said, he wanted just one special woman to spend his entire life with,"

"Those are the words that took your heart,"

"Yes they did and he did live up to his promise,"

"Ah…Ah…. how romantic," I said as I was teasing my mother.

While I was teasing mother at the table my father walked into the kitchen. We were staring at him as though he had done something wrong.

"What…?" Father said as he kissed my mother.

"Nothing," We said in unison.

"Something does smell good in here," Father said.

"It's mom's spaghetti sauce," I said.

"I can't wait…I am starving," Father said.

Mother remained quiet at the table, while my father went over to taste the sauce in the pot.

"Now that is delicious," Father said as he looks at the inquisitive faces at the table.

"What's going on?" He said.

Glancing over at mother I said, "Mother and I were just having a conversation about how you and she met,"

"She told you… that story?" Father said.

"Yeah…and… how you wanted that one special woman to spend the rest of your life with," I said.

"And I meant every word of it," Father said taking my mother in his arms and giving her a hug and a kiss.

"Honey… special words from your love, will carry you through hard times…you'll see," Mother said.

"But you two…never had hard times," I said.

"We have…but we remember the vows we took before the Lord… for better or worst…for richer or poorer…in sickness and health…so don't take your vows like a grain of salt…mean it when you say it," Father explained.

When father stated the words of a marital vow, the sincerity of them remained glued to my heart. My marriage had to be true and sacred before God. I only hope that Marcus feels the same about his marriage vows as I do. I wanted my marriage to be as honorable as my parents. I am sure they had some hard times but from what I have seen they managed to get through it all through the help of God.

CHAPTER 8

Later during the afternoon, I met Marcus at his condo. He was insisting that I come over. I was contemplating whether I should accept the invitation. It was strange how he had never invited me to his place before, but whatever Marcus wanted I adhered too. As a matter of fact, he even insisted on a specific time to appear. I thought I would surprise him by showing up a little early.

As I sat in my car outside the gated community I was beginning to think about how special I was to Marcus, because most guys would have taken advantage of a girl as innocent as me. I was engaged to Marcus although; I still felt that he had not given himself totally to me.

When I drove my car at the gate, the gatekeeper took one look at me, winked his eye signaling an okay. I parked my car next to Marcus's car not noticing his guest parking space was already taken. I walked slowly up to the entrance of the door, then I pressed the buzzer on the monitor that was in connection to Marcus's condo.

"Hello," Marcus answered.

"It's me, Marcus," I said.

"Oh…come on in," Marcus said surprised.

Marcus opened the door slowly. I could tell he was hiding something from me by the look upon his face. As I walked in Jesse was sitting on the bar stool at the counter. He was all sexy looking with his shirt off, showing all the muscular frames in his body. From the looks of it, they were having a marvelous time without inviting me.

"I thought you were coming over later?" Marcus asked as he pulled me a drink from the counter.

"No… Thank you…" I said as he placed the glass of wine in my face.

"Well… I thought I would surprise you…but I can come back," I replied looking around.

"Nonsense…stay…never mind Jesse, he and I were just chatting over some business," Marcus said as he kissed me on the forehead.

Their behavior didn't look like they were chatting over some business. Pondering in my mind were the words of unfaithfulness. I wouldn't put anything past Jesse, because he was jealous of Marcus and my relationship anyway. I walked around the apartment and started looking around the room. Marcus had a fabulous bedroom. The coordination was great. I could tell he had an eye for fashion and not just ordinary fashion, but the type you would see in the modern day magazines. Marcus noticed I was browsing around the place. I wanted to make sure there were no hidden surprises, especially in the bedrooms.

"Do you like it?" Marcus asked.

"Yes I think it is nice and very cozy," I replied. "Whose room is this?"

Marcus looked at Jesse in a strange way.

"Oh that's Jesse's room," Marcus replied.

"Oh yeah…Marcus said it was okay for me to move in since you two would be getting married soon," Jesse explained.

"So…in other words…?" I asked with a puzzled face.

"No…. Diamond…you got it all wrong, Jesse moved in so that I could move out," Marcus said.

"Why couldn't Jessie wait until we are married?" I asked.

"Well…it was convenient for Jesse and also he can save a little money by living here with me," Marcus explained.

I was contemplating on whether to believe that story or not. I didn't know what Jesse was up too. He was careful in not engaging into our little spout. I understood Marcus's explanation, but I didn't understand why he didn't inform me of the matter.

"Can you do me a favor…next time you want to make a decision like this one, can you at least tell me?" I asked.

"Sure baby, whatever you want…now… come sit down and have a drink with me," Marcus said as he sat on the sofa patting the space next to him.

"I don't want a drink…just tell me what was so important that you had to drag me over here for the first time," I said.

Jesse said interrupting with a distorted expression upon his face, "Well… I am going…I need to work on some of the tracks for the big tour,"

"You don't have to leave because of me," I said sarcastically.

Jesse ignored my behavior. He walked into the bedroom and put on his shirt notices I was watching every move he made. Finally, he took his car keys off of the counter and walked out the door. It was a sigh of relief, because I couldn't convey unto Marcus what I was feeling in front of Jesse.

"What's wrong?" Marcus asked trying to cheer me up by pitching my cheeks.

I smiled at Marcus and replied. "Nothing"

"You see I have nothing to hide…go look for yourself in the bedrooms and the kitchen…" He said.

Then Marcus took me by the hand and walked me over to the bathrooms.

"And now you are looking in the bathrooms…nothing," He said, as he pulled the shower curtain back.

I couldn't do anything but smirk at the way he was insinuating I did not believe his story. I turned around and there was Marcus pulling me closer to him by the bathroom door. I could feel he wanted to caress me into his arms, so I indulged into the moment and let him shuffle our bodies close together. There was warmth of heat steaming up between us. Suddenly I found myself connecting to the body chemistry that Marcus was bestowing upon me. It felt good and it felt right. The moisture from his lips began to incline to my tongue. His hands were deeply challenging the womanhood inside of me. I couldn't bare leading Marcus and not going to the finish line. I pulled quickly away from Marcus.

"Wait...Wait..." I said trying to pry Marcus's arms from around me.

He kept pulling and jerking me closer to him to satisfy his manly hormonal imbalance that was kicking in.

"Marcus...I can't do this," I said.

"Can't do what?" He said as he continued to smother me with kisses over my neck.

It was a battle trying to live up to my expectations of abstinence, especially when you have a man drooling all over you. I stood my grounds until Marcus backed off.

"I thought you said you loved me," Marcus said as I pushed him away from me.

"I do...but this is not the right time," I said.

"Right time...I was only trying to get a little loving for the brother!" He shouted.

"Your definition for little loving is a whole different ball game...I thought you told me you respected me and will wait for me," I said.

Marcus came to his senses and said, "You're right...I don't know what came over me, I guess... I just want you so bad,"

Watching Marcus's face, I couldn't do anything but forgive him. I wanted to take my man and hold tight, but I knew there was going to be more consequences. I went over and sat on the sofa. Marcus could feel that I was not in the mood for playing games. I could tell he wanted to continue but to soothe his conscious he changed the subject.

"Diamond...Have you thought about a date for the wedding?" He asked.

"Yes I was thinking a June wedding...it will give me some time to come back from the tour and do the finishing touches," I replied with relief.

"In the meantime, are you just going to put things on hold?" Marcus asked.

"No...No...my mother and your sister are already working on the wedding and they have hired a wedding planner," I said.

"Well at least you won't be stressed out with that,"

"I don't think a wedding stresses you out,"

"Baby I am only concerned about your well being and everything… by the way are you ready for the tour?"

"More than ready" I said.

"I hate to tell you this, but I won't be able to go with you on the winter tour, but you know my heart is with you,"

"Marcus I understand… I have come to realize in the music business that sometimes your personal life will have to be put on the back burner…we made that agreement when got engaged,"

"Now… that doesn't mean putting me on the back burner,"

"You know what I mean,"

"Baby it's all going to work out, you'll see…before you know it we will be married and making decisions on a house and family,"

The thought of a house was marvelous, but the thought of a family was not in my vocabulary at the moment. I didn't want Marcus to know this, so I just played along with his dreams.

"By the way when are we going to buy a house?" I asked trying to keep his mind off of families, raising children or even how many children we want.

"I have arranged for a realtor to give us a view of some beautiful property when you come back from the tour,"

"Oh really…you are becoming feisty on me,"

"I told you everything was going to work out fine…I want us to have a house before we get married, therefore we won't need to live in this condo with Jesse,"

"I think that would be a great idea," I said agreeing with Marcus.

The last thing I wanted to do was to live with Jesse. Before I could finish the consequences of my thinking, Marcus' demeanor on his face began to flourish with a desire of lust. His eyes begin to gleam directly into my pupils. I tried to avoid gazing into his eyes, because somehow my will of holding myself for my husband became weak. It was a constant battle for me.

There was a silence between us, as Marcus looked me into my eyes. It was as though a sudden stop of incredible sensation came over him.

"You know I love you…don't you," He said as we snuggled closely.

"I do know that," I said as I was drawn into his caressing arms.

This time he gave me a smack on the lips and slid slowly into my lap. I quietly kissed Marcus on the forehead. He took my hand to glide it up to his lips and continued to snuggle under me. While indulging into the romantic moment, I began to watch him close his eyes. I carefully fondled through his soft curly hair causing him to fall into a dreamland. Marcus seemed very comforting in my lap as he dripped off to sleep.

CHAPTER 9

Cold and windy were the attributes of my winter tour. I had become more and more dependent upon my career. Even though I was planning to stand before a preacher at the end of June, my success had to include my singing. Music was my destiny and the overshadowing intimacy in my life. I had become driven by the arrogance that competed with in my soul. The roots of my salvation were diminishing from my thoughts. Acknowledgment of "God" the ultimate person who bestowed the gifts I possessed was slowly becoming distant.. I was drifting into a meaningless world and no one could steer me differently. That is when my life was turning into a pool of vanity and I had no idea of how to swim out, so I began to sink. Marcus and singing began to become rational and humanistic idols for my purpose of living.

Today Marcus promised to meet me at the airport. I was disappointed he wasn't going to be with me on this tour, but it was understandable. Just before I boarded the plane Marcus called me on my cell phone to inform me that he was not coming. He had an emergency at the office that couldn't wait. I told myself I wasn't going to be upset because the music business has no certainties. I knew that the relationship that Marcus and I have will sometimes be distant when it came to me going on tours. I was delighted that Marcus trusted me. I didn't flatter myself, but I am a beautiful and attractive young lady. I am also multitalented, which most men adore when it comes to independent women.

Toni my assistant had prepared everything in advance. She made sure that I was professionally on time for every event. I thought it would be kind of fun being with Toni alone on this trip. Maybe she would get the idea that I was not giving up on Marcus because, Toni continues to manipulate many games around the office. One of her games was to always get everything approved by Marcus. This was her way of getting his attention. Her jealousy was beginning to become a flaming moment. Mostly everyone in the office knows that she is trying to figure out a way to get Marcus back or get back at him.

Toni was sitting next to me on the company's private plane. I notice she continued to hide behind her magazine in order not to conversate with me. It didn't bother me, because I indulged in conversations with her, especially when it came to talking about my relationship with Marcus.

I pulled on Toni's magazine and said, "Reading something interesting,"

For a moment she ignored me, then I yanked on the magazine as though I was trying to wake her up.

"Are you sleep or something?" I asked.

"No…busy," Toni replied.

"It can't be that interesting…it's just a regular tabloid…let me see if I am in there," I said as I pulled the top of the pages down.

Toni knew I caught on to her cover-up, because the magazine was upside down.

"It's just a magazine…and it doesn't even have my picture in it," I said ironically.

"I know it's just a magazine, but it has interesting stories…that don't focus on you," Toni said.

"Toni, are you still upset with me?" I asked.

"Why would I be upset?" Toni replied flipping the pages of the magazine.

I could discern by the way she was flipping the pages the timing was not right, because of my personality I wanted to egg her on until she answered me.

"What's the matter with you?" I kept questioning Toni's behavior.

"Diamond, maybe you don't have work to do, but I do," Toni said, taking a folder out of her briefcase.

"Toni, stop horsing around... tell me what's bothering you?" I asked.

"Diamond, you don't understand," Toni replied.

"Understand what?" I said. "I won't know unless you tell me.

Toni refused to tell me what was going on in her mind but I was purposely trying to dig it out. I took the folder from Toni's lap and said, "You are my assistant...you can talk to me about any thing,"

"You sure you want to hear what I have to say," Toni said as she gazed seriously into my eyes.

"Sure I want to hear," I said.

"I don't think so...never mind," Toni said as she reluctantly cancelled the conversation.

By the seriousness in Toni's eyes, I could tell she wanted to talk. I felt she was still having problems dealing with her intimate feelings for Marcus.

"Are you still in love with Marcus?" I said without thinking about her feelings.

Toni wouldn't respond to the question. She was handling the situation by ignoring me with her business papers. She was shuffling and flipping pages of paper like there was no tomorrow. I sense that there was deep tension in the seat next to me. It was like a time grenade about to explode and I was the pin that was about to be pulled. Toni's facial expressions were not pleasant to look at, even though she wasn't looking directly at me.

I didn't help the situation at all, because I kept agitating her.

"Toni..." I said.

"What Diamond!" Toni yelled.

"What's bothering you...must be PMS?" I said, trying to make her snap out of it. It didn't work because it put fuel on the fire. It was amusing to me seeing how she was being manipulated by my actions.

"Will you leave me along...I don't feel like talking...I have all this to go over!" She yelled shoving the papers in my face.

I decided to leave the conversation with her multi-personalities. Maybe she will get over it.

There was a quiet stigma between us throughout the time we were on the plane. I couldn't wait to arrive to our destiny.

Finally, the arrival to the British amphitheater was quick and unnoticeable. After I realized Toni had problems that were larger than mine, I began to use it as ammunition. I enjoyed every moment arousing her emotions.

While waiting to go out on stage, Toni helped me to prepare. I could hear the audience shouting my name. There was a sensation of awesome glee running through my veins. Toni was by my side telling me what to do and what not to do. It was a remarkable moment for me and a stepping stone toward winning a Grammy. I continued to hear the crowd shouting "Diamond," For a moment the voices began to fade out. I began to hear a soft voice saying, "This is all temporarily," I look around to see if someone was next to me, but there was no one there. Then the shouts from the crowd became loud again. A funny feeling came over me as I thought about the soft voices saying, "This is all temporarily", but because of the inspiring audience I thrust away from the thought. When I stepped out on the stage there were a multitude of people screaming. It was not a scream of fear, but of wholesome delight. There were signs all over the place honoring me. Most of them said, "Diamond We Love You," By surprise I heard a familiar voice.

I look at the side of the stage and there was Marcus cheering me on. Toni also was next to Marcus cheering also. By the excitement upon Toni's face I realized she wasn't upset with me. Toni probably carries other baggage yet to be revealed.

"I love you Diamond," Marcus said, as he blew a kiss toward me.

I could see in Toni's eyes that she was jealous with the way Marcus intimacy toward me. Toni tried to cover it up. I knew she was doing this to get through the night. She began to loosen up as the tour continued. Marcus wasn't able to stay through the entire tour. I was happy he was there on the opening night.

I song over twelve songs and the crowd kept wanting more. I had composed a special song for Marcus. I dedicated it to Marcus at the end of the show. It was so mystical and most of all fantastic reviews for paparazzi. This was a night that I would never forget. After this tour I sold over twenty million copies of my albums. It was the cap of my career. I knew it was time to put a crown on my relationship with Marcus. It was time for me to become his bride.

Finally, I was off tour and was able to focus on myself. I was excited about being home and away from the media. I needed a break especially with my June wedding arising. Mother and Sherrie had done most of the details with my wedding planner. My wedding dress was the only thing left to make a decision on. I spent an entire day going from shop to shop in every expensive town. My dress had to be the most exclusive and expensive. I was looking for the dress that would give Marcus a double take when I walk down the aisle.

"Let's look into this shop?" Mom said, as she opened the door of the store. Sherri and the Wedding planner named Gwen were very helpful, because my mother had an idea of a simple dress with lots of accessories mainly pearls. I didn't want a simple dress. I wanted to walk down the isle with a gown that was extravagant and had a personality of beauty and success.

As we walked into the store, the attendant recognized me abruptly. Because of the tabloids most of the bridal shops were looking to patronize me. They were bringing out all sorts of designer gowns.

"How about this dress..?" Gwen asked as she pulled out the most breathtaking dress I had ever seen.

I was speechless for a moment and then I shouted, "Where did you find this dress!"

"Oh, this is one of the gowns we had imported from Paris…we didn't know whether this was your taste," The sales attendant said.

"My taste….its…its…me, I meant me all the way…this dress I must have," I said.

"Honey… Are you sure…first try it on," Mom said.

"Yes this is me," I replied as I put the dress up to me and then looked into the mirror.

I looked at Sherrie. She shook her head in agreement. I rushed into the dressing room. I kept glancing at myself in the mirror. Sherrie yelled, "Are you okay?"

"I'm okay," I replied.

When I walked out toward the outer mirror in the shop, all eyes were on me, even the other customers were in awe.

"Yes that's you…don't you agree Sherrie?" Mom implied.

"Yes…yeah… I do…girl you are going to be the talk of the town," Sherrie said, as she pranced around me several times.

"Well I guess this will finalize our plans for today," Gwen stated.

"Yeah…this dress is signed sealed and delivered," I said.

While Gwen and Mother finalized the sale of my wedding dress, Sherrie and I decided to walk across the street to an ice cream shop. Before we could across the street we noticed Marcus's Porsche in front of it. I could tell his car from anyone else because he has his name on his tag with a playboy bunny on it. I plan to have that changed immediately after we are hitched.

Sherrie starting tugging on me to not go inside of the shop, but I was determined to get to the bottom of this. I walked inside of the shop pretending I was going to buy an ice cream sundae. I went up to the counter. I heard Sherrie whispering my name in the background trying to get me to leave and forget about the situation. Sherrie stood by the door out of sight, while I continued to act out my scene. I walked toward the counter trying to hide my face. I noticed Marcus was talking to someone in one of the booths, but I couldn't see the person because their back was against the back of the bench. At first, I thought I would just hang around and see what was happening, and then I began to feel an edge. I couldn't spare the moment any longer. I wanted to make sure Marcus was not cheating on me. So I started walking toward the booth, which is when Sherrie rushed in and called my name loudly.

"Diamond…did you get the ice cream?' Sherrie said hesitantly.

I looked puzzled for a moment, but when I turned around there was Marcus walking and behind him was Jesse. I had a sigh of relief come over me. Sherrie kept me from embarrassing myself.

Marcus heard Sherrie talking to me and said, "Well I guess we all had a taste for ice cream today,"

"Not really" I said.

Sherrie interrupted and said, "Yes we did" She took the sundae out of my hand quickly and started dipping into the ice cream like there was no tomorrow. She really knew how to play something off.

"So... Marcus what brings you and Jesse in here?" I said. It seemed like that was all that could come out of my mouth, because deep inside I felt Marcus was not keeping it real with me.

"Jesse and I were discussing some business, we thought we would change the atmosphere and get some ice cream," Marcus stated.

"It was just ice cream and business," Jesse explained.

"Well I can see that," I said.

"I thought you were going to look for your dress today?" Marcus asked.

"I did, but it doesn't take all day and besides, I found the most astounding dress," I said as Sherrie was attempting to shut me up before I spoil my wedding day.

"Okay...we got to go now," Sherrie said as she was pulling my arm away from Marcus.

"Okay...Okay," I said as I leaned toward Marcus and smacked him on the lips with a kiss.

"I'll call you later...or better yet; I will come by your house later," Marcus said, as he watched me being tugged by his sister out the door.

"Why not come for dinner, how about 8:00?" I asked.

"Okay...I'll see you then," Marcus replied as he was standing in front of the clerk's counter.

Sherrie continued to literally pull me out of the shop. I didn't know whether to take this as a positive or negative reaction.

"What's your problem?" I asked Sherrie as we attempt to cross the street.

"I have no problem...it's just you get excited too quick when you see Marcus with people," Sherrie replied.

"I don't get excited; I am just inquisitive, especially when he is not where he is supposed to be,"

"And where is that?"

"At the office, home… any of places that I have known are his whereabouts,"

"Girl you are going to have to get over this…don't you know who you are marrying?"

"I know…Marcus Singleton a top CEO," I replied being ironic with Sherrie.

"When are you going to start trusting Marcus?" Sherrie asked.

"I know…I trust him and everything…but deep inside I feel that there is something in between us," I replied.

"Have you talked to Marcus about this?

"No, but I don't want him to think I don't trust him,"

"Well you better talk to him before the wedding,"

I really didn't want to start up any tension in my relationship with Marcus. My heart wanted to accept whatever Marcus did, because I was remotely in love with him.

Finally, we were able to cross the street. Mother and Gwen were waiting outside the bridal shop for us.

"What took you so long?" Mother asked while looking at her watch with a sigh in her voice.

Before I could blurt out any words, Sherrie replied, "Oh we decided to be a kid again and try some ice cream,"

"Do me a favor…next time let me know," Mother said as we walked toward the car.

Little did she know there would never be a next time, especially picking out a wedding dress? This will be my first and last time, I promised myself.

CHAPTER 10

Waiting for Marcus to show up for dinner always gave me goose bumps, because he can sometime be full of surprises. He has a charm that could navigate any situation. I think that is one of his qualities that motivate me for the challenge. Since I am not the person anyone could ever want to meet, Marcus's characteristics balances our differences.

Even though Marcus was a great guy he was full of surprises, some that I didn't want to recognize. I anticipated Marcus was going to be late, because he always somehow had excuses. He would use Jesse as his escape goat most of the time. This particular night that he came over it was different.

Without notice the doorbell rang. I reluctantly looked at the clock on the wall. I just knew it wouldn't be Marcus, but low and behold it was him. When I opened the door he was standing in front of me with a glitter in his eyes just for me. He held in his hand my favorite, a yellow rose. Before I could say anything, he pulled me close to him and kissed me tightly in the mouth. I could hardly breathe. The sensation from the kiss was as though Marcus was truly in love with me.

"Well, Marcus…I didn't," I said.

"You didn't expect me on time," Marcus interrupted my thoughts.

"Well…" I said blushing from ear to ear, because of the powerful kiss we had just indulged into.

I took Marcus by the hand and walked him over to the living room. My father was sitting in his favorite lounging chair reading the newspaper.

"Hello Marcus," Father said, as he leaned his newspaper over to watch him sit down, then he looked at his watch.

"I know what you're thinking," Marcus said as he sat down.

My father ignored his statement and continued to read the newspaper.

"Mr. Oslo…did you hear what I just said," Marcus asked.

Father pulled the paper down from his face and replied, "I heard you, but as men we don't worry about time…just as long as we keep the women happy,"

"Oh dad, you do worry about time…you know if you don't come home on time for dinner you will have to hear mother's mouth," I said as mom was walking down the stairway.

"Hear… whose mouth?" Mother asked as she heard a portion of our conversation.

"Oh…Marcus you are here…I was hoping I would be finish with the roast before you came," Mother said surprise.

"That's okay… I thought I would start practicing being on time since after all… I have to make a good impression on my in-laws," Marcus smiled as the words were pouring out of his mouth.

"Tell me something Mr. Oslo?" Marcus asked.

"Why don't you call me Dad…since in a few weeks I will be your father-in-law?" Father replied.

"By the way, have you thought about investments for you and Diamond?

"I really haven't thought about it…but since you are on the subject, I was thinking to continue to let you handle Diamonds investments after we are married,"

I didn't want my father to mix this visit with finance so I walked over to Marcus and put my arms around him. He knew I wanted to change the subject by the startled look in my eyes.

"Okay, Dad…Why don't you hire a cook and maid for this large house, Mrs. Oslo wouldn't have to work so hard," Marcus asked.

Marcus didn't know he was intruding on my father's territory. My father didn't believe in having a maid or cook when the lady of the house can do the work herself. Even though my mother ran her own business, she was always doing her wifely duties.

"Janice doesn't need any help...she does fine...well... it's just the three of us, and Diamond is hardly home...and soon to be your wife," Father replied.

"Well I am going to make sure Diamond doen't have to lift a finger, especially when we start a family...isn't that right honey?" Marcus implied gesturing his eyes toward me.

I felt a lump in my throat as I squeezed out the words, "We'll... we'll... cross that bridge when we get there,"

"What bridge?" Marcus asked.

"Ah...Having a family," I replied desperately hoping that he would continue the conversation.

"I wasn't suggesting we start a family right away,"

"I didn't mean it the way it sounded,"

"Now Diamond...let's talk about this later,"

"It had better be later... and a lot later,"

By the look on my parent's faces, I could tell that they didn't enjoy Marcus and me quarreling in front of them. I was always taught to take the husband and wife disputes into your bedroom, unless the children needed to be involved. This was one of those moments I wished Marcus would have discussed things with me privately.

Mother deliberately interrupted and said," Well...Diamond, come on and help me set the table for dinner,"

I knew my mother was trying to gather a sensible evening without me having to ruin it with my selfish little ways. If she wouldn't have saved the faces, a cold atmosphere was about to happen between Marcus and me.

While we were setting the table for dinner, mother continued to give me some wisdom about my mouth. I was always forward when it came to giving my opinion. I guess it was because my parents always told me to be open with them about anything in my life. You kind of get used to being in control.

"Diamond, some things you just have to leave alone," Mom said, as she was placing the plates on the table.

"I was only speaking my mind," I replied.

"That's the problem…if you don't work on that now you are going to have a heap of heated days in your relationship," Mom stated.

"Why do you say that?" I asked while following mom around the table placing the napkins and silverware behind her.

"First, you must learn your spouse before you start running your mouth…there are some ways about Marcus you are not going to like… but first learn him and study his mood, then you will know when it is time to say or do certain things…that's how you keep peace in your home,"

"Tell me something…do you study daddy a lot?" I asked reluctantly.

"Why do you ask that?" Mom replied.

"Well…all my life you have been catering to his commands sometimes … then sometimes you control him," I said.

I could tell my mom didn't like me challenging her words by the way her lips were squirming trying to hold her composure.

"I know when to say certain things and the right time…that's what you call studying your mate," Mom said as she sat down at the table.

"Never take a man for granted…please…please don't think he is perfect," Mother implied.

"You been married too long…Marcus and I…we are a perfect couple," I said.

"Diamond there are no perfect couples…every marriage takes hard work, if you're not willing to work at it than don't take the job," Mom explained.

"But Marcus and I have known our problems…we seem to work things out fine," I said.

"For now…just wait until he has those matrimony papers on you… then you become a piece of property he doesn't have to worry about buying…you know what that means…child, I pray for our marriage daily…without it I don't think it would have lasted this long,"

"I thought you and daddy had a great relationship,"

"Great with Jesus…you don't know the many times I wanted to leave him, but I kept looking back at the moment we met…and my vows they are sacred to me.

"But you love daddy,"

"With all my heart…that is why I keep him before the Lord… not just him, but myself also, because women can be very determined sometimes,"

"Well… I guess I had better start praying now before any drama starts lashing toward us,"

"A marriage without God will not work…you will love each other, but bearing each other's differences will take the hand of God,"

"You know you are right mother, Marcus and I need to attend church together…ever since his mother died he refused to attend…and I am so tired all the time from rehearsals,"

"I notice you have been laying church down…don't forget the bridge that bought you over,"

"I won't," I said.

"…and another thing…keep folks out of your business…what goes on in your household stays in your household,"

"I try, but Toni is always watching everything we do and say,"

"You are going to have to get over Toni and realize that she wants to have…Marcus,"

"You know…Sherrie told me the same thing…this is a confirmation for me,"

"Diamond you are always busy, I don't know if we will ever get to talk like this again, but go into your marriage believing that it will work… if not, everything that happens wrong will lead you to think divorce,"

"Mom, I am so glad I got to talk with you…I feel much better knowing that marriage is something you have to work at…thanks for the advice," I implied.

"Baby, I love you…the truth is the only thing that can help," Mom said as she patted my shoulder,"

Mom was serious when she talked about marriage. She has been through so much, especially before I was conceived. I knew she wanted to tell me more by the remorseful look she had on her face. It was not the right timing.

Mom looked around to see if Dad and Marcus could hear our conversation. But before she could continue with words, she was interrupted by the entrance of Dad and Marcus.

"We decided to march right in here, since you two took so long to call us," Father said.

I took a double look at mom. I knew this was a moment she wanted to share with me alone.

Even though my talk with mom was short, it didn't matter as much because I will have a whole lifetime to talk to mom about men. Luckily, I have a mom who doesn't mind waiting for the perfect moment.

That evening the dinner was perfect and had a lasting moment that detailed Marcus's relationship with my parents. After all that's all that concerns me, was Marcus getting along with my parents, especially my dad. They were like two peas in a pod.

CHAPTER 11

Time was accelerating. It was finally the perfect day of my life. Where paparazzi, envy, jealousy and old flames will be able to finally close the Chapter in their books. I felt like it was a dream and I didn't want to be awakened. My prince was finally going to take his princess away.

The reflection of my beautiful brown skin illuminated as I stood in front of the tall floor mirror. I was admiring my beautiful self in the most remarkable and dynamite dress that anyone could ever wear on such a special occasion. It was one of those days that you wanted to be perfect and you didn't want even a pimple to surface your face. Nothing was more captivating than watching yourself and others prepare you for the most extravagant event that any woman would dare to dream. It was my wedding day and I wasn't about to let it self-destruct before my eyes. Staring in the mirror gave me the right to indulge into every given moment.

"Oh child... calm down, it will be over with soon," Mom said as she continued to fluff the slip under my wedding dress,"

"But mom, I feel so nervous" I said while looking in the stand-up mirror in the dressing room. I didn't realize how much of my life I was going to change. I won't be able to hang out with my friends on a regular basis and much of my time will be spent trying to live up to the expectations of my in-laws.

"Diamond you will be okay, remember this is your big day... everyone is nervous on their Wedding Day," Mom said attempting to keep me from feeling uptight.

I kept staring at myself in the mirror. I couldn't believe the transformation that was taking place before my very eyes. I am finally going to totally share my life with the one and only man that has been in my life since the day I laid eyes on him at the agency.

"What's the matter child?" Mother asked.

"Oh...Nothing" I solemnly replied.

"Oh...you'll be alright...stand still... so I can put on your headpiece," She said.

I glanced over at Sherrie my Maid of Honor sitting quietly in the chair next to the door. She had her hands up to her face and appeared to be daydreaming. She was not an ordinary Maid of Honor she was my groom's kid sister and had become my best friend.

"Sherrie, what are you sitting there staring at...come and help me?" Mom asked while trying to fit the bridal headpiece in a suitable place on my head.

"I wasn't staring...I was just wondering how I would look with such a beautiful gown on," Sherrie replied.

"Oh you will look gorgeous, and don't forget I have to be your Maid of Honor one day," I replied while giving her a smile.

"How are you going to be my Maid of Honor, you will probably be knocked up by that time," Sherrie said as she helped my mom to put on my bridal headpiece.

Some sparks had come into Sherrie's eyes as she adjusted the headpiece on my head.

"Knocked up...I am not planning on having children for at least five years," I replied.

"Yeah, that is what you say, child I tell you...you better have the children while you can, because the older you are, the chances of you becoming pregnant are slim," Mom said.

"Mrs. Oslo, don't pay Diamond any attention, she always feels she has her life map out," Sherrie said.

"Oh, I know she was like that since she started talking...but I must say... some things she did just happen...like her career in music," Mom explained.

"Now, that looks nice," Mom said as she stood behind me in the mirror admiring her baby girl standing tall and looking like a princess. I enjoyed every moment of the attention I was getting. I was known for getting my way, even if it meant destroying those in the way.

Finally there was a knock on the door.

"Come in" We shouted.

One of the bride maids came in and said, "Are you ready?"

"Of course she is ready," Sherrie replied.

"Is Marcus here yet?" I asked the bridesmaid as she was closing the door.

Marcus was known for not being on time, but he always had some lame brained excuse and I believed it every time. Attraction was his game and a woman was his fame.

"No, not yet" She replied, as she exited the room.

Mom looked at her watch and said, "Oh…he'll be here,"

Mom looked at me and saw the excitement in my eyes. I couldn't image the thoughts that were roaming around in her head. I grabbed her and gave her a big hug. Mom encouraged me by kissing me on the cheek and saying, "Baby it's going to be alright,"

The words, "It's going to be alright", gave me the assurance that it was really going to be okay.

I pulled up my gown so that I wouldn't step on the hem. Sherrie grabbed a hold of my train and placed it into my hand.

"We will be officially sisters as of today," Sherrie said.

"I know, and I am happy to be more than your best friend," I smiled as the sincere words released from my mouth.

Mom took my hand and squished it tightly. As she unleashed my hand it felt as though she was leaving me forever. But I knew she would always be there for me.

I stood in the room looking at the gown I was wearing and imagined the future with the only love of my life. I was in good spirits on the inside in which overshadowed my demeanor on the outside. I continued to look at the clock on the wall.

I could hear the orchestra melodies from inside the church pounding in my heart. It was around three-fifteen and there was no forewarning of Marcus being on time. The wedding was supposed to start at three o'clock. The waiting time brought about doubt and anticipation.

Finally it was the moment I was waiting for a knock on the door and I was headed down the road of matrimony. The white crispy chiffon dress was clinging to my butt as I walked down the isle of the church. The lasting accent on my dress were imported crystals and pearls, they reflected the lighting of the building. It was the longest distance I had anticipated on taking. Mom's florist shop did a stunning job on the decoration of the church. Each row of benches in the cathedra was dressed with flesh yellow roses and accented with baby breathes of flowers. I was slow in motion while the cameras were capturing a beautiful young black woman. I knew that I had everything perfect and destined to breed more perfection.

There were many people in attendance. Many I briefly knew, but who cared, I was the center of attraction today. As I came closer to the altar I could hear whispering voices stating how beautiful I was today. It was as though I was the queen of England.

Suddenly my ears tuned in to two women whispering, but it was loud enough for me to hear. One of the women said. "She is so beautiful"

"I wonder how much they spent on that gown?" another whispering voice asked.

"It doesn't matter, they have the money," A voice replied

"But she is too young for him…. maybe she tricked him?"

"I don't know, but it was a good trick,"

"No one can trick Marcus…there is more to this,"

"If only she knew,"

Then the snickering of laughter was trailing me from the corner of my eye as I watch my competition. It didn't bother me because I was the one wearing the expensive gown and I am the star. I was the one walking down the isle of the decorated Cathedral church.

The cameras couldn't stop flashing and the tabloids were destined to print the moment.

There was nothing like reading the headlines about the marriage of two prominent success people on the front page of the tabloids. I was excited about opening another Chapter of my life.

I glanced over at my mom wiping tears from her eyes. I looked at my dad as he walked me into the arms of another. His eyes were contradicting the; one moment it was watery eyes of joy and the next minute it was the eyes of sorrow. I didn't know whether he was crying because he was losing his baby girl. He smiled at me as I was taking the final step of leaving his nest into another man's nest. Dad held on to my hand tight as though he didn't want to let his baby girl go. Finally, I reached the altar of love and freedom. I had met the one and only man that I could spend my entire life with.

Dad whispered in my ear as he took my hand and placed it into my true love's hand, "I love you and will always be the first man in your life forever,"

I didn't know whether to take those words as a positive or a negative, but I had several confirmations that they were the truth. Flashbacks began to kindle my mind as I looked into my everlasting lover's eyes. His eyes were speaking "forever love" to me. I knew I had taken the right road in choosing a companion for the rest of my life. I kept staring in his eyes while the sweet melodies from the orchestra serenaded my soul.

When Marcus and I exchanged vows, I could feel the words sinking deep into my heart and passing into the soul of my body. This was real, and there was no turning back. Tears of joy kindled the both of us. My dad was trying to keep himself from getting emotional by holding a straight face. My mom face was drooling with tear drops and I could hear her continuing to blow her nose throughout the ceremony. Big Daddy was showing all thirty-twos with smiles. Jesse was the best man and he stayed close by to watch Marcus' every move. When Jesse gave Marcus the wedding ring, I could tell there was some rejection in Marcus's actions. I didn't know whether he was contemplating second thoughts or just jittery.

The minister said," You may now kiss the Bride,"

This was the moment I had been waiting for. All the competition in the world couldn't steal this Kodak moment from me. By the way, Toni didn't show up, she left a message stating "she had a family emergency," It was fine with me. It just made my day more peaceful. Before I could take a second thought I became Mrs. Marcus Singleton.

CHAPTER 12

Since I have become Mrs. Marcus Singleton, the tabloids have really made me a center of attraction. We were the headlines in the media. Most of the talk was about the reason Marcus married me. Some of the lies were: I was pregnant, Big Daddy made him marry me to save his career and so on. But it was just hearsay. I was not about to entertain those negative insinuations. I was happy and that was very important to me.

Marcus and I bought a beautiful mansion not too far from his father's domain. Well, I could say we bought it, but it was a gift from his father. He wanted to make a lasting impression on our marriage. Also, Marcus made sure I didn't lift a finger so he hired a maid, butler and chefs. I would say "The works!" He made sure I didn't get stressed out with daily household chores. Needless to say, a house does not keep a woman happy. Pure love is the center of happiness and I mean genuine true love.

My career was really in high peak now and I had a battle between being a fulltime wife or a fulltime dedicated singer. After I weighed my situation, it wasn't too difficult to make a decision. Even though, Marcus and I are married he is still an attraction to other women, I decided to continue to be a full-time artist so I could keep a grip on Marcus. I know Toni is still in love with him and who knows who else is involved. Hanging around Aseret would keep me apprised on what is going on. I realized if I became a housewife it would give Marcus enough space with excuses to come home late. By me hanging around the studio I can keep tabs on what is really going on. Not that I don't trust him. I just don't trust women.

I will never forget my first Christmas as being Mrs. Singleton. It was Christmas Eve; I decided that I would surprise Marcus and cook a grand Christmas dinner. Because most of the time my personal chef maintains our daily meals, I gave all of my helpers the holiday off to be with their families. I spent hours between being coached by my mom on the phone with different recipes. The kitchen looked like someone who was taking cooking lessons, but I knew this was going to be a special occasion for us.

While continuing to prepare my meal, I heard a voice coming from the entrance of my living room. It was Sherrie loaded down with presents in her hand. I walked out to greet her not noticing I looked like I had a battle in the kitchen. My forehead and chin had flour sprinkles on it. My apron looked like a kindergartener had just finish finger painting.

Sherrie stared at me for a moment and then said, "Lord… what in names have you been doing?"

"What does it look like I've been doing?" I replied as I reached over to help Sherrie with the presents in her hand.

"Looks like you've been fighting in the kitchen," Sherrie chuckled while she followed me toward the Christmas tree. She continued to talk as she handed me the presents to place under the tree.

"Well you can say it was a struggle…I have been back and forth on the phone taking cooking lessons for this grand dinner,"

"What grand dinner…I thought you and Marcus were eating dinner with us on tomorrow?

"No…we are eating dinner at home… this is our first Christmas and I want to be with Marcus alone,"

"Well…if you say so…but Marcus told Big Daddy that you two were coming over,"

"Oh, he did huh…when did this happen?"

"Big Daddy asked him weeks ago and he agreed…since he is trying to build his relationship back with him,"

Sherrie saw the way I was looking at her. She knew that I was not too keen on spending my first Christmas with the Singleton family, in that case I could have spent it with my own parents.

"Look Diamond, I didn't mean to spoil it for you," Sherrie said.

I spoke between my teeth, "You didn't spoil it…you just gave me a heads up about my husband,"

Sherrie knew by my tone of voice that I was furious.

"Look Sherrie I don't mean to make our visit short…but I have a lot to do…" I harshly stated while walking her toward the front door.

"Well…I hope to see you on tomorrow…and…Merry Christmas!" Sherrie shouted trying to save her face from the situation.

She didn't take the situation personally, because she knew I wasn't upset with her.

I closed the door quickly behind Sherrie and then I screamed to the top of the ceiling. I couldn't believe Marcus made plans without consulting me. I couldn't wait for him to come home. I was so furious until cooking became a hobby to keep the stress off of my mind. I kept looking at the clock on the kitchen wall. It was about seven o'clock p.m. when Sherrie left, now it was about 9:15 p.m. Marcus had not arrived. I didn't know whether to worry or continue to build my anger. I had completed my dinner about and hour ago and Marcus still was not to be found, not even a phone call. I decided to recline in the entertainment room. I begin to watch the late Christmas movie on the T.V. Before I knew it I had fallen asleep.

Without warning I felt a warm kiss on my forehead awakened me. I was startled for a moment. Marcus saw me open my eyes and he kissed me like he had never kissed me before. But that wasn't the problem. His breath had a scent of wine covered with Bianca mint. Even though I was indulged into his emotions, the thought of him not consulting me about our Christmas overshadowed the moment. I pulled away from him quickly. I notice his suit was wrinkled and his tie was untied from his shirt. It looked like he had an exciting night.

"Wait a minute!" I shouted, "Where have you been?"

"I was out celebrating with Jesse and some of the staff," Marcus replied.

"Celebrating....celebrating...do you know what time it is?"

"Yeah...time for you to give me some sugar," Marcus replied staggering to steal another kiss.

"Marcus...Stop it!" I shouted pulling his hands away from me.

"Baby you got something on your face...some white stuff," He said continuing to stagger in front of me.

"Yeah, I know..." I said while trying to wipe my face.

Tears began to flow from my eyes. I couldn't believe Marcus had no concern for my feelings.

"What's the matter baby?" Marcus solemnly asked.

"I have been it that kitchen almost all day trying to cook our first Christmas dinner," I replied.

"Why did you do that...I told you we were going to Big Daddy for dinner,"

"NO you didn't!"

"Well...I thought I did...aren't we...?" Marcus began to question his actions. Then he took me in his arms to sit down.

"I am sorry honey...I am so sorry," He said with regret.

I love Marcus so much, until I didn't know whether to forgive him or hit him.

"I tell you what... I will call Big Daddy right now...we can go over there later during the evening," Marcus said.

"Really... you would do that for me....but why didn't you tell me? I asked.

"I reckon I forgot...I thought I told you...please forgive me,"

"I forgive you for that, but what about not calling me...you know I worry when you don't call,"

"I am sorry about that too...I promise you it won't happen again,"

That night Marcus and I made up through our sexual fantasies. I was very vulnerable when it came to Marcus. He could tell a white lie and I would believe it. While Marcus was in the shower, his cell phone rang. I was not in the habit of answering his phone, because I felt that it was his way of having privacy from me, but I turned over in the bed and looked at the alarm clock it was almost one' clock in the morning. I kept contemplating if I should answer it. I took up enough nerves to just look at the caller's name on the phone. It showed "Jesse". I was at peace. I knew Jesse was probably calling about something that was about business. So I took the cell phone into the bathroom to Marcus. He looked at the name on the caller ID and smiled at me. Then he kissed me.

"Don't be too long honey," I said

"Oh…it's only Jesse…he probably needs to talk about some business deal," Marcus replied.

"I can call him tomorrow," Marcus said.

"No, honey call him tonight because tomorrow is our day together… no business please," I said as I headed toward the bed.

I could hear a lot of shouting coming from the bathroom as Marcus talked to Jesse. I ignored it, because this was a common practice between them. All I wanted to think about was spending tomorrow with Marcus alone. I didn't care about business. True love had overshadowed my critical thinking process.

CHAPTER 13

Refreshing and cool was the atmosphere on Christmas morning. When I awakened, Marcus was walking in the room with a tray of my favorite breakfast.

"I thought I would surprise you with breakfast in bed" Marcus said as he placed my pillow behind my head to prop me. Marcus then gave me a morning kiss, which always gave me a burst of energy.

"Oh…that is so sweet of you," I said as he placed the tray in front of me,"

"I cooked your eggs just the way you like them…and the…"

"Marcus honey…everything is great…you are going to spoil me,"

"That's what a wife is for…to be loved and spoiled,"

Suddenly, Marcus pulled out a black velvet box in front of me.

"Oh…Marcus…you didn't," I said with excitement.

"You didn't think I was going to let you have Christmas without a present," He replied.

"What is it?"

"Just open it,"

As I opened the box I became speechless. It was a beautiful string of pearls.

"Do you like it?" He asked.

Marcus went on to explain to me that these pearls were his mother's. I felt very special to have them.

"I love them," I replied.

"I wanted to give them to you on our wedding day…but I thought your first Christmas as my wife would be more appropriate,"

Marcus pulled my hair out of the way and clasped the pearls around my neck. My mind was immersing the moment of a queen being serenaded by her prince as he placed the pearls around my neck. Something special happened. I became special, because he gave me something that belonged to his mother. When a man gives you a family heirloom, it brings about a distinctive bond.

"You look beautiful," He said as he kept looking at the pearls around my neck.

I gave Marcus a big hug, and then said," I haven't forgotten about you,"

"You didn't huh…I was beginning to think this was a one-way gift giving…just kidding," He chuckled.

I reached over into the nightstands top drawer and took out a silver box and placed it in Marcus's hand.

"Now it's your turn for surprises…open it," I said.

Marcus opened the box. His eyes lighted up as he pulled out the platinum cuff links.

"These were my grandfather's,"

"These are…"

Marcus was short with words. I didn't know whether he didn't think he deserved them or not. I felt he deserved them and that was all that mattered. He was special to me and that specific bond was already in my heart.

"I love them," He said as he kissed me on the forehead.

"You do…I guess we were thinking the same page when it came to buying a gift,"

"Well you know, great minds always think the same,"

I didn't know where he picked up that saying from, but it sort of made since, especially at the moment.

Marcus was indulging into making me happy on this Christmas day. I didn't know whether to think he was trying to cover up from last night or he was just showing me his true affection.

The morning was great. Marcus and I enjoyed reminiscing about how we met and so on in front of the fireplace in our bedroom. We spent almost the entire morning enjoying each other's company.

That afternoon I began to prepare the table for our first Christmas dinner. Luckily we had no phone calls or doorbell ringing. We were enjoying the moment even if the paparazzi were sneaking around. For the moment it was a peaceful and lovely day.

While Marcus and I were sitting down at the dinner table the doorbell rang. We stared at each other in suspense. I was hoping it wasn't my parents. I stared at Marcus and Marcus responds back with his eyes. Neither one of us wanted to answer the door, but we knew it wouldn't stop ringing until one of us answered it.

We got up from the table and walked into the living room. I was right behind Marcus's footsteps, because I didn't want any surprises walking in on me. Low and behold, I couldn't believe who was standing at my front door.

"Toni!" Marcus said surprised.

I couldn't believe this woman had the nerve to come by my house, especially on Christmas Day.

I thought, "This better be good,"

"Happy Holidays…!" Toni cheerfully shouted as she entered into the room.

"Happy Holidays… to you!" Marcus replied looking toward me. He noticed I didn't say anything. He was gesturing with his eyes. I knew he wanted me to be cheerful, so I went along with his words.

"Toni, Merry Christmas," I said solemnly trying to keep a straight face.

"I didn't mean to interrupt your Christmas…I came by to drop off these important papers for Marcus…I figured he could go over them before he comes into the office on tomorrow,"

"Well, thank you Toni…but couldn't this wait until tomorrow?" Marcus asked.

"Marcus you know how you like to see contracts ahead of time before I negotiate," Toni replied.

Their conversation was beginning to be a two-way street. It was though I was invisible, so I made me a path into their two-way chat.

"Marcus probably won't be in tomorrow," I said trying to control the situation.

"Is that so Marcus?" Toni asked. "…Because I promised to have this contract rapped up by tomorrow evening,"

Marcus noticed that I was not keen on him spending today reading a contract, so he said, "Toni I will take care of it on tomorrow…today I am spending with my wife,"

Toni's face was beginning to feel tight as Marcus held me in his arms and kissed me. I could tell she was holding on to her past lust. I didn't believe she came by to bring papers. I felt she was trying to find a way to see what Marcus was doing for Christmas.

"Well…so that means you won't be in tomorrow?" Toni asked.

"You let me worry about the contract…why don't you go and enjoy your Christmas," Marcus replied as he escorted Toni toward the door.

"But…" Toni said.

"No buts…I will see you later," Marcus said as he closed the door.

I was so proud of my man. He stood up to that house wrecker.

"Marcus thanks for not ruining our day," I said.

"Honey, there is nothing in this world that can take me away from you today," He said.

"You really mean that?"

"No, I was just kidding…of course I meant that,"

Before I could really capture this moment as the truth, Marcus' cell phone rang. He looked at me as he glanced at the cell phone ringing on the table. I know he was contemplating on whether to answer it.

"Well go ahead…you know you want to answer it," I suggested.

"…you sure honey?" He asked.

"What will a phone call do…it won't take you out of the house," I replied.

As Marcus picked up the phone, he had a perplexed look upon his face.

"It's Jesse," He said as he looked at the caller ID.

Then he answered the phone.

"Hey man...what's up?" He asked Jesse.

"I can't do it today...I promised Diamond..."

"Well tough...not today man...I told you,"

Marcus was trying to keep his composure while watching my behavior as he spoke.

"Jesse...let me handle this...I will talk to you later!"

Marcus hurried to get off the phone. His mood had changed from the time we stood at the door hugging in front of Toni.

"Is everything okay?" I asked.

"Yes...everything is okay," Marcus replied trying to keep a straight face.

"What did Jesse want?" I asked knowing that I probably was invading on his privacy.

I covered it up by saying, "Never mind...don't tell me,"

"By the way honey...the dinner was delicious," He said covering his tracks.

I went along with his covering, "Really...I am glad you enjoyed it,"

Marcus took his hands and patted me on the butt and said, "Let's get ready to go and see Big Daddy,"

"But...what... about my parents?" I asked.

"Oh...we can stop by there on our way home from Big Daddy," Marcus replied.

"Well, okay" I replied.

"Then we can spend the entire night bringing in the day after Christmas," Marcus said piercing my eyes with seduction.

"That sounded like a plan to me," I said.

Marcus was the type of man that knew how to play his cards well. I just hope his luck didn't run out, especially with my deck.

When we arrived at Big Daddy's house, he was happy to see us. He had laid out the works when it came to the Christmas dinner. Marcus always told me his dad was a big show off and that he never really approved of anything he did. Marcus felt he was employed by Aseret so his dad could keep tabs on his life. At the dinner table I could feel the tension between the two of them. A person can only fake for so long. Eventually the true person will come out. Sherrie noticed the pressure building up in the room by the silence between Marcus and Big Daddy. So Sherrie initiated a conversation with me.

"So what did my big brother get you for Christmas?" Sherrie asked.

"He gave me something special...his mother's pearls...aren't they nice?" I implied as I was twisting the pears around my neck.

"Yes they are nice," Sherrie replied.

I saw how Marcus's dad was looking across the room at him. He was reluctant to comment on the matter.

"Marcus is so kindhearted," Sherrie said.

"Yes I know...that is why I love him," I said as I reached over to hold Marcus's hand on the table.

Marcus looked at me and smiled, but there was a coldest behind the gesture. I knew he wanted to hurry up and leave, but I wanted him to resolve his differences with his dad. Finally, Marcus spoke, "Dad I am really enjoying this meal,"

"Oh really" Big Daddy said.

"Yes, I really mean that," Marcus said.

Sherrie and I kept watching their conversation like it was a tennis match. We were anticipating the outcome. Suddenly, I was beginning to feel sick all of a sudden. My stomach was boiling and I felt like everything in my stomach was about to explode. While trying to keep myself from vomiting I said, "Will...you please excuse me," I rushed to the bathroom. Sherrie ran behind me to see what was going on.

"Are you alright?" Sherrie asked as she stood over me.

The gurgitation over the toilet continued, while she was agitating me with questions.

"Girl are you alright...you better get this checked out? Sherrie asked.

I turned around at looked at Sherrie and replied, "I'm okay...I felt sick...maybe I am exhausted,"

Then Sherrie said the words that I didn't want to hear for a long time, "Maybe girl you are pregnant,"

I tried to ignore the words that came in my thoughts. I couldn't be pregnant, not now. I couldn't see myself putting my tours on hold or even my career on hold for a baby. I kept thinking in my head maybe it was a virus.

"Sherrie…it could be a virus or something," I replied.

Sherrie wasn't too keen on that answer, but she knew there had to be more than a virus on the way I had been acting, especially my behavior in the past weeks.

"I think you need to get checked out by a doctor…you want me to go with you?" Sherrie asked.

"Oh…no…that's okay, I'll get checked out…trust me," I replied.

If I was pregnant, I didn't want Sherrie to know, in case I decided not to have it, which was an alternative I was contemplating.

"Just let's get back in there before they think something is seriously wrong," I said.

When we returned to the table Marcus and his dad were talking with laughs. I thought maybe they had settled their differences. But when I overheard the last words of the conversation they were only talking about business.

"Are you okay, honey?" Marcus asked looking over at Sherrie.

Before I could say anything Sherrie said, "Oh… she's okay…must be a virus or something,"

"Well, you probably better get that checked out as soon as you can," Marcus replied looking over at me.

"I will…but I think I am just exhausted," I said.

"Maybe she is not eating right," Big Daddy said.

"Yeah…honey are you eating?" Marcus asked.

"I told you I am okay…I will be fine," I replied.

I could tell by Sherrie's facial expressions that she was inquisitive about my answers. I believe she knew there was more to the sickness than a virus, but she always had my back. That's what friends are for. Even though I felt inside alone, I knew Sherrie would be by my side.

CHAPTER 14

After the holidays my career was back on a roll again. Marcus and I were spending less and less time with each other, but in my mind I didn't care, because I felt he wasn't going anywhere since we are married, little did I know about marriages. My career was at the top of the list when it came to making a decision. I continued to be fatigued, but I didn't take the time out to see if I really was pregnant. I was still seeing my menstrual cycle, so I felt it was nothing but exhaustion. Life was a bed of roses for me and I wasn't about to let it wither away.

I begin to indulge into things I had never even thought about. All the morals that my parents taught me were being overtaken with pride and greed. I can remember clearly when the seed of pride and greed took a total residency in me. Marcus and I had a few friends over from the office, of course Toni, and Jesse were included. I enjoyed flirting with Marcus around Toni. I could feel her itching inside to get back at me and I was ready to manipulate any scheme she could think of. It was funny to me because I hadn't felt that in a long time, because I had been so busy with my music. We were in the entertainment room watching T.V., playing the billiard or watching each other acting like clowns.. We were all letting off some steam from the office and getting loaded with alcohol. A habit I just recently picked up. I was sitting in the chair across from Toni. I made it my business to watch every move that she made. Later I found out she wasn't the only one I needed to watch, but for now she is my center focus for deceit. Then there was Cal, my choreographer, who was gay. I always received funny vibes from him, I don't think it's because he is gay; he just didn't jive with me.

"Hey Marcus have you ever had a real thrill?" Cal asked.

When he asked Marcus that question, the sip I had just taken from my wine cooler took a quick slurp in my throat. I thought, "What kind of a question to ask,"

Marcus was playing billiards with Jesse. He was stunned at the question. I could see that he was embarrassed by the question, because he tried his best to ignore him.

"Man…stop fooling around," Jesse replied.

"No…I really mean a thrill…not with women…or men," Cal said.

It was though the camera froze in the room. Everybody was staring at Cal as though he had lost his mind, especially since we knew his preferable gender.

In order to refrain Cal from making a fool out of himself, Marcus said, "Cal don't you see the ladies in here… have some respect,"

"You see…that's what I am talking about…the minute someone goes to talking about a thrill you think I am talking about sex…there are thrills in other things," Cal said.

"If they are coming from you, I rather not hear them," Marcus said as he continued playing his game with Jesse.

"Wait a minute Marcus…give the brother a chance to explain himself," Jesse implied.

"Okay…Cal…Explain yourself," Marcus said holding the pool table stick under his chin.

Cal began to reach into his backpack. He pulled out a clear plastic bag.

"Wait a minute…we are not about to do this in my house," Marcus explained. "I tell you what…I am going to act like I didn't see that,"

Marcus became furious about Cal pulling out a cocaine bag in our house.

"Okay…I catch your drift… you don't like real thrills…I get yah," Cal said.

Marcus was about to throw Cal out of the house, but I saved the day, by telling Marcus to let it go. I didn't want the afternoon ruined, especially when I knew the after affects would fall on me later.

I noticed Toni was very quiet during our office gathering. She was sitting and observing everyone, especially Marcus. She tried to play it off, but I could see her eyes jerking back and forth getting a glimpse of Marcus. When Marcus would lean over to shoot the ball on the table, she was watching his behind like it was her favorite ice cream. The obsession from her was being announced right before my eyes. I began to give her some ice cream to watch. I walked over to Marcus and started massages his shoulders while he was watching Jesse take his move on the table. Then he turned around toward me and we French kissed. I was looking straight into Toni's eyes as my lips and tongue caressed at the moment. Fire was kindling through Toni's eyes, but she played it off by walking over to the bar to get another drink. I decided to put fuel on the fire by going over to the bar. Toni ignored me as she put the ice into her drink. I stood next to her pretending I was waiting to make me a drink, a habit I wish I would have never entertained, because it opened up the door for more costly habits.

"Diamond, are you okay?" Toni asked.

I couldn't believe she had the audacity to ask me if I was okay.

"As okay as I would ever be," I smirked.

"Well good…then we both are okay," Toni said and she took a sip of her drink and trotted her body right in front of Marcus. She was desperate to get his attention. I sat at the bar waiting to see what was going to be her next move. Before I knew it, she was in Marcus' face like she was me.

I said to myself, "Oh know this whore didn't!"

I was even thinking words I never in my life thought to use. I notice Marcus was steady pulling her away, showing me he was not going to entertain her plot. She finally gave in and sat her body in a chair.

"Anybody, hungry?" Marcus asked.

Everybody was agreeing, somehow drinking enhances your appetite, especially in a tense situation.

"Honey, I will make us something from the kitchen," I replied.

"No…stay and enjoy I will tell George (butler) to get it," Marcus said as he walked out of the entertainment room to tell George.

Before I knew it, Toni was gagging from her drink. She looked like she was about to regurgitate. Quickly she ran toward the bathroom, which was outside the entertainment room. I chuckled, "The girl can't hold the hard stuff," What I didn't know, was that Toni was trying to figure out a way to be with Marcus alone.

I knew that regurgitating can take a while in the bathroom, but telling the butler to prepare some snacks was not a task.

I decided to check on Marcus. George the butler was walking toward me with refreshments.

"Where do you want them, mam?" George asked.

"Just take them into the entertainment room...by the way, where is Marcus?" I asked.

"Mam... he went into his office," George replied.

"Thank you, George," I said as I swiftly walked toward the office. Before I entered I heard someone talking. I thought it was Marcus on the phone, because sometimes he has a problem separating pleasure from business. I regressed whether I should enter or knock. Then I heard a female voice. It was Toni's voice. Marcus was in the room with Toni. I stood outside the office for a moment to listen.

"Toni...please leave it alone," Marcus said.

"But you promised me," Toni said.

"I didn't promise you anything but a job,"

"I can't stand the way you pretend around her,"

"Pretend...I love her...now leave me alone,"

"You don't love her...you love me," Replied Toni.

"I do love Diamond...and that's that,"

"Marcus, I never challenged you while you were sharing me with..."

"Look leave that alone...I love you...but I am in love with my wife,"

"Then what about the others...are you in love with them too!" Toni became loud and aggressive toward the conversation.

"Let's just leave that alone...you promised me you would wait," Marcus said.

"Do you know how it feels to wait?" Toni implied.

"I just want you to be patient...that's all,"

"Okay Marcus, we will continue to play your game for now…but sooner or later pay off has got to come forth!"

"I know…and it will be sooner than you think," Marcus said as I heard kissing and smacking lips.

I was furious and reluctant to open the door. When my hand took the doorknob, I felt a jerk from the other side of the door pulling it open.

My mouth could not refrain from saying, "What is this?"

"What is what?" Marcus implied.

"Diamond…it's not what you think," Toni explained trying to hurriedly walk away.

"Then what is it?" I asked.

"Diamond…I thought I would go over a few things with Toni for Monday," Marcus replied.

I didn't know whether to save the evidence for later or spill my guts now. So I decided revenge was a better way of handling Marcus.

"Next time Marcus, please don't mix pleasure with business…let's have some fun," I said as I hugged him.

Marcus' facial expression showed guilt. He didn't know whether I heard their conversation. I enjoyed the upper hand. Revenge became sweeter every minute.

It was getting late. I played the sweet innocent wife game the entire evening. Even though my heart was burning up, I didn't allow it to ruin the night. I began to flirt around with Cal. Knowing that it wasn't going to go any further sexually.

"Diamond, I got something that can ease your mind," Cal said as he eased closer to me on the sofa. He began to whisper softly as he pulled out the bag, "This right here can solve all your problems,"

I was a virgin when it came to any drugs, so I said, "What the heck…one time won't hurt,"

I scanned the room to see if anyone was paying attention to what Cal and I were about to do. Everyone was either on cloud nine or skating on ice, so it didn't matter what I was doing.

I whispered, "Cal not in here…let's go in the guest room,"

Cal replied, "Okay by me…but what if…"

"...don't worry about him, he has been induced to another time zone," I said.

I decided to use one of the guest rooms, because no one really uses it except the maids. If there is a whisk of tainted air no one would notice it.

Marcus was so intoxicated until he wasn't aware that Cal and I were in one of the guest rooms getting blazed. I began to establish a relationship with my marital problem through the white crystalline. From that night on, I was a slave to this costly companion "cocaine".

CHAPTER 15

The next morning I woke up in the bed of the guest room. My head felt as though a ton of bricks had fallen on it. I tried to recapture the night, but I could only remember Cal giving me something to sniff up my nose. I looked down at my clothing. My top was unbuttoned and my jeans were on the floor. I still had under garments on. I thought, "Oh my God…I hope nothing happened between Cal and me," I couldn't live with myself if something did.

Then I became weary and decided to pick up the phone next to the bed to call Cal.

I anticipated that his phone would probably ring for a moment and it did.

Finally he answered, "Hello,"

"Yes… Cal, look, about last night," I said.

"Diamond, don't worry… Nothing happened," Cal said.

"What about my clothes…they were…my buttons…" I said hysterically.

"Nothing happened…trust me…I left you in the room after you became so stoned," Cal explained.

I was relieved when Cal told me these words.

"When can we get together again…we had a great time?" Cal asked.

"I don't think we should…I…I… was wrong about last night," I said stumbling for words.

"Well if you change your mind you know where you can find me..,"

Cal was short and to the point. He hung up quickly and didn't bother to say goodbye. Even though Cal told me nothing really happened last night I was still perplexed about the situation. While putting on my jeans I heard a door close next to the room.

I went toward the door to see who was there. As I opened the door, Jesse was standing in the hallway with one of Marcus's robes on.

"Well, what are you doing here?" I asked.

"Marcus suggested Toni and I stay the night since the evening was such a blast," Jesse replied as he was walking toward the entertainment room.

"Where are Marcus and Toni?" I thought, but before I could complete the interrogation in my mind, Marcus was walking down the hall.

"Hey! Sleepy head," He said as he walked over to kiss me.

Marcus noticed that I was not myself, "Are you okay?"

He replied, "I'll be okay...just give me a few minutes to get myself together,"

I didn't notice I had slept until the afternoon. I wanted to ask Marcus about where Toni slept last night, but the answer probably would have kindled my soul.

"Come on down to the entertainment room...that's where everyone's at...we are going to work on some new lyrics for you to record before the Spring tour," Marcus said.

I speculated that Marcus had recommended Jesse and Toni to stay over for that reason. As I reopened my mind to the situation, I became paranoid about Toni staying the night. I was trying to pinpoint a positive result in my mind, but I could only imagine unfavorable reflections. In the mist of all the turmoil going on in my brain, my body was so irritable, I became nervous and fatigued. The headache was just a small portion of what was about to happen in my body.

I convinced myself that I could be normal for the day, because last night was last night. As I entered into the entertainment room, there was Toni sitting at the bar talking to Jesse and Marcus was watching the football game on T.V. It was one he previously recorded.

"There you are," He said as he turned his chair around, "Are you hungry...I'll have Susan get you something?"

"That's okay," I replied.

Eating food was not my cup of tea at the moment. My stomach felt like a butter churner was turning inside of me. On top of that, my sight was very blurry. I maintained my composure because I didn't want Marcus to be suspicious.

I thought out loud, "I don't have to take this crap!"

Everyone in the room paused in their positions.

"What's going on?" Marcus asked with a mysterious look upon his face.

"I am sick of…never mind," I replied rushing out the door.

I just wanted to be near my mother at this time. I decided to go by the house to see if she had time to spend with me today. I felt all mixed and messed up. I was beginning to believe I was falling apart. All the morals I was taught are beginning to be swallowed up with pride.

When I approached the door, mother was already coming out. I startled her.

"Well, what brings you around this neck of the woods?" Mother asked.

"Stop kidding mom…I just wanted to come and spend some time with you," I replied.

"Make it fast because I promised to meet a special customer at the florist…"

She said, "…I am already running a few minutes late,"

"Perhaps I can ride with you there, and then we can talk," I suggested.

"I guess we can… is there something wrong,"

"I…I don't know what is going on with me," I replied as we got into the car.

Mother was quiet for a moment as she was driving out of the driveway. Before she would give me advice, she was in the habit of meditating, especially when she wanted to say the right words at the right moment. She reminded me of a virtuous woman. Whether it was my father or me, she always wanted to do things that were pleasing in God's sight. My father on the other hand was the opposite, even though he attended church every Sunday, he believed that man should do and get all he can while he have a chance, no matter what's the cost. I resemble my father when it comes to functioning as a human-being.

I kept watching mother as she would thumb her fingers on the steering wheel. Finally' she began to verbally convey her opinion.

"You know Diamond…it's been a while since you been to church," Mother said.

"I know," I reluctantly said.

"You shouldn't be so busy that you can't give God some time,"

"It's not that…I just be so tired,"

"If it wasn't for Him you wouldn't be where you are today,"

"You sure it wasn't the lessons you and father paid for," I sarcastically said.

"It still took God to give us the money and the mind to guide you,"

I just knew my mother was about to get to the point of me needing to spend more time with God, so I said, "You know mother…I am sick and tired of this God stuff,"

"Can you do me a favor and attend church on Sunday…your father and I would really be happy…the Reverend also said he haven't seen you since the day of your wedding,"

"You think going to church will solve my problems?"

"It's a start,"

"Diamond…I don't really know how to say this…"

"Say what!"

"You seem very on edge today, what's wrong?"

"I told you… nothing!" I shouted as my arms were shaking.

"Diamond, you can talk to me,"

"Talk to you…so you can bring up attending church or this God thing!"

Mom perceived that something desperately was going on with me. I kept shaking and trembling. I was craving for an antidote. I continued to ignore it but I became more irritable.

"I am only trying to help," Mother implied.

"If you want to help me…be quiet…I am sick and tired of you telling me what to do…and…church is not for me…I sing R&B… gospel is not for me anymore!"

My behavior became unacceptable, but I had no remorse. I could tell my mother was disappointed in the way I was reacting, but she maintained her stability on her belief and modified the subject.

"Maybe you are coming down with something," Mother said.

"…Could… be," I reluctantly said trying to satisfy my mother's conscious.

"You need to call the doctor, when we reach the florist…it could be some flu or virus," Mother went on and on diagnosing my symptoms.

Being proactive about the situation, I called Cal. I had come to acknowledge that I needed a fix. I reached into my purse for my cell phone. His voicemail kept answering. I kept pressing the button to redial his number, still no Cal. Finally when we reached the florist shop I insisted I needed to see a friend. Mom agreed to let me borrow her car, since it was going to take some time with her customer's appointment.

I continued to try to reach Cal. When I called the agency, they told me he was not in today. I panicked with fear and anxiety. I realized I needed a fix and I needed it fast. The only place I could think of was the main street drag, where all the pips, whores and pushers hung out. I couldn't believe I was willing to stoop that low to feel that magical moment.

While being parked outside one of the main houses for hookers, a guy walked up to my car. My mother's car was a Mercedes. Most people who ride down the main street in a Mercedes are looking for either drugs or a one night stand.

I was frightened by his appearance, but I had a choice, to get fixed or be fixed. I rolled the window down slowly half way as he asked, "You got a dollar I can get?"

I began to manipulate the situation, "I will give you a dollar if you tell me where I can get some crystal,"

"You… not the cops… or sum-thing?" He asked reluctantly.

I rolled down my window all the way and said, "No,"

"Hey...I know you...you that chick...Diamond...I love your music,"

"I'm excited that you do...now who can I talk to,"

"You see that building on the right hand side...the one with the blue paint splashed all over it?"

I nodded, "Yes,"

"On the second floor number 23, tell him I sent you...his name is Shasta Baby Boy"

"Who are you?"

"I am Big James...be sure you tell him that,"

I reached into my purse to give him a dollar. Instead, I gave him a twenty. Big James was all grins. He grabbed the twenty and disappeared quickly.

I was indisposed about going to the building Big James recommended. As I walked up the stairs a creepy disoriented feeling came over me. There was a man sitting at the top of the stairway. His demeanor looked as though he was homeless. I became fearful as I heard frightening sounds coming from behind one of the doors.

I looked up at the man and asked, "Could you tell me where twenty-three is?"

He didn't say a word. I asked him again. Then he pointed to the door on his right that had a three on it. Apparently the two was missing. I was skeptical about knocking on the door, but my body was longing for a relief. A big guy opened the door slightly living just enough space to communicate to me.

"Can I help you?" He asked.

I was hesitated for words.

"Well speak up...I don't have all day," He said.

I felt like a large lump was caught in my throat as I said. "Big James sent me,"

He opened and closed the door quickly as I entered. I was devastated as I looked around the room and saw a young lady sitting at the base of a man's feet. Apparently, she was in her own little world. Also there was others sitting around with thier minds floating into Never land. Then I saw this peculiar looking man smoking a pipe, undressing me with his eyes.

Then I fearfully I said, "I am looking for Shasta Baby Boy,"

"You are looking right at him," The peculiar man stated.

His eyes kept scanning my body up and down. Even though I was almost twenty, I still looked I was fourteen without make-up.

"How old are you?" He said frantically.

"Almost twenty" I replied.

"I don't like having babies in my place…it's not healthy for my business,"

"Well, now you know I am not a baby,"

"What can I do for you?" He said.

"I need something…"

He noticed I was frequently scratching my arms and my legs were shaking unstoppable.

"I can see you need something," He looked at the big guy and chuckled.

"I have money," I stated as I pulled out a hundred dollar bill.

I was a virgin to this type of atmosphere. I didn't know you don't flash money like that, because than the supplier would attempt to drain you dry.

"Fix her up, Tyrease," He said to the big guy.

As Tyrease sat at the table with the white powder in front of me, my body was craving for the crystal as though it was my favorite chocolate food. I couldn't wait to put the taste of cocaine up my nostrils.

While I was snorting, the room began to swirl around as if I was on a merry-go-round. Immediately, I was between two worlds and voices in the room became distanced. I thought I was sailing on the ocean and finally the irritability had ceased. Before I knew it I was out like a lamp.

Hours had passed, before I had awakened. I was still sitting at the table with my head slumped over. I had fallen asleep at the table. As I looked around the room the business was same as usual. I didn't waste any time getting out of that building.

Luckily my mother's Mercedes was okay, especially in the area I had parked. I was trying to think of a legitimate excuse for being late. I went to the shop, but her manager told me my mother had already left. I dashed toward my parent's house.

There in front of her house was a patrol car, Marcus's car and my father's car. I thought, "My excuse is really going to have to be legitimate in order of me to get out of this one,"

When I opened the door, mother, Marcus and the police officer were sitting in the living room.

"Where have you been young lady...we were worried," Mother said.

"Oh...I was..." I said trying to make up a good one.

"I tried calling your cell several times," Marcus said.

"I was...shopping...you know me," I said.

"Well it looks like you won't need me," The Policeman said, as he placed his writing pad in his pocket.

I went to open the door for him. Then he turned around and said: "Young lady next time please call someone,"

"I will officer...thanks," I replied as I closed the door behind him.

Marcus noticed that I was acting strange. My mother kept looking at me without one word of speech.

"Honey, are you okay?" Marcus asked.

I gather they noticed I was reserved when it came to conversation. My mother knew something was wrong. Mothers always see beyond what's naturally in front of them.

"I am okay... please stop worrying," I replied.

In order to cease the coldness I was feeling in the room, I glanced at my watch and said, "Well I better get going,"

Then I rushed out noticing the coldest of my mother's eyes was tracking every step I was making. My good morals were steady declining. Not only was I an addict, now I am becoming a liar. It was scary especially when I had begun to become comfortable with my deceitful actions.

As I was getting into my car, Marcus yelled, "Wait Diamond,"

At the moment, I didn't want to converse with him, so I pretended I didn't hear him. Before I could pull the car out of the driveway he stood in front of the car. I knew then that I couldn't ignore him.

I stopped the car and got out.

"What's wrong with you Diamond?" He asked with a deeply concerned look in his eyes.

"Nothing...I just have things to do," I replied.

"I know something is wrong...you want to talk?"

"I told you...I am okay,"

Then Marcus took my hands and grasped them into his hands. He stared deeply into my eyes and said, "Honey I love you...I don't want anything to happen to you,"

"I love you too...I'm okay...I just went shopping...now everyone thinks something is wrong,"

"We are just concerned,"

"Marcus...really I am okay,"

"Okay...then let's go home...don't worry about the studio today... just...you and me alone today,"

"You really mean that...because lately you have been spending a lot of time with Toni, Jesse and who ever,"

"You don't have to worry about that...they have all left...I promise you I will consult with you next time," I implied.

Somehow Marcus was able to soothe my conscious for a moment. I was beginning to become someone I didn't even know myself. Personally, I was becoming immensely a Dr. Jekyll and Mr. Hyde.

CHAPTER 16

Even though I had acquired a taste for cocaine, this wasn't the only thing that was cultivating my conscious. I had come to a consensus that I needed to see a doctor, because for weeks, I was beginning to feel sick every morning. I was reluctant to go see my family doctor, because of the poison I was feeding my system daily. The only person I knew I could trust was mom. She gave me the name of a doctor that was not known for feeding the media. She didn't ask any questions, but I knew she probably already figured out my prognosis.

I visited the doctor and wasn't startled by the results of my testing. I was over four weeks pregnant. I couldn't tell by my body, because I had become very thin due to not eating. I didn't know whether to tell Marcus or get rid of it. I wasn't ready for a baby, nor was I ready to become a Mother. I began to think about ways of getting rid of the baby without anyone having knowledge I was pregnant. Even though I knew this thought was wrong, I didn't feel any remorse about it because it was all about me. If I kept this baby, I would have to put my career on hold, while Marcus continues with his life as usual. I couldn't take that chance. This was a difficult decision for me, so I decided to talk to mom about it, but I gave her the information as though it was someone else needing an answer to the situation. Somehow you can't fool Mother's instinct.

It was one of those days I didn't feel like being bothered by anyone, but the higher being knew that I needed some answers, so he sent mom by the house. We were sitting in the living room. The conversation was centered on me for the time being.

"Diamond what did the doctor say?" Mom asked.

"Oh…it's some virus or something," I replied.

"Are you sure…you look to be a little pale," Mom implied.

Little did she know; I was pale because I needed something, and I needed it bad. Cal usually supplied me with all the cocaine I needed but he was late delivering it today. My mind was focused on getting my antidote for this edgy feeling attacking my body. I wanted my mom to hurry up and get to her point, because I didn't want Cal to bump into her. I always knew the right time to have him come by. He always came when Marcus is at the office. Cal would call before he would come by. Anticipation was all over me as I listened to mom.

"Child you better take care of yourself," Mom said as she looked into my eyes strangely.

"I know this is more than a virus…you can't fool me," She said continuing to try to lure information.

"Your eyes look very gleam…are you sure you're telling me everything," Mom asked.

"Mom you're looking too deep into this," I replied as I got up to put a magazine on the coffee table. Mom was watching me closely as I stood up.

"I'll bet you are pregnant?" Mom stated with boldness.

When she said those words, I was astounded. She had hit the nail on the head.

"Why…do you say that?" I asked.

"Girl, you know I am aware of how a woman looks when she is expecting…with attitudes…and your body is looking frail," Mom replied.

"Okay…I admit…I am pregnant, but not for long," I said.

"What do you mean…not for long," Mom said.

"Just like I said…not for long,"

"You are not planning on doing what I think you…?"

"…Mom I can't have this baby," I replied.

"What does Marcus have to say about this?"

"He doesn't know,"

"Well, aren't you going to tell him?"

"No…well I don't know…I am not ready…I am just not ready,"

"You should have thought about that before you got married,"

"But I was taking precautions, the pill,"

"Don't you know the pill is not always security…but that is water under the bridge…I need to know what you're going to do."

We continued to go back and forth with words. I was extremely tired of battling about the issue.

"You know what mom, this is between Marcus and me…so let me handle this," I said trying to force my mom to drop the matter.

"You're right this is between you and Marcus…but it is going to be between you and God if you get rid of this child…because I know what you thinking,"

Before I could defend, the words that came out of mom's mouth, my cell phone rang. It was Cal. He was checking to see if the coast was clear. I knew if he came at this moment that my mom would be inquisitive about his visit, especially knowing his character. I decided to tell Cal to wait about thirty minutes before he came by, that would give me enough time to talk mom right out the door.

"Was that Marcus?" Mom asked.

"Mom!!!…," I replied.

"Oh, I am sorry…I keep forgetting that you are not a baby anymore,"

"Whether I am a baby or not, I don't think it is any of your business who is calling my cell phone,"

I could tell by the look on mom's face that she was surprised I was talking to her like that. But I was aggravated by her persistence. She didn't know that I was dealing with more than just being pregnant.

Mom ignored my behavior and said, "Baby, you need to get some rest…pray about the situation, I am sure God will give you the right answer…but you need to tell Marcus,"

As mom walked toward the door, I could sense she knew that I was determined to have it my way, no matter what God said. She kissed me on the jaw and walked out the door. I was relieved, not because she left, but because finally I can get the medicine I needed from Cal. Before I could call Cal the doorbell rang. I thought it was Cal but it was Sherrie.

She didn't give me a chance to tell her I was busy. She shoved the door open and walked in.

"Girl I got to tell you something," Sherrie said excitedly.

"What...I..." I said trying to tell her I really didn't have time to listen.

"Wait...let me get my thoughts together," Sherrie said walking over to the sofa to sit down. She was rambling through her purse.

"I got something to tell you," She said continuing to go through her purse.

"What?" I asked as I watched Sherrie pull out her compact to powder her face and refresh her lipstick.

"Give me a minute," She said.

I kept looking at the clock on the wall, because I knew Cal would probably be ringing the doorbell any minute.

"Hurry up...tell me, don't keep me waiting," I said.

"You know that dress I was looking at a week ago?" She said.

"Yes..." I replied.

"Well, after they sold that one, they finally got another one in, remember the dress that Cindy had on stage...well I got it...I finally had one imported to me,"

This was just like Sherrie, all this excitement about a dress.

"I know you didn't ride over here to announce about a dress," I said.

"It's not just a dress...it is the dress!" She said with her eyes bucked open.

"What is it with you and clothes?" I asked.

"I love clothes they make you feel like you are somebody,"

"You're already somebody...you are the daughter of Aseret's Talent Agency...what more do you need,"

"I need my own identity,"

"Well do something with your life other than shopping,"

"That's all I know...ever since I could remember that's all I was good at," Sherrie said.

"I know you have something you are good at...go to the college... or something," I said trying to rush the conversation.

"Sherrie I hate to rush you, but I have something I need to do," I said rubbing my arms with anxiety.

"Okay…we can get together later…if not I will call you," Sherrie said walking out the door.

While Sherrie was walking out the door Cal was driving up. Luckily Sherrie didn't see him bring in my package. I ran out to the car to meet him.

"You got it?" I asked as I leaned over the driver's window.

"Yeah" Cal replied as he handed me the package.

I was paranoid as I looked around the area of my neighborhood. I was making sure the area was clear of Sherrie and other bystanders. Then I reached into my pants pocket and handed Cal the money.

"See you later…enjoy," Cal said as he drove off.

The package in my hand felt like a million dollars, even though I was used to having millions this million was irreplaceable at the moment. I couldn't wait to go into my guest room and relieve my pain.

As I was walking into the house Susan the maid stopped me. I hid the bag under my blouse.

"Mrs. Singleton, could I ask you something?" She asked.

I hesitated to say yes, because I didn't know if the question was related to what I had under my blouse.

"Why…yes, go ahead," I replied.

"I was wondering if I could have the afternoon off, because my mother is ill and needs me to take her to the doctor," She said.

The perfect moment had come. I didn't have to hide in the guest room, especially today.

"Sure you can have the afternoon off…and don't hesitate to call me if you need anything…let me know how your mother is doing,"

"Thank you Mrs. Singleton," She replied as she walked toward the room to get her things.

I murmured, "Thank you…Susan!"

Finally, I was able to have the house to myself. I walked over to my stereo center and placed my favorite song on "Time over Ribbons," I sat at the table in my entertainment room and began to place the powder on the table and cut it with a razor blade. While placing the white powder in my nostrils, I couldn't think of anything but the moment. A hazed feeling came over me. It felt right and it felt good. I had no more mental pain attacking my mind. Every problem I had was diminishing into a fantasy world. The thought of me being three weeks pregnant didn't dawn on me at all. I didn't care. It was all about the moment I was indulging myself into and before I knew it I was slain into a world of delusional mischief. I could hear my cell phone ringing but I didn't have the strength to move quick enough to answer it. The music from the stereo was sounding like an antique recording on slow speed. I was physically and emotionally high.

I was able to get to the cell phone, but it had stopped ringing. A few minutes after that the house phone rang, I was fortunate to be right next to it.

"Hello" I said with a low-keyed voice.

"Are you okay?" Marcus asked on the other end of the phone.

"Yeah...I was sleeping," I replied trying to keep him from decoding something was wrong.

"I just wanted to let you know that I will be home early today...I want to take you out on the town to celebrate," He said.

"What?" I asked holding my head to keep it from falling.

"I said, I just...oh never mind...I'll see you when I get there,"

"What...get here..." I said. But before I could understand or finish my words Marcus had hung up the phone.

I was trying to decipher what Marcus was talking about, but all I could remember was the word "celebrate". Before I could attempt to call him back, my eyes were heavy and was pulled into the land of dreams.

CHAPTER 17

"Diamond, wake up!" Marcus shouted.

It was difficult for me to open my eyes. I could hear Marcus' voice repeatedly bouncing against my ears. He was trying to awaken me.

"Diamond, wake up.....what in God's name have you been doing!" Marcus shouted as he pulled my chin up and removed my hair from my face. My body was so limped until all I could do was lie down. Every attempt Marcus made to get me to sit up was useless. Finally, my eyes began to focus on his face.

"Diamond....what is this stuff doing in my house?" Marcus furiously asked as he removed the cocaine from the table and walked over to the sink across from the bar. He then washed the cocaine down the drain.

"What...what?" I asked groggily.

"I can't believe you are doing this to me," He replied as he stood over me with the empty bag in his hand.

"Will you leave me alone?" I asked.

"I'll leave you alone alright...I know it's that Cal...that is why he is always trying to see if I am going home," Marcus replied.

"It's not Cal's fault...I am able to handle my own decisions," I said.

"Apparently you don't ....especially with my child," He said abruptly.

I couldn't do anything but freeze in my thoughts. I was beginning to become angry at my mom. I knew she had to be the one to tell him.

"You don't know what you're talking about?" I said trying to throw the conversation in another direction.

"Yeah...well the doctor does," He replied.

"I don't know what you talking about....furthermore....I'm going to my room," I said as I walked past Marcus. Before I could take another step, Marcus jerked me by the arm and forced me to sit down.

"You are going to listen to what I have to say...you thought you could get over me, Marcus Singleton the CEO...don't you know that I know people...you have some explaining to do, and fast," Marcus said in a threatening tone.

"It was only a little coke," I said justifying my actions.

"A little...you probably been doing this for a while, that's why you are always fatigued and...look at you...you look like the wind is about to blow you down...are you going to let all of this go down the drain?" He asked as he looked around the room.

I was stunned for words. There was nothing I could do or say to correct what had just happened.

"Do you know you are poisoning our baby....by the way... the doctor called my assistant and left a message about your prenatal prescription...I did the pleasure of picking it up from the pharmacy?"

"Marcus...I don't know what to say,"

"You can start out by telling me how long you have been snorting cocaine,"

"How long...what you mean how long?"

"Ah...come on Diamond, who do you think you are kidding?" asked Marcus.

"Alright...it's been since December!"

"Well we better get you into a rehab before the tabloids get a wisp of this information...is anyone else other than Cal aware of this?"

"Not that I know,"

"What about your mom?"

"I...guess not...I don't know,"

"Well...think hard, you have just bought us into a fine mess... and you being knocked up doesn't help the situation," Marcus said as he paced around the room nervously.

"I don't know why you're worrying about it, you are the one who seemed to not find time to spend with me," I said.

"Don't try to place this distress upon me, don't you see that drugs can tear your career to shreds...not just your career, what about our child?" Marcus implied walking around the room rubbing his head continuously.

"What do you want me to do Marcus?" I asked.

"I don't...what do you want me to do? He replied.

"I...don't know...I just don't know!" I shouted with confusion having a ball game in my head.

"I tell you what...I got...never mind," Marcus shouted as he grabbed his keys off the table and quickly slammed the door.

I didn't know whether to think if Marcus was walking out on me or he was going to cool off. One thing for sure, I knew I was the problem. There was nothing for me to do but to call mom. I walked over to the bar to get a drink. When I poured the drink I felt a relief, but when I began to bring the glass to my lips I slammed it down on the table. I was adding fuel to the fire. I didn't need to add any bonuses to my situation. I reached over to the phone to call mom, but before I could pick up the receiver the doorbell rang. I could hear mom's voice talking to the butler. A sense of refuge was kindling my soul as mom reached the room.

"Well what's going on with you?" Mom asked.

I tried to pretend like I didn't know what she was implying.

"What you talking about?" I asked.

"Marcus called me on his cell and told me I needed to get over here...what's going on?" Mom implied.

"I'm okay...I'll be alright," I said.

"Well you don't look alright...and I know you are expecting," Mom said as she pulled me close to her to talk to her. As I was looking down trying to not let her look me into the eyes, mom pulled my chin up and stared directly into my pupils.

"You can fool anybody but a mother...you thought I didn't know you were pregnant, all those fatigue moments...and your face is shining like a full moon," Mom said as she continued to stare at me.

I couldn't lie to my mother, so I replied, "You're right...I am pregnant,"

"More than that…look to me, you are spaced out…you done got yourself hooked on the devil himself," Mom said.

"Ah…mom it's not the devil, everything that is not right is the devil to you…I just thought I would try a little coke for fun…,"

"For fun…don't you know that you are putting your career on the line…not to say what you are doing to my grandchild, you better get you some help… and fast?"

Tears were streaming down my face as I was begging my mother to help me. I had put myself in a bind and didn't know how to come out of it. I was on the edge of losing everything including my true love, Marcus.

"Mom, please help me," I said

"Honey, I can't help you until you help yourself," Mom replied.

"But what can I do?"

"First you need to admit you have a problem…looking at your condition, you have a serious problem,"

"Okay…Okay… I admit I have a problem,"

"Well that's a start, now what do you want to do about it?

"I want Marcus and me to be like we were before all of this,"

"Diamond, what are you going to do to get there…remember you have a baby inside of you, a life that God has given you and Marcus,"

"I will come clean,"

"And how are you going to do that?'

"I'll quit as of right now…I am done with the crystal,"

"Honey, you think it's that easy…don't you know you are now a junkie…without help junkies only come clean when they are found dead somewhere…you really need to go to a rehab,"

"But if I commit myself to a rehab my career could go down the drain,"

"And if you don't your career is already down the drain…it's not just your career…think about that child you are carrying…don't you know you can cause this child to be born with an addiction or even worse with a deformity?"

"I don't think Marcus will ever forgive me for what I have done,"

"In the state you are in now you can't worry about how Marcus feels…that man loves you…you need to show him how much you love him by getting your life back in order,"

"What should I do?"

"First thing to do is to call Marcus and talk to him, if you need me I will be a phone call away…I want you to know that I love you Diamond and I am not giving up on you…I trust you to make the right decision," Mom said as hugged me.

"I needed that, what would I do without you?" I asked.

"…Trust God," Mom replied as she led me to sit down on the sofa.

As I was wiping the tears from my face I said, "I thank God for you,"

It was as though my mom had read my mind as she said, "Don't worry about your dad I will handle him…just get well,"

While mother was walking out of the room I could feel the warmth of her spirit securing me like a blanket on a chilly day. Mother was the symbol of God giving me the assurance that everything would be okay. Reality kicked in and I was ready to do whatever it took to gain my integrity back.

The entire day I was anticipating Marcus entering the door. It was past midnight and there was no Marcus. I had prepared myself for bed when I heard the door downstairs open. I was reluctant about how to relate to Marcus, so I pretended that I was asleep in the chair next to my bed. I heard Marcus open the bedroom door. I expected him to not talk to me. Suddenly I felt him moving toward the chair, then he kneeled down in front of me pulling my hair from around my face. I opened my eyes while he was beholding the beauty he saw in me.

Then Marcus said sobbing, "We'll get through this honey…I love you,"

My eyes were becoming cloudy with water as I replied, "I love you too,"

I held Marcus's head in my lap close to the area where our baby was resting inside of me. I thought, "True love really covers a multitude of faults,"

CHAPTER 18

Life is like vapor. You have to grab it while it is still yet visible. That is what I decided to do when I entered a six month rehab program. I was now eight months pregnant and longing to be with my family again. My pregnancy was a great cover up while my career was on hold. Only the immediate family knew that I was in the rehab. Big Daddy had great connections which made sure everything about the rehab was sealed. My parents never ceased from writing and coming by to see me. The entire Singleton family was very supportive also, not because of my singing career, but because a new Singleton was about to enter the family. The ultra-sound showed that I was having a girl. The family didn't care whether it was a girl or a boy, as long as the child was healthy. The doctors said I was lucky to have received help when I did, because it could have damaged the fetus. I didn't take it as pure luck, but I know that the eyes of God were watching me, even when I am not aware of his divine care.

The day my little girl came into the world gave me another reason to believe that God never gave up on me. While I was in the delivery room going through all the life pains of giving birth, reality kicked in showing me how very vital life is to this world. As I held my baby girl in my arms, teardrops began to fall upon her face. The tears that I wiped were a shadow imitating my baby girl as a purification symbol. Marcus's face had a glow upon it that was unexplainable as he looked into our daughter's eyes. It was a Kodak moment for us and no one could steal the vibrate energy it bestowed upon us.

Marcus kissed me as he moved my sweaty hair from my forehead. I looked at Marcus as though we had produced the greatest product from our love. Marcus even laid a yellow rose next to my shoulder in the bed. As I looked at my daughter I would glance back and forth at Marcus and her beholding the beauty of the moment. I couldn't take my eyes off this beautiful gift that God had given us. My daughter had the cutest little ears and on her earlobes was a birth mark shaped like a heart, right in the place you would probably pierce them. She was the perfect baby made from true love. When the nurse took our daughter from us, I didn't want to cease the moment. I held on to her little body tightly as the nurse insisted to take her.

I sleep practically the entire day. I was exhausted and really into another world with meds. I couldn't believe that I would sleep the entire day without the nurses tugging on me to tend to my daughter. I hadn't even given her a name yet, but I am going to name her "Grace", because it was God's grace and mercy that brought me through. When I awakened I continued to watch the door for the nurses to bring my Grace in the room to be feed. I believed in the old fashion way, breastfeeding. It was strange how in every room I could hear babies crying or mother's talking baby talk to them, but my Grace was not in my room.

Finally, a nurse came into my room. I asked, "When can I see my daughter?"

The nurse was very reserved with her answer, "The doctor will be in soon,"

I wasn't asking about the doctor. I wanted to see my Grace.

Then I said again, "When am I going to feed my daughter?"

That is when the nurse rushed out for the doctor. I was beginning to become hysterical. My maternal instinct was initiating for the first time. I reached over the rail of the bed to call Marcus, but before I could touch the receiver, Marcus and the doctor walked in.

I didn't give them a chance to say anything. I blurted out, "Where is my baby?"

Marcus replied, "Calm down honey everything is okay,"

The doctor said, "There were some complications with your daughter,"

I didn't want to hear anymore. A lump in my throat implicated a warning of something bad has happened to my Grace. I didn't want to hear anymore. As the doctor spoke, I felt as though I was a million miles away from the situation.

Especially, when the doctor said that my daughter was not going to be normal, due to a lack of oxygen to her brain. The doctor walked out of the room to give Marcus and me space to visit the situation. But the thing that put the icing on the cake was that Marcus suggested that we put our daughter in rehabilitation for mentally challenged kids. I was devastated by the idea. I couldn't look at Marcus's mouth even when he said it.

Suddenly I felt the sympathy spirit kindle out of his soul for his satisfaction.

Marcus said, "Diamond, I know this doesn't feel good, but we can have other kids,"

I said, "Marcus you make this situation look like one of your business deals…if you don't get it right the first time to try again,"

Marcus sympathetically said, "I am thinking about you…and…"

I said, "No, you're not…my Grace is not the perfect child you wanted, so you give her up like that.

"Tell me something Diamond, do you have the time and energy to take care of a child like that,"

"Oh…now she is …a child like…don't' you know our love created this child,"

"Maybe if you would have kept your body away from that powder…,"

"….Don't you blame this on me…Grace is our blood, made from our love, or intimate moments," I implied.

"That's not what I am talking about…wait a minute…you already named her?" Marcus responded.

"Why not, she's our child,"

"You know what, I am done, done with the situation…I can't do what I want without permission from you"

As Marcus stormed out of the room, I began to cry. My insides felt like I had been crushed to the maximum. I didn't know where to begin when it came to praying, because I had failed God in so many ways. I wondered if God was punishing me for my past behavior. I sat in my bed flipping channels on the T.V. over and over. Even though my eyes were focused on the T.V. My mind was far from the picture. After a considerable length of time, I left my room to go and see my Grace. As I approached the window of the infants, I looked around for baby Singleton. I scanned the room carefully, but did not see my Grace. Finally I walked over to the nurses' station and asked, "Could you tell me where my baby is?"

The nurse replied, "What is your baby's name?"

I said, "Singleton...Singleton is the last name...but I am going to name her Grace,"

The nurse looked at the charts of the babies. Then another nurse came in. I saw her whispering to her. I watched every move they were making. Then the nurse called for the head nurse. While I was waiting, I could feel the tension coming from the staff. Then I overheard the nurse say, "This is a delicate situation...we'd better let the doctors take care of this,"

At that moment I felt an emptiness that I could not explain. I had discerned that Grace was far away from me. Without delay the head nurse and doctor confronted the situation with me. They told me that my daughter had been adopted immediately and the records were sealed. Marcus had declared me incompetent and was able to quickly connect to his personnel clouts to give up Grace for adoption without my permission. I was furious and crazed until the doctor gave me a sedative. All I could think about was my little girl being cared for by a stranger who knew not the love I possessed when she was conceived.

CHAPTER 19

During next day I was very gloomy, not because of the side effects of the sedative, but because my Grace was gone. I began to have a pity party with myself. My past events of selfishness were eating my soul alive. I was really getting angry with myself and especially God. I could not believe God would allow my baby to be taken from me. Most of all I didn't think Marcus would do such a thing to me. Because of the depression that began to possess me; a psychiatrist came to see me.

"Mrs. Singleton how are you today?" The psychiatrist asked.

"I really don't know," I replied.

"I am aware of your situation, so I am recommending that you seek counseling when you are discharged,"

"Can I ask you something?"

"Sure,"

"Why do I have to seek counseling for something I didn't do?"

"Because anytime someone goes through a severe trauma we are required to give them a follow-up…I know losing a child can cause a great set back on one's life, especially you…you see I know you are a career woman, my daughters love your CD's…but you can't let it get the best of you…that is why I am recommending you seek counseling,"

"Will I ever get over it?"

"Time can only tell, just seek counseling…now do you need me to prescribe you any medication to sleep?"

"No…I…I'll be alright,"

"What about…are you crying a lot?"

"Doctor if you were in my shoes, you probably would be crying too,"

"I am not saying that to be sarcastic, I am concerned…you just get some rest,"

"How long do I have to stay in here…since there is no baby?"

"I don't know, you will need to check with your physician…you take care of yourself, time has a way of healing the deepest things,"

As the psychiatrist was walking out the door, I was determined to get myself together and maybe find my Grace, but before I could start the plan, lightning struck my thoughts as Toni walked into my room with flowers in her hand. She had this look upon her that you just can't place your finger on it, but you just know there is a hidden agenda. As Toni placed the flowers on the counter next to my bed, she began fix up some words to say.

"Hey, girl!" Toni shouted.

"Hi," I said very quietly. I was on the look-out for snares and stuff.

"Well, you finally will be able to get back in shape…and get your music on a roll again," Toni implied.

She was going on and on. That was Toni she always had to get the center of attention.

"Yes…but right now I need to rest," I said.

"Girl, I heard you gave your baby up for adoption," She bluntly said.

That was just like Toni she could make you feel guilty in the midst of salvation.

"That was best…you know, you can't take care of that kind of a child with the career you have," She implied.

A kindle of fire was burning inside of me, until I wanted to extinguish it all over her body until she turned to ashes. Thank God, it was just a thought.

"Toni how do you know what I am capable of doing…have you any children?" I asked.

"No…and I don't want any, they just slow you down….that's what would have happened to you, trust me…I know," Toni replied.

"By the way, how did you know my baby was up for adoption?"

"Marcus told me he was upset and everything...so I soothed his pain by talking to him,"

Toni knew how to put spitting fire upon my soul. Just the thought of her soothing my husband, gave me a desire to take her skinny neck and choke it. I kept my composure while biting my tongue and I decided to be nice, considering she did take out time to visit.

"So what did Marcus tell you?" I asked.

"He said something like, the doctors said his daughter may not function as a normal child and he was hoping to be able to enjoy his child and not have to be concerned about a sick child," Toni replied, as if she had the upper hand with Marcus.

"Really...go on,"

"Listen Diamond, I have no right telling you what Marcus told me...talk to your man yourself!"

"Seem like you did all the talking for me!"

"Diamond I am not the one that came crawling to him, he came crawling to me...If I was you..."

"Well you're not me...you have anything else you want to say?"

"Not really, but then again...be careful because you could lose Marcus...he was looking out for your well-being,"

"And who's well-being are you looking out for Toni?"

Toni gave me a slick snicker as she said, "I just came by to check on you...I'll tell Marcus you are okay,"

I wanted to let Toni have it, as she pranced out of my room, but what would I have profited from it. It would only help her crawl back into the arms of Marcus, knowing this is the most vulnerable time in our relationship I wouldn't dare instigate it. Before I could think again the phone rang, it was Sherrie.

"Diamond, be strong girl," Sherrie said with a comforting voice.

"I'll try to," I softly replied.

"You know I don't like the hospitals and stuff, did you receive my flowers?"

"Of course I did, yours, Big Daddy and others…it kind of look like a funeral home in here,"

"I want to let you know that Big Daddy and I do not agree with Marcus's decision, but Marcus always had the big head…you take care of yourself…if you need me to do anything for you, I am a phone call away,"

"I know Sherrie, you are so good to me, you and your father…what I need now is your prayers, and I am really going through,"

"I'll make sure I pray for you…I know how it feels to lose someone you love, but I know that God is capable of filling the void,"

"Thanks again for being there for me…I got to go… I think I hear someone coming,"

"Love ya girl,"

"Love you too,"

Suddenly, I heard a knock on the wall of my doorway. A cheerful mist flew into my room as my dad and mom walked in. I thought, "What perfect timing". Tears began to form in my eyes as I saw my parents consoling demeanor. My mom rushed to hold me in her arms while my father beside her was holding the both of us. I could feel the disappointment they were withholding inside.

Mom kept whispering to me, "Its okay baby….it's okay,"

Finally, I was able to express the darkness I was feeling inside. Somehow when I am around my parents, especially my mother it felt like God was with me. Dad didn't have much to say. he was short for words. Mom is usually the one who has the comforting words that not only softens your pain, but also gives you the strength to endure. Heavy drops of tears were flowing from my eyes. I was pulling every pinch of hurting energy from my mind, until I couldn't do anything but let go.

Then I heard the voice of an angel say, "God's plan is in everything,"

I heard it again, "God's plan is in everything, but everything is not God's plan,"

By surprise the words of wisdom were coming from my dad not my mom.

Then he said it a third time, "God's plan is in everything, but everything is not God's plan," even mom was astounded at the words. It was as though we had heard from heaven. Then dad explained to me that some things that happen in our life are not God's divine will but his permissive will. God does not make us do anything. Even though we were born with a purpose for God, he doesn't make us do it. He gives us freedom of choice. Through the choices we make it gives God and opportunity to direct our path toward his will for our lives. The hurt and pain often comes to confirm God's will for our life. Hurt and pain are no more than compasses for our lives. While dad was explaining this to me, I began to realize that my baby has a purpose just like me.

Then I thought aloud, "Maybe God thought I wouldn't be a good mother,"

Mom replied, "Don't beat up yourself, you will come through this all…in due time you will come to know the reason for this very moment,"

"But Marcus didn't tell me he was going to do this to me," I said.

"I know honey…but you must focus on you…in due time all of the pieces will come together," Dad said.

"Your dad and I think it would be best, but it is up to you, if you came home for a little while until you and Marcus can iron this out," Mom said.

"I know you mean well, but I must face this with Marcus by myself, he is my husband and I must find a way to forgive his actions….because I love him," I said.

My parents knew how much love can cover a multitude of faults. They wouldn't dare come between the love and desire I have to be with my husband. My decision was to go home and face the demons I had stirred up in my home.

CHAPTER 20

The day I was released from the hospital, Dad and Mom came to pick me up. Marcus claimed that he had a business deal to wrap up. I knew he didn't want to face me, because of what he had done. Even though I told my parents that I wanted to go to my house, they kept insisting that I live with them for a while. I just couldn't see allowing Marcus with freedom to do what he pleased and I was standing alone in this situation. I believe, since he started my pain he should deal with it and not hide from it. That was my answer to the situation. So I returned home to my home. When I reached the door the butler was pleased to see me, and the maid was already prepared to take care of me. Marcus also hired a nurse to be with me 24 hours. By the look of things, Marcus already knew the outcome of my distress.

As I entered the entertainment room, I opened up the piano and began to place my fingers on the keys. Even though I was looking at the keys, my heart was far from the purpose. I sat at the piano and peck on the keys softly. I could not focus on anything but the pain that was protruding from my soul. A part of me was missing, it was though I had left something behind and there was nothing I could do about it. I continued to use my fingers on the piano to express my feelings inside. The more I pressed my fingers on the keys; I began to become the person consoled with melody that I was making with the keys. The energy that was releasing from my fingers had excelled any composition I had ever written. I felt the agony from my soul at liberty. I continued to indulge into the musical piece that was being created in my spirit. The atmosphere of the room portrayed an angel playing a harp while ministering to the heavenly body. It was the most powerful setting I had ever felt. It was though God himself was taking out time to heal the brokenness that had stolen the joy I had previously possessed.

While I continued being emersed into the melody, I could feel the presence of someone watching. As the feeling became stronger, I indulged into the moment stronger than ever. Suddenly, a hand rested upon my shoulder, and I glanced up. It was Marcus with tears in his eyes. Immediately, my fingers stopped playing and took a hold of Marcus's hand on my shoulder and I pulled it up to my jaw. The warmth of his hands kindled the fire that was trying to cease in my heart. I couldn't do anything but grab the moment with all sincerity. Before I knew it, we were feeling the moment of love with our lips smacking each other continuously. We couldn't pardon from the moment. The love we shared had dominated the ill feelings I had at the moment.

Marcus looked into my eyes and said, "Honey, I love you,"

I didn't want to hear any excuses. I just wanted Marcus to hold me in his arms, so I put my lips upon his lips and felt the ecstasy of intimacy flowing from the heated air from his nostrils upon my face.

Than Marcus pulled away and said, "I have to talk to you,"

He insisted that we talk. I wasn't ready to argue with Marcus about the situation. I really wanted to pretend it never existed.

"Not now…please not now!" I shouted

"Honey sooner or later you have to face the truth," Marcus said.

"I know…but…" I said.

"I understand honey, but I need to get this off of my conscious,"

"Well, if you insist,"

"Diamond, what can I say to make it better?"

"You can start by telling me why you gave our daughter away,"

"Well…I knew you couldn't take care of a sick child and I just don't have the time," Marcus replied.

"Sick child or not…she is our child…made from our love…how could you do that to me?"

"I was between a rock and a hard place when it came to making the decision,"

"That's not the point, don't you think you should have given me a chance to decide,"

"I guess I should have…but all I could think about was you trying to take care of a disabled child while trying to keep a very prominent career,"

"You know what Marcus…you're always thinking about yourself… How do you know if I wanted to continue singing, I could have composed and written lyrics for a while,"

"But it is not about that, it is about seeing you on stage, contracts, tours and all other assets that spring from the business,"

I became silent for a moment and said, "Now I see…it is all about you,"

"No baby…it's about you," Marcus implied.

"No, it is not…because if it was…you would have allowed me to make the decision with you!" I explained yelling from the top of my head.

"Well it's done! What you going to do about it!"

I was astounded at the attitude Marcus had about the situation. I could no longer look at him in the face without wanting to get revenge.

"I tell you what Marcus, You stay out of my way and I will stay out of your way!"

"So that's the way you want this to end, what are you trying to tell me?"

"I am saying I need my space…please just go,"

Marcus stormed out the room and slammed the front door. He slammed the door so hard to it sounded like the hinges fell off.

The strange thing about it, I really didn't mean the words I said out of my mouth. I was so much in love with Marcus until I could put syrup on his toes and suck them dry. I don't know why I came at Marcus in the way I did. Sometimes love will make you do strange things. I thought, "Now I have really made the ditch deeper than it was,"

Being angry can cause you to say things that you really don't mean, and it is going to take a lot to clear up.

This time when I sat at the piano, there was no melody, no pecking the keys and no atmosphere of success. I had nothing but remorse for what I had done, and Marcus really wanted to clear things up with me. I didn't realize I was giving him an opportunity to run into another woman's arms.

CHAPTER 21

It's has been two weeks since the moment of my distress with Marcus. We live in the same house but pretend to be strangers as we go about our daily activities. I couldn't wait until the month was over so that I can go back into the studio and become productive again. Again, it was all about me. Somehow I was no better than Marcus when it came to selfishness.

While I was reading in my bedroom, one of my past demons began to hunt me. I heard Cal downstairs talking to the butler. He had come by to pick up something Marcus had forgotten to take with him this morning. Just the thought of hearing Cal's voice rekindled a desire for my past habits. I hurried downstairs toward the door, hoping to catch Cal before he left. I had no such luck. But I knew he was just a phone call away.

I walked in the entertainment room and sat at the bar staring at myself in the glass mirrors on the wall. I began to look closely at my face. The beauty that was once flourishing was becoming a shadow fading away in the shade. My eyes were sunken in, as though I needed to have a long vacation. My eyes were not the only thing that was deteriorating from my body. My soul was deteriorating also; it was as though a part of my life had been snatched away from me quickly. I couldn't understand how or where it went. Was I moving too fast for my age? Could life have taken such a toll on me that I failed to realize how important it is? These were some of the torturing questions that were burning my conscience.

As I continue to torment myself on the outside there was a voice on the inside telling me that all was well and I just needed to start off from where I had finished. I kept trying to override that voice of possession with cheerful moments, but it kept riding me until I gave in. Finally, I picked up the portable phone off the coffee table and walked over to the barstool. Reluctantly, I started pressing the numbers on the phone. I was indecisive whether to go forward or hang up. I continued to try to press the numbers. Each time I would hang up. There was a part of me that didn't want to return to the past. I was nervous, until I took a drink from the bar. Then I pressed the numbers completely. There was a "hello" coming from the receiver. I startled for a moment, then I answered.

"Is that you Diamond?" Cal asked.

"Yes….it's me," I hesitated.

"Well, what's up?" Cal asked with a voice of confidence. I could tell by the sound of his voice that he knew what I was calling for.

"I…I…just can't go on like this…I nee…" I replied.

"…I know what you want…whatever you need I got it," Cal said.

"I don't know, what will…I promised Marcus, and …I just…"

"…leave Marcus to me, tell me what you need?"

"Could you please bring me something…I need it bad…I mean real bad…please,"

"You don't have to beg me twice, I am at your command….can you meet me somewhere?'

"I don't know…and what are you going to tell Marcus?"

"Baby, I have my lunch break in about forty-five minutes, I'll come by,"

"No, don't come by because Marcus seems to know about everyone who stops by…meet me at the ice cream shop…you know…the one we always go by,"

"Okay…but be on time I have things to do,"

As I hung up the receiver, I was indecisive on whether to go through with this. All of my thoughts were becoming confusing to me. One thing for sure, I knew I needed some comfort and at this moment, the only comfort I could see was the white powder. Even though I was taught to lean on God for comfort in the mist of my troubles; I didn't have the confidence in myself or God to trust those words. I was totally relying on the emotional feelings that were kindling a fire within my body. I began to think about how I had lost the very part of me...my child. I didn't know how to kick the memories out of my head. The best solution for me now is to let something else control my thoughts. The very habit I thought I had put into remote is now beginning to come out of remission.

Even when confusion was around, the taste for cocaine would always override my will. I drove to the ice-cream shop thinking about my relief Cal had waiting in his hand. When I entered the shop. I looked around but there was no Cal. So I sat in a booth in the back of the shop with my eyes staring on the entrance door constantly. I was on edge and very impatient and the hands on the clock on the wall couldn't move fast enough for me. Finally, Cal walks into the shop. His eyes began to scan around the room reluctantly. My guess, he was looking to see if there were any cops around. Then his eyes finally keyed in on me. He smiled and walked toward the back of the shop. I had severe anxieties attacking me. I didn't give him time to sit or say anything.

"You got it!" I shouted.

Cal looked around and gestured with his hands for me to keep my voice down. Cal sat next to me instead of in front of me. He was keeping a close watch on the audience.

"Yes, I got it?" Cal replied.

Cal had his hand under table passing the package to me. I passed the cash to him also under the table. I was beginning to pull it from under the table, when Cal said, "Wait until I leave, I do not want to get in trouble,"

I placed the package in my purse. A sigh of relief was in the atmosphere around me. I knew I was going to feel better now. Cal then got up to leave.

"Hey, where you going...you just got here!" I yelled.

"...and I am leaving, I will not be a part of this, Marcus is my boss and not just that, he is my friend," Cal explained.

"You didn't say that when you got me hooked," I replied.

"That was your choice, it's not like I held a gun up to your head," Cal said.

"Well...you're right...okay...I guess I will see you around," I remotely said.

"Diamond, my advice to you it to take it easy with this stuff... you're not making your situation any better,"

"I know...but I just need some peace...peace of mind,"

"And you think this is how you get it...look I just traffic the stuff, I don't snort it...I know what it can do to you,"

"Then why did you come here?"

"Baby, business is business...this is just a business deal, I don't look at you as no more than a ten cent hooker when it comes to business,"

"Oh yeah...but you love my money!" I shouted.

"Take it easy Diamond...it is only business," Cal continued to say as he walked out of the shop's door.

It didn't matter to me, what Cal thought of me. I knew who I was. I am Diamond, the famous R & B superstar. Everybody knew it, therefore one day of coke wasn't about to change it; but little did I know.

I was in a hurry to get to the house. I wanted to go into my guest room and have a one woman party. I locked the bedroom door and began to engage into my moment of success. The hardcover book next to my bed was my cutting table, while I place the white powder on it and put it into a position to snort. It felt so good to feel the crystal go up my nose and give me a high so powerful until I wanted it to be never-ending. I had completely forgotten about what more it could do to your body. My head felt like it was spinning around the room in circles. I was on a continuous merry-go-round that was not about to stop. The room kept spinning faster and faster until a deep darkness came upon me. I was into another world with no pain or hurt.

CHAPTER 22

I had a tremendous headache when I awakened. I could barely open my eyes and my body had this heavy feeling upon it. I could hear distant voices bouncing around the area. Suddenly, a woman was standing over me in a uniform talking to a man in white. My vision was very blurry, therefore I couldn't recognize who or what was going on. There was an odd and strange atmosphere around me. I tried to lift up from the bed, but something was restraining me. I kept trying to jerk my arms up, but they were held down. Within an instance, a hand was pressuring me to lie down. I could vaguely understand the conversation that was going on around me. I stopped wrestling with the hand that was pressing me down and began to key in on the situation around me. Without any further delay, my eyes began to have a clearer vision of the people around me. The room was very familiar as I focused on the surroundings. By surprise, I was back into the rehabilitation center for substance abuse. I became hysterical and began shouting loud profanity words at the people in the room; that is when the staff began to inject me with a sedative. Before by body could actually calm down; tears began to form in my eyes. Not one word could utter out of my mouth. My heart was filled with despair and disappointment. I just knew when I awakened from this horrible nightmare; the penalty was going to leave a lasting tattoo on my life.

Many changes came about in my life as I sat in the rehab for six months. Every week on Thursdays, missionaries were allowed to visit the rehab. I was able to sit and listen to them talk to us about making a change in our lives. There was one particular missionary that always sat next to me in the recreation room. Her name is Missionary Clara.

She would always observe me when I was reading or just listening to the television. God always has the right time, right moment and right person to help you deal with your storms. Missionary Clara was that person.

I will never forget how kind she was to me when I was very mean to her in the beginning. There was nothing I could say to get the best of her. Even though I would ignore the words she would say to me somehow this particular time something inside of me wanted to hear what she had to say. Missionary Clara held my hand; something she wouldn't normally do. My spirit was different within the connection this time; while Missionary Clara held my hand she began to speak words of wisdom to me.

"You are a beautiful person," Missionary Clara said.

I couldn't believe she was calling me beautiful, especially when my appearance was like a truck ran over me. I looked at her and smiled.

"You were born beautiful," Missionary Clara said.

"I know...everybody tells me that," I replied.

"It's not just the outer beauty...but there is something inside of you beautiful,"

"What do you mean...you don't know what type of a person I am?"

"I see your spirit...what is your name?"

"My name is Diamond...what do you mean... my spirit?"

"I see God has his hand on you...even from the day you were born,"

I couldn't argue with her on that. My birth in itself was a miracle. As I look at my life, I have had so many blessings trailing in my path, some I really didn't deserve.

"Diamond...I don't know how you are going to take this...but you have been going through a lot since your success," Missionary Clara said.

"Yes I have...sometimes it was all happening too fast," I said.

"Do you know God?"

"I used to go to church...but I have been so busy until, I didn't think about it,"

"I am not talking about going to church...do you know God as your personal savior?"

"I thought I did…but when I think of it, I think I just forgot about him," I replied.

"God hasn't forgotten about you…he loves you,"

"If God loves me, then why doesn't he stop all of this misery I am going through?"

"That's what I am talking about…your misery is a compass toward seeking God…misery in your life allows you to recognize that you can't handle all of the hurt and pain by yourself…let me ask you something… how did you handle recently your pain and hurt?"

I glanced around the room and said, "You see how I handled it,"

"Now that you know that you can't handle it, why don't you let God handle your situation?"

"How is he going to do it…you see where I am at…is he going to get me out of this?"

"God loves you Diamond…I can see you are still carrying past hurt and pain…this was not the answer," Missionary Clara replied as she looked around the room.

"Well when you talk to God tell him I need some help…since you seem to know him so well!"

"Diamond, I am going to have to leave, but I want you to call me when you need me…here is my card…take it,"

I took the card out of Missionary Clara's hand, while she gave me a hug. Missionary Clara really cared about my pain. She never missed a week coming to talk with me at the rehab. She also owned a restoration boarding house.

While I was in the rehab, Marcus refused to visit me. Somehow I believed that my fans were about to give up on me also. Marcus was spending a lot of time with Toni according to the cover on the tabloids. It was nobody's fault but mine. I played my cards with the wrong hand and lead my man into the arms of another woman; the woman who played the cards with a full deck. Our life was on display, therefore there was nothing I could do or say without the public interpreting negativity. The come back I was trying to gain through my marriage and success was going to take a lot of courage. My name was beginning to bd dragged in the mud with the paparazzi. Failure was taking a toll of me. The pride that I covet was intruded by disappointment, but I wasn't about to go down without a fight.

After the six months in the rehab, I returned back to the studios to make a new album. My career was all that I had left to keep me sane. Marcus and I lived in the same house but our hearts were in a duplex. I continued to recover the compassion that we had for each other, but cocaine left a scar on our marriage. In the public we would bandage the relationship with my success. I felt I had made a mountain out of a mole hill. It was time for me to step up to the plate and become a real woman; even if this meant fighting for my man and losing my dignity.

CHAPTER 23

Even though it was a tough fight; I finally won my audience back through my come back CD. Concerts were booked solid and I was on a roll. This is something no one could do but me. I knew I could do it. I had my in-laws in my corner, since they were the owner of my contract. It makes a difference when you are connected to someone. Not only was my career back in action, Marcus and I began to spend more time with each other. He realized I was serious about my career again. I had been clean from cocaine for four years and it was all about me again. Happiness was beginning to take root in my life. I had defeated my misery; at least I thought I did, until Pandora's Box began to open up.

Energy was bursting from Aseret's Agency. I was number one on the charts again, but a lasting imprint was about to conform. The seed of deception was about to burst into action. The memory of this day will forever kindle my soul with grief. This was my final concert for the year. I was feeling nausea and nervous while waiting backstage. Over the years I had lost a lot of weight, because I was so busy with my work, until I didn't think or desire to eat food; at least I thought that was the reason.

Toni and I were backstage preparing for me to make a lasting end of the year blast for my fans. I kept noticing Toni looking at me as I was standing near the entrance. I had to know what she was looking at.

"What's wrong?" I asked Toni.

"Nothing" Toni replied.

"Well…why are you looking at me like that?" I asked.

"Are you worried about something?" Toni implied.

"Why did you ask?" I asked her because I wanted her to say what was on her mind.

"You look a little pale and also you have become very thin," Toni bluntly said.

"Well, you know all the work and everything...its nothing,"

"Are you sure?"

"Why are you so concerned?" I said continuing to pull out more information from Toni.

"Diamond...I want you to know that there is nothing between Marcus and me anymore...I just had to tell you that,"

"What's wrong Miss Toni...is your conscience eating at you?"

"It's not my conscience...I have come to realize that there is no future with a married man, I was fooling myself that I could win Marcus back ...it is obvious his heart is somewhere else,"

"Why are you telling me this now...why couldn't you tell me this a month ago...a year ago..."

"I needed to come clean with you, I needed to get back at you for taking Marcus away from me...but it was never about you,"

"It was never about me...what are you saying Toni, let it out,"

"You will never understand, until you have been through what I have been through with Marcus,"

"What you and Marcus had is dead, so why are you trying to dig up dead things?"

"I am not digging up, I just want you to know that...well never mind...they are calling for you...give them your best shot!" Toni shouted as she gave a hug of compassion. I had never felt so much compassion coming from her until tonight.

The crowd was cheering and calling my name over and over, as I ran on stage to sing. I could see nothing but signs, cheers and the crowd screaming my success. I began to open my mouth to sing. I had never felt a sensation like I had felt that night. My dancers were all excited, as we stepped to the choreography. When I was in the middle of my concert, I began to feel lightheaded, but I thought it was from the excitement or maybe the lights. I continued to sing my next song, but I began to panic.

I noticed from the corner of my eyes, Toni was gesturing for Marcus to come on stage. Before I could open my mouth to sing another note, the room began to swirl around in circles. The voices from the audience were sounding like a record on slow motion. Finally, I tried to hold on to the microphone, but I fell to the floor.

When I opened my eyes, I was in an ambulance hooked up to an oxygen tank and IV's. Marcus was by my side squeezing my hand tightly. It was as though he thought I was leaving him. I could see his eyes becoming gleam. Then he took my hand, held it next to his mouth and kissed it. Marcus would not let go of my hand.

He kept repeating, "Hold on baby…please hold on for me,"

My heart could feel the empathy Marcus was overshadowed with. I was planning on holding on until I couldn't hold any more and I didn't want to die. I didn't know what was going on in my body, but I did know that I didn't want to die. My entire life was flashing before me as I was gasping for air. I didn't realize that death could come so soon. Tears began to form in my eyes as I was crying on the inside.

I thought, "I am so young, I have so much to live for…I am only twenty-five years old…I haven't even lived my life fully,"

All the foolishness I was catering to didn't even matter anymore. I was running for my life.

Suddenly I heard a paramedic say, "Her blood pressure is too high,"

"What is her temperature?" The other paramedic asked.

"104, but steady" He replied.

"How far are we from the hospital?" the paramedic asked.

"We are almost there," The driver replied.

I had never seen Marcus cry before, but he was literally in tears. At one point I was beginning to feel sorry for him, but then again this was payback for the pain he had caused me.

When we reached the hospital the media was already waiting at the emergency entrance. They were yelling and asking questions as Marcus ignored them and continued to hold my hand as they rolled the bed into the emergency room. Standing nearby were Toni and Jesse. Marcus yelled for them to wait in the waiting room until he could get further information. Toni called our parents, because the concert was in another state, therefore they would have to fly in.

As I lay on the bed, Marcus kept squeezing my hands. Then he began to pray to God. I had never seen him pray with so much sincerity.

He said, "God please don't take Diamond away from me…I will do better,"

He kept repeating the same prayer over and over. This probably is a wake-up call for him and also me.

The doctor walked into the room and said, "Mr. Singleton we are going to have to take some tests to see, what is going on,"

"Will she be alright? I mean is it serious," Marcus asked solemnly.

"I really can't say at this time…we need to take more tests," The doctor replied.

"What about the fever?"

"We are trying now to break the fever…the nurse will bring in some medicine…I will assure you Mr. Singleton we will do all we can for your wife,"

"Thank you, Doctor for your concern," Marcus said, as he continued to hold on to my hand.

It felt good having him catering to my needs. I haven't had this much attention from him since the day we went on our first date.

Marcus and I were anxious for the results of the test. Before the majority of the test came back, the doctor diagnosed me with pneumonia; therefore I was placed into an oxygen tank. My parents, Sherrie and Big Daddy finally came in from the airport. They were standing in the room with hopeless faces, but I stood on the Marcus's pray. I wanted God to strengthen me to come out of this situation. My family took turns sitting in the room with me. Marcus refused to leave my side.

Finally the doctor walked in with the test results. He asked my parents, Sherrie and Big Daddy to leave the room for a moment. While they were exiting, their countenance was discerning something was seriously wrong.

Then the doctor said to Marcus and me, "All of the test results were negative…"

"Great" Marcus replied.

"I meant… all of the test results were negative except one," The doctor implied.

"Which one" Marcus asked.

"The HIV test…showed positive with the virus,"

"What type… of virus?" Marcus hesitated to ask.

"According to the test results…Diamond has a positive result of HIV…AIDS,"

"That's got to be a mistake doctor…how could she have this?"

"HIV can be transmitted various ways through blood contacts…I can't tell you definitely how the virus was transported…you will have to talk to your wife," The doctor implied.

Marcus and the doctor were talking back and forth like I didn't exist in the room. I heard the entire conversation. I was devastated I had contacted AIDS. All I could think of is, Marcus and how he was running around on me.

"There is medicine out there that can keep the virus in remission… but Diamond's immune system is very weak, because of the substance abuse in the past," The doctor said.

"What can we do doctor?" Marcus asked.

"Continue to follow-up with medical care and make sure she takes her prescribed medicines…but first she is going to have to come out of the pneumonia, because her immune system is really weak," The doctor suggested.

"Meanwhile doctor, please do all you can to make her better,"

"Mr. Singleton, we are doing just that,"

The prayer that Marcus prayed for the pneumonia did work. I was out of the hospital within three weeks. Now I have started another battle the virus. I was wondering whether God was punishing me for all of my wrong doings.

As I lay in my bedroom I couldn't do anything but think about my life and how I had made a big mess of it. My mind kept wondering where the virus came from. I knew you couldn't catch HIV from snorting cocaine, because you don't use needles.

"Could Marcus have given me this virus?" I thought.

I was going to find out his results on today, because he went by the clinic to take the test. He wanted to make sure he wasn't the carrier. I was anxious to know his answer. I was hoping he was the one that gave me this disease, so that he can live with the guilt of giving me a deadly disease.

Before Marcus came home Toni stopped by to see how I was doing. She sat on the bed next to me and said, "Are you okay?"

"Yes...I'm okay," I replied.

"So when did the doctor says you can come back to work?"

"Not right now,"

"Why not"

"Toni, I need to ask you something...I don't know how to say this," I hesitated.

"Diamond, you can ask me anything, especially when you put up with my mess in the past," Toni said.

"Is Marcus sick?"

"What do you mean by sick?" Toni yelled.

"I mean the sick, sick...disease,"

"You mean herpes or some venereal disease...child that man is clean and always have been,"

"Then..."

"What are you trying to tell me Diamond...is something wrong?"

"I need to tell you something...I probably won't be coming back to work,"

"Girl, what's going on?"

"I have HIV,"

Toni's face was in shock and her mouth had a muzzle on it.

"I'm trying to tell you I have HIV...so if you know about something I don't know, please tell me," I implied with urgency.

"Diamond, I don't know how to tell you this, but remember when I told you that Marcus's heart is somewhere else, I was talking about another person.' Toni said.

"So there is another woman!" I shouted.

"I hate to burst your bubble girl…it's not another woman…it's a man," Toni said.

When she said a man, my heart felt like it dropped to my stomach. "No…No…that can't be true!" I yelled.

"I don't mean to get you upset…but it is Jesse," Toni replied.

"Huh…" I said gasping for breath.

"I thought you felt it…didn't you see the signs?"

I couldn't say anything. My mouth had become muzzled by the gay thought. Then I began to reminisce on the moments Marcus, Jesse and I were together. All this time I thought Jesse was keeping tabs on me instead he was keeping tabs on Marcus. I am finally seeing the big picture. I was astounded and blank with words.

"Diamond, please don't tell Marcus I told you," Toni begged.

I couldn't even tell her I wouldn't. I was lost for words. I was married to a down-low man. That is why he couldn't give me the true affection I needed as a man. All I could think of was what is next. Toni left me in a state of shock. I couldn't talk anymore to her so she left.

Marcus finally reached home. He didn't come into my bedroom right away, so I took a nap hoping he would come to me with the news of his test. It was later in the day before he came up to the bedroom. He walked in the room and sat in the recliner chair in the room and just stared for a moment. I was waiting for him to tell me he gave me AIDS.

Suddenly, some entertainment came into the room. Marcus walked over and sat on the bed next to me.

"So, how are you feeling today?" He asked.

"I'm okay," I replied kindling the flames about to extinguish out of my mouth.

"Well…I took the test,"

"And" I said waiting for him to burst the news with sorrow.

"It was negative"

"Negative!"

"That's what I said, negative,"

"That couldn't be so…I never slept with anyone but you!" I shouted.

"Well...what do you want me to say...I got AIDS...well I don't!" Marcus yelled

"Maybe your boyfriend Jesse has it and the test was not valid!"

"The test is valid...and...boyfriend Jesse, where did you get that from?"

"Don't worry...is it true?"

"What's it to you...you never around or satisfying me!"

"I want to know is it true...answer me, Marcus!"

Marcus hesitated for a moment and then said, "Yes...yeah...I love him,"

"So why did you marry me...why did you marry me?"

"Because my dad would not allow me to continue as a CEO until I found a woman to marry, he does not agree with my preference of a lover,"

"You took my dignity and my virginity,"

"It wasn't like you didn't want it...you forced this relationship on me, that is why I gave up our child, I didn't want any children by you... it was only a business deal,"

"So that is why you gave our daughter up for adoption,"

"I have nothing further to say...if you want a divorce then get it... because I don't know how you caught AIDS...must be some drug dealer you tricked for!"

I was furious at Marcus he had killed the little bit of intimacy left for him. Some people say love lasts forever, but love can be destroyed through deceit. Marcus deceived me for five years and all of the love that I felt a few minutes ago has now diminished into thin air. Maybe someone else will catch it.

I went into my closet to pull out my clothes. I kicked the luggage on the floor in the closet expressing my anger.

"You don't have to worry about me I am leaving!" I yelled toward Marcus.

Marcus ignored my words and walked out of the room to the entertainment bar to get a drink. It seemed to be the moment he was looking for. To finally get rid of me was on his agenda all the time. He was probably faking the caring and concerned spirit for the media.

The butler helped me to carry my luggage downstairs to the door. I walked into the entertainment room with Aseret's contract in my hand. I flicked a lighter open and burned the contract in his face. Then I said, "This is the last piece of property you will ever own of me,"

I walked out of the room and did not look back.

I moved in with my parents, just until I could get things settle between Marcus and me. I had no desire to run back into his arms, not this time.

CHAPTER 24

Marcus filed for a divorce by the request of his father. Aseret Agency was now suing me for breach of contract. The funds my father invested for me was wasting away daily until I had nothing left. I lost everything that I had worked hard for, but I did not lose my family. Even the dignity I prophesize on losing became a reality. Pride began to deteriorate my life and arrogance was drifting away into a deep depression. Success had taken me to rock bottom. One thing I learned from my life: success of this world is vanity…it will soon disappear and it did. I had become the common Diamond. No more media, stardom, or fans. It still was all about me to the public, but not the way I desired it to be. This is what happens when you soon forget the one who created you.

I lived with my parents for about eight months until they couldn't handle my illness anymore. One day while I was at the grocery store I ran into Missionary Clara, she offered to take me into her boarding house in the urban area. It wasn't what I was accustomed to, but it was clean. Even though it felt good reminiscing about the past, reality had finally kicked in and now I am alone. I have no one to blame but myself. As I looked over my life, I couldn't believe pride and greed was killing my intimacy, the true love that God had bestowed inside of me from the beginning. The most valuable lesson I learn through talking with Missionary Clara: There is a place in your heart that has a vacant sign, and until you occupy it with God it will always continue to be rented out with invaluable things. This is where I am right now.

I seldom have visits from Sherrie or Toni. My parents come by every now and then. Somehow people with AIDS are not popular not even among their relatives. But that's okay, Missionary Clara and her daughter Patience kept me with company. I usually stay in my room most of the time looking out of the window. Patience would sometimes peek into my room everyday to see if I was okay. I would often hear her reading books on the steps in the hallway and sometimes she would sing church songs. She reminded me of myself. I had never had a conversation with her until today. While she was on the steps reading her book, I walked in and sat next to her on the steps.

"What you doing?" I asked.

"Reading" Patience replied.

"Do you like to read?"

"Yeah…sometimes"

"Read to some of it to me,"

Patience began reading the book aloud. Then I would ask her questions. She was a bright young lady.

"How old are you Patience?"

"I'm six going on seven," She replied counting her fingers.

"I heard you singing the other day, do you like to sing?" I asked.

"Yeah…I love to sing…Missionary Clara told me I have a gift to sing from God," She replied.

When Patience said those words I began to recapture the moment when I was singing in church and the entire congregation was amazed at the maturity in my voice.

"What Missionary Clara said was true, keep singing… your gift will make room for you, but don't make room for your gift…because you might let anything come into the package,"

"What are you saying Miss Diamond?"

"Just listen to Missionary Clara, she will not steer you wrong,"

One Sunday morning Missionary Clara invited me to visit her church. It had been years since I had been inside of a church. She knocked on my room door.

"Diamond are you awake? She asked.

"Yeah, come in," I replied.

Missionary Clara had breakfast on a tray as she walked into the room. She took very good care of me even when my family and friends had abandoned me. God will always have a ram in the bush.

"How are you feeling this morning?' Missionary Clara asked.

"I am sort of weak this morning, but I will get by," I replied.

"Did you take your pills today?" She asked looking on the table next to my bed.

"Yes, I did…but I don't feel too well," I replied.

"Well, you just eat some of this and I will check on you later…I am going to church, I was going to invite you to come, but maybe next time…do you want me to leave Patience with you?"

"That's okay Miss Clara, I'll be alright,"

"Now if you feel like you need for me to stay with you, let me know,"

"I'll be fine," I said as I heard a knock on my door.

Missionary Clara opened the door. In front of the entrance was Sherrie standing with flowers in her hand. I was startled by her appearance.

"Well…looks like you'll have some company while I am gone," Missionary Clara said as she walked out the door.

I was short for words, then I said, "What storm blew you here?"

"Diamond, I will always be your friend, no matter what others think," Sherrie said, sitting on the edge of my bed.

"You sure you want to sit there?" I said coughing continuously.

Sherrie reached on top of the table next to my bed to hand me some tissue. Then she said, "Just because you're sick doesn't mean you are contagious,"

"What do you know about AIDS, you never had it?" I asked.

"No, but I have been reading about it…you can't catch it by air, it has to be by blood," She said.

I smiled at Sherrie and said, "Well looks like the little girl has been reading,"

"Now that's the Diamond I am use to," Sherrie said.

"Why do you keep holding those flowers? Put them on the dresser over there,"

Sherrie got up and placed the flowers on the dresser. She noticed the many pill bottles laying on it. I noticed the remorseful look upon Sherrie's face as she sat back on the bed.

"Don't feel sorry for me Sherrie, this was my fault," I said.

"It's not just that Diamond, Did you hear about what happen to Jesse?" Sherrie asked.

"No, but he probably was caught in the bed with Marcus by the paparazzi," I replied.

"I hate to tell you this…but Jesse is dead…they had his funeral two weeks ago," Sherrie said.

"Dead…how did he die?' I said, as I jumped up with despair.

"You really don't know,"

"No…I don't,"

"You haven't been reading the tabloids…he died from AIDS,"

"No…No…couldn't have"

"I am sorry to say, but he did…it was a big loss for all of us, because we were so close,"

"Why didn't someone tell me he was sick…I could have…"

"There was nothing you could have done,"

As I listened to Sherrie talking about Jesse's funeral, my mind recaptured all moments that he shared with Marcus and me. I didn't know that I was sharing my man with another lover. Then I thought to myself, "Could Marcus be lying to me about his test results,"

With a puzzle on my face, I asked Sherrie, "What do you know about Marcus and Jesse?"

"What about Marcus?" Sherrie asked.

"Come on girl, you know what I am talking about,"

"You talking about…"

"Yeah…that's what I'm talking about"

"That's how I know so much about the virus, didn't Marcus tell you about his results?"

"Yes he did, he told me it was negative,"

"I hate to tell you this…but Marcus' test results were positive, apparently you haven't been keeping up with the tabloids,"

When Sherrie told me the news, a lump began to form in my throat. Marcus had been lying to me and the guilt that I had band aided is now being uncovered. I couldn't discuss the matter any further with Sherrie.

"Sherrie I appreciate you coming by," I said.

"But, we haven't even talked about what's going on in your life," She said.

"You have, more than you know…I just want to get some rest…I haven't been feeling well,"

"Okay, I'll leave…but remember I am just a phone call away…I love you girl,"

While Sherrie was walking out the door, tears were rolling down my face. Once again Marcus was the leader of my failure. The scales that were covering my eyes was beginning to fall off, as I knelt down in front of my bed and looked up to heaven. I needed a breakthrough, because depression was taking a toll of me. I no longer wanted to eat or be in the company of other people. The window was my only place of warmth as I looked out of it. The sun that beamed on me through the window so often embedded hope for the moment. I needed help and I needed it soon. My soul was destined for a place of peace. I didn't want to live in this body anymore. Everything that I had coveted had backfired on me. In reality, I had detested everything I had accomplished in my life, including life itself.

Within an instance, I felt a warm sensation come over my body as I kneeled before Almighty God. At first I didn't know what to say and I started to forget about it and try to fall asleep but there was something inside tugging me to stay awake. I was wrestling with my will and God's will. Finally, a stream of tears began to run down my face.

My heart became heavy, that is when my mouth slowly opened uttering words unto God,

Heavenly Father, I need you
More than I ever needed you before,
I don't know what to do,
Everything I have touched has crumbled before my face,

I lost my dignity and my hope,
But I know you can rescue and restore my soul,
Please God do this for me,
Forgive me God for treating people as though they were dirt,
Forgive me Lord for using my body to defile your Holy Temple,
Give me the strength to forgive Marcus for the things he has done to me,
I realize this was a wake-up call for me,
Let me come back home Lord,
Teach me how to be your child,
I am tired of being the bastard,
I have been rebellious and didn't listen to your voice,
Even if you don't heal me,
Cleanse me up Lord,
Wash me,
Give me a pure and perfect heart toward you,
Then I will forever serve you in whatever state I am in,
Out of all my suffering,
I am learning that only you God know my purpose,
Only you God can give true success and happiness,
Remember me Lord,
For my victory has surpassed this earthly tabernacle,
I press toward the higher glory which is in Christ Jesus,
And God thanks for listening.

I couldn't stop talking to God. Suddenly I began to feel a calmness come over my body. Freedom and peace were occupying the room. Then I began to recognize God as my Father instead of God. This is when I knew I had taken ownership of His righteousness. God had finally become my Heavenly Father.

After I said this prayer my countenance was like Jesus when he was in the garden of Gethsemane. My clothes were wet from the tears and sweat that was dripping from body. I stayed on my knees for a while meditating on the peace God was giving me in my spirit and soul. Without delay, I heard a voice calling my name. I thought I was hearing things, so I continued to stay faced down on my bed. Then I felt a bright light shining on my bed. I looked up and saw a white mist in the light. The light had a different radiates about it. I knew this was a heavenly being and I was in awe. I couldn't utter a word.

Then I heard a whispering voice say, "I love you my child…go and sin no more,"

Immediately the light disappeared. Every ill feeling that I had felt before I prayed was lifted off of me. Depression was nowhere to be found. The sickness I felt this morning was gone. I had come to the conclusion that salvation had visited me today and now I am free.

CHAPTER 25

I was free in my spirit in soul, even though my body was still afflicted. I began to spend more time outside my bedroom. Sometimes I would sit on the steps of the porch with Patience, especially when Missionary Clara was out doing field work. We would read books and sing songs together. Patience helped me to realize I had another reason for living. I spent quality time with her. One day while Patience and I were sitting on the steps reading a man knocked on the door. I could see him through the window of the front door. I didn't know whether to open it or not. When he came closer, I could see that it was Marcus. I didn't want to let him see me this way. I hesitated for a moment. As Marcus came closer he no longer had the appearance of the handsome man I met years ago. His statue had diminished in sin.

"Who is it Diamond?" Patience asked.

"It's Marcus…my ex," I replied.

"You mean the man who works for the company you use to sing with,"

"Yeah"

"I want to meet him…let him in,"

When I opened the door he made a signal for a truck to back into the yard. I was holding on to Patience's hand as she was hugging me.

"Hi Diamond…I wanted to come by and see how you are doing and also to bring you something," Marcus said.

The guys were bringing me my piano from our entertainment room.

"I thought you could use this…I sold the house and is now living in a condo again,"

"Marcus, I am glad you stopped by…Patience go back in the house and wait for me," I said.

Patience was very protective of me. She was reluctant to go inside until I said, "I'll be alright…go on,"

After Patience went inside the house I began to talk with Marcus with a more serious tone.

"Marcus, I know you are the one, why did you lie to me?" I asked.

"I can't answer that Diamond, all I know is that I am sorry…it could have been my pride, but I didn't mean to hurt you," Marcus replied.

"It doesn't matter anymore it's over,"

"It doesn't have to be, we can start over,"

"Now you want to start over…after you took my life and shredded it into pieces, all this time I thought it was me, I thought I had done something wrong,"

"Diamond, please let me explain?"

"That's what I want you to do, go ahead and explain" I replied..

"I was selfish…I didn't realize what I had until it was gone…Can we start over? I can take care of you," He said in a forgiving tone.

"Marcus, what we have is gone…I don't believe it was ordained by God from the beginning, let's just let the past stay in the past,"

"Is this what you really want Diamond…Is this the way you want to live?"

"What's wrong with where I live…happiness is not in the things you possess, not even in your status…happiness is in God…I am going to do everything in my life, God's way from now on,"

"You can come live with me, can we start over?"

"Marcus, don't you know you are dying?" I implied.

"Why not start your life over with Jesus, because that's who is going to free you now,"

"We can start it over together,"

"I am starting over…the life you want me to live is no longer a desire in my heart anymore…I can't do it Marcus…it's not even about Jesse's death,"

"Baby, then what is it about?"

"It's about being in God's will…I don't feel any signals from God telling me to start over with you,"

"Diamond, I love you,"

"And you know what… I love you too…but not the way I used to…somehow I believe it was a lust thing from the beginning…we can always be friends…and I will always be here for you if you want to talk, but nothing more,"

"That's the way you want it…can you just think about it?"

"Marcus I have thought about it…what we had is over…the Chapters we had cannot be rewritten or added to…I am done,"

After those last words, Marcus came closer to me and kissed me on the jaw. I watched as he got into the car. He looked at me and then drove off. I did not feel guilty after he left. His kiss on my jaw had become cold and I knew right then that I had moved on.

When I walked into the house the piano was in the hallway. Patience was pecking the keys.

"You like that' I asked.

"Yeah, I do," Patience replied.

"Would you like for me to teach you how to play it,"

"Would you?"

"Sure it will give me something to do around here," I said, as Patience and I sat on the piano bench. I began to take her fingers and model some of the keys.

From that day forward, I began to teach Patience how to play the piano. She enjoyed the lessons and it brought about closeness in our relationship. She reminded me of my daughter Grace. Somehow there was a bond between us. She felt like I was her mom most of the time, because Missionary Clara was always going about her heavenly Father's business with the church.

Another year had passed by and with the Grace of God I outlived Marcus. He died a few months ago. Sadly Marcus did not die a peaceful death. The tabloids stated that Marcus committed suicide. He had shot himself in the head. Apparently he couldn't take the sting of death. When they found his body he was sitting in his favorite chair with my platinum plaque in his hand.

My body was rapidly declining, even though my soul was strong. I forced myself to teach Patience piano lessons. I gained strength in giving her those lessons. Each time she would play a melody it soothed my spirit. She was a miracle from Heaven and I believed she is the reason I am still alive.

One day while sitting in my room, Patience ran in my room with a piece of paper jumping up and down with excitement. It was a contest to compose a music piece. I had been working with her on composing for a while. You would be surprised with the creativity little one's can have.

"Do you think I can do it Diamond?" Patience said, as she lifted my head with a pillow.

"Sure you can…I believe you are ready," I said with a weak voice.

"What shall I compose?

"Remember that piece I taught you "Time over ribbons" I think should do that one,"

"You really think I can do it?" Patience said with excitement.

"Of course, now go tell your mom and work on the piece…practice brings perfection,"

"Diamond, will you come and sit by me on the piano…please,"

"Okay…just for a little while," I said, as I gathered enough strength to walk with her to the piano.

"Now don't move too fast, take your time," I said, while listening to her play the melody.

While Patience was playing the piano, I could see a reflection of me in her and she enjoyed the challenge of composing music. She didn't like to make mistakes, but I would always enlighten her to do more than she expected of herself.

We worked very hard on her musical piece and when the day came for her to perform I was too sick to attend. Missionary Clara and Patience left me in the room with a nurse. I was now in the last stage and could barely eat. The strength of God was keeping me alive to see my successor go to the next level.

I would lay in the bed thinking about the shadows of my life. I have finally realized what is my true purpose in life. The gift that God has given me was to be guided by Him and not by greed, pride or arrogance. You can't have it your way if you want God to cultivate the gift He has blessed you with. It's not what you want or desire; it is about what God has predestined you for. I failed in that area, by not seeking God for guidance. Some people come in your life for a season, some come for a reason, and some come to detour you off your path. I didn't recognize the value of my gift. Even though you have a gift it must be nurtured by God. A gift is only valuable if you take the time to unwrap it carefully, also you must know that without wisdom your gift can end up becoming vanity. I neglected to open my gift with gratitude…so it slipped into another person's hand, Patience my successor. Discipline plays a very important part in sustaining a gift. Discipline is only the only way you will really see the fullness of life. I was like a wild stallion in the wilderness, but because of the hardships I encountered I finally became tame. I have peace now that I know the true meaning and value of living: That is to use your gift to the glory of God and prepare to pass it on to the next person when your time is up. Pride, Greed and Selfishness can cause you to miss out on the true purpose of the Gift.

A few hours later I heard a commotion going on in the hallway. Patience was talking so fast in excitement. I could barely understand the words she was saying. She slammed my bedroom door open. The nurse told her to quiet down.

"Diamond…I just got to tell you!" Patience yelled with excitement.

"Calm down…calm down," Missionary Clara said.

"Okay, I'm calm…I won!" Patience screamed from the top of her head.

She showed me the trophy. I held it in my hand and gave her a big hug. I couldn't say much because my voice had become weak. The nurse was talking to Missionary Clara while I was hugging Patience. I hear the nurse telling Missionary Clara to contact my family. I knew I was dying it was just a matter of time.

When Patience looked at her mom and the nurse, she knew something was wrong. Tears began to run down her eyes.

"Diamond you can't leave," Patience said crying on Diamond's chest.

"Baby, I am going to a better place... I want you to know that you gave more value to my life than the platinum records I've ever had," I said with tears forming in my eyes.

"But, what about my music...you promised me you were going to be here for me," Patience said crying.

"I will...in your heart...it's your turn now...just remember to put God first....and..." I tried to continue, but death had come to visit me. I close my eyes and thought, "No matter what you accomplish in this world death will come whether rich or poor, but they both or soon forgotten.

As I drifted away, I heard Missionary Clara said, "Whether she knew it or not, Diamond accomplished her purpose in life,"

Patience did exactly what Diamond commanded her to do. She refused to compromise the gift God had bestowed upon her. At the age of twenty-three she became a phenomenal Gospel composer.

The End

Silent Predator

"Inspired by Actual Sleep Paralysis Events"

Dedicated to the restless souls.

ACKNOWLEDGEMENT

To The Holy Spirit,
who manifested the gift of writing upon me.

"What may seem hard today is just the answer for tomorrow"

Resa

CHAPTER 1

The storm was arousing more and more as the heavenly voices were speaking. Screeching sounds and strong weeping willow winds were pounding against the windowpane. The energy was progressing through the levels of sounds intruding the thunder that was roaming about the sky. Shadows of pain were reflecting on the wall of the bedroom. The storm was becoming more aggressive as the time passed by. Suddenly a loud crash vibrated the walls of the room capturing the figures that were reflecting all around me. I was frightened of the sounds; therefore, I immediately put my head under the blankets on my bed and shivered with a passion for safety. As the lightening continued, the reflections from it were attacking the outside of my blanket. Although I was in the room by myself, I could feel a presence of something or someone near the outside of my blanket. As I felt it coming closer fear was trampling upon my soul. I was scared to death.

I knew that the only secured place was either in my brother's room or my parent's room. Going into my brother's room was my unanimous decision, because I didn't want my parents to think I was being a baby. I waited for a few minutes and stirred up enough nerves to run into my brother's room. I finally dashed over toward my brother's bedroom door.

He was awakened by the jolted sound of the door opening.

"Daniel, are you awake?" I whispered as I slowly opened the door making sure I didn't disturb my parents in the other room.

"What's wrong Pam?" Daniel asked in a soft voice as he wiped his droopy eyes from a peaceful sleep.

"Can you sleep Daniel? I whispered to him, as I crept near the edge of his bed hoping he would move over.

"Yeah…I was asleep, until you woke me up." He said.

"Did you hear those creepy sounds?" I said.

"I heard the sound, that's what kept me asleep."

"The whispering sounds didn't scare you?"

"Pam, are you starting that again…go to sleep."

"I am serious Daniel, something is in this house."

"Pam go back to bed, it's nothing but nature expressing itself."

"That's what I am talking about…its scary."

"You want me to call mom?"

"No…please don't I am not a baby."

"Well you're acting like one…now go to bed."

"Please…can I sleep in here with you?"

"You need to learn to sleep in your room."

"But those things will get me."

"That's only in your imagination."

"Please…. Please Daniel let me sleep in here." I begged.

"Nope!"

"I'll give you a dollar out of my piggy bank."

Daniel stretched his arms out from under the covers and opened his palm faced up. He agreed to get my dollar out of my piggy bank.

"Hand it over now." Daniel demanded.

"I'm not going back in that room…not now…I'll give it to you in the morning." I said.

"Okay but please don't sleep close to me." Daniel said as he opened the covers for me to get into the bed.

"Can I sleep near the wall?"

"Oh, alright…but remember don't touch me." Daniel said as he pressed his arm on top of the covers between us.

I crossed over Daniel in order to sleep near the wall. The wall was a barrier for me on one side and Daniel's body was the other barrier. His arm pressing on the top kept the space between us secured. I felt safe on both sides. The use of the wall kept my eyes focused when I would awaken through the night. One thing I didn't want to see was some shadowing figures moving about the room. If anything comes into the room I won't have to see it.

Daniel abruptly turned to his side. I noticed him looking at me strangely.

"Pam, did you pray tonight?" Daniel asked.

"Yes I did." I replied.

"I was wondering.... now... go to sleep."

"Okay...but Daniel?"

"No Pam...please... go to sleep."

"Okay."

Even though the presence of Daniel comforted me deeply, the fearful activity didn't seize. For a while I was cuddled next to my brother secured by a warm body. Finally, my eyelids became heavy and I was beginning to doze off to sleep. Mysterious happenings were occurring while I was asleep. My body was beginning to have a strange feeling. I couldn't explain it in words, but I knew it existed. At first it felt like a normal sleep with dreams, but a battle between my dreams and awakening was occurring. I ceased fighting, that is when my body went into a trance. It was a battle trying to come out of it. I could hear the sounds of the storm outside and also feel my brother next to me, but I could not move. I became hysterical and tried to cry out, but my mouth wouldn't open. The cry from the inside of me could not vocally be heard outwardly.

It was a constant struggle for me to come out of the terrible feeling that had came over me. I began to hear hissing sounds in the room. I wouldn't dare open my eyes, even if I could. There was no movement from Daniel. I didn't know if he was aware of what was going on around us. It was the weirdest feeling I had ever felt before. Panic and perspire became the common attributes of my soul. Escaping out of the trance was my only rescue. I didn't know what was happening to me. I felt like I was in another world. Finally, I was able to use my vocal cords and mutter some words. Daniel awakened from the sound and shook me.

"Pam...Pam!" Daniel shouted as he continued to shake me.

"What!" I replied as he shook me out of the trance. I was shaking with fear.

"Are you okay?"

I couldn't utter any words because of the terror that had captured my soul.

Daniel watched as the shivering fear took a toll of me. I was in total shock as my body was trying to regain conscientiousness. I stood in the corner of the bed with the blanket up to my face shaking like a tree limb on a distorted windy night. Daniel sat on the bed just staring at me. He didn't know what to do or think. He was in total denial of the entire situation. Daniel finally came to a consensus that it was only a bad dream. This night initiated the predator that stalked me with no limitations.

Years have passed and I have frequently managed to keep silent of the terror that haunts me. I live in a mesmerized and secluded town called Sutton. It is an isolated and deceiving little town. Perfection was the breeder for the town's people. If you weren't perfect, you would be weeded out. What I mean by that is "you would never fit in". Some residents relocated, due to, the town being so prejudiced against deficiencies in people. But that is one of the ways the community eliminates you. That's part of their weeding process. The population was about 50,000 plus people. Everyone knew somebody and Success was a top priority.

I was born in this town and adaptation were not difficult for me to form. My parents have successful careers. My father, Richard Jones is the vice-president of our local bank, and my mother, Melissa Jones is an assistant principal at one of the elementary schools. I have two brothers, Daniel and Samuel. My parents are very proud of their children because my brothers and I are high achievers at the local Sutton schools.

I, Pamela Jones am determined to be the best that I can be in Sutton. Being the best meant there were going to be some challenges in my life; some that I couldn't afford to lose. I wouldn't dare let anyone know that I had encountered an unknown phenomena that attacks me mentally. The embarrassment would harm my family and me greatly.

Since the day I faced the night horrors it has become never-ending. My dreams have jeopardized my focus on reality. I called them night terrors, because they terrorize me mostly at night. During the day I am normal, as long as I am not fatigued from a day's work. Sometimes I feel this is a special gift, because I haven't met anyone who deals with this type of behavior. I wouldn't dare tell anyone about this dysfunctional matter in my life, because the imperfection in me will be revealed. Then I would be considered abnormal.

I have come to a consensus that the sleeping disorder I am dealing with will be a personal skeleton in my closet. My mother is the only one who covers the moments of secrecy in her heart. She is rather bothered by the fact that I don't sleep like normal people. She deals with the facts in her own way. I have been dealing with the terror since childhood and cannot shake it off for even a moment. I live in a town that uses secrets for ammunition, so if you want to stick around, it is best you keep quiet about things that don't make sense to the nature of man.

The town will conceal your faults for a while, to keep outsiders from getting into the town's affairs. The only time secrets are bought to the open is when the community wants to ex-communicate a family. Then the town councilmen would assemble together to make a unanimous decision. All sorts of darts are pointed at the victims to discredit them. This town has accumulated a bunch of humanistic hypocrites. In a way I think my parents are just as guilty of this scheme, because they have become blind to the reality of perfection.

I have high goals and expect to reach them by the age of 25 with no interferers. My plans are to become a doctor. I haven't decided on what type of doctor. I estimated, by the time I finish with my first pre-medical classes, then I will decide what field to specialize in.

Most of the people in this town are very competitive. If they weren't, somehow you would know it. If you live in this town, you have to be considered perfect to excel or become branded for life. That's where my aggressiveness comes from. In order to be accepted, success must be your top priority. It doesn't matter whether you are born smart or have a learning disability. Your best bet is to camouflage your deficiencies.

The people in this town assume you are perfect and will not think any differently.

Church has to be your ultimate goal on Sunday, even though most of the people in this town don't carry out moral standards. Most of the children in this town feel that going to church is like practicing to be a hypocrite, since the majority of the adults have some skeletons in their closet. No one dares to open up anyone's skeleton in the closet, because it would involve having your deep dark secrets revealed.

It is the season for our annual high school graduation; the town is decorated in a high mode and destined for more success stories. The community enjoys recognizing you for your achievements. High achievements in school are a top priority in this county. As long as I have known, there has not been one drop out in our community and ninety percent the people are college graduates.

Graduation became personable echoes before my very eyes as I stood before thousands of people to give my final farewell speech to my colleagues. The awesome feeling crawling on the inside began to rattle me, even though I didn't have much sleep last night. This was the big day and I am not going to let fatigue keep me away. The feeling of being reborn again had captured my soul.

Anticipation crept in as I was waiting for my final step toward my new destination. Finally, the dictation of my life is being set in stone. Looking around the audience, I spotted my parents sitting with great excitement. I looked a little further and saw my two brothers pointing at me.

All of the graduates had black and white attire on. We looked like penguins on and icy bed. Even though we probably didn't look that way, but we felt that way, especially with the entire town's people staring us down.

I am the valedictorian for this class and proud to be such a personal mascot. Of course, I enjoyed the high while it lasted even though I was hesitating on giving my valedictorian farewell speech. The eyes of the people looked manipulating waiting for this moment to happen. Some of the eyes had convinced themselves that they were perfect in everything and that this moment would be a Kodak moment. According to the town's records everything is marvelous here. If you have any problems you'd better not tell it, because once the rumor spreads you would become an outcast to our society.

I was called the queen of the campus. I practically participated in every activity on campus and won about every contest. Of course, I had lots of competition, but somehow they became invisible. Sometimes I felt my popularity won the ballots. Popularity was more important than moral standards. Unpleasant morals were hidden if you are one of the town councilmen. The town's councilmen handled all the decisions in Sutton. There is no limit to what can be done for the most valuable person in town.

Suddenly, I heard Principal Smith burst out with a proud voice, "Now we will hear from our Valedictorian, Pamela Jones!"

I was frozen to the chair. Even though I was popular and stuff, this moment is history for me. The guy next to me gave me a boost by tugging me on the shoulder.

"Pamela, that's you." He whispered.

I was totally in shock. I removed my butt from the chair, while listening to the crowd's cheers. I couldn't believe it, I was treading toward the doorway of success. The entire class of 1991 stood up and applauded me. Tears were streaming down my eyes as I walked toward the podium and shook Mr. Smith's hand. My family couldn't stop clapping. The entire audience was filled with high energy for the exciting moment.

As I stood there my mouth felt like it had frostbites on it. The words were slowly being delivered out of my mouth. Of all times, I chose this moment to become timid. Then I looked at my father as he looked directly in my eyes. The contact of his eyes to my eyes was a sensation of pure confidence being pierced directly into my pupils. The words from the speech began to utter out as though I was a famous poet delivering my Pulitzer poem. As I spoke with such dignity the audience was capturing the words as though they were vibrating their minds.

Finally, my speech was over. I was gratefully honored with a standing ovation. The never ending applauds filled the atmosphere. Tears continued to stream down my face like a waterfall. I could behold the beauty of Sutton being on one accord for this moment. This was only the beginning for the class of 1991.

Moving toward my seat, I kept thinking, this is the end of my days at Sutton High. As I moved closer to my row, my competition Amy, who sat in the same row, began to ponder her eyes up and down on me. Amy was a vicious and manipulating young lady. There were never-ending stories to what she is capable of doing. Amy has been trying to ruin my life since she moved to this town. She is a northern girl who thought New York was the best place to come from. Amy left New York at the age of 10, but she still thinks her English is better than everyone else, especially those who speak southern.

I tried to ignore her as I passed her chair. She politely put her leg in the way so that I couldn't get past her. Amy was always trying to gain attention and she didn't care how she obtained it. Like always, this was her way of getting attention, whether it was new hairdo or a new attraction to something on her body. She can be very surprising with new things.

Guy tried to keep us from turning the situation into a conventional confrontation.

I knew Guy was only looking out for my reputation. I looked back at him and smiled. Guy and I had been friends since childhood. Many people thought that we were related because we have the same last name. We have been friends for so long until our relationship couldn't be anything but friends.

As I was listening to the Principal announce our names to receive out diplomas, I heard my brother Daniel calling my name.

"Hey Pam, I can have your room, now!" He yelled.

That was just like my brother he didn't care where he was when he wanted something.

I took a quick glance at him and smiled. Daniel is two years younger than me, but Samuel is six years old and the youngest of the three of us. People used to tell my mother, she intentionally became pregnant because she missed having a baby in the house. My mother waited almost ten years to have another child. At least my father was able to recuperate from the childhood days of Daniel and me.

Suddenly I heard my name with great recognitions. My body felt like a lighted Christmas tree and my face became as radiant as the sun.

"Pamela Jones, graduated with high Honors!" shouted Mrs. Hebb, one of our Assistant Principals.

This was one of the happiest moments of my life. I just knew this was only the beginning of an eccentric life style.

Slowly, I walked toward the steps, taking one step at a time. Each step impressed in my mind the movement toward my goal in life. My feet became heavier each step I took. It was though I was moving in slow motion. I could hear my parents, brothers and peers, clapping and yelling my name. But before I could grasp the end of the diploma, a wavy movement flashed before my eyes. Blurriness began to suck in my eyesight. I tried to sustain my composure but my equilibrium was off. All of a sudden I saw myself falling to the ground and gasping for breath. Finally, everything was faded and looked like a television set about to blow a fuse. I could hear voices fading in and out. I could hear someone calling my name over and over. Finally, my body began to become unstable and everything became dark. It seemed as though I was in another world or time zone.

CHAPTER 2

Finally reality was beginning to kick in. My body felt weighed down and my head felt like a ton of bricks had hit me over the head. I could barely open my eyes.

Suddenly I hear a voice waken me.

I heard someone shouting, "Wake up young lady!"

It was a female's voice blasting my ears off. This time she was shaking me back and forth trying to gain some alertness from me. I tried to open my eyes but the light from the room was causing me to be in a daze. I abruptly closed my eyes, hoping that I would wake up in a sane world.

The female voice yelled again, "Wake up! Wake Up! You have been sleeping all afternoon."

That is when I gradually caught a hold of my senses and took a glimpse of what was before me. It was a woman staring me in the face as though she was my reflection in the mirror. As I awakened my motor skills were rapidly restoring to normal.

"What! I shouted.

"Where is my father?" I exclaimed.

"Young lady…you are going to need more than your father!"

As I squirmed, I recognized I was restrained with belts in a room with white walls.

"Where am I…and…" I asked, as I tried to speak, but the woman interrupted my thoughts.

"You are in a hospital and we are going to take good care of you." She said rudely.

She continued to waltz around the room trying to make me comfortable. She took the restraining belts off me and propped me up with a pillow.

"By the way, I am Miss Rawlins… I am here to help you… any way I can" she replied.

Watching Miss Rawlins move back and forth in the room, I asked, "What am I doing in here.

"You are here to get well young lady…you have a lot of work ahead of you." Miss Rawlins explained.

"Get well…lots of what?" I yelled trying to make sense out of all of this.

Miss Rawlins noticed the demeanor of my body and took me by the hand and looked into my eyes and said, "Don't you worry about a thing…you are in good hands."

She walked out of the door before I could get some answers as to why I was in this place. I noticed the interior of the room resembled a hospital room. I begin to recall in my mind the episodes that happened before I went up to the podium to receive my diploma. I kept pondering the moment over and over again in my mind. I became inquisitive about the room, so I went over to the window on the door and looked out. Outside the window didn't look like an ordinary hospital. It especially didn't look like Sutton Medical Center. There were people yelling, whining, and even butting their heads against the wall. In one corner I saw a young lady flicking at something in the air, but there was nothing in the air to flick at. I remember capturing a scene like this some time ago on television, but those people were in a mental institution.

Putting my hands up to my mouth, I felt like vomiting. Then a sensation of awe was wrapped around my head. I started holding my head with my hands.

"Oh…Oh No…can't be… am…crazy?" I shouted.

I began to become distraught with anger. The high self-esteem I had gained over the years was gradually being demolished.

While knocking on the door, I screamed as loud as I could

"Somebody please help me…plea-se…help!

The echoes of my cry for help bounced everywhere in the building. Without delay several nurses came through the door.

"What's going on in here!" The nurse shouted as she tried to pull my arms behind me to gain control.

Then another orderly came into the room. I had the strength of five people. They tried to calm me down by shaking me. The shaking method didn't work. It only made me scream more. The screaming made me delirious, until all I could hear were voices shouting back and forth.

"Who took the restrainer off of her?" The nurse asked.

"Hold her down...calm down young lady!" The orderly shouted.

"Take her to the bed and hold her down!"

"This time make sure the straps are tight!"

When I saw the nurse take out a large needle, I began to panic. I fought with the nurses for a while, until I was injected with the needle. My body began to calm down. I felt like I was on cloud nine. The hysterical moment was finally over. The lids of my eyes became heavy and I was drifting into la-la land. Sleep was not one of my favorite things and being forced to sleep is one of my worst scenarios. It is difficult to come out of night terrors when you are sedated with medications.

"Where am I?" I continued to speak in a daze as I was drifting into the land of sleep.

"You are at Central Mental Institution." She replied.

"Central Mental Institution...you have the wrong person...let me see the doctor!" I tried to scream, but because I was sedated the words would only come out with a slur.

"Oh, you will see the doctor in due time...now calm down young lady." She insisted.

I never thought I would end up in the Central Mental Institution. Central was outside of Sutton. The people in Sutton didn't feel they had the need for a mental hospital, because they often weeded out people with that type of mentality.

"Please ...please...don't put me to sleep.... please!" I was groggy and the words could barely utter out of my mouth.

Sleep had taken a toll on me.

It was late in the afternoon when I regain my consciousness. One of the orderlies came in the room with a nurse. They had a food tray for me. I didn't think they were going to sedate me again. They took the straps off with caution. I guess they thought I was going to be crazed again. The orderly left the room after the nurse indicating that it was safe. The nurse began to assist me in getting up. She raised my head upon my pillow and laid the covers below my waist.

"Okay young lady, time for you to eat something." The nurse demanded.

"Can you tell me why I am in here?" I asked, as my body was sinking down into the bed.

At first she wouldn't answer me, and then she picked up my chart at the end of the bed and glanced at me with a strange look.

"Your doctor will be here tomorrow you can get all that information then." She replied, as she walked toward the door.

I waited until she left the room before I began to investigate what was really going on. I looked around the room to see if I could feel a presence in my room. Coming out of a deep sleep sometimes leaves me paranoid, especially if there is an unknown presence in my room.

The phenomenon started when I was a child. The thought of going to sleep at night in the dark was my greatest fear. I would keep my nightlight on until daybreak. Sometimes I could feel my hair rising on my hand and a feeling of my body not being visible. My mother was the only human being that really understood the strange happenings that were occurring in my life. In order for me to feel secured at night, my mother would turn on my nightlight. Some nights she would sleep with me to give me the sense of comfort. Often she noticed me jerking in my sleep and would awaken me.

When we visited the family doctor, He confirmed to my mother it was just muscle spasms and fatigue from staying up all night studying. If I told the true reason that I had insomnia I probably would have been in Central Mental Institution sooner.

The episodes of sleepless nights and terrors were overwhelming for me. Sleeping became my worst enemy. Not even Amy could compare to the drama I received on terror nights. Sometimes daylight was my best friend. I can remember when I couldn't wait for daybreak to burst through the door cracks.

After the recapturing of some of my latest night terrors, I continued to watch the white walls in the room. Finally I dosed off into a deep sleep. It wasn't until about four o'clock in the morning when I awakened with a strange feeling arousing from my body. I was trying to keep my eyelids from getting heavy. The fatigue and daze was overshadowing me. Fighting sleep was a useless battle; because eventually my body was in the mode of comfort without hesitation.

Looking around the room I could see dark figures reflecting on the walls. Some of the figures formed into the shape of humans. Also, there were creepy hissing sounds coming from my surroundings. Later I could hear soft whispering voices trying to capture my attention. I began to panic and my chest felt like someone was standing on it. I thought shaking my legs would help me to retrieve consciousness, but it didn't work. Then I felt a weird presence of someone sitting on my bed. The fearful thing about night terrors is I can hear everything around me, but can only see the things in front of me, if my eyes are open. My body began to perspire heavily as the fear was taking me asunder.

Suddenly I heard the door open in my room. I was beginning to think that spirits were opening my door. I heard someone calling my name. I refused to accept that it was real. Then my name was called again. Finally the trance terminated immediately.

"Pam…Pam!" The voice shouted.

I still couldn't move. Then I felt someone shaking me.

"Pam…Wake up!" The voice shouted closely into my ears.

My body began to feel normal again. Sweat had drenched my gown and I was shaking like a leaf on a tree. When I noticed the moment was reality, I had a sigh of relief.

"Are you okay?" The nurse asked, as she continued to shake my arm.

"…Ah…ah…yes." I said while I startled.

The nurse saw my gown soaked with perspiration and my face was trenched with water, especially on my face. She put her hand on my forehead to check if I had a fever.

"Well…you don't seem hot, but let me take your temperature." The nurse insisted, as she reached in her pocket for the thermometer.

By the look on her face she implicated that my temperature was normal. Of course, I already knew that was going to be the result.

"You must have had a nightmare or something, you were shaking like the devil when I walked in…. are you sure you are okay?" The nurse inquired.

"Yes." I replied.

I couldn't have her thinking I was crazy, although I am admitted into a crazy place.

"I was checking to see if you needed anything." She said while looking into one of the dresser drawers to get me a fresh gown to put on.

"Here, put this on." She said.

I reached over for the gown with a face of despair.

"Are you sure you are okay?" She implied.

"Yes…I was just having a bad dream or something." I replied.

"Since you are awake, I will have them bring your breakfast."

"Thank you…I am starving." I said, insinuating I wanted her to leave.

"You have slept for three days from the first day you were admitted."

"Sleeping three days…can't be!" I thought, as I took off the sweaty gown.

"…I didn't see anything!" I exclaimed without thinking about what I was blurting out.

The nurse was very perplexed as she shook her head, then she bundled up the sweaty gown. She quietly straightened out my bed and then left.

I sat on the edge of my bed wondering where my parents were. I questioned myself over and over. The thought of someone knowing my mental state at this time began to traumatize me. The secret of my night terrors now lays between my mother and Guy Jones my best friend. Guy only knew I had nightmares that scared me to death. I would arouse him with some of my night stories just to scare him. But he never believed me.

The door jolted open. Miss Rawlins was in a jolly mood when she walked in. She was humming a familiar tune from church.

"Well I see you are up and about young lady." She said, as she walked toward my bed.

"Hey...I remember you." I said.

"Of course you do...I am the first thing you saw when you woke up from a three day rest." She said as she sat on the edge of my bed.

"You mean...I really was resting for three days...that's a record for me." I proclaimed.

"You not only rested ...you really slept like a silent lamb." She said, as she took my hand and held it for a moment.

This is the second time she held my hand. She wasn't even afraid of me.

"You be good and listen well." She insisted, as she looked me directly in the eyes.

"Listen well! She doesn't know half the stuff I hear especially at night." I thought as I smiled at her.

Miss Rawlins is a full-figured woman whose body impressions can be felt when she lifts off the bed. It gave me a flashback of the body impressions that were on my bed at night.

"I'm going now, you just be good...and listen well." She kept insisting as she left.

I smiled out of the corner of my face. Then I though about the words Miss Rawlins kept repeating to me. Before I could turn my back she was gone. Even though Miss Rawlins was a large woman she moved very swiftly.

It wasn't two minutes before the nurse came in with my breakfast.

"You must be starving; we got you whole wheat toast, cereal if you like...and..." She said, as she put the tray on the feeding tray across my bed.

"I can see for myself... you don't have to announce it," I said while lifting the top off of the tray of food.

"Well... you are a feisty little lady." The nurse implied.

"No...just hungry." I replied as I hurriedly took a bite out of toast.

"Did you see Miss Rawlins this morning?" I asked.

"Miss Rawlins?" The nurse replied.

"Yes...Miss Rawlins...the heavy lady, she has on a uniform." I explained.

"All the people in here wear a uniform, maybe she is on another shift."

"Yeah, but you can't miss her... she seems very different."

"There are a lot of different people here too...I tell you what, the next time you see her ask what shift she works, then maybe I can have some answers for you."

"Well maybe you can ask her... she left a few minutes before you came in."

The nurse paused for a second in her tracks with an inquisitive look upon her face.

"Make sure you eat all of your food." She insisted as she walked out of the door.

It seemed as though the nurse was trying to deviate from me questioning her.

After I ate my breakfast I laid the tray on the floor. Then I notice tennis shoe prints on the floor of my room. I didn't know if they were from the nurses or from my night terrors. I ignored it and rested across the bed for a moment. I just wanted to be back in my own bed. I was hoping the doctor releases me soon, but first I must find out why they have me in this ridiculous place.

Sanity became obsolete at the time and daydreaming became my security blanket. I began to think about when I first noticed the night dreams. I was about seven years old and it was a stormy night. I could hear the trees screeching against the windows. The thunder was roaring very loud. In my room I had a canopy bed, the poles on the bed resemble the legs of tall men in the shadows of the darkness. As the frightening sounds continued, I began to crawl up into a fetus position for security. If that didn't work, I would put my head under the covers.

One particular night I was under the covers and I could feel the pressure of someone's hands pressing my bed mattress. I was so afraid I would try to shiver my way out of it, but that didn't stop it. So, when the mattress began to relax, I peeped from under the covers. When the coast was clear I would run into Daniel's room and get into the bed with him. When morning came, my father would knock on the doors to awake us. He would find me in his room. The sad part about it, I wasn't in a trance when the activity in my room took place. I really was awake. Sometimes I would pinch myself to see if I was sleepwalking. Sanity was the highest goal I was trying to achieve I thought and maybe Central Mental Institution would help me to meet it.

CHAPTER 3

I thought meeting Dr. Susan Hunt, the great psychiatrist would conciliate my soul, but it only made matters more difficult to handle. She took pleasure in medicating her patients with antidepressants. I can recall the day she visited our school on Career Day. It was an honor to be chosen to escort her around to the classes for her presentations. As I was sitting in the chair across from her, I was hoping she didn't recognize me. She has top of the line credentials and has received so many honorary awards for much of her research. I could tell, by all the plaques on her wall. Sitting in her office made me uncomfortable. She was trying to figure out what was making me tick. She constantly stared at me while she shuffled papers on her desk. She had thick black glasses on with blonde hair. I thought, "What a combination."

Finally, she opened her mouth to conversate with me.

"Well Pam, how are you feeling today?" Dr. Hunt asked.

"I am okay." I replied, with my thumbs flicking around in my lap.

"Are you feeling fatigued?" She asked.

"I'm okay." I said, as I kept looking down in my lap at my thumbs.

"Tell me something doctor…do you think I am crazy or something?" I hurriedly inquired.

"That depends on what you call crazy." She replied distinctively.

"Well, you should know… Why am I here?"

"Pamela…or Pam…which one would you prefer I call you?"

"Pam…but it doesn't matter." I stated.

"Why do you think you are here?" She asked.

"Maybe because I fainted…I don't know." I replied.

Dr. Hunt continued to look at the records inside the folder. She kept flipping back in forth with the papers.

"According to your medical records you fainted at your graduation. Also, it states you were hysterical and delusional." Dr. Hunt stated.

"All I know…when I woke up, I was in this place." I said.

"Not according to my medical records." She said, as she handed them over to me to glance at.

"Pamela Jones was delusive and crazed upon entering the emergency room. She was panicky and seemed to be suffering from shortness of breath. Her skin was clammy and perspiration was pouring from her face." Dr. Hunt read from the records.

"Do you want me to go on?" Dr. Hunt implied with her pen tapping on the paper.

I couldn't let Dr. Hunt go on reading those lies.

"That can't be true…me… never…" I said weeping with tears.

Dr. Hunt handed me a tissue from the box on her desk. Then she came over and sat in the chair next to me.

"I can see that you are not up to talking." She said.

"I'll be okay…I need to talk…to someone." I said, while wiping the tears from my eyes.

"Have you been sleeping well?"

"Not as much as I would like to…but I did sleep for three days."

Dr. Hunt smiled at me and held my hand for a moment. She knew I was heavily sedated during those days.

"You know, I remember you from the Sutton High School…you were one of the students who took me on a tour around the school." Dr. Hunt said.

"I was hoping you didn't remember me." I said.

"I am here to help…looking at your records you were an honor student and very active in school and your community." She answered.

"Now that doesn't mean you won't get to attend college, it just means it is going to take some time." She said.

"But I have so many plans for my life doctor…. all…I did was faint." I stated.

I held my head down with shame of what I have become. Dr. Hunt took my chin and slowly pulled it up.

"You'll get back on track, but I need your help…I need to know what is causing you to have this neurotic behavior." She informed me with assurance.

Dr. Hunt gave me relative information about the episodes of hallucinations I was having when I first entered the hospital. My parents confirmed the fatigued behavior through my family doctor records that stated, I didn't have good sleep hygiene. He also suggested I get enough sleep, exercise regularly and reduce stress, which I know is difficult when you are in your last year of school.

"There were no medications prescribed?" She asked when she flipped through the records.

"Oh yeah…my parents didn't want me on any medications, because they thought it would interfere with my studies." I was reluctant to reply.

"Pam, I am going to ask you some personal questions, if you feel uncomfortable with any of the questions, please let me know."

"Do you wish you were never born?"

"No."

"Do you feel unworthy…. or feel like a failure?"

"Definitely…no!"

"What about seeing things?"

I was on edge and about to become unglued which she asked that question, but I kept my composure.

"What do you mean by seeing things?" I asked abruptly.

"Like …having hallucinations?"

"Sometimes I feel I am not alone." I answered in a way to turn the questioning technique.

"What do you mean by not alone…do you feel a presence around you"?

"Sometimes…it's…really not a presence just a sense of ….I can't explain it."

Dr. Hunt was never ending with her questions. She didn't give me a chance to take a breath before the next question. I felt like I was being interrogated.

Even though I wanted to talk, I didn't feel I could trust Dr. Hunt with this sort of information. She might use it as ammunition against me and I might never get out of this place, so I remained silent.

Then I remembered what Miss Rawlins said, "listen well".

Dr. Hunt finally received the clues that I didn't really want to talk about it. I wasn't going to blurt out answers without first checking her out.

"Pam, there are many people out there that are going through what you are going through...but you made a choice to get help." Dr. Hunt said.

"I didn't make the choice, my parents did." I replied with resentment.

"They only did it because they love you...tell me a little bit about what you like to do."

"Well...I like being popular."

"I can see that already."

"I...like being competitive...and I enjoy doing my best at everything."

"Do you have a friend...or boyfriend?'

"Don't have a boyfriend ...but I do have a close friend name Guy Jones...we grew up together."

"So... is he someone that you trust...or confine in?"

"Oh, yes...Guy is the only person I would tell my deepest secrets to?"

"And do you have any secrets now?"

"Yeah...yeah...I have secrets, don't everybody do?"

"Would you like to talk about one of them?"

"Yes...well no...I don't know."

"Let's talk about the day of your graduation, how did you feel?"

"I was excited...but sort...of tired"

"Why were you feeling tired?"

I had a gut feeling that if I didn't' give Dr. Hunt a little ammunition I would probably be sitting in this chair repeatedly. I began to open up to Dr. Hunt. I recalled the night before graduation. I was on the phone with my friend Karen. We were talking about not having to tolerate with our high school competitors since we were all attending different colleges. After my conversation with Karen, I prepared myself for bed. I was up pretty late, considering I had to get up early for tomorrow's occasion. My body was really tired and rundown from all the errands during the day. I laid across the bed for a while. I began to dose off to sleep, but in the mist of the sleep there was a feeling of not being in my body. It was like I was going into a trance. I tried to fight it by moving around in the room. Fighting wasn't helping me, because the more I fought, the sleepier I became. Suddenly I heard my bedroom door slam. I could vaguely see, but I could hear very clear.

There were voices whispering around me saying, "get her".

I was so scared, but I couldn't move. I tried to scream, but my mouth wouldn't move.

"God help me…God help…me!" Then I kept crying, "The blood of Jesus…" Then some relief was beginning to show up. I was able to tremble and shake my body to reality. I sprang up from the bed and walked around the room hoping that it was over. I was so tired and sleepy. But I detested going to sleep because of what would happen next. I remained awake until daybreak. When I finally came to my senses, I took a shower. In the shower I noticed these long scratch marks on my leg. There engraved into my skin were long nail impressions.

The scratch marks where beginning to fade because of the duration of time they appeared. But I stood up to show Dr. Hunt, so she wouldn't think I was making a fantasy story up.

"See…see…the markings! I didn't do this!" I shouted showing Dr. Hunt the print marks on my legs.

"I don't have nails…not long enough to scratch!" I continued to shout.

After telling the story to Dr. Hunt, she became very subdued. She had become completely indulged with my situation. Then she startled for a moment.

"I am going to request to have a test done on you for narcolepsy." Dr. Hunt said.

"What kind of a test is that"? I asked.

"Let me explain, Narcolepsy is a condition in which people are overcome with irresistible sleep attacks that occur unpredictably and at any time of the day." She explained clearly.

"Do you think I have that?"

"I can't say anything until I get permission from your parents … then we can perform the necessary test."

Dr. Hunt knew that I wanted to get this over as soon as possible. I really want to go back to living a normal life. She continued to record information on her note pad as she spoke to me.

"I am going to prescribe you some medications to help you sleep." She said as she wrote out a prescription on the chart.

I knew it wasn't long before she would be prescribing me antidepressants and psychotherapeutic drugs.

"Our next appointment will be next Tuesday…same time." She said as she jotted done more information in her notebook.

As I exited the room, I heard her pick up the phone and call someone.

"I need to speak to you about something…do remember the sleep disorder patient we had a year ago…. yes…I may have another case for our research on sleep paralysis." She said as she spoke on the phone.

The way she sounded on the phone, assured me that she was interested in helping me.

While walking down the hall to my room, I noticed a girl about my age sitting in a chair in the lounge area. There were other patients in the room also, but this girl stood out among all of them. She was about my age. She gazed at me as I walked past her. She implied for me to come over. At first I was hesitant, because I didn't know what loony tunes I would encounter in here. But she seemed like she needed a friend, so I walked over to her. She introduced herself as Nancy. She wasn't afraid to tell me she was diagnosing with schizophrenia. She continued to discuss her situation. I was amazed at her mentioning she heard voices talking to her. She was talking to someone or something when I approached her. It was a relief for me to be in acquaintance with someone with secrets like me. Nancy seemed very nice, but I wasn't looking for new friends, especially in here. I would rather remain unattached, especially in here. I didn't need anyone else's baggage, because it was too much carrying mine.

"You like it here?" Nancy asks, as she plays with something in her face.

I was trying to figure out what she was playing with.

"It's okay." I strongly replied.

Those words were beginning to become normal to my ears.

"How long you have been here." She asks, continuing to play with her invisible friend.

"About a week…but I hope to be out of here soon." I said with confidence.

"You hear that…sh…sh…?" Nancy asked.

"I know you heard that." Nancy kept insisting.

I began to feel nothing but remorse for Nancy, because she really felt that she was normal.

I was startled and wanted to get as far away as possible, but Nancy kept initiating the conversation. I decided to ignore her invisible friend. I knew that was one of the voices.

"After my test…I'm going home" I said.

"You can leave…but you can't hide…you will be back." Nancy said with a gloomy expression.

"I don't think so." I replied.

"I said the same thing two weeks ago…you see… I'm back." Nancy replied as she pointed toward herself.

"This place is not for me." I continued to be persistent.

"But you will be back…you will be back." She kept repeating.

Nancy was sort of weird, but I gather it was from her condition. I couldn't take the insanity any longer. Talking with schizophrenia was giving me the impression that I was sinking into a world of lunatics. I didn't hesitate to remain in her presence any longer. Quickly I proceeded toward my room.

CHAPTER 4

Yellow painted walls became my daily scenery. Lounging in the activity room was becoming a regular routine. On the day my parents were to visit me, the loud noise from the television was disturbing me. Dr. Hunt was discussing my condition with them in her office. The high anticipation of going home was frizzing my body. I was thinking I would probably be discharged since Dr. Hunt has me on antidepressants and panic attack medications. This type of meds I can administer at home with the help of my mother.

I was constantly glancing at the time on the clock on the wall. Time was moving slowly for some reason. My eyes began to become very heavy. I could barely keep them open. All of a sudden I began to feel drowsy. While I was watching the television daydreaming began to creep in.

My body began to feel funny; I thought, "Here it comes again".

But this time I couldn't see anyone. I could feel the presence of someone near, but no one was visible in the room. In order to fight off the trance I shook my legs continuously. Jerking my body back and forth in the chair was one of the ways I alleviate the trances.

Finally, a nurse walked into the room. She notices I had abrupt movements. She awakened me without asking any questions. I figured she was accustomed to moments like this.

I remember my church minister stating, "A lot of God's disciples are in the nut house, because people call them crazy for seeing things, when it is only a gift of discernment of spirits."

I thought, "I wonder if this is really true?"

Finally, my parents and Dr. Hunt entered the room. I rushed over to receive attention from my parents with a hug. I didn't waste any time asking if I were going home.

"So, I get to go home?"

"Wait a minute...come sit down." Father said.

We sat at the card table in the lounge. I could see by my mother's facial expression that there was no home coming for me today.

"Pam, we are willing to let you go home, but first you have to take a few tests for us." Dr. Hunt insisted as she looked across the room at my parents.

"Test...I don't need any..." I said.

Father was very concerned when he said, "Pamela, just listen to what the doctor has to say."

I listen as she discusses the sleeping tests that will be performed on my brain. Dr. Hunt referred us to a study she was doing on sleep paralysis. From the looks of my parents, she was very persuasive. I wouldn't be surprised if they had already given their consent.

"Tell me a little more about this sleep recording test that you are giving my daughter." Father asked.

"Well, this sleep recording is really called polysomnography, it will show the suppression of the skeletal muscle tone, a sleep onset REM period...which REM is the rapid eye movement, it and also it will check the dissociated REM sleep...I will explain all of these terms when we receive the test results." Dr. Hunt explained discretely.

"Will it hurt?" I asked with a frown on my face.

"Not at all...don't worry you are in safe hands." Dr. Hunt replied.

"Now the test will probably only take about four days..." She continued.

"Four days! You mean I have to stay here another week!" I shouted with anxiety.

"As soon as we get your test results back and go over the results with you and your parents, then we will go from there." Dr. Hunt said.

"Honey we will be right here for you while you take the tests." Mother said.

"I got a big surprise for you when you come home." Father said, trying to convince me to be cooperative.

Father could con me into doing anything, because he loves to show off. Even though I love them very much, my father tends to be the one who spoils me.

"Okay, if you insist." I stated.

"That's my girl." Mother confirmed as she took my hand and squeezed it tightly.

While my parents were embracing me with lots of love, Dr. Hunt looked over at me and smiled. I began to think that everything was working out for my good. Dr. Hunt has big plans for me with her research project. I hope I don't disappoint her.

Meanwhile, while I was finishing up my visit with my parents, Dr. Hunt was assertive with the plans for her new research project. "The sleeping disorder girl" "The sleep paralysis night hawk girl" is about to make history.

Dr. Hunt informed me that she has a research partner, Dr. Jim Stein. He was another renowned doctor destined for another honorary award behind his name. The information about my condition was studied also by to Dr. Stein. I believe they are planning on using me as a guinea pig. I wondered who their Frankenstein was a year ago. I was due to investigate, because I didn't want to be another lab specimen.

After my parents left, instead of going back into that lonely room, I remained in the lounge for lunch. It was very quiet and tranquil. My mind began to go back into time. When I was in the sixth grade, I experienced a moment that I will never forget. I was tired that day. I was about to take a test in math. I had been up all night studying, because I wanted to ace the test with flying colors. While I was watching my teacher review for the test at the chalkboard, I noticed a short man walking into the room. I looked around but no one noticed him. I kept raising my hand to let the teacher know that he was standing there mimicking everything she was doing, but she ignored me. Suddenly the man sat on her desk. I knew then that she and the class saw him, but no one responded. Then I yelled out the teacher's name and she answered me. I asked her if she knew we had a visitor. She thought I was trying to get out of doing my test. But I insisted that she recognize the man that was on her desk. My teacher became furious and sent me to the principal's office. I was embarrassed because the entire class was laughing at me and calling me a freak. The short man was smiling at me as I passed by the desk. I stopped for a moment and looked back and he was gone. Of course, my mother was called and the principal thought I was playing a prank in class. It was weeks later that I described the man to my teacher in a conference. She was astounded of the description I had given her. It was perfect match from the clothing to the smile of her dead father, who passed away before she graduated from college. The teacher thought I was trying to play with her emotions and refused to accept what I had told her. At that moment I was beginning to think I was a freak possessed by the devil. From that day on it was impossible for me to tell or reveal what I saw with my naked eye.

I needed to talk to someone that would believe what I was going through. Talking with my mother was not the answer, because she would brush it off and tell me she was praying for me. Prayer was okay but I needed to know what I was dealing with. Miss Rawlins seemed like the person that could understand me. I anticipated Miss Rawlins was working today so I could talk to her. I haven't seen her all day. Low and behold, here she comes now trotting along the hallway. She trotted right over to me.

Before Miss Rawlins could say anything, I yelled across the room.

"Hi Miss Rawlins", I shouted with enthusiasm.

"Hello lady, how are you today", She said.

"I am great and probably will be going home."

"Oh…yeah!"

"My parents were here today … they discuss with the doctor my situation …and after some test I will be going home."

"Well, that's a good reason to be happy." Miss Rawlins said with curiosity.

Before I could speak another exciting word, Miss Rawlins began to tell me about the tests.

"Having test done, sometimes prolongs it, especially if you are planning on getting out". She said trying to discourage me.

"Dr. Hunt explained to my parents it was going to take about four days."

Miss Rawlins continued going on with her conversation.

She didn't put a halt to her talking.

"I had a friend that went through those sleeping tests and the findings were zero..., more tests had to be done." She said.

Miss Rawlins continued to dampen my hope. My heart began to pound even more.

I thought, "Maybe Miss Rawlins is telling the truth... Why would she tell me these things?"

Miss Rawlins has always been helpful therefore I was beginning to become convinced that my stay could be prolonged by the tests.

I quickly changed the subject to block out any more disappointments at the moment.

"What shift you work on?" I asked to change the subject.

I notice she didn't have a nametag or anything that identified her as being staff.

"Sometimes I work all different shifts?" she replied.

"Where is your name tag...don't you have wear one for security purposes?"

She glanced at the pocket on her white uniform and exclaimed, "Oh...oh...that thing...everybody knows me around here, and I don't need one."

"With my reputation, I don't need identification" she replied.

Miss Rawlins was okay with me; she is probably the sanest person on the staff, with the exception of Dr. Hunt. I beginning to have some confidence in Dr Hunt.

Suddenly Miss Rawlins had vanished. Just like that. I looked down the hallway. She had completely disappeared from my sight.

That woman can move fast for her size. I walked a little further toward my room, but I still couldn't find her.

I passed Nancy on the floor shaking her head and staring at me as though she didn't know I existed. I tried to talk to her. But she would only twitch her lips and shake her head. This wasn't the Nancy I met. I remembered her telling me she was schizophrenic.

I thought, "Could this be one of the symptoms?"

I began to feel depressed as I stood watching Nancy in this delusional state of mind. When I realized I couldn't handle the situation, I ran to my room and sat in the corner with tears rolling down my face. I couldn't stop thinking about Nancy, because she was about my age.

My mind began to wonder, "Will that test help me?"

The thought of the test having a positive result oppressed my spirit deeply.

While sitting in the corner of my room weeping on the floor, I could only think about what my family must be thinking, especially my brothers, Samuel and Daniel. Not being their role models saddens me deeply. All of my accomplishments were perfect examples for them. I continued to weep until my eyes felt swollen. I didn't want to be in Central Mental Institution. I got up from the floor and walked toward the door. I became hysterical and peep out the window of the door.

"Somebody please help me…help…please…!" I yelled frantically.

Continuing to pound on the door, I knew someone would come to my rescue but there were no responses. The sad thing about it, the door wasn't locked. The nurses probably thought I was crazy. I slumped across my bed with deep thoughts of being in a daze. The last thing I remembered was getting my diploma, and then the insanity trip began.

Before I could go into dreamland, a woman came into the room. This time it wasn't Miss Rawlins. It was a nurse with a tray of pills in her hand. She didn't say much. It was though she was programmed to give out meds. She gave me a glass of water, handed the cup of pills to me and insinuated that I take them.

I knew the medication were a temporarily antidote in order to keep me tranquil for a while. I managed to put the medicine in my mouth but I didn't swallow it. With the tip of my tongue, I placed the pills under my tongue. I couldn't fool the nurse because she was accustomed to administering medication to patients. She pried my mouth open. Then she checked under my tongue. Of course, she saw the pills. I had to swallow them.

"I have to figure out away to hide those meds next time." I said quietly as the nurse left the room.

Before I faded into la-la-land, I tried to regain some of my memory. I fiddled around in my brain the dream I had about graduation. Suddenly I began to recapture some of the events. I remember early during the day of graduation, riding in the car with Guy and some friends. Guy was planning an after graduation party therefore, we were gathering up party supplies and food. During the latter part of the day, we stopped at a hamburger restaurant. I was very exhausted, so I remained in the car while they went in to buy burgers. Suddenly another episode of the trances began in daylight, which was unusual for me. There was a feeling of someone pinning me down in the back seat of the car. Sounds were penetrating around me, but I couldn't move. A frightening sense of evil surrounded me. It was as though I was being suffocated. I tried to shake myself out of it, but I couldn't seem to get a hold of myself. I could hear myself hear from within, but the sound was not physically heard. Then Guy returned to the car, slammed the door and awakens me. At that moment I realized, in some cases a loud noise can break up the monopoly. Before I could continue with my thoughts, I became drowsy.

Finally, tranquility kicked in and I was in" Dr. Medicine" world.

CHAPTER 5

"Wake Up!" the voice of a trumpet awoke me with blasting volume. It was the loud mouth of the morning nurse.

"Wake up Pam!"

She began to yell even louder.

"What...!" I shouted.

"I didn't mean to disturb you, but you have tests to be run in about an hour."

"Today...?" I asked.

"Yes today, so you will not be having any breakfast...maybe lunch." The nurse replied.

"So why did you disturb my sleep, do you know a lot of people would pay a lot of money to have slept like that?"

"That is why young lady you are taking the test, so you won't have to pay for sleep."

I don't know if she was being sarcastic or whether it was just her personality.

"Now stay up, someone will come in soon to transport you for the tests." The nurse demanded.

Before the test, Dr. Hunt and Dr. Stein visited me. This was the first time I had ever met Dr. Stein. He was another research genius. Dr. Stein's personal appearance resembles the real Dr. Frankenstein. He had been informed of my condition and was also known for mysterious research discoveries. Dr. Hunt used him as an assistant because of his phenomenon background in sleep paralysis.

"Good morning Pamela." Dr. Hunt greeted me with a smile.

"Good morning" I replied.

Dr. Stein was sitting behind her desk anticipating me sitting down.

"I want to introduce you to Dr. Stein; he will be assisting me through your entire process of testing."

"I am honored to meet you, I have heard so much about you." Dr. Stein said.

"He heard so much about me." I thought as he extended his hand for a handshake.

Dr. Hunt and Dr. Stein continued to ask me questions about my symptoms of the sleeping disorder. Dr. Stein was attentive as she wrote down my responses to the questions. I was debating on what to say without incriminating myself. I definitely didn't want to state any information that would cause more harm in the future.

"The nurse will be in soon to take you to the neurology lab to start your testing...are you ready?" Dr. Hunt asked.

"As ready as ever...I am ready to go home." I replied.

I began to interrogate Dr. Hunt with questions. I knew she probably couldn't answer until she received the test results.

"Dr. Hunt, do you think I will be okay after the testing." I asked.

"It depends on what okay are you talking about." She replied.

"I mean the okay...as...being sane or something...I don't want to be labeled crazy."

"You are not labeled crazy Pamela; you are just having some symptoms that are unexplainable at this time."

Dr. Stein continued to write down every response. He was very strange. He didn't say very much during the interview. I was sort of suspicious of him and didn't want to communicate verbally out of my mouth anymore. Dr. Hunt noticed that I was becoming withdrawn from the conversation.

"Pamela, I can't answer any questions until I have seen the test results...just be patient and relax during the tests so we can see the best results." Dr. Hunt said.

Dr. Hunt could convince anyone with her soft tone of voice, but me, I don't think so. I am sort of reserved when it comes to her. I really don't trust her, because first of all, she really gives me the creeps when she talks to me. It was as though she was using psychology on me to get answers. She doesn't know I am ahead of her game. I could always figure out when someone is trying to finagle an answer out of me. Maybe it's a gift. On the other hand, Dr. Stein was very calm person and was only looking for answers. Now I was on his side when it came to that.

I went along with Dr. Hunt's game and took the test. I just new she wasn't going to find anything. But you know researchers; if they have questionable results, then back to the drawing board.

While the nurse was wheeling my chair to the testing room, I noticed Nancy in the hallway. She was sitting on the floor in front of the door of her room,

"Wish you luck." Nancy said in a solemn tone of voice.

"Thank you." I replied.

"Pamela, I forgot to tell you about 911."

"911...that's an emergency number."

"It will help you." Nancy said as she held my hand tightly.

Somehow the nurse ignored my conversation with Nancy and continued to transport me to the testing room.

My thoughts of Nancy becoming a normal person were beginning to reverse. 911 is an emergency number. I didn't know if she was trying to tell me to call 911 or if it was a code to help her get out of this place.

In the testing room the machines looked very complicated. I was connected to a brain monitor that showed my brain waves. I was surrounded by a variety of neurotic equipment in the room. Dr. Stein and Dr. Hunt were watching the performance of the test on me through a glass window above the room. The nurse injected some sort of drug in me and before I knew it, I was out like a light bulb. The test lasted for a while, but I wasn't aware of it.

Finally, the test was over. When I regained consciousness, I was back into my room. Believe it or not, I was starving. It seemed like it took forever to finish. My lunch was already waiting on the table in my room. While eating my lunch, anticipation about going home was disturbing me deeply. The thought of being home in my own room and my own private area was clinging to my soul. The chances of me going home depended on Dr. Hunt getting negative test results. I was hoping to receive the results speedily, because I missed my family. But most of all, I miss hanging out with my best friends.

After I ate my lunch, I decided to read a magazine. We were allowed to read anytime. I enjoyed reading. Reading was a requirement in our home. Everyone had to pick up something to read during the day. Whether it was a newspaper or just an article that came in the mail. My parents believed that reading increases your knowledge and also enhances your vocabulary. It seems to be true. But in the town I live in, you really can't tell, because everybody is successful one way or another.

My eyes began to feel heavy as I read the magazine. The feeling of dizziness began to shadow me. Maybe it was from the medicine from the tests. Then all of a sudden the room began to feel like I wasn't there.

"Oh, know! Not again!" I thought.

I began to shake my legs and I started prancing around the room hoping this feeling would go away. It did for the moment. My eyelids were very heavy, but I couldn't go to sleep. Tears started streaming down my face. I am so tired of this life. What can I do? It seems like no one understands me except my mother. Dr. Hunt means well, but does she really doesn't understand what is going on with me. I was constantly trying to keep my eyes open. It was a task trying to stay awake when this transit feeling came over me.

There was a calmness overflowing the room, as the paranormal activity was escalating. Your body becomes relaxed as the night visions begin, but your mind wants to deviate from the situation. This particular time, I couldn't feel a presence, but I could hear sounds of everything going on outside my room. My body was paralyzed. I couldn't move anything. My mind was the only faculty of my body that I had control over. My mind kept saying over and over, "God help me…God help me."

I remember my mom telling me to call on God and He will help you. Sometimes it worked and sometimes it didn't. This time it worked. I wonder why sometimes it worked and sometimes it didn't. Was it because the presence in my room was evil?

Is it because the presence wanted to leave? My mother told me it was a gift from God. But would God torment his children? I need answers for these questions.

As I awakened, I laid in the bed for a moment with all sorts of crazy thoughts swimming through my head. The episodes of the sleeping disorder didn't happen regularly until I was on the medication. At home the sleeping disorder was happening rapidly. I was beginning to wonder if medication speeded up the episodes.

CHAPTER 6

While trying to gather the pieces of my life, my mind was meditating on what my friends and family could be feeling about me now. Although I wanted to go home, I really wasn't ready for the turmoil that was about to happen to my family. Admission into a mental institution can cause numerous of rumors and heartaches for your family. Even if Dr. Hunt released me on tomorrow, I don't know if I could handle going back to Sutton. The thought of disgracing my family places remorse in my heart. How were my brothers going to react to the news? What would Guy think of his best friend? I definitely didn't want to face Amy. She is the other nightmare I have to face daily. Amy can make you feel like you are as small as a grain of sand if she wanted too. The thought of me being locked up in a mental institution is all the ammunition she would need to destroy me for life. Running away could be a great solution to my problem. But where would I go. Sutton is all that I know. I am not familiar with Central City and who wants to live in a town with a bunch of unbalanced folks. I needed some answers and I needed them fast.

While I was lying across my bed and trying to figure away out of this, Miss Rawlins walks in. She came in with a piece of paper in her hand. She folded the piece of paper in my hand and closed my fingers around it tightly. Strangely that is all she came in to do. "Listen well." She said quietly. Then she smiled at me and trotted toward the door to exit. This was the first time Miss Rawlins didn't have a conversation with me. She wasn't upset with me because I notice a smile upon her face when she left. Maybe she was too busy to stop and talk today.

I opened my hand slowly and unfolded the piece of paper in my hand. Written on the paper was "Sleep tight…911…Nancy". Miss Rawlins had given me a message from Nancy. Does Nancy need help? Curiosity began to arouse in my head. I left my room and headed toward the activity, hoping that Nancy would be in there. While scanning the room and looking for Nancy, Miss Rawlins was in there watching TV. She knew who I was looking for.

"Looking for Nancy?" Miss Rawlins asked.

"Yeah, have you seen her" I replied.

"She is in the bathroom" (pointing toward the restroom).

Before Miss Rawlins could finish her words, Nancy came out the bathroom and sat beside me.

"Did you receive my message?" Nancy asked.

"Yeah…what's going on?" I replied.

"Nothing"

(Holding the note paper) "Nothing…you write me this strange note and…"

"I didn't mean any harm," Nancy said.

Miss Rawlins walked over to see the note and looked at me strangely.

"Listen well Pamela." Miss Rawlins said as she read the words off the note.

"What is this…listen well…are these some codes are something?" I asked.

"It's not codes…just listen." Miss Rawlins repeated.

"You two are strange…and when I say strange, I mean very strange!"

"Nancy sends me a note with "Sleep tight 911" on it and I am supposed to feel safe in this place!" I expressed deeply.

All of a sudden Nancy started crying. She was crying as though I had hit her.

"Nancy I am sorry…why are you crying?" I asked as I tried to restrain her from crying.

Miss Rawlins moved over to comfort her. I was content to see that there was no one in the room but us, because they probably would have put all of us in straight jackets.

"I am only trying to help you...please...you don't understand." Nancy tried to explain.

Suddenly a nurse came in and noticed the disturbing commotion.

The nurse said, "Is everything okay?"

"Yes...yes." I said.

The nurse walked out of the room after everyone proceeded to calm down.

Miss Rawlins and Nancy immediately left the room like nothing ever happened. I continued to sit in the lounge with anxiety over the commotion that happened. There were some suspicious events going on in this place.

Before I could get interested in watching television, I heard someone calling my name.

It was Dr. Hunt.

"Pamela, how are you doing today?" Dr. Hunt asks.

"Okay." I replied.

"I was looking for you, because we have a counseling session in about five minutes."

I really wasn't interested in her sessions about my sleep problem. I wanted to tell her to leave me alone.

"Dr. Hunt have you gotten the test results back yet?" I asked while trying to gain definite information on my case.

"I have received some of them, but I can't give you the prognosis until I have all of the results."

"So...if the results are good, I can go home and won't have to see you anymore?"

"Pamela, I wish it was that simple...we will still have to monitor your behavior consistently in order to make sure you are doing okay."

"You mean, keep me on medication and watch me act like a fool." I said as I noticed Dr. Hunt walking away.

While I was finishing that sentence, Dr. Hunt walked toward her office. I guess she didn't want to talk about my case in the activity room. I walked beside her as we entered her office.

The moment I sat down in the chair in her office, she began to inquire about my condition. I could tell by her responses, there were no real answers for me. The tests were not conclusive enough for her. Dr. Hunt was hoping that I would have some attacks while I was asleep, but it didn't concur to her research. I was a mystery to her, therefore she was going to release me the next day. Dr. Hunt promised me that she and Dr. Stein would do all that they could to further the research on my case. Meanwhile, I was told to continue on my daily medications and do my monthly office visits.

When Dr. Hunt told me she was going to release me there was not a feeling of excitement anywhere in my bones. I didn't know if my parents were ready for me to come home. Going home and facing the ridicules of the community was not my favorite activity for tomorrow.

CHAPTER 7

I sat solemnly on the bed, thinking about what my friends are thinking about me. All of a sudden, I heard a nurse and my parents walk into my room.

"Are you ready Pam?" Father asked.

"Of course she is ready." Mother answered for me.

"Not really." I replied letting my parents know that I could speak for myself.

"Why not?" Mother asks.

Both of my parents sat down on the bed as I explained to them the reason I was not ready.

"I am afraid…what will they think of me." I said.

"We have already taken care of what you are thinking…you see we were able to convince the neighbors and friends ….you were visiting with our relatives out of town." Mother explained as she huddled me under her.

"We were not going to let you go through the trauma the community would have caused…even your brothers think you are visiting relatives." Father said.

"But…what about the incident that happened at graduation?" I asked.

"We took care of that too…we told them you were in the hospital for fatigue ness…then we told them we sent you to our relatives out of town for rest." Mother replied.

"What about Guy and …"

"We took care of him also…he knows nothing but what we told the neighbors." Mother said.

"We have a surprise for you when you get home." Father said as he was searching for a way to comfort me.

"Honey, don't you worry about a thing…it's going to be okay." Mother exclaimed when she noticed the emptiness in my eyes.

Even though my parents did a cover-up, I continued to feel unwanted and uneasy about the situation. Thoughts were swimming around in my head. What if someone finds out I was in Central Mental Institution? What if I start having these sleeping episodes in the company of friends? I was afraid to go back, and didn't want to mention it to my parents, because of the confidence they had gained.

I couldn't leave without saying goodbye to Miss Rawlins and Nancy. I began to search for them as we exited through the halls. Father kept telling me we didn't have time for goodbyes. Mother was anxious to leave, because she didn't feel comfortable in a place like this. I searched for Miss Rawlins but she was nowhere to be found. Finally, I saw Nancy sitting in the activity room. She waved good-bye. While she was waving, I could see her mouth opening to say something.

"911" Nancy motioned her lips to say quietly.

Those words were very inquisitive in my mind as I left the center. They continue to take control over me especially during my travel home.

The ride home was peaceful, but isolated. My parents didn't say much in the car. I could sense it wasn't the same between them and me. Even though they did a cover up on my condition with the community, they didn't do a cover up with their personal feelings. Mother and I were very close; therefore, the quietness began to intimidate my relationship. She was always helping me to escape the sleeping episodes. Mother knew just what to say to soothe my anxiety. Some nights we would pray together to help me during the nights of fear.

There was an atmosphere of coldest in the car, until we reached our driveway. Father opened the car door for mother and me. He also helped me with my baggage and slowly opened the front door. When I opened the door, there standing in front of me were some of our friends from Sutton community.

"Surprise…!" They yelled with excitement.

The sight of a large banner was over the mantle of the living room a sign stood out stating, "Welcome Home Pamela Our Hometown Valedictorian."

I was astounded. I couldn't believe the town's people went out their way to make me feel at home. I was looking to be shunned by most of them. I looked around the room and noticed that most of my friends was smiling with glee. Then Karen ran over to give me a hug.

"I hope you got plenty of rest…because we have lots of things to do this summer." Karen spoke with much enthusiasm.

The atmosphere was filled with sincere warmth of security. Before I could scan the room there was Guy waiting for his turn to give me all of his attention.

"About time you came home…I was beginning to think you had lost your mind." Guy said while pulling me to give him a hug.

When he uttered those words out of his mouth, I began to think about that crazy mental place. My heart began to panic.

"I didn't mean any harm…I know you are all together…by the way I missed you." Guy explained when he noticed the expression on my face.

My baby brother Samuel came over and nearly knocked me down as he greeted me. He was my favorite of my brothers. He always made me laugh, especially when I had bad days. I can remember one morning when I was recuperating from a terrible nightmare; He walked in my room with his art supplies, sat on my bed and drew me a heart with a smiling face. Samuel was creative when it came to drawing pictures. Sometimes he would come up with some of the most original pictures to attract my attention. His art was always special, because his motive was to make me feel good. Somehow, I get the feeling Samuel is a special child.

Daniel was too busy talking to the girls. He had always been a lady's man since the day he was born. He had these big cheekbones that everyone likes to pinch and beautiful green eyes.

"Glad you could make it…just kidding." Daniel said while he was turning around from a conversation with a young lady.

I was so relieved to see the town had not given up on me. But not for long because in one corner of the room was my competition, Amy. She was staring at me up and down. I noticed she was having a great time whispering to the girl beside her.

Feeling uneasy was beginning to become a part of my demeanor. As I scanned the room of a community social hour, thoughts began to ponder around my head, "Will I ever be able to forget my past…. how long before this secret becomes a reality to other…are these people phony or not?"

Before I could complete my inquisitive suggestions, heavy hands leaned on my shoulder. It was father.

"You okay kid?" He said.

"I'll okay." I replied.

"It's going to be like this for a while…not knowing what to do or say because you don't know what others are thinking."

"I know dad…. but it feels so awkward…I don't know if these people are putting on a show or not."

"Pamela, you know the people in this community."

"Yeah, I know…but I feel as though they are covering up for me."

"How can they cover up something they don't know?"

"Daddy, you know they have ways of finding out things."

"I know…we are just going to have to pray that they don't"

By the look in father eyes, I knew he was concerned about me. His words were not adding up to his body language. I could see father had a heavy burden upon his shoulders. He is a prominent businessman with a problem child. This meant my family and I becoming alienated from this area. I didn't want this to happen, because anyone that becomes ex-communicated from Sutton becomes branded for life. Being branded denoted a miserable life outside of Sutton. I can recall a family that lived in this town about eight years ago that had problems with their son. He was a very handsome young man but had difficulty with his motor skills. This deficiency in his life caused his entire family to be banded from this town. The funny thing about it, the deficiency didn't become noticeable until he started hanging with some of the kids over in Central City. Keeping company with the kids in another town wasn't the problem. It was bringing the other town's children into Sutton. The people in Sutton don't want their children to mingle with outsiders. They informed us that bad habits could become permanent and those types of behaviors could infest our town. I felt it was necessary to mingle with other teens from different background, but it was a thought that I wouldn't dare speak out loud.

Even though I had been isolated for a while from my family, it did not put a gap into our relationship. My family still treated me like I was normal. While the party was going on for me, I began to realize that this was a special moment for me. I had to become grateful to the town's people.

I shadowed father the entire time. Everywhere he went I followed. I didn't feel like talking and daring to empty out my sickness.

As the evening passed, many of the guests began to diminish. I was happy because I needed some peace and quiet. I watched my family as they pampered the people in this town. It was as though they were really covering something. It was obvious to me and probably to others.

Amy didn't leave in the first nor second round. I figured she was hanging around to cook up some good gossip. It was funny how she would dip in and out of other's conversation in the room looking for a headline note for her next gossip group. So far no one gave her attention.

While I was sitting on the couch with my arms folded up, as I was anticipating Amy and her family to leave, she dashed over next to me.

"This is a nice party", Amy said.

I knew she was trying to initiate a conversation, so I started a round for her.

"Yes, it is nice." I replied picking up a sense of decoding from Amy.

"Are you feeling okay?" Amy asks.

"I'm fine." I replied with a firm tone of voice.

"You know…I was scared for when you passed out at graduation."

"Thanks for being concerned…Amy"

"Can I tell you something Pamela?"

"What?"

"Word is around that you got something wrong with you."

"Well that word is wrong...I was just fatigued and stuff!"

"Why are you so worked up about it anyway...I was just telling you the news around here."

"Maybe I don't want to hear the news around here."

"Pamela, for your own good...watch your back."

"There is...I don't have to watch my back...and furthermore Miss Amy you better watch your back."

"Pamela, I am only trying to be your friend by telling you this...if the town's people find out that it was more than fatigue this could be big trouble for you and your family...if you tell me..."

"If I tell you what...there is nothing more to tell."

Immediately I stormed away from Amy, because she was trying to dig for bones that were not there. Then Amy walked over to where Karen was and whispered something in her ear. I didn't worry, because Karen always told me the things Amy would say about me behind my back.

Finally the party was over and the entire guest had left except Guy and Karen. They continued to stay to help out with the after cleaning. It felt like old times having them around. Since we will be going our separate ways, I wanted to spend as much time with them during these last summer days.

While we were cleaning the kitchen, Karen and Guy began to empty their minds of all the latest gossip.

"Pam, we really missed you when you were away." Guy said.

"Yeah...we really did." Karen repeated.

I looked at Guy and Karen and a teardrop came from my eyes.

"I really missed you guys also." I said.

"I have to tell you Pam, lots of people are questioning your illness." Karen implied.

"They sure are...they are wondering why you had to go away...you know how this town is." Guy said.

"Pam...don't take it so personal...you know we will be there for you." Karen said continuing time to assure me.

Guy and Karen began to have a look of questioning above there heads. It was as though they were beginning to read my thoughts. I dried my tears so that they could not get personal with their questions.

"Come on ...don't get all mushy with me...I am okay...I just missed you all so much." I said while smiling at them.

"I tell you what Pam, lets hang out tomorrow at the mall, you can come too Karen." Guy suggested trying to mellow the conversation.

"As...if I have to ask." Karen said.

"Look you guys...I just got back home...I need some time ...but can we get together this weekend?" I asked.

"Fine with me...what about you Karen?" Guy asked.

"Okay...but call us or something and let us know you are still breathing." Karen replied.

Both of them grabbed me with the greatest love of concern. That evening began a permanent reconciliation for us with no shadow of doubt.

Even though there was no doubt about our friendship I couldn't say that about the sleeping disorder I had encountered. While I was preparing to go to sleep, I wondered if I really needed to take the medication that Dr. Hunt prescribed. I watched the bottle of pills sitting on my dresser. My eyes continued to stare at them. In my mind I was boggling whether I should take the medication or not. Then I focused closer on the bottles. I gazed at the Hospital name on the label. Just seeing the label gave me a sense of insecurity. Then my eyes scanned the entire row of pills I had to consume into my body. I knew those pills could put me into a world of sanctuary, but do I want to be totally dependent on these pills? Sometimes they cause the sleeping disorder to accelerate. I didn't want this to happen, but a good night's sleep was priceless to me. I knew the pills were only a temporally fix. Now it is up to me to decide whether I wanted a one-night stand or a cure that could last forever. Finally, I placed the pills in my hand and took one last look. I couldn't stand it anymore. I couldn't take the chance of having another tormenting night. This is one night I needed the quick fit.

"If I stop taking these pills maybe I can become normal again." I said quietly to myself.

I had convinced myself that it wouldn't work. I opened the bottle of pills and took one pill out. A glass of water was already prepared on the table for me, so I took the pill and slowly threw in the back of my throat. The process became less challenging as I opened each bottle of pills. I decided to take the one-night stand.

CHAPTER 8

The third night of peace was a resolution for me. That night my parents were going to a special meeting at the city hall. My brother Daniel spent the night with one of his friends, therefore I was left with babysitting Samuel. We watched television for a while in the living room. Then I helped him to draw a picture. It felt refreshing to be around him. All of a sudden a loud noise vibrated the house. It was thunder and lightning. Samuel was afraid of these acts of God. He was like a hinge on me. Whether he knew it, or not, I was just as fearful as he was, but I didn't let him know it.

"How long you think this will last...I'm scared?" Samuel said trembling with fear.

"Don't worry Sam its only thunder and lightening." I said.

Then a loud crashing sound shook the house. Samuel was glued to me like white on rice.

He began to shiver. I began to rock him like a baby in my arms. With no advanced notice, the lights went out. Samuel began to cry.

"Don't cry...I'm here...I'm here." I said holding Samuel close to me.

Samuel's body continued to shiver and tears were rolling down his face. I began humming a lullaby to him. His eyes were becoming heavy. I knew then that he was calming down. Before I could finish humming, he was knocking out in dreamland. I continued to hold Samuel in my arms. Watching him peacefully sleeping, indulged a spirit of peace within me. Then I sat there in the dark waiting for my parents to come home. It was early in the evening and their meetings sometimes go on all night.

I was hoping this would be one night the lights went out in the city hall, but with my luck they would probably have a generator. I began to feel awkward all over my body. I got up and laid Samuel on the other end of the sofa. I began to walk around in the dark, trying to keep that feeling off of me. It was the feeling of going into a daze. My eyes began to feel heavy.

"I need some light." I thought.

I waved my hand from wall to wall to get to the kitchen, so I could find some candles. I was in luck. Mom had left one of her scented candles out on the counter. Now I needed to find some matches. I was in luck again. The candle was right above the drawer that had the matches in it. This night seemed like it was all planned.

As I returned to the living room with the candle in my handle. I began to watch the reflection of the light of the candle on the wall. At first, I was frightened, until I convinced myself that it was only the shadow of the flame from the candle. I put the candle on the coffee table next to Samuels's art picture. Then I sat next to Samuel sleeping on the sofa. While watching the flame reflections on the wall make shapes, strange feeling began to haunt me again.

"What would I do to have a bottle of pills right now?" I asked myself quietly.

I reclined off the sofa and walked around the room again. I wanted to go to my room and pick up a bottle of my pills, but I was afraid that sleep would catch me in the room.

Finally, it came to a point where I had to sit down. My body was so fatigued. It seemed like the lights were going to take forever to come back on. My eyes became very heavy. At first, I was going into a peaceful sleep. Then I began to have a feeling of being in a trance. Before I knew it, I had stepped into sleep paralysis. I could see parts of Samuel's body sleeping peacefully on the sofa. The reflection from the candle's flame was still making shadowing pictures on the walls. The only thing that could move on my body was my eye. I felt a presence of someone in the room. Then I felt heaviness in the room. There was more than one presence was in the room. I was beginning to believe I was in the spirit world. All of my senses were in activation. I could hear sounds and feel impressions, but I could not move.

As I sat there in a paralyzed state, someone touched me. I couldn't see who it was because they were on the side of me and I could only see things that were in front of me. I continued to fight the parallelisms by trying to move my mobile physical factors. The more I tried to move the more sensitive I became to the surroundings. I was frightened to the point that I didn't care if I died at that moment.

"Just take me...take me...I am tired." I thought, as I was about to give up.

"Please leave me alone!" I screamed from the inside of my thoughts.

Then heaviness came upon my body. Someone was actually sitting between Samuel and me. I couldn't see them, but I knew they were there. I was hoping Samuel would awaken to bring me out of this condition.

"Just one touch...one human touch, would snap me out of this" I thought.

"Please let me awaken."

"Please God help me!" I cried on the inside.

"Please...God...is you...please help me!"

The spiritual battle went on for a while, until I remembered that if I try to shake, sometimes the presence would leave. Now this was a challenge, because sometimes it worked and sometimes it didn't. I tried to immobilize my legs. It didn't work the first time, so I constantly shook until there was a breakthrough. My leg began to shiver then I began to feel it shake. My body was finally returning to its normal state. I didn't feel the parallelism anymore. I was thanking God on the inside.

The lights were still out, but I was sane again, which was a blessing for me. I was tired from the horrible battle I had just encountered. I really wanted to get some normal sleep, but I was afraid of going to sleep. I continued to stare at the walls. Then I picked up Samuel's picture and looked at it for a while and before I knew it I had dosed off to sleep again.

I awakened to coughing and the smell of smoke! The entire coffee table was consumed with fire. I could hardly breathe. I looked over and saw Samuel gasping for breath. The only thought came to my mind was to get Samuel to safety. I ran over to the door and opened it. There standing at the door were my parents. Mother grabbed Samuel out of my arms. Father ran inside to try to stop the fire.

"Pam! What were you thinking?" Mother shouted as she clung to Samuel in her arms.

"But mom…!" I shouted trying to explain.

"You could have killed yourself and your brother."

"I didn't try…."

"Is this another one of your tricks to get attention?" Mother cried.

She didn't give me a chance to explain myself. Father finally was able put the fire out with the extinguisher in the kitchen. He came outside of the house to tell us everything was fine and that we were lucky to have been able to get out before the fire began to consume the sofa. Father knew that I wouldn't do anything to hurt Samuel. On the other hand, my mother still blamed me for being in the mental hospital. She was more of perfectionists than my father.

"Everything's okay…you will have to buy a new coffee table." Father said as he stood in front of mother with the fire extinguisher in his hand.

"That's all you can say…buy a new coffee table?" Mom expressed with anger.

"What else do you want me to say…you want me to say Pam was at fault?"

"You can at least let her know she was wrong."

"Wrong about what Melissa…everyone makes mistakes…aren't you happy your children are alive!"

Samuel and I were standing there watching them bicker at each other. Somehow my mother feels no one makes mistakes. It was late at night and my parents were in front of the house arguing back and forth.

"Richard, don't you think we should seek some more help for Pam?" Mother asked.

"Why…because the coffee table burned?" Father replied.

"No…that is not what I am saying… maybe she needs some more rest?"

"I know what you are implying…if she needs more rest she can get it at home!"

"Pam, Sam, get in the house…we have enough trouble around here…we don't need the neighbors adding anything else." Father exclaimed.

Both of my parents were furious. This time Mother didn't get the last word and most of all she didn't get her way. As we entered the house, father took the remains of the coffee table out the back door. I began to clean up the mess the fire left behind. Mother walked Samuel to his bedroom. Then she came into the living room to open up the discussion again. Mother was a wonderful woman, but she enjoyed having her ice cream and cake and eating it too.

"Mom please let me explain what happened?' I pleaded.

"Alright…sit down and tell me what happened." She said.

"Are you bothering this girl again?" Father said with anger about to explode.

"This time she wants to tell us the truth." Mother replied.

"She is always telling us the truth…you just have to believe her." Father said.

"Let me tell you what happened…for once!" I shouted to detest the feud between my parents.

"I was sitting on the sofa looking at Samuel's picture and I dosed off to sleep."

"So that's when the house caught on fire?" Mother said interrupting.

"Let her finish." Father stated.

"Thanks…all I know is that I woke up with flames looking at me." I said looking at father.

"See Richard, we just have to take her to get some more rest." Mother said.

"Tell me why we have to send her off to get more rest, Melissa?" Father asked.

"You know what happened at the meeting tonight…all the folks asking us, how has our daughter been doing…if they get a wisp of this, they will probably have the town investigating us."

"You worry too much about the people in this town…let's focus on our daughter right now."

"Pam does this have anything to do with you not sleeping?" Father asked.

"I can't lie to you daddy…I am still having these bad nights." I replied.

Mom wouldn't say anything; she knew I was suffering with this sleeping disease, but she is in denial.

"Are you taking your medication?" Father asked, continuing to try to get to the bottom of this.

"Yes, I am…but I have an appointment with Dr. Hunt in two days, maybe she would consider and alternative." I firmly replied.

"I don't know Pam…just don't walk in there telling the doctor what to do."

"I am so tried of taking medicine and seeing doctors…no one really knows what is going on with me."

"Baby, they will find out in due time…just keep praying, sooner or later there will be a remedy."

"You are going to be okay; Dr. Hunt is doing all she can for you." Mother said to comfort me.

"Mom I know that…you understand where I am coming from…I need to sleep, not the sleep that torments you at night…I am tired of wrestling in my sleep."

"Pam we love you…things will work out for your good." Father assured me.

"I hope so…if only you understood." I replied.

As I exited the room I could sense that my parents had the deepest concern for my condition. I was beginning to feel as though I had a terminal disease just waiting to come out of remission. Life with sleep paralysis alienates you from friends and from making new friends. I don't even want a relationship with a guy at this point; because I feel if I go into sleep world, he would think I am some kind of freak. When I think about it, this is only the beginning. If Dr. Hunt and Dr. Stein can't help me, I will find the solution myself even if it meant reaching out for spiritual help. I do attend church regularly and have a great relationship with our minister. So, if man doesn't help, I know God can help.

Going to my room seemed liked the most reasonable solution for the moment. Before I entered my room I passed Samuel's room and opened the door where he was sound asleep. I walked over to his bed and pulled the covers closer to his chin. He opened his eyes and smiled.

"Pam, I know it wasn't your fault, I shouldn't have drawn that picture." Samuel said.

"It had nothing to do with your picture…I love your pictures, you keep drawing those beautiful pictures for me…now go to sleep, you can draw another picture for me on tomorrow." I assured Samuel.

I kissed Samuel on the forehead and said good night to him.

"I love you Pam."

"I love you too, Sam."

One thing about Samuel, he could make your whole world feel at ease. He had this type of Spirit that reaches out to you and gives you hope. I really think God gave us Samuel for this reason.

While I was in my room getting ready for bed, my mind began to consider carefully whether I should take the pills tonight. I want to get well, but would taking the medications make me well? The medication was only keeping the disease in remission. I wanted a cure or else.

"Are sleeping disorders a curse or a gift?" I questioned myself. If it is a curse, I would like to know how to take it off. If it is a gift, I would like to know how to use it. The only one who would know these answers is God or a man of God. Maybe I will ask Minister Burke, he will probably have the answer.

I did my usual path of going over to the dresser and picking up my medication. This time I decided to place them back on the dresser. I picked a magazine off my nightstand to read. As I flipped the pages, I noticed there was an article in the magazine called; "Sleep Tight". I continued to read the introduction. The article was about the millions of people in the world that have a sleeping disorder called sleep paralysis. The topic captivated my attention. It discussed the many tests that were taken to help people with this disease. Then I noticed the research was done in a research center about 200 miles from us. The article also stated that a minister directed it. I became inquisitive about this research so I ripped the article out of the magazine. I noticed it had an 800 number, so I picked up the phone to call it, but father was on the phone. I took the paper and placed it in the top drawer of my nightstand. By then I heard a knock on my door.

"Come in." I said.

It was Father.

"Pam, do you need to use the phone?" He askd.

"Oh…that's okay."

"Alright…you have a good night." He said as he closed my bedroom door.

"You too, father."

I didn't want my parents to know that I was going to do my own little investigation on my own.

Meanwhile I was still contemplating on whether I should take the pills. I really wanted to seek other ways of getting help. I told myself, "I will not take those pills." I am not going to give Dr. Hunt that information until I feel it is time.

CHAPTER 9

I am now sitting in the waiting room at Central Mental Institution. In order to keep my mother from lying about where she had to go on today, she took a personal day from work to escort me to the doctor. I couldn't drive, because the medication stated no driving and if I drove to the doctor, Dr. Hunt would have questioned my ability to drive. I couldn't bear letting her know I wasn't taking the medication. We had a long wait due to Dr. Hunt having an emergency call. Meanwhile, I left mother sitting in the waiting area while I looked around for Nancy in the places I was allowed to travel. As I walked down the halls, I noticed a woman from the back that looked like Miss. Rawlins. I walked up to her. It was Miss. Rawlins.

"Hey…what you doing back here?" Miss. Rawlins said surprised.

"My doctor's appointment." I replied.

"You mean to tell me that you're still seeing that doctor."

"Yeah…for now."

"Can I ask you something Miss. Rawlins?"

"Now you know you can ask me anything…I'm your friend."

"Have you heard of anyone being cured from sleeping disorders?"

"No, I haven't, but I did know someone that was in here that went into a coma."

"In a coma…how did that happen?"

"No one seems to know."

I didn't want to hear anymore about that case, so I changed the subject.

"Have you seen Nancy?" I asked.

"No… not today." Miss Rawlins replied.

"Is she still in here?"

"I'm afraid very much so."

"Could you do me a favor Miss. Rawlins…tell her I asked about her and tell her hello?"

"Of course, I can do that for you."

"Well, I got a doctor I have to see…you have a good day."

"Oh…I plan on it young lady."

As I headed toward the waiting room I could feel the uneasiness in my body. I hated this place. I wanted to light a torch to it and destroy every doctor in the building. I have never seen so many mentally ill people in my entire life. The thought of Nancy still living in this place gave me the creeps. She needed some help and no one cares. All this place does is heavily sedate you for the next episode. I hope I never end up back in here. My mother was standing by the door of the waiting room.

"Dr. Hunt is waiting for you." She said.

"I was down the hall looking for the nurse who was so kind to me." I stated.

"Do you want me to go in there with you?" Mother asks.

"No, I am fine…just be here when I come out."

"I love you Pam."

"Oh mom…I am only going to see a doctor, but I love you too."

I could feel mother's remorse for my condition. She hated that I had this condition and felt it would ruin my life. I was grateful for her support.

I entered Dr. Hunt's office. She smiled as I walked toward the chair.

"How are you doing today?" She asks.

As usual she pulls out my medical file and grabs a note pad to write down my responds.

"I am doing fine." I replied.

"Is everything okay at home?"

"Sure."

"How are you adjusting to the medications?"

"Fine"

426

"Do you have any questions?"

"No."

"Pamela are you okay...you seem to be short with answers today."

"I'm okay; I just want to know if I can be cured?"

"I can't give you an answer to that until we have done all of our testing."

"But you did find out that I have a sleeping disorder?"

"Yes, but there are still more tests to run."

"Did you do a CAT scan on me?"

"Yes we did."

"Did you find anything wrong with my brain?"

"No, we didn't, but we did find out that you have a lot of stress attacking cells in the brain."

"What do you mean by a lot of stress attacking my brain?"

"Well Pamela, when you did the sleep test, we found out that your body is not properly resting."

"There are lots of people who don't rest, that doesn't mean they have to be crazy."

"I am not saying you are.... what I am saying is that you do have a problem with stress that can generate into something more serious if we don't find out the problem."

"I'm not stressed...you see I graduated with high honors."

"Pam, you must understand that stress can generate from a number of areas."

"Doc you are going to have to explain that to me."

"First of all Pamela, I don't feel you are telling me everything, I can't help you unless you help me."

"I am answering all the questions."

"It's not your answers, its what you are not answering...you have a sleeping disorder, now I need to ask you some questions that need straight answers.

"How long have you been having a difficult time sleeping?"

"Oh, I don't know...it could have been ever since I could remember."

"Are you afraid of the dark?"

"No!"

"Let me rephrase that; Are you afraid to fall asleep in the dark?"

I hesitated for a moment and replied, "Yeah… sometimes."

"Tell me why you are afraid sometimes?"

"Well because…it feels funny."

"What do you mean by feeling funny?"

"My body feels like it is slowly going into a trance."

"Can you hear your surroundings?"

"Yes, all my physical faculties are working except one."

"Which one?"

"I couldn't move my body."

"Tell me what else happens?"

"I began to feel like I am paralyzed."

"When we did the REM test on you, we noticed that your brain waves were in an awakened state while you were sleep."

"Were you able to see or visualize what was in the room?"

"Yes, many times."

"Pamela, don't be afraid to answer this next question."

"Do you see things?"

"Of course, everybody sees things."

"That's not what I am talking about…I am talking about seeing things that a normal person couldn't see."

"What are you trying to say Dr. Hunt? I am not normal, because I see things others don't see."

"Pamela, I'm not saying you are not normal…its just some people have the ability to tap in to zones that others cannot, this is one of the reasons Dr. Stein and I are doing a research on this particular disorder.

"Does this mean there is a cure out there?"

"Well, we are working on it, but until then we need your cooperation with some other tests that we will be running in the future…since you are now eighteen, we don't need your parents' permission."

"By the way Dr. Hunt… is this disease called "Sleep Paralysis"?"

"Yes, that is the medical name for it…but I am not saying you have this…I just see some symptoms."

"Pamela, are you taking all of your medications?"

Dr. Hunt began writing another prescription out for me. She said it was a drug to keep me from having the sleeping disorders regularly. I didn't want to take another pill in my life.

"So does this mean, I don't have to take the other medications?" I asked.

"No, you must continue taking the other meds." Dr. Hunt replied.

"Pamela on your way out the medical clerk will give you the release papers to have the other tests done."

"When will the tests start?"

"As soon as I can discuss it with Mr. Stein…I will have someone call you…do you have any questions for me?"

"No."

"Good, I will see you in two weeks and by then I should have some dates for testing."

"Thanks, Dr. Hunt."

"You have a good day and take your medications."

I didn't reply to that statement, because I didn't know whether I wanted to take any additional meds. My body was beginning to become a medicine cabinet. I signed the papers to take further tests whether I agreed or not. I just wanted some answers.

While driving home mother noticed how quiet I was.

"How was your appointment?" Mother said.

"It was okay…I have more pills to take." I replied showing her the prescription paper.

"Well Pamela, it's only for your good."

"Is it for my good or for your good?"

"Why would you say something like that?"

"The reason I am on these pills because you fail to deal with the truth."

"What truth?"

"Mother you can fool everybody except me."

"I have nothing to say." Mother said very nervously.

"Yes, you do. What about the times you saw me having the night terrors, you never told father?"

"Why should I tell him and put more burdens on him."

"Because he is my father…and he should know.".

"Mother, I know you have a secret, I can feel it."

"When I look at myself…I see you… the perfections…everything being perfect and but really happy."

"I'm happy."

"No you're not."

"Who are you to say young lady whether I am happy or not."

"You go on acting like there is nothing wrong with me…then when the least imperfection comes out you are ready to have me committed."

"I only want what's best for you."

"Yeah…me out of your life, so you want have to deal with this disease."

"This is not a disease."

"See…I knew you were hiding something!"

"Yes, Pamela! I suffer with the same thing you do!"

"So why did you let me go on thinking I was not normal…maybe you should be the one seeing the doctor."

"Pamela listen, throughout the years I have learned to adapt to this disorder."

I began to realize mother was in as much pain as me.

"How did you adapt mom…I don't see you afraid to go to sleep, I don't see you on medication."

"I am on medication, at first it was over the counter benadryl then it escalated to prescribed drugs."

"Is father aware of this?"

"Yes, he is and very supportive…that is one of the reasons your dad is so defensive when I agitate you."

"So, I gather the town does not know about you."

"No, and we plan to keep it that way."

"Now this Dr. Hunt, have you known her all the time."

"Yes, she has been my doctor for some time."

"So all the time she was just putting me on with questions?"

"Not really Pamela, according to Dr. Hunt Sleep paralysis can be hereditary, that is one of their research projects.

"Mother I didn't mean to get you upset and everything, I just wanted to know the truth."

"Now you know the truth…just leave it alone."

"Mother, I have something to show you when we reach home."

"What?"

"I think I can solve our problem."

Anticipation indulged inside of me as we pulled into the driveway. I just knew I stumbled over a remedy for mother and me. I ran to my room and grabbed the magazine clipping out of my nightstand drawer. Mother was in her room changing her clothes. I stormed into her room with excitement.

"What has come over you?" She asks.

"Remember when I said I have a solution." I said trying to rekindle her memory.

"Yeah…I remember."

Pulling out the magazine in front of her, I said, "Take a look at this."

Mother stared at the article's title. Then she went and sat on her bed and began to read the article.

"We can't do this." Mother said with eyes of disappointment.

"Why not?" I asked.

"Because if the town's councilman ever found out we went to a research center for testing we would be alienated for life."

"Who cares what the council says."

"I do, we can't start all over, your father has a great job and I am Assistant principal at a prominent elementary school…we can't stand to loose anything at this age."

"So why can't I go and do it…college doesn't start until September?"

"I don't know Pamela, let me think about it."

"Mother if you let me go…I can help both of us and if this disorder is hereditary…I will be helping our future generations."

"Just let me think about it."

Dr. Teresa

When my mother thinks about something, it could mean she is all for it. The problem is convincing father. He is not keen on me having research done on me. He doesn't even enjoy the conversation of me being in a mental Institution. He constantly defends me when my mother wants to have me committed. Sooner or later someone is going to have to surrender to the truth and pay for it.

CHAPTER 10

I had reached a decision not to take my medications. The thought of not having to take the pills gave me security blanket or false sense of healing. It wasn't the pills that were killing me softly, it was the frequent moods that kept me tapered to the bed.

I had been feeling great lately and felt I needed to be around people more. That is when I decided to take up the offer with my friends and hang out. I am excited about hanging out with Guy and Karen on tomorrow. We hadn't hung out with each other since the day of graduation. We had plans to go to the mall and shop for some college things for our freshman year. Even though Karen and I would be attending separate colleges, the schools are only a few miles apart. Guy and I will be attending Harvard University. It seemed like we are inseparable. Until I had the night terrors, in which Guy doesn't suffer with.

The night before the big day at the mall became my greatest horror night. It started out with me sitting at my dresser in front of the mirror. I began to brush my hair. I felt like pampering myself tonight. I even gave myself a homemade facial. Suddenly I heard a knock on the door. It was Daniel. We hadn't talked much with each other since the incident.

"I was wondering if I could borrow five dollars from you." Daniel asked as he peeped around the door.

"Sure, look in the top drawer of my nightstand." I replied.

I had forgotten that I kept the magazine clipping about the sleep tight article in that drawer. Before I could intercept Daniel opening the drawer, he noticed the article. The headline of the article was so bold until he couldn't miss it even if he wanted to.

"What's this Pam?" He asked as he pulled the paper out of the drawer.

"Oh… it's some article I tore out of a magazine."

"Have you read it yet?

"Yes…some of it."

"This seems interesting, I heard about this sleep paralysis, but not too many people like to talk about it."

"Would you if you were diagnosed with it?"

"I guess not…people will think you are some type of a freak or something."

I took the article out of Daniel's hand and said, "But future doctors like me want to gain all the medical knowledge they can."

"I guess so…hey, thanks for the five…I'll…"

"Don't worry…I'll get it back someway or another."

Daniel walked out of the room, while I continued to work on my facial. Suddenly my eyes began to glance at the bottle of pills on the corner of my dresser. It was strange because during the entire week I didn't notice those bottles. I thought I had placed them in the corner so I couldn't see them. Even though the bottles were like a billboard in my face, I refused to yield to them. I decided to listen to some music from the radio on my nightstand. Slowly my body was beginning to become tired and my eyelids became heavier and heavier by the moment. I was trying to fight it by moving around in the bed. It didn't work and I was too tired to get up and walk around like usual. Finally, I began to go into a trance and my body was immobilized to the point I could not move. The lamp was still on in my room and I could see everything that was in front of me. First, I heard a hissing sound in the background. Then there were voices talking all around me. Suddenly I saw a figure of a woman standing over me about to smother me to death.

I kept screaming inside of my body, "Help…help!"

No one could here me. Then I noticed other body shadows hovering over me. I realized there were spirits in my room. It was horrifying. I could not shout. I could not move. My eyes were my only defense at the time. On my bed was a movement of a heavy person sitting on my bed.

Heaviness began to burden my body as I fought for help. One thing I noticed was that they didn't touch me. They only looked at me and did a lot of muttering. I couldn't understand their conversation because the sounds were all cluttered together. I began to cry inside again.

"God please help me!"

"God please…please help me!"

I remember in the article that some of the people would call for Jesus. So, I began to call for him.

"Jesus please, help me!"

"Help… Help!"

Finally, I felt myself getting a breakthrough. All of the spirits had left my room, but I still couldn't get up. The heaviness was still on my body. It seemed like I was normal. I could still see the light from the lamp, the radio was still playing, but I was still in a paralyzed state. I didn't know what was going on. There was nothing in the room. I couldn't see all of the activity going on, because I was still in a trance state of mind. I waited there for a while hoping that I would come out of this at any time. When I thought it was all over, a paranormal activity started again. I closed my eyes immediately. A Spirit sat on my bed and started playing with my hair. This was the first time I had it to touch me. It felt like a woman's hand playing around in my hair.

I kept praying in my mind, "Lord please, don't let me open my eyes to see this person."

I refused to even peep at it. I was afraid I would see some hairy two-eyed woman looking me in the eye.

I started calling in my mind, "Help…please somebody help!"

"Jesus please… help me!" I said this over and over again until it left.

My body began to come out of the trance as I forced my legs to shake out of it. This time I didn't give myself a chance to go back into it again. I immediately jumped up when the heaviness left. My body was shivering and sweat was popping off of me like popcorn. I was so terrorized until I sat on the side of my bed with a stare. This was the worst terror I had ever had. It was a double dipper. I kept staring at my dresser of pills. I was so frightened until I didn't want to go to sleep unless

I had some pills. I reached over to my dresser and took all the bottles of pills and started taking one pill after another. I didn't care if it said once a day or twice a day. I needed help to sleep, and I needed it now. I didn't have any water, so I threw each pill one by one in the back of my throat and swallowed them dry. It was difficult without water, but it was worth it. The medicine didn't work automatically, so I stood up in the bed listening to the radio until my eyes became relaxed. I desired to be in dreamland regardless of what it took to get there.

When I awakened, I was very tired and did not want to deal with anyone. Antipressants began to become my best friend. It was eleven o'clock in the morning; my body was dominated by the will of staying in bed. Guy and Karen are supposed to pick me up around twelve o'clock to hang out at the mall. I could not face the day. Depression was beginning to creep into my senses. There was nothing that felt good to me than being under the influence of some type of substance. I kept my room door locked because I did not want Samuel to see me in this condition. Samuel would usually come into my room in the mornings and awaken me with one of his smiles or artistic works. He probably tried to come into my room, but I had the door locked. Samuel never intruded on my privacy. He knew if I had my door locked, it meant that I was busy or something.

Suddenly I heard a knock on the door it.

"Pam are you up!" Samuel said.

"Yeah" I replied.

"Can I come in?"

I hesitated to answer that question. I didn't want Samuel to see me sedated and delusional. I negotiated in my mind a good answer for him, because Samuel was very fragile when it came to our relationship. Then I thought, maybe he had one of his famous pictures he wants me to see.

"Samuel, give me a moment." I said.

I reached over my bed to go toward the dresser. I didn't want Samuel to see the medication bottles, so I placed them inside the dresser drawer. Then I wobbled across the room to open the door.

"What took you so long?" Samuel asked.

"You got to give a girl a chance to be presentable." I said.

As Samuel walked into the room, I could see he had drawn another picture for me. I took the picture and smiled. He was so happy I liked the picture. I had a wall full of pictures by Samuel. He had a wall of fame. I believe this is one of the reasons Samuel loved coming into my room.

Samuel and I chatted for a few minutes until I heard my mother calling my name. Then I could hear footsteps coming toward my room.

"Hey Pam, are you ready!" The voice said.

It was Guy's voice projecting through my bedroom door. Before I could reply, he opened the door and saw Samuel and I on the bed talking. Karen was right behind him.

"Are you still going with us today?" Karen asked.

I wouldn't dare tell them no, but on the other hand my heart wanted to be far away as possible when it came to indulging with company. This was the day I was supposed to hang with Guy and Karen at the mall.

"I don't know if I want to hang out today." I said.

I began to make up excuses for not going to the mall.

"I think I will stay home today and spend some time with Samuel." I stated.

Samuel was all smiles when I said that. But I really didn't mean I was going to saturate my entire day looking at him drawing pictures.

"You have all summer long to spend the day with Samuel." Guy said.

"No, she doesn't!" Samuel replied as he moved closer to grab my arm.

"You stay out of this you little whimper." Guy said.

"Hey…wait a minute, Guy… Samuel hasn't done anything to you." I said.

"Okay… guys lets' stop this…are you going or not?" Karen asked.

"Can we make it another day…I am really tired?" I replied.

Tired wasn't the word to use at this time, but it worked.

"Pam…okay go ahead and rest and everything…we'll call you later." Guy said as he looked at Karen with disappointment.

"You are really going to miss it, remember the guy name Tommy... he is going to be there." Karen stated as she began to manipulate me into going. It began to work, because my thoughts began to change about hanging out at the mall. Maybe I needed some adventure in my life or maybe it's just another fantasy. Why would a guy be interested in a freak like me? Then again, there could be someone out there made just for me. Even though these thoughts were sounded, I still had doubt about today. My father always told me, "When in doubt don't move".

I looked at the both of them. I didn't want to disappoint them, but I didn't want to be disoriented at the mall either. My final answer was "no". One thing about my friends they were apt to hear anything and not be offended.

CHAPTER 11

Even though I insinuated I was going to spend the entire day with Samuel, it didn't happen that way. I ended up spending the entire day in my room. I had become obsessed with being alone, until one day Guy and Karen came over and insisted that I go to the mall with them. They were very persistent. The both of them dragged me out of the bed and helped me to get dressed. I even put on a little make-up. I began to look seventy-five percent Pamela.

Even though seventy-five percent of me looked Pamela, this didn't take away my attraction from people at the mall. Almost everyone was greeting and smiling at me. Many of them came over and chatted with me. I was getting the center of attention again. Somehow there was not one doubt in my mind that I couldn't overcome this mishap in my life.

As we walked through the mall, I noticed Tommy sitting on one of the benches in the mall. He was talking with a young lady. I was hoping he would see me. Tommy was one of the most handsome guys in Sutton. Most young ladies called him a playboy. But I would say to myself, "If you got it, play it." I had always been attracted to Tommy, but because I have these night terrors, I was afraid to get into an intimate relationship with someone. I am afraid I might fall asleep on him and give him his worst nightmare. Sleep paralysis can put a brand on your relationship with someone if you are not careful. But I believed God has a special person out there for me.

Suddenly I felt someone from behind me touch my shoulder, it was Tommy. Karen looked at me and smiled. She looked at Guy with a look of; let's give her some space. Tommy and I began to chat.

"How are you Pamela" Tommy said as he stared at me up and down.

"I am fine." I tried to say bashfully.

"I'm sorry I didn't make it to your welcome home party."

"Oh…that's okay."

"How was your visit with your relatives?"

"It was okay."

"So…when are you leaving for college?"

I hesitated for a moment, because I really didn't know whether I would start college in the fall.

"…In about a month."

We continued on with divers of subject matters. Tommy treated me as though I was the only girl in the mall. Every time someone would stop to talk to us, he would speed the conversation up so that we could be on a one to one basis. I was beginning to feel wanted again by someone. It felt mighty good to have an attraction from the opposite sex. Even though I knew Tommy played his cards well. At this time, it didn't matter what cards or who cards he was playing.

Suddenly I began to perspire heavily above my forehead, while he was talking. I began to breathe rapidly. I tried to avoid attention from Tommy by turning around and pretending I was watching others passing in the mall. Tommy noticed the expressions on my face. He started walking me toward a bench.

"Are you alright?" He asked.

"I'll be okay." I replied as I sat on the bench.

Tommy continued to watch my face roll with sweat.

"Are you sure you are okay?"

I couldn't hold it any longer. I began to have a panic attack, one of the symptoms Dr. Hunt warned me about. I had shortening of breath and could hardly breathe. I felt as though the world was caving in on me.

"Pamela…you don't look to good." Tommy said as he continued to try to keep me balanced.

I couldn't reply back because of the dizziness that fluttered my face. I could tell Tommy didn't know how to handle the situation. He began to panic and started looking around for help. Then Tommy sat me on the bench and went looking for Guy and Karen. As he stepped away, my sight became blurry and I began to go into a trance. Tommy's visibility was like I was in a dream. I tried to keep my body from transforming, by shaking my legs and arms. The feeling of numbness came over my entire body. I couldn't do anything but lie there in a paraplegic state. Tears began to form on the inside of me, because I couldn't believe the episodes were happening while I was trying to build a relationship with someone.

Finally, I felt a hand touch my shoulder.

"Pamela…you okay." Karen said.

"Yeah…we rushd over as soon as we heard…" Guy said.

"Heard what?" I said.

"I heard you weren't feeling well." Guy replied.

"I'm okay…just, let's go home." I said.

"But we…" Karen said.

"No…let's take her home." Guy said.

"Where is Tommy?" I said.

We looked around and Tommy had disappeared. I didn't know if I had scared him off. I was afraid that the Dr. Jekyll and Mr. Hyde might come out in me and scare him off. After I was okay, Guy and Karen took me home. It was a while before they invited me to another public outing.

Days became longer and nights became shorter for me. Anti-depressants became part of daily diet. My body became weak spirited. I could barely hold my head up on my body. Food was not a priority any longer. I was destining for suicide.

Several times Guy and Karen came over to take me out, but I wouldn't take that chance. They even would come over sometimes and sit with me. Somehow, I knew that they knew something was not right. I was hoping they didn't spread the word around about me, especially in this town. The fear of Tommy spreading gossip about what had happened at the mall was relentless in my heart.

My daily routine was getting up take meds, lie in bed, and get up take meds and go to sleep at night. The night was really not sleep, because I continued to have night terrors and they became more aggressive. I began to sustain my sanity with more pills. My everyday attire became t-shirts and shorts. My personal hygiene was not becoming anymore. I would look into the mirror and become discouraged, wondering what has become of me.

I continued to make my appointments with Dr. Hunt, but there seemed to be no progress for me. Even though she and Dr. Stein were working on research that could possibly cure me. I hadn't seen any results yet. Every doctor visit either gave me more anti-depressants or experimenting with a new drug. It had become a never-ending story for me.

College was not a great priority in my life at that time. Even though I had been accepted into one of the top colleges in the United States, it was not a big deal to me anymore. I was one month away from stepping into my real reason for living and it was not a reality to me anymore. My goals had now become my dreams. My dreams had now become my goals.

My parents were having a difficult time adjusting to my new characteristics. Father would come home from work and not look me into the face. I overheard him and mother talking one day in the living room. They were discussing the matter of sending me back to Central Mental Institution. Both of them were having problems on their jobs with their colleagues. Father was mentioning how the customers in the bank would be whispering with the employees whenever he was present. Mother was concerned about the parents who were often complaining about her. She had never had any complaints on her job in the years she was employed. My parents were beginning to think that the community was getting suspicious about me, because I would never show up for functions that the town would have. I was always the center of attraction when it came to attending our town's functions. I was considered the number one girl in town. This all changed after one incident during graduation. Its funny how one flaw can disseminate your entire life?

I was deeply concerned about being sent back to Central Mental Institution. I did not want to be cooped in that place again. It seemed like there was no turning back for me. I needed some answers and I needed them now.

CHAPTER 12

I awakened one morning and had enough of this life. I did not want to be another outcast from this town. I waited until everyone left the house. Father left first, while mother took Samuel out for a day at the park. Daniel left to be with friends at the mall. It was the perfect moment for a great escape.

I began to think of a plan in my mind. Then I took out my overnighter and began to pack some clothes. I was determined to do something about my situation. When I glanced at the bottle of pills on my dresser, I refused to pack them into my bag. Although it was a challenge for me, I didn't give in. I needed a real life away from doctors and pills. Then I looked into my nightstand drawer for the magazine article and also took out the cash I had been saving. I dashed out of the room and exited my home. I didn't know where I was going, but it was a step toward redemption.

While I was walking, a sense of peace came upon me. It was as though I was gaining control over my life again. Before long I passed our church. My conscious kept pestering me to stop inside the church. I continued to wrestle with the voice on the inside, but it kept tugging at me rapidly. Finally, I gave in and walked inside the church. I sat on the bench for a while and began to pray to God for help. Distress was kindling my soul, because this was last resort, before I became totally loony. I felt this was my last resort before I became a loony.

As I was praying, I heard footsteps walking from the back of me. It was our community Pastor, Pastor Burke. Pastor Burke was a good man and willing to help anyone who asked for it. He was up in age and a faithful servant of God. He did not compromise with the hidden secrets that go on in Sutton. He knew there was too much pressure on success in this town, but he couldn't do anything about it. He would often tell us in Sunday services, "Success is planned by God and not run by man."

But the town's people didn't listen. He was only a Sunday voice to them. But I have always listened to him, because he has a lot of wisdom.

Pastor Burke waited until I stopped praying before he interrupted me.

"Pamela, how are you doing?" Pastor Burke asked.

"Fine...I guess." I replied.

I looked at Pastor Burke sincerely and said, "Can I ask you something?"

"Sure" He said.

"I mean ask you something...and you won't think I am crazy."

"Pamela I don't think you are crazy."

"You will when I finish with what I have to say."

"Pamela whatever you say in here stays between you, me and God."

"Well...I have been not sleeping at night."

"Go on." Pastor Burke said as he became interested.

"I have not been sleeping like normal people."

"Pamela, lots of people doesn't sleep normal...its called insomnia."

"Seeing things is not normal Pastor Burke."

"What sort of things do you see?"

"I mean things that ordinary people don't see."

"Pamela, you are just imagining things."

"How can I be imagining things...when I can hear and see what is going on."

Pastor Burke became very inclusive with his listening skills. He began to analyze every situation I was explaining to him. I could tell by his facial expressions that he somehow understood me but didn't want me to decode it. He didn't interrupt me with his interjections. By the expressions that were on his face I believe he had faith in my confession. When I recaptured some of the night terror events I experienced, He suggested we continue our conversation in the conference room. Pastor

Burke was a very respectful man and I trusted him. As we entered the room, he reached over to pick up his bible. He asked me to open it to Psalm 91.

Then he said, "Pamela this scripture was written for man to feel the safety in the presence of God."

"But what does it mean?" I said.

"Read it." He said.

I kept on reading it until I got to the fifth verse, then I paused.

"What are the terrors by night?" I said.

"It is the evil that is around." He said.

"Why would God allow evil to be around you?"

"Evil has been on this earth since the beginning of time…even more so today."

"But…why me?"

"I don't know Pamela."

"All that I know is that some things are unexplainable."

"So, you're telling me this could me normal?"

"I can't say…but I do no that David wrote this scripture and he was chosen by

God."

"So…this means I could be chosen?"

"I don't know."

I began to continue reading the scripture then I came to the sixth verse.

"What about the pestilence that walks in darkness…what are they?" I asked.

"These are the evil influences or agents that are in darkness." Pastor Burke replied.

"What do you mean evil influences…or agents?"

"I don't know for sure…it could mean evil spirits…diseases…I am not really sure."

"So, are you telling me that I could be cursed?"

"No, Pamela…I want you to know that you are not alone in this situation."

"Well I know that…but why me?"

"Pamela, I don't have the answer…but I am sure God has given the answer to someone."

As I finished Psalm 91, sleep paralysis was beginning to become alive to me. I wanted to know whether it was a gift or a curse. This is when my journey of the unknown began.

I pulled out the magazine clipping that was in my bag and showed it to Pastor Burke.

As he was reading it he said, "Yes…I heard of these people."

"Do you think these people can help me?"

"I don't know…and if I did…you know what kind of trouble you would be in."

"I don't care, I just want some answers."

"Sometimes some things are better off left alone."

"I know… but I got to find the answers…can you help me to contact them…there is a phone number on the bottom…you see? I asked as I pointed out the phone number at the bottom of the article.

"Yes…but I don't know if your parents would agree with me."

"I asked my mother, but she hasn't gotten back with me…I really want to talk to them."

"I don't know much about this research…but I have heard that it is legal…it also has helped lots of people."

"I just don't understand."

"Some understandings come in time… the silent predator that clinches my soul still gives me a sense of insecurity."

"So…can you help me?"

"I don't know these people…and look what town they are in, if the townspeople heard I was over in Central City it could mean a lot of talk here."

"Please…Please…. Pastor Burke, I need your help."

"Is that where you are going with that bag?"

"Yes…I need some answers…I need it fast, before I go off to college."

"I tell you what…let me get back with you on this…but I want you to go home and wait until I call you…I'll see what I can do."

CHAPTER 13

Days passed by and no call from Pastor Burke. He wouldn't look me in the eyes when he greeted me after Sunday morning services. I knew then the town had gotten to him. My parents wouldn't even talk about it. When I asked Mother what Father said about me going over to the research center in Central, she ignored me. Everyone was beginning to shun me. Samuel no longer drew pictures for me, and Daniel began to avoid my company. All hope was coming to an end. I was really beginning to believe that I was cursed.

It is one month away before I would be stepping on the university ground. I didn't know whether I should withdraw or continue to pursue my dreams. I didn't want to put my career on a stand still, but I couldn't attend college with this state of mind. Things began to take a turn for the worst for me. I isolated myself from society. My night terrors came day and night with no answers from man or God. I began to lose all hope. My parents were very adamant about me going back to Central Mental Institution. After one visit with Dr. Hunt, I was recommitted back into the institution.

For the very first time I didn't mind being in this place. I think I was beginning to adapt to this world on the other hand my parents would think differently. I could finally relate with people who really understand me, Nancy and Mrs. Rawlins.

Today I was in the recreational room watching TV alone. I could barely keep my eyes open because of all of the drugs my body was sedated with. I began to take a nap in the chair. Taking a nap was a daily routine for me. It felt so relaxing, until the moment of hallucinations crept in. I began to see all sorts of people walking around in the room. Some were even talking to me, but I couldn't talk back. It seemed as though my spirit was talking to them, because every time they would say something to me, I would respond from my mind. It was an actual communication from the mind. This was a new level in night terrors for me. There were no monsters or anything. The people were communicating with each other as if I was actually their audience in the room. My heart was pounding excessively with utmost desire to escape.

Suddenly, I heard a voice cry out to me. "Pam...Pam!

It was Nancy standing in front of me yelling my name. I couldn't awake until she shook me. That is when I came to reality.

"You okay Pam?" Nancy said.

"Of course I am." I said.

"Why are you still in here?" I said.

"Because... I need the help." Nancy replied.

"How long you are going to have to stay in here for help?"

"It won't be long...Dr. Hunt is helping me."

"Nancy how long have you been in here?"

"I don't know."

"Do you get to see your family?"

"Yeah...all the time."

"Well that's good...but don't you want to go home?"

"I don't know."

I didn't know what to think about Nancy. She seemed to think she is okay and this place is okay. Nancy has been on drugs so long until her brains had become fried. I couldn't bare the thought of being a twin to her condition. Getting out began to ponder my mind excessively.

"Nancy, I know someone who can help us." I said.

"But we are already getting help." Nancy replied.

"I'm talking about real help...maybe even get off of medication."

"But I need my pills...they help me to sleep."

"That's what I am talking about Nancy...we don't need pills to sleep."

"But I do...those bugs get me at night."

"Not if we get out of here."

"How are we going to do that?"

"I don't know but I will find a way."

Before long Miss Rawlins walked in.

"How is my girl today?" Miss Rawlins asked.

"I am okay." I said

"Just okay…what's the matter?"

"I want to get out of here."

"I was waiting for you to say that."

"Why would you say that Miss Rawlins?"

"Because I can see you are deteriorating in here."

Miss Rawlins sat next to me and began to tell me about a young lady that was in this place and died. She said the young lady came into this institution looking for the same help I was searching for. She informed me of the entire test they ran and also how she was heavily sedated all the time with medications. Miss Rawlins was furious when she talked about this young lady. It was as though she was her daughter are something. She said Dr. Hunt and Dr. Stein are nothing but hypocritical scientists. They make promises to you they can't keep.

That is when I asked, "Can you help me get out of here?"

"Help you…that is what I mean by "listen well"." Miss Rawlins said.

"I also want you to help Nancy also."

"What do you want me to do?"

"Have you heard of the Research called "Sleep Tight"?"

"Are you talking about the research center that is operated by a minister?"

"Yeah…he's a minister…I really want to meet him."

"Well…I don't know if I could do that."

"Come on Miss Rawlins please help me with this."

"I'll see what I can do."

Meanwhile, while Miss Rawlins was digging up answers for me, I declined taking my medications. I had trained myself to swallow the water without the pill. The nurse was accustomed to me taking my meds until she stopped checking my mouth to see if I had swallowed the pills. The night terrors were not as rapid, but I refused to be cultivated with medications. My body was beginning to weaken and fatigue was capturing my soul.

It was visiting day for me at Central Institution. I hadn't heard from my parents in over a week. Most of the time mother would come and she would make up excuses for father. It was as if father was avoiding me since my condition had taken a turn for the worst. Still the thought was in my mind to get to the research center. I felt that this was the answer for me.

CHAPTER 14

I sat in the activity room waiting for a visit whether it was mother or a stranger. I wanted to hear from someone in the civilian world. Nancy also was sitting in the activity room. I haven't seen one visitor come to see her since the day I was committed. But she tells me she sees her family all the time. Something about her doesn't add up.

I continued to wait for a visitor. The clock seemed like it was moving fast and still no sign of mother or somebody. Then I heard a voice called my name.

"Pamela."

I turned around and to my surprised it was Pastor Burke. Of all the people, he was the last person I expected to come and visit me. Most mental pavilions don't allow ministers in their sanctuary. I always thought medicine and ministers didn't mix when it came to mental illness. Possession by demons is the first thing that comes to ministers' minds when you are committed to a mental institution.

"Hello Pastor Burke…what brings you here?" I asked.

"I had to see you…I thought about what you and I talked about a few weeks ago." Pastor Burke replied as he sat next to me.

"I thought you were trying to avoid me…especially when I saw you at Sunday services."

"I wasn't trying to avoid you Pamela, I just couldn't let anyone be aware of what is going on. If I would have continued to talk to you about the situation, there would be some implications that I am involved with it."

"You could have told me or slipped a note to me, you lead me to believe that you didn't believe in me...now...see what happened to me."

"I am sorry Pamela, but there was no other way I could handle the situation...I'm here for you now."

Tears were filling my eyes, as I began to think of all the pain I must have been causing family and friends. Pastor Burke was the only soothing moment that was attacking my mind at the moment. I tried to manipulate Pastor Burke to get me out of this place.

"Are you going to help me get out of this place?" I asked.

"There is no way I can get you out of here without someone catching us." He said.

"I just want to go and get some help, you know...the place."

"You mean the research center that deals with sleeping disorder cases."

"Yeah."

"I have gone over this over and over in my mind...I don't know if it would be safe for me to take you there...and if I could, how would I be able to do that?"

"Pastor, you can visit me on Sunday and pretend that you are taking me to church...that would work."

"I don't know if it would work...you see that would mean I would have to lie about my whereabouts...I don't think you want me to do that."

At the moment I didn't care if he lied or not. I just wanted my sanity back. I wanted the real Pamela Jones back into my body. I couldn't bear another moment of pills and tests. Being away from my family was eating me up on the inside. The cry for help was unbearable.

Finally, Pastor Burke said, "Give me about two days; I will try to get you some answers."

"I don't know if I can wait two whole days...one night seems like a week to me." I said.

"I know Pamela, but I have to get some things in order first...trust me."

"Trust me" were the words that fill my soul with emptiness. From the time I have been in this sanctuary, people have been telling me to trust them one way or another. Pastor Burke began to indulge me with the things that were going on in Sutton since the day I was sent away. The town was getting suspicious with me going out of town visiting my relatives so frequently. Rumors about me were beginning to become very heavy in the town. Amy and her family were becoming the head instigator of the entire matter. I was even told that Amy was beginning to hang out with Guy and Karen.

The worst information that I could receive from Pastor Burke was my brother Samuel not being able to talk about me. Everyone knew him for his drawing, but Samuel was not even drawing any pictures anymore. What could be worst than that? I was a role model for Samuel and now I am destined for failure. I was a failure for my family, the entire community and me.

When Pastor Burke completed his summary of the opinions of people about me, pain as pins sticking me on the inside was hitting my chest. I was beginning to have a panic attack.

"Are you okay, Pamela?" Pastor Burke said.

"I will be okay." I said as I put my hands on my head.

"I knew I shouldn't have come." He said.

"No…that's okay…I needed to hear the truth…what better person to get it from." I replied.

I could see in Pastor Burke's eyes that he wanted to help me, but the manipulating town was getting to him.

"Pamela…I will do all that I can to help you." Pastor Burke said.

"You will?" I said excitingly.

"Yes, I will…it is about time someone stands up before those low life social aristocrats in Sutton."

"Pastor, watch what you are saying…you are a man of God."

"I believe God would agree with me on this one."

Pastor Burke was beginning to become furious as he discussed the townspeople.

"I really don't care what happens to me next." Pastor Burke murmured.

"What…?" I said.

"Never mind…you wouldn't understand."

"Thank you so much Pastor."

"Don't thank me yet…we've got to find away to get you out of here."

"Sunday would be a good day."

"Yes…it would."

"Pastor, I found out that I can be released for church."

Pastor Burke thought for a while then he said, "yes that will be a great idea…be ready for church on Sunday."

For a moment the idea was fantastic, but I was beginning to become selfish. I didn't think about the consequences for Pastor Burke.

"Never mind… about doing it." I said.

"Never mind…what has come over you…you are now about to get some help and you sound like you don't want it." Pastor Burke replied.

"I know…but what would become of you…your life could be destroyed in Sutton."

"I am being selfish when I let an entire town run the life of God's people…you just be ready on Sunday, I will be here thirty minutes before time."

I gave Pastor Burke a hug and whispered in his ear, "You are the best".

CHAPTER 15

As I sat in the chair across from Dr. Hunt and Dr. Stein, a million thoughts began to ponder my mind about whether they had a solution or whether I was another one of their projects about to go into finalization. Now this finalization didn't mean a solution, it probably was going to be another prolonged analogy of my diagnoses of sleep paralysis. Dr. Stein was not a man with a lot of words. He was more of the research type. Dr. Hunt was the one with all the answers piled up into my medical folder.

"Well Pamela, how are you doing?" Dr. Hunt said.

"Okay." I replied.

"Are you still waking up at night with night terrors?" She asked.

"Yes…but not as much." I replied.

Dr. Hunt didn't waste any time with her interrogations this time. She went straight to the point. Dr. Stein was standing there with his glasses elongating from his nose. He was documenting everything we discussed.

"Pamela what do you mean not as much?" Dr. Hunt asks.

"Well…I mean…I am sleeping better." I said.

"So…does that means you are taking your medications?"

"Yes I am." I replied knowing that I hadn't taken a dose of pills in weeks.

"Pamela, I am going to ask you some questions…some of them may be repetitious, but I still need you to answer them so that Dr. Stein can document that we had this conversation."

"Okay."

"Pamela…you have told me in the past that you could not sleep… tell me why?"

I looked at Dr. Stein so eager to write down my reply.

"Well sometimes I feel lightheaded."

"In what way?"

"It's like I am in another world or something."

"Are you able to move or speak?"

"At the beginning of the process I can."

"What do you mean by the beginning of the process?"

"At first you feel lightheaded, and then you feel like you are going into a daze, that is when the process begins to alter your mental faculties."

"Tell me about the altering of your mental faculties?"

"The inability to move or speak."

"How long does this last?"

"Sometimes a few minutes…sometimes it can last longer."

"How longer?"

"I have had them last for about an hour."

"Can you talk during this episode?"

"No…I have tried to speak but it is difficult."

I kept looking at Dr. Stein as he jotted down every detail. He was persistent. He would glance at Dr. Hunt if he needed a more simplex answer.

"Pamela, these questions are relating to what goes on when you are in this paraplegic stage." Dr. Hunt said.

"Okay…but does this mean you can help me?" I asked.

"Yes…we are getting there." Dr. Hunt replied.

"Now when you are unable to move can you see anything?" She asked.

"Yeah." I replied.

"Tell me what your surroundings look like?"

"It's normal…but I can only see whatever is in front of me and a little of what is on the sides of me."

"Can you tell me about some of the things you see…but not the normal things…the abnormal things?"

"You mean things that are not there?"

"I don't know…you tell me."

"Sometimes I can see shadows."

"Are they shadows of items in your room."

"No, because most of the time my room is very dark."

"What about since you have been here…have you seen anything?"

"I have seen people walking around in my room…and it is not the nurses…it's when everybody is asleep."

"Can you describe the people?"

I became antagonized with Dr. Hunt's questioning.

"I am not going to describe anymore…you think I am crazy!" I shouted.

"Calm down Pamela."

"I will not calm down…I have been in this place…and no one is helping me!"

Suddenly I heard a voice say, "We are helping you."

It was Dr. Stein. He had this authoritative voice until the entire room stood still to the sound of it.

"Yes, we are helping you." Dr. Stein repeated.

"In what way…pills…test…interrogations…when will you tell me the real diagnosis?"

"Pamela, can you relax and take a deep breathe?" Dr. Hunt asked.

I tried to refrain myself from getting out of the chair and turning over everything that was on her desk.

Finally, she gestured to Dr. Stein and said, "We will continue this at another time."

"No way, Dr. Hunt we need to finish this today!" I exclaimed.

"Not today Pamela…I feel you have had enough today…we will finish this session later."

My adrenaline was moving rapidly. I wanted this to be finalized today. I could have pounded myself over the head several times for having such an outrage over the questions. I slowly removed myself from the seat in front of Dr. Hunt and Dr. Stein. I could feel the presence of their eyes watching me as I left the room. I stood outside the door for a moment, because doctors always discussed their patients after they leave the office, either on tape recorder, paper or vocally.

I heard Dr. Stein say, "Well seems like she is like the case we had before."

"I know…but how are we going to convince her parents?" Dr. Hunt asks.

"She is eighteen."

"I know…but she insists that her parents okay everything."

"She will agree in due time…eventually her tolerates will become unbearable."

"So, what do we do in the meantime, Dr. Stein?"

"We wait…we just wait."

Time was running out for me. I did not want to be another statistical research number. Whatever they were planning I did not want to be a part of it. Even though they were the best doctors in town, the best doesn't mean they will always come through for you. I will never forget about what Miss Rawlins told me about the girl that was in a coma and later died. She was Dr. Hunt and Dr. Stein's latest research.

While walking toward my room, I built up some patience to wait until Sunday. Pastor Burke will take me to the research center and I will be cured. I thought if I became cured then I could return and help Nancy. Nancy was in the worst state of denial than I was. At least I can admit I am not the normal human being.

CHAPTER 16

Another episode of drugs and dragons was becoming my night on the town at the institution. While lying across my bed my eyes became very tired. I was negotiating back in forth in my mind whether I should take the medications. I didn't want to be on any sedative when Pastor Burke rescues me on Sunday. The medication wasn't doing me any good. The more pills I took the more delusional I became. I was beginning to think the medications were only used to pamper the disorder. No one really had the answer for this silent sleep disease.

My eyes were going into a trance. I began to become agitated with the sleeping disorders. I did not want another night terror. Even though it was mid day it still was a terror for me. It was as though the walls were caving in on me. Sweat was popping off my face like kernels of popcorn. My physical faculties could not move. I had the loudest buzzing and throbbing in my head.

Suddenly I felt a dark shadow smother my face. I closed my eyes quickly. I did not want to see what the shadow was beginning to form. There was a strange presence around me. I tried to move my body to another position so I couldn't indulge into the presence of whatever was in my room. This lasted for about three minutes.

Finally, I began to arise out of the trance, but my body was still immobile. I could recall this happening before, but I didn't come out of it right away. As I tried to shake my legs to regain conscience to the real world, I could feel the impressions of a body sitting on my bed. This was becoming remotely scary.

I heard someone open my door. I reluctantly opened my eyes. It was a relief to see it was Miss Rawlins. She was making her daily visitation rounds as usual. She came over and shook me. I regained my mobility again.

"What's wrong Pamela?" Miss Rawlins asked.

"I…. I…" I was startled for words.

"You were sweating and everything." She said.

"I know."

"What's going on with you?" She asked.

I began to cry. Miss Rawlins sat down on the bed and pulled me close to her, and then she hugged me.

"It's going to be alright." She said.

"I am so tired…so tired." I said.

"Tired of what?" She asked.

"I can't sleep…I can't nap…its miserable." I replied.

"Oh…Oh…it's going to be okay…aren't the doctors helping you?"

"Yes…but you know them."

"Well…yes I do…just trust me."

After Miss Rawlins comforted me, she headed toward the door. But before she could exit, she hesitated.

"Pamela…can I ask you something?" Miss Rawlins asked.

"You know you can ask me anything Miss Rawlins." I replied.

"Why were you shaking when I came in the room…and don't lie to me …you can trust me?" She asks.

"Miss Rawlins no one really understands."

"You can tell me."

Miss Rawlins and I sat on the bed. She held my hand as we talked.

"Please don't think I am crazy, but I see and hear things sometimes."

"Well we all do…some things we don't need to see or hear."

"That's not what I am talking about…I am talking about weird things."

"Go on."

"Sometimes it's shadows and the walls caving in on me."

"Pamela, can I share something with you?"

"Sure."

"You might think it is strange, but remember the young lady I told you about that was in a coma?"

"Yes."

"She was just like you."

"Really?"

"Yes, and she was in this same hospital."

"I wouldn't really say this is a hospital."

"Well…she was diagnosed with a sleeping disorder."

"That's what the doctors think I have."

"I am going to share something with you…but you can't tell anyone."

"I promise…who I can tell it to anyway?" I said as I looked around the room.

Miss Rawlins began to tell me about a young lady named Mary who had been diagnosed with sleep paralysis. When she first came in the mental institution she was a smart young lady just like me. Mary was a patient of Dr. Hunt's. She started out with test after test. When the tests didn't give answers, she was sedated with antidepressants. Dr. Hunt didn't give up on Mary. She continued to look for research pertaining to sleep disorders. There were many out there, but not one had a valid report of cures. Dr. Hunt became obsessed with finding a cure for Mary. Dr. Hunt began to work day and night, but there still was not enough validity to her research. Dr. Hunt was very fond of Mary, but Mary's case became beyond her abilities. The battle became too difficult for her to handle, Dr. Hunt sought for other physician's opinions.

During one of Dr. Hunt's medical conferences she met Dr. Stein. He was an answer to her prayer. At least that's what she thought at the time. Dr. Stein had been studying sleeping disorders for over three decades. He had the most prominent and updated research study reports. He was considered the president of sleep disorders. Dr. Stein agreed to come and work with Dr. Hunt on Mary's case. Sleep disorder was like a delicatessen to Dr. Stein. His entire life was surrounding by his research. He was a loner and didn't mind assisting when it came to research.

Dr. Hunt was delighted to have Dr. Stein come and assist her with Mary's case. The sad thing about it, with all that happiness Mary went into a coma the night before Dr. Hunt returned from her trip. Even though Dr. Hunt had a valid researcher it was too late for Mary.

As Miss Rawlins finished telling me the story, I gained the deepest sympathy for Dr. Hunt.

Then I asked, "Did Mary ever recover from the coma?"

"No…she died a week later." Miss Rawlins replied.

"I bet Dr. Hunt regrets she didn't find the solution in time."

"Yes…and that is why she is helping you."

"Do you think she can?"

"Remember what I said before…about her not being a good doctor…forget I ever said those things?"

"But…why?"

"I can't tell you…just believe me when I say, something good will come out of this."

"What about Dr. Stein?"

"He is one of the greatest doctors here at Central."

"Miss Rawlins…. have you heard of anyone he has cured?"

"Pamela I can't lie to you…all I know is he is a good doctor."

"So really he is taking a chance with me also?"

"Dr. Stein is not taking a chance with you…. Remember, he never got a chance to work on Mary's case."

"So then we really don't know if he can cure me are not?"

"…. I just know he is good, listen well…listen well young lady."

When Miss Rawlins walked out of my room, I knew that I had to go with Pastor Burke on Sunday. Dr. Stein was good and everything, but I had no validity of him curing some one from sleep paralysis.

I thought, "I will not give up the chance of getting help, even if it meant getting spiritual help instead of physical help."

I wasn't giving up on Dr. Hunt and Dr. Stein. I just didn't want to give up on my chances of becoming a normal human being.

Later I walked to the recreation room hoping to see Nancy. Nancy was there glued to the television.

"Hi Nancy." I said.

"Hi." Nancy replied.

Nancy's demeanor didn't look normal.

"Something wrong Nancy?"

"I'm just not feeling well today."

"If you stay off of those antidepressants you would feel better."

"It's not that."

"Then what is it?"

"I am going to be leaving soon."

"That's great!"

"Not for me...I will miss all my friends..."

".... But, you get to go home...just be happy you're not staying in this place."

Nancy wasn't happy. It was as though something was eating her up on the inside. According to our conversation, she didn't want to discuss the matter. To help change the mode of our conversation I began to talk to Nancy about the research center I was going to on Sunday.

"Nancy.... guess what?" I asked.

"What now Pamela!" Nancy shouted.

"Calm down girl...I got a plan...for the both of us, especially since you don't want to go home."

"Whatever plan you have, it wants work."

"Yes, it will."

"Not for you.... I mean for me."

"Why not.... just listen."

I sat closer to Nancy to inform her of my spectacular plan. She listens attentively. I told her that on Sunday Pastor Burke is coming to take me to church, but not only to church, but to the Sleep Tight Research Center. Also I told her that was am going to get well so that I can come back and get her so that she can be cured also.

"I still can't go." Nancy said.

"Why not?" I asked.

"I just can't"

"After I am cured...we can sneak you to church to be healed."

"You won't be able to sneak me to church, because I am leaving on Saturday."

"You can't do that...you will only come back more loony than before."

"This time I am going for good."

"You can't do that...act crazy...take more pills, so that you can stay longer."

"Pamela...I am proud of you.... listen well."

"Listen well...that's all you have to say to a friend who wants to help you."

"Listen well...Listen well!"

Nancy continued to say, "Listen well" as I continued to try to convince her to try to stay longer. Even though Nancy was destined to leave I knew in my heart she was put into my life for a reason.

CHAPTER 17

Nancy left yesterday without a good-bye. But I believe that she told me her good-byes when we last spoke in the recreation room. Miss Rawlins didn't have much to say to me about Nancy. Well, she never mentioned Nancy to me anyway. It was as though she was only here for me.

The sun was beaming on my face as I looked out the window. I was waiting for Pastor Burke to come and take me to my next step of freedom. The thoughts of freedom began to flourish in my mind. Curing is one thing but being set free is another. I believe that this is just the beginning for me. One day I will be helping someone else cope with sleep paralysis.

Suddenly Pastor Burke arrived. I was happy to see his face showed some confidence. In the past, I could tell if things were not going to work out by his facial expression. I didn't give him a chance to come over and greet me. I was more than ready to face the challenge that was before me.

"Pamela…you ready?" Pastor Burke asked.

"More than ready." I replied.

"It was sort of difficult to get away…I almost didn't make it, because our assistant pastor had an emergency…but he made it back in time." He said.

"Thank God for that."

"Remember…I didn't promise you this was going to be a cure."

"I know Pastor Burke…but we won't know unless we try."

"I am only going because you asked for my help…but in a sense it is easing my conscience also."

Pastor Burke signed me out for the day for church. It was an easy process because he was my pastor. As we walked out the door of the institution, I could see that Pastor Burke was uneasy about taking me out. He constantly browsed around the parking lot. I knew he was looking for some instigators. I was looking around for the church van, but it was not present.

Then I heard Pastor Burke say, "Right over here."

We were traveling in a meat van. I laughed on the inside but knew this was a cover up for our trip. I should have known Pastor Burke wasn't about to take the church van out of Sutton to an unknown research center.

"Where did you get the ride?" I ask.

"I have a cousin that lives in Central...he let me borrow it sometimes." Pastor Burke replied.

"Does he know what we are doing?"

"No...but again...he doesn't know what he is doing half the time." He said as he opened the door.

As we drove off the premises a sigh of relief came upon me. In order to keep the trip from being a long drawn out boring trip, I continued to talk about unrelated things."

"Pastor Burke...why aren't you married?" I asked.

"I guess I never thought about it." He replied.

"But there are a lot of nice women your age in our church."

"No offense...but I don't look at the faces...I have met some of them."

"You could have married someone from Central."

"And let the town disband me.... no way."

"Well, that would have been a great way of getting out of town."

"Where would I go."?

"I am accustomed to being a pastor.... I would need a recommendation."

"I guess you are right...that's why when I become cured, I am leaving."

"Where would you go Pam.?"

"I figured when I finish college I won't return to this God forsaken place."

"Do me a favor?"

"Keep that to yourself...you don't know how many times I had tried to leave."

"What happened?"

"Mistakenly I told someone and they told someone and so on...it was stopped."

"Well forget I ever said anything."

"I wasn't talking about me..." Pastor Burke smiled.

I dittoed his smile.

As the journey continued to Sleep Tight Research Center, Pastor Burke began to capture the events that were happening in Sutton. There was a lot of commotion going on in the town and it was all centered on me. My mother's assistant principal job was on the line and my father had been demoted to a loan officer. All because of a silly town that had a reputation of perfection. My parents were not allowed to attend the town's council meetings anymore until the truth about me is revealed. My parents refused to reveal the truth. They are still in denial and telling folks, "I am with relatives". The councilman wants the name of the relatives in order to get a valid claim on my visitation. The refusal of names is causing a lot of pressure on my family. One good thing about it my family will not give up. In a sense they are still fighting for me even if they don't visit me.

As we continued to ride along the road, my eyes began to become tired and sleepy. I was trying to fight it because I was excited about going to the research center. The fight didn't last long. My body was relaxed and went into a deep sleep. I dreamed a lot of silly things, sometimes I was laughing in my sleep. Before I could completely awaken from my sleep I felt a presence in the van. I could hear sounds from the back of my head, I couldn't cry out for help. I remembered that shaking my leg would help the situation. I shook my leg, but nothing happened, so I shook it again. Suddenly Pastor Burke shook me.

"Pam...are you okay?" He asked.

"Did you see that?" I asked.

"Yes, I did." He replied.

"Now you see what I have been going through."

"How often does this happen?"

"Frequently."

"How frequently?"

"Pastor...I don't know anymore...I am just tired."

He pulled my head onto his shoulder. "Just rest child...I will do all that I can."

But as I was resting on his shoulder, I kept mimicking over and over the twenty=third psalms. I overheard my mother telling my father this was her remedy if she felt a spirit or something was in her room. I slept like a lamb after that.

Finally I awakened and noticed a sign with the words "Sleep Tight Research Center". The arrow on the sign was pointing toward a wooden bridge. There were a lot of trees and the building was smothered with greenery. Then we pulled up to the Sleep Tight Research Center. It didn't look like a research center. The outside looked like and old cabin back into some wooded area. There were lots of cars in the parking area of the cabin. I gather that a lot of people either worked there or were patients like me. I really didn't think there were many people who suffered with sleep paralysis until I visited this center.

The door of the cabin opened. There was a young man around his twenties who greeted us.

He was too young to be a doctor; well at least I thought he was.

"Hello...my name is Brother Jonathan." He said.

I didn't hesitate to say hello. He was a handsome young man.

"Hello my name is Pamela.... and ...this is Pastor Burke...my pastor." I excitedly said.

I didn't give Pastor Burke a chance to introduce us. I was fully in control of the entire greeting, until we came to the medical part.

"Why yes...I am Pastor Burke, remember ..." Pastor Burke.

"Yes, I remember your call...this is the young lady you were talking about?" Brother Jonathan asks.

"Yes, I am…I am happy to meet you." I said.

Pastor Burke noticed I was getting frisky on him, so he told me he would handle everything from now on.

"Are you the one in control of this facility?" Pastor Burke asks.

"Why…no…Brother Jason Paul and Sister Tracy Paul manage this operation." Jonathan replied.

"And where are they?" Pastor Burke asked.

"Brother Jason had to run into town to pick up some supplies and Sister Tracy is in one of the rooms attending to a patient." Jonathan replied.

"This place is really big inside." I said looking around the facility.

"Oh yes it is…can I get you something to drink or eat?" Jonathan asked us as he continued to walk toward the waiting room.

"No thanks." Pastor Burke replied and looked over at me to say something.

"Oh…oh…nothing for me." I said.

We entered the waiting room; it was similar to the one at Central Mental, but not as large.

"Well, if you don't need anything I will let Sister Tracy know that you have arrived." Jonathan said.

Pastor Burke waited until Jonathan left the room and then opened up his briefcase. I noticed in his briefcase, he had a black folder. He pulled it out and started thumbing through the papers. It was a bunch of articles about the research center. I didn't know Pastor Burke was a fan of this place.

"What's that?" I asked

"These are articles I had been keeping about the center." Pastor Burke replied.

"Why do you have so many?" I asked looking at him thumb through them.

"I am looking for a particular article."

"What for?"

"Oh…it's nothing really particular." He replied.

I could tell Pastor Burke had something more to tell me but just was not able to at the time. After he searched through the papers, he put the folder back into his briefcase. I continued to look at the clock in the room. I was anxious to meet Sister Tracy. Somehow, I knew this place would be my solution to all of my problems.

CHAPTER 18

It wasn't long before Sister Tracy entered the room. She was a tall skinny brunette with spectacles that looked too large for her face. Her presence in the room brought about a sense of redemption to my soul. She walked over and introduced herself.

"Sorry I kept you waiting." Sister Tracy said.

"Oh… that's alright." Pastor Burke said as he stood up from the chair.

"I am glad you were able to find this place." Sister Tracy said.

"It wasn't difficult at all." Pastor Burke said with such confidence, knowing all the time I was the navigator for most of trip.

"So, this is Pamela?" Sister Tracy asked.

"Yes…I am glad to meet you, I have heard so much about this place." I replied.

"Yes, we have…can you give us more information?" Pastor Burke asked trying to detour me from talking too much.

"If you would follow me to my office, we can talk in there." Sister Tracy said.

"By the way, did you fill out the papers?" Sister Tracy asked.

"What papers?" Pastor Burke asked.

"We have routine forms that need to be filled out before we proceed…Sister Clara will get the necessary papers for you." Sister Tracy said while walking up to her receptionist desk.

"Sister Clara, will you please give them the necessary papers for entrance?" Sister Tracy said.

"Sure." Sister Clara said as she pulled the papers out of a drawer.

Sister Clara smiled as she handed the papers to Pastor Burke. I was assuming you didn't have to fill out papers to attend mission work.

Sister Tracy smiled and said, "As soon as you finish with the paperwork we can proceed."

"Does this mean I will have to wait?" I asked.

"Just a little bit…this is a normal procedure before we begin counseling…Pamela; I know Pastor Burke isn't your guardian, so we have to be very careful." Sister Tracy implied

"I want to thank you for being considerate of the situation." Pastor Burke said.

"I just hope we will be able to help you with no interruptions from outsiders." Sister Tracy said.

"Oh…I know you will!" I shouted to keep Pastor Burke from speaking any negative words that could spoil my hope.

"Just remember we have to be very cautious, because every time we try to help someone from Sutton, they tend to end up missing." Sister Tracy informed us.

I began to swallow hard as I looked at Pastor Burkes and Sister Tracy. I didn't want to be added to their statistics of missing persons.

"Don't worry, if you came this far without interruptions…you'll be fine." Sister Tracy said as she handed the papers to Pastor Burke.

"Pamela…you are going to be okay." He said trying to make me feel better.

At the moment the word "okay" was not the best choice of words for security. I could see Pastor Burke's hands trembling as he reached to get the papers from Sister Tracy. Then he paused for a moment. It was as if he was having a second thought. He had more to lose than me.

Sister Tracy recognized the anticipation that came over Pastor Burke, she said, "Pastor Burke, you can fill out those papers as we talk in my office."

While we were sitting in the office, I could see everything that was going on through a glass picture window within. Jonathan was staring from the outside at me. I was impatient and wanted Sister Tracy to skip the basic and go right into my therapy. I paced around the office for a moment and then headed toward Jonathan.

"Don't be scared." Jonathan said standing across the room.

"I'm not scared…just skeptical." I replied.

"What is there to be skeptical about…we are a religious group that wants to help God's soldiers." He said.

"I'm not his soldier."

"Whether you know it are not, you are."

"I am not!"

"That's why you have that special gift."

"What special gift…not sleeping disorders."

"Yes…you sure are special, only a few people in the world possesses it and the ones that have it are either living in a world of misery, locked up in a sanitarian, or doing the work of God, which is the least among all of them."

My inquisitive mind wanted to know what Jonathan was talking about. I moved closer to him to find out what he was talking about. Even though I was reluctant to get closer to him, I found myself drawn into his conversation.

"Listen Pamela, no one can help you now but God."

"But I have been crying to him for help, but nothing happens."

"He heard you…don't you think it was by chance you found us… you were lead to us."

"I don't understand what you are talking about." I said as Jonathan pulled me toward a seat.

I was highly interested in what Jonathan had to say, but I didn't know whether to trust him or not. I kept looking at the office door hoping Pastor Burke wouldn't rush out. Jonathan's conversation was idealistic in a way, but on the other hand it made sense.

"Pamela, can I ask you a question without you getting upset…I mean it is personal?" Jonathan asked.

"Sure…I have blurted out a lot of personal stuff lately." I replied.

"Well… are you a Christian?"

"I go to church every Sunday…I just haven't been lately…I am a faithful member."

"I'm not talking about going to church…I am talking about a personal relationship with God."

"You mean…like talking to him and he talks back…no…I think you are crazy…. I didn't mean it that way."

"I know you don't think I am crazy." Jonathan laughed because he knew what kind of crazy I was talking about.

Before our chat could go any further, Pastor Burke and Sister Tracy walked out of the office.

"Everything is set Pamela." Pastor Burke said as he walked toward me.

"You mean I get to stay…and get help!" I said excitedly.

"Yes, you're get to stay." Pastor Burke said wiping his face with a sigh of relief.

"But just for one week." Sister Tracy replied smiling at me.

I knew at that moment that there was some hope for me.

"But why one week…shouldn't it take longer?" I asked.

"That's all I can afford to give you without the town's people looking for you…I am already in this deep over my head…I don't even have the faintest idea of what I am going to say or do to keep you in here a week." Pastor Burke anxiously replied.

"Maybe you should tell them you have no idea what happened to me…that I ran away in your custody." I said.

"That would be lying Pamela, I have already broken many covenants with the church as of now." He said.

I began to feel really guilty for having Pastor Burke to put his career and moral standards with God into jeopardy. I didn't know whether to tell him to take me back or take a chance. I needed to hear confirmation from a divine voice.

"I think that is all we are going to need." Jonathan said interrupting the silent mode that was starring me in the face.

"I think so too." Sister Tracy commented with great assurance in her eyes.

"But what will you tell the town's people Pastor Burke?" I asked.

"Let me worry about that." He said as he hugged me goodbye.

Jonathan's words could have been the divine intervention I needed. During the first part of the night Jonathan gave me a tour of the place. There seemed to be a lot of praying and reading the word of God, as I glanced into each room. Jonathan informed me that an idle mind is the devil's workshop. Everyone in the building was to keep themselves productively busy at all times unless they were taking time to be with God. I was to help with the chores around the place, wherever I fitted in.

Later Jonathan took me to my room for the night. As we walked into the room, he looked around, and sat in a chair waiting. I scanned the room quietly. In the room was one twin bed and about four chairs in a circular fashion. In the far corner of the room was the entrance to the bathroom.

"What are you waiting for?" I asked.

"For your first therapy to start." He replied.

There was not one sight of treatment equipment in the room. I began wonder whether this place was legitimate. It was a little too late to think that way."

"What about treatments and all of those things?" I asked being skeptical.

"We are in the beginning of your therapy now." Jonathan said.

Jonathan noticed the doubt upon my face and began to explain the Sleep Tight research center method of treatment. He advised me to not be afraid and to listen well. I remember those words coming from Nancy's mouth. The research center didn't use any equipment, medical treatments or antidepressants. The energy that I was feeling around me was from a divine force. It was pulling me into a calm and peaceful state. Jonathan gave me bits and pieces of the research on sleep paralysis. He informed me of the theory of antidepressants resulting in putting up a wall that hindered spiritual help and increasing the brain's tendency to have hallucinations and delusional activity. One of the reasons many mental patients are on antidepressants was to keep them from coping with the real world. The sedatives were to keep them from being depressed and causing the patient to bring harm upon them. But there had been many cases of suicide behind sleeping disorders, especially when they were sedated with antidepressants and other types of medications. Sleep paralysis is a silent disease that cannot be cured, only placed into remission. There are only three ways to handle this silent predator, ignore it, become a pill popper, or get spiritual help which is believed to be the most effective way of dealing with it. Most of the time many of the patients are just asking for genuine sleep and unexplainable peace. The method the center used is from a divine force from heaven. Jonathan assured me that the method was safe and will give you a sense of peace without pills. The only thing he kept telling me was to "listen well", the famous words of Nancy and Miss Rawlins.

Suddenly Brother Jason walked into the room. He was a very tall and strange looking man, but his demeanor had a glow that was unexplainable.

"Hi Pamela...I am Brother Jason." He said.

My body was in a stunned condition therefore it was difficult for me to utter a word.

"I understand...I get this type of response all the time." Brother Jason said.

"No offenses...but you look..." I said.

"I know...Jonathan... will you tell Sister Tracy we are ready." Brother Jason said.

I had never seen God before, but from the way Pastor Burke explained his experiences, it seemed to be describable all over Brother Jason.

Jonathan left me in the room with Brother Jason. I was looking him up and down. He had a Holy Bible in his hand reading and meditating. He didn't say a word to me. I kept staring. I thought, "Maybe I need to escape...they could be in latter stage of loonies."

There was an explicit and mysterious atmosphere in the room. I was wondering what was about to happen next. I sat on the bed hoping what was about to happen would speed up. Sister Tracy and Jonathan walked into the room. A sigh of relief came upon my chest. I was wondering why there were so many chairs in the room. I thought maybe it was for the spirits that were going to visit me.

Sister Tracy handed me a Bible. I looked at it.

"Open it to Psalm 91." Brother Jason insisted.

I opened the bible to Psalm 91. I recalled the day I was at the church with Pastor Burke and how he told me about this amazing scripture. I had never read it before then.

"Read it." Brother Jason said.

I began to read the scripture quietly to myself.

"No…I insist you read it aloud." He said.

I didn't know where he was going, but I wanted some help, so I was obedient and read it out aloud. As the words blurted from my mouth, mystical force was inclining upon my soul.

"Don't you see now that what you have is not a curse?" Brother Jason asked.

"Yeah…but why me?" I asked.

"This comes from before time… God knew that there was going to be spiritual battles for his people, so he equipped some of us with the ability to see and feel the other side."

"So if what I have is a gift…then why do I see ghosts and weird things…even dead people?"

"Because Satan knows you have this gift, so he interferes with your ability by bringing entities from the dark side to block your confidence…. that is when fear takes over…God cannot work out of fear and doubt."

"So what can I do about this?"

"There is really nothing you can do about it… is a gift, and until people realize it, fear will always overshadow the wonders of it."

"Brother Jason, how can I stop seeing evil things?"

"There is only one way you can beat this…that is…knowing the real purpose of your gift."

"Not changing the subject or anything…so does this mean a lot of God's warriors are in mental institutions?"

"I'm not saying that everyone in the mental institution is one of God's warriors, because demons can possess people and cause them to go insane…I am saying some people don't know how to handle there gift. The feeling of being different and not understanding it can drive anyone insane.

"That is the reason I am fighting…I refuse to become schizophrenic."

"Schizophrenia is man's way of putting a label on the unknown."

"So that means some of the people at Central Mental Institution could be gifted?"

"That could very well be…you see, the natural man doesn't understand the spiritual things of God, because it takes God's spirit to discern them."

"So… what do I need to do?"

"What we are going to do tonight is spend time with you in the word and giving you a knowledge of who God is."

"But I already know him."

"Pamela, you think you know him…because if you did… you wouldn't have that fear that is hidden inside of you."

We all held hands and prayed a prayer of thanksgiving. All of a sudden, the two visible bodies that were sitting in the chairs decided to talk. I was wondering whether they ever going to say anything.

"Pamela…we know you don't understand…that is where we come in." Sister Tracy said.

"We are here to help you receive the word of God personally and to have Him as an intimate friend…I was once just like you, I couldn't sleep at night and was afraid to go to sleep, but when I found out who I really was, the night terrors became peaceful spiritual visions and dreams… sometimes they were even messages to help me and others understand the connection between the natural and spiritual world." Jonathan explained.

"Pamela, listen carefully, we are not saying that you won't have night terrors anymore, we are saying that you are safe in God's arms and He will protect you…" Brother Jason stated.

"Also, when evil is present…God will give you a sense of peace that will overcome the evil…therefore the evil will have to leave." Sister Tracy said. "I want you to memorize Psalm 23, because the evil presences do not like this scripture."

The information was astounding to me. I was practically shaking my head in agreement to the researcher's theory of sleep disorders.

"Do you have any more questions before we begin?" Brother Jason asked.

"Yes…do you mind telling me who was the last person that was missing from here?" I asked.

"We can't tell you that…but we can tell you that you are blessed to have Pastor Burke." Brother Jason said.

I was in the company of three religionist fanatics. The thought of escape was beginning to roam about my head, but where would I run. I couldn't return back to Sutton with the same state of mind and people calling me a freak. Returning to Central Mental Institution was not even an option, so I listened well through the night to what they were saying. One thing for sure it kept the hanks off of me.

The word of God was beginning to take a resident in my heart and soul. Such a sense of peace was surrounding me that I could not explain. When the left the room, I read Psalm 23 over and over again, trying to memorize the verses. I was preparing myself for the night terrors. This time I would be ready with my ammunition, the word of God. In a way, I was anxious about falling asleep, because I was willing to put Psalm 23 to the test. Because of the anticipation, it was impossible for me to rest. I read some more passages from the Bible and began to talk to God openly. At first, I felt inadequate about talking to someone I didn't see or know, but it was better than talking and seeing the evil spirits.

Suddenly my eyes became heavy and a source of energy came creeping in my room. My body was feelings as though I was not visible. Then I started quoting the Psalm 23 scripture, before the mode of the room captured me. Then I felt a rushing wind pass over my body. Before I could finish the scripture, I went into a deep sleep. It was the sleep of a peaceful lamb.

CHAPTER 19

It was five o'clock in the morning when I awakened to a knock on my room door.

"Time to get up." Sister Tracy said quietly at the door.

"Okay." I shouted trying to give myself a boost from the wonderful appealing sleep I had last night.

"Meet us in the dining hall in about fifteen minutes." She said.

Today was the best sleep I had in months. This was the type of therapy I didn't mind having, especially when you are not reluctant in awakening.

As I walked down the hallway, I noticed that it was very quiet. Even the others that were summoned to the dining hall were quietly strutting by me without a good morning. I had a strange feeling come over me as I walked into the dining hall. I stood by Jonathan and held his hand. We formed a circle and began to pray. Brother Jason was the leader of the prayer. This was a normal routine every morning before we scattered out to help with the daily chores.

Because of my many talents, which included cooking. I was placed in the kitchen with other sisters of the center to help cook breakfast. They were very funny and quite informative when it came to outside news. It was an enjoyable fellowship.

"I see you enjoying yourself." Sister Sue said, as she noticed me singing a tune while I was cooking the grits.

"Yes, I am…I slept so good last night." I said.

I sensed something was going on between the two sisters in the room, because they kept looking at each other with suspense every time I said something.

"Well, I am glad you slept good…because…" Sister Donna said as she was abruptly interrupted by Sister Sue shoving her shoulder.

"Leave it along." Sister Sue whispered to Sister Donna.

Sister Donna couldn't wait to burst out the latest news from town.

"I heard you are from Sutton." Sister Donna said.

"Yes I am." I replied quickly.

"That town is something else." She said.

"Well its okay." I said.

"Sister Donna leave the girl along." Sister Sue said.

"I want to know why everybody in that town thinks they are better than everybody outside." Sister Donna said.

"I don't know… I just lived there." I said.

"I see…" Sister Donna said trying to gather information out of me.

The room was like a time bomb about to happen. Sister Donna did not want to lighten up the conversation. I on the other hand was not about to pardon the peace that was surrounding me. I stirred every lump that was about to manifest itself in the pot of grits in order to keep myself from exploding.

While finishing the breakfast, the two sisters kept whispering behind my back. I could tell by their facial expressions they wanted more from me. But I wasn't willing to take down Sutton even if it were a deceiving little town.

As I walked over to set the table for breakfast, in the corner of my eye was Jonathan watching me. He signaled me to come outside on the porch. I was reluctant because of the nosey sisters in the kitchen. Then Jonathan opened the door waiting for me to follow. I looked over in the kitchen and observed that the sisters weren't looking and dashed out of the door.

"How long it was going to take you?" Jonathan said.

"Oh…I was waiting to see…" I replied.

"I know those two sisters…sometimes they can be pessimistic…pay them no mind." Jonathan said, as we sat on the steps of the porch.

"Can I talk to you about something?" He asked.

"Sure…but why me." I replied looking around with inquisitiveness upon me.

"I want you to know that I understand what you are going through."

"Really." I said being adamant about the situation.

I wasn't excited about Jonathan telling me he had experienced the things I have captivated in life, because I have heard it all before. What caught my attention was the sorrow that came upon him as he told me about the night terrors and the dead people who visited him. He also explained to me that some of the visits from the spirits were warnings of information to disseminate to people who were either close to him or who he had seen before. The connection between us began to bring about freedom of speech from me. I opened my heart out to him. I was and still am experiencing visits from the unknown. Jonathan even explained to me the first experience I had encountered with my naked eye. He told me when I saw the short man in my sixth grade class, he was coming to tell his daughter he was happy for her graduating from college. The smile on the short man's face was a message of happiness for his daughter. I was finally impressed with someone truly understanding the source that possessed me. My eyes were opening up and the pieces of the puzzle were about to be put into there proper places.

"Thanks for sharing that with me…I really needed that, you know…I slept good last night." I informed him.

"I knew you would…but that is not why I bought you out here." He said as he held my hand for comfort. "There is talk around town that you are missing."

"Oh no!" I shouted with fear coming over me.

"Yes…when I went into town this morning, I saw some cops at the store they were asking questions about you to the clerk."

"Did you tell Brother Jason?"

"I haven't had time to…because he spends hours in the mornings fasting and praying to God."

"What am I going to do?"

"I don't know…until I talk to Brother Jason."

"What about Pastor Burke…have you contacted him."

"According to the news in town, he was arrested for kidnapping you."

"I don't know what to do…I can't go back…what would the towns… what would my family think…I only wanted help." I said weeping with water forming in my eyes.

"All I know to do is to get you out of here and fast." Jonathan said holding me in his arms and trying to comfort me.

Jonathan had deep remorse for me. He decided to put his life on the line and not tell Brother Jason, because he didn't want the center to be closed. He implemented a plan to get me far away from the center as possible, but it had to be before the next night therapy of reading the Bible and prayer. Before nightfall, I packed my bag and waited by the bedside for Jonathan to come and rescue me. The time was passing swiftly. Suddenly I heard someone at the door.

"Pamela…are you in there?" She said.

"Yes." I replied.

"Open the door." She said.

I opened the door it was Sister Donna.

"Don't ask any questions, just follow me." Sister Donna insisted.

I followed Sister Donna to the back entrance of the building. The hallway was quiet as usual, because everyone was preparing for the nightly therapy. Sister Donna quietly opened the back door with her keys. I looked out the door but didn't see anyone. In the wooded area I saw a light from a car flicking.

"Go ahead Pamela…that's for you…God be with you." "Sister Donna said.

I ran toward the car thinking Sister Donna was helping Jonathan with my escape. When I came closer to the car, I didn't see Jonathan. There before my very eyes was Sister Sue in a car waiting for me. She quickly opened the door and took my bags and threw them in the back of the car and drove off in full speed. She didn't say anything she just put her right hand on top of my hand squeezing them tightly and smiled. The direction she was taking me was the opposite of Sutton. It was pitched dark and eerie. There was not one passing vehicle in sight. We drove for hours until we came to a road that was blocked by barricades. She stopped the car hastily on the side of the road and opened the passenger side of the car.

"This is as far as I can take you…you can walk from here." Sister Sue said.

"Where am I…I don't know what…" I said with my body shivering from the mystical atmosphere.

Sister Sue pointed toward a cabin hidden far into the distant woods, "That cabin can keep you safe for a while." She said.

Then she reached from the back seat and pulled out a brown bag. "I put you some sandwiches and drinks to carry you over…God be with you." She said as she extended her arms and gave me a warm hug.

As I was walking toward the woods, I could feel that Sister Sue didn't want me to be alone. She sat silently for a few minutes as I walked distantly into the woods. Then the headlights from her car disappeared like the stars in the morning. It was a mystical cold and dreary night in the woods. I felt more desolate than ever being left alone to solve the night terrors. I was prompt about listening to every word the research center instilled in me.

As I approached the cabin it was dusky and scary. I could hear the sound of owls hooting and crickets chirping. It was a creepy, broken-down wooden shack, but safe for now. When I opened the door, a musty odor attacked my nostrils. There was a fleshly made bed a waiting for me to rest. Also in the corner of the room was a lantern with oil and matches waiting on the table. Wood was already in the fireplace. It was as though someone had prepared this place for me. I lit the lantern and started the fire in the fireplace. From the looks of it the place had been well kept by someone. It was late and I was tired and hungry. My mind began to think about Sutton and the people. I was missing my family and friends. I was scared in the woods alone, but I knew this was the only means of safety until I could think of what to do next. I opened the bag of food Sister

Sue gave me. Inside the bag was also a Bible with markers of different scriptures. I took the lantern off the table and sat it next to the floor by the bed. I sat down and opened the Bible and pulled out a sandwich. Then I started reading the pages that were marked. Before I knew it, I was dripping into dreamland. Exhaustion was taking a toll on me. At first, I was sleeping very peacefully, until an eccentric was bestowed upon me. I kept saying to myself, "not again". My body had become drained and had a dazing feeling of not being there. I tried to fight it, but I kept dripping between two worlds. I couldn't see anything, but I could feel a foreign presence in the room. I tried to shake out of it, but it didn't work. Finally, my mind began to quote psalm 23 over and over again. The strange forces that were continuing to delay the delivery of the words from my mouth sealed my lips. Then I saw a bright light in the corner of the room and felt a rushing wind pass through my body. I kept trying to see where the light was coming from, but a force heavily pressed my body down. Suddenly my mouth was able to mumble the words. The funny thing about it, the evil spirit began to diminish as I repeated the chanted words of the scripture. A peaceful atmosphere captivated the fearful situation. Before I knew it, I was out of the trance and back into the world of normal dreams.

I awakened several times just to make sure daylight didn't creep upon me. I had realized that the divine being was protecting me. Waking up in the morning was another challenge for me. I needed a plan and I needed one before daybreak. I kept pondering ways to escape over in my mind. It was so peaceful inside the cabin until I turned the lantern off and got into the bed. I kept the fireplace going because it was chilly inside the cabin. The thought of a plan did not relinquish swiftly, because sleep took a toll of my thoughts. Finally, I dozed off into a quiet deep sleep. I slept hard. It was like I had done a day's work of severe labor.

Suddenly I saw a light shining into my face. I tried to keep it from awakening me by putting my hands up to my face, but the light continued. Before I knew it, I saw two policemen staring at me with a flashlight hovering over me.

"We found her." The policemen said.

"Are you Pamela?"

I studded for a moment and said, "Yes…I am Pamela."

"What…what's going on?" I asked.

"Young lady we have been looking all over for you." He said.

There at the door was a policewoman. She came over to help me prepare to leave.

I was frightened when I said, "I didn't do anything wrong."

"Well you were kidnapped…and considered a missing person." The policewoman said.

"I wasn't missing…I…." I said remembering that the Sleep Tight Center helped me. I didn't want to have them involved with this matter.

I realized that the police officers were going to take me back to Central Mental Institution. I didn't want to return to that insane place. I became distorted and crazed. I totally lost it. I didn't want to be depressed and pressed down with antidepressants and insane company. Before I knew it, there standing over me was a doctor from the institution.

"Hold her still?" The doctor shouted.

The policewoman tried to hold me down, but her strength couldn't do it. It took four policemen to bring my body under control. I was switching around aggressively. I didn't want to be sedated or institutionalized anymore. I felt I could handle the situation without drugs, pills or tests. Me fighting the situation didn't help any. Before I could scream again, the doctor had injected a sedative into my arm.

CHAPTER 20

Forced into accepting that I may never regain my sane identity again began to haze every thought. Just believing that I was at the crossroad of redemption gave me so much hope in faith. All of the faith I had was exhausted by the thought of not being able to visit the research center again. Sometimes it isn't the therapy that gives you hope, but the person who is administering the therapy. Brother Jason and his sister were those persons. Of course, there was also Brother Jonathan who was always by my side, but somehow I let my personal feelings put in remission the faith he was trying to get me to experience. I don't know if I will ever recover from the disease that I have inside of me, but I do acknowledge that faith in the higher being can take you a long distance, even if you don't have the answer.

I have come to realize that even when family leaves you desolate that there is someone who will never leave you. Brother Jonathan taught me the reality of true friends. He was very adamant about trusting in God. Faith was what I needed at the time.

Hope and faith kept kindling my mind as I sat on the bed. Just the thoughts I had began to ignite some hope into my soul. Finally, I was able to gain some confidence about by self and some hope to walk into Dr. Hunt's office. No matter what happened next, I knew that God was with me.

I sprung up from the bed and walked down the hall to Dr. Hunt's office. Even though I had this secret inside of me from the research center, a sense of dignity began to capture my soul. Eternal peace was flourishing over my body. I thought, "Is this the cure?"

The walk toward Dr. Hunt's office seemed very distant. I didn't know if this was an insinuation that something favorable was about to happen.

As I opened Dr. Hunt's door, the atmosphere of confidence began to diminish. There sitting at the desk was Dr. Hunt and standing next to her was Dr. Stein. They had an earnest demeanor clothed upon them.

"Have a seat." Dr. Hunt said.

I was hesitating to sit down as I watched their eyes with despair.

"How are you doing today?" Dr. Hunt asked.

"I am okay…can't you tell?" I said.

Dr. Stein said with a smile, "Looks can be deceiving sometimes."

That was all I needed was some nerdy doctor to knock down my line of confidence.

"Pamela…you look good." Dr. Hunt said.

"I feel good also." I replied.

Dr. Hunt began to shuffle through the medical file on her desk. She pulled out this paper with prognosis on it.

"I am going to be frank with you Pamela." Dr. Hunt said.

A deep swallow began to clog my throat as she continued to talk.

"Out of the entire test we have done we have not found one single thing physically wrong with you." She said.

"Really!" I said with excitement.

"Don't get me wrong…there is something going on abnormal with you, but it is not physical." She said.

"What do you mean abnormal?"

"Well, your brain waves or not normal, especially, when you are asleep."

Dr. Stein handed over a folder to Dr. Hunt and pulled out another paper. Dr. Stein wasn't talking much, but he had all of his ducks in a row.

"When we performed the REM test the first time it was normal… Do you know what the REM is?" Dr. Hunt asks.

"Yes, I no what it is…. rapid eye movement test." I replied.

"Well, we continued to perform these tests consistently…you are not totally asleep when you say you are asleep." Dr. Hunt explained.

"Dr. Hunt, do you mind if I go over the results with Pamela?" Dr. Stein asks.

"Sure... go ahead." Dr. Hunt replied.

Dr. Stein sat down in the chair next to me and began to explain my diagnosis. He continued to go on about the REM. I was not interested in this diagnosis and became crazed.

"What about Sleep paralysis!" I shouted.

"What about sleep paralysis?" Dr. Stein reluctantly asked.

"You go on about rapid eye movement...what about no movement at all!" I shouted.

"Calm down Pamela...just..." Dr. Hunt said.

"...Calm down, you people have been just playing games with me...I have over and over been letting you use me as your personal lab rabbit." I said.

"If you allow us to continue, we can talk about sleeping disorders." Dr. Stein explained.

"You can talk about sleeping disorders.... but what about sleep paralysis...I want to know about sleep paralysis." I said.

Suddenly a burst of water began to fill Dr. Hunt's eyes. She became very nervous after she pulled out a photo of a young lady from her desk drawer.

"This is why I don't like discussing sleep paralysis." She remorsefully said.

Pain and sorrow began to drain my body as I glanced at the photo. Then I took the photo out of Dr. Hunt's hand. The photograph was familiar to me. I looked deeper at the young lady in the picture. I couldn't believe my eyes. It was a photo of Nancy. An eerie feeling came over me. Nancy was related to Dr. Hunt. I became intrigued with the situation as Dr. Hunt talked about the young lady on the photograph. Dr. Hunt's soul was feeling with despair as she pulled another book out. It was a photo album flooded with pictures and events of Nancy.

"That's Nancy!" I shouted.

"Who...this person?" Dr. Hunt asked as she pointed to the picture.

"Yes...that's Nancy." I replied.

"Can't be, her name is Mary." Dr Hunt stated.

"But I have seen her before."

"Where did you see her?"

I couldn't tell Dr. Hunt I had seen this person before with my naked eyes because she would really think I am loony. So, I told her I saw her in my dreams. I really wasn't lying because they could have been delusional dreams.

"Did she tell you her name was Nancy?" Dr. Hunt asked.

"Yes…she did." I replied.

With a saddened face Dr. Hunt said, "Mary never really liked the name Mary…she insisted that I changed her name to Nancy, because she loved the Nancy Drew mystery books."

I thought "Maybe because she has become a mystery."

"Does she say much when you see her?" Dr. Hunt asked.

"Not much…but she seemed sad." I replied.

"Yes, I know…I could never really cure her…you know she had the same symptoms as you."

"I didn't know."

"Yes…she was my heart…that is why I want to help you so much…I feel I can repay my debt for the lost of Mary by saving you."

"I think Nancy…I mean Mary would like that."

Finally, after all of the pictures and reminiscing, I realized that Nancy had to be a ghost or something. I believe that is the reason no one talked about her to me, even Miss Rawlins. Was Nancy really a spirit or a figment of my imagination? Maybe it was an after-mass reaction of the medications I was taking. The pieces were coming together slowly as I listened to Dr. Hunt talk about the illness of her daughter. Nancy was an American model of a young girl destined for a successful life. According to the pictures, she was victorious in every contest she had ever entered. The pictures showed her in numerous contests. Nancy also loved horses. She had a horse that always won blue ribbon contests. Dr. Hunt also mentioned her daughter wanting to be one of her successors, but the sleep paralysis illness took a toll of her life. Nancy dealt with the same terrors I did. The worst was yet to be told. Nancy went into a coma before Dr. Hunt could relieve her night terrors.

As Dr. Hunt continued to talk about Nancy, I could see the hurt and agony that was attacking her spirit. Suddenly she ran out of the office bursting in tears. I was speechless. There was nothing that I could say to alleviate the distress that was intruding in Dr. Hunt's heart. Dr. Stein ran after Dr. Hunt to comfort her. I had come to the consensus that Nancy was trying to warn me about the institution. When I thought about it, I was really the only person that saw or communicated with her. Now that Nancy has left could be telling me her mission was over with me.

After a few minutes, Dr. Stein returned to the office. Dr. Stein continued to talk to me about the test he wanted to perform on me that could give leeway to a solution. He said it was a new test and had not had any validity yet. Dr. Stein assured me that it was not painful, but would have to be put under anesthetic, because it was dealing with my brain. When he mentioned my brain, I was in awe.

"My brain…" I exclaimed.

"Yes…but it is only to retrieve some liquid from the muscles in your brain." Dr. Stein explained.

"What if I don't make it through?" I asked.

"The test will only last about forty-five minutes." Dr. Stein said.

"Are you sure I will be alright?"

"Yes."

"Is this the test you ran on Nancy?"

"No…this is a different test…it is more advanced."

"Maybe I should ask my parents?"

"Don't bother…we have permission already from your parents."

"I need to see it."

Dr. Stein took out a paper out of my medical records. Both of my parents signed the permission for the tests on yesterday. They signed the papers on yesterday, but didn't have the audacity to visit their daughter. Their signature gave me confidence in Dr. Hunt and Dr. Stein. I knew that my parents wanted me cured.

CHAPTER 21

It was another awakening from night terrors again. I wasn't having them as frequently. After the visit from the research center, I had learned to adapt to the terrors and defend myself at night. Reciting the twenty-third Psalms really works now. I had to truly believe that there was a higher being keeping me safe. Faith was the key to having successful sleep. I remembered what Brother Jonathan told me about David in the book of Psalms 91. Ninety-one was a key number. I heard Nancy and Miss Rawlins mention it to me several times. I really didn't know the meaning of it until I met Jonathan.

It was time for me to prepare myself for testing. I had strong confidence this morning. Not just in myself, but also in the doctors. I was starting to believe that I was already cured even if the test didn't help me. I had a puissant feeling that some one higher was looking out for me.

An orderly walked in my room and asked, "You ready?"

"Don't I get to eat first…I am starving?" I asked.

"Not until after the test." He replied.

"By the way…where is the nurse with my meds?" I asked.

"You will take them after the test." He replied.

I really wasn't looking for the nurse with meds. I was prolonging the time, hoping for Miss Rawlins to walk into my room. I wanted to tell her about Nancy.

The orderly help me to get into the wheelchair. I really didn't need one, but it was hospital policy.

Strolling toward the testing room was a burst of freedom waiting to be born. It was a quiet morning. Every single hallway was in solitude.

Suddenly an outburst of noise began to come from the center of the next hallway. It was two orderlies tussling with someone. I couldn't believe my eyes. It was Miss Rawlins in a straight jacket. She was screaming.

"Let me go!" Miss Rawlins screamed.

"Hold her down for…!" one of the orderlies shouted.

"Leave me along!" She continued to scream.

As my wheelchair began to pass the commotion, she became hysterical.

"Pam…Pam…don't let them touch you!" She shouted.

"What's wrong Miss Rawlins?" I shouted.

"Don't …go for the test…!" She continued to scream.

Then I saw a nurse come over to her and inject her with a large syringe.

"Why are they treating her this way?" I asked.

"Who…Rawlins…this is normal for her." The orderly replied.

"Doesn't she work here?"

"Work here…are you kidding?"

"No…I am not kidding…she visits me all the time."

"You mean you let that crazy lady in your room?"

"Well, if she didn't work here…why was she wearing a uniform?"

"Wearing the hospital uniform is an incentive to keep her sane."

"You mean to tell me all this time I have been letting a loony into my room?"

"I wouldn't say loony…this is her first time in a long time having to be put her in a straightjacket."

"What's her problem?"

"She has hallucinations at night…some kind of crazy stuff."

When the orderly told me that, I knew then that someone was watching over me in another dimension. There was a reason Miss Rawlins didn't want me to take those tests.

My mind began to wonder if they tried this same test on her. Dr. Stein said there was no validity yet. Miss Rawlins was only trying to warn me. Fear began to overshadow the faith I had gained.

As we entered the testing room great agitation and anxiety pondered my heart. I glance around the room and saw Dr. Hunt and Dr. Stein preparing for the tests. Insecurity commenced, my body to perspire heavily. The sign of fear was boldly in my eyes.

Suddenly I changed my mind. I thought about Nancy and Miss Rawlins and the state they were in now. One patient was dead and one on the way. I looked at both of the doctors and panicked.

"Can we do this another time?" I said.

"Today is just as good." Dr. Hunt replied.

"Maybe…I'm not ready?" I said.

"Oh…you're ready." Dr. Stein replied.

As I was climbing on the table to lie down, I saw a hypodermic syringe being prepared to inject me. I also saw the anesthetic doctor waiting to put the IV in me to begin the process. I screamed with anxiety.

"Let me go…please let me go!" I screamed as loud as the room would allow me.

Before I could complete the thought of screaming again, I felt the pinch of a needle and behold I was fading into the land of dreams. But it wasn't the land of the dreams; it was the land of night terrors. My body was really numb because of the injection. I could only hear what was going on in the room. I heard the murmuring voices of the doctors. My eyes weren't open, but it was as though I had spiritual eyes. I wanted to cry out for help but my vocal cords wouldn't let me. I could see Nancy walking around the table. She was humming a song. Then she whispered in my ear, "Why did you let them do this to you?" I couldn't reply. She continued to repeat the same words over and over. Then she would hum a song again. This activity was going on while the doctors where sucking fluid from my brain. Then I heard other voices, coming from over my head. They were voices that sounded strange. I had never heard them before. I could see the shadows of the bodies, but they were not visible. I began to quote Psalms 23 in my body. I could hear the words profoundly capturing my soul. Finally, darkness came over me. Everything was insipid.

Suddenly I heard a voice say, "Looks like she is awaking."

My eyes slowly began to open.

"Pam...somebody call the nurse!" She shouted.

The voice had a familiar sound to it. It was my mother standing over me with a smiling face.

"Pam...Pam...its mother!" She shouted.

Then I heard other voices in the background of the room. There was a nurse disconnecting something from my throat. My body began to regain consciousness. There was a misty covering about the room. My eyes began to open slowly. I glanced at a shiny cross swinging back and forth above my head. Then the nurse smiled at me. She resembled Sister Tracy.

"Sister...Sister Tracy," I mumbled.

The nurse didn't utter a word. She moved from my presence so that I could see the view in the room.

There before me were my father, mother, and Daniel. I didn't see Samuel.

"Where is Samuel?" I asked in a sluggish voice.

"Here I am!" Samuel replied. He was on the floor drawing me one of his favorite pictures.

"We are so happy to see you back." My father said.

"Yeah...you scared us for a moment." Daniel said.

"How did I scare you it was only tests..." I said.

A voice next to my head said, "You're right a test."

It was Guy and Karen standing over my head.

"We are so glad you are back...I thought I would have to replace you with Amy." Karen said.

"College is waiting on us anyway Pamela...you couldn't miss that." Guy said.

I glanced around the room. There seemed to be millions of cards and flowers along the borders of my room. The room was unfamiliar to me. I haven't seen anything as exclusive as this in Central. The doctor came in to check my vital signs. Seems like the test was okay according to his gestures to the nurse.

"Was the test okay?" I asked.

"Where are Dr. Hunt and Dr. Stein...I want to thank them?" I continued.

Everyone in the room had an inquisitive look upon them. The doctor told my parents that it was not unusual for someone to talk strangely after what I had been through. But it was nothing. It was only a forty-five-minute test.

"Pam you really need to get some rest...you are a miracle." The doctor said.

"I know, thanks for everything...and let Dr. Hunt and Stein know that too." I said.

By the facial expressions of my parents, they didn't understand anything I was saying. Everyone gathered that I needed to rest so they gave me hugs and kisses and left. Then I heard the intercom announce, "Visiting hours will soon be over in ten minutes, thank you for visiting our patients here at Sutton Hospital and have a good evening." I looked over at the date on the wall it posted, "July 04, 1991".

The facial expression that came upon me could not be explained. A bright light shined in the corner of the room in the shape of a star. I was astounded at the radiation that was penetrating upon my face. There was a light that gave me a sense of peace that was unexplainable to man.

I stared continuously around the room as the warmth secured feeling captured my soul deeply. I finally realized it was only a vision full of dreams. I had awakened from a life-threatening profound sleep. Some predators have to remain silent in order to get your attention.

"Whether you believe it or not, I believe the vision had been a symbolization of an intriguing gift." I had been given a taste of life beyond this present time.

THE END

AUTHOR'S BIOGRAPHY

Dr. Teresa was born in Fort Pierce Florida. During her life, from childhood to adulthood she encountered a lot of adversities, but she endured through faith in God and the many gifts bestowed upon her. Dr. Teresa is an Educator (College Level, Elementary and Middle School), Certified Spiritual Christian Counselor, ordained Minister of Dr. Teresa Ministries LLC. and was a CEO of a faith-based Social Service for many years. She in inspired by writings that portray triumphs over obstacles through faith. Tragedies to Triumph collection of short stories includes the first four books she published.

LO QUE SE PERDIÓ

EN LAS

GUERRAS MUNDIALES

El amor de Dios sana todas las heridas

Autora

Hildegard Bonacker Bruni

SPANISH VERSION

CONTENTS

AGRADECIMIENTOS

Quisiera expresar mucha gratitud a mi madre y a mi padre por criar a mis hermanos, hermanas y a mí con valores cristianos y morales elevados. Estoy agradecida con mis hermanos y hermanas y sus cónyuges por ayudarme a recordar cómo vivíamos en casa antes y durante la Segunda Guerra Mundial. También estoy agradecida con todas las personas que nos cobijaron y nos dieron comida durante nuestra huida de Prusia del Este y con los soldados que nos ayudaron y protegieron.

Agradezco a mi difunto esposo, el Dr. Aldo R. Bruni, quien me amaba mucho y me ofreció un estilo de vida emocionante más allá de mis sueños. Atesoro el amor y el aliento de mi familia y estoy agradecida por los muchos amigos que conocí. Tengo el placer de reconocer la ayuda y amabilidad de mis amigos Kathryn Teitzel y David Long. Se tomaron el tiempo para leer y editar el manuscrito de mi libro, y su amor y amistad me han bendecido de muchas maneras.

Doy las gracias a Joachim Vonhoff, un operador de radio de la Marina Mercante. Residió en Berlín después de la Segunda Guerra Mundial. Él también contribuyó a mi historia. También mi amiga, Ilse Stritzke, que vivía en Prusia del Este después de que los rusos reclamaran parte de ella. Me contó cómo los soldados rusos maltrataban a su familia.

Sobre todo, agradezco a Dios que me perdonó la vida muchas veces y me permitió contar mi historia. A Él le doy toda la gloria y el honor por haberme protegido y guiado toda mi vida.

Donde mi memoria se quedó corta, la imaginación tomó el relevo para completar los hechos con la ficción.

INTRODUCCIÓN

M is padres, Gustav y Emilie (Schlikat) Bonacker, nacieron en Prusia del Este, al igual que sus cuatro hijas, Emma, Marta, Meta, Hildegard, y sus cuatro hijos, Georg, Edmund, Richard y Horst.

Los antepasados de mi padre vivían en Francia antes de la persecución de los hugonotes durante los siglos XVI y XVII. El rey Luis XIV y la Iglesia católica consideraban a los protestantes una amenaza para su país. Algunos huyeron a Salzburgo, Austria. Más tarde, los antepasados de mi padre se reasentaron en Prusia del Este.

Los antepasados de mi madre se remontan a la tribu prusiana original que vivía en una comuna junto al Mar Báltico. Mis antepasados prusianos cultivaban la fértil tierra, cazaban en los bosques y pescaban en los muchos lagos. Cada tribu hablaba un idioma diferente, pero todas practicaban la mitología pagana.

Durante el siglo XIII, los caballeros teutónicos alemanes ayudaron al duque polaco Conrad de Mazovia en una cruzada contra estos prusianos paganos. Después de una batalla de cuarenta años, los cruzados ganaron la guerra. El duque polaco recompensó a los cruzados que querían quedarse en Prusia con una tierra llamada Rittergut (Estado del Caballero). Más tarde, los cruzados se casaron con los prusianos conquistados y desarrollaron un Estado alemán cristiano de libertad, justicia y profundo amor por su país y Dios.

Mis abuelos maternos Jan August y Ana Schlikat, y mis padres crecieron durante la Primera Guerra Mundial, y sus ocho hijos durante la Segunda Guerra Mundial. Soportaron las tragedias de las dos guerras mundiales. En julio de 1944, mi padre fue reclutado por el ejército. El frente ruso se acercó rápidamente a la frontera con Prusia del Este y a nuestra ciudad natal de Wizajny. El 3 de agosto de 1944, el alcalde de nuestra localidad envió mensajeros a todos los vecinos, instándolos a escapar para evitar ser masacrados por el Ejército Rojo Ruso. Todas las personas debían reunirse en la plaza del pueblo a la mañana siguiente a las 9:00 a.m. Mamá no tuvo tiempo ni medios para avisar a nuestra hermana Marta, que trabajaba para la familia de un profesor en el cercano pueblo de Hellrau. Mamá emprendió un viaje de ocho meses en una carreta tirada por caballos con sus siete hijos. Horst, el hijo menor, tenía solo un año y nueve meses. Yo tenía siete años cuando empezamos nuestro viaje hacia el oeste sin un destino conocido. Soportamos diez semanas de un invierno muy frío, a veces siendo bombardeados. A menudo, pasamos hambre o nos enfermamos en el camino. Dormíamos en graneros, casas abandonadas, o en la carreta en los bosques o al borde de la carretera. Nos asentamos en Sophienhof, un enorme rancho en Schleswig Holstein, el 26 de marzo de 1945. Incluso allí, los británicos lanzaron bombas por la noche y los estadounidenses nos bombardearon durante el día. Vivíamos con el temor constante de que nos mataran. Un mes antes de que terminara la guerra, un grupo de soldados alemanes con prisioneros polacos se quedó en Sophienhof. Los soldados alemanes ayudaron a los civiles en todo lo que pudieron.

Después de que los generales alemanes se rindieran el 7 de mayo de 1945, terminó la Segunda Guerra Mundial en Alemania. Desafortunadamente, según el Tratado de Potsdam, los aliados acordaron y cedieron la región norte de Prusia Oriental a Rusia y la parte sur a Polonia. Después de 700 años, la hermosa tierra fértil a lo largo del Mar Báltico con una rica herencia alemana ya no pertenecía a Alemania. Por lo tanto, Prusia Oriental desapareció con la Segunda Guerra Mundial para siempre. Mis padres vivieron bajo cuatro gobiernos diferentes. Nacieron durante la Monarquía del Kaiser Wilhelm II, durando hasta el final de la Primera Guerra Mundial en 1918. Respetaron al Kaiser y vivieron en paz y bien. Kaiser Wilhelm II solo ayudó a Austria, que comenzó la Primera Guerra Mundial luchando contra Serbia. Los aliados declararon al Kaiser Wilhelm II culpable de crímenes de guerra y lo obligaron a abdicar y huir a Holanda. Después de la Primera Guerra Mundial, la República de Weimar existió desde 1918 hasta 1933. El Tratado de Versalles requería que Alemania pagara una fuerte restitución a los aliados, lo que resultó en caos, alto desempleo e hiperinflación.

Adolf Hitler llegó al poder y estableció el Tercer Reich, gobernando desde 1933 hasta 1945. Durante seis años, Hitler estuvo en guerra y el pueblo alemán sufrió humillaciones, los estragos de la guerra y pérdidas territoriales. Otros países perdieron muchos soldados, civiles y la destrucción de muchas ciudades pero ningún territorio o tierra.

Durante cuatro años, del 8 de mayo de 1945 al 24 de mayo de 1949, los cuatro aliados, Estados Unidos, Inglaterra, Francia y Rusia, dividieron a Alemania en cuatro secciones y gobernaron las zonas que ocupaban de acuerdo con las leyes de sus países.

Yo, Hildegard Bonacker, nací el 2 de enero de 1937 en el Tercer Reich. Viví toda la Segunda Guerra Mundial, durante la época en que Alemania no tenía gobierno propio y también en la República Alemana. La República Alemana (Deutsche Bundesrepublik) comenzó el 24 de mayo de 1949.

El Dr. Theodor Heuss se convirtió en el primer presidente de la República Alemana y Conrad Adenauer en el primer canciller. Crecer en una Alemania destruida por la posguerra nos presentó a mi familia y a mí muchas dificultades y desafíos . Obtener una educación y obtener una profesión fue difícil debido a la escasez de maestros e instalaciones escolares. Pero Dios, a quien encomendé mi vida en 1949, me ha ayudado a superar todos los obstáculos que enfrenté mientras crecía y durante toda mi vida.

Después de graduarme de la escuela de medicina como asistente médico comercial y práctico, trabajé en una clínica médica durante un año en Alemania. En diciembre de 1956 emigré a los Estados Unidos. Después de estar con el Dr. y la Sra. Jefferies durante seis meses en Des Moines, Iowa, me uní a la familia de mi hermano Edmund y mi hermana Emma en Chicago, Illinois. Mi conocimiento de los términos médicos en inglés era insuficiente para trabajar en un consultorio médico, así que comencé a trabajar como técnico de laboratorio en el Hospital Bethesda de Chicago. Estando allí, conocí al Dr. Aldo Bruni, quien estaba en el personal del hospital. Chocamos en una escalera mientras yo llevaba una bandeja de muestras de sangre del paciente al laboratorio. Encendió un profundo amor el uno por el otro.

Una vez que el Dr. Bruni y yo nos casamos, administré sus dos clínicas. Comenzamos juntos una vida emocionante, aventurera y, en ocasiones, desafiante. No solo disfrutábamos trabajando juntos, sino también yendo a representaciones de ópera, viajando, navegando, y explorando la belleza de la naturaleza. Nos hicimos amigos de médicos, profesionales y cantantes de ópera que daban lujosas fiestas y nos entretenían. En una de las reuniones musicales, tuve el placer de conocer al general estadounidense Healy. Hablamos de la Segunda Guerra Mundial. Mencioné que había escuchado una cinta que me regaló mi cuñado Gustav. En la cinta, los soldados y el pueblo alemanes fueron descritos como bárbaros y belicistas. Le dije que vivimos con soldados alemanes en una gran granja durante un mes antes de que terminara la guerra. Los soldados ayudaron en los campos, entretuvieron a la gente y siempre fueron amables y respetuosos con nosotros.

El general Healy respondió: "Bueno, Hildegard, fue así; teníamos propaganda escrita contra Inglaterra, Francia, Rusia y Alemania. Tendríamos que hacer quedar mal al país para justificar nuestra entrada en la guerra, dependiendo de con quién eligiéramos pelear. Sin embargo, si la propaganda se repite con suficiente frecuencia, se cree; el daño está hecho al país y al pueblo, y solo unos pocos se enteran de la verdad".

El comentario del General Healy me impulsó a comenzar a buscar la verdad sobre las dos guerras mundiales y los eventos históricos durante los años turbulentos antes y después de las guerras. La información sobre ambas guerras es interminable; también lo es la multiplicidad de razones y culpas de la Primera Guerra Mundial y la Segunda Guerra Mundial. Simplemente rasco la superficie de mi libro como fondo para mi historia y la de mi familia. Se necesita tiempo y dedicación para aprender a separar la verdad de las mentiras y los hechos de la ficción. La verdad sigue siendo la verdad, aunque nadie la crea. Una mentira sigue siendo una mentira, incluso si todos la creen. Solo Dios sabe toda la verdad. Él es el juez supremo de la gente y del mundo.

Doy gracias a Dios y a mi Salvador Jesucristo que protegió a mi familia para que sobreviviésemos a los peligros de la guerra y las dificultades de la vida. Tuve el privilegio de pasar por un espectro completo de experiencias físicas, emocionales, intelectuales y espirituales positivas y negativas. Probé la agonía y el éxtasis de la vida durante mi viaje peligroso y difícil, pero pacífico y emocionante. En Su misericordia, Dios me enseñó a comprender, amar, consolar y ayudar a otros que pasan por circunstancias difíciles. A mi Creador, le doy la gloria por enseñarme cómo usar todos los desafíos, sufrimientos y obstáculos a lo largo del camino de la vida como peldaños para acercarme a Él. Ahora estoy en mi último viaje aquí en la tierra a mi hogar celestial, sin saber cuándo terminará. Creo que terminará en el cielo. Dios me llevó triunfalmente a través de todas las tormentas de la vida, y confío en Él para seguir haciendo lo mismo hasta llegar al cielo, el destino final de mi viaje.

CAPÍTULO 1

Breve Historia de Prusia

A ntes de iniciar el viaje de mi familia, me gusta regresar en el tiempo y describir brevemente la historia de Prusia, el país donde nacieron mis abuelos y mis padres.2 Los ancestros de mi madre pertenecían a una antigua tribu prusiana, una de las diez tribus étnicas que vivían al principio del sigo en el Mar Báltico, al este del río Weichsel (Vistula). Ellos formaron comunas para protegerse de las amenazas humanas y naturales. Cada tribu hablaba un idioma diferente y practicaban mitología pagana. Ellos labraban el suelo fértil, cazaban en los abundantes bosques, pescaban en los numerosos lagos, y vivían de la tierra.

Mapa del este de Prusia, 1945

Durante el Siglo XIII, los Caballeros Teutónicos Alemanes, una orden militar alemana bajo el mando de Herman Salza, aceptaron asistir al Duque Polaco Conrad de Mazovia en la guerra contra los paganos prusianos. Aún cuando los cruzados tuvieron superar la resistencia con muchas batallas sangrientas contra los tenaces y vigorosos prusianos, lograron conquistarlos. El duque prometió a los cruzados que podrían quedarse en Prusia para mantener la paz, el gobierno y supervisar el desarrollo de los dominios recientemente adquiridos. El duque Conrad les otorgó a los cruzados que se quedaron títulos de nobleza y grandes parcelas de tierra --- el estado fue llamado Rittergut (Patrimonio de la Caballería).

Bajo el mandato del Rey Bohemio Ottokar II, los prusianos se casaron con los cruzados y los colonos. Ellos desarrollaron un Estado Alemán Cristiano de libertad, justicia, patriotismo, y un profundo amor a Dios. El rey construyó la conocida ciudad prusiana de Koenigberg (Colina del Rey), nombrada en honor a él, junto con 1,400 aldeas y noventa y tres pueblos.

Los colonos llegaron de diferentes lugares de Alemania y otros países europeos, construyeron ciudades, cultivaron la tierra, y convirtieron a los ateos al cristianismo. A su tiempo, los colonos, junto con los nativos prusianos, transformaron el país y pusieron en práctica un gobierno bueno y moderno, con libertad religiosa y tolerancia. Así, Prusia se convirtió en refugio para perseguidos religiosos y políticos.

Durante la Reforma, de 200,000 a 300,000 protestantes franceses (conocidos como Hugonotes),que eran considerados una amenaza para el trono del Rey Luis XIV y la Iglesia Católica, fueron perseguidos y exiliados de Francia. Muchos de los protestantes huyeron a Austria.

Cuando el Arzobispo Austriaco Leopold de Firmian expidió un decreto el 31 de Octubre de 1731, mandando que todos los protestantes y luteranos que no se reconvirtieran al catolicismo serian exiliados. Muchos tomaron sus biblias y libros religiosos, dejaron Austria y se asentaron en Prusia. Entre aquéllos que se asentaron en Prusia había banqueros, doctores, abogados, artesanos, trabajadores de fábricas y granjeros franceses que enriquecieron a su país anfitrión.

Prusia empezó a emerger en las finas artes y las ciencias. En 1544, el Rey Leopold II fundó la primera universidad en Koenigsberg, donde se enseñaba filosofía, ciencia y aprendizaje superior. El mundialmente reconocido filósofo alemán Emanuel Kant (1714-1804) nació en Koenigsberg (donde primero estudió filosofía) y después impartió clases en la universidad. "Crítica a la Razón Práctica" (Kritik der Praktischen Vernunft) y "Hacia la Paz Eterna" (Zum Ewigen Freiden) son dos de los muy conocidos libros que escribió y publicó. Él fomentó el idealismo alemán, al día de hoy sus trabajos inspiran e influencian la filosofía europea y mundial.

Prusia floreció bajo el reino de cuarenta y seis años de Frederick II, quien nació el 24 de enero de 1712, en la familia real de Hohenzollern. Mas adelante, Frederick II sería llamado Frederick El Grande. Él se consideraba un gobernante absoluto, un siervo del Estado de Dios. Viajó a cada rincón de su reino para conocer las necesidades de su gente y asegurarse de que los trabajadores y los pobres eran tratados justamente. Elevó el estándar de trabajo, pero también esperaba de cada hombre el cumplimiento de su deber, usó el sentido común y obedeció las leyes nacionales. Despojó a su corte de toda ostentosidad, él mismo trabajaba diariamente y practicaba una gestión financiera sólida. Se consideraba a sí mismo defensor de los pobres. La población le estimaba enormemente.

En Postdam, Berlín, mantuvo una vida disciplinada en su castillo "San Souci", tomando caminatas diarias en los magníficos jardines. Amaba el arte, la ciencia, la religión y la filosofía y otorgaba a sus súbditos la libertad de elegir su fe, contrario a otros gobernantes quienes forzaban su religión sobre sus gobernados.

La reina austriaca María Teresa amenazó con atacar el reino prusiano. Frederick El Grande defendió su país y se vio inmerso en una guerra de siete años (1756-1763). Con sus soldados de élite (Los Junkers Prusianos) y la ayuda del Zar Ruso Pedro II, ganó finalmente la batalla y la misma guerra. Después de que finalizara la guerra y de que su reino estuviera seguro, construyó iglesias, escuelas, teatros y pueblos; también desarrolló industrias.

Los historiadores aseguran que la grandeza de este reino no fue ganar batallas, pues también sufrió derrotas. Frederick El Grande tenía la habilidad y determinación de encontrar recursos para convertir los retos en ventajas. Su fe cristiana y su tolerancia a la religión de su gente contribuyó a su grandeza.

El reinó acorde a los principios cristianos. Se sintió responsable ante Dios por las decisiones y acciones que tomó. Un año antes de su muerte el 10 de septiembre de 1785, hizo un acuerdo con los Estados Unidos de América y fundó la Constitución del gobierno sobre principios cristianos. Las dos naciones jóvenes, Prusia y los Estados Unidos de América, firmaron un acuerdo de amistad y comercio que duró 132 años, hasta que América entró en la Primera Guerra Mundial en 1917.

Casi cien años después, Wilhelm I, séptimo rey de Prusia, (1871 – 1888), ayudado por su hábil estadista y consejero, Otto von Bismarck, unificó los numerosos reinos de Alemania. También se convirtió en emperador (Káiser) de la Alemania unificada. Durante su reinado, Alemania prosperó y se convirtió en el país mas fuerte y mejor administrado en Europa, así como en la envidia de Bretaña y Francia. Alemania y los países prósperos de Europa adquirieron colonias africanas y de otros lugares del mundo.

Mi madre y mi padre crecieron durante el reino de Wilhelm II, el noveno rey de Prusia, que se convirtió en el tercer káiser de Alemania el 15 de junio de 1888. Tomó el trono de su padre, el káiser Friedrich III, que murió de cáncer de laringe después de ser emperador de Alemania por solo noventa y nueve días.

Káiser Wilhelm II, Último emperador de Alemania

El Káiser Wilhelm II nació el 27 de enero de 1859 en Berlín. Su madre, Victoria, era la hija de la reina Victoria de Inglaterra. Tuvo un parto difícil con su primogénito y le nombró Wilhelm. Su dicha se desvaneció cuando descubrió que el brazo izquierdo de su hijo era deficiente. Los doctores hicieron uso de crueles tratamientos y métodos para estimular el desarrollo del brazo, con resultados negativos. Él intentó mas adelante sobreponerse a su discapacidad, pero el resentimiento de su demandante madre dejó una relación tensa entre ambos. De cualquier manera, él era muy cercano a su abuela, la Reina Victoria de Inglaterra.

El estricto educador del káiser Wilhelm II inculcó en él la creencia en Dios, el amor por la paz, la justicia, la belleza y el arte. También estudió ciencias políticas y leyes en Bonn, Alemania. Recibió su entrenamiento militar bajo el ojo vigilante del Comandante en Jefe y Canciller Otto von Bismark.

En 1881, mientras era rey de Prusia, se casó con la princesa Augusta Victoria de Schelswig – Holstein. Juntos tuvieron seis hijos y una hija.

El káiser Wilhelm II disfrutaba de la caza en Rominger Heide, un hermoso territorio de bosque y brezal, bien poblado con ciervos y vida silvestre. Aunque él mismo no podía cazar debido a su discapacidad, si disfrutaba de los rituales y celebraciones de cacería. Frecuentemente habitaba en Rominten, en su castillo de caza favorito, construido con madera en el estilo arquitectónico noruego. A un lado del alojamiento real mandó construir una iglesia. Rominten se encontraba tan solo a diez millas de Wizajny, nuestro lugar de nacimiento y hogar. Los bosques de Rominten se extendían cerca a nuestro pueblo. Los pobladores y familiares disfrutaban de recolectar hongos, avellanas y moras en Rominger Heide y los bosques que rodeaban nuestro rancho. El pueblo alemán reverenciaba a su rey y káiser, a quien consideraban justo y bondadoso para el bien del pueblo. Vivieron bien durante su reino.

Los káiseres Wilhelm I y Wilhelm II tuvieron un canciller y comandante en jefe competente, Otto von Bismarck. El nació como príncipe prusiano, Otto Eduard Leopold von Bismarck en Shoenhausen. El káiser Wilhelm I y Otto von Bismarck unieron los estados y reinos germanos para formar el Imperio Alemán, y él manejó responsable y justamente los asuntos nacionales e internacionales. Poseía una extraordinaria astucia política y habilidades diplomáticas, ganando la reputación de ser el "Canciller de Hierro".

Durante la monarquía, Alemania cambió a pasos acelerados de una sociedad agrícola a una nación industrial. El número de trabajadores incrementó rápidamente; formaron un partido político en 1875 y se proclamaron social -demócratas (en alemán: Sozialistische Arbeiterpartei Deutschland's, SPD abreviado).

Mientras sus números incrementaban, también lo hicieron su poder y sus demandas. El canciller von Bismarck inició programas sociales como seguro de salud, compensaciones para trabajadores y planes de pensión para los ancianos e inválidos con la finalidad de pacificar a los trabajadores.

En este tiempo, Alemania prosperó y estableció colonias en el Sudeste de África (ahora llamado Namibia), Camerún, Nueva Guinea, Archipiélagos Bismarck y las Islas Marshall. Inglaterra, Francia e Italia también colonizaron partes de África y Asia. El káiser Wilhelm II expandió su flota naval considerablemente bajo la dirección del altamente competente Almirante Alfred Tirpitz para proteger las colonias de agresores. Gran Bretaña buscó la supremacía naval y vio con desdén los avances de las flotas alemanas.

CAPÍTULO 2

Primera Guerra Mundial

Ciertos eventos llevaron al inicio de la Primera Guerra Mundial.3 El káiser Wilhelm II estaba celoso de la fama de Otto von Bismarck y los conflictos entre ellos se desarrollaron. El káiser forzó a Otto von Bismarck a retirarse en 1890. El káiser se convirtió en comandante en jefe de la milicia e implementó sus planes. Designó a Leo von Caprivi como su nuevo canciller. El káiser pasó mucho tiempo con los oficiales militares y navales. Cuando requería tomar decisiones significativas militares o políticas, primero pedía el consejo de sus generales y almirantes y después le presentaba los hechos al canciller. El káiser sentía desprecio por la opinión civil. Durante los treinta años de su reinado buscó el poder y dejó una marca de su influencia en Alemania y en el mundo. Alemania se convirtió en el poder industrial dominante de Europa, el único rival para Inglaterra.

No obstante, el káiser Wilhelm II olvidó renovar el tratado con Rusia que Bismarck había hecho bajo el mandato del káiser Wilhelm I. Francia llenó el vacío rápidamente firmando un tratado con Rusia. Ahora los tres aliados, Rusia, Francia e Inglaterra, llamados la Entente, rodeaban a Alemania.

Después, un desafortunado evento sucedió en Austria – Hungría. El Archiduque Franz Ferdinand, futuro heredero al trono de Austria – Hungría, fue asesinado el 28 de junio de 1914 por un estudiante, Gavrilo Princip, que pertenecía a la Mano Negra, una sociedad secreta serbia. El duque Berchtold de Austria – Hungría expidió un ultimátum a Serbia para llevar al asesino ante la justicia y anular la soberanía de Serbia. Serbia aceptó todos los términos del requerimiento, excepto que se negó a entregar su independencia. Austria- Hungría cesó sus relaciones diplomáticas con Serbia. Austria – Hunrgía ordenó primero una movilización parcial para destruir el movimiento nacionalista serbio y cimentar su influencia política en Bulgaria y Romania.

Si la guerra estallara, el káiser Wilhelm II prometió apoyo y otorgó a Austria - Hungría un cheque en blanco (Blankovollmacht), acción que fue malinterpretada por las otras naciones europeas, que acusaron a Alemania de querer acción. El káiser consideró el conflicto entre Austria – Hungría y Serbia como uno personal y esperaba evitar la guerra. Sin embargo, el tener un cheque en blanco alemán alentó a Austria – Hungría a declarar la guerra contra Serbia el 28 de julio de 1914. Rusia, obligado por un tratado con Serbia, anunció la movilización para defender a Serbia. El Zar Nikolaus II comprendió que su ayuda a Serbia implicaba una guerra indirecta contra Austria – Hungría y Alemania. Intentó detener la movilización, pero sus generales discreparon. El comandante ruso Sergei Doboroloski le dijo mas adelante al Zar que los generales habían decidido ir a guerra el 25 de julio de 1914. Tres días antes, incluso, de que Austria – Hungría declarara la guerra contra Serbia. Los generales rusos sabían que su movilización provocaría que Alemania entrara a la guerra, eso era lo que Rusia buscaba lograr. Alemania intentó detener el conflicto mandando un ultimátum para parar las preparaciones de guerra inmediatamente, pero Rusia no accedió. Alemania vio esto como un acto de guerra y el káiser Wilhelm II declaró la guerra contra Rusia el 1 de agosto de 1914.

Ahora, Francia, obligada por el nuevo tratado con Rusia, declaró la guerra contra Alemania e inició movilizaciones. Con guerra en los frentes este y oeste, Alemania esperaba asegurar la victoria sobre Francia a través del plan Schlieffen: marchar a través de Bélgica, derrotando rápidamente al ejército francés, y después concentrarse en pelear contra Rusia.

Cuando el ejército alemán marchó a través de la neutral Bélgica, el pueblo belga contraatacó. Siendo un aliado de Francia, Inglaterra fue provocado para declarar la guerra contra Alemania el 4 de agosto de 1914.

Después de que Inglaterra declarara la guerra contra Alemania, el káiser Wilhelm II apeló al pueblo alemán con un discurso el 6 de agosto de 1914:

"Desde el establecimiento de la monarquía alemana, ha sido el deseo de mis ancestros, así como mío, el mantener la paz y pacíficamente alcanzar nuestros objetivos. Sin embargo, nuestros oponentes están celosos de nuestro éxito. Hasta ahora, hemos tolerado la enemistad tanto abierta como secreta del Este, el Oeste y del otro lado del mar. Ahora, ellos quieren humillarnos. Ellos esperan que toleremos la invasión de nuestro aliado Austro – húngaro, quien está luchando por el reconocimiento como una potencia. Si permitimos esta humillación, habremos perdido nuestra fuerza y honor. Así que, ¡dejemos que el mundo decida! En tiempos de paz, el enemigo nos ataca. Por lo tanto, tomen sus armas y peleen. Cada duda e incertidumbre será traición a la madre patria. Es un asunto de existencia o extinción de nuestro Reich que nuestros antepasados establecieron, y un asunto de ser o no ser del poder alemán y la cultura alemana. Nos defenderemos hasta el último aliento de nuestra infantería y caballería. Lograremos superar esta batalla en contra de un mundo de enemigos. Nunca fue

Alemania asediada cuando estuvo unida. Hacia adelante con Dios, quien esté con nosotros, como lo estuvo él con nuestros ancestros.[14]

El ejército alemán empezó a marchar a través de Bélgica, rompiendo el acuerdo de neutralidad, y los civiles belgas atacaron a los soldados alemanes. Ambos países sufrieron grandes pérdidas de soldados y civiles. Muchos edificios también fueron destruidos.

Cuando el comandante de Gran Bretaña, Sir. John French, supo sobre Alemania ignorando la neutralidad de Bélgica, envió 100,000 soldados de sus cuerpos de infantería a Mons, Bélgica. El general Horace Smith – Dorrien intentó detener el avance del ejército alemán. Los fusileros ingleses explotaron el puente del canal Mons – Conde.

El 23 de agosto de 1914, Alexander von Kluck atacó el frente inglés. Aunque los soldados alemanes sufrieron grandes pérdidas debido al fuego de los rifles ingleses, el comandante en jefe, Sir. John French retiró a sus tropas al río francés Marne. Cuando el ejército alemán, ahora bajo el mando del General Falkenhayn, avanzó a Antwerp y Bruegge, las fuerzas aliadas ofrecieron una fuerte resistencia en Yepern. Para el 4 de septiembre de 1914, a pesar de que el ejército alemán rompió el frente y cruzó el río Marne, se retiraron debido a las grandes pérdidas humanas y abandonaron el plan Schlieffen de avanzar a París a través de Bélgica. Una guerra estacionaria, o guerra de trincheras se desató.

Los franceses introdujeron el uso de armas químicas: gas lacrimógeno y bromuro de Xylol. Sin embargo, ambos fueron ineficaces dado que se disiparon en el aire antes de alcanzar su objetivo. El 22 de abril de 1915 los alemanes usaron exitosamente cloropicrín en gas en la batalla de Yepern, matando a 5,000 enemigos. Las recientemente inventadas máscaras de gas previnieron muchas fatalidades. Mas tarde, un químico desarrolló el letal gas mostaza, también llamado gas amarillo. El 22 de abril de 1915 es considerado el inicio de la guerra química.

En el frente este, los rusos superaban en números al ejército alemán. Al principio, el ejército alemán sufrió contratiempos y grandes bajas cuando los rusos invadieron Prusia oriental. El ejército alemán perdió veinte mil soldados. Después, el general Erich Ludendorff y Paul von Hidenburg reemplazaron al general previo, Maximillian von Prittwitz. Se encontraron con el general ruso Alexander Samsonov y con su artillería en Tannenberg, Prusia oriental, con tropas reforzadas. Después de seis días de pelea intensa, Rusia sufrió importantes bajas. El general Alexander Samsonov intentó retirarse sin éxito, pues la mayoría de sus soldados fueron asesinados o capturados. De 150,000 soldados rusos, 92,000 fueron arrestados, 10,000 escaparon y el resto murieron. Tal derrota fue demasiado para el general ruso, quien cometió suicidio.

En los inicios de la Primera Guerra Mundial, todas las potencias construyeron planes débilmente, que se usaron preponderantemente para vigilar el frente occidental. Los pilotos reportaban la ubicación exacta y los avances del frente para que los ataques pudieran ser planeados con mayor precisión. Más adelante, al instalar ametralladoras en los aviones, tomaron lugar las batallas aéreas. Los pilotos alemanes superaban tácticamente a los franceses, ingleses y belgas. De hecho, en la batalla aérea llamada "Abril Sangriento" el Cuerpo Aéreo Aliado perdió 912 pilotos.

Manfred Albrecht Freiherr von Richtofen, conocido como el Barón Rojo, se convirtió en el As de Ases y en el ídolo de los pilotos alemanes. Sin embargo, el capitán Douglas Connell y Albert Woodbridge asestaron una herida de bala en su cabeza tras lo cual sufrió de severos dolores de cabeza y no pudo volar por un tiempo. Cuando volvió al aire el 21 de abril de 1918, se adentró demasiado en el territorio inglés, voló demasiado bajo, fue derribado y se estrelló en el suelo. Su cuerpo fue después recuperado y transportado a Wiesbaden, Alemania, donde fue sepultado con honores militares.

Hacia el fin de la Primera Guerra Mundial, los manufactureros equiparon a los aviones para llevar y soltar bombas. Los bombarderos se dirigían a destruir sitios militares y establecimientos industriales.

Desafortunadamente, con la esperanza de bajar la moral del enemigo, los bombarderos también mataron a muchos civiles en el camino.

A pesar de que el presidente Wilson prometió absoluta neutralidad de los Estados Unidos, fue atraído a la guerra por el Primer Señor del Almirantazgo Británico Winston Churchill. Los Estados Unidos entraron a la guerra y aportaron muchos aviones y pilotos bien entrenados a Europa. Incapaces de obtener repuestos aeronáuticos rápidamente, el escuadrón alemán superado en números comprendió que la victoria se decidiría en el mar o en la tierra, no en el aire.

Las flotas inglesas y americanas introdujeron un prototipo de portaaviones. Los hidroaviones despegaban de la plataforma de una nave, pero debían aterrizar en el agua para ser transportados al portaaviones con una grúa.

El submarino de guerra alemán, iniciado en 1915, se detuvo después de que el barco de pasajeros inglés "Lusitania" fuera hundido el 7 de mayo de 1915 por el submarino alemán U-20 en la costa sur de Irlanda. Mil ciento noventa y dos pasajeros murieron. Entre ellos había 128 americanos.

Cuando el señor Colin Simpson, corresponsal del *Sunday Times* de Londres, quien también estudiaba historia en la Universidad de Oxford, leyó reportes contradictorios sobre esta tragedia, comenzó una búsqueda de seis años por la verdad sobre el incidente del Lusitania, que describe en su libro El Lusitania.[5] El Señor Simpson descubrió la lista de inventario de la última carga en Nueva York el 30 de abril de 1915, de la Línea Cunard, diferida de la copia original que el presidente de los Estados Unidos de América, Woodrow Wilson tenía en su posesión.

El gobierno inglés informó al presidente de la Línea Cunard, el señor Alfred Booth, para que construyera una nave de pasajeros más rápida que la nave alemana llamada Káiser Wilhelm II que navegaba a 23.5 nudos por hora, la más rápida de ese tiempo. El señor Booth prometió construir dos naves, Lusitania y Mauretania, que alcanzarían 25 nudos por hora. En ese tiempo, el señor Winston Churchill, el ministro marino, visitó al señor Booth y le dio instrucciones y especificaciones para instalar el equipo necesario para transformarlas en navíos de guerra. El gobierno le pagaría una cierta suma y un costo anual de operación de 75,000.00 libras como compensación.

El 12 de mayo de 1913, el Lusitania fue puesto en dique seco con el pretexto de instalar la turbina más nueva, pero manteniendo en secreto los cambios que realmente se hicieron. Winston Churchill apremió al capitán del puerto para que instalara el equipo rápidamente pues la guerra con Alemania era inevitable. El Lusitania reasumió sus cruceros de pasajeros a Nueva York el 21 de Julio de 1913. El almirante ordenó equipar catorce barcos mercantes mas con armas.

Cuando Inglaterra declaró la guerra con Alemania el 4 de agosto de 1914, Inglaterra estaba bien preparada. El Lusitania tenia las armas instaladas y fue registrado el 17 de septiembre de 1914 como uno de los navíos de guerra armados de la flota principal del almirantazgo inglés.

Winston Churchill planeaba pasar a través de la patrulla alemana con banderas de países neutrales, especialmente de Estados Unidos. Los navíos de países neutrales no podían ser atacados. Winston Churcill también ordenó tratar a los capitanes alemanes, si fuesen capturados, como criminales y no darles el estatus de prisioneros. Para Winston Churchill era más conveniente dispararles que tomarlos presos. El almirantazgo inglés se rehusó a estas prácticas. Sin embargo, cuando el submarino alemán U-21 inspeccionaba el navío Ben Crauchan, descubrieron las órdenes del Almirantazgo Inglés de mantener banderas americanas y de embestir cuaquier submarinno, lo cual era contrario a la ley. El capitán alemán salvó a la tripulación británica y después hundió el Ben Crauchan.

Estas prácticas horrorizaron al gobierno alemán y a los oficiales submarinos. Demandaron remover el bloqueo, sosteniendo las normas de alta mar y permitiendo a la Marina Alemana atacar cualquier barco mercante sin advertencia. Alemania también declaró como zona de guerra a las aguas que rodean a Inglaterra e Irlanda, incluyendo el Canal Inglés. Los ingleses solo declararon al Mar Norte como zona de guerra.

El gobierno alemán envió una diligencia con esta práctica injusta y una copia de las órdenes del almirantazgo inglés al Secretario de Estado Americano William Bryan. En su ausencia, el señor Robert Lansing aceptó la diligencia. Escribió su respuesta y conscientemente omitió mencionar que él tenía una copia de la orden del almirantazgo inglés y que había expedido una advertencia a los pasajeros americanos para que no reservaran viajes de cruceros en navíos ingleses.

Cuando el señor William Bryan regresó y se enteró de las omisiones, se molestó. No obstante, el escrito y opinión del señor Robert Lansing prevaleció.

Para salvar la imagen neutral americana, los Estados Unidos advirtieron a Inglaterra, prohibiendo a los navíos ingleses portar banderas americanas. Alemania recibió aviso de que si atacaban otra nave neutral, Alemania sería llevada ante la justicia. Las consecuencias de tal acción llevarían a los Estados Unidos a entrar a la guerra.

En el incidente de Falaha, el almirante inglés nuevamente falló en reportar 13 toneladas de cargamento de pólvora. Omitió reportar que el capitán alemán le advirtió a todos los pasajeros abandonar la nave antes de hundirla. En su lugar, los medios retrataron al capitán alemán y a sus hombres como asesinos a sangre fría.

Muchos alemanes que vivían en Estados Unidos despreciaron estos falsos reportes. Un grupo de prominentes germano – americanos se reunieron en Nueva York. George Viereck, un editor de un periódico pro – alemán, The Fatherland, dirigió la junta. El dijo que si cualquier navío con pasajeros americanos fuera hundido, liberarían al diablo. Una persona presente dijo que el Lusitania estaba anclado en el puerto de Nueva York y partiría hacia Liverpool, Inglaterra el 1 de Mayo de 1915. El señor Viereck recibió aprobación unánime para publicar un artículo en cincuenta periódicos distintos para advertir a los pasajeros americanos, que habían reservado su lugar en el Lusitania, para que cancelaran sus reservaciones y consiguieran pasaje en algún navío americano. El Lusitania estaba cargado con munición para Inglaterra y podría ser atacado o hundido por submarinos alemanes.

Las advertencias, selladas en cincuenta sobres cerrados salieron de la oficina el 23 de abril de 1915 y tardaron una semana en llegar a los pasajeros. Debido al papeleo burocrático solamente un periódico, el Register of Des Moines, en Iowa, imprimió la advertencia. Tras una larga espera, el señor Viereck incluso fue a hablar personalmente con el Ministro de Asuntos Exteriores. El señor Viereck señaló al señor Bryan que el Lusitania estaba cargado de municiones para Inglaterra y que únicamente haría un viaje.

En Nueva York el oficial de aduana colaboró con el señor Ryan aceptando solo un listado parcial de productos comunes embarcados. Recibió la lista de real del material de guerra en el Lusitania cuatro o cinco días después de que dejó Nueva York. El señor Ryan prometió informar al presidente Wilson y advertir a la población americana para que cancelaran sus reservaciones de crucero en el Lusitania porque transportaba materiales de guerra. El presidente Wilson no hizo nada. Sin embargo, él debe haber sabido de la carga real y el peligro que los pasajeros podían afrontar. Cuando el presidente Wilson supo que el Lusitania fue atacado por un submarino alemán y que se había hundido, admitió saber el cruel destino de la nave. Le causó muchas noches sin dormir.

Mientras tanto, Winston Churchill y el Almirante Fisher se reunieron. Miraron el mapa donde se marcaba la ubicación de cada buque de guerra y submarino alemán y prestaron particular atención al U-20, que tenía curso hacia Fastnet Rock, Irlanda. Los cruceron recibieron protección superor de los buques de guerra antes de entrar a puerto. El buque de guerra Juno estaba en camino hacia el Lusitania. Winston Churchill se excusó en que Juno no podría resistir un ataque de un submarino; le ordenó a Juno vovler a Queenstown. Winston Churchill le mencionó esto al almirante Fisher y solicitó a un destructor de Milford para proteger al Lusitania. Aún así, no informó a su capitán, William Turner, de este hecho ni de que había un submarino alemán circundando las aguas. El capitán Turner también recibió una orden del almirantazgo de cambiar el curso y entrar al puerto de Queenstown, en lugar del de Liverpool, que era el destino original del Lusitania. El nuevo curso del Lusitania lo dirigía hacia el submarino U-20. Esta decisión llevó al catastrófico hundimiento del Lusitania el 7 de mayo de 1915. Al día de hoy, aún se desconoce quién dio la orden a las naves inglesas.

Sin embargo, Winston Churchill y el Almirante Fisher supuestamente arreglaron este desafortunada conspiración.

Cuando el capitán Hunter finalmente recibió la advertencia sobre el submarino, ya no podía cambiar de rumbo sin una orden del almirantazgo. El capitán Hunter solo redujo la velocidad a 15 nudos. Cuando el Lusitania se encontraba a 700m del U-20, el capitán Scheiger del submarino U-20 disparó un solo torpedo al estribor del buque. En su bitácora, escribió que una segunda explosión partió el puente en pedazos y causó que la nave se hundiera de proa. El capitán Hunter dio la orden de abandonar el barco inmediatamente. Debido a la incómoda posición de la nave, solo seis de los cuaretna y ocho botes salvavidas pudieron llegar a salvo al agua.

Muchos pasajeros saltaron del barco y nadaron entre los escombros, esperando ser salvados por otra nave. Sin embargo, 1,198 pasajeros se hundieron con el buque. Entre ellos había 128 americanos y el millonario Alfred Vanderbilt. Cuando el Almirante Fisher supo que el buque Juno casi alcanzaba a los sobrevivientes, ordenó al capitán del Juno a cambiar el curso y regresar al puerto. Los sobrevivientes aguantaron dos horas de miedo y pánico antes de que otros buques llegaran y los sacaran del agua y de los botes salvavidas.

Cuando el presidente Wilson recibió las noticias sobre esta catástrofe, procuró obtener una lista completa de la carga del Lusitania del oficial de aduanas. Esta lista reveló que casi toda la carga era contrabando de materiales de guerra y explosivos. El presidente Wilson y el señor Lansing, temerosos de ser descubiertos por ocutar la verdad al pueblo de los Estados Unidos, empañaron la verdad y expidieron una advertencia a Alemania, declarando que el gobierno alemán y el káiser Wilhelm II habían sido mal informados. El señor Bryan, que sabía la verdad, se negó a firmar tal advertencia. Winston Churchill, el Almirante Fisher y el pueblo inglés fueron decepcionados por el presidente Wilson cuando no declaró la guerrra inmediatamente contra

Alemania. Sin embargo, Alemania dejó de usar los submarinos en las batallas navales. Winston Churchill y el Almirante Fisher culparon al capitá Hunter de la tragedia del Lusitania para encubrir su involucramiento en este complot y evitar ser decubiertos.

Tres años después de este incidente, la cabeza de la Oficina de Aduanas de Nueva York entregó al presidente Wilson la lista original de embarque del Lusitania. La selló en un sobre y escribió en él "solo puede ser abierto por el presidente de los Estados Unidos", y después lo entregó a los archivos del Departamento de Tesorería. Permaneció intacto hasta 1940, cuando Gran Bretaña y los Estados Unidos se encontraron en una posición similar en mayo de 1945. En ese tiempo, el presidente Franklin D. Roosevelt, que también era subsecretario de la Marina, supo de este documento, lo abrió y lo hizo parte de su colección privada de Memorias Marinas. En este indicdente, se nos enseña como el destino de las personas está en las manos del gobierno, quien es capaz de sembrar intrigas y sacrificar vidas humanas si es conveniente para sus propósitos.

Winston Churchill sentía que estaba un paso más cerca de involucrar a Estados Unidos en la Primera Guerra Mundial. Otro incidente que usó el Servicio Secreto de la Marina Británica fue decodificar la diligencia Zimmerman y enviarla al presidente Wilson, quien la publicó en los periódicos americanos. En este telegrama del 16 de Enero de 1917, el káiser Wilhelm II le pedía al presidente mexicano Venustiano Carranza que se uniera como su aliado en la guerra contra Estados Unidos. A cambio, el gobierno alemán le ofrecía a México recuperar los territorios de Arizona, Texas y Nuevo México. Los generales mexicanos estudiaron la viabilidad de tal alianza y rechazaron la oferta.

El pueblo americano estaba devastado por las noticias, y el Congreso le dio al presidente Wilson aprobación para entrar en guerra contra Alemania. El 6 de abril de 1917 el presidente Woodrow Wilson declaró la guerra contra Alemania.

Mis abuelos y el pueblo alemán, pero mayormente el personal militar, estaba alarmado por estas noticias y temían que sucediera el peor escenrio. Alemania no tendría mas opción que ganar la guerra si las tropas americanas invadían Alemania.

En su desesperación, el káiser inició nuevamente la guerra con submarinos como útlimo recurso para conseguir un cambio favorable a Alemania. Sin embargo, provocó que otras naciones europeas se involucraran. Al principio, Italia evadió la guerra pero se unió al conflicto más adelante, rompió su alianza con Austria – Hungría y Alemania y unió fuerzas con la oposición de la Triple Entente.

Grecia, que se había mantenido neutral hasta ese momento, sintió presión de los gobiernos inglés y francés cuando asentaron un bloqueo en las costas griegas. Para quitar el bloqueo, se unió a los aliados el 27 de Junio e 1917. Anterior a ello, el comandante francés Jonnart le dio un ultimatum al Rey Constantino de Grecia para que abdicase, y lo consiguió. El gobierno nuevo en Grecia del presidente Venizelo cooperó con la Triple Entente y declaró la guerra contra Austria – Hungría y Alemania.

Mientras tanto, Lenin, que estaba en Finlandia, regresó a Rusia. Él y los bolcheviques asumieron el gobierno provisionalmente formado durante la revolución de Octubre. El 8 de Noviembre de 1917, Lennin expidió un decreto para finalizar la guerra, mismo que fue bienvenido por el káiser Wilhelm II y el Rey y comandante en jefe austriaco. Tomó lugar un amnisticio el 15 de diciembre de 1917, pero la propuesta de paz no tuvo éxito al comienzo. Finalmente, después de tortuosas negociaciones, Alemania logró un acuerdo de paz el 9 de febrero de 1918, primero con Romania y después, el 3 de marzo de 1918, con Rusia, mismo que Lenin firmó en Brest – Litovsk. Rusia sacrificó veinticinco porciento de su territorio europeo para detener las peleas en la guerra.

Ahora, los ejércitos alemanes, relevados del frente oriental, podían reforzar las batallas en el oeste. El 21 de marzo de 1918, los generales alemanes planearon una exitosa ofensiva de primavera, y el ejército alemán rompió el frente francés y avanzó al río Marne en Francia.

Rápidamente, las tropas americanas y francesas unieron fuerzas y detuvieron el avance alemán. El general americano Hunter Liggett ordenó 300 tanques, y el general William Mitchell trajo 500 aeronaves para contraatacar en la batalla de Amiens el 8 de agosto de 1918. Los soldados alemanes sufrieron importantes bajas en manos de las fuerzas aliads. La batalla fue llamada "El Día Negro" por el ejército alemán, que después tuvo que retirarse.

En su desesperación, el káiser reclutó a niños de diecisiete años. Mi padre se escapó del reclutamiento, pero sus hermanos mayores Matthew y Georg fueron reclutados por el ejército con antelación. Gracias a Dios, solo sufrieron heridas menores y regresaron a salvo a casa al finalizar la guerra.

A principios de Septiembre, las fuerzas aliadas también se penetraron en Bulgaria y conquistaron Macedonia. Los comandantes en jefe alemanes von Hidenburg y Ludendorff entendieron que una victoria contra los aliados, reforzados continuamente por tropas americanas frescas y equipo de guerra, era imposible. El 29 de septiembre de 1918, los generales alemanes sugirieron al káiser Wilhelm II y al imperio alemán que trabajaran en un acuerdo de amnisticio (Waffenstillstand). El presidente Woodrow Wilson pidió que el ejército alemán se retirara de todos los territorios inmediatamente.

El 7 de noviembre de 1918 iniciaron las negociaciones en un vagón de tren en el bosque de Compiegne, donde Francia, los Estados Unidos y Alemania llegaron a un acuerdo. Hicieron dieciocho demandas al káiser Wilhelm II y a Imperio Alemán. *1"Efectivo en seis horas después de la firma. 2. El despeje inmediato de Bélgica, Francia, Alsace – Lorraine debe concluir en catorce días. Cualquier tropa remanente en las áreas sera internada o tomada como prisioneros de guerra. 3. Entregar 5000 cañones y 30 000 ametralladores, 3000 morteros de trinchera, 2000 aviones, 4. Evacuar la orilla izquierda del río Rhine, Mayence, Coblence, colonia ocupada por el enemigo a un radio de 30 km. 10. Renunciar a los tratados de Brest – Litovsk y Bucarest, por mencionar solo algunas de las demandas de los aliados."* (Demandas de amnisticio publicadas en el Kreuz – Zeitung el 11 de Noviembre de 1918)

Todos los representantes firmaron el documento el 11 de noviembre de 1918 a las 5:00 am.[6] La tregua inició a las 11:00 am el mismo día.

Los encabezados de *El New York Times* decían:

Con el ejército americano en Francia, el 11 de noviembre, dejaron de pelear a las 11:00 en punto de esta mañana. En un parpadeo, cuatro años de masacres se detuvieron como si Dios hubiera pasado su dedo omnipotente a través de la escena de de matanzas y dicho, suficiente.

Cada año en los Estados Unidos, el día de los veteranos es celebrado el 11 de noviembre, conmemorando a los soldados que perdieron sus vidas en la Primera Guerra Mundial y en otras guerras. Un soldado no muere hasta que que es olvidado. Cada soldado de cada nación dio algo de sí mismo en las guerras, pero algunos sacrificaron su posesión mas valiosa, sus vidas. Los soldados de todos los países merecen respeto, honor y gratitud de sus patriotas.

El abuelo Heinrich y la abuela Marta recibieron las buenas nuevas del fin de la guerra y de que sus dos hijos mayores, Matthew y Georg, habían vuelto del campo de batalla solamente con heridas menores. Sin embargo, ellos y la mayoría de las personas alemanas se sentían tristes porque el káiser Wilhelm II fue forzado a abdicar. Él huyó de su cuartel general en Spa a Holanda el 10 de noviembre de 1918. Más adelante adquirió una casa en Doorn, en la provicia de Utrecht, donde vivió modestamente con su esposa Augustine Victoria y su familia. Y así, después de 300 años, el reinado de la familia real Hhenzollern terminó después de la Primera Guerra Mundial.

La Entente demandó que el káiser fuera entregado como prisionero de guerra, pero la reina Wilhemina de Holanda no cedió a las demandas y amenazas de la Entente. El káiser permaneció en Doorn. Después de la muerte de su esposa, Augusta Victoria, se casó con la princesa von Schoenach, Hermine von Reuss. Escribió y publicó sus memorias de guerra, absolviéndose de la culpa de la Primera Guerra Mundial. Se mantenía al día con las actividades políticas alemanas y aún esperaba ser renombrado Káiser, pero sus esperanzas se mantuvieron como esperanzas solamente. Murió el 4 de junio de 1941, durante la Segunda Guerra Mundial. Doorn honró al káiser con un elaborado funeral de Estado. Mas adelante el gobierno alemán regresó los restos del káiser Wilhelm II a Berlín.

Después de que terminara la monarquía, mis abuelos se preoocuparon por como el nuevo gobierno, denominado la República de Weimar, los afectaría a ellos y al pueblo alemán. Ellos habían atestiguado como la alianza con Austria – Hungría y la alianza entre otras naciones, con la esperanza de blindarse contra la guerra, detonaban un efecto dominó y englobaban a una nación tras otra en la Primera Guerra Mundial. Treinta y dos naciones participaron en esa guerra, llamada la primera guerra global, que reclamó 10 millones de vidas, hirió a 20 millones de soldados y 8 millones se convirtieron en prisioneros de guerra. El Imperio Alemán, el reino Pruso, y muchas moarquías europeas terminaron con la Primera Guerra mundial. Se fue la época de la elegante vida en las cortes de las familias reales. Con un régimen político diferente, surgió una nueva sociedad de masas. Las colonias africanas y asiáticas buscaron su independencia y los Estados Unidos se convirtió en una super potencia.

CAPÍTULO 3

El Tratado de Versalles

18 de enero de 1919 inció la infame conferencia de paz de la Liga de Naciones. Un representante de cada una de las siguientes naciones tuvo parte en esta asamblea: Los Estados Unidos de América, Bélgica, Bolivia, Brasil, Gran Bretaña, Canadá, Australia, Sudáfrica, Nueva Zelanda, India, China, Cuba, Ecuador, Francia, Grecia, Guatemala, Haití, Hedjaz, Honduras, Italia, Japón, Liberia, Nicaragua, Panamá, Perú, Polonia, Rumania, El Estado Serbo Croata-Slovenia, Siam, Checoslovaquia y Uruguay. Rusia decidió no enviar representante. Alemania, cuyo destino y futuro dependía del resultado de esta conferencia, tenía prohibido participar en las negociaciones por miedo a que el representante alemán pudiera poner a una nación contra otra para beneficiar a Alemania. Alemania solo podía responder por escrito, lo cual trajo resultados nulos.

El Primer Ministro Francés Gerge Clemenceau, presidió la asamblea; sus deseos de venganza hicieron demandas irrazonables a Alemania. Fue llamado el tigre, listo para despedazar a su presa. El presidente Woodrow Wilson de los Estados Unidos, el Primer Ministro inglés Lloyd George y el Ministro de Relaciones Exteriores Italiano, Victor Emanuele Orlando, también estuvieron presentes. El presidente Woodrow Wilson de los Estados Unidos sugirió mantener el tratado simple y combinar las demandas en catorce puntos, pero cedió el paso a otros representantes durante las negociaciones. En seis meses, redactaron cuatrocientos cuarenta artícuos con muchos anexos.

En el Anexo II, párrafo 12, CI-3 dice: Alemania está obligada a pagar por reparar, reestructurar y reconstruir la propiedad de las naciones invadidas. El costo será calculado cuando el trabajo termine. Anexo III:

1.- Alemania reconoce el derecho del Poder Aliado Asociado para reemplazar, tonelada por tonelada y clase por clase, los barcos mercantes, barcos pesqueros perdidos o dañados por la guerra.

2.- Alemania entrega a las Fuerzas Aliadas y a sus Gobiernos Asociados la propiedad de todos los barcos mercantes alemanes de mas de 1600 toneladas, la mitad de los barcos entre 1000 y 1600 toneladas, y un cuarto de todos los barcos pesqueros. Todos los barcos serán entregados en los dos meses en que este tratado entre en vigor.

Alemania podía tener un ejército de solamente 100,000 soldados. La construcción de tanques, submarinos y aeronaves estaba etrictamente prohibida. Alemania no podía alliarse con Austria nunca más.

La Liga de las Naciones ordenó a Alemania entregar todas sus colonias y ponerlas bajo su mandato. Parte del oeste de Prusia, incluyendo Poznan y el Corredor Polaco, y parte de Silesia fueron otorgados a Polonia. Danzing permaneció como una cuidad alemana libre. Bélgica se apoderó de Eupen y Malmedy, Dinamarca obtuvo parte de Schelswig – Holstein. Francia reclamó Alsace – Lorrain y la administración de Saarland por quince años. Alemania perdió un octavo del Imperio Alemán.

Los aliados presentaron los 440 artículos, anexos y sub párrafos del Tratado de Versalles al gobierno alemán el 7 de mayo de 1919, y la fecha del 28 de junio de 1919 fue puesta como límite para leer, absorber y responder a las demandas. Los aliados no bajaron las modificaciones solicitadas de los altos costos de reparaciones y restricciones que pidió Alemania. Tampoco removieron el artículo 231, en el que Alemania reconoce la culpa por la guerra.

Las fuerzas aliadas amenazaron con invadir Alemania y reanudar la guerra si no firmaban el documento como fue presentado. Con pesadumbre en el corazón y resentimiento profundamente arraigado hacia los redactores del Tratado de Versalles, los representantees alemanes firmaron el documento bajo protesta el 28 de junio de 1919.

Mis abuelos y el pueblo alemán se sintieron atormentados, humillados y resentidos de que la culpa de la guerra fuera adscrita únicamente a Alemania y no parcialmente a Austria- Hungría que inició la Primera Guerra Mundial. El pueblo alemán también pensaba que los costos de las reparaciones, el desmantelamiento de su industria, la reducción de las fuerzas militares, la entrega de ganado, otros bienes y la pérdida territorial eran injustas y excesivamente feroces.

El presidente Woodrow Wilson no entontraba aceptable el Tratado de Versalles, y los Estados Unidos no lo ratificaron. Dos veces se opuso el senado a la ratificación. Algunos senadores estaban a favor de aislamiento, otros se oponían a la Liga de Naciones y otros lamentaban las reparaciones excesivas. Marshall Ferdinand Foch, representante de Estados Unidos, firmó un acuerdo por separado el 25 de agosto de 1921.

El 10 de septiembre de 1919, los Aliados Europeos firmaron un Tratado de Paz y Austria tuvo que otorgar su independencia a Yugoslavia, Checoslovaquia, Hungría y Polonia. Los aliados le prohibieron a Austria unirse con Alemania. Otros tratados de paz entre Bulgaria, Hungría y Turquía siguieron. Al formar la

Liga de Naciones, el presidente Woodrow Wilson quería hacer del mundo un lugar seguro, discutir los problemas sin llegar a guerras. El Primer Ministro Británico David Lloyd George, que quería controlar los mares y expandir el comercio, pidió no ser tan duros con Alemania. Le dijo a los líderes que podría causarse otra guerra costal en el futuro si las demandas eran muy severas. Alemania pagó un precio prohibitivo injustamente por ayudar a Austria durante su conflicto con Serbia.

CAPÍTULO 4

República Alemana de Weimar

El reinado del káiser Wilhelm II terminó en 1919. El primer presidente, Friedrich Ebert, redactó una nueva Constitución para la República de Weimar, 8 nombrada en honor a la Ciudad de Weimar, donde los oficiales escribieron la nueva Constitución. Friedrich Ebert fue el primer, y Paul von Hidenburg el segundo presidente electo de la nueva República de Weimar.

La República de Weimar intentó reconstruir la patria, pero las enormes demandas de restitución quebraron su industria y economía. El gobierno empezó a imprimir mucho más dinero de lo que valía su fondo colateral para poder cumplir con estas obligaciones, lo que causó una super inflación de magnitudes nunca antes vistas en la historia. Imagine que en 1923 un dólar estadounidense valía 4.21 billones de marcos. En 1923, el marco real reemplazó al marco de papel en una tasa de cambio de 1:1,000,000.000.00 (un marco real a un millón de marcos de papel). En 1923, un huevo costaba 320 millones de marcos de papel. Las familias necesitaban barriles llenos de dinero para poder comprar la despensa. Después de que el marco real se convirtiera en la nueva moneda en Alemania, la economía mejoró y se estabilizó por un periodo corto de tiempo. La República de Weimar se dividió en tres fases: los años de crisis, los años de estabilidad y el decivle y disolución.

Cuando el marco real fue devaluado en 1923, la condición económica mejoró y se estabilizó un poco hasta 1928. De acuerdo con el Tratado de Versalles, en caso de que los altos pagos que Alemania tenía que hacer a Francia y Bélgica no fueran cumplidos, Francia y Bélgica invadirían el área industrial de Ruhr y tomarían lo que quisieran para ahogar la producción alemana de bienes y reducir los trabajos en las minas de carbón. Esta condición llevó a una depresión severa y puso una tremenda carga y dificultad sobre mi familia y las familias alemanas.

CAPÍTULO 5

El inicio de mi Familia

Mis abuelos vivieron durante el reino de Wilhelm II, el último káiser de Alemania. Ellos respetaban al káiser y vivieron con sus justas reglas para sus súbditos. Toda la familia prosperó.

Mis abuelos paternos, Heinrich y Marta Bonacker, vivían en un pequeño pueblo en Wirballen, al Este de Prusia; despúes se fueron a Wizajny. Tuvieron dos hijas llamadas Minna y Marta y cinco hijos, Matheus, Georg, Gustav, Otto y August. Mi abuelo era un excelente carpintero y se aseguró de que cada uno de sus hijos aprendieran un oficio. Mi padre, Gustav, se convirtió en albañil. Durante este tiempo, las hijas no necesitaban adquirir una profesión; ellas se casaban y críaban a sus familias. El abuelo Bonacker estaba agradecido de que sus tres hijos menores Gustav, Otto y August eran demasiado jóvenes para ser reclutados por el ejército de la Primera Guerra Mundial. Matheus y Heinrich regresaron con heridas menores después de haber servido como soldados en esta guerra.

Mis abuelos maternos, Jan August y Anna Schlikat tuvieron tres hijas: Marie, Lena y mi madre, Emilie, nacida el 11 de marzo de 1898. Desafortunadamente, agentes del gobierno ruso tomaron a los padres de mi madre por la fuerza para llevarlos a un campo de trabajo, dejando atrás a las tres hijas a su suerte.

Para sobrevivir, las tres hijas tuvieron que encontrar refugio y comida trabajando en hogares. Nunca supieron qué le pasó a sus padres ni a donde los llevaron.

Tía Katarina y su esposo

A la edad de veinte años, mi papá, Gustav Bonacker, se fue a Wizajny, a la granja de su tía Katarina. Cuando el esposo de la tía Katarina, Georg Klaus, murió repentinamente y su único hijo, Martin, inmigró a America, ella le pidió a su sobrino, Gustav, que la ayudara a manejar la granja. Siendo un granjero de corazón, Gustav trabajó diligentemente, labrando la tierra y criando animales para consumo propio y venta. Después de que terminara la Primera Guerra Mundial, la vida durante la República de Weimar fue dura. El gobierno restringió a los granjeros sobre cuántos animales podrían criar para uso personal y el ganado que debía ser entregado al gobierno. Esta severa restricción puso una enorme carga sobre los granjeros. Debido al alto costo monetario de la restitución, la inflación era desenfrenada.

Conforme pasaba el tiempo, la tía Katarina se hacía mas vieja y débil. Consideró conseguir ayuda para sus labores domésticas. Cada viernes los pobladores y rancheros iban a la plaza del mercado a vender y comprar mercancía. Los comerciantes del pueblo montaban sus puestos para vender sus mercancías y productos. Los granjeros llevaban en sus carretas cerdos, ovejas, producción y cualquier cosa que quisieran vender o cambiar, incluyendo los frutos de sus tierras. Muchas otras actividades sucedían en la plaza del mercado. Los trabajadores que necesitaban trabajo ofrecían sus habilidades y esperaban encontrar a un empleador. Un día, la tía Katarina fue con Gustav al mercado buscando a una ayudante doméstica. Después de caminar alrededor y buscar por un rato, sus ojos se detuvieron en una joven, una atractiva morena. Tía Katarina se acercó a ella para preguntarle su nombre y si estaría dispuesta a trabajar en su granja. Emilie Schlikat se presentó y aceptó ir con la tía Katarina a la granja para trabajar para ella.

Mientras viajaban a través de un entramado verde y trigales, la tia Katarina le preguntó a Emilie dónde vivían sus padres y porqué había dejado su casa. El mero hecho de que le recordaran la horrible escena de sus padres, a punta de pistola, siendo amenazados con matar a sus hijas si no se iban con los agentes rusos le hizo un nudo en la garganta. La escena pasó delante de sus ojos cuando, en la desesperación de salvar la vida de sus hijas, sus padres, agonizando emocionalmente, tuvieron que dejarlas e irse con los agentes rusos. Las lágrimas rodaron por sus sus mejillas y las de sus padres, y muchas permanecieron sin ser derramadas en sus adoloridos corazones cuando rogar por sus vidas fue en vano y los apartaron de sus hijas. Emilie explicó el horrible destino de sus padres brevemente. Emilie, revelando la experiencia traumática, empezó a llorar. La tía Katarina mostró mucha compasión por Emilie. La acogió y le pidió que olvidara el pasado. Animó a Emilie a mirar hacia el futuro con una mejor vida en su rancho en el campo. Sin embargo, ni Emilie ni la tía Katarina pudieron olvidar la tragedia de su familia y los horribles eventos de la guerra, las consecuencias y los tiempos difíciles que trajeron.

Emilie cumplió todas las tareas domésticas satisfactoriamente para tía Katarina. Con el paso del tiempo, Gustav se encariñó con Emilie y le pidió que se convirtiera en su esposa. El 28 de marzo de 1923, la primavera recién llegaba de acuerdo al calendario, pero la nieve aún cubría el suelo; Gustav y Emilie intercambiaban votos maritales en la Iglesia luterana de Wizajny. Una celebración familiar siguió en casa para los recién casados.

Iglesia Católica y Escuela de Wizajny

La tía Katarina se encariñó con Gustav y Emilie, los trataba como a sus propios hijos y los convirtió en herederos de su patrimonio. Creían en Dios y vivían en armonía entre ellos, los vecinos y la naturaleza.

Casi un año pasó, y los vientos invernales soplaron en los campos, formando montones alrededor de los edificios y los árboles. Gustav preparó el trineo y se apresuró al pueblo para traer a la partera a la casa. Emilie estaba por dar a luz a su primer hijo. Una vecina vino y mantuvo una olla de agua hirviendo en la estufa. A un lado de la cama de Emilie había una cuna que Gustav había construido para el nuevo miembro de la familia. La tía Katarina y Gustav se sintieron aliviados cuando la partera recibió a la bebé el 20 de febrero de 1924. Gustav hubiera preferido a un varón como primogénito, pero se consoló rápidamente, sabiendo que madre e hija se encontraban bien. Miró a su pequeña hija en la cuna y se sintió orgulloso de ser padre. Nombraron a su primera hija Emma.

Madre, Hermanas Marie, Lene e hija Emma

Un año y ocho meses después, el 3 de octubre de 1925, Emilie estaba esperando a su segundo hijo. Gustav silbaba mientras manejaba a través de los campos de barbecho y miraba a los gansos canadienses agruparse para su migración al Sur, en su camino hacia la partera. Esta vez él esperaba un hijo que lo ayudara con los campos y en casa. Gustav estuvo muy decepcionado cuando Emilie le presentó otra hija. Emma, sin embargo, dio la bienvenida a su hermana bebé. Caminó hacia la cuna y observo a su hermana, quien mas adelante sería llamada Marta. Gustav pronto se sobrepuso a su decepción y aceptó a su segunda hija como el nuevo miembro de la famillia. La tía Katarina adoraba a sus sobrinas nietas, Emma y Marta. Las trataba como si fueran sus nietas. Emilie se sentía aliviada de saber que sus hijas estaban en manos amorosas. Ahora ella acompañaba gustosamente a su esposo a los campos para ayudarlo a cosechar trigo, centeno o papas. En octubre, las plantas de papa se secaron en los surcos elevados. Todo el verano, pequeñas papas crecieron debajo de las plantas verdes. Cuando alcanzaban un tamaño específico, dejaban de crecer y la planta que sobresalía del suelo moría. Esa era la señal para removerlas del campo antes de que se congelaran y pudrieran. Mi padre guiaba el arado en cada una de las camas elevadas para voltear la tierra y exponer las papas. Emillie y algunos vecinos o familiares lo seguian, aflojando las papas de las plantas secas y del suelo, colocándolas primero en canastos y después vaciándolos en sacos. Gustav cargaba los sacos llenos en la carreta y los llevaba a casa. Puso suficientes en el sótano para el consumo en invierno y las demás las enterró bajo la linea de hielo en el suelo arenoso no muy lejos de la casa. Gustav rastrilló las plantas de papa muertas, poniendolas en grandes pilas y las quemó.

Gustav y Emilie aceptaron los frutos de las tierras fértiles con gratitud y agradecieron a Dios por la abundante cosecha. Cada temporada traía cierto ritmo natural, marcando el fin de una rutina y el inicio de otra.

Dos años pasaron rápido. Pronto Emilie dio a luz a un tercer hijo. Esta vez, las esperanzas de papá de tener un hijo eran altas. Sin embargo, una vez más fue decepcionado cuando el 8 de enero de 1928, Meta nació y no un hijo, como él esperaba.

Al fin, dos años después, el 15 de diciembre de 1930, su muy esperado hijo nació un frío dia de invierno. Lo nombró Georg en honor a su hermano. Georg era el orgullo y la alegría de su padre. Para su bautismo, invitó a toda su familia para celebrar con él este evento tan especial. No podía esperar a verlo crecer y trabajar con él. Emma y Marta cuidaban a su hermano pequeño y jugaban con él frecuentemente. Después de que George fuera capaz de caminar, Marta lo llevaba al lago. Mi padre había colocado una tabla larga en la parte mas estrecha, para que mi madre pudiera lavar la ropa ahí. Marta vio muy tentadora a la tabla y corrió sobre ella de un lado a otro. El pequeño Georg la siguió, se resbaló y cayó al agua. El corazón de Marta se detuvo cuando no lo vio emerger del agua inmediatamente. Temía que se hubiera ahogado. Finalmente, después de lo que pareció un largo tiempo, Georg salió a la superficie. Marta lo agarró y lo sacó del agua rápidamente. Él estaba tendido sobre el pasto sin vida, después empezó a toser agua y pudo respirar nuevamente. Marta se sintió aliviada de verlo con vida. Corrió a contarle a mamá lo que había pasado. Mamá la regañó y le prohibió llevar a Georg al lago.

Georg no tuvo que esperar mucho tiempo para tener un hermanito llamado Edmund, nacido el 14 de noviembre de 1932. Papá estaba encantado de tener dos hijos, que, cuando crecieran, le ayudarían con los campos y a cuidar a los caballos y vacas. Mamá estaba contenta de tener tres hijas con quiénes compartir las labores domésticas y cuidar a los hermanos pequeños.

Después de un año Edmund aún no podia camnar, su madre se preocupó cuando no vio desarrollo muscular en sus delgadas piernas. Ella temía que el niño tuviera polio y fuera inválido por el resto de su vida. En ese entonces, no había cura para la polio. Después de dos años el aún no podía pararse o dar unos cuántos pasos, su madre estaba segura de que tenía polio. Su corazón se rompía cuando lo veía arrastrarse hacia su hermano o hermanas. La abuela Katarina lo sentó a su lado, le masajeó los músculos en sus piernas y las movió hacia atrás y hacia adelante. Emma,

Marta y Meta ayudaron con los ejercicios. Finalmente, a la edad de tres años, y con la ayuda de sus heramanas, Edmundo dio sus primeros pasos y fue capaz de pararse por sí mismo. Gradualmente mejoró y pronto pudo caminar y correr con normalidad. Mamá lo consideró un milagro y agradeció a Dios por curar a su hijo y porque no quedó ninguna atrofia remanente en sus piernas.

Conforme la familia crecía, la casa se llenaba. En 1933 papa decidió construir una nueva. Mientras los campos y los bosques aún estaban cubiertos por una densa capa de nieve y los vientos invernales gemían su canción polar, papá amarró a los caballos al trineo y se dirigió al bosque. Seleccionó árboles jóvenes y rectos, con el grosor justo para servir como vigas de soporte para la casa. Papá recortaba todas las ramas y ponía los troncos limpios en pilas. Cuando tenía suficientes troncos, papá le pedía ayuda a un vecino para llevarlos al rancho, - la madera para las ventanas, los marcos de las puertas, el techo y los pisos la compró en el pueblo. Papá recogió la mejor paja para cubrir el techo.

Para finales de marzo, las primeras flores de campana de nieve se asomaban a través de la humedad del suelo y anunciaban la llegada de la primavera. Papá construyó alojamientos temporales en el establo cuando el clima era agradable antes de demoler la antigua casa. Los niños disfrutaban de dormir en el establo, pero la tía Katarina, mamá y papá estaban incómodos, soportaron las inconveniencias e incomodidades pacientemente.

Los hermanos de papá, Matheus, Georg, Otto y August ayudaron a cavar los cimientos y colocar los postes esquineros en la tierra. Los vecinos también vinieron a ayudar. Papá también tenía que labrar la tierra y sembrar trigo, centeno, avena y plantas de papa durante la construcción de una casa. Lentamente, las paredes emergieron, y con las vigas del techo puestas en su lugar, le dio a la estructura la apariencia de una casa.

Cuando papá y sus ayudantes aseguraron la última viga al techo, Emilie hizo una corona de flores, y Gustav aseguró la corona con listones de colores a la viga más alta del techo. Esta vieja tradición alemana es llamada "Richtfest" y es celebrada para pedir a Dios que bendiga la casa y expresar gratitud a los trabajadores. Tíos, tías, primos y vecinos se unieron a la celebración. Tío August tocó el acordeón de teclas y todos cantaron hasta altas horas de la noche. Mamá sirvió una variedad de sus salchichas caseras, pan recién horneado y pastel. Papá ofreció su cerveza hecha por él mismo y aguardiente, que había reservado para ocasiones especiales. Jugo de moras del jardín deleitaba las papilas gustativas de los niños.

Ahora comenzaba la carrera para cosechar los campos y terminar la casa antes de que llegara el invierno. Cuando los vientos cambiaron del sudoeste al noroeste a finales de septiembre y la temperatura comenzó a bajar, papá terminó de colocar el techo de paja en las vigas. Los vecinos ayudaron a aislar el exterior e interior de las paredes. Papá usó una mezcla de arcilla, yeso y pajilla finamente cortada en lugar de cemento para cubrir el interior y exterior de las paredes. Los gansos canadienses reuniéndose en los campos de trigo para migrar al sur indicaba la llegada del otoño. Papá se apresuró para instalar las ventanas y puertas para mantener el frio afuera. Papá aplicó varias capas de pintura blanca en el interior y exterior de las paredes y la familia se mudó a la casa. Qué día tan feliz para mamá y papá. Ellos agradecieron a Dios que nadie salió herido en la construcción y que la casa estaba terminada antes de la llegada del invierno. Noviembre llegó con un torbellino de nieve azotando los alrededores de la casa salvajemente, cubriendo todos los campos y prados con una cobija gruesa y esponjosa.

Ahora la casa necesitaba ser amueblada. Abuelo Heinrich Bonacker era un excelente constructor de gabinetes. Se ofreció a construir mesas, bastidores para las camas, bancas, y lo que fuera necesario para hacrla un cómodo hogar. Una semana antes de Navidad, papá fue en trineo al bosque, trajo un pino alto y lo acomodó en la sala. Papá calentó el horno de azulejos verdes para que Emilie y las niñas pudieran decorar el árbol cómodamente. Mamá abrió caja tras caja y entregó los bombillas de colores resplandecientes, estrellas de papel, guirnaldas, y muchos otros ornamentos, que Emma, Marta y Meta colgaron en el árbol. Como toque final, colocaron muchos candelabros y los ganchó a varias ramas.

En Nochebuena, después de que la oscuridad descendiera en la tierra cuibierta de nieve, mamá encendía vela por vela, que iluminaban la habitación y las llamas parpadeantes se reflejaban en las bombillas de colores. La familia entró y los niños se asombraban al ver este árbol mágicamente transformado. Mamá me contó la historia de Navidad sobre celebrar la remembranza del nacimiento de Jesucristo en Noche Buena. La familia se reunió alrededor del árbol de navidad y cantó: "Oh Tannenbaum, Oh Tannenbaum" (Oh, árbol de navidad, oh árbol de navidad), "Stille Nacht, Heilige Nacht" (Noche de paz, noche de amor) y otras canciones navideñas. Mamá le dio un regalo a cada niño, guantes tejidos a mano, o calcetas, después sirvió una pequeña cena antes de que papá atara los caballos al trineo y llevara a la familia a la iglesia para celebrar el nacimiento de Cristo con los feligreses en Wizajny. Mientras los caballos trotaban a través de la nieve, las campanas del trineo sonaban y el oscuro domo del cielo se llenaba de una miríada de estrellas. Los niños, acurrucados en pieles, miraban con asombro el mágico escenario invernal por el que pasaban. Una vez que papá llegó a la plaza de la iglesia, desató a los caballos del trineo, los ató a una viga y les ató una pequeña bolsa de avena a sus arneses. Eso los mantendría ocupados y calmados durante el servicio de a iglesia.

Mamá y los niños entraron primero a la iglesia, los siguió papá. La celebración de Navidad con el organista tocando una composición de Johann Sebastian Bach. Después los miembros de la iglesia cantaron una canción de navidad, seguido del sermón sobre el nacimiento de Cristo en Belén. Al final del sermón, dos niños encendieron todas las velas en los dos altos árboles de navidad, dejaron el altar y encendieron todas las otras luces. El coro de la iglesia cantó "Noche de paz, noche de amor" creando una atmósfera festiva para enaltecer la celebración. Después de la bendición, los monaguillos apagaron todas las velas con una pequeña copa en forma de campana en el extremo de una vara larga. Acompañados por música de órgano, los feligreses salieron de la iglesia. Los hombres fueron a atar los caballos a los trineos, encendieron las luces en los lados e iniciaron sus caminos a casa. La luz de la luna brillaba como diamantes en los prados y campos cubiertos de nieve bajo el cielo estrellado.

Al día siguiente cada niño encontró un plato de galletas, dulces y manzanas en la mesa. Le llamamos "Bunte Teller" en alemán. Santa Claus trajo los regalos durante la noche. Los niños devoraron rápidamente los dulces llenos de alegría. En la tarde, familiares vinieron a celebrar Navidad. Papá le mostró con orgullo a su familia su casa recién construida. Mamá preparó varios rostizados de ganso, col roja y albóndigas de papa. De postre ella sirvió strollen, relleno de mazapán que hizo ella misma. En el segundo día de Navidad, los vecinos vinieron a celebrar con la familia. La mágica Navidad en la casa nueva pasó rápidamente, y también lo hizo el año 1933. En la víspera de año nuevo, mamá y papá llevaron a la familia a casa del abuelo Heinrich; junto con otros miembros

de la familia, dieron la bienvenida al año 1934.

Durante los meses de invierno, nuestro padre construyó un horno en la cocina para que mamá pudiera hornear el pan y pasteles en casa. También construyó una banca rectangular de ladrillo de cuatro pies de alto, seis pies de profundidad y ocho pies de largo, canales abiertos debajo de la banca que conectaban a la estufa de la cocina. Cuando el fuego ardía en el hogar de la cocina, el humo se iba directamente por la chimenea exterior en verano. En invierno, papá abría la trampa que daba a la banca en la sala. El humo y el aire caliente corrían por los canales, calentando la banca de piedra y la habitación sin tener que lidiar con madera y ceniza en la sala. En invierno, era el lugar favorito de reunión. La abuela Katarina fascinaba a los niños contándoles cuentos o historias de su pasado. Mamá tejía calcetas, guantes o bufandas; también lo hacían sus hijas.

Papá hizo una estructura cuadrada de barro y paja en el ático que se hacía más estrecha en la punta y estaba conectada al corazón de la chimenea. Servía como ahumadero. Con una cortina, la cantidad de humo podía ser regulada o cortada por completo. Varillas de metal que cruzaban de un lado a otro servían para colgar salchichas o carne de cerdo para ser ahumada. Siendo un albañil, papá disfrutaba de trabajar en diferentes proyectos en la casa cuando los campos no requerían atención.

El primer invierno en la casa nueva pasó demasiado rápido y llegó la primavera. Emma, Marta y Meta ayudaban a mamá a preparar un jardín de hortalizas y camas de flores alrededor de la casa. Las flores estaban en pleno apogeo en julio y agosto y llenaban el aire con un agradable aroma. Para mediados de agosto de 1934, su madre anunció la llegada de un sexto hijo. El 15 de agosto, la partera recibió a otro bebé varón, quien sería llamado Richard. Richard era un bebé delicado, tenía unos grandes ojos azules, y la familia lo recibió con dicha y curiosidad. Papá y mamá estaban agradecidos de que todo habia salido bien y pensaban que tener tres hijas y tres hijos completaría la familia.

Emma, Marta y Meta ayudaron a criar a Richard, y pasado un año, fue capaz de caminar y decir algunas palabras. Edmund y Richard se sentaban en el suelo a jugar. A veces, su madre ponía una cobija en el jardín para que tomaran aire fresco y luz de sol. Al inicio de agosto de 1935, el cielo se tornó oscuro y sombrío, y las nubes embarazadas se reunían en el cielo. Truenos sonaron, retumbaron y sacudieron la casa entera. Los relámpagos zigzagueaban a través de la atmósfera mientras las masas de aire caliente y frío colisionaban. De repente, nuestro padre observó que el cielo permanecía iluminado por fuego. Vio la casa del vecino consumiéndose en llamas. Papá pensó que un rayo debia haberla alcanzado. Rápidamente, ató los caballos al trineo y se apresuró a la casa de la familia vecina Reinke. Para cuando llegó papá, las llamas habían consumido la mayor parte de la casa y de sus posesiones. El señor y la señora Reinke salvaron solamente algunos documentos, unos cuantos muebles y algunas pertenencias personales. Gracias a Dios, ninguno de los miembros de la familia fue alcanzado por un rayo o lastimado. De repente, los cielos se abrieron, y un aguacero inundó la casa en llamas y apagó el incendio lentamente. La familia, papá, y otros vecinos buscaron refugio en el establo. La tristeza llenó el corazón de la señora Reinke, y las lágrimas rodaron en sus mejillas cuando se dio cuenta de que el fuego había reducido su casa con sus preciosos contenidos a un montón de escombros carbonizados.

Papá sintió lástima por los veicnos y le pidió al señor y a la señora Reinke que se quedaran en nuestra casa hasta que hicieran otras provisiones para reconstruir su hogar. Ellos esperaron a que la lluvia pasara. Entonces papá le pidió a Alfred, Ophelia y sus tres hijos, Erwin, Oswald y Helmut subirse a la carreta y acompañarlo. Mamá recibió a los vecinos y los niños estaban felices de tener compañeros de juego temporalmente.

Al día siguiente, papá fue con el señor y la señora Reinke a su rancho para ver si algo podía salvarse de entre los escombros de la casa y para alimentar al ganado. Le pidieron a mi padre que regresara a su casa y que ellos lo alcanzarían en la tarde en su propia carreta. Alfred y Ophelia inmediatamente hicieron planes para reconstruir su casa. Estaban agradecidos de tener un lugar donde vivir mientras montaban una cocina provisional y cuartos en su establo. Los vecinos trabajaban en su casa en el día y solo venían a pasar la noche con nosotros. Sus familiares y otros vecinos ayudaron con la construcción de la casa. Completaron la estructura para hacerla vivible antes del invierno.

Pronto, una persona nueva se mudaría con nosotros. La hermana de mamá, Marie, trabajaba en la casa de una familia adinerada en Sudauen y sufría de tuberculosis ósea. El dolor severo y las heridas supurantes imposibilitaban que ella continuara en su trabajo. No tenía otro lugar a donde ir y le pidió a su hermana Emilie y a su cuñado Gustav si podía vivir con su familia. Ellos accedieron y papá manejó hasta Sudauen para recoger a la tía Marie. Le tomó algo de tiempo ajustarse a estar rodeada de seis niños todo el tiempo. Aunque la tía Marie era una mujer inteligente y hermosa, nunca se casó. Pronto se encariñó de sus sobrinos y sobrinas y estaba agradecida por el amor que le expresaban en sus muchos actos de bondad hacia ella. Emma y Meta la ayudaban a salir de cama todas las mañanas y Marta se encargó de limpiar y vendar sus heridas. Ella se sentía agradecida y nunca se quejó. El amor de sus sobrinas y sobrinos y la fe en Dios le dieron la fuerza para soportar su enfermedad incurable. Los niños se reunían alrededor de su cama en las tardes, y ella les contaba cuentos e historias, que los niños disfrutaban.

Mientras tanto, la tía Katarina, nuestra abuela adoptiva, se hizo frágil y su salud empeoró. Necesitaba ayuda para salir de la cama y llegar a su silla. Las niñas ayudaban todo lo que podían, y cuando estaban en la escuela, mamá cuidaba tanto a la tía Katarina como a su hermana Marie. La tia Katarina retomó algo de fuerza en el verano, pero dio su últmo aliento el 9 de septiembre de 1936 y se fue con su padre celestial, a quien había servido y adorado toda su vida. Antes de morir, dio a Emma su anillo de oro de compromiso como un recuerdo, que Emma atesoró toda su vida. La abuela Katarina dejó un gran vacío para Emma, Marta y Meta. Muchos familiares y vecinos vinieron para el funeral de tres días en casa. Cuatro días más tarde, una carroza fúnebre llevó el ataúd cerrado a la iglesia. El padre dio un sermón de despedida a todos los dolientes antes de que los asistentes fúnebres se llevaran el ataúd al cementerio mas cercano, donde su cuerpo fue enterrado para su eterno descanso.

Una vida se va y otra llega. Emilie le anunció a su esposo que la cigüeña pronto traería otro bebé. La Navidad pasó ¡y también el año 1936! El año 1937 llegó y también lo hizo la partera el día de Año Nuevo. Tres horas después de la media noche, el 2 de enero de 1937, una bebé lloró para ser aceptada en la familia y en el mundo al partir del vientre de su madre. Todos la recibieron con alegría y Emma eligió el nombre de Hildegard para ella. Así como una luz se apagaba, otra empezaba a brillar. El perpetuo ciclo de vida y muerte continúa --- están unidos como el día y la noche.

De acuerdo a mi hermana Emma, yo, Hildegard, era una bebé feliz y traje alegría a mis padres, hermanos y hermanas, quienes me cuidaron y jugaron conmigo. Desafortunadamente, nunca conocí a mi tía abuela Katarina, a quién todos amaban y llamaban abuela. Tampoco recuerdo a mi tía Marie. La infeccion de la tuberculosis lentamente deterioró sus huesos. Se marchitó como una hermosa flor en plena floración el Jueves Santo, 4 de abril de 1938, a la edad de treinta y ocho. Emilie, su hermana Lena, los sobrinos y las sobrinas mayores atesoraban los recuerdos de la Tía Marie. Yo solo recuerdo verla en una fotografía tomada mientras trabajaba para una noble familia en Sudauen. Se veía hermosa, con cabello chino y una bella sonrisa.

CAPÍTULO 6

El Tercer Reich

La República de Weimar duró quince años, de 1918 a 1933. El gobierno intentó reconstruir la patria, pero el enorme costo de restitución y demandas del Tratado de Versalles quebró su economía e industria.

¿Cómo fue que Adolf Hitler, nacido en Braunau, Austria, se convirtió en un ciudadano alemán y canciller de la República de Weimar?

Adolf Hitler nació el 20 de abril de 1889, en Braunau, Austria. Su padre, Alois, era un hijo ilegítimo de Maria Ana Schickelgrube y Leopold Frankenberger. Su madre, nacida como Klara Poelzl, era su prima. Avergonzado de la endogamia de sus ancestros, deshizo o destruyó todos los documentos e incluso las tumbas de sus ancestros austriacos. Los vecinos lo llamaban el niño judío cuando era un niño. En un artículo histórico, Jeannie Cohen declara que Jean-Paul-Mulders y Marc Vermeeren, un historiador belga, estudiaron las raíces de Hitler extensamente. Recolectaron saliva de treinta y nueve parientes distantes de Hitler. El estudio concluyó que entre los ancestros de Hitler puede haber sangre judía africana.

Cuando se suponía que debia ser reclutado por el ejército austriaco, voló a Munich. El 8 y 9 de noviembre de 1923, intentó derrocar al gobierno alemán. Esta desafortunada insurrección es conocida como el Putsch de la Cervecería. Hitler fue encontrado culpable de alta traición y sentenciado a cinco años en prisión. Antes de que fuera liberado nueve meses después, escribió el libro *Mein Kampf* (Mi Batalla).[23] En él, Hitler expresa su odio por los judíos. Dio elocuentes discursos sobre la desafiante posición en la que se econtraba Alemania e impresionó incluso a los jueces, quiénes lo liberaron después de nueve meses. Obtuvo la ciudadanía alemana y formó el Partido Nacional Socialista de los Trabajadores (que todos llaman el Partido Nazi).

Durante este tiempo caótico, los alemanes fueron desmoralizados y humillados. Para 1933, Adolf Hitler se convirtió en canciller del Reichstag, y en 1934, fue electo presidente de la República de Weimar; combinando ambos títulos, se llamó a sí mismo Fuehrer (líder). Renombró a la República de Weimer como el Tercer Reich.[10] El 12 de marzo de 1938, Adolf Hitler anexó Austria a Alemania. La matanza del 7 de noviembre de 1938 del diplomático alemán Ernst Rath a manos del judío Herschel Grynszpan detonó el inicio de las persecuciones de los judíos en la Noche de los Cristales Rotos (Kristallnacht). Primero le dio a los judíos alemanes la opción de irse de Alemania antes de eliminarlos de Alemania y después de Europa. Adolf Hitler tenía la idea de crear una raza pura Aria. Era exclusivamente su idea y no el deseo del gobierno o del pueblo alemán. También quería expandir el territorio del Tercer Reich. Sus elocuentes discursos jugaron con las emociones de los trabajadores en dficultades, y lentamente ganó poder. Adolf Hitler demandó absoluta obediencia y ser saludado por todos como "Heil Hitler" (Salve Hitler).

Hitler ignoró el Tratado de Versalles, restauró el orgullo alemán y reconstruyó la insfraestructura alemana, las escuelas e industrias. Al principio del Tercer Reich, parecía ser el líder más grande de Alemania. Entrenó soldados y construyó naves, aviones y armas destructoras, también misiles en fábricas subterráneas. Adolf Hitler creó Juventud Hitler para los niños de catorce a dieciocho años. Sus líderes los adoctrinaban con la ideología política de Hitler y los sometían a vigorosos entrenamientos físicos para prepararlos para ser buenos guerreros. Desafortunadamente, algunos miembros de Juventud Hitler fueron reclutados en el ejército antes de que terminara la Segunda Guerra Mundial, y muchos nunca regresaron.

Formó la Liga de las Damas Alemanas (BDM) para las jóvenes mujeres de la misma edad. Recibían instrucciones para ser competentes amas de casa, buenas esposas, y madres. También hacían ejercicios físicos y deportes para desarrollar cuerpos saludables. Antes de que finalizara la guerra, asistían a doctores y enfermeras para cuidar a los soldados heridos en los hospitales.

Desafortunadamente, después de alcanzar el pináculo del poder, se convirtió en un despiadado dictador. Cualquiera que se opusiera a él, sus ideas y su régimen era aprisionado o castigado con la muerte.

Empezó con conquistas militares para reclamar los territorios de Alemania perdidos durante la Primera Guerra Mundial. El 1 de septiembre de 1939, Hitler invadió Polonia y empezó la Segunda Guerra Mundial. Inglaterra y Francia, aliados de Polonia, declararon guerra contra Alemania el 3 de septiembre de 1939. Incluso el ejército de la Unión Soviética entró a Warsaw después de que fuera bombardeado y se rindiera. Entonces Hitler se concentró en conquistar los países Europeos del Oeste. Hitler alcanzó el climax de su popularidad cuando tomó París e invadió Francia.

Italia y Japón se unieron a Alemania el 27 de septiembre de 1940, y formaron una alianza llamada El Eje. El 13 de agosto de 1940, Hitler empezó el ataque aéreo a Inglaterra. Después de grandes pérdidas del Luftwaffe alemán, Hitler se sintió derrotado y dejó de bombardear Londres y otras ciudades inglesas. El primer ministro Winston Churchill buscó el apoyo del presidente Roosevelt, pero no fue hasta después del ataque japonés a Pearl Harbor el 7 de diciembre de 1941, que el presidente Roosevelt declaró guerra contra Japón tan solo cuatro días después. Adolf Hitler supo que América, aunque permanecía neutral, atacaba submarinos alemanes y Adolf Hitler declaró la guerra el 11 de diciembre de 1941 a Estados Unidos.

El pueblo alemán, los generales y la mayoría de los americanos reprobaban las decisiones de Adolf Hitler y cuestionaban su sanidad mental. Adolf Hitler cometió una insalvable atrocidad cuando inició la persecución contra los judíos. Llenó los campos de concentración, no solo con judíos, sino con cualquiera que se opusiese a él o a su régimen. Los prisioneros fueron obligados a hacer trabajos forzados y algunos murieron por desnutrición y enfermedades. Mucho se ha escrito sobre el genocidio por gas Zyklon; algunos son hechos y otros ficción.

Las topas americanas y británicas invadieron Sicilia en 1943 y terminaron el fascismo en Italia al remover a Benito Musolini del poder. El nuevo primer ministro Badoglio firmó el amnisticio incondicional con el General Dwight Eisenhower en julio de 1943.

El general Dwight Eisenhower, comandante de las Fuerzas Aliadas, invadió Normandía el 6 de junio de 1944 (Día D), con miles de aeronaves nuevas y barcos y aterrizando a más de un millón de soldados en las playas de Francia. Las tropas avanzaron a París el 26 de agosto de 1944, y el General Charles de Gaulle y los ciudadanos franceses recibieron a los libertadores americanos con gran júbilo.

Mientras tanto, tres millones de rusos del ejército rojo avanzaban hacia Berlín y se encontraban con las tropas americanas el 25 de Abril de 1945, rodeando Berlín. Después de que muchos soldados alemanes murieran en combate, Hitler reclutó hombres mayores, entre ellos mi padre, y adolescentes para reemplazarlos. Después de una horrenda batalla, Berlin se rindió el 2 de mayo de 1945.

Cuando Hitler se sintió derrotado y vio que no podía evitar ser capturado, el y Eva Brown se escondieron en un búnker en Berlín y se suicidaron el 30 de abril de 1945. Hitler primero tomó una cápsula de cianuro y después se disparó en la cabeza. Los generales alemanes acordaron dejar de pelear y se rindieron, y el General Alfred Jodl firmó la declaración de rendición en Reims, Francia. Los aliados demandaron la rendición de las fuerzas combatientes, y el General Wilhelm Keitel firmó el documento de rendición incondicional en Berlín el 8 de mayo de 1945, finalizando la Segunda Guerra Mundial en Alemania. Sin embargo, la guerra en el Pacífico continuó con Japón hasta que Estados Unidos, con el consentimiento de Inglaterra, soltó una bomba atómica en Hiroshima el 6 de agosto de 1945, y tres días después otra sobre Nagasaki. Mató instantáneamente a más de 200,000 civiles. Por meses, mucha gente murió por quemadures, radiación, enfermedades, desnutrición y heridas severas. Seis días después, el Emperador de Japón, Hirohito, se rindió. El 2 de septiembre de 1945, el Ministro de Relaciones Exteriores japonés Mamoru Shigemitsu y el General Yoshijiro Umezu firmaron sus nombres en los documentos de rendición USS Missouri, que formaron parte del Tratado de Postdam, en Misouri, EUA. El General Douglas MacArthur también estaba presente en esta sombría ceremonia cuando la Segunda Guerra

Mundial terminó oficialmente. Los aliados le permitieron al Emperador Hirohito permanecer en el trono pero restringieron su poder político en un gobierno japonés recién instaurado.

Los aliados forzaron a Alemania nuevamente a pagar costosas reparaciones y a renunciar permanentemente ciertos territorios de Alemania y otras regiones que Hitler había conquistado al inicio de la guerra. Como fue demandado en el Tratado de Paz de la Segunda Guerra Mundial de Potsdam, Rusia reclamó la parte sur de Prusia Oriental, Pomerania y Silesia. Dinamarca reclamó una parte de Schleswig del Norte y Francia una parte de Alsace Lorraine.

Se fue con ambas guerras mundiales un total de un tercio del territorio alemán. Catorce millones de personas tuvieron que dejar sus hogares y propiedades para huir al Oeste. Millones de alemanes étnicos que vivían en Rusia, Polonia, Checoslovaquia, Hungría y la Europa Oriental fueron expulsados de sus hogares, con frecuencia sometidos a violencia y terror, incluyendo homicidio, tortura y violación. Cientos de miles de alemanes terminaron internados en campos, que antes fueron campos de concentración.

Muchos habitantes alemanes, incluyendo mi propia familia, escaparon en 1944 antes de que los ejércitos rusos invadieran y rodearan Prusia del Este. Pero aquéllos que permanecieron fueron despojados de sus propiedades, tratados con brutalidad y transportados como ganado en camiones de carga al oeste de Alemania. Prusia del Este se convirtió en un enclave ruso. La población rusa, que se asentó en Prusia del Este, destruyó todos los monumentos históricos y reconstruyeron los pueblos y villas destruidos por la guerra. El gobierno polaco trató mal a los habitantes alemanes en Prusia del Este. Ellos, también, confiscaron sus propiedades y ordenaron que los alemanes se marcharan; sin embargo, le permitieron a algunos quedarse. Polonia anexó el área donde yo nací a su territorio.

Con la Segunda Guerra Mundial se fue el Tercer Reich y mi amada tierra natal (Heimat), Prusia del Este. Los cuatro aliados dividieron Alemania en zonas militares. El norte de Alemania fue ocupado por Inglaterra, el sur por Francia, Alemania central fue ocupada por los Estados Unidos y el este por Rusia. Por cuatro años Alemania no tuvo gobierno. Cada aliado regía su región ocupada de acuerdo a las leyes de su país.

El 23 de mayo de 1949, un gobierno nuevo, La República Federal de Alemania (BRD), tomó forma bajo el Presidente Theodor Heuss y el Canciller Conrad Adenauer. Con la ayuda del Plan Marshall americano, las secciones devastadas por la guerra del oeste de Alemania lentamente crecieron para convertirse en una nación próspera.

Tres años después del fin de la guerra, el reichsmark (marco real) fue reemplazado por el Deutsche Mark o D.M. (marco alemán) debido a la alta inflación.

Sin embargo, bajo la ocupación rusa en Alemania del Este, la llamada República Democrática Alemana (DDR), la parte oriental retrocedió. El gobierno ruso construyó una muralla (Cortina de Hierrro) y una zona desmilitarizada de cinco kilómetros de ancho para impedir que las personas se fueran de Alemania del Este. Cualquiera que intentara escapar de Alemania del Este sobre la frontera de manera ilegal, sería aprisionado o disparado en el momento.

Con la Segunda Guerra Mundial se fueron Prusia del Este y del Oeste y con ellos la cultura prusiana de setecientos años. Casi siete décadas han pasado desde que mi familia huyó del este de Prusia, yo aún lamento la pérdida de mi amada nación y cultura. El hecho de que nunca volveré a ver mi tierra natal de nuevo, de que Prusia del Este nunca será regresada a Alemania, ha emergido una profunda tristeza en mi corazón y lágrimas en mis ojos.

El país que una vez ofreció asilo a muchos perseguidos políticos y religiosos ahora ordenaba a sus habitantes irse para evitar que fueran masacrados por brutales ejércitos. Ellos escaparon, buscando refugio en otras regiones alemanas o extranjeras.

Qué extraña puede ser la vida; yo encontré un nuevo hogar en Norte América, que una vez firmó un tratado de amistad con el rey prusiano Frederick el grande, hace doscientos años. Amo a mi país adoptivo y soy una ciudadana naturalizada. Sin embargo, siempre atesoraré los recuerdos de mi natal Prusia del Este, lamentaré su pérdida y jamás olvidaré mis raíces.

La fuerte fe de mi madre nos ayudó a mis hermanos y a mi a pasar las tragedias de la guerra y las dificultades de la vida. Ella encontró consuelo en Dios, quien prometió que nuestra estancia en la tierra es solo temporal, pero nuestro hogar permanente está en el cielo, donde nos reuniremos con nuestros seres amados y viviremos por siempre con Dios, nuestro salvador, Jesús Cristo.

Después de un vistazo en los antecedentes históricos de Prusia y de Alemania, regresaré a mi lugar de nacimiento, la pequeña villa de Wiznajy, Prusia del Este, y recordaré mi infancia y la historia de mi familia.

CAPÍTULO 7

La vida en Casa

Papá se sentía contento, viviendo en el rancho con su familia grande. El 19 de noviembre de 1942, otro hijo, llamado Horst, fue añadido a sus siete hijos. Disfrutaba de la vida, bailaba, cantaba, y tenía un buen sentido del humor. Era un artesano en la albañilería. Era alto, rubio y tenía ojos azules. Mamá era morena, de ojos cafés, taciturna y muy religiosa. Ambos trabajaban diligentemente para labrar la tierra, producir cultivos, criar animales y alimentar a su gran familia, y vender el sobrante para comprar bienes para la casa y los niños.

Las estaciones crearon un patrón rítmico para nuestras vidas, y la naturaleza nos indujo a seguir su orden. La vida se empezaba a agitar bajo la nieve cuando las sombras del invierno se acortaban y los días se alargaban. Pronto las primeras flores de primavera atravesaban sus delicadas hojas y a través de la nieve florecían. Las frágiles campanas blancas de las gotas de nieve sonaban al inicio de la primavera.

Algunas gallinas mostraban señales de cambios en su comportamiento en primavera. Dejaban de poner huevos, perdían las plumas de sus pancitas, y hacían un extraño sonido crepitante.

Mi madre sabía cuando una gallina estaba lista para incubar huevos. Emma, Marta y Meta preparaban nidos en cajas de madera y canastas, las llenaban de paja y las forraban de plumas de ganso. Las colocaban en la entrada grande de la cocina porque el gallinero no tenía calefacción, y las frias noches podían impedir la incubación del huevo. Antes de que mi madre pusiera una docena más o menos en un nido, veía los huevos a contraluz para revisar si eran fértiles o no. Después ponía una gallina (Glucke, en alemán) sobre cada montón. Las niñas seccionaban partes en el establo, acomodando nidos para patos, gansos y pavos.

Vientos cada véz más cálidos soplaban cada día y derretían la nieve alrededor de la casa y el hielo del lago. Cerca de la orilla del lago, aparecían lirios acuáticos y otras flores y pastos. Los árboes y arbustos alrededor de la casa desplegaban sus delicadas hojas y bellos brotes. En la pradera crecieron abundantes pastos verdes y flores silvestres de muchos colores, y los campos de barbecho exponían su rico y oscuro suelo.

Papá estaba ansioso por labrar el suelo. Primero trajo cargas especiales de estiércol de vaca a los campos para distibuirlo con una horquilla por todo el suelo. Al día siguiente, papá llevó un arado al campo, lo ató detrás de un caballo, y comenzó a voltear una línea tras otra para cubrir el fertilizante natural y aflojar el suelo de la superficie. El silbaba o tarareaba una melodía alegrc mientras empujaba el arado dentro de la tierra al principio de una línea, manteniéndolo a cierta profundidad y levantándolo al final de cada línea. Iba de atrás hacia adelante hasta que la tierra del campo entero quedaba expuesta al sol y al aire fresco. Los cuervos lo seguian en busca de los gusanos gordos que quedaban expuestos. Una alondra trinaba una canción alegre mientras ascendía al domo azul celestial.

Papá esperó unos días para que el suelo se secara antes de rastrillarlo para deshacer los macizos y preparar la tierra para la siembra.

Al siguiente día, Georg le ayudó después de volver a casa de la escuela. Papá subió un costal lleno de trigo a la carreta y amarró el rastrillo en la carreta. Una vez que llegaron al campo, papá llenó medio saco con granos de trigo, con una tira atada a cada extremo y llevó la tira sobre su cabeza y hombro. Entonces caminó de un extremo del campo al otro, esparciendo puñado tras puñado de semillas en un movimiento de barrido sobre el suelo. Georg removió el rastrillo, lo ató a los caballos, y rastrillaba la porción donde papá había tirado las semillas. Georg fue de atrás hacia adelante varias veces para cubrir las semillas ligeramente con la tierra. Ahora, papá esperaba una lluvia ligera para acelerar el proceso de germinación.

Cuando la tarde cubrió la granja y los campos con oscuridad, mi mamá encendía la lámpara de aceite y la ponía sobre la mesa. (En el campo, el poder eléctrico no existía). Después de cenar, por dos o tres horas, Edmund y Georg hacian sus tareas. Richard y yo jugábamos juegos de mesa (Muehle, o Mensh Arger Dich Nicht), mientras mamá y Emma hilaban lana o cosían ropa para los hermanos más chicos.

Mamá, Emma y Meta prepararon el jardin de hortalizas, que papá había arado en el otoño el año anterior. Mamá preparaba las camas para varios vegetales con la punta de un rastrillo. Emma y Meta escarbaban un camino entre cada parcela, que Emma rastrillaba. Cada cierto tiempo, volteaba el rastrillo y daba un porrazo a un macizo de arcilla para romperlo. Una vez que la tierra estaba suave, mamá acomodaba surcos superficiales en las camas de vegetales. Ella acomodaba las semillas, que había salvado de cosechas previas, de zanahorias, rábanos, pepinos, rábanos picantes, betabeles, frijoles, guisantes, varios tipos de lechugas y repollos en ellas. Los nabos, remolachas y cebollas blancas servían como alimento a los cerdos y eran plantados en parcelas más grandes lejos de la casa. Yo no podía esperar a que las semillas brotaran y asomaran sus primeras dos hojas a través del suelo. Poco después de llegada la primavera, las aves migratorias volvían. Yo recibía con entusiasmo a las dos cigüeñas, que hacían nido en lo alto de nuestro establo. Disfrutaba de escuchar el traqueteo de sus picos. Corría al salir de casa para hablar con ellas en el dialecto de Prusia del Este "Storch, Storch, goder, bring me e kleenem Broder. Storch, Storch bester, bring mi e kleene Schwester" Traducción: Cigüeña, cigüeña, se buena y traeme un hermanito. Cigüeña, cigüeña, se la mejor y traeme una hermanita.

El graznido de un ganso salvaje volando al norte, el llamado del gallo, y la dulce canción del ruiseñor anunciaban la llegada oficial de la primavera y, con ella, la pascua. Todos esperábamos la pascua cuando nuestra hermana Marta vino a visitarnos. Después de que Marta se graduara de la escuela de gramática, a la edad de catorce años, encontró un trabajo en la aldea cercana de Hellrau con la familia de un maestro para ayudar con sus tres hijos. Había reunido suficiente experiencia en casa, ayudando a mamá a criar a los hermanos mas pequeños y disfrutaba de cuidar de los hermanos del maestro. Sin embargo, en las festividades especiales, como Pascua, Pentecostés, y Navidad, el señor Kessler, así se llamaba el maestro, le permitía tomar unos cuantos días para pasarlos con su familia.

Cada día, durante la semana previa a la Pascua, esperaba a Marta. Finalmente, la vi caminando en la colina hacia la casa, cargando paquetes en ambas manos. Corrí a saludarla. Puso sus bolsas en el suelo y me abrazó, me levantó y me dio vueltas en el aire: "Dios, has crecido" obervó, "Que bueno verte y estar de nuevo en casa". "¿Qué hay en esas bolsas?" pregunté.

"Tendrás que esperar hasta Pascua. No puedo decirte aún. Es una sopresa."

Salté y brinqué a su lado, sosteniendo una bolsa, preguntándome si habría una muñeca en ella. Todos la abrazaon en casa y la recibieron con muchas preguntas:

¿Te gusta trabajar para el maestro?

¿Te tratan bien?

¿Cuántos niños tienen?

¿Son tan obedientes como nosotros?

Las preguntas siguieron hasta que mi madre intercedió: "Dejen de hacerle tantas preguntas; Marta está cansada de la larga caminata. ¡Déjenla descansar un momento!"

Al día siguiente, celebramos Viernes Santo. Mamá nos contó la historia de la crucificción de Cristo, y por respeto al dolor de Cristo, no se nos permitía llevar a cabo conversaciones innecesarias. Mamá y papá, Emma, Marta, Meta y Georg ayunaron porque iban a tomar parte en la Sagrada Comunión en la iglesia.

Mamá insistio en que todos pidieran perdón por las palabras poco compasivas dichas o cualquier acto indebido. Mamá y papá se abrazaron, también lo hicieron las hermanas y Georg, quién primero pidió perdón para sus padres y después para cada uno. A veces, lágrimas expresaban el arrepentimiento que sentían por decir una pequeña mentira o desobedecer a mamá o papá. Todos se sintieron aliviados cuando papá ató el coche y nos llevó a la iglesia. Me acurruqué en el regazo de Marta. Ella me abrazó, pero no nos atrevimos a decir una palabra o romper el silencio.

Papá y Georg desataron a los caballos del coche en la plaza de la iglesia y los ataron a la viga grande donde los caballos de otros pobladores estaban ya atados. Todos entramos a la gran iglesia. Richard y yo nos unimos a otros niños en las filas delanteras mientras nuestros padres y los adultos se sentaban detrás de nosotros. Tres cruces estaban erguidas en la derecha del altar. Un velo negro cubría la cruz del centro.

Después de que los feligreses tomaron asiento, el organista tocó un preludio, seguido de una canción comunitaria. El pastor leyó la historia de la crucifixión de Cristo de la Biblia. El sermón siguio el tema: Cristo murió y sufrió por nuestra salvación, y nosotros debemos cargar nuestra cruz y la de otros. Cuando el pastor invitó a los feligreses a tomar parte en la Sagrada Comunión, ellos se acercaron al altar, se hincaron, recibieron primero la hostia y después el vino. Una canción mas siguió después de que el pastor sirvió la comunión al último participante; después, el pastor despidió a la congregación con una bendición. Todos partieron solemnemente de la iglesia.

De acuerdo a una vieja tradicion, comemos únicamente pescado en Viernes Santo. Después de la comida, Emma, Marta, y Meta prepararon los ingredientes para colorear los Huevos de Pascua. Cocinaron remolachas rojas, cáscaras de cebolla, musgo, y huevos en ollas separadas. Marta peló las remolachas rojas y las cortó en rodajas, para que el color púrpura rezumara en el agua caliente, después drenó el jugo de la remolacha en una olla más pequeña y suavemente puso, con una cuchara, los huevos en la olla. Después de algunos minutos, Marta sacó cada huevo del agua y los puso en un plato. Emma pintó huevos amarillos o ambar con el jugo de cáscara de cebolla y Marta, marrón verdoso con el líquido del musgo. Pronto, los huevos de varios colores llenaron el contenedor. Corrí a la pradera, recogí ranúculos, no-me- ovides, y larkspurs y se las entregué a Marta. Marta cortó los tallos y las arregló agradablemente en un plato hondo junto a los huevos coloridos en la mesa del comedor.

La mañana siguiente, mi mamá preparó la masa para el pan de trigo y centeno en dos cuencos de madera y lo dejó reposar para que se inflasen. Emma calentó el horno con leña. Cuando el horno estuvo listo, mamá dio palmaditas a la masa de trigo para darle formas alargadas y al de centeno en formas redondas.

Amasó un poco de masa de trigo en una charola para hornear y las dejó en la mesa para que se inflaran una vez mas. Una vez que la masa se infló lo suficiente, mi mamá colocó cada hogaza en un utensilio de madera (Schieber en alemán) y los introdujo en el horno. Emma mezcló harina, mantequilla y azúcar y esparció la mezcla sobre la masa en la bandeja de galletas, que nuestra madre puso en el horno más tarde. Un agradable aroma llenó la cocina despué de que mamá abrió el horno y tomó una hogaza tras otra. No podíamos esperar a que mamá las sirviera.

El sábado, cada uno de nosotros debía lustrar sus zapatos y preparar la ropa para el domingo. Le pregunté a mi hermana Marta: "¿Puedes elegir un vestido para mi?"

"Ven aquí, Hildke (así solía llamarme); tengo algo para ti." Ella fue a la recámara y volvió con una mano detrás de la espalda. "Cierra los ojos, Hildke", Apreté mis párpados rápidamente y los abrí cuando Marta dijo, "Ya puedes abrir tus ojos, mira lo que hice para ti". Vi un vestido rojo sin mangas con bordado alrededor del cuello.

"Es hermoso, ¿tú hiciste esto para mi? Gracias, gracias Marta," le dije mientras la abrazaba y la besaba en la mejilla. "Puede ser que necesites una blusa bajo el vestido mañana.

El aire aún es vigoroso", añadió Marta. Yo admiré el hermoso bordado y no podía esperar a usarlo para ir a la iglesia.

El sábado era día de baño. Mamá hervía una olla grande de agua, la vació en una bañera oval y añadió suficiente agua fría hasta que la temperatura del agua era la correcta. Marta me llevó de la mano, me ayudó a desvestirme y me metí a la bañera, situada en el medio de la cocina. Tomó una barra de jabón y me lavó primero el cabello y despué el resto de mi cuerpo mientras yo chapoteaba feliz en el agua. Marta me secó con una toalla grande, me ayudó a ponerme el camisón y me llevó a la recámara. Primero, se arrodilló conmigo para rezar una oración, antes de arroparme bajo el edredón de plumas y darme un beso de buenas noches. Mis hermanas, Emma, Marta y Meta tomaron su baño después. Cada una añadió más agua caliente antes de entrar en la bañera. Después, mis hermanos, Georg, Edmund y Richard tomaron sus turnos. Cuando terminaron, tiraron el agua del baño en el jardín. Mamá vació agua caliente y fría nuevamente para ella y su esposo.

Cuando el amanecer entró de puntillas en la tierra y llenó el campo de color, Emma se levantó para traer agua fresca del arroyo al día siguiente. Le llamamos agua de pascua. Se suponía que tenía poderes curativos. Todos lavaron sus caras en esta agua bendita y esperaban que hiciera un poco de magia. Marta escondió todos los huevos de colores en varios lugares alrededor de la casa y nos dijo, "el conejo de pascua tomó los huevos y los escondió para ustedes. Vayan a buscarlos". Mis tres hermanos y yo corrimos afuera y empezamos a buscar los huevos de pascua. "Encontré algunos", grité cuando vi un nido debajo de un arbusto.

"¡Mira donde descubrí huevos!" gritó Edmund, apuntando a la carreta en el establo. Georg encontró un nido en una caja en el frente de la casa. Richard descubrió huevos de pascua en una canasta cerca del establo. Corrimos a enseñarle a mamá, papá y nuestras hermanas nuestros tesoros recientemente encontrados. Aunque cada uno podía quedarse con los huevos que había encontrado, siempre los compartíamos con todos los miembros de la familia.

"Ahora, niños, es tiempo de arreglarse para la iglesia; nos vamos en diez minutos" Nos recordó mamá. Rápidamente, nos cambiamos con nuestra ropa de domingo. Cuando mi padre trajo el coche frente a la casa, todos saltamos dentro del coche. Mamá se sentó a frente, a un lado de papá. Hacia la iglesia manejó mi padre con su familia entera sobre el camino sin pavimentar del campo. De vez en cuando agitaba el látigo para hacer que los caballos trotaran más rápido. Me acurruqué en el regazo de Marta y disfruté viendo los campos verdes pasando a nuestra diestra y siniestra escuchando a las alondras trinar una feliz melodía mientras ascendían al cielo azul.

Hoy, el Domingo de Pascua, todos se unieron, celebrando la resurrección de Cristo con alegría. Emma cantaba con el coro de la iglesia antes de que iniciara el sermón. Al fin del sermón el pastor exclamó: "¡Cristo se ha levantado!" Los feligreses respondían con alegría "¡Ciertamente ha resucitado!". Después del sermón sobre la resurrección de Cristo y la bendición, todos se fueron de la iglesia. La gente se detenía en la plaza de la iglesia para visitar a amigos y vecinos. Georg y papá ataron los caballos al coche y manejaron directo a casa.

El domingo de pascua, los familiares vinieron a visitarnos. Mamá y mis hermanas prepararon pato con un plato especial de papa (Kugel en alemán) y repollo rojo para la comida. Como papá no podía costear el café real, café de nogal americano y pastel siguieron como postre. Dimos una especial bienvenida a la tía Minna Schloesser, la hermana de mi padre, con sus cinco hijos. Mis hermanas jugaron juegos de mesa con nuestras primas Greta, Wilma y Emma, mientras los niños y el primo Erich se entretenían jugando afuera. Herta, la prima mas joven, y yo nos entreteníamos con los huevos de pascua. Cada una rodaba un huevo en el montículo del jardín para ver cuál huevo iba más rápido. También jugamos con mi muñeca, que mi hermana Martha había hecho para mi el año anterior. Desafortunadamente, el tío Schloesser no nos pudo acompañar porque servía como soldado en la Segunda Guerra Mundial, al igual que los tíos Otto, August y Georg.

El día pasó muy rápido antes de que mi tía y mis primos volvieran a la villa, y nos fuimos contentos a dormir.

Los siguientes días pasaron felizmente, siguiendo a mi hermana Marta por la casa y afuera. Un día, mientras caminábamos por donde estaban las gallinas incubando huevos, escuchamos un piar. Suavemente Marta movió a la gallina, y vimos a un pequeño pollito rompiendo el cascarón del huevo. Corrí con mamá, tomé su mano, y le dije: "Mamá, mamá, ven rápido; ¡un pollito está saliendo de un huevo!" Mamá me siguió, y le enseñé el pollito en el cascarón roto.

"Aún es muy pronto para sacarlo del nido, pero vigilaremos los huevos de cerca desde ahora en adelante" Respondió mamá. Fue por una caja y la puso a un lado del nido. Más tarde mi madre y Marta recogieron un pollito tras otro, colocándolos con suavidad en la caja cerca a la estufa y tiró los cascarones rotos. Después de dos o tres días, todos los huevos habían eclosionado, y la gallina dejó el nido para estar con sus pollitos en un corral pequeño rodeado por malla gallinera. Desafortunadamente, también era tiempo para que Marta se fuera, lo que nos entristeció a todos.

"¿Te tienes que ir?" le pregunté, "¿Por qué no puedes quedarte con nosotros todo el tiempo?"

"Necesito ayudar a la señora Kessler con sus tres hijos" Contestó Marta, "Ven, vamos a despedirnos de todos antes de que me vaya." No solté su mano y caminé con ella hasta el fin de la coina. "Es mejor que corras a casa ahora" insistió Marta.

"¿Cuándo vas a volver?" le pregunté mientras Marta se agachaba para abrazarme.

"Muy pronto, ahora vete, vete." Di la vuelta y me apresuré a casa.

Unos cuantos días mas pasaron, y los patitos nacieron, y cuatro semanas después, los bebés gansos y pavos llegaron. Después de que Edmund llegó de la escuela, vió a los patitos, los gansos bebés, y los protegió de los cuervos y halcones que pudieran llevárselos. Ayudé a Richard con los pollitos. Cada mañana mamá contaba a cada bebé y hacía lo mismo por las tardes antes de guardarlas en el gallinero para pasar la noche. Un día, Richard y yo jugamos con una bicicleta vieja y nos alejamos demasiado del gallinero con los pollitos. Un cuervo bajó, nos arrebató un pollito y se fue volando. Le gritamos al cuervo, esperando que soltara a su presa, pero fue en vano. El resto de la tarde la pasamos con miedo al castigo que nos esperaba. Esperábamos que a mamá se le olvidara contar a los pollitos ese dia, pero no lo hizo – en su lugar, nos regañó y nos dio una nalgadas con el cinto de cuero de papá. Desde ese momento, siempre permanecíamos cerca del gallinero con los pollitos. Disfruté viendo a los patitos y a los gansos bebés chapoteando en el lago, saltando al agua, y nadando por primera vez, siguiendo a la mamá pato y ganso muy de cerca. Mientras mi hermano Edmund pastoreaba a los bebés pato y gansó cerca del lago, él pescaba con su caña y anzuelo hechos a mano. Ató un corcho a la linea como flotador. Cuando el corcho desaparecía dentro del agua, él sabía que había agarrado a un pez, levantaba el palo rápidamente y traía al pez a la orilla. A veces, se enfocaba más en pescar que en cumplir sus deberes. Un castigo le esperaba al final del día cuando descubría que faltaba un patito.

Una semana o un poco más después de Pascua, papá preparó el campo para plantar papas. Mamá y Emma cortaron cada papa a la mitad y las pusieron en canastos grandes. Después pusieron cada mitad con la parte cortada hacia abajo, con un pie masomenos de distancia entre ellas, en surcos superficiales. Papá cubrió las papas con un arado de cada lado, formando canales y filas de monticulos.

Pentecostés siguió a mediados de junio cuando la naturaleza luce su atuendo más festivo y colorido. Emma y Meta fueron a la arboleda cercana a cortar ramas de abedul. Yo iba con ellas y recogía las flores que me encontraba en el camino. Pusimos un arreglo de flores silvestres en el centro de la mesa del comedor. Tejimos una guirnalda con ramas verdes y la amarramos al marco de la puerta de la entrada. Todas las chicas jóvenes usaban vestidos blancos. Celebrábamos Pentecostés en casa, o íbamos a visitar a tíos, tías y sobrinos. La familia entera iba a la iglesia. Para gusto de todos, Marta volvió para celebrar esta memorable festividad con nosotros. No podíamos imaginarnos que esta sería la última Pentecostés que celebraríamos juntos como familia.

En julio, el pasto en las praderas era alto, y muchas flores sivestres, tréboles y otras plantas extendían una espesa alfombra sobre los campos. Cuando oímos el tintineo musical de la piedra de afilar y a papá afilando su guadaña, sabíamos que era tiempo de cortar el pasto en la pradera. Mamá y yo comimos con papá para que él no perdiera tiempo en volver a casa. Mamá extendió un pequeño mantel sobre el heno recién cortado y desenvolvió unos sándwiches hechos con salchicha hecha en casa. "Siéntate, Gustav, es tiempo de tomar un descanso y comer. Ya tienes una buena parte podada; ¿crees que podrás terminar para mañana en la noche?" Le preguntaba mamá mientras le entregaba un sándwich a papá junto con una botella de jugo de frambuesa.

"Debería terminar antees del atardecer" le respondió papá, después dio una mordida tras otra hasta que consumio dos sándwiches. Mamá y yo comimos uno cada una mientras estábamos sentadas en el pasto e respirábamos el agradable aroma del heno recién cortado y muchas flores que se encontraban en líneas ya desdibujadas. Corrí en el campo y recogí algunas flores silvestres antes de que mi padre las podara. Felices, mamá y yo nos dirigimos a casa.

Por varios días, el heno permaneció en el sol para secarse. Después, Emma, Meta y Georg fueron a la pradera a voltear el heno y formar filas. Después de que el sol secara el pasto por completo, papá, Emma, Meta y Georg llevaron la carreta a la pradera. Georg detuvo a los caballos. Emma permanecía sobre la carreta mientras papá y Meta levantaban el heno con horquillas. Emma juntó el heno al frente de la carreta al principio y después lo movía hacia atrás hasta que alcanzaba el final de la carreta. Meta rastrillaba el heno. Papá se quedó atrás. A veces, Edmund, Richard y yo tomábamos un aventón a casa en el suave heno de la carreta. Una vez en casa, Papá y Georg descargaban el heno y lo almacenaban en el establo.

El trigo se movía suavemente con la brisa y ondulaba en olas a través del campo. Papá sabía para finales de agosto que era tiempo de cosechar. Llamó a los hombres y mujeres jóvenes del vecindario para ayudar. En retorno, papá, Emma y Meta ayudarían a los vecinos a cosechar cuando sus plantíos estuvieran listos. Los hombres cortaban fila tras fila con sus guadañas.

Una mujer iba detrás de cada hombre, recogiendo dos puñados de tallos de trigo, haciendo un nudo al final para formar una cuerda. Juntaron una brazada de tallos de trigo y rápidamente ataron la cuerda alrededor para crear un manojo, que dejaban en el suelo.

Mamá permanecía en casa para preparar una comida sustancial, que llevaba al campo. Yo iba con ella y la ayudaba cargando un monton de platos. Todos recibían con agrado una pausa a medio día para descansar y comer y participar en conversaciones animadas. Los hombres discutían los eventos políticos más recientes, mientras las mujeres y las chicas platicaban sobre eventos familiares. Los hombres ayudaban a las mujeres a poner los conjuntos en sacos. Antes de que el sol pintara de dorado el cielo del oeste, los hombres ponían sus guadañas sobre el hombro y se marchaban a casa. Mujeres y chicas los seguían. Todos se apresuraban al lago para lavar el polvo de sus caras, brazos y piernas. Las mujeres y chicas no usaban medias, y sus piernas y pies sangraban por las cortadas sutiles.

Mientras todos se limpiaban y platicaban felizmente, yo estaba en la orilla observando a los alegres bañistas. Emma se me acercó con una piedra en su mano. "Ten, Hildke, toma esta piedra y lánzala al lago para salpicar a los vecinos". Yo tomé la piedra y la lancé al agua. Desafortunadamente, le pegó a la pierna de nuestro vecino Gustav Both en lugar de caer directamente en el agua. Él gritó "¿quién fue el canalla? Espera a que te atrape." Él cojeó fuera del agua, viendo la herida sangrando en su pierna. Cuando me vio corriendo, supo que había sido yo quién había lanzado la piedra.

Corrí colina arriba y me escondi en la letrina, esperando que no me encontrara ahí. Tampoco quería enfrentar a mamá, ella me castigaría también. Rápidamente aseguré la puerta con el gancho, me paré detrás de la puerta y me asomé a través del hoyo en forma de corazón para asegurarme de que nadie me seguía. Nadie lo hizo. Uno tras otro salieron del lago y entraron en la casa. Escuchaba las pláticas adentro en la cena mientras yo temblaba en la letrina, mi estómago rugía. Estaba hambrienta, muy hambrienta. Yo miraba y esperaba, miraba y esperaba. La oscuridad envolvió la granja; solo las luces de la casa iluminaban el patio tenuemente. Creo que nadie notó mi ausencia. El tiempo parecía haberse detenido. Tenia frío y esperaba ver a los vecinos marcharse, pero se quedaban y se quedaban. Parecía media noche cuando finalmente vi a los vecinos y a papá salir de la casa y decir buenas noches los unos a los otros. Esperé un poco más antes de atreverme a entrar en la casa.

"Fue tu culpa, Emma" la regañé. "No debiste haberme pedido que lanzara la piedra al agua."

"Lo siento mucho y te pido tu perdón," respondió Emma mientras me abrazaba. "¿Dónde estuviste todo este tiempo?"

"Me escondí en la letrina hasta que vi que se fueron los vecinos,"

"Todo este tiempo esperaste en la letrina, pobrecita, debes tener frío y hambre. Siéntate y come algo antes de que te lleve a la cama."

"Déjame tomar un vaso de leche y comer un sándwich," le dije, mirando a mamá, preguntándome si me reprendería. Me sentí aliviada cuando mi mamá no dijo nada, y salté a la cama y rápidamente me metí bajo el cálido cobertor de plumas. Tomó tres días más podar los campos de trigo. Pero desde ese entonces en adelante, yo siempre me escondia en algún lugar cuando nuestro vecino Gustav Both venía a visitarnos. Aún sentía remordimientos y temía su castigo.

Papá esperó hasta que los tallos con los granos se secaran en el campo antes de traerlos a casa. Descargaron los montones en el establo. Después de que la última carreta llegara a casa, Emma hizo una corona de cosecha. Con un hilo, ató tallos cortos de grano a una forma de corona hecha de alambre. La colgó en el techo de la cocina. Era una tradición anual para mostrar gratitud al creador por una cosecha abundante. Vecinos, familiares y familia celebraban con buena comida y bebida la buena producción de los campos.

Después de que todos los vecinos terminaran de traer todos los cultivos, se ayudaban entre ellos con el apaleo de trigo, avenas y centeno. No teníamos maquinaria ni eléctrica ni de gasolina; papá construyó un aparato especial (llamado Rosswerk en alemán) para mover las ruedas de la máquina de apaleo. Papá ató dos caballos más al extremo de una larga viga. Alguien debía guiar a uno de los caballos o montarlo para mantenerlo moviéndose a un paso continuo. Cuando los caballos se movían alrededor, ponían las ruedas y la campana en movimiento. A su vez, la campana movía el mecanismo de apaleo que separaba al grano de la paja. Una persona empujaba unos cuantos tallos a la vez para que no se atorara y detuviera. Tomó varios días para que el proceso de apaleo terminara en nuestra granja. Después mi padre iba con nuestros vecinos y familiares a ayudarles con sus propios prcesos.

Cortando Césped y Cosechando Lino

Cuando las flores silvestres esparcieron sus floraciones a través de las praderas y humedales durante el verano, papá preparaba una parte del pantano para cortar césped. Papá preparó un cuadrado de aproximadamente quince pies. Escarbó una trinchera angosta alrededor del área. Después cortó el césped pieza por pieza y lo arrojó al pantano adyacente. Después de que removió dos o tres capas de turba, el agua llenó el hoyo. Cavó una acequia para drenar el agua a un pantano más bajo. Cuando el montón alcanzó un tamaño específico, papá le dio tinas de agua a Emma y Meta, que vaciaron el agua sobre el césped. Papá salió del pozo, le pusó el arnés a los dos caballos, y pisoteó descalzo detrás del caballo hasta que las piezas de césped se rompieron y formaron una gruesa y negra arcilla semi-sólida. Papá se llevó una caja de la arcilla lejos de la pradera. Emma y Meta llenaron un molde seccionado en compartimientos del tamaño de un ladrillo con arcilla, lo levantaban, dejando la arcilla en forma de ladrillo en la tierra. Repitieron el proceso hasta que terminaron con toda la arcilla negra del césped. Después de unos días, mamá y mis hermanas mayores voltearon los ladrillos de arcilla para que se secaran completamente de ambos lados. Papá los llevó al rancho y los guardó en el cobertizo. Dado que la arcilla se quema más lento que la madera, mi mamá la usaba junto con la leña para cocinar en la estufa de leña y para calentar la estufa de azulejos (Kachelofen) en invierno.

Haciendo arcilla

La cosecha de lino comenzó cuando las delicadas flores azules se convirtieron en semillas. Papá, mamá y Emma caminaron por el campo para recolectar las semillas primero. Después, la familia entera arrancaba las plantas de raíz y las ataba en manojos. Papá cargaba la carreta con los manojos de lino y los llevaba a casa. Papá cavó un hoyo, construyó una estructura cuadrada de madera con postas delgadas alrededor, y puso los manojos de lino recargadas en ellas. Encendió una fogata dentro del hueco para secar los tallos de lino. Papá y mamá desataban manojo tras manojo, los colocaban en el piso del granero, y las golpeaban con un azotador de madera hasta que las vainas se rompían en pedazos pequeños y, cuando las agitaban, salían de las cáscaras. Mamá lavaba las fibras en otro baño de agua, y cuando estaban semi – secos, cepillaba un puñado tras otro con un fino cepillo de metal hecho de muchas filas de clavos delgados para remover cáscaras y dividir las fibras en delicados hilos. Una vez más, los hilos necesitaban secarse antees de que mi mamá los atara en pequeños manojos.

En invierno, los campos permanecían valdíos, y el trabajo empezaba en casa. Mamá, Emma y Meta tomaban turnos para hilar el lino en hilos finos. Más tarde, ellas tejerían tela de lino y cosían sábanas, camisas, y ropa interior del material tejido. La tela tejida en casa al principio era áspera al tacto, pero se suavizaba después de repetidas lavadas. Durante el verano mi mamá extendía las telas en el jardín para dejar que la luz del sol las blanqueara. A veces los gansos o los patos caminaban sobre las sábanas y dejaban manchas verdes detrás de ellos, lo que sea necesario volver a lavarlas.

Primer Día de Escuela

En 1943, la Segunda Guerra Mundial estalló alrededor de nosotros, pero aún nos sentíamos seguros en casa. Yo cumplí seis años en enero y me convertí en elegible para entrar a la escuela de gramática. En mi primer día mi papá me llevó junto con mis hermanos a la gran casa escolar en Wazajny. Yo bajé el paso para mirar a mi alrededor mientras mi papá me acompañaba al salón de clases, que la maestra me asignó. Primero la maestra se presentó: " mi nombre es Miss (Fraeulein) Brandt" miss Brandt llamó a cada estudiante por su nombre y les pidió que se pusieran de pie para que los compañeros de clases pudieran recordar sus nombres. Después la maestra entregó a cada pupilo un pizarrón rodeado de un marco de madera y una pluma hecha de pizarra gris. Una cuerda de un pie de largo atada a un hoyo en el marco con dos pequeñas esponjas que colgaban de las cuerdas.

Las esponjas servían para borrar lo escrito. En un lado del pizarrón, pequeños cuadros estaban grabados para escribir números y del otro lado líneas para escribir palabras. El primer día miss Brandt escribió los números del uno al diez en el pizarrón grande. Nos pidió que copiáramos cada número en uno de los pequeños cuadros y nos hizo repetir cada número después de ella. Después ella escribió las letras del abecedario en el pizarrón y nos dijo que las escribiéramos en las líneas del otro lado. Cuando completamente cubríamos nuestros pizarrones con números y letras, íbamos al frente y se lo enseñábamos a la maestra. Ella nos decía donde debíamos mejorar nuestra escritura. Remojábamos una esponja en agua, borrábamos las letras y los números, y secábamos el pizarrón con la otra. Y después volvíamos a escribir otra vez.

Mi hermano, Georg, que iba a la misma escuela, esperaba que mi clase terminara y caminaba a casa conmigo. Papá tenía mucho trabajo que hacer en el rancho como para recogerme en la escuela. Yo corría con mamá y le enseñaba las primeras letras y números que había aprendido a escribir.

"Mira, mamá, puedo escribir", exclamaba mientras le señalaba las letras en el pizarrón. Después de la comida me sentaba y practicaba y practicaba hasta que las letras fluían fácilmente y se veían mejor.

Al siguiente día con mi pizarrón debajo de mi brazo yo caminaba a la escuela con Georg, Edmund y Richard. Tomábamos un atajo a través de los grandes pastizales que nos ahorraba muchísimo tiempo. Yo disfrutaba aprender cosas nuevas cada día y conocer a mis compañeros de clase. Después de qué Fraulein Brandt trabajara con sus estudiantes por varios meses, separaba a los de aprendizaje rápido de los de aprendizaje lento. Para mi gusto, me colocó en el grupo de los de aprendizaje rápido. Ella enseñó a todos los estudiantes juntos al principio; después, ella le daba proyectos a los de aprendizaje lento mientras le enseñaba los de aprendizaje rápido temas más avanzados y viceversa. Yo satisfice mi curiosidad aprendiendo cosas nuevas cada día. Tampoco me molestaba caminar a la escuela sola una vez que conocía el atajo a Wizajny. No tenía clases ni sábados ni domingos.

Mientras el tiempo volaba, las cigüeñas también volaban lejos y dejaban los nidos en el techo del establo. Cuando Horst nació, le agradecía la cigüeñas la siguiente de primavera por habernos traído otro hermano bebé. Yo disfrutaba de jugar con él cuando regresaba a casa de la escuela. En octubre, parvadas de gansos salvajes se asentaban en los campos cercanos para alimentarse. Ellos graznaban y alzaban su salas para emprender el vuelo. Se acomodaban en formaciones V y migraban al sur para pasar el invierno en un clima más cálido. Muchas otras aves migratorias se fueron, y noviembre marcó el final del otoño.

Papá y Georg se apresuraban al bosque cercano para cortar leña para el invierno. Sí, el invierno llegó rápidamente y transformó el escenario, cubriendo nuestro camino a la escuela con nieve. Nos tomó mucho más tiempo atravesar la densa nieve en las pasturas para llegar a la escuela. Una vez quedé atrapada en una tormenta de nieve. No podía ver ningún punto de referencia y me perdí. Simplemente seguí caminando mientras el viento empujaba los copos de nieve en mi cara y ojos y me cegaba. Cuando empecé a subir la colina, la única en nuestra área, sabía que estaba cerca de nuestra casa, y mi mamá me recibió en casa enseguida. Después de ese episodio, mi papá o un vecino nos llevaban a la escuela en trineo cuando había una tormenta de nieve a través de nuestra área.

Nuestras calcetas de lana tejidas a mano, guantes, y suéteres evitaban que nuestros huesos titiritaran. Los abrigos hechos del material tejido en casa protegían a nuestros cuerpos del viento y del frío. Antes de entrar al salón de clases, nos teníamos que quitar nuestros abrigos, capas, y zapatos y ponernos pantuflas hechas de paja. Y durante el intermedio, la escuela proveía de zanahorias frescas, nabos o col fermentada para alimentarnos.

Debido a la guerra, las mercancías eran escasas; sólo la escuela poseía libros, que los estudiantes podían usar en clase. No se nos permitía llevarnos ningún libro a casa. Formábamos oraciones con las diferentes palabras que habíamos aprendido.

También copiamos oraciones en nuestro pizarrón y las leíamos repetidamente hasta que sabíamos las oraciones de memoria. Sin embargo, sobrevivíamos con lo poquito que teníamos. Después de qué habíamos aprendido los números, la maestra nos enseñó a resolver adiciones matemáticas simples y problemas con sustracciones.

Antes de Navidad, nuestra maestra nos llevó a deslizarnos en tobogán. Llevábamos nuestros trineos a las cima de una pequeña colina, después dos estudiantes se sentaban juntos, y con un empuje de nuestro pie, empezábamos a deslizarnos hacia abajo.Rápido y más rápido,nos deslizábamos colina abajo hacia el lago congelado. Los toboganes seguían avanzando por algún tiempo en el hielo antes de que se detuvieran completamente. Rápidamente, subíamos a las cima de la colina para deslizarnos una y otra vez colina abajo hasta que la maestra nos pidió que fuéramos a casa. ¡Que vigorizante! Cuando llegué a casa estaba exhausta y me acurruqué bajo el cálido cobertor muy pronto después de la cena.

Edmundo y Richard cada uno tomaron dos tablas curvas de un barril grande,les pusieron tirantes de cuero arriba para amarrar sus zapatos en las tablas, y esquiaron hacia la colina cercana. A veces, se tropezaban y rodaban varias veces y se resbalaban por un tiempo antes de qué pudieran pararse en sus esquís hechos en casa y completar la carrera. Edmund hizo patines de hielo para mi hermano Richard y para mi clavando dos grandes cables en la suela de nuestros zapatos de madera. Patinábamos de ida y de regreso en el lago congelado, viendo quién podía ir más rápido. Mayormente, Richard ganaba las carreras.

El invierno y el año 1943 llegaron al fin, y 1944 trajo muchos cambios. Habían pasado casi cinco años desde que Alemania empezó la Segunda Guerra Mundial. Durante la primavera, los soldados alemanes cavaron trincheras cerca de nuestra villa y prepararon el terreno para pelear contra el ejército rojo ruso que se acercaba lentamente a la frontera de Prusia del Este.

Para la mitad del verano, muchos civiles, jóvenes varones que pertenecían a la juventud Hitler, y jóvenes mujeres, fueron ordenados a cavar profundas y anchas trincheras a lo largo de la frontera oriental para prevenir que los tanques rusos avanzaran hacia Prusia del Este.

A mediados de julio de 1944, mi papá fue reclutado en el ejército. Con el corazón roto, dejó a mi madre y a sus ocho hijos atrás. Lágrimas rodaban por sus mejillas cuando abrazaba a cada uno de sus hijos para despedirse. Yo nunca había visto a papá llorar antes. Yo me preguntaba ¿qué había pasado? Mamá nos explicó más tarde que papá había sido reclutado en el ejército. No tuvo que pelear como un soldado combatiente pero se le ordenaba a preparar el campo de batalla, cavar trincheras, construir estructuras, o destruir puentes.

Sólo por un corto tiempo pudieron los soldados alemanes prevenir que el ejército ruso llegara la a la frontera a invadir Prusia del éste. Hitler y su comandante local, Erick Koch, no tomaron previsiones para los civiles en caso de una ofensiva rusa. Su orden era sostener el frente prusiano bajo cualquier circunstancia y no permitir que la gente se fuera. Quería mantener las autopistas y caminos libres para que los soldados pudieran pelear contra los rusos si invadían Prusia del Este. Sin embargo, muchos alcaldes tomaron la iniciativa de ordenar a sus ciudadanos abandonar sus casas e irse al oeste.

CAPÍTULO 8

Escape de Prusia del Este

Sucedió el 3 de agosto, 644, un mensajero de Whitney vino en bicicleta. Toco la puerta a medianoche. Mamá se despertó y se apresuró a la puerta, pensando que tal vez algún vecino necesitaba ayuda. Y en su lugar, cuando abrió la puerta, le sorprendió ver a un extraño parado frente a ella. Él le anunció, "¡los rusos vienen! rápido, rápido, ¡deben irse!. Vayan a la plaza de la villa a las 9:00 am esta mañana". Antes de qué mi madre tuviera la oportunidad de hacer alguna pregunta, el extraño montó su bicicleta y se fue.

Mamá, impresionada por las noticias tan lúgubres, se precipitó en la habitación, gritando, "Niños levántense rápido; tenemos que irnos en unas cuantas horas; los rusos están llegando". Saltamos de la cama y seguimos las órdenes de Mamá: Georg, tú prepara la carreta, alimenta los caballos, y lleva contigo mucha avena. También, dale suficiente heno a las vacas. Emma, tu junta todas las salchichas y el jamón del ahumadero. Empaca los alimentos enlatados del sótano y toma un saco de harina del ático. Meta, tu empaca ropa para todos. También, toma abrigos de invierno, suéteres gruesos, calcetas de lana, y guantes. Edmund, Richard, ustedes alimenten a los pavos, gansos, patos, y gallinas. Hilda, Tu baña y viste a Horst. Desde la medianoche hasta el amanecer, nos apresurábamos de un lado a otro para estar listos lo más rápido posible. Mamá descubrió solamente dos hogazas de pan en la despensa.

Inmediatamente, encendió el horno y preparó masa para pan. Mientras la masa se alzaba, ella reunió toda su vajilla fina, cubiertos de plata, y otros artículos domésticos valuables en una caja de madera. Mamá le pidió a Georg y a Edmund cavar un hoyo grande en el jardín para enterrar la caja, esperando encontrar sus cosas cuando regresáramos a casa. Mamá logró tener listas cinco Ogassa de pan más antes del amanecer. Aún calientes, las puso en un saco limpio para que se enfriaran y después las colocó en la carreta. Nos apresuramos sin parar iluminados por una linterna hasta el amanecer, empacando todas las cosas que pensábamos que podríamos necesitar.

El sol salió y esparció sus rayos dorados alrededor de nuestra casa y sobre los campos como cualquier otro día. Rápidamente, Mamá reunió la familia alrededor de la mesa del comedor, y después de dar las gracias, sirvió una sopa hecha de albóndigas de harina hervidas en leche. La llamamos "Klunkersupper" en el dialecto del de Prusia del Este. También frío algunos panqueques, hechos mayormente de huevo con un poquito de harina. Ema los junto en un plato de metal, los envolvió en un trapo limpio, y los puso en la carreta con todos los otros alimentos. "Meta, llena una lechera con agua y átala a la carreta", demandó mamá.

Yo también mi casa de muñecas, corrí con mi mamá: "¿me puedo llevar mi casa de muñecas también?" "No, Hildke, no tenemos suficiente espacio en la carreta; sólo llévate la muñeca" Aunque estaba triste de dejar mi hermosa casa de muñecas, obedecí la petición de mi madre.

Todos nos reunimos afuera en la carreta. Mamá fue una vez más de un cuarto a otro y tomo una última mirada a las cosas que ella atesoraba. La tristeza estrechó su corazón y llenó sus ojos de lágrimas mientras ella se despedía de su amada casa, donde habían nacido sus ocho hijos, y donde encontró a su marido y la felicidad al criar su familia. Ella no sabía cuándo o si volvería a ver su casa una vez más.

También estaba preocupada por Marta. Mamá no le podía mandar un mensaje. A todos nos preocupaba lo que podría pasarle. ¿Sería ella capaz de huir a tiempo con la familia del profesor? Estos pensamientos entristecían a mamá. Ella unió sus manos, levantó sus ojos al cielo, y encomendó su seguridad en las manos de Dios. Ella llamó a Ema y Meta y les pidió: tomen toda la ropa de camas de plumas y pónganlas arriba de la carreta también. Mamá caminó rápidamente en el establo y le dio una última mirada sus vacas, terneras, y cerdos. Abrió la puerta del gallinero y dejó salir a las gallinas, gansos, patos y pavos. Les esparció suficiente comida afuera para durar varios días.

Emma corrió con nuestra pastor alemán Senta, la abrazó, y la liberó de su cadena. "Hildke, y Richard, súbanse a la carreta". Ella también se subió con Horst en el frente, a un lado de Emma, quien tomó las riendas. Emma agitó el látigo, y nuestros dos caballos Kastan y Kobel, empezaron a jalar nuestra cargada carreta hacia nuestro pueblo, Wizajny. Meta, Georg, y Edmund caminaban a un lado colina arriba hasta que llegamos a la cima. Emma detuvo a los caballos y dejó que todos se subieran a la carreta. Mamá volteó una vez más a ver a su amado hogar. El pensar que no sabía cuándo o si volvería a ver su casa de nuevo llenó su corazón con una profunda tristeza. Estaba preocupada por el destino de Marta. También se preocupaba por el paradero de su esposo.

Cuándo Emma vio a Senta, nuestro perro fiel, siguiéndonos, se bajó de la carreta. Ella tomó su cabeza, la miró a los ojos, y con lágrimas le pidió: "Senta, debes volver y vigilar la granja. Tú no puedes venir con nosotros; ve, regresa, Senta entendió; obedientemente, regresó y trotó lentamente hacia casa. Emma subió a la carreta y nos fuimos. Pasamos los dorados campos de trigo y centeno listos para ser cosechados en dos o tres semanas. Pasamos pasturas verdes llenas de ganado de pastoreo. Un poco antes de las 9:00 a m., llegamos a Wizajny.

Carreta tras carreta llenaron la plaza del pueblo. Mujeres, niños, y adultos mayores sentados arriba de sus artículos domésticos, cargados rápidamente en sus carretas. "Formen una línea y vámonos",gritaba el alcalde,señalando a la siguiente carreta a entrar a la línea y una larga procesión empezó a moverse.

Nuestro viaje hacia un destino desconocido empezó el 4 de agosto de 1944, y nadie sabía qué tan largo sería o cuando terminaría.

El sol de agosto extendía sus cálidos rayos sobre la sombría travesía de las personas sentadas en sus carretas cargadas. Los niños platicaban y hacían muchas preguntas, pero los adultos no encontraban palabras, pues sus corazones estaban llenos de pena y melancolía por tener que dejar sus casas tan repentinamente. Los caballos trotaron en el polvoriento camino por varias horas antes de detenerse en el bosque de Rominter Heide. Hicimos una pausa para alimentar a los caballos y les dimos agua,la gente comió sandwiches o cualquier cosa que hubieran traído. Mamá nos dio panqueques caseros y un vaso de agua para tomar. Georg empacó avena en los pequeños sacos de alimentar y los ató al freno de cada caballo para que pudieran comer sin desperdiciar nada. Después de qué removió la bolsa de alimento, les dio un balde de agua. Ahora Georg tomó las riendas, y mamá y Horst se sentaron a su lado; yo me senté atrás de Horst mientras Emma, Meta, Edmund, y Richard caminaban a los lados de la carreta.

Las carretas rodaron hasta que el atardecer envolvió lentamente el paisaje; era tiempo de detenernos y buscar refugio en el bosque. Las carretas se movieron a la derecha lo más posible para dejar suficiente espacio para los camiones que pasaran. Mientras mamá y Emma hacían sandwiches, Edmund, Richard, y Yo explorábamos el bosque. "Manténganse cerca de las carretas", nos advertía mamá. "Lo haremos", contestaba Edmund. Nos fuimos. Qué bien se sintió poder correr después de estar sentada en la carreta todo el día.

"Está oscureciendo; deberíamos regresar a la carreta". Edmundo indicó que lo siguiéramos, y lo hicimos. Durante el atardecer, comimos nuestros sandwiches y nos preparamos para dormir en la carreta abierta entre las cobijas de plumas. Cuatro de nosotros alineados al frente y cuatro en la parte de atrás de la carreta, todas las piernas hacia adentro. Las mamás consolaban a los niños que lloraban mientras los ayudaban a dormir. Mis ojos miraban a la luz que disminuía en el cielo y miraban a una estrella tras otra, llenando la oscuridad. Pronto, la lula llena emergió detrás del bosque, expendió un pálido velo sobre el paisaje y los cansados viajeros, y borró a muchas de las estrellas. De vez en cuando, el llanto de un niño, el quejido de un anciano, o el aullar de los lobos rompía el silencio. Finalmente, después de mi oración nocturna, me dormí.

Tan pronto como el sol rompié la oscuridad de la noche y besó la creación de la vida, nos levantamos. Las aves trinaban felizmente en el bosque, mientras las tristes y asonoras melodías resonaban en los corazones de las madres y los viejos. Después de que comimos y de que los caballos devoraran sus avenas, Georg ató los caballos a la carreta y seguimos la marcha. El golpeteo de las herraduras de los caballos creaba un sonido rítmico mientras jalaban su preciosa carga de personas, comida y artículos domésticos hora tras hora hasta el atardecer. Los rayos dorados barrían suntuosamente los campos y prados mientras nos aproximábamos al pueblo de Goldap.

Entramos en la plaza del pueblo, rodeada de una hermosa iglesia y otros edificios importantes. Los soldados asignaron las carretas a varias calles y casas para pasar la noche. Algunos residentes ya habían escapado, dejando atrás sus casas vacías. Otros aún esperaban en casa, con la esperazna de que el ejército alemán pudiera detener el avance de los rusos por Prusia del Este. Encontramos refugio junto con otras dos familias en una hermosa granja vacía en las afueras de Goldap. Georg desató la carreta y fue a buscar algo de forraje para los caballos. Las madres entraron primero para revisar donde dormiría cada familia. Dado que éramos la familia más grande de ocho, decidieron ocupar una habitación para mamá, Horst y yo; y el resto podría dormir en la sala.

Ambas de las otras familias Kirstein se acomodarían cada una en los cuartos más grandes. Las mamás se reunieron en la cocina. Buscaron y econtraron algo de fruta enlatada en la despensa y papas en el sótano. Decidieron cocinar sopa de papa y servir la fruta como postre.

Los niños fueron a explorar otros edificios en la granja. Trepamos a la cima del pajar y descubrimos un gran toro rodeado de paredes de heno. El dueño quería asegurarse de que sobriviera por su cuenta durante un largo tiempo con una cantidad tan amplia de heno. Estábamos intrigados por su tamaño y aspecto rudo e intentamos provocarlo aventándole heno en la cara. Él se sacudió y empezó a rascar el suelo con su pata derecha. Entre más forraje aventábamos a su cabeza, más rápido rascaba, mirándonos con una ferocidad que me dio escalofríos en la espalda.

"Es mejor que regresemos a la casa antes de que alguien caiga al corral del toro" le pedí a mis hermanos. Bajamos y regresamos a la casa, donde nos esperaba la cena. Cargamos nuestras cobijas de plumas adentro de la casa y nos acomodamos para pasar la noche.

La mañana siguiente, cuando el brillo dorado del sol iluminaba el horizonte, empezamos nuestro viaje hacia Angerburg. Ahora, los soldados acompañaban la marcha. Montaron cocinas exteriores en ubicaciones estratégicas para ofrecer un sandwich o sopa de vegetales con una pequeña ración de carne a los viajeros. Hoy el aire se sentía denso. En el oeste, oscuras nubes se aproximaban a nosotros con prisa. Vimos destellos de luz atravesando el cielo. El trueno sonaba cada vez mas cerca. Mamá se ocupó, sacando una pieza grande de lona que había empacado en la carreta. Con la ayuda de Emma, la expendió sobre las cobijas de plumas.

"Niños, es mejor que se suban a la carreta y se metan debajo de la lona antes de que la lluvia empiece."

"¿Puedo caminar?" Preguntó Emma, "Amo sentir la lluvia tibia corriendo bajo mi cara y brazos."

"Es mejor que subas; no sabes cuándo podrás cambiar tu ropa mojada," Le insistió mamá.

Tan pronto como todos habían encontrado refugio bajo la lona y la lluvia cayó a cántaros. Emma se sentó a la derecha de Georg, Mamá en el medio con Horst, y Meta en la izquierda. Emma y Meta sostenían la lona sobre nuestras cabezas y las suyas. Georg sostenía las riendas para mantener estables a los caballos. Emma y Meta habían atado las esquinas traseras de la lona a la carreta para evitar que el viento la volara.

Poco a poco retrocedí hasta la parte de atrás de la carreta, levanté la lona y saqué mis manos. Las gotas cálidas acariciaron mis manos. Volteé ambas palmas, formé una cuenca, y la dejé llenarse de agua, hasta que se derramó creando una pequeña cascada. Sin embargo, cuando vi el destello de un relámpago y escuché el estruendo del trueno cerca, metí mis manos rápidamente. Temía que el relámpago pudiera alcanzarlas. Los pequeños pozos se llenaron de agua. Cuando las gotas de lluvia tocaban la superficie de los charcos, creaban pequeñas fuentes. Mis pies morían de ganas de bajar y correr en los charcos de agua. La lluvia escurría por la espalda de los caballos y bajaba por sus crines. De vez en cuando, sacudían sus cabezas para liberarse rápidamente del agua. Sus pieles se veían limpias y brillantes mientras trotaban sobre el camino enlodado. La lluvia cayó por lo que pareció ser un largo tiempo. Los campos y los bosques recibían la lluvia que lavaba el polvo de sus follajes.

Poco a poco, los truenos se oían cada vez mas distantes, los relámpagos se atenuaban y se hacían mas pequeños, y pronto la lluvia se detuvo por completo. Un hermoso arcoiris cubría el cielo al mismo tiempo que el sol salía. Emma y Meta jalaron la lona, y mi mamá les ayudó a sacudir el agua que se había juntado en la lona. "Mamá, mamá, ¿me puedo bajar ahora?" Le pregunté emocionada. "Puedes bajarte, pero quédate del lado derecho, cerca de la carreta."

Antes de que pudiera terminar la oración, salté de la carreta. Edmund y Richard me siguieron. Dejamos nuestros zapatos en la carreta. Qué emocionante era cruzar los charcos de agua tibia. Richard levantó su pie derecho fuera del agua y me salpicó. Rápidamente lo salpiqué de regreso. Edmund se unió a nosotros. Correteamos por un rato. Se sentía tan bien correr después de estar sentados en la carreta por lo que pareció un largo tiempo. Vimos otro charco grande. Richard y Edmund empezaron un concurso de salpicadero. Richard levantaba su pie derecho, moviéndolo hacia atrás, y con la planta aventó un chorro de agua al aire. "A ver si puedes llegar más lejos que yo," Richard retaba a Edmund.

"Por supuesto que puedo," Respondió Edmund. Levantó su pie y lo movió hacia atrás. Perdió el equilibrio y se cayó al agua, creando una gran salpicadura. Me reí a carcajadas, lo que lo apenó y lo hizo enojar.

"No te rías de mi, pequeña Biskraet (sapo feo, en dialecto). Te voy a alcanzar," me gritó. Salí corriendo antes de que él se levanara. Temía que me castigara por haberme burlado de él. Me sentí culpable y me disculpé con él. Cuidadosamente, me escondí detrás de Richard mientras esperaba su respuesta. Cuando dejó de perseguirme, supe que había aceptado mis disculpas. Toqué a Richard en el hombro, "Vamos a jugar a las traes", y corrí lejos de él. Richard corrió a tocar a Edmund y lo metió en el juego también.

Emma y Meta se bajaron de la carreta para estirarse y disfrutar de una caminata ligera, al igual que muchos otros viajeros. Horst se durmió en el regazo de mamá. Ella tomó una de las almohadas cuadradas, la acomodó en forma de cuna, y colocó a Horst en ella para que continuara su siesta.

A medio día, llegamos a la villa de Budden. Todos esperaban detenerse para un descanso breve. Sin embargo, el líder mandó la orden de carreta en carreta de continuar para llegar al siguiente pueblo antes de que cayera la noche.

Mamá nos llamó a la carreta. Ella preparó un sandwich con salchicha casera para cada uno de nosotros. Sabía muy bien en el campo. Cansada de jugar, me acosté y me dormí.

Para cuando desperté, podía ver el pueblo de Angerburg a la distancia. La aguja de la iglesia, la torre y el castillo, que se erguía en una clina, formaban una silueta placentera. Recorrimos el río Angerapp por un tiempo corto antes de llegar a la plaza del mercado del pueblo.

Los habitantes del pueblo alcanzaron las carretas y ofrecieron sus hogares a los viajeros para pasar la noche. Cuando llegó nuestro turno, el oficial que designaba lugares preguntó "¿Quién tiene espacio para una madre con siete hijos?" Un caballero viejo dio un paso al frente, "Yo los tomaré". Cuando se acercó a la carreta, se presentó como el señor Lemke y nos invitó a su casa. Georg le pidió que subiera a la carreta. El saludó a toda la familia y mi madre le agradeció por hospedarnos en su hogar. El señor

Lemke y mi mamá hablaron todo el camino. El le preguntó a mi madre de donde venía y hacia dónde pensaba ir.

"Me gustaría quedarme tan cerca de Wizajny como sea posible, para que cuando la guerra acabe, pueda volver a mi hogar" le respondió mamá.

"Yo escuché la radio esta mañana; el ejército ruso avanzó 1000 kilómetros en las últimas seis semanas y no está muy lejos de la frontera de Prusia del Este. Hasta ahora, Prusia del Este era un oasis de paz, pero ahora me temo que el ejército rojo invadirá nuestra área. No sé por cuánto tiempo puedan los soldados alemanes detener el avance de los rusos. En este punto, no me importa si ganamos o perdemos la guerra. Solo quiero que termine antes de que Prusia del Este caiga en manos de los rusos. Temo por mi esposa; tiene una artritis incapacitante y está en cama. En su condición, no puede viajar. Así que, no tengo otra opción más que permanecer aquí. El solo pensar que ella pueda ser torturada o asesinada por los soldados rusos me hace temblar" expresó consternado el señor Lemke a mi mamá.

"Yo estaría aterrorizada de ver a mis hijas ser brutalizadas por soldados rusos también. Esuché que violan mujeres sin importar su edad. Dios no permita que lleguen a lastimar o matar a mis hijas," mamá dijo mientras su expresión se tornaba siniestra, y encogía sus hombros.

"Esperemos que eso nunca suceda", respondió el señor Lemke. Después él señaló a la granja al frente, "Esa es mi casa. Niños, pueden bajarse y correr. Pero sean silenciosos, mi esposa está enferma y puede estar dormida."

Edmund, Richard y yo saltamos de la carreta y corrimos a la casa. Calladamente, miramos alrededor mientras la carreta llegaba al patio. "Esperen, niños, primero quiero mi esposa los conozca a todos." Con esas palabras, él esperó a que todos estuviéramos agrupados en la puerta principal, después nos pidió que entráramos. El señor Lemke tocó la puerta del dormitorio primero, "Traje a una madre con siete hijos a quedarse con nosotros por un tiempo. Querida, (Liebchen),

¿se puede pasar?" Cuando la escuchó decir "Si, pasen," abrió la puerta del dormitorio. La señora Lemke usaba un camisón tejido rosa y descansaba en cama. Nos recibió con una sonrisa cuando el señor Lemke nos la presentó "esta es mi esposa, Erna Lemke," después, señalando a mi madre, "y esta es la señora Bonacker y sus siete hijos. Dejaré que la señora Bonacker te presente a sus niños." Mamá nombró primero a mis hermanas mayores, después los tres niños, después a mi y al último a Horst, a quien llevaba en brazos. Las niñas sonrieron e hicieron una reverencia, los niños inclinaron sus cabezas y sonrieron cuando mi madre los presentó uno por uno.

La señora Lemke nos dio la bienvenida. Después el señor Lemke nos mostró la sala, donde se suponía que dormiríamos. También llevó a mi mamá a la cocina. "Esta es nuestra cocina. Tendremos que tomar turnos para cocinar. Ahora puedes usarla. Nosotros ya comimos antes de que yo fuera al pueblo. Tus hijos deben tener hambre. Adelante, instálense."

Mamá estiró su mano y, con un apretón de manos, respondió. "Muchas gracias por compartir su hermoso hogar con nosotros." Después mi mamá nos dijo: "Vayan por las cobijas de plumas y sábanas y tráiganlas a la casa. Emma y Meta, ustedes preparen la cena." Emma y Meta tomaron las provisiones de comida a la cocina y prepararon sandwiches de salchicha para nosotros.

Después de la cena, Richard y yo salimos para explorar la granja. Encontramos al señor Lemke ordeñando a la vaca. Investigamos el jardín de vegetales a lado del establo. No nos atrevimos a recoger unpepino o a sacar una zanahoria del suelo. Las manzanas rojas y las peras en su punto que nos veían desde los árboles nos tentaban aún mas. Mamá nos había prohibido estrictamente el tomar nada que no nos perteneciera. Así que, solo pasamos de largo, añorando el sabor de una jugosa manzana o una dulce pera. Mientras corríamos por el gallinero, las gallinas saltaban y cacaraqueaban ruidosamente. Georg y Edmund habían atado a los caballos junto con los del señor Lemke y puesto una paca de heno frente a ellos. Pronto, mi mamá nos llamó a la casa. Era hora de dormir.

El segundo día, el señor Lemke me permitió visitar a la señora Lemke. Entré en la habitación bellamente decorada y saludé a la señora Lemke con una reverencia y un "Buenos días, señora Lemke."

"Acércate, pequeña", me invitó a acercarme a ella. Tomó mi mano y me preguntó mi nombre.

"Hildegard," le respondí.

"¿De dónde vienes?"

"De Wizajny," le respondí.

"¿Hacia dónde vas?"

"No lo se," le respondí, encogiendo mis hombros.

La señora Lemke no hizo mas preguntas; en su lugar, me invitó a sentarme en la cama a su lado: "Te voy a contar una historia. ¿Conoces el cuento de Hansel y Gretel?"

"¡No!"

"Entonces te lo contaré,"

Ella empezó, "Hansel y Gretel vivían en el bosque. Un día, mientras recogían bayas, se perdieron. Encontraron una casa de galleta de jengibre en donde vivía una bruja, que quería matarlos y comérselos. Pero Hansel era valiente; empujó a la bruja dentro del horno. Encontraron su camino de regreso a casa. Sus papás los recibieron con gran alegría cuando volvieron ilesos del bosque."

"Ves, Hildegard, nunca debes alejarte sola de tu casa; o si no, una bruja podría atraparte a ti también" me advirtió.

"No, no, yo nunca me alejaré de mi madre," le aseguré mientras pensaba en la bruja malvada. Ella soltó mi mano y me dejo ir.

"Puedes volver mañana si quieres."

"Gracias; lo haré. ¿Puedo traer a mi hermano Richard también?" le pregunté.

"Claro."

Corrí de regreso con mamá y le reporté que la señora amable me había contado un cuento. Ella nos había invitado a Richard y a mi a volver mañana por otra historia.

"Eso está bien, puedes ir otra vez," me informó mamá. Yo estaba muy feliz de que mamá lo aprobara. Esperaba con ansias mi siguiente visita a la señora Lemke.

Después de la comida, Edmund nos invitó a Richard y a mi a ir al pueblo. Caminamos a lo largo del lago y llegamos a la plaza del pueblo donde estaba el ladrillo rojo de la iglesia de San Pedro y Pablo. La iglesia había sido construida en un estilo arquitectónico romano simple. El colosal reloj en la torre tocaba la una. Edmund quería ver el interior de la iglesia. Empujó la pesada puerta. Para su desmayo, la encontró cerrada. Caminamos a través de una parte del pueblo y descubrimos el antiguo castillo. Exploramos el patio y buscamos puertas abiertas, pero no tuvimos suerte al mirar adentro. Después caminamos por el lago antes de regresar a la granja.

Cuando Georg vio a Edmund, le pidió que lo ayudara a limpiar el pesebre de la vaca. Richard y yo buscamos para ver si podríamos encontrar un pedazo de un plato de porcelana para jugar a "la escuela." Cuando no pudimos encontrar ninguno, él agarró dos pequeñas piedras planas y me dio una, "esto servirá."

El agarró un palo y dibujó un gran rectángulo en el suelo. Después lo dividió en seis cuadros iguales de aproximadamente un pie y medio de ancho. Dibujó un semicírculo en uno de los extremos del rectángulo, que se llamaba cielo (Himmel).

Richard me ofreció empezar el juego que llamábamos clase (Klasse). Tomé mi piedra y la tiré hacia atrás. Si caía fuera de las líneas o en una línea, perdía mi turno. Cuando caía adentro de un rectángulo o en el cielo, podía empezar a empujar la piedra a la siguiente casilla con el pie derecho mientras levantaba el izquierdo del suelo. Mi piedra cayó en el segundo cuadro, así que lo empuje al tercero. Sólo podíamos empujarla una vez por turno.

Richard aventó su piedra hacia atrás justo en el cielo y luego la empujó directamente a la cuarta clase. El objetivo era pasar por todos los cuadros (clases) sin fallas tan rápido como fuera posible para ganar el juego. También podías empujar a tu oponente fuera de la clase o en una línea con tu piedra. Entonces él tendría que empezar desde el principio otra vez. Jugamos cuatro juegos. Richard ganó tres juegos y yo solamente uno.

Cuando vimos al señor Lemke, le preguntamos, "¿podemos visitar a la señora Lemke ahora?" Cuándo dijo que sí, entramos a la casa y tocamos la puerta de la habitación. "Entren" respondió la señora Lemke. Abrimos la puerta y caminamos hacia ella. Después de una reverencia, le presenté a mi hermano Richard; ella nos pidió que nos sentáramos en el piso al lado de la cama. "¿Cuál cuento quieren oír hoy, Rumpelstilzchen o La Caperucita Roja?"

Antes de qué Richard tuviera la oportunidad de hablar, respondí rápidamente, "la caperucita roja, por favor". No sentamos ahí en silencio mientras ella nadaba como la caperucita roja llevaba una canasta llena de comida a su abuela que vivía en el bosque. Caperucita roja encontró que el lobo grande y malo se había comido su abuela y que para su horror, dormía en la cama de su abuela. Ella corrió por el cazador. El vino, abrió el estómago del lobo, y sacó a la abuela, que aún estaba viva. El cazador llenó el estómago con piedras y lo cosió. Cuando el lobo despertó de su sueño tenía sed. Fue al río a tomar agua, se agachó, y se ahogó. Caperucita roja y su abuela vivieron felices por siempre.

Eso es todo por hoy; pueden volver mañana. Richard y yo nos levantamos. Nos dimos un apretón de manos.

Yo le expresé nuestra gratitud con las siguientes "palabras gracias, muchas gracias por contarnos tus historias; te veremos mañana."

Corrimos de regreso a la cocina, donde mamá y la cena nos esperaban. El señor Lemke trajo una lechera llena de leche tibia, algunas salchichas, y pan recién horneado. Señaló a los gabinetes de la cocina, "pueden usar los platos de porcelana y las tazas que están ahí."

Después de qué Mamá agradeció al señor Lemke, Emma y Meta pusieron la mesa con los coloridos platos de porcelana. La mesa se veía festiva. Sin embargo, un ramo de flores frescas la hubiera mejorado. Después de qué todos los niños nos sentamos y juntamos nuestras manos, mamá agachó su cabeza y agradeció a Dios por la seguridad de sus hijos, el generoso casero, y sus regalos. Tan pronto como ella dijo "Amén", todas las manos alcanzaron un pedazo de pan y algo de salchicha. Sabía muy bien con un vaso de leche fresca. El aire tibio de agosto, lleno con el aroma de las flores, entraba a través de la ventana abierta. El sol empezaba descender y pintaba el horizonte de naranja y dorado. Una suave brisa llevaba la melodiosa canción de un ruiseñor a través de la ventana. La noche expandió su suave y oscura capa gentilmente sobre la tierra y puso a la naturaleza y a las personas a dormir. Sin embargo, no pude dormir por un tiempo, pensando en el lobo grande y malo y esperando que no viniera a devorar a ninguno de nosotros.

Al día siguiente, mientras comíamos el desayuno, escuchamos una voz masculina gritando, "Atención, esto es una orden." Todos salimos corriendo de la cocina y vimos a un mensajero montado en un caballo. Cuando nos vio, continuó anunciando a través de su megáfono, "la pastura está llena de vacas que necesitan ser ordeñadas. Vengan y traigan tantos contenedores como puedan. Vayan a la plaza del pueblo y alguien los llevará a la pastura." El mensajero bajo el megáfono con estas palabras y se fue para entregar el mensaje al siguiente rancho.

"Mamá, mamá, podemos ir Richard y yo", le rogué a mamá. "Solo si prometes mantenerte cerca de Emma y Meta y ayudarlas," respondió mamá.

Yo respondí, "lo haré; lo haré, lo prometo," saltando arriba y debajo de la emoción. Richard y yo corrimos con Emma y Meta, que juntaban y lavaban tinas y lecheras. Nos fuimos. Emma y Meta llevaban las lecheras y una tina; al igual que Georg y Edmund. Richard y yo los seguíamos mientras mamá y Horst se quedaron en casa.

Llegamos al mercado donde la gente pasaba hacia las pasturas designadas. Pronto después de que nos fuimos del pueblo, escuchamos el mugir de las vacas en la distancia. Entre más nos acercamos al campo más fuerte se escuchaba. "Guau, mira todas esas vacas," exclamó Georg, impresionado.

Edmund añadió asombrado mientras miraba el vasto número de vacas en dos pasturas separadas, "nunca había visto tantas vacas antes. ¿De dónde vinieron?"

Las vacas que necesitaban ser ordeñadas estaban reunidas en una pastura, y las que ya habían sido ordeñadas llenaban el campo adjunto.

Muchas mujeres ya habían ordeñado, y muchas más llegaban a llenar sus contenedores con leche fresca. Emma y Meta encontraron cada una a una vaca. Le dieron palmaditas a la vaca primero en su cabeza y después en la panza antes de sentarse en las tinas y empezar a ordeñar. Escuchamos el chorro ruidoso golpear el metal del fondo del balde, mezclado con el mugir de las vacas. Algunas vacas que no habían sido ordeñadas por varios días tenían las ubres extendidas y sentían dolor cuando las tocaban. Al principio pateaban y mugían en agonía pero después se calmaban cuando la presión en sus ubres se había liberado, y la última gota de leche estaba en el balde.

Emma nos pedía que nos mantuviéramos cerca a ella. Emma y Meta llenaron un balde tras otro, después lo vaciaban en las lecheras. Cuando la lechera estaba llena la mitad, Emma les pedía a Georg y Edmund que le llevaran de regreso a la granja para que mamá la vaciara.

"Asegúrense de volver lo más rápido posible," ella insistía. "Lo haremos," le aseguraba Georg.

Cuando Georg y Edmund traían la leche, mamá la vaciaba en una tina portátil de metal. Lavaba la lechera y mandaba a los niños de regreso a la pastura con seis sandwiches en un plato de metal envueltos en un trapo limpio de cocina. Se los dio a Georg, advirtiéndole, "asegúrate de no comértelos en el camino."

Las campanas del reloj de la iglesia tocaron 12 veces cuando Edmund y Georg pasaban a través del pueblo. Ellos sabían que era hora de comer y se apresuraron a la pastura. Les tomó un tiempo encontrar a Emma, Meta, Richard y a mí entre la multitud. Todos estábamos felices de llenar nuestros estómagos vacíos con sandwich de salami acompañado de un trago de leche tibia.

Después de una breve pausa para comer, Emma y Meta continuaron ordeñando hasta que llenaron las dos lecheras y los baldes. Después todos regresamos a la granja con nuestra leche fresca.

"Estoy feliz de que el día ha terminado. Me duelen las manos," Remarcó Emma.

Meta añadió "las mías también están a doloridas. Nunca había ordeñado a tantas vacas en un día. Algunas vacas no habían sido ordeñadas por algún tiempo. Sus ubres estaban extendidas al punto de explotar."

"Sí, las pobres vacas sufren sin nadie las ordeña frecuentemente."

"Vezs que afortunados son los toros; ellos no necesitan ser ordeñados," interpuso Georg y rió.

Ema y metas rieron también," sí, seguro que son afortunados, tampoco dan a luz a sus crías."

Para cuando llegamos a la granja, el sol estaba abajo y le daba a nuestras cejas un brillo dorado. Mamá nos recibió con la cena. Utilizando la leche fresca, hizo una sopa con albóndigas en ella. Ella tomó de nosotros los botes llenos y los vació en la tina de metal. Colocaron las dos lecheras en la despensa, que no tenía ventanas y era más fresca que los otros cuartos. Pronto después de la cena, Emma y Meta fueron a dormir. Todos nos sentamos alrededor de la mesa y hablamos por un rato antes de unirnos a ellas, y el sueño vino rápidamente, y cerramos nuestros ojos.

Cuándo el suave rosado del amanecer entró a través de la ventana, nos levantamos e iniciamos otro día ocupado. Mamá les pidió a Emma y a Msta que ayudaran a ordeñar y le dio leche a alguien más. Teníamos suficiente por el momento. Así que, fueron a la pastura con los baldes vacíos y mis hermanos y yo las seguimos.

Mamá esperaba hasta que suficiente crema se asentaba en la superficie de la leche. La removía y la vaciaba en un barril para hacer mantequilla. Mamá después se sentaba al lado del barril, colocando el vástago con el disco redondo de madera adentro. Ella cerraba el barril con una tapa de madera y empujaba el disco interno vigorosamente hacia arriba y hacia abajo para mover la crema rápidamente alrededor. Después de un tiempo se formaban grandes grumos. Mi mamá removía los grumos de mantequilla y los colocaba en una olla de agua fría. Los movía para enjuagarles la leche. Repetía el proceso hasta que el agua salía limpia. Después ella exprimía todos los pequeños grumos juntos y formaba una gran bola de mantequilla. La colocaba en una olla y la llevaba a la bodega fría. También guardaba mantequilla en el sótano para evitar que se tornara rancia. Mamá también dio al señor y la señora Lemke un gran pedazo de mantequilla para expresar su gratitud por cobijar a su gran familia y darle todos los utensilios necesarios. La ordeña y la mantequilla siguieron por un corto periodo de tiempo antes de qué un mensajero viniera y nos dijera que nos alistáramos para dejar el pueblo en dos días.

Mamá, Emma, y Meta lavaron todas las sábanas y ropa y hornearon pan para el camino. George y Edmund cepillaron a los caballos y le pidieron al señor Lemke algo de avena para los caballos para el camino. Richard y yo pedimos permiso para visitar una vez más a la señora Lemke y escuchar tal vez otra historia. La señora Lemke que disfrutaba contar historias a los niños y agradecía la oportunidad de entretenernos. Nos dijo algunas bromas de Max y Moritz de libro de Wilhelm Busch para alegrarnos. Al final, la señora Lemke que nos advirtió que no repitiéramos esas travesuras. Aunque la tristeza ensombrecía su amable cara porque ella sabía que no volvería a vernos, ella aún quería que fuéramos felices durante las breves horas que compartíamos con ella.

Después del desayuno, todos llevamos nuestras pertenencias y cobijas de plumas a la carreta.

"¿Puedo correr con la señora Lemke y despedirme de ella?" le rogué a mamá.

"Hazlo rápido; tenemos que irnos y alcanzar a las otras carretas en unos minutos."

"lo haré; lo haré," le prometí y corrí con la señora Lemke. "Vine a despedirme."

Tome su mano y ella tomó la mía. Sostuvo mi mano en la suya por un tiempo antes de decir con lágrimas en sus ojos, "Adiós, pequeña, que Dios te proteja de todo mal."

"Adiós, señora Lemke," le contesté mientras le di un beso en la frente. Salí corriendo cuando escuché a mi madre llamándome. Mamá entró a la habitación para agradecerle a la señora Lemke y despedirse de parte de toda la familia. Después todos le agradecemos al señor Lemke por dejarnos quedarnos con él y por la buena comida que nos dio para llevarnos en nuestro viaje.

Nos fuimos. Nos unimos a los otros refugiados en la plaza del pueblo y comenzamos nuestro camino. Viajamos por la costa este del lago Mauer, después continuamos hacia el oeste. Sólo hicimos una rápida parada para comer y continuamos hasta el atardecer. Cuando llegábamos a un estado grande ya vacío, decidíamos pasar la noche ahí, y seis carretas nos acompañaban.

Algunos niños se bajaban de las carretas y se conocían entre ellos. La señora Marta Kirstein, una viuda de guerra, tenía una bebé de nueve meses llamada Renate, además de un hijo Waldemar. Ernst Hein era tan sólo un niño de dos años como mi hermano Horst, y Ewald Heisel tenía cinco, El esposo de la señora Heisel había muerto en combate durante la guerra. También conocimos al octagenario padre de la señora Helen Hein. Lo llamamos señor Maschat. Fritz Kirstein, un soldado herido con licencia, acompañaba a su familia.

Mis hermanas conversaban con Grete Kirstein, Wanda y Greta Liedke, y Erna Ambrosat mientras las madres atendían a las necesidades de los niños pequeños. Las mujeres se reunían en la cocina. Revisaban la despensa, esperando encontrarse con algo de comida. Desafortunadamente sólo veían repisas vacías

"Tal vez haya un sótano debajo de la casa. Por qué no buscamos, a ver si podemos encontrar la entrada al sótano, estoy segura que deben tener alguno en alguna parte," ponderó Emma.

"Buscaré afuera de la casa para ver si puedo encontrar la entrada", se ofreció Meta a investigar. Salió y caminó alrededor de la casa, se tropezó con, lo que parecía ser una ventana de una noria, pero tenía una puerta de metal en lugar de ventana. Corrió de regreso a la cocina, anunciando: "creo que encontré la entrada al sótano, pero necesito ayuda para bajar por el pozo. Mi hermana Ema y Greta siguieron a meta a la ubicación."

"Necesitamos una escalera para bajar al pozo. ¿Dónde podemos encontrar una escalera? Verbalizaó Emma.

"Vamos a hacer esto, Meta, Tu ve hacia atrás, agárrate del borde y Greta y yo tomaremos tus manos y te bajaremos."

Así lo hicieron. Meta abrió un poco la puerta y vio una grande y oscura habitación. Afortunadamente, ahí había una escalera que llevaba al sótano.

Meta, sin miedo, pisó la escalera y bajó al sótano. Lentamente, sus ojos se acostumbraron a la semi – oscuridad, y vio algunos barriles en las repisas inferiores. Levantó una de las tapas y olió col fermentada. Después fue hacia el siguiente y descubrió cueritos de cerdo. "Encontré comida," gritó Meta, "Vayan por contenedores. Meta observó a su alrededor y se tropezó con un saco de papas. Tomó una papa tras otra y empezó a aventarlas al pozo, y algunas caían en la tierra.

Mientras tanto, Emma y Greta volvían con unos botes grandes. "Deja de aventarnos papas; sube y toma los botes," le gritó Emma. Meta subió y se llevó uno de los botes, después el siguiente y llenó uno con carne y el otro con col fermentada. "Greta, lleva la carne a la cocina y trae un contenedor para las papas."

Después recogió las papas sueltas y las puso en un montón. "¿Tienes suficientes papas?" preguntó Meta.

"Avienta unas cuantas mas, nos apartaremos del camino."
Cuando Emma consideró que eran suficientes, gritó, "Sube, ya
tenemos suficiente."

"OK," Meta respondiño, "voy a subir". Después de que
Meta aventara suficientes papas del sótano al suelo, subió la
escalera del pozo, cerró la pierta del sótano y Emma y Greta la
ayudaron a salir.

Las madres y sus hijas mayores se reunían en la cocina para
pelar las papas, y preparaban una gran olla de col fermentada,
cueritos de cerdo y papas. Todos devoraron la comida con gusto.
Después de la cena, los hombres fueron a alimentar a los caballos.
Los adultos se reunieron en la sala y conversaban mientras los
niños jugaban afuera. Entramos cuando la noche abrazaba a la
tierra y dejaba caer su oscuro manto sobre la granja.

Las madres y los niños pequeños dormían en la casa mientras
que los jóvenes pasaban la noche en el establo en el henil. Yo
me acurruqué junto a mi madre y mi hermano pequeño. Recé
y me quedé dormida.

Cuando la noche dio a luz a un nuevo día, y el los rayos del
sol atravesaban las nubes y dibujó largas sombras en la tierra,
empezamos nuestro camino. Las aves trinaban, y la canción de
las alondras, ascendiendo al cielo, nos acompañaban. Las nubes
se iban a la deriva, y el sol brillaba sobre los campos dorados
de trigo listos para ser cosechados. Cruzamos el río Angerapp
que decantaba en el Lago Mauer. El río murmuraba su antigua
canción, ignorando la gran caravana de carretas pasando sobre
el puente. De vez en cuando, echábamos un vistaso al lago
Mauer antes de que entráramos al denso bosque de Goerlitz.
Mamá señalaba que Hitler había construido un búnker para él
mismo y su equipo en este denso bosque para esconderse de las
batallas de la guerra.

Pasamos por el famoso búnker, Wolfschanze, que Hilter construyó en 1941 en el bosque de Goerlitz, entre Angerburg y Rastenburg. Hasta 1944, Prusia del Este no había entrado en el fuego directo, y Hitler y su equipo encontraron un lugar seguro en esta región. El búnker consistía en edificios para el mismo Fuehrer y sus generales, comandantes, altos oficiales del gobierno, y asociados cercanos. Tenía hoteles y un casino para entretenimiento del equipo y sus invitados. Los diferentes edificios incluian una estación de gas accesible a través de caminos pavimentados. Un tren diario de de Angerburg hacía una parada en el camino en la estación del búnker antes de llegar a Berlín. Hitler tenía uno de los regimientos más antiguos de Prusia, originario de los tiempos de Federico el Grande, protegiendo su búnker. Después de un atentado de asesinato fallido contra la vida de Hitler el 20 de julio de 1944, por el General y Duque von Stauffenberg, Hitler se volvió mas siniestro y brutal y ordenó a todos los habitantes de Prusia del Este quedarse en sus hogares, incluso si eso significaba la muerte para ellos.

Yo observé alrededor, esperando mirar a un soldado haciendo guardia en el búnker; sin embargo, no vi ninguno. En su lugar, las pisadas de las herraduras de los caballos, el rechinar, y el cascabeleo de las ruedas de las carretas perforaban el silencio del denso bosque.

Atravesamos el pueblo de Rastenburg, que fundaron los cruzados en el siglo XIV al construir un castillo para descansar y protegerse de los guerreros prusianos.

Después de algunos días de viajar a través de campos maduros de trigo y papa, praderas, y bosques, llegamos al pueblo de Allenstein. Entramos a través del arco de la torre alta del castillo, que llevaba a la parte vieja del pueblo. Vimos a la imponente iglesia de St. Jacob dominando el paisaje. Una estatua del astrónomo polaco – germano Nicolás Copérnico guardaba la entrada al castillo.

Hicimos una breve parada en la plaza del pueblo y esperamos instrucciones. El alcalde del pueblo nos dijo que nos quedáramos en Allenstein hasta que hubiera otras indicaciones. Después dirigió a cada familia a una granja o residencia diferente.

Terminamos en un terreno bellísimo administrado por tres hermanas. Sus esposos, reclutados en la Segunda Guerra Mundial, aún eran soldados activos en combate. Nos recibieron cálidamente y nos asignaron habitaciones, con un porche cerrado que daba vista al jardín. Mi mamá le agradeció a las damas y le pidió a Emma y Meta que trajeran nuestras cobijas y ropas adentro de la casa. Georg desató a los caballos, los llevó a los establos y les dio heno y agua. Edmund y Richard empezaron a explorar los alrededores de la granja. Me les uní mas tarde. Los manzanos y perales estaban cargados de frutas maduras. Miramos las peras y anhelamos tener una con ansias. Una de las hermanas debió habernos visto mientras veíamos la fruta; ella comentó: "No agarren ninguna fruta del árbol, solo pueden comer de la fruta que ha caído al suelo." "Si," le respondimos al unísono. Cada día revisábamos el peral para ver si alguna pera había caído al suelo. Cuando vi la primera en el pasto, grité de alegría mientras iba a recogerla. Cada hermano le dio una mordida. Siempre esperábamos por los vientos fuertes o por que las peras maduras cayeran del ábol. Si encontrábamos varias peras en un día de tormenta, le llevábamos una a mamá y a mis hermanas también.

Después de unos días, nos ajustamos a la rutina de las tres hermanas. Emma y Meta fueron con las hermanas a ordeñar vacas en las pasturas cercanas cada mañana y arde. Edmund, Richard y yo fuimos con ellas y juntamos a las vacas en un pequeño corral. Georg se hacía cargo de los caballos, limpiaba los establos y los chiqueros. Nunca supe el nombre de las tres hermanas; nos referíamos a cada una como Liebe Frau (querida dama).

Mamá se quedaba en casa, cuidaba a Horst, y preparaba el desayuno, comida y cena.

El alcalde de Allenstein envió un mensajero a caballo para todos los refugiados, informándoles que el Frente Oriental no había avanzado y que podíamos quedarnos hasta nuevas indicaciones. Recibimos las buenas noticias. Emma le preguntó a mamá si podría ir con su amiga Martha a nuestro hogar en Wizajny y ver si podrían hacer algo para salvar los cultivos en nuestra granja. Mamá no consideró que fuera seguro para dos jóvenes mujeres el viajar solas. Pero Emma insistió en que regresarían inmediatamente si se encontraban con algún peligro. De mala gana, mamá la dejó ir.

Al día siguiente, mamá preparó sándwiches para su viaje. Con lágrimas en los ojos, mamá abrazó a Emma, y con estas palabras:"Que Dios te cuide, hija mía, y que te traiga de regreso a salvo." Emma tomó el paquete de sándwiches y una botella de jugo y rápidamente se encontró con su amiga, Martha.

Emma y Martha caminaron hacia Allenstein. En una hora llegaron a la estación del tren. Después de esperar un rato, tomaron un tren hacia Ratensburg, donde cambiaron a un tren hacia Goldap. Llegaron por la tarde. No había trenes de Goldap a Wizajny. Decidieron pasar la noche en la estación del tren de Goldap para descansar un poco. Muy temprano al día siguiente, cuando la luna llena aún traspasaba el bosque, iniciaron su largo camino a casa. Pronto, el sol comenzó a deslizarse a través de los árboles y dio a luz a un nuevo día. Emma y Martha cubrieron los siguientes cuarenta kilómetros (veinticinco millas) a pie, pasando a través de Rominten, donde se detuvieron por un tiempo breve.

"¿Tú sabías que el Káiser Wilhelm II tenía su castillo de caza en Rominten?" le preguntó Emma a Martha.

"Si, recuerdo que mi madre me contaba sobre los frecuentes viajes de caza que el Káiser hacía a esta área."

Emma respondió: "aunque el Káiser no podía cazar por sí mismo, disfrutaba de las afueras y del ritual de caza con sus amigos."

"Emma, ¿no sería emocionante ver el castillo?" "Si, Martha, pero no tenemos tiempo; vamos."

Dejaron de platicar cuando entraron al bosque y miraron alrededor con precaución buscando soldados escondidos detrás de los árboles. El cacaraqueo de una gallina, el crujido de las ramas y el zumbido de los aviones rompieron el silencio. Exhasutas, cansadas y hambrientas, llegaron a Wizajny antes del atardecer. Una hora mas tarde, partieron hacia la casa de Martha, y unos minutos después, Emma entró al patio de nuestra granja. Emma estaba sorprendida de escuchar voces cuando se acercó a la entrada. Su corazón estaba acelerado al pensar que podría haber soldados rusos en la casa. Emma se quedó parada frente a la puerta y escuchó cuidadosamente, intentando descifrar el idioma que hablaban las personas que estaban adentro.

Cuando abrió la puerta, un soldado alemán, con cara de sorpresa e increduidad, la recibió, "Fraeulein, ¿qué estás haciendo aquí? ¿De dónde vienes?"

"Mi nombre es Emma; soy la hija del dueño de esta granja. Quería revisar y ver si podía preservar los vegetales del jardín para el invierno y cosechar algo de trigo para tener comida en caso de que podamos regresar a casa." El soldado bajó la cabeza igeramente, diciendo, "mi nombre es Hans; por favor, pasa y conoce a mis otros camaradas." Ella entró a la cocina y fue al comedor, donde vio a tres soldados mas sentados en la mesa, comiendo sus cenas. La miraron con gran sorpresa como si fuera un fantasma aparecido del cielo. Señalando a cada soldado, Hans presentó a sus tres camaradas, Erich, Dieter y Peter.

"¿De dónde vienes?" preguntó Erich.

"Vengo de Allenstein, donde mi familia se está quedando temporalmente."

"¿Cómo llegaste aquí? Inquirió Dieter.

"Mi vecina Martha y yo tomamos el tren a Goldap y luego caminamos el resto del camino," respondió Emma, después vio la comida y de repente se sintió hambrienta.

"Debes estar hambrienta, ven y come con nosotros," Peter hizo un gesto para invitar a Emma a sentarse, después fue a traer un plato y cubiertos para ella y llenó su plato con estofado de puerco y vegetales.

"Gracias", le dijo ella y comió con gusto, pues no había comido nada en todo el día. Los soldados esperaron antes de bombardearla con preguntas y advertencias:

"¿Qué te hizo regresar?" "¿Acaso no sabes que es muy peligroso que estés aquí?" El frente ruso está tan solo a veinte kilómetros de aquí. Algunos soldados rusos ya merodean en esta area, es mejor que permanezcas en la casa y no te aventures a ir a los campos."

Emma escuchó y después respondió: "Permaneceré dentro de la casa." Después empezó a recoger la mesa y ayudó a lavar los platos.

"Debes estar cansada. Puedes tomar mi cama por esta noche, yo dormiré con mis camaradas en la sala," le aseguró Hans.

Se sentaron en la mesa por un rato, conversando antes de decir "buenas noches" el uno al otro.

Cansada de la larga caminata, Emma se hundió en la cama sin desvestirse y cayó profundamente dormida.

Emma se levantó cuando salió el sol en el horizonte oriental y pintó las nubes en muchas sombras rosas, naranjas y doradas.

Tomó una toalla y bajó al lago a lavarse la cara, después peinó su cabello con sus dedos antes de volver a casa. Los soldados se ocuparon, preparando el desayuno y la saludaron amigablemente: "¿Dormiste bien?".

"Oh si, muy bien. ¿Puedo ayudarlos en la cocina?" respondió Emma cuando vio a Hans frente a la estufa de leña, poniendo mas leños en las brazas.

"Puedes freír los huevos si quieres; nosotros vamos a calentar leche y a cortar pan. Erich, Dieter y Peter también entraron en la cocina a saludar a Emma y a comer el desayuno. "Emma, no creo que debas quedarte aquí; deberías regresar con tu familia lo mas pronto posible," enfatizó Erich. "El panorama no es bueno para nuestra patria. Hitler huyó a su búnker en Berlín. Hasta Hitler teme que Alemania sufrirá

una derrota." Añadió Dieter,

"El frente ruso está avanzando cada día hacia el oeste y rodenado Prusia del Este. No se cuánto tiempo pueda detenerlos nuestro ejército. Los soldados rusos ya rompieron el frente alemán y se escondieron en el bosque durante el día. Por la noche cometieron actos de vandalismo, dispararon a los alemanes y violaron a las mujeres," advirtió Dieter. "Debes irte mañana. No hay nada que puedas hacer aquí de cualquier manera." Añadió Peter.

Emma escuchó atenta y respondió, "Déjenme descansar un día o dos y ayudar donde ppueda antes de que regrese con mi familia." Todos acordaron que lo más que podría quedarse serían dos días. "Si ustedes insisten, me iré el día después de mañana," respondió Emma. "¿Puedo ayudar de alguna manera mientras estoy aquí?" preguntó.

"Tal vez puedas ayudar a cocinar" respondió Peter. "Déjame ver que puedo hacer," con estas palabras, ella se levantó de la mesa, levantó los platos y los lavó.

Los soldados se levantaron y fueron al establo para alimentar y cepillar a los caballos.

Emma caminó sobre la alfombra del comedor, la movió y levantó las tablas que cubrían la entrada al sótano. Despacio bajó la escalera mientras sus ojos se acostumbraban a la oscuridad. Emma se sorprendió al encontrar un barril casi lleno de col fermentada y otro de cueros de cerdo que su madre había dejado atrás. Pensó que volveríamos pronto y tendríamos algo que comer. Un pequeño saco de papas viejas y con brotes estaba en el piso del sótano. Los soldados no habían descubierto la entrada secreta al sótano.

Emma subió para agarrar contenedores y tomó un plato entero de col fermentada, un costillar y algunas papas para llevarlas a la cocina. No le gustó el aspecto de las papas. Emma recordó que su madre siempre plantaba una parcela de papas en el jardín de hortalizas a inicios de la primavera. Emma fue al jardín y removió el suelo alrededor de las plantas de papa para revisar si podría encontrar papas nuevas lo suficientemente grandes para ser comidas. Ella estaba encantada de encontrar, aquí y allá, algunas grandes, junto con montones de otras mas pequeñas. Se apresuró al establo a buscar un azadón. Después escarbó en el sueño y removió la tierraa lado de algunas plantas de papa cuidadosamente. Sin perturbar el crecimiento de la planta, recogió solamente las papas mas grandes de cada planta y las colocó en una canasta hasta que tuvo suficientes. Sacó un puñado de cebollas y bajó al lago a lavar los vegetales. Puso el costillar y la col fermentada en una olla en la cocina y añadió algo de agua. Colocó mas leños y hierba en el hogar para cocinar la comida. Más adelante añadió las papas peladas y la cebolla picada y lo dejó hervir a fuego lento.

Después ella salió a revisar cuantas vacas estaban cerca en la pastua. Contó solo cinco y se preguntó qué le habría pasado a las otras seis. Todos los gansos y patos se habían ido, solo quedaban agunas gallinas en el gallinero, y un cerdo acostado en un montón de paja en el chiquero. Hans vio a Emma salir del chiquero y se le acercó: "Debes preguntarte qué le pasó a los otros cerdos y vacas, ¿no es cierto?"

"Si," le respondió ella.

"Se los vendimos a tu vecino, que decidió quedarse aquí, aunque los rusos invadan el área"

"Quisiera poder decirte que la guerra acabará pronto, y que podrán regresar a su hogar, pero las condiciones se ven muy lúgubres para la patria. Después de que el General Americano Dwight Eisenhower, con la participación de los aliados, invadió Normandía el 6 de junio de 1944, nuestras defensas fueron debilitadas. Los generales alemanes Erwin Rommel y Gerd von Rundstedt mantuvieron sus posiciones, aunque les quedan menos de un cuarto de los recursos humanos y menos aviones que sus oponentes para defender a sus tropas. Miles de americanos, sus aliados, y soldades alemanes ya han perdido sus vidas peleando en la guerra," dijo tristemente.

"No sabemos por cuánto tiempo podrá la milicia alemana mantener sus posiciones." Hans pausó por un momento y miró la expresión sombía de Emma. Después continuó, "quisiera darte esperanza en lugar de dudas sobre el futuro de tu casa."

Emma lo miró, conteniendo las lágrimas y dijo: "No sabía que el destino de nuestro país estaba perdido."

Olas de pánico pasaron en su mente mientras pensaba en perder su amada granja.

"Vamos, vamos, jovencita, no estés triste. Vamos a ver qué están haciendo los camaradas," intentó en vano Hans para animarla.

"Tu adelántate, tengo que poner una olla en la estufa. Será mejor que regrese a la cocina y revise la comida," contestó

Emma. En el camino a la cocina, las lágrimas brotaron de sus ojos y corrieron por sus mejillas. Salió y recogió un montón de asteres y las puso en la mesa. Las flores animaban su sombrío humos y añadían algo de belleza a la habitación.

Ella meneó la comida y puso un poco mas de madera en el hogar antes de sentarse en la mesa. Después se caminó de una habitación a otra y recordó sucesos de su niñez y juventud. Miró la cuna que su padre había hecho y vio a su madre mecer a sus ocho bebés. Siendo la mayor de los ocho, Emma recordó haber mecido a sus hermanos más pequeños para arrullarlos mientras les cantaba una canción de cuna. Ahora estaba vacia y abandonada en la sala.

Caminó por la rueca en la esquina y giró la rueda con su mano. Pensó en todo el hilo fino que hbaía hilado de lana para tejer calcetas, guantes y suéteres para sus hermanos y hermanas menores. La melancolía y la nostalgia llenaron su corazón mientras sus pensamientos habitaban su pasado. En el alféizar de la ventana estaba una planta de mirto que ella había cuidado por muchos años para tejer una diadema para su velo de boda algún día. Ella no se atrevía a pensar en lo que podría pasar si los soldados rusos invadieran su casa.

Las voces de los soldados trajeron sus pensamientos de regreso al presente. Dejó la sala y fue a la cocina a recibirlos. Ella anunció que la comida estaría lista en una hora.

"Iremos a caballo a revisar el área," recomendó Peter.

"Es peligroso que Emma se quede aquí sola, alguien debe quedarse con ella," sugirió Erich.

"Ustedes vayan, yo me quedo aquí," contestó Hans.

"Tal vez puedan cabalgar hacia la granja de mi vecina y decirle a mi amiga, Martha, que debe estar lista para partir mañana. Les diré donde vive."

"Podemos hacer eso." Confirmó Peter antes de que él y sus dos camaradas fueran al establo y montaran a sus caballos. Emma los siguió y señaló la granja de la familia de su amiga. Ellos dijeron "Auf Wiedersehen (adiós)," y se fueron a caballo.

Una vez que llegaron al rancho del vecino, desmontaron de sus caballos, los aseguraron a un árbol, y tocaron a la puera: "Hola, te traemos noticias de tu amiga Emma", gritó Peter para asegurarse de que el sonido penetrara la puerta. El sonido en la puerta sobresaltó a Martha. Se apresuró a la puerta, y antes de abrir, preguntó:

"¿Quién es?"

"¡Te traemos un mensaje de tu amiga, Emma!"

Repitió Peter. Cuando escuchó el nombre de Emma, abrió la puerta: "Buen día, soldados, ¿qué pasa con Emma?"

"Buen día, Fraeulein, tu amiga Emma quiere que sepas que debes estar lista para partir mañana temprano en la mañana. ¡Es demasiado peligroso para las dos quedarse aquí!" le aseguró Peter.

"El frente ruso está solo a 20 kilómetros (veinte millas y media) al este de Wizajny, y no sé por cuánto tiempo nuestros soldados sean capaces de detener a los rusos," añadió Erich.

"¿Podemos hacer algo mientras estamos aquí?" inquisió Dieter.

"Gracias por ofrecer su ayuda, pero estoy bien," respondió Martha.

"Por qué no vienes a casa de tu amiga hoy y pasas la noche ahí para que puedan irse juntas mañana en la mañana. No es seguro para ti estar aquí sola. Hemos visto soldados rusos en el área," le advirtió Dieter.

El pensar en que soldados rusos podían aparecer durante la noche puso miedo en la mente de Martha, y respondió: "Voy a hacerme cargo de algunas cosas, cerrar la casa y después voy. Muchas gracias por su preocupación y por traerme el mensaje de

Emma. Adiós. Nos vemos mas tarde." Los soldados regresaron a sus caballos y se fueron.

"Aún es temprano; ¿por qué no cabalgamos a la villa?" sugirió Peter.

"Si, podemos hacer eso," afirmó Erich. Tomaron un atajo y pasaron a través de las praderas, galoparon cerca del cementerio y llegaron a la villa de Wizajny.

Usualmente, los vendedores que intentaban vender sus bienes caseros, ganado, y hortalizas, llenaban la plaza del mercado en sábados y domingos. Hoy solo un pequeño número de granjeros polacos ofrecían sus bienes a pocos compradores prospecto. La mayoría de los residentes alemanes ya se habían ido.

Peter y Erich se reunieron con otros soldados a caballo con quienes conversaron. Les preguntaron sobre algún cambio en las órdenes del comandante y sobre si el frente ruso habría avanzado. Uno de los soldados contestó: "Cada día, el frente ruso se mueve un kilómetro mas o menos hacia adelante. Nuestras defensas son demasiado débiles como para hacerlos retroceder. Solo podemos intentar ralentizar la invasión rusa, para que nuestra gente pueda salir de manera segura."

"Si, se ve desolador para nosotros. Ya no hay esperanza de ganar la guerra. Todo lo que podemos hacer ahora es detener a los rusos el mayor tiempo posible para evitar que asesinen civiles," añadió otro soldado. Erich se estremeció al pensar en civiles cayendo en las manos de os brutales soldados rusas, y dijo "Que el cielo ayude a todas las víctimas y a nosotros de esta guerra inútil." Erich y Peter se despidieron con un saludo militar y empezaron a moverse con la cadencia de los caballos. Cuando llegaron a la cima de la colina, llamada Fuchsenberg (Colina del Zorro), hicieron una pausa. El sol estaba en su cénit y exetendia un velo dorado sobre el enrollante campo carpeteado con campos de trigo maduro y verdes pasturas.

"¡Qué hermoso campo! Qué triste que los dueños que han cultivado y trabajado el suelo todas sus vidas hayan tenido que irse." Expresó Peter.

Erich añadió, "Tengo mucha compasión por Emma, así como por todos los residentes que tuvieron que abandonar sus hogares. Quien sabe si algún día puedan regrsar. Odio lo que el Fuehrer ha hecho con nuestro país y nuestra gente. Su grandiosa idea de ser el gobernante supremo de Europa ha derramado tanta sangre, sacrificado tantas vidas humanas, y traído tanta devastación no solo a nuestro país, sino también al mundo. Y aún así, el no quiere rendirse, aunque ganar la guerra sea impensable."

"No, no va a rendirse, su lema es: `Victoria o meuerte.` No escuchó a sus generales cuando le sugirieron rendirse, salvar mas vidas humanas y prevenir la destrucción de nuestra amada patria." Peter citó con desdén, "Si, ¿por qué estamos luchando los soldados?"

"Yo dejé de luchar por el Fuehrer hace mucho tiempo; yo peleo por mis compatriotas y para proteger sus vidas de las brutalidades de la guerra. Espero que todos salgamos vivos de este combate," acordó Erich.

Cuando pensaron en la inminente invasión rusa y en el destino de su amado país, el silencio se apoderó de sus corazones como las garras de un ágila agarrando la garganta de su presa. Un silencio que hizo brotar lágrimas, proclamando el peligro inminente. Después jalaron las riendas para mover a los caballos. Cuando llegaron a la granja, Emma puso la mesa y les pidió que se sentaran para comer.

"¿Dónde encontraste col fermentada y puerco? No los he comido desde que dejé mi casa. Sabe tan bien." Erich comentó después de que comió varios bocadillos.

"Mamá dejó un poco en el sótano. Hay más. Les enseñaré donde está la entrada al sótano."

"Sugerimos que Martha viniera a pasar la noche aquí contigo. Es demasiado peligroso para ella quedarse sola. Ella accedió y vendrá en la tarde." Le informó Peter a Emma.

"Me alegra saber que viene; ella estará mas segura aquí," respondió Emma.

Comieron con gusto y le agradecieron a Emma el haber preparado tan deliciosa comida. Despoués se excusaron con estas palabras: "Vamos a inspeccionar el área."

"Creo que prefiero quedarme aquí con Emma para protegerla," informó Hans a sus camaradas y empezó a ayudarle a Emma a limpiar la mesa mientras sus camaadas montaron a sus caballos y se fueron a inspeccionar el área.

Cuando terminaron con los platos, Emma le dijo a Hans que le gustaría ver qué vegetales podría encontrar en el jardín para la cena. Tomó una canasta de la cocina y caminó al cobertizo por un azadón. "¿Puedo ir contigo?" le preguntó Hans. "Por supuesto," respondió Emma. Emma sacó un manojo de zanahorias, les sacudió la tierra y las colocó en el suelo.

"También quiero sacar mas papas para esta noche."

"Déjame escarbar y tu juntas las papas." Emma le entregó el azadón a Hans, y el removió la tierra de ciertas plantas. Hans hizo muchas preguntas sobre la familia. El admiraba el coraje de Emma de dejar a su familia para regresar a cuidar la granja. A él le gustaba Emma. No solamente tenía ella un carácter fuerte y bueno, además era atractiva, rubia, de ojos azules y de buena figura también. El miró afectuosamente a Emma y le dijo: "No solo eres hermosa, sino también valiente y de buen corazon. Me gustas."

A Emma esto le cogió completamente desprevenida y se sonrojó. Cuando Hans vió que se sonrojaba, el miró al suelo y siguió cavando. Llenaron la canasta con papas en poco tiempo. Emma también sacó algunos nabos y cebollas.

"Vamos a lavar los vegetales al algo. Nos ahorra el tiempo de ir a buscar agua al pozo y llevarla hasta la casa. Hans cargó la canasta con papas mientras Emma cargaba el manojo de zanahorias, cebolla, y nabos a la tabla que cubría la esquina del lago.

"Dame las papas; yo las lavo," le dijo a Hans.

Hans le entregó la canasta. Ella la sumergió y la sacó el agua para quitar la tierra de las papas. Para limpiar las zanahorias, nabos y cebollas, ella sacudió los manojos de atrás hacia adelante.

"¿Por qué no dejamos todo aquí y vamos a caminar? El día es muy bello como para quedarse adentro." Emma accedió. Caminaron alrededor del lago y pasaron los campos dorados de trigo maduro, listo para ser cosechado.

"Desearía que hubiera algo que pudiera hacer para evitar que estos hermosos cultivos se desperdiciaran." Emma remarcó con tristeza.

"Si, es descorazonador. Tuviste que abandonar tu hermosa granja. ¿Quién sabe qué pasará a nuestro país y nuestra gente? Si sobrevivimos a esta guerra, tal vez pueda volver y ayudarte a volver a cultivar tu granja," Con estas palabras, se acercó a Emma, tomó su mano, se detuvo, y la miró a los ojos, esperando una expresión de aceptación. Emma se sonrojó nuevamente y no pudo decir ni una palabra. Ella solamente asintió con la cabeza. Continuaron caminando. Ambos estuvieron en silencio por un rato; pensaron en el futuro y en una posible reunión después de la guerra. Finalmente, Hans rompió el silencio, "no tienes que responder ahora; te daré la dirección de mi casa, y puedes contactarme si quieres una vez que la guerra haya terminado."

"Espero que podamos volver a nuestro hogar después del final de la guerra. Amo el lugar donde nací y he pasado aquí toda mi vida." Continuó Emma.

"Yo nací en Palmnicken, cerca del mar Báltico. Yo, también, amo a Prusia del Este. Mi padre es un pescador y mi madre, una maestra de secundaria. No he visto a mis padres por un tiempo. Espero que hayan podido escapar y que no hayan caído en las manos del ejército ruso." Añadió Hans.

Y Hans vio un montón de flores de anciano en los campos de trigo. Se agachó a recogerlos. Después, se los entregó a Ema con las palabras: "flores hermosas para una adorable Fraeulein." Emma las aceptó con una sonrisa y un "gracias." Hans llevó su mano a su oído y si susurró, "escucha, escucha, las Alondras cantan una dulce serenata para para ti."

"la alegre canción de la Alondra expresa mis afectos por ti," dijo Hans mientras se movió más cerca de Emma e intentó abrazarla. Aunque el corazón de Ema expresaba afecto por él, también, dio un paso atrás y añadió, "mañana tengo que dejarte, quién sabe, si sobrevivimos a esta guerra, no hagamos que despedirnos sea más difícil para nosotros." Hans respetó sus deseos y le soltó la mano.

"Regresemos a la casa; es tiempo de preparar la cena," sugirió Emma. Casi no hablaron el resto del camino. Cada uno estaba absorto en sus pensamientos sobre el desesperanzador destino de la guerra, su destino, y el destino y futuro de su país. Tan pronto como llegaron, Ema puso las flores de anciano en un florero, las colocó en la mesa, y preparó la cena. Ella quería sorprender a los soldados y hacer algo especial para ellos, panqueques de papa. Después de qué Emma peló suficientes papas, las ralló. Mientras tanto, Dieter y Peter también volvieron a casa. Cuando vieron a Emma trabajando tan duro, Dieter ofreció ayudarle. Emma aceptó su ayuda. Ella buscó en la cocina por algo de aceite o de manteca pero no puedo encontrarlo. "¿Qué puedo usar para freír los panqueques?" se preguntó.

"Ah Sí, puedo saltear los cueros de puerco y usar esa grasa para freír los panqueques de papa. Eso está muy bien; todavía tenemos más en el sótano."

"Ven, te voy a enseñar dónde está la entrada al sótano, para que puedan usar el resto de la comida que se quedó ahí." Cuando llegaron al comedor, ella dobló la alfombra y removió las tres tablas que formaban la puerta. "Déjame bajar y encontrar lo que buscas y familiarizarme con las cosas como están ahí abajo." Se ofreció Dieter.

"Por favor, tráeme un costillar de puerco," le pidió Emma. "Está bien, te traeré uno," respondió Ditter. Bajo la escalera, esperó un momento a que sus ojos se ajustarán a la semi oscuridad antes de caminar hacia los dos barriles. Dieter levantó una de las tapas y vio col fermentada al fondo del barril. Cuando abrió el segundo barril tomó un costillar salado de puerco. Ella le agradeció a Ditter antes de qué subiera la escalera al piso. Después colocaron las tablas sueltas sobre las vigas y acomodaron la alfombra sobre el área otra vez para ocultar la entrada al sótano.

"Es bieno saber que aún tenemos algo de comida extra en caso de que no tengamos suficiente provisiones del ejército."

Remarcó Dieter antes de regresar a la cocina para terminar de rallar las papas.

Emma lavó la sal de la carne, la secó, cortó el costillar en tiras, y las frió. Ella removió las tiras de tocino frito y virtió la grasa en una olla ahsta que tuvo suficiente. Emma caminó hacia Dieter y le agradeció por su ayuda. Tomó el recipiente con las papas ralladas, añadió huevos, y unas pizcas de sal. Batió la mezcla y la dejó reposar por un rato.

Mientras tanto, Martha llegó, y saludó a Emma con un abrazo. Le preguntó:"¿Qué estas cocinando? Huele muy bien."

"Estoy friendo tocino y voy a usar esa grasa para los panqueques de papa," respondió Emma. Martha se ofreció a ayudar. "Puedes poner la mesa, Martha, y después ayudarme a

freír los panqueques," le pidió Emma

Martha puso la mesa y ayudó a Emma a freír conjuntos de panqueques de papa. Después, Emma puso piezas nuevas de arcilla en el hogar, calentó col fermentada y sobras de puerco del almuerzo, y esperó a los soldados.

Ya casi eran las 6:00 p.m cuando Peter y Dieter volvieron de su cabalgata de vigilancia. "Tengo mucha hambre", dijo Peter.

"Yo también. Huele muy bien. ¿Qué prepararon las damas?" preguntó Dieter.

Antes de qué Emma tuviera la oportunidad de responder, Peter miró a la estufa, anunciando con alegría: "panqueques de papa, mi platillo favorito No recuerdo cuando fue la última vez que nos comí. Fue hace tanto tiempo "

Unos minutos después, Hans y Erich entraron, y se sentaron a disfrutar de su comida casera.

"Gracias, Emma, por consentir nuestros paladares esta noche. Eres una gran cocinera," Hans elogió a Emma.

"Gracias, Hans, me place hacer algo para ti y tus camaradas," contestó Emma, "Ustedes dan su vida para defender nuestra amada patria, y preparar sus platillos favoritos es lo menos que puedo hacer bajo estas circunstancias," respondió Emma. Todos disfrutaron la cena. Sin embargo, Peter se volvió sombrío cuando anunció: "el frente oriental ruso avanza diariamente; están a menos de 15 km. Desafortunadamente, nuestras limitadas defensas no van a poder repeler al ejército ruso. Pueden sobrepasarnos en cualquier momento."

No sólo eso, la fuerza aérea Rusaa mando 1,400 aeroplanos a 25 millas al noreste de aquí. Quién sabe por cuánto tiempo nuestra división 28 de infantería podrá detener a los rusos. Jóvenes damas, arriesgaron sus vidas al regresar a sus casas. De verdad espero que puedan regresar a salvo con sus familias.

Después de qué todos terminaron de cenar, los soldados se excusaron de la mesa:

"¿Por qué no nos acompañan en el jardín? es una tarde hermosa," sugirió Hans.

"Lo haremos una vez que limpiemos la mesa y lavemos los platos," accedió Martha.

Los soldados caminaron alrededor de la casa para revisar que no hubiera intrusos merodeando cerca del vecindario antes de sentarse en el jardín bajo un árbol de manzanas. Emma y Marta los alcanzaron más tarde. El aroma de las flores reseda llenaba el aire y añadía belleza a la tarde de verano. En el lago, las ranas empezaban a croar su concierto enaltecido por la melodiosa canción del ruiseñor. Todo absorbía un momentáneo interludio de paz en la naturaleza antes de qué sus sueños fueran destrozados y enfrentará en la brutal realidad de la guerra.

Hans rompió el silencio y empezó a lamentar al aire su compasión por su pueblo y su país: "qué diferente sería el destino de Alemania ahora, si el plan de matar a Hitler en el búnker Wolfschanze, en Rastenburg, Prusia del Este hubiera sido exitoso. Claus Schenk Graf von Sauffenberg colocó una bomba en el búnker durante una conferencia el 20 de julio de 1944. Desafortunadamente, no mató a Hitler; solo chamuscó sus pantalones, mató a tres miembros de su equipo, y lastimó a otros presentes. Altamanete custodiado, Hitler huyó del búnker en Rastenburg al de Berlín."

Dieter reveló, "¿tú sabes lo que le pasaría a todos los generales y los miles de civiles que participan en el movimiento de resistencia? Serían cazados y ejecutados por Hitler. Muchos generales y sus familias cometerían suicidio antes de ser colgados o disparados por la Gestapo de Hitler o los soldados SS. ¿Quién sabe, cuantos más inocentes tendrán que sacrificar sus vidas debido a las acciones brutales del Fuehrer y la falta de cooperación de los aliados?"

"A partir de 1938, 1939, y durante la guerra, los generales alemanes, liderando el Wehrmacht (ejército civil), intentaron negociar con los gobiernos británico y americano para derrocar el régimen nazi de Hitler. Sin embargo, ni el primer ministro Churchill ni el presidente Roosevelt cooperaron con el movimiento de resistencia y sus generales," reveló Erich. "Ellos temían que un nuevo gobierno militar en Alemania pudiese ganar poder. Su meta no es solamente erradicar a Hitler y su régimen nazi, sino destruir a Alemania. Los aliados publicaron propaganda de qué los alemanes son crueles nazis. Pintaron al enemigo de su elección, el ejército alemán, y la gente alemana como malos y viciosos para justificar su entrada en la guerra contra Alemania."

"Carl Friederich Goerdeler, uno de los muchos emisarios de la resistencia, intentó convencer a los aliados de qué los alemanes pensaban diferente, que eran personas decentes, y que odiaban el régimen nazi de Hitler, e imploró la cooperación de los aliados para matar o apresar a Hitler. La resistencia planeaba reemplazar la brutal dictadura de Hitler con un gobierno pacífico. La resistencia ya había preparado secretamente una lista de nombres para el nuevo presidente y las otras cabezas de Estado para un gobierno alemán nuevo. Desafortunadamente, todas las negociaciones diplomáticas fallaron," reveló Peter.

Mientras tanto, Emma y Marta entraban al jardín. Peter y Erich se pusieron de pie y les ofrecieron sus lugares. "Por favor, siéntense y acompáñennos."

"Gracias, lo haremos. Que tarde tan serena," remarcó Ema. "Espero que la guerra termine pronto, y que mi familia pueda volver a casa."

Peter fue al establo y trajo consigo dos baldes. Los colocaron enfrente de la banca y se sentaron en ellos. Por un rato, todos permanecieron en silencio, encantados por la serenidad y la belleza de la tarde.

Hans rompió el silencio, "jóvenes damas, a qué hora les gustaría irse mañana."

"Tal vez a las 7:00 a.m.," respondió Martha.

"Creo que deberían empezar antes, para que puedan llegar a Goldap antes de qué oscurezca. Ahí pueden tomar el tren a Angerburg. Estarán más seguras en la estación del tren en la noche que en el camino," les instruyó Hans. "Tal vez 5:00 o 6:00 a.m. sería más ventajoso."

"¿Tienen suficiente dinero para un pasaje de tren?." Les pregunto Erich.

"Tengo 10.00 RM." Le respondió Emma. "Yo tengo 15.00 RM," añadió Martha.

Los soldados consideraron que no sería suficiente para el largo camino de regreso a Allenstein. Cada camarada buscó en sus bolsillos y les dio algo de su dinero.

Con las palabras, "muchísimas gracias," Emma y Martha expresaron simultáneamente su gratitud y añadieron "que generoso de su parte, pero ¿tendrán ustedes suficiente?".

"Tenemos suficiente para nuestras necesidades," respondió Dieter.

Nadie habló por un rato; todos pensaban en sus casas, sus familias, y el profundo afecto que tenían por su país con tan bellos paisajes. Se preguntaban qué pasaría antes de que es la guerra terminara y después de que terminara. Este momentáneo silencio proclamaba la tempestad por venir en el Este.

Previendo la invasión rusa y la tragedia de su gente y su país, Hans quería saborear estos pequeños momentos de paz con sus camaradas y las jóvenes damas. Sacó una pequeña armónica de su

119

bolsillo y empezó a tocar la canción folklórica prusiana "Tierra de bosques oscuros y lagos de cristal." Sus camaradas al principio tararearon, después cantaron un verso tras otro, acompañados de Emma y Martha. Para cuando alcanzaron el cuarto verso, lágrimas habían brotado de los ojos de Emma y de Martha, y en lugar de cantar las palabras, sollozaban. Pensaban en los rusos destruyendo sus hermosas casas y su amada Prusia del este.

Hans entendía sus sentimientos y espero un rato hasta que Emma y Martha reganaron su compostura. Empezó a tocar melodías más alegres para animarlas. Cantaron canciones folclóricas familiares y conversaron hasta que la noche embelleció los cielos con estrellas y una media luna, que ascendió sobre los campos.

Hans se puso de pie con las palabras: "damas, es mejor que duerman un poco," caminó hacia Emma y Martha, estrechó sus manos y les deseó una buena noche.

Con la respuesta, "buenas noches," ambas damas se excusaron y caminaron hacia la casa.

"Creo que me voy a acostar vestida como estoy, en caso de que tengamos que salir a prisa de la casa," sugirió Emma.

"Yo haré lo mismo," respondió Martha. Ambas se acomodaron en la misma cama, cerraron sus ojos, y esperaron a quedarse dormidas.

Afuera, los soldados decidieron que Peter tomaría la guardia en la noche, y que los otros intentarían dormir, también. Por un rato, una lechuza en el establo rompió el silencio con su sonido angustiado.

Repentinamente, pasada la medianoche, despertadas por el estruendo de disparos, Emma y Martha saltaron de la cama y corrieron fuera de la casa. Asustadas, le preguntaron a Peter, quien estaba de pie en la entrada, "¿qué está sucediendo?" "vuelvan a la casa inmediatamente," les gritó Peter mientras se paraba frente

a ellas, añadiendo, "los partidistas polacos nos están atacando."
Hans, Erich y Dieter salieron de la casa y se unieron a Peter.
Todos ellos abrieron fuego. Emma y Martha, una vez adentro
en la sala, se tiraron al suelo. Emma miró al cielo y le pidió
a Dios proteger a los soldados y a ellas mismas de cualquier
daño. Mientras las balas atravesaba en el aire, ellas escuchaban
intensamente. Los soldados se cubrieron en el cobertizo para
desviar la balacera de la casa.

Después de un rato, los disparos se detuvieron. Los soldados
esperaron fuera hasta que consideraron seguro el volver a entrar
a la casa. Sin embargo, Peter y Erich se ofrecieron a quedarse
afuera por si los partidarios estuvieran escondidos cerca y
decidían atacar nuevamente. Afortunadamente, ninguna bala le
dio a los soldados. Hans y Dieter entraron a la sala anunciando,
"El peligro parece haber terminado, al menos por el momento,"
anunció Hans.

"Intenten dormir ahora."

"¿Salió alguien herido?" inquirió Emma. "No, escapamos a
las balas," le aseguro Hans.

"Gracias a Dios las balas no les dieron a ustedes ni a nosotras."

"Escuché a uno de los partidarios quejarse. Una de nuestras
balas debe haber dado con un intruso," añadió Hans. Hans y
Dieter les desearon buenas noches y fueron a su habitación a
descansar mientras Emma y Martha regresaron a su habitación.
Ambas dieron vueltas en la cama por algún tiempo, pensando
en la reciente confrontación con los partidarios y los peligros
que las damas podrían encontrarse en su camino de regreso
a sus familias. Finalmente, después de rezar y pedirle a Dios
su protección, se durmieron por algunas horas. Una tenue luz
entraba por la ventana cuando Emma y Martha se despertaron.
Se levantaron, lavaron, y prepararon panqueques y huevos para los

121

soldados antes de iniciar su camino de regreso. Hans se ofreció a acompañarlas lo que Emma y Martha apreciaron mucho.

Mientras tanto, el sol había ascendido sobre el establo y daba una resplandeciente brillo sobre los campos dorados.

"Qué tristeza llena a mi corazón al ver los campos de trigo desperdiciarse cuando tanta gente no tiene suficiente para comer" remarcó Hans.

"Desearía haberme quedado y pedirle a los vecinos ayuda para cosechar el trigo," respondió Ema en un tono de voz desesperado.

"¡Es imposible que te quedes! Simplemente no sabemos por cuanto tiempo podremos detener el frente Ruso. Desde que América entró a la guerra, Stalin recibió tanques, aviones, y otros suministros militares del presidente Roosevelt y del primer ministro Churchill también." Hans ventiló su miedo a la derrota.

"Nuestros soldados están superados en número, y los suministros de guerra han disminuido. No hay manera de qué peleemos por mucho tiempo y ganar es imposible. Mi principal preocupación ahora es ver que ustedes dos regresen a salvo con sus familias de la manera más rápida."

"Ambas estamos muy agradecidas por tu ayuda. Espero que no sufras ninguna consecuencia por tomar tiempo de tus deberes." Remarcó Martha.

Mis camaradas y yo supervisamos la excavación de trincheras cercanas; nadie sabrá si no estoy ahí por unas cuantas horas," respondió Hans. En lugar de tomar el camino, tomaron un atajo y cruzaron rápidamente la larga pastura para llegar más rápido a la villa. Usualmente, la plaza de la Villa rebosaba de vida; hoy, no había gente; la mayoría de los residentes ya se habían ido. Sólo algunos tanques y camiones de transporte militar estaban en el Ayuntamiento de la villa. Hans, Emma, y Martha caminaron hacia uno de los camiones. Hans le preguntó al conductor si alguien estaba por manejar hacia Goldap y podría llevar a dos damas con ellos. "No sé si alguien más vaya, pero yo no tengo ninguna asignación todavía; yo podría llevarlas a Goldap," le respondió el conductor. Se presentó a si mismo como Heintich Schulz. Hans respondió mientras estrechaba la mano del conductor. Mi nombre es Hans Gudat, y ella es Emma Bonacker y Martha Thomas.

"Gracias por ofrecer tu ayuda, para que las damas puedan regresar con sus familias más rápido," después volvió con Emma y Martha: "este conductor las llevará a Goldap, donde pueden alcanzar el tren," Hans le informó a las damas. Después se volteó con Emma, la abrazó, le dio un beso en la frente, y le dijo: "que Dios te proteja y te permita llegar a salvo a tu destino. Me importas. Hasta luego, querida." Emma miró a Hans, sus ojos se encontraron, y expresaron su afecto el uno por el otro. Ella lo abrazó y se despidió con estas palabras,

"Adiós, Hans. Gracias por protegernos. Si Dios quiere, nos veremos otra vez después de que la guerra termine. Que Dios te proteja."

Él le entregó un pedazo de papel, "aquí está la dirección de mi casa; puedes escribirme una vez que llegues a tu destino, y si Dios quiere, tal vez nos veamos otra vez."

Después Hans se volvió con Martha y estrecho su mano: "adiós, Martha, que tengan un viaje seguro. Espero que te reúnas con tu familia a salvo en Allenstein."

"Muchas gracias por tu ayuda. Que Dios te proteja del peligro y de la muerte." Han se despidió con la mano, y después empezó a caminar prontamente de regreso a la granja.

Heinrich se bajó del asiento del conductor, le dio la vuelta al camión y le abrió la puerta a Emma y a Martha. Ellas se subieron al camión y se sentaron a un lado del conductor. Heinrich puso la palanca de velocidades en marcha y se fueron. Después de un tiempo, ellos llegaron al camino principal de Rominten; pasaron a un lado del camino de hecho por los refugiados. Heinrich les hizo a las damas muchas preguntas, como porque habían vuelto a casa, donde estaban sus familias, hace cuanto habían dejado sus familias, y otras. Mientras hablaban, de repente,un avión voló sobre ellos. Lo que parecieron segundos después, escucharon las detonaciones de las balas perforar el aire y alcanzar a un caballo y una carreta a una corta distancia frente a ellos. Heinrich detuvo abruptamente el camión, saltó, y ayudó a Emma y a Martha a bajarse.

"Corran al bosque, rápido; otro avión se aproxima," gritó Heinrich. Apagó la máquina y siguió a las damas. Finalmente, todo el tráfico se detuvo, y la gente corrió al bosque en busca de cobertura. Se tiraron al suelo y esperaron a que el bombardero pasara.

"Dios mío, espero que no bombardeen la estación de tren de Goldap o las vías del tren a Rastenburg. Espero que puedan regresar a salvo con sus familias," remarcó Heinrich.

Emma suspiró, "Le pido a Dios, que lo logremos."

Un tercer avión se acercó al camión. Afortunadamente el aeroplano pasó sin abrir fuego. Todos esperaron y esperaron hasta que no escuchaban sonidos de los engranes de los aeroplanos.

Heinrich rompió el silencio, "Creo que ya es seguro; vayámonos."

Se puso de pie y ayudó a Emma y a Martha a pararse, también. Caminaron de regreso al camión y entraron en la cabina. Heinrich encendió la máquina, puso la palanca de velocidades en marcha y comenzó a manejar. "Gracias a Dios, mi camión no fue alcanzado. Aún funciona."

Heinrich manejó con prisa a la estación de tren, donde Emma y Martha esperaban tomar el siguiente tren.

"Ustedes dos quédense adentro del camión, voy a averiguar cuando sale el siguiente tren a Rastenburgo," se dirigio Heinrich a las Fraeuleins y fue a la taquilla para ver el horario del tren.

Regresó rápidamente, "El siguiente tren sale a las 11:30 a.m. a Rastenburg." Mirando su reloj, continuó, "tienen una hora y media antes de que el tren parta. ¿Tienen suficiente dinero para comprar los pasajes?".

Antes de que Emma o Martha respondieran, Heinrich buscó en su bolsillo y sacó veinte marcos reales, y se los entregó a Emma, que no quería aceptarlos.

"Muchas gracias; creo que tenemos suficiente para los pasajes" respondió Emma.

"Solo tómenlo; pueden necesitarlo para comprar algo de comida."

Heinrich insistió. A regañadientes, Emma aceptó el regalo. "Tengo que dejarlas ahora y regresar a mi puesto. Espero que regresen a salvo con sus familias y que vivan para ver el final de la guerra." Con estas palabras, Heinrich se despidió de sus pasajeras.

Emma y Martha estrecharon su mano y expresaron su profunda gratitud por su ayuda; "Muchas gracias por traernos aquí. Que Dios te cuide y a tus camaradas, te protega de ser herido, y te lleve a casa a salvo cuando termine la guerra."

Heinrich regresó a su camión y manejó hacia su puesto para reportarse a sus deberes.

Una larga linea se formó en la taquilla, madres con hijos de todas las edades, hombres ancianos, y mujeres que no tenían medios propios de transporte intentaban subirse al tren. Algunos llevaban mochilas, otros jalaban pequeños carros cargados con maletas, sacos, cobijas, pertenencias personales y comida. Algunas personas empujaban carriolas llenas de cosas y cargaban a los bebés en sus brazos. Algunos habían llegado caminando después de horas de las villas cercanas. Aunque estaban exhaustos de jalar sus cargas, esperaban con gran anticipación al tren y la oportunidad de escapar de caer en manos de los brutales soldados rusos, que estaban a una corta distancia de la frontera de Prusia del Este.

Emma y Martha se sintieron afortunadas de que el tren aún estaba en servicio y de obtener boletos para la partida de las 11:30 a.m. Los bombarderos rusos habían explotado muchas estaciones de tren y caminos ara detener el transporte de soldados y de civiles.

La gente se enfilaba a lo largo de las vías del tren, esperando pacientemente la llegada del tren. Finalmente, el humo de la locomotora apareció en el horizonte. El resoplar de los engranes rítmicos de la locomotora y el sonido de las ruedas se hacía cada vez más alto conforme el tren se aproximaba a la estación. Pronto, el tren se detuvo. Las puertas se abrieron, pero extrañamente, ningún pasajero se bajó.

La prisa de entrar al tren comenzó. Las madres con hijos pequeños y otros adultos ocuparon la mayoría de los asientos, lo que obligó a Emma y Martha a permanecer de pie durante todo el viaje.

Pronto después de que el tren llegara a su siguiente destino, un conductor pasó por la multitud, revisando los pasajes de los pasajeros, y anunció que Angerburg era la siguiente parada.

Mucha gente se alineó en las vías, pero solo un pequeño número pudo subirse. El resto, decepcionados, tenían que esperar al siguiente tren.

El resoplar de la locomotora se hizo mas lento, llevando un tren grande y sobrecargado de gente y equipaje. Tomó mucho tiempo alcanzar el siguiente pueblo de Allenstein, donde Emma y Martha se bajaron.

"Gracias a Dios, lo hemos logrado hasta ahorita. Muero de hambre," anunció Emma.

"Yo también," respondió Martha. "Esperemos a salir de la ciudad antes de comer. Me siento culpable de comer frente a niños hambrientos y adultos."

"Esa es una buena idea." Coincidio Emma.

Pensar en comida y en sus familias, aceleró su paso y las hizo ignorar la belleza arquitectónica del pueblo.

Después de caminar a lado de muchas carretas fuera del perímetro de la ciudad, tomaron un pequeño sendero, encontraron una piedra como una banca y se sentaron. Emma sacó una línea de salchichas y una pieza de pan, la partió a la mitad y se la entregó a Martha.

"Ten, Martha, estoy segura de que tu también tienes hambre."

"Gracias, Emma, sí que la tengo." Se siente bien sentarse después de estar paradas tantas horas en el tren," respondió Martha.

Devoraron su comida, se levantaron, y empezaron el último trecho de camino a la granja donde había dejado a su madre y a sus seis hermanos.

Llegaron a un cruce de caminos, donde se despidieron con un abrazo. "Esperemos que encontremos a nuestras familias aquí."

"En verdad espero que no se hayan ido aún. "¡Adiós!"

"¡Adiós!" respondió Emma. Apresuró sus pasos, ansiosa de reunirse con su familia.

Mientras Emma se acercaba a la granja, vio a Hilde y a Horst jugando afuera. Se sintió aliviada.

Tan pronto como Horst y yo vimos a Emma, corrimos hacia ella. Emma se agachó y nos abrazó.

"Qué feliz soy de encontrarlos aquí todavía," suspiró Emma, aliviada.

Cuando Emma entró a la cocina, donde mamá y meta limpiaban la mesa del comedor, mamá casi deja caer los platos que llevaba en sus manos. Los puso rápidamente en el fregadero y abrazó a Emma.

"Gracias a Dios estás de vuelta." No podía decir mas palabras; lágrimas de alegría expresaban más de lo que las palabras hubieran hecho. Meta, Georg, Edmund, y Richard todos se apresuraron hacia ella y le diern un gran abrazo. Incluso los ojos de Emma se llenaron de lágrimas de gratutid al reunirse con su familia. Mamá miró al cielo y envió una plegaria, sin palabras, a nuestro padre celestial, agradeciéndole por retorno seguro de su hija mayor.

"Debes estar hambrienta; Meta, calienta la sopa de borscht y tráeselo a Emma," mamá le dijo a Meta. Mamá volteó con Emma otra vez y le dijo, "cuando termines de comer y descanses por un rato, tienes que contarnos todo sobre tu viaje y cómo encontraste las cosas en casa."

Emma asintió con la cabeza.

"Sí, mamá, lo haré." Después de disfrutar la sopa caliente, ella se excusó y fue a la cama. Emma agradeció a nuestro padre celestial por traerla a ella y a su amiga de regreso a salvo con sus familias, después, exhausta por el largo viaje, cayó en un largo sueño.

Al día siguiente, la familia se reunió en la mesa y escuchó a Emma responder pregunta tras pregunta sobre nuestro hogar. Mamá expresó su gratitud al saber que la casa permanecía sin daños y que no había sido bombardeada o quemada. Mamá se preocupó cuando Emma nos dijo que el frente ruso estaba avanzando rápidamente. Ahora estaba solamente a 20 kilómetros (12 millas y media) de nuestra granja. Los soldados alemanes construyeron trincheras cerca de nuestra casa para parar a los tanques rusos. Los soldados alemanes no sabían cuánto tiempo podrían retener la invasión rusa. Los soldados nos instaron a salir de Prusia del Este tan pronto como fuera posible, pues los soldados rusos tratan a las mujeres alemanas con brutalidad.

Mamá escuchó atentamente, después le pidió a Emma que fuera con Mister Kristein, que se había convertido en el líder del grupo, y le informara sobre la lúgubre situación en casa.

Después de ayudar a ordeñar las vacas en el establo, Emma caminó rápidamente a través de los campos abiertos hacia la casa donde la familia Kristein había encontrado refugio. Vio al señor Kerstein en el porche, fumando su pipa. Lo saludó cortesmente y le dijo sore la situación en casa y el mensaje de los soldados de dejar Pusia del Este lo más pronto posible. El señor Kirstein agradeció a Emma por las noticias pero no dio una respuesta definitiva sobre lo que pretendía o podía hacer.

Después Ema tocó a la puerta, entró, y saludo al resto de la familia. Después de una corta conversación, se excusó y dijo "AufWiedersehen (adiós)" a la familia Kirstein y se apresuró de regreso a su propia familia.

Consternado por el rápido avance del frente ruso, el señor Kristein mandó a sus tres hijos, Fritz, Edmund, y Georg, a notificar a los miembros de nuestro grupo para alistarnos porque teníamos que irnos rápidamente. El señor Kristein estaba agradecido de tener a sus tres hijos con él. Fritz, el mayor era un soldado herido en licencia cuando la familia tuvo que dejar su hogar. Edmund y Georg eran demasiado jóvenes para ser reclutados. Sin embargo, Gustav, el segundo hijo, todavía estaba activo en combate. Por algún tiempo, el señor Kristein no había escuchado noticias sobre su hijo, Gustav, y esperaba que aún estuviera vivo. Ahora él y todas las otras familias pensaban solamente en prepararse para salir rápidamente.

Sin embargo, nadie podía irse sin el permiso del oficial del gobierno (Gauleiter).

El mes de agosto terminó, y septiembre empezó. Con el otoño aproximandose, el clima podía tornarse frío repentinamente. El señor Kristein considero sabio instalar cubiertas en las carretas.

El notificó a todos los hombres capaces en nuestro grupo para ayudar a cada familia a cubrir las carretas.

Un día el grupo llegó a nuestra granja. Trajeron ramas pesadas de sauce y de otros árboles. Los hombres ataron los postes, lo suficientemente largos para formar un arco sobre la carreta, de cada lado de la carreta.

Mamá y Emma buscaron material para cubrir los arcos. No encontraron suficientes cobijas de lana. Mamá le preguntó a la mayor de las hermanas del rancho si tenía algo de tela o más cobijas de sobra.

"Déjame buscar." Con estas palabras, se excusó. Después de un rato, volvió, cargando una brazada de telas y cobijas.

"Toma todo lo que necesites."

"Muchas gracias; creo que esto es más que suficiente."

Cuando Emma volvió, apresuró a su madre para preparar la carreta para la salida. Junto con la carreta, mamá, Emma, y Meta, extendieron las telas en la carreta, empalmando algunas pulgadas. Emma levantó uno de los postes que aún estaban en el suelo y lo usó como regla para medir el ancho y largo de la cubierta. Consideraron un poco de material extra para cada lado y suficiente para cubrir la apertura al frente y atrás.

Mamá, Emma, y Meta las cosieron con hilo grueso, que las hermanas les dieron. Los hombres ataron una cuerda a cada esquina y jalaron las telas sobre los arcos. Una vez que estaban acomodadas apropiadamente, ajustaron las telas con cuerdas a los lados derecho e izquierdo de la carreta. Usaron una tabla delgada y angosta para clavar la tela a las escaleras en cada lado de la carreta. En unas cuantas horas, terminaron el trabajo y fueron a ayudar a la siguiente familia.

Al día siguiente, mamá me encontró llorando en la cama. "¿Qué pasa, Hildke?" me preguntó mamá.

"Tengo dolor en las ingles y detrás de las rodillas." "Déjame ver."

Levanté mis sábanas y le enseñé a mi mamá dónde me dolía. Ella notó enrojecimiento e hinchazón en las ingles.

"Parece que estás desarrollando absesos. Es mejor que te quedes en cama. Te pondré una compresa calienta para aliviar el dolor."

"¿Puedo levantarme para desayunar, mamá?"

"Supongo que puedes, pero después debes volver a la cama."

"Si mamá, lo haré."

Cuando di el primer paso, el dolor aumentó. Sin embargo, logré desayunar y volver a la cama a intentar dormir otra vez, pero no pude porque las pulsaciones incrementaron.

Emma vino y puso toallas calientes sobre el área. El calor calmó un poco el dolor, y pude dormir por un rato.

Por unos días, Emma continuó con las compresas calientes. En el segundo día, escuché al viento aullando, y le pedí a Emma que me llevara al porche cerrado, donde podía mirar hacia afuera. El peral se movía de un lado a otro. Miré con atención por si acaso, alguna pera se caía. De repente, dejé salir un chillido de alegría, "Yippy, una pera se cayó al suelo." Pensé en correr afuera para recogerla antes de que mis hermanos la vieran. Traté de levantarme y di unos cuantos pasos, pero tuve que regresar a mi asiento rápido. El dolor era demasiado severo.

Llamé a Richard. Él no vino. Después llamé a Edmund; el tampoco estaba cerca de la casa. Cuando Emma volvió para cambiar mi compresa, le señalé el lugar donde había caído la pera. Le pedí que fuera por ella. Emma salió y buscó alrededor. Finalmente, encontro no una, sino dos peras y me las trajo. Yo estaba encantada de morder una jugosa y madura pera. Temporalmente, olvidé el dolor mientras masticaba la deliciosa fruta.

El viento trajo lluvia y temperaturas mas frías. Pero mi temperatura se elevó. Cuando mamá vino y tocó mi frente, remarcó alarmada, "Tienes fiebre." Mamá fue con las tres hermanas y les preguntó si tendrían alguna aspirina.

No tenían.

"¿Hay algún arbusto de baya de saúco cerca?" "Si, por las pasturas."

"Bien. Muchas gracias."

Mi mamá llamó a Emma inmediatamente y le dio instrucciones para recoger algunas bayas de sáuco.

Emma tomó una tina y se apresuró hacia la pastura, donde encontró el arbusto de bayas de sáuco cargado con bayas maduras. Ella pizcó racimo tras racimo, llenando la tina a la mitad y caminó apresuradamente a la granja.

Mmi mamá puso una olla de agua en el hogar. Ella y Emma removieron las bayas de los tallos y las pusieron en el agua hirviendo. Esperó un rato, después las aplastó para exprimirle todo el jugo a cada una. Ella coló las bayas con un trapo, llenó un vaso con el jugo, le puso algo de azúcar, y me lo trajo.

"Toma esto. ¡Te ayudará a bajar la fiebre!"

Me tomé el vaso entero. Sabía bien. Traté de dormir de nuevo pero sentía calor primero y después frío. Mi cuerpo temblaba de los escalofríos. Llamé a mi madre y le pedí que se quedara conmigo.

Cuando mi mamá miró los absesos, decidió exprimirlos. Mamá le instruyó a Emma que esterilizara un cuchillo filoso y puntiagudo en agua hirviendo y que trajera una sábana limpia. Mamá cortó la sábana y después rompió algunas tiras y pedazos rectangulares.

"Emma, tráeme el cuchillo. Pon algo de agua en la olla, después sumerge estos trapos en el agua. Espera hasta que se enfríen, y después me los traes."

Emma siguió las instrucciones de mi mamá. Mamá jaló el cobertor y me pidió que me pusiera boca abajo. Limpió cada abceso detrás de mi rodilla con uno de los trapos húmedos en agua con sal. Después tomó el cuchillo y rápidamente picó la cabeza de cada abceso y exprimió el pus a través de la abertura. Mi cuerpo se sacudió y lágrimas rodaron en la almohada cuando sentí el dolor de cada incisión.

Emma dobló el trapo cuadrado y lo colocó en la abertura de los abcesos. Usó las tiras como vendas y las usó para rodear las rodillas y sostener la tela en su lugar.

"Puedes voltearte sobre tu espalda y descansar un momento."

Sentí el dolor pulsátil detrás de mis rodillas y no pude encontrar una posición cómoda. Pronto, mamá y Emma regresaron y me hicieron el mismo procedimiento tortuosoen los abcesos de las ingles. Mi cuerpo ardía en fiebre, y yo temblaba. Estaba exhausta y finalmente encontré algo de alivio en un inquieto estupor y dormí.

Mi mamá le instruyó a Emma que quemara los trapos mjados de pus y sangre para que nadie pudiera infectarse. Al día siguiente, la fiebre aún estaba alta. Sin embargo, cada día la temperatura bajaba, y el dolor pulsante disminuía poco a poco. De vez en vez, Emma me llevaba al porche y me acomodaba en la silla cómodamente. Disfrutaba de ver a las aves y escuchar su trinar y sus canciones. De vez en cuando, una ardilla me entretenía mientras saltaba de rama en rama y mordía una pera.

Después de una semana, los abcesos dejaron de supurar y empezaron a cerrarse. La fiebre se fue, también. Finalmente, podía salir. Se sentía tan bien poder caminar y correr otra vez. Mientras tanto, agosto pasó, también lo hizo septiembre, y no llegaron órdenes de evacuación del comandante, Erich Koch, para que los refugiados se movieran. Sin embargo, el frente ruso avanzaba diariamente, del Este hacia Koenigsberg y del

Oesta hacia Osterode y Allenstein, donde nos quedábamos. Los rusos ya habían invadido mi pueblo natal, Wizajny, y la parte noreste de Prusia del Este mientras el ejército marchaba hacia Koenigsberg. El objetivo ruso era rodear Prusia del Este completamente y cortarlo del resto de Alemania.

En una tarde aún cálida de septiembre, el señor.y la señora Kirstein estaban sentados en el porche cerrado. La señora Kirstein tejía un suéter, y el señor Kirstein disfrutaba de fumar su pipa mientras estaba absorto en sus pensamientos. De vez en cuando, miraba a través de la ventana hacia el camino. En la distancia, el señor Kirstein notó a una persona en bicicleta aproximándose a la casa. Intentó ver su cara y reconocer a la persona.

"¿Podría ser mi hijo Gustav?" pensó por un segundo, "no, no podría; ¿cómo sabría él donde estamos?" corrigió sus pensamientos momentáneamente, pero luego miró más de cerca al ciclista mientras él reducía la velocidad al acercarse a la casa. "Si, se parece a Gustav. Si, es Gustav." Jaló a su esposa del brazo.

"Mira, mira, es Gustav, viene hacia nosotros," gritó de alegría. Al principio, ella pensó que su esposo estaba fantaseando. Cuando ella miró de cerca reconoció a su hijo, aventó su tejido, jaló a su esposo de la silla, y los dos corrieron a encontrarlo en el camino.

El señor.y la señora Kirstein gritaron, "Gustav, Gustav, gracias a Dios estas vivo y nos encontraste." Lágrimas de felicidad llenaron sus ojos mientras abrazaban a Gustav y lo recibían.

"Ven, ven; debes estar cansado y hambriento. Te prepararé algo de comer, y después nos puedes contar como nos encontraste aquí."

"Incluso trajiste tu acordeón contigo," remarcó la señora Kirstein cuando vio el estuche del acordeón amarrado a la parte trasera de la bicicleta.

"¡Qué feliz soy de haberlos encontrado!" Gustav expresó su dicha al reunirse con su familia, también lo hizo su madre, su hermana Greta y sus hermanos Fritz, Edmund y Georg.

Todos lo inundaron con preguntas.

"Niños, niños, dejen que Gustav descanse primero. Mañana él podrá responder a todas sus preguntas."

Después de que la familia consumió sus huevos y panqueques de desayuno al día siguiente, se quedaron sentados alrededor de la mesa, esperando ansiosamente escuchar la historia de Gustav.

"Aún no puedo creer que fui capaz de econtrarlos vivos y a salvo. Ahora les contaré donde serví en el ejército. Me uní a la Fuerza Aaérea. Sufrí de severa congelación en mis manos y en mis pies, lo que me descalificó. Como sé de carpintería, los oficiales militares me mandaron nueve meses a Checoslovaquia para entrenar como ingeniero militar. Nuestro trabajo era construir puentes por donde los tanques y ejércitos alemanes pudieran pasar y destruirlos una vez que hubieran cumplido su propósito, para que los enemigos no pudieran usarlos.

Los ciudadanos checos y los ciudadanos polacos y rusos formaron grupos de resistencia y se denominaron partidarios. Estos civiles sin entrenamiento pelearon por sus países. Se escondían en los bosques, en las cimas de los árboles, zanjas, edificios abandonados, o cualquier lugar en el que pudieran. Disparaban y mataban en el acto a cualquier soldado que estuviera a la vista. Cuando los soldados alemanes les pidieron que se rindieran, no lo hicieron. Los capturaron y los encerraron en búnkers. Incendiaban los búnkers. Algunos con ropas en llamas salían corriendo, y con los brazos al aire, se rendían, clamando piedad solo parar ser acribillados a muerte. Era algo horrible de ver; nunca lo olvidaré.

El ejército ruso trató de rodear Prusia del Este. Mientras se movían hacia el sur, y al oeste, yo estaba envuelto en una batalla contra los rusos. Afortunadamente, los soldados alemanes pudieron sostener sus posiciones y no permitieron el avance del ejército ruso, salvando a los ciudadanos alemanes de la masacre.

Fui herido y enviado al hospital militar, donde fui tratado y liberado y dado licencia de abandonar esa batalla. Fui a casa en tren, camionesmilitares, o a pie, dormí en cualquier lugar que considerara seguro. Llegué a casa solo para decepcionarme al descubrir que ya se habían ido. Tenía que reportarme con la Gestapo en Wizajny. Tomé algo de salchichay schnapps (alcohol) caseros que encontré en casa y se los dí al comandante a cargo. En lugar de mandarme a otro campo de batalla, me dijo que esperara órdenes. Fui a la oficina del mayor y le pregunté cuándo y a dónde se habían ido los pobladores. Empaqué un poco de ropa, comida, y mi acordeón en la bicicleta y empecé a buscarlos. A veces era los suficientemente afortunado de encontrar un tren detenido en las vías de alguna estación y saltaba en él. A veces encontraba un camión de transporte cargado con soldados que me llevaban por un pedazo del camino. Una vez, cuando iba en un tren, la locomotora se desenganchó del vagón y me quedé en el bosque. Cuando me di cuenta de que la locomotora y el resto del tren se movían sin el vagón en el que yo estaba, tomé mi bicicleta y pedaleé.

Dormí en graneros, casas abandonadas, bosques o comapos, con el peligro acechándome. Siempre tuve que estar alerta. Me agachaba cuando una granada o una bala volaban sobre mi cabeza o cerca de mi. Muy seguido tuve que esconderme en el bosque cuando los bombarderos rusos pasaban sobre mi y soltaban bombas en quien fuera y lo que fuera que se moviera. Partidarios rusos y polacos, que habían penetrado Rusia del Este, abrieron fuego contra mi. A veces pensaba que una bala o una bomba me mataría, pero gracias a Dios; escapé ileso.

Hubo vecesen que pensé que moriría de hambre. Pepené comida y maté cerdos, conejos o lo que fuera que encontrara vivo." El señor y la señora Kirstein, que escuchaban atentamente, interrumpieron brevemente, mirando al cielo, "Gracias Dios por salvar a nuestro hijo y traerlo a nosotros ileso."

Después Gustav continuó, *"Una vez, mientras me estaba recuperando de mis heridas en el hospital, conocí a un soldado que peleó en la batalla de Stalingrado y sosntenía heridas.*

Me dijo que a el Wehrmacht, soldados que no pertenecían a los Nazis, (Partido Nacional Socialista), no le gustaba Hitler y sus soldados SS, así como a los generales de Wehrmacht. El conflicto y la desarmonía existían entre ambos grupos de soldados. Los soldados SS se quedaban atrás y dejaban que el Wehrmacht entrara en combate activo.

El general Paulus, quien comnadó al ejército alemán en Stalingrado, se rindió voluntariamente ante los rusos y no perdió la batalla debido a la falta de suministros de comida o amunición, como se anunció al público en los periódicos. El general Paulus prefirió convertirse en prisionero de guerra antes de ser un siervo bajo las órdenes del despiadado dictador Hitler quien comanda a sus generales y soldados a pelear hasta el final y nunca rendirse. "Victoria o muerte" es su slogan.

Después de que los rusos ganaron la batalla en Stalingrado, el ejército avanzó rápidamente. Están intentando rodear Prusia del Este en su marcha hacia Berlín. Si queremos seguir vivos, es mejor que nos dirijamos al sudoeste, donde aún hay un paso hacia el corredor polaco. Creo que debo ir con todas las otras familias a notificarles que deben estar listos para partir en dos días."

"Si, hijo mío, esa es una buena idea" respondió su padre. "Iré contigo; yo se donde viven todas las familias." Se ofreció su hermano mayor Fritz para acompañar a Gustav.

Fueron de familia en familia hasta que informaron a las seis. Las noticias de una partida súbita alarmó a mi madre, pero el temor de que sus hijas pudieran ser violadas y torturadas por soldados rusos era mas doloroso que irse. Así, nuestra estancia en la granja terminó. El otoño y la escarcha llegaron y tintaron a los árboles con colores brillantes, y el bosque rodeaba las doradas praderas. Los días se hicieron más cortos, y las sombras mas largas.

Desafortunadamente, mientras la naturaleza se preparaba para su largo sueño de invierno, nosotros no vimos forzados a terminar nuestra estancia y a iniciar nuestro viaje. Muchas lágrimas rodaron mientras nos despedimos de las tres hermanas en el día de partida.

No pudimos agradecerles suficientemente por habernos alimentado, resguardado y por tanta amabilidad mientras nos quedamos con ellas. Las hermanas nos ofrecieron llevarnos una vaca para que tuviéramos suficiente leche para Horst y la familia. Mamá aceptó este generoso regalo. Georg ató a la vaca a la carreta con una cuerda, y nos fuimos. Todos nuestros ojos estaban enfocados en la granja hasta que la distancia se tragó los contornos de los edificios y los árboles.

Llegamos a la plaza de Allenstein, llena de muchos caballos y carretas, y buscamos a las familias de nuestra aldea. Nos alineamos una detrás de otra y empezmos un nuevo segmento de nuestro viaje. El alcalde del pueblo nos dijo que fuéramos hacia el sudoeste, donde los rusos aún no habían cerrado el perímetro alrededor de Prusia del Este y donde aún se mantenía erguido un puente para cruzar el río Weichsel.

Hacia adelante rodaron las carretas por el día y se detenían al atardecer para que los cansados viajeros pudieran alimentarse y con suerte un poco de descanso. Los caballos, también cansados de jalar su pesada carga todo el día, necesitaban un bien merecido descanso y forraje fresco para continuar, al igual que nuestra vaca. Cada día nos quedábamos en un lugar diferente, en una granja o acampábamos al aire libre en los bosques. A veces dormíamos en casas abandonadas, establos, graneros o donde fuera que encontráramos edificios vacantes. Una vez, encontramos una escuela abandonada. Una habitación grande tenía paja en el suelo a lo largo de las dos paredes opuestas. Tomamos nuestras sábanas y almohadas y nos acomodamos para pasar la noche. Tan pronto como pusimos nuestras cabezas en las almohadas, escuchamos un crujido en la paja. Me desperté varias veces y sentí algo trepando por mi cuerpo. Comencé a rascarme. El extraño ruido también despertó a mi madre y a mis hermanos y hermanas.

Al día siguiente, vimos piojos sobre nosotros. Nos dimos cuenta de que los piojos infestaban la paja en donde nos habíamos dormido. Mas tarde, alguien nos dijo que los prisioneros rusos habían dormido ahí y nadie se había molestado en cambiar la paja cuando se fueron.

Mamá juntó todas las sábanas y las sacudió con la esperanza de que remover a los piojos. También nos hizo cambiarnos de ropa. Hizo un nudo con las ropas infestadas en una sábana con la esperanza de que cualquier piojo remanente no se saliera de ahí y se no se asentara en la carreta. Sin embargo, nuestros esfuerzos de librarnos de los piojos fallaron. Algunos tomaron residencia en nuestras cabezas y se convirtieron en indeseados compañeros de viaje. Los piojos dejaban sus huevecillos en nuestros cabellos para asegurar la continuidad de su especie. Su picazón y caminar en nuestras cabezas nos fastidiaba sin fin.

Tan pronto como encontramos una casa abandonada con agua corriente, mamá y Emma hirvieron todas las sábanas infestadas y nuestras ropas, matando a muchos de los piojos, pero aún, nuestras cabezas eran su sitio favorito para vivir y reproducirse.

Avanzábamos lentamente. A veces alguna carreta se rompía, o camiones de transporte militar detenían el tráfico. En una ocasión, nos quedamos en un hermoso terreno, donde los dueños se habían ido recientemente. Fritz y el señor Kirstein forzaron la puerta de la entreda y encontraron todo adentro aún intacto y muy ordenado. Decidieron pasar la noche ahí y anunciaron, "Pasaremos la noche aquí."

Después de alinear todas las carretas en el piojo, todos se bajaron. Las mujeres fueron directamente a la cocina, donde todo estaba aún en orden y bellamente acomodado. Cuando entraron a la despensa, se maravillaron de encontrar las repisas bien surtidas con alimentos enlatados. Después exploraron todas las otras habitaciones y decidieron dónde dormiría cada familia esa noche. Marta Kirstein se acomodó con su bebé, Renata, y su hijo, Waldemar, en una habitación, y la señora Heisel con sus tres hijos, Helmut, Edna, y Gustav, en otra habitación. Con su padre anciano, joven hijo, Ernst, hija, Elfriede, y Oswald, el señor Hein tomó otra habitación. Mi mamá y sus siete hijos se asentaron en una habitación grande. La familia Kirstein de seis miembros, se acomodaron en la sala y la familia Liedke, de cinco, en la biblioteca. La señora Ambrosat y su hija, Greta, usaron las bancas del comedor como camastros para esa noche.

Mientras los hombres desataban a los caballos de las carretas y buscaban forraje, encontraron un cerdo en uno de los chiqueros. Decidieron sacrificarlo para que todos pudieran cenar algo de carne fresca.

Elfriede, Edna, y yo, subimos corriendo las escaleras y descubrimos una pequeña habitación en el ático con dos baúles. Los abrimos y encontramos que uno de ellos estaba lleno de muñecas y otro de juegos y juguetes para niño. Tomé una muñeca con una hermosa cara de porcelana y largas trenzas en un adorable vestido de rayas verdes con rojo y flores blancas.

"Yo tomaré esta," le anuncié a Elfriede y a Edna, "hay más en el baúl para ustedes."

"Ok, puedes quedarte con esa. Yo tomaré esta otra," enseñándome otra muñeca bonita.

Edna escogió otra muñeca también bonita. También tomamos una pequeña para Renata. Le dijimos a los niños sobre los juegos en el ático. Ellos corrieron hacia arriba, escogieron un ajedrez y un tablero de damas, y le trajeron un caballo de peluche a mi hermano Horst y otro animal a Ernst. Jugar con estos juguetes nos hizo muy felices a los niños. Olvidamos todas las dificultades de la guerra esa tarde. Después de que las madres cocinaran algo de carne de cerdofresca, papas y col fermentada, alimentaron a los niños antes de que los adultos consumieran su cena. Nosotras tres niñas llevamos nuestras muñecas a la sala y jugamos con ellas hasta que nos fuimos a la cama. Gritos repentinos de voces de hombres me despertaron. Me laventé y me asomé por la puerta. Vi a Fritz con un cuchillo en su mano persiguiendo a su hermano Gustav mientras gritaba palabras obscenas. Cerré la puerta rápidamente, me metí nuevamente en la cama, y me cubrí la cabeza con la cobija mientras temblaba del miedo de que pudiera entrar a mi habitación y lastimarme a mi o a alguien mas. Esperé por lo que pareció un largo tiempo a que mi mamá viniera. Tan pronto como la escuché entrar en el cuarto, mi miedo se mitigó, y le pregunté "¿Qué pasó con los hermanos Kirstein?".

Mamá me respondió: "Se emborracharon y empezaron a pelear entre ellos. Puedes volver a dormirte. Fritz. Y Gustav dejaron de pelear e hicieron las paces."

Aunque mi madre se escuchaba segura, me tomó algo de tiempo volver a dormirme.

Después del desayuno, cargamos todas nuestras pertenencias en las carretas la mañana siguiente, nos reunimos con nuestro grupo de siete, y empezamos nuestro viaje con dirección hacia el sudoeste. Esperábamos poder pasar a salvo a través de la apertura en el frente ruso.

Para inicios de octubre de 1944, los ejércitos rusos irrumpieron la frontera prusiana en la región de Memel por primera vez. Los tanques abrieron fuego contra las personas que escapaban, rodaron sobre ellos y sus carretas jaladas por caballos, y las cadenas rechinaban mientras aplastaban y masacraban a todos y todo en su camino. El ejército alemán estaba debilitado y no podía forzar al frente ruso a retroceder; se retiraron y ayudaron a los civiles prusianos a escapar tanto como les posible. Después de que los rusos rompieron la frontera noreste de la región de Memel, empezaron a rodear Prusia del Este por completo. Goldap, la ciudad cerca de nosotros, cayó en manos de los rusos para fines de octubre.

Escalofríos recorrían las mentes de las personas cuando las noticias sobre la invasión rusa a Prusia del Este se esparcieron, que hasta ese momento era considerado un santuario seguro para líderes políticos, sus familias y civiles por igual.

Incluso ganar la guerra parecía futil; Hitler movilizó a cada hombre entre las edades de dieciséis y sesenta y cinco y los envió al campo de batalla. Este grupo de hombres inexpertos y sin entrenamiento, llamado "Volkstrum," no ayudó a la causa. Al contrario, dejaron a niños, mujeres y adultos mayores defenderse a si mismos mientras huían de los rusos y abandonaban sus amados hogares. Todo por lo que generaciones habían trabajado y cultivado por muchos años tuvo que dejarse atrás. Trajo mas sufrimiento, dificultades y caos a las familias.

La marcha de refugiados avanzaba cada día muy despacio. Camiones de transportes llenos de soldados y los recién reclutados Volksturm se apresuraban a los campos de batalla orientales y desaceleraban la marcha. Algunos días sólo viajábamos cinco millas o menos. Sin embargo, nuestras siete familias fueron afortunadas al tener dos soldados, Fritz y Gustav, con nosotros, aunque su padre y el señor Liedke, ya pasaban de los sesenta y cinco, aún eran físicamente capaces de ayudar y proteger a nuestro grupo. Mamá agradeció a Dios que Georg, su hijo mayor, de ahora catorce años de edad, no tenía que enlistarse en el Volksturm. Georg asumió la responsabilidad de cuidar de los caballos y la carreta. Sin embargo, Fritz y Gustav, hábiles en las artes de la carpintería y equipo agrícola, reparaban las ruedas rotas de las carretas, arneses, o lo que fuera que necesitara reparación. También buscaban provisiones de alimentos y nos protegían. Reemplazaban herraduras y arreglaban equipo desgastado o dañado.

En noviembre, el cielo se turnó gris, y la niebla se asentó en el suelo. Algunos días la lluvia empapaba las cubiertas de las carretas, y el agua goteaba sobre nosotros por dentro. Creaba charcos en los caminos rurales sin pavimentar. Personas a pie y los caballos trotaban sobre ellos, salpicando de agua sucia a los lados, no habia tiempo para hacer pausas. Debíamos seguir adelante.

Noviembre terminó, y cubrimos solo distancias cortas cada día. Diciembre abrió con temperaturas bajo cero y con nieve. Los días se hicieron mas cortos y las noches mas largas y mas frías. El hielo extendía una manta de cristal sobre los campos, arbustos y árboles. Éstos brillaban en la mañana cuando los rayos del sol vertían sus dorados rayos sobre ellos. Algunos días, tormentas de nieve azotaban furiosamente contra el patético grupo de marchantes y frenaban a los caballos y las carretas. El viento se arrojaba contra las cubiertas de las carretas que se movían de atrás hacia adelante como si estuvieran listas para arrancarse y salir volando. La ráfaga enufrecida encontraba hasta la mas mínima abertura en las cubiertas, y sentíamos el frío adentro. Mamá cubrió a sus cuatro hijos menores con las cobijas de plumas para evitar que nos congeláramos. Se unió a Georg, quien supervisaba y manejaba la carreta. Para aligerar la carga a los caballos, Emma y Meta caminaban junto a la carreta. Entre mas nieve se acumulaba, se hacía más difícil para los caballos jalar la carreta. Los caballos resollaban y resoplaban con cada movimiento para avanzar, también lo hacían Emma y Meta.

Solo cuando la oscuridad se asentaba, tratábamos de buscar cobijo para los viajeros y descanso para los caballos. Esperábamos conseguir una comida caliente para las familias y forraje para los caballos. Dormíamos en casas abandonadas, establos, heniles, o cualquier estrucura en la que pudiéramos resguardarnos del frío. En una ocasión, para salir de una tormenta de nieve, pasamos la noche con vacas en un establo. Mientras nuestras madres preparaban el área para dormir apilando suficiente paja en el piso de concreto donde no había vacas, Emma, Meta y las otras damas jóvenes ordeñaban algunas vacas para obtener leche fresca y tibia para los niños pequeños y hambrientos. Después de que tomábamos la leche tibia, que sabía tan bien, mi madre traía las sábanas y las cobijas de plumas de la carreta y nos cobijaba para dormir. Yo no podía dormir. El hedor de las heces de las vacas era nauseabundo. Cerré mi nariz. No ayudó mucho tampoco. Di vueltas por algún tiempo antes de jalar las cobijas para cubrirme la cabeza para mantener el hedor fuera y al fin poder dormir. En la madrugada, el mugido de las vacas nos despertó. Reunimos nuestro equipo y continuamos el viaje.

Cuando no había ninguna granja ni aldea a la vista, teníamos que seguiur avanzando o morir de frío. Era un continuo alto y avance, y la marcha batallaba para avanazar solo unos kilómetros y mantenerse con vida. Mientras tanto, los mediados de diciembre se aproximaban, y con ellos, Navidad. Los hombres a cargo decidieron encontrar un lugar para quedarnos por un tiempo y pasar Navidad en una casa.

Encontramos a una viuda polaca, la señora Grabowski, dispuesta a acogerns y a compartir parte de su casa con nosotros.

Después de buscar en granjas adyacentes, las otras seis familias también encontraron rancheros disponibles a acomodarlos.

La dama de la granja, donde nos quedamos, nos ayudó a acomodarons en una recámara pequeña con una estufa y asignó la sala grande como dormitorios. También compartió algo de sus provisiones de comida con nosotros. Estábamos muy agradecidos de estar en un lugar cálido y comer comida caliente otra vez. Antes de dormir, mamá hervía agua y preparaba un baño en un gran barril para nosotros. Primero, bañaba a Horst. Después era mi turno. Que bien se sentía sumergirse en agua tibia y ser tallada y limpiada de la cabeza a los pies. Mamá mantenía una olla de agua hirviendo en la estufa. Después de cada baño, ella añadía mas agua caliente a la tina. Después de que todos se bañaron y habían ido a dormir, ella se limpiaba. Antes de irse a dormir, ella agradecía a Dios por tener a su familia resguardada y a salvo.

Al día siguiente, aprendimos que la dama tenía un hijo llamado Janek y una hija llamada Stella. No conocimos a Janek hasta que oscureció. Tenía mas de dieciocho y era elegible para ser reclutado por el ejército polaco. Su madre lo tenía escondido en el granero para evitar que fuera a la guerra. Se quedaba en un gran cubiculo donde una gran paca de heno, que servía como puerta, podía ser empujada desde adentro cuando su hermana le llevaba comida o cuando él quería venir a la casa después de que oscurecía. La pobre madre vivía en un constante temor de que un agente del gobierno apareciera para llevarse a su único hijo.

Emma y Meta ayudaron a ordeñar las vacas y en todo lo que la dama les pedía que hicieran en la casa. Georg y Edmund alimentaban a los caballos y a las vacas. Richard, Horst y yo nos quedábamos con mamá en la cocina, ayudándola a pelar papas, y otras labores de cocina pequeñas.

La Navidad se acercaba rápidamente. Emma y Meta decidieron poner un árbol de Navidad. Les pidieron a Georg y a

Edmund que fueran al bosque a buscar un pino de talla mediana. Los chicos tomaron un trineo y fueron al bosque cercano. Después de encontrar un pino bien formado y simétrico, lo cortaron, lo amarraron al trineo y lo jalaron de regreso a la granja. Emma estaba encantada cuando vio la forma y el tamaño del pino. Le ayudó a sus hermanos a hacer un pie de pino con algunas tablas viejas que encontraron en el establo. Lo llevaron a la sala y lo acomodaron en la esquina.

"¿Qué haremos con los ornamentos?" preguntó Meta. "Haremos algunos," respondió Emma, "Vne, vamos al establo y consigamos algo de paja. Haremos estrellas de paja; te voy a enseñar a armarlas."

Fueron al establo y recogieron un puñado de pajillas gruesas y largas. Les cortaron las partes delgadas y los nudos y las remojaron toda la noche en un plato con agua para hacer a las pajillas flexibles y evitar que se rompieran. Después de que terminaron sus labores el siguiente día, sacaron las pajillas del agua y las secaron con un trapo. Después las partieron por la mitad y las aplanaron con un cuchillo.

"Mira, Meta, ahora tu dobla la paja, para que el lado brilloso quede por fuera y el opaco por dentro. Haz que un extremo quede de una pulgada de largo, así," Emma le enseñó a Meta como hacerlo.

"Haz lo mismo con las cuatro pajillas. Después las vas a entretejer así para formar un cuadrado. Ahora dobla las pajillas mas largas, para que tengas ocho paijllas, dos de cada lado, y entrelázalas así." Emma esperó hasta que Meta completó sus instrucciones.

"Ahora corta todas las pajillas a la misma longitud, después haz un bucle y asegura cada extremo en el centro, así. Ves, y ahora tienes un bonito ornamento." Después de que terminaron varios de los mismos ornamentos, Emma le enseñó a Meta otras variaciones de ornamentos de paja. Yo me senté calladamente a su lado y observé cada movimiento que hacian. Después de un tiempo, le pregunté a Emma si yo podía hacer una estrella también.

"Ven, déjame empezar una para ti, y tu puedes terminarla."

Emma dobló cuatro pajillas y las entrelazó en un cuadrado antes de entregármelo con las instrucciones que seguían.

"Ves, a continuación, doblas cada pajilla, para que tengas ocho pajillas, dos de cada lado."

Ella esperó hasta que terminé de doblar cada una de las pajillas.

"Ahora, las cortas todas a la misma longitud, así de largo." Ella cortó las primeras y yo el resto.

"¿Así está bien?" le pregunté.

"Si, ahora toma cada extremo y asegúralo en el cuadrado del centro, así," me instruyó mientras doblaba y aseguraba el primero.

"Okey, lo intentaré," le respondí. Después doblé cada pajilla hasta que terminé con todas.

"Mira, Emma, hice mi primer ornamento. ¿Puedo hacer más por mi cuenta ahora?" le dije a Emma mienstras le presentaba orgullosamente mi primer manualidad.

"Claro, tu puedes," respondió Emma.

Me sentí muy madura contribuyendo y ayudando en una arte tan fina. Los primeros ornamentos estaban algo flojos y los moños desiguales, pero se veían cada vez mejor con un poco de práctica. No podía esperar a colgarlos en el árbol. Cada día después de comer o de cenar, nos sentábamos alrededor de la mesa y hacíamos ornamentos. Un día, Emma anunció que había obtenido algo de papel de la dama de la casa. Les voy a enseñar como hacer estrellas de papel con el. Lo cortó en tiras anchas e iguales y las dobló hasta que parecieron estrellas. Para mi, era más retador trabajar con papel que con paja.

Sin embargo, después de varios intentos y errores, finalmente entendí como hacer estrellas de papel.

"¿Tienes algunas velas?" preguntó Meta.

"Le voy a preguntar a la señora Grabowski; talvez pueda darnos algunas de las suyas," le respondió Emma.

Al día siguiente, Emma anunció alegremente, mientras me enseñaba un puñado de velas, "mira lo que la señora Grabowski me dio. ¿No es maravilloso que tenemos velas reales para poner en el árbol?"

"Es maravilloso; no puedo esperar; ¿cuándo vamos a ponerlas en el árbol?"

"Primero, tenemos que poner hilo en todos los ornamentos. Haremos eso hoy. Tal vez, mañana podemos empezar a colgarlos en el árbol."

Emma le pidió a mamá algo de estambre. Mamá nos trajo hilo blanco en un carrete con dos agujas. Los trajo consigo, sabiendo que siempre iba a tener que enmendar las ropas de niños.

"Aquí está el carrete blanco, pero no usen demasiado," nos advirtió mamá.

Emma cortó un montón de hilos de cuatro pulgadas de largo aproximadamente y me los entregó. Después tomó una hebra y me enseñó como atravesarla en el moño y hacer un nudo. Miré con cuidado y después seguí sus instrucciones. Emma y Meta ensartaron una aguja, jalaron el estambre a través de la esquina de cada estrella de papel, y después hicieron un nudo. Trabajamos toda la tarde para poder terminar.

Después de la cena, Emma instruyó a Georg y a Edmund para que fueran a invitar a las seis familias a la celebración de Noche Buena.

"Georg, pídele a Gustav Kirstein que traiga su acordeón." Después de alimentar a los caballos y las vacas al día siguiente, Georg y Edmund pisotearon a través de la profunda nieve de una granja a otra, donde se quedaban los refugiados, y los invitaban a reunirse parala celebración de Noche Buena a las 5:00 pm.

Exhaustos, congelándose y hambrientos, regresaron por la tarde antes de que el sol lanzara sus últimos rayos en la blanca nieve y se desvaneciera en la oscuridad de la noche.

La Navidad se acercaba rápidamente. Nuestra anticipación crecía con cada día que pasaba. Finalmente, unos días antes de Navidad, Emma dijo, "Vamos a decorar el árbol esta tarde. Primero, debemos calentar la habitación. Ve y pídele a Georg y a Edmund que traigan algo de leña y troncos a la casa."

Corrí al establo, donde ambos juntaban heno para llevar a los caballos y las vacas.

"Emma quiere que lleven algo de madera adentro. Ella quiere calentar la habitación donde vamos a poner el árbol de Navidad. Apúrense para que podamos empezar," añadí.

Ellos detuvieron sus labores y cumplieron la petición de Emma con prontitud.

Yo misma llevé algo de palitos a la casa para acelerar el proceso. Emma colocó los pedazos delgados de madera en el fondo, después hizo una pirámide con los troncos en el horno (Kachelofen). Tomó una vara larga y delgada de madera, fue a la cocina, y encendió la varita en el hogar. Después protegió la pequeña llama con su mano mientras la llevaba a la sala. Pronto el fuego crujió en el horno y consumió los leños simultáneamente mientras irradiaba calor a través de las aberturas del horno. Esperamos hasta que el lugar estaba lo suficientemente tibio antes de colgar nuestras estrellas hechas a mano en el árbol.

"Ahora, pongamos las velas. Ten, sosténlas por mi, y yo las voy a amarrar a las ramas," Emma me instruyó.

Pronto terminamos de decorar.

"Se ve hermoso," expresé mi alegría mientras daba un paso atrás para darle un buen vistazo al árbol decorado. Corrí a lacocina, agarré a mi madre de la mano, y grité, "Mamá, mamá, ven a ver nuestro adorable, decorado árbol." Ella me siguió a la sala.

"Si, es muy bonito, pero sería más bonito si le añadiéramos ornamentos de color de nuestra casa", comentó mamá.

Me sentí triste al ver que mi mamá no compartía mi entusiasmo y remarqué, "Pero mamá, nosotras mismas hicimos los ornamentos, y para mi, se ven hermosos en el árbol."

"Supongo que podemos estar agradecidos de tener un árbol de Navidad y de estar en un lugar cálido y no en el camino en el drío," mamá me respondió mientras regresaba a la cocina a preparar la cena.

Afuera, el invierno desataba toda su furia. Los enbravecidos vientos del norte rugian y sonaban en los cristales de las ventanas. Grandes copos de nieve danzaban al rápido ritmo del viento silbante antes de caer exhaustos en el suelo. Al amanecer, cuando el sol quemaba al último remanente de la noche, revelaba la mágica transformación en un paraíso invernal. La cobija de blanco puro de neve cubría echos, borraba pisadas, ranuras y surcos. El suelo parecía casi sagrado mientras los copos de nieve resplandecían en la luz del sol. Tan pronto como mis hermanos descubrieron la nieve recién caída, se vistieron, corrieron afuera y comenzaron una pelea de bolas de nieve. Me apresuré afuera a unirme a ellos. La mayoría de mis bolas de nieve no dieron con mis hermanos pero las suyas no fallaron.

"Hagamos un muñeco de nieve," sugerí después de que estaba cubierta de nieve. Ellos accedieron, y empezamos a rodar la nieve en forma de bolas. Me ofrecí a hacer la cabeza, que era la más pequeña. Pronto pusieron una gran bola de nieve abajo, una mediana en el centro, y la mas pequeña arriba, representando la cabeza. Corrí dentro de la casa y le pedí a mi mamá una zanahoria, que necesitaba para hacer la nariz.

Ella respondió, "no tengo zanahorias, pero puedes usar un palito de los que usamos para encender la madera." Se lo llevé a Edmund.

"Aquí hay un palito para la nariz," dije mientras le entregaba el palito.

"¿Qué tal un sombrero?"

"Moldearé uno con turba," Edmund respondió y fue al establo a conseguir algunos cuadros de turba y unos palos. Primero clavó palos finos en dos piezas de turba para formar un cuadro perfecto. Después Edmund cortó otra pieza rectangular a la mitad y puso ambas piezas arriba del cuadrado. Después rompió las esquinas del cuadrado y lo redondeó. Edumnd removió algo de nieve de la coronilla con la ayuda de Georg y de Richard y amaró el sombrero a la cabeza del muñeco de nieve con mas palos. Tomó segmentos de turba, les dio la forma de pequeñas pelotas, y presionó dos en la cabeza a manera de ojos. Hizo un surco curveado bajo la nariz. Georg hizo una línea de agujeros redondos en las dos bolas de abajo y colocó turba en ellos, que servían como botones negros. Habíamos colocado al muñeco de nieve a lado de la entrada, para que todo el que nos visitara lo viera.

"Que bonito muñeco de nieve," grité de alegría. "Pero ahora voy adentro de la casa, mis manos se están enfriando." Invité a todos a ir afuera a ver al muñeco de nieve. Mamá salió, sonrió al ver nuestra creación, y después le pidió a los chicos que escarbaran caminos hacia el granero y el establo. Trabajaron duro cavando dos caminos de la entrada de granero y del establo antes de empezar sus labores diarias de limpiar el establo y alimentar a los animales.

Dos días antes de Noche Buena, Emma y Meta limpiaron la sala y la prepararon para la celebración con nuestros compañeros viajeros. El alcalde de la ciudad envió a cada familia refugiada una mitad de una porción de mantequilla del tamaño de un ladrillo, y la dama de la casa le dio a mi madre algo de harina, azúcar y huevos para hornear galletas para sus hijos y los invitados. Cuando supe las buenas noticias, me quedé en la cocina con mamá y me ofrecí a ayudarla. Primero, mamá puso la harina en la mesa, hizo una hendidura en el centro, y puso un pedazo de la mantequilla, algo de azúcar y dos huevos en ella. Después mezcló la harina lentamente con los ingredientes en una masa y la amasó antes de extenderla con un rodillo en una lámina en la mesa. A continuación, mamá tomó un vaso, cubrió el borde con harina, y luego lo presionó en la lámina de masa. Movió el vaso de atrás a adelante unas cuántas veces hasta que cortó una galleta perfectamente circular. Finalmente, lo levantó y colocó el círculo en la charola de galletas.

"Mamá, mamá, ¿puedo cortar las galletas?" le pregunté. "Si, si puedes, pero ten cuidado de no presionar demasiado

fuerte. El vidrio puede romperse. Ten, inténtalo," mamá me instruyó mientras me entregaba el vidrio que había cubierto de harina.

"Gracias, mamá, seré cuidadosa," respondí y me ocupé en presionar las galletas circulares. Al principio, no pude cortar por completo la masa, y las galletas no se separaban bien de la masa. Sin embargo, después de unos cuantos intentos, salieron bonitas y redondas. Mamá colocó las galletas en charolas para hornear, después las puso en el horno pre calentado. Pronto el aroma de las galletas horneadas llenó la cocina. No podía esperar a probar una.

"Mamá, ¿puedo comer una galleta?" supliqué.

"Espera a que se enfríen, después puedes comer una." Así, esperé por lo que pareció un muy largo tiempo. Finalmente, mi madre levantó una galleta y me la entregó. Rápidamente le di una mordida, "Um," que bien sabía. No había comido una galleta en mucho tiempo.

Mamá colocó una galleta para cada uno de nosotros en la mesa y después puso el resto para Noche Buena y Navidad. No podía esperar a que llegara Noche Buena y Navidad. Finalmente, estaba aquí, y también la nueva nieve que había caído el día anterior y había transformado el paisaje en un paraíso invernal. El día pasó lentamente, y mi anticipación por celebrar la tarde en compañía de nuestros compañeros viajeros crecía cada minuto. No quité mis ojos de la ventana todo el día.

De repente, al atardecer, escuché campanas de trineos sonar. Corrí afuera mientras las familias Kirstein y Liedke llegaban. Pronto después, el trineo de Hein y Heisel se estacionó, también. Estaba encantada de ver a Gustav traer su acordeón con él y añadir música a esta celebración especial. Después de que todos llegaron, Emma y Meta encendieron las velas en el árbol de Navidad. Nos reunimos alrededor del árbol iluminado y cantamos primero "Oh Tannenbaum, oh Tannenbaum wie gruen sind deine Blaetter" (Oh árbol de Navidad, Oh árbol de Navidad, que verdes son tus ramas) acompañados de Gustav en su acordeón. Cada canción navideña levantaba el humor festivo y encendía una chispa en los ojos de los que celebraban.

Mientras cantábamos "Noche de paz, Noche de amor, todo es paz alrededor," no pensamos en los horrores de la enfurecida guerra que nos rodeaba. En su lugar, pensábamos en los escenarios pacíficos de Belén, donde Jesús, el Salvador y Príncipe de la paz, nació. Todos anhelábamos el fin de la guerra y estar de regreso en nuestros hogares viviendo en paz y armonía. Después de que terminamos de cantar canciones navideñas, Emma y Meta extinguieron las velas del árbol y encendieron las lámparas de aceite. Mamá pasó un plato con las galletas caseras. Todos se quedaron un rato mas, conversando alegremente. De vez en cuando, Gustav tocaba canciones tradicionales familiares e invitaba a todos a cantar. A media noche, la festividad terminó, los visitantes dijeron, "Buenas noches," se subieron a sus trineos, y se deslizaron de regreso en la noche estrellada acompañados del sonido de las campanas en los trineos. La magia de la tarde se mantuvo viva en mis pensamientos después de que fui a la cama y me mantuvo despierta por un tiempo. Finalmente, el sueño me cerró los ojos, y soñé con Santa Claus, preguntándome si podría trarnos algo esta Navidad. Extrañábamos a mi hermana Marta y nos preguntábamos dónde habría celebrado Navidad y si estaría a salvo.

El día de Navidad, cuando entramos a la cocina, encontramos siete platos en la mesa con tres galletas en cada uno.

"Mamá, mamá, Santa Claus no se olvidó de nosotros; nos encontró incluso aquí," grité de alegría cuando vi los platos con las galletas. Mmaá no quería decepcionarnos; quería que creyéramos que Santa Claus nos había encontrado ahí, también. Ella puso los siete platos (Bunte Teller) en la mesa durante la noche. No tenía mas que galletas para ofrecernos. Aunque no podíamos ir a la iglesia a celebrar el nacimiento del niño Cristo, nos vestimos en nuestras mejores ropas en su honor. Mamá, Emma, y Meta pasaban la mayor parte de la mañana en la cocina, preparando la tracidional cena de Navidad de ganso, col roja, y papas, un regalo para la dama de la casa. El aroma del ganso rostizado y su calor llenaron la cocina, donde todos nos reunimos, esperando a que estas especialidades fueran cocinadas y servidas.

Finalmente, Emma trajo el ganso rostizado a la mesa y Meta los vegetales. Mamá cortó y sirvió un pedazo de ganso en cada plato, y Meta añadió los vegetales. Mamá dio las gracias y agradeció a Dios por la comida y el nacimiento de nuestro Salvador y que estábamos todos juntos en una cálida casa. ¡Qué festín! ¡Qué maravillos sabía! Todos disfrutamos de la extraordinaria comida. Después de que Emma despejara la mesa, ella leyó la historia del nacimiento del bebé Jesús en un establo en Belén. Cantamos algunas canciones navideñas y agradecimos a Dios el estar dentro, protegidos de los fríos del enfurecido invierno afuera. Nuestros pensamientos sin embargo, nos regresaron a la última Navidad en casa, preguntándonos cuando y si podríamos celebrar la Navidad en casa otra vez.

Al día siguiente, mi mamá, Emma y Meta se sentaron cerca de la estufa de la cocina y tejieron bufandas, guantes, y calcetas para sus hermanos mas pequeños. La amable dama de la casa recogió todos sus sobrantes de lana y se los dio a nuestra madre. Mamá estaba muy agradecida por su generosidad porque ella no había traído suficientes ropas cálidas para el invierno. La semana entre Navidad y Año Nuevo pasó más bien despacio, recibimos el año de 1945 calladamente en nuestro hogar temporal. Mamá, Emma y Meta prepararon las tradicionales donas, pero esta vez con mermelada por dentro. Sin embargo, las rodaron en azúcar para darnos algo dulce. El resto de la Navidad la pasamos calladamente en la cocina. Mamá estaba preocupada por el futuro de su familia y le rezaba a Dios por su protección.

En Año nuevvo, el señor Kirstein mandó a sus hijos Fritz y Gustav a nuestro grupo para actualizarnos sobre el frente ruso. Nuestra villa y región fue invadida y saqueada en Octubre de 1944. En enero de 1945, invadieron el Rominter Heide y Goldap y marcharon hacia Gumbinnen y Tilsit rápidamente. Cada vez, los hermanos Kirstein nos advertían que estuviéramos listos para partir en cualquier momento. Georg se aseguró de que el herrero local le pusiera las herraduras de invierno correctas a los caballos. Revisó la carreta y las cubiertas y reforzó los arcos donde era necesario. Mamá, Emma y Meta remendaron calcetas y medias. Ellas lavaban ropa más frecuentemente, para que siempre estuviéramos listos para irnos en el momento.

155

El sábado 7 de enero, Gustav vino y anunció que el ejército rojo planeaba un ataque significativo pronto. Debíamos irnos el viernes 12 de enero de 1945. Deben estar en el rancho donde nos estamos quedando nosotros a las 8:00 am. Se marchó cabalgando rápidamente y desapareció en la tormenta de invieno para llevar el mensaje urgente a la siguiente familia. Mi mamá fue inmediatamente con la señora Grabowski y le informó que debíamos irnos para el viernes. Mamá le preguntó, "¿Podría darnos algo de harina y otra comida que le sobre para llevarnos en el viaje? Algunas cobijas y ropas cálidas ayudarían, también."

"Si," contestó ella, "Revisaré y te daré aquello de lo que pueda prescindir." Mi mamá le agradeció a la señora Grabowski y volvió a la cocina. "Emma y Meta, reúnan toda la ropa sucia y empiecen a lavarla. Georg y Edmund, ustedes revisen que los arneses de los caballos y la carreta estén bien reparados."

La tarde del martes, Gustav y su hermano, Fritz, vinieron. Trajeron herraduras especiales de invierno de un herrero local y se ofrecieron a ponérselas a nuestros caballos. También trajeron todas las herramientas consigo y en poco tiempo habían removido las herraduras viejas y puesto las nuevas. Después se fueron a ayudar a herrar a los caballos de las otras familias.

En los siguientes d´ñias, todos cooperamos para alistarnos para la partida. Para la noche del martes, el termómetro bajó a -21ºC (-6ºF). Mamá nos levantó temprano, preparó el desayuno para nosotros, y para las 7:00 a.m., fuimos a decier "adiós" a la señora Grabowski. Mi mamá la abrazó primero y le agradeció por compartir su hogar y comida con nosotros por varias semanas. Lágrimas de gratitud brotaron de los ojos de mamá y después de los de la señora Grabowski. Ella miró a cada uno de nosotros con gran compasión mientras nosotros movíamos la cabeza, despidiéndonos, preguntándonos como sobreviríamos el invierno y cuál sería nuestro destino. Georg ató los caballos a la carreta.

Mamá puso a Horst, Richard y a mi en la carreta y nos cubrió con las cobijas de plumas para mantenernos calientes. Mamá se subió del lado derecho del asiento de la carreta y Georg en el izquierdo para tomar las riendas. Emma, Meta y Edmund decidieron caminar para liagerar la carga a los caballos. Georg sonó el látigo para hacer que los caballos se movieran. La nieve seca crujía mientras los caballos avanzaban para jalar la carreta a través de la nieve endurecida. Vientos frígidos se arrojaban contra las cubiertas, y ráfagas frías soplaban a través de las aberturas.

La fuerza de los vientos hacía mas lentos los pasos de Emma, Meta y Edmund. Ellos envolvieron bufandas alrededor de sus cabezas para no inhalar el aire frígido. La humedad de sus alientos se convertía en critales de hielo al minuto que exhalaban. Se encorvaban para sobreponerse a la resistencia del viento.

Para las 8:00 a.m., todas las siete carretas se reunieron en la granja donde se quedaba la familia Kirstein. El señor Kirstein, la cabeza de nuestro grupo, puso su carreta en movimiento, y las seis carretas lo siguieron. La parte mas demandante, dura y larga de nuestro caminó empezó sin saber cuando y dónde terminaría.

La reciente nevada, temperaturas frías, y fuertes vientos, nos detenian considerablemente. Habíamos cubierto solamente una distancia para el atardecer antes de que el señor Kirstein decidiera que pasáramos la noche en una granja abandonada. Las madres juntaron algo de sus provisiones de comida e hicieron sopa caliente para los niños y los adultos. Trajeron sus cobijas de plumas a la casa y prepararon las camas para la noche. Al día siguiente, empezamos temprano, pues el señor Kirstein quería que llegáramos al pueblo de Plock, donde esperaba cruzar el río Weichsel.

Antes de medio día, alcanzamos y nos unimos a una larga fila de carretas con las mismas intenciones, solo para que nos informaran que los puentes sobre el Weichsel habían sido explotados para evitar que los tanques enemigos cruzaran. Qué hacer ahora se volvió una cuestión urgente. El alcalde del pueblo envió mensajeros a redirigir el tráfico al noreste a lo largo del lado derecho de la ribera. Después de atravesar el pueblo y detenerse en el área boscosa, el mensajero señaló a un estrecho y empinado camino que llevaba diagonalmente al río. Las frígidas temperaturas de la semana anterior cubrían el río con una densa capa de hielo, lo suficientemente gruesa para permitir que las carretas pasaran sobre ella. Ahora abrazábamos al invierno como a un amigo que extendió un puente de hielo a través del río para que cruzáramos. Nos detuvimos en la ribera. Muchas de las carretas que intentaron bajar el empinado camino congelado nunca llegaron a cruzar el río. Algunos caballos se resbalaron y cayeron, deslizándose ribera abajo junto con las carretas a las que estaban atados. Algunos se lesionaron severamente o murieron por las carretas que habían caído sobre ellos. Caballos muertos, carretas rotas, y artículos domésticos estaban esparcidos sobre el terraplén y el río congelado creaban una escena catastrófica. Yo estaba horrorizada con esta vista cuando pensé que lo mismo podría pasarnos a nuestros caballos y carreta.

El señor Kirstein y sus dos hijos mayores, Fritz y Gustav, analizaron la peligrosa situación y planearon para minimizar el riesgo de bajar las carretas por el congelado camino empinado. "Necesitamos dos postes gruesos del doble de ancho de la carreta. Podemos ponerlos entre los rayos de las ruedas traseras de las carretas oara evitar que ganen velocidad al descender.

Vayan y corten dos árboles lo suficientemnte gruesos y fuertes para este trabajo."

"Si, padre, encontraremos a los árboles de la talla indicada para nuestro propósito."

Tomaron una hacha y una sierra y se adentraron en el área boscosa para seleccionar dos árboles de la anchura correcta.

Optaron por tener un poste extra para el caso de que uno de los postes se rompiera. Mientras tanto, el señor Kirstein y su hijo menor Edmund fueron de carreta en carreta e instruyeron a las personas sobre como sus hijos les ayudarían a bajar la colina y todo eso, incluso niños pequeños y adultos mayores, debían baja de las carretas y cruzar el rió a pie.

Pronto Fritz y Gustav retornaron con dos grandes y esbeltos troncos de árbol. Empujaron uno de ellos a través de las ruedas traseras, cortando la parte mas delgada a la longitud deseada, y después cortaron el segundo del mismo tamaño. Preparaon la carreta del señor Kirstein primero empujando los postes entre los rayos de las llantas traseras. Fritz y el señor Liedke agarraron la viga de un lado de la carreta, y Gustav y Edmund fueron del otro lado mientras que el señor Kirstein sostenía firmemente las riendas de los caballos. Cuando todos estabanlistos, el señor Kirstein ordenó a los caballos moverse, jalando detrás de ellos la carreta. Las ruedas delanteras giraron, pero las traseras se deslizaron sobre el hielo. Los hombres tuvieron que tirar hacia atrás con fuerza, para que la carreta no ganara velocidad, se estrellara contra los caballos, y los tumbara. Una distancia segura tenía que mantenerse entre la carreta y los caballos para mantenerlos estables. Entre más bajaban, más empinado se volvía el camino y más difícil era detener la carreta.

A excepción de los niños muy jóvenes y el señor Maschat de ochenta años de edad, que permaneció en su carreta, todas las demás personas se bajaron de sus carretas y miraron como cada carreta hacía su camino para bajar a la ribera y hacia el hielo. Al principio, los caballos patinaron un poco cuando pisaron sobre el hielo pero se movieron establemente y jalaron la carreta sobre la superficie helada del río. Todos sostuvimos el aliento hasta que la carreta llegó al otro lado del río. Aunque la ribera oeste era mas baja, no había camino diagonal que fuera colina arriba.

Fue una ardua prueba para los caballos el jalar la carreta colina arriba sobre la ribera congelada. La señora Kirstein, su hija Greta y su hijo más joven Georg habían bajado lentamente el camino hasta el río congelado. Cuando su carreta llegó al otro lado del río, unieron sus manos, formando una línea para cruzar el río, y treparon al otro lado. Todos estábamos agradecidos de que los hombres hubieran ayudado a bajar la carreta a salvo.

La siguiente carreta en bajar fue la de la familia Kiedke y la nuestra, con Georg a cargo de los caballos y la carreta. Mamá miraba ansiosa como Georg maniobraba la carreta con la ayuda de Gustav y Fritz colina abajo hacie el hielo. Después los hombres removieron las vigas de las ruedas y las llevaron colina arriba para ayudar a la siguiente carreta a bajar. Gustav nos indicó que bajáramos la colina y siguiéramos la carreta a distancia. Emma trajo a Horst colina abajo, y la seguimos. Cuando todos nos reunimos en la superficie congelada del río, Emma, con Horst en sus brazos, tomó la delantera; mamá, tomando mi mano, seguía. Yo tomé la mano de Richard, después mi hermano mayor Edmund y Meta seguían al final.

Empujé un pie tra sotro hacia adelante, escuchando por si el hielo se rompía. Llegamos al otro lado del río y subimos a la ribera. Nuestros caballos batallaron y patinaron una y otra vez al jalar la carreta en el camino ribera arriba. Kastan y Kobel sudaron, y espuma salía de sus hocicos. El señor Kirstein y el señor Liedke vinieron a ayudarnos y empujaron la carreta desde atrás cuando los caballos la jalaban colina arriba. Después de muchos intentos, al final tuvieron éxito. Cuando nuestra familia, nuestros cabalos y la carreta estuvieron seguros del otro lado de la ribera, mamá agradeció a Dios. Todos esperábamos que el resto de nuestro grupo y todas las carretas pudieran cruzar a salvo el río congelado. Miramos como una carreta tras otra bajaban de forma segura por el empinado camino helado mientras esperábamos. Cuando todas las personas y sus carretas llegaron a la orilla oeste, el sol extendió sus últimos rayos sobre el paisaje cubierto de nieve. La oscuridad y el aire frígido nos abrazó y nos hizo temblar. El habmbre rugió en nuestros estómagos.

Fritz y gustav habían traído algunos ladrillos y troncos para el caso de que no pudiéramos encontrar un lugar donde pasar la noche. Fritz y Gustav encendieron una fogata. Le dieron una olla grande a Edmund y Rudlf y les pidieron que la llenaran con nieve fresca, que derritieron en e fuego. Edmund y Rudolf tomaron un balde, seguían trayendo nieve, y la vaciaban en la olla hasta llenarla tres cuartos. Las mamás y las hijas mayores tomaron un poco de agua antes de que estuviera caliente y la mezclaron con harina para formar pequeñas albóndigas (Klunker en dialecto prusiano oriental). Las abóndigas de harina eran añadidas al agua hirviendo y meneadas para que no se pegaran entre si. Fritz y Gustav partieron la mitad de un pedazo de panza de cerdo. Echaron las piezas pequeñas junto con algo de sal en la olla. Todos nos reunimos alrededor de la fogata. Aunque el aire cálido no nos acariciaba, nos sentíamos más cálidos al ver las llamas danzar. Después de que la sopa estuvo lista, el señor Kirstein le pidió a todos que vinieran a comer sopa caliente. Corrimos a la carreta y nos formamos y esperamos hasta que Fritz y Gustav vaciaron un cucharon de sopa en nuestros platos. Aunque la panza de puerco estaba dura como el cuero, estábamos agradecidos de tener algo caliente para llenar nuestros estómagos vacíos. Emma y Meta recogieron nuestros platos sucios y los limpiaron con nieve para remover los restos de comida.

Mamá nos pidió que nos quitáramos los zapatos pero que nos dejáramos las ropas puestas antes de meternos bajo las cobijas de plumas para dormir. Edmund, Richard, mi hermana Meta y yo nos acostamos con nuestras cabezas en la parte de atrás de la carreta. Mamá, Horst, y Emma se acomodaron en la parte delantera de la carreta. Georg se nos unió después de alimentar a los caballos. Arrojó una cobija sobre sus lomos para mantenerlos calientes y los desató de la carreta. Los ató a un árbol cercano. Nos acurrucamos debajo de las cobijas, no solo para calentarnos con las cobijas de plumas, sino para beneficiarnos de nuestro calor corporal. Yo exhalaba el aire caliente debajo de la cobija levantada para calentarme más rápido. Rápidamente la bajaba cuando inhalaba.

Apenas cerré mis ojos cuando el sonido de los aeroplanos acercándose se hizo cada vez más alto. Cada vez soltaban una bomba, la explosión causaba un estruendo tan ruidoso que yo rápidamente metía mi cabeza bajo la cobija y mis manos en mis oídos para reducir el nivel de ruido. Las bombas causaron no solo destrucción, sino también incendios. Las llamas danzaban en la oscuridad de la noche, y su luz penetraba hasta la cubierta de nuestra careta. El fuego antiaéreo alemán siguió a una balacera de cañones en la ribera este, esperando derribar o asustar a los aeroplanos rusos para que se retiraran. Ninguno de nosotros pudo dormir. Mamá intentó consolarnos y le rezó a Dios que salvara nuestras vidas evitando que una bomba cayera sobre nosotros. Pasada la media noche, el sonido de los aeroplanos se detuvo conforme los aviones de guerra rusos regresaban a su base y el fuego del cañón del flanco defensor alemán cesaba. Sin embargo, la terrible noche parecía no tener fin.

Al fin, el dorado orbe del sol apareció en el horizonte oriental e iluminó nuestras carretas. Fritz y Gustav fueron los primeros en levantarse y prender una fogata. Llenaron una gran olla con nieve, la pusieron en el fuego para derretirla y ponerla a hervir, de manera que todos tuvieran una bebida caliente para llenar sus estómagos. Algunos tomaron café de nogal; mi mamá preparó una gran olla de te de hierbabuena para nosotros. Después nos preparó un sándwich con salchicha casera para cada uno de nosotros.

Georg puso forraje, consistente de avena mezclada con paja molida, para los caballos en dos bolsas y las colgó a sus arneses. También les dio un balde de agua. Después de que las familias y los caballos estuvieron listos, las seis carretas se alinearon detrás del señor Kirstein, y los caballos comenzaron a jalar las carretas a través del camino secundario cubierto de nieve. Las mamás con los niños mas pequeños se mantenían cobijadas en las cobijas de plumas dentro de las carretas mientras que los adultos pisoteaban a través de la nieve a un lado de sus carretas. Otras carretas cubiertas y abiertas se unieron a la trágica marcha. El viento silbaba y agitaba la cubierta mientras los caballos tiraban y pisoteaban en la nieve para jalar las cargadas carretas lentamente para avanzar. El rechinar de las ruedas mezclado con la detonación distante de los cañones creaba una lamentable y triste melodía. Aunque el son se levantaba en el horizonte, las temperaturas se mantenían bajo cero grados centígrados.

Así seguimos. Antes del atardecer, llegamos a una granja. El señor Kirstein decidió que nos detuviéramos y le diéramos a los caballos y a las personas que iban a pie un descanso. Se acercó al granjero y le preguntó si las carretas podrían encontrar refugio en su granja para pasar la noche. Primero, el granjero refunfuñó pero le permitió al señor Kirstein quedarse. Todas las madres con sus hijos se apresuraron adentro de la casa para escapar del frío y calentar sus congelados cuerpos. Mientras tanto, el granjero nos permitió poner a los caballos en su establo. También les dio agua y heno.

La compasiva esposa del granjero preparó sopa y la repartió en platos a los hambrientos viajeros. Cada uno saborearon cada cucharada de sopa y estaban agradecidos por tener algo caliente en sus estómagos. Después de que la señora de la casa designara un lugar para cada familia, mamá le pidió a Emma y Meta que trajeran las cuatro cobijas de plumas y que las pusieran en la cálida sala de estar. Meta puso primero una sábana, puso dos cobijas de plumas para que sirvieran como colchón, y dos encima para cubrirnos. La señora Hein hizo lo mismo para su familia a lado de la nuestra. Después de un rato, todos nos metimos debajo de las cobijas. Mi mamá, Horst, Richard, y yo nos acurrucamos hacia la pared, y Emma, Meta, Georgg y Edmund estaban en el lado opuesto. Aunque había muchas personas que llenaban el espacio en la habitación, el solo estar calientes se sintio muy bien.

Fritz, Gustav y Edmund Kirstein tomaron turnos vigilando a los caballos y la casa y se despertaron antes del amanecer para alistar todo y empezar temprano. Las temperaturas cayeron bajo cero, creando hielo bajo la nieve, dificultando a los caballos el jalar las carretas. Tenían que pisotear con fuerza a través de la nieve para que los clavos en sus herraduras perforaran el hielo y no se resbalaran. Su aliento se convertía inmediatamente en cristales de hielo tan pronto como entraban en contacto con el aire gélido; también lo hacía el aliento de las personas que caminaban o que estaban sentadas al frente de las carretas. Emma, Meta y Edmund caminaban a lado de nuestra carreta. Cruzaron sus brazos rápida y contínuamente sobre sus pechos para evitar que sus manos y dedos se congelaran. Sacudían sus dedos dentro de sus zapatos para mantener la circulación de la sangre. Alrededor de sus caras, habían envuelto bufandas de lana para evitar que el aire bravío golpeara sus pieles.

La patética marcha se movía por el día y buscaba refugio por las noches. Si la suerte nos acompañaba, encontrábamos alguna casa abandonada o algunas granjas donde la gente, que aún no había huído, nos daba refugio y comida por una noche. Los alcaldes de algunas aldeas que pasábamos nos proveían de lugares para quedarnos y servían comida caliente para los cansados viajeros. Algunos días, comimos solo un sándwich; por varios días, nos quedamos sin coemr. Entonces el hambre ceñía sus garras en el estómago y lentamente drenaba y debilitaba a sus cansadas víctimas. Los huesos estiraban la delgada piel, y el aire soplaba las entrañas vacías. Motivados por el miedo a la muerte, debíamos movernos o perecer.

Incluso mamá y Horst se meteron a la cubierta de la carreta y buscaron calor bajo las cobijas de plumas. Emma y Meta tomaron las riendas de los caballos de vez en cuando para darle un descanso a Georg. Mamá agradecía a Dios cada día que sus hijos estuvieran aún con vida. Muerte, caballos congelados, y algunos cuerpos humanos yacían al lado del camino. Las familias que habían perdido a un ser querido no podían cavar una tumba en el suelo congelado para enterrar a sus muertos.

Los aeroplanos rusos habían distribuido folletos para el ejército rojo para añadir a la miseria de la gente y de los refugiados. Algunos cayeron en manos de soldadoes alemanes y civiles, también, y leían:

"Rotarmist: Du stehst jetzt auf deutschem Boden. Die Stunde der Rache hat geschlagen. (Soldado del ejército rojo, estás en suelo alemán. La hora de la vengaza ha llegado.)

Wir vernichten de Feind. (Destruiremos al enemigo)

Wir werden alle totschlagen (Los golpearemos a todos hasta matarlos)

Die Deutschen sind keine Menschen. (Los alemanes no son seres humanos),

Wir werden nicht sprechen. (No hablaremos)

Wir werden uns nicht aufregen. (No vamos a deteriorarnos)

Wir warden töen. (Mataremos)

Brenne verfluchtes Deutschland. (Quemen, condenen a Alemania)

Joseph Stalin, que era ateo, despachó a los generales rusos y a los soldados rusos a que violaran a las mujeres alemanas, destruyeran sus aldeas, y mataran, mataran, mataran. Ilya Ehrenburg, una periodista judía rusa, y el ministro de propaganda de Joseph Stalin, expresaron su odio en muchos periódicos rusos. Adoctrinaron a los soldados rusos, "Maten a los alemanes --- esto lo pide tu madre anciana mata a los alemanes --- esto lo piden tus hijos, mata a los alemanes, así lo ordena tu patria. No abandones tu deber --- mata, mata, mata. Después de que mates a un alemán, mata a uno segundo para nosotros. No hay nada mas entretenido que ver cadáveres alemanes.

Bombardeo de Berlín SGM

Sabiendo lo que le esperaba a los civiles alemanes, los soldados alemanes en la frontera de Prusia del Este pelearon tenazmente, incluso dando sus vidas para contener al ejército rojo ruso. Ahora, ya no pensaban en la victoria de su Fuehrer o en salvar a su país. Sus únicos pensamientos eran salvar tantas vidas de su gente como fuera posible, a menudo sacrificando sus propias vidas. Ellos ayudaron siempre que pudieron a evacuar gente. Los soldados rusos trataban a los alemanes, especialmente a las mujeres alemanas, por venganza por haber matado rusos y destruido algunas de sus ciudades durante los últimos años de batallas en Rusia.

Las carretas rodaron a través de la nieve y el hielo. Algunos días, la marcha de los lastimosos viajeros solo avanzaba unos kilómetros; otros días, un poco más. Algunos días, teníamos comida; otros días, nos aguantábamos el hambre. El clima era brutal durante el resto del mes de enero de 1945, y las temperauras raramente subían sobre cero durante el día y se hundían bajo cero durante la noche. El frío torcía los labios sobre los dientes titiritantes, y los ojos miraban lastimosamente hacia la nada. Caballos y humanos soportaron por igual las dificultades. La fe en Dios y el miedo de ser atropellados por tanques rusos o ser asesinados por bombas nos forzaban a seguir adelante y aguantar los sufrimientos y peligros que cada día traía consigo.

Al principio de febrero, la temperatura subió. Aún era demasiado frío como para abrir la cubierta al frente y en la parte posterior de la carreta, o para sentarse afuera al frente de la carreta. Conforme los días se alargaban y el sol calentaba, vimos la luz filtrándose a través de la cubierta. Incluso sentimos la calidez del sol cuando sacamos las manos sobre las coberturas del amanecer. La nieve empezó a derretirse, las ruedas de las carretas rodaban en suelo firme y calles pavimentadas otra vez.

Pasamos pueblos pequeños en el camino. Sin embargo, la ciudad mas emocionante por la que atravesamos hasta ahora era Stettin, la capital de Pomerania. Afortunadamente, algunos puentes aún estaban erguidos, y pudimos cruzar el río Oder, que fluye a través del lago Dammscher (Dammscher See) y más adelante se vacía en el mar Báltico. Pasar sobre el puente y ver las torres en ambas riberas y ver las torres de la iglesia y otros edificios esenciales fue una experiencia emocionante. También atravesamos secciones donde las bombas habían destruido la mayoría de los edificios. Solo paredes parciales e irregulares, con los huecos de las ventanas, permanecían entre pilas de escombros --- que imagen tan deprimente nos encontramos de lo que una vez fue una hermosa ciudad. Cada vez que pasábamos una hermosa estructura que aún estaba intacta, yo la señalaba para asegurarme de que mis hermanos no se la perdieran.

Después de pasar Stettin y alejarnos lo mas posible del centro de la ciudad, el señor Kirstein decidió encontrar refugio antes de que la oscuridad se asentara, para el caso de que la Fuerza Aérea Real decidiera soltarunas cuantas bombas mas sobre Stettin durante la noche. Cuando el señor Kirstein vió una casa aún intacta en las afueras de Stettin, decidió que nos quedaríamos ahí. Las seis carretas lo siguieron. Afortunadamente, una pareja de ancianos vivía ahí. Fueron lo suficientemente amables para permitirnos pasar la noche en su hogar. No tenían suficiente comida, así que todas las familias compartieron lo que aún poseían.

Febrero pasó. Marzo llegó, y también lo hicieron temperaturas más cálidas. Las carretas rodeaban un poco más rápido ahora. Georg recogía las cubiertas del frente y detrás de la carreta en la tarde, y el aire húmedo y fresco vigorizaba de alguna manera nuestros cuerpos débiles y delgados.

La nieve se había derretido, y las praderas empezaban a reverdecer. Incluso los árboles y los arbustos daban señales de la primavera y empezaban a brotar. La alondra volaba alto y emocionaba a todos con sus dulces y melódicas canciones, que no habían sido afectadas por la destrucción en el suelo. Las cigüeñas también habían vuelto. Muchas encontraron sus nidos en los techos destruidos y tuvieron que encontrar nuevas ubicaciones para reconstruir sus nidos. Acechaban en las praderas para recoger un bocado por aquí y por allá. Después de que los niños pasaran dos meses acosados y sentados en las carretas cubiertas, añoraban mover sus delgadas piernas. Querían correr por las praderas y jugar con los rayos del sol y perseguir a las cigüeñas. Los niños solo podían soñar con jugar; debían permanecer en la carreta y seguir con el viaje. Nadie sabía por cuánto mas la marcha tendría que seguir ni cual sería su destino.

Viajamos a través de las hermosas provincias de Mecklenburg y llegamos a las afueras de la ciudad de Schwerin. Afortunadamente, la ciudad soportó solamente cuatro ataques y pocos daños estructurales porque no tenía industrias esenciales. El romántico palacio permanecía sin cambios en uno de los siete lagos que rodeaban la parte vieja de Schwerin.

Como la marcha estaba en las periferias del pueblo, los viajeros solo podían ver la distante silueta del horizonte y del palacio. Sin embargo, los niños se emocionaban cada vez que veían un castillo, una elegante torre, o una torreta de iglesia aún intacta.

La marcha continuó viajando a través del adorable escenario pastoral de Mecklenburg, después pasó por Ratzenburgg hacia Luebeck. La ciudad sufrió terribles ataques aéreos durante Marzo de 1942, cuando Arthur Harris de la Fuerza Aérea Real de Inglaterra atacó áreas civiles y creó una tormenta de fuego. Destruyó tres de las iglesiasa mas importantes y causó daños masivos a las partes históricas del antiguo ueblo de Luebeck. Afortunadamente, la famosa Torre Holsten permaneció intacta. Los niños se emocionaban cuando pasaban por estructuras antiguas, góticas, de ladrillos rojos.

"Miren, miren," llamé la atención de mis hermanos mientras señalaba las dos masivas torres antes de pasar a través de la entrada. En la entrada, los oficiales le dijeron a los líderes de la marcha cuál sería su destino. Le dijeron al señor Kirstein, que el destino de su grupo era Pratjau. Entonces el señor Kirstein la pidió a su hijo Gustav que fuera a cada carreta y que les dijera que iríamos por Eutin hacia Pratjau. Todos suspiraron con alivio porque el viaje pronto terminaría después de estar en el camino dentro de una carreta cubierta por casi diez semanas seguidas.

Pasamos el río Trave antes de llegar a la vieja sección del pueblo.

"Que triste, las bombas dañaron algunos de los edificios medievales," remarcó Edmund.

"Si, definitivamente es una pena, los antiguos edificios se mantuvieron erguidos por cientos de años, y en un ataque aéreo destruyeron tantas estructuras en minutos," yo remarqué. "Yo espero que la guerra y la destrucción terminen pronto, y que podamos ir a casa," añadió Richard. Edmund contestó, "Yo también lo deseo. Desafortunadamente, nadie sabe cuando acabará la guerra."

Sin embargo, sabíamos que nuestro arduo viaje terminaría pronto.

Aún era de día cuando pasamos Luebeck. El señor Kirsetin decidió manejar lo mas lejos posible del centro de la ciudad para evadir un posible ataque aéreo. Cuando vimos una granja, se detuvo y fue a preguntar al dueño si él y las otras familias podrían pasar la noche en su granja. La esposa del granjero también salió de la casa y ofreció que las familias se asentaran para pasar la noche.

"Pasen, y les mostraré donde pueden quedarse; las madres y los niños pueden dormir en la casa, y los hijos más grandes y hombres pueden dormir en el granero. También pueden usar heno para los caballos. Cocinaré algo de sopa para todos ustedes, para que tengan algo caliente en sus estómagos."

El señor Kirstein agradeció a los granjeros y le dijo a los viajeros que nos quedaríamos ahí por la noche y que nuestro destino sería Pratjau, al que deberíamos llegar en unos pocos días. Todos se bajaron de las carretas y estaban contentos de escuchar las buenas nuevas de que el viaje casi terminaba.

Las madres y sus hijas mayores llevaron las cobijas de plumas adentro de la casa donde la esposa del granjero les había designado que podían dormir. Los hombres y chicos mas grandes desataron a los caballos, les dieron forraje y agua. Los niños se reunieron en el patio y jugaron a las atrapadas entre ellos hasta que mamá nos llamó para cenar y para alistarnos para dormir.

A la mañana siguiente la señora cocinó algo de avena con leche fresca para todos los niños y sirvió pan y mermelada para los adultos con café hecho de nogal. Las madres le agradecieron a la esposa del granjero por su generosidad y amabilidad, y el señor Kirstein le agradeció al granjero por dejarnos quedarnos una noche y por proveer forraje para los caballos.

Georg, y mi madre, con Horst en su regazo, se sentaron en el frente de la carreta. Edmund, Richard y yo nos movimos a la parte de atrás de la carreta; colgamos nuestros pies a través de los rayos de la escalera, abrazando a la viga superior. Queríamos asegurarnos de que no se nos pasara nada. Emma y Meta eligieron caminar por un rato a lado de la carreta.

La primavera había llegado, no solamente de acuerdo al calendario, ¡sino también de acuerdo a la naturaleza! Finalmente, las temperaturas subieron lo suficiente como para usaar ropas mas ligeras y no queadrnos bajo las cobijas de plumas todo el día. Pasamos a través de verdes praderas de pastoreo embellecidas con las flores primaverales. Delicadas hojas verdes adornaban los arbustos y árboles a lo largo del camino. Las aves migratorias volvieron. Las cigüeñas acechaban los campos, esperando atrapar alguna rana.

"¿Tú crees que las cigüeñas también hayan regresado al nido en la cima de nuestro establo?" preguné.

"Espero que si. Como quiesiera estar en casa y ver a las golondrinas construir sus nidos bajo los techos," respondió Edmund.

"Qué emoción escuchar el canto de la alindra y la llamada de la gallina," remarcó Richard.

"¿Crees que encontremos las mismas aves a dónde vamos que las que teníamos en casa?" pregunté.

"Tenemos que esperar y ver qué nos encontramos en Pratjau," respondió Edmund.

Los niños miraban de izquierda a derecha y no querían perderse nada. Estar absortos con el adorable escenario hacía que el tiempo pasara mucho más rápido para los niños. De vez en cuando, Emma y Meta subían a la carreta y tomaban las riendas para darle un descanso a Georg y la oportunidad de caminar, para aflojar sus piernas.

El señor Kirstein se detuvo alrededor de medio día en otra granja grande para pedir algo de forraje para los caballos, darles un descanso, y pedir algo de comida, principalmente para los niños.

En la tarde, la silueta de Eutin apareció en el horizonte con el majestuoso castillo de Eutin y los dos campanarios de sus iglesias resaltaban sobre el resto del pueblo. Conforme nos acercábamos a la ciudad, las estructuras de ladrillos rojos estaban cada vez más cerca. Pronto el lago se hizo visible.

"Que bien se ven los edificios de ladrillo rojo entre el delicado verde de los árboles en brote," yo exclamé.

"Si, en realidad es bonito ver un pueblo que no ha sido destruido por bombas," remarcó Edmund.

"Me pregunto cómo se verá el lugar donde nos vamos a quedar" questionó Richard.

"Espero que tengamos mucho espacio para correr y jugar."
"Yo también. Estoy tana cansada de estar sentada
todo el día."

"Si, estaé contento de dormir en una cama de verdad otra vez en lugar de apretado en la carreta o dormir en el piso."

"Esperaremos a ver donde aterrizamos."

El señor Kirstein vio un camino estrecho que llevaba a una granja grande, dirigió a su grupo hacia allá. Afortunadamente, el granjero tuvo piedad de nosotros, los viajeros de aspecto patético.

"Pueden quedarse aquí por esta noche," dijo la esposa del granjero, "le diré a mi cocinera que prepare algo para ustedes." La esposa del granjero llamó a su cocinera y le instruyó que preparara comida para las familias. La granja empleaba a muchos trabajadores que dormían y comían en la granja durante la semana. En fines de semana, los trabajadores iban a sus casas con sus familias. El comedor y sus habitaciones estaban vacantes sábados y domingos. La dama de la casa le pidió a la cocinera que nos enseñara donde estaban las habitaciones de los trabajadores, donde podríamos dormir esa noche.

"Prepara la mesa en el comedor para la gente."

Mientras cocinaban la comida, las mamás llevaron a sus familias a los edificios donde dormirían. Aunque dos personas debian compartir una cama, había suficientes para los treinta y cinco viajeros. Una vez que los niños supieron donde iban a dormir y comer, corrieron afuera para explorar y ver qué podrían descubrir. A una distancia corta del establo, los niños vieron un estanque.

"Veamos quién puede llegar ahí primero," dijo Richard. "Fórmense aquí."

Frieda, Edna, Helmut y yo formamos una línea a un lado de Richard. Cuando Richard dijo, "Uno, dos, tres, va," todos arrancaron hacia adelante. Richard levantó sus manos y anunció que él era el ganador. Los niños se acercarom al estanque y pusieron sus manos en el agua para ver si estaba lo suficientemente tibia para quitarse sus zapatos y caminar en el estanque.

"Está muy frío para mi, y no me quiero meter en el agua," Frieda le informó a sus compañeros. Decidieron caminar alrededor del estanque para ver si podían encontrar ranas o peces pero no vieron nada.

"Corramos alrededor del estanque unas cuantas veces."
"Miren, hay algunas violetas en el pasto," llamé a Frieda y Edna.

"Frieda, quiero recoger algunas; ¿quiéres quedarte conmigo?"

"Claro, dejemos que los niños corran y jueguen mientras nos quedamos atrás."

"Yo también me quedaré contigo," dijo Edna.

Las tres buscamos en la pradera y estábamos encantadas cada vez que encontrábamos un racimo de violetas. Cuando tuvimos un puñado de violetas, decidimos regresar a la casa. Frieda, Edna y yo corrimos a nuestras adres para darles nuestro atesorado regalo.

"Qué hermosasson las flores; ¿Dónde las encontraron?" "Las encontré cerca del estanque. ¿Podemos ponerlas en la mesa del comedor para que todos las disfruten?"

"Por supuesto, querida. Ve y pregúntale a la señora de la casa si está de acuerdo en darte un contenedor para ponerlas."

Corrí hacia la casa, toqué la puerta, y esperé a que la señora saliera.

"Buenas tardes," sosteniendo el bouquet de violetas, le dije, "mire lo que encontré cerca del estanque. ¿Está bien si las ponemos en la mesa del comedor, y podría darme un florero?"

"Por supuesto, esper, te traeré uno,"

"Toma este," dijo mientras me daba un florero.

Le agradecí a la señora y corrí al comedor para enseñárselo a mis amigas.

"Miren, Frieda y Edna, podemos poner todas nuestras flores juntas." Edna y yo le dimos nuestras violetas a Frieda. Ella las acomodó y las puso en una de las mesas de comedor en la gran habitación.

Aunque el bouquet se veía pequeño en la gran mesa, le añadía un toque de belleza y le recordaba a los viajeros la llegada de la primavera.

La cocinera llamó a las personas a la mesa y le pidió a las chicas mas grandes que sirvieran la comida. Los hombres estaban muy contentos de sentarse a comer, ser servidos, y no tener que esperar en una fila por un largo tiempo.

Después de que todos habían comido, el señor Kirstein se levantó. Se dirigió a su grupo de compañeros viajeros, "Esta será probablemente la última vez que estemos todos juntos antes de que cada familia vaya a un lugar diferente. Sé que hemos soportado grandes dificultades, hambre, frío, y peligros, pero todos tenemos una razón para estar agradecidos con Dios, que nos guió y protegió, sin cuya ayuda nunca lo hubiéramos logrado. Levantémonos y cantemos juntos,"

"Ahora, agradezcamos todos a Dios."

Después de que todos se pusieran de pie, el señor Kirstein empezó a cantar y todos se le unieron:

Ahora agradezcamos todos a Dios, con corazones, manos y voces,

Quién ha hecho cosas maravillosas, en quien este mundo se regocija.

¿Quién nos ha bendecido a través de los brazos de nuestras madres en nuestro camino?

Con incontables regalos de amor, y aún es nuestro el día de hoy.

Emma, las dos Getas y Wanda se sabían las palabras de los tres versos de memoria. El resto tarareaban la melodía. Después de que terminamos de cantar, el señor Kirsetein les deseó a todos buenas noches y mencionó que debíamos empezar temprano en la mañana para llegar a nuestro destino con luz de día. La esposa del granjero le pidió a la cocinera que preparara un desayuno de avena caliente para los niños y que hiciera pan, mantequilla y sandwiches de miel para los adultos.

Cuando el gallo cantó temprano en la mañana, mi mamá nos despertó y nos dijo que nos alistáramos para el viaje.

"Gracias a Dios, estos serán nuestros últimos dos días en el camino; me pregunto donde nos quedaremos ahora," mamá le remarcaba a Emma. "Ve y ayuda a Georg a alimentar a los caballos."

"Meta, tu toma todas las cobijas de plumas y llévalas a la carreta, después desayunemos y pongámonos en marcha."

La esposa del granjero y su marido salieron a las 6:00 a.m. a despedirse de nosotros. El señor Kirstein y todas las madres le agradecieron por permitirnos pasar la noche en la granja y proveernos con comida. Pasamos una noche mas en una escuela de una aldea pequeña antes de llegar por la tarde a Pratjau.

Cuando llegamos a la aldea, el señor Kirstein llegó a un lugar con un gran patio, y las seis carretas lo siguieron. El primer edificio estaba vacío, pero una familia vivía a un lado. El señor Kirstein tocó la puerta y una persona amigable salió. "Buenas tardes, yo soy el señor Kirstein; mi grupo de refugiados y yo fuimos instruidos asentarnos en Pratjau.

¿Podría indicame donde vive el alcalde, para que nos diga a dónde debe ir cada familia?"

"Buenas tardes, yo soy el señor Sabrow, el maestro de gramática de la escuela. Espere aquí, llamaré a mi criada, ella puede mostrarle dónde vive el alcalde."

"Ella es Olga; los llevará con el alcalde" "Que tenga buen día, señor Kirstein."

"Podemos ir todos juntos con las carretas. Hay suficiente espacio en la plaza de la aldea para todos ustedes," dijo Olga. "Bien, entonces súbete a mi carreta, Iremos ahí juntos. A una distancia corta de la escuela, las carretas se detuvieron en la plaza de la aldea. Olga señaló la casa donde vivía el alcalde.

El señor Kirstein fue, tocó la puerta, y un hombre de mediana edad salió.

El señor Kirstein se presentó y dijo su razón para contactarlo. El alcalde lo saludó y le dijo que mandaría a su hijo a cada carreta de cada familia designada.

"Sin embargo, tres de las familias tendrán que ir a Sophienhof. Está a solo una milla de aquí."

El señor Kirstein le agradeció a Olga y la despachó. Se volvió para hablar con la familias Hein, Marta Kirstein y la familia Bonacker y les dijo que fueran a Sophienhof, un rancho enorme. Agradecidas, tres familias partieron de los otros viajers y se dirigieron a su destino asignado en Sophienhof.

CAPÍTULO 9

La Vida en Sophienhof

El administrador de estado, el señor Otzen, se reunió con las tres familias y les enseñó dónde iban a vivir. Ocho de nosotros compartíamos un departamento de una habitación con cinco de la familia Hein, trece en total. La familia Hein ocupó la habitación y nuestra familia, la sala. Todos usábamos la cocina. La señora Martha Kirstein y sus dos hijos compartían un apartamento de una habitación con cuatro otras personas en la puerta siguiente. El dueño del terreno había construido los dos edificios triples de ladrillo rojo para sus trabajadores y sus familias.

"Les mostraré dónde pueden poner a sus caballos y carretas," el señor Otzen señaló al establo. Antes de que descarguen las carretas, pueden dejarlas afuera, en frente del establo por el momento," informó el señor Otzen a las familias, "vayan al gran comedor, a un lado de la mansión. La cocinera y su ayudante han preparado una comida para ustedes."

Georg se bajó de la carreta primero, después ayudó a mamá y a Horst a bajar. Todos los niños siguieron a mamá hacia el comedor, también lo hizo la familia Hein y Martha Kirstein con sus dos hijos. La cocinera había preparado una sopa de guisantes partidos con pedacitos de carne de puerco en ella.

Cada uno podía comer también un pedazo de pan. Los cuatro niños pequeños recibieron un vas de leche.

Mi mamá y la señora Hein entraron a la casa primero. Un pequeño pasillo llevaba a tres habitaciones, una cocina a la izquierda, una pequeña recámara a la derecha, y la sala al frente.

"Dios mío, ¿catorce personas tienen que vivir en estas dos habitaciones? ¿Cómo va a funcionar eso?" cuestionó la señora Hein.

"Seguro estaremos apretados, pero debemos hacer lo mejor que podamos," respondió mamá. "Es mejor que vivir en la carreta; también creo que estaremos más seguros aquí," añadió mamá mientras entraba en la sala.

"Espero que así sea," respondió la señora Hein. Miraron el contenido de las habitaciones.

Tres marcos de madera primitivos, cada uno con un saco grande lleno de paja, estaba a lo largo de las paredes y servían como camas. Una mesa grande y algunas sillas estaban en el centro de la habitación. Un horno, cubierto de azulejos brillantes de color verde, estaba empotrado en la esquina a un lado de la entrada de la sala. Iba desde el suelo hasta el techo. Cuando estaba encendido, proveía de suficiente calor para calentar la sala y la recámara.

Los muebles de la cocina consistían en una mesa grande con una larga banca en cada lado. Baldes llenos de agua utilizaban una banca mas pequeña contra la pared. No había agua corriente en la casa. Debíamos acarrearla de un pozo o de un arroyo cercano a la casa. Contra una pared había una estufa de madera para cocinar. Los pisos de la entrada y de la cocina eran de concreto y paneles de madera cubrían los pisos de la recámara y la sala.

El señor Anderson, el asistente del administrador del terreno, vivía con su familia en la puerta siguiente a donde nos mudamos. La señora Anderson vino a saludar a las familias.

"Yo se que el apartamento es demasiado pequeño para dos familias, pero no hay nada mas que esté vacante."

"Haremos lo mejor que podamos. Estoy feliz de que ya no vivamos en la carreta ni estemos en un lugar diferente cada día," respondió mamá. "Quiero que conozca a mis dos hijas mayores, Emma y Meta."

Después de que el señor Anderson estrechara sus manos, se excusó y dejó que mi mamá y sus hijas continuaran desempacando primero las cobijas de plumas, después la ropa y otras pocas pertenencias que llevaban a la casa hasta que la carreta estuvo vacía. Después Georg trajo los caballos, los ató a la carreta y la jaló hacia el lugar designado. Después, llevó a los caballos al establo, les quitó los arneses, y los ató con un collar de cuero y una cuerda a un poste junto al lugar donde se alimentaban. Después Georg consiguió un balde de agua del pozo y heno del granero para los caballos.

Edmund, Richard, y yo hicimos rondas, nos familiarizamos con los alrededores con la esperanza de conocer a mas niños de nuestra edad. Un niño y una niña de la casa vecina salieron a vernos.

"¿Quiénes son? ¿qué hacen aquí?" nos preguntó el niño a nosotros, extraños.

"Mi nombre es Edmund; él es mi hermano Richard y mi hermana Hilde. Somos refugiados y se supone que vivamos aquí. ¿Cuáles son sus nombres?"

"Mi nombre es Hans, y esta es mi hermana Lisa," respondió el niño.

Todos estrechamos manos.

"¿Quieren que les enseñe los alrededores?" preguntó Hans.

"¡Oh si! Déjame ver si Frieda quiere acompañarnos."

Fui adentro y llamé a Frieda, "¿Quieres ir con nosotros y ver la granja?"

"Ahora no, debo ayudar a mi mamá a desempacar," respondió ella.

"Okey, entonces iré sola."

Hans y Lisa se dirigieron a la mansión primero. Edmund, Richard, y yo los seguimos.

Señalando a la casa, "Aquí es donde vive el señor Jessen, el dueño del terreno. Es muy estricto y no quiere que los niños jueguen dentro del establo o de otros edificios."

"El interior debe ser hermoso, juzgando por las cortinas de encaje en los ventanales", remarqué.

"Si, los muebles también son exquisitos, pero la señora Jessen casi nunca sale de la casa y el señor Jessen cojea. Miren detrás de la casa al maravilloso jardín. En el verano, los árboles están cargados con frutos. Sus manzanas y peras son dulces y jugosas."

Después cruzaron la calle, "Aquí es donde viven el señor Diercks y su familia. El señor Diercks es el administrador del ganado. Puede ser malo si te ve haciendo algo que no le gusta. La señora Diercks distribuye la leche todos los días para los hijos de las familias. Ella también recibe y distribuye el correo cada semana."

Pasamos el establo de las vacas. Frente al establo había un enorme tanque de cemento. Los trabajadores recolectaban y vaciaban el abono de las vacas en un pozo de cemento abierto durante el invierno y lo esparcían como fertilizante sobre los campos en la primavera. Después, pasaron el granero y el chiquero y llegaron a la casa del señor Otzen y su familia con un hermoso jardín a su lado.

"Deben cuidarse del señor Otzen. El reporta cualquier acto indebido al señor Jessen y puede meterlos en problemas. Sin embargo, sus hijos, Heike y Willie son muy buenos."

"Ahora, los llevaré al estanque detrás de los establos de las vacas. No pueden nadar en el estanque. El agua para lavar los establos se ensucia y se drena en el estanque. Se enfermarán si se les mete agua a la boca mientras nadan. Sin embargo, en invierno, pueden patinar en el."

"Qué pena; me gusta nadar," Edmund remarcó. "A mi también," añadió Richard.

"Cuando queremos nadar vamos al lago Selenter. Está a una distancia corta de aquí. Vamos frecuentemente en el verano. Pueden venir con nosotros si quieren"

"Es mejor que regresemos con mamá. Se estará preguntando dónde estamos," remarqué mientras volteaba a la casa donde nos quedaríamos.

"Adiós, Hans y Lisa. Gracias por mostrarnos los alrededores. ¿Podemos verlos mañana?" Remarcó Richard antes de que se fueran a su departamento.

Mientras tanto, el sol empezó a ponerse, y las madres se preocupaban por conseguir la cena para sus hijos. La señora Anderson se sintió mal por los niños y mandó una hogaza de pan, un pedazo pequeño de mantequilla, y salchicha casera a la señora Hein y a mi madre. Como la cocina era demasiado pequeña para alimentar a las catorce personas al mismo tiempo, la señora Hein estuvo de acuerdo en dejar que mi mamá y su familia cocinaran y comieran primero.

Emma encendió el fuego en la estufa de leña para calentar una olla de agua para el te y lavar las manos y caras de sus hermanos y hermanas. Antes de alistarnos para la cama, pregunté, "¿Mamá, donde está el baño?"

"Está en el chiquero en frente de la casa," respondió mamá. "¿En el chiquero?"

"¡Eso se oye horrible! Si tengo que ir en la noche, ¿tengo que caminar afuera en la oscuridad hacia el chiquero?"

"Te acostumbrarás," respondió mamá.

Pensé que nunca me acostumbraría a ello, pero no me atreví a decírselo a mamá.

Fui al otro lado del chiquero a revisar el baño. No estaba muy entusiasmada con la ubicación ni con el olor. Ciertamente tampoco me acostumbraría a usarlo.

El resto de la tarde pasó en desorden. Mamá asignó los lugares para dormir para las tres camas que estaban contra la pared.

"Emma, Meta y Hildke, ustedes duerman en esta cama en la esquina. Georg, Edmund, y Richard, ustedes duerman en la cama a lado de sus hermanas. Horst y yo tomaremos la primera cama."

Aunque a nosotros como niños no nos gustaba la idea de tres personas durmiendo en una cama pequeña, obedecimos a nuestra madre.

La primera noche fue incómoda para mi. Cada vez que Emma o Meta se daban la vuelta, me despertaban al patearme en un costado o en la barbilla. Vestirme en la presencia de mis hermanos y no saber cuándo algún miembro de la familia Hein podría pasar me apenaba. Estoy segura de que lo mismo les pasaba a mis hermanas.

Cuando le dije a Emma y Meta sobre mi incomodidad, ellas encontraron una solución sosteniendo una de las cobijas de plumas hacia la pared, para que nadie me viera vestirme o desvestirme a la hora de dormir. Yo hacía lo mismo para ellas también.

Tomó varios días acostumbrarnos a nuestros nuevos cuartos y arreglos de vivienda. Pronto, Emma arregló una cama en la recámara más pequeña, Georg se instaló en la despensa, para que solo dos hermanos durmieran en cada cama. Mamá y la señora Hein arreglaron el uso de la cocina. Cocinábamos y comíamos el desayuno, comida y cena primero, y la señora Hein y su familia después. A cada familia era asignado un día de baño en una tina grande en la cocina --- nuestra familia en viernes y la familia de la señora Hein en sábado. De alguna manera, desarrollamos una rutina tolerable y lentamente nos familiarizamos con todos los vecinos y familias del terreno.

El señor y la señora Anderson, nuestros vecinos de la izquierda, le dieron trabajo a Georg cuidando a los caballos y trabajando en los campos cuando se necesitaba. El señor Diercks le pidió a Emma y a Meta que ordeñaran a las vacas, que ya pastaban en las pasturas. La paga era mínima, pero en retorno, la familia recibía leche fresca cada día, algo de grano y otros alimentos. Una parcela para un jardín también fue asignada, misma que compartíamos con la familia Hein.

En unos cuantos días, el 1 de abril de 1945, celebraríamos la primera Pascua lejos de casa. Mamá estaba preocupada por ir a la iglesia y con qué alimentar a su familia en esta memorable festividad.

Le preguntó a la señora Anderson donde estaba la iglesia más cercana.

"Usualmente vamos a la aldea vecina, Fargau, a la iglesia. En ocasiones especiales, el servicio religioso se da en el castillo de Salzau, también, pero no en esta Pascua."

"¿Van a ir a la iglesia? Como no sabemos dónde está Fargau, ¿podríamos seguirlos?"

"Claro que si, el señor y la señora Jessen y otras familias también van a ir. El servicio empieza a las 9:00 a.m. Estén listos a las 8:30 a.m. Está sólo a unas millas de aquí. Pero nos gusta llegar temprano, para que podamos encontrar un buen lugar para asegurar a los caballos."

"Gracias; se lo haré saber a Georg. Mi familia estará lista a las 8:30 a.m."

"Por cierto, ¿tienen alguna comida especial para la Pascua? Si no la tiene, le pediré a mi esposo que sacrifique algunos pollos extra para tu familia."

"Gracias; es muy amable de tu parte ofrecerme pollo fresco. Mi familia estará muy agradecida y feliz de tener carne."

"También mandaré papas y nabos con el pollo." "Muchas, muchas gracias."

"También tenemos una costumbre de Pascua aquí de ir por agua al arroyo. Se supone que cura distintas enfermedades después de que te lavas con ella. Pero la persona que va por el agua no puede mirar a la izquierda ni a la derecha ni hablar; de otra manera, el agua pierde sus poderes curativos. Espera, te daré una docena de huevos. Tus hijas pueden colorearlos para los niños."

"Seguramente aprecien un huevo colorido para Pascua."

La señora Anderson le entregó a mamá un recipiente lleno de huevos. Mi mamá le agradeció de nuevo y llevó los huevos a la casa.

"Miren lo que tenemos aquí," enseñando el recipiente de huevos a la familia.

La señora Anderson me los dio. También sacrificará a algunos pollos para nosotros. La señora Anderson también me dijo que habrá servicio religioso en la iglesia de Fargau el Domingo de Pascua. Georg, iremos a la iglesia de Fargau. Ten los caballos y la carreta listos para las 8:30 a.m.

"Ten, Emma, tu puedes hervir los huevos y colorearlos para nosotros."

"¿Qué usaré? ¿No tenemos color?"

"Ve al bosque cercano; puede ser que encuentres flores. También puedes usar musgo o cortezas viejas. Pon cada cosa en un recipiente individual, después hierve agua y vacía el agua caliente sobre ellos. Déjalo reposar por un rato o toda la noche

antes de que remuevas las flores, musgo y cortezas, y tendrás unas soluciones coloreadas para pintar los huevos." "Esa es una idea inteligente. Iré ahora mismo al bosque
cercano y veré qué puedo encontrar ahí." "¿Puedo ir contigo, Emma?" le pregunté.

"Si, puedes venir conmigo; consigamos un balde primero."

Nos fuimos. Yo saltaba alegremente hasta que llegamos al bosque.

"Mira a todas esas hermosas primaveras amarillas," dije mientras las recogía un racimo tras otro mientras Emma juntaba algo de musgo y recogía corteza pulverizada, que encontró junto a la cepa podrida de un árbol. Caminamos con cuidado por el bosque para no pisar las primaveras y las anémonas que cubrían el suelo como una alfombra mágica.

"¿Puedo también recoger algunas flores para la mesa?" "Claro que si, sería lindo tener flores frescas en la mesa."

Recogí algunas flores de anémonas blancas primaverales y no-me-olvides silvestres que encontré en la orilla de un pequeño estante y las mezclé con las primaveras.

"¿Está bien si corro para adelantarme? Quiero sorprender a mamá"

"Si, puedes correr. Yo te seguiré."

Corrí a la casa a presentarle el ramo a mamá.

"Mira, mamá, lo que encontré para ti, ¿no son hermosas?" remarqué mientras le entregaba las flores a mamá.

"Gracias, son hermosas. Déjame ver dónde puedo conseguir un contenedor para las flores."

Mamá entró en la cocina y encontró una taza con el asa rota. Me la dio.

"Ten, usa esto. Pon las flores en la sala por ahora, y el Domingo de Pascua, podemos ponerlas en la mesa de la cocina con nuestra comida."

"Muy bien. Así lo haré."

Mientras tanto, Emma volvió con el balde lleno. Fue a la cocina y puso una olla de agua en el hogar Después Emma puso el musgo, la corteza y las florecillas en tazas individuales y le vertió agua hirviendo a cada una. Las dejó reposar por la noche.

Después de que nuestra familia desayunó la mañana siguiente, yo inmediatamente me ofrecí a ayudar a Emma a colorear los huevos.

"Tenemos que esperar a que la familia Hein tome su desayuno primero antes de que podamos usar la cocina. Ve a jugar afuera; te llamaré cuando esté lista."

Corrí afuera. Vi a dos niñas jugando con sus muñecas en los escalones de una casa vecina. Me acerqué lentamente.

"Mi nombre es Hildegard. Todos me llaman Hilde. Mi familia y yo llegamos aquí hace cuatro días. Mamá nos dijo que nos quedaríamos aquí por un tiempo." Después de que las dos niñas me miraron, se presentaron como Katie y Brigitte. "Ven, siéntate, y cuéntanos de donde vienes," me

invitó Katie.

Respondí todas las preguntas que me hicieron las niñas. Brigitte y Katie estaban sorprendidas de escuchar que mi familia y yo veníamos de Prusia del Este a caballo y carruaje; y que incluso viajamos durante el invierno.

"Mamá tiene la esperanza de que la guerra termine pronto, para que podamos volver a nuestro hogar en nuestra granja en Prusia del Este," añadí.

"Si, nuestros padres y nosotras tenemos la misma esperanza. Últimamente, la escuela ha cerrado por los ataques aéreos."

"¿A qué escuela van?"

"Vamos a Pratjau; está a una distancia corta a pie de aquí," añadió Katie.

"Espero que puedan reabrir la escuela pronto. A mi me gusta ir a la escuela," remarqué.

"Espero que nos den un maestro nuevo. No me gusta mucho el actual. Es muy estricto y nos castiga severamente si hacemos algo mal," comentó Brigitte.

"Fue lindo conocerlas. ¿Puedo venir mas tarde a jugar con ustedes? Debo ayudar a mi hermana a colorear huevos." Cuando escuché a mi hermana Emma llamándome, me excusé. Emma había removido las florecillas, el musgo y la corteza de las tazas. Esperó un poco mientras el sedimento se asentaba en el fondo de las tazas. Puso el primer huevo en el

líquido verde.

"Déjame poner el siguiente huevo en el líquido color amarillo," le dije.

"Claro, ¡adelante! Puedes hacer los huevos siguientes también."

Con mucho cuidado metí un huevo en la solución amarilla y otro en la café. Después esperamos y miramos como los huevos tomaban distintos colores. Después esperamos y miramos a los huevos teñirse de los diferentes colores. Con una cuchara, Emma sacó el primero huevo del líquido café y lo secó.

"Está lo suficientemente oscuro; puedes poner otro."

Cuando todos los huevos estuvieron coloreados, los pusimos en un plato, los llevamos a la sala y los colocamos a un lado de las flores. Era un símbolo, nos recordaba a la Pascua en casa.

Emma le ofreció las soluciones con color a Frau Hein, pero ella no estaba interesada en colorear huevos de Pascua.

El viernes era día de baño. Después de que ambas familias cenaron, Emma puso una gran olla de agua en el hogar. Meta y Georg acarreaban baldes de agua del pozo a la cocina. Georg le había preguntado al administrador si podía tomar prestado uno de los contenedores de metal, que tenía agua para las vacas mientras ellas estaban en las pasturas. El administrador le dio uno, y lo trajo a casa como tina de baño para nuestra familia. Emma vació primero una olla entera de agua caliente en la tina, después suficiente agua fría para hacerla cómodamente tibia al tacto. Después llamó a Horst, lo desvistió, y lo sentó en la tina. Él estaba tan feliz, golpeaba el agua con ambas manos salpicando por doquier. Pero cuando llegó el momento de lavar su cabeza con jabón casero, no le gustó y empezó a llorar. Cuando Emma terminó con Horst, era mi turno. Emma añadió mas agua caliente a la tina.

"Se siente muy bien tomar un baño; lava solo mi cabello, Emma, el resto lo puedo lavar yo."

"Como quieras, pero hazlo rápido; el resto de tus hermanos y mamá necesitan tomar un baño también."

"Esta bien, me apresuraré."

Me salí de la tina, froté mi cabello para secarlo primero, después el resto de mi cuerpo antes de ponerme mi ropa interior y camisa. Corrí a la sala, salté en la cama, y me metí bajo la cobija. Me apenaría mucho que alguien me viera en mi ropa interior. Le pedí a mamá un peine. Envolví la cobija de plumas a mi alrededor mientras cepillaba mi cabello mojado. Después me arrodillé en la cama y dije mis oraciones antes de dormir.

Después de que los niños tomaran sus baños, Emma cambió el agua para nuestra madre, Meta y ella misma. La familia Hein pasaba por el mismo ritual el sábado.

La noche del sábado, me desperté en varias ocasiones por miedo a dormir más allá del amanecer; quería asegurarme de ser la primera persona en estar en el arroyo. Aún estaba oscuro cuando me levanté silenciosamente, me puse mi vestido, mis zapatos, tomé un balde y fui al arroyo. Todos dormían aún. Eso era bueno, pensé. Cuando llegué al riachuelo, sumergí la apertura del balde en el agua corriente hasta que lo llené a tres cuartos. Lo levanté y comencé mi regreso a casa. Justo entones, vi a nuestra vecina, Lisa, salir de la puerta. Me apresuré detrás del otro lado de la casa y entré antes de que Lisa pudiera verme. Estaba feliz y llevaba el agua mágica a la sala, para que nadie más que nuestra familia pudiera usarla. Después me quité mi vestido, me metí sin ser notada bajo las cobijas, y esperé a que mi mamá despertara a todos.

El llamado de mamá hizo que todos salieran de sus camas. "Mamá, mira, traje agua de Pascua para nosotros del arroyo." Señalando al balde en la esquina de la habitación. "Muy bien, mi niña, es suficiente para que cada uno de nosotros se lave su cara." Mamá había puesto para cada uno de sus hijos las mejores ropas que pudo encontrar en el montón amarrado en una sábana y nos las dio a mi, Richard, Edmund, y Georg. Emma y Meta escogieron las suyas. Los vestidos, sin planchar, se veían arrugados y desaliñados, pero tendrían que ser suficientes por el momento.

A las 8:30 a.m. puntualmente, Georg tenía a los caballos en sus arneses y atados a la carreta; también lo hicieron así las otras familias que querían ir a la iglesia. Ese día, incluso los dueños, el señor y la señora Jessen, tenían su carruaje elegante dispuesto para ir a la iglesia el Domingo de Pascua. Todas las carretas siguieron al carruaje.

Era un hermoso día de primavera. La alondra subía tan alto que difícilmente podía verse, pero podía escucharse su alegre canción. Las primeras flores de primavera aparecieron entre las frescas praderas verdes; que encanto de ver. Llegamos a tiempo para desatar a los caballos de las carretas y atarlos a la viga. El cochero del señor Jessen se quedó con los caballos para vigilarlos y al carruaje. La señora Jessen lucía elegante en un traje brillante con un sombrero a juego, caminado a un lado de su esposo que cojeaba. Todos los seguían. Cuando entramos a la iglesia, los pobladores locales nos veían de pies a cabeza como diciendo, "¿De dónde vinieron esos gitanos?" Nos sentimos incómodos de que nuestra ropa, así como la de los otros refugiados, se viera tan patética.

Tan pronto como el órgano comenzó a tocar y cantamos la primera canción de Pascua, nos olvidamos de nuestra apariencia y solo cantamos junto con la congregación. El pastor dio un alentador sermón sobre la crucifixión y resurrección de Cristo y recordó a sus feligreses que estaban sirviendo a un Dios vivo y Señor. Cerró con las palabras: "Tengan valor; Dios los ayudará a atravesar esta guerra sin sentido y las dificultades que el país enfrenta." Después de la bendición, el pastor despidió a los fieles.

Me apresuré a la carreta para escapar de las miradas curiosas y degradantes de las personas. Mi familia me siguió y esperó a que el señor y la señora Jessen encabezaran el tren de carretas de regreso a Sophienhof.

Mamá, Emma y Meta empezaron a preparar pollo, papas, y repollo. Yo ayudé a poner la mesa. Puse los huevos coloreados alrededor del ramo como centro de mesa. Edmund y Richard fueron con Georg a poner a los caballos en el establo y les dieron algo de agua y heno. Cuando todo estuvo listo, mi mamá me mandó a llamar a los niños a la mesa. Todos nos sentamos en las dos bancas; mamá juntó sus manos, y también lo hicieron todos sus hijos. Mamá agradeció a Dios por la comida y por traer a sus hijos a salvo a través de las últimas traicioneras diez semanas de viaje. También rezó por la protección de su marido y de su hija, Marta, sin saber donde estaban o si aún estaban con vida.

Fotografía Familiar

La familia entera saboreó la comida. Emma dejó que cada quien escogiera un huevo de color. Los niños más pequeños tuvieron uno extra cada uno, y Emma pidió que los guardáramos para mañana. En la tarde, los niños salieron a revisar en las distintas áreas de los edificios. También conocieron a niños de las casas adyacentes, Uwe, Brigitte, y Hans. Platicaron, jugaron a las atrapadas, y disfrutaron de correr y moverse antes de sentarse o acostarse en las carretas por mucho tiempo.

El segundo día después de Pascua aún se consideraba día festivo y nadie trabajaba excepto los sirvientes que cuidaban animales y las personas que debían ordeñar a las vacas.

El día siguiente era 3 de abril de 1945, mientras las madres e hijas lavaban ropa y se asentaban, de repente, las sirenas penetraron el aire en la tarde. Los niños corrieron de afuera hacia adentro de la casa.

"Mamá, mamá, ¿qué está pasando?"

"Suena como la alarma de un ataque aéreo. Déjame correr con el vecino para preguntarle qué debemos hacer. Tu quédate adentro."

Mamá caminó a la casa del señor Anderson y le preguntó porqué sonaban las sirenas y qué debían hacer ella y su familia. "Suena como un ataque aéreo en Kiel; no tenemos búnker.

Corremos al bosque y esperamos ahí a que termine. A veces, solo nos quedamos en casa y esperamos a que el peligro pase. Nunca se sabe dónde o cuándo puedan soltar sus bombas"

"¿Deberíamos correr al bosque en este momento?"

"Creo que el día de bombardeo no va a durar mucho. Solo quédense en casa hasta que la alarma suene otra vez, anunciando el fin del ataque. Sin embargo, dígale a los niños que tengan cuidado con los bombarderos en picado durante el día. Atacan personas, trenes, carros o cualquier cosa al azar. En la noche, asegúrese de cubrir la ventana con una cobija gruesa cuando prendan la luz, para que los pilotos no puedan ver donde hay gente viviendo. Cuando suene la alarma por mucho tiempo o durante la noche, todos corremos al bosque a cubrirnos."

"Gracias por la información. Nunca pensé que las bombas pudieran matarnos después de haber sobrevivido el largo y extenuante camino," dijo mamá.

Mamá regresó a su familia y les advirtió del peligro y de que se cuidaran de los bombarderos en picado que disparaban y mataban a individuos cuando los veían al descubierto.

La señora Hein vino a la habitación y le preguntó a mamá porqué sonaban las sirenas. Nuestra madre pasó la información que recibió del señor Anderson. Todos esperamos callados y escuchamos con atención. Podíamos escuchar el distante sonido de los aeroplanos. Una vez, el sonido de los aeroplanos se volvió ensordecedor. Todos corrimos a mamá, pensando que una bomba caería sobre nosotros. Gracias a Dios, solo volaron sobre nosotros. La sirena sonó nuevamente unas horas mas tarde, dejándonos saber que el ataque con bombas había terminado por ahora.

Todos respiramos con alivio de que los aeroplanos no soltaran bombas sobre nosotros, y de que podíamos salir otra vez.

Al día siguiente Georg escuchó al señor Otzen mencionar al señor Anderson lo mal que estaban los muelles de Kiel, incluyendo los navíos de guerra, estaban destruidos, y muchas personas perdieron sus vidas.

Georg nos pasó las malas noticias en la comida. Vivíamos en peligro constante. El sonido de un escuadrón o de un aeroplano nos hacía temblar del miedo, y corríamos ya sea hacia adentro de la casa o del establo, lo que estuviera mas cerca de nosotros.

El 9 de abril de 1945, Kiel sufrió un gran ataque donde cientos de aeroplanos soltaron sus bombas en los puertos, áreas industriales y secciones residenciales.

La alarma sonó por un tiempo mientras yo aún dormía.

Mamá supo del peligro y nos despertó a todos.

"Vístanse rápido; debemos correr al bosque." Todas las otras familias se alistaron para ir a cubrirse al bosque también. Apenas habíamos llegado al estanque cuando una bomba perforó el aire con un chillido agudo antes de explotar con un gran estruendo. La tierra se sacudió por el impacto, mientras la bomba explotó entre los árboles a una corta distancia más adelante del estanque. El fuerte sonido de la explosión nos hizo cubrirnos los oídos y temblar de miedo de que fuéramos el siguiente objetivo. Mamá nos dijo que nos quedáramos ahí en el estanque y que nos acostáramos y nos cubriéramos con cobijas. La fresca noche de abril nos hizo estremecernos de frío y temblar por miedo a las bombas. Pasaba la media noche después de que ya no escuchamos más aeroplanos volando sobre nosotros. Todas las familias recogieron sus pertenencias, y nos regresamos a las casas.

"Gracias Dios por vigilarnos y protegernos del daño," expresó mamá. "Si hubiéramos llegado al bosque como planeábamos, todos hubiéramos sido asesinados."

Aunque fuimos de nuevo a la cama, me aferré fuerte a Meta, temiendo que mas bombarderos regresaran.

A la tarde siguiente, escuchamos mucha conmoción en el patio de la granja. Un grupo de soldados vino en camiones de guerra. ¡Se detuvieron! El conductor de uno de los camiones se bajó y fue a la casa del dueño. Después de que regresó, les ordenó a los soldados bajarse.

"Instalaremos cuarteles temporales aquí hasta que tengamos otras órdenes," les dijo a los soldados. Después todos se bajaron. Un grupo de soldados se veían un poco harapientos en sus uniformes caqui y verde oliva. Después nos enteramos de que eran prisioneros de guerra polacos y rusos. Mas niños se reunieron para ver lo que estaba pasando.

Nadie se atrevía a dirigirse a los soldados, pero platicaban entre ellos por un tiempo y externaron su curiosidad. Después se fueron.

Edmund fue a bosque detrás del estanque al día siguiente a ver el daño causado por la bomba. Vio un hoyo profundo y grande y mucha metralla alrededor. Conforme empezó a retroceder, Edmund notó una bomba que aún no explotaba. Estaba enterrada a la mitad en el suelo. Se acercó mucho para inspeccionar la bomba sin tocarla. Miró alrededor para ver si podía hallar más bombas. Edmund se regresó a casa cuando no encontró más y le dijo a mamá sobre la bomba que había encontrado. Mamá le advirtió que no debía tocarla ni levantarla. Podría explotar y matarte.

Mientras tanto, soldados alemanes y un grupo de prisioneros establecieron un campamento temporal en el terreno. Algunos soldados fueron lo suficientemente afortunados de conseguir una habitación, y otros levantaron tiendas de campaña en el bosque. Algunos incluso dormían en el establo. Después de limpiar y lavar los establos de las vacas, los prisioneros polacos los usaron como sus dormitorios; cubrieron el piso con paja a manera de colchón.

Los soldados instalaron una cocina móvil a un lado de la leñera, no muy lejos de nuestra casa. La cocina y sus al redores se volvieron mi campo de juegos favorito. Yo estaba encantada de oler los maravillosos aromas que venían de la cocina cuando preparaban las comidas para los soldados y los prisioneros.

Pronto, conocí a las dos hijas de la familia Diercks, Katie, la mayor y Elisabeth, la menor, que era de mi edad.

Para el sábado, vimos a algunos soldados construyendo una mesa en las praderas. Teníamos curiosidad sobre lo que los soldados harían con ella. Ambas caminamos hacia donde estaban los soldados, y Elisabeth les preguntó por qué estaban poniendo una mesa en el medio de la pradera.

"Mañana es domingo. Estamos intentando construir un pequeño altar. Nos gustaría tener un servicio religioso para los soldados y todos los residentes del terreno. Dile a tus padres y a todos los residentes sobre el servicio. Empezaremos a las 9:00 a.m. Pídeles que traigan sus propias sillas. Nosotros armaremos algunas bancas con tablas para los soldados."

"¿Podemos ayudar?" pregunté.

"Pregúntale a tus padres si pueden prestarnos un mantel blanco para ese día. Algunas velas y flores también se verían apropiadas."

"Le preguntaré a mi madre si puedo traerte uno de nuestros manteles," respondió Elisabeth.

"¿Cuándo lo necesitarás?"

"Hasta mañana a las 8:00 a.m. pero vuelve hoy mismo y dime qué es lo que puedes traer."

"Lo haré."

"Yo recogeré flores silvestres," añadí.

"Le preguntaré a mi madre si podemos recoger algunas de nuestro jardín," dijo Elisabeth.

"Bien, avísanos. Las veo después,"

Corrí al bosque, recogí un gran ramo de anémonas y primaveras, y me apresuré con los soldados, que aún estaban armando las bancas.

"Mira lo que encontré; ¿Puedes usar estas?" le entregué las flores al soldado.

"Muy bonitas; ahora necesitamos un contenedor donde ponerlas."

"Correré a casa y traeré uno."

Me apresuré de regreso con una taza de metal llena de agua. Puse el ramo en la taza y lo coloqué en la mesa. Elisabeth llegó con las buenas noticias de que su madre prestaría un mantel para mañana y dos candelabros con velas.

"Dile a tu madre que apreciamos su gentileza. Espero que pueda venir también al servicio."

"Creo que lo hará. Nuestra familia entera vendrá. Los veo mañana a las 8:00 a.m."

Me apresuré a casa a decirle a mamá y a mis hermanos sobre el servicio dominical que los soldados celebrarían en la pradera. Ya construyeron un altar y acomodaron una fila de bancas frente al altar.

"¿Iremos todos al servicio mañana?" "Por supuesto, iremos."

"¿A qué hora será?"

"A las 9:00 a.m., pero me iré una hora antes para ayudar a decorar el altar."

"Muy bien. Asegúrense todos de preparar sus ropas para mañana para que no se nos haga tarde."

A la mañana siguiente, me fui a las 8:00 a.m. para ayudar a Elisabeth a poner el mantel blanco, las velas y las flores en el altar. Después de apresurarse en el desayuno, mamá tomo a Horst de la mano y les pidió a sus seis hijos que la siguieran al servicio al aire libre.

"Georg, lleva una silla para mamá," dijo Emma. "Nosotros podemos sentarnos en el pasto."

Los soldados y los residentes se reunieron frente a un altar simbólico al aire libre con gran anticipación. Un hermoso mantel de encaje que llegaba hasta el suelo cubría la mesa. Un soldado había hecho una cruz con dos palos en un soporte, unidos por una delgada cuerda. Había dos candelabros a los lados izquierdo y derecho de la cruz, después dos ramos de lilas de distintos colores, y al final, mi pequeño ramo de flores blancas y amarillas.

Aunque era simple, les recordaba a todos a un altar de iglesia real, simbolizando un lugar de alabanza.

Un soldado vestido con uniforme se paró detrás del altar, les dio la bienvenida a los asistentes, y les pidió que cantaran "Más cerca mi Dios de ti."

Otro soldado vestido con uniforme de la marina se sentó a un lado del altar y tocó la melodía en un piano-acordeón.

Cuando cantábamos el segundo verso:

"Aunque igual que un viajero, el sol se ha escondido,
La oscuridad me cubra, mi descanso una piedra,
Aún así, en mis sueños, estaré más cerca, mi Dios, de ti."

Si, todos sentíamos la oscuridad, el peligro y el sufrimiento de la guerra y añorábamos la paz.

Después leyó el salmo 25, empezando: *"Hacia ti, elevo mi alma. Oh Dios mío, confío en ti; no me dejes avergonzarme. No dejes que mis enemigos triunfen sobre mi."*

Terminó con los últimos dos versos:

"Deja que la integridad y la rectitud me preserven,
Pues espero en ti. Redime a Israel,
Oh Dios, de todos estos problemas."

Y el pastor añadió, así como Dios liberó a Israel de toda dificultad, le rezamos a Dios que nos proteja de la guerra y todas las dificultados que nos ha causado. Después de que habló de las dificultades del Rey David y de su fe en el señor, tomó el tema de los problemas actuales de su gente y los animó a confiar en Dios, ser pacientes, y en su debido tiempo Dios nos salvará de esta guerra malvada y nos traerá paz.

"Terminemos nuestro servicio con el himno: *"Befiehl du deine Wege"* que se traduce al español: *"Encomienden sus actos al Señor."*

El soldado que tocaba el piano-acordeón empezó a tocar la canción, y todas las personas que recordaban la letra se unieron cantando:

"Encomienda lo que te aflige
En el corazón, y todos tus actos
A él que nunca te abandona,
A quién hizo la creación.
Quién libremente hace caminos
Para las nubes, el aire y el viento,
Y se preocupa por quien alguna vez toma
Un camino para que lo encuentres."

Pocas personas sabían la letra del último verso. Eran adecuadas, y el acordeonista las cantó a manera de oración:

"Oh Señor, no alargues más
Nuestro tiempo de miseria,
Nuestras manos y pies ahora se fortalecen,
Y hasta la muerte, Que seamos
vigilados y cuidados Por Ti,

En fidelidad y amor,
Así venimos donde preparado para
Nosotros es nuestra bendición. Morada. ”[11]

Las lágrimas que se habían acumulado en el corazón de mamá brotaron de sus ojos mientras escuchaba las reconfortantes palabras de la canción. Otras madres también lloraban pidiendo paz. El pastor oficiante cerró con una oración, y la bendición a los fieles, movidos por el inspirador sermón, lentamente, dejaron el campo abierto.

Después del servicio, Elisabeth y yo fuimos al altar a recoger el mantel, las velas y las flores. Yo pregunté si podíamos tener otro servicio religioso el siguiente domingo.

“Dios mediante, ese es nuestro plan.” “Bien, entonces traeré mas flores frescas.”

“Y yo traeré el mantel y las velas otra vez.” Añadió Elisabeth.

“Ten, también puedes llevarte uno de los ramos de lilas, pues se marchitarían rápidamente en el sol.” Tomé las lilas y los dos contenedores pequeños con las flores silvestres. Coloqué las lilas en la sala y las dos más pequeñas en la mesa de la cocina.

Los residentes esperaban deseos otro servicio religioso. Los soldados planearon mas eventos para la comunidad e incluso uno especial para los niños. Los niños seguían a los soldados para ver en qué podrían ayudar. Los soldados le preguntaron al señor Jessen si podían hacer un espectáculo en el granero, donde había un espacio amplio vacante que podía servir como escenario. Los niños ayudaron a preparar los asientos de pacas de heno para los adultos. Los niños se subieron al loft y vieron hacia abajo al escenario provisional en el que los soldados actuarían. Había mucha emoción en el aire mientras veíamos las preparaciones para el gran evento. El viernes, los niños fueron de casa en casa para anunciar el show el sábado a las 3:00 p.m. Alguien incluso fue a la alcaldía de Pratjau unos días antes para informarle a los aldeanos sobre el evento venidero.

El sábado al fin llegó. La mayoría de las personas locales del terreno y de la aldea llenaron los asientos en el granero. Y los niños subieron al loft.

El 21 de abril, a las 3:00 p.m., el acordeonista empezó el espectáculo con la canción: Freut Euch des Lebens so lange das Laempchen glueht (Disfruten la vida mientras la lámpara aún brille). Tocó una pieza de música alegre, tratando de llevar alegría a las personas cansadas por la guerra. Después anunció el primer acto, un malabarista, usando huevos. Cuando añadió mas y mas huevos, fue cada vez más rápido, conteníamos nuestra respiración, pensando que se le caerían uno o dos huevos. Pero era muy hábil y no dejó caer ninguno. Después usó botellas sin dejar caer ninguna. Terminó su acto de malabarismo con tres antorchas encendidas. La audiencia aplaudió con entusiasmo. Siguieron varias manibras acrobáticas con bicicleta. Los soldados incluso pusieron una cuerda tensa, y un acróbata caminó sobre ella sin una red debajo. Los niños disfrutaron especialmente al payaso, Bobby, con una gran nariz roja y una enorme boca. Usaba un ríado traje multicolor. Además de hacer acorbacias graciosas, se tragó un reloj e incluso un cuchillo y los hizo desaparecer. Cuando abrió su boca, estaba vacía. Los niños estaban fascinados por el payaso y sus actos.

Al final, el acordeonista tocó y cantó algunas canciones populares alemanas y le pidió a la audiencia que cantaran con él. El administrador del terreno le agradeció a los soldados por su actuación. Le trajeron alegría a las personas durante un tiempo en el que la guerra aún era violenta en Alemania. La tranquilidad no duró mucho; dos días después, tuvimos otro breve ataque aéreo durante la noche. Ni siquiera tuvimos tiempo de dejar la casa antes de que terminara. Al día siguiente escuchamos que varias bombas cayeron en el Mar Selenter (Lago de Selent) y en las afueras de la aldea.

Afortunadamente, las bombas no mataron a nadie.

Dado lo sobrepoblados de los dormitorios, desarrollamos una rutina específica. Con cada departamento venía un jardín de hortalizas. Nosotros compartíamos nuestro jardín con la familia Hein. Emma y Meta disfrutaban de hacer jardinería. "¿Dónde crees que podamos conseguir algunas semillas de vegetales?"

"Tal vez, el jardinero del dueño pueda darnos algunas." "Esa es una buena idea. Le preguntaré al jardinero cuando lo vea."

Al día siguiente Emma vio al jardinero trabajando en el jardín. Antes de entrar, le pidió permiso para hacerlo.

"Buenos días, mi nombre es Emma. Soy la hija de la señora Bonacker, la familia de refugiados que se acaba de mudar recientemente."

El le extendió su mano a Emma, "Mi nombre es señor Schroeder; ¿en qué te puedo ayudar?"

"Me gustaría plantar algo en nuestro jardín pero no tengo semillas. ¿Podría darnos algunas semillas de vegetales que le sobren?"

"Vuelve mañana, revisaré qué puedo encontrar para ti."

Emma estrechó la mano del señor Schroeder mientras dijo, "Muchas gracias, señor Schroeder. Lo veré mañana."

Al día siguiente el jardinero le dio algunas semillas a Emma. Ella fue a la casas y le dijo a Meta las maravillosas noticias sobre las semillas de vegetales que había recibido.

Emma y Meta inmediatamente se apresuraron al jardín y empezaron a remover el suelo pala tras pala y rompieron todos los macizos. Después dividieron una sección del jardín en parcelas y las rastrillaron hasta que el suelo estaba flojo y suave. Emma dibujó una línea con un pequeño zurco con el mango del rastrillo en el cual Meta puso un pequeño puñado de semillas cuidadosamente. Después Emma cubrió cada pequeño hueco delicadamente con tierra. Emma marcó cada fila con los nombres de zanahoria, rábano, lechuga, betabel, escritos en un pedazo de papel que puso en un palo al final de cada fila.

"Mamá, hoy plantamos todas las semillas de vegetales.

¿No es fabuloso? ¿Que tendremos vegetales frescos de nuestro jardín?" Anunció Meta cuando regresó de plantar.

"Eso está muy bien. ¿Puedes conseguir algo de papas de alguien para plantar?"

"Le preguntaré a la señora Anderson si le sobran algunas."

Un poco mas tarde, Meta regresó con una pequeña canasta llena de papas arrugads, que ya habían brotado.

"Bien, dame una papa. Verás, si partes cada papa en cuatro partes, y las pones con el corte hacia abajo y brote hacia arriba, tendrás cuatro veces el número de plantas."

"Eso haré. Le diré a Emma que ya tenemos papas. Nos ocuparemos preparando la tierra."

Meta le llevó las buenas noticias de las papas a Emma. "Déjame ver si puedo conseguir una pala del vecino y te ayudaré a remover la tierra."

"Haremos eso mañana. Ya hicimos suficiente por hoy."

Al día siguiente mientras Emma y Meta empezaban a remover el suelo pala por pala, un soldado se les acercó, y se presentó. "Mi nombre es Albert. ¿Puedo ayudar?"

Antes de que Emma tuviera oportinidad de contestar, él dijo, "déjame usar la pala, esto es demasiado duro para usted." Estiró su mano y tomó la pala.

"Gracias. Por cierto, mi nombre es Emma, y esta es mi hermana, Meta." Emma le entregó la pala y tomó el rastrillo. Meta, tu usa el azadón y rompe los macizos de tierra antes de que yo rastrille. Platicaron y trabajaron y en poco tiempo tuvieron una parcela grande preparada.

Después de que Albert se enterara de que Emma y su familia eran refugiados de Prusia del Este, le hizo muchas preguntas sobre su historia. El le dijo que era de Setting, Pomerania. Tenían vívidas conversaciones que siempre terminaban en las mismas notas de esperanza de que la guerra acabara pronto, y que todos pudieran volver a sus hogares.

Los otros soldados ayudaban a labrar los campos o con cualquier cosa que vieran que necesitara reparaciones. Los prisioneros Rusos y Polacos estaban excentos del trabajo.

Mis hermanos y yo conocimos a los niños de los vecinos. Ellos disfrutaban de ver todas las actividades que hacían los soldados. Supimos que los soldados consiguieron permiso del señor Jessen, el dueño, de hacer un baile en la leñera el 28 de abril de 1945. Esparcimos el rumor e invitamos también a los jóvenes de Pratjau. Edmund, Richard, y yo corrimos de Pratjau a la pequeña tienda de abarrotes de la familia Lill. Anuciamos el baile venidero y le pedimos a la señora Lill que invitara a sus clientes al evento. También fuimos donde estaban las familias Kirstein, Liedke y Heisel para informarles del baile próximo.

Los soldados preparaon los asientos en la leñera; tomaron troncos sin cortar, los acomodaron hacia arriba y con algunos pies de separación y colocaron tablas sobre los bloques. Al final había algunas sillas.

La muy anticipada tarde de sábado finalmente llegó, y también llegaron muchos jóvenes y los soldados. Le pregunté a mamá si podía desverlarme e ir con mis hermanos al baile. Primero, dudó en decir que si, pero después Georg, Edmund, y Richard prometieron ir conmigo. Además, ambas hermanas irían también.

El aroma de las lilas llenaba el aire, así como el sonido de la música. El piano-acordeonista empezó con un vals. Los soldados miraron alrededor buscando jóvenes que no estuvieran acompañadas y se apresuraban a invitarlas a bailar. Yo miré a mis hermanas Emma y Meta, preguntándome con quién bailarían. Reconocí al amable soldado, Albert, invitando a Emma un baile. Otro soldado bailó con Meta prácticamente toda la tarde. El acordeonista empezó a cantar "Oh, querida Augustina." Los soldados asistentes se le unieron primero y después los que bailaban también. Todos cantaron, bailaron y disfrutaron de un breve hiato de la guerra. Aunque yo solo tenía ocho años, soñaba con aprender a bailar cuando creciera. La magia de la tarde se desvaneció demasiado pronto, y todos volvieron a la dura realidad de la vida.

Mamá y los otros refugiados recibían estampillas para alimentos para cada miembro de la familia y una pequeña cantidad de dinero para las necesidades esenciales. Georg trabajaba en los campos y cuidaba de los caballos. Emma y Meta ayudaban a ordeñar a las vacas a cambio de una miserable compensación monetaria y medio litro de leche para cada niño por día; por lo menos, no moríamos de hambre. Teníamos un pequeño lugar para vivir y nada de privacidad, teníamos un techo sobre nuestras cabezas. De vez en cuando, el dueño de una tienda de comestibles del siguiente pueblo más grande, Bendfeld, venía con un pequeño camión y vendía un poco de sus productos. Cuando se nos acababa alguna cosa, íbamos a su tienda en Bendfeld. Usualmente, Emma se ofrecía a ir en la mañana, y yo siempre la acompañaba.

Emma y yo empezábamos temprano las mañanas de los martes con bolsas vacías en nuestras manos y pasábamos por plantas de mostaza y hermosos campos amarillos y verdes praderas. De reprente, un avión se vino en picada hacia nosotras.

"Hilde, corre detrás de los setos y agáchate." Emma me siguió rápidamente y se tumbó a mi lado. Unos minutos mas tarde, escuchamos una balacera de metralletas donde estaríamos de no haber corrido detrás de los setos. Yo temblé de miedo.

"¿Aún quieres ir a Bendfeld? ¿No crees que deberíamos regresar? ¿Qué tal si el aeroplano vuelve y nos dispara otra vez?" "No creo que vuelva por aquí." Emma intentó consolarme.

Tomó mi mano, me ayudó a levantarme, y continuamos la caminata de una hora para llegar a Bendfeld. Tanto Emma como yo mantuvimos nuestros ojos no solo en el camino, sino también en el cielo por posibles aeroplanos. Llegamos a la tienda y el señor y la señora Puck nos saludaron cálidamente, estaban detrás del mostrador, ayudando a otros clientes.

Emmma esperó su turno, después le dijo a la señora Puck lo que necesitaba comprar. Antes de entregarle los artículo a Emma, crecó la tarjeta para ver si tenía suficientes estampillas para alimentos para cubrirlos. Teníamos estampillas nuevas para mantequilla, azúcar, harina, pan, carne y otros artículos cada mes. Ya que estábamos a finales de Arbil, le pidió a la señora Puck que le diera todas las cosas que aún estaban disponibles antes de que las estampillas expiraran. Cada vez que la señora Puck ponía algo en el mostrador, cortaba la estampilla correspondiente hasta que todas se habían ido. Emma pagó por los artículos antes de colocar el azúcar, mantequilla, harina, salchicha, y pan en la canasta y bolsa. Antes de dejar la tienda, la señora Puck me dio una golosina. Le agradecí a la señora Puck, y luego Emma estrechó manos con el señor Puck y se despidió.

Los productos nos hacían ir mas lento. De repente, me detuve, "Escucha, Emma, una alondra está cantando. ¿No es simplemente hermoso?" Emma tambié se detuvo. Puso su canasta en el piso por un momento y miró hacia arriba para ver si podía encontrar la alondra. Cuando vio un punto negro, la señaló para mi, "Mira, mira, ahí está la alondra." Yo miré encantada hacia arriba.

"Si, ahora puedo verla también." Nos mantuvimos quietas y escuchamos el canto de la alondra por un ratito. Tocó una fibra sensible en el corazón de Emma, y ella empezó a cantar una canción de primavera. Yo no sabía la letra, así que solo tarareé. Estábamos felices de ver y escuchar a la alondra en lugar de aeroplanos volando sobre nosotras. Regresamos justo a tiempo para la comida.

Cada mañana y tarde, Emma y Meta se ofrecían a ordeñar a las vacas en las pasturas. Una carreta plana, estirada por caballos, con las lecheras de metal vacías en el centro recogía a todas las personas que iban a ordeñar a las vacas y las traía de regreso con las lecheras llenas. Naturalmente, yo esperaba a que la carreta regresara al rancho. Cuando veía la carreta con las lecheras, corría con mamá y agarraba el contenedor para recoger nuestra ración diaria de leche. Una lechera de metal, que no estaba llena, se ponía frente a la casa del señor y la señora Dierck bajo un techo entre la residencia y el cuarto donde guardaban la leche. La señora Dierck o su hija mayor Katie, vaciaban la leche en el contenedor de cada persona. Los medios litros de Katie siempre eran mas generosos. Los niños menores a seis años recibían un litro, y los niños de hasta catorce años recibían medio litro por día. Los trabajadores guardaban el resto de la leche en un cuarto especial opuesto a la casa. A la mañana siguiente, un camión venía y recogía las lecheras de metal y las llevaba a una planta procesadora de lácteos en Schoenberg, el pueblo más cercano a Sophienhof. Los adultos y los niños llegaron a conocer a los residentes que vivían en el rancho. Un día Liselotte, Lisa y Brigitte me preguntaron si me gustaría hacer dulce.

"Claro," respondí. El dulce no era fácil de encontrar. "Debes traer dos cucharadas de azúcar y venir mañana después de que mamá y papá vayan a ordeñar," me dijo Liselotte.

"Déjenme ver si puedo conseguir algo de azúcar," respondí yo y me fui, pensando en como conseguir azúcar sin que mamá notara que faltaba. Yo sabía que mamá nunca me daría para hacer dulce. A la tarde siguiente, vigilé cada paso de mamá y busqué la oportunidad de meterme a escondidas a la despensa y tomar algo de azúcar del contenedor de azúcar.

Emma y Meta ya se habían ido también. Observé a mamá tomar a Horst e ir al jardín.

"Ahora era la oportunidad de conseguir el azúcar y correr a la casa de los vecinos antes de que mamá regresara. Toqué en la puerta de los vecinos; Liselotte me pidió que entrara.

"Pensé que no vendrías, así que ya empezamos a derretir nuestra azúcar," me informó Liselotte.

"Aquí está el azúcar que tomé sin que mamá lo notara." "Déjame añadirla a la que está en el sartén y derretirla," me dijo Liselotte.

Miré el azúcar disolviéndose y lentamente volverse café mientras inhalaba el dulce aroma. Finalmente, todo el azúcar se derritió y se convirtió en un pegajoso globo de color café claro. Liselotte tomó el sartén del fuego y esparció la sustancia en un recipiente para hornear cuadrado para que se enfriara.

Nos sentamos alrededor del sartén, mirando y salivando. Al fin, Liselotte tomó la lámina de azúcar endurecida, la rompió en cuatro pedazos y nos dio un pedazo a cada una de nosotras. "Ahora, es mejor que lo coman todo aquí y que no le digan a nadie sobre nuestra hechura de dulce, de otro modo, nos meteremos en problemas."

"Oh no, no lo haremos," todas prometimos mientras tomábamos un bocado tras otro del dulce y crujiente caramelo hasta que lo consumimos todo. Liselotte lavó el sartén y tostó algo de trigo para eliminar el olor del azúcar derretida, para que su madre no la cuestionara.

Liselotte nos informó a Brigitte y a mi, que nos diría cuándo podríamos hacer dulce otra vez. Le agradecí a Liselotte y me fui. Después de hacer dulce en tres ocasiones mas, La mamá de Liselotte se enfermó mientras ordeñaba vacas en la pastura. Regresó temprano a casa y descubrió nuestro secreto. Nos prohibió estricamente usar de su azúcar para hacer dulce y nos amenazó con castigarnos. Yo temía que la mamá de Liselotte le dijera a mi mamá de nuestra actividad secreta, así que pensé que sería mejor decirle a mamá que había tomado azúcar sin su consentimiento. Esperé la oportunidad adecuada cuando estuviera sola con mamá en la cocina.

"Mamá, hice algo malo; tomé algo de azúcar sin pedirte permiso primero. Hicimos dulce con Liselotte y su hermana en su casa. Lo siento mucho, fui yo."

"Es algo bueno que te hayas dado cuenta de que hiciste mal y que pidieras perdón. Te perdono. Pero si algún día te escucho o te atrapo haciendo algo a mis espaldas de nuevo, tendrás tu merecido castigo."

Corrí hacia mi madre y agarré su mano.

"Gracias por perdonarme y por no enojarte conmigo."

Estaba aliviada de mi culpa y continué felizmente ayudándole a mamá a pelar papas para la comida.

Desde que los soldados llegaron a la granja, volvió a la vida con diferentes actividades. Ya sea que los soldados trabajaran en los campos, ayudaran a ordeñar las vacas, o cortaran madera, se juntaban en la tarde y cantaban. Un guapo soldado, vestido en un uniforme de la marina azul y blanco, tocaba el acordión y acompañaba a los cantantes. Nosotros abríamos la ventana y escuchábamos la bella música.

En domingo, jubileo, al final del servicio religioso al aire libre, el pastor oficiante anunció que ese sábado, 28 de abril de 1945, los soldados darían una presentación musical a las 3:00

p.m. Le pidió a los niños que invitaran a sus familias y a las personas de Pratjau. Qué emocionante tener una presentación musical justo aquí en la granja, pensé. No podía esperar a que llegara el día.

"Edmund y Richard, ¿quieren ir a Pratjau esta tarde a decirle a la almacenista sobre el concierto para que pueda esparcir el rumor a sus clientes?"

"Vamos a preguntarle a mamá si piensa que está bien," respondió Edmund.

Mientras comíamos, Edmund le pidió permiso a su madre para que los tres fuéramos a Pratjau a informar a la señora Lill sobre el concierto.

"¿Podemos también visitar a la familia Heisel mientras estamos en Pratjau?"

"Pueden ir, pero asegúrense de estar en casa antes de las 5:00 p.m." respondió nuestra madre.

"Gracias, mamá; estaremos de regreso antes de la cena," respondí.

"Vamos, Edmund y Richard, ¡vamos!"

Caminamos rápidamente a donde la señora Lill y anunciamos la fecha y la hora del concierto próximo.

"Por favor, divulgue las noticias a sus clientes y amigos," le pedí antes de visitar a la familia Kirstein, que vivía en las premisas de la alcaldía. Edmund preguntó si el señor Kirstein podría hablar con el alcalde para que sus mensajeros anunciaran el evento a todos los residentes del pueblo. Después de que el señor Kirstein prometió hacerlo, fuimos a visitar a la familia Heisel. Le dije a Edna, que era de mi edad, del concierto, y Richard le informó a Helmut y a su hermano Gustav.

Edmund habló con el señor Heisel mientras Helmut, Richard, Edna y yo jugábamos un juego de agravación antes de volver a Sophienhof.

Toda la semana, vimos cada actividad en la granja. Tres días antes del concierto, los soldados empezaron a ensamblar el escenario. Colocaron una carreta plana frente a la leñera. Después armaron un marco de madera del largo de la carreta y siete pies de alto sobre la plataforma. Clavaron el marco a la carreta. Varios niños se acercaron y preguntaron si podían ayudar. Bobby, el payaso, también estaba entre los trabajadores. Él entretenía a los niños haciendo graciosas expresiones faciales para verlos reír. Algunos niños le tenían miedo a Bobby y lloraban cuando lo veían. Bobby le pidió a los niños que le pidieran permiso a sus padres para traer algunas sábanas para usarlas como telón de fondo, diciendo, "las necesitaremos para el domingo; nos gustaría que trajeran flores recién cortadas para decorar el frente del escenario el martes." Bobby y otros tres soldados tomaron algunas tablas de la leñera y construyeron tres jardineras cuadradas, del largo del frente y los lados de la plataforma y las clavaron en el escenario improvisado. La tarde del viernes, varios niños trajeron suficientes sábanas para cubrir el marco cuadrado de la parte posterior.

El sábado después de la comida, corrí al jardín de flores para ver qué podía usar para decorar el escenario. El arbusto de lilas había terminado de florecer, pero se podía usar el follaje como relleno. Las peonías estaban en flor. Después de pedirle permiso a mamá, recogí un ramo de peonías y algunas ramas de lilas y se las llevé a los soldados. Otros niños vinieron con flores primaverales y las entregaron a los soldados, quienes añadieron los toques finales al escenario improvisado.

"Necesitamos contenedores con agua para mantener las flores frescas," le dijo uno de los soldados a los niños. Rápidamente, los niños corrieron a sus casas y volvieron con tazas, vasos, latas, o lo que pudieran agarrar. Bobby tomó un balde y llenó todos los contenedores con agua antes de acomodar las flores en las jardineras. Se veía atractivo.

Para las 2:30 p.m., las primeras personas de la aldea llegaron; para las 3:00 p.m., muchas personas llenaban las bancas. Algunos incluso trajeron sus sillas para estar más cómodos. Guardé lugares para mi familia cerca del escenario. No se querían perder ninguna parte de la presentación.

El ansiado momento llegó. Un acordeonista entró al escenario. Le dio la bienvenida a la audiencia y anunció que la primera aria eran extractos de la opereta *El Barón Gitano* (Der Zigeiner Baron) de Johann Strauss, Jr. Empezó tocando la apertura para El Barón Gitano. Qué música de vals tan encantadora. Muchos siguieron el ritmo golpeteando con los pies. Otros movían la parte superior de sus cuerpos a la derecha y a la izquierda al ritmo de la música. Después, un soldado de uniforme condecorado, representando a un hombre noble, entró al escenario cantando:

"Como un espíritu vivo y terminado: todo es un honor, y yo se mas." (Als flotter Geist Ja, das alles ist Ehr, das kann ich und noch mehr).

Después, un cantante entró vestido de gitano. Usaba una camisa blanca desabotonada y un largo cinto rojo atado a la cintura y pantalones sueltos levantados por arriba de las rodillas. Cantó la aria: Escribir y leer nunca fue mi fuerte (Das Schreiben und das Lessen ist nie mein Fach gewesen).

La aria terminó con el refrán: mi propósito ideal en la vida es criar cerdos y curar jamón" (Mein idealer Lebenszweck, ist Borstenvieh und Schweinspeck.)

En la tercer aria, "Quién nos casó" (Wer runs getraut), el mismo soldado representando al hombre noble cantó. El acordeonista cerró la primera parte tocando la Marcha Radetzky. Invitó a la audiencia a aplaudir al ritmo de la música. La alegre música hizo que las personas olvidaran momentáneamente que la guerra seguía embravecida en Alemania, y estaban encantados de escuchar hermosa música en un escenario tan inusual.

El acordeonista anunció tres arias de Franz Lehar de la Opereta: *El Zarevich*, La Canción Volga. Primero tocó la introducción a la canción, después el soldado con voz de barítono empezó a cantar: *"Solo, solo otra vez, tan solo como siempre"* (Allein, wieder allein, einsam wie immer). La melancólica pero hechizante canción hizo que algunos padres, cuyos hijos aún peleaban en la guerra, se sintieran tristes.

Un tenor cantó la siguiente aria: *"Por qué cada primavera tiene solo un Mayo"* (Warum hat jeder Fruehling ach nur einen Mai). Esta canción melódica cambió el humor sombrío de la audiencia por uno mas alegre. La tercer aria: "Mi corazón es solamente tuyo" (Das Land des Laechelns) de Franz Lehar. En esta aria, un amante promete su corazón a su amada. Después de que el aplauso entusiasta se desvaneciera y de que el tenor abandonara el escenario, el acordeonista anunció que habría un breve intermedio.

Después de aproximadamente quince minutos, el acordeonista regresó con un grupo de soldados al escenario y anunció que conmemoraríamos a los soldados caídos cantanto, "Yo tenía un camarada" (Ich hatte eienen Jameraden). Pongámonos de pie todos para dar tributo a los valientes soldados que perdieron sus vidas peleando por nuestra patria.

Después de que todos se pararon, el acordeonista empezó con los soldados, y todo el que sabía la canción se unió. Muchos de los que habían perdido a un miembro de la familia o pariente derramaron lágrimas; yo vi a mi madre también limpiarse las lágrimas de los ojos, pensando en papá y si aún estaría vivo. Ya casi era un año que no teníamos noticias de él. Yo también pensaba en mi padre ausente y esperaba que aún estuviera vivo y que volviera pronto a casa.

Después de terminar esta emotiva canción, todos se sentaron.

"Ahora nuestros soldados cantarán canciones alemanas tradicionales, y ustedes pueden cantar con ellos. Empezaremos con la canción: "Una vez que vuelva a mi hogar otra vez" (Kehr ich eins zur Heimat wieder). Por la siguiente hora, el soldado y la audiencia cantaron varias canciones tradicionales alemanas. Cuando el canto paró, el soldado, que oficiaba como pastor, dio un paso adelante. Se dirigió primero a los soldados. "Muchas gracias a todos, mis camaradas, por su talentosa presentación y por iluminar la vida de estas personas.

Estoy seguro de que ellos también están muy agradecidos con ustedes."

Después de que el largo aplauso se desvaneciera, continuó, "Lamentablemente, aún estamos en guerra, pidamos a nuestro Padre celestial que la guerra termine rápidamente, y que nuestros soldados puedan volver a casa. Encomendamos nuestras vidas en las manos de Dios y le pedimos que nos cuide. Recemos juntos "Padre nuestro que estás en el cielo". La presentación terminó con la canción: "Toma mi mano y guíame" (So nimm den meine Haende). La emotiva presentación musical conmovió a todos. Calladamente, las personas se pusieron de pie y fueron a casa.

Después de la cena, Edmund, Richard, yo y muchos otros niños, fuimos al escenario y ayudamos a desmantelar las sábanas y las jardineras. Las niñas que trajeron las sábanas y flores se llevaron las mismas a casa. Antes de irme, le dije a un soldado, "Que maravillosa presentación musical," después le pregunté, "¿Tu crees que vayan a dar otra presentación antes de irse?"

"Mi querida pequeña, no sabemos cuánto tiempo vayamos a quedarnos aquí o a donde nos vayan a enviar," respondió con tristeza en su voz y se fue; yo también y los otros niños nos fuimos.

El 1 de mayo de 1945, todos los soldados estaban inquietos; habían recibido la noticia de que el Fuehrer había cometido suicidio el 30 de abril de 1945, en su búnker en Berlín, un dia antes de que el ejército ruso llegara a Berlín. Eva Braun, con quien se había casado un día antes de su muerte, había muerto con él.

Los soldados también informaron a los civiles que el 30 de abril de 1945, Hitler había muerto al tomar cianuro y después haberle disparado primero a Eva Braun y después a él mismo. Los soldados sabían que la guerra terminaría pronto pero temían el cómo los Aliados penalizarían a Alemania por haber iniciado la guerra.

Los bombardeos y las batallas continuaron por una semana antes de que los generales alemanes firmaran los documentos de rendición incondicional el 7 de mayo de 1945 en los cuarteles de Eisenhower en Reims, Francia. El presidente Truman declaró el fin de la Segunda Guerra Mundial con Alemania el 8 de mayo. Alrededor de todo el mundo, excepto en Japón y Alemania, la gente celebraba la victoria sobre Alemania con júbilo. El pueblo alemán, que había sufrido mas, vio a su país destruido. Lloraron la muerte de millones de soldados y civiles asesinados o que habían muerto por hambruna o enfermedad. Las fuerzas aéreas británicas y americanas bombardearon las principales ciudades grandes, y se veían como el infierno en la tierrra. Los alemanes, que lentamente emergían de los escombros de las ciudades, batallaban para mantenerse con vida, comiendo lo que sea que pudieran encontrar. Algunos caminaron por millas fuera de las ciudades y rogaron a los granjeros por comida. Vivían en sótanos o entre las ruinas hasta que pudieron construir refugios temporales de ladrillo y escombros. Ahora temían nuevamente sobre cómo se castigaría a su país por los crímenes de guerra, mientras que los vencedores, aunque algunos también habían cometido muchos crímenes de guerra, serían celebrados como héroes, y recompensados mediante tratados.

Mi madre estaba agradecida de que nuestra familia tenía refugio, aunque muy inadecuado, y de que tenía suficiente comida para alimentar a sus hijos en crecimiento. Los niños y todos los residentes de la granja se sintieron muy tristes cuando se enteraron de que los soldados debían irse. La mayoría de los soldados de nuestra granja se fueron el 9 de mayo. Todos estábamos agradecidos con los soldados. Fueron tan solidarios, buenos y útiles a nostros. Algunos, que vivían en los estados orientales, que habían sido ocupados por los rusos, no querían convertirse en prisioneros rusos. Decidieron quedarse en la granja.

Albert, que se había encariñado con mi hermana Emma, se fue a regañadientes. Tenía que volver con su familia para ver si habían sobrevivido pero prometió volver si las circunstancias se lo permitían. A Emma le gustaba Albert, y la tristeza llenó su corazón cuando se despidieron mientras trabajaban en el jardín un día antes de que él se fuera. Yo disfrutaba de estar cerca de ellos y siempre encontraba una razón para hacerlo, como ayudar con el trabajo del jardín, para poder oír sus conversaciones y mirar sus expresiones felices cuando se veían a los ojos.

"Emma, eres afortunada de estar en una granja, donde tienes comida. Piensa en los millones de personas de las grandes ciudades cuyos hogares fueron destruidos, y deben mendigar y negociar comida con tiendas aledañas y granjeros para sobrevivir."

"Si, le gradezco a Dios, no solamente por la comida sino por salvar a mi familia de ser asesinados por bombas o morir de hambre o enfermedad. Supongo que tendremos que quedarnos aquí hasta que nos permitan volver a Prusia del Este."

"No eleves mucho tus esperanzas; no sabemos que parte de nuestros país regalarán los Aliados. Prusia del Este es una parte rica y fértil de Alemania. Rusia y Polonia pueden reclamar una parte o la totalidad de ella."

"En verdad espero que eso no suceda. Amo mi hogar y espero regresar pronto al lugar donde nací."

"Ciertamente deseo para ti y para todos nosotros que siga siendo parte de nuestra patria."

Después de que Albert terminara de desenhierbar, le dio su mano a Emma y la levantó. Después la abrazó, le besó la frente, y dijo, "Adiós, querida Emma, y tal vez, Dios mediante, nos veamos nuevamente."

"Adiós, Albert. Que mi Dios te proteja."

Tristemente se separaron. A la mañana siguiente, el 10 de mayo, Albert se fue con otros soldados. Muchas personas llegaron, no solo para despedirse, pero también para agradecerles por su servicio y ayuda mientras estuvieron aquí. Nos mantuvimos en silencio y nos despedimos con un gesto de la mano, entristecidos por su partida, pero los recuerdos de su amabilidad hacia nosotros permanecerán.

Unos días después, dos tanques británicos llegaron y se estacionaron a lado de la casa del señor Dierck. Un montón de niños y yo corrimos hacia los tanques. Nunca habíamos visto un tanque. Veíamos sorprendidos al vehículo tan extrañamente construido. Nosotros, los niños, nos movimos a un lado por miedo a que los tanques nos atropellaran. Dos soldados negros emergieron de uno de los tanques y dos soldados blancos del segundo.

No podía apartar mis ojos del soldado negro. Nunca había visto a una persona negra antes. Me preguntaba cómo es que se habían vuelto negros y de dónde venían.

Saludaron con un ademán a los niños, después se bajaron del tanque y les ofrecieron goma de mascar. Los niños temían aceptar cualquier cosa de extraños y se apartaron cuando las personas de color se les acercaron. Después uno de ellos desenvolvió una goma de mascar, lo puso en su boca, y lo masticó.

"Ten, toma uno; es dulce," dijo el soldado mientras le ofrecía la goma de mascar otra vez a los niños.

Sabiendo que era algo comestible, un niño tras otro aceptó un pedazo de goma de mascar. Nunca antes habían probado la goma de mascar. Después el soldado sacó su goma de mascar de su boca y la tiró. Quería demostrarle a los niños, que no debían tragarla, sino escupirla. Yo mastiqué y me gustó el dulce sabor a menta. Cuando intenté tirarla, el soldado mencionó que la masticara mas tiempo. Asi que, los niños masticaron y se rieron entre ellos, y también lo hicieron los soldados.

Después de un tiempo, los dos tanques se fueron con las cadenas haciendo un extraño sonido crepitante. Sin embargo, en lugar de manejar sobre el camino, pasaron a través de los campos de trigo, dejando dos senderos de plantas aplastadas detrás de ellos. Nunca pude entender porqué los soldados tenían que destruir plantas cuando pudieron haber usado los caminos.

Corrí rápidamente a casa, exclamando, "Mamá, mamá, vi a una persona negra. ¿Porqué algunas personas son negras?"

"Hija mía, Dios los hizo así. Todos son hijos de Dios, sin importar el color de su piel."

"Si, madre. Supongo que tengo mucho que aprender; por cierto, ¿sabes cuando iniciará la escuela?"

"Mi vecino me dijo que no empezará hasta el otoño. Están buscando a un maestro nuevo. El maestro de Pratjau se fue."
"Espero que la aldea pueda encontrar a un maestro pronto.

Me gusta ir a la escuela a aprender cosas nuevas."

Mayo pasó, y llegó el verano. Edmund y Richard se hicieron amigos de los niños de la granja y yo de las niñas. Los niños jugaban soccer u otros deportes con pelotas, mientras que las niñas jugaban con sus muñecas, saltaban la cuerda, o jugaban juegos de mesa, como Agravio y muelle (Muehle)

Una tarde, una gran camioneta llegó a la granja. La camioneta pertencecía a un circo, y el conductor llegó a recoger heno para los animales. Le pidió al dueño una carga de heno y ofreció, como pago parcial, boletos gratis para los niños de la granja. Cuando los niños se enteraron de estas noticias, inmediatamente le pidieron permiso a sus padres para ver el circo. Mamá nos permitió a Georg, Edmund, Richard y a mi ir. Le dio a Georg órdenes estrictas de mantenerme a la vista, para que no me perdiera entre la multitud.

La carga pareció tomar un tiempo muy largo mientras esperábamos alrededor de la camioneta. Finalmente, la camioneta estaba cargada; el conductor le dio la señal a los niños para que treparan y se acomodaran en el heno. Todos se apresuraron al centro para no caerse. Nos sentamos cerca los unos de los otros para caber todos. La camioneta rodó por el irregular camino sin pavimentar por media hora hasta llegar al circo en Schoenberg. El conductor dejó que los niños se bajaran en la carpa y les dijo que esperaran adentro mientras llevaba el heno a las jaulas de animales para alimentar a los caballos antes del espectáculo.

Con gran anticipación, esperamos y esperamos. Dos horas que parecieron largas. La gente empezó a llenar la carpa, una señal de que el espectáculo estaba por iniciar. Cuando todas las bancas estuvieron ocupadas, la música empezó a sonar. El maestro de ceremonias salió y anunció el primer acto. Cuatro jinetes a caballo entraron en la carpa. Mientras los caballos galopában rápidamente alrededor de la arena, los jinetes se bajaban de un salto, hacían algunos trucos, y después saltaban otra vez sobre el lomo de su caballo. Todos aplaudieron cuando uno de los jinetes se paró sobre dos caballos y cabalgó velozmente alredor del círculo. Siguieron mas artistas ecuestres de doma en hermosos caballos blancos. Cuando los trabajadores construyeron rápidamente una jaula, entró un león con el domador de leones, contuvimos el aliento. Muchas veces, el león rugió y enseñó sus dientes cuando el domador agitaba el látigo. Afortunadamente, el león terminó todos sus trucos sin atacar al domador, lo que fue un gran consuelo para la audiencia. Tres payasos entraron girando a la arena y realizaron todo tipo de trucos para hacer reír a todos. Después, los trapecistas mantuvieron a todos en suspenso hasta que saltaron a la red y bajaron al suello, acompañados de un explosivo aplauso. Las artes acrobáticas en bicicleta también recibieron muchos aplausos, también el que caminó en la cuerda floja y el acto del elefante. Nos entristecimos cuando terminó el espectáculo. Pudimos haberlo visto una y otra vez por un largo tiempo. Nuestro grupo de niños se mantuvo junto afuera de la carpa hasta que el conductor de la camioneta llegó a recogernos. Había dejado un poco de heno en la caja de la camioneta, para que no tuviéramos que sentarnos en lo duro del fondo.

"Que espectáculo tan emocionante, ¿no crees?" le pregunté a Frieda.

"Realmente lo fue; el que más me gustó fue el trapecista." "El domador de leones me hizo contener el aliento cada vez que el león rugía a su domador. Pero disfruté de todos los actos."

Mientras tanto, el sol retrajo sus dorados rayos y cubrió la tierra con un abrigo suave y oscuro. Me acosté en el heno y pronto entré al mundo de los sueños. Georg me despertó cuando la camioneta llegó a la granja. Mamá nos esperaba y estaba contenta de que todos hubiéramos regresado a casa a salvo. Los niños estaban fascinados con los diferentes actos del circo. Al día siguiente, imitaron a los artistas e intentaron hacer volteretas mientras saltaban del henil a la carreta que aún tenía paja, sin darse cuenta del peligro.

Durante el resto de la primavera y el verano, cultivamos el jardín y esperamos ansiosos para cosechar los primeros rábanos y lechugas. Cuando las hojas de la zanahoria crecieron lo suficiente, revisábamos, removiendo la tierra alrededor de la planta, para ver si podíamos encontrar una zanahoria lo suficientemente grande para sacarla y comerla. Por supuesto, la lavábamos primero junto con las hojas. Que bien sabía fresca del jardín. A lo largo del jardín corría un arroyo. Solíamos bajar el corto camino para ir por agua para las plantas. Pensé que era el sitio perfecto para construir un lugar pequeño para pasar tiempo en soldedad. Estar lejos del sobrepoblado departamento sería un gusto. Primero, cavé un área del lado del jardín en el arroyo y apilé la tierra en el fondo para hacer la base. Busqué algunas piedras y las acomodé alrededor de los cimientos cuadrados. Corté ramas de un sauce cercano y las clavé en los lados frente a las piedras. Dejé las hojas en las partes de arriba para formar una pared.

Al día siguiente, busqué hasta encontrar una tabla angosta y bloques de madera para formar una banca. Después puse una tabla mas grande sobre dos postes para formar una mesa y aseguré la tabla con dos clavos. No le dije a nadie sobre mi lugar secreto. Cada día, cuando no tenía deberes por hacer, iba a mi sitio secreto, me sentaba ahí, escuchaba el sonido crepitante del arroyo, el cantar de las aves, y soñaba despierta. Estaba asombrada de que las hojas de las ramas de sauce aún estuvieran verdes después de una semana o más. Ahora tenía una pared viviente. Recogí algunas flores silvestres, las puse en una taza y la coloqué en la mesa. Me sentía tan feliz en mi escondite secreto. Lo compartía solo con mi muñeca. Ni siquiera mi madre sabía dónde estaba mi escondite. Cuando me olvidaba del tiempo y me quedaba más tiempo del debido, le decía que estaba en el jardín. Todo fue bien por un tiempo. Un día, tuvimos una severa tormenta con una precipitación cuantiosa que duró toda la noche. A la mañana siguiente, fui a mi lugar secreto. Me encontré con un desastre; el arroyo creció, y se llevó el suelo y las paredes de mi escondite. Me sentí tan triste por perder mi llugar secreto, pero la vida siguió.

CAPÍTULO 10

EVENTOS IMPORTANTES

Un evento placentero sucedió. **El** tío August, el hermano mas pequeño de papá, vino a nosotros desde Noruega, donde estaba apostado como soldado hasta que terminó la guerra. Nos había encontrado a través de la Cruz Roja donde nuestra familia se quedaba. El tío August esperaba encontrar a su hermano, nuestro padre, con nosotros. Estaba decepcionado de que su hermano Gustav aún estuviera detenido en algún lugar. El tío August solía tocar el acordeón y cantar en todas las celebraciones familiares. Desafortunadamente, tuvo que dejar su acordeón en casa cuando se unió al ejército. Al tío August también le gustaba dibujar. Cada vez que nos escribía una carta, dibujaba hermosas flores con lápices de colores en el encabezado. Mis hermanos, hermanas y yo admirábamos y amábamos al tío August y a todos los tíos y tías del lado de mi padre. Tenían un gran sentido del humor y entusiasmo por la vida, amaban la música y el baile. Su alegre disposición hacía felices a todos los que los rodeaban. También sabían como contar historias serias y divertidas. Desafortunadamente, el tío Otto, el mas joven de cinco hermanos, ya había muerto como un soldado de la Segunda Guerra Mundial. El tío August había traído un pequeño balde de arenques encurtidos de Noruega. Que gusto era para nosotros morder el jugoso y salado arenque. El tío August se quedó con nosotros por aproximadamente dos semanas. Ayudaba con el azadón en el jardín o con cualquier cosa que se necesitara hacer, Cómo partir leños de madera para la estufa de leña.

Emma compartió la cama conmigo y Meta para que el tío August pudiera tener algo de privacidad y la cama en la recámara más pequeña. Con gusto compartíamos los vegetales frescos del jardín. Nos sentimos tristes cuando nos despedimos de él. El mes de mayo se fue junto con las hermosas flores silvestres en las praderas y bosques. Yo disfrutaba de correr en las pasturas y recoger lo que encontrara en flor. Mi flor silvestre favorita eran los no-me-olvides, que crecían a un lado del arroyo y duraban un largo tiempo en un florero. Sin embargo, no se nos permitía recoger la flor amarilla de canola que cubría los grandes campos, tampoco se nos permitía entrar a los campos de trigo a recoger brotes de aciano o amapolas.

Para finales de junio o principios de julio, la flor amarilla se convirtió en semillas negras en una pequeña y redonda vaina. Era tiempo de cosechar las semillas y de podar las plantas. Mi hermana Emma, Elfriede, y yo caminábamos detrás de la podadora y recogíamos cualquier planta seca que se quedara atrás. Rápidamente aplastábamos las vainas y poníamos las semillas en nuestras bolsas, atadas a nuestras cinturas. La planta seca la tirábamos. Probablemente recolectábamos una o dos libras de semillas en un día. Caminando entre los tallos recién cortados, nos cortábamos las piernas al punto de sangrado y rozaduras. Después de descansar por la noche, estábamos afuera en los campos recogiendo cada día hasta que los campos estuvieron podados. Después Georg llevaba las semillas al molino, donde el dueño ponía las semillas negras en una prensa para liberar el aceite. Si obteníamos dos litros de aceite de canola de la cosecha, estábamos agradecidos.

Mamá lo usaba en los aderezos para ensaladas y para freír panqueques y otras comidas.

Después tocaba la cosecha de trigo. La podadora cortaba el trigo. Otras mujeres que vivían en la granja, Emma y Meta incluidas, juntaban un manojo de trigo, lo ataban con tallos torcidos de trigo, y los ponían en el suelo. Los hombres juntaban los gavillas y los ponían de pie uno contra otro formando pilas en forma de trapecio. Elfriede y yo fuimos a recoger cáscaras de trigo. Recogíamos cada tallo cortado que se quedaba atrás, frotábamos las cabezas rápidamente con nuestras manos para remover el grano del tallo, y lo poníamos en nuestro costal. Cuando teníamos más de medio costal lleno, lo llevábamos a casa con nuestras madres. Regresábamos al campo hasta que los trabajadores terminaban de cortar el trigo.

Los gavillas permanecían de pie en los campos por dos semanas o más hasta que los tallos se hicieran blancos, y las espigas del trigo estuvieran secas. Una carreta vacía tras otra llegaba del campo y volvían a la granja cargadas de gavillas. En el último día de traer los gavillas, las mujeres tejieron tallos de trigo alrededor de un marco de metal con forma de corona, ataban listones de colores en la parte de abajo del círculo, y lo llevaban de regreso a la granja. Temporalmente, la colgaban en el granero. El fin de semana siguiente, el dueño ofreció una gran cena baile para todos los trabajadores en el Gasthaus de la familia Lill en Pratjau. Un empleado aseguró la corona en el techo, en el centro del salón. El administrador del terreno le agradeció a Dios por la buena cosecha y a todos los trabajadores que trajeron el cultivo, les sirvieron de cenar. La música empezó a sonar después de que los sirvientes despejaron las mesas. El administrador y su esposa empezaron el primer vals, y todos se les unieron. Los niños no estaban permitidos ni en el salón ni en las mesas. Pero Elfriede, otros niños de la aldea y yo nos subimos a un loft adyacente al salón de baile, nos sentamos calladamente, y escuchamos la música del acordeonista. Cómo deseé poder bailar con un niño de mi edad. Tal vez con mi amiga Elfriede, que era tres años mayor que yo. Calladamente, estaba escuchando la música y viendo los movimientos rápidos de los pies y esperando que un día yo pudiera bailar así. La celebración siguió hasta la media noche, pero yo tenía que estar en casa para las 9:00 p.m.

En agosto recibimos las buenas noticias de que la escuela empezaría pronto. Todos los niños entre seis y catorce años debían ir a registrarse para entrar a clases. El maestro, cuyo nombre era señor Sabrow, recibió a todos los estudiantes en la escuela de un solo salón de clases. Le preguntó a cada niño en qué clase se quedaron. Después puso a los estudiantes de cada clase en secciones. Como mis hermanos Edmund, Richard y yo no teníamos boletas de calificaciones porque tuvimos que huir antes de que las expidieran, el maestro nos hizo exámenes. El señor Sabrow colocó a Edmund en quingo grado, a Richard en cuarto grado, y a mí en segundo grado. Instruir a todos los alumnos en el mismo salón era todo un reto para el maestro. Asignaba tareas escritas a los estudiantes a quiénes no podía enseñarles en persona. Daba cada clase en aproximadamente cuarenta y cinco minutos. Todos los estudiantes iniciaban a las 8:00 am, tenían media hora de recreo, y se marchaban a casa a la 1:00 p.m. Los cuadernos y papel escaseaban. Teníamos pizarras y lápices para pizarras para escribir, que eran fáciles de borrar con una esponja húmeda.

Una escuela de un solo salón de clases presenta una oportunidad fascinante para escuchar las clases de materias avanzadas que se impartían a los estudiantes más grandes y obtener conocimiento más rápido. Yo disfrutaba de escuchar las presentaciones de geografía e historia de los niveles más altos.

Como mis hermanos Edmund y Richard iban a la misma escuela, también podía aprender de ellos. Se sentía muy bien estar de regreso en la escuela y estudiar tantas cosas nuevas. El señor Sabrow era muy estricto con nosotros. Si un estudiante no hacía su tarea o molestaba a otro estudiante, el maestro castigaba a ese estudiante en consecuencia. Recibían un reglazo en los dedos o varias nalgadas con un palo. Todos mostrábamos nuestro mejor comportamiento para evitar el castigo.

Después de un año, el señor Sabrow se mudó a Schoenberg para enseñar en la secundaria. El señor Reimers y su familia lo reemplazaron.

Clase de Gramática

Agosto se fue muy rápido, y septiembre nos trajo muchas alegrías inesperadas. Mi hermana Emma y mi hermano Edmund disfrutaban de recolectar hongos en el bosque cercano. Encontrar un hongo nos emocionaba, y corríamos con Emma cada vez para saber si era comestible o venenoso. Emma podía diferenciar entre un hongo comestible y otro venenoso. Pronto aprendimos a diferenciarlos y recogíamos solamente los buenos. También recolectábamos zarzamoras en los bordes del bosque y frambuesas silvestres en un claro localizado en el bosque. Edmund se adentró en los arbustos en busca de frambuesas y después salió corriendo, gritando mientras manoteaba su cabeza y cuerpo. Corrimos para revisar qué había pasado. Cuando pisó un nido de avispas, las avispas atacaron y lo picaron. Lo llevamos a casa rápidamente. Emma buscó los aguijones, removió algunos, después puso vinagre sobre las áreas inflamadas para calmar el dolor.

Frieda, Brigitte, y yo disfrutábamos de pizcar avellanas. También juntábamos las nueces de las ramas de los árboles, que crecían en el bosque cercano. Tiraban sus vainas en el otoño. Usualmente, tres o cuatro nueces están en la misma vaina. Sólo las hayas, que tenían más de cuarenta años de edad, daban numerosas semillas de hayuco cada siete años. Fuimos varias veces a recogerlas. Cubrían el suelo después de un vendaval, y no llevaba mucho tiempo llenar una arpillera de semillas de hayuco. Georg las llevaba al molino para exprimirles el aceite, que mamá usaba para cocinar.

La cosecha de papa empezaba en octubre. Como la pequeña producción de papa que cultivaban nuestras madres en el jardín no alimentaba a su gran familia durante un invierno entero, Emma y Meta fueron a los campos cultivados de papas a recoger papas. En la tarde, Frieda y yo también fuimos a desenterrar papas después de salir de la escuela. Removíamos mucha tierra antes de encontrar una papa o dos, pero logramos llenar una canasta en una tarde. Cansadas de escarbar, pero agradecidas con lo encontrado, íbamos a casa a presentarle a mamá los productos recolectados.

Mamá, Emma y Meta preservaron tantas cosas de nuestro jardín como pudieron. Llenaban un barril de col, añadían los ingredientes necesarios para iniciar el proceso de fermentación, y convertirlo en col fermentada. Mi madre guardaba papas, zanahorias, y betabeles en el sótano frío para el invierno;

hizo mermelada de varias bayas. Recogimos las manzanas, las colocamos en cajas y las cubríamos de paja, y las guardábamos en el ático para el invierno. Después del atareado otoño y el sombrío mes de noviembre llegó el anticipado mes de diciembre y las épocas navideñas. Recibimos alegremente los primeros copos de nieve con la anticipación de deslizarnos y patinar. En la escuela, aprendimos varias canciones de Navidad y las cantamos alegremente en el camino de regreso a casa. En casa, mamá, Emma, y Meta se ocuparon en tejer calcetas y guantes para los niños.También me enseñaron a tejer. Yo tejía la parte recta de las calcetas, y Emma hacía el talón y terminaba cerrando la punta del calcetín. Disfrutaba de tejer. Como no teníamos decoraciones para el árbol de Navidad, hicimos estrellas de tiras de papel y paja. Nuestros vecinos nos dieron unas cuantas velas con los candelabros para iluminar el árbol en Noche Buena. Una semana antes de Navidad, Georg y Edmund fueron al bosque cercano y cortaron un pino de talla mediana. Edmund buscó unas cuantas tablas pequeñas e hizo un pie para el pino. Emma, Meta, y yo colgamos todas nuestras decoraciones hechas a mano en el árbol y aseguramos los pocos candelabros con las velas blancas en las ramas. Se veía muy elemental, Pero era el símbolo de la Navidad. Mi madre se veía sombría. Yo sabía que extrañaba a papá y a Marta que no estaban con nosotros. Todos los extrañábamos también.

En Noche Buena, nos poníamos nuestras mejores ropas y nos reuníamos alrededor del árbol de Navidad. Emma contó la historia sobre el nacimiento de Cristo, que conmemorábamos ese día. Después todos cantábamos nuestra canción navideña favorita, "Noche de Paz, Noche de Amor," y otras cuántas canciones antes de que Emma y Meta le entregaran a mamá y a cada uno de sus hermanos un par de calcetas y guantes tejidos a mano y tomaran lo mismo para ellas mismas. No teníamos papel para envolver los regalos, pero estaban hechos con amor y nos mantendrían calientitos en la fría temporada de invierno que estaba por llegar.

El día de Navidad, Georg y Edmund ataron los caballos a la carreta, y toda la familia fue al Castillo de Salzau para asistir al servicio religioso. Nevó lo suficiente para convertir el paisaje en un paraíso invernal pero no quedó nieve suficiente en el camino como para usar un trineo. Un enorme y bellamente decorado árbol permanecía a un lado del púlpito en el espacioso salón designado para los servicios religiosos. El servicio inició con la canción *"Oh, Tú, alegre, oh, Tú, maravillosa, Navidad que revela la gracia."* Después de la bendición, abandonamos el salón y platicamos con la mayoría de los refugiados con los que viajamos durante nuestro escape de Prusia del Este. Conversamos por un tiempo, después nos deseamos una feliz Navidad y regresamos a Sophienhof.

Celebrábamos la segunda Navidad lejos de casa. Todos extrañábamos a papá y a Marta, que siempre se vestía como Santa Claus y nos traía regalos hechos a mano para cada uno de nosotros. Aún así, estábamos contentos porque la guerra había terminado, y porque teníamos comida, una cama donde dormir, un techo sobre nuestras cabezas, las tres necesidades básicas. Todo lo demás era considerado un lujo en ese tiempo.

Pollo horneado reemplazó al tradicional ganso rostizado en la cena de Navidad con col roja y papas. Cada uno recibió una galleta y una manzana como postre. Agradecimos a Dios y estuvimos contentos.

El ganado permaneció dentro del establo durante el invierno y Emma y Meta ya no tenían que ir a las pasturas a ordeñar las vacas. Les daba más tiempo para ayudar a mamá con las tareas domésticas. Edmund, Richard y yo probamos la fuerza del hielo en el estanque. Cuando ya no crujía al pisarlo muy fuerte, sabíamos que estaba lo suficientemente grueso, y que era seguro para patinar. Por supuesto, no teníamos patines elegantes. Edmund ponía dos alambres en las suelas de nuestros zapatos, lo que nos ayudaba a deslizarnos cómodamente sobre el hielo. Si pasábamos sobre alguna irregularidad, caíamos, pero nos levantábamos y seguíamos patinando. Los hijos de los vecinos se unían a la diversión hasta que oscurecía o hasta que nos llamaban para regresar a casa. Por supuesto, solo podíamos ir a patinar después de comer juntos y hacer nuestras tareas de la escuela y domésticas primero.

Todos los niños nos quedábamos en casa con nuestra madre en la víspera de Año Nuevo. Ella había horneado las tradicionales donas rellenas de mermelada y le dio una a cada uno de nosotros después de cenar. Georg fue a visitar a su amigo Hugo. Emma se hizo amiga de Gustav Kirstein y Meta, de Ernst Siedel, y fueron todos juntos a un baile en el Gasthaus de la familia Lill en Pratjau. Volvieron a casa después de dar la bienvenida al año de 1946. Me quedé despierta por un largo tiempo, pensando en casa y en el paseo en trineo bajo el claro cielo estrellado, cuando íbamos a casa de los abuelos y jugábamos con mis primos, que también nos visitaban. Me preguntaba quién viviría ahora en nuestra casa y si algún día podríamos volver a nuestro hogar en Prusia del Este.

Dos días después, yo celebraba mi noveno cumpleaños. Mamá consiguió suficientes ingredientes para hornear un pastel sencillo, que compartimos todos en la tarde. Mi madre y todos mis hermanos me felicitaron, pero no hubo velas ni me cantaron "Feliz Cumpleaños". Emma me dio un par de guantes tejidos, que necesitaba. Mis hermanos y yo nos reunimos con los niños vecinos en el estanque, patinamos hasta el oscurecer.

El invierno pasó lentamente. Mantener la habitación y la cocina calientes fue todo un reto para Emma y Meta. Yo ayudaba a mamá con las labores de lavandería para toda la familia. Traía balde tras balde de agua del pozo. La ropa se dejaba en remojo toda la noche en una gran olla de agua y jabón. Al día siguiente hervíamos la ropa por un tiempo. Esperábamos a que el agua se enfriara. Mi mamá o Emma lavaban cada prenda a mano y las enjuagaban en agua fresca. Después colgaban la ropa afuera en una cuerda. Cuando la temperatura era bajo cero y Emma colgaba la ropa en la cuerda, se congelaban inmediatamente y se volvían tiesas. Esperaban a que el sol saliera y descongelara la ropa y la secara de alguna manera. En un día nublado de invierno, Emma y Meta ponían varias cuerdas de ropa alrededor del horno (Kachelofen) y esperaban hasta que cada prenda se secara. Solo planchaban los vestidos, pantalones y camisas para el domingo. Brasas encendidas, colocadas dentro de la plancha, la calentaban. La temperatura de la plancha siempre variaba. Cuando Emma o Meta ponían brasas nuevas en la plancha, estaba ardiente; ella siempre tenía un trapo mojado a un lado de la plancha para revisar la temperatura y evitar quemar un hoyo en un vestido o camisa.

El invierno era el tiempo de sacrificar uno de los cerdos que criábamos en el pequeño chiquero que estaba frente a la casa. Los adultos trabajaban arduamente en cortar al cerdo, haciendo salchichas y jamón encurtido. Ponían pancetas de cerdo en grandes barriles, las salteaban y las guardaban en el sótano. Marcábamos cada cadena de salchichas con una tira de tela, las contábamos y después las llevábamos con el carnicero de la aldea más cercana para que las ahumara. El carnicero mandaba un mensaje cuando el cliente podría pasar a recoger las salchichas ahumadas. Para compensar al carnicero por sus servicios, la gente le daba salchichas o le pagaba la cantidad requerida. Casi no podíamos esperar a que Georg nos llevara donde el carnicero para recoger los productos ahumados. Era un verdadero placer morder un sándwich con salchicha recién ahumada (Metwurst). Emma sabía exactamente qué cantidad de sal y otras especias usar para realzar el sabor.

Nuestro primer invierno en Sophienhof pasó relativamente lento, pero recibimos la llegada de la primavera con mucho entusiasmo. En el camino a casa de la escuela, escuché a la primera alondra cantar y la vi ascender alto en el cielo; me regocijé y empecé a cantar canciones de primavera silenciosamente. También nos aprendimos poemas de primavera de memoria, que yo recitaba mientras saltaba y corría a casa de la escuela. Me había hecho amiga de Elisabeth Diercks, la hija del administrador de lácteos. Ella estaba conmigo en segundo grado; nos gustaba deambular por los bosques.

Yo disfrutaba la escuela. Me fue bien en matemáticas, geografía, historia y religión. Mi ortografía en alemán necesitaba mejorar para ser perfecta. El verano llegó, y mucho entusiasmo creció en la escuela para preparar una celebración especial llamada Popinjay (Vogelschiessen en alemán). De acuerdo con el tamaño y patrón designado, los niños de sexto grado se ocuparon en cortar un pájaro de una tabla de madera. Lo ataron a un palo de cincuenta pies de alto, cavaron un hoyo afuera en las premisas de la escuela, y clavaron el palo con el pájaro. Las niñas de sexto grado pusieron doce botellas del mismo tipo a cierta distancia de separación en un cuadrado marcado. Su competencia consistía en lanzar anillos de metal alrededor de las botellas. La festividad tomó lugar pronto después de que empezaran las vacaciones de verano. Los niños llegaron con sus arcos y flechas con punta redonda. A la orden del maestro, empezaron a dispararlas. Los niños pudieron dispararle al pájaro, que se rompía con cada impacto, y las piezas bajaban volando. El niño que tirara mas piezas sería coronado rey por el día. El segundo mejor ganaba un primer premio y el tercero también ganaba un premio.

Mientras tanto, cada niña de sexto grado recibía aproximadamente diez anillos. Tenía que pararse detrás de una línea, a cierta distancia de las botellas, después aventar cada anillo sobre el cuello de las botellas y esperar que no cayeran a un lado de las botellas en el suelo. Un anotador marcaba cuántos anillos había lanzado correctamente cada niña. La niña que tuviera el conteo más alto se convertía en reina, y las que se habían quedado cerca recibían premios. La reina usaba una corona de flores frescas, simbolizando una corona. El maestro colocaba un listón ancho sobre el hombro izquierdo del rey y lo aseguraba del lado derecho sobre la cadera. Un pequeño desfile en la aldea encabezado por el rey y la reina seguía a los juegos. Dos niñas altas llevaban un lazo decorado con flores frescas sobre el rey y la reina y las parejas que quedaron en primer y segundo premio.

El desfile fue de la escuela a la Gasthaus de la familia Lill donde una celebración, en honor al rey y a la reina tomó lugar. Los adultos montaron suficientes mesas y sillas para todos los alumnos y el maestro. Los padres trajeron pasteles caseros para los estudiantes. Las hermanas mayores de los estudiantes servían leche junto con el pastel. El maestro presentó al rey y a la reina a todos los estudiantes. Gerd Schluensen tocó el piano-acordeón: el rey y la reina, y las parejas que habían ganado primer y segundo premio empezaron a bailar el vals "Ach du Lieber Augustine" (Oh querida Augustine).

Después Gerd tocó un foxtrot y les pidió a todos los estudiantes que bailaran. Mis pies se empezaron a mover bajo la mesa al ritmo de la música. Cómo deseaba que un niño me pidiera que bailara con él. Ni siquiera me atrevía a mirar al chico, Gottfried Keller, que me gustaba. Pero qué sorpresa cuándo el se paró frente a mi, inclinó la cabeza, y me pidió que bailara con él. Me sonrojé al principio, pero rápidamente acepté, me levanté y lo seguí a la pista de baile. Me sentí algo incómoda y torpe al principio, pero pronto seguí su guía y disfruté de mi primer baile con un niño. Aunque Gottfried bailó con otras niñas, me pidió varias veces que bailara con él. Me hizo sentir muy feliz y madura, y tomé interés por el. Como bailó más frecuentemente conmigo que con otras niñas, pensé que yo también le gustaba. Edmund y Richard, que eran buenos bailarines, les pidieron a las niñas mas grandes que bailaran con ellos. Después de los festejos de los niños, él baile para los adultos empezó en la tarde, al que Emma, Meta con sus amigos, y mi hermano mayor Georg asistieron. Todos bailaron bien con la música del piano-acordeón, tocado por Gustav, y Hugo en la tarde.

Un poco después del evento de Popinjay, recibí mi primera boleta de calificaciones, y las vacaciones de verano iniciaron. Mis calificaciones eran todas buenas, y avancé a tercer grado. El maestro me dijo que debía mejorar mi ortografía en alemán. Mi madre hablaba el dialecto de Prusia del Este en casa, que era muy diferente al alto alemán literario (Hochdeutsch). De vez en cuando, usaba una palabra prusiana incorrectamente o deletreaba mal otras.

Pasamos las vacaciones de verano ayudando a mamá en el jardín, recogiendo bayas, juntando leña para el invierno, o haciendo cualquier labor que mamá nos asignaba, como recoger trébol fresco para los conejos que mamá criaba. Sin embargo, siempre encontrábamos tiempo para juegos de pelota, jugar al escondite, u otros juegos.

A inicios de agosto, la señora Hein anunció que ella y su familia se mudarían a una casa llamada Lehmhaus, donde tendrían más espacio. Mamá recibió con gusto su mudanza. Ahora, su familia tendría más espacio. Meta movió su cama a la recámara vacante. Más tarde, mandó hacer una base para cama para mi. Ya no tenía que dormir con mi hermana, apretadas en una pequeña cama; me estiraba y me movía con libertad. Ya no compartíamos la cocina. Emma pintó las paredes de blanco. Usando un trapo doblado, mojado en pintura verde, ella pintó un diseño en las paredes. Se veía limpio y alegre. Podíamos comer al mismo tiempo todos los días. La vida parecía menos caótica ahora.

A veces, corría a la pradera, donde Emma y Meta ordeñaban vacas y esperaba para regresar con ellas en el camión de la leche. A Ernst Seidel, quien llegó como un soldado herido a Sophienhof, y que se quedó en la granja después de que la guerra terminó, le gustaba Meta, y se enamoraron mientras ambos ordeñaban vacas. Él siempre se sentaba a su lado mientras regresaban de la pastura a la granja. A Ernst le gustaba hablar con ella y tomar su mano. En su día libre, el le ayudaba a Meta en el jardín. Disfrutaban de trabajar juntos. Meta hacía muchas preguntas sobre la familia de Ernst Seidel y como había terminado en Sophienhof.

Meta y Ernst Seidel

Ernst le contó a Meta que su madre, Agnes, murió cuando él tenía solo cinco años de edad. Él tenía dos hermanas, Klara,

235

y Frieda, y un hermano, Alfred. Su padre, Gustav, se volvió a casar en 1922, y tuvieron una hija, Else. Después de que Ernst se graduara de la escuela de gramática, trabajó en una fábrica de vidrio por algunos años. En 1937, a la edad de veintidós años fue reclutado en el ejército de Hitler y fue sometido a un riguroso entrenamiento militar. Cuando empezó la Segunda Guerra Mundial el 1 de septiembre de 1939, Ernst peleó en las batallas de Checoslovaquia, Francia y Polonia. Cuando el ejército ruso invadió y rodeó Prusia del Este, Ernst se unió a la 64va división de artillería bajo el comando de O. Steebler. Ernst cuidó de los caballos de oficiales de alto rango y comandantes, además de también participar en los combates. Le contó a Meta sobre un ataque aéreo desgarrador donde él y tres otros camaradas se escaparon de la muerte. Una bomba cayó a un lado de la trinchera, donde saltaron para cubrirse. Afortunadamente, la bomba no explotó; de otra manera, el hubiera volado en pedazos.

Meta tomó la mano de Ernst, "Gracias a Dios que salvó tu vida. ¿Dónde fuiste herido?"

"Cuando luché en Rusia de 1941 a 1945, en la última batalla, un pedazo de metralla me pegó arriba del codo izquierdo y me lastimó el brazo. Mis camaradas y yo tratamos de conseguir ayuda en el hospital. Pero los rusos avanzaron, y el ejército movió el hospital a una isla. Mi unidad y yo peleamos para atravesar el círculo ruso, y llegamos al puerto de Pilau. Una nave alemana con rumbo a Noruega llevaba a otros soldados lesionados y a mí a bordo. Nuestra nave también llevaba prisioneros rusos y polacos que habían sido capturados por el ejército alemán. Los navíos británicos patrullaban el Mar Báltico y capturaban las naves alemanas, y los soldados se convertían en prisioneros de guerra. Sin embargo, el almirantazgo británico permitía que las naves llegaran a Kiel, en Schleswig-Holstein. Los pasajeros de nuestra nave consistían mayormente en alemanes, prisioneros polacos y rusos; algunos de ellos y yo fuimos enviados a

Sophienhof en lugar de a Inglaterra, que se convirtió en mi fortuna; de otra manera, nunca te hubiera conocido."

"Sí, estoy muy agradecida de que fueras liberado de los británicos y llegado aquí. ¿Quieres volver con tu familia en Schlesien algún día?"

"Desafortunadamente, Schlesien ya no pertenece a Alemania; de acuerdo al Tratado de Paz de Postdam, los cuatro aliados se la dieron a Polonia. En caso de regresar a mi pueblo natal en Schlesien, la policía polaca me capturaría. Los polacos me enviarían a una mina de carbón o a alguna fábrica a trabajar en horribles condiciones. Muchos soldados alemanes que fueron a buscar a sus familias nunca volvieron."

Ernst tomó las manos de Meta, la miró a los ojos, y le imploró, "Me quedaré aquí contigo si te casas conmigo."

Meta se sonrojó de la emoción, después apretó firmemente las manos de Ernst y dijo, "Sí, lo haré."

Sellaron su promesa con un beso.

Meta llevó rápidamente a Ernst con su madre para compartirle las emocionantes noticias.

"Madre, Ernst y yo queremos casarnos. ¿Tenemos tu permiso?"

"Pero niños, ¿dónde van a vivir? No hay ni apartamentos ni casas vacantes aquí en Sophienhof ni en Pratjau."

"Madre, podemos poner una estufa de leña en mi cuarto y vivir ahí."

"Si, señora Bonacker, no nos molestaría vivir en una habitación,"

Interpuso Ernst.

"Está bien por mí si están satisfechos con ese arreglo. ¿Ya tienen pensada una fecha?"

"Aún no, pero talvez esta Navidad sería un buen tiempo para tener una boda."

"Navidad es una ocasión de reunirnos todos con los familiares, así que tendremos dos razones para celebrar."

"Tenemos cuatro meses para hacer las preparaciones necesarias, ¡que deben ser suficientes! ¿Eso está bien por tí, Ernst?"

"Está bien por mí," respondió Ernst.

Meta y Ernst fijaron la Navidad como su fecha de boda. Emma y Gustav Kirstein se encariñaron y enamoraron durante él largo y arduo trayecto, y el la visitaba frecuentemente en Sophienhof. Gustav le pidió a Emma que se casara con el. Emma obtuvo él permiso de nuestra madre antes de que fijaran la fecha de su boda. Discutieron los días y escogieron el día de Navidad, miércoles, 25 de diciembre de 1946, como una boda doble. Emma y Meta anunciaron sus próximas nupcias a sus hermanos y hermana, quienes recibieron con gusto las noticias.

"¿También van a tener una despedida de soltera (Polterabend en alemán)?"

"Ya veremos, caería en Noche Buena, que no es un buen día para una despedida de soltera. Tendríamos que moverla un día," Emma le dijo a su hermana y a nosotros.

"Aún hay suficiente tiempo; no nos preocupemos por eso ahora. Deberían pensar en alistarse para la escuela ahora," terminó la conversación Meta.

Para mediados de agosto, regresamos a la escuela. El señor Wilhelm Reimers, el maestro nuevo, nos recibió. También nos presentó a su hijo, Willie, a quien colocó en segundo grado, y a su hija, Anneliese, en tercer grado. Yo estaba sorprendida de que el señor Reimers le pidiera a Hannelore, con quien yo compartía mi escritorio, que se moviera y pusiera a su hija, Anneliese, a mi lado. Era un honor para mi sentarme a lado de la hija del maestro. Nos llevábamos bien, y conforme pasó el tiempo, nos hicimos buenas amigas. Siendo el único maestro, el señor Reimers tendía que enseñar alemán, matemáticas, geografía, historia, religión, música, arte, y algunos ejercicios físicos a los diferentes grados.

Mientras enseñaba a un grado, les instruía a los otros estudiantes que trabajaran en una materia en silencio. Debió haber sido un reto para Él maestro el dar instrucciones en varias materias, pero manejaba bien a los estudiantes y presentaba cada tema con facilidad y profundo conocimiento. Desarrolló una buena relación con los estudiantes, y ellos se encariñaron con el. Sin embargo, disciplinaba a los estudiantes que no se portaban bien o que no hacían la tarea haciéndolos quedarse una hora mas tarde haciendo una asignación particular o recibiendo un reglazo en la palma de la mano. El peor y más vergonzoso castigo era recibir varias nalgadas con un palo en frente de la clase. Los niños normalmente recibían este tipo de castigo. Aunque dolía, también le enseñaba la lección al estudiante que no olvidaría muy rápido.

El señor Reimers acordó con la señora Hoffman para que fuera a la escuela una vez a la semana a enseñar a las niñas como coser, tejer, bordar, remendar calcetas y otras prendas. En el verano, nos sentábamos afuera en un gran tronco de árbol mientras seguíamos las instrucciones de hacer distintas puntadas de bordado en una tira de tela; como disfrutaba de aprender todas las distintas manualidades. Ahora podía ayudar a mamá a remendar calcetas y fondos prolijamente.

No teníamos cuadernos, solíamos cortar mapas en cuadros y escribir los exámenes en la parte blanca del reverso. Escribíamos nuestra tarea o trabajo en la escuela en nuestra pizarra.

Una vez al mes, el maestro despedía a la clase y nos llevaba a una excursión llamada (Wandertag en alemán) un día de caminata. El caminaba con nosotros a sitios históricos y nos contaba la historia de cada lugar. Caminábamos por praderas y bosques en otras excursiones, y él señalaba los distintos tipos de plantas y nos daba los nombres de las plantas. Nos enseñó varias canciones, y todos nos uníamos cantando.

Una de mis excursiones favoritas era pasear en una carreta abierta a la playa de Schoenberg. Los trabajadores habían atado tablas a través de la escalera para que los estudiantes se sentaran. Temprano en la mañana, atábamos flores a los lados entre las tablas. Mi hermano mayor Georg manejaba una de las tres carretas. Nos íbamos cantando todo el camino hasta que llegábamos a la playa. Desempacábamos las cobijas y nuestros trajes de baño. Cada niña se cambiaba a su traje de baño, mientras otra niña sostenía una toalla a su alrededor. Los niños se ayudaban entre ellos, también. Corrimos al agua. Al principio, se sentía fría, pero nos ajustamos rápidamente a la temperatura fría. Los niños salpicaban a las niñas con agua y viceversa. Los niños y niñas que sabían nadar, nadaban muy lejos. Yo no podía mantenerme a flote por el tiempo suficiente para sentirme segura en aguas profundas, así que caminaba mar adentro hasta que ya no podía sentir el suelo bajo mis pies, después nadaba de regreso a la orilla. De esta manera, siempre podía tocar el suelo y mantener mi cabeza fuera del agua si me daban calambres o experimentaba alguna emergencia.

A medio día, el maestro nos llamaba para hacer una pausa y comer. Los sándwiches que traíamos de casa sabían muy bien al aire libre; los devorábamos rápidamente para regresar a nadar, construir castillos de arena, o jugar a las atrapadas. A las 3:00 p.m., el maestro nos llamaba para alistarnos para regresar a casa. Estábamos exhaustos pero felices después de un emocionante día en la playa.

Estudiar al día siguiente era algo problemático; el pensamiento volaba de regreso a la excursión de la playa y la estimulante experiencia. Pero en poco tiempo, puse atención cuando el maestro nos leyó el poema Otoño de Johann Wolfgang von Goethe. El señor Reimers nos explicó en qué palabra poner el énfasis y cuántas estrofas debe tener cada verso. La manera en que él nos leía el poema sonaba tan melódica. Tener mi primer libro de poesía titulado *Der Bluetenbaum* (El árbol en floración) me dio la oportunidad de familiarizarme con los diferentes poetas y sus trabajos. Siempre admiré como los poetas pueden expresar sus pensamientos, ideas, observaciones e historias de una manera tan conmovedora en pocas palabras. Cuando tenía la oportunidad de leer un poema, creaba una imagen o veía fotografías de los personajes descritos por el poeta. A menudo, también soñaba con la historia que el autor expresaba en versos.

Agosto y septiembre pasaron rápidamente. El maestro me dio una segunda boleta de calificaciones, que era lo suficientemente buena para pasar a cuarto grado. Mi hermano Edmund pasó a sexto grado y Richard a quinto grado. Al principio de octubre, recibimos dos semanas enteras de vacaciones. Ayudamos a mamá a desenterrar las papas del jardín y recogimos manzanas de los árboles. También fuimos al bosque a juntar ramas secas para encender la leña en invierno. El dueño le permitía a cada familia cortar un árbol de cierto grosor. Georg y Edmund removieron las ramas y cortaron el tronco en leños de un pie de largo. Esperaron a que los leños secaran, después los partieron y los juntaron en el cobertizo para que tuviéramos suficiente leña extra para el invierno. La cantidad de carbón que el gobierno había asignado a nuestra familia no era suficiente para calentar la sala y cocinar en la estufa todo el invierno.

Los lúgubres días de noviembre nos dieron una probada del invierno que se aproximaba, y por supuesto, nuestros pensamientos se centraban en la próxima despedida de solteros y en las bodas. Edmund y Richard recolectaban baldes de metal rotos o cualquier pieza de metal que pudieran encontrar para hacer ruido. Yo me dediqué a buscar pedazos rotos de platos de porcelana o cerámica, que se supone traen buena suerte a los recién casados. Emma y Gustav decidieron tener la despedida de solteros un día antes de Noche Buena, lunes, 23 de diciembre. Meta no quería participar en esta costumbre, que llamaba un evento pagano. Sin embargo, Emma y Gustav no querían decepcionar a sus hermanos, hermanas, amigos y vecinos.

La tarde del lunes, el día antes de Noche Buena, todos los niños de los vecinos y los adultos solteros se reunieron frente a la casa, llevando varios pedazos de metal o piezas rotas de cerámica o porcelana. Heinz Steinbeck, un amigo de Emma y Gustav, puso primero un arado roto y otras piezas de metal grandes frente a la puerta. Después todos los demás empezaron a aventar sus objetos contra el metal, intentando hacer el mayor ruido posible. Entre mayor era el ruido, más reían los niños. El ruido y las risas duraron más allá del atardecer. Gustav abrió la puerta. Se abrió paso a través de los escombros y les dio la bienvenida a las personas. Les ofreció algunas bebidas alcohólicas caseras (Aguardiente) a los adultos, y Emma vino detrás de el con galletas para los niños. Todos ayudaron a la pareja a despejar el desorden de la puerta.

Como regla, celebrábamos la Noche Buena asistiendo al tradicional servicio religioso. Este año todos iríamos a la iglesia para la ceremonia de matrimonio en Navidad. El señor Jessen prestó su privado y elegante carruaje junto con los caballos para llevar a las dos parejas a Salzau, donde el gran salón del castillo servía como iglesia. A las 8:00 a.m., el hermoso carruaje se detuvo frente a la puerta para recoger a Emma y a Meta. Ambas usaban vestidos negros, con un velo blanco y corto cubriendo sus cabezas y caras. Una corona de mirto sostenía el velo en su lugar. Mamá, Horst, Elsa, la hermana de Ernst y yo pudimos irnos con las novias en el elegante carruaje. Nos cubrimos con cobijas para mantenernos calientes.

Varias carretas regulares se adelantaron a las novias y los novios; otros familiares, amigos y vecinos los siguieron. Había caído apenas suficiente nieve para transformar el aburrido escenario otoñal en una pintoresca escena invernal, acorde a la Navidad. Cuando nuestro carruaje llegó, Edmund y Fritz, el hermano de Gustav, que también era padrino de honor, vinieron a llevar a las novias a la iglesia, donde los novios, Gustav y Ernst, las esperaban junto con sus dos damas de honor, Wanda y Greta. Desafortunadamente, nuestro padre no estaba presente para entregar a sus hijas para casarse. Los novios se encontraron con las novias en el vestíbulo y entraron con la corte nupcial un poco antes de que iniciara el servicio religioso. Se pararon frente al altar, esperando al pastor. Ambas familias y familiares se sentaron en las filas delanteras. Los feligreses regulares llenaron el gran salón.

Cuando entró el pastor, saludó a la corte nupcial con una sonrisa y una inclinación. Después se dirigió a los feligreses, "Hoy, no solamente celebramos la Navidad, también celebramos la ceremonia de matrimonio de dos parejas. Primero, levantémonos y cantemos la canción navideña. "Oh tu alegre, oh tu maravillosa Navidad."

Boda de Emma y Gustav

Después el pastor hizo que la corte nupcial diera un paso al frente. Les dio un pequeño sermón sobre los deberes cristianos del esposo y de la esposa, después hizo que intercambiaran votos, puso los anillos en sus dedos, y los pronunció marido y mujer. Después los esposos besaron a sus esposas para confirmar sus votos maritales. Después de que la corte nupcial se sentó, el pastor dio un vívido sermón sobre la importancia del nacimiento de Cristo, que conmemoramos ese día. Después elaboró en cómo sería el mundo de gris si Cristo no hubiera nacido. Todos los fieles cantaron "Noche de paz, noche de amor" antes de que el pastor despidiera a los feligreses dando la bendición y deseando a todos una bendita Navidad.

Todos los miembros de la familia fueron con los recién casados para felicitarlos antes de irse del edificio. Ahora, ambas parejas iban de regreso a Sophienhof en él mismo carruaje, y Mamá, Horst y yo nos unimos al resto de nuestra familia en la carreta de Georg. Mamá, Emma y Meta habían horneado pan fresco para la comida con salchicha casera y jamón ahumado. Ofrecieron pastel casero y café de nogal o té de hierbas en la sala. Después de que mamá sirvió una modesta cena de puerco

244

asado, col roja y papas hervidas, los hombres sacaron las mesas de la sala. Nuestro tío August, el hermano más joven de mi padre, vino también. El tocó música para cantar y bailar en el piano-acordeón. El sabía como hacer a otros felices con su música y personalidad entusiasta. Los invitados que no bailaron usaron algunas bancas y camas para sentarse. Mis hermanos Horst, Richard, Edmund y yo nos subimos a una cama y vimos a los adultos bailar. Cantamos las canciones que nos sabíamos de memoria. Siempre me preguntaba si tan solo pudiera bailar como mis hermanas y tal vez casarme como ellas algún día. La celebración siguió hasta la media noche, pero yo me quedé dormida mucho antes arriba de la cama. Mamá tuvo que despertarme después de que los invitados se fueron para prepararme para ir a la cama. El segundo día de Navidad también es un día festivo. Usualmente, amigos y vecinos vienen por pastel y café en la tarde. Esta vez vinieron mas personas de las usuales para felicitar a los recién casados. Ahora Ernst y Meta iban a ordeñar las vacas al establo.

La señora Jessen necesitaba una ayudante extra para preparar comida para los trabajadores y le pidió a Emma que la asistiera como su mucama regular. Gustav fue empleado por el señor Jessen como carpintero y empleado de mantenimiento haciendo todo tipo de trabajo de reparaciones en carretas, equipo, o cualquier cosa que necesitara arreglo. Vivir en una pequeña habitación no era fácil para ninguna de las parejas, pero hacían lo mejor que podían. Estaban agradecidos de tener refugio y comida y suficiente madera y carbón para calentar la habitación. Meta y Ernst decidieron recibir el año de 1947 en casa, también lo decidieron así mamá y nosotros sus hijos más jóvenes. Emma y Gustav fueron a Pratjau con la familia de Gustav para celebrar con ellos. Gustav tocó el piano-acordeón, y los vecinos y amigos se les unieron, y recibieron el Año Nuevo con música y bailando.

El invierno pasó lentamente en la granja y en la escuela. Desde que los británicos habían ocupado Schleswig- Holstein, hicieron obligatorio que los niños en la escuela de gramática estudiaran el idioma inglés en quinto y sexto grado. Yo completaría mi cuarto grado para finales del verano y, con esperanza, pasaría y entraría al quinto grado. Ansiaba aprender un idioma nuevo y aprender sobre algunas costumbres de Inglaterra. Mis hermanos no compartían mi entusiasmo; en su lugar, ellos preferían trabajar con sus manos, arreglando cosas o haciendo juguetes para nuestro hermano menor Horst.

El 2 de enero de 1947, yo celebraba mi décimo cumpleaños. Mi madre no tenía ingredientes para hornear galletas para mí. Solo horneó pan francés. Batió mantequilla para incrementar la pequeña cantidad que nos daba el gobierno. Mamá puso una pequeña cantidad de mantequilla en un pedazo de pan blanco y le untaba un poco de miel encima, sustituyendo a un pastel. Sabía delicioso. Solo comíamos este manjar en ocasiones especiales. El señor Diercks criaba abejas y nos daba un frasco de miel de vez en cuando.

El resto de enero y febrero transcurrió sin eventualidades. Para finales de marzo, las temperaturas subieron, y la gloria del sol naciente filtrándose a través de las cortinas de nubes pintaba el cielo con muchos tonos de colores pasteles. La alondra volvió y llenó el aire con sus trinos elevándose alto en el cielo para cantar pianísimo y fortísimo otra vez mientras descendía. Las campanillas ya asomaban sus puntiagudas hojas a través del suelo y enseñaban sus bonitas campanas blancas. La naturaleza despertaba, y la primera señal de hojas enroscadas aparecía en los árboles. Las praderas marrones se tornaban en un frondoso verde, y los trabajadores llevaban las vacas a las pasturas. Todos ayudamos a nuestra madre a preparar el jardín para plantar, que sería a principios de abril. Cuando llegó mayo, la naturaleza floreció, y Meta anunció que estaba esperando a un bebé en noviembre. La familia entera estaba feliz y ansiaban recibir a una nueva vida en el mundo. Gustav prometió construir una cuna para el bebé. Emma buscó lana delicada para tejer una cobija de bebé. En la escuela, yo había aprendido a tejer cosas simples, como el tubo de una calceta. Le pedí a Emma un ovillo de lana para tejer un simple tubo de calceta. Noviembre ya es frio, y de esta manera, yo quería dar calcetas para mantener los pies del bebé calientes. Todo el verano, pensamos en la nueva llegada. El 8 de noviembre, Ernst y Georg fueron en carruaje de caballo a Schoenberg para informarle al Dr. Berman, que había cuidado a Meta durante su embarazo, que Meta ya tenía dolores de labor de parto. El Dr. Berman despidió a sus pacientes en la oficina, les dijo que volvieran mañana, y se fue con Ernst y Georg a Sophienhof. Mamá y Emma se quedaron con Meta, mantuvieron una olla de agua hirviendo en la estufa, y prepararon la cuna y la ropa de bebé. Edmund, Richard, Horst y yo esperamos tras puertas cerradas a escuchar el primer llanto del bebé. Cuando Ernst, que no quería ver el parto, se nos unió, supimos que el bebé llegaría a este mundo pronto. Alrededor de diez minutos pasaron cuando escuchamos el primer llanto del bebé. Emma gritó, "¡Es un niño!"

Ernst sonrió y estuvo orgulloso de que su primogénito era un varón. Después de que Emma bañó al bebé, vendó el ombligo, y lo vistió, nos llamó para que viéramos al pequeño. Ernst fue con Meta y la besó en la frente, "Estoy agradecido de que todo haya salido bien y de que tenemos un hijo." Aunque Meta estaba exhausta, estaba feliz de que todo había ido bien, y de que Dios le dio un hijo. Mis hermanos y yo fuimos a la cuna y admiramos al bebé.

"Sabes, Hilde, ahora eres una tía, y yo un tío y el es nuestro pequeño sobrino," me dijo Edmund.

"Yo pensaba que los tíos y tías debían ser mucho mayores a lo que somos nosotros; yo solamente tengo diez años. ¿Qué hay de Horst? El solo tiene cinco años; ¿el también es un tío?" bromeé.

"Tío Horst, si, tu eres un tío." "Eso suena gracioso."

Ernst levantó a su hijo y lo presionó gentilmente a su corazón, "Bienvenido, mi pequeño hijo. Te llamaremos Manfred. Que seas una bendición para nosotros."

Me hubiera gustado cargarlo, también, pero se veía tan pequeño y frágil; no me atrevía a tocarlo.

"Vengan, niños, ¡dejemos a los padres a solas con su hijo recién nacido!" Mamá tomó a Horst de la mano y salió de la habitación con él. Todos la seguimos. Disfrutamos mucho viendo al pequeño Manfred crecer y hacerse más fuerte. Cuando el sostuvo su cabeza erguida, Meta nos dejó cargarlo por un breve tiempo. Cuando llegó diciembre, cayó la primera nevada, pensamos en Navidad, y nos ocupamos haciendo regalos. Le pedí a Emma algo de estambre y un gancho para tejer. En la escuela, Fraeulein Hoffman me enseñó a tejer. Ella me ayudó a empezar un pequeño gorrito para Manfred. Yo tejí en círculos hasta que tuve un gran tubo de más o menos medio pie de largo. Junté uno de los extremos y lo cerré. Después le pedí a mi maestra de economía doméstica que me enseñara como hacer un pompón. Lo aseguré a la parte de arriba del gorro. Terminó siendo bastante bonito. Casi no podía esperar a dárselo a mi hermana para Manfred.

En la escuela, también aprendimos mas canciones navideñas y otra obra, esta vez, el cuento de Rumpelstilzchen.

La actuábamos para nuestros padres antes de que empezaran las vacaciones navideñas el 21 de diciembre de 1947. Tener un bebé en la familia hizo que Noche Buena y el día de Navidad fueran muy especiales y nos recordaba al nacimiento del bebé

Jesús, cuya remembranza celebrábamos. Intercambiamos regalos como siempre en Noche Buena. Le di a Meta el gorrito, "Mira, Meta, ¡lo que hice para Manfred!"

"Lo hiciste tu misma. Es muy lindo. Gracias."

"¿Podrías ver cómo le queda?" Meta removió el gorro que estaba usando y le puso el mío.

"Es justo la talla correcta y se ve muy bonito. Debemos ponerle un listón de cada lado, para que podamos atarlo y evitar que se caiga de la cabeza del bebé."

"Puedo tejerlos y ponerlos. Ya puedes quitárselo. Lo arreglaré después."

Emma había tejido una pequeña chaqueta para el y mi mamá una cobija de bebé. Meta estaba agradecida de tener ropas más cálidas para él para el invierno. Enero de 1948 inició con una tormenta de nieve, y el viento sacudió las ventanas, y la nieve se arrojaba contra los cristales, creando un sonido espeluznante. Todo el mes de enero fue gélido, y era difícil mantener las habitaciones cómodamente cálidas, especialmente durante la noche. Las brasas brillantes se mantenían calientes bajo una pila de cenizas, pero no calentaban suficientemente la habitación entera. Nos metíamos bajo las cobijas de plumas para mantenernos calientes.

Mamá despertaba primero en la mañana, removía las cenizas, y ponía unos palitos en las brasas encendidas. Esperaba hasta que los palitos se encendieran antes de colocar leños mas gruesos sobre ellos. Iba a la cocina y hacía lo mismo en la estufa para estar lista para cocinar el desayuno. Emma y Gustav no tenían horno ni estufa en su recámara. Cada uno tomó un ladrillo caliente a la cama para mantener sus pies calientes durante la noche. Meta y Ernst solo tenían una estufa para cocinar que mantenían encendida todo el día.

Meta dejó de ordeñar vacas por un mes y medio. Cuando regresó a trabajar, mamá cuidaba a Manfred. Yo también le ayudaba a cambiar pañales o jugar con el después de que volvía de la escuela. En febrero, Manfred se enfermó y empezó a llorar. Cuando Meta volvió de ordeñar, Manfred tenía una fiebre muy alta y dificultad para respirar. Meta sospechaba que era neumonía. No había ningún doctor en el área. Meta inmediatamente le pidió a Ernst que los llevara a la Clínica Infantil en Kiel. El le preguntó al vecino si podía prestarle un caballo y un carruaje para ir a Schoenberg. Georg fue con Ernst para llevar a Meta a la estación de tren en Schoenberg. Ella tomó a Manfred en sus brazos envuelto en una cobija. Después de que se subió al tren, Ernst y Georg volvieron a la granja porque tenían trabajo al día siguiente.

Meta descubrió la cabeza del bebé y tocó su frente; se sentía aún más caliente que antes. La respiración era débil, y después de un rato, dejó de respirar. Meta dejó salir un grito de desesperación, "Dios mío, Dios mío, no lo dejes morir." Era muy tarde. Manfred no volvió a respirar, y entonces cerró sus ojos, se volvió pálido, y falleció. Devastada, Meta enterró su cabeza en la cobija y lloró hasta que llegó a Kiel. El conductor se acercó a Meta y le preguntó dónde quería bajarse. Meta aún quería ir al Hospital Infantil y pedirle al doctor que revisara a Manfred. El conductor del tren ayudó a Meta a bajarse, cerca del Hospital Infantil. Ella llegó con su hijo sin vida al hospital. Después de dar toda la información al oficial de admisiones, una enfermera los llevó a una habitación. Ella destapó al bebé y lo colocó en una cama. Después ella llamó al doctor para que examinara al bebé. El doctor revisó los pulmones y el pulso, no encontró signos de vida en ellos, y pronunció al bebé muerto. Expresó sus condolencias y dejó a la afligida y doliente madre con la enfermera.

"¿Qué voy a hacer? No puedo llevar al bebé muerto de vuelta a la granja. No hay un lugar donde lo pueda enterrar." Esa y otras preguntas cruzaron la mente de Meta. La enfermera le dijo a Meta; que mandaría traer al pastor del hospital y él la ayudaría. Meta esperó alrededor de una hora, que pareció larga antes de que la enfermera volviera con el pastor. La enfermera le había explicado las circunstancias al pastor, quien expresó sus condolencias y después vio al pálido bebé sin vida con una expresión de compasión.

"Lamento mucho la pérdida de tu hijo. Tenemos una iglesia y un cementerio cercano. Puedes enterrar a tu hijo en nuestro cementerio; sin embargo, no tenemos lugar para cuidar el cuerpo. Debes hacer arreglos para que se quede en el hospital hasta el funeral. La enfermera te asistirá. Podríamos tener el funeral el domingo por la tarde. ¿Eso sería tiempo suficiente para que avises a tu esposo, familia y parientes?"

"Creo que será suficiente. Mi familia puede estar aquí para la 1:00 p.m. y aún regresar a la granja antes de que oscurezca.

¿Es una buena hora para usted, pastor?"

"Sí, te veré a tí y a tu familia el domingo, 14 de noviembre de 1948. Que Dios te consuele." Estrechó su mano al despedirse y se marchó. Mientras tanto, el sol descendía, y la oscuridad no solo se asentaba en la ciudad, sino también el corazón de Meta mientras veía el cuerpo sin vida de su primogénito. Después enterró su cabeza en la cobija y las lágrimas rodaron por sus mejillas. La enfermera le dijo a Meta que tenía que llevarse al bebé y ponerlo en la morgue. Meta le dio un beso más en la fría frente antes de que la enfermera tomara al bebé y se lo llevara. La enfermera le dijo a Meta que volvería pronto. Cuando la enfermera volvió, le dijo a Meta que no estaba en condiciones de volver a la granja esa noche. Te conseguiré una cobija para mantenerte caliente, puedes quedarte en el vestíbulo. La enfermera tomó a Meta del brazo y la llevó al vestíbulo.

"Siéntate en el sillón. Tal vez, incluso puedas dormir. ¿Puedo conseguirte algo de comer o beber? Debes tener hambre."

"No tengo ganas de comer, pero tal vez una taza de te me ayude a relajarme."

"Bien, pediré que te traigan una taza de té."

Meta se sentó en el sillón. Alguien le trajo una taza de té. La tomó lentamente, después se cubrió y continuó sollozando y sonándose la nariz por un tiempo hasta que colapsó en el sillón y se quedó dormida. El flujo de los pacientes dentro del hospital despertó a Meta. Le tomó unos minutos reorientarse a sí misma sobre donde estaba y por qué estaba ahí. La enfermera, que había cuidado de Meta, se le acercó. Le dijo a Meta que volviera a casa para planear el funeral con la familia. Meta le agradeció a la enfermera por la cobija y le dijo que volvería el domingo por la mañana.

Meta, con el corazón roto, caminó hacia la estación del tren y consiguió un pasaje de tren. Cuando el tren llegó, Meta se subió a la plataforma, entró en el vagón del tren, se hundió en el asiento, y lloró. Cuando el conductor revisó los pasajes, ella le contó sobre su pérdida y le pidió que le avisara cuando el tren llegara a Schoenberg. Aproximadamente una hora mas tarde, el conductor vino y le dijo a Meta que la siguiente parada sería Schoenberg. Meta dobló la cobija de bebé que se había llevado con ella y se bajó del tren. Meta no tenía medios para comunicarse con su esposo, así que tuvo que caminar de regreso a Sophienhof por el camino rural irregular y sin pavimentar. Algunas veces, ella se tambaleaba, pisando un gran bache. Su corazón estaba inundado de pena. Después ella miró al cielo y gritó, "Dios, ¿por qué mi primero hijo murió?"

Después pensó por un tiempo. Dios debió haber sufrido al ver a su hijo ser colgado en la cruz para morir por nuestros pecados, aún cuándo él era libre de pecado. Ella pensó, "Mi bebé también estaba libre de pecado, y tú te lo llevaste, lo que es difícil de aceptar para mi." Entonces el pasaje bíblico vino a su mente de no dejar que su corazón se turbara, que confiara en Dios, y en debido tiempo él la consolaría. Estas palabras calmaron su mente, aunque su corazón permaneció lleno de dolor.

Para mediodía, ella llegó a Sophienhof. Ernst aún trabajaba en el establo. Mamá y sus cuatro hijos y yo estábamos sentados en la mesa y comíamos nuestro almuerzo cuando Meta entró. "Manfred murió antes de que pudiéramos llegar al hospital."

Mamá se levantó, abrazó a Meta, y expresó su simpatía. Ambas lloraron antes de sentarse a comer con nosotros y contarnos la historia completa, que me hizo llorar a mi también. Entonces Meta fue a su cuarto y esperó a que su esposo regresara de trabajar. Cuando Ernst entró, Meta se levantó, lo abrazó, y empezó a llorar. Ernst supo sin que Meta dijera una sola palabra que su hijo se había muerto. Por un rato, nadie fue capaz de decir una palabra. Entonces Meta le dijo a Ernst sobre los arreglos que había hecho para el funeral de Manfred.

"Sí, es una buena idea enterrarlo en Kiel, donde la funeraria puede cuidar su tumba. Cuando nos vayamos de Sophienhof, que lo haremos eventualmente, el cementerio local abandonaría su tumba. Tomaste la decisión correcta."

"Podemos pedirle a Gustav que haga un ataúd para Manfred. Emma y yo prepararemos los cojines. Puedo usar su ropón de bautismo para vestirlo. No tenemos mucho tiempo; por favor, ve con Gustav de inmediato." Ernst había visto a Gustav arreglando la rueda de una carreta. Ernst, que no podía creer que había perdido a su pequeño hijo, fue con Gustav, le dijo sobre la muerte de su hijo, y le pidió que hiciera un pequeño ataúd para él de dos pies de largo. Lo necesitamos para el domingo."

"Lamento mucho tu pérdida. Buscaré donde puedo encontrar buenas tablas de madera que pueda usar. Te haré saber cuando esté listo."

Solo podíamos comunicarnos con familiares por correspondencia o mensajeros personales; ambas maneras tomarían demasiado tiempo y no podrían llegar a tiempo. El domingo en la mañana, Georg ató los caballos a la carreta y nos llevó a Ernst, Meta, Emma, Gustav, Mamá, Edmund y a mi a la estación de tren en Schoenberg. Richard tuvo que quedarse a cuidar a Horst. Ernst llevaba el ataúd en un saco, y Meta llevaba las ropas para Manfred. Después de que llegamos a Kiel, fuimos al hospital para alistar a Manfred en el ataúd. Meta buscó a la misma enfermera que la había ayudado antes. La enfermera llevó a Meta y a Ernst a la morgue. Las lágrimas brotaron de sus ojos cuando vieron el pequeño cuerpecito sin vida en una pequeña mesa de hospital en la morgue. Los esperamos en el vestíbulo del hospital. Cuando Ernst llegó cargando el ataúd bajo sus brazos, Gustav lo libertó tomando el ataúd, "Tú sostén de Meta; ella necesita de tu apoyo. Vámonos, Meta, guíanos a la iglesia."

El pastor nos esperaba en la capilla del cementerio. Después de que Gustav colocara el pequeño ataúd en la mesa frente al altar, abrió la cubierta. Manfred parecía un angelito dormido en su ropón blanco de bautismo. El pastor expresó sus condolencias a Ernst y a todos nosotros.

"Si, es muy duro perder a tu primer hijo, pero él ahora está en el cielo, donde no hay sufrimiento, y Dios les dará consuelo también."

El pastor dio un corto sermón sobre las temporadas de la vida y lo frágil que la vida es. Si tenemos fe, nos uniremos a

Manfred algún día y viviremos eternamente. El pensar en verlo en el cielo nos dio un destello de consuelo y esperanza. Después del sermón, fuimos al ataúd para verlo por última vez y dar nuestra última despedida al pequeño Manfred. Meta y Ernst lo besaron en la frente mientras las lágrimas llenaban sus ojos, y algunas incluso cayeron en su frente. El resto de nuestra familia tocó sus manitas heladas, cruzadas en su cuerpo. Entonces Gustav cerró el ataúd. El pastor dijo una oración antes de que Gustav y Ernst llevaran el ataúd al sitio de entierro y lo bajaran en la tumba cavada. Estaba muy frío, así que el pastor solo dijo unos pocos pasajes antes de echar la primera pala de tierra sobre el ataúd. Meta y Ernst hicieron lo mismo. El pastor dijo otra oración, estrechó sus manos y les dio una bendición antes de despedirse de todos.

Recogimos nuestras pertenencias en la capilla y nos encaminamos a la estación del tren, esperando tomar el tren de Schoenberg.

Cuando llegamos a Schoenberg, Georg nos esperaba afuera de la estación del tren. También había traído más cobijas para mantenernos calientes. Antes de llegar a Sophienhof, el sol se había puesto, y la oscuridad cubría no solamente el paisaje, sino también empapaba a nuestros corazones. Pero un destello de esperanza quedaba, que si creíamos en Dios, él no solamente nos consolaría, también veríamos de nuevo a Manfred en el cielo. Emma y su madre prepararon algunos sándwiches para todos nosotros antes de que nos fuéramos a la cama. Esperábamos encontrar descanso de un largo y emocionalmente exhausto día. El espíritu de Meta había sido golpeado por la pena esa noche; ella no fue capaz de dormir por un largo tiempo. Al día siguiente, ella estaba demasiado exhausta y con el corazón roto como para ir a trabajar. Se puso un vestido negro, que era una costumbre alemana cuando un familiar cercano moría. Las mujeres usaban únicamente vestidos negros por un año entero, y los hombres usaban un listón negro en la parte superior de las mangas de sus chaquetas. Meta y Ernst siguieron esta tradición. El invierno pasó lentamente para nosotros. Apenas teníamos suficiente carbón y leña para calentarnos durante el invierno. Recibimos a la primavera con los brazos abiertos. Estábamos felices de explorar el campo abierto otra vez, correr por las praderas y los bosques, jugar a la pelota, y otros juegos con los niños de los vecinos.

Antes de tener nuestras vacaciones de verano, dos eventos sucedieron el 3 de abril de 1948; el presidente Truman firmó el Plan de Recuperación Europea. También es conocido como el Plan Marshall,[13] nombrado en honor al Secretario de Estado, George Marshall. Los Estados Unidos designaron billones de dólares y bienes a dieciséis naciones europeas para restaurar la infraestructura económica y crear estabilidad política en Europa. Los Estados Unidos e Inglaterra pensaban que era necesario bloquear el comunismo para que no se infiltrase en Europa. La Unión Soviética no aceptó el Plan Marshall; temían que pudiera debilitar su influencia en sus estados satélite. Sólo cinco por ciento de los subsidios económicos eran requeridos en pago por cada país para implementar el programa. Durante y después de la guerra, la economía alemana había colapsado. Los precios estaban fijos, la comida era racionada, los bienes eran difíciles de conseguir, lo que creó un mercado negro incontrolable una tasa de inflación alta. La producción industrial y de comida había bajado considerablemente. La gente de las ciudades había tenido que ir al campo a hacer trueques de comida. El presidente Truman se dio cuenta de que Alemania necesitaba una reforma monetaria que eliminara el racionamiento y creara un mercado libre.

El 20 de junio de 1948, la reforma monetaria inició, que cambió la vida de las personas en Alemania, así como las nuestras.

La relación entre los gobiernos americano, británico y ruso se deterioró después de la Segunda Guerra Mundial. El presidente Truman y el Primer Ministro Churchill se dieron cuenta de que una Alemania y una Europa económicamente fuertes eran necesarias para mantener a Rusia al margen. Ambos aliados ingeniaron la idea de crear una nueva moneda para Alemania, llamada Marco Alemán, que remplazaría al inflado Marco Estatal y al Marco Militar. El presidente Truman imprimió el Marco Alemán en los Estados unidos. Quinientas toneladas de moneda empacadas en 23,000 cajas, picaportes marcados, fueron enviados en secreto a Bremerhaven. Este evento secreto fue llamado Operación Ave Perro.[14] De Bremerhaven, 800 camiones transportaron las cajas de moneda a Frankfurt. Ludwig Erhard, quién políticamente se oponía a Hitler y que se había rehusado a aceptar una economía centralizada bajo el gobierno de Hitler, había sido designado para trabajar en los detalles de la nueva moneda. Los oficiales le informaron a las fábricas que debían retener la entrega de productos hasta que la nueva moneda tuviera efecto.

El 20 de Juno de 1948, 40.00 MA (Cuarenta Marcos Alemanes) fueron asignados a cada persona. Mi madre recibió 240.00 MA para su hogar de seis personas y 20 MA más por persona en una fecha posterior. Emma fue al día siguiente a la aldea, donde recogía las estampillas de ración para recoger el dinero para ella y Gustav, y nuestra familia.

Los oficiales ya tenían toda la información de cada familia, que ayudó a implementar el programa rápidamente.

De repente en toda Alemania, una abundancia de bienes y comida llenaron las tiendas y estantes vacíos. Por primera vez, desde el principio de la Segunda Guerra Mundial, casi nueve años atrás, las personas podían comprar sin límites lo que desearan sus corazones. Una ola de júbilo recorrió al país. Emma llevó a Edmund, Richard y a mí de compras a Kiel. Muchas ruinas de estructuras bombardeadas fueron desmanteladas, algunas demolidas y surgieron nuevos edificios entre las ruinas del centro de la ciudad. Los negocios reabrieron. Los estudiantes empezaron a plantar árboles en las zonas de escombros. La administración de la ciudad reconstruyó la estación de tren, reparó las vías y los trenes volvieron a funcionar. Después de bajarnos en la estación de tren, Emma buscó una tienda de telas. Compró algunas telas para un vestido para ella y también para mi madre y para mí. Emma me dejó elegir el material que me gustaba. Luego fuimos a una tienda de ropa, donde compró un par de pantalones cortos para Georg, Edmund, Richard y Horst. Antes de irnos a casa, nos invitó a un helado que nunca habíamos comido antes. Tenía un sabor delicioso. Tomamos el tren de regreso a Schoenberg. Desde Schoenberg, caminamos a casa llevando nuestros paquetes a Sophienhof. Aunque cansados de las compras del día en la gran ciudad, estábamos emocionados de mostrar nuestras compras a madre. Le dimos la tela que compramos para ella. Todos esperábamos con ansias un nuevo vestido de nuestra elección.

El señor Puck y su camioneta, cargada de comida, dejaron de venir. Ahora tenía tanta mercancía que ya no cabía en su pequeña camioneta. Todos caminamos a su tienda en Bendfeld. A partir de entonces, las cosas comenzaron a avanzar. Con el dinero del Plan Marshall y el valor estable del marco alemán, Alemania reconstruyó la infraestructura, limpió los escombros y reconstruyó ciudades y pueblos. Aunque Alemania era país más destruido y recibía la menor cantidad de dinero per cápita, los alemanes reconstruyeron rápidamente su país. Comenzó el milagro económico, también llamado Wirtschaftswunder.

Muchas personas que vivían entre las ruinas encontraron o construyeron apartamentos o casas. Lo más importante es que pudimos comprar suficiente comida una vez más.

Sin embargo, Rusia no aceptó la ayuda del Plan Marshall ni permitió que el Marco Alemán circulara en la zona de Alemania ocupada por los rusos. Temían que esto debilitara su influencia sobre sus estados satélites. A pesar de que Berlín, la capital de Alemania, estaba en la zona ocupada por los rusos, los cuatro aliados dividieron Berlín en sectores americano, inglés, francés y ruso. El inconveniente de que Rusia no permitiera que el Marco Alemán fuera la moneda en su zona ocupada dividió a Alemania en Alemania Oriental y Alemania Occidental. Todos los productos y bienes provenientes de Alemania Occidental debían ser transportados a través de la zona ocupada por los rusos en camiones o trenes hasta Berlín, ubicada en la principal ruta de transporte a cien millas de la frontera de Alemania Occidental. Cuatro días después de que Rusia se negara a aceptar el Deutsche Mark en la zona oriental, intentaron expulsar a los tres aliados de Berlín. Los rusos bloquearon todas las carreteras, vías férreas y vías fluviales que entraban en Berlín. Rusia intentaba hambrear a los dos millones de habitantes de Berlín Occidental para que los aliados occidentales cedieran y se retiraran de Berlín. El bloqueo de Berlín fue la primera gran crisis internacional y el primer conflicto entre Rusia y sus aliados que se intensificó en la Guerra Fría. Rusia también cerró la base aérea controlada por los aliados.

Los aliados tenían tres opciones: abandonar su parte ocupada de Berlín y permitir que Rusia se hiciera cargo, lo que significaba dejar que Rusia tuviera su camino y permitirles hacer más demandas en el futuro, o usar la fuerza militar para prevenir el bloqueo, lo que podría provocar una tercera guerra mundial, otra tragedia. Decidieron mantenerse firmes y no ceder ante las demandas de Rusia. El General William Turner diseñó un plan que no pondría en riesgo la posición firme de los estadounidenses y sus aliados. Organizó lo que más tarde se llamaría Operación Vittles. El General William Turner diseñó un plan para utilizar 220 aviones bombarderos C 54 para volar toneladas de alimentos, carbón, gasolina y otros materiales sin parar hasta Berlín para evitar que la gente muriera de hambre. Pronto, los pilotos de Gran Bretaña, Francia y otros países se unieron a la operación, y todos los aviones aterrizaron en la zona británica porque la base aérea controlada por los aliados estaba cerrada. De día y de noche, en tormentas o mal tiempo, los aviones llevaron a cabo su misión. Los civiles se unieron para ayudar a descargar la mercancía, para que los aviones pudieran despegar rápidamente y hacer espacio para que aterrizaran otros aviones. Pilotos militares y privados y aeronaves se unieron a la Operación Vittles. Entre los suministros llevados por aire a Berlín, se entregaron 500,000 paquetes de ayuda.

Cuando el piloto Gail Halverson aterrizó en el aeropuerto de Tempelhof, se encontró con niños vestidos con harapos parados detrás de una cerca de alambre de púas. Cuando les preguntó qué querían tener, respondieron "paz". La respuesta de los niños le despertó compasión. Solo tenía una tira de chicle, que rompió en cuatro piezas y le dio a un niño con el papel. El niño cortó el papel en pedazos y se lo entregó a los niños para que pudieran oler la menta del papel. El piloto Halverson quedó tan impresionado por el comportamiento de los niños que quiso hacer algo por ellos. Decidió recolectar dulces y tirarlos desde el avión para los niños. Sabía que necesitaba permiso de las autoridades apropiadas, pero no había tiempo para obtenerlo. La noticia de su operación se difundió y sus amigos y personas de todo el mundo le enviaron dulces para los niños. Les dijo a los niños que agitaría las alas cuando se acercara al aeropuerto.

De esta manera, identificarían su avión y estarían listos para ir a recoger los dulces. Ató los dulces a pañuelos blancos, que sirvieron como pequeños paracaídas y facilitaron encontrar los dulces. El capitán Halverson se hizo conocido como el Bombardero de Caramelos y Tío Alas Temblorosas.

Durante el invierno de 1948 y 1949, la operación se volvió temporalmente difícil, y algunos días, ningún avión podía despegar debido al mal tiempo. La Operación Vittles continuó y se convirtió en el logro más destacado en la historia de los vuelos de suministro. Stalin se dio cuenta de que los aliados no abandonarían Berlín a ningún costo, y levantó el bloqueo el 12 de mayo de 1949. Antes de que el Piloto Halverson y otros pilotos dejaran el Aeropuerto de Tempelhof, cientos de niños y adultos llegaron al aeropuerto de Tempelhof, algunos con ramos de flores, otros con notas para agradecer a los pilotos por su amabilidad y ayuda humanitaria en evitar que se murieran de hambre. Los aliados y personas de todo el mundo mostraron tanta humanidad hacia los ciudadanos alemanes en Berlín. Pilotos y personas trabajando juntos para salvar a los residentes de Berlín del hambre comenzaron a curar los traumas y heridas de la posguerra.

Incluso nuestro grupo de refugiados recibió paquetes de ayuda de los estadounidenses en Sophienhof. Cada vez que llegaba el Yellow Mail Coach, corríamos para ver al cartero descargar el correo. Si veíamos un paquete de ayuda, nos poníamos muy contentos. Corríamos a casa para decirle a nuestra madre que había llegado un paquete. Podíamos recoger el correo entre la 1:00 y las 2:00 p.m. La Sra. Diercks, quien manejaba el servicio de correo, desempacaba los bienes, colocando toda la comida en un lado de la mesa y la ropa en el otro lado. Para la 1:00 p.m, un grupo de personas y niños se paraban frente a la mesa, observando todas esas cosas hermosas expuestas. La Sra. Diercks permitía que solo una persona a la vez escogiera un artículo. Ella distribuía la comida a cada madre.

Una vez me emocioné al encontrar una falda con hermosas flores rojas y blancas rodeadas de hojas verdes. Se convirtió en el tesoro que solo usaba los domingos, yendo a la iglesia. Mamá, Emma y Meta recibían vestidos. Los niños a veces recibían pantalones y otras veces suéteres o camisas. Cuán preciados eran esos artículos y cuán agradecidos estábamos con el gobierno y las personas estadounidenses por su generosidad. Se decía: "Cada paquete de ayuda es una contribución personal a la paz mundial que nuestra nación busca. Expresa la preocupación y la amistad de Estados Unidos en un lenguaje que todos entienden". Ciertamente entendíamos el lenguaje de tener suficiente comida para comer y recibir algo especial, lo que llamábamos ropa de lujo. Qué orgullosa me sentía yendo a la escuela con una falda nueva que recibí de un paquete de ayuda.

Alemania necesitaba resolver muchos problemas políticos. Después de que Alemania perdiera la Segunda Guerra Mundial, el Tercer Reich se derrumbó. Alemania no tuvo un gobierno central desde 1945 hasta 1949.

Durante la posguerra, los aliados dividieron Alemania en cuatro zonas de ocupación controladas por administraciones americana, británica, francesa y rusa. Los cuatro aliados también dividieron y ocuparon la ciudad de Berlín, ubicada en la zona rusa. Cuando surgieron conflictos entre la Unión Soviética y Alemania, los tres socios, Estados Unidos, Gran Bretaña y Francia, decidieron el resultado y gobernaron Alemania.

El 23 de mayo de 1949 se reunió el primer Consejo Parlamentario de Alemania Occidental y declaró formalmente el establecimiento de la República Federal de Alemania. Conrad Adenauer, presidente del Consejo, anunció: "Hoy nace una nueva Alemania". La gente se convirtió en libre de unirse al partido de su elección y votar por un presidente de su elección. El 12 de septiembre de 1949 eligieron al Dr. Theodor Heuss como el primer presidente de la República Federal de Alemania.

Konrad Adenauer se convirtió en un líder justo y humanitario con una educación cristiana y familiarizado con las ideologías políticas. Desarrolló una buena relación con los tres aliados de Alemania Occidental. Su ministro de economía, Ludwig Erhard, abolió el programa de racionamiento después de la reforma monetaria de 1948. El nuevo gobierno alemán buscó equilibrar programas sociales para trabajadores y civiles con oportunidades de inversión de capital para industriales, comerciantes y empresarios. Los planes meticulosamente diseñados de Ludwig Erhard tuvieron éxito en la recuperación económica. Tomó varios años de trabajo duro para beneficiar a Alemania y Europa. Más tarde fue llamado el "milagro económico" (Wirtschaftswunder).

El canciller Adenauer también se reunió en 1952 con el ministro de relaciones exteriores de Israel, Moshe Sharett, y firmó un acuerdo de reparación para compensar a los sobrevivientes del Holocausto por su sufrimiento durante la Segunda Guerra Mundial. Este acuerdo sigue vigente hoy en día. El gobierno soviético respondió rápidamente a la acción de Alemania Occidental formando en octubre de 1949 la República Democrática Alemana o DDR en Alemania Oriental. Estas acciones alejaron la reunificación de la Alemania dividida. Dividieron a Alemania y al mundo, crearon animosidad y avivaron la Guerra Fría entre el Este, los países controlados por los comunistas, y el Oeste, el mundo libre.

La economía en Alemania del Este empeoró y la vida se hizo difícil bajo la dictadura comunista de Rusia. Muchos alemanes del este huyeron a Alemania del Oeste. En 1961, el gobierno ruso construyó un muro, más tarde llamado la cortina de hierro, desde el mar Báltico a lo largo de toda la frontera, visiblemente dividiendo Alemania del Este y del Oeste. Una zona militar de cinco millas de ancho a lo largo de la frontera se encargó de patrullar y prevenir que las personas cruzaran la frontera sin permisos especiales. Cualquiera que fuera capturado intentando escapar sería disparado en el acto o capturado y castigado. Solo ciertos puntos de control abrieron con restricciones severas para los viajeros de Alemania del Este a Alemania del Oeste y viceversa.

Sin embargo, la prohibición de viajar libremente, la escasez de bienes y otras restricciones llevaron a la gente a rebelarse y a celebrar manifestaciones. En primer lugar, se relajaron las restricciones de viaje. El 9 de noviembre de 1989, miles de ciudadanos se reunieron en Berlín Oriental y se dirigieron hacia el muro con martillos y picos, y rompieron partes del muro. Los guardias ya no podían controlar a la multitud enojada y los dejaron cruzar hacia Berlín Occidental. Más tarde, el presidente ruso Mikhail Gorbachev, quien también introdujo la "perestroika" de apertura al pueblo ruso, permitió la eliminación de la cortina de hierro y la unificación de Alemania Oriental y Occidental.

Finalmente, con el consentimiento de los Estados Unidos, Francia, el Reino Unido y la Unión Soviética, las dos Alemanias se unieron y recuperaron su soberanía. El Acuerdo Dos más Cuatro firmado en Moscú el 12 de septiembre de 1990 selló la reunificación de Alemania Oriental y Occidental. Los cuatro términos esenciales fueron que las fuerzas aliadas retiraran sus tropas y devolvieran plena soberanía a Alemania. Se permitió un límite de 370,000 fuerzas armadas alemanas. Alemania tuvo que jurar no hacer reclamaciones futuras sobre el territorio que pertenecía a Alemania antes de 1945. Desafortunadamente, un tercio de Alemania, incluyendo mi querida Prusia Oriental, desapareció para siempre después de terminar ambas guerras mundiales.

Permítanme retroceder a mi escuela primaria en 1949. Cuando el Sr. Reimers nos despidió para nuestras vacaciones de verano y nos dio nuestras boletas de calificaciones, les dijo a los estudiantes que terminarían sexto grado el próximo año que podían postularse a una escuela secundaria en Schoenberg. No sería fácil entrar. Debido a la escasez de profesores y a una pequeña instalación de enseñanza, solo se podía acomodar a unos pocos estudiantes. Los estudiantes tendrían que someterse a un examen intensivo escrito y oral durante dos semanas. La escuela secundaria solo aceptaba a los mejores estudiantes. Sabiendo que terminaría sexto grado el próximo año, inmediatamente pensé en ir a la escuela secundaria. ¿Serían mis calificaciones lo suficientemente buenas como para aprobar los exámenes? Pero, ¿cómo llegaría allí? ¿Mi madre me permitiría ir? Muchos pensamientos pasaron por mi mente. También esperaba que otros niños o niñas estuvieran interesados en ir.

Corrí a casa y le conté a mi madre sobre la posibilidad de ir a la escuela secundaria y le pregunté si me permitiría asistir si pasaba las pruebas requeridas.

"Déjame pensarlo por un tiempo, cómo podríamos hacerlo posible. Necesitarías una bicicleta porque no hay transporte público disponible hacia Schoenberg. También necesitarás más y mejores prendas de vestir. No podemos permitirnos comprar todas estas cosas para ti en este momento. También podría haber matrícula que pagar."

"Por favor, por favor, Madre, déjame ir. Tú puedes hacerlo posible."

"Sólo se paciente; we will see what we can do."

Por ahora, tuve que conformarme con que mi madre no respondió con un rotundo no. Actualmente, ni siquiera sabía cómo andar en bicicleta muy bien. Necesitaba más práctica. Siempre que veía a alguien andando en bicicleta, preguntaba si me dejarían montar en ella. Al principio, arrancar y mantener el equilibrio en la bicicleta me hacía caer con frecuencia. Pero pronto, me sentí más segura y salí sin tambalearme.

Durante el verano de 1949, los escarabajos de la papa infestaron las plantas jóvenes. El Sr. Jessen decidió emplear a los niños para recoger los escarabajos de las plantas y salvar la cosecha de papas. Él, a su vez, pagaría algunos centavos por hora a cada niño. Un grupo de mis vecinos y yo nos ofrecimos como voluntarios para que yo pudiera ganar algo de dinero para comprar una bicicleta. Uno de los trabajadores de la granja llevaría un registro de cuántas horas trabajaba cada niño y los pagaría al final de la semana. Llevaría a casa mis pocos marcos y se los daría a mi madre.

"¡Mira, madre! Esta semana gané algo de dinero. Podemos usarlo para comprar una bicicleta para ir a la escuela."

"Sí, Hildke, así me llamaba en el dialecto de Prusia Oriental, lo guardaré para ti."

Me sentí tan animada por contribuir a la compra de la bicicleta, que podría convertirse en realidad si no era este año, tal vez el próximo.

En el otoño, mi hermano menor, que tenía seis años, comenzó la escuela primaria. Lo llevé a la escuela y lo presenté al Sr. Reimers. Al principio, era tímido, pero se volvió más sociable una vez que conoció a sus compañeros de clase. Sobresalió en deportes y disfrutó corriendo y jugando partidos de fútbol.

Después de que Edmund se graduó de la escuela primaria, comenzó a trabajar para la familia Groth en Fargau. El señor Groth era el alcalde de Fargau y también tenía una pequeña finca. Edmund administraba la granja para el señor Groth, quien también compró nuestros dos caballos. El señor Jessen, dueño de Sophienhof, ya no quería proporcionar comida para nuestros caballos, lo que nos obligó a venderlos. Todos estábamos tristes por separarnos de nuestros valientes caballos, Kastan y Kobel, quienes salvaron nuestras vidas durante el largo y peligroso viaje desde Prusia Oriental hasta nuestro lugar actual en Schleswig-Holstein.

Mamá aceptó algunos cambios, pero otros no. Ella se aferró a sus valores cristianos y esperaba que todos sus hijos siguieran su ejemplo. Emma y Meta lo hicieron aceptando a Jesucristo como su Salvador personal. Un día, Meta me dio un folleto de Werner Heuchelbach que describía cómo ser salvo. Después de leerlo con gran interés, me arrodillé y le pedí a Jesús que lavara todos mis pecados y entrara en mi corazón. Sentí una cálida luz que me envolvía y una gran alegría llenó mi corazón. Corrí a mi madre y a Meta y compartí esta maravillosa experiencia con ellas. Se regocijaron conmigo. A partir de entonces, escuché cuidadosamente al predicador en la iglesia, porque quería aprender más sobre las enseñanzas de Cristo y cómo poner en acción las palabras que él enseñaba. Al ser un cristiano renacido, mi fe en Dios de repente cobró vida y significado y ya no era solo un ritual religioso. Ahora obedecía a mi madre no solo por deber sino porque Dios nos manda a honrar a nuestro padre y madre. Obtuve un catecismo compilado por Martin Lutero, un libro que se usaba en las escuelas para enseñarnos las reglas básicas de nuestra fe y que debíamos memorizar antes de la confirmación a los catorce años. Contenía los Diez Mandamientos, la Oración del Señor, la confesión de fe, las explicaciones de los Sacramentos sagrados y algo de historia de la iglesia. Los catecismos luteranos y católicos difieren en algunos puntos porque los luteranos, la denominación de nuestra familia, no creen en el papa y su infalibilidad.

El domingo antes de la confirmación, a los estudiantes se les harían preguntas al azar del catecismo para responder frente a la congregación y recitar versículos bíblicos, historia religiosa y letras de himnos. Siempre que tenía un momento libre, leía una página o dos y memorizaba los contenidos. Emma y Meta, ambas cristianas nacidas de nuevo, respondieron muchas de mis preguntas sobre el crecimiento en la fe.

Meta estaba esperando otro bebé, y el 1 de junio de 1950 dio a luz a una niña saludable. Meta, Ernst y todos nosotros dimos la bienvenida a la nueva integrante de la familia con alegría y la llamaron Agnes. Siempre que tenía un momento libre, iba a la habitación de Meta para ver y tocar a la bebé. Esta vez, Meta se quedó en casa por más tiempo para cuidar a su pequeña hija.

Mi hermano Richard se graduó de la escuela primaria y comenzó a asistir a una escuela de oficios en Schoenberg. Era muy talentoso en la fabricación de cosas de metal. Quería estudiar la artesanía del trabajo del hierro, o herrero, como se le llama en alemán. Richard asistió a un año de clases en una escuela de oficios antes de convertirse en aprendiz en un taller de maestros herreros. La escuela de oficios resultó estar en Schoenberg en el mismo edificio que la escuela secundaria a la que yo quería asistir.

Durante el verano, trabajé en la granja siempre que pude para ganar algunos marcos. Para finales del verano, había acumulado algo de dinero y le pregunté a mi madre si era suficiente para comprar una bicicleta.

"Realmente no, pero agregaré el resto para comprarte una bicicleta, y podrás ir a la escuela secundaria", respondió mi madre.

Corrí hacia mi madre, la abracé y grité: "¡Gracias, gracias, eso es maravilloso! ¿Cuándo vamos a comprar una bicicleta?" "Esperaremos hasta el próximo año, durante tus vacaciones de verano".

"Eso está bien, puedo esperar".

No podía esperar a volver a la escuela y contarle la excelente noticia a mi maestro. Cuando regresé a la escuela y entré al sexto grado, le dije al maestro que mi madre me había permitido inscribirme en la escuela secundaria. El maestro respondió: "Me alegro por tí también". Luego preguntó si había otro estudiante que quisiera asistir a la escuela secundaria. Cuando nadie respondió, supe que tendría que ir sola. Pero eso no me importaba. Iría a pesar de ser la única estudiante de mi clase de la escuela primaria. El otoño y el invierno pasaron lentamente y sin eventos. Estaba contando los meses hasta las vacaciones de verano.

El día antes de que comenzaran nuestras vacaciones, recibimos nuestras boletas de calificaciones. Yo no recibí la mía y me preguntaba por qué. Entonces, el Sr. Reimers me dijo que esperara en el aula, quería hablar conmigo. Después de que todos los estudiantes se fueron, se acercó a mi escritorio, me mostró mi boleta de calificaciones con mis notas y dijo: "Ves, Hildegard, sabiendo que vas a la escuela secundaria, bajé tus calificaciones a propósito. Te diré por qué, cuando los maestros de la escuela secundaria vean tus calificaciones, no esperarán mucho de ti, pero tú los sorprenderás y les darás lo mejor de ti, lo que será más de lo que presumen. Sé que lo harás bien. Eres una buena estudiante y tienes muchas ganas de aprender".

Al principio, estaba perpleja. Luego pensé por un momento y dije: "ciertamente haré lo mejor que pueda".

Luego me entregó mi boleta y una hoja de papel con el nombre de la escuela secundaria, la dirección, la fecha de registro y el comienzo del período de prueba de dos semanas.

"Recuerda, también, madura y mantente pura".

"Lo recordaré; muchas gracias por todo lo que me has enseñado".

Con un apretón de manos y una reverencia, me despedí y me fui. Me sentí algo triste porque el Sr. Reimers ya no sería mi maestro, porque aprendí mucho de él en los últimos cuatro años. Él nos enseñó a sus estudiantes y a mí no solo materias sino sabiduría para la vida. Mientras caminaba lentamente a casa, reflexioné sobre su acción y comentario, y comencé a entender su motivo. El Sr. Reimers intentó enseñarme una lección vital, ser o hacer más de lo esperado. El verso que escribió en mi álbum me vino a la mente: "La verdadera belleza es la luz que irradia a través de tus ojos desde el espíritu interior".

Cuando llegué a casa, le conté a mi madre la razón del maestro para bajar mis calificaciones. Ella estuvo completamente de acuerdo con él. Le pregunté cuándo podríamos comprar la bicicleta. Ciertamente voy a la escuela secundaria. Le di la fecha de registro y cuando comenzarían los exámenes de dos semanas.

"Tal vez Richard te lleve a Schoenberg en su bicicleta. Le pediré que averigüe primero el precio. También puede llevarte a registrarte".

Tan pronto como vi a Richard entrar por la puerta, corrí hacia él y le dije: "Richard, Mamá quiere que me lleves a Schoenberg a comprar una bicicleta. ¿Lo harás?"

"Lo haré si mi madre lo permite. Déjame hablar primero con ella".

Richard se acercó a mi madre, que estaba limpiando la lechuga. "Madre, ¿quieres que compre una bicicleta para Hilde?"

"Sí, ella decidió ir a la escuela secundaria y necesita una bicicleta. Cuando vayas a Schoenberg mañana, busca una tienda de bicicletas y averigua cuánto cuesta una bicicleta de mujer."

"Ves, Richard, mamá quiere que tenga una bicicleta, y yo la quiero lo más pronto posible."

"Está bien, averiguaré el precio mañana." "Gracias, Richard."

También le dije la buena noticia a Horst y Georg sobre conseguir una bicicleta. Horst terminó el primer grado y comenzó el segundo grado en otoño. Georg fue el único hermano que no pudo aprender un oficio porque tenía que trabajar en la granja para proporcionar alimentos a nuestra familia.

Cuando llegó la hora de acostarme, estaba demasiado emocionada por ir a la escuela secundaria y tener una bicicleta nueva que no pude dormir por mucho tiempo. Cuando me desperté al día siguiente, Richard ya había ido a la escuela. No podía esperar hasta que regresara a la finca; caminé hacia él para encontrarme con él. Tan pronto como vi a mi hermano a lo lejos, corrí para saludarlo.

"¿Encontraste una tienda de bicicletas? ¿Cuáles son los precios?"

"Sí, encontré una tienda de bicicletas muy bonita en Schoenberg, donde puedes conseguir una bicicleta de mujer decente entre 60,00 MA y 100,00 MA."

"Eso es bueno. Ya gané alrededor de 25,00 MA durante el verano que le di a mamá. Estoy segura de que ella compensará el resto del dinero."

"Creo que lo hará."

"Vamos a decirle las buenas noticias a nuestra madre." Richard se acercó a nuestra madre y le habló sobre el precio de una bicicleta de mujer y le preguntó si podía comprármela. "Te daré 100,00 MA, y puedes llevarla mañana para comprar una bicicleta para Hildke".

Estaba cerca y dejé escapar un grito de alegría: "¡Eso es maravilloso, gracias madre y gracias a ti, Dios, por hacer realidad mi sueño!"

A la mañana siguiente, me levanté temprano, me puse mi mejor atuendo de domingo y nos fuimos a Schoenberg conmigo en el manubrio de Richard. Fue un viaje difícil para Richard, que tuvo que pedalear muy fuerte, llevando mi peso extra, y para mí, sentada en la barra de hierro dura durante más de una hora también fue incómodo. Cuando entramos en la tienda de bicicletas, nos olvidamos del dolor del viaje. Miré alrededor y luego fui a cada bicicleta de mujer para escrutarla antes de hacer mi elección. Una bicicleta llamó mi atención, y volví a ella varias veces y la revisé cuidadosamente. Era una bicicleta Victoria roja de 1950. Incluso tenía un protector de falda de ganchillo y dos resortes en el asiento. Le dije a Richard que quería comprar esa bicicleta en específico. Richard preguntó cuánto costaba, luego pagó al vendedor 75,00 MA, quien a su vez me la entregó con estas palabras: "Hiciste una buena elección, y si cuidas bien la bicicleta, te durará mucho tiempo".

"Gracias, seguro que cuidaré bien de ella".

Feliz como una alondra de ser dueña de una bicicleta, la empujé fuera de la tienda. "¿Quieres que vaya contigo a la escuela y espere allí? El edificio de la escuela está en la periferia de la ciudad. También puedo comprobar dónde tendrás que registrarte para los exámenes".

"Puedes venir conmigo para verificar el lugar de registro, sin embargo, no tienes que esperar en la escuela. Terminaré mis clases a las 2:00 p. m. Puedes volver a la ciudad y mirar las tiendas".

"Eso es una idea maravillosa. Lo haré".

"Solo asegúrate de no llegar tarde. Aquí tienes 2,00 MA, cómprate algo para almorzar".

"Gracias. No llegaré tarde. Nos vemos a las 2:00 p. m."

Dejé mi bicicleta junto a la de Richard y entré al edificio para preguntar dónde estaba la oficina de registro de la escuela secundaria. Una señora me mostró la oficina. Entré para verificar qué documentos necesitaría y cuándo era la fecha límite. Después de obtener la información necesaria, regresé felizmente a la ciudad. Me detuve en cada tienda de ropa para dama y admiré hermosos vestidos, faldas y blusas. Las zapaterías también me atrajeron, esas sandalias de cuero delicadas en diferentes colores para el verano. Pero cada vez que deseaba algún artículo, miraba mi bicicleta nueva y no deseaba nada más. Escuché los relojes de las torres de las iglesias sonar doce veces. Sabía que era hora de conseguir algo para comer. Cuando vi una panadería, entré y compré un pretzel fresco de tamaño considerable. Unas pocas mesas con sillas permiten que los clientes se queden y consuman sus pasteles en la panadería. Hice una pausa y comí mi pretzel antes de decidir caminar lentamente de regreso a la escuela para encontrarme con Richard. Por ahora, estaba cansada de caminar. Encontré un lugar, me senté y esperé a Richard. A las 2:00 p. m., la puerta de entrada principal se abrió y salieron los estudiantes. Cuando vi a Richard, tomé mi bicicleta y caminé hacia él.

"Hola, Richard, ya ves, llegué a tiempo".

"Muy bien, pongámonos en marcha. Tengo mucha tarea que hacer".

Richard recogió su bicicleta y nos dirigimos hacia Sophienhof por el camino rural sin pavimentar lleno de baches y llegamos aproximadamente una hora más tarde.

Puse mi bicicleta frente a la entrada y corrí hacia la casa de mi madre. La tomé de la mano y la llevé a mi nueva bicicleta. "Mira, madre, ¿no es una bicicleta hermosa? Muchas gracias."

"Sí, seguro que es una bicicleta bonita. Hiciste una buena elección."

"¡Gracias! ¿Puedo llevarla adentro? No quiero dejarla afuera durante la noche".

"Pónlo en la entrada detrás de la escalera; estará fuera del camino. Hice lo que mi madre me dijo.

Al día siguiente, recorrí el rancho, les mostré a todos los vecinos mi bicicleta nueva y les dije que solicitaría el ingreso a la escuela secundaria el miércoles.

El miércoles por la mañana, tomé mi boleta de calificaciones y mi tarjeta de identificación y fui con Richard a Schoenberg para registrarme para el exámen de ingreso para asistir a la escuela secundaria. Cuando llegué, ya había una larga fila en el pasillo. Después de esperar lo que pareció mucho tiempo, se abrió la puerta de la oficina, salieron una madre y una hija, y una señora me pidió que pasara.

"Buenos días, hice una reverencia; Soy Hildegard Bonacker; Aquí está mi boleta de calificaciones y mi identificación".

"Buenos días, señorita Bonacker; por favor tome asiento mientras reviso su boleta de calificaciones y lo ingreso en el registro".

Dije: "Gracias", y me senté.

La secretaria miró primero la identificación, ingresó mi nombre, fecha de nacimiento y dirección en su libro. Luego revisó mi boleta de calificaciones, tomó notas de mis calificaciones y me devolvió ambos documentos. La secretaria me dijo que los exámenes comenzarían el lunes 10 de julio a las 8:00 a. m. y finaliza el 24 de julio de 1950.

"Traiga algunos cuadernos, un lápiz y una pluma estilográfica. Le notificaremos una semana más tarde si pasó las pruebas y será aceptada o no. Las clases regulares comenzarán el 7 de agosto de 1950, para los alumnos que hayan aprobado los exámenes".

"Adiós, señorita Bonacker. Nos vemos el 10 de julio". Me levanté, hice una reverencia, me despedí y salí de la oficina. Mientras tanto, no tuve suficiente tiempo para ir a la ciudad, así que esperé afuera a Richard. Cuando terminó sus clases, nos reunimos y cabalgamos juntos a casa. Le dije que me registré y que comenzaría las pruebas el 10 de julio de 1950.

El domingo 9 de julio, toda la familia, y varios vecinos se dirigieron a la iglesia del castillo de Salzau. Después de almorzar, yo inmediatamente comencé a poner mi cuaderno, lápiz y pluma estilográfica, llena de tinta, en una bolsa para las pruebas de secundaria del lunes para asegurarme de que no olvidaría nada. Al día siguiente, me levanté muy temprano. Mamá me preparó el desayuno. Luego preparó un sándwich con mantequilla y salami casero para llevar en el almuerzo. Me dirigí a Schoenberg mientras el sol acababa de salir y arrojaba sus brillantes rayos sobre los campos, y también iluminaba mi día. Llegué media hora antes y me registré en la sala designada para que los estudiantes fueran evaluados.

El director de la escuela se presentó como el profesor Foerster. Luego le pidió a cada estudiante que se pusiera de pie individualmente y dijera su nombre. Había algunas chicas más que chicos en la habitación. El profesor, a su vez, nos dijo en qué materias nos pondría a prueba. Los profesores enseñaban matemáticas, alemán, lecciones de inglés, historia y geografía durante las próximas dos semanas y luego nos evaluaron en cada materia. Aprendimos sobre todas las plantas y criaturas inusuales de Australia. La maestra nos mostró imágenes de un ornitorrinco, un oso koala, canguros, los habitantes aborígenes de los desiertos y las formas y tamaños únicos de los árboles botella. Estas diferentes criaturas y plantas me fascinaron. De camino a casa, repetí todos los nombres para asegurarme de no olvidarlos. Un día, el profesor Foerster salió de la escuela al mismo tiempo que yo salía con mi bicicleta. Me invitó a caminar con él a su casa, que no estaba muy lejos de la escuela. Me sentí honrada y empujé mi bicicleta mientras caminábamos y hablábamos. Me dijo cuánto le gustaban las rosas y qué variedades ya cultivaba. Escuché atentamente, y de vez en cuando, Le di una respuesta a una pregunta sobre dónde nací, dónde viví y qué flores me gustaban. En poco tiempo llegamos a su casa, y vimos las rosas multicolores en flor que llenaban su jardín,

"Qué hermosas son tus rosas", dije, admirando la variedad de los colores. Luego dijo: "Adiós, señorita Bonacker". Hice una reverencia y dije con una sonrisa: "Adiós, profesor Foerster".

Felizmente, monté mi bicicleta y volé a casa rápidamente para contarles a mi madre y hermanas sobre mi caminata con el profesor; la primera semana transcurrió sin dificultad. Hicimos exámenes escritos en la segunda semana, los profesores de las distintas materias nos dieron exámenes orales. La primera vez que tuve que pararme frente a la clase y responder preguntas en presencia de un grupo de profesores, mis nervios se tensaron y mis respuestas llegaron lentamente, pero me relajaba más y más con cada pregunta que me hacían. Los maestros tomaron notas después de que cada estudiante hubiera respondido las preguntas. Esperaba haber dado respuestas correctas a la mayoría de las preguntas. Cuando el profesor nos despidió el último día, nos dijo que recibiríamos el aviso por escrito antes del 31 de julio y que las clases comenzarían el 7 de agosto para los estudiantes que serían aceptados. Pedaleé a casa, preguntándome si lo había hecho lo suficientemente bien como para que me admitieran o no.

Cada vez que llegaba el vagón de correo, corría de inmediato para verificar si llegaba una carta para mí de la escuela secundaria en Schoenberg. Pasaron tres días y no llegó ningún correo. Al no haber llegado la carta a fines de julio, comencé a preocuparme por no aprobar los exámenes. Cuando para el martes 1 de agosto no recibí ninguna notificación, estaba desesperada. ¿Reprobé los exámenes o pasó algo con el servicio de correo? ¿Qué debo hacer? ¿Debo aceptar que no pude ir a la escuela secundaria o ir y averiguar qué pasó? Pasé una noche inquieta y oré a Dios para que me mostrara lo que debo hacer. No podía comprender que mi sueño se rompiera y enfrentar la vergüenza de mi maestro de escuela primaria y decirles a todos los estudiantes que no pasé las pruebas. La oficina de la escuela probablemente estaría cerrada durante la semana antes de que comiencen las clases. ¿Qué puedo hacer? Oré a Dios, ¿qué debo hacer para saber qué pasó?

Entonces pensé en el profesor Foerster. Recordé dónde vivía. ¿Por qué no voy a él y hablo con él? Sí, eso es lo que haría mañana, miércoles 2 de agosto. Me levanté temprano pero no me fui enseguida. Si llego a su casa a las 10:00 am, pensé que ya habría desayunado, y tal vez lo encontraría trabajando en el jardín. Esperé hasta las 9:00 a. m. antes de irme Cuando llegué a la casa del profesor Foerster, lo encontré recortando los capullos de rosas muertas de los arbustos. Me detuve en la puerta y le di mi nombre, y antes de que me invitara a entrar al jardín, le expresé mis disculpas por haber venido a su casa, pero necesitaba hablar con él con urgencia.

"¿Qué pasó, señorita Bonacker? Por favor entra." Entré al jardín,

"Por favor, continúe con su trabajo, profesor Foerster. Recuérdeme tomando todos los exámenes, solo faltan cinco días antes de que comiencen las clases, y no he recibido ninguna notificación si pasé las pruebas y si fui aceptada o no". Con gran anticipación, esperé su respuesta: "Por supuesto, señorita Bonacker, usted pasó bien todas las pruebas y ha sido aceptada".

"¿En realidad?" Medio incrédula pero luego emocionada, alargué la mano hacia la mano derecha del profesor Foerster. Nos dimos la mano mientras yo exclamaba: "Gracias, gracias, profesor. No sabe lo feliz que me hizo su respuesta. Estaré allí el lunes por la mañana para comenzar las clases". Luego me despedí y me fui. Le agradecí a Dios que pregunté personalmente si aprobé los exámenes y fui aceptada. Mi espíritu me levantó y sentí que volé en alas de águila de regreso a Sophienhof. Corrí a la cocina para contarle a mi madre las buenas noticias, lo que también la hizo feliz. Después del almuerzo, Fuí a la escuela primaria para decirle a mi maestro, el Sr. Reimers, que aprobé los exámenes y comenzaría la escuela secundaria la semana siguiente. Estaba encantado. "No tenía dudas de que serías aceptada. Te deseo lo mejor." Le agradecí por haberme enseñado el currículo educativo y la sabiduría y los valores morales necesarios para desarrollar un carácter noble. Me fui con emociones encontradas, triste por separarme de mi excelente maestro y compañeros de clase, pero feliz de comenzar la escuela secundaria. De camino a casa, los cinco años que pasé en esta escuela de un salón con un maestro tan sabio y conocedor pasaron por mi mente. También recordé el verso que escribió en mi álbum: "La verdadera belleza es la luz que irradia a través de tus ojos desde el espíritu interior". También nos enseñó: "Nada en este mundo es constante, excepto el cambio". Más adelante en la vida, pensé en lo que significaba la madurez para mí, y escribí el siguiente poema:

¿Qué es la madurez?
Sin duda es una meta piadosa y noble
Madurar y permanecer siempre puro.

La madurez es más que adquirir conocimientos, años,
es elegir sabiamente lo que uno piensa, hace y oye.
Es saber cuándo escuchar cuándo hablar.
Respeta al fuerte, al manso y al débil.
Perdonar a las personas que ofenden de nuevo
y decir lo siento cuando es debido.
Cuando cumplo mi promesa y mi palabra,
la confianza y el honor serán una gran recompensa.
Para terminar las tareas que comencé a hacer
A pesar de que es un sacrificio seguir.
Uso sabiamente mis bienes, mi tiempo
Confío y obedezco la palabra de Dios, sublime.
Él me muestra cómo hacer lo correcto y lo mejor,
por lo tanto, yo y otros seremos ricamente bendecidos.
Amar a Dios, a mí mismo, a mis amigos, a mis hermanos

e inspirarme para hacer el bien a los demás.
Seguro que es una meta piadosa y noble,
madurar y permanecer siempre pura.

Me di cuenta de que mi vida encontró un cambio. Al principio, me llenó de cierta tristeza dejar atrás lo familiar. Entonces acogí la nueva oportunidad de estudios superiores con entusiasmo y la alegría llenó mi corazón. Sólo quedaban tres días antes de que comenzara una nueva etapa de mi vida. Lavé y pulí mi bicicleta y lavé y planché mi mejor atuendo. Llené mi estilográfica con tinta y afilé mi lápiz. Llevé dos cuadernos, uno con cuadrados y otro con líneas. El 7 de agosto me levanté a las 5:00 a. m. y a las 6:30 a. m. comencé mi viaje a la escuela. Quería asegurarme de llegar al menos media hora antes de que comenzaran las clases.

Otros estudiantes comenzaron a llegar, y pronto el patio se llenó. Uno de los maestros alineó cada clase en fila antes de ingresar al edificio y al salón de clases designado. Los estudiantes mayores ingresaron primero; nuestra fila ingresó en último lugar. Otro profesor nos esperaba en el aula y asignó dos alumnos por pupitre. Dos filas de diez pupitres con niños y dos filas con niñas. Cuando todos los estudiantes se sentaron en sus asientos asignados, un estudiante tras otro se puso de pie y se presentó por su nombre. Inge Dunger y yo nos sentamos en la primera fila central. La señorita Bond se presentó y nos dijo que cada estudiante tenía que tomar "alemán, matemáticas, álgebra, geografía, historia, biología, química y arte. Estas materias eran obligatorias. Dado que Schleswig Holstein fue ocupado por los británicos, el inglés también es obligatorio".

"Sin embargo, también ofrecemos clases de latín y francés como materias voluntarias. Puede inscribirse en estas clases al final de esta sesión". La señorita Bond entregó el horario de la semana y a qué hora un maestro enseñaría cada materia específica. Después de la guerra, debido a la escasez de maestros, cada maestro enseñaba más de una materia. La primera semana demandó mucha atención el aprender los nombres de los maestros y qué materia enseñaron en qué salón de clases. También necesitábamos familiarizarnos con los nombres de nuestros compañeros de clase. Después de dos semanas, desarrollamos una rutina específica y nos sentimos cómodos y bien ajustados.

El profesor Foerster enseñó inglés, francés y latín. Aprendimos los nuevos sonidos nasales en francés y escribimos y pronunciamos correctamente las palabras en francés, latín e inglés. Disfruté mucho de sus clases y trabajé duro para no decepcionar al Prof. Forster. Cada vez que escribíamos una prueba, y no cometía un error de ortografía, sonreía mientras me entregaba el cuaderno. Una vez cometí un error de ortografía, y me regañó delante de toda la clase, "esperaba más de tí", me dijo y me bajó la nota un punto. Me sentí avergonzada y trabajé aún más en los tres idiomas para no decepcionar al profesor y evitar la humillación.

Otra sorpresa agradable vino a mi camino; nuestro profesor de matemáticas, el Sr. Sabrow, fue el mismo profesor que tuve el primer curso en la escuela de gramática de Pratjau. Me reconoció y supo que me gustaban las matemáticas. Me llamaba de vez en cuando a la pizarra para explicar una fórmula de álgebra o un problema de matemáticas a los alumnos.

El profesor Augustine instruyó geografía e historia. Sufrió una lesión durante la Segunda Guerra Mundial en la pierna derecha, lo que provocó que cojeara y usara un bastón. Sin embargo, cuando hablaba con una voz suave pero firme, no podías evitar que te gustara. Primero, aprendimos de memoria los nombres de las capitales de cada país europeo, las ciudades importantes, los ríos, las montañas, la flora y la fauna y lo que producía cada país.

Comenzamos nuestra lección de historia con el Imperio Romano, seguido por la migración de las diversas tribus a las diferentes partes de Europa. El profesor Augustine presentó la historia vívidamente y escuchamos con atención los nombres de las tribus y dónde se asentó cada tribu. Al final de cada lección, él citaba un proverbio para enseñarnos sabiduría. Todavía recuerdo una de sus citas: "Quien miente una vez no será creído incluso después de que diga la verdad más tarde", La señorita Bond enseñó gramática, ortografía y literatura alemanas. Ella nos familiarizó con los dos poetas épicos, Johann Wolfgang von Goethe y Friedrich Schiller, y muchos otros poetas y autores famosos de varios países. También teníamos que aprender poemas de memoria y recitarlos frente a la clase. Disfruté aprendiendo nuevas materias y andando en bicicleta a la escuela todos los días.

Un día, mientras conducía por una parte sinuosa de la carretera, un adolescente cortó la curva y chocó conmigo. Me caí y me golpeé la cabeza contra el manillar. El chico me ayudó a levantarme, me enderezó el manubrio y continuó cabalgando hacia su destino en la dirección opuesta. Continué mi camino a la escuela a pesar de que desarrollé un dolor de cabeza terrible. Cuando el profesor Foerster me miró, supo que no me sentía bien. Incluso antes de comenzar a enseñar, me preguntó qué pasó. Le conté sobre el accidente.

"No estás en condiciones de quedarte en la escuela. ¿Sabes quién puede llevarte a casa?"

"Mi hermano Richard está aquí en la escuela de oficios". "Bien. Enviaré a alguien a la clase de Richard y le pediré permiso al maestro para llevarte a casa. No andes en bicicleta; podrías marearte y caer de nuevo." "Gracias, profesor Foerster".

Varios minutos después, llegó Richard y comenzamos a empujar nuestras bicicletas a casa. Mi dolor de cabeza se intensificó. Apenas logré volver a casa. Cuando mi madre vio mi ojo izquierdo ensangrentado, le conté lo sucedido; inmediatamente me acostó. Puso un paño frío y húmedo sobre mi ojo izquierdo. se sintió mejor, y me quedé dormida. Mi estómago rugiente me despertó al final de la tarde.

"Mamá, tengo hambre. ¿Puedes traerme algo de comer?" Mi madre volvió con un bocadillo y un vaso de leche. Me senté, le di un mordisco y cuando comencé a masticar, cada movimiento de la mandíbula me dolía.

Le entregué el sándwich a mi madre.

"Lo siento, es demasiado doloroso comer el sándwich.

Tomaré otro vaso de leche para llenar mi estómago ahora." "Te haré un poco de sopa más tarde".

"Gracias Madre."

Mis hermanas Emma y Meta se sorprendieron al encontrarme en la cama, al igual que mi hermano Horst cuando llegó de la escuela y Georg cuando terminó de trabajar. Expresaron su compasión por mí. Mamá preparó una sopa ligera con unas albóndigas diminutas, que tragué sin masticar. Pasé una noche inquieta y solo pude dormir del lado derecho. La más mínima presión en la mejilla izquierda dolía. Cuando me levanté al día siguiente y me miré en el espejo, la sangre cubría todo el ojo y se formaron manchas negras y azules en la parte superior de la mejilla izquierda. Después de la rutina de la mañana y un tazón de sopa de leche ligera, volví a la cama. Esta vez llevé mi libro de poesía conmigo, con la esperanza de poder leer mientras mantenía la cabeza quieta. Leí el poema, "El rey de los Elfos (Der Erlkoenig)". Expresa el dolor emocional de un padre que lleva a caballo a su hijo enfermo al médico, y el hijo muere en el camino. Leer tantos poemas me hizo apreciar y admirar la habilidad del poeta para pintar una imagen mental vívida con pocas palabras. Pensé, si tan solo tuviera esa habilidad, sería maravilloso. También aproveché el tiempo para estudiar el

Catecismo Luterano y leer la Biblia. Me quedaba despierta más y más cada día y caminaba por el rancho para ver a mis amigos y vecinos. El dolor disminuyó. Después de una semana, le dije a mi madre que iba a volver a la escuela. No quería perderme muchas clases.

"Creo que es demasiado pronto, todavía". "Iré despacio y estaré bien".

"Me sentiré mejor si Richard te lleva el primer día. Si te mareas, puedes caerte; él estaría allí para ayudarte."

"Está bien, madre, iré con Richard".

El lunes siguiente, nos fuimos a la escuela. Sentía un dolor punzante en la mejilla izquierda cada vez que golpeaba un bache en el camino rural sin pavimentar lleno de baches. No me atrevía a mencionárselo a Richard por miedo a que se lo contara a mamá y ella me obligara a quedarme más tiempo en casa. En mi clase de inglés, el profesor Foerster me dio la bienvenida y me pidió que pasara al frente para poder mirarme el ojo de cerca.

"Se ve descolorido, pero ¿te sientes bien?"

"Oh, sí, estoy bien", respondí rápidamente, para que no sospechara que todavía sufría de dolor y malestar. La decoloración se desvanecía cada día, y el ojo se aclaraba, pero el dolor no desapareció por completo. Después de dos semanas, de camino a casa desde la escuela, decidí ver al Dr. Schmidt en Bendfeld. Le conté sobre el accidente; me examinó. Cuando hizo presión en el pómulo izquierdo, sentí un dolor agudo, como un cuchillo que me apuñala en la mejilla.

"Creo que tu pómulo está fracturado", dijo; sin embargo, no hay nada que pueda hacer. Tomará algún tiempo para sanar por sí mismo. Mientras tanto, evite los deportes y cualquier ejercicio extenuante como correr y saltar. Tome una aspirina cuando el dolor sea demasiado intenso. Asegúrate de no participar en actividades deportivas durante el próximo mes más o menos".

"Gracias, Dr. Schmidt. Lo haré."

Fui a casa. No le dije a nadie sobre el diagnóstico del médico. No quería faltar a la escuela. Después de un mes, el dolor disminuyó y me sentí cómoda participando nuevamente en deportes.

Me gustaron especialmente las excursiones cuando el profesor Foerster nos llevó a lugares históricos específicos. Un día fuimos en tren a Laboe, situado en el Mar Báltico. Aquí visitamos el Memorial Naval, que se inició en 1927 y se completó en 1936. Originalmente fue construido en memoria de los marines reales, que murieron en la Primera Guerra Mundial. Más tarde, en 1945 se agregaron al monumento los nombres de los infantes de marina muertos en la Segunda Guerra Mundial. Desde Laboe, tomamos un barco a Kiel; qué emocionante deslizarse sobre la superficie del agua y sentir el viento acariciar las mejillas. Cuando llegamos al puerto de Kiel, el profesor Foerster nos contó la triste historia de la destrucción masiva de Kiel durante la Segunda Guerra Mundial. Más tarde, las Fuerzas Aéreas británicas y estadounidenses bombardearon intensamente la zona industrial porque era un puerto esencial para la construcción naval marítima. Afortunadamente, se reconstruyeron muchos edificios, infraestructuras y fábricas, y algunos todavía estaban en construcción.

El Kaiser Wilhelm II había ordenado un canal para conectar el fiordo de Kiel en Holtenau con el Mar del Norte en Brunsbuettel. Fue nombrado Kaiser-Wilhelm-Kanal en honor al Kaiser Wilhelm I, el padre del Kaiser Wilhelm II, quien inició la construcción del canal y lo terminó en 1895. Ahorró más de 250 millas náuticas de distancia navegando alrededor de la península de Jutland y evitó pasar por mares propensos a tormentas. Más tarde, pasó a llamarse Nord- Ostsee-Kanal (Canal del Mar Báltico del Norte). Nos informó sobre la antigua y prestigiosa universidad de Kiel, la más grande de Schleswig-Holstein, fundada en 1665. También mencionó la Semana de Kiel (Kieler Woche); El evento comenzó con veinte participantes de vela en 1882, se cerró durante la Segunda Guerra Mundial, se reabrió en 1948 y se convirtió en una de las competencias de vela y festivales folclóricos más grandes del mundo. Me quedé tan cerca del profesor Foerster; No quería perderme ninguno de sus comentarios. Cuando tuve la oportunidad, le hice preguntas, a las que siempre respondió educadamente. Los estudiantes, y sobre todo yo, desarrollamos una gran admiración y simpatía por el profesor Foerster. Estudiamos mucho para no decepcionarlo, y las niñas compitieron y trataron de superar a los niños, lo que lográbamos con frecuencia. Ya fuera en el verano o el invierno, nunca llegué tarde ni perdí un día de clases debido al mal tiempo. Durante las tormentas de nieve, tenía que levantarme temprano y, en la oscuridad, empujaba la bicicleta por el camino congelado y lleno de baches con la nieve y el viento azotándome la cara.

Después de que todos los estudiantes se conocieron, algunos me invitaban a pasar la noche en sus casas. También averigüé dónde vivían mis parientes lejanos en Schoenberg. Tenían hijos de mi misma edad. Después de visitarlos y presentarme, me invitaron a pasar un fin de semana aquí y allá con ellos. Disfruté mucho de su compañía y tener solo un corto paseo en bicicleta a la escuela al día siguiente fue una ventaja.

Todos estudiábamos mucho; nadie quería quedarse atrás para repetir un año o ser expulsado después de reprobar el segundo año. La señorita Bond, que enseñaba alemán, exigió que memorizáramos poemas de poetas alemanes famosos. Mi poema favorito, escrito por Friedrich Schiller, fue Das Lied von der Glocke "La Canción de la Campana" (La campana) Es el poema más largo (430 versos) y más conocido jamás escrito en la literatura alemana. Solo necesitábamos aprender secciones individuales de memoria. En este poema, Friedrich Schiller describe la fabricación de una campana en versos conmovedores y cómo el sonido de la campana acompaña a una persona desde el nacimiento hasta la muerte a través de la alegría o la tristeza. Expresa que todas las cosas terrenales se desvanecen y cambian continuamente. Esperaba que el primer sonido de la nueva campana proclamara la paz.

Todo el pueblo alemán anhelaba una paz duradera para reconstruir sus vidas y su país. Sin embargo, ¿Comenzó la paz real después de que los generales alemanes se vieran obligados a rendirse incondicionalmente hace cinco años, o fue solo una tregua para poner fin al combate? ¿Qué precio se vio obligada a pagar Alemania y qué sacrificios adicionales se exigieron a los ciudadanos alemanes?

El presidente Franklin D. Roosevelt y el primer ministro Winston Churchill tenían buenas intenciones cuando se reunieron el 14 de agosto de 1941 en el acorazado Príncipe de Wales y redactaron el documento de la Carta del Atlántico.[17] Definieron los objetivos del mundo de posguerra en ocho párrafos que todos los aliados y Once países europeos confirmaron y aceptaron en una reunión el 24 de septiembre de 1941, en el Palacio de St. James, en Londres. Todos prometieron realizar estas declaraciones lo mejor que pudieran. En enero de 1942, un grupo de veintiséis naciones aliadas prometieron su apoyo.

1. Sus países no buscan engrandecimientos, territoriales, u otros.
2. No desean ver cambios territoriales que no concuerden con los deseos libremente expresados de las personas involucradas.
3. Respetan el derecho de todas las personas a elegir la forma de gobierno bajo la cual vivirán, y desean que se

restablezcan los derechos soberanos y el autogobierno de quienes han sido privados de ellos por la fuerza.

4. Se esforzarán, con el debido respeto de sus obligaciones existentes, para que todos los Estados, grandes o pequeños, vencedores o vencidos, disfruten aún más del acceso, en igualdad de condiciones, al comercio y a las materias primas del mundo que necesitan para su economía. prosperidad.

5. Desean lograr la más completa colaboración entre todas las naciones en el campo económico con el objeto de asegurar, para todos, mejores estándares laborales, progreso económico y seguridad social.

6. Después de la destrucción final de la tiranía nazi, esperan ver establecida una paz que brinde a todas las naciones los medios para vivir en seguridad. grandes o pequeños, vencedores o vencidos del acceso, en igualdad de condiciones, al comercio y a las materias primas del mundo que necesitan para su prosperidad económica.

7. Tal paz debería permitir a todos los hombres atravesar los mares y océanos sin obstáculos.

8. Creen que todas las naciones del mundo, por razones reales y espirituales, deben abandonar el uso de la fuerza. Dado que no se puede mantener una paz futura si las naciones que amenazan o pueden amenazar con una agresión fuera de sus fronteras, continúan empleando armamentos terrestres, marítimos o aéreos, creen, hasta que se establezca un sistema más amplio y permanente de seguridad general, que el desarme de tales naciones es esencial. Asimismo, ayudarán y fomentarán todas las demás medidas practicables para aligerar la abrumadora carga de los armamentos para las personas amantes de la paz.

Otra reunión tuvo lugar entre el presidente Franklin D. Roosevelt, El primer ministro Winston S. Churchill y Joseph V. Stalin del 3 al 11 de febrero de 1945, para discutir el destino de Alemania después de la Segunda Guerra Mundial. En esa reunión resolvieron nuevamente defender el contenido de los ocho párrafos de la Carta del Atlántico y tratar a vencedores y vencidos con la misma dignidad y respeto.

¿Qué pasó? ¿Por qué no se cumplieron las promesas de las reglas escritas en los ocho párrafos de la declaración propuesta de la Carta del Atlántico? ¿Por qué el pueblo alemán, en contra de su propia voluntad, se vio obligado a ceder una gran parte de Alemania Oriental, Pomerania, Newmark (Mark Brandenburg) y Silesia (Schlesien) a Polonia? ¿Por qué el sur de Prusia Oriental, la región de Memel y la ciudad de Danzig también fueron arrebatados a los alemanes y entregados a Polonia? Por qué los tres aliados y las Naciones Unidas permiten que Joseph Stalin tome la parte norte de Prusia Oriental con el puerto y la Ciudad Universitaria, Koenigsberg, ahora llamada Kaliningrado? ¿Por qué al pueblo alemán no se le permitió gobernar su propio país? Después de la capitulación de Alemania, terminó el Reich alemán. Los gobiernos estadounidense, británico, francés y ruso dividieron Alemania en cuatro zonas, las ocuparon con sus tropas y establecieron su cuartel general principal en Berlín y un cuartel general satélite en cada zona. Durante cuatro años, Alemania no tuvo gobierno. Los cuatro representantes que firmaron la Declaración de Berliner fueron el General Dwight Eisenhower, EE.UU.; Marshall Georgi Schukow, Rusia; General Bernhard Montgomery, Gran Bretaña; y el General Jean de Lattre de Tassigny, Francia. Los cuatro aliados no pusieron límite a la duración de la ocupación. Gobernaron Alemania desde sus respectivos países. Los cuatro socios establecieron todos estos reglamentos sin un representante o la aprobación del pueblo alemán.

¿Por qué los aliados y los representantes de las Naciones Unidas no hicieron cumplir sus propias reglas y permitieron que el gobierno ruso maltratara y utilizara a las mujeres y jóvenes alemanes que no pudieron escapar a tiempo como esclavos en condiciones inhumanas? ¿Por qué se permitió a los rusos despojar a los habitantes alemanes de todos sus bienes y propiedades y ser expulsados de sus hogares o enviados en trenes de carga como ganado a la zona de Alemania ocupada por los rusos? ¿Por qué se permitió que muchos prisioneros de guerra alemanes fueran llevados a Siberia para trabajar en condiciones y tratos inhumanos? ¿Por qué el general Dwight Eisenhower quitó el estatus de prisionero de guerra a los soldados alemanes capturados y los trató como fuerzas enemigas desarmadas (DEF)? De esta forma, los DEFs no tenían protección bajo el derecho internacional de la Convención de Ginebra. Estaban a merced de los caprichos de los vencedores. Al incumplir las normas internacionales, los aliados también cometieron crímenes de guerra.

Rheinwiesenlager, Fotografía de dominio público

¿Por qué se permitió a Polonia retener a los prisioneros de guerra como trabajadores esclavos mucho después de que terminó la guerra, haciéndolos trabajar en condiciones horribles, con poca comida, golpeándolos y mutilando sus cuerpos?

Mi padre se convirtió en prisionero de guerra en Polonia en 1945. Después de que terminó la guerra el 8 de mayo de 1945, con la rendición incondicional de Alemania, regresó a su hogar en Prusia Oriental, con la esperanza de encontrar allí a su familia. Desafortunadamente, la policía polaca lo atrapó y lo metió en prisión durante ocho años. Tuvo que trabajar en canteras y minas de carbón durante esos ocho años. Incluso después de ser liberado de la cárcel, tuvo que permanecer cuatro años más en el área antes de recibir el permiso en noviembre de 1957 para reunirse con su esposa Emilie y su hijo menor, Horst, en Essingen, Alemania.

¿Por qué el general Dwight Eisenhower estableció y supervisó los campos de prisioneros a lo largo del río Rin? ¿Por qué puso a los prisioneros detrás de cercas de alambre de púas en campos abiertos sin ningún refugio para que los prisioneros tuvieran que cavar hoyos para mantenerse calientes? Cuando llovía, los huecos se llenaban de lodo y no tenían instalaciones para lavar la ropa. Tuvieron que pararse en fila durante diez horas para conseguir un vaso de agua clorada del río Rin para saciar su sed. ¿Por qué les dio poca comida y agua y dejó que cientos y miles murieran de desnutrición, fiebre tifoidea y disentería? ¿Por qué no permitió que la Cruz Roja y los suministros privados de alimentos fueran entregados a los prisioneros cuando el abundante suministro de alimentos del ejército estadounidense estaba disponible?

¿Por qué las Naciones Unidas no intervinieron y detuvieron estas atrocidades en los campos del prado del Rin?

¿Por qué la población de Alemania fue sometida a un trauma físico y psíquico sin precedentes en la historia? ¿Por qué el sufrimiento y los sacrificios del pueblo alemán, principalmente de Alemania Oriental, permanecieron desconocidos para el mundo? ¿Por qué solo se publicitan los crímenes del Führer y su ejército y, a menudo, incluso se magnifican y tergiversan, y los crímenes de los aliados pasaron por alto como si no ocurrieran? ¿Por qué los aliados, que condenaron los crímenes de guerra y dijeron que vencedores y vencidos debían ser tratados por igual, cometieron también crímenes de guerra, algunos incluso peores? ¿Por qué la prensa no informó al público de estos crímenes de guerra? En cambio, el pueblo estadounidense trató con respeto a los prisioneros alemanes, que tuvieron la fortuna de ir a Estados Unidos, y los ayudó. Les dieron trabajo a cambio y los acogieron como buenos y responsables trabajadores y personas.

En Inglaterra, bajo la dirección de Norman Cross, el gobierno británico hizo todo lo posible para tratar a los prisioneros de guerra con humanidad y proporcionarles el mismo tipo de comida que la población local. Heinz Kraemer, prisionero de guerra en Inglaterra, fue invitado por el pastor británico Small a pasar la Navidad en su casa. La esposa del pastor Small era alemana y quería celebrar la Navidad con canciones navideñas tradicionales alemanas. Mi amigo estaba abrumado por la experiencia emocional de celebrar la Navidad en una casa particular siendo prisionero de guerra en Inglaterra. Sin embargo, en algunos campos de prisioneros ingleses, los prisioneros tenían que trabajar en campos de trabajo y eran maltratados.

En cambio, la Wehrmacht alemana, que invadió París en junio de 1940 y capturó a muchos soldados franceses como prisioneros de guerra, dividió los campos de prisioneros por rangos, Oflags (Offizierslager) para el campo de oficiales y Stalags (Stammlager) para los campos de prisioneros de guerra ordinarios. Los prisioneros vivían en cuarteles, fortalezas, asilos o instalaciones especialmente construidas y podían trabajar en los campos o fábricas de Alemania. El tratamiento de los prisioneros variaba según el comandante a cargo. Sin embargo, muchos eventos culturales tuvieron lugar dentro de la mayoría de los campamentos. Los presos formaron clubes, bandas y equipos deportivos, y escucharon conferencias. Muchos prisioneros no vivían en campos; algunos vivían entre los civiles y eran tratados de acuerdo con la Convención de Ginebra. Recibían una pequeña parte de su salario; parte de su salario se destinaba a la Operación Wehrmacht alemana. Los oficiales a veces estaban exentos de trabajar.

¿Por qué, cuando los cuatro aliados no establecieron un límite de tiempo para la duración de la ocupación, los ocupantes exigieron a los estudiantes que aprendieran el idioma de sus países?

Como vivíamos en la zona británica, era obligatorio estudiar inglés en quinto y sexto grado de la escuela de gramática y durante todo el bachillerato y la universidad.

Con el paso de los meses, aprendimos a citar algunas partes de César en latín, leímos algunas historias sencillas en francés y escribimos ensayos en inglés. Disfruté mucho, no solo de los idiomas extranjeros, sino también de todas las demás materias. Desde que comencé la escuela secundaria y tenía mucha tarea todos los días, me quedaba poco tiempo para jugar con mis amigos de mi antigua escuela primaria y en la granja.

Un día de primavera, cuando llegué a casa de la escuela, mi madre me anunció la gran noticia que la Cruz Roja notificó a ella que encontraron a su hija Marta después de muchos años de búsqueda. Vivía en Silkerode en Thüringen, estaba casada y tenía dos hijos. La Cruz Roja nos dio la dirección de Marta y nuestra dirección a Marta. Emma le escribió inmediatamente a Marta y le pidió que viniera a visitarnos. Marta respondió diciendo que ella y su familia vendrían en tren a Schoenberg el sábado 13 de mayo de 1950. Todos estábamos emocionados de ver a nuestra hermana Marta después de tantos años y conocer a nuestros dos sobrinos. Desafortunadamente, no pude conducir con mi hermano Georg a la estación de tren; Tenía que estar en la escuela ese día. Mamá, Emma y Horst iban en el carruaje, que el Sr. Jessen permitió que Georg usara. Mamá y todos nosotros estábamos encantados de verla a ella y a sus dos hijos, Erhard y Bernhard. Corrí a casa desde la escuela lo más rápido posible para abrazar a mi querida hermana Marta y conocer a mis dos sobrinos. Después de abrazarme, dio un paso atrás, me miró bien y exclamó: "¡Vaya, has crecido desde que te vi hace seis años! Ya no pareces un niño; pareces una joven."

"Gracias; Yo también iré a la escuela secundaria", anuncié con orgullo.

"Está bien; Ojalá hubiera podido ir a la escuela secundaria. Estaba agradecida de terminar la escuela primaria; después, tuve que ir a trabajar. Hubiera preferido ser costurera, pero la guerra cambió todos mis planes".

"Lamento mucho que no hayas podido seguir tú carrera deseada. Siempre cosiste ropa tan hermosa para mí y mis muñecas".

"Todavía coso para mis hijos y para mí. Me gusta ser madre y ama de casa."

"Me alegra que te guste tu papel como ama de casa; También me gusta coser, hacer crochet y tejer. Tal vez, algún día, me casaré y tendré una familia como tu."

"Solo espera hasta que obtengas una buena educación antes de pensar en casarte".

"Me gustaría ser maestra después de graduarme de la escuela secundaria".

"Siempre se necesitan buenos maestros".

"Disculpa, tengo que hacer mucha tarea para mañana. Me gusta terminarla antes de la cena."

Mamá exigió que todos comiéramos al mismo tiempo. Esperamos hasta que Georg llegara a casa del trabajo a las 5:00

p. m. Le dio suficiente tiempo para que se aseara y, a las 6:00 p. m., todos teníamos que estar sentados en la mesa. Hoy, mi madre puso sobre la mesa sus mejores embutidos para la ocasión especial junto con su pan casero. Incluso había horneado un pastel sencillo, que fue un verdadero placer para todos nosotros. Después de que mamá inclinó la cabeza y dijo una bendición, comenzamos a comer.

"Sé que todos estamos ansiosos por saber sobre la fuga de Marta y cómo terminó en Silkerode", dijo mamá. "Esta noche, ella está cansada. Esperaremos hasta mañana para escuchar su historia". Nos sentamos en silencio y consumimos nuestros deliciosos sándwiches de salchicha.

Todavía tenía clases el sábado por la mañana, esperé ansiosamente a que terminaran las clases y luego corrí a casa. Después del almuerzo, pregunté si podía llevar a Erhard y Bernhard a dar un paseo y mostrarles algunos animales de granja. Les advertí que no pasaran más allá de la cerca hacia el prado; hay un toro malo, y podría lastimarlos. Cuando regresamos a la casa, ambos estaban cansados y tomaron una siesta mientras yo hacía mi tarea. Mamá y Emma prepararon pollo, repollo rojo y puré de papas para la cena. Todos disfrutamos del regalo, especialmente Edmund, quien llegó a casa ese fin de semana desde Schoenberg, donde trabajaba como aprendiz haciendo barriles. Después de que mi madre, mis hermanas y yo recogiéramos la mesa y laváramos los platos, todos nos sentamos en la mesa de la cocina y bombardeamos a Martha con preguntas sobre los eventos de los últimos seis años en que estuvimos separados. Meta y Ernst también se unieron a nosotros.

"Ahora, niños, cállense y dejen que Marta nos cuente su historia".

Mientras todos los ojos la miraban, ella comenzó a contarnos: "Como saben, en 1944, trabajé para el maestro Sr.

Kessler en Hellrau. Ayudé a su esposa a criar a sus tres hijos y una hija. El niño más pequeño acaba de empezar a caminar. Pasaba las tardes en mi habitación arriba de la escuela y cosía faldas, guantes de punto o suéteres para mi hermana menor, Hilde. A menudo, después de que los niños se acostaban, también jugábamos algunos juegos de mesa. A fines de julio de 1944, escuchamos en la radio que los habitantes de Wizajny tuvieron que huir porque el frente ruso avanzaba rápidamente hacia nuestra zona. Celebramos el cumpleaños del hijo mayor el 1 de agosto y partimos al día siguiente a caballo y en calesa y nos unimos a la larga caminata de refugiados."

"¿A dónde fuiste?" preguntó mamá.

"Nuestra caminata condujo a través de Rominter Heide, pensando que estaríamos más protegidos de los ataques con bombas entre los espesos bosques. No fue así; todas las noches oíamos el zumbido de los aviones sobre nosotros, el ruido penetrante de las bombas cayendo y explotando, sin saber si la próxima bomba caería sobre nosotros. Fue extremadamente aterrador. Al día siguiente tuvimos que conducir alrededor de los cráteres de las bombas. Caballos muertos, vacas y cuerpos humanos yacían entre carros rotos. Algunas personas enganchaban vacas a sus carretas para tener leche fresca para sus hijos. Lentamente atravesamos Angerburg y Loetzen y llegamos a Allenstein. Aquí, dejamos nuestros caballos y carro y todas nuestras pertenencias y continuamos en tren a Bunzlau, Schlesien, donde el Sr. y la Sra. Kessler tenían algunos amigos. Nos quedamos allí hasta febrero. Se suponía que íbamos a continuar en autobús a Dresde, pero el autobús nunca apareció. El señor Kessler decidió tomar el tren. cuando llegamos a la estación de tren, encontramos el tren completamente lleno. Incluso afuera no había más espacio para estar de pie. En una vía diferente había algunos vagones vacíos. Toda la gente corrió hacia ellos y entró en los vagones

sin locomotora. Fuimos afortunados; el conductor del tren
sacó el tren completamente ocupado de la ciudad, desconectó
la locomotora y regresó a la estación de tren para recoger los
vagones adicionales. Cambió las vías, luego conectó los otros
vagones al tren y se fue. Apenas salimos de la estación de tren
cuando una bomba golpeó y voló la estación de tren. Qué horrible
espectáculo ver los escombros del edificio volando por los aires,
seguidos de una explosión y un incendio. Era aún peor pensar; si
el conductor no hubiera regresado por los vagones adicionales,
también habríamos volado en pedazos. Dimos gracias a Dios
por salvarnos la vida".

Bombardeo de Dresden de 1945

El rostro de Marta se puso pálido y tenso mientras hablaba y
revivía esta aterradora experiencia. Me senté al lado de Marta y
temblé. Agarré su mano y traté de consolarla, "Alabado sea Dios
por salvarte a ti y a todas las personas en el tren. ¿Llegaste sana y
salva a Dresde? "Si lo hicimos. Decidimos quedarnos en Dresde,
pero las bombas destruyeron la mayor parte de la ciudad y apenas
podíamos movernos; el señor Kessler y su familia encontraron

un lugar para quedarse fuera de la ciudad. Me ofrecí como voluntaria para ayudar en un hospital temporal que se instaló para soldados heridos. Conocí a Edith, una enfermera que también trabajaba allí. Nos hicimos buenas amigas y ambas vivíamos en un campo de refugiados cercano. Edith estaba comprometida con un soldado. Cuando terminó la guerra y el hospital cerró sus puertas, Edith se fue a Juetzenbach, donde vivía su prometido. En su camino, pasó por Silkerode, donde se detuvo para preguntar direcciones. La persona que le dio las instrucciones resultó ser un jardinero. Después de que Edith tuvo una larga conversación con el jardinero, se presentó como Karl Spitzer, y le preguntó si ella y su amiga Marta podían venir a trabajar para él. Él le dijo que Juetzenbach, donde vive su prometido, estaba a solo diez millas de Silkerode. Edith le dijo al jardinero que no podía trabajar para él, pero que le preguntaría a Marta. Después de que Edith visitara a su novio, regresó al campamento en Dresde y me contó sobre la oferta de trabajo de jardinero. Me alegró salir del campamento, acepté la oferta y comencé a trabajar para el Sr. Spitzer en septiembre de 1945. Poco a poco llegué a conocer a la gente de este pintoresco pueblo. Cuando conocí a Hermann Volz, nos atrajimos el uno al otro y disfrutábamos de una buena conversación y baile. Cuando su madre murió en 1946, me pidió que me casara con él. Con mucho gusto acepté su propuesta e intercambiamos votos el 21 de abril de 1946. Al año siguiente, en agosto, nació mi hijo Erhard, y un año después, Bernhard se unió a nuestra familia." Mamá se levantó, abrazó a Marta; lágrimas de alegría brotaron cuando dijo: "Mi querida hija, estoy muy contenta de que Dios te haya protegido, de que nos hayamos encontrado, de que te casaras con un buen esposo y de que tengas a dos adorables hijos."

"Yo también", dijo Marta mientras lágrimas de alegría rodaban por sus mejillas.

"¿Cuál es la profesión de su esposo?" preguntó mamá. "Es un secretario municipal y trabaja para el alcalde de Silkerode".

"Eso es muy bueno."

Marta continuó: "Desafortunadamente, Herman sufrió una lesión en la cabeza durante la Segunda Guerra Mundial, mientras suministraba granadas de mano a los soldados en Kalinin, Rusia. Después de estar en coma durante seis semanas, recuperó el conocimiento pero perdió el ojo izquierdo. Hermann debe usar anteojos especiales para cubrir la cavidad del ojo faltante. Sufre de frecuentes dolores de cabeza. Sin embargo, es muy amable con los niños y conmigo. Todos nos llevamos bien y estoy agradecida de tener un esposo amoroso. Ahora, déjame saber cómo y cuándo llegaste a Sophienhof.

Entonces mamá comenzó a decirle: "A mediados de julio de 1944, papá fue reclutado. El frente ruso avanzó rápidamente en la frontera oriental. Antes de la medianoche del 2 de agosto, vino un mensajero del alcalde de Wizayny y nos dijo que estuviéramos listos para salir de la plaza de la ciudad a las 9:00 am". Emma, Meta, mis hermanos y yo interrumpíamos de vez en cuando y describíamos escenas gráficas que nos dejaban horribles impresiones. Solo le contamos la primera parte de nuestro escape.

"Te diremos más mañana por la noche. Ahora es el momento de que los niños se bañen, una tradición de los sábados por la noche, y se acuesten".

No fuimos a la iglesia el domingo por la mañana porque queríamos pasar mucho tiempo con Marta y nuestros sobrinos, pero aun así vestimos nuestras mejores galas. Mamá era todo sonrisas hoy, sabiendo que sus ocho hijos estaban reunidos a su alrededor. Gustav y Ernst también se unieron a nosotros para almorzar.

Después del almuerzo, nuestros sobrinos, Richard, Horst y yo dimos un paseo hasta el bosque cercano llamado Kaelberholz. en primavera, una abundancia de flores cubría el suelo bajo hayas gigantes. Iris amarillos estaban cerca de la orilla del estanque. No pude resistirme a recoger algunas flores de iris para mi madre. También ayudé a Erhard a elegir un ramo de flores silvestres para su madre. Los pájaros trinaban y otros cantaban mientras la brisa se deslizaba entre las ramas, agregando un relajante sonido de fondo al concierto del bosque. Regresamos contentos, y Erhard y yo entregamos alegremente las flores a nuestras madres, quienes nos agradecieron y pusieron un ramo en la mesa de la cocina y el otro en la sala de estar. Erhard y Bernhard se acostaron en la cama de mi madre y tomaron una larga siesta. Mamá, Emma, Meta, Marta y yo nos sentamos alrededor de la mesa de la sala, y Marta quería saber cuándo salimos de casa, por dónde viajamos, cómo y cuándo llegamos a Sophienhof. Mamá, Emma y Meta respondieron una pregunta tras otra hasta la hora de la cena. Martha, Al ver a Meta embarazada, le preguntó cuándo esperaba a su bebé.

Meta le dijo en dos semanas a principios de junio. "Espero que todo vaya bien y que des a luz a un bebé sano", "Rezo para que Dios me dé un niño sano y que siga vivo esta vez. Desafortunadamente, mi primer hijo, Manfred, murió de neumonía cuando tenía sólo tres meses de edad."

Continuaron su conversación después de la cena hasta que llegó la hora de irse a la cama. Cada día compartimos nuestras experiencias de los últimos seis años. La semana que pasó con Marta y su familia pasó rápido. Llegó el día triste en que tuvimos que despedirnos de ellos. Las lágrimas llenaron los ojos de mamá y Marta cuando se separaron. Georg le había pedido al Sr. Jessen si pudiera usar el carruaje para llevarlos a la estación de tren de Schoenberg. Insistí en ir con ellos. Mi madre finalmente dio su consentimiento. Disfruté sentarme en el elegante carruaje detrás del cochero con mis dos sobrinos y ver pasar el paisaje. No me importaron los baches en el camino rural sin pavimentar. Llegamos temprano y esperamos hasta que abordaron el tren y partió. Me entristeció verlos partir. Me senté con mi hermano delante y disfruté del paisaje desde la perspectiva del cochero de camino a casa.

Todos volvimos a nuestra rutina. el primero de junio, Meta anunció que estaba teniendo dolores de parto. Ernst condujo rápidamente hasta Schoenberg para llamar a la partera. La partera había visto a Meta varias veces antes y se aseguró de estar disponible en su fecha de parto. Emma y mi madre se quedaron con Meta. Mamá y Emma esperaron para ayudar a la partera. Mi madre revisó la cuna y se aseguró de que la ropa, los pañales y las frazadas estuvieran allí. Dejaba que Meta le apretara la mano cada vez que el dolor era demasiado intenso. Con frecuencia llamaba a Ernst, quien finalmente llegó con la partera dos horas después. La partera puso sus instrumentos en la olla de agua hirviendo, esperó unos quince minutos, luego los colocó en una toalla limpia sobre la mesa. Se sentó frente a Meta y esperó. Ernst pasó a la otra habitación y se quedó allí. Finalmente, la bolsa de agua se rompió y la partera ayudó al bebé a ingresar al nuevo mundo. Cortó el cordón umbilical, sostuvo al bebé boca abajo y le dio una palmada suave en las nalgas para hacerla llorar. Luego le entregó el bebé a Emma, lo bañó, lo vistió y lo puso en la cuna. Emma fue a la otra habitación y le anunció a Ernst: "Es una niña".

Ernst corrió hacia Meta, la besó en la frente, "Me alegro de que todo haya ido bien, y de que tenemos una hijita". Luego se acercó a la cuna y miró a su hija recién nacida con una gran cara sonriente. Mamá estaba orgullosa de ser abuela nuevamente, y mis hermanos y hermanas disfrutaron de su nueva sobrina. Esta vez, Ernst no dejó que Meta volviera a trabajar. Quería evitar perder a su pequeña hija si se enfermaba durante la ausencia de su madre. Después de ser bautizada y lo suficientemente fuerte, Meta nos permitió cargar a Agnes y jugar con ella. Meta volvió a disfrutar de su rol de madre.

A mediados de julio comenzaron las vacaciones de verano, que todos los estudiantes esperaban con ansias. El último día de clases, la señorita Bond, nuestra profesora de alemán, nos entregó nuestra primer boleta de calificaciones. Rápidamente abrí la mío y revisé mis calificaciones en cada materia. Cuando leía (versetzt), pasé del primero al segundo grado, haciéndome muy feliz. Dos niños no tuvieron tanta suerte. Tuvieron que repetir la misma clase un año más. Un niño incluso tuvo que dejar la escuela por completo porque había reprobado la misma clase por segunda vez. Me sentí terrible por él. Las lágrimas rodaron por sus mejillas cuando se despidió de nosotros, sabiendo que no regresaría en agosto. Corrí a casa y le dije a mi madre que mi boleta de calificaciones era buena y que comenzaría el segundo año de la escuela secundaria a fines del verano. Por supuesto, Tuve que anunciar con orgullo a mis compañeros de la escuela primaria que me fue bien en la escuela secundaria y que avanzaría al siguiente grado.

En el verano, ayudaba a mi madre a recoger frambuesas, bayas y grosellas que crecían en el jardín. Emma nos llevó a un seto de un campo donde crecían moras. Cuando teníamos una cubeta mediana llena, íbamos a casa y se los dábamos a nuestra madre, que hacía mermelada o jugo con ellos y las bayas de la huerta. A veces, mi amiga, Elisabeth, se unía a nosotros. Hablamos de coser y que me gustaba coser. Me dijo que tenía una máquina de coser y me pidió que le cosiera un vestido.

Pensé que podría intentarlo. Elisabeth trajo un sobre grande con el diseño del vestido en el exterior y grandes hojas de papel fino con varias líneas en el interior. Teníamos que averiguar qué líneas tenía el patrón de su vestido, luego trazarlo con una rueda pequeña con dientes en otra hoja de papel. Trazamos todas las secciones con las mismas marcas de línea. Después de verificar y asegurarnos de tener todas las partes del vestido, cortamos cada forma del papel. Luego coloqué el patrón sobre el material. la tela negra tenía líneas blancas y pequeñas flores rojas entre las líneas. Colocamos la tela de modo que todas las líneas quedaran rectas, luego fijé el patrón al material y corté el material una pulgada más grande, dejando espacio para la costura.

Primero, cosí el corpiño, luego le pegué la falda. Llamé a Elisabeth para probárselo. Los lados del corpiño necesitaban ser reducidos un poco; de lo demás, le quedaba bien. Ahora venía la parte más desafiante: ajustar las mangas cortas. Luché hasta que lo puse bien, luego lo cosí a mano primero y luego con la máquina de coser. No sabía coser la cremallera con la máquina, así que lo hice a mano en la parte superior de la falda y en la parte inferior del lado izquierdo del corpiño. Cuando terminé, me acerqué a Elisabeth, le entregué el vestido y le pedí que se lo probara. Le quedó. El estilo se le veía precioso. Las dos estábamos contentas. Me animó a coser más cosas en su máquina de coser.

También permitimos algo de tiempo para la diversión de verano, nadando en el lago Selenter con Frieda, Elisabeth, Katie y otros amigos. No sabía nadar muy bien. Caminé lo más lejos que pude, toqué el fondo y luego nadé de regreso a la orilla. Una vez, me alejé demasiado y, de repente, golpeé un agujero en el fondo del lago y caí rápidamente. Me asusté y rápidamente saqué la cabeza del agua y nadé de regreso a la orilla. Elisabeth me dijo más tarde que una bomba cayó en el lago, creando un gran agujero. A partir de entonces, evité ir en esa dirección.

A mediados de agosto terminaron las vacaciones de verano y comenzaron las clases. Ver a los compañeros de clase y compartir nuestras aventuras de vacaciones fue emocionante. Luego comenzamos a estudiar las diferentes materias nuevamente y a leer más historias de Julio César en latín. En inglés, nos deleitó la novela Daddy-Long-Legs de Jean Webster y extractos de Le Malade Imaginaire (El enfermo imaginario) de Moliere. La profesora, Miss Bond, que enseñaba alemán, nos familiarizó con el conocido autor Thomas Mann, quien escribió *Los Buddenbrook* que describe la vida de una familia de Schleswig-Holstein en Alemania y varios otros autores. También tuvimos que aprender de memoria varios poemas de los conocidos poetas Johann Wolfgang von Goethe, Friedrich Schiller, Theodor Storm, Heinrich Heine y Herman Hesse. Junto a Friedrich Schiller, Johann Wolfgang von Goethe fue considerado el poeta y autor alemán más importante. Tuvimos que aprender varios de sus poemas de memoria, como "La canción nocturna de Wander del aprendiz" y "El Erlking". Todavía recuerdo el primer verso del poema:

"Wer reitet so spät durch
Nacht und Wind? Es ist der
Vater mit seinem Tipo:
Er hat den Knaben wohl
in dem Arm, Er fasst ihn
sicher, er hält ihn warm.

Traducido
¿Quién cabalga tan tarde por la noche
y el viento? Es el padre con su hijo.
Tiene al niño en sus brazos
Lo sostiene con seguridad; lo mantiene caliente.[21]

Franz Schubert compuso melodías para muchos de los poemas de Johann Wolfgang von Goethe. Ludwig von Beethoven compuso música para algunas de las obras que escribió Goethe, como Fausto. Ludwig von Beethoven también compuso una melodía para el poema de Friedrich Schiller, "La Oda a la Alegría", cantada por coros de todo el mundo. Siempre admiré a los poetas que crean imágenes con pocas palabras selectivas y conmovedoras. Conocer diferentes partes del mundo y aprender sobre su historia y culturas me fascinó, especialmente el vendaje de pies de Japón. También me gustaban las matemáticas y el álgebra. Recordar las fórmulas de todos los elementos en química me aburría. Sin embargo, disfruté la biología y aprendí más sobre el medio ambiente. Llegó el otoño. Todos los árboles mostraban sus coloridas hojas antes de que la helada las arrancara de las ramas. El viento las hizo girar y girar antes de dejarlas caer al suelo. Bandadas de gansos canadienses aterrizaron en los campos segados antes de migrar al sur a un clima más cálido. Siguió el invierno con temperaturas muy frías y andar en bicicleta contra el viento frío redujo mi velocidad. Tenía que levantarme mucho antes del amanecer para llegar a tiempo a clases, especialmente cuando tenía que empujar la bicicleta en la carretera helada en lugar de andar en ella. Pero independientemente de lo malo que fuera el tiempo, nunca perdí un día de clases por el mal tiempo.

Llegó la Navidad y tuvimos dos semanas de vacaciones. Esta Navidad fue única, con la bebé Agnes deleitando a la familia cuando nos reunimos alrededor del árbol de Navidad. Sus ojos brillaban al mirar las velas encendidas y escucharnos cantar canciones navideñas. Emma había tejido una hermosa chaqueta rosa para Agnes. Le hice una gorra rosa a crochet y mi mamá le regaló una mantita de bebé que ella misma tejió. No sabíamos que esta sería la última Navidad que pasaríamos con ellos. Emma y Gustav anunciaron que les gustaría emigrar con su familia a Estados Unidos. Ya habían solicitado sus visas. Se siguió un procedimiento de un año para completar todos los documentos necesarios, someterse a exámenes médicos y verificar sus antecedentes para recibir el permiso de inmigración final. En agosto de 1951, partieron con sus familias desde Bremerhaven en barco a Nueva York. Luego continuaron en tren a York, Pensilvania, donde se instalaron a vivir.

Mamá y todos mis hermanos y yo sentimos pena al verlos partir. Me encariñé con Emma. Debido a la diferencia de edad de trece años, La consideraba como mi segunda madre. Ernst y Meta le dijeron a mi madre que también les gustaría emigrar a los Estados Unidos. Antes de solicitar sus visas, preguntaron si a mi mamá y al resto de la familia les gustaría ir con ellos. Mamá le dijo a Meta que quería quedarse en Alemania, con la esperanza de que nuestro padre regresara algún día. Sin embargo, mi madre recibió un aviso de que podía mudarse al sur de Alemania. El gobierno alemán trató de trasladar a los refugiados de las regiones más pobladas a las menos pobladas.

CAPÍTULO 11

MUDANZA Y VIDA
EN ESSINGEN

Mamá se dio cuenta de que no había futuro para sus hijos en una granja. Ella nos preguntó si nos gustaría mudarnos. Georg, Edmund y Richard dieron la bienvenida a un cambio. En cambio, yo hubiera preferido terminar la escuela secundaria en Schoenberg.

Los meses de invierno pasaron lentamente. En primavera, Meta anunció que esperaba otro bebé. El 26 de noviembre de 1951, una partera dio a luz a una niña. Meta y Ernst la llamaron Ilse y estaban felices de que Agnes tuviera una hermanita. Todo el tiempo, estuvieron trabajando para asegurar sus documentos de inmigración. En abril recibieron sus visas y el 10 de abril de 1952, Ernst, Meta y sus dos hijas volaron de Hamburgo a Nueva York. Continuaron en tren hasta Prairie du Chien y en autobús hasta una granja familiar en Froehlich, Iowa. Una vez que llegaron a su destino, Meta escribió que Ernst trabajaba en la finca por un pequeño salario de $90.00 qué? por mes más algo de comida para su familia. Fue un comienzo humilde. La barrera del idioma añadió dificultades para comunicarse con el agricultor, pero vivían solos en una pequeña casa y estaban contentos. Todos extrañamos a nuestras hermanas Emma y Meta y a nuestras sobrinas.

Mientras tanto, el alcalde de Pratjau hacía todos los trámites necesarios para la mudanza de nuestra familia. En junio de 1952, mi madre recibió un aviso de que podíamos mudarnos a Landau, Pfalz, en julio.

Le rogué a mi madre que esperara hasta que comenzaran las vacaciones de verano, así no perdería muchos días de clases y también podría obtener mi boleta de calificaciones de todo un semestre. Mamá estuvo de acuerdo. El siguiente fin de semana lo pasé con mis parientes lejanos en Neu Schoenberg. Le dije a Waldi y a su hermana menor, Greta, que esta era mi última visita porque mi familia se mudaba. Sentían pena de verme partir. Yo también me sentí triste. Siempre esperábamos pasar un fin de semana juntos y jugar diferentes juegos.

Cuando regresé a la escuela, esperé hasta una semana antes de que comenzaran las vacaciones para decirle al profesor Foerster que mi familia se mudaría al sur de Alemania a fines de julio.

"Hildegard, siento mucho que te vayas".

"Profesor Foerster, lamento mucho dejarlo a usted y a su escuela".

"Te daré mi dirección; me puedes escribir."

"Eso es tan amable de tu parte. Seguramente lo haré.""Me gusta saber a dónde irás y a qué escuela asistirás en la ciudad". Luego les dije a mis otros compañeros de clase la última semana de clases que mi familia y yo nos mudaríamos a Landau en la región del Palatino. Algunos estaban tristes, otros indiferentes a mi salida de la escuela. Inge, quien se sentó a mi lado y se convirtió en mi amiga, me dijo que ella y su familia también planeaban mudarse ese verano. Su padre alquiló una casa en el conocido balneario de Timmendorfer Strand en el Mar Báltico.

Inge me dijo que le gustaba nadar y que anhelaba la vida en la playa.

El último día de clases, el profesor Foerster llamó a cada estudiante por su nombre para que avanzaran y recibieran sus boletas de calificaciones. Cuando me dio mi boleta de calificaciones, las lágrimas brotaron de mis ojos y rodaron por mis mejillas. Solo pude pronunciar "Danke" (Gracias). Tomé mi boleta de calificaciones y me senté en mi escritorio para secarme las lágrimas, que seguían fluyendo. Después de que cada estudiante recibió sus boletas de calificaciones, el profesor Foerster le dijo a la clase que se sentía triste al ver que dos de sus estudiantes favoritas, Inge y Hildegard, salían de la escuela simultáneamente. Luego se acercó a Inge ya mí. Nos estrechó la mano y nos deseó lo mejor para el futuro.

Muchas más lágrimas brotaron al despedirme de Inge y de algunos otros queridos compañeros de clase. A regañadientes, tomé mi bicicleta y emprendí el camino a casa. Esta vez empujé mi bicicleta por la ciudad, solo para ver por última vez todos los escaparates de las tiendas y los hermosos jardines. También me detuve en la casa del profesor Foerster y miré las diversas rosas en flor. Una profunda gratitud llenó mi corazón por la maravillosa experiencia de aprendizaje en la escuela secundaria. El profesor Foerster me enseñó no solo francés, latín e inglés, sino también principios morales. Él y todos los demás maestros nos alentaron a ser y hacer siempre lo mejor posible en la vida, independientemente de las circunstancias. De camino a casa, monté mi bicicleta lentamente, y en determinados tramos, empujé mi bicicleta para disfrutar por última vez de las impresionantes vistas de jardines y campos que se habían vuelto tan familiares y queridos para mí. Esa tarde y noche, apenas hablé. Mi corazón se desbordó con la tristeza de haber dejado la escuela secundaria. Los días siguientes brotaron lágrimas al despedirme de muchos de mis compañeros de juegos y amigos de Sophienhof y Pratjau. Georg, Edmund y Richard tuvieron que notificar a sus empleadores que estaban consternados por perderlos. Mis tres hermanos trabajaron duro e hicieron bien su trabajo. Sin embargo, Georg dio la bienvenida a la mudanza. Anhelaba algo diferente a cuidar de los caballos y trabajar en los campos del rancho del Sr. Jessen.

A la semana siguiente, mi madre me recordó que revisara mi ropa, regalara la que le quedaba pequeña y lavara el resto. Deberíamos tener todo empacado para el domingo 20 de julio y estar listos para partir el lunes 21 de julio de 1952. Cada hermano y yo solo podíamos llevar una maleta llena de ropa, boletas de calificaciones, libros y artículos personales. Mamá puso la ropa de Horst y la suya propia en una maleta más grande. Mandó hacer una gran caja de madera para sus pocos enseres domésticos y los edredones de plumas. Insistió en que cada uno de nosotros debería tener su edredón y su almohada, que ella, Emma y Meta rellenaron con las plumas de ganso que criamos en nuestra casa en Prusia del Este. El lunes por la mañana, mamá también tomó la ropa de cama, los platos y los cubiertos y los envolvió en la caja grande entre los edredones de plumas. Después de que Edmund cerró la caja clavando las tablas sueltas al marco, escribió la dirección de nuestro destino en el baúl del campamento asignado en Queichheim-Landau/Pfalz.

A las 8:00 am, Rudi, nuestro vecino, llegó con el carruaje fuera de la puerta. Nos ayudó a cargar nuestras pertenencias en la parte trasera del carruaje. Georg cabalgaba con Rudi al frente mientras nuestra madre, Edmund, Richard, Horst y yo nos sentamos en los asientos traseros del carruaje. Por lo general, estaría emocionada de viajar en el prestigioso carruaje del Sr. Jessen, pero hoy mi corazón estaba lleno de tristeza, dejando atrás a mi escuela secundaria y mis amigos. Una fase terminó y comenzó una fase desconocida. Todos nos sentamos en silencio, cada uno absorto en sus propios pensamientos hasta que llegamos a la estación de tren en Schoenberg. Un empleado del alcalde de Pratjau había comprado nuestros pasajes de tren antes y nos los trajo. Rudi comprobó de qué vía saldría nuestro tren. Luego nos ayudó a llevar todas nuestras pertenencias a esa pista. Esperamos el tren para ir a Preetz, una pequeña ciudad situada entre Lanker y Post Lake. Llegamos a la estación de tren, ubicada en el centro de la ciudad, aproximadamente una hora después. Desde allí, continuamos a Hamburgo, Hannover, pasando por Frankfort, y luego a Landau. Ver las grandes ciudades y el paisaje del interior de Alemania con sus colinas, valles y muchos bosques pasando por las ventanas nos fascinaba. Llegamos a la estación de tren de Landau a altas horas de la noche. Allí nos esperaba un conductor de autobús y nos llevó a un Gast Staette (Posada) llamada Wirtschaft zum Lamm en Queichheim, un suburbio de Landau. Estábamos hambrientos y exhaustos por el largo viaje. El posadero preparó un sándwich para cada uno de nosotros, que comimos en el restaurante. Luego nos llevó a un gran salón, donde los colchones colocados en el piso servían para otras familias y para nosotros como dormitorios temporales. Con una linterna nos mostró dónde estaba el baño y qué seis colchones debíamos ocupar. No queríamos despertar a las otras personas. Pusimos nuestras maletas a nuestro lado, nos quitamos los zapatos, nos acostamos en nuestros colchones y nos quedamos dormidos rápidamente.

A la mañana siguiente, nos despertamos relativamente tarde. La mayoría de la gente ya se había ido al restaurante. Rápidamente nos lavamos la cara, nos cepillamos los dientes y nos unimos a los otros refugiados para desayunar. Nos sentamos junto a una familia con cuatro niños y una niña. También se habían escapado de Prusia Oriental y esperaban que se les asignara un nuevo lugar para establecerse. Nos presentamos y nos hicimos amigos de la familia Ehrlich. El señor Ehrlich tenía asma. Después de cada oración, respiraba con fuerza para tener suficiente aire para la siguiente oración. La señora Ehrlich era una dama delicada y refinada, y los cuatro niños, Wolfgang, Freddie, Juergen y Dieter, obedecían a sus padres y eran respetuosos con las demás personas y con nosotros. Me hice amigo de su hija Inge, que era unos años menor que yo. Cuando los niños exploraban el vecindario, caminábamos y hablábamos sobre nuestros pasatiempos y las escuelas a las que asistíamos.

Mi madre hablaba de su casa en Prusia Oriental, y también la Sra. Ehrlich. Los niños se enteraron de que había carruseles y otras atracciones en el pueblo. Una noche, los chicos decidieron ir a la ciudad de Landau. Ellos pidieron permiso a sus padres, y nosotros a nuestra madre, e Inge y yo fuimos. Georg, que tenía algo de dinero, nos invitó a dar un paseo en un carrusel. Inge y yo decidimos sentarnos en uno de los asientos redondos mientras los niños montaban los caballos.

Cuando todos estuvieron a bordo, la música comenzó a sonar y nuestros asientos comenzaron a girar más y más rápido. Sentí náuseas y mi pobre estómago quería vomitar su contenido. Puse una mano frente a mi boca y apenas podía esperar hasta que el carrusel se detuviera. Me tambaleé fuera de mi asiento y traté de encontrar un lugar discreto donde liberar el contenido de mi estómago. Luego volví con Inge y los chicos. Supongo que los carruseles y otras atracciones giratorias no me sentaron bien. Afortunadamente, me recuperé rápidamente. Después de la puesta del sol, cuando el cielo se oscureció, de repente escuchamos un gran estruendo y los fuegos artificiales iluminaron el cielo. Miramos con asombro todas las diferentes configuraciones y colores de la pantalla. Nos hipnotizó. Nunca habíamos visto tal espectáculo en el cielo. Después de que terminó, volvimos al campamento y les contamos a nuestros padres sobre los maravillosos fuegos artificiales que vimos.

Al día siguiente, vino un empleado de la ciudad y nos dijo que un autobús llegaría a las 2:00 p. m. y a llevarnos a Essingen y a la familia Ehrlich, a Edesheim. Empacamos todas nuestras pertenencias y poco antes de las 2:00 p. m. las sacamos a la calle donde se detenía el autobús. La familia Ehrlich hizo lo mismo. El conductor del autobús cargó nuestro equipaje en el autobús y nos llevó primero a Essingen, un pequeño pueblo a unas cinco millas al noreste de Landau, y luego continuó a Edesheim, a unas ocho millas y media al norte de Landau. Estábamos tristes por separarnos de la familia Ehrlich, pero prometimos que nos veríamos pronto. El señor y la sra. Ehrlich y los niños tomaron nota de la apariencia y la ubicación de la casa a la que nos mudamos, para que pudieran venir a visitarnos. Le dimos las gracias al conductor del autobús antes de que se marchara con la familia Ehrlich. Georg y Edmund subieron la caja grande al apartamento.

Luego regresaron y llevaron las otras maletas a la sala de estar. Los paneles de madera marrón de las paredes hacían que la habitación pareciera oscura, pero el apartamento estaba limpio y tenía dos dormitorios, una cocina y una amplia sala de estar. La gente del pueblo aportó el mobiliario imprescindible, una mesa con seis sillas en la cocina, un sofá, con dos mesillas y luz en el salón, y dos camas individuales con colchones en cada dormitorio. Un armario de madera independiente en cada dormitorio sirvió para colgar nuestro armario y guardar la ropa de cama. Estábamos agradecidos por la mejora significativa con respecto al estrecho apartamento de una habitación que compartíamos con Emma y Meta. Mi madre desempacó primero las sábanas y los edredones y los artículos del hogar, y luego mis hermanos desempacaron su ropa, zapatos y las pocas pertenencias personales que habían traído. Nuestra madre le dio dinero a Georg y le pidió que buscara una tienda de comestibles y comprara pan y salchichas.

Georg salió de la casa y le preguntó a la primera persona que encontró dónde estaba una tienda de comestibles. El hombre señaló la calle donde la tienda de Bender vendía comestibles, salchichas, productos agrícolas y otros alimentos. En unos días nos acomodamos.

Otras dos familias vivían en el mismo edificio, que se llamaba La Casa del Maestro. La señora Wistof y sus cuatro hijos, Edelmut, Freimut, Wismut y Hartmut, vivían en el lado izquierdo de la entrada, y el Sr. y la Sra. Buchert, su hijo pequeño Willie y una hija adolescente, Carla, ocupaban el apartamento del centro y nosotros el apartamento a la derecha de ellos. Tuvimos que ir a la oficina del alcalde para registrar a nuestra familia y nuestra dirección de residencia actual. Georg preguntó si alguien en el pueblo necesitaba ayuda. Como no tuvo la oportunidad de adquirir un oficio debido a la guerra, aceptaría cualquier trabajo. Horst, con solo diez años, necesitaba terminar la escuela primaria. Pregunté dónde estaba la escuela secundaria más cercana. La escuela equivalente, Neusprachliches Gymnasium (gimnasio para nuevos idiomas), estaba en Landau. Tomé el tren a Landau, luego pregunté por la dirección y encontré el edificio de la escuela. Yo pregunté cuándo y dónde podía inscribirme antes de que comenzaran las clases el lunes 11 de agosto de 1952.

Edmund encontró un lugar para continuar su formación en carpintería en Herxheim, un pueblo a diez millas al sur de Essingen. Richard buscó un herrero, donde pudiera terminar su aprendizaje y obtener su certificación de maestro.Un herrero en Ramstein contrató a Richard. Ramstein, también una base militar estadounidense, se encuentra aproximadamente a doce millas al oeste de Kaiserslautern. Georg encontró trabajo en el viñedo del Sr. Feldman en Essingen. Después de que terminaron las vacaciones de verano, Horst asistió a la escuela primaria local y yo fui al Neusprachliches Gymnasium en Landau. Mi madre se quedaba sola en casa todas las mañanas. Hizo las compras en el supermercado local y en la carnicería, preparó la comida para Horst y para mí, y se encargó de todas las tareas del hogar.

En el primer día de clases, Me puse mi mejor vestido de domingo, una falda negra con rayas rosas en el corpiño. Salí de casa relativamente temprano, caminé hasta la estación de tren en Knoerringen-Essingen y tomé el tren a Landau. La escuela estaba aproximadamente a quince minutos a pie de la estación de tren. Las clases comenzaron a las 8:00 am. Cuando vi el letrero del salón de clases de cuarto grado, entré. Lentamente, la habitación se llenó. Todos tenían un asiento designado; como era nueva, me puse de pie y esperé a que el profesor me asignara uno. Finalmente, el maestro entró al salón de clases. Todos los alumnos se pusieron de pie y saludaron al profesor quien les devolvió el saludo y les pidió que se sentaran. Permanecí de pie. El maestro se volvió hacia mí y me preguntó mi nombre y dónde vivía. Entonces el maestro se presentó como el Sr. Gritzan y me asignó para sentarme al lado de Barbara Bliemel en la segunda fila a su izquierda. Movió a la otra estudiante, sentada a su lado, al escritorio vacío en la parte de atrás. Recibimos un cronograma para la próxima semana con las materias y en qué aula se impartirían. Me tomó un poco de tiempo familiarizarme con los maestros y los estudiantes.

Un sacerdote instruía la doctrina católica a estudiantes católicos, y un pastor enseñaba la doctrina evangélica a estudiantes protestantes. Mis clases de francés me resultaron difíciles ya que tenía dos años de atraso. Los franceses ocuparon el estado de Palatine (Pfalz); era obligatorio comenzar el francés en el sexto grado de la escuela primaria.

Como procedía de una parte de Alemania ocupada por los británicos, estaba dos años adelantada en mi clase de inglés y dos años atrasada en francés. Dejé el latín para ponerme al día con mi francés. Luché y pasé mucho tiempo extra ampliando mi vocabulario en francés y aprendiendo nuevas reglas gramaticales. Con todas las demás materias, no tuve ningún problema, y me fue bien.

También conocí a las personas que iban todas las mañanas a la estación de tren Knoerringen-Essingen. Edelmut Wistof, que vivía en el mismo edificio, fue a la escuela de oficios, al igual que Herman Jaeger, que vivía en la casa en la plaza del pueblo cerca del final de la ciudad. Su hermana Heidrun asistió a una escuela de niñas en Landau. Entablamos vívidas conversaciones durante la caminata de quince minutos hasta la estación de tren y el viaje en tren de media hora hasta Landau. De camino a casa, caminé con algunos estudiantes que tomaron el mismo tren que yo. Viajar en tren a Landau y ver pasar las montañas Hardt a la derecha fue mucho más placentero y más cómodo que ir en bicicleta sola a la escuela por el camino rural lleno de baches a Schoenberg. Mi profesora de inglés, la señorita Kleiner, también vivía en Essingen. A veces nos encontrábamos en el tren.

Pronto conocí a la directora de la escuela, la Sra. Stelzemueller, y los profesores y sus asignaturas. Me caían bien todos los profesores, pero el Dr. Freitag, quien se unió al personal más tarde y enseñó alemán e historia, se convirtió en mi favorito. Era estricto y exigía mucho de los estudiantes pero presentó cada episodio histórico vívidamente y cautivó nuestra atención. Al final de cada clase nos contaba una anécdota o una cita de algún autor o filósofo famoso para darnos consejos prácticos para la vida. Se me quedó grabada una cita: "Una gota constante penetra incluso una roca" (Steter Tropfen huellt den Stein), equivalente al dicho, la persistencia vale la pena. Tuvimos que escribir un ensayo sobre este tema. También presentamos una reseña de un libro o una charla sobre una experiencia de la vida real frente a la clase. Elegí hablar de nuestra huida de Prusia del Este. Al principio, estaba nerviosa por levantarme para presentar mi triste y personal encuentro de la vida real frente a la clase. Las palabras fluyeron sin esfuerzo cuando vi como los compañeros escuchaban atentamente e incluso se limpiaban las lágrimas de los ojos. Recordando algunos episodios, Tuve que tragarme el nudo en la garganta y limpiarme las lágrimas de los ojos antes de terminar mi reseña. El maestro, así como mis compañeros de clase, se sintieron conmovidos por mi historia real, pero trágica. Siguió un breve silencio antes de que incluso el maestro pronunciara un agradecimiento y pudiera regresar a mi asiento.

Cuando llegamos a la historia de la Segunda Guerra Mundial, también nos contó lo injusto que los Aliados trataban al pueblo alemán. Wernher von Braun, quien desarrolló la ciencia espacial, se vio obligado a divulgar los nombres de los principales científicos. Los estadounidenses y los rusos tomaron las patentes de los cohetes, los principales científicos y otros importantes descubrimientos científicos en la exploración espacial de Alemania. El gobierno estadounidense seleccionó a Wernher von Braun además de muchos otros científicos, técnicos y equipos para trabajar para el gobierno estadounidense. El gobierno ruso hizo lo mismo. Dr. Freitag nos dijo varias veces: "El hombre aprende de la historia que el hombre no aprende nada de la historia".

Hacer gimnasia en el hermoso gimnasio con la señorita Letterle a veces era extenuante pero sobre todo divertido. Exigió que realizáramos todos los movimientos en el caballo, la barra o el piso correctamente.

La Señora Setlazek dio lecciones de música y nos enseñó a recordar todos los nombres de las notas musicales y sus sonidos y los diferentes signos. Cuando nos enseñaba una canción, primero la tocaba en el piano y luego repetía las palabras de la partitura y nos hacía cantar la melodía. Ella nos enseñó sobre los diferentes tipos de música, la estructura de las composiciones, como una sinfonía, rondó, ópera sonata, opereta y varias otras piezas musicales. También aprendimos muchas canciones populares de memoria. Landau ofreció actuaciones musicales en el teatro llamado Festhalle. Cuando escuché que la ópera Otello se representaría en el Festhalle, decidí comprar boletos y asistir a la función.[22] Sabía que mamá no me dejaría ir solo por la noche. Le pregunté a mi hermano Edmund si me acompañaría. Estuvo de acuerdo y obtuve dos boletos a bajo precio. Apenas podía esperar a que llegara el día de septiembre en que vería mi primera representación de ópera. Me puse mi mejor vestido y Edmund su mejor traje, y nos fuimos en su pequeña motocicleta a Landau. Tuve que aferrarme a mi ropa así como a mi hermano.

Cuando llegamos al Festhalle, Edmund puso su motocicleta en un área designada. Entramos al teatro, mostramos nuestras entradas al ujier, nos señaló el balcón superior por donde íbamos y nos sentamos. La emoción aumentó cuando se apagaron las luces y se abrió el telón. El trueno retumbó y los relámpagos salpicaron cuando Otello entró al escenario. Regresó victorioso del campo de batalla. Fue recibido por la gente así como por su bella esposa, Desdémona. Expresaron su amor en un dueto conmovedor y estaban felices de estar juntos. Las arias dramáticas y la música me conmovieron. Pero mi hermano se durmió. Gracias a Dios que no roncaba, me hubiera dado mucha vergüenza. En el siguiente acto, Yago, un soldado, trama un complot para hacer creer a Otello que su esposa le fue infiel a él y su amigo Cassio lo traicionó en el último acto, Otello acusó a Desdémona de serle infiel, la arrojó sobre la cama y mató a Desdémona. Después de que su amigo Cassio le dijera a Otello que no era cierto, Otello se suicida. Herido de muerte, se acerca a Desdémona, la besa y cae sin vida al suelo junto a Desdémona. Se me formó un nudo en la garganta mientras veía el final trágico de la ópera. El telón se cerró. Cuando los artistas llegaron frente al telón, los aplausos llenaron el teatro y Edmund se despertó.

"¿Dónde estamos?" dijo mientras se limpiaba el sueño de los ojos.

"Estamos en el teatro y la ópera acaba de terminar. Ven, vámonos a casa ahora."

Salimos del teatro, montamos nuestra moto y volvimos a casa. Pensé en la actuación dramática de camino a casa y recordé la escena del amor, la traición y el final trágico durante muchos días.

Al día siguiente en la escuela, la Sra. Gritzan impartió clases de religión para los estudiantes evangélicos y luteranos. Un sacerdote enseñaba a los estudiantes católicos. Estudiamos la reforma que comenzó cuando Martín Lutero, un monje católico, que luego se convirtió en profesor de teología, vio que la Iglesia Católica bajo el Papa León X se aprovechaba de sus seguidores.[23] Vendían la absolución de los pecados no solo para los vivos sino también para los los muertos. El profesor Martín Lutero escribió sus "95 tesis", expresando las prácticas corruptas de la Iglesia Católica. Clavó su carta en la iglesia del castillo de Wittenberg el 31 de octubre de 1517. El profesor Martín Lutero creía que, según la Biblia, el hombre se salva solo por la gracia y no por las buenas obras. El Papa León X leyó las llamadas "95 tesis" Declarando al Prof. Martín Lutero un hereje, y lo excomulgó el 3 de enero de 1521. El Papa León X le dio una oportunidad de renunciar a sus críticas y acusaciones a la iglesia católica en presencia del emperador Carlos V (Kaiser Karl V), duques y obispos en Worms el 17 de abril de 1521. Cuando el Prof. Martín Lutero se negó desafiante a retractarse de sus escritos y se adhirió a las enseñanzas de la Biblia, el emperador lo declaró hereje y fuera de la ley. El elector de Sajonia, Federico III el Sabio (Kurfuerst Friedrich III der Weise) le dio protección al Prof. Martín Lutero en su castillo de Wartburg. Se casó con Katharina von Bora y tuvo seis hijos. Durante su encierro, tradujo la Biblia, escrita en latín, al idioma alemán. Le tomó diez años de trabajo. Ahora todo el pueblo alemán podía leer la Palabra de Dios y no sólo los líderes religiosos privilegiados y educados. profesor Martín Lutero escribió varios libros y un catecismo, un libro condensado para enseñar a los jóvenes los Diez Mandamientos, el significado de los Santos Sacramentos, y la doctrina luterana fundamental. Teníamos que saberlo de memoria antes de ser confirmados. El profesor Martín Lutero murió de un derrame cerebral el 18 de febrero de 1546, a los sesenta y dos años, y la ciudad lo enterró en la Iglesia del Castillo de Wittenberg.

Dado que existían muchas denominaciones y religiones, a menudo me preguntaba cuál era la correcta. Durante una clase, le pregunté a la Sra. Gritzan, "Dado que cada denominación y religión enseña una doctrina diferente y afirma ser correcta, ¿puede decirme cuál es la correcta?"

"Así es, Hildegard", dijo, "la Biblia, que es la Palabra de Dios, contiene las respuestas a todas las necesidades humanas; si necesitas consuelo, en ella encontrarás consuelo. Si necesitas orientación, encontrarás orientación en ella. Si buscas la salvación, la encontrarás en ella. Desafortunadamente, algunos líderes religiosos de varias denominaciones tomaron parte del contenido de la Biblia y lo convirtieron en ley para que los miembros de su iglesia la obedecieran. Dios mira el corazón de cada individuo y no la forma exterior de adoración".

"Señora Gritzan, muchas gracias por tu explicación. Ahora entiendo cómo aplicar la Palabra de Dios en la vida diaria".

El esposo de la Sra. Gritzan enseñaba matemáticas y álgebra. Disfruté aprendiendo a resolver diferentes problemas matemáticos y familiarizándome con fórmulas de álgebra.

La señorita Kist nos introdujo en el arte de la caligrafía y la pintura con acuarela. Usábamos bolígrafos y tinta especiales para escribir palabras en la forma inglesa antigua. Ella no nos dio instrucciones definidas sobre cómo pintar un tema. Quería estimular nuestra imaginación y dejarnos usar nuestro diseño y combinación de colores. Mis dibujos se veían muy rudimentarios en comparación con los de otros estudiantes. Admiré las pinturas de Heidi Hartung y Hildegard Weigel. Sin embargo, con cada clase, las pinceladas fluían con menos esfuerzo y las combinaciones de colores mejoraban. al igual que la composición general de cada tema. Crear imágenes capturó mi interés, tanto que elegí pintar como mi pasatiempo más adelante en la vida. Cuanto más aprendía sobre las diversas formas de arte y los artistas, más apreciaba las pinturas de los grandes maestros.

La señorita Walker enseñaba física y química. Memorizar todas las abreviaturas de todos los elementos y combinar varios elementos para crear una nueva sustancia no me interesó al principio. Pero la señorita Walker supo captar nuestra atención, y me fue bien en ambas materias. La geografía me fascinó, principalmente cuando el Dr. Stumbaum disertó sobre África. Tuvimos que memorizar los diferentes estados, sus capitales, lo que cada estado producía industrialmente y en agricultura. Imágenes de elefantes, jirafas, leones y otros animales exóticos encendieron en mí el deseo de viajar y conocer el mundo. Cuando el Dr. Stumbaum también nos habló de la labor misionera del Médico Misionero alemán Albert Schweitzer en Lambarene en el África Ecuatorial

Francesa y de las exploraciones y la labor misionera de David Livingston desde Escocia, incluso alimenté la idea de ir como ayudante misionera en África. Me fascinó aprender sobre los diferentes climas, zonas horarias, topografía y vegetación de todos los continentes de la tierra. Me aseguré de hacer todos mis exámenes de geografía a satisfacción del Dr. Stumbaum. Me premió con la nota más alta en geografía.

La calificación más baja que recibí fue en francés. El señor Euler, nuestro profesor de francés, sabía que yo estaba dos años atrasada en francés. No importó cuánto lo intenté y pasé más tiempo leyendo y escribiendo en francés, no podía alcanzar a los estudiantes que estaban dos años por delante. En ese momento, tampoco pudimos obtener libros de los últimos años. Me esforcé por obtener una calificación aprobatoria, lo cual hice. El inglés, enseñado por la señorita Kleiner, era demasiado elemental ya que comencé a estudiar inglés ya en la escuela primaria, estaba muy por delante de mi clase. Se volvió bastante aburrido. Me agradaba la señorita Kleiner. Ella también vivía en Essingen, y la veía de vez en cuando en eventos especiales en el pueblo. Di gracias a Dios cada noche que la vida mejoró para todos nosotros después de mudarnos a Essingen.

A medida que me familiarizaba con los maestros y mis compañeros de clase, disfrutaba ir a la escuela. Conocimos a niños y niñas de otras escuelas mientras íbamos a la estación de tren, a aproximadamente 1 kilómetro del pueblo. Entablamos conversaciones significativas durante los viajes en tren y continuamos discutiendo eventos históricos y el futuro de Europa.

El año 1952 trajo muchos cambios en nuestras vidas. Georg disfrutó trabajando para el dueño de un viñedo, el Sr. Feldman, en Essingen. En primavera, cultivó los viñedos, ayudó con la cosecha en otoño y mantuvo limpias las enormes barricas de roble. También transfirió la vid fermentada de un barril a otro. Luego se deshizo de todo el sedimento del fondo de los barriles.

Controlaba con frecuencia el proceso de fermentación para asegurar la calidad de la vid.

Edmund avanzó con su formación en carpintería. Richard se volvió hábil y aprendió a fabricar objetos con hierro en bruto y otros metales. Horst, el hermano menor, tenía algunos años más para asistir a la escuela primaria antes de elegir una profesión u oficio.

Además de ir a la iglesia evangélica local en Essingen, teníamos un pastor, Armin Schlender, que visitaba a los refugiados luteranos de Europa del Este una o dos veces al año. No sólo predicaba sino que también enseñaba a los jóvenes antes de confirmarlos. El domingo 31 de agosto de 1952, el pastor Armin Schlender me confirmó solo a mí en la iglesia local. Por lo general, cada joven debía responder dos o tres preguntas aleatorias. Tuve que responder todas las preguntas que me hizo el pastor Schlender sobre la historia de la iglesia, citando versículos de la Biblia, recitando los Diez Mandamientos, y tantos más durante al menos de veinte minutos a media hora. Al principio, me sentí intimidada, sola frente a toda la congregación. Tenía miedo de dar una respuesta incorrecta a algunas preguntas. Después de proporcionar las respuestas adecuadas varias veces, gané confianza y respondí todas las preguntas correctamente. El pastor Schlender asintió y dijo: "Bien hecho, Hildegard". Me entregó mi certificado de confirmación con estas palabras del Salmo 37:5 "Encomienda todo lo que hagas al Señor. Confía en Él, y Él hará que suceda." Me estrechó la mano y me felicitó. Luego regresé y me senté con mi familia mientras el pastor Schlender se sentaba en la primera fila para el servicio regular de la iglesia realizado por el pastor Bruenings. Después del servicio, muchos feligreses me felicitaron. Nosotros fuimos a casa. Un amigo nos preparó el almuerzo. Pastor Schlender, algunos familiares y amigos cercanos se unieron a nosotros para celebrar el feliz evento de mi confirmación.

Otro evento que vale la pena mencionar fue la formación de un grupo de jóvenes para refugiados de Alemania Oriental llamado Deutsche Jugend des Ostens, DJO. Heinz Equart, el líder de un grupo de niños en Landau, me pidió que formara un grupo de niños en Essingen. El objetivo era mantener viva la historia, la cultura y la música de Alemania Oriental. Por supuesto, dije que no al principio, afirmando que no tenía experiencia organizando y dirigiendo un grupo de niños. Sin embargo, después de una larga conversación, el Sr. Equart me convenció de estar de acuerdo cuando se ofreció como voluntario para realizar las primeras reuniones y proporcionaría el material necesario para las reuniones. Empecé a reclutar niños de entre seis y doce años. Los niños locales también fueron bienvenidos. Después de que tres refugiados locales y nueve se unieran al grupo, obtuve permiso para usar una sala de construcción comunitaria. Le notifiqué al Sr. Equart. Vino un miércoles por la tarde para hacer la primera reunión, explicando el propósito de nuestras reuniones, que era aprender y mantener viva la historia de las regiones perdidas de Alemania y aprender sus canciones y bailes populares. En el medio, presentó algunos juegos que podríamos jugar para mantener a los jóvenes interesados en regresar.

El señor Equart trajo una flauta de madera, en la que tocaría la melodía de una canción. Luego decía una línea a la vez y nos hacía repetir las palabras varias veces antes de que pudiéramos cantar toda la canción. Nos reuníamos todos los miércoles a las 3:00 p. m. durante una hora o más después de llegar a casa de la escuela. Los niños disfrutaron aprendiendo nuevas canciones y juegos. En la tercera reunión, el Sr.

Equart trajo a Willie, que tocaba el acordeón de piano, para enseñarnos un baile folclórico. Como teníamos cinco niños y siete niñas, una niña tenía que hacer el papel de baile de un niño. El señor Equart caminaba con un bastón debido a una lesión que sufrió durante la Segunda Guerra Mundial, por lo que no pudo demostrar físicamente los movimientos del baile, pero les dio instrucciones precisas a los niños y niñas. Ellos observaron cada paso y trataron de recordarlos. Los niños aprendieron rápido y disfrutaron saltando y girando al ritmo de la música. Cerramos esa reunión, cantando la canción de Prusia del Este: "Tierra de bosques oscuros y lagos cristalinos". Sonaba mucho mejor, acompañado por la música de acordeón de Willie. Conocí mejor a los niños y, con el tiempo, cultivamos amistades duraderas.

En octubre, el Sr. Equart trajo una obra de teatro y sugirió que practicáramos y actuáramos para nuestros padres y los habitantes del pueblo en Navidad. La obra se llamaba "La muñeca perdida". El señor Equart explicó brevemente la historia: "Un niño perdió una muñeca y dos niños se dispusieron a buscarla". Me dio el guión y la tarea de elegir a la persona adecuada para cada papel, lo cual hice en la siguiente reunión. Decidí que la niña más pequeña de seis años, Gudrun, fuera nuestra muñeca. Mi hermano Horst y Peter serían los dos niños que buscarían la muñeca. Todos los demás niños interpretaron el papel de personas con las que se encontraron los dos niños mientras buscaban la muñeca perdida. Durante la primera sesión, le pedí a cada niño que leyera su parte. En la segunda sesión, les hice poner más sentimiento en cada palabra que decían, la próxima vez; esperaba que se supieran la mayoría de sus partes de memoria. Luego practicamos representando sus roles una y otra vez. Tomó tiempo, paciencia, persistencia y práctica repetida hasta que sonó y se vio satisfactorio. También jugamos juegos y cantamos canciones folklóricas después de cada ensayo para que los niños también se divirtieran. Llegó diciembre. Le pedí al Sr. Equart que viera nuestra obra y nos hiciera saber dónde podíamos mejorar la actuación. En general, le gustó la forma en que los niños interpretaron sus papeles. Solo de vez en cuando, se detuvo e hizo algunas correcciones. El domingo 14 de diciembre de los niños actuaron en el gimnasio del pueblo. Fuimos media hora antes para ponernos los disfraces de los niños y estar listos a las 5:00 p.m. El gimnasio comenzó a llenarse con los padres de los niños así como con muchos residentes del pueblo.

El ponente anunció el programa de inicio con varios cantos navideños seguidos del grupo infantil DJO presentando la obra de teatro "La muñeca perdida", bajo la dirección de la señorita Hildegard Bonacker. Las mariposas revoloteaban en mi estómago, pero no podía mostrarles a los niños que estaba nerviosa. Cuando terminó la canción "Oh Árbol de Navidad, Oh Árbol de Navidad", comenzó nuestra obra. Horst y Peter subieron al escenario tímidamente pero pronto ganaron confianza e interpretaron bien sus papeles, al igual que la muñeca encontrado y todo el elenco. Cuando escuché el aplauso entusiasta de la audiencia cuando todos nos reunimos en el escenario al final de la presentación, respiré aliviada. El orador agradeció a todos los niños por su excelente desempeño. Estaba orgullosa de mi grupo y también les agradecí.

La primavera siguiente, nuestro pueblo de Essingen tuvo una celebración especial y nuestro grupo representó la obra para la ocasión. Desafortunadamente, me enfermé de sarampión, y los niños tenían que actuar solos. El público disfrutó de la obra y yo estaba orgullosa de que los niños actuaran sin mi presencia.

Yo respetaba las opiniones de Heinz Equart y su amigo, Heinz Kraemer, a quien me presentó. Heinz Kraemer dirigía un grupo DJO de adultos de Landau. Se convirtieron en mis asesores para ayudarme a elegir una carrera. Ambos vivían en el camino de la escuela secundaria a la estación de tren.

Frecuentemente los visitaba, especialmente cuando tenía algún tema que tratar con ellos.

Cuando se acercaba el momento de graduarse de la escuela secundaria, Heinz Equart me preguntó: "¿Qué profesión quieres elegir?"

Le dije: "Estaba pensando en ser enfermera. Me gustaba la profesión médica".

"Serías casi como una prisionera trabajando en diferentes turnos en el hospital y estudiando al mismo tiempo. Amas demasiado la vida como para estar encerrada en el hospital.

¿Por qué no te conviertes en asistente médico, trabajas en el consultorio de un médico durante la semana y tener los fines de semana libres? Serás mucho más feliz que siendo enfermera".

"Creo que es una excelente idea, pero estoy segura de que la matrícula es costosa. Yo no tengo dinero, y mi madre tampoco".

"Dado que tu padre no regresó de la guerra, podrías solicitar asistencia financiera del gobierno. Buscaré en el periódico para encontrar una facultad de medicina".

"¿Dónde solicitaría fondos educativos?"

"Hay una oficina del gobierno aquí en Landau donde puedes pedir ayuda. Vuelve la próxima semana y te daré la dirección".

"Muchas gracias, Sr. Equart. Volveré pronto."

Le estreché la mano, me despedí de él y de su esposa y me fui a la estación de tren. Mientras estaba sentada en el tren, la idea de convertirme en asistente médico me atraía cada vez más. y comencé a pensar en cómo podría hacerlo posible. Necesitaría un nuevo guardarropa también. Los pocos vestidos y pares de zapatos que poseía no serían suficientes. Pero el pensamiento se arraigó en mi mente y reflexioné sobre cómo podría hacerlo realidad.

La semana siguiente fui de nuevo al departamento del señor Equart. La señora Equart siempre fue amable y me ofrecía un bocadillo si almorzaban cuando yo llegaba. Inmediatamente pregunté: "¿Obtuviste la dirección de la oficina financiera (Finanzamt)?" El señor Equart se levantó de la mesa, tomó una hoja de papel de su escritorio y me dijo mientras me la entregaba: "Aquí está el nombre y la dirección de la oficina del IRS", mientras me entregaba la hoja de papel.

"Todavía no encontré el nombre de la escuela de medicina, pero lo conseguiré para ti".

"Muchas gracias. No puedo quedarme mucho tiempo hoy; Tengo mucha tarea que hacer", y con estas palabras me despedí.

Le conté a mi madre sobre mis planes. Ella no se opuso, pero me dijo que no tenía medios para pagar mi educación superior. Mencioné que podría solicitar una posible ayuda del gobierno.

"Adelante, si puedes obtener ayuda del gobierno".

"Te agradezco, Madre, que apruebes mi plan".

Durante la próxima visita al Sr. Equart, me presentó el nombre y la dirección de una escuela de medicina en Essen. La escuela del Dr. Glaeser capacitaba a estudiantes en el campo de los negocios y la medicina para ser asistentes médicos. Estaba muy agradecida por la información. Inmediatamente le escribí a la escuela del Dr. Glaser, preguntando sobre los requisitos para asistir a su escuela de medicina. También tuve que averiguar cuánto sería la matrícula antes de solicitar fondos del gobierno. Sabiendo cuán lentas operan las agencias gubernamentales, tuve que pensar qué hacer durante el período de espera. Decidí buscar trabajo después de graduarme de la escuela secundaria. También me daría algo de dinero para comprar ropa nueva. Todos los días esperaba ansiosamente una carta de la escuela de medicina. Finalmente, llegó, indicando que la matrícula era de 350.00 marcos alemanes (aprox. $83.00 dólares estadounidenses) por mes. Al día siguiente, fui a la institución financiera, presenté la carta en la oficina y expliqué mis intenciones de asistir a la escuela de medicina. Pregunté si sería elegible para recibir alguna ayuda del gobierno. Me dijo que tendría que cumplir con requisitos específicos para recibir fondos del gobierno. Le pregunté qué documentos eran necesarios para presentar con la solicitud. Me dio un formulario para llenar. También me dijo que trajera un certificado de que mi padre todavía era un prisionero de guerra y que mi madre tenía que criar sola a ocho hijos. Le di las gracias al funcionario y le dije que regresaría en cuanto tuviera los documentos. Al día siguiente fui con alcalde de Essingen y obtuve la declaración requerida. Llené la solicitud y la llevé a la institución financiera. El funcionario me dijo que procesaría la solicitud y que regresara en un mes. Volví en un mes. El funcionario me preguntó si tenía un hermano mayor que trabajara. Le dije que sí. Entonces tráigame una carta de su jefe sobre cuánto gana por mes y regrese en un mes. Se prolongó una y otra vez, cada vez pidiendo diferentes papeles y posponiendo una respuesta definitiva y positiva.

Mientras tanto, me gradué de la escuela secundaria a fines de la primavera de 1954. No hubo celebración especial ni en la escuela ni en casa. El Dr. Freitag, nuestro profesor de Historia y Alemán, nos entregó a cada uno de nosotros nuestra boleta de calificaciones, que sirvió como diploma, y nos deseó lo mejor. Menos de la mitad de los compañeros continuaron durante otros tres años para terminar el Abitur, equivalente a un título universitario. Bárbara, que estaba sentada a mi lado, también se quedó. Estaba triste por dejar a todos mis compañeros de clase, sin saber si ir a la escuela de medicina se convertiría en una realidad. Le rogué a Dios que así fuera. Sabía que no podía quedarme en casa y esperar indefinidamente una respuesta del gobierno, así que busqué trabajo.

Primero, fui a una boutique de moda, donde vendían ropa elegante para damas. Presenté mi diploma de escuela secundaria y un breve currículum (Lebenslauf). Después de que la gerente revisó mis credenciales, me dijo que estaba buscando a alguien para comprar la ropa de la boutique. Como no tenía ninguna experiencia en el campo, me ofrecerían la oportunidad de aprender el oficio. Le dije al gerente que solo buscaba un puesto temporal mientras esperaba la ayuda del gobierno para asistir a la escuela de medicina. Agradecí su oferta, pero no sería justo capacitarme cuando no podría ocupar el puesto de forma permanente. Ella me agradeció por ser honesta. Antes de irme, a su vez, le di las gracias por ofrecerme un trabajo.

A continuación, solicité un trabajo en una fábrica de bombillas eléctricas ubicada en las afueras de Landau. Fui con el director de la planta y le pregunté si podía contratarme. Mencioné que acababa de salir de la escuela y que no tenía experiencia trabajando en una fábrica, pero que estaba dispuesta a aprender lo que fuera necesario para hacer el trabajo. Me envió con el Sr. Becker, el gerente del laboratorio, que necesitaba un trabajador adicional. Después de una breve entrevista, el Sr. Becker me contrató y se ofreció a capacitarme en el trabajo. Antes de irme, le pregunté al Sr. Becker cuando debo empezar.

"Puedes empezar el martes 1 de junio de 1954 a las 8:00 a. m.".

"Muchas gracias, Sr. Becker. Estaré aquí el martes."

Me fui con un apretón de manos y un corazón lleno de gratitud, y me fui feliz. De camino a la estación de tren, me detuve en el departamento del Sr. Equart para contarle las buenas noticias sobre ser contratada por la fábrica de bombillas. Mencioné que trabajaría allí temporalmente hasta que recibiera fondos del gobierno para inscribirme en la escuela de medicina.

"Entiendo que es bueno para ti trabajar mientras esperas. Por cierto, ¿podrías contactar a suficientes niños y niñas mayores para formar otro grupo de jóvenes en Essingen?"

"Déjame ver cuántos de mis amigos estarían dispuestos a unirse a nuestro grupo".

Después de que empecé a trabajar, tenía que viajar en tren. Durante el camino a la estación de tren, le pedí a Hermann Jaeger y a su hermana Heidrun que formaran un grupo DJO y que me sugirieran otros amigos. También solicité amigos de otros pueblos. En un período corto, teníamos trece adultos jóvenes comprometidos a establecer otro grupo. El Sr. Equart trabajó junto con el Sr. Kraemer, quien dirigió el grupo de adultos en Landau. El señor Kraemer llevó a cabo las primeras reuniones en el aula de la escuela de gramática local. Hermann obtuvo permiso del director para usar una habitación. El señor Kraemer hizo que las reuniones fueran agradables. Sin embargo, preguntó quién estaría dispuesto a celebrar futuras reuniones y establecer programas para el grupo. Hermann Jaeger se ofreció como voluntario. Era un joven inteligente con altos valores morales y formación musical, tocando el violín. Sus hermanas Heidrun y Helga, que tocaban el piano, también se unieron al grupo. También se unieron mi hermano Richard, dos amigos nuestros, Anneliese y Fritz Gutzler, dos hermanos Edelmuth y Freimuth Wistof, Barbara y Brigitte Maywald, Inge Hoffman y Fritz Hunzinger. Solo ocho jóvenes eran refugiados de Alemania Oriental; los otros eran residentes nativos de Essingen y pueblos de los alrededores.

Ambos grupos de jóvenes DJO

El señor Kraemer explicó el propósito de DJO (Deutsche Jugend des Ostens—Juventud Alemana del Este), los Grupos DJO formados en toda Alemania y un seminario en Bad Kissingen enseñó a los jóvenes cómo ser buenos líderes. Hermann asistió al taller. Se convirtió en nuestro destacado líder, quien nos dirigió no solo en el canto sino también en el baile folclórico. Hermann también compartió su conocimiento histórico de Alemania. Nos familiarizó con la belleza y los lugares de interés histórico de nuestro entorno. Una vez al año, grupos de todas partes de Alemania se reunían y competían en canto, baile folclórico y deportes. Nuestro grupo solía ganar el primer premio en canto. Después de que terminaron las competencias, los jóvenes se sentaron alrededor de una fogata por la noche y cantaron mientras observaban las estrellas iluminar el cielo oscuro y aterciopelado. En otras ocasiones, Hermann organizaba un viaje en tren a un castillo o sitio histórico; caminábamos durante varias horas a través de los hermosos bosques caducifolios, observando las flores que cubrían el suelo y escuchando cantar a los pájaros mientras cantábamos. Comenzamos a cantar desde el momento en que subimos al tren y cantamos hasta el momento en que llegamos a casa. Nos sabíamos muchas canciones de memoria. Cuando parábamos en un restaurante para almorzar, dedicábamos más tiempo y Hermann invitaba a los clientes a cantar con nosotros. Siempre disfrutaron la oportunidad de expresar su alegría a través de la música. Desarrollamos una camaradería significativa y respetuosa entre los niños y niñas, y el Sr. Kraemer también estaba satisfecho con nuestro grupo Essinger. Planeó ciertos eventos junto con su grupo de Landau. Para la víspera de Año Nuevo de 1954, nuestros dos grupos se unirían a otros en Boppard, una pintoresca ciudad ubicada en el río Rin, al sur de Koblenz. Hermann, el líder de nuestro grupo de jóvenes, varios otros miembros y yo nos reunimos con el grupo Landau, dirigido por el Sr. Kramer. Tomamos el tren a Boppard y nos registramos en un albergue juvenil ubicado en la cima de una colina con vista a Boppard y al río Rin. Después de que los grupos de otros pueblos se registraron el viernes 31 de diciembre de 1954 y cenaron, nos reunimos en el gran salón alrededor de la chimenea.

Primero, cantamos algunas canciones, luego la narradora, Ursula Winters, nos contó el cuento de hadas de "La gallina de los huevos de oro",[27] escrito por los hermanos Grimm.

Ursula Winters, la narradora, pidió voluntarios dispuestos a interpretar los papeles de los diferentes personajes de la historia. Después de tener suficientes personas, primero preguntó qué papel quería jugar cada uno y asignó el resto a los voluntarios. Luego mencionó que cada persona tendría que escribir y recitar su guión y confeccionar sus disfraces. La función de cuento de hadas tendría lugar al día siguiente frente a la chimenea a las 6:00 p. m. Los actores podían reunirse en la habitación detrás de la chimenea antes de que comenzara el espectáculo.

A continuación, alguien recitó un poema sobre la víspera de Año Nuevo. Luego cantamos canciones folklóricas hasta poco antes de la medianoche. El posadero del albergue juvenil proporcionó champán. Brevemente, antes de la medianoche, miramos el reloj. Cuando ambas manijas señalaron la medianoche, levantamos nuestras copas y gritamos "Prosit Neujahr" (Feliz Año Nuevo). Luego abrazamos a nuestros amigos más cercanos y les deseamos personalmente un Feliz Año Nuevo. Después de dejar el salón para retirarme por la noche, salí. Me paré en la colina, mirando la ciudad iluminada. Escuché las campanas de la iglesia sonar en el año 1955.

Mis pensamientos se dirigieron a mi familia. Entonces miré al cielo y agradecí a Dios que me había dado un año más. Oré pidiendo guía, protección y Su ayuda con mis planes para mi carrera. Unos cuantos copos de nieve empezaron a caer suavemente, como una lluvia de bendiciones, como si fueran mensajeros de Dios diciendo: "La paz os dejo. No dejes que tu corazón se turbe. No tengas miedo. Yo estoy contigo, siempre." Tal paz descendió sobre mí. Me quedé allí hipnotizada por la belleza escénica y por la solemnidad del momento divino. En silencio, regresé a la habitación y puse el Año Nuevo en las manos amorosas de Dios, oré por mi familia y me quedé dormida.

El día siguiente, las personas que se ofrecieron como voluntarias para actuar trataron de encontrar o confeccionar los disfraces adecuados para sus personajes y crearon y recitaron sus papeles. Sigrid, del grupo Landau, se ofreció como voluntaria para ser payasa. Me pidió que le prestara mi colorida pijama verde con flores rojas y blancas. Le quedaba holgadamente. Ató una cinta alrededor de cada muñeca y tobillo y alborotó las mangas y las piernas del pijama. Doblamos una bufanda, luego la colocamos alrededor de su cuello y atamos la cinta alrededor. Lo junté uniformemente en volantes. Ahora, Sigrid parecía un verdadero payaso. Su papel consistía en poner expresiones faciales graciosas y realizar algunas acrobacias para hacer reír a la princesa.

"¿Qué pasa con los zapatos grandes?"

"Tendremos que hacerlos con calcetines. Podemos preguntarle al Sr. Kramer si está dispuesto a prestarnos un par de sus calcetines."

Sigrid se quitó el disfraz y fue a preguntarle al Sr. Kramer si pudiera prestarle un par de calcetines. Él lo hizo. Rápidamente rellenamos cada calcetín con papel higiénico fino y atamos una cinta alrededor de la punta, formando una bolita. La segunda parte era más prominente, y la última era lo suficientemente larga como para parecer la punta larga de un zapato. Sigrid se los probó y se los amarró a los pies para no perderlos al caminar. Tuvimos que ajustar la firmeza del papel higiénico para que las puntas no se doblaran cuando caminaba. Sigrid estaba satisfecha con su apariencia. A continuación, quería recitar algunas de sus líneas en privado. Los niños y niñas se ocuparon todo el día, confeccionando disfraces apropiados para sus papeles y tranquilamente inventando las letras que encajaban con sus personajes. La emoción llenó el albergue juvenil y todos esperaban ansiosos el espectáculo.

Los actores, un padre anciano, una madre y tres hijos adultos se sentaron alrededor de la chimenea a las seis en punto. El padre se lamentó: "Nuestro suministro de leña es casi nulo. Tenemos que ir al bosque a cortar un poco de madera." Dirigiéndose al niño mayor, "Hijo, quiero que vayas al bosque y cortes leña".

La madre agregó: "Horneé un pastel para ti, para que no tengas que morirte de hambre mientras trabajas; También te daré una botella de vino." El hijo tomó su bolsa con la comida, el vino, vio y se fue al bosque. Los padres y los dos hijos bajaron del escenario. La siguiente escena cambió rápidamente. Dos niños llevaban una rama representando un árbol en el escenario y lo erigió entre troncos. El hijo comenzó a cortar el árbol con una sierra improvisada hecha con una ramita y una cuerda. Mientras hacía una pausa para comer, un viejecito se acercó y le preguntó: "Tengo hambre. ¿Puedes darme un poco de tu comida?"

"¡No, no lo haré!" respondió. Después de que terminó de comer, continuó cortando el árbol. La sierra resbaló. Se lastimó la pierna. Gritando, tiró la sierra y corrió a casa. El árbol desapareció del escenario, y los padres con los otros dos hijos aparecieron nuevamente. El hijo herido entró cojeando en la habitación, gimiendo. La madre corrió hacia él, lo abrazó, "Hijo mío, mi querido hijo, ¿qué te pasó?"

"La sierra resbaló y me cortó la pierna".

La madre inmediatamente lo puso en la silla, limpió la herida y envolvió una venda alrededor de la pierna.

"Solo descansa hasta que sane."

Luego se dirige al segundo hijo mayor: "Ve tú a cortar leña, se acerca el invierno y no tenemos suficiente leña".

"¡Sí, Madre, iré!".

Su madre también le proporcionó un delicioso pastel y un buen vino. El segundo hijo se despidió y salió a cortar leña. Los padres y el hijo herido abandonan la escena. Un niño puso rápidamente una rama en una pila de troncos. El segundo hijo pone la sierra contra el vástago. Un viejecito apareció mientras movía la sierra de un lado a otro, tratando de cortar el árbol.

"Joven, ¿tienes algo de comida que puedas compartir con un anciano hambriento como yo?"

"No quiero compartir mi comida contigo, miserable criatura; vete y no interrumpas mi trabajo", grita el niño y trata de empujarlo hacia un lado. En ese momento, la sierra resbaló y se cortó la pierna izquierda. Gritó y maldijo al viejo y cojeó hacia casa.

La escena cambia nuevamente a la casa de los padres. "Madre, madre, mira lo que me pasó, traté de ahuyentar a un mendigo y la sierra me golpeó la pierna".

"Mi pobre hijo, hasta tú tuviste mala suerte. Ven, déjame cuidar tu herida."

El padre se sentó junto a la chimenea. levantó la mano derecha con desesperación y golpeó la mesa con el puño. "¿Qué vamos a hacer ahora? Seguro que no podemos enviar a Simpleton. Él no sabe cómo hacer nada, ¿verdad?"

"Sí, es un dilema", dirigiéndose a su esposo, continuó: "Es posible que tengas que ir tú mismo".

En ese momento, Simpleton entró en la habitación. Cuando vio que sus dos hermanos estaban heridos, se ofreció a ir al bosque a cortar leña.

Al principio, la madre rechazó su oferta, "¿Qué te hace pensar que puedes hacerlo si tus hermanos no pudieron terminar la tarea?".

"Déjame ir, madre. Trataré de hacer lo mejor que pueda."

La madre todavía dudaba de su capacidad para lograr algo que valiera la pena.

Ella sólo le preparó un pastel horneado en cenizas y le dio una botella de cerveza agria.

"Aquí, hijo, toma esto y vete". Ni siquiera lo abrazó como lo hizo con sus dos hijos mayores preferidos.

La escena cambió. La rama, que representaba el árbol imaginario, apareció nuevamente en el escenario. Los troncos rodeaban la rama en la parte inferior. Simpleton silbó mientras aserraba el árbol. Después de que pasó un tiempo, el viejito pasó cojeando.

"¿Estoy hambriento? ¿Puedes prescindir de algo de tu comida?"

"Por supuesto, ven y siéntate, y comeremos juntos", responde Simpleton,

Simpleton se sentó junto al anciano, desenvolvió su pastel, lo partió por la mitad y le ofreció la mitad al anciano.

"Toma esto; No quiero que pases hambre."

"Gracias", dijo el anciano y le dio un mordisco al pastel simple.

"Aquí hay una bebida para ti también".

El hombre mayor tomó un gran trago de la botella que Simpleton le entregó. Terminó su pedazo de pastel, le dio las gracias a Simpleton y se fue, diciendo: "Sigue cortando; te traerá buena suerte."

Simpleton continuó cortando el árbol. Cuando el árbol cayó al suelo, vio un ganso dorado en el tronco. Lo recogió y comenzó a reflexionar sobre qué hacer a continuación.

"¿Qué tengo que hacer? No tengo ganas de ir a casa. Mi familia solo se reirá de mí. Creo que iré a la taberna cercana y tomaré una copa, una buena comida y pasaré la noche en la posada".

Simpleton salió del escenario, silbando una melodía alegre. Los muchachos quitaron el árbol y los troncos de madera y rápidamente armaron una escena de taberna que constaba de una mesa larga y dos bancos. Los niños se sentaron en ambos bancos levantando sus copas y cantando una canción de bebida. Tres jóvenes camareras, que eran las hijas del posadero, volvieron a llenar los vasos vacíos. Cuando Simpleton entró con la gallina de los huevos de oro bajo el brazo, las tres hermanas sintieron curiosidad. Se acercaron a él y le preguntaron.

"¿Qué tienes ahí?" apuntando a la gallina de los huevos de oro.

"Esa es mi gallina de los mágica de los huevos de oro".

"Un ganso todo hecho de oro puro", dijo la hermana menor. Luego pensó, si sólo pudiera tener una pluma, sería rica y ya no necesitaría trabajar en la taberna. Las dos hermanas mayores pensaron lo mismo.

Después de un rato, los clientes abandonaron la taberna. Las luces se atenuaron, y Simpleton se acostó en el banco y puso el ganso sobre la mesa. Simpleton roncaba, fingiendo dormir.

Primero, la hermana mayor se acerca de puntillas al ganso y trata de arrancarle una pluma. Cuando trató de quitar la mano, se le pegó a la gallina de los huevos de oro. Lo mismo les sucedió a las otras dos hermanas. Esperaron hasta que Simpleton se despertó y le rogaron.

"¡Suéltanos! ¡Suéltanos!"

"No tengo poder sobre la magia de la gallina de los huevos de oro. Lo siento, tendrán que venir conmigo."

Simpleton terminó de desayunar y salió de la taberna con la gallina de los huevos de oro. Las tres hermanas lo siguieron mientras el padre observaba con gran angustia la partida de sus tres hijas.

"Libera a mis hijas, ahora mismo", exigió, agitando el puño hacia Simpleton.

"Lo siento, no tengo poder; tendrán que venir conmigo", respondió mientras salía de la taberna.

Dos muchachos limpiaron los muebles de la taberna y transformaron el escenario en un camino que conducía a través de un campo a un pueblo.

Llegó un párroco. Cuando vio a las tres niñas siguiendo a un joven, gritó:

"Qué vergüenza, niñas traviesas; ¿Por qué corren detrás de un joven?

Caminó hacia ellos, tratando de alejar a las chicas, "Vamos, suéltense", ordenó. Pero en lugar de soltarlas, también se atascó y tuvo que seguir a donde quiera que fuera Simpleton.

Entonces llegó un custodio. Cuando vio que el párroco seguía a Simpleton y a las tres niñas, se asombró y gritó: "Señor párroco, ¿a dónde va? ¿No sabes que tenemos un bautizo hoy? Corrió tras el párroco y agarró su abrigo, tratando de separarlo. Desafortunadamente, él también se quedó atascado. La misma tragedia también les sucedió a dos trabajadores que querían liberar al párroco. Los siete que siguieron a Simpleton salieron del escenario, lamentándose y gritándole con enojo.

El escenario cambió rápidamente. Los dos chicos erigieron dos ventanas hechas de cartón, pusieron una torreta a cada lado, asemejándose a un castillo. Un rey y su hija se sentaron detrás de la ventana. La hija estaba tan seria y nunca sonreía. El rey anunció:

"Quien pueda hacer reír a mi hija, la tendrá por esposa".

Primero fue el payaso, que hizo todo tipo de muecas y acrobacias, pero la princesa no sonrió. Muchos otros pretendientes se esforzaron pero también sin éxito.

A lo largo llegó Simpleton con su séquito. Cuando la princesa los vio, comenzó a reír tan fuerte que no pudo parar.

Simpleton, que conocía la promesa del rey, fue a pedirle al rey la mano de su hija en matrimonio. El rey estaba enojado de que un simple leñador se casara con su hija. Esperaba a un noble como yerno y no a un leñador común.

El rey trató de desanimar a Simpleton al hacer tres demandas desafiantes que pensó que no podría cumplir.

Cuando cumplió con las tres demandas, el rey no pudo negarle a su hija como esposa. El rey y su hija salieron del castillo al escenario, y el rey colocó la mano de su hija en la mano de Simpleton. La belleza de la princesa hipnotizó a Simpleton. Todavía no podía creer que ella iba a ser su esposa.

El rey salió del escenario, seguido por la princesa sosteniendo la mano de Simpleton, y toda la gente caminó detrás de ellos. El público aplaudió. Los actores subieron al escenario e hicieron una reverencia. El público de jóvenes aplaudió de nuevo. Entonces Ursula Winters, la narradora, subió al escenario.

"Gracias a todos; interpretaron bien tus papeles. El vestuario, dadas las circunstancias, fue creativo. Espero que hayan aprendido la lección del cuento de hadas; Dios recompensa las buenas acciones y castiga las malas acciones." Después de la obra, los participantes se cambiaron y regresaron a la sala principal de reuniones; cantamos algunas canciones folklóricas más antes de retirarnos por la noche. A la mañana siguiente, un grupo de niños se reunió debajo de mi ventana y cantaron la canción de Prusia Oriental, "Aennchen von Tharau". Miré por la ventana y vi a Herman dirigiendo a los niños dándome una serenata por mi cumpleaños. Su consideración me conmovió; después de cantar la canción de cumpleaños alemana, "Hail to the birthday child", Hermann me felicitó personalmente por mi decimoctavo cumpleaños. Cuando bajé a desayunar, alguien había puesto un arco de flores alrededor de mi plato. Heinz Kraemer, el líder del grupo Landau, y Hermann, el líder de nuestro grupo, se sentaron a mi lado. Cada vez que Hermann me miraba, sus ojos expresaban afecto por mí. Cada vez que nuestros ojos se encontraban, se desbordaban de aprecio el uno por el otro. En lugar de decir una oración, cantamos una canción para expresar nuestra gratitud a Dios por sus bendiciones y la comida. Antes de que empezáramos a comer, Heinz Kraemer se levantó y me felicitó, y todo el grupo volvió a cantar la canción de cumpleaños. Ser honrada de una manera tan increíble por mi cumpleaños número 18 me conmovió profundamente. Sentí que había alcanzado un hito de independencia. Pensé que podía tomar más de mis propias decisiones ahora como adulto. Después del desayuno, nuestro grupo y el de Landau salieron del albergue juvenil en autobús y se dirigieron a la estación de tren para tomar el tren a casa. Todos estábamos absortos en nuestros pensamientos sobre la forma maravillosa en que recibimos el año 1955. Reviví cada momento de la forma extraordinaria en que celebré mi cumpleaños número 18.

Me tomó algunos días volver a la rutina diaria: ----- trabajar cinco días a la semana, dirigir el grupo de mis niños todos los miércoles y reunirme con el grupo mayor una vez a la semana los jueves. Nos sentimos recompensados por aprender nuevas canciones o bailes folclóricos bajo la dirección de Hermann y disfruté de conversaciones estimulantes sobre diversas formas de arte, literatura y la historia de nuestro propio país y de otros países.

En febrero, el primer domingo, Hermann pasó por la casa y me pidió que fuera a deslizarme en trineos con él. Con el permiso de mi madre, acepté unirme a él. Tiramos del trineo detrás de nosotros a través de los campos sobre la nieve recién caída, transformando el paisaje en un paraíso invernal mágico y blanco. En las afueras del pueblo, nos acercamos a una pequeña colina. Juntos tiramos del trineo cuesta arriba. Entonces Hermann me dejó sentarme al frente. Empujó el trineo para ponerlo en movimiento, saltó sobre el trineo y se sentó detrás de mí. Me aferré a la parte delantera del trineo con ambas manos. Hermann se agarraba al trineo con una mano y me sostenía con el otro brazo. Corrimos cuesta abajo, gritando de alegría. A veces, Hermann se acostaba en el trineo y se deslizaba cuesta abajo solo. Yo hice lo mismo, y juntos recorrimos felizmente un tobogán hasta el anochecer.

Mientras tanto, la noche entró de puntillas en el pueblo y envolvió las casas en un manto oscuro. La luna llena se elevó y esparció una suave luz sobre todo el paisaje. Dejamos de andar en trineo y empezamos a ir a casa. La magia y la paz del momento trascendieron nuestros pensamientos. Hermann comenzó a

cantar, "La rosa de la luna" (Der Mond ist aufgegangen). Me
uní a él suavemente. Cantamos juntos hasta llegar al pueblo,
tirando del trineo detrás de nosotros. Cuando llegamos a nuestra
casa, le estreché la mano y le dije: "Gracias, Hermann; buenas
noches." Me acercó a él, me abrazó y dijo: "Hilde, te quiero
mucho. Me gustaría que fueras mi esposa." Luego me besó en
los labios. Ese beso descansó solo un momento en mis labios
pero sería un recuerdo para toda la vida.

Yo estaba perpleja y no podía decir una palabra. Quería
a Hermann como a un amigo, pero aún no había pensado en
convertirme en su esposa. me liberé; sin pronunciar una palabra.

Rápidamente corrí hacia la casa, cerré la puerta y lo dejé
sin palabras al aire libre. Estoy segura de que no esperaba que
yo respondiera a su pedida de manera tan negativa. Me tomó
mucho tiempo conciliar el sueño. Los pensamientos dieron
vueltas en mi cabeza. En un momento me sentí feliz de que
pensara tan bien en mí que quisiera casarse conmigo. Al minuto
siguiente pensé que era demasiado joven para estar atada y me
sentí terrible por decepcionar a Hermann. Primero, quería
obtener una profesión, trabajar por un tiempo y luego pensar en
casarme. Al día siguiente tomamos el tren a Landau; Hermann
parecía aplastado. Sentí ganas de consolarlo y explicarle por qué
actué de la forma en que lo hice. Ninguno de nosotros dijo una
palabra porque muchas otras personas también caminaron hacia
el tren. Hermann tardó algún tiempo en superar mi reacción
adversa a su propuesta de matrimonio.

INSCRIPCIÓN EN LA ESCUELA DE MEDICINA

En el presente, tenía que enfrentar la realidad y continuar solicitando ayuda financiera del gobierno. Había aplicado hace varios meses sin obtener una respuesta positiva. Cada vez que iba a la Oficina de Rentas Internas (Finanzamt), la secretaria me pedía otro documento en lugar de darme una respuesta positiva. ¡Se volvió frustrante! Sentí que el secretario prolongó el procesamiento de mi solicitud, esperando que me desanimara, me diera por vencida y me olvidara de mi solicitud de ayuda educativa. Estaba decidida a poner micrófonos ocultos en la oficina hasta que el gobierno me otorgara la asistencia que tenía derecho a recibir. Pasó enero y febrero. Hice varios viajes más a la Oficina de Rentas Internas sin un compromiso de su parte para ayudarme siquiera con la matrícula de la facultad de medicina. El 1 de abril de 1955 fue la fecha límite para inscribirse en La Escuela Vocacional del Dr. Glaeser para asistentes médicos prácticos-comerciales en Essen. El 1 de marzo todavía trabajaba en la fábrica de bombillas. ¿Qué tengo que hacer? ¿Debería dejar de ir a la escuela de medicina este año por completo? La idea de seguir trabajando un año más en la fábrica no me atraía. Oré para que Dios me ayudara a tomar la decisión correcta. Me pareció claro que debía inscribirme independientemente del compromiso del gobierno de otorgarme asistencia financiera. Pensé que había ahorrado suficiente dinero para los primeros meses de matrícula y alojamiento y comida.

El lunes 7 de marzo fui con el director de la fábrica. Le dije que me gustaría inscribirme en una facultad de medicina antes del 1 de abril y que tendría que dejarla antes del 21 de marzo.

"Lamento que te vayas. Has sido una buena empleada. Entiendo que con tus calificaciones quieres adquirir una profesión diferente. Te deseo lo mejor."

Le agradecí al Sr. Becker por la oportunidad de trabajar para él y la capacitación en el trabajo.

Durante las próximas dos semanas, fui dos veces a la Oficina de Rentas Internos, con la esperanza de recibir un compromiso positivo. Cada vez salí de la oficina decepcionada. Independientemente de no recibir ayuda económica del gobierno, decidí inscribirme en La Escuela de Medicina Vocacional del Dr. Glaeser.

En mi último día de trabajo, fui nuevamente con el jefe para despedirme y obtener una carta de referencia. Me complació el contenido de la carta cuando leí la descripción de mi buena conducta y calidad de trabajo. Separarme de mis compañeros de trabajo, con quienes había desarrollado una relación cortés y de confianza, fue difícil para ellos y para mí. Fue demasiado doloroso para mí despedirme de los niños y niñas de mi grupo juvenil. En la última reunión del grupo de jóvenes adultos, me sentí triste al despedirme de los niños y niñas. Nos habíamos tomado cariño y habíamos desarrollado una extraordinaria camaradería entre nosotros. Principalmente sentí el dolor emocional al separarme de Hermann. Echaría de menos nuestra especial amistad y nuestras vívidas conversaciones.

Ahora tenía que concentrarme en ir a Essen para inscribirme en la Escuela Profesional de Asistentes Médicos Comerciales-Prácticos. El Dr. Ernst Glaeser era el director de la escuela. El miércoles 30 de marzo me despedí de mamá y de Emma. Mamá y Emma me tuvieron mucho tiempo en sus brazos y lloraron. Yo también. Tomé el primer tren de Essingen a Landau, donde compré un pasaje a Essen. Cambié de tren en varias ciudades. Afortunadamente, llegué a tiempo para encontrar la oficina de la escuela de medicina todavía abierta. Llamé a la puerta, una señora, que supuse que era la secretaria, me invitó a pasar. Me presenté. Entonces le dije que me gustaría inscribirme en La Escuela de Medicina del Dr. Glaeser.

"Tendrás que hablar con el Dr. Glaeser; él le hará saber si es posible agregar otro estudiante tan tarde.

La secretaria me presentó al Dr. Glaeser, "Fraeulein Bonacker quisiera saber si todavía podemos aceptar a otro estudiante para este semestre".

"Buenas tardes Dr. Glaeser; Lamento no haber presentado la solicitud formalmente antes, esperé y esperé la asistencia del gobierno, que no aprobaron. Pero tengo suficiente dinero ahorrado para la matrícula de los primeros meses. ¿Todavía podrías aceptar a un estudiante más?"

"Déjame ver la lista de cuántos estudiantes ya están inscritos. Veo a un estudiante cancelado en el último minuto. Supongo que puedes tomar su lugar."

"Gracias, Dr. Glaeser¡, eso es maravilloso!"

"Tal vez puedas quedarte con la dirección Mohrmann, quien se ofreció a dar alojamiento y comida a cuatro estudiantes. Debido a la última cancelación, solo ha tomado tres hasta ahora".

El Dr. Glaeser me entregó un papel con la Sra. La dirección de Mohrmann,

"Aquí está su dirección. Toma el tren a Essen- Rellinghausen, y desde allí puede caminar; no está demasiado lejos de su casa. Si ella no quiere tomar un estudiante más, regresa y encontraremos otro lugar para ti".

El Dr. Glaeser me entregó varias hojas con el programa de la escuela, dónde darían las clases los profesores y qué materia enseñarían.

"Familiarízate con los nombres de los maestros y las ubicaciones de las clases. Debes estar aquí en el salón de clases de al lado el viernes 1 de abril para conocer a todos los estudiantes y obtener la lista de las clases para la próxima semana".

Tomé la hoja de papel, me levanté, le estreché la mano, "Dr. Glaeser, gracias, muchas gracias. Estaré en clase el viernes."

Hice una reverencia y salí de la oficina. Sólo Dios, a quien agradecí de inmediato, y yo sabremos cuán agradecida y contenta estuve en ese momento de ser aceptada en la facultad de medicina. Recogí mi maleta, salí de la oficina y comencé a balancearla de un lado a otro con alegría. Seguí las instrucciones y encontré Hauptstr. 79, en Rellinghausen, un suburbio de Essen. Busqué a la entrada del complejo de apartamentos el nombre de la señora Mohrmann. Subí al segundo piso y llamé a la puerta. Una señora de mediana edad abrió la puerta y preguntó:

"¿En qué puedo ayudarla?"

"Soy Hildegard Bonacker. Acabo de inscribirme en La Escuela de Medicina del Dr. Glaeser. El Dr. Glaeser me dijo que aún podrías tener espacio para un estudiante más."

"Sí, aún tengo espacio."

"¿Considerarías acomodarme?" Dejó que sus ojos se deslizaran sobre mí de pies a cabeza y luego dijo:

"Supongo que puedo. Pero se supone que tú y los otros tres estudiantes vendrán mañana."

Le expliqué a la Sra. Mohrmann mis circunstancias y le pregunté si podía quedarme en su casa ya hoy. Ella fue comprensiva y me dejó entrar. Primero, me presentó a su anciana madre. Luego me mostró el dormitorio donde dormiría.

"Pero tendrás que compartir una cama con otra estudiante".

La cama parecía bastante espaciosa y tenía dos cobertores de plumas.

"No me importa en absoluto; gracias." Ella me mostró el resto de su apartamento.

"Puedes desempacar tus cosas ahora y unirte a nosotros en una hora para cenar".

"Gracias, es muy amable de su parte; Lo haré."

Miré mi reloj de pulsera; indicaba las 6:00 p.m. No había comido en todo el día. estaba muerta de hambre.

A las 7:00 p.m. entré al comedor donde me esperaban la señora Mohrmann y su madre en una mesa repleta de pan, queso y fiambres variados. Qué fiesta para los ojos de una persona hambrienta como yo. Esperé para sentarme y obtener permiso para comenzar a servirme. Cogí una rebanada de pan, le unté mantequilla, le puse varios trozos de salami encima y saboreé cada bocado. Luego comí otra loncha de jamón y queso. Podría haber comido tres sándwiches más, pero no quería parecer descortés y crear una impresión equivocada, así que dije no, gracias cuando la Sra. Mohrmann me pidió que me sirviera de nuevo. Cuando la Sra. Mohrmann y su madre terminaron sus sándwiches, me hicieron muchas preguntas sobre mis antecedentes. Después de que se levantaron, me ofrecí a ayudar a limpiar la mesa y lavar los platos. Terminé los platos, luego me excusé y fui al dormitorio. Mi corazón se desbordó de aprecio por haber sido aceptada en la escuela de medicina y haber encontrado un lugar tan agradable para quedarme. Me arrodillé y oré, expresando mi gratitud por la ayuda de Dios y le pedí que me guiara en el futuro. Todas mis preocupaciones se desvanecieron y la alegría pura llenó mi corazón. Dormí bien. Al día siguiente, después del desayuno, salí a caminar para familiarizarme con el vecindario circundante. Encontrar un bosque cercano me encantó. Disfruté paseando por el bosque y escuchando el canto de los pájaros. Ese día, mi corazón cantó un canto alegre con los pájaros pero sin palabras. Cerca encontré una iglesia a la que planeaba asistir los domingos.

El jueves 31 de marzo llegaron Gertrud, Gerda y Friedel. Después de que la Sra. Mohrmann nos presentó, las asignó a los dormitorios. Gertrud y Gerda compartirían una habitación con dos camas, y Friedel y yo seríamos compañeras de habitación y dormiríamos en la misma cama. No me importó en absoluto. Cuatro señoritas viviendo juntas debería ser fascinante.

Durante la primera cena, comimos juntas; compartimos nuestros antecedentes y nuestras historias familiares. Las tres eran las únicas hijas de sus familias. Solo yo venía de una familia de ocho hijos. Gerda era adoptada. Al día siguiente, todas salimos temprano y tomamos un tren hacia el centro de la ciudad de Essen, donde estaba la escuela. La habitación contigua a la oficina se llenó rápidamente. Cuando el Dr. Glaeser entró, todos nos levantamos. Después de saludarnos, pidió a cada estudiante que, al ser llamado por su nombre, se levantara, se presentara, y dijera brevemente de dónde venía y sobre sus antecedentes familiares. Luego nos dio un horario con los nombres de los maestros y las materias que enseñarían durante la próxima semana. El Dr. Glaeser nos despidió antes del mediodía y aun así regresamos a casa de la Sra. Mohrmann a tiempo para el almuerzo.

El sábado, después del desayuno, Friedel, mi compañera de cuarto y yo salimos a caminar por el bosque. Ese día, la gente no trabajó, y más personas caminaron por el bosque de lo habitual. Sin embargo, disfrutamos viendo las frescas hojas verdes de los árboles y las flores de primavera que cubrían el suelo. Hablamos un poco. Ella también disfrutaba mucho de la naturaleza. Me alegré de que tuviéramos algo en común. Cuando me dijo que no permite que nadie conozca su ser interior, me quedé perpleja y me pregunté: "¿Por qué?". Luego me advirtió que ni siquiera intentara explorar sus pensamientos. En cambio, Le dije que no tenía secretos; Pienso y actúo igual, y todos pueden ver quién soy. Supongo que intentó evitar que le hiciera preguntas personales en el futuro. Pensé, siempre que alguien quiere ocultar información, algo no debe estar del todo bien, pero lo que ella decidiera estaba bien por mí.

El domingo siguiente, les pregunté a las tres niñas si querían ir a la iglesia cercana. Cada una encontró una excusa; querían escribir a sus padres. Pensé que debería escribir a casa también. Prefería ir a la iglesia por la mañana y esperar hasta la tarde para escribir. El pastor predicó el sermón sobre el hijo pródigo. Un hijo se fue de casa y derrochó su riqueza en los placeres del mundo. Desilusionado y desvalido, regresó a la casa de su padre para pedir perdón y ser el sirviente de su padre. El padre no sólo perdonó a su hijo, sino que lo vistió con ropa fina, le preparó un banquete y restableció los lazos familiares. El hijo mayor se sintió estafado y celoso. Se había quedado fielmente en casa y había hecho la voluntad de su padre, y nunca recibió tal honor. Dios se regocija cuando un pecador, que estaba perdido, encuentra el camino para volver a Dios. Luego agregó el pastor, el celoso sólo se hace daño a sí mismo. Pero cuando los celos se convierten en admiración y amor, ambas personas se sienten recompensadas con alegría.

Esa fue una buena lección para recordar. Cuando conozco a alguien, pienso que es más inteligente y hermosa que yo; No debo estar celosa sino expresar mi admiración.

Abril y mayo exigieron mucha disciplina y concentración para recordar todos los nombres de los profesores y las materias que impartían. Rápidamente elegí a mi maestro favorito, la Dr. Dreisine, una doctora que enseñaba ginecología. Me gustó la forma en que el Dr. Reiche presentó Cirugía Menor. Dr. von Grabe impartió clases de Medicina General y Patología de una manera ilustrativa que exigió el 100 por ciento de atención. Los médicos no solo enseñaban en la escuela sino que también tenían prácticas privadas. A menudo traían ejemplos de sus interacciones con sus pacientes para mostrarnos cómo aplicar nuestra teoría en la práctica con los pacientes.

La materia que menos me gustó fue mecanografía impartida por la Sra. Weber. Durante los exámenes, me perdía palabras cuando intentaba escribir rápido o escribía mal las palabras. Destaqué en la clase de estenografía del señor Puersten y lo hice satisfactoriamente en alemán, instruido por el Sr. Dietrich. No me importaba mucho la correspondencia comercial, ni la instructora Sra. Schmitz Hartmann.

Todavía había escasez de edificios, y el Dr. Glaeser no tenía una escuela propia; los profesores impartieron clases en diferentes lugares para cada materia. A veces las cuatro asistíamos a los mismos cursos, a veces a cursos separados. Varias clases duraban medio día, otras todo el día. A veces no fue fácil para la Sra. Mohrmann para preparar el almuerzo para nosotras. Tuvimos que darle el horario de cada día para preparar sándwiches para llevar cuando los necesitara. Todas cenamos juntas. Disfrutamos de nuestro café y pastel (Kaffeeklatsch) por la tarde los fines de semana e intercambiamos experiencias memorables de la semana.

También escribí una carta a la Oficina de Impuestos Internos (Finanzamt). Les informé que me había inscrito en la Escuela Vocacional de Asistentes Médicos Prácticos Comerciales y que enviaran los fondos asignados, cuando se otorgaran, a mi dirección en la casa de la Sra. de Mohrmann. A principios de junio todavía no había recibido una respuesta positiva. Las cartas que escribía cada mes seguían sin respuesta. Mis finanzas disminuyeron lentamente. Estaba muy preocupada por pagar el resto de la matrícula, el transporte y el alojamiento y la comida si no recibía ninguna ayuda. Desesperada, le escribí a mi hermano Edmund y le pedí dinero. También mantuve correspondencia con Hermann y le expliqué que apreciaba su afecto por mí. Aún, por el momento, quería concentrarme en obtener mi profesión y tal vez trabajar durante algunos años antes de pensar en casarme. Tal vez sería mejor para los dos olvidarnos y no comunicarnos más. esperé ansiosamente por su respuesta a mi carta. Esperé en vano todos los días un mensaje de Hermann y de mi hermano Edmund.

Intenté aún más concentrarme en mis estudios y no pensar en mi grave situación financiera. Friedel, Gerda, Gertrude y yo a menudo llevábamos nuestros cuadernos cuando dábamos un paseo por el bosque. Cada una buscaba un lugar tranquilo para estudiar. En un momento específico, nos reuniríamos en un área designada, haríamos preguntas sobre el tema que se enseña en la escuela para estar preparadas para repasar en clase al día siguiente. No siempre podíamos estudiar sin ser molestadas. A veces entablamos conversaciones con personas que conocimos en el camino.

A veces, nos uníamos a un grupo de jóvenes de estudio de la Biblia el miércoles. Cada semana el Sr. Pfeiffer nos enseñaba capítulos de la Biblia y la historia de varias arquitecturas de iglesias. Conocimos a los asistentes del grupo. Peter, Karl-Heinz y Ferdi vivían en el vecindario y Werner vivían en el mismo edificio de apartamentos en el piso inferior. Siempre nos trataron con respeto y cortesía. Salíamos a caminar por el bosque o asistíamos juntos a eventos locales especiales. Durante nuestros paseos, Peter mostró una personalidad diferente cada vez. Uno nunca sabía cuál era actuación o cuál era la realidad. También tenía sentido del humor y nos hacía reír. En junio, después de que el agua del lago Baldeney se calentara, las cuatro niñas íbamos a nadar los fines de semana. Aunque no era una buena nadadora, disfrutaba jugando en el agua fría y refrescante.

A finales de junio, el calor y la humedad me incomodaban. Algunos días iba sola a clases. No me importaba estar sola con mis pensamientos. Un día, cuando me bajé del tren en Stadtwald, No podía creer lo que veía. Vi a Hermann parado en la estación de tren. Miré, una y otra vez, para ver si era él. Nunca esperé encontrarlo aquí. Cuando me vio, me saludó con una sonrisa. Probablemente estaba tan sorprendido de encontrarme en la estación de tren como yo. Yo había esperado o una carta, y ahora estaba aquí en persona. ¡Increíble! Me dijo que solo tenía unos minutos antes de que saliera su tren. Intercambiamos algunas palabras sobre nuestro bienestar. Con un abrazo rápido y despidiéndose, me prometió verme el martes siguiente. Subió al tren, que se puso en marcha. Él se había ido. Por un momento, me quedé perpleja y estupefacta junto a las vías del tren antes de regresar al apartamento, absorta en mis pensamientos. Después de la cena, no podía concentrarme en hacer ninguna tarea. Pensé toda la noche en Hermann. ¿Qué me dirá cuando venga el martes? ¿Intentará convencerme de que cambie de opinión y me case con él?

¿Seré lo suficientemente fuerte para resistirlo si lo hace? Esos y otros pensamientos similares llenaron mi mente. Antes de irme a la cama, Oré a Dios para que me mostrara Su voluntad y me guiara para decir las palabras correctas y tomar la decisión correcta.

El sábado, Elisabeth nos había invitado a Renate y a mí a un pastel y un café. Disfrutamos compartiendo nuestra fe cristiana y hablando de varios temas, también de nuestros hermanos y el matrimonio. Todas teníamos un hermano; éramos cercanas. Elisabeth se sintió herida cuando su hermano se casó y la descuidó por completo. Les dije lo agradecida que estaba con mi hermano, que aún no estaba casado pero me cuidaba y me ayudaba. Nunca podría decepcionarlo. Renate dijo que su hermano se sentía más cerca de ella que de su esposa. Ella me preguntó ¿qué diría Cristo? No pude darle una respuesta apropiada. Sin embargo, no estuve de acuerdo con su siguiente declaración. Ella sintió que el matrimonio era la muerte del amor. Ella tampoco quería tener hijos. Pensé justo lo contrario: el matrimonio es la realización del amor, y los hijos son una bendición adicional.

Después de que terminamos de saborear el delicioso pastel y el café, dimos un largo paseo por el bosque y encontramos un lugar donde nos sentamos. Sin pronunciar una palabra, simplemente disfrutamos de la belleza del paisaje y el reflejo de la luz de la luna en el lago. Una música lejana de acordeón interrumpió el silencio como si estuviera tocando una canción de cuna para la naturaleza. Mis pensamientos regresaron a mi hogar en Prusia del Este, donde nuestra familia había vivido felizmente y de dónde nos habíamos ido hace casi once años.

¿Quién habitaba nuestra casa ahora? ¿Cómo se veían la casa y el jardín? ¿Seríamos capaces de volver alguna vez? Podría haberme sentado allí durante horas, soñando con la vida en casa; sin embargo, momentáneamente, estaba en un pueblo extraño sola con mis pensamientos.

El lunes 27 de junio, de camino a la estación de tren, me encontré con una gran multitud. Tuve que abrirme paso a empujones para subir al tren. Los entusiastas del deporte dieron la bienvenida al equipo de fútbol de Essen que había ganado la Copa de Alemania. La multitud les arrojó flores y celebró su victoria con gritos estruendosos.

Al día siguiente, martes 28 de junio, como había prometido, Hermann llegó a primera hora de la tarde. Perdí mis clases de la tarde para poder pasar el tiempo juntos. Elegimos un lugar tranquilo en el bosque cercano, desde donde teníamos una vista del lago. Primero, me dijo que tomó un curso en la Universidad de South Westphalia en Educación y Pedagogía. Describió brevemente dando ejemplos prácticos de los aspectos más destacados de los temas. También hablamos sobre diferentes puntos de vista de la vida. Admiré su profundo conocimiento y sabiduría de la naturaleza humana y el análisis del carácter. También me dijo que soy muy diferente de mis hermanos y hermanas. Debo haber heredado algunos rasgos de carácter de mi padre.

"Me gustaría conocerlo".

"Tal vez, algún día, cuando regrese a casa desde Polonia, donde fue capturado como prisionero de guerra. Sí, heredé su entusiasmo por la vida y su sentido del humor".

Ambos hicimos una pausa por un momento, luego se volvió hacia mí y me abrazó, y me dio un largo beso. Mi sangre corría por mi cuerpo y mi corazón latía más rápido. Pero no traté de liberarme a la fuerza esta vez. cuando me soltó, tomó mis dos manos, me miró a los ojos y expresó sus sentimientos por mí:

"Hildegard, ¿pensaste que el contenido de tu última carta me impediría amarte y me haría olvidarte a ti y a nuestra relación por completo? No, eso es imposible. Tu última carta me molestó."

Sacó la carta del bolsillo de la chaqueta. Se lo quité de la mano, lo rompí en pedazos y lo tiré a un arbusto cercano.

"Lo siento, me da vergüenza haber escrito esa carta negativa".

Luego me besó de nuevo.

"Ahora, te necesito aún más. Después de que llego a casa del trabajo y me siento solo en mi habitación por la noche, anhelo estar cerca de ti".

En ese momento, me di cuenta de cuánto significaba para mí también su amistad y su amor, y cuánto había aprendido de él.

"Hermann, estoy tan feliz de que hayas venido, y de que todavía me amas, incluso después de decirte que no me casaría contigo."

Siguió otro beso al que respondí. "El beso ya no pertenece a nuestra amistad."

"Tonterías, ¿entonces quieres decir que todo estuvo mal?"

"No, pero nuestros pensamientos eran diferentes antes". "¿Por qué no se me debe permitir dar un beso a la persona que amo?"

Escribiste que deberíamos olvidarnos el uno del otro y detener todas las comunicaciones entre nosotros", respondió Hermann. "Me parece ridículo evitar vernos. Entonces el amor podría convertirse en odio, lo cual es perjudicial para ambos. Todo lo contrario, me gustaría que pudiéramos vernos lo más seguido posible y nutrir nuestra amistad. Por cierto, te deseo un esposo que te entienda".

Su respuesta desinteresada me tomó por sorpresa. Aprecié aún más su pensamiento maduro y carácter noble en ese momento.

"Te deseo lo mejor para tu futuro y también una buena esposa", le dije. Siguió otro beso y otro abrazo.

Por un momento, reflexioné sobre nuestra inusual pero hermosa amistad. Nuestros caminos se cruzaron de vez en cuando, y siempre nos dimos cuenta de cuánto se enriquecían nuestras vidas al compartir esos momentos especiales, respetando los sentimientos y pensamientos de los demás, y viviendo bajo el mismo principio moral: *madurar y permanecer puros.*

La tarde pasó demasiado rápido. La puesta de sol detrás de las colinas en la orilla opuesta del lago extendía un velo translúcido de color naranja pálido sobre la superficie lisa. Era hora de irse. Volvimos al apartamento. Comimos un tazón de sopa que la Sra. Mohrmann había guardado para nosotros. Luego acompañé a Hermann sólo un corto trecho hasta la estación de tren. Nos despedimos sin saber cuándo y dónde nos volveríamos a ver. Hermann fue a Essingen, y me quedé en Essen. Di gracias a Dios por haber pasado juntos una tarde tan agradable y significativa. Estaba soñando despierta y absorta en mis pensamientos. Todavía no podía comprender que una amistad mental y espiritual tan hermosa pudiera existir entre un joven y una joven. Según el filósofo griego Platón, Hermann y yo fuimos bendecidos con una amistad amorosa, llamada amor platónico (espiritual), que enriqueció nuestras vidas con virtud, alegría, misterio, angustia y sacrificio.

Al día siguiente me desperté y me sorprendió no ver a mi compañera de cuarto Friedel en la cama. Estaba preocupada por lo que podría haberle pasado. Entonces recordé que había ido a dar un paseo con Werner. Quería preguntarle dónde estaba. Fui a la habitación de Werner y llamé a la puerta. Me sorprendió aún más encontrar a Friedel en el lugar de Werner. Había pasado la noche con Werner. Dijo que Werner y ella se habían ido a dar un paseo. Llegaron tarde a casa, y cuando llamó a nuestra puerta, nadie le abrió la puerta, así que bajó a la habitación de Werner y durmió allí. Por suerte, la Sra. Mohrmann no estaba en casa esa mañana y no sabía lo que había pasado. Esperábamos que nunca se enterara.

Friedel estaba nerviosa y paseaba de un lado a otro; ella temía que la Sra. Mohrman la desalojaría si descubriera su mal comportamiento. Aunque desaprobé la conducta de Friedel, no pude reprenderla. Unos días después, la madre de Werner le dijo a la Sra. Mohrmann lo que pasó. La Señora Mohrmann estaba furiosa y la regañó terriblemente. Sentí pena por Friedel. Después de que las cosas se calmaron un poco, fui con la Sra. Mohrmann y le pedí que perdonara a Friedel y que no le mostrara animosidad. En cambio, la traté con amabilidad y la ayudé a superar este percance. La Señora Mohrmann fue comprensiva y accedió a hacerlo. Con la ayuda de Dios, yo hice lo mismo, y nos hicimos más cercanas la una a la otra de lo que éramos antes. Dios me mostró cómo sana nuestras heridas cuando podemos perdonar y tratar a un ofensor con amor en lugar de odio. Si dejamos de lado los pensamientos negativos sobre una persona y otros sentimientos negativos y los reemplazamos con compasión y bondad, crecemos y maduramos. Agradecí a Dios por mostrarme Su manera de actuar en esta situación.

En la semana que siguió, Friedel y yo íbamos con frecuencia al bosque para estudiar y hablar. A menudo, pensaba en nuestro hogar en Prusia del Este, en mi padre, cuándo y si regresaría de Polonia. Pensaba en mi hermana Emma y su hijo de tres años, Bernhard, que vivían con nuestra madre, Edmund y Horst en Essingen. Entonces pensé en mi futuro. ¿El gobierno aprobará la asistencia monetaria para que pueda terminar mi educación médica? ¿Dónde encontraré un puesto? ¿Con quién me casaré algún día?

¿Podría ser Hermann? Estos y otros pensamientos cruzaron por mi mente. Deseaba amar a una persona de todo corazón y hacer feliz a mi futuro cónyuge. Sin embargo, ahora tenía que dar toda mi atención a estudiar y escribir los mejores exámenes que pudiera. Recibimos una boleta de calificaciones provisional para presentar con nuestras solicitudes de empleo. De vez en cuando, Friedel y yo, y a veces Gertrud y Gerda, nos reuníamos y veíamos una buena película juntas. Gerda disfrutaba escribiendo historias. Una vez escribió una historia sobre la viuda alegre y los cuatro estudiantes. Sabía exagerar las cosas y poner mucho humor en su escritura.

Gerda tenía miedo a los animales. Cuando íbamos a caminar, y un insecto se arrastraba por el suelo, o pasaba un venado, ella saltaba y gritaba. En su lugar, nos reíamos. Un día intentamos jugarle una mala pasada. Friedel y yo salimos al jardín y atrapamos una rana. Lo escondimos en un paraguas y la llevamos a su habitación. Queríamos envolver a la rana en su camisón. En ese momento, ella entró en la habitación. Cuando vio que la rana saltaba de su cama, gritó tan fuerte que todo el vecindario pudo oírla. Pensamos que iba a tener un ataque al corazón. Gracias a Dios la Sra. Mohrmann había ido de compras esa tarde; de lo contrario, nos habría reprendido. De ahora en adelante, no le jugaríamos tales trucos. Aceptamos su fobia a los animales como parte de su personalidad.

Pasó una semana y el cartero entregó una carta de Hermann. Abrí el sobre rápidamente y leí:

Son las 9:15 PM. Estoy sentado en mi oficina y escucho la canción The Moon Ascended. Me trae recuerdos de cuando estaba solo en mi habitación. Todas las noches abría la ventana, miraba la luna y las estrellas, y pensaba en ti y en nuestra felicidad y futuro. Hoy pienso en ti también pero en circunstancias diferentes. El amor apasionado que te tenía antes disminuyó y dio lugar a nuestra cálida amistad inicial. Está bien, tal vez incluso mejor así.

Él estaba en lo correcto. Admiraba su sabiduría y comprensión. Sin embargo, el contenido de su carta también me trajo dolor emocional. Me di cuenta de que me preocupaba por él aún más ahora que antes. ¿Quizás su visita alimentó mi amor por él? ¿Habría sido mejor que no hubiera venido? Pero ahora creo que es mejor así. Contesté la carta de Hermann al día siguiente; Le dije lo agradecida que estaba por su amistad y comprensión.

No mencioné cuánto me importaba él ahora. También me dolió haberlo decepcionado al no aceptar su propuesta. Pero en ese momento, mi sentido común anuló mis emociones y pensé que había tomado la decisión correcta. Le pedí a Dios que me enseñara a elegir sabiamente en el futuro y que mi conducta le agradara. Nuestro Padre celestial nos envía desafíos y dificultades en la vida, pero si, con la ayuda de Dios, los encontramos victoriosos, aun haciendo sacrificios para agradarle, Él siempre nos recompensa con alegría, paz interior y crecimiento espiritual.

Edmund me envió un paquete con algunas cosas que necesitaba y 150 MA (marcos alemanes). Solo pude agradecerle en ese momento y esperar algún día; poder devolver su amabilidad y generosidad. También recibí una carta de mi amiga Lore. Adjuntó una foto de sí misma. Se veía tan solemne y algo triste. Deseaba poder estar con ella para consolarla y animarla. Le preocupaba mucho el deterioro de la salud de sus padres y se sentía sola por ser hija única. Le hubiera gustado tener un hermano o una hermana para planear eventos juntos o compartir pensamientos. Respondí ambas cartas de inmediato. Mi corazón se desbordó de gratitud por mis cuatro hermanos y tres hermanas, a quienes amaba mucho. Me sentí más cerca de mi hermana Emma y de mi hermano Edmund. Cada vez que pensaba en el futuro y el matrimonio, siempre quería tener muchos hijos. Me preguntaba por qué la Sra. Mohrmann no tuvo hijos. Una tarde me dijo que había tenido dos abortos espontáneos. Su marido Luego fue asesinado durante la Segunda Guerra Mundial y no quería volver a casarse para formar una familia.

Sí, el instinto y deseo de la mayoría de las mujeres es tener hijos y tener un matrimonio feliz. No todas las mujeres logran ese objetivo. Sin embargo, hay una meta superior: ser salvos por la sangre de Jesucristo, servir y amar a Dios primero y a nuestro prójimo como a nosotros mismos, independientemente de nuestra procedencia.

Sí, muchas veces me planteé con quién me casaría y cuál sería mi destino. Pero en ese momento, tenía que concentrarme en estudiar y aprobar los exámenes tomados en todas las materias. Tuve que disciplinarme para no desviarme. Pero mi compañera de cuarto, Friedel, tenía una manera de entrometerse en mi vida personal al hacer muchas preguntas sobre un tema que me sentía incómodA al revelar. Ella inquirió.

"¿Tu madre te escribe alguna vez?" "No."

"Por qué, ¿Tu madre y tú no os lleváis bien?"

"Me da vergüenza decir que mi madre no sabe escribir. Creció cerca de la frontera rusa. Los funcionarios rusos se llevaron a sus padres cuando era joven y no pudo ir a la escuela. Sin embargo, aprendió a leer la Biblia. Ella estaba satisfecha con eso".

"Lamento oír eso. Pero, ¿Tú y tu madre tienen una relación cercana?"

"No muy cerca; mi madre rara vez expresa sus sentimientos o su amor a mis hermanos, hermanas y a mí. Nunca nos pregunta cómo nos sentimos o qué pensamos. Ella sólo nos reprende si no la obedecemos. Si es necesario, usa un cinturón o una ramita para golpearnos si hacemos algo que ella cree que está mal".

"¿Debe ser horrible no sentirse amado o no ser comprendido por tu madre?"

"Sí, a veces, es doloroso. A veces me pregunto, ¿no soy digna de ser amada por mi madre, o mi madre no tiene la capacidad de expresar su amor a sus hijos?

Sentí lágrimas brotar. Levanté la almohada a un lado, para que Friedel no pudiera verme llorar. Me dije a mí misma que fuera fuerte. Le dije buenas noches a Friedel, para que dejara de hacer más preguntas. Pero mis pensamientos sobre mi madre continuaron ocupando mi mente hasta altas horas de la noche.

Cuando dejé de llorar, pensé en lo difícil que debe haber sido para mi madre separarse de sus padres durante la Primera Guerra Mundial y criar ocho hijos durante la Segunda Guerra Mundial. Luego, perdió su casa y todo lo que alguna vez tuvo. Mi padre fue reclutado como soldado antes de que terminara la guerra. Durante muchos años no supo si su esposo aún vivía o no. La guerra terminó hace once años, y sin embargo no volvió a casa. Tal vez todo el sufrimiento por el que pasó mamá la hizo taciturna. Sentí compasión y gratitud hacia mi madre por criarnos a los ocho con valores cristianos y morales elevados. También estaba agradecida de que me permitiera ir a la escuela secundaria y estudiar para ser asistente médico. Sentí vergüenza por lo que le había dicho a Friedel sobre mi madre. En casa, en Prusia del Este, éramos felices como familia y anhelaba volver a casa. Mi madre mostró su amor por sus hijos ocupándose de sus necesidades. Ahora me sentía sin hogar, preguntándome quién vivía en nuestra granja y si alguna vez se nos permitiría regresar a nuestro lugar de nacimiento. ¿Debo estar descontenta con mi suerte? No, me volví a Dios en oración. Después de pedir perdón, sentí que Su amor me rodeaba. Agradecí a Dios por ayudarme a superar todos los desafíos de mi vida y le pedí que me enseñara a vivir en armonía con las personas y amarlas incondicionalmente. Caí en un sueño profundo y al día siguiente estaba lista para enfrentar nuevos desafíos.

Durante los últimos dos días, la Sra. Mohrmann nos regañó y criticó. Ella hirió nuestros sentimientos. Pero sellé mis labios y seguí siendo cortés con ella. No podía entender lo cambiante que podía ser. Hicimos nuestro mejor esfuerzo para acomodarla. Cada vez que la situación en el apartamento se volvía desagradable, buscábamos refugio en el bosque. El aire fresco y la belleza de la naturaleza tuvieron un efecto calmante sobre nosotros y le dieron a la Sra. Mohrmann la oportunidad de ordenar sus pensamientos y cambiar su actitud gruñona.

Después de regresar de nuestro paseo, encontré una carta de Hermann.

La abrí rápidamente y leí el contenido con emociones encontradas; me impresionó la siguiente parte:

Justo ahora, escucho los comentarios deportivos sobre la carrera de kayak en el lago Baldeney. El Mar Baldeney aparece de nuevo frente a mí, y te veo sentada a mi lado. Son hermosos recuerdos y, aún sin una foto, video o descripción, siempre permanecerán vívidos para nosotros. En este lugar, ambos nos volvimos más maduros. PERMANECER PURO Y MADURO ES EL ARTE MÁS HERMOSO Y TAMBIÉN EL MÁS DIFÍCIL DE LA VIDA. (Rein bleiben und reif werden ist die schoenste und schwerste Lebenskunst) Es una meta a alcanzar no sólo durante la juventud, sino a lo largo de toda nuestra vida.

Cuanta razón tenía Hermann. Respondí y le dije cuán feliz estaba de que ambos tuviéramos altos valores morales y viviéramos de acuerdo con ellos. Cuando pasé por el lugar donde ambos pasamos tiempo juntos, pensé en él y deseé estar con él para disfrutar de una conversación animada y absorber la belleza del paisaje juntos. Cada vez que escuchaba ciertas canciones, mis pensamientos viajaban hacia él. También le agradecí por comprenderme y respetar mis sentimientos. A pesar de que mi respuesta negativa hizo añicos su sueño de pasar nuestras vidas juntos, actuó de manera tan honorable. Le agradecí que decidiéramos ser amigos y mantenernos en contacto. Luego también escribí sobre cuánto tenía que estudiar momentáneamente para los próximos exámenes. Cada vez que le escribía una carta, ya esperaba su respuesta. Sus dos hermanas, Helge y Heidrun, también mantuvieron correspondencia conmigo. Heidrun todavía estaba en el grupo de jóvenes y me informó sobre la próxima reunión de los grupos de jóvenes de Renania-Palatino en Bingen. Esperaban que nuestro grupo ganara otro premio en canto y baile. Cuánto deseaba poder estar con nuestro grupo. Helge tampoco pudo unirse a ellos. Estudió para ser enfermera y simultáneamente trabajaba en el hospital para su formación práctica. Pensé en dónde haría mi capacitación en el trabajo algún día. Después de aprender todas las teorías en las diversas materias médicas, sería necesario ponerlas en práctica.

Después de un duro día de exámenes y estudios bíblicos sobre la creación, Friedel y yo decidimos dar un paseo por el bosque. Era una tarde clara y tranquila. La luna se elevó y extendió una cinta plateada sobre el lago. Las luces de las casas en la orilla opuesta del lago se reflejaban en la superficie del agua oscura. Encontramos un lugar tranquilo y, sin decir una palabra, nos sentamos y absorbimos la belleza del paisaje. De repente sonó una trompeta y tocó una canción y más tarde se le unió una orquesta. Agregó mucho al estado de ánimo festivo del momento, principalmente cuando tocaron el himno cristiano, "Oh, el poder de Dios, todo lo demás trasciende". Cuando terminaron el concierto tocando el Himno Nacional Alemán, mi pensamiento ascendió a Dios y le agradecí por haberme guiado y protegido tan maravillosamente hasta ahora. Entonces mis pensamientos volaron de regreso al mundo mágico en Prusia del Este. Sentí nostalgia y me costó mucho evitar que las lágrimas no lloradas se desbordaran de mis ojos. Mientras ambas estábamos en silencio, dos jóvenes se nos acercaron y quisieron unirse a nosotros. Al principio, rechazamos su solicitud. Se presentaron como Heinz y Franz. Empezaron a hablar de música y que les gustaría cantar para nosotros.

Sus modales corteses nos convencieron de que les dejáramos acompañarnos. Ambos tenían voces agradables y se comportaban con respeto. Heinz mencionó que tocaba el acordeón y se ofreció a entretenernos el sábado. Acordamos encontrarnos en el mismo lugar y esperamos un interludio musical.

Durante el resto de la semana, estudiamos y escribimos exámenes en varias materias. Todavía cometía demasiados errores tipográficos y me preocupaba no obtener una calificación aprobatoria en mi boleta de calificaciones. Dr. Reiche, que enseñaba cirugía menor, supo cómo presentar su tema para cautivar nuestra atención. De vez en cuando, daba ejemplos de su práctica e interacción con sus pacientes. Parecía estricto pero justo. Como paciente, confiaría en él completamente. Poseía el conocimiento y la personalidad para ser el cirujano ideal que sabía cómo tratar a los pacientes ya las personas.

El sábado después de la cena, fuimos al Lago Baldeney a escuchar al acordeonista Heinz ya su amigo Franz, el cantante. Llegaron tarde, pero llegaron. Primero, Heinz tocó canciones que deseábamos escuchar. Luego escogió canciones o piezas musicales al azar. Friedel y yo nos sentamos en el banco y escuchamos con atención. Cuando cantó la canción "Madre querida, dame un potro" (Mamatschi schenk mir ein Pferdchen). Esta canción debe haberle traído recuerdos dolorosos. Se atragantó y dejó de cantar. Luego, Heinz nos dijo por qué esta canción lo puso tan triste.

"Yo solo tenía cinco años. Mi madre no creía en el régimen de Hitler. Un día expresó su opinión negativa sobre Hitler. Alguien la denunció a la Gestapo. Al día siguiente vino la Gestapo a la casa, la agarró y se llevó a mi madre a un campo de concentración. Nunca supe de ella, y nunca la volví a ver.

Me sentí muy mal y expresé mi compasión por él.

"Qué cruel estar separado de tu madre a una edad tan temprana. Sí, cuánto sufrimiento se infligió a innumerables personas inocentes de todas las edades y nacionalidades durante la Segunda Guerra Mundial. Solo Dios sabe toda la angustia y el sufrimiento que soportó la gente. Perdí mi hogar en Prusia del Este y mi padre aún no ha regresado después de haber sido tomado como prisionero de guerra en Polonia".

"Lamento escuchar sobre la tragedia de su familia".

Heinz tocó algunas canciones más mientras Franz cantaba antes de que empezáramos a regresar a casa. En el camino, Heinz nos dijo que podía analizar personajes. Le pedimos que analizara el nuestro. En la siguiente farola, nos detuvimos. Heinz comenzó conmigo colocando mi cabeza debajo de la farola para ver mi rostro. Me miró directamente a los ojos y comenzó a decirme.

"Hildegard, amas el arte y la naturaleza. No piensas mucho en el arte moderno. Eres abierta y honesta pero firme. No permites que nadie se acerque demasiado a ti. Si alguien te ha hecho mal, no lo puedes olvidar fácilmente. Eres una persona muy leal y cariñosa. Sin embargo, tus altas aspiraciones no siempre se cumplen. Debes exigir tu derecho con más frecuencia y evitar que la gente se aproveche de tu amabilidad. No estás del todo sana. Deberías ver a un médico y que te examine".

Entonces Friedel se puso bajo la luz y Heinz comenzó a decirle.

"Friedel, eres abierta y honesta, pero no siempre leal. Sólo serás leal a la persona que creas que cumple con tus expectativas. También amas la naturaleza y el arte. Todos tus deseos tampoco se cumplirán para ti. Tienes el don de extraer información secreta de las personas sin revelar tus pensamientos o secretos. Estás apegada a algunas personas pero no eres firme; deberías ser tan firme como Hildegard."

Luego me miró y dijo: "Posees la capacidad de evaluar los caracteres humanos, pero te lleva mucho tiempo. Sin embargo, ambas son jóvenes inteligentes." Ambas estábamos perplejas por el análisis preciso de los personajes por parte de un extraño que nos conocía solo por unas pocas horas. Agradecimos a Heinz y Franz por entretenernos antes de despedirnos. Se fueron al día siguiente y nunca más los volvimos a ver.

Al día siguiente recibí una larga carta de mi hermano. Le pregunté qué debía hacer si no puedo obtener un puesto en el consultorio de un médico de inmediato. Me dijo que tuviera paciencia y encontraría un lugar para ejercer mi profesión recién adquirida. Luego me escribió que mi hermano Georg se había casado con una mujer que tenía un carácter problemático además de ser mayor y discapacitada. Edmund me dijo que Georg se arrepentiría de haber hecho tal elección sin proyectar las consecuencias futuras. Sentí pena por mi hermano Georg. Era amable, trabajador y siempre dispuesto a ayudar a los demás. Se merecía una buena esposa y una vida feliz. Edmund me dijo que le gustaría enviarme algunos obsequios como recompensa por aprobar todos los exámenes intermedios.

Necesitaba muchas cosas, pero él ya había hecho mucho por mí. Me sentiría culpable de pedir más. Le respondí que ya había hecho mucho por mí y que no era necesario enviarme un regalo especial ahora. El mismo día recibí una tarjeta de Hermann sobre la reunión de DJO en Bingen. Escribió que nuestro grupo juvenil ganó el primer premio en canto y el tercer lugar en danza folclórica. Ambos debíamos estar encantados con su actuación. Es en parte el resultado de nuestro trabajo conjunto en el grupo. Disfrutamos trabajar juntos, establecer altos estándares y lograr resultados. Extrañaba a nuestro grupo y especialmente a Hermann.

Todos los días esperaba una respuesta de la Oficina del Oficina de Rentas Internas. El gobierno todavía no me había notificado si recibiría ayuda financiera de ellos. Me estaba quedando sin fondos. le rogué a mi hermano que me enviara algo de dinero. Un día no me alcanzaba ni para pagar el billete de tren. Friedel me prestó 1.00 MA para que pudiera ir a clase. Después de que pasó un tiempo, se dio cuenta de que no podía devolverlo; me dijo que me perdonaría la deuda si me comía una rebanada de pan con sardinas y mermelada. La sola vista me dio náuseas. Tomé un bocado y tuve dificultad para tragarlo. Sabía horrible. Cuando terminé el último bocado, dijo, pagaste tu deuda. Me disculpé, corrí al baño y descargué el contenido del estómago en la taza del inodoro. Cada vez que mis compañeras de cuarto compraban una Coca-Cola, recibían cuatro popotes por compartirla, así que no me sentía tan mal.

A principios de agosto, recibí mi boleta de calificaciones provisional para enviar con cada solicitud de puesto. Estaba agradecida de tener calificaciones aprobatorias en todas las materias, incluso al escribir. Los médicos que buscaban asistentes enviaron sus nombres, direcciones y el tipo de práctica que tenían. Inmediatamente, copié los nombres y direcciones de ocho médicos. Escribí ocho cartas. Incluí un currículum y mi boleta de calificaciones, con la esperanza de que un médico me ofreciera un puesto. La misma noche, cuando fui al estudio bíblico, el Sr. Pfeiffer me dijo que también revisaría y vería si podía recomendar a un médico que buscase un asistente. Le estaba agradecida. Oré a Dios para que me ayudara a encontrar una posición y fortalecer mi fe.

Al día siguiente el Sr. Pfeiffer me dio las direcciones de dos médicos.

La misma noche, fui con el Dr. Kelt. Después de esperar una hora y media, me preguntó si tenía alguna experiencia práctica. Mi respuesta fue no. Todavía voy a la escuela.

"Que escuela"?

"La escuela del Dr. Glaeser."

"Mi asistente actual es de la misma escuela. Mi esposa y yo nos vamos de vacaciones en breve. Otro médico se ocupará de mi práctica durante mi ausencia. si ella no cumple con la aprobación de mi colega, es posible que puedas comenzar a trabajar para mí el 1 de noviembre de 1955. Ponte en contacto conmigo a finales de octubre."

Agradecí al Dr. Kelt y salió de su oficina con un rayo de esperanza. También me dio un billete de autobús, pero opté por volver andando al apartamento y pasar con el Sr. Pfeiffer. Le hablé de mi entrevista con el Dr. Kelt y que iría con el Dr. Hinterleitner mañana. Al día siguiente, después de que el Dr. Grabe enseñó la patología de los órganos respiratorios superiores, Gertrud y yo tomamos el tren a Essen-West para buscar al Dr. Hinterleitner. Cuando llegamos, la Dra. Hinterleitner me dijo que ya había contratado a alguien recientemente, pero tuvo la amabilidad de darme la dirección de un amigo, un oftalmólogo. Agradecí al Dr. Hinterleitner por su recomendación. Decepcionada, salí de su oficina.

Tomé un tranvía a la parte de la ciudad donde se encontraba la oficina del Oftalmólogo Dr. Baberowski. Un joven entró en la siguiente parada y se sentó a mi lado. Me dijo que era un futbolista muy conocido. Murió su esposa y tuvo dos hijos. Sus hijos también fueron futbolistas. Tenía treinta y ocho años y buscaba esposa. Me dio su dirección y me pidió que lo visitara.

Lo Rechacé. Me alegré de bajarme en la siguiente parada. Apenas entré a la oficina del Dr. Baberowski cuando cayó una fuerte lluvia que golpeaba las ventanas. Esperé un rato hasta que el Dr. Baberowski me llamó a su oficina privada. Me preguntó sobre mis antecedentes, mi experiencia médica y si sabía escribir a máquina. Sin darme una respuesta, se excusó. Tenía que ver a más pacientes. Me pidió que volviera después del horario de oficina a las 5:00 p. m. el lunes siguiente. Me agradó el Dr. Baberowski, pero no su oficina pequeña, oscura y anticuada, que estaba ubicada en una zona deteriorada de la ciudad. Dudaba si estaría satisfecha trabajando en su oficina. La lluvia paró. Cansada, llegué al departamento. Antes de quedarme dormida, oré a Dios para que me ayudara a encontrar un puesto con el médico adecuado.

A mediados de agosto recibí la primera respuesta a mis solicitudes laborales del Dr. Jerg en Wendlingen; ya había contratado a un asistente. Entristecida, decidí volver a la entrevista con el Dr. Baberowski. Después de hacer más preguntas, se tomó el tiempo para probarme en el archivo de registros y la escritura. La máquina de escribir obsoleta me dio problemas y no me fue tan bien. Dijo que compraría una nueva. También comprobó mi letra haciéndome copiar una parte de un artículo. También tuve dificultad para escribir con su estilográfica. Cuando le pregunté cuánto sería el salario si decidía contratarme, no me dio una respuesta definitiva, pero me aseguró que no era un tacaño. También habló sobre un plan para construir una nueva oficina. Me trató con cortesía e incluso me llevó en su carro a la estación de tren. Mientras estaba sentado en el tren, pensé que no usaría todo el conocimiento médico que acabo de adquirir si trabajaba para un oftalmólogo. Cuanto más lo reflexionaba, menos me parecía aceptar el puesto del Dr. Baberowski. Si no pudiera encontrar un lugar en la medicina familiar, ¿consideraría aceptar su oferta?

De camino a casa, me reuní con mis compañeros de cuarto, Gertrud, Gerda y Friedel, para ver la segunda parte de la película, *Los caballos de mi padre*. En la primera parte de la película, un niño enfermo, estando hospitalizado, renuncia a las ganas de vivir. Durante una visita al hospital, una novia le leyó el diario de su padre. Revivió vívidamente los eventos pasados que tuvo con su padre. El recuerdo de su padre lo animó a vivir. Su salud mejoró, y encontró un propósito para vivir de nuevo. En la segunda parte, el productor de cine transmitió mucha sabiduría para vivir una vida gratificante. Varias citas me impresionaron y las anoté.

"Trata tanto a las mujeres como a los caballos con amor. La vida no siempre es un juego limpio. La honestidad supera todo. Sin embargo, la persona que para siempre permanece honesta tiene una experiencia de vida desafiante pero más gratificante. Cuando se necesita ayuda, Dios siempre la proporciona en el momento adecuado".

Estaba agradecida por los excelentes consejos que me dieron y estoy segura de que otros también lo estaban. Dios a menudo me ayudó en situaciones difíciles y que amenazaron mi vida en el pasado; Confié en Él entonces y hago lo mismo ahora y lo haré en el futuro. La vida es una batalla continua, y para salir victorioso al enfrentar todos los desafíos, le pedí a Dios que me diera Su guía, fortaleza y sabiduría para tomar las decisiones correctas ahora y en el futuro.

Al día siguiente el Dr. Glaeser me llamó a su oficina; me dijo que recibió una carta del Dr. Mossen, a quien había visto en Landau antes de asistir a la Escuela de Medicina del Dr. Glaeser. El Dr. Mossen preguntó por mis calificaciones; si le parecían buenas, ofrecería un puesto como aprendiz de técnico de rayos X. Pagaría $30.00 MA por mes. El Dr. Glaeser estaba indignado por el salario que el Dr. Mossen propuso pagar a un asistente médico. Dijo que planeaba enviarle una respuesta apropiada a su carta insultante. Agradecí al Dr. Glaeser. Me disculpé por no haber pagado la matrícula de agosto. Mencioné: "Solicité hace más de un año asistencia educativa. Mi padre aún no ha regresado de haber sido capturado y retenido por el gobierno polaco. Al ser considerada medio huérfana, tenía derecho a la asistencia del gobierno para la educación. Sin embargo, no había recibido ningún dinero. Usé todo el dinero que ahorré y el dinero que me había enviado mi hermano. Por favor, Dr.

Glaeser, déjame terminar la escuela. Tan pronto como encuentre un trabajo, pagaré mis deudas".

"Tráigame la dirección del oficial del IRS y le enviaré una carta rígida. Es vergonzoso que no te asignaran los fondos antes de que empezaras la escuela".

"Gracias, Dr. Glaeser, por su comprensión y por comunicarse con el funcionario del IRS. Le traeré la dirección y el nombre del gerente de la oficina".

Cuando regresé al departamento, encontré una carta de mi hermana Emma. Ella escribió que mi madre había experimentado una hemorragia uterina masiva. El ginecólogo la hospitalizó y programó una histerectomía. Rogué a Dios que la operación saliera bien. Agradecí a mi hermana Emma que estuvo con mi madre para ayudarla durante el período de recuperación postoperatoria. Me preguntó si ya había encontrado un lugar para trabajar. Desafortunadamente, tuve que responderle que aún no lo había hecho. El mismo día recibí dos respuestas negativas más, una de un médico en Muensingen y Giessen. Fue muy decepcionante.

El jueves 18 de agosto fue el cumpleaños de Gerda. Gertrud, Friedel y yo le compramos un libro. La señora Mohrmann le regaló una hermosa vela y un cervatillo de peluche. Ella estaba encantada. La señora Mohrmann también horneó un pastel para ella y preparó un impresionante ponche para una celebración. Sin embargo, cuando le pedimos a la Sra. Mohrmann que celebrara con nosotros por la tarde, nos dio un contundente *no* por respuesta. También se negó a beber el ponche que le ofreció Gerda. Gerda se sintió herida y comenzó a llorar. Sentí pena por ella. Le pregunté a la Sra. Mohrmann por qué se negó a celebrar con nosotros. Ella respondió sarcásticamente: "Tengo mis razones". Entonces me pregunté por qué los cambios repentinos de humor. Sin embargo, no queríamos que el humor de la señora Mohrmann estropeara el cumpleaños de Gerda. Les habíamos comentado a los chicos del grupo de jóvenes sobre el cumpleaños de Gerda. Se ofrecieron a celebrar con nosotros. Empacamos los utensilios, el pastel y el ponche en una canasta y lo llevamos por la noche al salón donde se llevó a cabo el estudio bíblico. Pedro, Ferdi, Werner, y Karl-Heinz fueron considerados y le dieron algunos obsequios, que Gerda agradeció. Peter me deleitó con un ramo de rosas. Disfrutamos el pastel y el ponche y cantamos juntos varias canciones folclóricas. Todos estaban felices. Agradecí que Gerda se animara y disfrutara de su celebración especial de dieciocho años.

La señora Mohrmann hirió mis sentimientos cuando me culpó por no haberle pedido que celebrara con nosotros, lo cual no era cierto. Ella descargó sus quejas sobre nosotros a Gertrud. También le dije a la Sra. Mohrmann que no tenía dinero para pagar el alojamiento y la comida de agosto. Le informé que esperaba que mi hermano Edmund me enviara algo de dinero y que fuera paciente. Sin embargo, la Sra. Mohrmann les dijo a las otras chicas que me despediría si no pagaba pronto. Me sentí avergonzada y humillada y profundamente herida. ¿No fue suficiente con decírmelo?

¿Tenía que hablar a mis espaldas con mis compañeras de cuarto sobre mi deuda? Desesperada, volví a escribir a mi hermano y al Sr. Dobereiner en el Servicio de Impuestos Internos, instándolo a enviar la asistencia a la que tenía derecho, o no podría terminar la escuela de medicina. Sí, no es fácil tratar con funcionarios gubernamentales indiferentes, ni comprensivos ni altruistas. Me hizo darme cuenta de que mi vida sería un desafío. Tendría que enfrentar muchas dificultades en el futuro. Entonces razoné, es bueno, porque las dificultades y el sufrimiento me hacen pensar. Pensar me hace sabia y fuerte. La sabiduría da alegría en la vida. Aunque sufría dolor emocional hoy, estaba agradecida con Dios porque me enseñó cómo vivir según Sus reglas. Dios siempre me da el consuelo y la fuerza adecuada para cada día. Sí, todavía tengo mucho que aprender. Le pedí a Dios que me proporcionara una mente receptiva, un corazón amoroso y un espíritu recto.

El último sábado de agosto no tuvimos clases. Gertrud y yo fuimos al río Ruhr donde muchos jóvenes acamparon, navegaron en kayak y nadaron. Algunos campistas cantaron canciones folklóricas acompañados de un guitarrista; Gertrud y yo nos sentamos en un banco cercano y cantamos. Nos sentimos felices cantando y continuamos cantando de camino a casa también. Cuando llegamos a casa, encontramos a la madre de Peter, la Sra. Haertel, esperándonos. Ella estaba angustiada y nos dijo que su hijo estaba desaparecido desde ayer. Se fue de casa sin despedirse y sin llevarse nada consigo. Ella nos preguntó si él nos había mencionado algo sobre irse de casa o adónde quería ir. Aunque lo recordaba hablando de convertirse en soldado e ir a la Legión Extranjera, pensé que era solo una fantasía. ¿Cómo podría causarle más dolor a una madre preocupada hablándole de la Legión Extranjera? Opté por no decir nada. Gertrud, Gerda y Friedel no le dieron ninguna pista definitiva a la Sra. Haertel tampoco.

Recordé que Peter actuó de manera extraña y distraída últimamente. Tal vez, estaba fabricando el plan para irse de casa. La Señora Haertel se fue desconsolada y llorando. No pudimos darle pistas de adónde fue.

Reflexioné sobre cuál fue la razón por la que se fue de casa. Nos dijo que su madre le impuso reglas estrictas y lo trató como a un niño. Se olvidó de que ahora es un adulto y merece algo de libertad y respeto por su forma de pensar. La madre, que perdió a su marido en la Segunda Guerra Mundial, solo tuvo un hijo, Peter. Ella lo trató como a un niño y se aferró a él con tanta fuerza que al hijo le molestó su completo control. Se fue de casa con la esperanza de liberarse y vivir como un adulto. Ciertamente esperaba que no se hubiera unido a la Legión Extranjera Francesa. Sus soldados no fueron bien tratados. Oré para que Dios, que conocía el paradero y los pensamientos de Peter, lo protegiera y lo llevara a casa sano y salvo con su afligida madre, para quien él significaba todo. Le pedí a Dios que consolara el corazón sangrante de la madre y enjugara sus lágrimas mientras esperaba el regreso de su hijo. Mi espera por una respuesta positiva a las muchas solicitudes de trabajo finalmente me dio su recompensa. El Dr. Samietz de Gelnhausen y el Dr. Flaecher de Waibstadt pidieron más información. Al día siguiente, envié por correo el material solicitado con una foto mía—al fin, un rayo de esperanza para conseguir un puesto antes de que terminara la escuela. También recibí 150.00 MA de mi hermano Edmund. Fui inmediatamente con la Sra. Mohrmann y pagué el alquiler de agosto. Ella dijo: "Sabes que también vence el alquiler de septiembre".

"Sí, lo sé. Le pagaré tan pronto como tenga más dinero. Por favor sea paciente; este es todo el dinero que tengo en este momento."

Me entristeció que ella no entendiera mi terrible situación financiera; tampoco el Sr. Doebereiner de la Oficina del Oficina de Rentas Internas. Escribió una carta con otra excusa pero sin dinero. Aunque me sentía mal siempre pidiéndole dinero a mi hermano, le escribí pidiéndole que me enviara más cada vez que pudiera. Todavía debía dos meses de matrícula y un mes de alojamiento y comida. Cuando fui al estudio bíblico por la noche, hablé de mi problema financiero con el Sr. Pfeiffer. Tuvo la amabilidad de ofrecerse a escribir una carta al Sr. Doebereiner rogándole que pague al menos la matrícula y el alojamiento y la comida de los últimos dos meses. Le dije Dr. Glaeser ya había escrito a la oficina del IRS; esperemos hasta que obtengamos una respuesta primero. Estaba emocionalmente agotada. Antes de quedarme dormida, oré a Dios: "Tú conoces mi situación desesperada; nada es imposible para Ti. Confío en ti de todo corazón en que resolverás todo lo mejor para mí. Cuida a mi madre, dale fuerzas para que se recupere bien de la cirugía. Consuela a la madre desconsolada de Peter. Evita que Peter cometa un error del que se arrepentirá por el resto de su vida. Padre Celestial, Tú conoces las necesidades de cada persona y las satisfarás en tu tiempo". Después de comprometer a todos y mi vida al cuidado amoroso de Dios, me quedé dormida en paz.

Llegó el último mes de clases. Recibí septiembre con emociones encontradas. Disfruté de la escuela, pero me sentí terrible y avergonzada de pedirle dinero continuamente a mi hermano Edmund, principalmente cuando Emma escribió que él no ganaba demasiado mucho últimamente. Tampoco mis hermanos Georg o Richard. Richard todavía era un aprendiz y ganaba solo 30,00 MA por mes, viviendo en las instalaciones del herrero. Mi madre apenas recibía lo suficiente para pagar el alquiler y comprar alimentos para ella y mi hermano menor, Horst, de solo doce años.

Una carta de Hermann me hizo feliz. Incluyó un hermoso verso en la carta.

Así como las estrellas giran eternamente en armonía,
¿Así serán también nuestras vidas?
En lo inmenso y diminuto aparece Dios.
Toda la creación se mueve en ritmo
La alegría es su noble canción.
Sólo los humanos no aprecian su belleza
Y buscan fatigosamente otros placeres.
Amigos busquen el sentido en las maravillas de Dios
Para que la alegría llene sus corazones.

Hermann cerró con el dicho:

"Mira hacia las estrellas y presta atención a tu camino".

Me di cuenta de que teníamos mucho en común. Ambos disfrutamos de la naturaleza y las maravillas de Dios con los cambios perpetuos, complaciendo nuestros sentidos. Amábamos la música clásica y folclórica que nos levantaba el ánimo y la buena literatura, especialmente la poesía, que nos hablaba al corazón. Ambos no sólo habíamos establecido altos estándares morales para nuestras vidas, sino que nos adherimos a ellos sin importar el sacrificio que tomara. Cada carta profundizó mi respeto y admiración por él. Los recuerdos de los pocos momentos que pasamos juntos siempre serán apreciados por los dos. Yo simplemente no estaba lista todavía para comprometerme con el matrimonio. Le pedí a Dios que me guiara para poder tomar la decisión correcta en el momento correcto.

El tiempo que pasé en Essen terminaría en menos de un mes y comenzaría una nueva etapa de mi vida. Cada momento que tuve libre, fui al lago. Siempre llevaba mis cuadernos y tenía buenas intenciones de estudiar. Sin embargo, algunas veces agradables interrupciones me impidieron hacerlo. Un sábado por la tarde, me senté en la orilla del lago, salpicando el agua de un lado a otro con los pies. Un viento hizo olas rodando hasta la orilla. Escuché el sonido rítmico y observé las olas blancas rompiendo en la playa de arena. estaba soñando despierta. Cuando miré hacia arriba, un velero se acercó a la orilla y una voz llamó:

"Fraeulein, ¿quieres navegar con nosotros?" Primero, estaba sorprendida y reacia. Entonces pensé que nunca había tenido la oportunidad de navegar antes. ¿Por qué no?

"Sí, con mucho gusto", respondí antes de darme cuenta de que los dos marineros habían aterrizado el bote en la playa junto a mí. Un joven salió del bote y me ayudó a subir. Después, caminó con el velero hasta que estuvo en aguas más profundas, luego subió a bordo él mismo. Un marinero manejaba las velas, el otro el timón. El viento hinchó las velas y despegamos hacia el centro del lago. Qué estimulante para mí deslizarme tranquilamente sobre la superficie del agua. Siempre había querido ir a navegar. Ahora mi deseo se había hecho realidad. Disfruté de la experiencia que los dos marineros me presentaron de una manera tan inesperada. Ambos marineros estaban tan absortos en maniobrar el barco que apenas hablaban. Solo sonrieron cuando me miraron y vieron lo mucho que disfruté navegando con ellos. La tarde pasó demasiado rápido. Me llevaron de regreso al mismo lugar donde me recogieron. Nos presentamos antes de separarnos. Sin preguntas, sin demandas, solo disfrutando de la tarde navegando juntos en el hermoso lago Baldeney. No podría agradecerles lo suficiente por cumplir uno de mis sueños.

Otro sueño se hizo realidad cuando recibí la primera respuesta positiva a mis muchas solicitudes. El Dr. Samietz de Gelnhausen me ofreció 200.00 MA por mes, una habitación con calefacción central y diez días de vacaciones pagadas el primer año. Podía empezar el 10 de octubre de 1955. Inmediatamente le respondí que aceptaría su oferta y que podría comenzar a la hora sugerida. Confirmó mi aceptación con una carta cortés. Agradecí a Dios por permitirme poner en práctica todos los conocimientos que había adquirido en el La escuela del Dr. de Medicina de Glaeser. También estaba encantada de tener nueve días para pasar en casa antes de empezar a trabajar. Compartí las buenas noticias con mis compañeras de cuarto. Ellas también se alegraron por mí.

Hacia la noche, Gertrud y Gerda entraron en nuestra habitación. Todas nos sentamos en la cama y contamos historias divertidas. Nos reímos fuerte. La señora Mohrmann abrió la puerta, nos gritó y nos reprendió por sentarnos en la cama. Me sorprendió el lenguaje duro que usó y todo mi cuerpo tembló. No dijimos una palabra y esperamos hasta que se fue. Luego Gerda y Gertrud se fueron a su habitación. Después de calmarme, decidí ir a la clase de Biblia. El señor Pfeiffer habló sobre cómo lidiar con las deficiencias de otras personas. Si hay un conflicto entre usted y otras personas, revise su conciencia antes de acusar a la otra persona; ese fue el mensaje correcto para ese día. Pensé en cómo manejar el incidente con la Sra. Mohrmann. Le pedí a Dios que me perdonara si hacía algo malo. A su vez, también la perdonaría y la trataría con la misma cortesía que antes. Gerda creó una situación más desagradable, habló mal de nosotras tres y luego se quejó de la Sra. Mohrmann. Estaba enfadada con nosotros y era descortés. Durante el último mes de clases, me entristeció que se desarrollara tal discordia entre nosotras cuando teníamos que estudiar intensamente para los exámenes finales.

Un día tuvimos una hora y media de descanso entre clases. Christel, de quien me había hecho amiga, y yo fuimos a la habitación donde estaban las máquinas de escribir. Practiqué mecanografiar. Christel recitó algunas citas. Me gustaron mucho y le pedí que me las escribiera.

1. *No pidamos una carga ligera sino una espalda fuerte.*
2. *Quien quiera llegar a las alturas tiene que descargar peso.*
3. *Nuestro anhelo de felicidad es tan ilimitado que solo puede ser satisfecho en el cielo.*
4. *Si quieres conocerte a ti mismo, actúa y sabrás quién eres.*
5. *Mi corazón, te preguntaré ¿qué es el amor? Dime,*
6. *Dos almas y un pensamiento. Dos corazones y un latido".*

Después de las clases, volví al apartamento y la Sra. Mohrmann todavía nos reprendió durante la cena. Me sentí tan mal de que nuestra estadía terminara de una manera tan poco armoniosa. Oré a Dios para que me mostrara dónde había hecho algo malo y que me perdonara, y yo perdonara a la Sra. Mohrmann por herir mis sentimientos. La señora Mohrmann también expuso los rasgos negativos del carácter de Friedel y me hizo responsable por no corregirla y ser amable con Friedel. También se quejó de Gerda y Gertrud por no seguir todos sus deseos. Todas nos sentimos terribles, nos disculpamos con la Sra. Mohrmann, nos perdonamos mutuamente y esperamos que se restableciera la paz y la armonía.

Cada día traía más estudio y exámenes. Los pensamientos de regresar a casa con mi familia me ocupaban cada vez más a medida que se acercaba el final de la escuela. Tenía muchas ganas de ver a mi madre, Emma, Edmund, Horst y Bernie, el hijo de mi hermana Emma. Hermann también escribió que planeaba unas vacaciones durante octubre y que pasaría algún tiempo con su familia en Essingen. También mencionó que su madre estaba organizando una reunión familiar cuando él estuviera en casa y que estaba ansioso por verme.

Una semana antes de que terminara la escuela, recibí una carta del gobierno con un cheque adjunto. Estaba agradecida de que el Sr. Dobereiner, finalmente, después de aproximadamente un año y medio, respondió positivamente a la carta del Dr. Glaeser, que escribió hace algún tiempo. Al día siguiente, fui a la oficina del Dr. Glaeser, pagué el saldo de mi matrícula y le agradecí por haberme ayudado a completar mi educación médica. Pagué el saldo por alojamiento y comida. Le agradecí a la Sra. Mohrmann por ser paciente, y esperar el dinero. Volvió a ser cortés, lo que me hizo feliz de que la paz y la armonía regresaran entre nosotros. Antes de quedarme dormida, le di gracias a Dios, tenía suficiente dinero para pagar mis deudas, terminé la escuela con buenas notas y tenía un puesto asegurado en el consultorio de un médico. Le pedí a Dios que me diera un corazón amoroso para cuidar a los pacientes de la Clñinica del Dr. Samietz. Mi gran deseo era servir y honrar a Dios con todo mi corazón y alma de la mejor manera posible.

Despedirme de nuestros instructores y compañeros de clase, por quienes había desarrollado un cariño, llenó mi corazón de emociones encontradas. Estaba triste porque probablemente nunca los volvería a ver, pero me alegró haber obtenido una profesión y un trabajo en la clínica de un médico para practicar mis habilidades médicas y prácticas recién adquiridas. Tenía muchas ganas de ver a mi familia. Empaqué mis pertenencias en mi maleta de madera y compré mi boleto de tren con dos días de anticipación.

El 30 de septiembre de 1955, todos los estudiantes se reunieron en un gran salón y el Dr. Glaeser entregó las boletas de calificaciones finales y luego nos deseó lo mejor. Cada estudiante estrechó su mano antes de salir del salón de clases. Expresé mi profunda gratitud al Dr. Glaeser por ayudarme a obtener la ayuda del gobierno y terminar el seminario. Al revisar mi boleta de calificaciones, estaba satisfecha con recibir principalmente buenas calificaciones, una muy buena en taquigrafía y una satisfactoria en cirugía menor. Me gustó la materia, pero no sabía por qué saqué una calificación tan baja y cómo pude haberlo mejorado. El jueves por la noche, todos fuimos una vez más a través del bosque hasta el lago Baldeney, que atesoramos durante nuestra estancia en Essen. Todo el tiempo que pasamos en el lago quedarían como recuerdos inolvidables de nuestra juventud y parte de nuestra vida.

El viernes 30 de septiembre, Friedel, Gerda y Gertrud se despidieron de la Sra. Mohrmann y de mi. Se fueron un día antes. Yo estaba contenta de que la Sra. Mohrmann mostró sus mejores modales y les deseó lo mejor para el futuro. Abracé a Gerda, Gertrud y Friedel y expresé mis mejores deseos para su futuro también. Intercambiamos direcciones por si acaso queríamos mantener correspondencia. Les pedí perdón si había herido sus sentimientos sin querer. Friedel hizo lo mismo. Todas nos separamos armoniosamente. Me fui al día siguiente, y la Sra. Mohrmann fue muy amable conmigo. La disputa temporal había pasado, y el aire volvió a ser claro. Me disculpé por haber herido sus sentimientos sin querer. Me abrazó y me dijo: "Todo está olvidado y no estoy enfadada contigo".

Me fui sintiéndome aliviada y contenta. Tomé mi maleta y mi bolso, bajé las escaleras y fui a la estación de tren para tomar un tren temprano a Duisburg donde conectaría con otros trenes a Landau/Palatine y Knoeringen/Essingen, mi destino final. El viaje en tren tomó menos de veinte minutos hasta Duisburg, donde tuve que bajarme para tomar el tren a Koblenz. Tuve poco tiempo para cambiar a la vía donde saldría el tren para Koblenz.

Después de embarcarme en el tren y acomodarme en el vagón, solo un anciano entró en el mismo vagón de tren.

Cojeaba y caminaba con bastón. Llevaba un estuche de violín que colocó cuidadosamente a su lado en el asiento. Debe haber sido un instrumento valioso que no quería que se dañara al caer del compartimento superior. Nos sentamos en bancos opuestos en silencio y esperamos que el tren saliera de la estación. Vimos las casas pasar más y más rápido hasta dejar atrás la ciudad de Duisburgo. Después de un rato, el caballero pasajero se presentó como Karl Berger con un apretón de manos. Respondí y dije mi nombre.

Empezamos una animada conversación sobre música. El señor Berger me dijo que tocaba el violín en la Orquesta Sinfónica de Essen y que iba a visitar a su hijo Charles en Koblenz. Su hijo era un virtuoso del piano y ambos disfrutaban tocar juntos. Le gustaba especialmente tocar composiciones de Mozart, Schubert y Beethoven. Le dije que apreciaba la música de los tres compositores, pero que también disfrutaba de las representaciones de ópera, especialmente de las óperas de Giuseppe Verdi. Él, por su parte, prefería la música instrumental. También hablamos de literatura e historia. Su disposición alegre se transformó en tristeza cuando habló de la Segunda Guerra Mundial. Despreciaba las crueles acciones y el régimen de Hitler, pero no le gustaba cómo los aliados humillaban y maltrataban al pueblo alemán. A pesar de que el presidente Roosevelt y el primer ministro Winston Churchill habían prometido que vencedores y vencidos serían tratados por igual, acordaron ceder algunas de las regiones orientales de nuestro país a Rusia y Polonia como parte del tratado de paz. Le dije al Sr. Berger que yo había vivido¿? / nacido¿? en Prusia del Este, y ahora Polonia reclamaba la parte sur de Prusia del Este. Probablemente nunca podré volver a mi lugar de origen. Hicimos una pausa por un momento, reflexionando sobre las nefastas consecuencias de la Segunda Guerra Mundial, que nos entristecieron. Entonces el Sr. Berger inició nuestra conversación sobre literatura y los poetas y autores favoritos de Alemania. Estábamos tan envueltos en la conversación que prestamos poca atención al pasar por Cologne y Bonn, La actual capital de Alemania. Cuando llegamos a Koblenz, ambos desembarcamos, nos despedimos y nos deseamos lo mejor para el futuro.

Tuve apenas unos minutos para encontrar la vía por donde saldría el tren rumbo a Mainz. Los trenes en Alemania son principalmente puntuales, pero llegué a tiempo. el vagón se llenó con pasajeros. Tuve la suerte de conseguir un asiento junto a la ventana. Esta vez quería observar el paisaje y no involucrarme en conversaciones. Miré por la ventana y disfruté del hermoso paisaje del valle del Rin ubicado entre las cadenas montañosas de Hunsrueck y Taunus. Los viñedos estaban cambiando a sus coloridos tonos de amarillo, naranja, rojo y óxido. La recolección de las uvas había comenzado temprano. La gente se reunía en los campos para recoger las uvas. Mis ojos se deleitaron con los brillantes colores del otoño. Parecía como si Dios hubiera pintado una obra de arte exquisita usando pinceles gigantes y todos los colores de la paleta. Los alemanes celebraron el Día de Acción de Gracias el 1 de octubre. Los granjeros y otras personas llevaron algo de su trigo cultivado en casa al altar de la iglesia, agradeciendo a Dios por una cosecha abundante. Los pobres de la comunidad recibieron las ofrendas y los alimentos. Dado que el 1 de octubre cayó en sábado este año, el Día de Acción de Gracias se celebró en la iglesia el domingo, 2 de octubre. Estaría en casa a tiempo para celebrar este día especial con mi familia.

Llegamos a Mainz, situada en la confluencia de los ríos Rin y Meno. Mainz es la capital de Renania-Palatino. Es conocida como la casa natal de Johannes Gutenberg, quien inventó la primera imprenta con letras metálicas móviles. En 1454 imprimió las primeras cuarenta y dos páginas de la Biblia y completó la impresión de toda la Biblia en 1455. Como cada página contenía cuarenta y dos líneas, la llamó la Biblia de cuarenta y dos páginas. Algunas páginas las había adornado con diseños artísticos. Johannes Gutenberg también hizo su propia tinta. Después de terminar de imprimir casi doscientas Biblias, también imprimió un Libro de Salmos, que revolucionó Europa y el mundo. Por primera vez, el público podía leer libros impresos. Antes, todos los manuscritos eran escritos a mano por monjes y solo eran accesibles para los papas, el clero y los intelectuales. Cuando el editor alemán trajo la primera Biblia a los Estados Unidos en 1847, los oficiales de aduanas se quitaron los sombreros en reverencia a la Santa Biblia, la palabra de Dios. 1946, un año después de la Segunda Guerra Mundial, Mainz construyó, nombró y dedicó una universidad en honor a Johannes Gutenberg.

Tuve que cambiar de tren en Mainz y luego viajar a través de Schifferstadt, Neustadt y Landau a Knoerringen-Essingen. Viajando a lo largo de Vine Road (Weinstrasse), observé los coloridos campos de uva y los bosques de la montaña Haardt. Entre las hayas y los robles crecían abundantes castaños. El sol de la tarde hizo brillar los colores otoñales del bosque. Y los recuerdos de las muchas caminatas que solíamos hacer con el grupo de jóvenes cobraron vida cuando recogíamos castañas maduras en el bosque.

Sólo un cambio de tren más en Landau a Knoerringen-Essingen, y estaría en casa. Como no teníamos teléfonos para avisarles a mis hermanos la hora de mi llegada, nadie me recibió en la última estación de tren. Me bajé del tren y llevé mi maleta a casa. Cuando llegué al pueblo, me encontré con algunos aldeanos parados en la calle conversando. Los sábados, todos barrían la calle frente a sus casas o comercios. Mis pasos eran cada vez más rápidos a medida que me acercaba al lugar donde vivíamos. Dejé mi maleta, abrí la puerta y corrí hacia mi madre para abrazarla primero, luego mi hermana Emma y los hermanos Edmund, Richard y Horst, que estaban en casa este fin de semana. Luego recogí a mi sobrinito Bernie y le di un gran abrazo.

"¡Vaya, cómo has crecido, Bernie!"

"Sí, tengo tres años y no tengo esposa",

Respondió Bernie. Sonreí,

"Joven, todavía puedes esperar un tiempo hasta que encuentres una esposa". Todos me recibieron con cariño. Edmund trajo mi maleta y la puso en el banco de la cocina. Saqué los dulces y le di algunos a Bernie y le ofrecí algunos a mi familia. Mamá y Emma habían preparado un plato especial, Sauerbraten, albóndigas de patata rellenas y col lombarda. De postre, Emma hizo strudel de manzana. Seguro que sabía bien. Después de la cena, hablé sobre la escuela y de que el lunes 10 de octubre comenzaría a trabajar para el Dr. Samietz en Gelnhausen. Edmund y Emma expresaron sus sentimientos al estar contentos de que hubiera terminado la escuela con éxito y obtenido un puesto en el consultorio de un médico. Mamá permaneció taciturna. Sin embargo, cuando me miró y sonrió, lo acepté como su aprobación. Habría apreciado aún más su consentimiento verbal.

El domingo, después de escuchar las campanas de la iglesia sonar tres veces, todos caminamos a la iglesia para celebrar el día de Acción de Gracias. La iglesia estaba a solo media cuadra del apartamento. Después de la liturgia de apertura del servicio, los campesinos trajeron frutos de sus cosechas al altar. El coro de la iglesia cantó la canción "Ahora, agradezcamos todos a nuestro Dios", expresando gratitud a Dios por una buena cosecha. El mensaje del sermón enfatizó las bendiciones de dar y las abundantes recompensas recibidas a cambio. Después del servicio de la iglesia, conocí a varios miembros del coro y al pastor Bruenings, nuestro vecino. El pastor Bruenings me saludó:

"Me alegro de verte de nuevo. ¿Has vuelto para quedarte?"

"No, me iré el próximo domingo. Conseguí un puesto en el consultorio de un médico en Gelnhausen".

"Dios te bendiga y te deseo lo mejor".

"Gracias, Pastor Bruenings; Volveré de vez en cuando."

El lunes, Edmund y Richard regresaron a su lugar de trabajo. Dijeron que estarían alrededor del siguiente fin de semana. Los siguientes días, lavé y planché toda mi ropa y clasifiqué todas mis cosas. Entonces, el jueves por la noche fui a la reunión del grupo de jóvenes DJO. Me abrazaron y expresamos nuestra alegría de vernos de nuevo. Hermann, quien pasó sus breves vacaciones en casa, también asistió a la reunión; su abrazo duró más. Ver a Hermann nuevamente llenó mi corazón de alegría y recordé todos los momentos felices de nuestra maravillosa amistad. Nuestras miradas se cruzaban con frecuencia expresando nuestra admiración y cariño. Habíamos desarrollado un cariño el uno por el otro, y la separación entristeció nuestros corazones. Pero nos prometimos mantenernos en contacto en el futuro. Cerramos la reunión con la canción: "Ade zur guten Nacht jetzt wird der Schluss gemacht, das ich muss scheiden". (Adiós, buenas noches, ha llegado la hora de partir). Se me hizo un nudo en la garganta cuando nos despedimos de cada persona. Traté de sonreir cuando Hermann se me acercó. Me invitó a unirme a su reunión familiar el próximo sábado 8 de octubre a las 3:00 p. m. También estaría su tío Heiner, que era artista.

"Gracias; Me encantaría ir contigo. Tengo muchas ganas de ver a tu tío y a tu familia".

"Me alegra que te unas a nosotros. Nos vemos el sábado a las 3:00 pm"

El jueves, di un paseo rápido en bicicleta a Landau. Visité a los dos líderes juveniles, Heinz Kraemer y Heinz Equart, para agradecerles por haberme dirigido y ayudado a obtener un título como médica y asistente médico práctico. También les comenté la dificultad que tuve para recibir ayuda del gobierno. Finalmente se concedió el último mes de clases. Ambos se alegraron de saber que todo salió bien al final y que había asegurado un puesto. También pasé por mi boutique favorita y compré una blusa blanca y una falda negra para ir a la iglesia en ocasiones especiales. Era un día frío pero soleado, y disfruté de la brisa fresca que acariciaba mis mejillas mientras pedaleaba de regreso a Essingen. Envié oraciones de agradecimiento a Dios por haberme guiado tan maravillosamente a través de todas las dificultades. Pronto tendré la oportunidad de servirle ayudando a pacientes en una clínica médica.

El sábado por la tarde, caminé hasta la casa de Hermann. En el patio, el tío Heiner había instalado una colección de pinturas. Las ofreció en venta y ya había vendido algunas a la gente del pueblo. Admiraba mucho sus pinturas al óleo y sus pinturas al pastel. Me llamó la atención un óleo con una cruz sobre un cerro rodeado de bosques al atardecer. Me hubiera gustado comprar el cuadro, pero claro, no tenía dinero. Este cuadro despertó en mí el deseo de pintar. Pensé:

"Si tan solo pudiera pintar así, sería muy feliz".

Después de que terminó la exhibición pública, la Sra. Jaeger invitó a la familia, parientes y amigos cercanos a su gran comedor en el piso de arriba para tomar un pastel y un café. La señora Jaeger horneaba deliciosos pasteles y tocaba bien la guitarra. El tío Heiner era un virtuoso del arpa, Helge tocaba el piano y Hermann el violín. Limpiamos las mesas y luego nos reunimos alrededor del piano y comenzamos a cantar canciones folklóricas acompañadas por el piano, la guitarra, el violín y el arpa. La alegre música llenó la habitación y mi corazón, así como los corazones de todos los presentes. De vez en cuando, el tío Heiner cantaba un solo mientras tocaba el arpa. Me recordó mucho al rey David cantando uno de sus salmos. Expresó mucho sentimiento en sus canciones. Su personalidad irradiaba amor y paz. El solo hecho de estar en su presencia me hizo sentir alegre y serena. También escribió poesía inspiradora. Viajó a varios lugares para pintar escenas pintorescas. Amaba los paisajes montañosos de los Alpes, que plasmó magníficamente en sus óleos. Después de que terminó la sesión de música, me despedí de la Sra. Jaeger y su hermano, el tío Heiner, y todos los miembros de la familia e invitados. Hermann me acompañó hasta la puerta. Le agradecí por permitirme pasar este evento especial con su familia y parientes. Le di la dirección del lugar donde trabajaría. Prometimos seguir en contacto. Me deseó lo mejor cuando nos despedimos con un abrazo que expresaba nuestra profunda amistad, que prometíamos mantener. Me dijo que aún tenía vacaciones hasta el miércoles de la próxima semana. Desafortunadamente, tuve que irme el domingo y comenzar a trabajar el lunes.

"Lamento que no podamos viajar juntos hasta Frankfurt.
Me pregunto cuándo podremos volver a vernos".

"Ojalá pudiéramos; tal vez tengamos la oportunidad de encontrarnos nuevamente durante nuestras próximas vacaciones." Me abrazó una vez más y me besó en la frente,

"Adiós". Dije "Adiós" y me fui.

Cuando regresé a nuestro apartamento, mamá, Emma, Bernie y mis cuatro hermanos me esperaban. Todos cenamos juntos. Emma nos dijo que ella y Bernie podrían emigrar a los Estados Unidos. Gustav, que se quedó en Aalen con sus padres y su familia, quería que ella también lo acompañara. Desafortunadamente, su esposo estaba más apegado a sus padres y hermanos que a su esposa e hijo. Él y su familia no trataron a Emma con amabilidad. No se sentía cómoda volviendo con ellos, pero no tenía muchas opciones. Me dio mucha pena escuchar sobre su sufrimiento emocional y que nos dejaría. Pero amaba a su hijo, Bernie, y quería que él también creciera con su padre. Gustav, su esposo y toda su familia ya habían solicitado la visa de inmigración para ellos y también para mi hermana y Bernie. Todos esperaron a que se aprobaran los documentos finales de inmigración.

El domingo por la mañana no pude ir a la iglesia. Después de despedirme de mi madre y mis hermanos, mi hermana Emma y Bernie, mi hermano Edmund me llevó a mí y a mi maleta de madera en su motocicleta a la estación de tren de Landau. Elegí un tren temprano para poder llegar a Gelnhausen por la tarde. Tuve que cambiar de tren en Mannheim y Frankfurt para conectar con Gelnhausen. El tren viajó a lo largo del río Main. Fui al vagón donde estaba el restaurante del tren, donde me di el gusto de una taza de café y un trozo de pastel. Vi pasar el hermoso paisaje. Poco después de regresar a mi asiento, el tren se detuvo y llegué a Gelnhausen.

PRIMERA POSICIÓN EN UNA CLÍNICA MÉDICA

Un caballero me ayudó con mi maleta. Me preguntó adónde iba.

Le dije: "Voy a Ir a la clínica del Dr. Samietz."

"Voy en esa dirección y te mostraré dónde vive. ¿Qué te lleva a él un domingo?"

"Soy asistente médica y comenzaré a trabajar para él mañana".

"Buena suerte. Dr. Samietz es un poco duro, pero es un buen médico".

"Gracias por decirme que el Dr. Samietz es rudo; Tendré que adaptarme a su personalidad".

Charlamos unos minutos y antes de que me diera cuenta llegamos a la calle Barbarroja 6. El caballero señaló la casa de piedra color terracota, "Aquí es donde el Dr. Samietz vive. Tiene su clínica en el mismo edificio."

Le agradecí al caballero por su ayuda. Entonces llamé a la puerta grande. En breve una señora abrió la puerta. Nos presentamos.

"Soy Fraeulein Bonacker, la asistente del doctor."

"Soy Frau Samietz. Adelante. Te estábamos esperando."

Tomé mi maleta y entré en un inmenso pasillo con una escalera de color marrón oscuro que conducía.

"Sígueme; Te llevaré a la habitación donde te hospedarás." Recogí mi maleta y seguí a la Sra. Samietz. Abrió la puerta de una pequeña habitación con una cama, una mesa y dos sillas, y una cómoda.

"Esta es la habitación para ti. Te mostraré la clínica mañana por la mañana antes de que empieces a trabajar a las 8:00 a. m. Ahora, solo desempaca tus cosas. Te veo mañana."

"Gracias señora Samietz; Nos vemos abajo mañana por la mañana.

La señora Samietz agregó: "Por cierto, el inodoro y la ducha están al frente a esta habitación. Tendrás que compartirlo con mi hija Úrsula".

"Gracias; eso está bien."

Primero, miré por la ventana. Vi parte de la ciudad a la izquierda y una colina con las ruinas de un castillo a la derecha. Me complació tener una linda vista. Luego levanté la maleta sobre la cama y desempaqué mis pertenencias. Colgué los vestidos, blusas y faldas en el perchero y coloqué el resto en diferentes cajones. Empujé los tres pares de zapatos que traje debajo de la cama y también mi maleta de madera. Un radiador de vapor calentaba la habitación. Junto a la puerta había un fregadero de cerámica con agua corriente fría y caliente. La habitación era sencilla, pero estaba satisfecha de tener mi propio lugar por primera vez. Todavía no estaba segura de qué arreglos podía hacer para mis comidas. Comí algunas galletas que había traído conmigo para esta noche y bebí el agua del grifo solo para satisfacer mi sed. Antes de acostarme, leí un rato. Puse la alarma que había traído conmigo a las 6:00 a. m. Entonces oré y agradecí a Dios que tenía un lugar para quedarme y trabajar. Le pedí a Dios que me mostrara Su camino en el nuevo capítulo de mi vida, trabajando en una clínica médica.

Me levanté a las 6:00 am. al día siguiente. Comí algunas galletas más y bebí un vaso de agua caliente del grifo. Me cepillé los dientes, me lavé, me vestí y bajé a las 7:45 a. m. La puerta de la clínica todavía estaba cerrada. Encontré la puerta de la cocina abierta, donde vi a una señora lavando platos. Entré y me presenté. Me dijo que se llamaba Lioba y que trabajaba para el Dr. y la Sra. Samietz como empleada doméstica y cocinaba para ellos. La cocina era toda blanca, fundamental, sin adornos. Hablamos durante unos minutos. Cuando escuché que alguien bajaba las escaleras, fui al pasillo a saludar a la Sra. Samietz. Me dio los buenos días y abrió la puerta de la clínica.

"Esta es la sala de examinación, donde el Dr. Samietz revisa y trata a los pacientes. Aplicarás inyecciones y harás algunas pruebas a los pacientes aquí".

En el centro de la habitación había una mesa de examen. Una pequeña mesa con dos sillas estaba cerrada a la puerta preparada con los elementos necesarios para aplicar inyecciones intravenosas. En el lado opuesto había armarios montados en la pared y otros en el suelo. Una cama también estaba contra una pared. La señora Samietz abrió la puerta de la sala de consulta. Un escritorio con una silla grande detrás para el médico y dos sillas más pequeñas para los pacientes al frente. La señora Samietz señaló un escritorio más pequeño con una silla en el lado opuesto. Sobre el escritorio había una vieja máquina de escribir.

"Aquí es donde te sentarás. Los registros de los pacientes están en los cajones. No trabajamos con cita previa. Cada vez que un paciente ingresa a la sala de espera, sacas su expediente. Llamarás a los pacientes para que vean al médico en la secuencia en que llegan. Luego, colocarás el historial en el escritorio del médico. Antes de que el paciente se vaya, asegúrate de ingresar cada procedimiento o inyección administrada en el cuadro. Luego los archivas en orden alfabético".

Luego, abrió la puerta de la gran sala de espera con sillas colocadas a lo largo de todas las paredes. Una mesa baja cubierta con material de lectura estaba en el centro de la habitación. Abrió la puerta que conducía al exterior, por donde entrarían los pacientes. El primer paciente ya estaba esperando. La señora Samietz la saludó, "Buenos días Sra. Fehl; Quiero que conozcas a nuestra nueva asistente médica, la señorita Hildegard Bonacker." La saludé también y le respondí:

"Es un placer conocerla, Sra. Fehl. Entre y tome asiento en la sala de espera".

Entonces la Sra. Samietz me mostró otra habitación con una colosal máquina de rayos X, "Esta es la sala de rayos X. ¿Sabes cómo tomar radiografías?

"No, no aprendimos a operar una máquina de rayos X, pero estoy dispuesta a aprender a tomar radiografías".

Escuché pasos bajando las escaleras. Dr. Samietz se reunió con nosotros en el pasillo después de que salimos de la sala de rayos X. Lo saludé, "Buenos días Dr. Samietz."

"Buenos días, señorita Bonacker. Bienvenida a nuestra clínica."

"Gracias."

Su aspecto físico me sorprendió. Pesaba mucho más de trescientas libras. El peso de sus mejillas caía prácticamente hasta la barbilla. Seguimos al Dr. Samietz a la sala de consulta. Se puso su bata blanca antes de sentarse detrás de su escritorio. Su barriga protuberante descansaba sobre la silla. Sin embargo, su sonrisa era genuina y amistosa. La señora Samietz sacó el expediente del primer paciente, la Sra. Fehl, y me dijo que la llamara para que entrara. Coloqué el expediente del paciente en el escritorio del Dr. Samietz. Me enteré de que la Sra. Fehl tenía diabetes y necesitaba volver a surtir una receta. Dr. Samietz escribió la receta, le preguntó cómo se sentía y luego le dijo que volviera en un mes. La sala de espera comenzó a llenarse. La señora Samietz me dijo el nombre de cada paciente, luego saqué sus gráficos y los alineé en la secuencia en la que venían. Vimos un paciente tras otro, y antes de que nos diéramos cuenta, era mediodía; La señora Samietz cerró la puerta exterior de la sala de espera. El Dr. y la Sra. Samietz tomarían un descanso para almorzar hasta las 4:00 p. m. Permanecí en la oficina hasta que archivé todos los gráficos y ordené las cosas en la sala de examen. La señora Samietz me indicó que comenzara a las 3:00 p.m. para familiarizarme con los nombres de los pacientes y los artículos en la sala de examen.

Para entonces, mi estómago gruñó. Pero me quedé la hora extra, archivé todos los gráficos, ordené todas las revistas en la sala de espera y revisé el contenido de los gabinetes en la sala de examen. Fui a la cocina, donde Lioba estaba lavando los platos, y le pregunté dónde estaba la tienda de comestibles más cercana. Luego subí las escaleras, tomé mi bolso, me puse una chaqueta y me fui de compras. Compré seis rollos, 100 gramos de salchicha suave (Metwurst), lo suficiente para untar en los rollos. También compré un tarro pequeño de mermelada, 100 gramos de mantequilla, un cartón de leche y pan de centeno para el desayuno. Comí dos de mis panecillos y bebí parte de la leche para el almuerzo. El primer mes tuve que ser frugal con el dinero que me dio mi hermano. Una vez que recibiera mi salario, podría pagar más alimentos y tal vez algunas frutas también. Pero por ahora, me alegré de tener algo para poner en mi estómago hambriento. A las 3:00 p. m., volví a bajar. Mi habitación estaba en el tercer piso. Lioba me dijo que el comedor, la sala y el dormitorio del Dr. y la Sra. Samietz estaban en el segundo piso; también estaba una habitación privada del Dr. Samietz donde guardaba sus libros de medicina y se ocupaba de su correspondencia y llamadas telefónicas. Tanto la Dr. como la Sra. Samietz tomaban una siesta todos los días después del almuerzo. La comida, preparada por Lioba, era enviada con un montaplatos manual desde la cocina hasta el comedor. Los platos sucios se enviaban de nuevo a la cocina para lavarlos y guardarlos en los armarios de la cocina.

A las 4:00 p.m., el Dra. y la Sra. Samietz bajaron las escaleras. Ya había abierto la sala de espera poco antes. Saqué el historial del primer paciente y lo puse primero en mi escritorio y en el escritorio del médico después de que se sentó. La mayoría de los pacientes venían por renovaciones de recetas, gripe, otros problemas de salud menores y algunas inyecciones. La señora Samietz me mostró las jeringas y ampollas esterilizadas con el medicamento que recibía el paciente. Observé con mucha atención y pude aplicar la tercera inyección intermuscular por mí misma. La señora Samietz le dio al paciente la opción de recibir una inyección en el brazo o en el trasero. Yo hice lo mismo. La señora Samietz demostró cómo administrar una inyección intravenosa de calcio. La señora Samietz me preguntó si había puesto alguna inyección intravenosa. Le dije que no aprendimos a poner inyecciones intravenosas.

"Hoy, tenemos un paciente que viene para una inyección de calcio. El médico te mostrará cómo aplicar inyecciones intravenosas. Solemos dejar que el paciente se acueste en la cama. Si inyectas el calcio rápidamente, el paciente puede desmayarse. Se presenta en ampolla de 10 ml. Rompió la parte superior de la ampolla y llenó la jeringa con el calcio líquido. Dejó la aguja con la jeringa adjunta en la ampolla. Luego tomó una bola de algodón, la empapó en alcohol y la colocó junto a la jeringa y el torniquete.

"Cada vez que vas a poner una inyección intravenosa, tienes que mostrarle al médico la ampolla con la jeringa llena y decirle cuál es el medicamento y quién recibirá la inyección. Esta precaución evita errores."

"Sí, señora Samietz, así lo haré."

"Ahora, el médico le mostrará cómo aplicar la inyección intravenosa. Llama al paciente y dile al médico que todo está listo".

"Sí, señora Samietz. Lo haré."

Llamé al Sr. Krueger y luego le dije al Dr. Samietz que todo estaba listo. Después de que el paciente se tendiera en la cama, el Dr. Samietz se sentó en la silla junto a él. El puso el torniquete en la parte superior del brazo, lo apretó y comenzó a buscar la vena en la El pliegue interno del codo. Una vez que encontró una vena, me dejó sentirla también. Luego esterilizó la zona con un algodón empapado en alcohol, metió la aguja en la vena y retrajo el émbolo de la jeringa hasta que una pequeña cantidad de sangre entró en el líquido. Una vez que aseguró que la aguja estaba en la vena, soltó el torniquete y comenzó a inyectar la solución lentamente.

"Solo avíseme si tiene calor", le pidió el Dr. Samietz al paciente. Si decía que sí, el médico se detenía un rato y luego continuaba.

Como puede ver, señorita Bonacker, las inyecciones de calcio hay que ponerlas muy despacio; de lo contrario, el paciente se calienta mucho y se desmaya".

"Sí, Dr. Samietz, inyectaré el calcio muy lentamente."

Una vez que el médico terminó, regresó a la sala de consulta. Llamé al siguiente paciente por él. La señora Samietz permaneció en la sala de examen con el Sr. Krueger un poco más para asegurarse de que estaba bien. Luego lo dejó salir por la puerta lateral a través del pasillo. No quería molestar al médico ni al siguiente paciente en la sala de consulta. A las 6:00 p. m., la sala de espera estaba vacía. La señora Samietz me pidió que cerrara la puerta y archivara todos los registros antes de subir, lo cual hice. Aunque el primer día fue un desafío, le agradecí a Dios que todo salió bien. Consumí mis dos bollos con la salchicha y leí el Nuevo Testamento por un rato. Me hundí cansada pero contenta en mi cama y dormí bien y en paz.

El día siguiente fue casi una repetición del primer día. Las cosas volvieron a salir bien. Tuve la oportunidad de conocer a más pacientes cuyos nombres traté de recordar. El miércoles era mi día libre. Después del desayuno, fui a familiarizarme con el pueblo y alrededores. Subí a la colina para explorar las ruinas de lo que parecía haber sido una vez un castillo. En el patio, una profesora explicaba la historia del castillo a sus alumnos. Me quedé cerca de ella y escuché.

"El castillo fue construido en el siglo XII por Friedrich Barbarossa en el estilo arquitectónico románico. Gelnhausen también se llama la ciudad de Barbarossa. Friedrich Barbarossa fue coronado rey de Alemania en Aquisgrán, Alemania, emperador romano en Roma y rey de Italia en Pavía. Reinó desde 1155 hasta 1190. Durante la guerra de treinta años con Francia, España, Suecia y Alemania desde 1618 hasta 1648, el castillo fue destruido por una emboscada sueca. Solía ser un municipio independiente; una vez disuelto a finales del siglo XIX, pasó a formar parte de la ciudad de Gelnhausen. Las ruinas se convirtieron en una atracción turística y una inspiración para los estudiosos amantes del arte. El Emperador también construyó un lugar en la isla del río Kinzig, llamado Lugar Imperial (Kaiserplatz)".

La maestra señaló cuesta abajo:

"Desde aquí, tienen una hermosa vista de Gelnhausen y del río Kinzig. Avancemos más cuesta arriba, donde nos adentraremos en el bosque. Daremos un pequeño paseo por el bosque cercano, que también pertenecía al castillo."

La clase se fue. Me quedé atrás por un tiempo y observé la vista dominante de la ciudad del valle del río Kinzig. Luego caminé cuesta arriba y paseé por el bosque. El sol se deslizaba entre las ramas parcialmente desnudas de hayas y robles mientras algunas hojas aún caían. Las hojas secas crujieron cuando las pisé. Busqué hayucos que esperaba que las ardillas aún no se hubieran devorado. Aquí y allá, encontré uno. Disfruté de su sabor. Al mediodía volví al pueblo, Fui a la tienda de comestibles y compré salchichas y bollos para el almuerzo. Después del almuerzo, tomé una siesta, leí mi Nuevo Testamento, escribí una carta a casa y otra a mi amiga, Lore, en Niederbexbach. Antes de retirarme por la noche, agradecí a Dios por la belleza del bosque y un hermoso día.

Los siguientes días también fueron bien. La señora Samietz destacó la importancia de obtener un formulario de seguro para cada paciente que consulta al médico.

"Siempre que venga un paciente, verifique si tiene un formulario de seguro (Krankenschein) del gobierno. Si no, pídales que la traigan la próxima vez. Tendremos que listar todos los servicios del médico y enviarlos a la Oficina de Seguro de Salud para el cobro del pago al final de cada trimestre del año. Los pacientes también necesitarán un formulario nuevo cada tres meses".

"Sí, señora Samietz, revisaré y me aseguraré de que los pacientes hayan traído sus formularios".

El viernes llegó un paciente con dificultad para respirar. El Dr. Samietz quería una radiografía de tórax. La señora Samietz llevó al paciente a la sala de rayos X. La seguí, observé cómo configurar los diales en la máquina de rayos X, colocar la película en el casete y colocarla en un soporte. Luego colocó al paciente frente al casete y colocó ambos hombros contra el casete. Le indicó al paciente que respirara profundamente y lo sostuviera. Luego presionó un botón en la máquina de rayos X. Cuando escuchó el clic, le dijo al paciente que volviera a respirar y que se sentara mientras revelaba la película. Ambos entramos en el cuarto oscuro. La señora Samietz retiró con cuidado la película, la colocó en una percha especial y luego la sumergió en un tanque lleno de una solución.

"Este es el desarrollador. Mueva la película suavemente hacia arriba y hacia abajo hasta que vea que la imagen del objeto radiografiado aparece claramente en la película. Luego, lave el revelador en el tanque de agua y colóquelo en el fijador por unos minutos. Esta solución deteiene el proceso de develación y retiene la imagen tomada. Al final, vuelves a sumergir la película en el agua y la dejas secar. Sin embargo, puedes mostrárselo al médico antes de que se seque".

Ella tomó la película húmeda y se la mostró al médico. Miró la película, notó algo anormal y le dijo a la Sra. Samietz que le gustaría hacer una fluoroscopia de los pulmones del paciente. El Dr. Samietz entró en la sala de rayos X, se puso el delantal de plomo y se sentó en la silla. Le pidió al paciente que se parara detrás de la oscura pantalla móvil de rayos X y colocó al paciente detrás de la pantalla. El médico movió al paciente y la pantalla para ver los lóbulos de los pulmones desde diferentes ángulos para detectar anomalías. Este procedimiento tomó de diez a veinte minutos. Cuando terminó, le dijo al paciente que tenía un tumor. El Dr. Samietz completó un formulario particular (Ueberweisung) para admitir al paciente en el hospital local para una biopsia y una evaluación y tratamiento adicionales. El sábado, la oficina estuvo abierta solo medio día. La Señora Samietz me informó que todos los fines de semana, cuando los consultorios médicos están cerrados, uno de los médicos locales está de guardia para emergencias. El último fin de semana del mes, la Dra. Mantel sustituiría a su marido. Tendrás que tomar las llamadas telefónicas de los pacientes. Escuché atentamente. Sin embargo, todavía tenía dos fines de semana libres para conocer más lugares en la ciudad y sus alrededores.

Lioba me había hablado de un café llamado Little Castle (Das Schloesschen), ubicado en la colina. Mencionó que el propietario toca el piano y, a veces, la gente también canta. Además, sirve buena comida y sabrosa repostería. Pensé que podría derrochar un poco el domingo y comprobarlo por mí misma. También me informó cuál y dónde estaba la Iglesia Evangelística para informarme sobre los servicios. Planeaba ir allí el domingo siguiente. Hoy, quería satisfacer mi antojo de algo dulce. El camino hacia el Café pasaba por un huerto de manzanos. A estas alturas, el dueño del huerto había recogido las manzanas y las hojas se habían caído de las ramas. Aquí y allá, una manzana arrugada colgaba del árbol. Habría arrancado uno o dos si estuvieran en las extremidades inferiores cerca de la carretera. Una manzana habría sabido bien, incluso algo seca al sol. Llegué al café a última hora de la tarde. Un mesero me sentó junto a la ventana en una mesa pequeña, cubierta con un mantel blanco y un pequeño jarrón con flores frescas decorándola. El café se veía muy acogedor y me sentí bien sentada junto a la ventana con vista a la ciudad. El mesero trajo el menú.

"¿Quieres tu café ahora o con el postre?" "Con postre, por favor."

El menú ofrecía una variedad de pasteles exuberantes. Me gustó el Black Forest Cake (Schwarzwaelder Kirschtorte), pero el precio era demasiado alto para mi escaso presupuesto actual. Me conformé con el pastel de manzana menos costoso (Apfeltorte). El mesero regresó:

"Fraeulein, ¿está lista para ordenar?"

"Sí, Quisiera la Apfeltorte y una taza de café con crema, por favor."

"Gracias, ¿eso es todo?"

"Sí, eso sería todo".

Hoy, solo unos pocos clientes visitaron el café temprano, pero más personas entraron después de las 3:30 p. m. Luego entró el dueño, se sentó en el banco frente al piano y comenzó a tocar la "Serenata" de Schubert. Entonces una pareja se levantó, se acercó al piano y le preguntó al dueño si podía acompañarlos al aria de The Gypsy Baron, "¿Quién nos casó?". (Wer Uns Getraut). El pianista hojeó sus partituras. Luego dijo: "Aquí está; podemos empezar."

La pareja se tomó de la mano, mirándose a los ojos, expresando tanto amor el uno por el otro, y cantó el hermoso dúo de la Opereta, The Gypsy Baron, compuesto por Johann Strauss. Sus voces sonaban celestiales. También cantaron algunas canciones de Schubert y duetos de otras operetas. La música me absorbió por completo. le di un mordisco a mi tarta de manzana y un sorbo de café para que durara lo máximo posible. Cuando dejaron de cantar, terminé mi postre. Pagué al mesero y felizmente bajé la colina. Observé cómo el sol se hundía más y más, arrojando un velo gris sobre la montaña y la ciudad. Regresé antes de que la noche sumergiera la ciudad en tinieblas. Di gracias a Dios por la música estimulante. Me quedé despierta durante algún tiempo. Soñé que algún día conocería a mi príncipe azul, me enamoraría como los cantantes y viviría más eventos musicales maravillosos.

La semana siguiente, la Sra. Samietz me dejó trabajar sola en la clínica. Todo fue bien. El miércoles hice mis compras para el resto de la semana. El Dr. Samietz me informó que estaría de guardia este fin de semana, y la Dra. Mantel lo sustituiría. Mi deber era contestar el teléfono, tomar el nombre y la dirección del paciente, y la emergencia médica del paciente. El sábado al mediodía, terminamos el horario de oficina. Llegó la Dra.

Mantel. El Dr. Samietz me la presentó. Luego me dijo que llevara el teléfono arriba, lo conectara al tomacorriente afuera de mi puerta y lo colocara sobre la mesa pequeña.

"La Dra. Mantel estará cenando con nosotros. Pasará la noche en mi habitación privada en el segundo piso. Cada vez que reciba una llamada de emergencia, toque la puerta y dele la información del paciente".

"Sí, Dr. Samietz, lo haré", respondí antes de recuperar el teléfono y llevarlo arriba. Dejé mi puerta abierta día y noche para no perder una llamada telefónica. Comí mi sándwich. Luego me senté frente a la puerta abierta, leyendo una traducción al alemán del libro de Anne Murrow Lindbergh, El Regalo del Mar. En él, ella describe lo que el mar y las conchas individuales le han enseñado. Le gustaban especialmente las conchas de ostras. La incansable adaptabilidad y tenacidad atrajeron su asombrada admiración. La ostra se siente cómoda en su sencillez y familiaridad. Me gustó su frase sobre el amor de pareja. Me impulsó a escribirlo en su totalidad:

"Cuando cada uno de los cónyuges ama tan completamente que se ha olvidado de preguntarse si es o no amado a cambio; cuando solo sabe que ama y se mueve con su música entonces, y solo entonces son dos personas capaces de bailar perfectamente en sintonía con el mismo ritmo."

La otra cita me impresionó y me recordó a Dios creando tanta belleza en las flores. "Arreglar un plato de flores por la mañana puede dar una sensación de tranquilidad en un día lleno de gente, como escribir un poema o rezar una oración".

Siempre me gustó un ramo de flores silvestres frescas en mi mesa. Las considero las sonrisas de Dios.

En primavera y verano, las recogía en el bosque o en los senderos. Corté hierbas secas, pequeñas ramas con hojas de colores, o cualquier cosa que pudiera encontrar que se vería bonita en otoño. Compartí mi pasión por las flores con Anne Morrow Lindbergh. Mientras continuaba leyendo su libro, sonó el teléfono. Dejé el libro y corrí al pasillo para contestar el teléfono, "Esta es la asistente del Dr. Samietz; ¿Le puedo ayudar en algo?" Una madre preocupada me informó por teléfono que su hijo tenía fiebre alta y que le gustaría que el médico viera a su hijo enfermo. Anoté toda la información necesaria y le aseguré a la madre, que la Dra. Mantel estaría allí lo antes posible. La madre se sintió aliviada al saber que la médica haría una visita a domicilio en breve. Era ya tarde, por la tarde. La Dra. Mantel todavía estaría abajo con el Dr. y la Sra. Samietz. Inmediatamente bajé y llamé a la puerta: La Sra. Samietz vino a abrir la puerta. Me disculpé por entrometerme, pero le dije que una madre acababa de llamar y quería que el médico viera a su hijo enfermo. Le entregué la hoja de papel con el nombre y la dirección del paciente a la Sra. Samietz. Ella me agradeció y me dijo que la Dra. Mantel estaría en camino en breve.

Subí las escaleras de nuevo para asegurarme de que no perdería una llamada telefónica. Tomé mi libro y comencé a leer. Hice una breve pausa para tomar un sándwich para la cena. Seguí leyendo hasta altas horas de la noche. No me atrevía a ir a la cama. A medianoche, el teléfono volvió a sonar. Una hija preocupada me informó que su anciana madre se había caído y tenía mucho dolor. ¿Podría el doctor venir a verla? Después de haber anotado toda la información, fui y llamé a la habitación donde la Dra. Mantel dormía, "Lamento molestarla, Dra. Mantel, tengo otra llamada para usted. Llegó a la puerta, "¿Qué le pasa al paciente que necesito ver?"

"Una señora mayor se cayó y está con mucho dolor; aquí está su nombre y dirección."

Le entregué la hoja de papel y regresé a mi habitación. Me senté a la mesa y comencé a leer de nuevo. A estas alturas, estaba cansada y me costaba mucho mantenerme despierta. Debo haberme quedado dormida. Cuando el teléfono volvió a sonar, salté y rápidamente corrí hacia el teléfono. Una señora angustiada me dijo que su esposo estaba teniendo un ataque de vesícula biliar y tenía mucho dolor. Le aseguré que la Dra. Mantel estaría allí tan pronto como pudiera. La esposa se calmó un poco, sabiendo que su esposo tendría ayuda. Cuando le di la información a la Dra. Mantel, me pidió que trajera una ampolla de morfina y una jeringa de abajo, lo cual hice. Pronto, la Dra. Mantel se dirigía a ver al paciente. El lunes por la mañana, tan cansada como estaba por no haber dormido casi toda la noche, tenía que estar en la oficina a las 8:00 a.m. La Dra. Mantel también bajó para informarme qué servicios brindaba a los pacientes que visitaba. Le puso una inyección de penicilina al niño que tenía mucha fiebre y redactó un formulario de hospitalización para la señora que se cayó. La Dra. Mantel sospechaba de una fractura de cadera. Le dio una inyección intravenosa de morfina al paciente que tuvo un ataque de vesícula biliar. Tuve que hacer un cuadro para cada paciente e ingresar la visita domiciliaria y las inyecciones administradas. Luego tuve que llamar a los pacientes para que trajeran los formularios del seguro para cobrar la tarifa por los servicios prestados. Antes de que la Dra. Mantel se fuera, me agradeció y dijo que volvería en un mes.

Me gustaron sus modales corteses y esperaba trabajar con ella nuevamente el próximo mes. Al mes siguiente, conocí a más pacientes, y algunos de ellos me querían lo suficiente como para invitarme a almorzar ó a un pastel y un café el domingo por la tarde, lo que me hizo sentir apreciada y disfruté de su amabilidad. Aprendí a hacer pruebas de tolerancia a la glucosa, controlar los niveles de azúcar en la sangre, hacer un CBC, tomar muestras del líquido estomacal, hacer radiografías y desarrollar películas. Empecé a ganar confianza en mí misma y me sentía cómoda trabajando con el médico y especialmente con los pacientes. Después de las horas de oficina de la mañana, el Dr. Samietz me dictó una carta y tuve que taquigrafiarla. Dictó con bastante rapidez. Desafortunadamente, me perdí ciertas palabras. Pero no me atreví a pedirle que las repitiera. Supuse que completaba las palabras adecuadas cuando escribía la carta. Después de que el Dr. Samietz se fue a almorzar, yo me quedé en la oficina escribiendo en la vieja máquina de escribir. Tuve que empujar lentamente cada letra en el teclado; de lo contrario, dos barras se entrecruzarían y se atascarían. Tuve que parar y desconectarlos, lo cual fue una pérdida de tiempo. Algunas letras no estaban claras, como la a y la e, porque se les había acumulado demasiada tinta de la cinta. Cuando llegué a los espacios en blanco, Los llené con palabras que pensé que encajarían. Dediqué parte de mi hora del almuerzo a terminar la carta. Lo puse en el escritorio del Dr. Samietz para que pudiera leerlo a su conveniencia.

Estábamos ocupados por la tarde y él no pudo leer la carta hasta que todos los pacientes se fueron. Contuve la respiración, con la esperanza de haberlo escrito a su entera satisfacción. Después de que terminó de leer, tiró la carta sobre el escritorio y me gritó: "Esto no es lo que te dicté, eres una estúpida y nunca llegarás a nada". Sus palabras fueron como un cuchillo apuñalándome en el corazón. Mi cuerpo tembló y me puse pálida. Me ahogué. El Dr. Samietz escribió sus palabras sobre las mías sustituidas, me arrojó la carta: "¡Escríbela de nuevo correctamente!".

Sin pronunciar una palabra, puse la carta en mi escritorio. Todavía estaba sorprendida por los comentarios despectivos y groseros del médico. Después de que se fue, me senté y lloré por un rato antes de volver a escribir la carta. Me costó mucho concentrarme en el contenido de la carta. Sentí ganas de poner la carta sin corregir en su escritorio con una nota que dijera: "No me gusta que me traten así. ¡Renuncio!"

Hablé con Dios para que me mostrara cómo actuar en esta situación de una manera que lo honraría. Razoné que Dios no querría que me escapara de un problema. Le gustaría que fuera fuerte y enfrentara el desafío, que hiciera todo lo posible para resolverlo y que confiara en Dios para ayudarme a encontrar la manera de actuar correctamente. Volver a escribir la carta me agotó emocionalmente. Pero la terminé, la leí varias veces, la puse en el escritorio del Dr. Samietz y subí las escaleras. Era pasada la hora de la cena. Perdí temporalmente el apetito. Me tiré en la cama y muchos pensamientos pasaron por mi mente.

Renunciar y huir de un problema es como ser un cobarde y me perseguiría en el futuro. Devolver grosería por grosería sería anticristiano y me haría sentir mal. ¿Cuál sería la mejor solución para este problema según la voluntad de Dios? Me quedaría y practicaría taquigrafía todos los días hasta que fuera competente para tomar dictados. Yo prometí, con la ayuda de Dios, convertirme en la mejor persona que posiblemente podría ser. Varias veces repetí la frase, "Voy a llegar a algo. Te lo mostraré; ¡Voy a llegar a algo! Dios, ayúdame a convertir este desengaño humano en una cita divina". Juré que si alguna vez tuviera empleados en el futuro, nunca sería grosero con ellos ni los degradaría.

Los trataría con el mayor respeto y cortesía. Antes de irme a dormir, recuperé mi paz interior al creer que con la ayuda de Dios había tomado la decisión correcta. Di gracias a Dios por mostrarme Su voluntad y esperaba que todo saliera bien. Todas las mañanas me levantaba una hora antes y practicaba taquigrafía para tomar dictados cada vez más rápido. Cada vez que el Dr. Samietz me dictó una carta, me puse nerviosa y tuve miedo de equivocarme. A su debido tiempo, escribí las cartas a su satisfacción y evité sus comentarios groseros y confrontaciones desagradables.

Se acercaba el final de octubre. Las iglesias luterana y evangélica protestante celebran cada año el 31 de octubre el Día de la Reforma. Es una conmemoración del día de 1517 cuando Martín Lutero, un monje alemán, clavó las famosas noventa y cinco tesis en la puerta de la iglesia del castillo de Wittenberg. No estuvo de acuerdo con la enseñanza de la Iglesia Católica de que una persona puede ganar la salvación a través de las buenas obras. El Dr. Lutero no creía en la compra y venta de indulgencias. Consideró que por la fe en Dios y aceptando a Jesucristo como Salvador, una persona obtiene la salvación como un regalo de Dios. El Dr. Lutero reconoció la Biblia como la autoridad religiosa. Este año, celebrábamos el Día de la Reforma el domingo 30 de octubre. Decidí ir a la Evangélica Marienkirche.

Caminé por la parte antigua de la ciudad antes de llegar a la iglesia, construida en estilo románico tardío y gótico temprano de piedra arenisca rosa de dos tonos con torres oscuras y altas. Entré por la enorme puerta enmarcada por columnas de piedra adornadas, estatuas talladas colocadas sobre el arco de la puerta. El interior, especialmente el altar, me impresionó aún más con todas las alturas, exquisitas esculturas y pinturas: la luz que penetra en las altas vidrieras arqueadas que arrojan un suave resplandor sobre el altar y las paredes de piedra. Estatuas, cuadros y candelabros decoraban los vestíbulos y todas las áreas. Después la iglesia se llenó y me senté, el organista empezó a tocar. Qué maravilloso e inspirador sonido llenó toda la iglesia. El pastor, vestido con una túnica larga y negra, se colocó detrás del altar. La congregación se levantó. Después de la liturgia, los fieles cantaron: "Castillo fuerte es nuestro Dios". Luego, el pastor predicó sobre el significado de la reforma y el papel de Martín Lutero en el comienzo de la reforma. Después del sermón, la congregación cantó una canción más antes de que el párroco despidiera a los feligreses con una bendición.

Regresé a mi apartamento, satisfecha de haber encontrado una iglesia a la que asistir tan a menudo como podía. El 1 de noviembre recibí mi primer sueldo en efectivo. A pesar de que fue solo por tres semanas, aprecié poder comprar algunos de los artículos que consideraba de lujo, como una estufa eléctrica, una olla, y una cacerola para prepararme comidas calientes para el almuerzo. Ahora comería sándwiches solo para la cena. Como no tenía refrigerador, tenía que ir de compras varias veces a la semana para comprar carne fresca o salchichas. Me las arreglé para estirar mis fondos hasta el próximo día de pago.

Una noche, escuché un golpe en mi puerta, "Fraeulein Bonacker, apúrate a bajar. El Dr. Samietz tiene mucho dolor; está teniendo un ataque de vesícula biliar. Toma morfina y ven y dale una inyección".

"Sí, señora Samietz, lo haré."

Me puse la bata rápidamente, tomé la jeringa y la ampolla de morfina, el torniquete, empapé una bola de algodón en alcohol y corrí escaleras arriba. Encontré al Dr. Samietz gimiendo y gimiendo. Estaba en un dolor severo. Cuando me vio entrar en la habitación, estiró su brazo izquierdo, "Rápido, dame la inyección; ¡Tengo mucho dolor!"

"Sí, Dr. Samietz, lo haré."

Extraje la morfina en la jeringa, luego puse rápidamente el torniquete en su brazo izquierdo y le pedí que cerrara el puño. Cuando pude sentir la vena, esterilicé la zona con alcohol, y empujé la aguja en la vena. Por suerte, no perdí la vena en el primer intento. Estaba aliviada. Luego comencé a inyectarle la morfina lentamente. Saber que la morfina aliviaría el dolor lo hizo relajarse. Le agradecí a Dios que no me faltó la vena y no provoqué que se enfadara conmigo. La señora Samietz me dio las gracias antes de salir de la habitación. Bajé todas las cosas a la clínica antes de volver a la cama. El día siguiente era miércoles, por lo que el médico pudo recuperarse de la noche agotadora y dolorosa. Para el jueves, el Dr. Samietz estaba de regreso en la clínica, viendo pacientes nuevamente. Incluso me dijo que aplicaba buenas inyecciones intravenosas. Me alegró oírlo decir eso. A medida que pasaba el tiempo, nos sentimos cómodos trabajando juntos. Sabía lo que esperaba de mí y traté de cumplir con sus expectativas siempre que pude. Durante mis compras semanales de comestibles, dos o tres soldados estadounidenses a menudo me seguían y querían entablar una conversación. Fingí que no entendía inglés y seguí caminando. Cuando veía una tienda, entraba, miraba alrededor y esperaba a que pasaran, y me sintiera segura, no siendo vista por ellos. Una guarnición estadounidense ocupó Gelnhausen y muchos soldados vivían en la ciudad. Algunos de los soldados contrajeron gonorrea. No les gustaba ir a la oficina médica en la base para recibir tratamiento. Se avergonzarían de tenerlo registrado en sus registros médicos. Optaron por ir a médicos locales para sus inyecciones de penicilina. Teníamos soldados llamando a la puerta principal con frecuencia, solicitando inyecciones de penicilina. Los llevaba directamente a la sala de reconocimiento para ponerles la inyección de penicilina en el brazo. Pagaban 20.00 MA por inyección, que le daba de inmediato al médico. Era un ingreso adicional no registrado.

Un día, el Dr. y la Sra. Samietz salieron por el día. La criada se había ido. Sólo yo me quedé sola en la casa. Escuché un golpe en la puerta. Cuando bajé para abrir la puerta, un soldado de color muy alto se paró frente a mí y dijo: "Penicillin Spritze, bitte, (inyección de penicilina, por favor)".

Me sorprendió e intimidó completamente al principio. No estaba segura de si debía cerrar la puerta, decir que el médico no estaba aquí o simplemente dejarlo entrar y ponerle la inyección. Opté por dejarlo entrar en lugar de hacerle saber que el médico no estaba en casa. Oré por la protección de Dios mientras me preparaba y le daba la inyección en el brazo. Me entregó los 20.00 MA y se fue. Le agradecí a Dios que no me molestara. Los soldados regresaban para recibir inyecciones de penicilina hasta que desaparecían los síntomas. Cuando el Dr. y la Sra. Samietz regresaron, le entregué el billete de 20.00 MA al médico.

Un domingo, la Sra. Fehl me invitó a almorzar. Me presentó a su hijo Hans y a su nuera, Helen, y a un amigo, llamado Franz, que era organista. Todos apreciaban la música clásica y de órgano, al igual que yo. Franz, el organista, me dijo que iba a la iglesia a practicar de vez en cuando. Me preguntó si estaría interesada en unirme y escucharlo tocar.

"Estaría encantada de escucharte tocar. Podría hacerlo en mi día libre el miércoles".

"Puedo verte el miércoles a las 4:00 p.m." "Muy bien; Te veré entonces en la iglesia."

Pasamos una tarde agradable juntos. Le agradecí a la Sra. Fehl y su familia por el delicioso almuerzo. También agradecí al organista su invitación para escucharlo tocar.

El miércoles por la mañana, después de practicar taquigrafía, limpié mi habitación, preparé chucrut, salchichas y estofado de papas para el almuerzo, leí hasta las 3:30 p.m., caminé hasta la iglesia y me senté en el banco de la última fila. La iglesia permaneció sin calefacción en otoño e invierno. Me alegré de llevar un abrigo grueso y guantes. Mientras miraba a mi alrededor y admiraba todas las exquisitas decoraciones religiosas, Franz, el organista, vino a saludarme,

"Buenas tardes Fraeulein Hildegard. Es bueno verte aquí, y llegaste puntual también. Comenzaré a tocar en breve".

"Buenas tardes, Sr. Franz. Estoy ansiosa por escucharte tocar".

Caminó hacia el órgano, se sentó y comenzó a tocar. Cuando Franz tocó las teclas, el sonido abandonó los tubos del órgano y flotó por la iglesia vacía. Cuando las melodías sagradas llegaron a mis oídos y tocaron mi corazón y mi espíritu, reverberaron con gran alegría. La música conmovedora y la belleza circundante de la decoración de la iglesia elevaron mi alma. Me senté extasiada en mi asiento, olvidándome del tiempo y de todo lo demás. Cuando la música se detuvo, sentí que desperté de un sueño placentero. El señor Franz se acercó a mí. Le dije cuánto disfrutaba escuchando la música que tocaba en el órgano.

"Me alegra que te haya gustado la música. ¿Quizás puedas venir de nuevo?"

"Ciertamente me gustaría escucharte tocar de nuevo".

Le di las gracias y nos despedimos con un apretón de manos. Regresé a mi habitación y leí hasta la hora de acostarme. Di gracias a Dios por esta experiencia musical edificante.

Los tristes días de noviembre, cuando las ramas desnudas lloraban la pérdida de sus hojas, pasaron lentamente. El anterior domingo 27 de noviembre celebramos el primer día de Adviento, una tradición cristiana para preparar el nacimiento de Jesús. El miércoles anterior, fui al bosque, rompí algunas ramas de pino, hice una corona y le puse cuatro velas. Lo coloqué sobre mi mesa y cada domingo por la noche encendía una vela más. Miraba la luz parpadeante de las velas, meditaba, y leía mi Biblia o algunos poemas de mi libro de poesía Bluetenbaum. Empecé a pensar en la Navidad. Sabía que el Dr. Samietz no me concedería tiempo libre después de que solo trabajé dos meses para él. Significaba que no podría ir a casa. El Dr. y la Sra. Samietz no me habían invitado ni una vez a cenar ni a ninguna comida; probablemente tampoco me invitarían en Navidad. No me gustaba la idea de pasar estas memorables vacaciones sola en mi habitación. Esperé pacientemente a que alguien me invitara.

Mientras tanto, escribí mis tarjetas navideñas a mi mamá, mis hermanas Marta y Meta, mis parientes cercanos, mi amiga Lore y Hermann. A mediados de diciembre, Lioba me pidió que pasara la Nochebuena y el día de Navidad con su familia. Acepté su invitación con alegría y le agradecí por ser tan amable. Haber recibido solo dos salarios hasta el momento no me permitió comprar regalos de Navidad para Lioba y sus padres. Decidí comprar unas hojas de papel firme y hacer estrellas para colgar en el árbol de Navidad, que toda la familia pudiera disfrutar. Todas las noches, corté tiras de papel y las doblé en forma de estrellas. Mi hermana Emma me había enseñado a hacer estrellas con tiras de papel y paja. Seguro que extrañaría estar en casa con mi familia en Navidad. Ni siquiera pude llamarlos porque no tenían teléfono. Cerca de Navidad, recibí una tarjeta navideña y una carta de mi hermano Edmund. Incluyó 50,00 MA en la tarjeta para que yo pudiera comprar un regalo para mí. Le estaba muy agradecida. Mis zapatos marrones se veían desgastados y solo tenía unos pocos vestidos. Me compré un par de zapatos marrones y un vestido marrón claro que usaría para Navidad. Algunos pacientes detallistas me trajeron cajas de dulces para Navidad. Una carta y una tarjeta de Hermann estaban entre las tarjetas y cartas que recibí con deseos de Feliz Navidad. Agradecí ser recordada en este tiempo festivo y especialmente por Hermann. Su mensaje me recordó los preciosos momentos que compartimos, animándonos mutuamente a vivir de acuerdo con nuestros elevados ideales.

El viernes 23 de diciembre aún teníamos horario de oficina. Pero en Nochebuena, Navidad y el 26 de diciembre, el Dr. Samietz cerró la oficina. En Nochebuena, Lioba llegó temprano para preparar la comida para la Nochebuena y el día de Navidad. Al mediodía estaba lista para partir. Viajaba en bicicleta desde Biebergemuend a Gelnhausen. Me dijo que su hermano mayor,

Peter, vendría en motocicleta a recogerme, lo cual hizo. Había empacado mi bolsa de viaje y lo esperé abajo en la cocina con Lioba. En diciembre, el invierno entró con fuerza. La temperatura descendió por debajo de cero. Me envolví en mi pesado abrigo, me puse un pañuelo en la cabeza y me lo envolví alrededor de la cara antes de montarme en la motocicleta. Me dio pena que Lioba anduviera en bicicleta, incluso en el frío invierno, de Biebergemuend a Gelnhausen, media hora en cada sentido. llevaba medias de nailon, y mis piernas se congelaron durante el viaje. Afortunadamente, estaba a solo seis millas de distancia. El señor y la señora Krack me recibieron en su casa modesta pero decorada con buen gusto en Biebergemuend. También conocí al hermano menor Erhard. Todos esperamos hasta que llegó Lioba. A las 3:00 p.m., la Sra. Krack sirvió pastel y café mientras disfrutábamos charlando.

En Nochebuena, la Sra. Krack sirvió una carpa con ensalada de patatas, que disfruté mucho. A las 11:00 p.m., todos caminamos hacia la iglesia católica y celebramos la misa festiva de medianoche. Sin embargo, tuve dificultades para mantenerme despierta tan tarde en la noche. Lioba tuvo la amabilidad de dormir en el sofá y dejarme dormir en su cómoda cama. Dormí muy bien y llegué bastante tarde; no necesitábamos ir a la iglesia ese día. La señora Krack sirvió un almuerzo elaborado de ganso asado, repollo rojo y albóndigas de patata para el almuerzo. El aroma del ganso asado me recordó a la comida casera de mi madre; Extrañaba estar con mi familia pero estaba agradecida con la familia Krack por invitarme a celebrar la Navidad con ellos. Después de que comimos pastel y café por la tarde, Peter me llevó de vuelta a Gelnhausen. Principalmente agradecí a Dios por su gran amor por nosotros que envió a su único hijo Jesucristo, cuyo cumpleaños conmemoramos cada año en Navidad. Pensé en el viaje de Cristo desde el pesebre hasta la cruz y cómo dio su vida para que podamos tener salvación y vida eterna. También agradecí a Dios que no tuve que estar sola en esta celebración especial.

El viernes 30 de diciembre de 1955, la sra. Samietz me mostró cómo llenar los formularios de seguro para el último trimestre del año. Ingresé en el formulario de seguro de cada paciente todas las visitas al consultorio, las inyecciones y los servicios médicos prestados. Me tomó más tiempo de lo que esperaba y terminé la última entrada el sábado por la noche, a pesar de que la oficina estaba cerrada ese día.

La víspera de Año Nuevo, sábado 31 de diciembre de 1955, opté por quedarme en casa. Leí mi Biblia y medité en todos los eventos del año pasado y cuán maravillosamente Dios me había ayudado a superar todos los desafíos y pruebas. Confié en Dios. Él nunca me defraudó. Dios llenó mi corazón de alegría y paz. Me acosté relativamente temprano. A medianoche, las campanas de la iglesia anunciaron la llegada del nuevo año 1956. El sonido de las campanas me despertó. Me quedé despierta por un tiempo, preguntándome qué tenía Dios reservado para mí este próximo año. Tenía la costumbre de elegir un versículo de la Biblia para cada año. Este año fue Marcos 4:39, "Y levantándose, reprendió al viento, y dijo al mar: Enmudece. Y cesó el viento, y hubo una gran calma."

Reflexioné sobre cómo se aplicaría esto a mi vida. Sí, Dios y mi Salvador calmaron muchas tormentas en mi vida y me ayudaron en tiempos difíciles. Confié en que Él haría lo mismo en el futuro. Fui a la iglesia el domingo por la mañana. Por la tarde, decidí ir temprano al Castle Café para darme un gusto con un pedazo de pastel y café. Ese día, el dueño tocaba el piano, pero ningún artista cantaba para deleite de los clientes. Acababa de recibir mi tercer salario mensual. Tenía ganas de cumplirme un capricho con un trozo de pastel de la Selva Negra. Estaba delicioso. Regresé temprano antes de que oscureciera. Al día siguiente, en mi cumpleaños, tenía que trabajar. Durante mi descanso para almorzar, fui a la oficina de correos para enviar los formularios de seguro del gobierno. No hice nada especial para mi cumpleaños. El Dr. y la Sra. Samietz no recordaban mi cumpleaños. Solo le dije a Lioba que mi cumpleaños número 19 era el 2 de enero. Me trajo un trozo de pastel al día siguiente. Estaba muy agradecida por su amistad y amabilidad y que viniera cinco días a la semana con el Dr. y la Sra. Samietz. Si quisiera hablar con ella, iría a la cocina, donde trabajaba la mayor parte del día.

A veces se llevaban a cabo seminarios especiales para agricultores u otros grupos especiales en Gelnhausen. En Enero, un joven de un grupo llegó a la clínica con una infección de las vías respiratorias superiores. El Dr. Samietz le ordenó una inyección de penicilina. Mientras le ponía la inyección en el brazo, entabló una conversación conmigo. Me dijo que era un refugiado de Prusia Oriental. Asistía al seminario de productos lácteos y eventualmente quería emigrar a Alberta, Canadá. Le dije que también había nacido en Prusia Oriental y que mi familia escapó de los rusos en 1944. Me preguntó cuál era mi nombre y si podía invitarme a almorzar o cenar un día después de recuperarme. Me presenté y le dije que estaba permitido que me llamara durante el horario de oficina y que mis días libres eran los miércoles y los domingos.

"Tal vez podamos encontrarnos un domingo. No tengo conferencias los domingos."

"El domingo por la tarde estará bien para mi".

"Muy bien, Fraeulein Bonacker; Te llamaré cuando esté bien. Adiós."

"Adiós, Sr. Gollnick. Nos dimos la mano y se fue.

Dos semanas después, Horst Gollnick me llamó y me pidió que lo acompañara a caminar en el Bosque Buedinger el domingo. Le dije que podía llegar temprano en la tarde después de los servicios de la iglesia. Quedamos en salir a la 1:00 p. m. Puntualmente a la 1:00 p.m., tocó a la puerta. Bajé las escaleras y abrí la puerta. Nos saludamos cortésmente y luego comenzamos a caminar cuesta arriba hacia el castillo, charlando sobre los eventos de las últimas dos semanas.Cuando entramos en el bosque, dejamos de hablar. Observamos la hermosa transformación del bosque por la nieve recién caída. Los ojos se deleitaron, observando el paisaje invernal mágico de color blanco puro. Oímos el crujido bajo nuestras botas mientras caminábamos sobre la nieve. De vez en cuando, un montón de nieve caía de un árbol y rompía el pacífico silencio del bosque. Mis pensamientos viajaron en el tiempo a Prusia del Este, donde nací y crecí de niña rodeada de bosques. Horst rompió el silencio preguntándome dónde nací y dónde vivimos después de la guerra. Le hice las mismas preguntas ya que él también nació en Prusia del Este. Intercambiamos varios eventos de la guerra. Ambos habíamos sobrevivido a muchas situaciones peligrosas y estábamos agradecidos de seguir vivos. No nos dimos cuenta de cómo había pasado el tiempo tan rápido.

Cuando llegamos a un restaurante en el bosque, Horst me invitó a acompañarlo para comer algo. Después de haber estado afuera en el frío por un tiempo, algo caliente para comer sonaba bien. Nos sentamos en el restaurante rústico y pedimos sopa de guisantes caliente. Pedí un té para beber y Horst una taza de café. Disfrutamos del ambiente acogedor junto con nuestra comida y bebida antes de regresar a la ciudad. El sol de la tarde se deslizó a través de las ramas desnudas, y las sombras de los árboles se hicieron más y más largas. Llegamos a la ciudad justo antes del atardecer. Algo cansados pero a la vez eufóricos, nos despedimos. Estar en la naturaleza tuvo un efecto calmante en mi cuerpo y alma.

Antes de despedirnos, Horst preguntó: "¿Puedo llamarte de nuevo? Disfruté de tu compañía."

"Si puedes. También me gustaba recordar nuestros hogares en Prusia del Este".

Con un apretón de manos, nos separamos. Me gustaron los modales corteses y respetuosos de Horst. En las próximas semanas, muchos pacientes contrajeron gripe y neumonía. Apliqué muchas inyecciones de penicilina. El Dr. Samietz admitió a los pacientes con infecciones pulmonares graves en el hospital, donde los médicos del personal del hospital continuarían tratando a los pacientes. Disfruté los fines de semana cuando la Dra. Mantel vino a atender las llamadas de emergencia del Dr. Samietz. Cualesquiera que fueran las preguntas que tenía, ella siempre las respondía sin hacerme sentir estúpida. Apreció que yo quisiera aprender cosas nuevas en el campo de la medicina. Desarrollamos una relación cordial entre nosotras y con los pacientes. Durante enero, el mes más frío del año, me vino la gripe. No me atrevía a salir del trabajo. Aunque tenía fiebre, todavía trabajaba en la clínica. Dr. Samietz debió notar que no me sentía bien, y la fiebre me había sonrojado la cara.

"¿Qué pasa, fraeulein Bonacker? No te ves bien." "Tengo fiebre y me duele el cuerpo".

"Ven, déjame revisarte".

Me acerqué al médico. Puso su mano en mi frente y dijo: "Seguro que tienes fiebre. Toma una aspirina y sube a descansar. Llamaré a mi esposa para que me ayude en la clínica".

"Gracias, Dr. Samietz; eso haré"

Me disculpé y subí las escaleras. Me preparé una taza de té, comí un sándwich y me fui a la cama, aunque solo era temprano en la tarde. Sudé toda la noche. El día siguiente era miércoles, mi día libre. Solo me levanté para comer, luego pasé el resto del día en la cama. Para el jueves, me sentí mejor. Fui a trabajar el resto de la semana. El domingo volví a descansar. Me llevó una semana más recuperarme completamente de la gripe.

El miércoles siguiente por la tarde, escuché un golpe en la puerta. Después de que Lioba abrió la puerta, me llamó: "Hay un caballero en la puerta; él quiere verte."

Bajé corriendo las escaleras para ser recibida por Horst Gollnick.

"Buenas tardes, Fraeulein Bonacker."

"Buenas tardes, Sr. Gollnick. ¿Qué puedo hacer por ti?"
"¿Puedo invitarte el domingo a ir conmigo a Frankfurt a ver la obra El enfermo imaginario de Moliere?"[28]

"Gracias; Creo que puedo ir contigo. ¿A qué hora?"

"Te recogeré a las 10:00 a.m. El viaje en tren no dura más de una hora. Podemos almorzar antes de que comience la obra."

"Muy bien; Te veré el domingo."

"Adiós, hasta el domingo." "¡Adiós!"

Felizmente, subí corriendo las escaleras pensando en ver una obra de teatro en Frankfurt.

Llegó el domingo, y también el Sr. Gollnick puntualmente a las 10:00 a. m. Después de un breve saludo, caminamos hacia la estación de tren. El señor Gollnick compró los billetes de ida y vuelta. Sin embargo, preferí pagar por el mío. Solo tuvimos que esperar un poco antes de que saliera el tren. Tuvimos la suerte de encontrar un tren que no hacía ninguna parada. El paisaje pasó volando. Llegamos relativamente temprano a la estación principal de ferrocarril y comenzamos a caminar. El señor Gollnick preguntó cómo llegar a Willy Brandt Platz, donde estaba la Casa Grande del Teatro Municipal. Caminamos por Taunus Street hasta Willy Brandt Platz. El señor Gollnick preguntó cómo llegar a un buen restaurante cerca del teatro. El señor le dijo que el Restaurante Francais en el Hotel Frankfurter Hof tenía una excelente comida. Estaba localizado a una corta distancia de ahí sobre el Kaiser Platz.

Como teníamos tiempo de sobra antes de que comenzara la obra, el Sr. Gollnick me invitó a almorzar. Caminamos hasta el Hotel Frankfurter Hof, donde encontramos el lujoso restaurante. Un mesero elegantemente vestido nos sentó en una mesa cubierta con un mantel blanco. Un pequeño ramo de flores frescas con dos velas estaba en el centro. Parecía tentador. El camarero nos trajo el menú escrito en francés. El señor Gollnick y yo nos miramos sin saber qué pedir. Ninguno de nosotros estaba familiarizado con los platos franceses que figuraban en el menú. Miré la mesa a mi lado y le mostré al mesero que quería ese plato en particular. El señor Gollnick miró a otra mesa y ordenó señalando el plato. La etiqueta y los modales en la mesa son esenciales en Alemania y Europa. Uno no quiere ser criticado o sentirse humillado en la sociedad. Observábamos cómo las personas comían la comida que pedíamos para que la comiéramos correctamente. De vez en cuando, nos mirábamos y sonreíamos. El señor Gollnick también pidió una botella de vino. El camarero trajo las copas y las llenó con el vino. El Señor Gollnick levantó la copa, "Fraeulein Bonacker, hago un brindis y propongo que nos llamemos por nuestros nombres. Por supuesto, ¿solo si estás de acuerdo?"

"Señor Gollnick, estoy de acuerdo." Levantamos nuestras copas suavemente, luego nos tocamos las copas y Horst dijo: "¡Prost! (A tu salud), Hildegard."Yo respondí. —¡Prost, Horst! Luego, Horst comenzó a hablarme en un tono menos formal sobre sus planes de ir a una granja lechera en Alberta, Canadá, y dijo: "Trabajaré allí por un tiempo, y tal vez algún día pueda adquirir una granja lechera propia". "¿Tienes algún plan para el futuro, Hildegard?" preguntó.

"Aún no. Seguiré trabajando para el Dr. Samietz por un tiempo. Esta primavera, mi hermano mayor vendrá a visitarme. Veré lo que tiene en mente".

"Quizás, algún día, podrías considerar unirte a mí en Canadá. No espero que me des una respuesta ahora. Es solo un pensamiento para el futuro".

"Gracias por preguntarme, pero no puedo comprometerme ahora. Prefiero que sigamos siendo amigos sin ataduras".

El camarero trajo la comida: un soufflé de espinacas para mí y una tortilla rellena con muchos ingredientes que Horst había pedido. Nos miramos, sonreímos, nos deseamos buen provecho en francés y empezamos a comer. Solo necesitábamos un tenedor para comer nuestros platos y usamos el cuchillo para untar la mantequilla en los croissants. Nos sentíamos muy correctos, mezclándonos con todos los demás invitados mientras disfrutábamos de nuestra comida francesa. Era demasiado temprano para ir al teatro. Decidimos dar un paseo por el río Meno en la calle Mainkai. Aunque todavía era invierno, no se sentía demasiado frío con el sol en el horizonte. Llegamos al teatro y conseguimos cómodos asientos en la sección central del teatro. La decoración del teatro no era elaborada sino agradable, y el escenario era relativamente pequeño. A las 2:00 p.m., todos los asientos estaban ocupados y se levantó el telón del escenario.

Acto I: En medio del escenario había una cama con un paciente acostado; un médico examinó al paciente con su estetoscopio. La segunda esposa Beline, la hija Angelique y la criada Toinette también están presentes. Lamenta que el médico y el farmacéutico, el hermano del médico, lo lleven a la quiebra. Toinette se esfuerza por convencer a Aragan, el nombre del paciente, de que no estaba enfermo pero que no tiene éxito en hacerlo. Sin embargo, Beline y el médico se confabulan para obtener dinero de Aragan. Para que la hija no interfiera con su plan, intentan convencer a Aragón para que la enviara a un convento. Pero Aragan quiere ver casada a su hija con Thomas, el hijo del médico; de esta manera, tendrá un médico de cabecera que le brindará un servicio médico gratuito. Angelique, sin embargo, ama a otra persona llamada Cleante. Ella regaña a su padre por tratar de obligarla, en contra de su voluntad, a casarse con alguien a quien no ama. Mientras se discute de un lado a otro, se cierra el telón en el Acto I. El público, contento con la excelente actuación, aplaude. Una breve pausa antes de que se levante el telón de nuevo.

En el Acto II, Toinette simpatiza con Angelique. Ella le dice a su amigo Cleante que se supone que Angelique se casará con Thomas, el hijo del médico. Cleante se disfraza de amigo de la profesora de canto de Angelique para pasar tiempo a solas con Angelique. Él encuentra a Thomas no muy brillante. Cleante no puede imaginarse a Angelique casada con Thomas. Ella le ruega a su padre que le dé tiempo para pensarlo. El padre le da cuatro días para casarse con Tomás o para ir al convento. Beralde, el hermano de Aragan, aparece en el escenario y suplica en nombre de Angelique, pero es en vano. Beralde despide al médico y al farmacéutico. El telón se cierra. Siguen los aplausos.

En el Acto III, Beralde y Toinette diseñan un plan para engañar a Aragan. Toinette se disfraza de doctora y le dice a Aragan que el doctor anterior lo trató por la enfermedad equivocada. Los pulmones están enfermos y no los intestinos. Ella sigue y sigue mientras el público se ríe. Beralde le ruega a Aragan que no meta a Angelique en el convento que fue idea de Beline. Beralde y Toinette tienen una solución para convencer a Aragan de cuánto lo ama Beline. Le dicen a Aragan que se acueste en el sofá y finja que está muerto. Beralde se esconde detrás de una pantalla. Cuando Beline sube al escenario, encuentra a Toinette llorando. Ella le dice a Beline que Aragan está muerto. Beline no derrama una lágrima. Ella lo insulta y quiere su dinero. En ese momento, Aragan se levanta del sofá y Beline sale corriendo del escenario, todavía maldiciéndolo. Toinette le dice a Aragan que se acueste de nuevo en el sofá y finja estar muerta. Angélica entra en escena. Cuando se entera de que su padre murió, se derrumba y llora. El amor de su hija mueve al padre. Él se levanta del sofá, la abraza y le dice que se puede casar con Cleante, pero que él debe estudiar para ser médico.

Geralde tiene una idea mejor. Sugiere que su hermano sea médico. Conoce una facultad que puede convertirlo en médico de la noche a la mañana. Invitan a bailarines gitanos al escenario. Realizan la ceremonia y declaran que Aragan es médico.

El telón se cierra. El público aplaude. Los actores se acercan al telón y se inclinan ante el público.

"Horst, esa fue una obra encantadora. Disfruté tanto de la actuación como de la historia cómica. ¿Te gustó?"

"Sí, también me gustó. Moliere nos da una idea de cuán poderosa es la mente para crear enfermedades imaginarias".

"También demuestra cómo ciertas circunstancias revelarán el verdadero carácter de una persona", agregué.

"Sí, Moliere lo demostró también en su obra".

Salimos del teatro y caminamos hasta la estación de tren para tomar el próximo tren a Gelnhausen, donde llegamos poco después del atardecer. Paseando de regreso a la casa del Dr. Samietz, Horst me dijo: "Terminaré el seminario pronto. Una celebración formal de despedida con música y baile se dará a todos los participantes al final. ¿Podrías acompañarme?"

"Dependiendo de la fecha. ¿Cuándo será?"

"La fiesta será una semana después de Pascua".

"Después de Pascua, estaré encantada de acompañarte. Sin embargo, No bailo durante la temporada de Cuaresma. Tampoco escucho música durante los cuarenta días de Cuaresma para conmemorar el sufrimiento de Cristo".

"Me alegra que la fiesta no sea durante la Cuaresma y que puedas asistir a esta celebración especial. Les daré la fecha, la hora y el lugar poco antes del evento".

"Muy bien."

"¿Puedo llamarte antes?"

"Puedes."

"Buenas noches, Hildegard. Gracias por pasar un día encantador conmigo."

"Muchas gracias. También disfruté el viaje a Frankfurt y nuestra asistencia al teatro. Buenas noches, Horst."

Nos dimos la mano y se fue.

Al día siguiente la sala de espera estaba repleta. Tratamos a la mayoría de los pacientes por infecciones de las vías respiratorias superiores, gripe y resfriados. Algunos recibieron inyecciones para la anemia u otras enfermedades crónicas. Terminamos las horas de oficina de la mañana relativamente tarde. No tuve tiempo de ir a comprar comida. Un sándwich con mantequilla y salami tenía que ser suficiente para el almuerzo. Llegaron menos pacientes por la tarde. Por la noche, Estaba cansada y me acosté temprano después de haber consumido otro sándwich. Cada mes que pasaba, me sentía más cómoda tomando dictados. Practicar taquigrafía todas las mañanas ayudó. Cometí menos errores. Estaba agradecida por ello.

Disfruté ser invitada por los pacientes, conocerlos personalmente y, por supuesto, compartir sus deliciosas comidas y pasteles caseros. La señora Fehl me invitó para Semana Santa, que fue el 1 de abril de ese año. La clínica estaba cerrada por el Viernes Santo. Decidí hervir unos huevos y decorarlos con lápices de colores. Dibujé narcisos, violetas y tulipanes en los huevos para la Sra. Fehl, su hija y su yerno. Decoré tres huevos con amapolas rojas, aciano azul y tulipanes rosados, que coloqué sobre la mesa. Una tradición de Viernes Santo que teníamos en casa era que no se nos permitía hablar. Mientras estábamos en silencio, mamá nos recordaba pensar en el dolor que Cristo sufrió en la cruz. Como pasé el día sola, seguí fielmente las instrucciones de mi madre. El Domingo de Resurrección llegó con un amanecer glorioso. Fui a la iglesia para celebrar la resurrección de Cristo con los fieles de la Marienkirche. El coro de la iglesia cantó el coro Aleluya del Mesías de Haendel. Antes y después del sermón sobre la resurrección de Cristo de la tumba, los asistentes cantaron canciones alegres del salvador resucitado. No sólo celebramos la resurrección de Cristo sino el despertar de una nueva vida en la naturaleza. Con alegría, caminé a casa.

Esperé hasta poco antes del mediodía. Tomé mis huevos de Pascua y fui con la Sra. de Fehl. Después de un saludo amistoso, entregué a cada persona uno de mis huevos autodecorados. Me dieron las gracias y los pusieron sobre la mesa. Entonces la Sra. Fehl me pidió que me sentara en una mesa bellamente decorada con flores frescas de primavera y huevos de Pascua de colores. La hija sirvió un asado de cordero, espárragos frescos y ensalada de patata alemana. Hacía mucho tiempo que no disfrutaba de una comida tan deliciosa. A las 3:00 p.m. saboreamos el postre, una tarta Frankfurter Kranz rellena de buttercream y decorada con huevos de Pascua de colores y un conejito de chocolate en el centro.

Siendo maestro, el yerno explicó cómo el conejo de Pascua y los huevos, que son símbolos de fertilidad y vida, se remontan al siglo XV de una celebración pagana alemana de la diosa teutónica Eostre. Los conejos son un signo de fertilidad y huevos de nueva vida. Estos símbolos fueron absorbidos y se convirtieron en parte de nuestra tradición cristiana. También coincide con la celebración judía de la Pascua, una conmemoración de la liberación de los judíos de la esclavitud en Egipto. Me fascinó conocer otros antecedentes históricos de la Semana Santa. Pasamos una tarde deliciosa. Le agradecí a la Sra. Fehl y su familia por incluirme en su celebración familiar. Felizmente, regresé a mi apartamento. Agradecí a Dios por resucitar a Cristo y por permitirme celebrar este día especial con una familia cristiana y no sola. También oré a mi Señor y Salvador viviente para que me ayudara a vivir mi vida de tal manera que reflejara Su imagen. El Lunes de Pascua también se celebraba, sobre todo con familiares, amigos o vecinos, y nadie trabajaba. Como tenía el día libre, decidí ir durante la tarde al Berg Schloesschen Café. Qué delicia pasear por el huerto de manzanos, ver brotar las hojas de los manzanos y preparando las flores para que se abran en breve. La alondra ascendió y gorjeó una alegre melodía. Me llenó el corazón de alegría, no solo escuchando a la alondra y otras aves, sino también viendo el despertar de la naturaleza después del largo y triste descanso invernal. Mucha gente caminó hasta el café en este hermoso día de primavera y se detuvo para comer algo. Por suerte, encontré una pequeña mesa vacía.

Ese día un fresco ramo de violetas decoraba la mesa. Siendo un día de fiesta, pedí una torta de avellanas con una taza de café. El mesero también trajo un pequeño huevo de chocolate en un plato para la ocasión especial. El dueño puso el interludio de "Cavalleria Rusticana". Más tarde se levantó un tenor y cantó arias de la opereta, "El Príncipe Estudiante". Cuando cantó la canción de beber, los invitados se unieron, levantando sus copas o copas de vid y balanceándolas felizmente de un lado a otro. Cuando el tenor hizo una pausa, el propietario tocó algunas composiciones de Mozart, Schubert y Beethoven. Podría haberme quedado toda la noche y haber escuchado la hermosa música después de no haberla escuchado durante cuarenta días. El sol comenzó a ponerse y tuve que regresar antes de que la oscuridad lo tragara por completo.

Como la clínica estuvo cerrada por dos días, el martes, la sala de espera estaba repleta de pacientes que padecían problemas estomacales, alergias, artritis y otras enfermedades. Terminamos las horas de oficina de la mañana tarde. Durante las próximas dos semanas, pensé en qué ponerme para el banquete de la fiesta de graduación de Horst. Yo no poseía un formal o elegante Vestido de noche. Mi prima Emmi, de Alemania del Este, me había enviado un vestido beige con flores negras. Quería que lo tiñera de verde esmeralda. En Alemania del Este, ella no podía comprar tinte, así que me pidió que se lo tiñera. Lo llevé a un lugar para que lo hicieran profesionalmente. Resultó muy bien. Me probé el vestido. Me quedó bien y se veía atractivo en mí. Entonces, pensé que a ella no le importaría si lo usaba para esta ocasión especial. No pude telefonearla, pero le explicaría en una carta que me puse su vestido una vez para una ocasión especial. Opté por no cobrarle el teñido del vestido como muestra de agradecimiento.

El sábado 14 de abril solo trabajamos por la mañana. Gracias a Dios, no tuvimos ningún servicio de llamadas de emergencia para ese fin de semana. Tuve tiempo suficiente para prepararme para el banquete. Me puse mis tacones altos y hasta me puse lápiz labial. También creé un peinado más elegante.

A las 5:00 p.m. llegó Horst. Se veía elegante, vestido con un traje negro, camisa blanca y corbatín.

"Buenas noches, Hildegard. Te ves encantadora. También me gusta tu nuevo peinado".

"Gracias."

"Te ves muy elegante también".

"Gracias. ¿Crees que te sentirás cómoda caminando con tacones altos al restaurante Kauffmann?"

"Creo que puedo arreglármelas."

Horst me ofreció su brazo. Acepté caminar del brazo para sujetarlo en caso de que tropezara. Veinte minutos después, llegamos al restaurante y entramos en un salón de banquetes. Las mesas estaban dispuestas en forma de herradura y bellamente decoradas con diferentes ramos de rosas amarillas, tulipanes rojos y nube con una vela en el centro. Horst se acercó a un amigo y me presentó. Ambos nos sentamos en la mesa al lado de su amigo. Ya habían llegado muchos otros jóvenes y sus acompañantes. Después de que los camareros trajeran vino y aperitivos, sirvieron la cena, que consistió en un escalope vienés, albóndigas de patata y col lombarda. El postre consistía en un vaso de fruta, cubierto con crema batida, chocolate rallado y decorado con una hoja de menta fresca.

"Qué deliciosa comida."

"Sí, el restaurante Kaufmann's es conocido por su comida de calidad. Ya he comido aquí un par de veces." añadió Horst. Tan pronto como los meseros despejaron las mesas, llegó una pequeña banda compuesta por un acordeonista, un violinista y un guitarrista. Comenzaron a tocar música para bailar.

Horst se levantó y me invitó a bailar el vals con la melodía de la alegre vida gitana. Hacía tiempo que no bailaba. Me sentí encantada de poder girar y girar al ritmo de vals de la música. Horst sabía cómo liderar bien, y seguí cada uno de sus movimientos con prontitud. Ambos disfrutamos de los diversos bailes hasta la medianoche cuando la música se detuvo, y todos nos levantamos y cantamos la canción: "Aufwiedersehn, Aufwiedersehn, Bleib Nicht So Lange Fort" (Adiós, adiós, no te quedes demasiado tiempo). Les dijimos buenas noches a algunos de los invitados a la mesa antes de irnos. Sobre nosotros, la luna nueva y las estrellas tachonaban el cielo oscuro, y junto a nosotros, las tenues luces de la calle nos ayudaban a ver el camino de regreso. A estas alturas, me dolían los pies de caminar por el camino de cemento. Cuando llegamos a la puerta de la casa del doctor, le agradecí a Horst por la hermosa velada.

"Disfruté mucho bailando contigo también. Me siento triste porque mi tiempo en Gelnhausen terminará pronto y me dirigiré a Alberta, Canadá. ¿Puedo escribirte?"

"Si puedes. ¡Sabes mi dirección!"

"Bueno, Hildegard, te deseo lo mejor para el futuro. Tal vez, nos volvamos a ver.

"Te deseo buena suerte en Canadá. Todavía no sé qué me depara el futuro. En este momento, no puedo hacer ningún compromiso".

Me abrazó y me besó en la frente, "Adiós, Hildegard".

Le respondí: "Adiós, Horst. Que Dios te bendiga en el futuro."

Y así nos separamos, sintiéndonos tristes, sin saber si nos volveríamos a ver.

Al día siguiente, domingo, me levanté relativamente tarde. Descansé mis pies doloridos para estar en condiciones de trabajar al día siguiente. El lunes, revisando el correo comercial, encontré una carta de mi hermano Edmund. Me escribió que quería visitarme el domingo 29 de abril y quedarse hasta el martes 1 de mayo. Tenía muchas ganas de volver a verlo. Pero, ¿dónde iba a dormir? Mi habitación tenía solo una cama pequeña y un baño compartido con Úrsula, la hija del médico. Tendría que encontrar una habitación de hotel razonable para él. El miércoles, caminé a algunos de los hoteles de la ciudad y verifiqué cuáles eran de bajo precio. Por ahora, estaba feliz de que viniera. Fui al Hotel Altstadt cerca de Marienkirche en Kaiser Platz. Como mi hermano ahora trabajaba como carpintero, pensé que podría pagar una pequeña habitación de hotel. Le escribí que me alegraba de que pudiera visitarme y que le haría una reserva en un hotel de la ciudad. Limpié mi habitación a fondo, así como la ventana. Me sentí terrible por no tener un horno para hacer un pastel para él.

El domingo por la mañana me quedé en casa sin saber a qué hora llegaría Edmund. Cociné un guiso de chucrut, codillo de cerdo y patatas. Con frecuencia miraba por la ventana para ver si podía verlo en la motocicleta. Finalmente, al mediodía, llegó. Corrí escaleras abajo para saludarlo con un gran abrazo, "¡Me alegro de verte! ¿Espero que tengas un buen viaje?"

"El tráfico denso en Frankfurt me retrasó, pero me alegro de haber llegado a salvo".

"Yo también"

"¿Dónde puedo poner mi motocicleta?"

"El Dr. Samietz sugirió ponerla detrás del garaje en el jardín. Estará a salvo allí."

Después de que estacionó la motocicleta, subimos las escaleras.

"Bienvenido a mi habitacion; aquí es donde vivo ahora. Es pequeña, pero estoy contenta. Lo único que extraño es no tener una estufa con horno. No puedo cocinar comidas completas. Por favor, siéntate en la mesa. Te hice un estofado de chucrut y jarrete de cerdo con patatas."

Encendí mi quemador eléctrico de una bobina para recalentar la comida. Puse la mesa con anticipación con un mantel de encaje y flores frescas.

"Debes estar hambriento. Déjame llenar tu plato." Después de dar gracias, comimos el estofado y, de postre, compré un pastel de picadura de abeja (Bienenstich Kuchen), relleno de crema de mantequilla y cubierto con almendras tostadas y caramelizadas. Disfrutamos la comida pero especialmente el pastel con una taza de café instantáneo.

Le pregunté cómo estaban nuestra madre, Horst, Emma y Bernie. Me dijo que Emma y Bernie regresarán a los Estados

Unidos en breve con su esposo y su familia. Edmund estaba preocupado por ellos y quería ir también.

"No me gusta dejarte atrás. ¿Considerarías irte conmigo?" Esta pregunta me sorprendió.

"No tengo edad para tomar mi propia decisión. Necesitaría el permiso de mi madre. Ni siquiera estoy segura de que ella estaría dispuesta a dejarme ir. Meta ya se fue. Emma se irá en breve y Marta vive en la zona desmilitarizada lejos de ella".

"Déjame ese asunto a mí. Veré que puedo hacer." "Si puedes obtener el permiso de nuestra madre, puedo irme contigo por algunos años. Quiero conocer los Estados Unidos.

Sin embargo, me gustaría volver a Alemania nuevamente y encontrar otro lugar para trabajar."

"Cuando regrese a casa, comenzaré a solicitar mis documentos de inmigración. Hablaré con nuestra madre y le haré saber tu decisión.¿Qué futuro tienes aquí, viviendo en esta pequeña habitación y trabajando duro por un salario exiguo?" "No creo que me gustaría quedarme aquí por mucho tiempo. Tal vez, algún día, me casaré y tendré mi propia familia y tal vez incluso mi propia casa. Hermann estaría encantado si le dijera que cambié de opinión".

"Por favor, no pienses en el matrimonio ahora. Piensa en ir a América conmigo. Podrías tener un mejor futuro allí."

"Está bien, iré contigo si obtienes el permiso de mamá".

Qué emocionante sonaba el plan, pero no quería elevar mis esperanzas demasiado todavía. Después de limpiar la mesa y lavar los platos, Le pregunté a Edmund si quería tomar una siesta. Viajar a través de las ciudades congestionadas debe haber sido agotador.

"Sí, creo que tomaré una siesta corta. Se sentirá bien estirar las piernas".

"Bien, me callaré y leeré".

Me senté a la mesa y abrí la Biblia. Me costaba mucho concentrarme en el texto que tenía delante. Mis pensamientos vagaban en todas direcciones, pensando en un posible viaje a América. ¿Cómo reacciónará el Dr. Samietz cuando le diga que renunciaré? ¿Dónde y cómo terminaría viviendo en Estados Unidos? Y muchos otros pensamientos cruzaron por mi mente. Después de orar y poner este asunto al cuidado de Dios y pedirle que me ayudara a tomar la decisión correcta de acuerdo a su voluntad, recuperé mi paz interior.

Edmund se había quedado profundamente dormido. A las 4:00 p. m., lo desperté. Era hora de ir al hotel y registrarlo.

"Será mejor que vayamos al Hotel Altstadt ahora. ¿Crees que quieres dejar tu moto en el jardín? Creo que es seguro aquí. El hotel está a poca distancia de la casa."

"Está bien, solo llevaré mi maleta. Vayamos." Caminamos hasta la parte antigua de Gelnhausen,

pasando por la hermosa Marienkirche y la Pastelería del Pueblo Viejo, donde compré pan y pasteles. Antes de que llegáramos al hotel, le dije a Edmund que no era un hotel elegante pero era de precio modesto y muy limpio. Pensé que sería suficiente para una noche. Cuando llegamos al Hotel Altstadt, entramos en el vestíbulo. Un amable recepcionista nos recibió.

"¿Qué puedo hacer por ustedes?"

"Soy la señorita Bonacker. Hice una reservación para mi hermano Edmund para esta noche."

"Un momento, por favor, déjame mirar el registro de invitados. Sí, reservé la habitación 305 para Edmund Bonaker. Mientras señalaba la escalera, nos indicó cómo llegar a la habitación. Está arriba en el tercer piso. Puedes subir estas escaleras."

"¿Quieres que te pague ahora?" preguntó Edmundo. "Lo que prefieras, ahora o mañana, cuando te vayas." "Prefiero pagar ahora. ¿Cuanto cuesta el cuarto?" "100.00 MA o 24.00 dólares americanos."

"Pagaré en MA. Aquí esta el dinero." Edmund le entregó dos billetes de 50,00 MA. "Gracias. Espera, te daré el recibo."

"Aquí está el recibo y la llave".

Edmund tomó el recibo y la llave. Subimos las escaleras hasta la habitación; estaba modestamente amueblada pero limpia y tenía una hermosa vista de la ciudad.

"Estará bien por una noche", comentó Edmund.

"¿Te gustaría cenar en mi casa? Compré salchichas y pan, ¿o preferirías comer en un restaurante?"

"Creo que podemos comer en un restaurante. ¿Conoces a uno bueno en la ciudad?"

"Sí, comí una vez en Kaufmann's; su comida es excelente." "Entonces vayamos allí", le dije a Edmund lo bien que sabía el wiener schnitzel, que comí en el restaurante Kaufmann. Me gustaría probar un asado de venado que vi en el menú. Disfrutamos tanto de la comida como del rápido servicio. Disfrutamos de la indulgencia inesperada y nos fortaleció la música que tocaron. Sin embargo, no podíamos quedarnos demasiado tarde. Edmund tenía que regresar mañana y necesitaba descansar bien por la noche antes de regresar a casa. Me acompañó de regreso a mi casa y volvería mañana por la mañana para el desayuno. Esa noche, no tardé mucho en conciliar el sueño; Estaba demasiado cansada como para pensar en el futuro. Como el 1 de mayo era fiesta nacional, el Día del Trabajo alemán, tampoco trabajábamos. Me alegré de tener tiempo extra para pasarlo con mi hermano. Quería irse el lunes para no quedar atrapado en el pesado tráfico de las vacaciones. Preparé café, puse la mesa con todas las salchichas. Tan pronto como llegó Edmund, comimos un abundante desayuno.

Hablamos un rato sobre los planes de inmigración. Edmund me escribiría inmediatamente después de obtener el permiso de nuestra madre. Mencionó que ya había iniciado el proceso migratorio para obtener una visa para ir a los Estados Unidos. Sin duda, no quería dejarme atrás. Tampoco me gustaría estar separada de mi hermana Emma y mi hermano Edmund. La decisión final recayó en mi madre. Recé para que ella fuera comprensiva y me dejara ir. La idea de que estaríamos tan lejos el uno del otro si mi madre no me daba permiso me entristecía.

El 1 de mayo celebramos el Día del Trabajo. Muchas personas disfrutaron de caminatas en los bosques, dando la bienvenida al nuevo despertar de la naturaleza. El sol me rogaba que saliera de casa y saliera a caminar. Después del almuerzo, paseé por el huerto de manzanos, con los árboles en flor. Las abejas zumbaban de flor en flor mientras los pájaros cantaban alegremente, volando de árbol en árbol, atrapando insectos. Me hizo olvidar mi preocupación por la inmigración por el momento. Después de una caminata de dos horas por el bosque, fui a mi café favorito, Berg Schloesschen (Castillo de la Montaña). Como era una fiesta memorable, muchas personas vinieron y llenaron el café. Sin embargo, el mesero y el dueño me conocían como una cliente regular; me acomodaron en una mesita junto a la ventana. Pensé en pedir un postre especial, crepas, para la ocasión. El mesero trajo un plato no solo con una crepa sino también adornado con fresas frescas, arándanos, frambuesas y una bola de helado. Ciertamente se veía apetitoso y sabía celestial con una taza de café. Tomé un bocado de cada uno pero terminé el helado primero. Comí lentamente, recogiendo un trozo de fresa u otra baya para que durara mucho tiempo mientras escuchaba la música del piano. Después de un rato, una señora se levantó y cantó canciones populares. La audiencia cantó alegremente, y yo también. Me fui a casa antes del atardecer, todavía tarareando algunas de las melodías en mi cabeza.

Un flujo constante de pacientes en la oficina nos mantuvo ocupados. A medida que me volví más competente en la clínica, el Dr. Samietz me trató con más cortesía. Sin embargo, cada día que pasaba pensaba en emigrar con mi hermano a los Estados Unidos. Esperé ansiosamente el correo de mi hermano. Finalmente, después de una semana, llegó una carta de Edmund. No podía esperar para abrirlo. Sin embargo, No podía leerlo en presencia del médico o de los pacientes. Me excusé diciendo que tenía que ir al baño. Rápidamente, abrí el sobre y mis ojos recorrieron la carta para encontrar la palabra permiso. Vi la frase en la que mi madre decía que sí. Eso es todo lo que quería saber por ahora. El resto de la carta la leería después del horario de oficina. me apresuré a regresar a la sala de recepción para ayudar a cuidar a los pacientes. Esta buena noticia hizo que mi corazón se acelerara. Me costaba mantener la calma y concentrarme en mis deberes. Después de que terminaron las horas de oficina, corrí escaleras arriba. Primero, leí la carta en su totalidad antes de preparar el almuerzo.

¿Había entendido bien? ¿Mi madre me dio su consentimiento para unirme a Edmund y emigrar a Estados Unidos? Luego también escribió que tuvo un accidente con su motocicleta en el camino a casa desde Gelnhausen. Mientras pasaba un camión, el pistón se recalentó, la motocicleta se detuvo y él cayó con la motocicleta en la banqueta de la calle. Afortunadamente, cayó sobre la banqueta blanda delante del camión. Si se hubiera caído en la carretera, el camión lo habría atropellado y lo habría matado. Gracias a Dios, eso no sucedió, y no se lastimó gravemente. Esperó hasta que el pistón se enfriara y continuó lentamente a casa, procurando no rebasar a ningún otro vehículo. Ahora pensé en cómo solicitar los documentos de inmigración. Todavía no podía contarle a nadie sobre mi plan. Debía manejar todo el proceso en secreto. No quería poner en peligro mi trabajo ni sentirme avergonzada si no me concedían la visa. Inmediatamente le respondí a Edmund que comenzaría el proceso el próximo miércoles, lo cual hice.

Tomé un tren temprano a Frankfurt para llegar cuando abriera la oficina del Consulado Americano. El empleado de la taquilla me dijo que el Consulado Americano estaba en el número 30 de la calle Giessener y me dio instrucciones sobre cómo llegar. Un amable empleado me llamó y me preguntó qué podía hacer por mí. Le expliqué que yo era una refugiada de Prusia del Este y que mis dos hermanas ya habían emigrado a los Estados Unidos y que a mi hermano Edmund y a mí también nos gustaría unirnos a ellos. El empleado me explicó que la cuota de Estados Unidos todavía estaba abierta y que podía solicitar una visa de inmigración. Luego me entregó una lista con todos los documentos necesarios y una solicitud de visa permanente.

"Cuando tengas todos los documentos requeridos, regresa; Comenzaremos a trabajar en tu solicitud. Si todos los documentos están en orden, toma aproximadamente medio año obtener el aviso de aprobación o desaprobación".

"Gracias; Le enviaré los documentos necesarios lo antes posible. Adiós."

Cuando salí de la oficina, era mediodía. Me detuve en un pequeño restaurante y me comí un sándwich de bratwurst con chucrut. Paseé por los escaparates de las tiendas textiles. Por ahora, solo podía soñar con tener ropa cara y elegante. Caminé hasta la estación de tren, abordé el tren y llegué a Gelnhausen a última hora de la tarde. Inmediatamente le escribí una carta a mi hermano Edmund. Primero, le pedí que le agradeciera a mi madre por permitirme ir a América, y le agradecí a Edmund por obtener su permiso. Luego enumeré todos los documentos que necesitaba que me enviara. Sólo había llevado conmigo mi tarjeta de identificación. Sin embargo, también necesitaba solicitar un pasaporte alemán. En mi día libre del miércoles siguiente, fui a la Oficina de Ciudadanía en Gelnhausen para preguntar qué documentos necesitaba para solicitar un pasaporte. Requerían fotos seleccionadas y mi tarjeta de identificación. Pregunté dónde estaba la cabina de fotos más cercana. Me tomaron fotos, luego regresé a la Oficina del Ciudadano y les di las fotos y mi tarjeta de identificación. El empleado copió toda mi información de mi tarjeta de identificación y me dijo que tomaría de cuatro a seis semanas obtener el pasaporte.

Cada día esperaba correo de mi hermano Edmund. Finalmente, llegó el paquete que contenía mi certificado de nacimiento, certificado de confirmación, boletas de calificaciones de mi escuela secundaria y del Dr. Glaeser, y la carta de recomendación de mi primer trabajo. El miércoles siguiente, tomé un tren a Frankfurt y presenté todos los documentos requeridos a la Oficina de Inmigración del Consulado Americano. Después de que el empleado comprobara los documentos, me informó que necesitan tener los originales traducidos al inglés y ser aprobados por el director del Departamento de Inmigración. Tomaría alrededor de un mes para el procedimiento. Puede recogerlos en su próxima visita en un mes. Si todos los informes están en orden, también deberá realizarse un examen médico completo.

"Adiós, señorita Bonacker; vuelva en un mes." "Adiós señor; Le veré en un mes".

Así, comencé un largo procedimiento de ir y venir al consulado estadounidense, recoger los documentos originales, tomar nuevos y esperar hasta que la oficina verificara mis antecedentes. Me sometí a un examen médico completo, incluyendo radiografías de tórax y un electrocardiograma. Mientras tanto, seguí con mi trabajo en la clínica sin dejar que el Dr. y la Sra. Samietz o pacientes o amigos supieran de mis planes de emigrar a Estados Unidos. Solo le escribí cartas a mi hermano y le conté sobre el progreso de mi solicitud de visa. Cada vez que tenía un miércoles libre, iba de excursión al bosque. Escuchar el canto de los pájaros y el susurro de la brisa entre las ramas me encantaba. Me di el gusto de un cuarto de libra de dulce de coco, que consumí lentamente. Los hice durar todo el tiempo que caminé. En el camino de regreso, me detenía y compraba comestibles para los próximos tres días, principalmente pan, panecillos y salchichas, una o dos chuletas de cerdo y un frasco de chucrut. Continué visitando el castillo de la montaña para mis golosinas dominicales. Cada domingo, el dueño tocaba música semiclásica o popular para deleite de los invitados. De vez en cuando, las divas de la ópera o algunos cantantes famosos se levantaban y entretenían a los visitantes. Algunos cantantes folclóricos invitaron a los invitados a cantar. La mayoría de las personas tenían un repertorio bastante extenso de canciones folklóricas y estaban felices de unirse al cantante o al pianista. Siempre disfruté la tarde del domingo en el café y la caminata cuesta arriba y cuesta abajo, cubierta de manzanos.

Mientras tanto, mi hermano Edmund escribió que mi hermana Emma, su esposo Gustav y su hijo Bernard irían a los Estados Unidos a mediados de julio. Me sentí triste por no poder ir a casa a despedirme de mi hermana Emma y mi sobrino Bernie. Pero sabía que el Dr. Samietz no me daría tiempo libre antes de cumplir con mis requisitos de vacaciones. Edmund me envió una foto de Bernie vestido con un conjunto azul marino y blanco alemán, incluida la gorra con las dos cintas en la espalda. Se veía adorable en él. Cuando alguien le preguntaba cuántos años tenía, respondía: "Tengo tres años y no tengo esposa". Su respuesta haría reír a la gente. Mi hermana, su familia y sus suegros volaron en un avión de transporte de la Compañía de

Transportes Tigres Voladores. Salieron de Hamburgo y volaron a Nueva York, luego continuaron en tren a Chicago. Decidieron quedarse en Chicago, donde vivían muchos alemanes. Encontrar trabajo en una gran ciudad debería ser más fácil que en un pueblo pequeño.

Edmund se entristeció al ver que nuestra hermana se iba de casa. Esperaba unirse a ella pronto. Ya había solicitado sus documentos de inmigración en Munich y esperaba su visa. Ambos nos quedamos a la espera de la aprobación final. Pasó el verano y el otoño, con todo su colorido esplendor, llegó a los campos y bosques. Los manzanos de la huerta llevaban sus frutos maduros listos para ser cosechados. De camino al castillo de la montaña, recogía alguna manzana que se hubiera caído al suelo. Cuando los fuertes vientos peinaban las copas de los árboles, arrancaban más manzanas y las arrojaban al suelo y al borde del camino. Quería juntar lo suficiente para hacer manzanas fritas como un regalo. Sin embargo, mi alegría llegó al saber que mi hermano Edmund había recibido su visa. Durante mi último viaje a Frankfurt, supe que cumplía con todos los requisitos de inmigración, y que mi visa también había sido aprobada. Ahora estaba segura de que pronto nos reuniríamos con mi hermana Emma y su familia en Chicago El 16 de diciembre de 1956 fue mi fecha de salida designada de Bremerhaven con el barco de transporte militar estadounidense llamado General Harry Tayler.

Por su parte, Edmund eligió volar a los Estados Unidos. Se suponía que su avión saldría de Hamburgo a principios de noviembre. Hubiera preferido ir con mi hermano en avión que viajar en barco. El océano puede estar agitado en invierno. Por ahora le agradecí a Dios que no nos separáramos y que ambos pudiéramos irnos a Estados Unidos. No importaba que cada uno saliera en una fecha diferente. También esperábamos ver a la hermana Meta y su familia, quienes ya habían vivido en

Iowa durante algunos años. Le escribí a mi hermana que me gustaría quedarme con ellos hasta que encontrara un puesto médico. Pregunté dónde le sería más fácil venir a recogerme. Ahora venía la pregunta difícil: cómo y cuándo le diría al Dr. Samietz mi plan y le daría el aviso para terminar el trabajo con él. ¿Cómo reaccionaría? Oré para que Dios me diera las palabras correctas y me mostrara el momento correcto. Tuve que decirle al Dr. Samietz primero y después a mis amigos y pacientes. Esperé hasta haber cumplido un año trabajando en la clínica. El sábado 13 de octubre, después de ver a todos los pacientes, me acerqué al escritorio del Dr. Samietz y le dije, Dr. Samietz, me gustaría decirle que he recibido mi aprobación para emigrar a los Estados Unidos.

"¿Quieres ir a dónde? ¿Quieres ir a América? "

"Sí, mi hermano Edmund se irá en noviembre. Mi salida en barco está prevista para el 16 de diciembre".

"¿Cuánto tiempo puedes seguir trabajando?"

"Creo que puedo quedarme hasta finales de noviembre. Pensé en avisarte con anticipación, para que tuviera tiempo suficiente de encontrar una nueva asistente."

"Supongo que, si ese es el caso, no puedo evitar que te vayas. Ahora que has aprendido a realizar todo el trabajo a mi entera satisfacción y a los pacientes les gusta, esperaba que te hubieras quedado más tiempo. Pero no puedo retenerte aquí en contra de tu voluntad."

"Gracias, Dr. Samietz. ¿Serías tan amable de escribirme una carta de recomendación? Estoy segura de que si solicito un puesto en los Estados Unidos, al nuevo empleador le gustaría saber cómo desempeñé mis funciones en mi trabajo anterior".

"Lo haré. Sé que mis pacientes te extrañarán. Les caes bien."

"Sé que también los extrañaré. Me encariñé con muchos de sus pacientes. Pero todos tenemos diferentes destinos que seguir".

"Supongo que tengo que dejarte ir".

"Gracias, Dr. Samietz, por ser tan comprensivo."

Agradecí que todo salió bien, y el Dr. Samietz no me reprendió. Fue comprensivo y muy educado. Supongo que los pacientes que me dijeron que el Dr. Samietz parece rudo por fuera pero es amable por dentro estaban en lo correcto. Mi respeto por él creció. Me quedé en la oficina y archivé los registros de los pacientes. Terminé de poner todos los artículos en orden en la sala de espera y la sala de examen antes de subir las escaleras. Respiré aliviada de que el Dr. Samietz aceptara mi renuncia cortésmente y sin enfado. Al día siguiente, le conté a Lioba, su criada, mis planes. Con el paso del tiempo, compartí mi intención con los pacientes a los que me había encariñado. Algunos estaban tristes, otros indiferentes a mi salida de la clínica.

Antes de irme de Alemania, quería ver a mi hermana Marta y su familia, que vivían en la zona militar de cinco millas de ancho en Alemania Oriental. Los viajes dentro y fuera de su región estaban restringidos, y el consulado de Alemania Oriental, bajo el dominio ruso, concedía pocos permisos. A las personas que vivían en Alemania Oriental tampoco se les permitía viajar a Alemania Occidental. Me preocupaba si habría posibilidad de visitarla antes de que emigrara a América. Fui con un agente de viajes local y le expliqué mi posición. Luego pregunté cómo obtener un permiso de viaje para visitar a mi hermana en la zona militar de Alemania Oriental. El agente de viajes me preguntó cuándo vi a mi hermana por última vez. Le dije que fue hace más de diez años.

"Existe una pequeña posibilidad de que el consulado de Alemania Oriental pueda cumplir con su solicitud y permitirle verla. ¿Tienes tu DNI y pasaporte contigo?

¿Cuándo te gustaría ir y cuánto tiempo te gustaría quedarte con tu hermana?"

"Me gustaría quedarme con ella diez días, desde el lunes 4 de diciembre hasta el viernes 14 de diciembre". Le entregué mi pasaporte y mi tarjeta de identificación personal. Copió toda la información necesaria en una solicitud. "Enviaré la solicitud a Berlín para su aprobación. Puede tomar alrededor de tres a cuatro semanas recibir una respuesta". "Gracias; Volveré en tres semanas. Adiós." Seguro que esperaba y oraba a Dios para que mi deseo fuera concedido. Mi hermana y su familia estarían encantados de que pudiera pasar al menos unos días con ellos antes de partir a otro país. Sólo me quedaban seis semanas más de trabajo en la clínica. Escribí a mi madre y a Edmund que quería visitar a mi hermana Marta y su familia en Alemania Oriental y que había solicitado un permiso de viaje. Sin embargo, no tenía la seguridad de recibirlo. También les hice saber que estaría en casa el 1 de diciembre. Edmund respondió que volaría el martes 13 de noviembre de Hamburgo a Nueva York y luego tomaría un tren a Chicago, donde vivía nuestra hermana Emma y su familia. Me escribiría tan pronto como llegara a Chicago. A menudo, me sorprendí distraída, pensando en todas las cosas que aún tenía que preparar antes de irme. Pensamientos de emoción acerca de ir a otro país zumbaban como un enjambre de abejas en mi cerebro. Tuve que obligarme a concentrarme en mi trabajo. Le pedí a Dios que no cometiera un error, como aplicar una inyección equivocada o causar dolor o sufrimiento innecesario a un paciente. Di gracias a Dios que hasta el momento no había ocurrido ningún incidente traumático. Esperaba que durante el resto del tiempo que trabajara no pasara nada. También les escribí a mis tías, tíos, a mis amigas y a Hermann que saldría en diciembre para ir a los Estados Unidos de América. En este punto, no tenía idea si sería una visita por tiempo limitado o una estadía permanente. Me preguntaba qué pensaría Hermann de que me fuera de Alemania y si aún tendría la oportunidad de verlo. También notifiqué a la administración de la ciudad de Gelnhausen, que exigió que me registrara la fecha en que tomé residencia en la ciudad y la fecha en que abandoaba la ciudad. Tres semanas y media después, fui a la agencia de viajes. Cuando entré en la oficina de viajes, el empleado me saludó con una sonrisa tranquilizadora.

"Fraeulein Bonacker, tengo buenas noticias para usted. Le conseguí el permiso de viaje." Luego miró entre su correspondencia y me entregó mi visa con estas palabras: "Solo asegúrate de notificar a la estación de policía del pueblo cuando llegues a Silkerode y cuando te vayas. Limite los viajes a otras ciudades. Si necesita ir a otro lugar, lleve siempre consigo su permiso y pasaporte para evitar confrontaciones desagradables".

"Gracias por obtener la visa a tiempo. Seguiré de cerca tus consejos. Adiós."

Felizmente, regresé a mi habitación y le escribí una carta a mi hermana Marta, sabiendo que ella y su familia estarían encantados de escuchar las buenas noticias sobre mi visita.

El último domingo de noviembre di mi paseo habitual hasta el Mountain Castle Café. Era un día frío y sombrío de otoño. Las ramas de los manzanos lloraron la pérdida de sus hojas y frutos. También lamenté la partida de mi café favorito en la ciudad. El propietario, el sr. Krueger, siempre me saludaba amablemente como una de sus fieles invitadas. Ese día notó la tristeza de mi expresión y me preguntó qué me preocupaba. Le dije que esta era mi última visita y que planeaba emigrar a Estados Unidos el próximo mes.

"Lamento que te vayas, pero te deseo buena suerte en Estados Unidos. Ven, ven, ahora anímate. Les tocaré música especial que compuse recientemente. Te lo dedicaré como mi regalo de despedida."

Después de que me senté en una mesa, el pianista propietario se acercó al piano y tocó su composición. El señor Krueger me abrumó con la belleza de la música y su gesto de dedicarme su composición. Me levanté y le di las gracias con un apretón de manos. Luego regresé a mi mesa y pedí un strudel de manzana con salsa de vainilla caliente, una de las especialidades del café, y mi taza de café habitual. La salsa caliente sabía tan bien en este día húmedo y sombrío. Siendo frío, no aparecieron muchas personas ese domingo. Pero los presentes disfrutaron de sus delicias mientras escuchaban una variedad de música. Después de que terminé de comer, esperé hasta que el Sr. Krueger terminó de tocar la "Serenata" de Schubert. Luego me acerqué a él y le dije: "Sr. Krueger, lo siento, tengo que irme ahora. Quiero agradecerte por tu composición y por todo el deleite que me brindaste con tu música y, por supuesto, todos tus deliciosos pasteles y postres especiales. Siempre atesoraré los recuerdos de mis visitas aquí." "Señorita Bonacker, también extrañaré verla todos los domingos. Fuiste una clienta encantadora."

Se levantó, me abrazó y se despidió. Luego les dijo a los clientes que la señorita Bonacker los deja para irse a América; cantémosle todos "Adiós" (Aufwiedersehn). Mientras los clientes cantaban a capella, me conmovieron hasta las lágrimas. Cuando terminaron de cantar, me sequé las lágrimas rápidamente, agradecí a la gente y al sr. Krueger, y me fui. Mi corazón se desbordó de mezcla emociones de tristeza y alegría mientras bajaba la colina a través del huerto de manzanos por última vez.

Dos días antes de terminar mi trabajo, el Dr. Samietz me dio una carta de recomendación con estas palabras: "Aquí está la carta de recomendación. En general, lo hiciste bien y te deseo buena suerte para encontrar el puesto adecuado en Estados Unidos".

"Gracias, Dr. Samietz; Seguro que lo haré. Gracias también por enseñarme tantos procedimientos médicos mientras trabajaba para usted".

Apenas podía esperar para ir a mi habitación y leer el contenido de su carta. Aquí hay una traducción de lo que escribió:

Dr. en medicina Walther Samietz Gelnhausen, 28.
Noviembre de 1956
Calle Barbarossa. Número 6 Tel 24 56

Informe de la señorita Bonacker, Hilde, nacida el 2 de enero de 1937

Contraté a la señorita Hilde Bonacker como asistente comercial y médica desde el 10 de octubre de 1955 hasta finales de noviembre de 1956. Durante ese tiempo, realizó todas sus tareas requeridas en la clínica. Se desempeñó como mi asistente médico y realizó todos los análisis de laboratorio ella misma. Podía confiar en los resultados de sus estudios gástricos, hemogramas, glucosa y otras pruebas de laboratorio, porque era competente y hacía bien las pruebas. La señorita Bonacker también tomó radiografías. Manejaba todos los registros médicos, la correspondencia y cobraba los honorarios médicos del gobierno. Ella ejecutó todo su trabajo asignado concienzudamente y para mi gran satisfacción.

La señorita Bonacker también vivía en mi casa y era una inquilina agradable y cortés. Sus modales y su comportamiento siempre fueron impecables.

La Srta. Bonacker termina su empleo conmigo porque quiere emigrar a Estados Unidos. Lamento haberla perdido, pero le deseo todo lo mejor para el futuro.

Dr. Walther Samietz

El contenido de la carta del Dr. Samietz me asombró al principio. Muy rara vez me mostró que apreciaba mi trabajo excepcional y mis modales impecables. Me demostró de nuevo que bajo la apariencia áspera había un corazón gentil. Di gracias a Dios por esa noche y al Dr. Samietz a la mañana siguiente por la carta de tan alta recomendación. Él solo respondió con una gran sonrisa, y yo también. Todos los malos sentimientos del pasado se desvanecieron en el olvido. El jueves y el viernes hice las maletas de última hora y limpié la habitación. Quería dejar todo impecable y en orden. Después de ver al último paciente el viernes, me despedí del Dr. Samietz y también la señora Samietz bajó a la sala de recepción para despedirse de mí. Me agradecieron por haber sido una asistente médico tan capaz y cortés. A su vez, agradecí al Dr. Samietz por la oportunidad de haber adquirido experiencia práctica trabajando para y con él. Me desearon lo mejor, y yo también. Lioba, su doncella, se sintió muy triste porque me iba. Nos habíamos encariñado y sabía que la extrañaría. Úrsula, la hija del Dr. y la Sra. Samietz, vino a despedirse el viernes por la noche. Ambos habíamos desarrollado una relación cordial y ella expresó cuánto disfrutaba confiar en mí y lamentaba verme partir.

El sábado por la mañana, caminé con dos maletas hasta la estación de tren para tomar el primer tren de Frankfurt. Me detuve una vez en el camino para echar un vistazo más a la Marienkirche, las ruinas del castillo, el Castillo de la Montaña y otros lugares familiares que había disfrutado mientras residí un año en Gelnhausen. Nunca olvidaré mis caminatas de los miércoles por el bosque mientras consumía lentamente mi dulce de coco y escuchaba el canto de los pájaros. Acogí con beneplácito los cambios de estación en los bosques, especialmente el despertar de la naturaleza en primavera. Observé la nieve que cubría las hojas secas y los restos del otoño con multitud de copos blancos, transformando el bosque en un pacífico paraíso invernal. Siempre me sentí cerca de Dios y Su creación en el bosque. Después de cada caminata, la belleza, la vida silvestre y las maravillas del bosque refrescaron mi mente e inspiraron mi alma.

En ese momento mi mente volvió rápidamente a mi caminata hacia la estación de tren. Llegué justo a tiempo para tomar el tren temprano a Frankfurt. Tuve que cambiar el tren de Frankfurt, yendo a Mannheim y Neustadt antes de llegar a Landau a última hora de la tarde. En Landau, tomé el tren local a Knoerringen-Essingen. Desde allí, solo había que caminar un poco hasta Essingen, donde todavía vivían mi madre y mi hermano Horst. Viajar en tren y ver los diversos paisajes que pasaban por la ventana me atraía; también lo hizo conocer interesantes compañeros de viaje. Pero hoy, mis pensamientos ya viajaban a mi hermana Marta en Alemania del Este, y no presté mucha atención al paisaje que pasaba.

Agotada, finalmente llegué a casa. Mi hermano Richard había venido a casa el fin de semana; cuando me vio por la ventana, vino a ayudarme a llevar mis maletas a la casa. Verlo me trajo todos los recuerdos de la infancia de Prusia del Este, y me alegré de que tuviera el fin de semana libre. Mi madre y Horst estaban felices de volver a verme después de un año. Por la mañana, todos fuimos a la iglesia. Sucedió que era el primer domingo de Adviento. Después de que nos sentamos, recordé cuando me paré sola frente al altar el día que me confirmaron y respondí correctamente todas las preguntas que me hizo el pastor Armin Schlender. Luego miré hacia el balcón, donde estaba sentado el coro de la iglesia. Mi hermano Georg y yo nos unimos al coro poco después de llegar a Essingen. El señor Jaeger, el director de orquesta, nos enseñó muchos himnos religiosos y siempre esperábamos con ansias el picnic anual. Muchos recuerdos pasaron por mi mente antes de que el pastor diera la bienvenida a los feligreses, y comenzamos a cantar el cántico de Adviento, "Ven, ven, Emmanuel".

Después de que terminamos la liturgia tradicional, el coro de la iglesia cantó: "Hija de Sión, regocíjate, regocíjate, mira que tu rey viene a ti". Miré al balcón. Vi a todos los cantantes familiares y me despedí de ellos en silencio. El pastor Bruenings predicó el sermón sobre cómo preparar nuestros corazones para la venida del Salvador. Después del sermón, los feligreses se dirigieron al altar para recibir la sagrada comunión. Luego cantamos los tres primeros versos, "Encomienda tu camino y lo que aflige a tu corazón al cuidado más fiel". La canté con tan celosa confianza en el camino desconocido que Dios me conduciría en el futuro. El párroco dijo la bendición y nos despidió. Le dije a mi madre que quería esperar y despedirme del pastor Bruenings. Mamá, Richard y Horst dijeron que se irían a casa, a solo media cuadra de la iglesia, y prepararían el almuerzo. Mientras esperaba al pastor, hablé con los vecinos y también con algunos miembros del coro de la iglesia. Estaban contentos de verme pero tristes de verme dejar el país. Cuando el pastor Bruenings se me acercó, le dije que pronto iría a Estados Unidos, pero que primero planeaba visitar a mi hermana Marta en Alemania Oriental.

"Lamento que te vayas, pero deseo que Dios te acompañe y te proteja siempre y donde quiera que estés".

"Gracias, Pastor Bruenings; Les deseo a usted y a su familia también las bendiciones de Dios."

"¿Cuándo te vas?"

"El martes; Viajaré con mi hermana Marta que vive en Silkerode, y mi barco sale de Bremerhaven el 16 de diciembre".

"Adiós, Hildegard y que Dios te bendiga. Le diré a mi hija Gudrun que te vea mañana".

"Gracias; dele mi despedida a la Sra. Bruenings y a su familia también.

Adiós, pastor Bruenings."

Nos dimos la mano y caminé a casa. Cuando entré en la cocina, podía oler el pato asándose en el horno. Mamá preparó mi comida favorita. De postre, había horneado un pastel de manzana. Saboreé su cocina; mis tres hermanos también.

Georg, que trabajaba para el viñedo local del Sr. Feldmann, se unió a nosotros en la iglesia y para el almuerzo. Con solo catorce años, mi hermano menor, Horst, parecía muy triste porque me iba de Alemania pronto y, con tristeza, mi madre vio a su tercera y menor hija partir a otro país. Intenté incansablemente animarlos hablando con gran entusiasmo sobre Estados Unidos. También dejé abierta la posibilidad de volver si, por cualquier motivo, no me gustaría vivir allí. Se obligaron a ser más alegres, pero solo por apariencia. El domingo por la noche, Richard tuvo que regresar a su lugar de trabajo, al igual que Georg, que vivía en el viñedo. Las lágrimas brotaron cuando nos despedimos. Le di las gracias a Georg por haber asumido el papel de su padre durante nuestra huida de Prusia Oriental. Él alimentó a los caballos y nos ayudó a sobrevivir los setenta y cuatro días de viaje a caballo y en carreta a través de un invierno muy frío a través de las terribles condiciones y peligros de la Segunda Guerra Mundial. Siempre estaré en deuda con él y con los hermanos Kirstein, Fritz y Gustav, quienes nos ayudaron valientemente con las reparaciones de las carretas, proporcionándonos comida y forraje para los caballos. Pero sobre todo, siempre agradeceré a Dios que Él nos protegió y nos mantuvo vivos a través de los peligros y los bombardeos de la Segunda Guerra Mundial. Ahora le pedía a Dios que me protegiera y me guiara mientras comenzaba un nuevo viaje a otra parte del mundo.

El domingo por la tarde visité a la familia Wistof. Tres hermanos. Edelmut, Freimut, y Hartmut pertenecía a nuestro grupo de jóvenes, al igual que las dos hermanas, Helge y Heidrun de Hermann Jaeger. Yo también esperaba ver a Hermann. Pasé brevemente para ver a Gudrun y Norbert Kleinschmidt y Heidi e Ingrid Freytag, que se habían unido a mi grupo de jóvenes. Estaba agradecida por el tiempo que habíamos pasado juntos y los muchos eventos hermosos a los que asistimos y triste por dejarlos atrás. Regresé a tiempo para la cena. Después de la cena, nos sentamos cerca del radiador y recordamos la vida en Prusia del Este. Antes de irme a dormir, agradecí a Dios que me permitió ver a tantos amigos y vecinos antes de irme. También agradecí a Dios por su guía y amor hasta ahora. Con confianza pongo todas mis preocupaciones futuras en Sus manos amorosas.

El lunes, planeé hacer dos maletas, una con mi ropa para visitar a mi hermana en Alemania del Este, y una de madera más grande que enviaría directamente a Bremerhaven al barco General Harry Taylor. Mientras revisaba afanosamente mis libros, mi madre sugirió: "También, llévate un edredón de plumas, que rellené con plumas de ganso de nuestra granja en Prusia del Este. Siempre te mantendrá caliente. También traerá recuerdos de cómo las cobijas de plumas nos salvaron en la Segunda Guerra Mundial de congelarnos durante la huida de Prusia del Este".

"¿Cómo puedo meter uno en mi maleta?" Pensé. Pero luego reflexioné sobre las palabras de mi madre: "Siempre te mantendrá abrigada y te recordará tu hogar". Decidí llevarme uno.

Mamá fue al armario, donde había guardado el de los niños, "Toma, toma este y las sábanas también".

"Lo haré, madre, ¡Gracias!»

Luego revisé todos mis libros, boletas de calificaciones y cuadernos. Tuve que ser muy selectiva con un espacio tan limitado. Tomé todas mis boletas de calificaciones, cartas de referencia, mi libro de poesía llamado El Árbol en Flor (Der Bluetenbaum), Un diccionario o y mi Biblia. También tomé tres platos de postre con tazas y platillos. Los amigos me los habían dado para mi confirmación. Siempre me recordaría la amabilidad de mis amigos y esa celebración especial. Embalé cada pieza individualmente en papel y lo coloqué entre la cubierta de plumón para asegurarme de que no se rompieran. Metí todos los demás artículos que había seleccionado para llevar y la manta de plumas antes de cerrar la maleta. Escribí la dirección de la compañía naviera encima del baúl y lo llevé a la oficina de correos a última hora de la tarde. Horst, que había regresado de la escuela, vino conmigo y me ayudó a llevar la maleta de madera a la oficina de correos. Corrimos a casa. Revisé mi guardarropa y elegí algunas prendas abrigadas para llevar también. Guardé todos mis documentos de inmigración, pasaporte y tarjeta de identificación en mi bolso de gran tamaño y algunos Marcos Alemanes que había guardado mientras trabajaba en la clínica.

Después de la cena, hablamos un rato. Expresé mi gratitud a mi madre por hacer posible que yo fuera a la escuela secundaria y permitirme emigrar a los Estados Unidos. Sabía que era un gran sacrificio para ella dejarme ir, pero ella no quería hacer nada contrario a los planes de Dios y mis aspiraciones. Cuando me acosté tarde y físicamente cansada, mi mente permaneció despierta durante mucho tiempo. Pensamientos del pasado y el futuro corrían de un lado a otro en mi cabeza. Pasada la medianoche finalmente me quedé dormida por unas horas. A las 5:00 a.m. sonó el despertador. Era hora de levantarse y prepararse. Mi madre también se levantó para hacer el desayuno. Horst se despertó una hora después. No tenía que ir a la escuela hasta las 8:00 a.m. Dejé mi maleta y mi cartera junto a la puerta antes de sentarnos a desayunar. Ninguno de los dos podía poner nuestros pensamientos y emociones en palabras; solo nuestras expresiones faciales revelaron los sentimientos de nuestros corazones. Llegó el momento de decir adiós. Solo nos miramos, luego nos abrazamos y dejamos que nuestras lágrimas fluyeran. Entonces tuve que dejar ir a mi madre. Ella pronunció: "Que Dios te acompañe y te proteja siempre".

"Gracias Madre; él lo hará Que Dios esté contigo y te consuele."

Agarré mi bolso y Horst la maleta, y nos fuimos. Sin embargo, una parte de mi vida se quedó atrás.

Amaneció cuando Horst y yo llegamos a la estación del ferrocarril. Lentamente llegaron más personas. La mayoría iba a Landau. Tuve que ir en dirección contraria a Neustadt. Me despedí de Horst cuando llegó mi tren. Lo abracé y le pedí que cuidara de nuestra madre, diciendo: "Ella te necesitará aún más ahora que todas tus hermanas están lejos de casa". Contuve mis lágrimas y me embarqué rápidamente en el tren. Afortunadamente, ninguna otra persona entró en el vagón. Me senté, puse mi maleta a mi lado, saqué mi pañuelo y me sequé las lágrimas. El maquinista hizo sonar el silbato y puso en marcha el motor de la locomotora. Las ruedas comenzaron a girar mientras el vapor y el humo se escapaban por la chimenea de la locomotora y dejaban atrás una banda de vapor blanco.

Los bosques mixtos cubrían las montañas Haardt y rodaban por la ventana. Ese día, los árboles de hoja caduca sin hojas exponían los castillos y otros puntos de referencia, que pude reconocer desde la distancia. El Bosque Palatino era un paraíso para los excursionistas, que los recompensaba con pequeños ríos y estanques para relajarse y refrescarse. Una rica flora cubría el suelo en primavera y creaba una colorida alfombra viva de musgo y varias flores silvestres. En otoño, cosechamos castañas en abundancia. Recuerdo las muchas caminatas vigorizantes que hicimos en el bosque mientras cantábamos canciones folklóricas.

En otoño, recogíamos las castañas caídas y las tosábamos en un fuego abierto mientras saboreábamos la vid blanca opaca recién fermentada. Después de que nuestros estómagos estuvieran satisfechos, nos sentábamos alrededor de la fogata y cantábamos. En invierno, buscábamos una colina para deslizarnos en trineos o esquiar. Recordé cuando me puse un par de esquís por primera vez y bajé de la montaña. No sabía cómo parar. Simplemente me caí de lado, me levanté, subí la colina y pregunté cómo detenerme correctamente en la próxima carrera. Recogiendo bayas y setas en el bosque también eran uno de mis pasatiempos favoritos. Ahora, el pasado era solo un recuerdo atesorado. El futuro era solo un misterio y un sueño. Cuando el conductor vino a revisar el pasaje, me devolvió al presente. Cuando miró mi boleto y vio todos los nombres de las ciudades donde tenía que cambiar de tren, comentó:

"Fraeulein, tiene un largo camino por delante. A continuación, debe cambiar el tren en Neustadt que va a Mannheim".

"Gracias. Lo haré."

El conductor pasó por el pasillo cuando llegamos a Neustadt y gritó: "Próxima parada, Neustadt". Me preparé para desembarcar. Llevé mi maleta a la taquilla y le pregunté al empleado en qué vía salía el tren a Mannheim. Cuando llegó el tren, me subí. En Mannheim, cambié el tren que iba a Frankfurt. Como había viajado por Frankfurt varias veces, Ya estaba familiarizada con la estación de ferrocarril allí. Tuve tiempo de sobra para conseguir un pretzel y una Coca-Cola mientras esperaba el tren que iba a Hanau. En Hanau, tomé el tren a Eisenach, que estaba en la frontera con Alemania Oriental. Aunque el tren se detuvo en las grandes ciudades del camino, no tuve que cambiar de tren hasta llegar a Eisenach. Cuando me subí al tren en Hanau, elegí un compartimento en medio del vagón menos ruidoso y tambaleante. En las paradas, algunas personas bajaron del tren;

otros se subieron. Algunas personas disfrutaban conversando con los viajeros; otros leyeron libros, periódicos o incluso tomaron siestas. Mi pasatiempo favorito mientras viajaba en tren era ir al vagón comedor, comer o simplemente un postre y una taza de café mientras observaba el paisaje que cambiaba rápidamente.

En la próxima parada en Schuechtern, un distinguido caballero entró al auto y se sentó frente a mí. Después de quitarse el abrigo, el sombrero y los guantes y poner su maletín en el compartimiento de almacenamiento superior, comenzó una conversación y me preguntó sobre mi destino de viaje. Le dije que mi último objetivo era Nueva York por barco. Ahora voy de camino a visitar a mi hermana en Silkerode, Alemania Oriental.

"Pero Fraeulein, espero que no tenga todos sus documentos de inmigración con usted".

"Sí, los tengo."

"Creo que no es seguro llevarlos contigo a Alemania Oriental. En caso de que uno de los guardias en la frontera sea rencoroso, podría quitártelos y arruinar todos tus planes."

"No pensé en esa posibilidad. ¿Qué sugieres que haga?"
"¿No puedes enviarlos a casa y luego volver a recogerlos?" "Ojalá pudiera, pero no tengo tiempo para ir a casa;

también está fuera de mi camino. Me quedaré con mi hermana en Silkerode hasta el 14 de diciembre. Luego tengo que viajar a Bremerhaven para tomar el barco a Nueva York el 16 de diciembre".

"¿No tienes un pariente o un amigo en el camino a Bremerhaven, ¿dónde podrías enviar los documentos y luego recogerlos a tu regreso?"

Reflexioné por un momento. Entonces pensé que tal vez debería enviar los documentos a Hermann en Hamburgo. Podría parar de camino a Bremerhaven para recogerlos.

"Sí, señor, tengo un amigo en Hamburgo donde podría enviarlos y luego recogerlos después de visitar a mi hermana".
"Eso es una buena idea. La siguiente parada es Fulda.

Tenemos alrededor de media hora. Puedes ir a la taquilla y enviar los documentos desde allí. Mi destino es Bad Hersfeld. Puedo vigilar tu equipaje."

"Gracias, señor, es muy amable de su parte. Lo haré.

¿Tendrías una hoja de papel en blanco de la que pudieras prescindir?"

"Sí. Espera, te lo consigo." El caballero tomó su maletín, lo abrió y me entregó una hoja de papel. "Lo siento, no tengo un sobre grande; de lo contrario, te lo daría."

"Gracias; Tengo los documentos en un sobre grande en blanco. Puedo usar el mismo para el correo", Me excusé mientras le escribía una nota a Hermann. Luego puse la visa y los documentos de inmigración en el sobre y se los dirigí a Hermann. Como no tenía residencia, puse la dirección del remitente de mi madre en el sobre. Luego lo puse en mi bolso.

"Ahora puedo enviar la carta en Fulda. Espero que llegue antes que yo; de lo contrario, literalmente perderé el barco".

"Creo que lo hará. Aquí el servicio de correo es confiable.

¿Puedo preguntar cuál es su razón para ir a Estados Unidos?" "Uno de mis hermanos y dos hermanas ya están en los Estados Unidos. Quiero unirme a ellos. Estados Unidos, Canadá, Australia y América del Sur tienen una cuota para aceptar solo a unos tantos refugiados. Como soy una refugiada de Prusia del Este y mi hermano y mis dos hermanas ya están allí, elegí unirme a ellos en Estados Unidos". "¿Cuándo te fuiste de Prusia del Este?"

"Mi madre, con siete hijos, huyó a caballo y en carreta en agosto de 1944. Viajamos en caminatas durante ocho meses haciendo varias paradas en el camino antes de detenernos en Schleswig Holstein poco antes de que terminara la guerra".

"¿Dónde estaba tu padre?"

"Mi padre fue reclutado en el ejército dos semanas antes de que saliéramos de Prusia del Este. El ejército polaco capturó a mi padre y lo mantuvo como prisionero y luego como trabajador forzado en una cantera de piedra y minas de carbón. A la fecha no ha regresado".

"Lamento oír eso; Sí, La Segunda Guerra Mundial trajo tanta destrucción y sufrimiento insuperable a tantas familias. Tuve suerte de sobrevivir. Vi a muchos de mis camaradas heridos y asesinados. Tuve la suerte de sufrir sólo heridas leves y me recuperé por completo. En Bad Hersfeld, tuvimos un campo de prisioneros estadounidense en abril y mayo de 1945. El profesor Ernst Hermann Ruebsam vivía en Bad Hersfeld y estuvo prisionero en el campo durante doce días. Aunque la guerra ya había terminado, los estadounidenses lo mantuvieron prisionero en el campo. ¿Quizás no debería contarte sobre su horrible experiencia ya que te vas a Estados Unidos? ¿No quiero pintarles una imagen negativa de Estados Unidos?".

"Mis hermanas, al igual que mi hermano, solo tienen cosas buenas que decir sobre cómo las tratan los estadounidenses. Espero que me traten con respeto también. Puede decirme lo que sucedió en el campo de Bad Hersfeld. Estoy muy interesada en las historias personales de soldados y civiles que sobrevivieron a la Segunda Guerra Mundial".

"Cuando el profesor Ernst Hermann Ruebsam entró por primera vez en el campamento, no podía creer lo que veía. Soldados heridos con miembros amputados envueltos en vendas ensangrentadas yacían en el suelo desnudo y fangoso. Ningún refugio o incluso una tienda de campaña los protegía de los elementos o para mantenerlos calientes. Yacían detrás del alambre de púas en las llamadas jaulas. Los soldados hambrientos y helados pidieron ayuda desesperadamente, pero no llegó ninguna ayuda. Los heridos deben haber sido traídos de un hospital y arrojados a las jaulas. Los soldados cavaron hoyos en el suelo con sus propias manos, una cuchara o cualquier cosa que les quedara después de ser despojados de sus pertenencias personales antes de que los guardias los persiguieran como si fueran ganado dentro de las jaulas. Este campamento estaba en un pantano, y si los soldados cavaban demasiado profundo, el agua subterránea llenaría el agujero. Luego salieron del hoyo y caminaron alrededor, tratando de entrar en calor. Dormir en el suelo húmedo y frío era casi imposible por un período más largo. Cuando el lado que toca el suelo se enfría demasiado, la persona se despierta y gira hacia el otro lado o se levanta y camina. Los reflectores brillantes que se movían sobre el campamento durante toda la noche también impidieron que los soldados durmieran. Cada mañana tenían que hacer fila para conseguir medio vaso de agua. Algunos incluso colapsaron mientras esperaban en la fila. Al mediodía, los soldados pobres, vivos, desnutridos y débiles tenían que hacer fila nuevamente para recibir una comida por día. Consistía en dos galletas saladas puestas en una mano desnuda y cuatro ciruelas enlatadas en la otra mano. No hay agua corriente ni duchas o baños regulares; sólo se excavó una letrina para cada jaula. Muchos presos murieron de desnutrición, neumonía y diarrea. Soldados y civiles sospechosos de ser miembros de las SS de Hitler o considerados culpables de crímenes de guerra fueron ejecutados en el acto sin juicio. Si no corrían por su propia voluntad al lugar de la ejecución, eran golpeados. Gritos de desesperación precedieron al sonido de las balas, luego silencio. Los cuerpos fueron recogidos y transportados en camiones. Nadie notificó a los familiares, solo cadáveres registrados sin nombre. Incluso después de que terminó la guerra, la matanza en estas jaulas continuó. Matar o dejar morir era la política del general Eisenhower. Prohibió a cualquier civil o militar llevar comida a los presos. El castigo para cualquier persona atrapada en el acto de ayudar al soldado hambriento era la muerte, independientemente de si se trataba de un niño, una mujer o un guardia estadounidense. La Cruz Roja tenía trece millones de paquetes de alimentos, muchos artículos de tocador y hasta material para nuevos uniformes. Los guardias negaron haber entregado los bienes a los prisioneros en este campo. Cuando la Cruz Roja trató de exponer la verdad, rápidamente fue cubierta por mentiras".

Negué con la cabeza con incredulidad, se me formó un nudo en la garganta al escuchar este increíble informe. Traté de contener mis lágrimas de compasión por esos pobres prisioneros. Saqué mi pañuelo y me sequé las lágrimas que se escapaban. Muchas lágrimas quedaron sin derramar. Me preguntaba qué tipo de historias tendría que contar mi padre si alguna vez salía de la prisión polaca. Entonces mis pensamientos rápidamente regresaron al presente.

Me di cuenta de que incluso para el caballero, era doloroso hablar sobre este tema como lo reveló su expresión facial sombría.

Pregunté: "¿Cómo podría permitirse ese trato a los prisioneros? Según la Convención de Ginebra de 1929, ¿se supone que los prisioneros deben ser tratados con el mismo respeto que los soldados del ejército vencedor y liberados después de que termine la guerra? "

Si eso es verdad. Pero para no obedecer a la Convención de Ginebra, el general Eisenhower, con el permiso del presidente Roosevelt y del gobierno estadounidense, rebautizó a los prisioneros de guerra como Fuerzas Enemigas Desarmadas DEF, lo que no les otorgó la protección de la Convención de Ginebra".

"Eso es realmente cruel y muy perjudicial para las pobres víctimas de la Segunda Guerra Mundial. Espero que no en todos los campamentos los CEF hayan sido tratados con tanta crueldad".

"No, en algunos campamentos, los soldados estadounidenses que custodiaban los campos eran más compasivos y ayudaban a los soldados alemanes o permitían que la Cruz Roja o los civiles llevaran comida a los campos. Sin embargo, ese no fue el caso en Bad Hersfeld. Los camiones estadounidenses recogieron a los habitantes del campo y los transportaron al campo de Bad Kreuznach a mediados de mayo, donde las condiciones eran aún peores. Al principio, los presos tenían un atisbo de esperanza de ser llevados al cuartel para ser liberados. Pero cuando aterrizaron en Bad Kreuznach, la desesperación reemplazó su esperanza. Se suponía que los millones de prisioneros tomados después del 8 de mayo, el día de la capitulación, serían liberados. Pero los aliados ya habían planeado mantenerlos como trabajadores forzados. Usaron el argumento de que los aliados nunca firmaron un tratado de paz con Alemania. El prisionero de guerra alemán (POW) no tenía derechos ni protección después de cambiar su estado a Fuerzas enemigas desarmadas, DEF. Tampoco se registraron sus nombres en los campamentos. Quitaron todos los rangos de oficiales o generales. Los que sobrevivieron a estas atrocidades no tenían derecho a reclamar ninguna compensación. Por eso de los tres millones y medio de presos no se pudo contabilizar un millón".

Le pregunté al caballero: "¿Cómo podría permitirse ese trato? ¿Dónde estaban las Naciones Unidas que habían escrito la Carta del Atlántico de que vencedores y vencidos debían ser tratados por igual? ¿Por qué la Prensa no denunció estas prácticas desleales?".

"Fue muy trágico después del colapso del Tercer Reich. Alemania no tenía un gobierno central para defenderse. Los cuatro aliados dividieron Alemania en cuatro partes; Rusia ocupó

Alemania Oriental, Inglaterra la parte norte, Francia la parte occidental y Estados Unidos la parte central y sur de Alemania. Los aliados gobernaban cada zona por sus leyes militares. Alemania estaba a su merced. Francia también se hizo cargo de ocho campos de Rhein Meadow. Enviaron muchos prisioneros a Francia. Dos mil de ellos estaban en tan malas condiciones físicas que murieron en el camino. Un tercio de ellos eran solo esqueletos vivientes y demasiado débiles para trabajar. Se supo que la División del general Philippe Leclerc roció a los prisioneros alemanes con gasolina y luego los vio quemarse vivos. También corrió con sus tanques sobre los prisioneros y los aplastó hasta la muerte. El teniente Gallay condujo a quinientos prisioneros a un granero. Luego arrojó una granada de mano en el granero y observó después de la explosión, extremidades y partes del cuerpo humano volaron por el aire. Los guardias dispararon a los sobrevivientes con ametralladoras.

"Sí, poco se sabe cuán inhumanamente los cuatro aliados, Estados Unidos, Gran Bretaña, Francia y Rusia, trataron no solo a los prisioneros de guerra sino también al pueblo alemán. Como usted, los refugiados de la parte oriental de Alemania perdieron sus hogares y tuvieron que escapar del sufrimiento. Las familias o ancianos que quedaron fueron despojados de sus pertenencias y expulsados de sus hogares como animales por los rusos y polacos. Nunca se les permitió regresar. Las víctimas quedaron con los cuerpos quebrantados, el corazón sangrando, el espíritu destrozado y sumidos en la oscuridad de la noche y el olvido; pero no olvidados por Dios y por las personas que aman a Dios, familiares, amigos y personas que aman la verdad. Buscarán la verdad y la encontrarán".

Cuando el caballero hizo una pausa, agregué: "Solo Dios sabe toda la verdad. Encontramos fragmentos mientras buscamos la verdad. Tratamos de poner el conocimiento que adquirimos en la perspectiva correcta. Obtenemos una imagen diferente a la que nos dijeron originalmente la propaganda, la prensa, los periódicos o los informes blanqueados que cubren la verdad con mentiras".

El caballero continuó: "Eso es cierto. A menudo se necesitan generaciones para sufrir el estigma de la propaganda injusta difundida por el país que quería entrar en guerra. La propaganda pinta un cuadro horrible del país contra el que elige como enemigo para justificar la entrada en la guerra y luchar y conquistar al enemigo retratado. Sin embargo, la propaganda mundial permanece en la mente de la gente; solo los sobrevivientes lo saben, y los buscadores de la verdad obtendrán una imagen más clara de la realidad. James Bacque, un periodista canadiense, visitó esos campamentos y describió las condiciones deplorables que encontró. Sin embargo, el profesor Ernst Hermann Ruebsam vivió del 9 al 21 de mayo de 1945 en el campo de Bad Hersfeld, y nos contó las mismas historias. Él dijo: *'Es la gracia de Dios haber sobrevivido a estas crueldades y la gracia de no haber sido afectado por ellas'.* El 21 de mayo, un guardia estadounidense se llevó al Prof. Ruebsam a un cuartel para darle de alta. Tuvo el lujo de tomar una ducha por primera vez en doce días y dormir una noche bajo techo en lugar de en el frío suelo desnudo bajo el cielo abierto. Antes de que él y otros camaradas fueran liberados, la guardia estadounidense los llevó afuera con vista a su ciudad y les dijo: *'No vinimos a liberar a Alemania. nosotros no ocupamosAlemania para liberar a los alemanes. Alemania será ocupada como una nación enemiga conquistada,'* El Prof. Ruebsam se sintió humillado por estos comentarios".

"Qué comentario tan humillante. Tú y yo todavía somos considerados enemigos de Estados Unidos porque han pasado once años desde que Alemania todavía está ocupada por Estados Unidos y los tres aliados. ¿Crees que llegará el momento en que los aliados abandonen nuestro país y Alemania recupere la soberanía?"

"Eso esperamos, pero no sé si eso sucederá o cuándo. Otra trágica explotación de Alemania fue la *Operación Paperclip*. Incluso dos años antes de que Alemania se rindiera, Estados Unidos llevó a cabo en secreto programas de recolección de datos y patentes técnicas y científicas. Los agentes secretos recopilaron nombres de los principales científicos alemanes. Tan pronto como terminó la guerra, los principales científicos, incluido Wernher von Braun, un ingeniero aeroespacial, y cualquiera que fuera útil para promover el programa de cohetes, fue llevado a América. También hubo otros equipos para explotar a Alemania, confiscando documentos científicos, instalaciones de investigación y aviones. Rusia tenía un programa similar llamado *Ossawakim*.

Tan pronto como los rusos ocuparon Alemania Oriental, su gobierno reunió a dos mil científicos y especialistas Para servirse de ellos y los transportó a ellos y a sus familias a la fuerza a Rusia. También desmantelaron muchas fábricas y enviaron la maquinaria y el equipo a Rusia.

Inglaterra tuvo la Operación *Epsilon*. Diez científicos alemanes fueron capturados en 1945 y llevados a Farm Hall cerca de Cambridge para ser interrogados durante seis meses. Farm Hall interfirió las habitaciones de los científicos para escuchar las conversaciones de los científicos y determinar qué tan avanzada estaba Alemania en la construcción de la bomba atómica. Inglaterra trató con lujo a estos científicos. Sin embargo, los prisioneros alemanes regulares también fueron renombrados CEF (Fuerzas Enemigas Civiles) y despojados de sus derechos de la Convención de Ginebra. Los presos trabajaban como trabajadores forzados, sin recibir suficiente comida; fueron desnutridos y maltratados por el gobierno británico, que también capturó a civiles que pensaban que eran comunistas".

"Heinz Kraemer, el líder del grupo juvenil DJO al que me uní, me dijo cuán respetuosamente lo trató el guardia de la prisión inglesa. Lo invitó a celebrar la Navidad con su familia. Su esposa era alemana y quería volver a escuchar canciones navideñas alemanas, que él cantaba para ellos. Nunca olvidará su acto de bondad y consideración".

"Sí, la gente de cada país suele ser diferente y más compasiva que los funcionarios del gobierno o sus comandantes militares. Uno nunca debe generalizar. El bien y el mal coexisten y siempre lo harán. La guerra permitirá que la persona malvada actúe en su ansia de poder y codicia y elimine o torture a los que se interpongan en su camino. Incluso en las circunstancias más trágicas, una buena persona actuará con compasión y amabilidad, ayudando a los demás humanos sin importar su religión, raza o nacionalidad. Sería ideal si las personas en todo el mundo vivieran según la regla de oro: "*Trata a los demás como deseas que te traten a ti*".

"Eso ciertamente transformaría el mundo si cada persona viviera según la regla de oro. Eliminaría las guerras y mucho sufrimiento humano. El mundo sería un lugar más civilizado y seguro para vivir. Dios nos mandó amarlo a Él primero y a nuestro prójimo como a nosotros mismos. Si podemos tratar a nuestros semejantes como Cristo trató a la gente y amar y perdonar a los demás, coexistiremos y viviremos en paz; y aborreceremos el mal."

"Yo agregaría, como cristianos, podemos trascender la regla de oro. Podemos aprender a actuar como Jesús nos enseñó a actuar amando incondicionalmente".

El conductor atravesó el pasillo y anunció: "Fulda, próxima parada".

Me disculpé y me dispuse a desembarcar para enviar la carta. Inmediatamente me acerqué a la ventanilla de venta de entradas y pregunté cuánto tardaría en llegar una carta de Fulda a Hamburgo. El empleado de la ventanilla me aseguró que demora aproximadamente una semana o menos. Le entregué el sobre con todos los documentos al secretario y lo envié por correo. Ciertamente esperaba que la carta llegara a Hamburgo antes que yo. También tuve que cambiar mi billete de tren de Hannover a Hamburgo y de Hamburgo a Bremerhaven. Estaba agradecida de tener suficiente dinero para pagar el franqueo adicional inesperado y la tarifa. Regresé a mi vagón y agradecí al caballero por cuidar mi maleta.

"Espero que el correo llegue a tiempo".

"Creo que sí; el servicio de correos es bastante puntual."

Después de pasar por Huenfeld, el tren se detuvo en Bad Hersfeld, donde se bajó el señor.

"Adiós, Fraeulein, fuiste una agradable compañera de viaje y te deseo lo mejor en Estados Unidos".

"Gracias Señor. Me alegro de que me haya advertido de que no llevara conmigo mis documentos de inmigración a Alemania Oriental. Gracias por describir el destino de los prisioneros alemanes en Bad Hersfeld, Inglaterra, Francia y Rusia. También te deseo lo mejor para el futuro. ¡Adiós, señor!" Nos dimos la mano y nos separamos. Permanecí en mi compartimiento del tren, y los pensamientos del trágico destino de los prisioneros alemanes se asentaron en mi mente, y no pude borrarlos. Miré por la ventana sin ser realmente consciente del paisaje que pasaba. Bebra fue la siguiente parada antes de llegar a Eisenach y la frontera con Alemania Oriental.

En Eisenach, todos los pasajeros tenían que bajarse del tren. Las personas que querían continuar en tren hacia Alemania Oriental caminaron hasta un puesto de control de la frontera fuertemente custodiada. Cuando llegué a los guardias, revisaron mi pasaporte, el permiso especial, y mi DNI. Luego me pidieron que abriera mi maleta. Revisaron cada artículo no solo en la maleta sino también en mi bolso. Cuando encontraron todo en orden, me preguntaron adónde iba y cuánto tiempo me quedaría con mi hermana. Continuó: "Asegúrate de ir a la estación de policía inmediatamente cuando llegues a Silkerode y también cuando te vayas. Si deseas ir a otro pueblo, debe notificar a la policía también a dónde irá y cuánto tiempo permanecerá allí".

"Sí, señor, eso haré".

Empujé mi ropa hacia abajo en la maleta y la cerré. Luego le pregunté al guardia dónde podía tomar el tren a Erfurt. Seguí sus indicaciones, y después de esperar un rato, me embarqué en el tren a Erfurt. Seguro que me alegré de no tener mis documentos de inmigración conmigo. Tan minuciosamente como los guardias revisaron todo, los habrían encontrado y podrían haberlos confiscado. Di gracias a Dios que un extraño caballero me aconsejó que los enviara por correo antes de ingresar a Alemania Oriental.

Noté tal diferencia entre Alemania Occidental y Alemania Oriental. Los trenes en Alemania Occidental estaban bien mantenidos, pero en Alemania Oriental, casi nada se hizo a los trenes ni a los edificios desde que terminó la guerra. Los edificios eran grises, algunos en extrema necesidad de reparación. Incluso las expresiones faciales de las personas aquí eran sombrías. Casi nadie hablaba entre sí. Yo también permanecí en silencio, y mis pensamientos no podían liberarse de la mala suerte de los prisioneros de guerra alemanes y de cómo el gobierno militar ruso controlaba la vida de cada persona aquí. El paisaje invernal también se veía gris y lúgubre. De vez en cuando, las cimas de las montañas cubiertas de nieve crearon una vista agradable. En Erfurt, tuve que cambiar de tren para ir a Nordhausen. Incluso la estación de tren de Erfurt parecía deteriorada, y las paredes necesitaban urgentemente pintura. No podía creer la diferencia que hace un gobierno en el país y en la vida de las personas. Cuando llegué a Nordhausen, encontré las mismas condiciones. Desde Nordhausen, tomé el tren local a Zwinge y llegué al final de la tarde. Desde allí, tuve que caminar hasta Silkerode. Como no tenía forma de hacerle saber a mi hermana mi hora de llegada, nadie podía venir a buscarme a la estación de tren. Tuve que caminar más de dos millas desde Zwinge hasta Silkerode. Al principio, me sentía bien para moverme después de estar sentada la mayor parte del día en trenes o estaciones de ferrocarril. Pero después de un tiempo, me dolían los pies y mis brazos se cansaron de llevar la maleta.

CAPÍTULO 14

VISITANDO A MI HERMANA MARTA

Mientras tanto, el sol descendía más y más bajo. Traté de aumentar mi ritmo para llegar a la casa de mi hermana antes de que oscureciera por completo. Me sentía exhausta pero feliz de que finalmente llegué a la casa de mi hermana poco después del atardecer. Mi hermana Marta, mi cuñado Hermann, mis sobrinos Erhard y Bernhard, y mi sobrinita Beate, a quien aún no conocía, se emocionaron al verme, y yo también. Tras la afectuosa bienvenida, Marta me invitó a sentarme en la mesa del comedor, que ella misma había puesto con antelación. Sirvió pan y salami casero, y salchicha de hígado. Como tenía hambre, saboreé la salchicha y el pastel caseros. Después de ayudar a limpiar la mesa, me excusé.

Hermana Marta y su familia

Sobrina Beate

Estaba cansada y esperaba con ansias una buena noche de sueño. Antes de que Marta me llevara arriba a un loft con una cama en una habitación pequeña, me mostró dónde estaba el baño de abajo. Me preparé y subí al dormitorio. Antes de desvestirme en la habitación fría, me arrodillé frente a la cama para orar. Di gracias a Dios que el viaje en tren salió bien y pude visitar a mi hermana Marta y su familia después de muchos años de estar separadas. Después de ponerme el camisón, rápidamente me metí debajo de la cobija de plumas y me quedé dormida. A la mañana siguiente, me levanté relativamente tarde. Cuando bajé, encontré a Marta sola en la cocina. Hermann había ido a trabajar para la administración del pueblo en el ayuntamiento local. Erhard y Bernhard fueron a la escuela primaria y Beate fue al jardín de infancia. Marta limpiaba la cocina y juntaba todos los ingredientes para preparar el almuerzo. El almuerzo es la comida principal del día y generalmente se come al mediodía o después de que los niños regresan a casa de la escuela. Dado que la oficina de administración del pueblo estaba a poca distancia de la casa, Hermann también vendría a casa a almorzar. Pelé las papas y limpié y corté las verduras que ella guardaba en el sótano. Mientras trabajábamos, hablábamos. Le pregunté cómo era la vida en la zona fronteriza de cinco kilómetros.

"Al principio, no fue tan malo; Pudimos viajar a los pueblos de los alrededores, pero ahora los guardias son muy estrictos y no podemos cruzar la frontera con Alemania Occidental. No podemos obtener permiso para visitar a nuestra familia en Alemania Occidental a menos que estemos jubilados. El gobierno ruso teme que un trabajador no regrese a Alemania Oriental. Si atrapan a alguien cruzando la frontera ilegalmente, le disparan en el acto".

"Qué trágico; No puedo creer la diferencia que hay entre Alemania Oriental y Occidental. Aquí todo está deteriorado, mientras que muchos edificios se reconstruyen y ya se reparan en Alemania Occidental".

"Sí, es difícil conseguir material, también tener suficiente dinero para permitirse comprar material cuando está disponible. Nuestra casa es vieja y necesita mucho trabajo, pero solo podemos hacer un poco a la vez. Estoy agradecida de que tengamos espacio para criar dos cerdos y aves de corral, para que mi familia tenga suficiente para comer. Vendemos un cerdo para obtener dinero extra para comprar otros artículos necesarios. También tenemos una gran huerta. Conservo en vasos y latas muchas frutas y algunas verduras para el invierno que guardamos en la bodega."

"¿Todavía tienes que tener estampillas para la mantequilla, la harina y el azúcar?"

"Sí, todavía lo hacemos y algunos otros artículos también. Me alegro de que podamos obtener pan de centeno y panecillos sin estampillas y de buena calidad también".

"¿De dónde saca todo el forraje para sus cerdos y aves de corral?"

"Somos afortunados de tener cuatro acres de tierra. Lo labramos y sembramos centeno, avena y trigo. Lamentablemente no contamos con maquinaria. Hacemos todas las cosas a mano. Es un trabajo duro. Los muchachos tienen que ayudarnos a Hermann y a mí a labrar la tierra y cosechar el grano y las papas".

"Ese es un trabajo duro para niños de ocho y nueve años".

"Es un trabajo duro, pero todos los miembros de la familia tienen que colaborar, incluso los niños más pequeños. Ojalá pudieran evitar trabajar tan duro a una edad temprana, pero es una cuestión de supervivencia. Los vecinos también se ayudan entre sí cuando es necesario".

No me di cuenta de lo rápido que había pasado la mañana. Ya era mediodía cuando Hermann entró por la puerta, seguido de los niños. Ayudé a los niños a quitarse los pesados abrigos de invierno, gorros y bufandas y les di un fuerte abrazo a cada uno. Ya se habían quitado los zapatos en la entrada y se habían puesto pantuflas para mantener limpio el interior de la casa. Marta preparó un guiso de conejo, puré de papas y una ensalada de remolacha roja para el almuerzo que todos disfrutamos. Hermann tomó una siesta corta antes de que volviera a trabajar. Los chicos fueron a dar de comer a los conejos. También trajeron más leña a la casa. Beate, tan pequeña como era, ayudaba a recoger la mesa y a lavar los platos. Erhard y Bernhard hicieron su tarea para la escuela. Después de que Marta y yo termináramos de lavar los platos, ella se sentó junto a la estufa de azulejos (Kachelofen) en la sala y tejió un par de calcetines. Le pregunté a Beate si quería que le contara un cuento de hadas. Ella felizmente asintió. La tomé en mi regazo. Nos sentamos junto a la estufa de azulejos para calentarnos. Mientras las llamas crepitaban y bailaban entre los leños, le conté el cuento de hadas de Hansel y Gretel. Ella escuchó atentamente, y cuando mencioné a la bruja en la historia, sus ojos se agrandaron y temió que la bruja arrojara a Hansel y Gretel al horno ardiente. Pero cuando Hansel empujó a la bruja al horno, ella respiró hondo y exclamó: "Qué bueno que la bruja malvada murió, y Hansel y Gretel encontraron el camino a casa nuevamente". Llegué al final. "y ellos vivieron felices para siempre."

Antes de la cena, Marta, Beate y yo pusimos la mesa para tener todo listo para el regreso de Hermann. Tuvimos una animada conversación mientras cenábamos. Erhard y Bernhard le contaron a su madre y a su padre lo que habían aprendido en la escuela hoy. Beate expresó su alegría de que la tía Hilde le contara un cuento de hadas de Hansel, Gretel y la bruja malvada. Después de la cena, los chicos jugaron algunos juegos de mesa; luego los niños se fueron a la cama.

Marta siguió tejiendo. Hermann llevaba un parche en el ojo. Tenía curiosidad y le pregunté cómo Hermann sufrió su lesión en el ojo.

"Cuando el ejército me reclutó, Me ordenaron construir muros de refuerzo en la costa de Francia y Noruega. En 1941, cuando los rusos invadieron Prusia Oriental, mi batallón fue enviado al Frente Oriental y terminé en Stalingrado. En una de las batallas, una bala me entró en el cráneo por el lado izquierdo. La dirección del proyectil cambió y escapó por la abertura del ojo izquierdo, destrozando completamente el ojo. Me internaron en el hospital de Berlín, donde permanecí durante mucho tiempo. Al ser declarado no apto para pelear, el médico me envió a casa. Estoy agradecido de que los rusos no me hayan capturado, pero muchos de mis camaradas se convirtieron en prisioneros de guerra. La mayoría de ellos fueron enviados a Siberia como trabajadores forzados y nunca regresaron a casa. El ejército me premió con la cruz de hierro por salvar la vida de un compañero herido.

"¡Es tan trágico que hayas perdido el ojo! ¿No te pusiste un ojo artificial por razones estéticas?"

"Sí, me hicieron un ojo artificial. Estaba unido a los anteojos. Cuando voy a trabajar, me pongo las gafas con el ojo. En casa me quito los anteojos y solo me pongo un parche en el ojo".

"¿Sigues teniendo dolor o malestar?"

"Sí, especialmente cuando cambia el tiempo. También tengo dolores de cabeza frecuentes si trabajo demasiado físicamente. Pero aprendí a vivir con este problema".

"Sí, muchas personas tendrán que aprender a vivir con los problemas que les trajo la Segunda Guerra Mundial. Me pregunto si mi padre volverá alguna vez de Polonia. Fue capturado hace once años como prisionero de guerra y todavía no está en casa".

"Sí, es una tragedia que a los prisioneros de guerra alemanes no se les diera la protección de la Convención de Ginebra como se merecían".

"Durante el viaje en tren, conocí a un caballero de Bad Hersfeld, donde se encontraba un campo de prisioneros estadounidense de soldados alemanes en campos abiertos detrás de alambre de púas. Me contó cuán infrahumanos eran los campos y la crueldad con que los guardias estadounidenses trataban a los pobres soldados capturados. Siempre pensé que los generales estadounidenses eran los más humanos".

"Desafortunadamente, la guerra saca a relucir los mejores o los peores rasgos de carácter en las personas, especialmente en los funcionarios de alto rango".

"Olvidémonos de la guerra ahora y pensemos en algo más agradable. ¿Cuáles son tus ocupaciones favoritas?"

"Me gusta tejer canastas y hacer escobas, así como reparar zapatos u otros artículos para los vecinos para ganar un poco de dinero extra. La pensión de veterano que recibo y el pequeño salario que recibo de la ciudad no son suficientes para formar una familia y cuidar los edificios".

"Ese es un trabajo duro para ti y para Marta".

"Sí, los niños ayudan después de que llegan a casa de la escuela y hacen su tarea. Obtienen verduras frescas para alimentar a los conejos y limpiar sus jaulas. Son buenos chicos y ayudan mucho. Incluso Beate, con lo pequeña que es, trata de ayudar a su madre en la cocina".

"Me alegro de que tengas suficiente comida para tu familia. Muchas familias que viven en las grandes ciudades pasan hambre".

"Sí, los habitantes de las ciudades de Alemania Oriental tienen dificultades para obtener un suministro suficiente de cualquier cosa, especialmente alimentos. A veces hacen cola durante horas para conseguir carne, frutas o verduras frescas.

Tenemos al menos un jardín para cultivar verduras y podemos criar aves y cerdos. Marta sabe enlatar y conservar muchas cosas, para que no pasemos hambre. Los cuatro acres de tierra que tenemos son suficientes para cultivar trigo, avena y centeno para alimentar a las vacas, los cerdos y las aves de corral".

"Me alegra oír eso. ¿Cómo cultivas tu tierra?"

"Atamos a la vaca al arado para remover la tierra y luego antes del rastrillo para romper los terrones de tierra".

"¿Qué hay de cosechar los campos?"

"Yo siego con una guadaña a mano, y Marta recoge las gavillas. Los muchachos apilan las gavillas en montones para que el grano se seque. Uno de nuestros vecinos tiene una trilladora. Viene a ayudarnos a trillar. También guardamos la paja y la mezclamos en el pienso de los animales.

"Eso seguro es una tarea difícil y tediosa".

"Sí, eso es, pero no pasamos hambre. Estoy agradecido por eso."

Miré a Marta, que estaba muy ocupada tejiendo. Ya tenía un calcetín terminado y la segunda mitad terminada. Yo le pregunte a ella.

"Marta, ¿a ti también te gusta tejer crochet? ¿Quizás puedas mostrarme un nuevo patrón para tejer bordes alrededor de pañuelos?"

"Mañana, te mostraré algunos patrones que puedes elegir. Tengo algunos pañuelos sencillos que puedes usar." "Gracias, eso es bueno, entonces puedo estar haciendo algo también".

Hablamos hasta que las llamas del horno de azulejos quedaron sepultadas bajo las cenizas. Nos acostamos y nos enterramos bajo nuestras cobijas de plumas.

Al día siguiente el sol nos trajo alegría, y los alrededores se veían más brillantes. Los chicos iban a la escuela y Beate al jardín de niños. Ayudé a Marta a ordenar la cocina y a preparar algunas verduras para el almuerzo. Marta también hizo una tarta para el fin de semana, que decoraríamos el sábado.

Después del almuerzo, Marta sacó los pañuelos. Ella me dio un poco de hilo blanco y rosa claro. Con el ganchillo fino, Marta me enseñó a tejer un borde a modo de encaje alrededor. Cuando terminé una fila, me mostró el siguiente paso. Cuando Hermann llegó a casa del trabajo, cenamos. Los niños disfrutaron pasar tiempo con su padre antes de acostarse. Marta tejía con agujas y con gancho. Hermann siempre estaba dispuesto a ayudar a los vecinos cada vez que podía. Esa noche, reparó un par de zapatos para su vecino. Primero cortó los patrones de las suelas y tacones de una pieza de cuero grueso, luego usó pegamento y clavos cortos para unirlos a las suelas y tacones de los zapatos. Marta disfrutaba mucho de la música. Hermann le había comprado una radio. Por la noche, sintonizó una estación que transmitía melodías de opereta. Ella felizmente tarareaba. También me gustaban las canciones de los diferentes compositores, las óperas y las zarzuelas; a Hermann también. Mientras nuestras manos se afanaban, nuestros corazones se regocijaban con la música, y las llamas crepitaban y bailaban en el horno hasta que llegó la hora de acostarse. Como los niños no tenían escuela el sábado, dormían hasta más tarde, y Beate también. Solo los tres desayunamos juntos. Marta y Hermann me preguntaron qué me motivó a ir a América. Les dije que decidí unirme a mi hermano Edmund y mis dos hermanas Emma y Meta. Edmund no quería dejarme atrás. Convenció a mi madre para que me permitiera ir también. Sin embargo, como ambos aplicamos en diferentes consulados estadounidenses, Edmund en Munich, yo en Frankfurt, no pudimos irnos juntos. Partió en avión en noviembre y yo partiría el 16 de diciembre en barco desde Bremerhaven.

"¿Ya tienes un lugar donde te quedarás o trabajarás?"

"No aún no. Primero iré con mi hermana Meta y su familia. Más tarde podría reunirme con mi hermana Emma y mi hermano Edmund en Chicago. Veré cómo van las cosas". "¿Quieres quedarte allí de forma permanente o volver a Alemania de nuevo?"

"Yo tampoco lo sé. confío en Dios; Él me mostrará Su camino. Te escribiré y te haré saber dónde estaré y qué haré."

"Ciertamente espero que no te decepciones".

"Yo también lo espero."

Mientras tanto, los niños se levantaron y estaban listos para el desayuno. Marta les hizo panqueques de harina con huevos revueltos y tocino y una taza de chocolate caliente. Lo devoraron alegremente en poco tiempo. Luego los niños fueron con su padre a dar de comer a la vaca, los cerdos y las aves de corral, mientras Beate se quedaba en la cocina y limpiaba la mesa. Beate no quería salir de la cocina hoy. Sabía que su madre haría el relleno para el pastel Bundt especial que horneó ayer. Marta cocinó una generosa porción de budín de vainilla. Lo dejó a un lado para que se enfriara. Cortó el pastel en tres capas, luego untó un poco de mermelada de cereza en dos capas. Marta fue añadiendo poco a poco pequeñas porciones de mantequilla cuando el budín estuvo lo suficientemente frío mientras lo batía con un batidor de huevos. Cuando la consistencia estuvo firme, la puso entre las tres capas y sobre el exterior del bizcocho. Luego espolvoreó avellanas molidas sobre el pastel, lo decoró con pequeñas estrellas de crema batida y colocó cerezas enlatadas en la parte superior de cada estrella. Se veía delicioso. Marta dejó un poco de crema de mantequilla en el bol para que Beate lamiera. Sus ojos se iluminaban cada vez que se ponía un poco de crema de mantequilla en la boca. Incluso se me hizo la boca agua al ver el hermoso pastel. Pero teníamos que esperar un día más.

El sábado por la noche era la hora del baño para la familia. Después de que la familia se bañara, Marta tiró el agua de la bañera y llenó la bañera de aluminio con agua fresca. Primero me arrodillé y me lavé el cabello con jabón, luego usé una solución de vinagre como acondicionador. Se sentía bien sumergirse en el agua tibia. Marta calentó una toalla al lado de la estufa para secar mi cabello y mi cuerpo. Me sentí tan renovada y limpia. Nos lavamos la cara en un recipiente con agua tibia durante la semana y tomamos lo que llamamos un baño ruso, cada uno usando una toallita húmeda para limpiar nuestros cuerpos.

El domingo por la mañana, todos nos pusimos nuestras mejores galas. Sólo Hermann iba a la iglesia. Este fue el único domingo que pasaría con mi hermana, Marta; quería preparar una cena especial de Navidad. Marta asó un ganso, descuartizado dos días antes. También hizo albóndigas de papa y repollo rojo. Todos ayudamos a Marta a pelar y rallar patatas para las albóndigas. Beate y yo pusimos la mesa. Utilizamos la mejor mantelería y porcelana para esta ocasión especial. Pusimos la corona de ramas de pino, llamada corona de Adviento, con las cuatro velas sobre la mesa. Encendimos dos velas por el segundo domingo de Adviento. Hermann dijo una bendición, y todos pudimos saborear el ganso asado y las deliciosas guarniciones.

Qué placer fue eso para mí, y ni siquiera era Navidad todavía.

"Estoy tan feliz de que pudieras venir a visitarnos antes de ir a Estados Unidos", dijo Marta.

"Yo también."

Esperamos ansiosos el pastel que disfrutamos a las 3:00 p.m. Marta sintonizó una estación de radio con canciones de Adviento que pudimos cantar. Fue tan festivo y me recordó a mi hogar. El pastel sabía delicioso. Ahora entendía por qué amigos y vecinos le pedían a mi hermana que les hiciera este delicioso pastel para sus ocasiones especiales. Pensar en mi madre estando sin sus hijas decorando el árbol de Navidad y preparando la cena, hizo que la tristeza entrara en mi corazón.

También me preguntaba cómo pasaría la Navidad este año en el barco. No quería que nadie notara mi tristeza. Miré a los niños felices y me regocijé con ellos. Agradecí a Dios ya mi hermana y cuñado por celebrar este día en particular, conmemorar el nacimiento de nuestro Señor y Salvador Jesucristo y traerme muchos recuerdos de la infancia.

Al día siguiente, cuando me desperté, encontré nieve en el desván. Noté que el techo tenía un agujero por donde entraba la nieve. Los niños dieron la bienvenida a la nieve. Podrían ir en trineo en la colina en su patio trasero. Le dije a Beate que la recogería del jardín de niños. Esperamos hasta que los niños salieron de la escuela y caminamos juntos a casa. La nieve ya se había acumulado unas pocas pulgadas, y Erhard reunió suficiente nieve para convertirla en una bola de nieve. Me lo arrojó suavemente. Les dije que estaba bien conmigo si nos metíamos en una pelea de bolas de nieve. Cada vez que me pegaba una pelota, se reían. Le pedí a Beate que me ayudara a luchar contra los chicos. Formó las bolas rápidamente y luego golpeó a uno de sus hermanos, gritando: "¡Te tengo!".

Después del almuerzo, los niños hicieron sus labores y tareas rápidamente para poder ir a pasear en trineo. Hermann había hecho un trineo para cada niño. Beate se turnaba para subirse junto con sus hermanos. Cuando los niños terminaron su tarea, me preguntaron si quería ir y verlos deslizarse en trineo. Subieron la colina tirando del trineo. Luego se sentaron en los trineos y bajaron corriendo la colina. Observé cómo giraban o frenaban el trineo con los pies. Después de algunas carreras cuesta abajo, me preguntaron si quería intentarlo. Estuve de acuerdo y subí lo que me pareció una colina empinada. Entonces Erhard me entregó su trineo. "Aquí, Tante Hilde, siéntate en el trineo. Agárrate a la cuerda y al lateral del trineo. Cuando bajes, baja el pie derecho si quieres girar a la derecha y el pie izquierdo si quieres ir a la izquierda".

"Si lo haré. Bernhard, espera y baja después de mí. No quiero chocar contigo."

Me senté en el trineo, Erhard me dio un empujón para arrancar y bajé corriendo la colina; Apenas tuve tiempo de darme la vuelta y casi choqué contra el granero al pie de la colina.

"Bien, Tante Hilde. Espérame al pie de la colina. Bajaré a buscar el trineo. ¿Quieres ir una vez más?"

"No, gracias, será mejor que entre. Se está poniendo demasiado frío para mí."

"Solo deja el trineo allí. Bajaré con Bernhard y lo agarraré."

"Bien, te veo luego adentro".

Encontré a Marta tejiendo y a Hermann comenzando a tejer una pequeña canasta. Después de calentarme las manos, tomé mi pañuelo y comencé a tejer. Tenía curiosidad sobre el tipo de trabajo que estaba haciendo Hermann.

"Hermann, ¿puedo hacerte una pregunta sin distraerte de tu tejido?"

"No, adelante. ¿Qué te gustaría saber?" "¿Qué tipo de trabajo haces para el pueblo?"

"Nuestro pueblo tiene poco más de cuatrocientos habitantes, y no todos tienen o pueden permitirse comprar una radio. Escucho las noticias todos los días. Recorro el pueblo y anuncio a través de un altavoz las noticias importantes. Mantengo informada a la gente. También hago contabilidad. Cuando veo calles u otras infraestructuras que necesitan reparación, se lo comunico al alcalde, y envía una cuadrilla para hacer el trabajo. También me aseguro de que los propietarios paguen sus impuestos inmobiliarios. Si una persona es morosa, voy a su casa a cobrar los impuestos o le doy una advertencia si no puede pagar de inmediato o arreglo un plan con el que se sienta cómodo".

"Puedo ver que tienes una posición bastante responsable en la administración del pueblo".

"Sí. Sin embargo, lo más frustrante es no conseguir material para reparar calles o edificios o esperar mucho tiempo para la entrega. Desafortunadamente, cuando los rusos ocuparon Alemania Oriental, desmantelaron la mayoría de las fábricas y se llevaron maquinaria y equipos a Rusia. Están apilados en Rusia sin ser utilizados. No entiendo por qué el gobierno ruso no continuó fabricando productos de Alemania Oriental como lo hace en Alemania Occidental. Sería mucho más fácil mantener las carreteras y los edificios". "Sí, es una tragedia que los cuatro aliados hayan ocupado Alemania. Parece que la gente de Alemania Oriental bajo la ocupación rusa es la que está peor. Espero que algún día cesen las cuatro ocupaciones militares y podamos volver a tener nuestro propio gobierno".

"Todos lo esperamos, especialmente para nuestros hijos; ahora, ellos y nosotros somos como prisioneros en nuestro propio país, especialmente donde vivimos, la llamada zona fronteriza de cinco kilómetros. En algunas zonas, la frontera atraviesa un pueblo y separa familias y vecinos. Los guardias matan a muchas personas que intentan escapar con minas ocultas o con armas de fuego automáticas. Ni siquiera se nos permite visitar a nuestros familiares en Alemania Occidental. Al menos tú puedes viajar libremente en las tres zonas ocupadas. En Alemania Occidental, la economía es mucho mejor que aquí".

"Eso es verdad. Deseé por su bien que su área hubiera estado en la zona estadounidense también en la zona fronteriza de cinco kilómetros de la ocupación rusa".

"Ciertamente habríamos estado mucho mejor bajo la ocupación estadounidense que bajo la ocupación rusa. Mi sueño para mis hijos es volver a tener una Alemania libre, no gobernada por un dictador comunista, sino por un gobierno democrático gobernado por su propio pueblo y que les permita elegir a sus líderes".

"Sí, todos esperamos y deseamos que suceda algún día". "Es extraño cómo los pensamientos de Karl Marx en sus dos manifiestos sobre el capitalismo y el socialismo causaron la Revolución Rusa de 1917 treinta años después de su muerte. Vladimir Lenin derrocó el gobierno zarista de tres siglos y lo reemplazó con un nuevo gobierno proletario basado en la creencia del ateo Karl Marx. Karl Marx nació en Trier, Alemania, de padres judíos. Se instaló en Londres y se hizo conocido internacionalmente por sus ideas socialistas y comunistas."

"Desafortunadamente, los dictadores comunistas solo esclavizan a las personas, haciéndolas dependientes del gobierno. Puedes ver la marcada diferencia entre Alemania Oriental y Occidental. Es fácil ser comunista en un país libre, pero no una persona libre en un país comunista", agregó Hermann.

"Qué cierto es eso. Todos esperamos que algún día todas las tropas abandonen Alemania y pueda recuperar su soberanía como un país libre gobernado por su pueblo".

"Ciertamente haría que su vida y la de su familia fuera mucho más fácil".

Habiendo visto las dificultades de la familia de mi hermana y la grave condición de Alemania Oriental, recé para que cesaran las ocupaciones militares de Alemania y los refugiados pudieran regresar a su lugar de nacimiento. Deseaba que todos los ciudadanos pudieran viajar en su propio país y en el extranjero sin restricciones. Recé para que los prisioneros que aún estaban detenidos en otros países, como mi padre, fueran liberados y regresaran con sus familias. Pronto tuve que pensar en mi viaje a Hamburgo. Sólo quedaban tres días. Durante el día, hacíamos los quehaceres y cocinábamos. Mi sobrina disfrutó que la recogiera todos los días del jardín de niños. A veces, también salía a caminar con los niños después de que habían hecho sus deberes y tareas. Por la noche, nos relajamos haciendo trabajos manuales y recordando la vida en casa en Prusia del Este. El jueves empaqué mi maleta y el viernes por la mañana estaba lista para partir. Me sentí triste al despedirme de los niños antes de que fueran a la escuela. Los niños también lo sintieron.

Preguntaron: "¿Cuándo volverás, tía Hilde?".

Lamentablemente, tuve que responder: "No sé".

Mi cuñado se fue del trabajo el viernes, para que él y mi hermana pudieran acompañarme a Zwinge. Cuando llegamos a la estación de ferrocarril, me despedí de Hermann y le agradecí su presencia. Entonces abracé a mi hermana Marta. Una profunda tristeza llenó nuestros corazones, sin saber cuándo o si nos volveríamos a ver. Nuestras lágrimas y nuestro fuerte abrazo demostraron más amor de lo que las palabras podrían haber expresado. Me sostuvo en sus brazos por un tiempo antes de que pudiera encontrar palabras para decir adiós.

"Que Dios vaya contigo y te proteja. Escríbenos tan pronto como llegues a América. Adiós, mi querida hermana, Hilde."

"Adiós, mi querida hermana Marta. Que Dios te proteja a ti y a tu familia siempre hasta que nos volvamos a ver."

Rápidamente abracé a Hermann antes de que él y mi hermana Marta salieran de la estación de tren. Me quedé a esperar el tren. El tren llegó en breve. Primero puse mi maleta en el andén y luego subí los escalones del tren. Encontré un vagón vacío, donde entré y me acomodé. No vinieron otros pasajeros, lo cual era preferible para mí. Todavía estaba desconsolada por despedirme de mi hermana y de su familia. El tren se balanceó, cabalgando a través del sinuoso valle montañoso en las estrechas vías del tren. De vez en cuando, miraba por la ventana, observando las montañas nevadas de Harz y los bosques oscuros que se extendían desde el valle hasta la mitad de los picos. El invierno transformó el paisaje en un cuadro mágico y pacífico. También calmó mi mente antes de llegar a Nordhausen media hora más tarde.

Allí cambié el tren que iba a Hannover. Cuando el tren llegó a la frontera, los guardias de Alemania Oriental vinieron y revisaron todos los documentos nuevamente. También me preguntaron qué artículos había comprado. La porcelana fina de Meissen estaba prohibida para sacar del país y algunas otras cosas también. Me dejaron cruzar la frontera hacia el Oeste cuando no encontraron artículos prohibidos en mi maleta y todas mis identificaciones y permisos en regla. Sin embargo, se aseguraron de que todos los ciudadanos de Alemania Oriental y los conductores permanecieran en Alemania Oriental. Sólo los pasajeros de Alemania Occidental podían desembarcar, cruzar la frontera, y viajar en otros trenes a través de Alemania Occidental. Le agradecí a Dios que no tuve ningún problema con los guardias de la patrulla y volví a entrar en Alemania Occidental a salvo. No podía creer la diferencia entre Alemania Oriental y Occidental. No parecía que alguna vez fuera el mismo país. Me di cuenta de cómo un gobierno puede hacer o deshacer una nación.

El tren pasó por el hermoso tramo de las montañas Harz, dejando atrás el pico más alto (3743 pies) llamado Brocken. Disfruté viendo el paisaje invernal de montaña que lentamente se transformó en colinas ondulantes. A veces, las vías del tren seguían el lecho del río Leine. Ramas y rocas formaron hermosas esculturas de hielo en ambas orillas del río mientras el agua aún fluía en el centro. Casi tres horas después, llegamos a Hannover, donde tuve que cambiar de tren. En octubre de 1943, durante la Segunda Guerra Mundial, el edificio de la estación de tren fue fuertemente bombardeado y destruido en su mayor parte. Recién en junio de 1945 se restableció el primer servicio de trenes de pasajeros. En 1948 se inició la reconstrucción de los edificios y vías. Noté la diferencia drástica entre las estaciones de tren en ruinas en Alemania Oriental y la estación de ferrocarril reconstruida y bien mantenida en Hannover. Ahí tomé el tren que iba a Hamburgo. Después de instalarme, le pregunté al conductor que vino a revisar los boletos para la ubicación del vagón comedor.

Fui allí, me senté en una mesa pequeña y pedí salmón ahumado con todas las guarniciones en un panecillo especial y una taza de té de menta. El cálido vapor de la taza de té se sentía tan acogedor al mirar el frío paisaje invernal que pasaba por la ventana. Saboreé cada bocado de salmón ahumado lentamente. Cuando volví al vagón del tren, Me sentí relajada y me quedé dormida. Solo cuando escuché al conductor gritar: "¡Siguiente parada, Hamburgo-Altona!" Me desperté. Me puse el abrigo, bajé la maleta y me dispuse a bajar del tren, al igual que muchos otros pasajeros.

CAPÍTULO 15

El tiempo en Hamburg

Cuando **el tren redujo la velocidad** y se detuvo en Hamburgo, busqué a Hermann. No lo ví. El pensamiento corría por mi mente, "¿Qué pasa si la carta con los documentos no llega? ¿Qué haré entonces? Decidí quedarme en un lugar y esperar hasta que todos los pasajeros se fueran. Supuse que si Hermann estuviera aquí, haría lo mismo para poder verme. Finalmente, todos los pasajeros habían despejado las vías y vi a Hermann parado al comienzo del tren. Qué alivio. Ahora sabía que él había recibido mi carta con mis documentos de inmigración. Primero, saludé, él también. Agarré mi maleta y corrí hacia él y Hermann hacia mí.

"Qué agradable sorpresa verte". Dejé mi maleta para saludarlo. Me abrazó y expresó su alegría de verme de nuevo. "No tienes idea de lo feliz que estoy de verte aquí,

Hermann. Ahora sé que llegaron mis documentos".

"Sí, acaban de llegar ayer. Seguro que tienes suerte." Cogió mi maleta con una mano y tomó mi mano con la otra. Caminamos de la mano con alegría a través de la estación de tren, siendo completamente ajenos a nuestro entorno. Hermann pidió un taxi y me llevó al lugar donde vivía. Había arreglado con su casera dónde podría pasar la noche. Tan pronto como llegamos, Hermann me presentó a su casera, la Sra. Holz. Ella fue muy cortés. Como era tarde, nos ofreció pastel y café. Entablamos una conversación. Me hizo muchas preguntas sobre mi viaje a los Estados Unidos y cuál era mi propósito. Le pregunté sobre su familia y si vivió en Hamburgo durante la Segunda Guerra Mundial.

"Sí, es un milagro que sobreviviera al gran ataque del 25 de julio de 1943. Sir Arthur, a quien llamaban Bomber Harris, odiaba a los alemanes y envió 792 aviones un minuto después de la medianoche y arrojó 8.000 toneladas de bombas sobre Hamburgo, destruyendo la mayor parte del centro de la ciudad. Usó largas tiras de aluminio, llamadas ventanas, captadas por radar en lugar de los aviones del atacante. La Fuerza Aérea Real atacó Hamburgo por la noche y la Fuerza Aérea Americana durante el día, destruyendo fábricas y edificios públicos y matando a miles de personas. en su mayoría mujeres y niños. Algunos se quemaron vivos y muchos quedaron discapacitados por el resto de sus vidas. Los ataques y tormentas de fuego continuaron durante diez días más. Esos días y el año 1943, nunca los olvidaré. Cuando salimos de entre los escombros, las llamas y el humo cubrían la mayor parte de la ciudad medio destruida. Esqueletos de casas y edificios se elevaban como fantasmas entre los escombros humeantes. Las bombas destruyeron parte de mi casa; mi cocina y sala de estar se podían usar hasta que encontré la manera de reconstruir el resto de la casa. Mucha gente lo había perdido todo y tuvo que abandonar la ciudad o construir un refugio temporal con los escombros".

Pude sentir su angustia mientras recordaba el trágico bombardeo de Hamburgo. Habiendo pasado por ataques aéreos yo misma, expresé mi simpatía por ella.

"Siento mucho que hayas tenido que pasar por esta horrible experiencia. Gracias a Dios que no fue durante el invierno; de lo contrario, muchas personas habrían muerto congeladas. Me alegro de que hayas sobrevivido a toda la carnicería y de que los habitantes hayan reconstruido la mayor parte de Hamburgo de nuevo."

Hermann sólo escuchó.Terminamos nuestra conversación y agradecimos a la Sra. Holz por el pastel y el café antes de ir a nuestras habitaciones.

"Olvidémonos de la guerra por ahora y pensemos en cosas más agradables. ¿Qué te gustaría hacer esta noche?"

"Hace tiempo que no bailo. ¿Podríamos ir a un lugar donde toque una banda en vivo?"

"Sí, hay un restaurante llamado Zwick's en St. Pauli cerca de Reeperbahn, donde una banda toca música dance los sábados por la noche. ¿Te gustaría ir allí?"

"Si crees que la banda es buena, por mí está bien". "También sirven comida. Podemos ir pronto para conseguir una buena mesa y cenar allí."

"Eso suena tentador. ¿Necesito cambiarme o este vestido es adecuado para la ocasión?"

"Estás bien. No es un lugar elegante; la gente se viste casualmente. Si quieres refrescarte, aquí está el baño."

"Gracias; así lo haré." El baño y su habitación tenían las necesidades básicas, pero Hermann los mantuvo limpios y ordenados, lo que me gustó. A las 06:30 p.m. salimos a buscar un taxi. Cuando uno pasó, Hermann alzó la mano e hizo que el conductor se detuviera. En poco tiempo, llegamos al restaurante Zwick's en St. Pauli. Muchas mesas ocupadas rodeaban la gran pista de baile. El camarero nos asignó una pequeña mesa cerca de la plataforma de baile. Luces de colores e instrumentos musicales decoraban las paredes, ventanas y techos.El dueño también colgó muchos carteles de celebridades en las paredes. Parecía acogedor pero desordenado. Hermann me aseguró que la comida que servían era excelente. Pedí wiener schnitzel y

Hermann pidió sauerbraten. Mientras esperábamos nuestra comida, Hermann me miró, "Aún no puedo creer que te hayas detenido en Hamburg para verme. Estoy tan encantado de pasar momentos memorables contigo antes de que te vayas a Estados Unidos. ¿Quién sabe cuándo tendremos la oportunidad de volver a vernos?".

"También estoy feliz de que el destino nos haya dado la oportunidad de estar juntos, aunque sea por poco tiempo".

"Tienes que prometerme escribirme y mantenerme en contacto. Debemos continuar alimentando nuestra amistad especial. Siempre atesoraré los recuerdos de la época en que pertenecimos al grupo de jóvenes, todas las caminatas que hicimos en los bosques con nuestro grupo mientras cantábamos en el tren, en restaurantes o en competencias".

"Sí, bajo tu liderazgo, nuestro grupo siempre se destacó, especialmente en el canto. Y como disfruté hacer bailes folclóricos contigo y bailes de salón también. Me alegro de que me hayas llevado a bailar esta noche. ¿Quién sabe cuándo podré volver a bailar?".

"Siempre me gustó bailar contigo. Estoy agradecido por tener otra oportunidad inesperada de bailar contigo esta noche. Siempre atesoramos las llamadas casualidades inesperadas de la vida".

"Ciertamente lo hacemos. Reunirme contigo en la estación de tren de Essen fue una grata sorpresa. Nunca olvidaré todos los maravillosos conciertos en tu casa; tú tocabas el violín, tu hermana Helge el piano y tu madre tocaba la guitarra, y todos cantábamos".

"Sí, extraño las reuniones musicales con mi familia y amigos mientras estoy aquí en Hamburgo. Sin embargo, cada vez que voy a casa, tenemos una reunión familiar con música. Me iré a casa por Navidad. Espero estar con mi familia. Mi tío Heinrich prometió venir también."

"Cómo admiré las exquisitas pinturas de tu tío Heinrich en las que expresaba tanto amor por la belleza de la naturaleza. Cuando tocaba el arpa y cantaba, Pensé en la presencia del Rey David, deleitándonos, cantando salmos de alabanzas. el irradió tanta paz y amor. Solo estar en su presencia me hizo feliz. Mi gran deseo era y sigue siendo aprender a pintar como tu tío Heinrich."

"Nunca se nota porque tienes buen ojo para la belleza. Tal vez, algún día aprenderás a pintar también. Estudié música y amo la música, pero soy un gran apreciador de las bellas artes."

"¿Te gusta el arte moderno?"

"No en particular. A algunas personas les gustan los diseños abstractos, pero yo prefiero motivos y pinturas realistas."

Mientras tanto, el camarero nos trajo la comida. Mi wiener schnitzel estaba cocinado a la perfección; estaba húmedo y tierno por dentro con el empanado marrón y crujiente por fuera. Las verduras también estaban deliciosas.

«¿Cómo está tu sauerbraten?"

"Es delicioso."

Disfrutamos nuestra comida.

"¿Qué hay del postre?"

"Gracias, tal vez, más tarde. De momento, estoy muy satisfecha."

La banda llegó y preparó sus instrumentos. Terminamos de consumir nuestra comida; la banda empezó a tocar el vals, "En la Calle de los Cordeleros" (Auf der Reeperbahn). Hermann se levantó y me invitó a bailar. Me dio la mano, me levanté y pronto bailamos alegremente dando vueltas y vueltas. Luego siguió una polca. Ni siquiera nos sentábamos entre bailes. Sabíamos muchas letras de las canciones que tocaba la banda. Cantamos y bailamos alegremente hasta la medianoche sin pausa.

"¿No crees que deberíamos irnos ahora?"

"Si lo crees, nos iremos. Disfruté muchísimo la velada. ¿Quién sabe cuándo podré volver a bailar?".

La banda tocó el tango, "La Paloma". ¿Podemos bailar este tango y luego irnos?"

"Si te hace feliz, seguro que podemos".

Mis pies ya deberían estar cansados, pero bailar el tango y escuchar la letra de la canción levantó mi espíritu hasta las nubes.

Sabiendo que este era el último baile, agradecí a Hermann por llevarme a este animado restaurante.

"¡Espero que hayas disfrutado la noche tanto como yo!"

"Ciertamente lo hice. Debes estar cansado a estas alturas."

Fuimos a recoger nuestros abrigos.

"Quédate adentro. Saldré y conseguiré un taxi."

Después de un corto tiempo, Hermann regresó y me llevó al taxi, esperándonos en el restaurante Zwick's. Cuando llegamos al apartamento, era pasada la medianoche.

"¿Te gustaría retirarte ahora mismo? Entonces iré a la sala de estar de mi casera. Se ofreció a dejarme dormir en su sofá por esta noche.

"Todavía no estoy demasiado cansada. Si quieres, podemos quedarnos un rato y hablar."

"Está bien."

Hermann me preguntó quiénes eran mis poetas favoritos. Le dije: "Wolfgang von Goethe, Friedrich von Schiller y Heinrich Heine".

"Sí, esos poetas nos dejaron un caudal de sabiduría. Friedrich von Schiller admiraba los poemas de Wolfgang von Goethe. Eran amigos."

"Me gusta la cita de Goethe, *'Si quieres escribir en un estilo directo, primero tienes que concebirlo claramente en tu alma. Si alguien quiere escribir magníficamente, tiene que tener un carácter magnífico.*"[29]

"Eso es muy cierto; sólo podemos expresar lo que concebimos en nuestra mente y alma y sentimos en nuestro corazón. Me gusta la cita de Friedrich von Schiller, *¡Sé de mente noble! Nuestro propio corazón, y no las opiniones de otros hombres sobre nosotros, constituye nuestro verdadero honor*".

"*La dignidad de la humanidad está en vuestras manos; protegedla. Se hunde contigo; ascenderá contigo. El hombre valiente no piensa en sí mismo. Ayuda a los oprimidos y pon tu confianza en Dios.*"

Hermann agregó: "Me gusta la cita de Wolfgang von Goethe: *"El hombre no solo se crea para sí mismo sino también para su país. Cuanto más fácil es el camino, menos se requiere de los hombres. Cuanto más compleja es la tarea del pueblo, más alto asciende el pueblo*".

"Sí, mi profesor de primaria me dijo que eligiera el camino más desafiante; requerirá más de tí. Me lo tomé en serio. Dejar a mi familia, mi país e incluso a ti atrás e ir a un país extranjero y enfrentarme a lo desconocido es un sacrificio excepcional para mí. Confío en Dios, quien resolverá todas las cosas para bien."

"Para mí es igual de difícil, o tal vez más, renunciar a ti y verte dejarme a mí y a tu país natal. Eso me recuerda una cita de Emanual Kant, el gran filósofo de la Razón Pura y la Moralidad de Prusia del Este: *"No eres rico por lo que posees, sino por lo que puedes entregar con dignidad"*. Según Emanual Kant, podemos considerarnos ricos entregándonos unos a otros con dignidad y adhiriendo a nuestros valores morales". "Trataré de recordar esto, y otra cita suya, *"Así como lo bello es limitado, lo sublime es ilimitado, de modo que la mente en presencia de lo sublime que intenta imaginar lo que no puede, tiene dolor en el fracaso pero placer contemplando la inmensidad del intento."*

Contemplemos lo sublime para enriquecer nuestras vidas."

"Eso me recuerda otra cita de Friedrich von Schiller, *"Para que alguien esté comprometido con la verdad y la libertad en la más alta búsqueda de la belleza, un artista debe encontrar una manera de equilibrar lo existente en el espacio y el tiempo, pero siempre esforzarse por trascender las limitaciones de su sociedad secular en una búsqueda constante de lo eterno".*

"Sí, tenemos que mirar hacia el cielo y el Universo pero también mirar nuestro camino en la tierra y apreciar la belleza que nos rodea".

Por un momento, pensé en la definición de belleza de la creación de Dios. Un poema que escribí más tarde se ajusta a este tema.

Dios creó por amor
Hombres, el universo, la tierra.
Para compartir la belleza de sus obras y artes,
Dios llenó de sabiduría los corazones humanos.
Él nos pidió que vivamos en paz los unos con los otros,
Y que amemos a Dios primero y luego a cada hermano.
Si amamos incondicionalmente tendremos un atisbo de eternidad.
Dios nos enseña a afrontar cada desafío
Con fe en Él y valor digno.
Viviremos con entusiasmo y trataremos de hacer lo mejor que podamos,
Entonces dejemos a Dios las preocupaciones y el resto.
Dios nos bendecirá sobremanera
Y nos recompensará con Su tesoro.

Pongo toda mi confianza en Dios y disfruto de la belleza de Su creación, así como de hermosas obras de arte, música, literatura y arquitectura".

"Yo también disfruto de las obras creativas de los artistas y especialmente de la música. Mis compositores favoritos son Beethoven, Mozart y Schubert, y tantos otros compositores alemanes de operetas. Tenemos una gran cantidad de canciones folklóricas que también me gustan".

"Además de los compositores que nombraste, también me gustan las óperas de Giuseppe Verdi. Presentan varios solos, dúos, coros y ballets, captando la atención del público durante toda la actuación. No soy demasiado aficionado a las óperas de Richard Wagner. Solo me gustan algunas arias y oberturas suyas."

"Nuestro país aportó tanto al mundo en el arte, la música, la literatura y sobre todo la ciencia. Que trágico, que nuestro pueblo y país tuvieron que ser humillados después de la Segunda Guerra Mundial por las atrocidades de Hitler.

¿Crees que la ocupación terminará algún día y recuperaremos nuestra soberanía?".

"Seguro espero eso. Deseo que los países europeos se unan y formen una alianza para protegerse de ser tomados por Rusia y el comunismo. Solo podemos esperar lo mejor."

Antes de que nos diéramos cuenta, amaneció, era hora de prepararme para mi viaje en tren a Bremerhaven.

A las 7:00 a. m., Hermann me dijo que la casera nos serviría el desayuno en breve.

"Vamos a refrescarnos antes de irnos. Tendremos que irnos a la estación de ferrocarril después del desayuno."

Cuando entramos a la cocina, encontramos la mesa ya puesta. Nos esperaba un surtido de panecillos y variedad de embutidos, quesos y huevos duros.

"Buenos días señora Holz. Qué amable de su parte habernos preparado el desayuno."

"Buenos días, señorita Bonacker. Buenos días, Hermann, ¿durmieron bien?"

"No dormimos nada. Hablamos toda la noche después de que volvimos del restaurante", respondió Hermann. La señora Holz nos pidió que nos sentáramos y nos sirviéramos. Disfrutamos de los panecillos calientes con fiambres y mermelada y un huevo hervido.

Antes de irnos, le agradecimos su hospitalidad y el delicioso desayuno que nos preparó. Me deseó un buen viaje y buena suerte en Estados Unidos antes de despedirnos.

Hermann había pedido un taxi para las 8:30 a.m. Cuando llegó el taxi, Hermann le dijo al conductor que nos llevara a la estación principal de trenes. Ambos nos subimos al auto, nos sentamos cerca uno del otro y apenas pronunciamos una palabra. Nuestras emociones de separarnos eran demasiado profundas como para expresarlas con palabras. Hermann tomó mi mano y la apretó con fuerza como diciendo, quédate aquí conmigo; encontraremos nuestro destino juntos. De vez en cuando, nos mirábamos y veíamos la tristeza en nuestros ojos y expresiones faciales. Cuando salimos del taxi, Hermann pagó al conductor y llevó mi maleta a la estación de tren. Fuimos a la ventanilla y compré el boleto a Bremerhaven. Hermann me acompañó hasta la vía de donde partía el tren. Después de dejar la maleta, primero me estrechó la mano y me deseó un buen viaje y buena suerte en Estados Unidos. Luego me abrazó con fuerza y susurró: "Me entristece dejarte ir, pero recuerda, siempre te querré".

"Siempre serás mi querido amigo. Siempre atesoraré nuestra amistad y los momentos memorables que hemos pasado juntos" susurré.

"Yo también recordaré los maravillosos momentos que pasamos juntos y te admiraré por tus altos valores morales y tu noble carácter. Me facilitó mantener nuestros altos estándares morales en todas las circunstancias".

"Gracias. Te respeto mucho por ser honesto y honorable en todas tus acciones. Ambos *maduramos y permanecimos puros.* Dios te bendiga siempre."

"Adiós, mi querida Hilde. Dios esté contigo también." Solo pude decir: "Adiós, Hermann". Me soltó y se alejó.

Me quedé de pie viéndolo alejarse más y más. Mi corazón dijo: "Renuncia a tu plan y síguelo", pero mi cabeza dijo que continuaras con tu viaje. Obedecí a mi cabeza y me subí al tren. Me alegré de encontrar un compartimiento de tren vacío y no entablar una conversación con extraños. Me apoyé en la esquina junto a la ventana y agradecí a Dios que mis documentos de inmigración hubieran llegado a la dirección de Hermann y de que tuvimos otra oportunidad de compartir nuestros pensamientos e ideas. Puse mis planes y preocupaciones en las manos de Dios y me fui. Me desperté unas tres horas después cuando escuché al conductor llamar. "Bremerhaven, última parada, todos desembarcan".

CAPÍTULO 16

Viaje en Barco a Nueva York

Después de bajarme del tren, contraté un taxi para que me llevara al puerto, de donde partían los barcos estadounidenses. El taxista se detuvo en una oficina en un gran complejo de barracas. Me presenté al empleado y le dije que se suponía que debía partir mañana con el barco de transporte de soldados General Harry Taylor. Sacó la lista de pasajeros y dijo: "Sí, estás en la lista. Pero el barco parte un día más tarde de lo previsto".

"No sabía eso. ¿Dónde puedo quedarme el día extra?" "Puedes quedarte en una habitación de las barracas.

"Espera aquí; Llamaré a alguien para que te lleve allí. Aquí también hay un horario para la salida del barco. Asegúrate de llegar allí con dos horas de anticipación."

"Gracias, es muy amable de su parte dejarme quedarme aquí un día más. Estaré en el puerto a tiempo. Por cierto, había enviado mi equipaje antes de tiempo. ¿Llegó? ¿Hay algún restaurante en el complejo?"

"Sí, hay un restaurante en el edificio grande, donde se sirve el desayuno a las 7:00 a.m., el almuerzo a mediodía y la cena a las 6:00 p.m. El empleado revisó otra lista y me dijo que llegó mi equipaje. A los pocos minutos, vino un joven, recogió mi maleta y me pidió que lo siguiera. Me llevó a un cuartel cercano, abrió la puerta y me mostró la habitación en la que se suponía que me iba a quedar dos noches. Le agradecí al joven antes de que se fuera. Estaba más cansada que hambrienta y opté por tomar una siesta. Me desperté justo a tiempo para cenar. Di un largo paseo después de salir del restaurante. Luego regresé a la habitación, que tenía solo las necesidades básicas pero estaba limpia. Desempaqué algo de ropa para el día siguiente. Después de ducharme, saqué el pequeño Nuevo Testamento que guardaba en mi bolso. Lo abrí al azar y leí Mateo 14: 24 -33.

Jesús les pidió a los discípulos que subieran a la barca mientras Jesús subía a la montaña a orar. Cuando el bote estaba en medio del mar, una tormenta creó olas altas y sacudió el bote. Jesús caminó sobre el mar hacia la barca. Los discípulos no reconocieron a Jesús y tuvieron miedo. Jesús les dijo: "Tened buen ánimo. No tengáis miedo; Soy yo, le respondió Pedro. "Caballero, si eres tú, ordéname que camine sobre las aguas hacia ti. Y Jesús dijo: "Ven". Pedro lo hizo. Cuando vio el fuerte viento y las grandes olas, comenzó a hundirse y gritó: "Señor, sálvame". Jesús extendió su mano y lo salvó, diciendo: "Hombre de poca fe, ¿por qué dudaste? Cuando subieron a la barca, el viento cesó. La gente en la barca adoró a Jesús, diciendo: "Verdaderamente, eres hijo de Dios".

Reflexioné sobre esas palabras y las tomé como un mensaje personal para mi próximo viaje por mar: "No temas incluso si te encuentras con mares agitados; Estoy contigo y siempre te protegeré." Antes de acostarme, oré y agradecí a Dios por su mensaje de consuelo.

El lunes 17 de diciembre de 1956, un trabajador me llevó al puerto, donde me reuní con mucha gente en un gran salón. En un muelle cercano se encontraba el barco de transporte del ejército llamado H. M. S. General Harry Taylor, el barco en el que me asignaron viajar a través del Atlántico a Nueva York. Parecía más un acorazado gris que un crucero. Pero no me importaba, siempre y cuando estuviera en condiciones de navegar.

Barco MS General Harry Taylor, 1956

Después de que un empleado de inmigración revisara los documentos de cada persona, nos embarcamos en el barco. Un infante de marina me llevó a una habitación enorme y me mostró mi litera. Cuando todos los pasajeros estuvieron a bordo, el barco se preparó para partir. Una gran multitud se había congregado en el muelle para despedir a familiares y amigos. Yo, en cambio, subí a cubierta para despedirme de mi país natal. Mientras una banda tocaba "Adiós, Adiós" (Aufwiedersehn, Aufwiedersehn), un sentimiento triste llenó mi corazón. Me quedé en cubierta hasta que la música se desvaneció y la costa se desvaneció en la distancia cuando el barco partió hacia las aguas abiertas del Mar del Norte. Luego regresé a la habitación grande y llena de gente que me habían asignado y encontré mi litera. Miré alrededor buscando los baños y las duchas. Conocí a una joven encantadora que tenía la litera a mi lado. Decidimos explorar el barco para averiguar dónde estaban el comedor y otras instalaciones. Fuimos a almorzar y cenar juntas en el gran comedor. Con tanta gente en un solo lugar y familias enteras con niños pequeños viajando, no pude conciliar el sueño hasta altas horas de la noche. El Mar del Norte estaba relativamente tranquilo. Después de pasar por el Canal de la Mancha y entrar en el Océano Atlántico, los vientos levantaron olas altas, sacudiendo el barco ferozmente, y los pasajeros se marearon. Un joven vestido con un uniforme azul marino se me acercó y se presentó como James Chambers.

"Vimos en sus registros que usted es una asistente médico. Nuestros médicos necesitan intérpretes que hablen alemán e inglés. ¿Estarías dispuesta a ayudarnos?"

"Aunque hablo inglés, no conozco la terminología médica en inglés. Intentaré ayudar si el médico me considera adecuada."

"Ven conmigo. Te llevaré al consultorio del médico; Dejaremos que el médico decida".

Después de presentarme al Dr. Strom y teniendo una breve conversación, el Dr. Strom me pidió que estuviera en su oficina a las 2:00 p. m. El señor Chambers también me informó que podía quedarme en una de las habitaciones de la sección del hospital, cerca del consultorio del médico. Me llevó allí y me mostró la habitación que me habían asignado. Le agradecí mucho al Sr. Chambers y estaba contenta de tener un lugar para mí. Después de regresar con mi equipaje, me encontré con otra señora en el hospital. Nos presentamos. Su nombre era Olga. Era una enfermera de Rusia que hablaba inglés, alemán y ruso. El Dr. Weiss, el segundo médico a bordo del barco, le pidió a Olga que fuera su intérprete.

Ambas nos sentimos afortunadas de tener una habitación propia y una cama más cómoda y pudimos dormir sin niños llorando y sin gente lamentándose. Todos los días nos reuníamos con los médicos durante el horario de oficina. El primer día que asistí al Dr. Strom y a su enfermera, el Dr. Strom trató sólo a unas pocas personas mareadas. El médico recetó Dramamine para las náuseas y los vómitos, y luego les dijo a los pacientes que bebieran muchos líquidos para evitar deshidratarse. Aprendí las palabras en inglés rápidamente para los síntomas más comunes del mareo y algunas otras enfermedades y qué medicina y tratamiento me recetó el médico. Si no sabía un nombre, usaría el lenguaje de señas para hacer llegar el mensaje del médico al paciente.

Cuanto más viajábamos en el Océano Atlántico, más agitado se volvía el océano. Enormes olas golpeaban contra el casco, salpicaban la cubierta y sacudían el barco con fiereza. Más y más pacientes acudían al médico cada día, y menos personas se presentaban en el comedor. Yo también me mareé. El Dr. Strom me dio Dramamine, lo que me hizo sentir mejor. Opté por continuar asistiendo al Dr. Strom. De vez en cuando, tenía que disculparme e ir al baño para vaciar el contenido de mi estómago. Algunos pacientes deshidratados tuvieron que ser hospitalizados y recibir una inyección intravenosa o intramuscular de Dramamine junto con fluidos electrolíticos para reemplazar el líquido, los minerales, el sodio y el potasio agotados. Siempre que tenía tiempo libre, tejía bordes alrededor de pañuelos para distraerme del mareo. Después de una semana de luchar contra el mar embravecido y surcar las olas espumosas, la velocidad del viento disminuyó un poco y calmó las aguas turbulentas.

El 24 de diciembre celebramos la Nochebuena. La tripulación del barco había colocado un árbol de Navidad en la capilla. A las 10:00 p.m. horas se realizó un servicio para los pasajeros evangélicos, y a la medianoche una misa para los pasajeros católicos. Seguí la pista de la hora alemana, que estaba seis horas adelantada con respecto a la hora de Nueva York. A las 6:00 p.m., que sería medianoche en Alemania, salí a cubierta. Pensé en cómo mi familia celebraría la Navidad mañana y cómo Hermann y su familia me cantaron a medianoche la canción: "Noche Divina de Estrellas Brillantes" (Hohe Nacht der Klaren

Sterne)[30] y otras hermosas canciones navideñas acompañadas por Hermann al violín, Helge al piano y la Sra. Jaeger la guitarra. En mi imaginación, canté y sentí que estaba en medio de ellos. Fue una hermosa manifestación de la Navidad. Reflexioné sobre la verdadera razón por la que celebramos la Navidad, el nacimiento de nuestro Salvador Jesucristo. Mis pensamientos no se quedaron solo con mi familia y amigos en Alemania, sino que mis pensamientos viajaron a Belén. Vi al niño Jesús en el pesebre con María y José cuidándolo. Los pastores estaban arrodillados frente al pesebre y adorando al recién nacido Rey y Salvador del mundo. Yo también adoraba al Rey recién nacido.

Después de la cena, Olga y yo fuimos al servicio de Navidad de las 10:00 p. m. en la capilla. Escuchamos el cuento de Navidad y cantamos varios villancicos. Eran pasadas las 11:00 p. m. cuando el capellán despidió a los fieles con una bendición. Antes de acostarme, agradecí a Dios que incluso en medio del océano y entre extraños, podía celebrar el nacimiento de Cristo de una manera cristiana significativa. En Cristo, nos sentimos unidos como hermanos y hermanas y no como extraños.

Al día siguiente después del desayuno. El señor Chambers llamó a la puerta. Cuando lo abrí, anunció con alegría: "Feliz Navidad, Hildegard, tengo un regalo para tí". Luego me entregó un pequeño paquete. Lo abrí y encontré un brazalete en él.

"Esto es encantador. Gracias. También tengo un pequeño regalo para ti, pero no tenía papel de regalo".

Le di un pañuelo con un borde azul que había tejido durante el viaje. "Eso es muy lindo. Lo guardaré como un recuerdo tuyo. Hildegard no cambies nunca; sigue siendo como eres. En unos días, abandonarás el barco. No sé si volveré a verte. Te deseo lo mejor en mi país. Espero que encuentres un nuevo hogar y felicidad en Estados Unidos. Te daré mi dirección; puedes escribirme y hacerme saber dónde estarás y como es tu vida en los Estados Unidos."

"Señor Chambers, primero permítame agradecerle por ser tan considerado y darme un regalo de Navidad y por su amabilidad hacia mí durante el viaje. Aprecio mucho ambas cosas. Una vez que encuentre un lugar para quedarme, les haré saber dónde viviré y si he encontrado trabajo".

"Muy bien. Te deseo una feliz navidad."

"También le deseo una Feliz Navidad y un futuro lleno de bendiciones".

El señor Chambers se fue. Su amabilidad y obsequio hicieron que mi Navidad en el mar fuera muy especial.

El día de Navidad, el capitán habló por el altavoz. Deseó a la tripulación y a los pasajeros una Feliz Navidad. También anunció que llegaríamos a Nueva York mañana a primera hora de la tarde. Más avanzada la tarde, siguió una celebración civil de Navidad. Los pasajeros de varios países cantaron canciones navideñas y tocaron música. Olga y yo asistimos al evento especial. También tuvimos juntos la tradicional cena americana de Navidad: pavo relleno, patatas y judías verdes. El pastel de calabaza y nuez terminó la deliciosa comida. Antes de retirarme a dormir, subí a cubierta para mirar el cielo repleto de estrellas. La luna había disminuido a un cuarto, oscureciendo la noche y haciendo más brillantes las estrellas. El zumbido de los motores y la proa cortando las olas rompieron el silencio. Me sentí cerca de Dios, de mi familia y de mis amigos. Di gracias a Dios por una celebración especial de Navidad en el mar y una travesía segura hasta el momento, a pesar del océano agitado. Agradecida y alegre, me retiré por la noche.

Al día siguiente en la clínica, el Dr. Strom me preguntó a dónde iba y si ya tenía un lugar para trabajar. Le dije que mi padrino vivía en Des Moines, Iowa, y que planeaba ir a ver a mi hermana en Garnavillo, Iowa.

"Tengo un amigo en Des Moines en la Clínica Beaverdale. Te daré una carta de recomendación para él. Tal vez pueda ayudarte a conseguir un puesto en la clínica."

"Gracias por su amabilidad. Le agradezco que me recomiende a su amigo y que me permitiera asistirlo en la clínica."

A la mañana siguiente, empaqué todas mis pertenencias antes de ir al consultorio del médico. Como prometió, el Dr. Strom me dio la carta. Después de ver al último paciente, le agradecí por dejarme trabajar con él y la carta de recomendación. También me agradeció por ayudarlo como intérprete. Antes de ir a la cabina, subí a cubierta. El horizonte de Nueva York apareció en la distancia, y al frente se encontraba la Estatua de la Libertad. Su antorcha encendida nos dio la bienvenida con las famosas líneas de Lázaro: "Dame a tus cansados, tus pobres, tus masas amontonadas que anhelan respirar libertad".

Mientras nos acercábamos a Nueva York, me quedé allí fascinada, viendo la luz de la antorcha brillando más y más y la Estatua de la Libertad y los rascacielos cada vez más altos. De repente, el barco se detuvo cuando estábamos cerca de la entrada del puerto. El capitán anunció que no podíamos entrar al puerto porque los estibadores estaban en huelga. Tendríamos que esperar hasta que volvieran al trabajo. Pasamos la tarde y la noche del miércoles, esperando el permiso para entrar al puerto. El jueves por la noche, el capitán anunció que podríamos ingresar al puerto el viernes 28 de diciembre por la mañana. No me cansaba de ver el horizonte de Nueva York durante el día y me fascinaba por la noche cuando las luces regulares y navideñas transformaban la ciudad en una imagen mágica de cuento de hadas. Muchos pasajeros subieron a cubierta para tomar aire fresco y observar el horizonte de Nueva York. También tuve la oportunidad de despedirme de personas que conocí durante el viaje.

El viernes por la mañana, la tripulación levó el ancla y el barco comenzó a moverse. Aproximadamente una hora más tarde, entramos en el puerto de Nueva York. Todos los pasajeros desembarcaron y esperaron su equipaje, que una grúa descargó en una gran red. La tripulación transportó las maletas y cajas a un almacén cercano donde pudimos reclamarlas. Los pasajeros que necesitaban continuar su viaje eran recogidos por autobuses y transportados al aeropuerto o a las estaciones de tren. Después de que conseguí mi equipaje, alguien llevó mi gran maleta de madera al autobús que iba a la estación de tren. Conseguí un boleto para ir a Chicago y luego continuar a Prairie Du Chien, Wisconsin. Los paisajes pastorales y las estructuras de la ciudad pasaban rápidamente por la ventana del tren durante el día. Durante la noche traté de dormir, pero el ruido del tren no me dejaba dormir. Al día siguiente, cambié de tren en Chicago, crucé campos agrícolas cubiertos de nieve, hermosos bosques y pasé lagos en Illinois e Iowa antes de llegar a Prairie Du Chien. Llamé a mi hermana, y al poco tiempo, mi cuñado y mi hermana me recogieron en la estación de ferrocarril.

Condujimos sobre el poderoso río Mississippi y, después de un viaje corto, llegamos a Garnavillo, Iowa, donde mi cuñado trabajaba en una granja enorme. Mi hermana cuidaba de sus tres hijas, Agnes, Ilse y Christa, y vivía en una casa espaciosa y cómoda. Qué maravillosa sorpresa: mi hermana Emma, mi sobrino Bernie y mi hermano Edmund vinieron de Chicago para darme la bienvenida a Estados Unidos. Estábamos tan felices de estar unidos de nuevo. Meta me entregó una carta dirigida a mí pero enviada a la dirección de mi hermana.

La abrí rápidamente y encontré una foto de una hermosa familia con tres niños pequeños. No podría estar más sorprendida de leer que el Dr. y la Sra. Jefferies, que vivía en Des Moines, Iowa, me preguntaran si me gustaría residir en su casa y ayudarlos con los niños. Agradecí a Dios por esta oportunidad de vivir con la hermosa familia de un ortodoncista estadounidense. Inmediatamente compartí las buenas noticias con mi familia. También mencioné que el Dr. Strom del barco me había dado una carta para su amigo médico que administraba una clínica en Des Moines. Quizá pueda contratarme. Eso no me dejó más remedio que ir a Des Moines. Me sentí terrible al decepcionar a mi hermana Emma y mi hermano Edmund porque no me fui con ellos a Chicago, como esperaban que hiciera.

El año nuevo acaba de pasar; celebramos mi vigésimo cumpleaños el miércoles 2 de enero de 1957. Meta preparó un ganso asado con todas las guarniciones y de postre una torta alemana de chocolate. Para mí fue una alegría compartir sus experiencias de vida en Estados Unidos y mis eventos del año pasado. El miércoles llamé al Dr. y la Sra. Jefferies y les dije que aceptaría su oferta. Pregunté si podía verlos el 3 de enero de 1957. Acordaron reunirse conmigo en persona el jueves. Antes de que mi cuñado Ernst me llevara a Des Moines, llevó a mi hermana Emma, mi sobrino Bernie, y hermano Edmund a la estación de ferrocarril en Prairie Du Chien. Sentí tristeza por no ir con ellos, pero Dios tenía otros planes para mí.

Dr. Y Sra Jeffries, con Jon, Kim & Jill

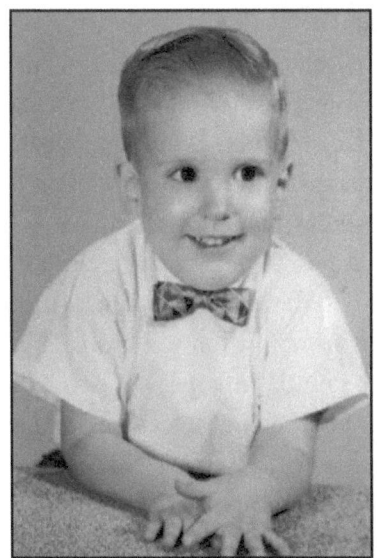

Kent Jeffries

Cuando llegué a la residencia del Dr. y la Sra. Jefferies, me saludaron calurosamente. Hablamos un rato y la Sra. Jefferies explicó lo que esperaban de mí. Después de que acepté, me aceptaron para quedarme con su familia. Mi cuñado se fue, luego de saber que fui aceptada para quedarme con la familia Jefferies. También le mencioné al Dr. y la Sra. Jefferies que había trabajado con el Dr. Strom a bordo del barco como intérprete. El Dr. Strom me había dado una carta de recomendación para un amigo médico de la Clínica Beaverdale. El lunes siguiente, 7 de enero de 1957, la Sra. Jefferies me llevó a la Clínica Beaverdale. Presenté la carta del Dr. Strom al gerente. Después de leerlo, me ofreció un puesto temporal en el departamento de rayos X y luego en el laboratorio por medio día. No podía agradecerle a Dios lo suficiente por la manera maravillosa en que me había proveído de un lugar especial para quedarme y trabajar cercanos en el mismo pueblo.

La familia Jefferies y yo desarrollamos una rutina cómoda. El Dr. Jefferies comenzó su horario de oficina a las 8:30 a.m. en el centro de Des Moines. Empecé a trabajar en la clínica a las 8:00 a.m. Cada mañana, el Dr. Jefferies preparó un suntuoso desayuno de tostadas, tocino o salchichas y huevos, jugo de frutas y café. Luego me dejaba en la clínica antes de ir a su oficina. La señora Jefferies se levantaba más tarde y preparaba el desayuno para los niños. Jon y Kim iban a la escuela, Jill, de cuatro años, al jardín de infantes, y Kent, de ocho meses, que no aparece en la foto, se quedaba en casa. Al mediodía, la Sra. Jefferies me recogía en la clínica. Hacía el almuerzo para todos nosotros. Después del almuerzo, Kent y Jill tomaban una siesta. Cuando se despertaban, salían a caminar con Kent en la carriola y, a veces, llevaban a Jill.

Ayudaba a levantar la mesa, limpiar la casa, y hacer ropa y planchado. Me trataron como parte de su familia. Nunca lo había pasado tan bien en mi vida. Di gracias a Dios cada día por la bondad de toda la familia. También agradecí la oportunidad de aprender inglés conversacional. La señora Jefferies, habiendo sido una ex azafata, hablaba un inglés literario hermoso. También lo hacía el Dr. Jefferies. Ambos eran muy inteligentes. Siempre teníamos un diccionario alemán-inglés en la encimera de la cocina. Si yo no supiera una palabra en inglés, la buscaría en el diccionario. También tomé clases avanzadas de inglés en la universidad, donde conocí a otras señoritas de las que me hice amiga.

CAPÍTULO 17

Yendo a Chicago

Todo parecía tan perfecto, y yo estaba muy contenta con la vida. Sin embargo, mi hermano Edmund y mi hermana Emma querían que fuera a Chicago. Al principio, la idea de renunciar a mi maravillosa vida con la familia Jefferies no me atraía. Oré por la guía de Dios. A medida que pasaba el tiempo, parecía más evidente que debía unirme a mi familia. Un día, cuando la Sra. Jefferies mencionó cómo conoció a su esposo en Chicago y agregó: "Hildegard, nunca te dejaré ir a Chicago".

"Siento decepcionarte. Les prometí a mi hermano y a mi hermana que me reuniría con ellos en Chicago".

"Pero no puedes simplemente dejarnos. ¿No eres feliz aquí?"

"Estoy encantada de vivir con usted y su familia, y me cuesta dejarlos, pero mi familia me necesita en Chicago".

"Supongo que tengo que dejarte ir, aunque estaremos tristes de verte partir y te extrañaremos.¿Cuándo te quieres ir?" "Tal vez en dos semanas. También quiero dar un aviso de dos semanas a la clínica. Podría salir el lunes 1 de julio".

Esa noche la Sra. Jefferies le dio la noticia a su familia de que me iría el 1 de julio.

"¿Por qué nos dejas tan pronto?"

"Estoy complacida con su familia y agradecido con todos, pero mi familia quiere que me una a ellos en Chicago".

"Supongo que si ya hiciste la promesa, tenemos que dejarte ir". Jon y Kim también expresaron su tristeza y me pidieron que me quedara. Me había encariñado con los niños y dejarlos también me hacía infeliz. El personal de la Clínica Beaverdale se entristeció al verme partir; yo también. Todos me trataron con mucho cariño. Disfruté trabajar con los técnicos y las enfermeras.

El lunes 1 de julio fue el último desayuno que tuve con el Dr. Jefferies. Ambos nos sentimos tristes, pero él me deseó lo mejor antes de irse solo a su oficina. Luego ayudé a la Sra. Jefferies a llevar a los niños a la escuela antes de llevarme a la estación de tren.

"Hildegard, me siento desanimada de que te vayas, pero escríbenos y cuéntanos cómo te va en Chicago".

"Le escribiré. Muchas gracias por haber sido tan amable de aceptarme como parte de su familia. Siempre estaré agradecida con todos ustedes". Las lágrimas comenzaban a brotar de mis ojos cuando la Sra. Jefferies me abrazó y nos despedimos.

Una vez que llegué a Chicago, mi hermana Emma y mi hermano Edmund me recibieron con los brazos abiertos. Edmund había alquilado un apartamento en la calle Racine, cerca del barrio alemán. También me presentó a una iglesia oficiada por un pastor alemán. Conocí a muchos jóvenes feligreses alemanes y nos unimos al coro de la iglesia. Encontré un empleo temporal en Bankers Life and Casualty Insurance Co. en el departamento de reclamaciones. Durante ese tiempo, aprendí los términos médicos en inglés de muchas enfermedades. Sin embargo, sentarme detrás de un escritorio durante ocho horas todos los días no me satisfacía por completo. Extrañaba el contacto con los pacientes.

Papá regresa de Polonia, 1957

Otro evento importante tuvo lugar. En septiembre de 1957, después de más de doce años de cautiverio, mi padre regresó de Polonia. Deseé poder regresar rápidamente a Alemania para darle la bienvenida personalmente, pero económicamente no podía pagar el pasaje aéreo a Alemania. Sabía que tenía que buscar un trabajo mejor pagado para viajar a Alemania a visitar a mi padre, a quien no había visto en trece años. Mi hermano Horst me envió un informe escrito de mi padre y sus experiencias de los últimos doce años, que traduje al inglés:

Yo, Gustav Bonacker, nacido el 4 de septiembre de 1902 en Wizajny, Kreis Sudauen, Prusia del Este, resido en Essingen, Alemania, Landauerstr. 184.

Fui reclutado en julio de 1944 por el ejército alemán (Wehrmacht). Me enviaron a la División de Construcción en Modlin, Polonia. Estuve con esta División hasta mayo de 1945. Después de que terminó la guerra, Me convertí en un prisionero de guerra estadounidense y me enviaron al campo francés de Chalon, donde permanecí hasta que me liberaron en octubre de 1945. Como supuse que mi familia todavía estaba en Prusia del Este, quería regresar a nuestra casa en Prusia del Este. Cuando otros soldados y yo llegamos en tren a Sudauen, los otros soldados alemanes y yo fuimos capturados y convertidos en prisioneros por la policía polaca. Después de varios días de interrogatorio por parte de la policía polaca, fui encarcelado cerca de Sudauen. Aquí me retuvieron hasta octubre de 1946. Luego me condenaron a seis años más en el campo de prisioneros de Bialystock.

Cuatro semanas después, me transportaron a la cárcel en Warthenburg, Prusia Oriental. Permanecí allí hasta julio de 1947. De allí fui enviado a la prisión de Rawitch, donde permanecí hasta 1950. Después de un examen médico, fui enviado con otros presos que aún podían trabajar a Gross-Strenlitz. Aquí trabajamos en una cantera de piedra hasta que me transfirieron en 1951 o 1952 a la mina de carbón de Katowich. Allí trabajé hasta el 17 de marzo de 1953. Terminó mi condena y me liberaron. Tres semanas antes, el oficial a cargo de la prisión me preguntó qué pensaba hacer después de mi liberación. Cuando le dije que quería reunirme con mi familia en Alemania Occidental, me prohibió estrictamente ir allí. Sólo se me permitió vivir en la provincia de Sudauen. Estuve de acuerdo, feliz de salir de la prisión. Hasta abril de 1956 trabajé como peón libre en el bosque. Después, busqué trabajo en Treuburg, Prusia Oriental, donde trabajé en el bosque hasta septiembre de 1957, cuando me permitieron salir de Polonia.

Me siento obligado a mencionar que hasta el año 1947 fuimos tratados con mucha brutalidad. Nos golpeaban con frecuencia y nos maltrataban, lo que resultó en una oreja mutilada y un dedo índice dañado en mi mano derecha. En diciembre de 1947, me golpearon tan brutalmente que tuve que ser hospitalizado durante casi cuatro semanas. Todo mi cuerpo estaba hinchado y me dolían todas las articulaciones. La alimentación también era muy pobre. Muchos compañeros murieron por desnutrición o maltrato.

Leer el informe de mi padre me entristeció considerablemente. Quería correr a casa lo antes posible para verlo. Primero, tuve que encontrar un trabajo mejor pagado para ahorrar lo suficiente para el viaje. En la víspera de Año Nuevo, fui a una agencia de empleo en el centro de Chicago. El empleado me envió a una entrevista en el Hospital Americano. Aunque le dije al patólogo, Dr. Eisenstadt, que me entrevistó, que nunca había trabajado en histología, me contrató. Él dijo: "La técnica, Irene, te enseñará. Necesitamos un técnico de laboratorio en histología para el Hospital Bethesda, que se inaugurará en febrero de 1958".

Acepté el puesto. Dos semanas después, Irene me enseñó los procedimientos de histología y comencé a trabajar en el Hospital Bethesda a principios de marzo. Margaret, la directora de laboratorio del Hospital Bethesda, también me enseñó cómo realizar pruebas de química, serología, hematología y bacteriología. Disfruté trabajar con los técnicos de laboratorio y la gerente Margaret, y conocer al administrador, el Sr. Glass, las enfermeras, otros empleados y algunos médicos del personal del hospital de Bethesda. Le di gracias a Dios por trabajar nuevamente en el campo de la medicina, lo cual disfruté mucho.

En 1958 volé a Frankfurt, Alemania, y luego tomé el tren a Landau. Mi hermano Horst y mi padre vinieron a buscarme a la estación de tren. Aunque todavía reconocía a mi padre, él no me recordaba. Me había visto por última vez cuando yo tenía siete años. Había cambiado más allá del reconocimiento durante los últimos trece años. Exclamó con incredulidad: "Tú eres mi pequeña Hildchen. Creciste para convertirte en una hermosa y joven Fraeulein. Nos conectamos de inmediato y disfrutamos recordando la vida en casa en Prusia del Este antes de la guerra. También describió las condiciones deterioradas después de que el pueblo polaco se apoderara de nuestra tierra. Hablamos de tantas celebraciones familiares del pasado. No había perdido su sentido del humor y su sonrisa a pesar de los trágicos años de encarcelamiento. Las dos semanas pasaron demasiado rápido, recordando la vida en casa en Prusia del Este antes y después de la Segunda Guerra Mundial y contándome algunas experiencias de los últimos doce años. Desafortunadamente, tuve que regresar a Chicago nuevamente. Sin embargo, me alegró ver a mi padre y renovar nuestro vínculo familiar.

Todo parecía ir bien. Sin embargo, un año después, mi hermano Edmund fue reclutado por el ejército estadounidense a pesar de no ser ciudadano estadounidense. Después del entrenamiento de campo de entrenamiento en Fort Worth, fue enviado a Alemania. Me quedé atrás. Recientemente había comprado un automóvil a crédito. Mi salario por sí solo era insuficiente para hacer los pagos mensuales, así que busqué otro trabajo de medio tiempo.

No muy lejos de donde vivía, otro pequeño hospital había abierto recientemente. Después de que la administradora del Roosevelt Memorial Hospital, la Sra. Jones, me entrevistó; me contrató. Birute, el jefe de técnicos de laboratorio, trabajaba en la mañana, el Sr. Chapman, en la tarde, y yo cubría las horas de la noche. El Dr. Robert Stein, un brillante patólogo, venía varios días a la semana a describir las piezas quirúrgicas macroscópicas y examinaba y diagnosticaba microscópicamente las láminas que le había preparado de las secciones quirúrgicas anteriores. Durante el día, trabajaba en el Centro de Investigación del Laboratorio Abbot. Además de ser el patólogo del Roosevelt Memorial Hospital en Chicago, el Dr. Stein también trabajaba algunas tardes en el Hospital Mc Henry en McHenry. Estudió patología forense y realizó seminarios en ese campo. Disfruté preparando las diapositivas para sus conferencias. También me dejó hacer todas las autopsias con él, donde aprendí cómo las diferentes enfermedades afectaban los órganos del cuerpo humano.

El Dr. Stein fue un excelente maestro y un ser humano humilde y amable, contrastando con la personalidad exigente y autoritaria del Dr. Eisenstadt en el Hospital Bethesda. De vez en cuando, el Dr. Eisenstadt examinaba mi conocimiento médico haciéndome preguntas específicas sobre un frotis de sangre o pruebas de laboratorio anormales. Sin embargo, parecía satisfecho con mis respuestas.

Un día, después de tomar muestras de sangre de un paciente y bajar las escaleras hacia el laboratorio, conocí al Dr. Bruni. Subió las escaleras para ver a sus pacientes. Era importante para mí dirgirme a cada médico por su nombre. Lo saludé cortésmente, "Buenos días, Dr. Bruni; ¿cómo está hoy?" El Dr. Bruni me lanzó una mirada tan penetrante que me sobresaltó. Me sonrojé, luego me congelé y casi dejé caer mi bandeja. A partir de ese momento, se convirtió en una atracción mutua que floreció en un compañerismo y un amor vitales.

Siempre que el Dr. Bruni visitaba a sus pacientes en el hospital, se detenía en el laboratorio para revisar la sangre de sus pacientes u otros análisis y siempre me dedicaba una mirada afectuosa. Un día, el Dr. Bruni me preguntó si estaría interesada en trabajar en su oficina. Hizo una cita para una entrevista. Después de recogerme para la entrevista, me llevó primero a cenar a un restaurante y luego a bailar en el elegante Aragon Ballroom de Chicago, donde tocó una gran orquesta esa noche. ¡Con qué elegancia bailaba el vals el Dr. Bruni, el foxtrot, y sobre todo el tango!. Ambos disfrutamos inmensamente del baile de salón. Dr. Bruni nunca me entrevistó para trabajar para él en su clínica de Chicago. Más tarde, me dijo que ya había encontrado una enfermera.

¿Quizás tenía otros planes para mí?

Trabajar doce horas al día afectó mi salud. Le escribí a mi hermano Edmund y le dije que tendría que dejar un trabajo.

Le pregunté si podíamos vender el auto para eliminar los pagos de la hipoteca. Con el consentimiento de mi hermano, vendí su auto. Dado que trabajar en el Hospital Roosevelt Memorial reduciría mi tiempo de viaje a la mitad, opté por solicitar empleo completo allí. Después de hablar con la administradora del hospital, la Sra. Jones, me contrató para cubrir las horas de la tarde y la noche. Le di aviso al Dr. Eisenstadt en el Hospital Bethesda que me gustaría renunciar. Quería trabajar a tiempo completo en el Roosevelt Memorial Hospital. El Dr. Eisenstadt estaba enojado porque me fui tan pronto después de que me permitió entrenarme en histología. Sin embargo, el Dr. Stein me dio la bienvenida como empleada de tiempo completo en el Roosevelt Memorial Hospital. Mi salud mejoró y me sentí vigorizada. también encontré un apartamento a poca distancia del hospital. Le di gracias a Dios por el cambio. Desde que el Dr. Bruni ya no me veía en el Hospital Bethesda, venía cada vez que su horario se lo permitía por la mañana. Visitaba a sus pacientes hospitalizados por la mañana y asistía al cirujano durante las operaciones de sus pacientes. Su horario de oficina en la clínica comenzaba a la 1:00 p. m. y finalizaba a las 9:00 p.m. horas con una hora de descanso para cenar entre las 5:00 p.m. y 6:00 p. m. Con cada visita, nuestra atracción mutua crecía y comenzó un cortejo romántico y emocionante. Empezamos a llamarnos por nuestros nombres de pila. Aldo me llamó Hilda en lugar de Hildegard. No tenía horas de oficina el miércoles. Me llevaba a navegar en el lago Michigan, o íbamos a pescar en el lago Shangri-La, Wisconsin. Descubrimos muchas hermosas regiones escénicas de Wisconsin. Disfrutamos de conferencias en el Planetario de Chicago, el Museo de Ciencia e Industria o los Museos de Arte. Compartimos muchos intereses y disfrutamos de la música de ópera.

Mientras tanto, mi hermano Edmund se enamoró de una hermosa joven llamada Karin mientras estaba en Alemania. Se casaron el 6 de agosto de 1960 en la famosa Catedral de Ulm. Al año siguiente regresó a Chicago con su encantadora novia.

515

CAPÍTULO 18

Contrayendo Matrimonio con el Dr. Aldo Bruni

Fijamos el día 2 de abril de 1966 como la fecha de nuestra boda. Aldo y yo nos alegramos no sólo de reunirnos físicamente, sino también eufóricos por unirnos en santo matrimonio.

Casándome con el Dr. Aldo Bruni

El pastor Edwards nos casó en la Iglesia Luterana La Santa Cruz en Wheatridge, Colorado. Dio un sermón sencillo pero profundo sobre los deberes del marido y la mujer en el matrimonio. A la noche siguió una elegante recepción con nuevos amigos en el Brown Palace de Denver, donde pasamos la noche en una de sus suites de lujo. Al día siguiente, nos fuimos de luna de miel a Vail, Colorado. Renuncié a mi trabajo, dejé mi apartamento y empaqué mis pertenencias personales en la camioneta antes de conducir de regreso a Chicago.

Nos deleitamos al ver llegar la primavera a las Montañas Rocosas y cubrir las praderas con pasto exuberante y flores silvestres. Con emoción, planeamos nuestro futuro juntos. Nos quedamos en Chicago por un tiempo en el apartamento de una habitación, donde Aldo vivía solo durante la separación de su ex esposa y su familia. Abrimos un segundo consultorio médico en Island Lake, que yo administraba. También compramos una nueva casa en Barrington Harbor Estates con un apretón de manos del Sr. Hubschman, el desarrollador del área. Vivía al otro lado de la calle. El señor Hubschman se convirtió no sólo en un paciente nuestro, sino en un amigo de toda la vida. Cuando la oficina de Island Lake nos quedó pequeña, Aldo construyó un centro médico en Barrington, a solo cinco minutos de nuestra residencia. Contratamos una secretaria médica y una enfermera. Dirigí el Centro Médico Barrington y trabajé medio tiempo en la clínica. También alquilamos consultorios para médicos y un dentista.

Cuando la práctica de Barrington floreció, Aldo vendió el centro médico y el edificio comercial en Touhy Avenue en Chicago y ejerció solo en Barrington. Ahora teníamos más tiempo para navegar en el lago Michigan. Disfrutamos paseando por las orillas del lago Michigan, observando los cambios durante las diferentes horas del día y las estaciones. Frecuentábamos teatros y exhibiciones en varios museos y escuchábamos conferencias inspiradoras en el Planetario y otros lugares. Asistir a funciones de ópera en el Lyric Opera House de Chicago y escuchar a los artistas favoritos alegró nuestros inviernos. Durante el verano, nos reuníamos con cantantes de ópera y amigos para participar en conciertos en el hermoso Ravinia Park en Highland Park. En uno de los cruceros de Roma, Italia, a Nueva York, Aldo se hizo amigo del famoso tenor lírico Ferruccio Tagliavini, quien estaba comprometido para cantar en la Ópera Metropolitana de Nueva York. Ferruccio Talgliavini se hizo amigo de Aldo y de la familia Bruni. Cada vez que escuchábamos música de ópera, Aldo cantaba junto con los artistas. Conocía la letra de muchas arias famosas.

Otro punto culminante de cada invierno era la cena con baile de cada hospital en un elegante restaurante o club. Exquisitos arreglos florales decoraban las mesas y realzaban el hermoso ambiente. Los médicos vestían esmóquines y sus esposas o acompañantes vestían vestidos largos y elegantes y lujosos abrigos de piel. Aldo y yo disfrutamos de la deliciosa comida, los bailes de salón y las animadas conversaciones con sus colegas.

Admiraba los modales de Aldo junto a la cama con sus pacientes. A veces, cuando los especialistas perdían la esperanza, Aldo luchaba por la vida de sus pacientes alentándolos a mejorar. Recuerdo a la paciente, Clara Cernocky, con fiebre alta y problemas cardíacos además de un abdomen distendido. Mientras estaba en el hospital, una radiografía mostró que un pequeño hueso de pollo perforó el intestino y le provocó una peritonitis aguda. Aldo la programó inmediatamente para la cirugía. Apenas sobrevivió a la cirugía y el cirujano no pensó que se recuperaría. la misma tarde, después de que terminamos el horario de oficina a las 9:00 p. m., nos dirigimos al Hospital de la Sagrada Familia para ver a Clara. Yacía pálida y sin vida, conectada a tantos monitores y botellas intravenosas. Incluso estaba demasiado débil para hablar. Después de que Aldo revisó la ingesta de líquidos intravenosos y los monitores, tomó su mano y dijo, "¡Clara, lo lograrás!" Ella lo miró y sonrió. Aldo la besó en la frente. Volvió a sonreír cuando nos despedimos, y desde ese día su recuperación mejoró día a día. Después de dos semanas, dejó el hospital y vivió muchos años más. Su esposo estaba tan agradecido con Aldo por salvar la vida de su esposa que él y su esposa se convirtieron en buenos amigos nuestros.

Disfruté trabajar con Aldo en la clínica, cuidando a sus pacientes. Al conocer a los pacientes y los procedimientos de la oficina, ayudé a aliviar el estrés profesional. Quería ser la mejor esposa posible y también crear un ambiente relajante en casa. Siempre que encontraba un buen consejo, lo leía y lo copiaba. Cada tres meses recibimos un pequeño folleto de la A. H. Compañía farmacéutica Robins, llamado Robins Readers. Copié las cinco reglas de un matrimonio feliz del reverendo J. H. Randolph Ray: [31]

1. *Tener un objetivo común para su matrimonio.*
2. *Mire los actos de todos los días y deje que las grandes ocasiones se ocupen de sí mismas.*
3. *Tener los mismos derechos financieramente.*
4. *Cuida tus modales. La cortesía es el ángel guardián del Amor.*
5. *¡Sea amable! La bondad es la sangre de la vida, el elixir del matrimonio. Esta es la regla de oro del matrimonio y el secreto para hacer que el amor perdure a lo largo de los años.*

Traté de seguir estas reglas para hacer feliz a mi esposo. La vida parecía contenta en el exterior, pero ambos echamos de menos tener hijos propios. Ser padre de fin de semana no cumplía los deseos de Aldo ni los de los niños. Después de que pasaron varios años y no podía concebir, descubrimos que la exposición a los rayos X sin la protección adecuada había dañado mis ovarios mientras trabajaba en el consultorio del médico en Alemania. Ambos nos sentimos desilusionados. Me sentí triste por no cumplir el deseo de Aldo de tener un hijo o dos para él. Incluso pensamos en adoptar un niño y una niña, pero los orfanatos con los que contactamos lo complicaron demasiado.

Los hijos de Aldo, Gilda, Christine, Joanne, Frank

Oré para que Dios me mostrara una manera de acercarme a los cuatro hijos de Aldo. Al principio, me consideraban una intrusa en su familia y estaban resentidos conmigo, lo cual era comprensible. A medida que pasaba el tiempo, esperaba que desarrolláramos un afecto mutuo espontáneo, lo cual hicimos. Con el hijo Frank y la hija mayor Joanne, cultivé un profundo vínculo familiar y de amor. No podría haber pedido mejores hijos para mí. Las hijas menores, Christine y Gilda, me respetaban como la esposa de su padre, pero no llegaron a ser tan cercanas a mí como Frank y Joanne. Acepté sus sentimientos espontáneos hacia mí, aunque Aldo y yo deseábamos que hubiera sido más amistoso. Aprendimos a vivir en el presente y a dejar que el trabajo de cada día absorbiera nuestros intereses, energía y entusiasmo.

Cuando Joanne y Frank se casaron y tuvieron hijos, disfrutábamos pasar tiempo con los nietos. Cada vez que teníamos un fin de semana libre, íbamos a la casa de Joanne y recogíamos a Patricia y Paul. Tenían sus maletas listas y siempre estaban emocionados de pasar la noche con el abuelo y Omi (abuela en alemán). Aldo llevaba a Paul a pescar en el río Fox mientras Patricia y yo horneábamos un pastel o preparábamos comidas juntas. Disfrutaba montando a Red, nuestro Setter Irlandés. También disfrutábamos pasar tiempo con los hijos de Frank, Julia, Carla y Phillip, quienes tenían una imaginación vívida. Incluso llevamos a Paul con nosotros en un viaje de dos semanas a Florida y Key West.

Celebrábamos nuestro décimo aniversario de bodas el 2 de abril de 1976. El mismo año Estados Unidos conmemoró el 200 aniversario de su fundación. Quería darle a Aldo algo especial. Aprendí a escribir poesía. Durante un año, escribí en secreto 100 poemas sobre nuestra vida personal y la naturaleza, la fe y otros temas. Para celebrar este evento especial, volamos a Las Vegas y nos alojamos en el Hotel MGM durante una semana. Antes de ir a cenar en nuestro aniversario, Aldo me entregó una tarjeta, "Para mi esposa en nuestro aniversario", expresándome su amor y gratitud.

La tarjeta decía:

Te amo por ser tan maravillosa Querida,
cada día de la semana y cada mes del año,
y cuanto más estemos juntos, más sé
que siempre seré feliz de amarte así.

Aldo escribió:

Y ahora, querida, déjame expresarte mi gratitud por tu amabilidad,
paciencia, sinceridad y todas las demás cualidades que he encontrado
en ti. Estos son los mejores regalos que me puedes ofrecer, ya que

estos son regalos que no se pueden obtener con dinero y son difíciles de encontrar en este mundo pervertido y corrupto. Solo con estas cualidades podemos estar seguros de un futuro feliz y contemplado sin importar los obstáculos pasados y futuros que han obstruido y obstruirán nuestros caminos. Solo armados con estas cualidades, podemos esperar el éxito.

Gracias de nuevo, querida, por cada pequeña cosa que has hecho por mí, y perdona mi ceguera si, en ocasiones, he condenado tus acciones.

Que tus esperanzas y sueños se cumplan porque solo en el cumplimiento de los tuyos puedo ver los míos hechos realidad. Tu Aldo

Las palabras de Aldo llenaron mi corazón con un amor aún más profundo por él. Me levanté, lo abracé y le agradecí su exquisita tarjeta y sus nobles pensamientos. Entonces le di el libro de mis 100 poemas escritos a mano. Apenas podía esperar a ver su reacción.

Abrió el libro y leyó el primer poema. Luego me preguntó: "¿Dónde encontraste este poema sobre nuestro primer encuentro?"

"Escribí todos los poemas durante el último año."

"¿Tú escribiste todos estos poemas? ¿Cuándo los escribiste sin que yo lo supiera? "

"Cada vez que estabas fuera, o me escapaba de la habitación durante la noche para escribir. Quería sorprenderte y hacerte un regalo muy personal e inesperado para hacerte feliz."

"Gracias cariño. Tu consideración ciertamente me hizo feliz. Vamos a comer ahora. Leeré más tarde."

Con alegría cenamos en el comedor más elegante del MGM Hotel-Casino. Después de regresar a nuestra habitación, Aldo leyó algunos de mis poemas en voz alta. Cuando Aldo me dijo cuánto le gustaban, me sentí animada a seguir escribiendo más poesía. Disfrutamos viendo programas, probando suerte en las máquinas de póquer y explorando las afueras de Las Vegas durante una semana.

Cada año, hacíamos un viaje a diferentes partes de los Estados Unidos o un crucero a países o islas extranjeras. Para nuestro aniversario de bodas de plata, reservamos un crucero por el Pacífico Sur. Nos hicimos amigos del capitán y su familia y tuve el honor de cenar en la mesa del capitán. Mientras navegábamos cerca de las islas hawaianas, vimos la erupción del volcán, arrojando lava fundida al aire. La lava resplandeciente se deslizó por la montaña, se estrelló contra el océano y creó una fuente de espuma y fuego. Durante uno de nuestros viajes a Roma, asistimos a una representación de la ópera "Aida" en el famoso Teatro al aire libre de Caracalla en Roma. El gran escenario permitía que incluso los animales entraran en la plataforma. Disfrutamos de la hermosa aria "Celeste Aida" (Divina Aida), y de la espectacular (Marcha Triunfal). Pero el aria que nunca olvidaré es cuando Aida, la princesa etíope capturada, cantó O patria mia te vedro mai piu (Oh, patria mía, no te volveré a ver). Un camello vivo yacía junto a ella, y detrás de una palmera, la luna se elevó y creó el escenario perfecto para el aria nostálgica de la princesa Aida. Compartí los sentimientos de Aida, preguntándome si alguna vez volvería a ver mi hogar. Siempre atesoraremos la excelente actuación en el mágico escenario. La noche siguiente, vimos Cavalleria Rusticana con un caballo vivo en el escenario, que también se destacó.

A veces, la vida nos presentó desafíos. Aldo trabajaba duro. Tratar con pacientes, realizar cirugías y visitar pacientes en el hospital genera mucho estrés. Aprendí a lidiar no solo con el estrés profesional sino también con un temperamento italiano explosivo. Me callaba o me iba de la escena hasta que Aldo se calmara y estuviera de mejor humor. Hacía todo con una pasión, que aprendí a apreciar; el sufrimiento y la alegría, la agonía y el éxtasis son parte de la vida, y los acepté como tales.

Como me gustaba el arte, tomé clases en varios momentos de pintura al óleo, acuarela y pintura en porcelana. Aprendí a entender viendo las cosas con ojos de artista. Me gustó especialmente pintar flores con todas sus diferentes formas de capullos de colores. Asistir a la Academia de Arte en el centro de Chicago o a clases en Harper College me recompensó con mejores composiciones y obras de arte. Clementyna Porzak me introdujo en el fino arte de la pintura en porcelana. Pinté todo un juego de vajilla de porcelana para ocho con un diseño de rosas.

Pintura al óleo de flores

Otra aventura nueva y emocionante comenzó cuando buscamos un lugar para jubilarnos en Oregón. Después de no encontrar ningún lugar que cumpliera con todas nuestras expectativas, nos dirigimos al Parque Nacional de Yosemite. De camino, paramos en el lago Tahoe. La belleza del lago cristalino y las montañas circundantes nos encantaron a ambos. Aldo, siendo dinámico y ambicioso, decidió retirarse en South Lake Tahoe. Inmediatamente compró un lote residencial con una vista panorámica del lago y las montañas. Aldo dibujó un plano de planta para la casa y se lo dio a un arquitecto. La Agencia de Planificación Regional de Tahoe emitió sólo unos pocos permisos de construcción cada año. Éramos afortunados de obtener uno, y Aldo contrató a un contratista para que pusiera los cimientos entre las rocas gigantes. Al año siguiente, el contratista completó la casa.

Aldo sorprendió a todos cuando anunció que quería retirarse dentro de un año. Incluso yo pensé que era demasiado pronto, tal vez en cinco años sonaba más aceptable para mí. Me entristeció dejar a mi familia, amigos y también a los pacientes que aprendimos a apreciar. No quería mostrarle a Aldo cómo me molestó su decisión de jubilarse anticipadamente. En el camino a casa desde la iglesia, que no quería dejar, encontré un lugar apartado con vista al paisaje pastoral donde estacioné y lloré para liberar mi angustia emocional. Una vez, un policía se detuvo y preguntó si podía ayudar. Rápidamente me limpié las lágrimas y le dije: "No, gracias, solo estoy meditando."

En poco tiempo me olvidé de sentir lástima por mí misma y comencé a prepararme para la gran mudanza a South Lake Tahoe. Aldo encontró un médico a quien presentó a sus leales pacientes de mucho tiempo. Aldo y yo trabajamos durante un año con el Dr. Leony antes de que se hiciera cargo de nuestra práctica. El día del cierre de la clínica vimos muchos pacientes y terminamos tarde. Los últimos pacientes eran cuatro generaciones, que habían seguido a Aldo desde que abrió su primer centro médico en Chicago. Aldo trató a la madre, a su hija, y dio a luz al hijo Frank, quien también tuvo un hijo. Cuando Aldo les dijo que pronto nos mudaríamos a California y les agradeció su lealtad, la Sra. Gugliani abrazó a Aldo y empezó a llorar; también lo hizo la hija, la Sra. Mariani. Fue un momento muy emotivo para todos nosotros despedirnos de nuestros fieles pacientes y dejar el centro médico.

Lentamente, con la ayuda de Dios, todo encajó. Despedirnos de familiares y amigos nos entristeció a ambos. También nos entristeció dejar nuestra primera casa, donde disfrutamos de muchas espléndidas fiestas. En la celebración del último cumpleaños de Aldo, cantantes de ópera y un acordeonista entretuvieron a nuestros invitados. Nuestra familia, amigos y doctores la pasaron de maravilla. Atesoro la cinta que grabé de este evento especial. Muchos buenos recuerdos pasaron por nuestras mentes antes de que cerráramos la casa vacía y nos fuéramos.

CAPÍTULO 19

Mudanza a Lake Tahoe

Con la mudanza a **South** Lake Tahoe y la jubilación, comenzó un nuevo capítulo de nuestra vida. La emoción de mudarme a una nueva casa y decorar cada habitación alivió mi tristeza por dejar Barrington. Aldo creó entre las rocas enormes una plataforma con varias vías de tren y pueblos iluminados. Aldo diseñó un escenario de cuento de hadas alrededor del jacuzzi. Decoré las habitaciones superiores, lo que complació a Aldo. La vista panorámica del lago cristalino y las escarpadas montañas nos encantó.

Vista panorámica de la casa de Lake Tahoe

Navegamos, hicimos caminatas, pescamos en lagos más pequeños y nos familiarizamos con la belleza y las maravillas naturales del lago Tahoe. Sin embargo, el primer invierno nos tomó por sorpresa: nevó no pulgadas, sino pies y llegó hasta el techo del garaje. Aldo cavó un túnel para salir del garaje. Conducir arriba y abajo de la colina empinada también presentó un desafío. Aldo hizo planes para comprar una casa rodante e ir al sur la próxima invierno. Pasamos algún tiempo en el pintoresco Palm Springs y continuamos hasta el Baja California. Decidimos pasar el resto del invierno en Posada RV Park al sur de Mulegé en la Bahía Concepción. Nos gustó la ubicación, alquilamos un lote cerca de la playa y construimos una casa el siguiente invierno.

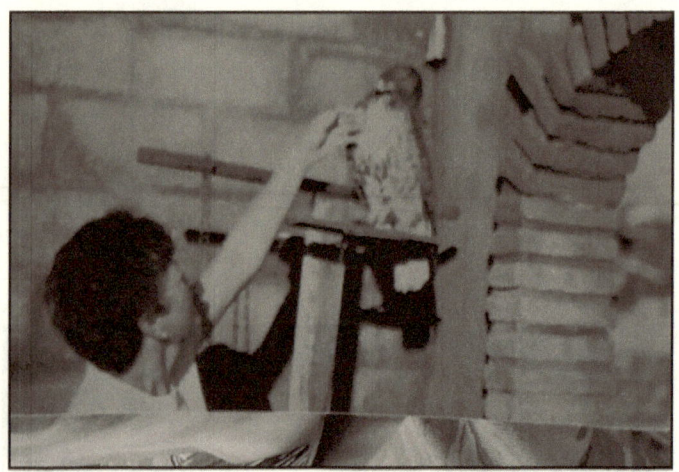

Nuestro halcón Pedro

Un trabajador le trajo un halcón herido a Aldo durante la construcción y le pidió que lo cuidara. Aldo le inmovilizó el ala lesionada con un trozo de media de nailon y colocó una férula en la pierna lesionada. El halcón se recuperó por completo. Antes de regresar a los Estados Unidos, liberamos al halcón.

Voló a la playa y se sentó. varias gaviotas lo atacaron. No podíamos imaginar dejar que las gaviotas mataran a nuestro halcón, al que llamamos cariñosamente Pedro. Decidimos llevarlo con nosotros a Lake Tahoe, aunque eso significaba pagar una multa alta o ir a la cárcel. Por suerte, cruzamos la frontera sin que la patrulla fronteriza descubriera a Pedro. Una vez liberado, Pedro se adaptó bien al cambio de clima y medio ambiente. Nos trajo alegría por más de treinta años volviendo cada año y dando vueltas sobre la casa o volando por el patio cuando estábamos afuera.

Disfrutamos de navegar, pescar, pescar almejas y nadar en la Bahía de Concepción durante tres años. Sin embargo, conducir el camino sinuoso y peligroso de La Baja dos veces cada temporada se volvió engorroso. Un vecino nos dijo que tomáramos el ferry de Santa Rosalía a Guaymas. Desde allí, podríamos tomar la carretera de peaje recién construida a Nogales y los Estados Unidos, lo cual hicimos. Una vez que llegamos a Guaymas, recorrimos la zona y descubrimos San Carlos. Nos gustó el pueblo y la ubicación y buscamos una casa. Después de que encontramos un hogar a nuestra satisfacción, Aldo hizo una oferta. El propietario aceptó nuestra oferta, así que dos semanas después vendimos la casa en La Baja y comenzamos a remodelar la casa de San Carlos. Dios hizo todo perfectamente. Di gracias a Dios; ya no necesitábamos conducir por la traicionera carretera a través de La Baja hasta la Posada. Ahora podríamos conducir a Nogales y tomar la carretera de peaje de cuatro carriles a San Carlos, México. Así, San Carlos se convirtió en nuestra residencia de invierno en septiembre de 1989.

CAPÍTULO 20

La vida en San Carlos

Nuestra casa en San Carlos, a la que llamamos nuestra residencia de invierno, ofrecía una vista panorámica de 360 grados con un puente conectado a una torre alta a la casa. En cada momento del día, la imagen cambiaba. Al despertar al amanecer, pudimos ver el sol naciente con todos sus vivos colores pastel sobre Honeymoon Island. La puesta de sol mostró brillantes nubes rojas, naranjas y amarillas sobre la montaña Tetakawi. Durante la noche observamos con telescopio o binoculares las diferentes constelaciones de las estrellas. El clima, donde se juntan el desierto, la montaña y el mar, nos acompañó.

Vistas escénicas de la casa en San Carlos

Disfrutamos de navegar, nadar y pescar en el pintoresco Mar de Cortés. Hicimos muchos amigos, nos unimos a la Iglesia Comunitaria de San Carlos, una iglesia cristiana de muchas denominaciones. El pastor no seguía preferencias religiosas sino que predicaba solamente la Palabra de Dios de la Biblia. La iglesia no sólo apoyó a muchos misioneros, sino que también ayudó a la gente local dondequiera que fue necesario. En el pequeño vestíbulo de la iglesia se ofrecieron a los feligreses libros expuestos en estanterías. Un día tomé un libro llamado The Case for Easter de Lee Strobel.[32] Lee Strobel, un periodista de investigación del Chicago Tribune, se dispuso a negar la resurrección de Jesucristo. Para concluir su tarea, el Sr. Strobel entrevistó a patólogos, médicos, científicos, físicos y otros. Para mi asombro, encontré la primera entrevista del Sr. Strobel con el Dr. Robert Stein, con quien trabajé durante seis años en el Roosevelt Memorial Hospital de Chicago. El conocimiento del Dr. Stein impresionó al Sr. Strobel hasta el punto de que lo llamó una enciclopedia ambulante. Estuve totalmente de acuerdo en que el Dr. Stein no solo era brillante en su profesión de patología forense sino también una persona amable y humilde y un excelente maestro. El Dr. Stein se convirtió en el médico forense del condado de Cook, y la instalación recién construida se llamó Instituto Dr. Robert Stein. Después de que Lee Strobel terminó sus entrevistas e investigaciones, llegó a la siguiente conclusión: "Dios es el Creador del universo y de muchos sistemas complejos funcionales".[33]

El cuerpo humano consta de miles de sistemas complejos que funcionan perfectamente. Surge con la influencia externa de la inteligencia, y la función se interrumpe sin una guía continua. La inteligencia externa (pensamiento o idea) primero tiene que imaginar los objetos o sistemas y luego reunir todos los elementos y componentes para construirlos. Cuanto más complejo es el sistema, más inteligencia externa se requiere. La inteligencia humana puede crear máquinas y objetos, pero Dios, quien creó la naturaleza con sus millones de sistemas en funcionamiento, tiene una inteligencia mucho mayor que la mente humana.

El señor Strobel observó que ningún sistema de funcionamiento complejo se origina nunca sin la guía continua de la inteligencia externa; debe haber una inteligencia externa que creó innumerables sistemas funcionales en la naturaleza. Estas dos realidades son profundas e innegables pruebas científicas de Dios. La verdad siempre permanecerá: La ciencia sin lugar a dudas prueba que Dios existe, no importa cuántos se opongan a la verdad con la teoría de la evolución, una teoría no probada. En cambio, la ciencia prueba a Dios y niega la evolución. A la mayoría de las personas se les hace creer que la fe en Dios no es científica, y que la creencia en la evolución es científica. No todo lo que aprendemos en la escuela y los medios de comunicación es cierto. Crean la ilusión de que la ciencia hace superfluo a Dios, mientras que lo contrario es cierto. La ciencia es adquirir nuevos conocimientos a través de la observación de realidades e integrando o corrigiendo conocimientos previos. Una fuerza sobrenatural reemplaza a la naturaleza. Muchos médicos fueron testigos de la sanación a través de la intervención divina en casos desesperados.

El científico inglés, Sir Isaac Newton, afirma:

Este hermosísimo sistema de sol, planetas y cometas sólo podría proceder del consejo y dominio de un Ser inteligente. Y si las estrellas fijas son el centro de otros sistemas similares, estos siendo formados por el mismo sabio consejo, deben estar todos sujetos al dominio de Uno. Este Ser gobierna todas las cosas no como un alma del mundo sino como un Señor de todo.

El científico Albert Einstein expresa así la existencia de Dios:

Todo aquél que está seriamente involucrado en el estudio de la ciencia se convence de que un espíritu se manifiesta en las leyes del Universo – un espíritu bastamente superior al del hombre y uno ante el cual nosotros, con nuestros modestos poderes, debemos sentirnos humildes.

Max Karl Planck, ganador del Premio Nobel de Física, escribe:

Tanto la religión como la ciencia requieren la creencia en Dios. Para los creyentes, Dios está en el principio, y para los físicos, Dios está al final de todas las consideraciones. Para los primeros, Él es el fundamento, para los segundos, la corona del edificio de toda cosmovisión generalizada.

La mayoría de nosotros creemos lo que queremos creer mientras estamos en un país libre, pero la verdad es que a menudo pensamos en la forma en que los medios de comunicación y la educación secular imponen en nuestras mentes. El ateo cree que eres considerado un ser humano inteligente si niegas la existencia de Dios. Si te atreves a pensar siquiera en la posible presencia de Dios, serás etiquetado como ignorante, religioso y acientífico.

La experiencia que cambió la vida de Lee Strobel de ser ateo a convertirse en un evangelista cristiano lo impulsó a escribir muchos libros cristianos y dar conferencias cristianas y de otras instituciones. Uno de sus libros más conocidos es The Case for Christ. Leí el primer libro escrito de Lee Strobel, The Case for Easter, con gran interés no sólo por sus habilidades de escritura sino también porque entrevistó al Dr. Robert Stein, quien me enseñó no solo conocimientos médicos, sino también sabiduría de la vida durante el tiempo que trabajé con él.

Mi esposo continuó utilizando sus habilidades médicas. Una vez al mes, donaba su servicio médico a los indios Yaqui en Bacum. Los niños del pueblo saludaban al Dr. Bruni con entusiasmo cuando repartía vestidos, pantalones o juguetes que yo coleccionaba para ellos. Yo le agradecía a Dios que Aldo continuara usando su conocimiento médico para ayudar a los pobres que no tenían medios para ir a ver a un doctor.

Incluso después de jubilarnos, continuamos tomando un crucero o un viaje a diferentes partes del mundo. Cuando visitamos Nueva Zelanda, Aldo se enamoró de su belleza escénica y pensó en pasar los inviernos en Nueva Zelanda. Por impulso, compró una granja de cincuenta acres con vista al océano en Orewa, cerca de Auckland. Cuando regresamos de nuestro viaje, Aldo puso a la venta la casa en San Carlos. Me sentí desconsolada; No sólo me gustaba nuestra casa, sino sobre todo los maravillosos amigos que hicimos en San Carlos. Oré a Dios para que me mostrara qué hacer. Le prometí a Aldo que solo me mudaría con una condición: viviríamos en la finca por un tiempo para ver si lo hacía feliz.

Cuando regresamos a Nueva Zelanda,pasamos noviembre, diciembre y parte de enero en nuestro rancho. Aldo contrató a un contratista para reparar y pintar la casa. Fuimos a tiendas de antigüedades y ventas de garaje para comprar muebles y utensilios de cocina. Dispusimos los muebles de manera atractiva y cosí cortinas para las ventanas. Empezó a llover. Llovió y llovió. El sol brilló solo unos pocos días durante nuestra estadía en la finca. Aldo contrajo gripe y fiebre alta, y yo desarrollé culebrilla en el ojo izquierdo y en la cabeza. Al acercarse la Navidad, ambos pensamos en la celebración llena de alegría en el soleado San Carlos y sentimos nostalgia. Aldo, en su desesperación, gritó: "Vámonos de este país".

Estas palabras sonaron como música dulce para mis oídos. Inmediatamente arrendamos la propiedad a la señora y sus dos hijos quienes nos vendieron la propiedad y volamos de regreso a México. Dimos gracias a Dios que la inmobiliaria no había vendido la casa en San Carlos. Vendimos la granja de Orewa después de las dificultades con los inquilinos de Nueva Zelanda que no pagaban el alquiler a tiempo y arruinaban la propiedad. Di gracias a Dios por poner fin a la aventura de Nueva Zelanda dos años después.

Aldo se estableció y comenzó a escribir sus memorias. Tenía una manera tan clara y conmovedora de expresar sus pensamientos. Con la vista panorámica del océano y las montañas escarpadas, la torre se convirtió en su lugar favorito para escribir. Terminó de escribir sus memorias en 2001. Edité su guión y lo mandé publicar en el 2002. Al mismo tiempo, recopilé los poemas que había escrito para mi esposo, los que escribí para el 200 aniversario de los Estados Unidos y muchos otros y los publiqué al mismo tiempo. Llamé a mi colección "Una canción en la noche" con el subtítulo "Cuanto más oscura es la medianoche, más brillante es la luz de las estrellas".

Desafortunadamente, un año después, la salud de Aldo se deterioró. Un día apenas podía respirar. El Dr. Canale, al ser llamado, acudió de inmediato a la casa y le salvó la vida. Estuve y sigo estando muy agradecida con el Dr. Canale por su pronta ayuda. Ingresó a Aldo al Hospital CIMA de Hermosillo, donde recibió un excelente tratamiento en la unidad de cuidados intensivos durante diecisiete días. Físicamente se recuperó, pero mentalmente decayó. Fue desgarrador para mí ver que su mente brillante le fallaba gradualmente. Cada día presentaba nuevos desafíos. Agradecí a mi bondadosa empleada doméstica Rosalba (apodada Chava), quien me ayudó a cuidar a mi esposo enfermo.

Mi empleada doméstica Chava & sus hijos, Fernando y Adelyte

Caminaba con Aldo todos los días mientras él todavía podía moverse. Cantaban juntos y simplemente eran joviales. Su hermana Sulma también nos ayudó cuando fue necesario. También aprecié la amabilidad de la familia y muchos amigos amables. Entendieron, apoyaron y se quedaron con mi esposo cuando iba a la iglesia, de compras o a otras funciones. Después de casi cuarenta años, Dios contestó mi incesante oración cuando Aldo se convirtió en un cristiano confeso al comienzo de su enfermedad. Aldo se volvió más paciente, amable, amoroso y nunca se quejaba. Siempre sonreía y se sentía seguro en mi presencia. Me llamó su ángel, como al principio de nuestro noviazgo. Cada vez que notaba una disminución en la capacidad mental de Aldo, lamentaba su pérdida. La gracia de Dios y el profundo amor mutuo nos ayudaron a enfrentar los complejos desafíos de la vida y nos recompensaron con paz interior y alegría.

En el verano de 2009, su hija mayor, Joanne, y su esposo, el Dr. David Trotter, nos visitaron en Lake Tahoe. Aunque sabían que era la última vez que lo verían, estaban agradecidos de que su padre aún los reconociera y pudiera expresar su amor por ellos y ellos su amor por él. En septiembre, su hijo Frank y su nuera Peggy nos visitaron en Lake Tahoe. Aldo de repente se puso muy enfermo y respiraba con dificultad. Llamamos a la ambulancia, que lo llevó al Barton Memorial Hospital. El médico tratante y las enfermeras compartieron nuestro dolor al dar el último adiós a mi amado esposo y Frank y Peggy a su padre. A la 1:00 am Al día siguiente, Aldo respiró por última vez y su alma ascendió al cielo, pero su amor y los recuerdos de nuestra vida juntos florecerán continuamente en mi corazón y mente. Siempre estaré agradecida con Frank y Peggy por estar conmigo durante este momento difícil de duelo por la pérdida de mi esposo y su padre. Aprecié la compasión y el consuelo de familiares y amigos, pero principalmente que Aldo aceptó a Cristo y se separó en paz sin sufrimiento prolongado. Los pacientes, a quienes atendió sinceramente, siempre recordarán al Dr. Aldo Bruni. Su dedicación y compasión por sus pacientes trajeron esperanza y coraje a los casos más desesperados. Terminaré este capítulo con las palabras de Aldo de su libro, *Mis memorias:*

Cuando finalmente esta vida, como todo lo demás en este mundo, llegue a su etapa final, deje que estos breves recuerdos míos, tan simplemente expresados en mi trabajo, sean revelados a mis hijos y a todos los miembros íntimos de mi familia con la esperanza de que sean llevados por las generaciones por venir como un recuerdo del pasado y para estimular un mejor futuro,

Así como la última rosa del verano se marchitó, así lo hizo la vida de mi amado esposo Aldo después de florecer por ochenta y cinco años.

CAPÍTULO 21

La vida como Viuda

Perder a un esposo es desgarrador, pero cambiar todos los documentos necesarios es un proceso largo y difícil. Mi abogado, el Sr. R. Alling, preparó todos los documentos legales con prontitud. Me permitió volver a San Carlos un mes después. Aprecié el excelente y rápido asesoramiento y servicio profesional del Sr. Alling. Necesitaba cambiar documentos legales en México, lo cual no salió tan bien como en los Estados Unidos. Tomó varios años transferir el fideicomiso a mi nombre.

Sin embargo, todos mis amigos en San Carlos de la Iglesia Comunitaria de San Carlos me consolaron invitándome a sus casas para las fiestas o cenas. Mi consuelo más increíble vino de Dios. Él me dio nuevas fuerzas para cada día manejar todas las transiciones y ajustes que necesitaba hacer como viuda. Continuamente agradecí a Dios desde el fondo de mi corazón y confié en Él por suplir cada necesidad en Su tiempo perfecto.

Llené el vacío de la pérdida de mi esposo consolando y ayudando a otros. Transmitir el amor de Dios y el amor que tenía por mi esposo para hacer felices a los demás curó mi dolor. Cada desafío que enfrenté, lo usé como un trampolín para desarrollar una relación más cercana y significativa con Dios, la familia y los amigos.

Familiares y amigos vinieron a visitarme. Siempre pasábamos días deliciosos juntos. Una vez mi hijastro Frank y Peggy y mis amigos, Sue y Ed de San Diego, me visitaron en Lake Tahoe al mismo tiempo. Me invitaron a un viaje de rafting en el río Truckee. Para mí, fue una experiencia emocionante balancearme de un lado a otro mientras pasaba por rápidos o rocas. Por suerte, solo me caí en el bote de goma tres veces y no salí del bote. Disfruté pasar tiempo con mi hijastra Joanne y su esposo, el Dr. David Trotter, en su hermosa casa en Laguna Beach. Vimos el Desfile de los Maestros, un espectáculo espectacular que recrea una pintura, una estatua o un evento con personas reales cada tres minutos. Una orquesta en vivo toca música apropiada para cada exhibición. "La Última Cena" de Leonardo Da Vinci remata el magnífico espectáculo. Antes de que comenzara el espectáculo, vimos la exhibición de varios tipos de arte y joyas y disfrutamos de una cena juntos en el ambiente del parque. A veces, Frank y Peggy o mis amigos de San Diego disfrutaban de la amable hospitalidad de Joanne y Dave al mismo tiempo que yo.

Teniendo más tiempo libre, me concentré en escribir mi libro, que había comenzado hace varios años, no solo escribiendo sino investigando hechos sobre la Primera y la Segunda Guerra Mundial. Busqué respuestas a muchas preguntas. Quería saber la verdad y no lo que la propaganda y los medios publicitaban. Haber vivido en Alemania durante la Segunda Guerra Mundial y hablar alemán e inglés me ayudó a encontrar información variada. En ocasiones, los medios o los líderes exageraron hechos, blanquearon algunos, sacaron algunos de contexto u omitieron hechos para mantener una buena apariencia pública. Los líderes o personas incluso crearon mentiras si sirvieron a su causa. El bien y el mal han existido desde la creación del hombre. Algunas veces el criminal culpará a la víctima por sus crímenes para cubrir o minimizar su culpa.

CAPÍTULO 22

El Holocausto y otros Crímenes de Guerra

Escribir sobre el Holocausto y los crímenes de los aliados fue el tema más desafiante para mí. Cuando el líder de un país comete un crimen, yo le adscribo el crimen al líder y no llamo criminales a todos los habitantes del país. Algunos líderes y muchas personas y documentos de finales del siglo XX y principios del XXI se hicieron públicos, y aquellos que digan la verdad no serán encarcelados ni castigados por revelar la verdad. Sólo Dios conoce toda la verdad y las intrigas del trasfondo de los hechos históricos. Leí numerosos artículos en alemán e inglés sobre diversos temas y encontré información contradictoria sobre ambas guerras. A menudo me preguntaba cómo y quién contó los seis millones de judíos asesinados en los campos de concentración. No solo yo, sino profesores, historiadores y personas de todos los ámbitos de la vida y de muchos países partimos en una misión de investigación. Encontré un sitio web llamado Beforeitsnews.com, Parte 1, "Emperador de todas las mentiras". El Holocausto de los seis millones de judíos enumera diez periódicos que mencionan primero la cifra de los seis millones. "El Holocausto es el modelo del sufrimiento judío y se trata como si estuviera más allá del escrutinio".

Nunca sabremos todos los hechos sobre las atrocidades de la Segunda Guerra Mundial y los crímenes de lesa humanidad cometidos por todos los países involucrados, pero tenemos un atisbo de la verdad aquí y allá. Solo Dios sabe toda la verdad. Según el artículo, la cifra de los seis millones existía mucho antes de que Adolf Hitler llegara al poder. Durante la Primera Guerra Mundial, el gobierno británico acordó apoyar la Declaración de Belfour para establecer una patria en Palestina para los judíos. A cambio, pidieron asegurar un lobby judío en Estados Unidos y unirse a ellos como aliados. Después del final de la Primera Guerra Mundial, el gobierno británico no cumplió su promesa. Desde 1919 se había publicado que seis millones de judíos habían sido amenazados con ser exterminados en Europa a menos que obtuvieran una patria, Palestina. Mientras estaba en el cargo, el primer ministro británico Stanley Baldwin difundió la mentira de que seis millones de judíos fueron gaseados en Alemania. Posteriormente admitió que las cámaras de gas no existían en ese momento; era sólo propaganda. Se disculpó públicamente con el pueblo alemán por su insulto racista hacia ellos. Aún así, el daño ya estaba hecho y la propaganda permaneció en la mente de la gente, dañando la reputación del pueblo alemán. Esto sucedió catorce años antes de que Hitler llegara al poder en 1934. Después de la muerte del presidente Paul von Hindenburg, el pueblo alemán votó por Adolf Hitler. Eliminó al presidente de la República de Weimar y se declaró Líder (Führer) y rebautizó la República de Weimar como Tercer Reich. Según un informe de Carl Nordling del 27 de mayo de 2013, solo 563.733 judíos vivían en Alemania durante la dictadura de Adolf Hitler entre 1933 y 1945. A doscientos sesenta y seis mil se les dio la opción de quedarse o irse. Sólo 297.733 judíos permanecieron en Alemania. Carlos O. Nordling da una cifra de 4.830.000 (+/-300.000) viviendo en toda Europa, de los cuales

2,7 a 3,6 millones sobrevivieron a la Segunda Guerra Mundial y al Holocausto, lo que deja solamente 1,230,000 que murieron en todos los campos de concentración de Europa, incluyendo Auschwitz, Polonia.

Más recientemente, después de que el líder soviético Gorbachov devolviera a la Cruz Roja Alemana los registros confiscados del Holocausto de Auschwitz, el número de judíos que murieron allí fue de solo 30.000. El resto eran internados de toda Europa u opositores políticos al régimen de Hitler. Ningún documento habla de una programa de exterminio, matanzas masivas o gaseamiento. Una señora judía, Marika Frank, llegó allí desde Hungría cuando se suponía que 25.000 judíos habían sido gaseados diariamente. No vio nada de lo que le habían dicho. Después de que cumplieron sus sentencias, fueron puestos en libertad y pudieron irse a casa. Yehuda Bauer afirma que si hubiera sido un campo de asesinatos en masa, como se hizo creer a la gente después de la guerra, ¿por qué alguien sería liberado para exponer las atrocidades que ocurrieron? El químico investigador William B. Lindsay, después de un cuidadoso examen in situ de las "cámaras de gas" en Auschwitz, Birkenau y Majdanek, declaró: "He llegado a la conclusión de que nadie fue asesinado intencionalmente o deliberadamente con Zyklon B (gas de ácido cianhídrico) de esta manera. Lo considero absolutamente imposible."

Después de una meticulosa investigación e investigación en el lugar, un judío estadounidense, David Cole, descubrió que la cámara de gas se creó en 1947, dos años después de que terminara la guerra. Se quitaron algunas paredes para crear una gran sala. Se abrió un hueco en el techo para arrojar el gas sobre las víctimas. Esta llamada "cámara de gas" se inventó para hacer plausible la historia del gaseo masivo para el público, y aún hoy, para los muchos turistas que vienen a visitar las instalaciones, ahora convertidas en museo. El director y los guías turísticos del Museo de Auschwitz reciben instrucciones sobre qué decir a los visitantes para camuflar parte de la verdad. Miles de presos fueron liberados después de la guerra y fueron entrevistados por la Cruz Roja para ver si presenciaron el presunto gaseamiento. Respondieron negativamente. Cuando las nuevas víctimas llegaron a las instalaciones, se vertió una pequeña cantidad de polvo de Zyklon B a través del orificio del techo para desinfectar a las personas.

Entonces, ¿cuál era el verdadero propósito y función de los llamados campos de concentración? En uno de sus artículos "La verdad de la Segunda Guerra Mundial", John Torell afirma: *Ya en 1870, hubo una guerra entre Alemania y su aliado Japón en la planificación contra Inglaterra, Francia, la Unión Soviética y los Estados Unidos. Albert Pike, el general estadounidense, fue comisionado por el Gobierno Mundial para diseñar un plan de grandes guerras, para crear una condición en la que todas las naciones pudieran ser gobernadas por un Líder Mundial. Ya en 1934, la estadounidense Ford Motor Co. y la International Telegraph Co. (ITT) construyeron fábricas en Alemania y Rusia donde se fabricaban tanques, camiones y aviones para Hitler y Stalin. Los directores de estas fábricas de guerra tenían dudas sobre emplear solo trabajadores alemanes, temiendo perderlos cuando estallara la guerra. Sabían que la mayoría de los hombres alemanes serían reclutados como soldados durante la guerra. Para resolver este problema, se les ocurrió la idea de trabajos forzados y campos de esclavos. Hitler vio la ventaja de deshacerse de todas las personas que se oponían a su régimen. Adolf Hitler nombró a Heinrich Himmler y Adolf Eichmann, ambos judíos, para supervisar y administrar los campos. Los líderes del partido comunista, el partido socialdemócrata, los pastores alemanes y los cristianos que se oponían al régimen de Hitler fueron sentenciados en secreto y puestos en estos campos. Más tarde llegaron los gitanos, y recién en 1938 se formó el primer grupo de 20.000 judíos. No es cierto que estos campos fueran construidos y usados para exterminar judíos como la propaganda del Holocausto quiere que todos crean. Los financieros estadounidenses y las empresas industriales alemanas como Krupp y otras desarrollaron estos parques industriales y campos de trabajo que pertenecían al World Leader Group para asegurar productos y máquinas de guerra para la Segunda Guerra Mundial. La mayoría de las personas que murieron en los campos de concentración eran prisioneros de Alemania o de otros países y no solo judíos, como se le hace creer al público.*[36]

Según un artículo reciente de Independent News:

Dan Plesch, autor de Los derechos humanos después de Hitler, Las potencias aliadas *conocían la escala del Holocausto judío dos años y medio antes de lo que generalmente se supone. A pesar de esto, comentó que las potencias aliadas hicieron muy poco para rescatar o brindar refugio a quienes estaban en peligro de muerte.*

En extensos estudios sobre el Holocausto y el tratamiento de los prisioneros de guerra alemanes, los autores escribieron sobre muchos hechos desconocidos antes. Solo recientemente, al obtener documentos originales de archivos e información disponible en Internet fue posible tal compilación de datos. Desafortunadamente, tantas víctimas inocentes sufrieron, y algunos villanos fueron celebrados como héroes. Un crimen es un crimen, independientemente de quién lo cometa. Los criminales deben ser llevados ante la justicia, y no todos los ciudadanos del país deben ser llamados criminales y ser castigados por los crímenes de su líder.

En un resumen sobre la persecución de los judíos de 1933 a 1945, y el destino de los prisioneros de guerra y civiles alemanes después de 1945, muchos autores recopilaron información y hechos nuevos recientemente sobre los campos de concentración. Las fotos de los cadáveres apilados que tomó el general Eisenhower eran cadáveres de prisioneros alemanes del campo de prisioneros estadounidense Rhein- Wiesen. Según un informe, el productor de cine Alfred Hitchcock dispuso los cadáveres de tal manera que pareciera que todos eran judíos. Al crear una imagen de asesinato masivo de judíos, el general Eisenhower encubrió sus propias actividades criminales de dejar morir intencionalmente a los prisioneros de guerra alemanes. Incluso Stalin envió judíos a los gulags (campos de trabajos forzados) y mató a más de un millón, porque no encontró ningún uso para ellos. Desafortunadamente, estas fotos manipuladas también se usaron contra los llamados criminales de guerra en los juicios de Nürnberg.

Al final de la Segunda Guerra Mundial, no solo los prisioneros de guerra, sino también los ciudadanos alemanes y los ciudadanos de todos los países involucrados en la guerra, sufrieron lesiones y enfermedades físicas, pero también traumas emocionales. No solo murieron millones de judíos como consecuencia de la Segunda Guerra Mundial, sino también millones de niños y familias inocentes de todos los países donde la guerra se desató.

Nunca debemos *olvidar* el Holocausto y la persecución de los judíos durante la Segunda Guerra Mundial.

Sin embargo, siempre debemos *recordar* el sufrimiento de todas las personas inocentes y víctimas de todos los países de ambas guerras mundiales y exponer a los verdaderos criminales de la humanidad, que encubrieron sus crímenes culpando a otros. Ningún civil o soldado fue sometido a un trato más inhumano que los alemanes a través del bombardeo de las ciudades y los japoneses quemados vivos y mutilados por las bombas atómicas.

Las personas que nunca han estado en una guerra no conocen los sacrificios de los soldados y cuántas heridas y traumas emocionales soportan. Las personas que nunca han vivido en una zona de guerra nunca sabrán cuántas atrocidades sufrieron los civiles y los prisioneros y qué sacrificios se vieron obligados a hacer.

Un documento de Michael Palomino, publicado en 2003 y actualizado en 2015, resume algunos datos desconocidos sobre la persecución de los judíos y algunas de las atrocidades de los aliados que Hollywood llevó al cine, difundiendo por todo el mundo. Nadie habló sobre el trato inhumano de los soldados alemanes asesinados en los campos de Rhine Meadow u otros campos de trabajos forzados de los cuatro aliados. Solo recientemente, historiadores, sobrevivientes de guerra y buscadores de la verdad escriben sobre los 14.000,000 de civiles desplazados alemanes de Alemania Oriental y el tercio de los territorios alemanes entregados a Polonia y Rusia después de ambas guerras mundiales. Algunos residentes que no pudieron escapar antes de que terminara la Segunda Guerra Mundial tuvieron que trabajar duro por tan solo un poco de comida. Los rusos abusaron sexualmente mujeres y jovencitas. En condiciones inhumanas, fueron despojados de sus pertenencias, expulsados de sus propiedades y enviados en vagones de tren abarrotados hacia el oeste. Sin embargo, los prisioneros de guerra alemanes que trabajaban para agricultores o fábricas privadas en los Estados Unidos, Francia e Inglaterra eran bien tratados y respetados. Los líderes y personas a cargo ejercieron su odio y venganza en grupos particulares y los gobiernos de los aliados contra los prisioneros de guerra y civiles alemanes. Toda la población de Alemania fue responsabilizada por los crímenes de Hitler, en este caso, condenándolos a maltratarlos y humillarlos. Los generales y soldados de los aliados que ocultaron sus crímenes del público fueron celebrados como héroes por sus países. En cambio, la mayoría de los generales y soldados alemanes que se convirtieron en prisioneros de guerra fueron tratados como fuerzas enemigas desarmadas y no como prisioneros de guerra según las normas de la Convención de Ginebra. Los generales y soldados de todos los países que luchan o mueren en el cumplimiento del deber deben ser tratados con respeto; por lo tanto, los civiles de cada país deben ser tratados con dignidad después del final de una guerra. Los comandantes en jefe de cada país comenzaron las guerras, no los civiles. El presidente Roosevelt y el primer ministro Winston Churchill establecieron reglas según las cuales los vencedores y los derrotados deben recibir el mismo trato.

"¿Por qué no siguieron sus propias reglas después del final de la Segunda Guerra Mundial?"

Tantas preguntas están y tal vez permanecerán sin respuesta. Solo vislumbramos documentos y hechos desclasificados a medida que se descubre y publica más información en Internet, libros y medios públicos. Solo Dios conoce toda la verdad, y Él tiene el control de la gente en la tierra y toda Su magnífica creación del universo. Incluso Dios se arrepintió a veces de haber creado a los humanos al ver el mal que cometían. Sin embargo, Dios, en su misericordia sin límites, los salvó una y otra vez de la extinción. Sabiendo lo difícil sería obtener la salvación cumpliendo la ley, Dios sacrificó a su amado hijo Jesucristo para que las personas puedan salvarse solo por gracia y no por buenas obras.

Mi corazón está con todas las personas inocentes de todos los países que sufrieron atrocidades en ambas guerras mundiales. Condeno el crimen pero no odio a los criminales. Rezo para que la gente de todos los países haga lo mismo. Recuerdo muchas cosas compasivas y honorables, como el puente aéreo de Berlín y el Plan Marshall estadounidense que ayudó a reconstruir Alemania y los países y economías de Europa. Esperemos que hayamos aprendido a trabajar juntos con los países del mundo y resolver las diferencias a través de la diplomacia y el entendimiento en lugar de las guerras.

Antes, durante y después de las guerras, se difundió propaganda y mentiras para promover las causas de los líderes mundiales. Se necesitan años de investigación meticulosa y recopilación de información para separar la ficción de los hechos, el mito de la realidad y las mentiras de la verdad.

"Solo cuando sepamos la verdad, y debemos buscar diligentemente la verdad, seremos libres y más capaces de interpretar las intrigas de los eventos históricos. Entonces, con suerte, también aprenderemos a perdonar a los criminales de la humanidad y a vivir en paz con nuestros habitantes globales."[18]

Una vez, en una cena en Londres, surgió la pregunta: "¿Quién dominará el futuro?".

El profesor Huxley declaró: La nación que se apega a los hechos. Señores, a todos los hechos, y el hecho más grande de la historia es Dios. Dios es la respuesta a todas nuestras preguntas. Él revela sus respuestas a todas las preguntas humanas en su Santa Palabra, la Biblia".

CAPÍTULO 23

Crucero Báltico y Otras Visitas

Desde que aprendí la historia de la princesa prusiana Catalina la Grande en la escuela secundaria, deseaba visitar Rusia algún día y ver la influencia que dejó en su país adoptivo, Rusia. Su reinado como zarina de toda Rusia me fascinó, y siempre quise ver dónde gobernaba. Catalina la Grande nació el 2 de mayo de 1729 en Stettin, Prusia, como princesa de Anhalt-Zerbst. Atrajo a muchos alemanes a Rusia dándoles algunas tierras, prometiéndoles libertad religiosa y otros privilegios. Se convirtió a la iglesia ortodoxa oriental, gobernada por el ejemplo de Prusia, y llevó el arte y la cultura europeos a Rusia. Desde que el crucero por el Báltico hizo escala en St. Petersburgo, decidí unirme a un crucero en agosto de 2011 para visitar siete países en el Mar Báltico. Parando en St. Petersburgo y ver la influencia de Pedro el Grande y Catalina la Grande deleitó mis ojos y mi mente. Pedro el Grande envió artesanos, escultores y arquitectos de todo el mundo para estudiar los diseños de palacios, fuentes y estatuas para los planes de San Petersburgo de construir una ciudad. Pedro el Grande construyó un fuerte en mayo de 1703 para protegerse de los suecos que invadían la ciudad. Posteriormente, el arquitecto suizo Tressini continuó construyendo la ciudad, y miles de trabajadores forzados murieron al levantar los edificios de la ciudad en un pantano.

Las estatuas doradas, las cascadas y el paisaje me impresionaron así como a los demás turistas. Todas las fuentes funcionaban con agua a presión procedente de depósitos construidos a diferentes niveles. No se necesitan motores eléctricos para operar las muchas fuentes.

Cuando vi la elegancia del palacio de verano de Catalina la Grande, quedé abrumada y también por el esplendor de la sala de ámbar restaurada. La decoración original de la habitación de ámbar desapareció durante la Segunda Guerra Mundial. La restauración de la sala de ámbar comenzó en 1979 y tomó veinticuatro años a un costo de once millones de dólares. El presidente ruso, Vladimir Putin, y el entonces canciller alemán, Gerhard Schroeder, dedicaron la sala de ámbar restaurada, con motivo del 300 aniversario de St. Petersburgo Sin embargo, la desaparición de los muros de ámbar originales desmantelados sigue siendo un misterio. El hijo de Federico el Grande, rey de Prusia, entregó la sala de ámbar original en 1716 como regalo a Pedro el Grande, Zar de Rusia, quien expresó su admiración por la exquisita obra de arte durante una de sus visitas. También fue conmemorado por un tratado entre los dos gobernantes contra Carlos XII de Suecia. Ahora es considerada la octava maravilla del mundo. Ver la colección de arte y antigüedades rodeada por el ambiente y la elegancia del Museo del Hermitage me dejó sin palabras. Me gustó especialmente la pintura de tamaño natural del Regreso del hijo pródigo de Rembrandt. Pararme frente a la obra de arte original de Leonardo da Vinci, la Madonna Litta, me hizo sentir humilde. Las pinturas de Tiziano con efectos de luces y sombras tan bellamente equilibrados siempre me fascinaron. Un empresario inglés, James Cox, creó el Golden Peacock animado con tres pájaros de tamaño natural, un pavo real, un gallo y un búho. Se enciende solo una vez por semana los miércoles a la 1:00 p.m. Uno de los admiradores de Catalina la Grande quería impresionar a la zarina con este regalo único. En 1764, Catalina la Grande adquirió su primera colección de arte en Berlín de manos de Johann Gotzkowski, quien había adquirido la Obra de arte para el rey Federico II de Prusia. Quería traer cultura y prestigio al trono y tenía la intención de mostrárselo solo a sus amigos y al círculo cercano de la corte en su palacio de invierno. Mientras reinaba el zar Nicolás II, abrió el museo al público. Durante la Revolución de 1917, el museo se convirtió en propiedad pública y el estado opera la colección de arte más extensa del mundo, tres millones de obras de arte, de las cuales solo un millón se exhiben permanentemente. El reinado de Catalina la Grande trajo prestigio a Rusia y entre los países europeos. Asistir a un espectáculo de ballet ruso y ver a las elegantes bailarinas bailar con la música de Cenicienta de Sergei Prokofiev, terminó mi memorable visita a St. Petersburgo.

Cuando el crucero se detuvo en Warnemuende, Alemania, Organicé una reunión con el exlíder de nuestro Grupo Juvenil DJO, Heinz Kraemer, y su yerno Michael Glueber. Ambos vivían en Harsefeld, al suroeste de Hamburgo. Hacía más de cincuenta años que no nos veíamos. Admiré cuánto contribuyó a los grupos de jóvenes de los refugiados. Perdió su casa en Pomerania, Alemania, que fue entregada a Polonia después de la Segunda Guerra Mundial. Recordamos diferentes eventos del pasado y los muchos cambios en el presente. Aunque ya había cumplido los noventa años, todavía escribía informes y poemas para ocasiones especiales y daba conferencias en escuelas sobre sus experiencias en la Segunda Guerra Mundial. Nuestra vívida conversación y la alegría de vernos después de tanto tiempo seguirán siendo inolvidables. Estuvimos en estrecho contacto todo el tiempo. Desafortunadamente, falleció unos años después de que nos vimos.

Tres años más tarde volé a Alemania para visitar a mi hermano menor, Horst, en Offenbach. Asistimos a la confirmación de mi sobrino bisnieto Ramón Martín en Herleshausen. Mi hermano organizó una reunión con varios ex miembros del Grupo de Jóvenes DJO jóvenes y mayores y sus cónyuges. Nos entretuvo el hijo de mi amiga, Bernd Russy, y un acordeonista. Todos cantamos e intercambiamos muchos eventos del pasado y del presente. Nos mantuvimos en contacto durante más de cincuenta años. Nos detuvimos en el camino para ver a algunos amigos más del antiguo Grupo Juvenil DJO. También hice una reserva por diez días en el Hilda Stift en Wiesbaden. Pensé que era un balneario para turistas. En cambio, resultó ser un hogar para personas mayores. Tenía muchas ganas de asistir a una función de ópera. Desafortunadamente, durante ese tiempo no se programaron óperas ni conciertos. Sin embargo, mi sobrina nieta, Jana Martin, vino a quedarse conmigo unos días. Exploramos la ciudad y los parques y saboreamos la deliciosa comida en los restaurantes italianos. Además, Hildegard Kleinschmidt, una compañera de la escuela secundaria, y su esposo, el profesor de Pedagogía, Gottfried Kleinschmidt, me visitaron en Wiesbaden. Pasamos juntos un día memorable. También disfruté de una presentación musical en el Hilda Stift, conociendo a los residentes y saboreando su buena comida todos los días, principalmente los sabrosos pasteles que se sirven cada tarde.

Al año siguiente, volé a Naples, Florida, visité a los hijos de mi esposo y celebré el cumpleaños de Frank con su familia y amigos. Gigi, Christine y Frank decoraron sus casas maravillosamente y vivieron en una zona prestigiosa de Naples. Disfrutamos de la deliciosa comida que prepararon Frank y Peggy, siendo ambos excelentes cocineros. También disfruté conocer a sus amables vecinos y amigos, así como un paseo con Frank en su motocicleta por el hermoso vecindario paisajístico. Juntos, navegamos por la Bahía de Naples, para ver las magníficas mansiones de los políticos ricos y los magnates de los negocios.

En el camino, me detuve en Hot Springs para celebrar el cumpleaños de mi amiga Ilse Stritzke el 15 de marzo.Paseamos por Hot Springs, miramos todas las exquisitas antigüedades exhibidas en las ventanas e incluso reservamos un masaje. Ilse también nació en Prusia del Este. Nos conocimos en Chicago mientras asistíamos a la misma Iglesia Luterana. Su familia no escapó antes de que los rusos invadieran Prusia del Este y vivieron durante tres años con los ocupantes rusos. Los soldados rusos trataron atrozmente a las mujeres y niñas. Ella me contó cómo su hermanito murió de desnutrición y cómo encarcelaron a su hermana por traer a casa una papa del campo. Murió en prisión. Hablamos de muchos temas y experiencias y de cómo Dios nos ayudó durante la guerra y los tiempos incomprensibles de la posguerra.

Toda mi vida deseé ver la colección de arte del museo más grande del mundo, el Louvre, en París. En la primavera de 2016, plancé combinar una visita al Louvre y un crucero por el río Danubio. Planeaba volar a Bruselas para visitar a mi amiga Elisabeth Bruns, que vivía en Oudenaarde, Bélgica, y luego un viaje en tren a París. Elisabeth también reservó una visita a la exhibición de Hieronymus Bosch en Hertogenbosch. En ese momento, llegaron a casa obras de arte de todo el mundo. El artista pintó principalmente temas religiosos al óleo sobre grandes paneles de madera. Se hicieron famosos los paneles del Jardín de las delicias y del Juicio Final, que pintó en el siglo XV. Ambos lamentamos haber tenido que cancelar la visita a mi amiga, Elisabeth. Mis planes cambiaron en el último minuto cuando los terroristas atacaron el aeropuerto de Bruselas, destruyeron parte de la estructura y provocaron su cierre. Volví a reservar mi vuelo de Bruselas a Frankfurt, Alemania, y me quedé la semana adicional con mi sobrina Beate Martin y su esposo Gerald en Silkerode. Ella estaba encantada, y después de que superé mi decepción, yo también lo estaba. Me trataron como realeza y me presentaron a algunos de sus amigos. Cuando le mencioné sobre la cancelación de mi viaje al Louvre, dijo: "No hay problema, podemos ver la exhibición de arte en la pantalla grande". Mi sobrina y su esposo disfrutaban viendo películas sobre la naturaleza e instalaron una pantalla de televisión gigante en toda la pared. Vimos el magnífico Palacio del Renacimiento con las obras de arte y las pinturas, esculturas y estatuas de fama mundial durante dos noches.

Por supuesto, ver la famosa Mona Lisa de Leonardo Da Vinci siempre es impresionante. Cuando miré de cerca a Mona Lisa, noté que el artista no le había pintado las cejas. Leonardo Da Vinci creía que la simplicidad era la máxima sofisticación. Vimos la pintura original, The Swing, de Fragonard de 1766, de la cual poseemos una copia de un artista italiano. Vimos Liberty de Eugene Delacroix 1830 y muchas otras obras maestras famosas en la comodidad de su hogar sin luchar contra la multitud. Originalmente, el palacio del Louvre sirvió como residencia de los reyes franceses. Cuando el rey Luis XVI decidió residir en el palacio de Versalles, el rey transformó el castillo en un museo que visitan más de diez millones de personas cada año.

La amiga de mi sobrina, Sabine Scheideman, que enseñaba inglés, ruso y arte en la escuela de Bischofrode, me pidió que me uniera a ella y le diera una conferencia en su clase de inglés. Aunque no tuve tiempo para prepararme, los estudiantes hicieron varias preguntas sobre mis experiencias pasadas. Los estudiantes absorbieron todos mis comentarios con atención y mostraron interés en mi libro de poesía y escritura. Al final de la clase, un estudiante me obsequió un ramo de tulipanes como muestra de agradecimiento. Cuando los estudiantes se graduaron y se fueron de excursión, me escribieron una postal, firmada por cada estudiante. Aprecié su consideración. Yo a su vez envié a la maestra y a cada alumno un libro de mis poemas, llamado Una canción en la noche.

Me uní a la agente de viajes Melissa Porzak de San Diego y su grupo en un crucero por el Danubio una semana después. Primero, nos reunimos todos en el lujoso Hotel Aria en la hermosa ciudad de Praga. A continuación, cogimos un autobús hasta Vilshofen, donde nos embarcamos en el crucero Ama. Después de que Melissa, nuestra directora de viajes, nos presentara a todos, nos convertimos en una gran familia para el resto de las excursiones y comidas por tierra. El viaje en autobús a través de la región del lago del sur de Baviera se detuvo en Mondsee, Austria, para visitar la iglesia colegiada de San Michaels. La ceremonia de matrimonio de Maria y Georg von Trapp en el musical La Novicia Rebelde fue filmada en la iglesia. El altar exquisitamente decorado muestra en la sección inferior reliquias de los antiguos gobernantes austriacos, decorado con joyas preciosas. Mientras filmaba la escena de la boda de Julie Andrews y Christopher Plummer para La Novicia Rebelde, el fotógrafo cubrió algunas de las reliquias. La abadía histórica medieval adyacente de Mondsee alberga una destacada colección de libros, incluyendo algunas partituras originales de las composiciones de Ludwig von Beethoven. Admiré el concepto de belleza, los artistas que crearon todas las estatuas doradas ornamentadas entre columnas, no solo en el altar sino también a ambos lados de la iglesia. Durante todo el día, los ojos se deleitaron no solo con la obra de arte hecha por humanos, sino también con la creación de Dios de un paisaje tan hermoso.

Al visitar Viena, la capital de Austria, vimos la influencia de la emperatriz María Teresa (1740-1780) y el emperador Francisco José (1848 -1916), quienes crearon muchos edificios monumentales de estilo barroco. Visitamos el castillo del emperador y la estructura frente a él, el establo de los famosos caballos lipizzanos de la Escuela Española de Equitación. Solo vislumbramos algunos caballos y, desafortunadamente, no vimos su magnífica actuación. Viena se jacta de muchos eventos culturales y musicales y atrae a artistas de todo el mundo. La Orquesta Sinfónica de Viena, la Orquesta Filarmónica de Viena, el Coro de Niños de Viena y las Galas de Ópera son de renombre mundial; también lo son los festivales de música en el Castillo Schoenbrun. Afortunadamente, asistimos a un concierto en el Orchestra Hall. recuerdo un incidente que me sucedió antes del comienzo de la actuación. De camino al baño de arriba, me encontré con un músico con un violín. Le pregunté: "¿Tengo suficiente tiempo para ir al baño?" Él respondió cortésmente: "Sí". Cuando regresé, descubrí que el músico con el que hablé era el director de la orquesta. Esperó hasta que me senté y luego comenzó a dirigir y tocar el violín, un Walz de Viena, "El Danubio Azul" de Johann Strauss. Un tenor y una soprano cantaron arias de ópera y dos bailarines, hombre y mujer, bailaron para el público. Recompensamos a todos los artistas con un estruendoso aplauso. Por supuesto, no podíamos irnos de Viena sin ver la noria gigante del Parque de Atracciones Prater y degustar un auténtico strudel de manzana vienés con salsa caliente de vainilla.

La siguiente ciudad por la que navegamos fue Budapest. Navegando por Budapest de noche con el Parlamento y todos los edificios históricos iluminados terminó el memorable crucero con un gran final. Cierta tristeza llenó mi corazón al separarme de mis compañeros de viaje quienes me mostraron amabilidad e interés en mi libro. Todos me dieron sus direcciones de correo electrónico para que les avisara cuando mi libro fuera publicado. Desde Budapest, volé a Londres, San Francisco y de regreso a Reno. Durante el verano tuve muchas visitas; incluso la maestra Sabine Scheideman vino con su esposo y su hija de Alemania, dos sobrinas, Christa e Ilse con sus esposos, Rick y Ron, y los amigos Sue y Ed Guzek de San Diego. Todos disfrutamos de la compañía de los demás y de la belleza escénica del Lago Tahoe.

Más tarde ese verano, en la mamografía anual de rutina, el radiólogo descubrió un bulto en mi seno izquierdo. La biopsia confirmó un crecimiento canceroso, que la cirujana Dra. Evans extrajo poco después de la biopsia. Durante mis preparativos para la cirugía, vi a la Dra. Evans apoyada contra la pared con las manos cruzadas. Pensé que estaba orando y yo también me sentí en paz. Más tarde supe que la Dra. Evans era una cirujana cristiana y oraba por sus pacientes antes, durante y después de la cirugía. El Dr. Alexis Carrel, ganador del premio Nobel en 1912 y cuya investigación allanó el camino para los trasplantes de órganos, dijo lo siguiente sobre la oración:

La oración es el único poder en el mundo que parece vencer las "Leyes de la Naturaleza". Bien entendida, la oración es una actividad madura indispensable para el pleno desarrollo de la personalidad, la integración última de las facultades más elevadas del hombre. Sólo en la oración logramos esa unión completa y armoniosa de cuerpo, mente y espíritu, que le da a la frágil caña humana su fuerza inquebrantable.[34]

Mi amiga, Carol Miller, me esperaba en el vestíbulo. Después de que me levanté sin marearme de la camilla en la sala de recuperación, me llevó a casa. Unas horas más tarde, todavía no tenía dolor y me sentía muy bien, por lo que Carol decidió irse a casa en lugar de quedarse a pasar la noche. El vendaje de plástico en spray me permitió ducharme y nunca sufrí molestias ni dolor. Agradecí a Dios por los resultados de la cirugía, realizada por un cirujano cristiano, y que el oncólogo no recetó quimioterapia.

CAPÍTULO 24

Celebraciones Especiales

Dado que mi esposo, el Dr. Aldo Bruni, falleció el 28 de septiembre del 2009, quería honrarlo con un evento especial celebrando su vida. Cada año, cuando pensaba en prepararme para el evento, el dolor me abrumaba y las lágrimas corrían por mis mejillas y detenían mis planes. Siete años después, pensé, por qué no hacer un doble evento, celebrar la vida de mi esposo a fines de enero de 2017 y mi octogésimo cumpleaños al mismo tiempo. Hablé con la mi familia y la de mi esposo, y estuvieron de acuerdo. Entonces comencé a diseñar la invitación y el programa para el evento en el Country Club de San Carlos. Como recuerdos, creé separadores con una rosa para las damas y flores de aciano para los caballeros, con un poema que escribí sobre amigos. También imprimí una breve biografía de mi esposo para cada pareja o para un solo invitado. Trabajé diligentemente durante varios meses; mis amigos y mi empleada doméstica Chava me ayudaron en todo lo que pudieron.

El evento semi-formal dio inicio el domingo 29 de enero a las 3:00 p.m.

Había contratado a cuatro jóvenes de la familia McLean para llevar a los invitados a las mesas, decoradas con ramos de rosas rosadas, pequeñas flores azules, margaritas blancas, crisantemos verdes y nube. Durante la cena, Valeria, soprano de ópera, interpretó canciones populares acompañada de su prometido, Roberto, en el piano. Además, un sacerdote vestido con un elegante traje bordado y un sombrero a juego cantó acompañado de guitarras. Mi familia, Peggy, Frank, Joanne y Dave me deleitaron con su presencia. Mis maravillosos vecinos Kelly y Ron de South Lake Tahoe, mi amiga Marcia Bogan de Bakersfield y Penny de Phoenix. El Dr. Benda y el Dr. Patterson, Mark y Curt, parte del equipo médico de Bozeman, Montana, celebraron conmigo, al igual que el pastor Glenn Driedger y Jeannine y más de cien invitados. Después de que los camareros sirvieran una cena temprana de filet mignon y camarones al coco, mi maestro de ceremonias, David Long, dio la bienvenida elocuentemente a los invitados y anunció el comienzo del programa, en honor a mi difunto esposo, el Dr. Aldo R. Bruni.

Cumpleaños 80 y memorial para el Dr. Aldo R. Bruni

Jenny Navarra tradujo la biografía y los discursos al español. El Padre Rogelio comenzó el programa cantando

"Amor Eterno" de Juan Gabriel mientras yo estaba de pie en el escenario frente al gran retrato de mi esposo junto a mi amiga María de los Ángeles. Juan Gabriel escribió esta emotiva canción cuando su madre murió en 1984. Entonces mi maestro de ceremonias, David Long, comenzó a leer la biografía de mi esposo. David puso tanta emoción en su excelente presentación que captó la atención de la audiencia por completo. Durante una breve pausa, Valeria cantó una de las arias favoritas de mi esposo y mía, "Casta Diva", de la ópera "Norma" de Bellini. Monserat cantó "Tú me levantas", y Ricardo "Non ti scordar mai di me" (Nunca te olvides de mí), una de las canciones populares favoritas de mi esposo. A continuación, Joanne y Frank expresaron su amor por su padre, mencionando algunos eventos importantes compartidos. También mostraron su gratitud hacia mí y cuánto contribuí a sus vidas y la vida de su padre. Sus discursos me conmovieron; también lo hizo el de Tato, un niño de trece años cuya abuela y madre eran amigas mías. Tato me preguntó si también podía dar un breve discurso. Acepté sin saber qué esperar. Su madre, a quien amaba mucho, tenía cáncer y otros problemas de salud, y compartiendo su dolor, lo maduró prematuramente. Tato expresó su cariño por mí y aprendió de mí a vivir el presente, apreciar el bien de cada momento y amar incondicionalmente. Por lo general, adquirimos esta lección más adelante en la vida, y él la había aprendido de mí cuando aún era un adolescente. Me sentí humilde. Después del discurso de Tato, mi empleada doméstica Chava comenzó a leer sus notas. Empezó a llorar y no podía terminar de expresar su aprecio y admiración por la forma en que la tratábamos. Luego, Valeria, Monserat y Aubrey cantaron "La última rosa del verano". Cada jovencita me regaló una rosa rosa para simbolizar que la vida sigue, incluso si un ser querido fallece, y volvemos a encontrar la belleza a lo largo del camino cambiado de la vida.

Después de una breve pausa, Nancy Dreiling trajo el pastel decorado con buen gusto con las mismas flores que los centros de mesa y dos velas que decían 80 encima. Todos cantaron "Feliz Cumpleaños" en inglés primero y luego la canción mexicana de cumpleaños "Las Mañanitas", traducida: Es el día es la mañana en que te tratan como a un rey porque esta mañana es tu cumpleaños y tus alabanzas cantaremos.

Mientras tanto, los bailarines folclóricos de Obregón, vestidos con impresionantes trajes coloridos, subieron al escenario y realizaron danzas mexicanas durante más de una hora. Al final de la actuación, los invitados salieron para soltar globos iluminados inflados y miraron los fuegos artificiales que un amigo preparó como regalo. La mayoría de los invitados se fueron. Sin embargo, Marcello, que había traído su acordeón, entretuvo a mi familia y amigos cercanos durante una hora más. Cantó canciones italianas y cantamos con él. Seis horas después, a las 9:00 p. m., todos nos fuimos a casa cansados pero contentos de que todo salió bien. Agradecí a Dios por toda su guía y bendiciones.

Antes de que mi familia y amigos de los Estados Unidos se fueran, organicé una cena mexicana y, como sorpresa, contraté una banda de mariachis para entretenerlos. Justo cuando todos terminaron de comer, la puerta se abrió y los músicos entraron a la habitación. Todos salimos al patio y escuchamos la música del mariachi bajo el cielo estrellado. Antes de que todos se fueran, agradecí a mi querida familia y amigos por hacer que el evento fuera memorable para todos nosotros.

Mi hermano Edmund y mi cuñada me visitaron en Lake Tahoe durante el verano. Disfrutamos recordando nuestra infancia en Prusia del Este, saboreando la comida que solía cocinar nuestra madre y el hermoso paisaje del Lago Tahoe. A pesar de que Prusia Oriental desapareció con las dos guerras mundiales, los recuerdos de nuestra infancia siempre permanecerán.

Otro evento agradable fue la celebración de la boda mexicana de mis amigos, Valeria y Roberto, el 19 de noviembre de 2017, que me dio a conocer la tradición mexicana. Valeria me preguntó si su cortejo nupcial podría alistarse en mi departamento. Estuve de acuerdo. El domingo por la mañana, cuatro estilistas llegaron primero y transformaron el lugar en un salón de belleza. Luego vinieron las madres de los novios y las ocho damas de honor. Cada dama de honor lució una chaqueta de raso de colores que les había regalado la novia, indicando el color del vestido que usarían para la ceremonia en la playa del Hotel San Carlos Plaza. Las estilistas crearon peinados elegantes y diferentes para cada dama, incluyéndome a mí. Después de ponerse sus vestidos, todas se veían impresionantes. Una dama de honor se olvidó de traer su vestido formal con ella; alguien Tenía que traerlo de Guaymas. Retrasó el inicio de la ceremonia una hora. Los trabajadores instalaron una plataforma de madera en la arena de la playa con sillas blancas para los invitados detrás de un altar decorado. El párroco también incluyó a los padres de los novios en la ceremonia cuando colocó un gran rosario sobre los hombros de los novios mientras se unía a ellos como marido y mujer. Los padres y los invitados felicitaron a los recién casados. Después de la ceremonia, las familias e invitados se sirvieron aperitivos, vino y refrescos de una mesa bellamente dispuesta en la playa. A la noche siguió una recepción en un salón de banquetes con música de mariachi que entretuvo a familiares y amigos hasta altas horas de la noche. Como regalo de bodas, dejé que los recién casados se quedaran en mi departamento por una semana. Antes de que se fueran, invité a sus familiares y amigos a cenar. Más tarde, les presenté el siguiente poema que escribí para ellos:

"El amor es una canción"

El amor es una canción que nunca necesita terminar.
Tiene la melodía más dulce para otorgar.

El hermoso amor de los recién casados sólo es
Un prólogo de una dicha amorosa más fuerte.
Después de compartir años de alegría y tristeza,
Su amor se hace más profundo; entonces mañana
Reflejará el infinito amor divino de Dios,
Y será desinteresado, generoso y sublime.
Sus corazones rebosarán de melodías
Que durarán aquí y por las eternidades.

El amor es una canción que nunca necesita terminar,
Tiene la melodía más dulce para otorgar.

Tanto a Valeria como a Roberto les gustó tanto el poema que Roberto le compuso una melodía. Valeria cantó la nueva canción con mucho sentimiento en nuestra próxima reunión; me conmovió profundamente. Todos disfrutaron de nuestros eventos musicales, así que decidimos tener uno cada año en mi casa. Valeria, Roberto y su padre Louis nos trajeron mucha alegría a mis amigos y a mí; atesoramos nuestras amistades.

Cuando regresé a Lake Tahoe la primavera siguiente, tuve el placer de conocer a mis nuevos vecinos, la Dra. Tatjana, su marido Keith, y sus dos hijas Erika y Evelina, así como algunas de sus amigas y sus vecinos Rayna y Dan Currier. También nos reunimos con mis vecinos y amigos inmediatos Kelly y Ron. Todos disfrutábamos de la compañía de los demás y nos ayudábamos cuando era necesario. Pasar el 4 de julio con Kelly y Ron y sus amigos, disfrutar de la deliciosa comida y la amable hospitalidad de Kelly, y ver el espectáculo de fuegos artificiales en el lago desde su hermosa casa siempre es un placer. Ambos no sólo son vecinos cariñosos, sino también amigos preciados.

Al año siguiente, conocí a una doctora, Connie Hahn, que vino con el equipo médico de Bozeman, Montana, a San Carlos, México. Durante su visita al lago Tahoe, la Dra. Hahn me presentó su amiga doctora, la Dra. Pattie Francis, que vivía en el lago Tahoe. La Dra. Francis y la Dra. Hahn pertenecen a la organización cristiana llamada Mujeres Médicas Cristianas por Cristo (CWPC). Cuando quince miembros se reunieron en casa de la Dra. Francis para planificar la agenda de los próximos cinco años, también me incluyeron en su círculo. Admiré su misión de donar su tiempo para ayudar a pacientes necesitados en países extranjeros, que no tienen los medios para pagar los servicios médicos.

Para el 4 de julio de 2019, invité a la Dra. Francis y a su familia. También tuve una pareja de Idaho visitándome. Todos pasamos una tarde memorable viendo los fuegos artificiales sobre el lago desde el balcón de mi casa. Cientos de barcos con sus luces rojas y verdes rodearon las barcazas desde las que se lanzaron los fuegos artificiales. Añaden un efecto especial a las coloridas exhibiciones cerca del agua y en el cielo. Al final, cuando se lanzan muchos fuegos artificiales simultáneamente, mis invitados estaban asombrados, y yo también.

Desafortunadamente, me caí cuando traté de poner un cartón de huevos en el basurero al día siguiente. Pensando que era solo una lesión muscular en la parte superior del brazo, tomé algunas pastillas para el dolor y esperaba que sanara pronto.

En agosto, mis amigos Sue y Ed de San Diego vinieron a visitarme. Dan y Rayna nos invitaron a mis amigos Sue, Ed y a mí a un viaje en barco de un día de duración, observando la belleza de la costa del lago Tahoe con todas las magníficas mansiones. Dan es un excelente capitán que maniobra bien el bote en curvas cerradas, pero también explica la historia de los lugares únicos del lago Tahoe, como un guía turístico profesional.

Cuando Sue y Ed regresaron a San Diego, fui con ellos. Nos detuvimos en Bakersfield y visitamos a mi amiga Marcia Bogan, quien recientemente se había sometido a una cirugía de columna y usaba un yeso en todo el cuerpo. Ella y su hijo Gene nos recibieron en el conocido restaurante vasco, los Woolgrowers. A pesar de estar incapacitada, Marcia parecía de buen ánimo, y estábamos felices de volver a vernos. Ella me llama su hermana en Cristo. Nos conocimos en San Carlos hace muchos años. Sin embargo, después de que su esposo falleciera, ella y su hijo regresaron a Bakersfield para estar cerca de su madre. Manejamos directamente a Laguna Beach desde Bakersfield para ver a mi hijastra Joanne y su esposo, el Dr. Trotter.

Ed tenía un compromiso a la mañana siguiente, así que regresó a San Diego. Al día siguiente, Mary Ellen, la hermana de Sue, se unió a nosotros para ver el Desfile de los Maestros. El tema del año fue "La máquina del tiempo", combinando el arte y la ciencia en la exhibición. Además, el productor del concurso incluyó un alunizaje recreado con un astronauta en vivo, muy impresionante. Finalmente, por supuesto, la "Última Cena" de Leonardo Da Vinci con la música de fondo apropiada de la orquesta en vivo es la culminación del espectáculo, que todos disfrutamos.

Cuando regresé de San Diego, el dolor de mi hombro derecho había disminuido, pero noté algunos movimientos limitados de mi brazo derecho. Decidí ver a un cirujano ortopédico. La resonancia magnética del hombro derecho mostró un desgarro completo del tendón del húmero y cambios artríticos. El cirujano ortopédico sugirió un reemplazo total de hombro. Le dije al médico que tenía planes de irme a México el próximo mes y pensaría en operarme. Inmediatamente envié el informe por correo electrónico a mi yerno David, un excelente cirujano ortopédico, y le pedí su opinión. Me llamó y me hizo una sola pregunta: "¿Tienes mucho dolor?" Cuando lo sorprendí con la respuesta, "No". Él respondió: "Con la severidad de tu informe, deberías sentir mucho dolor. Como no tiene ninguno, le sugiero que no se opere." "Seguí su consejo y aprendí a vivir con la función limitada del brazo derecho. Le agradecí a Dios que no tenía dolor y no necesitaba reemplazo de hombro ni tratamientos específicos. Un mes después, mi empleada doméstica Chava y yo partimos felices a México.

Poco después de llegar a San Carlos, la trágica muerte de mi querida amiga Carol Miller me conmocionó a mí, a su familia y a sus amigos cercanos. Todos extrañamos su amistad amable, amorosa y generosa. Su hijo, James, y su familia, que viven en Reno, se hicieron amigos míos y también me visitaron en Lake Tahoe. El mismo año también perdí a otras dos queridas amigas, Betty Barengo y María Esther Morales. Cuando nos mudamos a San Carlos, Betty me presentó al Club Recuerdo, trabajamos juntas durante muchos años y donamos el dinero que recaudamos a organizaciones benéficas y personas necesitadas. María Esther también falleció después de sufrir durante mucho tiempo cáncer y problemas en la columna. Monserat, la hija de María Esther, y sus hijos Tato y Ricardo, tres niños superdotados e inteligentes, me dieron mucha alegría cantando o cocinando juntos.

Desafortunadamente, También perdí a mi hermana Meta Seidel, de noventa años. Ella fue al encuentro de su Señor a quien sirvió fielmente toda su vida. Antes de que mamá se encontrara cara a cara con su Salvador, nos enseñó con el ejemplo los valores cristianos y que el sufrimiento es necesario en la vida para desarrollar un carácter cristiano noble. Tratamos de vivir de acuerdo con sus valores morales y cumplir con sus expectativas. Mi padre, mis hermanas mayores Emma y Marta, así como mis hermanos Georg y Richard también fallecieron. Como resultado, nuestra familia se redujo a mis hermanos Edmund, Horst y yo.

El autor libanés, Kahlil Gibran, mejor conocido como "El profeta", cita: "La tristeza ensancha el corazón para que pueda contener más alegría". La pérdida de una vida trae tristeza, pero un bebé recién nacido trae alegría a los padres, familiares y amigos. Mis amigos Katie y Denver Janz dieron la bienvenida a su hija, Noel y Valeria y Roberto, a su hijo Roberto. Valeria dio a luz a su bebé por cesárea y su esposo tocó el piano en la sala de operaciones durante todo el parto. Esperan que su hijo se convierta en cantante o pianista. Cuando Valeria y su familia vinieron a la celebración del cumpleaños de tres de mis amigas y mío en enero del 2020, Robertito pateaba rítmicamente sus piececitos mientras su madre cantaba hermosas arias y canciones populares mexicanas. Los cumpleaños de mis amigas, Judy Long y Maggie Snell, fueron el 1 de enero, el mío el 2 de enero y el de Sahsha Sturt el 10 de diciembre. Decidimos celebrar con nuestros amigos mutuos en casa. El padre de Valeria, Luis Quijada, tocaba la guitarra y cantaba solo o con su hija. Todos disfrutamos de una deliciosa tarde musical.

En febrero se propagó la infección por el coronavirus COVID-19, provocando una pandemia mundial. Inmediatamente se hizo obligatorio el distanciamiento social y el uso de mascarillas. Los líderes mundiales restringieron los viajes internacionales y ordenaron el cierre de muchos negocios, como hoteles y restaurantes. Los artistas intérpretes o ejecutantes cancelaron conciertos en vivo y eventos públicos. En detrimento de los aficionados al deporte, no podían ver sus juegos favoritos en persona. Muchas familias no pudieron celebrar sus bodas y otras reuniones debido a la rápida propagación de las infecciones. Las universidades, escuelas e iglesias cerraron, creando una norma social completamente diferente para las personas en todo el mundo. La producción reducida temporalmente de artículos de papel y otros artículos provocó escasez y largas filas en los supermercados. Lo peor de todo es que muchos de los que contrajeron COVID-19 murieron y las familias ni siquiera pudieron reunirse para sus funerales. Mi corazón se conmovió y oré por las personas desafortunadas que perdieron a sus seres queridos, trabajos y hogares en países donde el gobierno no les brindó ninguna asistencia financiera como lo hizo el gobierno estadounidense.

Durante todo el verano, los incendios ardieron alrededor de la cuenca del lago Tahoe, y el denso humo hizo que las montañas y el lago fueran invisibles. Afortunadamente, Podría volver a México en otoño otra vez. Mis amigos Kathryn y Harvey Teitzel, dueños de un condominio en Seattle y San Carlos, México, me recogieron camino a San Carlos. Kathryn condujo mi auto y su esposo el de ellos. Disfrutamos de vívidas conversaciones sobre su trabajo misionero en Rusia y mis experiencias pasadas durante la Segunda Guerra Mundial. Siempre agradecimos a Dios por ayudarnos victoriosamente a través de nuestras tormentas de la vida y bendecirnos más allá de toda medida.

Cuando llegamos a San Carlos, mi empleada doméstica, Rosalba (Chava), vino a la casa en su día libre para ayudarme a desempacar el auto. Me recibió con los brazos abiertos y puso flores frescas en las mesas para mi deleite. Estoy agradecida por su amabilidad, consideración y lealtad. Siempre me anima a escribir. El día que le digo que escribí algunas páginas, aplaude y exclama alegremente: "Eso es bueno". Ha trabajado para mí durante catorce años. Sucesivamente, Siempre cumplí y sigo manteniendo la promesa que le hice a Dios hace sesenta y cuatro años de tratar a los empleados con respeto y nunca menospreciarlos, sino elogiarlos y ayudarlos donde sea indicado.

El distanciamiento social está vigente en San Carlos; Se sintió extraño ver algunos de los servicios de nuestra iglesia en Internet en lugar de reunirnos con los feligreses en la iglesia.

También evitamos muchas reuniones sociales. Sin embargo, me mantengo en contacto con toda mi familia y amigos llamando y enviando mensajes de correo electrónico. Nos consolamos y animamos unos a otros a permanecer enfocados en Dios, y he aprendido de las dificultades de este tiempo caótico para convertirme en una mejor persona.

CAPÍTULO 25

Mirando hacia atrás con Gratitud

Mientras escribía mi libro, miré hacia atrás en mi vida con gratitud hacia Dios primero. Jesús me salvó por gracia cuando aún era una niña. Él nos guió a mi familia y a mí victoriosamente a través de ambas guerras mundiales. Dios nos ayudó a superar los peligros, los sufrimientos, el hambre, las dificultades, el dolor, las desilusiones y las enfermedades mientras confiábamos y obedecíamos Su voluntad. Me maravillo de cuántas veces nos arrancó de las garras de la misma muerte durante la guerra y nos salvó la vida. Cuando la oscuridad emocional nos rodeó, Dios trajo luz y alegría a nuestras vidas, a menudo de manera milagrosa. La vida es como un lienzo en blanco. La obra de arte final depende de si contratamos a un artista divino o secular. Dios usará todas nuestras desilusiones y sufrimientos como sombras y las alegrías y felicidades como puntos culminantes de la pintura. Confié en Dios con mi vida. Agregó Sus gráciles trazos dorados para dar belleza y resplandor a la obra maestra terminada, deleitando y trayendo alegría a la gente.

Por otro lado, si hubiera dejado que la influencia y el mal del mundo crearan una pintura, se vería sombría y deprimente y disgustaría o incluso molestaría a los espectadores. Como individuo, tuve la opción, independientemente de las circunstancias, de qué trabajo de vida crearía. Estoy agradecida de que mi madre nos criara a mí ya mis hermanos con principios cristianos. Los maestros me enseñaron no solo su currículo asignado sino también valores morales y sabiduría práctica para la vida. Valoro a los muchos amigos que Dios me envió para compartir las experiencias de la vida. Una alegría compartida la multiplica; un dolor compartido lo disminuye. Dios, me dejó probar la agonía y el éxtasis de la vida. Aprendí que la tranquilidad protegida no es la condición de vida más favorable.

Por el contrario, las dificultades y la fe en Dios crean un carácter fuerte y noble. Estoy agradecida con Dios por llevarme por arduos e increíbles viajes a través de muchos mares tormentosos y peligros y también apacibles cimas de montañas. Aún así, Él siempre me llevó a salvo y triunfalmente a Sus brazos amorosos, enriquecida y bendecida sin medida. Dios cumplió todas las promesas que pedí y especialmente la de Romanos 8:28 "A los que aman a Dios, todas las cosas les ayudan a bien."

Ahora mi objetivo es vivir según las reglas de Dios y reemplazar la regla de oro con lo que llamo mi regla de platino, pensando y actuando de la manera que mi Señor y Salvador me enseñó con Su ejemplo. Sé que tengo defectos, pero confío en la gracia, la guía y la ayuda de Dios para superar algunos. Quiero darle a Dios toda la gloria y llevar consuelo y alegría a los demás.

Aunque sé que con las guerras mundiales se fue mi natal Prusia del este y mi hogar, Dios ha preparado un hogar eterno en el cielo para todos Sus hijos fieles y para mí. Qué esplendor inimaginable y grandioso será ver a Dios Padre y a Su Hijo Jesucristo cara a cara y escuchar las voces del ángel glorioso cantando. Me reuniré con todos mis seres queridos, amigos y creyentes de todas las naciones del mundo que fueron al cielo antes que yo. El amor de Dios sanó todas las heridas y enjugó todas las lágrimas. Él los reemplazará con gozo eterno. adoraré, alabaré, y glorificaré a mi Padre celestial, Señor y Salvador Jesús Cristo por siempre.

Notas Finales

1.   Capítulo 1, Página 8
Ostpreussen.de Geschichte, Landsmannschaft Ostpreussen, e.v. Hamburg, Alemania
https://ostpreussen.de/Ospreussen/geschichte.htm

2.   Capítulo 1, Página 9-11
El Reino de Prusia – Wikipedia, https://enWikipedia.org

3.   Capítulo 2, Página 14
Resumen de la Historia de la Primera Guerra Mundial
https://Britannica.com/event/world/war

4.   Capítulo 2, Página 15-16
Káiser Wilhelm II, Ansprache zum Ausbruch des 1 Weltkrieges (Balkonreden 31. Juli und August 1914) Wilhelm II, discursos de guerra
https://wwi.lib.buy.edu>index.php>Wilhelm_II's.war...

5.   Capítulo 2, Página 18-23
Reseña del Lusitania por Colin Simpson, publicada por Reason (1976)
(61-63) Reseña del Libro por Roger Hummel
jeff@jrhummel.com

6.   Capítulo 2, Página 24
Día de Armisticio: fin de la Primera Guerra Mundial –
Historia
https://www.history.com>this-day-in-history>world-...

7. Capítulo 3, Página 28-30
El Tratado de Versalles, Editorial A&E Canal de TV,
originalmente publicado el 29 de octubre de 2009; actualizado
el 3 de marzo de 2020
https://www.history.com<topics>world-war-I>treaty

8. Capítulo 4, Página 30-31
La República de Weimar – Historia, publicado el 4 de
diciembre del 2017 por A&E Canal de TV; actualizado el
4 de Marzo del 2021
https://www.history.com/topics/Germany/Weimar-Republic

9. Capítulo 6, Página 44-45
Tercer Reich / Hechos e historia / Britannica
https://www.britannica.com > ... > Historical Places

10. Capítulo 6, Página 46-48
(Segunda Guerra Mundial Hechos y Resumen) Historia,
Fechas, Combatientes, resumen de 2 minutos, 27 de septiembre
del 2021 – Segunda Guerra Mundial
https://www.britannica.com > events > World-War-II

11. Capítulo 10, Página 226
Plan Marshall – Historia; history.com Editores, originalmente
publicado el 16 de diciembre del 2009, actualizado el 5 de
Junio del 2020
https://www. histor y. co m/topics/w or ld-war-ii/marshall-plan-1..

12. Capítulo 10, Página 227
LAS NACIONES: Operación Ave Perro – TIME
Article/0,9171,779865,000.html 28/06/1948
https://content.time.com > magazine > article

13.   Capítulo 10, Página 229 – 230
El Bloqueo de Berlín – La Guerra Fría
Autor: Brian Dorn (BA, MA, Dip, Tch) & Jennier Llewellyn,
BA, MA, Di Ed John Rae (MA, Med) Steve Thompson (BA,
M Lit. Dip. Ed.) Australianos
 https://alphahistory.com/coldwar/berlin-blockade

14.   Capítulo 10, Página 231
Formación de la República Federal Alemana / Britannica
Artículo originalmente publicado el 13 de Noviembre del
2009, actualizado el 20 de mayo del 2020
https://www.history.com > this-day-in-history > federal ...

15.   Capítulo 10, Página 251 -252
Contenido y análisis, Atlantic Charter de Wikipedia la
Enciclopedia Libre. Atlantic Charter – Wikipedia.
https://en.wikipedia.org/wiki/Atlantic-charter

16.   Capítulo 10, Página 253
La Conferencia de Postdam, Texto bajo licencia CC – BY – SA
https://en.wikipedia.org>Postdam_Agreement

17. Capítulo 10, Página 254
Die Wahrheit über den Zweiten Weltkrieg – Europa La
Verdad Sobre la Segunda Guerra Mundial, por John Torell,
página 1, 2. http://www.eaec-de.org/Wahrheit_ueber_ den_2.
Weltkrieg

18. Capítulo 10, Página 254
Tribuna Renegada Artículo publicado el 24 de Marzo del 2018 por John Wear ¿Los aliados superaron a los Alemanes en crímenes y atrocidades?
www. renegadetribune. com/allies-outdo-germans-crime-atrocities

19.	Capítulo 10, Página 255
El Oscuro Secreto de la SGM Campo de Muerte Alemán Artículo publicado el 13 de enero del 2017 por Richard Stockton, revisado y actualizado por John Kuroski el 20 de julio del 2017
https://allthatinteresting.com>Rheinwiesenlager

20.	Capítulo 11, Página 278
Martin Lutero/Biografía/Reforma/Logros Líder religioso alemán por Hans Hildebrand
http://www.britannica.com>biography>Martin-Luther

21. Capítulo 14, Página 399 – 402
Segunda Guerra Mundial, Francia, Adolf Hitler, Sophie Scholl Artículo publicado el 08.05.2020 por Andreas Noll después de la Segunda Guerra Mundial, POWs Alemanas fueron enlistadas para reconstruir Francia
https://www.dw.com>a533374941

22. Capítulo 14, Páginas 403 – 414
Mein Heimatland Zeitschrift fuer Geschichte, Volks-und Heimatkunde Mai 1945, Kriegsgefangene im amerikanischen Lager (POWs en los campos americanos) In den Hersfelder Haunewiesen bei Prof. Ernst-Hermann Rübsam, Bad Herslfeld, Alemania

23.   Capítulo 14, Páginas 414-415 Nichts ist vergessen.
Nothing is vergotten
Gespräche von deutschen un russischen Kriegsgefangenen
Discursos de prisioneros de Guerra alemanes y rusos
http://nanopdf.com>anzeigen-634-hb_19-Nano-PFG

24.   Adendum, Página 489
Tabelle über die Judenverfolgung bei Michael Palamino,
publicado en el 2003, actualizado en Agosto del 2015 Resumen
sobre la persecución de los Judíos 1933 – 1945
http://www.hist.com/judentum-aktenlage/hd/6-mio-
partition-GB.htm

25.   Libros leídos:
1. El Caso para Pascua de Lee Strobel
Originalmente publicado en el 2004 por Zondervan, lanzado
el 15 de diciembre del 2009, ISBN 97803 108 65858

26.   Imágenes de Ciencia y Dios en bing.com images ...
Artículo de Lee Strobel publicado el 26/11/2012

2. Mein Kampf
Por Adolf Hitler, publicado el 18 de Julio de 1925, en Alemania

3. Freund so du etwas bist
Por Heinrich Tieck en Editorial Walther Scheuermann en
Wien, Austria. 22da Edición impresa en 1960 por R.Kiesel
en Salzburg, Austria.

4. Der Kampf um Ostpreussen
Autor Dieckert, Kurt y Grossman Horst (Pasta dura) Editorial
Lindenbaum Verlag, GmbH 201
ISBN 97839 381 76160, Versión Alemana

5. Arroyos en el Desierto
Por Sra. Chas. E. Cowman, Vigésimo Primera Edición
Publicada por Oriental Missionary Society, Los Angeles,
Calif. 1941, Mil novecientos cuarenta y uno.

6. Robins Reader No. 1, 1972 por Médicos y Pacientes Como
ser Feliz en el Matrimonio por Reverendo J.H. Randolph
Ray, de Little Church around the Corner de Nueva York.

7. Robins Reader Primavera de 1986 de Médicos y Pacientes
Un doctor mira a la oración, Dr. Alexis Carrel, Premio Nobel
de la Medicina de 1912

8. El cuento del Ganso de Oro
Por Jacob Grimm y Wilhelm Grimm originalmente publicado
en 1812. Grupo Arne – Thompson.
ATU571 (Episodio de tipo 513 B0

9. EL ENFERMO IMAGINARIO – Comedia de tres actos
Por Jean-Baptiste Moliere estrenado el 10 de febrero de
1673 en el Teatro du Palais-Royal en Paris, originalmente
coreografeado por Pierre Beauchamp

10. Ópera de Otello
Compuesta por Giuseppe Verdi, basada en la obra de
Shakespeare Otelo. Representada primero en el Teatro Alla
Scalla Milan el 5 de Febrero de 1887

27. Letras de canciones
1. Capítulo 9, Página 177
Entrega lo que te aflije, Autor Paul Gerhardt 1867
http://hymnary.org/text/commit_whatever_grieves_the

2. Capítulo 10, página 266
El rey de los elfos o El rey de los alisos, poema de Johann Wolfgang con Goethe, Escrito en 1782 y publicad el mismo año que Der Erlkoenig
https://www.britannica.com>Literature>Poetry

3. Capítulo 12, Página 328
Canción: Hohe Nacht der klaren Sterne (Alta noche de las estrellas claras) compuesta por Hans Bauman (1914-1988) Publicada en 1936
https://de.Wikipedia.org>wiki>Hoh...

Ver también:

waykiwayki.com Emperador de todas las mentiras (Parte 1) publicado el 8 de octubre del 2014

http://www.thetruthseeker.co.uk/article.asp?ID=135> (web13) Crímenes de guerra de los Aliados 1941 – 1950

https:www.nationsonling.org>one world>Federal – Repu ... Formación de la Primera República Federal de Alemania

https://www.deutschland.de/en/topic/politics/germany-europe/two-plus-four-treaty
Términos del Tratado Dos por Cuatro

Título: Lo que se perdió en las Guerras Mundiales: El Amor de Dios Sana Todas las Heridas
Autor: Hildegard Bonacker Bruni
Editorial: Hildegard Bruni Publishing
Género: Biografías Alemanas Históricas / Consciencia y Pensamiento
Revisado por: Jack Chambers

Hollywood Book Reviews

Se dice comúnmente que la historia está escrita por los vencedores. En esta cuestión, comúnmente son aquéllos que emergen victoriosos o alcanzan sus metas en la vida quiéenes son admirados de la manera más favorable en cualquier situación. Hay muchos ejemplos de esto, como muchos consideran a Roma uno de los imperios más grandes jamás construidos a pesar de la falta de moralidad que comúnmente ocurría en los altos niveles de la sociedad, o cuando los Estados Unidos "ganó" la carrera espacial en los 1960s a pesar de que Rusia tenía un programa espacial igualmente avanzado. Uno de los casos más infames de esto debe haber sido durante ambas guerras mundiales, en las cuales muchos ciudadanos alemanes y de naciones vecinas fueron al agrupados junto con aquellos que pelearon y llevaron la propaganda de los gobernantes de ese tiempo.

En el libro *"Lo que se perdió en las Guerras Mundiales: El Amor de Dios Sana Todas las Heridas"* de la autora Hildegard Bonacker Bruni, la autora comparte la compleja historia de su familia al sobrevivir a la Segunda Guerra Mundial y el impacto que ambas guerras mundiales tuvieron en muchas de las familias dentro y cerca de Alemania. Al relatar la historia de sus propias experiencias y las de su familia, y el impacto que su fe compartida tuvo en ellos mientras luchaban por sobrevivir, la autora explora las causas de las guerras, la diferencia entre aquellos que crearon los problemas que llevaron a la guerra, y aquellos que fueron forzados al conflicto, y la tragedia que resultó para las personas inocentes desplazadas por la guerra al final.

La autora hace un trabajo maravilloso al equilibrar el libro con registros históricos y discusión a través de narración de memorias. El detalle que proporciona la autora es asombroso, tanto para la historia y genealogía de su familia como para el corazón del conflicto durante ambas guerras mundiales. Los trágicos eventos que trajeron caos y pérdida a tantos en todo el mundo, a menudo se centran en las diversas culturas y personas que perdieron la vida durante la guerra fuera de Alemania y sus países vecinos. Sin embargo, raramente los amantes de la historia y los lectores de no ficción, tienen la oportunidad de escuchar de primera mano cómo las personas en estas áreas se enteraron del conflicto y lucharon por sobrevivir durante esos tumultuosos tiempos en medio del conflicto. El trasfondo prusiano de la autora y el impacto que la guerra tuvo en su familia fueron abordados de manera profunda y plasmados en este libro, lo que mantendrá a los lectores concentrados en las luchas personales de la autora.

Esta lectura es perfecta para aquellos que disfrutan de libros de no ficción, en particular para aquellos que disfrutan de la historia, los viajes filosóficos e introspectivos, y los libros con un trasfondo cristiano en los temas de las memorias. Las luchas emocionales y espirituales y los logros que la autora detalla en este libro son inspiradores y muestran la fortaleza del espíritu humano cuando se enfrenta a estos eventos aplastantes. El equilibrio que se encuentra en estos temas y el enfoque honesto del estilo de escritura, realmente permite a los lectores sentir la conexión emocional de la autora y su familia, y sus experiencias compartidas durante ese tiempo.

Memorable, esclarecedor y cautivador, *"Lo que se perdió en las Guerras Mundiales: El Amor de Dios Sana Todas las Heridas"* de la autora Hildegard Bonacker Bruni es un libro de no ficción e histórico que los lectores no podrán dejar de leer. El estilo de escritura orientado a los detalles y el trasfondo emocional de la familia de la autora y sus experiencias culminan en un libro lleno de tragedia y triunfo, y la curación general que viene al confiar en la fe durante estos tiempos difíciles.

Título: Lo que se perdió en las Guerras Mundiales :El Amor de Dios Sana Todas las Heridas
Autor: Hildegard Bonacker Bruni
Editorial: Hildegard Bruni Publishing
Género: Memorias
Revisado por: Ephantus M.

Pacific Book Review

"Lo que se perdió en las Guerras Mundiales: El Amor de Dios Sana Todas las Heridas", es un intrincado relato de la travesía exultante de la familia de la autora Hildegard Bonacker Bruni a través de las dos Guerras Mundiales, y cómo el contar con las inquebrantables misericordias de Dios les permitió eludir amenazas, sufrimientos, hambre, desgracias, miseria, desánimos y enfermedades.

Crecer en una Alemania postguerra destruida presentó a la familia de Hildegard muchos problemas, y obtener educación fue difícil debido a la falta de maestros y facilidades escolares. Por la gracia de Dios, se graduó de una escuela de medicina como asistente médica comercial y práctica, y posteriormente se casó con el Dr. Aldo Bruni, un caballero que la apoyaría y con quien experimentaría una vida de profunda alegría y felicidad.

Los lectores encontrarán su narración minuciosa con datos históricos y políticos sobre su origen ancestral, Prusia. Ella es cuidadosa al revelar cómo el país se convirtió en refugio para perseguidos religiosos y políticos, y cómo finalmente llegó a la nada después de la horrenda Segunda Guerra Mundial, que cobró diez millones de vidas, hirió a veinte millones de soldados y convirtió a ocho millones de personas en prisioneros de guerra. También ha compartido sus encuentros en diferentes lugares, así como la desgarradora temporada de perder a su querido esposo, después de lo cual retomó la investigación y escritura de este libro.

Este es un texto que motiva poderosamente el consuelo y el aliento para las personas que atraviesan momentos difíciles, como un medio a través del cual podemos sanar nuestras propias tristezas y heridas mentales. Es un libro que también pone de manifiesto muchas falsedades cronológicas que se han transmitido a lo largo de los años, y a través de las cuales muchos villanos han sido celebrados como héroes. Los lectores no dejarán de notar la devoción de la autora hacia la verdad, la formulación de notable decencia y el albergue de una confianza absoluta en Dios, como el patrón auténtico que conduce a una vida segura y triunfante. De hecho, es una lectura que verá a su audiencia anticipar el cumplimiento de las promesas de Dios, así como su confiabilidad cuando todo lo demás falla.

En general, *"Lo que se perdió en las Guerras Mundiales: El Amor de Dios Sana Todas las Heridas"* revela los efectos insondables de la guerra, y también logra afectar una actitud agradecida a través de su valioso contenido. Es un texto que vale la pena leer tanto para cristianos como para no cristianos, y cuyas lecciones tomarán años olvidar. ¡Recomiendo encarecidamente este libro!